mom's Book!

# OPEN A WINDOW

# OPEN A WINDOW...

# TO EXCEPTIONAL LITERATURE

Lead your students to appreciate literature across time and cultures with an unparalleled collection of classic and contemporary selections.

# OPEN A WINDOW...

## TO LANGUAGE ARTS INTEGRATION

*U*se literature as a bridge to teaching skills mastery: critical reading, writing, grammar, speaking and listening... solid instruction at the teachable moment.

# OPEN A WINDOW...

## TO GROUND-BREAKING TECHNOLOGY

**D**iscover a remarkable multimedia Writing Studio that integrates literature and writing:

writing software, hand–held Electronic Grammar Handbook, Literature Videodiscs, Transparencies for Writing, Audio Prose Library.

# OPEN A WINDOW...

## TO PRENTICE HALL LITERATURE

### WHERE GREAT IDEAS HAPPEN

Student Text

Annotated Teacher's Edition

Teaching Portfolio
(with Computer Test Bank)

Multicultural Library

Great Works Library

Study Guides

Library of Video Classics

Listening to Literature
Audiocassettes

**The Prentice Hall Literature
Writing Studio:**

Bank Street Writer Software

Writer's Helper Software

Franklin Language Master 6000

Literature Videodiscs

Audio Prose Library Audiocassettes

Transparencies for Writing

Front cover art: Interior with a Table, 1921, Vanessa Bell,
Tate Gallery, London, Art Resource, New York

PRENTICE HALL LITERATURE Copper

PRENTICE HALL LITERATURE Bronze

PRENTICE HALL LITERATURE Silver

PRENTICE HALL LITERATURE Gold

PRENTICE HALL LITERATURE Platinum

PRENTICE HALL LITERATURE The American Experience

PRENTICE HALL LITERATURE The British Tradition

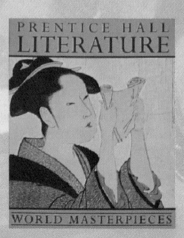
PRENTICE HALL LITERATURE WORLD MASTERPIECES

# Annotated Teacher's Edition

# PRENTICE HALL

# LITERATURE
## SILVER

### PARAMOUNT EDITION

**TAOS VALLEY, 1932–1935**
*Victor Higgins*
*Snite Museum of Art, University of Notre Dame*

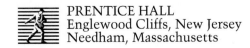

PRENTICE HALL
Englewood Cliffs, New Jersey
Needham, Massachusetts

PRENTICE HALL
A Division of Simon & Schuster
Englewood Cliffs, New Jersey 07632

## ACKNOWLEDGMENTS

Grateful acknowledgment is made to the following for permission to reprint copyrighted material:

**Doubleday, a Division of Bantam Doubleday Dell Publishing Group, Inc.**
From "Prologue: Dedication to Peace" in *When Heaven and Earth Changed Places* by Le Ly Hayslip with Jay Wurts. Copyright © 1989 by Le Ly Hayslip and Charles Jay Wurts. Excerpt from *The Diary of Anne Frank, The Critical Edition,* prepared by the Netherlands State Institute for War Documentation, translated by Arnold J. Pomerans and B. M. Mooyaart, edited by David Barnouw and Gerrold Van Der Stroom. Used by permission.

**National Council of Teachers of English**
From *SLATE Starter Sheet*, June 1987, "Guidelines for Using Journals in School Settings." Approved by the NCTE Commission on Composition, November 28, 1986. Reprinted with permission of the National Council of Teachers of English.

**Random House, Inc.**
Excerpt from "Hannah Elisabeth Pick-Goslar: from *The Last Seven Months of Anne Frank,* by Willy Lindwer, translated from Dutch by Alison Meersschaert. English translation Copyright © 1991 by Random House, Inc.

Note: Every effort has been made to locate the copyright owner of material reprinted in this book. Omissions brought to our attention will be corrected in subsequent editions.

# CONTENTS

# WHAT IS INTEGRATED LANGUAGE ARTS?

## Sharon Sorenson
formerly with Evansville-Vanderburgh School Corporation
Evansville, Indiana

Those of us who have been in the classroom for more than a few years recall the time when there were separate literature, composition, and grammar classes. We were reasonably satisfied teaching literature. We lectured, occasionally asking questions and seeking discussion. The students listened, and, for the most part, were successful on the tests we gave on literature. Beyond that, however, we could say little about our students' understanding and even less about their enthusiasm. We were frustrated, for instance, by students who, even though they were superior literature students, wrote miserably poor compositions chock full of grammatical errors. Why, we stormed, couldn't students see the connection between all those grammar rules and their own writing? Why couldn't they write successful, thoughtful, coherent essays about literature? Some of us even cast blame on one another. "If the teacher across the hall really did a good job of teaching grammar last semester, students would know where to put commas this semester," we fumed behind closed doors.

Later, we took a bold step: We decided to do away with some of those separate classes and teach grammar and composition together. We believed integrated grammar and composition classes would be the answer to our prayers. Now, at last, we could have the same students for grammar and composition and know full well that students had been taught the rules and could apply those rules to their writing. Unfortunately, in spite of our hopes, combined grammar and composition classes weren't the answer, either. For the most part, student writing was little improved.

## The Writing Process

Next, the writing process took the language arts teaching profession by storm. We began working more carefully with students, taking them through prewriting activities, giving them supervised time to write, modeling the revising process, and talking about proofreading in terms of grammar, usage, and mechanics rules. We increased classroom emphasis on peer editing, cooperative learning, and editorial boards, moving away from transmission of information to transaction, from a teacher-centered classroom to a student-centered one. Suddenly, those old grammar handbooks came off the shelves as students struggled to find rules to support whatever error a proofreader found. Grammar, usage, and mechanics became a relevant part of the writing process as students began to see the purpose behind the rules.

The research had been there all along. "Don't teach grammar in isolation," studies said. "It has no meaning to students if not couched in the context of something useful—like writing."

Let's face it. Would anybody except an English teacher expect Ernest Hemingway to describe the use of gerund phrases in his writing? Would Mark Twain have passed a test that asked him to identify the tense and form of verb phrases such as *could have been revising*? What, then, is the relationship between understanding grammar and writing well? That was the question research posed. Of course, we know now that a student's thorough understanding of grammar is no guarantee that he or she will write well. Accurately, maybe, but not well. Writing, the researchers said, is far more than nouns, commas, and participles that don't dangle.

## What Makes Good Writing?

Ah, that was the rub! If writing well takes more than applying grammar rules, what makes good writing? We know the answer: We expect our students to say something when they write! But, we argued, given the tools of grammar, usage, and mechanics, shouldn't they be able to just say it? Apparently not. The problem is that grammar rules don't teach students to think like writers. Or to create sentences, paragraphs, and pages like writers. In fact, to think like writers, students need to study writers. Regularly. Daily. All kinds of writers. Then students can identify with the process of writing as a form of thinking. To write is to think. Bingo! This was the first step toward recognizing the importance of integrated language arts.

## Integrated Language Arts and Whole Language

About the same time that this first step started marching in the minds of middle-school and high-school language arts teachers, our colleagues in elementary schools began talking about whole language. Depending on whose definition you acept, whole language can be a thematically structured curriculum or a literature-driven curriculum. In either case, all content areas—language arts, science, social studies, math, art, music—spring from a central theme or a central piece of literature. A story about an ugly duckling, for instance, will lead to a science lesson about why duck feathers repel moisture, a math lesson about the incubation of their eggs, a social studies lesson about their semiannual migratory routes, a language arts lesson about using quotation marks when writing narrative, and similar music and art lessons.

However, we middle- and high-school teachers teach mainly language arts, so the term *whole language* didn't seem entirely appropriate. As a result, most of us began talking about integrated language arts. We followed the same philosophy as our elementary-school colleagues—that the parts should come from the whole—but we framed it in the context of our own teaching world. Thus, the term *integrated language arts* has come to refer to a literature-driven language arts curriculum. We start with a piece of literature—a short story, poem, play, essay, or novel—and incorporate instruction in all of the other language arts skills within its framework: reading, writing, grammar, usage, mechanics, spelling, vocabulary, critical thinking, and speaking and listening. We rely heavily on the teachable moment, teaching, for instance, a vocabulary word the moment it pops up in the literature, teaching critical thinking skills as part of the response to literature, teaching grammar as it springs from the discussion of the writer's style, teaching writing as students prepare written responses to the literature, and teaching usage and mechanics during the proofreading process of that written response.

## A Changed Classroom

The result is a changed classroom. Some of the changes are hard for us; all of them are proving successful for students. For instance, lesson plans are harder to write because content pops up at unexpected and unanticipated moments, changing the direction of the best laid plans. Curriculum guides must necessarily become more flexible because we address skills within the context of the literature and at the teachable moment. Classroom strategies and management techniques change because we focus on student-centered activities that meet varying ability levels and respond to individual needs. While the changes are sometimes hard for veteran teachers, the results are changed classrooms that excite students, promote learning, and improve test scores.

What does an integrated language arts classroom look like and sound like? Here's a mythical classroom. As students settle in their seats, they find a learning log prompt on the overhead projector. Its purpose is to serve as a prereading activity. The prompt asks students to think about an experience they have had in nature. Maybe they have watched a sunset, hiked in the desert, crossed a glacier, or witnessed a severe storm. What did they see? Students begin writing in response to the prompt. The teacher roams the room reading over shoulders, checking for prior knowledge and individual interests, while also preparing students for the experience they will have reading M. Scott Momaday's poem "New World." A few minutes later, the teacher asks students to name the five senses, to give examples of each, and then to return to their learning logs to add the other senses to their descriptions. The teacher gives them three minutes. Afterward, students are asked to reason logically about what the term *sensory language* must mean, and, without discussion, to write a one-sentence definition in their logs. The teacher is setting students up for the literary focus of Momaday's poem, using another kind of prereading activity but also employing critical thinking skills. Simultaneously, the teacher is engaging students as active learners. To write is to think. And everyone is participating.

Next it is time for an initial choral reading of the poem. Students simply listen for overall impression. On a second reading, however, the teacher stops—at the teachable moment—to ask students to define an unusual word. It is the vocabulary lesson for the day.

Then, to begin getting at the poem's meaning, students do what they were prepared to do before the reading: look for sensory words, an activity completed individually, cooperatively, or in a whole-class setting. After the choral reading of the poem (to say is to think), students read about the author and indicate how understanding his background helps them understand the poem. After further discussion, moving through as complicated an analysis of the literature as makes sense with the given class, the teacher surprises students by asking them to name the verbs in the poem and to identify their tense. After students identify the verbs as present tense, the teacher asks them to substitute the past tense as he or she rereads the poem. Many students recognize that the change in verb tense affects the meaning of the poem—dramatically. So there's the grammar lesson for the day: Use consistent verb tense and use it to convey your message.

Now, back to those learning logs. The prereading activity also functions as a prewriting activity, because the teacher now asks students to use their learning log ideas (with the sensory language already in place) to create one or two products: a poem modeled after ''New World'' or a narrative description of their experience. In the course of students developing their written products, the teacher may refer to the poem to model structure, sensory language, punctuation, even grammar. Not only does that teaching technique reiterate the elements of the author's style, but it stimulates students' thinking. In the course of revising, students cope with unity, coherence, supporting details, transitions, and the other techniques of clear writing. In the course of proofreading, peer editors tackle grammar, usage, and mechanics problems and find their solutions. Students who are writing at computers may even use a style checker to analyze their sentence lengths, sentence structure, and readability indices. The lesson is finished in about two days.

## What Happens in the Integrated Classroom?

What happened during that integrated language arts lesson? Students addressed all of the language arts skills within the context of the literature. All of the parts came out of the whole. They studied literature—a poem—and literary concepts, including sensory language. They practiced active reading skills —predicting, analyzing, clarifying, visualizing, summarizing. They wrote—in their learning logs to promote active learning and in response to the literature to produce a formal written product. They studied grammar—the use of consistent verb tense and its effect on meaning. They referred to usage and mechanics rules, employed critical thinking skills, and engaged in speaking and listening activities.

Integrated language arts classrooms are as varied as the teachers and students who inhabit them, and the activities are equally varied. They are exciting places where skills, not drills, are taught when the students need them. Some teachers, however, feel frustration because they believe that the teachable moment lacks structure. There is no guarantee, they say, that we will actually cover everything we're supposed to cover; it's just too hit or miss.

Those of us who are highly structured will continue to feel this tugging at our professional consciences.

However, look at it this way: If the student isn't using dangling participles, why teach him not to? If he is using them, then teach him, not his classmates, at the teachable moment, referring to his own writing. Or if most of the students face the same problem, do a five-minute minilesson, and then let the practice come in their own writing. Remind yourself what the research tells us: Students don't learn skills in isolation. We can best approach skills from the context or their use—in the literature and in the student's own writing at the moment the student needs them.

## The Test

Two teachers told me recently that they put these integrated language arts ideas to the test. They had evenly matched classes, so one teacher taught the traditional grammar units and intersperesed them with writing, and the other teacher taught the integrated language arts approach, letting all of the language arts skills spring from the literature. At the end of the year, both classes took the same test (it happened to be a state-mandated one). The class whose teacher had used the integrated approach attained much higher scores than those whose teacher had pounded rules and skills all year.

''Why do you think that happened?'' I asked. ''Simple,'' was one teacher's response. ''The kids learn best at the moment they have a need for the knowledge. That's when it makes sense to them, and that's why they remember it.'' ''You know,'' she went on, ''it's like someone telling you how to change a flat tire. Only when you really need to know do those instructions matter. I just applied that little analogy to my language arts classroom.''

Lots of teachers who faced flat tires in their classrooms have turned to an integrated language arts approach. They like what they find. ''It's refreshing,'' one teacher said, ''to find students who really have something to say. The literature discussions provoke thought, the literature itself provides for structure and style, and the writing process makes sense after students see how other writers put it into effect. It's the complete cycle. We read writing to write reading.''

Right!

# The Prentice Hall Literature Program
## OVERVIEW

The *Prentice Hall Literature* program is an integrated language arts program, offering high-quality, appealing, traditional and contemporary literary selections, writing instruction and activities, and study aids that will guide students into, through, and beyond the literature.

## The Student Book
### Organization

The selections are organized by genre to encourage comprehensive study of the types of literature. The following list shows the units and the sections within each unit into which the selections are organized.

**The Short Story:** Plot, Character, Setting, Theme
**Drama:** Two plays
**Nonfiction:** Biographies and Personal Accounts, Essays for Enjoyment, Essays in the Content Areas
**Poetry:** Narrative Poetry, Figurative Language and Imagery, Lyric Poetry, Facets of Nature, Perceptions, Choices
**The American Folk Tradition:** In the Beginning, Heroes and Legends, Tall Tales
**The Novel:** A Complete Novel

The number and variety of selections offer choice and flexibility in meeting curriculum requirements as well as student needs and interests.

### Unique Features

Because the *Prentice Hall Literature* program puts emphasis on the reading and appreciation of literature, it offers several unique features to help students become active readers.

### Reading Preparation and Support

**Reading Actively** Each unit begins with a feature called Reading Actively, which includes a set of strategies for effectively reading the literature in the unit. The strategies involve the reader in the text before reading and while reading. Such involvement and reaction are necessary if students are to learn.

In the short story, nonfiction, and poetry units, this feature is followed by a Model, which is annotated by a student to demonstrate how a good reader might use the active reading strategies to understand a selection. Students are encouraged to use these strategies as they read other selections in the unit. This feature provides a method of scaffolding—giving students help and support while they acquire the skills to become successful readers of literature. To give students further practice with this process, there is an additional selection in the Teaching Portfolio, which students can annotate themselves.

**Guide for Reading** All other selections begin with a Guide for Reading. This page, which precedes the selection, contains useful prereading information. The Guide for Reading prepares students for successful reading in four ways:

- A biography of the author provides insight into how the author came to write the selection.
- A literary focus section introduces the literary concept that is taught with the selection.
- A reading focus feature activates students' prior knowledge, involves them in the reading process, and provides a specific goal for reading.
- A vocabulary list presents, in glossary format, words from the selection that might present difficulty in reading.

This Guide for Reading provides the background to encourage comprehension, motivate students to read, and give them technical support to read successfully.

**Theme Bar** At the top of the beginning of each selection, you will find a label identifying the theme. This feature makes it easy to thumb through the book and connect selections with similar themes.

**Reading and Responding** The short story, nonfiction, and poetry units also end with a feature called Reading and Responding. This feature serves as a summary for reading and analyzing the particular types of literature and comprehending the literary elements and devices that are in them. For example, Reading and Responding for Short Stories shows a student responding to plot, character, theme, and setting, and analyzes the application of these elements in a particular story. In the Teaching Portfolio, there is an additional selection that the students can annotate themselves.

Each selection is self-contained and complete so that you can use the selections in any order.

### After Reading

Features at the end of the selection are designed to foster comprehension and encourage constructive response, either personal or literary. These features encourage the growth of skills needed by students to become independent readers. These features comprise five areas:

**Responding to the Selection** These study questions are built upon four levels of comprehension: the personal response, the literal, the interpretive, and the applied. The questions are grouped by four levels of increasing complexity: your response, recalling (literal), interpreting (inference, analysis), and applying (generalization, extension, judgment). The different levels may be used as appropriate for different ability levels, or may be used to take all students through different levels of thinking.

**Analyzing Literature** This section develops and reinforces the literary concept or skill introduced on the Guide for Reading page and applies it to the selection. It helps students to understand literary concepts and appreciate writers' techniques, thereby enabling them to respond appropriately to literature.

**Critical Thinking and Reading** This section introduces students to those critical thinking and critical reading skills that are necessary for understanding literature. It gives them an opportunity to apply these skills to the literary selections.

**Thinking and Writing** This is a composition assignment arising from the selection. This assignment, which may be creative or analytical, is process-oriented, suggesting steps for prewriting, drafting, and revising.

**Learning Options** This section provides activities that address a variety of learning styles and helps facilitate a student-centered approach.

## Other Special Features

**One Writer's Process** This feature is always connected to a selection in the anthology. In it, the process used by the writer of that selection is explained, allowing students to gain insight into how writers think and write and to see the writing process in action.

**Multicultural Connection** Using a literature selection as a springboard, this feature helps students to appreciate connections among cultures.

## End of Unit

**Your Writing Process** Each unit ends with two complete writing lessons. Each lesson focuses on a form of writing and guides students through the writing process.

## End of Book

Three handbooks are provided at the end of *Prentice Hall Literature:* Handbook of the Writing Process, Handbook of Grammar and Revising Strategies, and Handbook of Literary Terms and Techniques.

**Handbook of the Writing Process** This handbook presents three lessons focusing on the writing process. One lesson concentrates on prewriting, another on drafting and revising, and the third on proofreading and publishing.

**Handbook of Grammar and Revising Strategies** This handbook presents strategies for revising common writing problems, with examples of good usage from the literature selections. It also contains a brief overview of the grammar of a sentence, punctuation rules, and correct usage.

**Handbook of Literary Terms and Techniques** This handbook provides an alphabetical guide to the literary terms introduced on the Guide for Reading page and taught in the Analyzing Literature activities at the end of selections. Each entry provides a full definition of the term or technique with one or more examples. The handbook can be used for preteaching, for review, or as a support for students as they work on individual Analyzing Literature activities.

# TEACHING SUPPORT

## The Annotated Teacher's Edition

The Annotated Teacher's Edition of *Prentice Hall Literature* is designed to be used both for planning and for actual in-class teaching. It offers planning aids and specific teaching suggestions for all selections. This planning and teaching material appears in the side columns next to the reduced student pages of each selection. These annotations, which correspond to the student material on that page, help you give your students positive and relevant experiences with literature by asking the right questions at the right time and by pointing out what is significant.

## Preparation

The annotations in the margin next to the Guide for Reading page help you prepare your students to read. These annotations provide the groundwork for reading, help you deal with different ability levels, and often call upon students' prior knowledge. You will find the following notes:

**More About the Author** These notes extend the information about the author given in the student book. Often they contain a quotation, anecdote, or question that helps personalize the writer.

**Literary Focus** These notes provide tips for teaching the literary element introduced on the Guide for Reading page.

**Prereading Focus** These notes provide tips for teaching the Focus activity on the Guide for Reading page.

**Vocabulary** These notes provide tips for teaching the vocabulary words. When appropriate, a **Spelling Tip** also accompanies the vocabulary words.

**Objectives** This boxed material lists the instructional objectives for the selection. These objectives are keyed in to the end-of-selection material.

**Support Material** This section lists all the support material for the selection found in the Teaching Portfolio and other program components.

## Presentation

You may use the notes throughout the pages of the selection to direct your discussion in class. As you and your students read the selection, you will find additional notes that enable you to customize the lesson for your class. They let you increase your students' involvement in the work and enrich their reading of it, while enabling them to deal with the particular genres. The following kinds of notes may direct your class discussions:

**Motivation/Prior Knowledge** These notes contain questions and tips for calling upon students' prior knowledge in order to motivate them to read the selections.

**Purpose-Setting Question** These notes provide a focus for reading.

**Master Teacher Notes** These classroom tips from master teachers give an approach, a strategy, or a very special bit of information that enlivens the selection or increases appreciation.

**Humanities Notes** For each piece of fine art in the student book, there is a humanities note giving information on the work of art and the artist. These notes generally point out features of the piece of art that relate it to the work of literature with which it is presented. Additionally, the humanities note concludes with questions that you may use if you wish to discuss the art as part of your discussion of the work.

**Thematic Focus** These notes connect to the Theme Bar at the top of every selection. They provide suggestions for teaching the theme.

**Making Connections** These notes connect the particular selection with other selections in the anthology having similar topics, ideas, situations, or characters.

**Enrichment** Enrichment notes provide the additional information on points of interest that arise in the selection. You may use this information to enrich your students' knowledge of the background of a selection and appreciation of it.

**Reading Strategies** Strategies to promote student comprehension of the literary text reinforce the emphasis on enabling students to read literature.

**Clarification** Words, phrases, or ideas that might be obstacles to student understanding are clarified to ensure comprehension.

**Discussion** Throughout the selection, you will find additional questions and points for discussion. These help you proceed through the selection with students, eliciting their understanding and appreciation of significant passages.

**Literary Focus** To promote understanding of the writer's techniques, literary focus annotations direct attention to those aspects of the selection that reflect the literary concept presented with it.

**Critical Thinking and Reading** These notes reinforce the critical thinking and reading skills developed throughout the program.

**ESL Teaching Strategy** These notes suggest ways to make the selection accessible to students.

**Multicultural Focus** These notes connect cultural information in the selections with other cultures and the students' own experiences. At times, they contain tips on teaching sensitive material.

**Alternative Assessment** These notes provide alternative assessment suggestions for many selections. At times they provide strategies for assessing students' understanding of the selection; at other times they are tied to end-of-selection activities.

**Technology Notes** These notes show when and how to use the components of the Prentice Hall Literature Writing Studio. An icon, printed in blue, indicates which component would be useful at this point.

**Cooperative Learning** These notes provide cooperative activities that help students better understand the selection and move beyond the selection.

**Thematic Response** These notes ask students to respond to the theme of the selection. This theme was identified in the Theme Bar.

**Reader's Response** These notes ask a question designed to prompt the students' personal response to the selection.

**Grammar in Action** Grammar in Action notes integrate language arts skills. These notes demonstrate the writer's use of particular grammatical or style points. They present a direct link between grammar and writing.

Occasional **Commentary** and **Primary Source** notes add background or insight to the selection.

There are probably more notes than you need for presenting any given selection. We emphasize the importance of selecting those annotations that are best suited to your classes and to your course of instruction.

## Closure and Extension

Answers are provided for all questions in each feature following the selection. Where questions are open-ended, we present a suggested response or we suggest points that students should note in their answers.

The annotations after the selection also include the following:

**Challenge** These questions take students beyond those given with the instruction.

**Publishing Student Writing** For many selections, notes suggest ways to publish the writing students have done in the Thinking and Writing feature.

**Writing Across the Curriculum** Where appropriate, you will see suggestions for additional assignments or suggestions for relating the Thinking and Writing assignment to student's work in another discipline.

**Learning Options** These notes explain how the options address various learning styles.

In addition, you will find teaching suggestions for the special features in the student book.

## The Teaching Portfolio

The Teaching Portfolio provides support for teaching and testing all of the selections and skills in *Prentice Hall Literature.*

## Fine Art Transparencies

Twenty fine art transparencies with blackline masters are provided in the Teaching Portfolio. These can be used to introduce selections and motivate students to read, or they may be used as additional writing assignments in response to art. The fine art is keyed into the selections through Master Teacher Notes in the Annotated Teacher's Edition. In the Portfolio, each transparency is accompanied by a writing assignment for students and a lesson plan for teaching that assignment.

## Beginning of Unit

Each unit begins with a list of objectives and a skills chart listing literary elements and skills covered in the unit. The skills chart also identifies all the blackline masters in the Teaching Portfolio that correlate to each selection.

## The Selections

Full teaching support is provided for each selection. This support material is organized by selection for your convenience. The support for each selection consists of the following: Teacher Backup, Grammar in Action Worksheet, Usage and Mechanics Worksheet, Vocabulary Check, Analyzing Literature Worksheet*, Critical Thinking and Reading Worksheet*, Language Worksheet* (there are always two of the starred three), and a Selection Test.

**Teacher Backup** Teacher Backup material is provided for each selection. This material consists of more information about the author, a critical quotation about the author, a summary of the selection, and a list of other works by the author. In addition, there is a Check Test that you can use to check if students have read the selection. Help in teaching and evaluating the writing assignment in the student text is provided as well as three alternative composition assignments for the students. One of these is less challenging than the assignment in the student text, one is more challenging, and one requires the student to write in response to literary criticism. Finally, answers to all worksheets and tests are provided.

**Grammar in Action Worksheets** These worksheets provide additional instruction and practice on the topic presented with a selection in the Annotated Teacher's Edition.

**Usage and Mechanics** The Usage and Mechanics Worksheets provide sentences dealing with the selection that contain errors in usage and mechanics. They provide additional practice with the skill presented in the Grammar in Action worksheet. Such common problems as run-on sentences, sentence fragments, and subject-verb agreement are incorporated into these sentences as well as errors in spelling and punctuation. We suggest you have your students correct these sentences orally so that they can discuss each problem.

**Vocabulary Check** The Vocabulary Check tests mastery of the vocabulary words listed on the Guide for Reading page before each selection. This blackline master can be used as a test or as an in-class or at-home assignment.

**Worksheets** The Analyzing Literature Worksheet, Critical Thinking and Reading Worksheet, and Language Worksheet support and expand upon the skills taught at the end of the selection in the student book.

**Selection Test** A Selection Test is provided for each selection. This test requires students to demonstrate comprehension and interpretation of the selection and to apply the skills taught at the end of the selection. The test includes an essay question and a reader's response question.

**Annotated Models** For each selection that is annotated as a model in the student book (at the beginning of the short story, nonfiction, and poetry units), a selection is provided in the Teaching Portfolio for students to annotate themselves.

## End of Unit

Each unit ends with two unit tests: a short-answer test and an essay test, with guidelines for evaluating student responses to the essay test questions. In addition, a list of suggested projects, a bibliography, and list of audio-visual aids are included.

## End of Portfolio

At the end of the Teaching Portfolio are models of strong and weak student writing, a guide to evaluating student writing, and writing process activities.

## Computer Test Bank

Information about the Computer Test Bank and instructions for receiving the appropriate version are included in the Teaching Portfolio. The Computer Test Bank provides the selection test and unit tests from the Teaching Portfolio on computer disks. The program allows you to modify the selection tests by deleting items from the short-answer selection tests supplied, choosing a different essay question, and writing your own test questions. You can save your test for future use.

## Library of Video Classics

The Library of Video Classics provides videotapes of films made of major works in this level. Each tape is accompanied by a Viewing Guide, which gives background on the film or director, a planning overview for the film, and previewing and after-viewing questions and activities.

## Study Guides

Study Guides for major novels and plays are available with *Prentice Hall Literature.* These guides will help you teach many of the works of your choice as part of your total literature program. Each guide contains an overview of the novel or play, chapter-by-chapter lessons, assignments leading to essays and imaginative writing, guidelines for dealing with provocative themes, a bibliography, and blackline masters of skills and a test for the work.

## Multicultural Library

This library contains twenty young adult novels by acclaimed writers from diverse backgrounds. The books will have particular appeal in Grades 6–10. Each title is accompanied by a Study Guide

## Great Works Library

This library contains unabridged editions of time-honored classics by major writers. The books will have particular appeal to high-school students. Each title is accompanied by a Study Guide.

## Listening to Literature Audiocassettes

A series of audiocassettes is available for each level of *Prentice Hall Literature.* The audiocassettes provide professional readings of selections to enliven classroom learning. Each level is accompanied by a teacher's guide.

## Prentice Hall Literature Writing Studio

The Writing Studio provides tools that help the teacher integrate writing instruction with the literature program and facilitate the writing process. Tips on how and when to use the Writing Studio are provided in the Annotated Teacher's Edition for *Prentice Hall Literature.* We suggest teachers customize their program from the following components:

**Bank Street Writer** software
**Writer's Helper** software
**Franklin Language Master 6000**
**Literature Videodiscs**
**Audio Prose Library** audiocassettes
**Transparencies for Writing**

# Skills Chart for Selections in Each Unit

The following chart shows the literary elements and integrated language arts skills covered with each selection. An asterisk (*) indicates that a worksheet appears in the Teaching Portfolio.

**SHORT STORIES**

| Selection | Analyzing Literature | Critical Thinking and Reading | Thinking and Writing | Learning Options | Grammar in Action | Understanding Language |
|---|---|---|---|---|---|---|
| **Reading Actively** | | | | | | |
| "Tears of Autumn," Yoshiko Uchida, p. 3 | Understanding motivation* | Making predictions* | Writing an extension of the story | Art Writing | Using vivid verbs* Using coordinating conjunctions* | |
| **Plot** | | | | | | |
| "Rain, Rain, Go Away," Isaac Asimov, p. 13 | Understanding plot* | Understanding the sequence of events* | Writing a short story | Writing | Understanding dialogue* | |
| "Christmas Day in the Morning," Pearl S. Buck, p. 21 | Understanding a flashback* | Understanding time order | Writing an extended definition | Writing | Understanding compound-complex sentences* | Using context clues* |
| "The Adventure of the Speckled Band," Sir Arthur Conan Doyle, p. 27 | Examining conflict | Understanding logical reasoning* | Understanding your thinking | | Using who and whom* Understanding adjective clauses* Understanding compound sentences* Understanding passive voice* | Choosing the meaning that fits the context* |
| "The Captain and His Horse," Beryl Markham, p. 47 | Investigating suspense* | Making predictions | Writing about suspense | Cross-curricular connections | Using demonstrative pronouns* | Interpreting metaphors* |
| "A Retrieved Reformation," O. Henry, p. 61 | Understanding the surprise ending* | Recognizing allusions | Writing about a surprise ending | Art Writing | Using dashes* Understanding pronouns and antecedents* | Finding meanings to fit the context* |
| "The Finish of Patsy Barnes," Paul Laurence Dunbar, p. 69 | Understanding climax in plot* | Examining details important to plot* | Writing about the story's climax | Writing Speaking and listening | Varying sentence length* | |

| Selection | Analyzing Literature | Critical Thinking and Reading | Thinking and Writing | Learning Options | Grammar in Action | Understanding Language |
|---|---|---|---|---|---|---|
| "Charles," Shirley Jackson, p. 79 | Investigating point of view* | Making inferences about the plot | Writing from another point of view | | Understanding dialogue* | Using the suffix -*ly* to form adverbs* |
| **Character** | | | | | | |
| "The White Umbrella," Gish Jen, p. 85 | Understanding character traits* | Understanding figurative language* | Exploring point of view | Writing | Using complex sentences* | |
| "Gentleman of Rio en Medio," Juan A. A. Sedillo, p. 93 | Identifying major and minor characters | | Comparing and contrasting cultures* | | | Understanding words from Spanish* |
| "Raymond's Run," Toni Cade Bambara, p. 97 | Recognizing round and flat characters* | Identifying reasons | Writing an extension of the story | Writing Language Cross-curricular connection | Understanding parallelism* Using consistent verb tense* | Understanding idioms* |
| "A Canary's Ideas," Joaquim Maria Machado de Assis, p. 107 | Understanding characterization* | Making inferences about characters* | Writing a journal entry | Art | | |
| "The Day I Got Lost," Isaac Bashevis Singer, p. 113 | Understanding narrator* | Understanding caricature | Writing a story | Multicultural activity | Understanding verb tenses* | Understanding synonyms and antonyms* |
| **Setting** | | | | | | |
| "The Land and the Water," Shirley Ann Grau, p. 119 | Understanding setting* | Making inferences about setting | Describing a setting | Art Writing | Using semicolons* Understanding sentence fragments* | Choosing meaning to fit the context* |
| "Tears of the Sea," Olive Senior, p. 129 | Understanding descriptive details* | Analyzing the effect of setting on plot* | Using descriptive details | Cross-curricular connection Writing | Punctuating items in a series* | |
| "Crime on Mars," Arthur C. Clarke, p. 137 | Understanding time as part of setting | Identifying scientific details* | Continuing a science-fiction story | Cross-curricular connection Art | Using adverbs* | Recognizing new words* |

| Selection | Analyzing Literature | Critical Thinking and Reading | Thinking and Writing | Learning Options | Grammar in Action | Understanding Language |
|---|---|---|---|---|---|---|
| "The Tell-Tale Heart," Edgar Allan Poe, p. 145 | Describing atmosphere or mood | Choosing words to create atmosphere* | Writing to create atmosphere | | Appreciating connotations* | Choosing the meaning that fits the context* |
| "The Drummer Boy of Shiloh," Ray Bradbury, p. 151 | Recognizing historical details* | Identifying appropriate historical details | Writing about a historical setting | Cross-curricular connection | Understanding dialogue* Understanding active voice* | Understanding synonyms* |
| **Theme** | | | | | | |
| "The Smallest Dragonboy," Anne McCaffrey, p. 159 | Understanding theme* | Identifying realistic details* | Writing about rites of passage | Writing | Recognizing degrees of comparison* Using transitional words and phrases* | |
| "The Six Rows of Pompons," Toshio Mori, p. 173 | Understanding key statements* | Comparing and contrasting attitudes* | Writing a letter about theme | Writing Art | | |
| "Thank You, M'am," Langston Hughes, p. 179 | Using character to understand theme | Identifying generalizations* | Writing about a character | Speaking and listening | Understanding compound predicates* | Understanding compound words* |
| "The Man Without a Country," Edward Everett Hale, p. 185 | Recognizing symbols | Paraphrasing* | Writing about theme | | Understanding action verbs* Using sentence variety* | Choosing the meaning that fits the context* |
| "Flowers for Algernon," Daniel Keyes, p. 201 | Understanding point of view and theme* | Comparing and contrasting views | Writing about theme | Performance Writing | Understanding first-person narration* Understanding adverb clauses* Understanding second-person point of view* Understanding participles and participial phrases* | Understanding synonyms and antonyms* |

| Selection | Analyzing Literature | Critical Thinking and Reading | Thinking and Writing | Learning Options | Grammar in Action | Understanding Language |
|---|---|---|---|---|---|---|
| **Reading and Responding** | | | | | | |
| "The Medicine Bag," Virginia Driving Hawk Sneve, p. 225 | Reviewing the short story* | Evaluating a story* | Continuing a story | Writing | Using descriptive words* Using transitions* | |

**DRAMA**

| Selection | Analyzing Literature | Critical Thinking and Reading | Thinking and Writing | Learning Options | Grammar in Action | Understanding Language |
|---|---|---|---|---|---|---|
| *The House of Dies Drear,* Acts I and II, Richard Wesley, p. 245 | Understanding a screenplay* | Visualizing a screenplay* | Taking a character's point of view | Performance | Using informal language in dialogue* | |
| *The House of Dies Drear,* Acts III–V, p. 263 | Understanding suspense* | Appreciating atmosphere* | Writing a report | Cross-curricular connection | Using participal phrases* | |
| *The House of Dies Drear,* Acts VI and VII, p. 279 | Understanding setting* | Understanding setting and plot* | Writing a story | Art Cross-curricular connection Community connections | Using prepositions and prepositional phrases* | |
| *The Diary of Anne Frank,* Act I, Frances Goodrich and Albert Hackett, p. 303 | Appreciating the use of flashback | Predicting outcomes* | Writing as a character in a play | | Understanding simple sentences* Connecting ideas of equal weight* Understanding infinitives* Understanding imperative sentences* | Recognizing words from German* |
| *The Diary of Anne Frank,* Act II, p. 345 | Understanding characters and theme* | Finding support for opinions* | Writing a letter to the editor | | Using contractions* Understanding ellipses* | |

**NONFICTION**

| Selection | Analyzing Literature | Critical Thinking and Reading | Thinking and Writing | Learning Options | Grammar in Action | Understanding Language |
|---|---|---|---|---|---|---|
| **Reading Actively** | | | | | | |
| From *One Writer's Beginnings*, Eudora Welty, p. 377 | Understanding the informal essay | Comparing and contrasting opinions* | Writing about beginnings | Language | Understanding complex sentences* | Tracing word histories* |
| **Biographies and Personal Accounts** | | | | | | |
| "Harriet Tubman: Guide to Freedom," Ann Petry, p. 383 | Understanding biography* | Recognizing subjective details* | Writing a biography | Performance | Understanding subordinate clauses* Subject-verb agreement* | |
| "Roberto Clemente: A Bittersweet Memoir," Jerry Izenberg, p. 393 | Understanding the memoir* | Identifying primary sources | Writing a memoir | Speaking and listening Cross-curricular connection | Understanding dashes* | Using prefixes and suffixes to determine meaning* |
| From *I Know Why the Caged Bird Sings*, Maya Angelou, p. 403 | Understanding autobiography | Inferring the author's purpose* | Writing an autobiographical sketch | Art Speaking and listening | Using vivid adjectives* | Choosing the meaning that fits the context* |
| "Cub Pilot on the Mississippi," Mark Twain, p. 411 | Understanding conflicts* | Separating fact from opinion | Writing about conflict | Writing Cross-curricular connection | Appreciating dialect* Using precise, carefully selected verbs* | Using contrast clues* |
| "Fathers and Daughters," Le Ly Hayslip, p. 421 | Understanding the narrator in autobiography* | Recognizing the effect of point of view* | Writing from another point of view | Cross-curricular connection Art | Using punctuation marks in dialogue* | |
| **Essays for Enjoyment** | | | | | | |
| "Sancho," J. Frank Dobie, p. 431 | Understanding a narrative essay* | Putting events in chronological order* | Writing a letter | Art | Understanding prepositional phrases* | |
| "Debbie," James Herriot, p. 439 | Understanding characters in an essay | Comparing and contrasting characters* | Comparing and contrasting cats | Speaking and listening | Using quotation marks* | Understanding technical words* |
| "Animal Craftsmen," Bruce Brooks, p. 445 | Understanding the reflective essay* | Analyzing perspectives* | Writing about the wonder in nature | Writing Cross-curricular connection | Understanding pronoun case* | |

| Selection | Analyzing Literature | Critical Thinking and Reading | Thinking and Writing | Learning Options | Grammar in Action | Understanding Language |
|---|---|---|---|---|---|---|
| "Forest Fire," Anaïs Nin, p. 453 | Understanding descriptive essays* | Separating fact and opinion | Writing a descriptive essay | Writing | | Identifying word origins* |
| "The Indian All Around Us," Bernard De Voto, p. 457 | Understanding an expository essay* | Identifying main ideas* | Writing an expository essay | Multicultural activity | Using commas to separate items in a series* | |
| "The Trouble with Television," Robert MacNeil, p. 463 | Understanding the persuasive essay* | Recognizing connotative language | Writing a persuasive essay | Art | Using topic sentences* | Choosing the meaning that fits the context* |

**Essays in the Content Areas**

| Selection | Analyzing Literature | Critical Thinking and Reading | Thinking and Writing | Learning Options | Grammar in Action | Understanding Language |
|---|---|---|---|---|---|---|
| "Shooting Stars," Hal Borland, p. 469 | Understanding observation* | Recognizing observation and inference* | Observing | Writing | | |
| "The Sounds of Richard Rodgers," Ellen Goodman, p. 473 | Setting a purpose for reading | Recognizing subjective details* | Writing about an artistic person | Cross-curricular connection Multicultural activity | | Appreciating music terms* |
| "Dial Versus Digital," Isaac Asimov, p. 477 | Varying your rate of reading | Finding main ideas* | Writing about technology | Performance | | Using the prefix counter-* |
| "Hokusai: The Old Man Mad About Drawing," Stephen Longstreet, p. 481 | Taking notes* | Finding implied main ideas | Writing about art | Art | | Appreciating art terms* |
| "Talking About Writing," Ursula K. Le Guin, p. 485 | Understanding outlining* | Sequencing events | Writing advice about performing a skill | Community connections | | Using dictionary terms* |

**Reading and Responding**

| Selection | Analyzing Literature | Critical Thinking and Reading | Thinking and Writing | Learning Options | Grammar in Action | Understanding Language |
|---|---|---|---|---|---|---|
| "A to Z in Foods as Metaphors," Mimi Sheraton, p. 491 | Understanding an essay's purpose* | Interpreting metaphorical language* | Writing about language arts | Language | Understanding parenthetical expressions* | |

| Selection | Analyzing Literature | Critical Thinking and Reading | Thinking and Writing | Learning Options | Grammar in Action | Understanding Language |
|---|---|---|---|---|---|---|
| **Reading Actively** | | | | | | |
| "Drum Song," Wendy Rose, p. 503 | Appreciating imagery* | Understanding repetition* | Using imagery in writing | Writing Cross-curricular connection | | |
| **Narrative Poetry** | | | | | | |
| "Paul Revere's Ride," Henry Wadsworth Longfellow, p. 509 | Understanding a narrative poem | Sequencing events* | Summarizing the events in the poem | Speaking and listening Cross-curricular connection | | Using a thesaurus* |
| "Runagate Runagate," Robert Hayden, p. 517 | Understanding allusions* | Understanding how allusions affect meaning* | | | | |
| "Columbus," Joaquin Miller, p. 521 | Understanding rhythm and refrain | Making inferences about theme* | Writing a poem about a historical figure | Cross-curricular connection | | Appreciating old-fashioned words* |
| "Barbara Frietchie," John Greenleaf Whittier, p. 525 | Creating characters* | Making inferences about characters | Writing a definition of a hero | Cross-curricular connection | Understanding verb tense* | Choosing meaning to fit context* |
| **Figurative Language and Imagery** | | | | | | |
| "Lyric 17," José Garcia Villa, p. 532 | Understanding similes  Understanding similes, metaphors, and personification* | | Writing similes | Speaking and listening Art | | Appreciating diction* |
| "O Captain! My Captain!" Walt Whitman, p. 534 | Understanding metaphors | | | | | |
| "Jetliner," Naoshi Koriyama, p. 537 | Understanding personification | | Writing about figurative language | | | |
| "The Term," William Carlos Williams, p. 540 | Understanding imagery | | | Writing | | |
| "Reflections Dental," Phyllis McGinley, p. 542 | Understanding humorous images | | | Writing | | |
| "Ring Out, Wild Bells," Alfred, Lord Tennyson, p. 544 | Recognizing and interpreting imagery* | | Writing a patterned poem | Multicultural activity | | Recognizing denotations and connotations of words* |

| Selection | Analyzing Literature | Critical Thinking and Reading | Thinking and Writing | Learning Options | Grammar in Action | Understanding Language |
|---|---|---|---|---|---|---|
| "Old Man," Ricardo Sánchez, p. 548<br><br>"Southern Mansion," Arna Bontemps, p. 550<br><br>"Taught Me Purple," Evelyn Tooley Hunt, p. 551 | Understanding symbolism<br><br>Interpreting symbols carefully* | | Writing about a symbol<br><br>Writing about symbolism | | | Understanding synonyms and antonyms* |

**Lyric Poetry**

| Selection | Analyzing Literature | Critical Thinking and Reading | Thinking and Writing | Learning Options | Grammar in Action | Understanding Language |
|---|---|---|---|---|---|---|
| "Four Little Foxes," Lew Sarett, p. 556<br><br>"Harlem Night Song," Langston Hughes, p. 558<br><br>"Blue-Butterfly Day," Robert Frost, p. 559<br><br>"For My Sister Molly Who in the Fifties," Alice Walker, p. 560 | Understanding lyric poetry | Making inferences about mood* | Writing a lyric poem | Writing | | Recognizing sensory language* |
| "Silver," Walter de la Mare, p. 564<br><br>"Forgotten Language," Shel Silverstein, p. 565<br><br>"Blow, Blow, Thou Winter Wind," William Shakespeare, p. 566 | Understanding alliteration*<br>Understanding parallel structure | | | Performance | | Understanding poetic language* |
| "Hog Calling," Morris Bishop, p. 569<br><br>"I Raised a Great Hullabaloo," Anonymous, p. 569 | Understanding limericks* | | Writing a limerick | Art<br>Speaking and listening<br>Language | | Using rhythmic language* |

**Facets of Nature**

| Selection | Analyzing Literature | Critical Thinking and Reading | Thinking and Writing | Learning Options | Grammar in Action | Understanding Language |
|---|---|---|---|---|---|---|
| Two Haiku, Bashō and Moritake, p. 573 | Understanding haiku* | | Writing a haiku | | | Choosing words* |

| Selection | Analyzing Literature | Critical Thinking and Reading | Thinking and Writing | Learning Options | Grammar in Action | Understanding Language |
|---|---|---|---|---|---|---|
| "January," John Updike, p. 576<br>"Winter Moon," Langston Hughes p. 578<br>"Song of the Sky Loom," Tewa Indian, p. 579<br>"New World," N. Scott Momaday, p. 580 | Recognizing sensory language* | Paraphrasing a poem | Using sensory language<br>Writing a poem | Speaking and listening<br>Writing<br>Cross-curricular connection<br>Art | Recognizing verb tense* | Writing sensory language* |

**Perceptions**

| Selection | Analyzing Literature | Critical Thinking and Reading | Thinking and Writing | Learning Options | Grammar in Action | Understanding Language |
|---|---|---|---|---|---|---|
| "The City Is So Big," Richard García, p. 586<br>"Concrete Mixers," Patricia Hubbell, p. 587<br>"Southbound on the Freeway," May Swenson, p. 588 | Understanding free verse* | Reading free verse* | Writing Free verse | | | |
| "400-Meter Free Style," Maxine Kumin, p. 591 | Understanding concrete poetry* | | Writing a concrete poem | Writing<br>Cross-curricular connection | | Choosing the meaning that fits the context* |

**Choices**

| Selection | Analyzing Literature | Critical Thinking and Reading | Thinking and Writing | Learning Options | Grammar in Action | Understanding Language |
|---|---|---|---|---|---|---|
| "Identity," Julio Noboa Polanco, p. 598<br>"The Road Not Taken," Robert Frost, p. 600 | Hearing the speaker's voice* | Interpreting differences in metaphors | | | | Finding synonyms* |
| "Woman With Flower," Naomi Long Madgett, p. 603<br>"The Other Pioneers," Roberto Félix Salazar, p. 606 | Understanding tone* | Making inferences about a speaker* | Experimenting with tone | | | |

## POETRY (continued)

| Selection | Analyzing Literature | Critical Thinking and Reading | Thinking and Writing | Learning Options | Grammar in Action | Understanding Language |
|---|---|---|---|---|---|---|
| **Reading and Responding** | | | | | | |
| "The Story-Teller," Mark Van Doren, p. 609 | Understanding rhyme* | Defining poetry* | Retelling a story | Art<br>Writing | | |

## THE AMERICAN FOLK TRADITION

| Selection | Analyzing Literature | Critical Thinking and Reading | Thinking and Writing | Learning Options | Grammar in Action | Understanding Language |
|---|---|---|---|---|---|---|
| **In the Beginning** | | | | | | |
| "The Four Elements," José Griego y Maestas and Rudolfo A. Anaya, p. 621 | Understanding a myth* | Appreciating personification* | | | | |
| "The Spirit Chief Names the Animal People," Mourning Dove, p. 623 | Understanding creation myths* | Understanding cause and effect* | Writing a myth | Performance | | |
| "How the Snake Got Poison" p. 629<br>"Why the Waves Have Whitecaps," Zora Neale Hurston, p. 630 | Understanding African American folklore* | Appreciating imagination* | Writing an imaginative folk tale | Art<br>Performance | | |
| **Heroes and Legends** | | | | | | |
| "The Girl Who Hunted Rabbits," Zuñi Indian Legend, p. 635 | Understanding a legend | Making inferences from a legend* | Retelling a legend | Cross-curricular connection<br>Art | Understanding conjunctions*<br>Understanding prepositional phrases* | Choosing meaning to fit context |

## THE AMERICAN FOLK TRADITION (continued)

| Selection | Analyzing Literature | Critical Thinking and Reading | Thinking and Writing | Learning Options | Grammar in Action | Understanding Language |
|---|---|---|---|---|---|---|
| "Hammerman," Adrien Stoutenberg, p. 643<br><br>"John Henry," Traditional, p. 650 | Understanding the folk hero<br><br>Understanding the oral tradition* | Making inferences about characters* | Writing another adventure | Performance<br><br>Cross-curricular connection | | Choosing effective synonyms*<br>Determining word meaning from Latin roots |
| "Johnny Appleseed," Rosemary Carr Benét, p. 655 | Understanding characterization* | Making inferences about characters* | Comparing and contrasting | Community connections<br>Art | | |
| "Chicoria," José Griego y Maestas and Rudolfo A. Anaya, p. 659 | Appreciating the clever character* | Making inferences about culture* | Writing a folk tale | Speaking and listening | | |
| **Tall Tales** | | | | | | |
| From "The People, Yes," Carl Sandburg, p. 665 | Understanding a yarn* | | Writing a yarn | Art<br>Writing | | Appreciating compound words* |
| "Paul Bunyan of the North Woods," Carl Sandburg, p. 669 | Understanding a folk tale | Making generalizations about a folk tale* | Writing a response to critical comment | Writing | | Appreciating homophones* |
| "Pecos Bill: The Cyclone," Harold W. Felton, p. 673 | Understanding conflict in a folk tale* | Identifying reasons* | Writing a description of a conflict | Cross-curricular connection | Using precise words* | |
| "Davy Crockett's Dream," Davy Crockett, p. 681<br><br>"Tussle with a Bear," Davy Crockett, p. 683 | Understanding a tall tale* | Recognizing exaggeration<br><br>Appreciating dialect | Creating a tall tale | Art<br><br>Cross-curricular connection | | Appreciating dialect* |

*T21*

| Selection | Analyzing Literature | Critical Thinking and Reading | Thinking and Writing | Learning Options | Grammar in Action | Understanding Language |
|---|---|---|---|---|---|---|
| *The Pearl,* Chapters 1–3, John Steinbeck, p. 695 | Understanding characters in a parable<br>Understanding character and point of view* | | Writing from Juana's point of view | Writing<br>Art | Using dashes*<br>Understanding intensive and reflexive pronouns* | Appreciating words from Spanish* |
| *The Pearl,* Chapters 4–6, p. 717 | Understanding plot and theme | Recognizing cause and effect* | Responding to literary criticism | Writing<br>Cross-curricular connection | Understanding gerunds*<br>Understanding participles*<br>Using specific verbs* | Appreciating vivid verbs* |

# THE READER'S RESPONSE JOURNAL

## Dr. Charles R. Cooper

University of California
San Diego, California

A Reader's Response Journal can be a very important component of a literature course using *Prentice Hall Literature.* Along with a wide range of other writing activities catalogued later in this section, many of the writing activities in the text can be collected in a student's Reader's Response Journal. For example, students could enter into their Reader's Response Journals the text's writing-prior-to-reading activities; the Critical Thinking and Reading activities requiring writing; prewriting, notes, and drafts of revised essays written for the Your Writing Process assignments.

A Reader's Response Journal is a place for students to write often and informally about their reading. They may write nearly every day. Each time, they may write only a few sentences, a page, or more. The writing must be legible, so that you and other students can read it; but it does not have to be entirely correct. It is rarely revised. It is usually not planned carefully. Instead, students start writing quickly and let their ideas or examples develop *as they write.* This kind of writing can best be considered exploratory. Though it should be honest and engage the reading seriously, it can also be playful.

A collection of journal entries can provide the basis for later, carefully planned formal essays, of course, but that does not have to be its primary purpose. Most teachers who assign Reader's Response Journals consider their primary benefits to be engagement with literature, testing and clarifying of responses and ideas through writing, experimentation with various kinds of writing about literature, a record of students' progress through the course, and a repository of material to be used in later assignments.

Though many school and college teachers assign Reader's Response Journals—they are also called reader's logs or learner's journals or academic journals—some teachers remain skeptical. It is not unreasonable to assume that unplanned, exploratory, unrevised writing leads only in circles, rather than toward shaped, formal essays. A teacher might ask: Doesn't casual writing involve only casual thinking? If students' errors are accepted in any of their assigned writing, won't they be practicing error rather than perfecting their prose? How can time be found in an already full course for a major new strand of work? How will reluctant student writers respond to demands for still more writing? How can time be found to evaluate such large amounts of writing? If all students keep journals, what unforeseen problems of classroom management result?

Some of these appropriately skeptical questions can be answered here, the answers coming from reported practices of many classroom teachers. (Perhaps the best source is *The Journal Book,* edited by Toby Fulwiler and published by Heineman Educational Books, 70 Court Street, Portsmouth, N.H. 03801. Teachers' journals, like *English Journal,* now regularly report teachers' experiences with Reader's Response Journals.) Teachers who advocate the use of Reader's Response Journals rely on a fundamentally important idea about writing: Writing fulfills two different but complementary functions—exploratory and expository (or expressive and transactional). These teachers, supported by current researchers and theorists of language, believe that better expository writing results from the kind of exploratory writing that fills students' journals. These teachers also believe that even brief journal writings require critical thinking. They know that over several months of personal choice and assigned journal writings, students will practice a wide range of thinking and writing activities.

## Getting Your Students Started

The most representative advice for getting started comes from the Commission on Composition of the National Council of Teachers of English (NCTE). Here are their "Guidelines for Using Journals in the School Setting," published in 1986:

1. Explain that journals are neither "diaries" nor "class notebooks," but borrow features from each: Like the diary, journals are written in the first person about issues the writer cares about; like the class notebook, journals are concerned with the content of a particular course.
2. Ask students to buy looseleaf notebooks. This way students can hand in to you only that which pertains directly to your class, keeping more intimate entries private.
3. Suggest that students divide journals in several sections, one for your course, one for another

course, another for private entries. When you collect the journal, you need only collect that which pertains to your own course.

4. Ask students to do short journal writes in class; write with them; and share your writing with the class. Since you don't grade journals, the fact that you write too gives the assignment more value.

5. Every time you ask students to write in class, do something active and deliberate with what they have written: Have volunteers read whole entries aloud; have everyone read one sentence to the whole class; have neighbors share one passage with each other, etc. (In each case, students who do not like what they have written should have the right to pass.) Sharing the writing like this also gives credibility to a nongraded assignment.

6. Count but do not grade student journals. While it's important not to qualitatively evaluate specific journal entries—for here students must be allowed to take risks—good journals should count in some quantitative way: a certain number of points, a plus added to a grade, as an in-class resource for taking tests.

7. Do not write back to every entry; it will burn you out. Instead, skim-read journals and write responses to entries that especially concern you.

8. At the end of the term, ask students to put in (a) page numbers, (b) a title for each entry, (c) a table of contents, and (d) an evaluative conclusion. This synthesizing activity asks journal writers to treat these documents seriously and to review what they have written over a whole term of study.

Some teachers ask students to keep a spiralbound notebook, which can be more easily carried around by the student, gathered up in quantity by the teacher at evaluation time, or filed more readily somewhere in the classroom for classes or students reluctant to do homework. Other teachers prefer looseleaf notebooks (recommended in Point 2 of the NCTE guidelines) because they can take up and evaluate just a few pages at a time.

Write with your students at first: They may never have seen anyone writing in a journal. You can help them see what you expect in a journal entry by reading yours aloud. They will be reading some of their entries aloud in class, but you may also want to duplicate exemplary entries for the class to examine more carefully. You could share with them selections from published journals.

## Evaluation

To persist at the frequent writing required in a Reader's Response Journal, students will need rewards and encouragement. Let them know at the start how you will read and evaluate their journals. Inform them of the contribution of their journal work to their total grades.

Some teachers make a certain grade (perhaps a "C") contingent on completion of all Reader's Response Journal assignments. Some give points for completing each entry, with bonus points for especially insightful entries. Some teachers base as much as half of the course grade on journals.

It is important to look fairly soon at the journals for the first time so that you can ensure that everyone is off to a good start.

## Reader's Response Journal Activities

Following are several classroom-proven journal writing activities. You can choose from among them to devise an appropriate Reader's Response Journal plan for any of your classes.

**Prewriting for Essays** A Reader's Response Journal can be a valuable repository of students' prewriting for essays and other writing activities. The early writing activities up to the draft could be entered into the journal, where they are immediately available for class or small-group sharing and discussion.

**Answering Prepared Questions** During or after reading a work, students can answer specific questions that you assign. These can be especially valuable frequent journal assignments when students are reading a longer novel or play. These questions can very well be designed as prewriting for essays, or they can have the purpose of exploring and clarifying important passages in the reading, perhaps as preparation for class discussion.

Students must understand that answering questions in the Reader's Response Journal is different from answering questions on a test. In the journal, they should write in an exploratory (even playful) way. They should be taking risks, expecting to be surprised by what they write, knowing they will make discoveries *during* the writing. They do not have to find the answer and plan their response carefully before writing, as though they are answering an essay question in a test. They should just start writing and let the writing lead them to an answer.

Occasionally you may want students to revise their answers to important questions. At the beginning of class, in small groups, students can compare and discuss their answers to a question. They can then bring problems and questions to the teacher and other students in the class for discussion. Students then revise their original answers as homework.

**Writing Questions About Puzzling Passages** Students can list questions they have about puzzling passages. This activity can encourage students to be active, questioning readers. The questions are good discussion starters.

**Predicting What Comes Next** From research on the process we know that skilled readers are always making predictions about what comes next. You can encourage students to make predictions by asking them, especially with longer works, to write down their predictions in the Reader's Response Journal. You can assign predictions at timely points in the reading of a work.

**Writing Alternative Beginnings and Endings to Stories** Students may be asked to write alternative beginnings and endings to stories or chapters in novels, alternatives based on a careful reading of the story and relying on the story's characters and plot. Students may also usefully be asked to write a justification (an argument with reasons) for their alternative beginnings and endings.

This activity leads to productive class discussions about the structure of stories. Students invariably enjoy sharing their alternative beginnings and endings for a story read in common.

**Participating in Class Meetings** The Reader's Response Journal can be useful in class. Students can write to focus their energy and attention at the beginning of class. They can write at various moments during class—to summarize a discussion, quietly argue a point in a debate too hot for further rowdy class discussion, react to part of a work read aloud, analyze the style of a brief passage, or contrast two brief passages just before small-group or whole-class discussion. They can reflect on a class meeting. In all of these ways, the Reader's Response Journal becomes a valuable adjunct to class discussion.

**Copying and Commenting on Favorite Passages** Students can copy out brief passages and comment on the passages in any way they like. They can explain why they like a passage (its style or art), or they can write about what it evokes in their personal experience. Copying (old-fashioned as it seems) remains a useful way of learning about syntax and style.

A variation on copy/comment is an activity Phillis Brooks at the University of California at Berkeley calls "persona paraphrase." In this activity, students imitate a sentence or a paragraph in their reading by supplying their own content to the exact syntax of the original.

**Making Personal Responses** Personal response and evaluation are central to literary study. Personal response to literature is a natural first step toward analysis and interpretation. A Reader's Response Journal gives response a prominent place in your course. The various activities that follow are valuable in their own right, and they can also lead to personal or reflective essays on assigned readings. All of these activities are generic: They can be used repeatedly in just the form below with any kind of literary work. Consequently, you could select a few of them to use as continuing response activities in a course.

**Responding to the Most Important Word, Sentence, and Passage** Ask students to select what seems to *them* to be the most important word, sentence, and brief passage in a work. They copy their choices into the journal and then explain why they chose them. The choices are theirs, but they must have reasons for their choices. These journal entries can lead to interesting class discussions.

**Associating Personal Experiences** Students can connect what they've read to their own experience. You tell them, "Briefly describe a part of the work that reminds you of something in your own experience. Tell the story of what you were reminded of."

**Expressing Identification With Characters** Identifying with characters is central to the process of reading fiction. Two teachers in British Columbia have suggested the following questions to help students express responses to characters in the Reader's Response Journal (G. L. Sampson and N. Carlman, "A Hierarchy of Student Responses to Literature," *English Journal,* 71 [January 1982], 54–57).

Questions to initiate student responses:

1. What do you think of the main character?
2. Why do you like or dislike him or her?
3. What do you think of the antagonist?
4. Why do you like or dislike him or her?

Questions for reflection on overt characteristics:

1. What similarities are there among the characters you like?
2. What similarities are there among the characters you dislike?
3. What generalizations can you make now about why you like or dislike certain characters?

Questions for reflection on inferred characteristics:

1. What are the values of the characters you like?
2. How do these values compare with your values?
3. What are the values of the characters you dislike?
4. How do these values compare with your values?
5. What generalizations can you make now about how characters' values affect the way you feel about them?

**Giving Unguided Responses** You can simply invite students to write about anything at all in response to the reading, perhaps giving them guidelines as general as "Write at least a half [or one] page." Or you can offer suggestions for students' unguided responses. A California teacher (D. Cookston, "This Guy Can Really Write," in M. Barr, P. D'Arcy, M. K. Healy, eds., *What's Going On*, Boynton/Cook, 1982, pp. 196–217) provides suggestions like the following for Part II of John Steinbeck's *East of Eden*.

You might respond to
—nostalgia for the past.
—hope for the future.
—Adam's blindness to Cathy's flaws.
—the decency of the Hamilton family.
—Kate's plot against Eve.
—Samuel's advice to Adam: "Act out being alive, like a play. And after awhile, a long while, it will be true."
—"And I guess a man's importance in the world can be measured by the quality and number of his glories."

**Reflecting on Earlier Journal Entries** In this variation, sometimes called "double-entry" or "dialectical" journal writing, students write only on the right of two facing pages about their reading as they read, reserving the left page for commentary, reflection, and interpretation afterward. Here are one teacher's instructions about what to put on the right page.

1. Times when your reading changes:
   You see something you didn't see before.
   You recognize a pattern—the images start to overlap, gestures or phrases recur, some details seem associated with each other.
   The story suddenly seems to you to be about something different from what you thought.
   You discover that you were misreading.
   The writer introduces a new context or new perspective.
2. Times when you are surprised or puzzled:
   Something just doesn't fit.

   Things don't make sense—pose explicitly the question or problem that occurs to you.
3. Details that seem important and that make you look again.
4. Way in which the story makes you speculate about life.
5. Your first impression of the ending—what "ended"?

And on the left page:

Whereas the right-hand pages involve your direct reactions to the text, your first gestures at making meanings out of it, the left-hand pages are for a completely different activity. When you finish a story or a group of stories by the same writer, go back and use the facing pages to comment on your original observations and to make something of them. Is there a pattern to the changes you experienced? Does the ending tie them together? Why did you misread when you did? Then reflect on yourself as a reader—what do you focus on? What do you care most about? What do you disregard? Where do you have to strain to follow the story sympathetically? Finally, as you make these reflections on your reading experience, discuss your emerging sense of how the story works and what it's about. (Gary Lindberg, "The Journal Conference: From Dialectic to Dialogue," in Toby Fulwiler, *The Journal Book*.)

Some teachers rely solely on the double-entry journal, giving no specific assignments like those in many other activities catalogued here.

**Reflecting on the Course** Students can use the Reader's Response Journal for a very important task—reflecting on their own learning. They can describe and evaluate their development as readers and writers in the course. Questions like these would be appropriate:

—Do your own personal reading interests seem to be changing? If so, explain how.
—At what moment during the reading [of a particular text] did you feel your own attitudes most challenged? How did you react to that moment? What do you make of your reaction?
—As a result of your reading [of a particular text] have you changed any of your beliefs, attitudes, or values? If so, explain what happened and how it happened.
—What have you learned about reading literature (as a special form of reading) during this course? Describe what you have learned.
—Think about the way your Reader's Response

Journal influenced your development as a reader and writer during this unit. Describe what you learned by keeping a Reader's Response Journal.

—What kinds of writing about literature have you most enjoyed in this course? Least enjoyed? Describe specific writings and say why you feel as you do about them.

—As a reader and writer, what can you do now that you couldn't do before this course began?

—What one writing assignment was most valuable to you during this course? Describe this assignment and what you wrote. Explain why it was valuable.

## Summary of Reader's Response Journal Activities

You will want students to vary the writing in the Reader's Response Journal. This summary of writing activities can be a checklist to help you evaluate the variety of journal assignments you are giving.

Prewriting for Essays
Answering Prepared Questions
Writing Questions About Puzzling Passages
Predicting What Comes Next
Writing Alternative Beginnings and Endings to Stories
Participating in Class Meetings
Copying and Commenting on Favorite Passages
Making Personal Responses
Responding to the Most Important Word, Sentence, and Passage
Associated Personal Experiences
Expressing Identification with Characters
Giving Unguided Responses
Reflecting on Earlier Journal Entries
Reflecting on the Course

The Reader's Response Journal activities may be summarized in another way—as specific thinking and writing strategies. The following list illustrates the surprisingly wide range of intellectual activity required in a Reader's Response Journal. (Mary Weber, a high-school English teacher and curriculum consultant in the San Diego schools, prepared this summary.)

Listing of
  actions or events in a plot sequence
  different versions of a story
  differing points of view
Responding to prepared questions on content
Questioning a puzzling passage

Summarizing
  a class discussion about a work
  plot in a work
  findings in log writings
  information or ideas in an article or book about a literary work
Predicting development in a longer work
Imitating the style of a passage
Commenting on a passage copied from
  the work
  its style
  its art
  its relevance to its historical context
  its relevance to the present
Reacting personally to
  a passage (as a key scene, as illustrative of the writer's art, theme, etc.)
  a character or characters (values, personality, actions)
  a work's content, theme, structure, etc.
  a group or class discussion on a work
Categorizing
  characters by qualities they have in common
  actions in a plot
  different works by elements they have in common
Analyzing an aspect of a work
  style
  characterization
  plot
  theme
  setting
  meanings of selected quotations
Analyzing similarities and differences in
  literary works
  characters
  events
  settings
  passages
Justifying the selection of a
  word
  line
  sentence
  passage
Arguing about ideas in a work
Reflecting on learning accomplished in
  reading a work or several works
  writing about literature
Evaluating
  a work as a whole
  the theme, characterization, language, etc., of a work
  writing about literature as an activity

# SUCCESS STRATEGIES FOR THE AT-RISK STUDENT

## Dr. Ellen Lees Backstrom
Former English Department Chair
Wm. F. Hart Union High School District
Santa Clarita, California

Who is the at-risk student? How will we have to adapt to meet the needs of this student? For example, will we have to alter our lesson plans to facilitate the at-risk student's learning in our classrooms? Will expectations and/or assessment have to change in order to accommodate at-risk students? In order to examine possible answers to these questions, we must develop a working vocabulary: When you think of an at-risk student, what characteristics come to mind? What characteristics would you add to the list below?

### Characteristics of At-Risk Students

- Bored—short attention span
- Excessive absenteeism
- Fears failure
- Low self-esteem
- Discipline problem
- Health problems
- Inattentive—lack of motivation
- Less able
- Language impaired
- Disadvantaged
- Prone to drop out
- Dependent

These characteristics describe certain behaviors. They are not necessarily the causes of the student's being at risk. These behaviors can be changed. We all know of individuals who have overcome these behaviors. We know of specific teachers who have motivated students to change and schools that have dedicated themselves to the success of all. Therefore, our working definition of an at-risk student is simple: The at-risk student is anyone who is not working up to potential.

## A Suitable Environment

The story of the at-risk student can be turned into a tale of success, not failure. Student success will be achieved if there is a supportive learning environment that takes into consideration the following:

- Appropriate learning outcomes
- Specific content that engages students
- Communication of expectations
- Model task related thinking and problem solving
- Lesson strategies that address individual needs
- Learning activities that address learning styles
- Instructional materials that motivate
- Authentic assessment that links assessment with curriculum and instruction

How can we provide a supportive environment? To start, teachers must believe that underachievers can achieve. They must provide learning options that will help the underachievers succeed. These options are keys to success.

## Creating a Program for Success

Keeping in mind the qualities of a supportive learning environment, the teacher can create a program for success by setting realistic, attainable goals and by utilizing authentic assessment strategies such as performance-based assessment and portfolio assessment. In addition, the teacher can help students to recognize the connection between effort and outcome. All too often, students do not see that they can turn failure into success simply by working a little "smarter," not necessarily a little harder. Rewards also help. The teacher can motivate students by supplying both extrinsic and intrinsic rewards.

### Extrinsic Motivators

- Provide rewards/incentives
  - Positive postcards home or phone calls
  - Time in class to pursue special interests
- Provide prizes
  - Play money to bank for prizes
  - Raffle tickets
  - Free homework passes
- Create an atmosphere of healthy competition

### Intrinsic Motivators

- Adapt tasks to interests
- Vary activities
- Allow choices, individual responses, and decisions
- Provide immediate feedback
- Allow enough time to finish projects
- Include higher-level objectives always

As teachers, we must stimulate students to learn. If we show interest in learning, students can and will use our behavior as a model. If we project enthusiasm, students will believe we have something interesting and valuable to teach. If we clearly communicate our expectations, students will strive to meet those expectations. In our classrooms, we must minimize anxiety, or fear of failure, and stimulate creativity and curiosity by making students feel safe enough to make mistakes. All too often, students don't try because they feel their answers will be wrong. In addition, we must make students responsible for their own learning by collaborating on goals and objectives and maintaining a balance between teacher-centered and student-centered learning.

## Special Problems

We find at-risk students everywhere. They run the gamut from AP classes to regular classes to remediation classes. Whatever the placement, we find that at-risk students usually have academic and/or social difficulties. Disorganization may be the first weakness to strengthen. Providing strategies for students to become organized will lead to improvement in their academic performance. For example, some teachers have students use a daily planner to get themselves organized. Others have them create "To Do" lists at the end of each day and then refer to these lists at the start of the next day. They can create their own "To Do" list on the computer. The idea is to empower the students so that they take responsibility for themselves. Another strategy is to have students take a partner to keep each other on track, especially if one partner is absent.

Another problem is dependency. At-risk students often grow dependent on the teacher or on the class routine. They may not have had enough successful experiences to enable them to rely on and trust their own abilities. Collaborative learning strategies often help students build their confidence and overcome feelings of dependency. And breaking the routine or doing something unexpected not only stimulates interest but also weans students away from dependency.

At-risk students also may process information differently—and their way of processing information may be in direct opposition to the ways in which you structure your lessons. Rather than focusing on what these students cannot accomplish, it might be easier to concentrate on a methodology that will help these students grasp the material. Whatever methods you choose, keep in mind that one of your objectives should include activities that meet the needs of all learning modalities (visual, auditory, and kinesthetic). Remember that a 100% diet of one item may be deadly. The activities must balance with the instruction. There is a big difference between looking at students as a problem and labeling them, and looking at your classroom as part of the problem and finding ways to improve the classroom through a balance of heterogeneous groupings, equal interactions, and student-centered activities.

## Activities for Success

Here is a list of sample activities that create success in the classroom. Many of these activities can be based on literature, using as a springboard the plot and characters of selections students have read.

### Writing and Illustrating

For a specific audience
  young readers
  older readers
  cross-generational
For television and/or
  movies
Letters to famous people, authors, or
  penpals in other
  countries
Surveys
Questionnaires and
  interview guides
Advertisements and
  commercials
Diary entries
Cartoons
Obituaries
Headlines
Bumper stickers
Maps
Timelines
Adapted classics and
  mixed-up classics
Songs, rap music
Storyboards
Dear Abby columns
Postcards
Literary report cards
Wanted posters
Crossword puzzles
Collages
Mobiles
Time capsules
Murals
Fine-art re-creations

### Creative Dramatics

Skits
Readers theater
Scenarios
Inventions
Role-playing
Soap operas
Singing telegrams
Videotapes
Audio tapes
Scavenger hunts
Five senses
Debates
Mime
Puppets
Dance
Poses
Simulations
Line ups
Hot Seat (Twenty
  Questions)
Who Am I?
Pictionary
Win, Lose, or
  Draw
Charades

Activities like the ones above allow teachers to move in three directions. First, they allow the teacher to create an environment of active learning. Next, they allow the teacher to link active learning with higher-level thinking skills. Third, they provide the opportunity for the teacher to tie it all together with cooperative learning. Thus the teacher can provide choice, balance, and control in order to create a classroom with a learning environment that invites student success.

# ASSESSMENT AND EVALUATION IN PRENTICE HALL LITERATURE
## Ruth Townsend

former English Teacher and Teacher Coordinator
Yorktown High School
Yorktown Heights, New York

> Education . . . Helping the child realize
> his [her] potentialities.
> —Erich Fromm

There are many valid ways to educate students, to help them achieve success as readers and writers, speakers and listeners. However, the way students' learning is assessed and evaluated often determines the quality of that learning. *Prentice Hall Literature* offers a variety of assessment and evaluation strategies to promote students' progress toward mastery of language arts outcomes.

## LEARNING OUTCOMES

The goal of language arts instruction is to make students successful readers, writers, speakers, and thinkers who can demonstrate the following learning outcomes:

1. As readers, students
   - respond personally, aesthetically, and critically to diverse texts
   - collect facts and ideas, discover relationships, and make inferences
   - make critical judgments, analyze, evaluate, and draw conclusions.
2. As writers, students
   - express personal feelings and ideas in a variety of modes
   - communicate information, ideas, and beliefs to a variety of audiences
   - express their ideas critically and evaluatively express their ideas persuasively and provide support for those ideas.
3. As speakers and listeners, students
   - express themselves orally to entertain and to inform
   - interpret information and apply it
   - evaluate ideas according to personal and/or objective criteria.

## ASSESSMENT AND EVALUATION OPTIONS

Measuring student growth begins with assessment, an ongoing process of gathering information to meet many different evaluation purposes. *Prentice Hall Literature* provides a wide range of assessment strategies and procedures, including testing.

## Testing Options

### Selection Tests

1. Part A of the Selection Test contains multiple-choice questions. These types of test items play a role in the initial stages of the assessment and evaluation of your students' growth toward mastery of the learning outcomes. You may use tests on content knowledge as reading checks and as the basis of discussions; you may also use them for collaborative reviews of reading and to prompt personal and critical responses. You may choose to have students work independently or collaboratively to frame their answers to each question and to justify them with textual evidence. You may want students to extend their discussion of the story beyond the printed questions to develop their own questions and to evaluate the universal relevance of the story.

2. Part B of the Selection Test is an essay question. Essay questions offer your students the opportunity to go beyond the limited responses of the multiple-choice items to explore an idea in some depth.

3. Part 3 of the Selection Test is a Reader's Response question. This type of question elicits a personal response to literature.

## Other Testing Options

*Prentice Hall Literature* offers a number of writing assignments and expressive activities that may be used as tests to assess and evaluate your students' mastery of the learning outcomes.

## ALTERNATIVE ASSESSMENT OPTIONS

Testing is only one way to measure comprehension of ideas, reasoning processes, or problem-solving skills. Assessment is a continuing process linked with curriculum and instruction.

In a student-centered classroom, you assess and evaluate growth in many ways, each of which motivates your students to use language for effective communication. The student-centered classroom enables students to perceive themselves as partners with you in the learning process. That process includes their ability to assess their own competence, determine goals for their own achievement, and judge their own performance. As your students learn to assess and evaluate their own work, they become empowered to take increasing responsibility for their own learning.

You can assist your students in developing self-assessment skills by involving them in the following activities:

Reader's Response Journals
Alternative and Expressive Assignments
Protocols
Peer Review
Collaborative Assessment
Student Portfolios

## Reader's Response Journals

Reader's Response journals help students become conscious of their own thinking processes by asking them to make observations of what they read and to respond personally based on those observations. Making observations about a text requires readers to be as objective as possible. Of course some personal judgment is involved in deciding which details of the text are relevant and appropriate to "observe." However, when making observations students concentrate on factual information and cite concrete details of language or description to back up their observations.

Responding personally to a text is also an important part of active reading. After students have recorded each observation, they react personally, making inferences and predictions, evaluating details, and raising questions. They may question the significance of details they have observed, the meaning of events they have recorded, or the reasons for human behavior they have noted. They may also explore the implications of the connections between what they have read and their own experiences, other pieces of literature, and the world in which they live. Because students' questions are generated by their personal responses to what is otherwise objective and concrete, they can see the relationship between logical inferences and concrete details.

A student's response journal may look like this sample based on a reading of John Steinbeck's *The Pearl.*

| *Observations* | *Personal Responses* |
|---|---|
| Steinbeck says this story is a parable and that everyone can take his own meaning from it. | I know parables are stories with moral lessons, that according to the "Guide for Reading" illustrate a universal truth. I don't usually like that kind of story, and I bet there's a hidden meaning in this story we're all supposed to get. |
| Kino and his family live in a house on the beach and sleep on mats. And their baby, Coyotito, sleeps in a hanging box. | These people seem poor but happy. Maybe they don't know any better. I can't imagine being happy and poor, but I guess money can't buy happiness either. |
| When Kino beats and stamps the scorpion, "The Song of the Enemy roared in his ears." | This is a very strong contrast to the "Song of the Family" that filled Kino's heart just a few minutes earlier. |

## Alternative and Expressive Assignments

Alternative assignments challenge students to present their critical reading responses imaginatively. They make judgments about character development, the significance of plot details and stylistic techniques, including characteristics of diction, imagery, and syntax. Judgments about literary elements may lend support to students' ideas of theme and the universal significance of a text, or they may cause students to rethink or re-envision their initial responses to the reading. These are sample alternative assignments:

Writing letters to real and imagined audiences
Writing in the persona of a character in the text
Comparing literary figures to real people
Writing investigative reports
Writing editorials
Writing human interest stories
Creating speeches in various personae
Creating commercials or advertisements

You will find examples of alternative assignments throughout the student text under Thinking and Writing, in the Annotated Teacher's Edition, and in the Teaching Portfolio. For example, here is an Alternate Composition Assignment from the Teaching Portfolio for *The Pearl:*

Imagine that you are the doctor. You have just heard the news about Kino's discovery of the giant pearl. How do you feel about having turned him away from your door? Why do you decide you will go to his family? Keeping in character, freewrite to explore your feelings about the event. Then write a letter to a friend telling about the event and what you plan to do. Make sure that you use a tone that reflects the doctor's character.

Expressive assignments stimulate creativity by encouraging students to re-envision the text and to re-create portions of it. Here are some examples of expressive assignments:

Writing a new ending for a selection
Adding scenes
Changing the point of view
Writing a modern version or a parody
Conducting a trial of a character
Holding elections for literary characters
Inventing a newspaper or magazine based on a selection
Writing a poem based on the selection
Making a video

You will find examples of alternative and expressive assignments throughout the student text, in the Teaching Portfolio, and in the Annotated Teacher's Edition. The Thinking and Writing assignment for *The Pearl* on page 715 of the student text is an expressive assignment.

> Choose an incident in the story and rewrite it from Juana's point of view. First, review Chapters 1 through 3, concentrating on aspects of Juana's character. Next, imagine that you are Juana and freewrite about the incident, describing your thoughts, feelings, and actions. Then use this information to rewrite the incident from her point of view.

## Protocols

Protocols are descriptions of the thinking and writing process. They enable your students to assess their own learning by providing them with the opportunity to describe the processes they follow in writing, reading, and speaking. Thus, students begin to monitor their progress toward mastery. To prompt the writing of protocols, students answer questions such as these:

What were your content and stylistic goals in this piece?
How successful do you feel you were in meeting those goals?
What gave you difficulty in this assignment?
What new learning came out of writing this piece?

You may adapt this basic protocol to fit your specific assignments. For example, if students are writing a response to the expressive assignment for *The Pearl,* they will be rewriting the story from the point of view of Juana and might respond in a protocol to questions like these:

On what incident in Chapters 1–3 did you focus?
What personality did you give Juana?
What thoughts and feelings did you wish to convey about her in regard to the incident?

What effect did writing the story from Juana's point of view have on the first three chapters?
What did you learn about point of view from this assignment?

## Peer Review

Peer review offers your students another opportunity to develop their metacognition skills as they learn from each other. Working in pairs or in small groups, students review each other's work and make suggestions for revision of content, form, and mechanics. However, the emphasis of the review changes, depending on what stage in the writing process the peer critique occurs. For example, in the drafting stage students focus on content and development, answering questions like these:

What do you see as the writer's purpose?
For what audience is this piece intended?
What specific details did the writer include to accomplish that purpose?
What additional information would enhance the piece?
What, if anything, would you suggest the writer delete?

In the editing stage the review questions may focus more on form and mechanics. Your students may consider these questions:

What is the topic of each paragraph?
Are the supporting details presented logically?
Are the verb tenses appropriate and consistent?
What corrections do you suggest for improving the language and mechanics of the piece?

You may tailor the peer reviews to fit specific assignments. For example, if your students have written a response to the Thinking and Writing assignment on page 715 for *The Pearl,* the peer review might include questions like these:

On what incident did the writer focus?
What personality did the writer give to Juana?
What thoughts and feeling of Juana did the writer convey?
What did the change in point of view do to your understanding of the story?
What concrete suggestions do you have for the writer to make the story more effective?

To validate the peer review, you may have your students revise their work, incorporating those suggestions they believe will enhance their final product. Thoughtful peer reviews have a value not only for the students whose pieces are reviewed but for the reviewers who in the process of assessing other students' work are practicing their active reading skills.

## Collaborative Assessment

Collaborative assessment offers yet another opportunity for your students to develop an awareness of their thinking and writing processes, enabling you and your students to work together to determine the criteria for evaluating student performance. These criteria, usually identified in the initial stages of an assignment, may change as your students develop their competence as language users. Because they have helped define the criteria for evaluation, your students have a clearer understanding of how to complete the assignment successfully. These criteria form the basis for the writing of their protocols and for peer reviews. Criteria vary but may include these factors:

Accuracy of content
Relevance of detail
Appropriateness of form
Consistency of voice
Variety of sentence structure
Correctness of language mechanics

Collaborative assessment helps your students gain confidence in their ability to participate in evaluating their individual mastery of the learning outcomes.

## Student Portfolios

One of the most powerful assessment options available to you and your students is the portfolio. Portfolios are collections of students' work. You may choose to have portfolios contain various drafts of students' work so that you can assess growth during the process of writing a paper, examples of students' best work so that you can assess growth during the year, or a combination of both. For portfolios to be effective learning tools, students must be trained to take responsibility for their own learning. That means they must develop skills for self-assessment.

Once students have taken responsibility for their own learning by working through reader response and critical response activities, they have developed the skills necessary to create portfolios. What makes portfolios effective is that they involve students even further in the assessment and evaluation process. To prepare their portfolios, students review a body of their work and select those performance pieces they believe best represent their growth toward mastery of the learning outcomes. They may create several different kinds of portfolios:

**Individual Performance Portfolios** Your students may create individual portfolios reflecting their performance on a particular unit of study. Students collaborate with you in determining the number and type of pieces to include in the portfolio. Your students also help establish the criteria for evaluation of the portfolio. Individual portfolios may be a collection of videotaped dramatic presentations or speeches, stories, memoirs, poems and/or responses to poems, and personal and analytical essays on a particular theme or literary work.

A sample portfolio for *The Pearl* might include student responses to the following assignments:

The Reader's Response Journal
The Selection Test
The Thinking and Writing assignments
The Essay Question in the Teaching Portfolio
Any of the Alternate Composition assignments in the Teaching Portfolio
One of the Unit Projects in the Teaching Portfolio

From these assignments, you and your students may decide to include three pieces. By selecting those pieces they believe best reflect their growth toward mastery of the learning outcomes, students reveal their ability to assess their own work. You may also give your students the opportunity to revise any of their selections and to enhance their portfolio with additional pieces that reflect their appreciation and understanding of the text.

**Project Portfolios** Working collaboratively, your students may create project porfolios that reflect their performance on a particular project. Here too students help define the direction and scope of the product or activity. They work together with you to establish the criteria for evaluation of the project. Project portfolios may be written products such as newspapers, news magazines, or handbooks based on a particular literary work, or they may be performance oriented such as trials, elections, game shows, interview shows, or videos.

**Mastery Portfolios** At the end of a course your students may compile a mastery portfolio that reflects their best work in the course. You and your students may decide how many pieces to include, what modes to have represented, and whether to include early pieces as well as later pieces to demonstrate growth. Creating the portfolio also offers your students an opportunity to revise any work in order to demonstrate mastery.

**Portfolio Protocols** The most valuable step in the creation of a portfolio is the writing of the protocol in which students describe the rationale behind their portfolio selections, the learning demonstrated in each piece, and their awareness of their strengths and weaknesses as language users. To prompt the writing of the protocols, your students may consider questions like these:

What pieces did you include in your portfolio?
Why did you select these particular pieces?
What learning does each piece reflect?

What insights did you gain about yourself as a reader, writer, speaker, and listener from creating this portfolio?

## Evaluating Portfolios

Even though students have been active participants in the creation and assessment of their portfolios, ultimately it is your responsibility to evaluate the work and assign a grade. Just as your students are guided by clearly defined criteria as they develop their portfolios, you are guided by these same criteria as you evaluate their performance. In general, these criteria reflect concern for content, form, and presentation.

Evaluation of content focuses on the students' abilities to reflect their understanding of or insight into the literature studied, the concepts explored, the issues considered, as well as their facility with modes of writing. Mastery is characterized by each student's demonstration of skill in analytical thinking, that is, the ability to summarize, compare, and synthesize.

Evaluation of form focuses on students' mastery of the modes of response, including logical and appropriate organization and sequence, coherence, unity, sophistication of style, and control of language use.

Evaluation of presentation deals with the appearance of the final product—its attractiveness and its appropriateness for the focus of the content.

## MASTERY OF LEARNING OUTCOMES

Evaluation of student mastery requires consideration of the desired outcomes for reading, writing, speaking, and listening. The extent to which your students meet the desired outcomes determines their level of mastery of English/language arts skills.

**Competent:** The students who demonstrate competence in reading, writing, speaking, and listening can deal with a wide range of subject matter in a variety of forms. They reveal an ability to see relationships; they can emulate models; they can apply knowledge in a limited number of contexts.

**Excellent:** Students who demonstrate excellence in reading, writing, speaking, and listening can deal with complex and sophisticated subject matter. They discriminate among language forms for specific purposes and make appropriate stylistic judgments. They synthesize their insights in a variety of contexts.

**Superior:** Superior students are characterized by their originality and creativity. They reveal depth of perception, imaginative insights, and authority in all aspects of language use.

## CONCLUSION

As an English/language arts teacher you have a wide variety of assessment and evaluation options available to you in *Prentice Hall Literature*. These assessment and evaluation strategies, including testing, alternative assessment options, and student portfolios, offer you and your students choices for measuring growth toward mastery of the learning outcomes. Even more important, these strategies afford you the opportunity to respond to the individual needs of your students.

## Bibliography

Benson, Barbara. "Effective Tests: Let Them Write!" *The English Journal,* Feb. 1991.

DeFabio, Roseanne. "Outcomes Projects." State Education Department. Albany, N.Y., 1991.

English Language Arts Syllabus K–12. State Education Department. Bureau of Curriculum Development. Albany, N.Y., 1988.

Johnson, D.W., and Johnson, R. *Circles of Learning: Cooperation in the Classroom.* Alexandria, Va.: ASCD, 1984. New York State English Language Arts Syllabus.

Neubert, Gloria, and McNelis, Sally. "Peer Response: Teaching Specific Revision Suggestions." *The English Journal,* Sept. 1990.

Perrone, Vito. *Expanding Student Assessment.* Alexandria, Va.: ASCD, 1991.

Rosenblatt, L. *The Reader, the Text, and the Poem.* Cambridge, Mass.: Harvard University Press, 1978.

Schwartz, Jeffrey. "Let Them Assess Their Own Learning." *The English Journal.* Feb. 1991.

Shaughnessy, Mina. *Errors and Expectations.* New York: Oxford University Press, 1977.

Tchudi, Stephen. *Planning and Assessing the Curriculum in English Language Arts.* Alexandria, Va.: ASCD, 1991.

Tierney, Robert J., Carter, Mark, and Desai, Laura. *Porfolio Assessment in the Reading-Writing Classroom.* Norwood, Mass.: Christopher Gordon Publishers, 1991.

Wiggins, Grant. "A True Test: Toward More Authentic and Equitable Assessment." *Phi Delta Kappan,* May 1989.

Wolf, Denny P. "Portfolio Assessment: Sampling Student Work." *Educational Leadership,* April 1989.

# MULTICULTURALISM AND THE LANGUAGE ARTS CLASSROOM
## Dr. Rose Duhon-Sells
Founder and President of National Association for Multicultural Education

## Why Do We Need Multicultural Education?

Increasingly, the nation's classrooms are becoming more culturally diverse. The 1990 census revealed that one of every four people who live in the United States is a person of color; by the turn of the century that figure will be one out of every three. Students of color constitute a majority in twenty-five of the nation's largest school districts and in California, our most populous state. Furthermore, people of color will make up nearly half (46 percent) of the nation's school-age youth by the year 2020 and about 27 percent of these students will be victims of poverty. The percentage of people of color in our schools will continue to rise throughout the early decades of the next century.

In a nation as culturally, racially, and linguistically diverse as ours, the need for intergroup knowledge, understanding, and respect is critical. Multicultural education is a fundamental element in the restructuring of our educational systems. We need to prepare our young people to meet these goals:

- to understand the pluralistic nature of our country
- to recognize and appreciate connections between cultures
- to view our nation's diversity as a rich resource

Recognizing and appreciating the richness, rareness, and similarities and differences of each cultural group contributing to the American mosaic benefits us all. With this in mind, multicultural education endeavors to actualize the concept of "*e pluribus unum*," while encouraging a society that recognizes and respects the cultures of its diverse groups.

## Teachers Are the Key

Teachers can lead students to celebrate the diversity of our nation. As teachers help students understand the cultures of different groups, they break down students' hostility toward those unlike themselves. We all remember what it was like to be young—the awkwardness, the insecurity. To the young, to be different is wrong. The young need their teachers' support, not only to accept diversity but to celebrate it. Multicultural education helps students in these ways:

- They affirm their own culture.
- They free themselves from cultural boundaries.
- They widen their own perspective.
- They accept individuals whose views are different from theirs.

## The Language Arts Classroom

The language arts classroom is the ideal arena for celebrating diversity. Literature teaches us to walk in another's shoes and see through that person's eyes. As students read, they see the similarities among people of various cultures across time and place. They identify with characters whose backgrounds are quite unlike their own and see that we are together striving to find answers to the human predicament. They come to acknowledge that whatever they have felt or feared or hoped, someone else has experienced similar fears and dreams. Literature teaches us that in this vast world, we are all connected: We are not alone.

In your language arts classroom, encourage students to see literature as a window on life. As they talk about literature, have them make connections with their own experiences. Try book talks: Establish weekly discussion sessions where students from varying cultures read and review books about each other's culture. By guiding students to see cultural connections, you will help them move from a simple awareness of diversity to acceptance and support.

## Infusing Multicultural Education in the Curriculum

The following stages will help to infuse multicultural education in the school curriculum:

**Stage 1:** At the university level, the teacher education curriculum must reflect the quality and value of cultural diversity of this country. Student teachers should have opportunities to participate in field experiences, such as classroom observations and peer training in schools with mixed-group student populations. Professors in colleges of education must be required to be knowledgeable about the contributions to this nation by people of varous cultures. There is a critical need for educators to accept and understand the value of multicultural education and its significance to the survival of all Americans.

**Stage 2:** Our educational policymakers must emphasize the need for multicultural education and accept no delays. They must evaluate programs effectively; for example, a project funded in the name of multicultural education that deals only with food and dress practices does not further multicultural goals. Kroeber and Kluckman (1952) emphasize stressing the intangible aspects of culture in a multicultural program—ideas, ways of thinking, values, symbols, etc. It is these factors that distinguish cultural groups in the United States.

**Stage 3:** Teachers and the general public must appreciate the pyschological cost on human beings who are forced to assimilate in order to be accepted by the dominant culture. Assimilation may lead to self-denial and rejection of family and ethnic ties. The demands of assimilation run counter to democratic goals and equality of opportunity (Banks, Cortes, Gay, Garcia, Ochoa). On the other hand, multicultual education fosters self-esteem by appreciating differences and celebrating diversity.

As teachers come to understand the historical development of stereotypes of various ethnic groups, they can recognize them in written works and popular culture and take practical steps to help students avoid reinforcing or perpetuating these stereotypes. For example, when studying Native Americans, supplementing works written in the 1800's with contemporary portraits will help students form a more balanced picture (Charles, 1991).

Literature helps readers build self-respect and encourages the development of positive values. However, in the past, not all groups have been presented well. For example, African Americans have not always been presented in a positive fashion. Fortunately, books today are bringing about more positive outlooks.

It is anticipated, or at least hoped that the goals of multicultural education will be reached as teachers and others responsible for educating our children include multiculturalism in their plans as they restructure our education system.

## References

Banks, James. "Curriculum Guidelines for Multicultural Education." Prepared by the NCSS Task Force on Ethnic Studies Guidelines. Adopted by NCSS Board of Directors, 1976.

Caldwell-Wood, Naomi, and Mitten, Lisa A. " 'I' Is Not for Indian: The Portrayal of Native Americans in Books for Young People." *Multicultural Review*, Vol. 1, Number 2, April 1992.

Charles, Jesus. "Combating American Indian Stereotypes Through Literature Study." In Carl A. Grant (ed.), *Toward Education That Is Multicultural*, Proceedings of the First Annual Meeting of the National Association for Multicultural Education, 1991.

Garcia, Jesus. "Multicultural Education Teacher Preparation Programs: A Political or an Educational Concept?" *Phi Delta Kappan*, November 1991.

Gay, Geneva. "Culturally Diverse Students and Social Studies." In James P. Shaver (ed.), *Handbook of Research on Social Studies Teaching and Learning* (pp. 144–156). New York: Macmillan, 1991.

Kroeber, Alfred, and Kluckman, Clyde. *Cultures: A Critical Review of Concepts and Definitions.* New York: Vintage, 1952.

---

### Prentice Hall Literature

"Literature—the mystery of the human heart moving through time."
Hugh Dinwiddy

*Prentice Hall Literature* is firmly committed to the goals of multicultural education. We believe these goals can be accomplished when students and teachers are provided with literary selections that are sensitively chosen to reflect the diversity of our nation and to move students to an appreciation and acceptance of cultures other than their own. Key elements of the *Prentice Hall Literature* program are

- A Multicultural Review Board to advise on the appropriateness of selections
- Literature written by authors from a broad spectrum of times, cultures, and backgrounds
- Literature reflecting the diversity of our nation and of the world
- Multicultural Connection features in the student anthologies that help students see connections between cultures and appreciate cultures other than their own
- Multicultural Focus notes in the Annotated Teacher's Editions that create an awareness of cultural connections with almost every selection
- Questioning strategy that helps students apply literature to their own lives and that leads to deeper understanding and affirmation
- *Prentice Hall Literature* Multicultural Library of fine young adult literature
- *Prentice Hall Literature* Audio Prose Library containing interviews with authors from a variety of backgrounds and cultures and readings by those authors

# TECHNOLOGY IN THE LANGUAGE ARTS CLASSROOM

**Bonita C. LaBelle**
Director of English
Shrewsbury High School
Shrewsbury, Massachusetts

English teachers want to share their enthusiasm for reading and writing with students. That is why looking through the table of contents of a literary anthology excites the feelings and intellect of a truly committed English teacher. When teachers see Cather's short stories and Hughes's poetry, for example, they imagine stimulating classroom discussions and enlightening analyses of writing form and style. But even the most dedicated and creative classroom teacher runs up against the students of the 1990's: young people who like stories but don't necessarily want to read and write about literature. How, then, does today's English teacher actively involve students in reading and writing?

## Involving Students by Using Technology

We know that students learn best when they are actively involved in the learning process, interacting with each other, and when they have opportunities to show what they already know. Students today are visual learners who have been brought up in a world of technology. At home, many use computers, calculators, VCRs, CD players, camcorders, video games, and a variety of advanced appliances and machines. After school or in the summers, students work with database inventories at the local lumberyard or doctor's office. Today's typical young person comes to school with good technological skills and a real interest in video, graphics, and sound. Why not capitalize on these skills and interests by teaching reading and writing using the tools of technology?

By using technology, ranging from writing software to multimedia databases, English teachers can maximize student involvement and bring literature and writing to life. The ideal English teaching environment is a classroom with an area for student discussion and sharing, and another space equipped with a computer for each student. More realistically, however, effective integration of technology often takes place in school-shared writing labs. Even one to five computers in any individual classroom provide English teachers with the opportunity to teach with technology. Writing software, hand-held grammar checks, laserdiscs, videos, and audio tapes can all contribute to improved student understanding of writing and literature.

## Writing Software

When writing software was first introduced into schools, no one could have anticipated the impact technology would have on writing programs across the country. Writing software packages now provide teachers with a way to teach writing. There is no better way to improve student writing than by sharing student examples with the class, focusing on mechanical issues under study, and discussing style and content with actual student examples. By using a liquid crystal display (LCD) unit attached to one computer, with the flick of a switch, an English instructor can easily project any sample student writing. No longer is it necessary to stand in a long line to make multiple copies of student writing on duplicating machines. With just one LCD and a box of students' disks, the teacher has a writing lesson at his or her fingertips. This technology helps create a writing workshop atmosphere where students gain confidence in their writing skills and grow adept at discussing writing techniques. They love to see their own work projected up on the screen; shared writing motivates them to try harder and to improve. As one lower-level student wrote in an evaluation of his ninth-grade English class: "Computers helped me become a better writer. Sharing my work in front of the class and seeing how other kids liked my ideas and images made me realize I'm a pretty good writer—and knowing that is half the battle."

Similarly, tenth-grader Joanne Schnare reflected back on the experiences of tenth-grade English class this way: "I walked into Room 319 on the first day of school, shy and still looking for the piece of self-esteem I lost along the way. Even though I had heard many good things about both the English teacher and the computer lab, I still had a clear vision of a class like I had last year . . . boring. But this year's English class made me think about what I read and pushed me to read more carefully and write more effectively. We used word processors and shared our writings and reading responses frequently on 'the big screen.' I gained so much confidence because kids wanted to see my thoughts . . . they'd say, 'Read Jo Jo's!!' I may have walked in shy, but I walked out . . . Jo-Jo Schnare."

Computers make the writing process possible. English teachers who take students to writing labs to create rough drafts provide kids with an "on disk" copy of their writing that will ultimately go through multiple editing changes based on peer editing and teacher conferencing. Word processing has made editing easier by providing tools for correcting spelling, reorganizing and rearranging sentences and paragraphs, running grammar checks, etc. Before word processing, students were hesitant to spend time editing their work. By word processing first drafts, students see first attempts as simply beginnings and willingly progress through additional drafts until they complete an acceptable final piece.

Therefore, students are eager to word process and edit their writing; they like to write with computers, becoming very focused on their work. Students who hate to hand write compositions become avid word processor writers who enjoy creating and sharing their ideas and feelings. The student with atrocious handwriting can finally understand his or her own thoughts and successfully share them with others. Spelling improves. Self-esteem improves. Also, students become more concerned about accuracy and correctness. Learning-disabled students carry work begun in English class on disk to the resource room where support staff continue and expand upon lessons in writing and mechanics. If an electronic network exists in the school, special and regular education teachers can communicate about students' process and share examples of work and assignments.

## Laserdiscs

Laserdisc technology provides the English teacher with focused looks at specific video footage. Thousands of movies and plays are available on laserdiscs, and many excellent historical presentations. *Letter From the Birmingham Jail* and *The Gettysburg Address* are now available. Given the limited class time in a typical high school, sharing full-length films has become virtually impossible. While students might be given videos to take home and review for homework, spending two to three hours of classroom time watching a movie or documentary is counterproductive.

What laserdisc technology allows the teacher to do is key in on selected segments of a given presentation. By using a remote control and a publisher-provided segment guide, the teacher can focus in on a specific passage by simply inputting chapter or track numbers. Without winding and rewinding videotape, the teacher has immediate control of the presentation. This technique provides students with key passages for analysis, comparison, and contrast. (For *Prentice Hall Literature*, bar code access through the Annotat-

ed Teacher's Edition is provided for all laserdiscs in the *Prentice Hall Literature* Writing Studio.

For example, when reading Shakespeare's *Romeo and Juliet*, students are able to read descriptions of certain characters and events and, then, with laserdisc technology, key in on just those passages that help illustrate specific ideas or descriptions. Mercutio's street fight and death scene are difficult for students to imagine; they are often confused as to how Romeo was involved. Keying in on the corresponding videodisc footage clarifies the scene and brings Shakespeare's words to life.

Laserdisc technology helps teachers promote thinking skills, particularly comparison and contrast. In reading *Great Expectations*, for example, students need not watch the entire film to write a comparison and contrast paper. Using the laserdisc, the students can focus on and analyze specific portions of the novel and film versions. They can note parallel scenes, changes in chronology, and deliberate changes by the filmmaker to highlight their own understanding of Dickens's purpose.

## Integrating Technology in Your Lesson Plans

Technology helps students get actively involved in reading and writing. The following paragraphs delineate the integration of technology in teaching Fitzgerald's *The Great Gatsby*. Before reading the novel, students view an art transparency of life in the 1920's, and, then, using the details they see in the painting, write descriptive pieces of what life might have been like at that time. Using the LCD and the student writing, the teacher then shares sample writing, highlighting quality student work and recognizing good uses of mechanical points studied in class.

Continuing to ready students for a reading of the book, the teacher shows students Chapter 2 of the *History in Motion* videodisc (easily available through many media centers), comparing daily life in the 1920's with their own speculations written the day before. They gain additional real-life details from audio tapes, including jazz performances and speeches from the 1920's. Students now have a feel for the time period of the novel, and their minds have been activated to become more intensely involved in Fitzgerald's book.

After reading Chapters 1 and 2 of the novel, cooperative learning groups of students (four students in a group works well) gather around a common computer and generate lists of character descriptions. Each group is responsible for a single character: Daisy, Tom, Myrtle, Nick, or Wilson. In presenting their character to the rest of the class, each group is responsible for reviewing information given by Fitzgerald and speculating on the character's future actions.

As students progress through the novel and the teacher continues to emphasize the interrelationship between history and literature, students might use a piece of software like the "Mac TimeLiner" to bring Gatsby's life and the events of the 1920's together. By creating their own timelines of Gatsby's life, students are forced to use the text to verify dates and chronology. Printouts are available on a single page or banner-length display. However, before printing, students might call up some of the events of the 1920's that appear on the prepared American History timeline available in the software package. By creating a merge between their own Gatsby timeline and the prepared events of 1920's, students see clearly the interrelationship of history and literature.

Multimedia projects can be used as a culmination activity for studying a piece of literature such as *The Great Gatsby,* or they may be interjected at any point in the unit. Using software packages like "Point of View" or "Media Text," students can expand their knowledge base of the 1920's by doing additional research. For many students, writing the traditional research paper is not a valuable experience. Students frequently plagiarize and often lose their own voice, writing in a style that is clearly not their own. English teachers have to wonder if the weeks and weeks spent on form and documentation are worth the effort. The multimedia research project allows students to integrate information from printed materials, various videodiscs, and audio sources, and to become more personally involved.

For example, after reading *The Great Gatsby,* students brainstorm for ideas to research. Fitzgerald's book is loaded with wonderful topics, from Prohibition to the movies. After brainstorming, students might choose to investigate something like the World Series of 1919. Using details about the fictional character of Meyer Wolfshiem from *The Great Gatsby* as an opening, students could go on to write about the importance of baseball in America by adding an audio portion from Lou Gehrig's or Babe Ruth's farewell to baseball speeches (*Great Speeches of the 20th Century*). They could include primary sources based on oral history in both textual and audio formats. Students could then go on to Eliot Asinof's *Eight Men Out* for more textual material and scan any related still photos into the report. Finally, they would share the project with the rest of the class. Other students and teachers would assess the relevance of the included multimedia materials and comment on the effectiveness of the piece. By compiling such a research project, students become actively involved thinkers: They must read new material; they must watch and listen to audio and visual materials; and, above all, they must make critical decisions about the selection of appropriate textual, audio, and visual components.

## Personalizing Students' Experiences

Contrary to popular opinion, the integration of technology into the English curriculum personalizes students' reading and writing experiences. Rather than distancing students from their teacher and classmates, technological learning tools foster interactive experiences.

Several years ago, a student of mine created a multimedia project that was an outgrowth of an oral history project she had completed: a ten-page biography about her grandfather. Because her grandfather had fought in World War II, Rachel decided to investigate further some history about the war, specifically the bombing of Hiroshima. Using a multimedia database that supplied information through timelines, texts, pictures, and video sequences, Rachel gave her grandfather's memories accurate and expanded historical perspective. As part of the presentation, Rachel recorded her grandfather's comments, integrating them into the report; she scanned in original photographs of her grandfather in uniform with his battalion. Her presentation of the project to the class was a moving experience. As Rachel described it, the multimedia approach was rigorous but fun and "I learned more about World War II, my grandfather, and me than I ever dreamed I would. The class's response to my work made me feel like I really accomplished something important in school."

## Preparing Students for the Twenty-first Century

As we prepare students for the twenty-first century, we must think about our current teaching and learning paradigm. The teacher-centered classroom must be viewed as a model of the past. Student interaction, collaborative learning groups, and the tools of technology are important parts of today's learning styles. Students today need individualized approaches to learning; it is no longer possible to maximize student learning without using technology. Because English teachers most directly prepare students for successful communication in the technologically advanced world beyond high school, we must capitalize upon the feelings, goals, and skills students bring to our classrooms. We can do so by integrating technology into the English curriculum.

# HOW SCIENCE, PHYSICAL EDUCATION, MATH, AND HISTORY CAN MAKE YOUR STUDENTS LOVE ENGLISH

**Terri Fields**
English Teacher
Sunnyslope High School
Phoenix, Arizona

The bell rings before you can answer a student's question about a story the class has been reading, so you're pleased to see the student in the hallway after school. You walk over to him and begin to explain the point about which he'd asked earlier in the day. He looks at you blankly. "Uhh, let's see; which story was that?" he finally mumbles.

You remind him that the class has been discussing the same short story for the past three days.

"Oh, yeah, right," he says sheepishly. "Well, it's been a long time since English this morning. . . ."

As a teacher you have probably asked yourself how you can get students to remember what they have learned in English. You've also asked an even more basic question: How do you get them to care about learning the literature at all?

A solution to both questions may be found in bringing other content material into the English classroom, for literature is not something separate from life but instead an integral part of life. As an English teacher, you can see this truth so vividly that you may not realize how many students have never made the connection. In fact, few students see any application of their literature study to any other class work.

Therefore, if you really want literature to matter to your students, if you really want to involve them in its study, it is your responsibility to relate literature to the rest of the curriculum and to current events. The more knowledge students apply to their reading, the more they can enjoy the reading. By the same token, the more they learn to apply the details, themes, and characters of literature to life and its problems, the more they can develop insightful answers.

If you believe that an interdisciplinary approach makes sense, you must ask how you can best make it a reality in your classroom. The answer begins in mapping out your literature units by asking yourself, "How might these stories/poems/plays/novels apply to other classes students are taking?"

For example, suppose you are going to cover a story in which the protagonists endure bitter cold to survive. Consider assigning the story while the students' science teacher is talking about the effects of temperature on the body. If you can't coordinate timing precisely, you can assign the story some time after the science teacher's unit on body temperature. Then you can tell students you expect them to use their science books and notes to explain how the author of this story used scientific knowledge to make the story both suspenseful and believable. Not only will this assignment allow students to see that there is relationship between science and English, but it will also help them to appreciate the research a writer undertakes.

Suppose you are going to study a poem in which the theme centers on oppression. You might ask students to select a person they have studied in history class and write a short paper discussing how that historical figure would have reacted to the meaning and mood of the poem. Such an assignment allows students a variety of learning experiences. They must reread and interpret the poem. They must review their history notes to decide on a particular figure. They must review what the figure believed and then decide how that would affect their interpretation of the poem.

You might present copies of some of the best papers to the history teacher. Imagine this teacher's surprise on discovering that another teacher is helping to review the history material with students. You may find the teacher saying, "Thanks! Is there something I can do in my class to help you with English?"

At that point, you have a perfect opportunity to suggest that the teacher intersperse a few of your vocabulary words in lectures. You might also offer to provide a list of all the selections your students will be reading. If the teacher remembers any of them, you would appreciate the teacher mentioning his or her enjoyment of them during class.

In interdisplinary learning's most ideal form, teachers from all disciplines would reinforce one another's teaching. Teachers would plan units together so that students could see the same concept covered from historical, literary, and scientific viewpoints.

While that may not be feasible at your school, you can get a taste of the idea and its impact on student learning by planning even one unit with a teacher from a different discipline. If logistics prevent that, you can still bring interdisciplinary learning to your classroom by helping students apply the material they are learning in other classes to your literature units and the literature they are learning in English to material being covered in other classes. The more purpose students see in knowing material, the more likely it is that they will learn, retain, and apply it.

# PRENTICE HALL

# LITERATURE

COPPER

BRONZE

SILVER

GOLD

PLATINUM

THE AMERICAN EXPERIENCE

THE BRITISH TRADITION

WORLD MASTERPIECES

# PRENTICE HALL

## LITERATURE
### Silver

#### PARAMOUNT EDITION

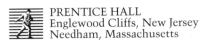

**TAOS VALLEY, 1932–1935**
*Victor Higgins*
Snite Museum of Art, University of Notre Dame

PRENTICE HALL
Englewood Cliffs, New Jersey
Needham, Massachusetts

## Humanities Note

Fine art, *Taos Valley,* by Victor Higgins (1884–1949). An American artist, Higgins was a member of the original Taos Society of Artists established in Taos, New Mexico, in 1914. The natural beauty of this dusty pueblo town and the surrounding countryside attracted painters, writers, and other assorted characters, making it an artists' colony unique in the United States. Victor Higgins first came to Taos to fulfill a commission, given to him by Carter Harrison, the former mayor of Chicago, to paint the magnificent countryside. He was so taken with Taos that he stayed and built himself a small adobe "castle" with a tower that commanded a view of the valley. Higgins then devoted his life to painting the New Mexico landscape and the Native Americans who inhabited it. After his death his daughter discovered a quantity of lovely watercolor and oil paintings in his abandoned studio. He was saved from obscurity by a posthumous exhibition of his work mounted by the Santa Fe Museum.

*Taos Valley* was painted in the early 1930's and may have been the view from Higgins's tower. He paints this landscape with lush color and lively brushstrokes that are reminiscent of the impressionists. The angular sprawl of the mountains is repeated in the glowing rocks in the foreground. The thick clouds appear weighty and solid, almost like mountains themselves. This charming landscape is executed with a sensitive familiarity that tells the viewer the artist has painted it many times. This beautiful vision of the desert terrain takes the viewer into the landscape and opens his imagination to what might lie beyond the mountains.

ISBN 0-13-722414-1

1 2 3 4 5 6 7 8 9 10   97 96 95 94 93

Art credits begin on page 815.

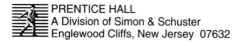

PRENTICE HALL
A Division of Simon & Schuster
Englewood Cliffs, New Jersey  07632

## STAFF CREDITS FOR PRENTICE HALL LITERATURE

**Publisher:** Eileen Thompson

**Editorial:** Ellen Bowler, Douglas McCollum, Philip Fried, Kelly Ackley,
Eric Hausmann, Lauren Weidenman

**Multicultural/ESL:** Marina Liapunov, Barbara T. Stone

**Marketing:** Mollie Ledwith, Belinda Loh

**National Language Arts Consultants:** Ellen Lees Backstrom, Ed.D., Craig A.
McGhee, Karen Massey Riley, Vennisa Travers, Gail Witt

**Permissions:** Doris Robinson

**Design:** Susan Walrath, Carmela Pereira, Leslie Osher, AnnMarie Roselli

**Visual Research:** Libby Forsyth, Emily Rose, Martha Conway

**Production:** Suse Bell, Joan McCulley, Elizabeth Torjussen, Amy E. Fleming,
Lynn Contrucci, Garret Schenck, Lorraine Moffa

**Publishing Technology:** Andrew Black, Deborah J. Jones, Monduane Harris,
Cleasta Wilburn, Greg Myers

**Pre-Press Production:** Laura Sanderson, Natalia Bilash, Denise Herckenrath

**Print and Bind:** Rhett Conklin, Gertrude Szyferblatt

## ACKNOWLEDGMENTS

Grateful acknowledgment is made to the following for
permission to reprint copyrighted material:

**American Way**
"Dial Versus Digital" by Isaac Asimov. Reprinted by
permission of *American Way*, inflight magazine of
American Airlines, copyright 1985 by American Airlines.

**Rudolfo A. Anaya**
"Chicoria" and "Los cuatro elementos/The Four Elements,"
translated by Rudolfo A. Anaya, from *Cuentos: Tales
From the Hispanic Southwest*, selected by and adapted in
Spanish by José Griego y Maestas, retold in English by
Rudolfo A. Anaya. Copyright © 1980 by the Museum of
New Mexico Press.

**Arte Publico Press**
"Old Man" by Ricardo Sánchez is reprinted with
permission of the publisher from *Selected Poems*
(Houston: Arte Publico Press–University of Houston,
1985).

(Continued on page 812.)

*iv*

# CONTENTS

*v*

## DRAMA

## NONFICTION

*vii*

# THE AMERICAN FOLK TRADITION

*ix*

## THE NOVEL

## ADDITIONAL FEATURES

# PRENTICE HALL
# LITERATURE
## *Silver*

*One of the pleasantest things in the world is going on a journey; but I like to go by myself.*

—*William Hazlitt*

**CHILDREN AND PIGEONS IN THE PARK, CENTRAL PARK, 1907**
*Millard Sheets*
*Photograph Courtesy of Kennedy Galleries, New York*

# SHORT STORIES

A short story is one of the most popular forms of literature. Even though it is fiction, a product of the author's imagination, you may become interested in reading it because it deals with people, places, actions, and events that seem familiar. At other times it may stir your imagination because it deals with the fantastic—or unusual. Whatever your reason for enjoying a particular short story, you will find that because it is short, you can usually read it in one sitting.

A short story is made up of elements: plot, character, setting, point of view, and theme. The plot is the sequence of events in the story. The characters are the people, and sometimes the animals, that play a role in the story. The setting is where and when the events take place. Often the plot, characters, and setting work together to reveal a theme, or insight into life.

Adventure stories, mysteries, science fiction, animal tales—these are just a few of the varied types of short stories that authors write. In this unit you will encounter many of these types, and you will learn strategies to help you understand and appreciate short stories more thoroughly.

## Humanities Note

Fine art, *Children and Pigeons in the Park, Central Park,* by Millard Sheets. Millard Sheets, an American painter, designer, illustrator, and graphic artist, was born in 1907 in California. He studied art in Los Angeles at the Chouinard Art Institute and at the University of Southern California. His travels throughout the world broadened his artistic perceptions. Millard Sheets has made diverse contributions to the art world. He has taught, designed murals, illustrated for *Life* magazine, created architectural designs, designed movie sets in Hollywood, and won many awards for his outstanding watercolor paintings.

*Children and Pigeons in the Park* is a watercolor. The style can be called impressionistic and the subject lighthearted. The activity suggests stories in progress. Quick, lively brush strokes give a bright spontaneity to the scene. The fresh and diverse color lends to it an appropriate sun-dappled appearance. This painting has the same familiar appeal today as it did when it was painted.

**Alternative Assessment** *Portfolio Assignment:* To enable you and your students to assess their learning, ask them to create a portfolio of their written responses as they read selections in the Short Stories unit. They may select the best pieces from among their written work on the short stories:

Reader's Response Journals
Learning Options assignments
Thinking and Writing assignments
Your Writing Process assignments
Alternative Composition assignments (in the Teaching Portfolio)
Essay question from the Unit Test (in the Teaching Portfolio)

Have your students then write a protocol for their portfolios in which they explain their reasons for selecting the pieces they chose to include in their portfolios and the learning that is reflected.

## Preparation

**Reading Actively** Research has shown that effective reading requires an active process on the part of the reader. The strategies listed here enable students to become thoughtful, active readers of fiction.

To introduce the process outlined on this page, ask students to discuss the ways in which they normally read a story. What strategies have they found that work for them? You might ask your students what difficulties they have encountered while reading. Then discuss the strategies listed here. Explain that these strategies help students become more effective readers. The model on the following pages contains an active reader's questions, visualizations, predictions, connections, and responses. Have students pay attention to these notes as they read. Also ask them to create their own questions, visualizations, predictions, connections, and responses. For further practice with the process, use the selection in the Teaching Portfolio, "The Baroque Marble" by E. A. Proulx, page 8, which students can annotate themselves. Encourage students to continue to use these strategies when reading other stories.

**Cooperative Learning** After students have annotated the selection in the Teaching Portfolio, have them form small groups of mixed ability levels to compare their questions, visualizations, predictions, connections, and responses. Then with the whole class, review the sample to demonstrate and validate the variety of possible reactions.

# READING ACTIVELY

## Short Stories

A short story is fiction—a work of literature in which the characters and events are imagined by the author. Fiction allows you to explore new worlds, share the joys and sorrows of characters, and learn from the invented experiences of others.

Reading short stories is an active process. It is a process in which you use your imagination to picture what is happening in the story and then derive meaning from that picture. You do this through the following active-reading strategies:

QUESTION What questions come to mind as you are reading? For example, why do characters act as they do? What causes events to happen? Why does the writer include certain information? Look for answers to your questions as you continue to read.

VISUALIZE Try to visualize what is happening by using details from the story to create a picture in your mind. While reading, change your picture as the story unfolds and your understanding grows. Use your visualization to help clarify any confusing parts.

PREDICT What do you think will happen? Look for clues in the story that seem to lead to a certain outcome. As you continue reading, you will see whether your predictions are correct.

CONNECT Bring your own experience and knowledge to the story. Make connections with what you know about similar situations or people in your own life.

Also make connections between one event and another in the story. Try to figure out how all the pieces of the story fit together.

RESPOND Think about what the story means. What does it say to you? What feelings do you experience as you read? What has the story added to your understanding of people and the world around you?

Try to use these strategies as you read the stories in this unit. They will help you increase your enjoyment and understanding of literature.

On pages 3–9 you can see an example of active reading by Matt Frary of Rampart School in Colorado Springs, Colorado. The notes in the side column include Matt's thoughts and comments as he read "Tears of Autumn." Your own thoughts as you read may be different because each reader brings something different to a story and takes away something different.

*2   Short Stories*

# MODEL

# Tears of Autumn

Yoshiko Uchida

Hana Omiya stood at the railing of the small ship that shuddered toward America in a turbulent November sea. She shivered as she pulled the folds of her silk kimono close to her throat and tightened the wool shawl about her shoulders.

She was thin and small, her dark eyes shadowed in her pale face, her black hair piled high in a pompadour that seemed too heavy for so slight a woman. She clung to the moist rail and breathed the damp salt air deep into her lungs. Her body seemed leaden and lifeless, as though it were simply the vehicle transporting her soul to a strange new life, and she longed with childlike intensity to be home again in Oka Village.

She longed to see the bright persimmon dotting the barren trees beside the thatched roofs, to see the fields of golden rice stretching to the mountains where only last fall she had gathered plum white mushrooms, and to see once more the maple trees lacing their flaming colors through the green pine. If only she could see a familiar face, eat a meal without retching, walk on solid ground, and stretch out at night on a *tatami* mat[1] instead of in a hard narrow bunk. She thought now of seeking the warm shelter of her bunk but could not bear to face the relentless smell of fish that penetrated the lower decks.

Why did I ever leave Japan? she wondered bitterly. Why did I ever listen to my uncle? And yet she knew it was she herself who had begun the chain of events that placed her on this heaving ship. It was she who had first planted in her uncle's mind the thought that she would make a good wife for Taro Takeda, the lonely man who had gone to America to make his fortune in Oakland, California.

It all began one day when her uncle had come to visit her mother.

"I must find a nice young bride," he had said, startling Hana with this blunt talk of marriage in her presence. She

**Question:** *What is Hana on the boat for? Is she sure she wants to be on it?*

**Respond:** *This sounds like a beautiful place. Hana seems so lonely.*

**Connect:** *Maybe Hana is bitter because she changed her mind about leaving Japan, and she can't turn back.*

**Predict:** *Hana doesn't seem to know Taro Takeda very well—I don't think she will end up marrying him.*

1. *tatami* (tə tä′ mē) **mat** *n.*: A floor mat woven of rice straw, traditionally used in Japanese homes.

*Tears of Autumn*   3

**2 Reader's Response** It is part of the close-knit Japanese family structure that the eldest child remain on the homestead, living with the parents and taking care of them as long as they survive. How might you react if this were your family's cultural tradition?

**3 Enrichment** The cities named in this story are all very near each other in the south central part of Japan. You might want to show your students the locations of Osaka and Nagoya on a map of Japan.

**4 Discussion** The age difference seems not to bother Hana. Why? What other information about him might balance out the age difference?

**5 Clarification** These are Japanese food staples.

**Connect:** *Maybe Hana is upset because she is being forced to marry a man who is not really suitable.*

**Question:** *Does the husband take the wife's name in the Japanese culture?*

**Connect:** *Hana doesn't seem too interested in getting married. If she does get married, it will probably be because her family wants her to.*

blushed and was ready to leave the room when her uncle quickly added, "My good friend Takeda has a son in America. I must find someone willing to travel to that far land."

This last remark was intended to indicate to Hana and her mother that he didn't consider this a suitable prospect for Hana, who was the youngest daughter of what once had been a fine family. Her father, until his death fifteen years ago, had been the largest landholder of the village and one of its last samurai.[2] They had once had many servants and field hands, but now all that was changed. Their money was gone. Hana's three older sisters had made good marriages, and the eldest remained in their home with her husband to carry on the Omiya name and perpetuate the homestead. Her other sisters had married merchants in Osaka and Nagoya and were living comfortably.

Now that Hana was twenty-one, finding a proper husband for her had taken on an urgency that produced an embarrassing secretive air over the entire matter. Usually, her mother didn't speak of it until they were lying side by side on their quilts at night. Then, under the protective cover of darkness, she would suggest one name and then another, hoping that Hana would indicate an interest in one of them.

Her uncle spoke freely of Taro Takeda only because he was so sure Hana would never consider him. "He is a conscientious, hardworking man who has been in the United States for almost ten years. He is thirty-one, operates a small shop, and rents some rooms above the shop where he lives." Her uncle rubbed his chin thoughtfully. "He could provide well for a wife," he added.

"Ah," Hana's mother said softly.

"You say he is successful in this business?" Hana's sister inquired.

"His father tells me he sells many things in his shop—clothing, stockings, needles, thread, and buttons—such things as that. He also sells bean paste, pickled radish, bean cake, and soy sauce. A wife of his would not go cold or hungry."

They all nodded, each of them picturing this merchant in varying degrees of success and affluence. There were many

---

**2. samurai** (sam′ ə rī′) *n*.: A Japanese army officer or member of the military class.

## Grammar in Action

Yoshiko Uchida uses vivid, exact verbs to create mental pictures for the reader. A **vivid verb** is one that shows action clearly. For instance, Uchida writes that "she [Hana] . . . tightened the wool shawl about her shoulders." The verb *tightened* gives the reader a vivid picture. If Uchida had written "she put the wool shawl about her shoulders" instead, the mental picture would not have been as strong. Notice the kinds of verbs that Yoshiko Uchida uses in these sentences:

She *shivered* as she *pulled* the fold of her silk kimono close to her throat and *tightened the wool shawl about her shoulders*.

Japanese emigrating to America these days, and Hana had heard of the picture brides who went with nothing more than an exchange of photographs to bind them to a strange man.

"Taro San[3] is lonely," her uncle continued. "I want to find for him a fine young woman who is strong and brave enough to cross the ocean alone."

6 "It would certainly be a different kind of life," Hana's sister ventured, and for a moment, Hana thought she glimpsed a longing ordinarily concealed behind her quiet, obedient face. In that same instant, Hana knew she wanted more for herself than her sisters had in their proper, arranged, and loveless marriages. She wanted to escape the smothering strictures of life in her village. She certainly was not going to marry a farmer and spend her life working beside him planting, weeding, and harvesting in the rice paddies until her back became bent from too many years of stooping and her skin was turned to brown leather by the sun and wind. Neither did she particularly relish the idea of marrying a merchant in a big city as her two sisters had done. Since her mother objected to her going to Tokyo to seek employment as a

7 teacher, perhaps she would consent to a flight to America for what seemed a proper and respectable marriage.

Almost before she realized what she was doing, she spoke to her uncle. "Oji San, perhaps I should go to America to make this lonely man a good wife."

"You, Hana Chan?"[4] Her uncle observed her with startled curiosity. "You would go all alone to a foreign land so far away from your mother and family?"

"I would not allow it." Her mother spoke fiercely. Hana was her youngest and she had lavished upon her the attention and latitude that often befall the last child. How could she permit her to travel so far, even to marry the son of Takeda who was known to her brother?

But now, a notion that had seemed quite impossible a moment before was lodged in his receptive mind, and Hana's uncle grasped it with the pleasure that comes from an unexpected discovery.

"You know," he said looking at Hana, "it might be a very good life in America."

---
**3. San:** (săn): Japanese term added to names, indicating respect.
**4. Chan** (chăn): Japanese term added to children's names.

**Visualize:** *Suddenly we see rebellion brewing in the normally obedient girl. We see Hana as she pictures herself, bent and worn from years of labor, and we know why all she wants is out, no matter what it costs.*

**Connect:** *It is ironic how Hana's mother has been pushing her to marry, yet refuses to let her marry Taro. Maybe that makes Taro more appealing to Hana.*

**6 Discussion** This paragraph tells what Hana wants from life. How do you think her own thoughts influence what she thinks of Taro?

**7 Discussion** Why do you suppose Hana's mother objects to her taking a teaching job?

---

Neither did she particularly *relish* the idea of marrying a merchant. . . .

She *clung* to the moist rail and breathed the damp salt air deep into her lungs.

On the pier black umbrellas *bobbed* here and there. . . .

**Student Activity 1.** Find five more examples in the story of sentences with vivid verbs. What makes the verbs vivid?

**Student Activity 2.** Write a brief paragraph in which you describe how you would feel if you were Hana. Choose one of three settings: in Japan anticipating your journey, on the steam-ship anticipating your arrival, or on the pier meeting Taro. Use vivid verbs. As a class, prepare a list of the vivid verbs used in your paragraphs.

**Electronic Handbook** You may want students to review verbs before completing the Grammar in Action activities. If students have access to the Language Master 6000, have them enter *verb* and press the GRAMMAR key.

**8 Discussion** Is escape a good reason for marrying Taro Takeda? Why or why not?

**9 Enrichment** In the traditional Japanese culture, family background determines one's status, no matter what one's personality, skills, or other merits. The Japanese cherish the family and make sure of its solidarity. Before Hana can marry into Taro Takeda's family, her relatives must make sure his background is acceptable and of equal status to their own.

**10 Discussion** Why is Taro's letter so formal and impersonal?

## Humanities Note

*Untitled,* 1990, by Kinuko Y. Craft. Artist Kinuko Yamabe Craft was born in Japan in 1940. She spent her early years on a tree farm near Kanazawa where she practiced painting. At age 24, she came to the United States to study commercial art at the Art Institute of Chicago. During these years she met and married fellow artist Mahlon Craft. Kinuko Craft now lives and works in Norwalk, Connecticut.

Kinuko Craft is an artist of great versatility. Her commercial style ranges from contemporary studies of sports figures to delicate reproductions of an eighteenth-century Japanese scroll. This untitled illustration was produced in 1990 for a collection of novellas entitled *Behind the Waterfall*. Her style here is that of antique Japanese prints with soft faded colors, an artist's seal, and a figure in traditional garb. The use of a mirror as the focal point of the painting is a clever and poignant device. A woman of another century sees herself reflected as a modern, westernized woman. This speaks of the problems faced by immigrants caught between two worlds, that of their tradition and their new life in America.

**Respond:** *Women definitely don't seem to be considered equals.*

UNTITLED ILLUSTRATION, 1990
*Kinuko Y. Craft*

You may ask your students these questions:
1. Do you think the woman in the painting is feeling the same conflicts as the woman in the story?
2. What do you think the artist is saying about change?

Hana felt a faint fluttering in her heart. Perhaps this lonely man in America was her means of escaping both the village and the encirclement of her family. **8**

Her uncle spoke with increasing enthusiasm of sending Hana to become Taro's wife. And the husband of Hana's sister, who was head of their household, spoke with equal eagerness. Although he never said so, Hana guessed he would be pleased to be rid of her, the spirited younger sister who stirred up his placid life with what he considered radical ideas about life and the role of women. He often claimed that Hana had too much schooling for a girl. She had graduated from Women's High School in Kyoto, which gave her five more years of schooling than her older sister.

"It has addled her brain—all that learning from those books," he said when he tired of arguing with Hana.

A man's word carried much weight for Hana's mother. Pressed by the two men, she consulted her other daughters and their husbands. She discussed the matter carefully with her brother and asked the village priest. Finally, she agreed to an exchange of family histories and an investigation was begun into Taro Takeda's family, his education, and his **9** health, so they would be assured there was no insanity or tuberculosis or police records concealed in his family's past. Soon Hana's uncle was devoting his energies entirely to serving as go-between for Hana's mother and Taro Takeda's father.

When at last an agreement to the marriage was almost reached, Taro wrote his first letter to Hana. It was brief and proper and gave no more clue to his character than the stiff **10** formal portrait taken at his graduation from middle school. Hana's uncle had given her the picture with apologies from his parents, because it was the only photo they had of him and it was not a flattering likeness.

Hana hid the letter and photograph in the sleeve of her kimono and took them to the outhouse to study in private. Squinting in the dim light and trying to ignore the foul odor, she read and reread Taro's letter, trying to find the real man somewhere in the sparse unbending prose.

By the time he sent her money for her steamship tickets, she had received ten more letters, but none revealed much more of the man than the first. In none did he disclose his loneliness or his need, but Hana understood this. In fact, she

## Grammar in Action

Uchida uses **coordinating conjunctions** to make her sentences flow and to create vivid pictures. Coordinating conjunctions like *and, but,* and *or* join two or more parts. They may join nouns, verbs, adjectives, adverbs, or even whole sentences. Read these sentences to see how Uchida uses conjunctions.

She was thin *and* small. (compound adjectives)

On the pier black umbrellas bobbed here *and* there. (compound adverbs)

would have recoiled from a man who bared his intimate thoughts to her so soon. After all, they would have a lifetime together to get to know one another.

So it was that Hana had left her family and sailed alone to America with a small hope trembling inside of her. Tomorrow, at last, the ship would dock in San Francisco and she would meet face to face the man she was soon to marry. Hana was overcome with excitement at the thought of being in America, and terrified of the meeting about to take place. What would she say to Taro Takeda when they first met, and for all the days and years after?

Hana wondered about the flat above the shop. Perhaps it would be luxuriously furnished with the finest of brocades and lacquers,[5] and perhaps there would be a servant, although he had not mentioned it. She worried whether she would be able to manage on the meager English she had learned at Women's High School. The overwhelming anxiety for the day to come and the violent rolling of the ship were more than Hana could bear. Shuddering in the face of the wind, she leaned over the railing and became violently and wretchedly ill.

By five the next morning, Hana was up and dressed in her finest purple silk kimono and coat. She could not eat the bean soup and rice that appeared for breakfast and took only a few bites of the yellow pickled radish. Her bags, which had scarcely been touched since she boarded the ship, were easily packed, for all they contained were her kimonos and some of her favorite books. The large willow basket, tightly secured by a rope, remained under the bunk, untouched since her uncle had placed it there.

She had not befriended the other women in her cabin, for they had lain in their bunks for most of the voyage, too sick to be company to anyone. Each morning Hana had fled the closeness of the sleeping quarters and spent most of the day huddled in a corner of the deck, listening to the lonely songs of some Russians also traveling to an alien land.

As the ship approached land, Hana hurried up to the deck to look out at the gray expanse of ocean and sky, eager for a first glimpse of her new homeland.

**11**

**Respond:** *Hana seems too concerned about what he will give her. Is she thinking about him as a person or a way to escape?*

**Question:** *What is in the basket, and why won't Hana touch it?*

**Connect:** *These songs may make Hana feel that other people are in the same situation.*

---

5. **brocades** (brō′ kādz′) **and lacquers** (lak′ ərz) *n.*: Rich cloths with raised designs, and highly polished, decorative pieces of wood.

*Tears of Autumn* 7

**11 Discussion** Hana feels excited and terrified. Why do you think Hana feels these conflicting emotions?

**Multicultural Focus** The Japanese writer Yoshiko Uchida sketches a series of cultural practices very different from those found in the United States. One of the customs is the arranged marriage, in which parents select the marriage partners for their children, choosing people they believe to be suitable in status and temperament. In this story, the marriage exemplifies not only the ceremonial reserve between men and women but also the restricted life of many Japanese women in rural areas. Having ideas of one's own, expressing opinions, or even graduating from a high school in a major city—all these are considered somehow unfitting for a young Japanese woman in the traditional setting depicted here.

Alert students to the cultural implications of this story. Point out that, for immigrants to the United States, the notion of freedom and America often go hand in hand. How will such ideas be tested for Hana, as compared with an immigrant from another country? How do her notions of freedom go along with or contradict her ideas about love and marriage?

---

This last remark was intended to indicate to Hana *and* her mother that he didn't consider this a suitable prospect for Hana. (compound subject)

The letter eased her anxiety for a while, *but* as soon as she was released *and* boarded the launch for San Francisco, new fears rose up. (compound sentence and compound verb)

**Student Activity.** In these sentences from the story, identify what the conjunctions join.
1. I want to find for him a fine young woman who is strong and brave enough to cross the ocean alone.
2. In none did he disclose his loneliness or his need, but Hana understood this.
3. She would suggest one name and then another.
4. Hana knew she wanted more for herself than her sisters had in their proper, arranged and loveless marriages.
5. She leaned over the railing and became violently and wretchedly ill.

**Electronic Handbook** You may want students to review conjunctions before completing the Grammar in Action activities. If students have access to the Language Master 6000, have them enter *conjunction* and press the GRAMMAR key.

**Respond:** *The immigrants were treated more like dogs than people.*

**Visualize:** *The picture of the black umbrellas and the dreary day goes with Hana's feelings of dread and desperation.*

**Connect:** *Hana is still thinking of Taro in a superficial way.*

"We won't be docking until almost noon," one of the deckhands told her.

Hana nodded, "I can wait," she answered, but the last hours seemed the longest.

When she set foot on American soil at last, it was not in the city of San Francisco as she had expected, but on Angel Island, where all third-class passengers were taken. She spent two miserable days and nights waiting, as the immigrants were questioned by officials, examined for trachoma[6] and tuberculosis, and tested for hookworm.[7] It was a bewildering, degrading beginning, and Hana was sick with anxiety, wondering if she would ever be released.

On the third day, a Japanese messenger from San Francisco appeared with a letter for her from Taro. He had written it the day of her arrival, but it had not reached her for two days.

Taro welcomed her to America, and told her that the bearer of the letter would inform Taro when she was to be released so he could be at the pier to meet her.

The letter eased her anxiety for a while, but as soon as she was released and boarded the launch for San Francisco, new fears rose up to smother her with a feeling almost of dread. **12**

The early morning mist had become a light chilling rain, and on the pier black umbrellas bobbed here and there, making the task of recognition even harder. Hana searched desperately for a face that resembled the photo she had studied so long and hard. Suppose he hadn't come. What would she do then?

Hana took a deep breath, lifted her head and walked slowly from the launch. The moment she was on the pier, a man in a black coat, wearing a derby and carrying an umbrella, came quickly to her side. He was of slight build, not much taller than she, and his face was sallow and pale. He bowed stiffly and murmured, "You have had a long trip, Miss Omiya. I hope you are well."

Hana caught her breath. "You are Takeda San?" she asked.

He removed his hat and Hana was further startled to see that he was already turning bald.

---

**6. trachoma** (trə kō′ mə) *n.*: A contagious infection of the eyes.
**7. hookworm** (hoŏk′ wŭrm′) *n.*: A disease caused by hookworms, small worms that attach themselves to the intestines.

## Primary Source

In her writing, Uchida moved from looking strictly at Japanese culture as she does in "Tears of Autumn" to focusing on the Japanese-American culture. She said, "I want to dispel the stereotypic image still held by many non-Asians about the Japanese and write about them as real people. I hope to convey the strength of spirit and the sense of hope and purpose I have observed in many first-generation Japanese. Beyond that, I write to celebrate our common humanity, for the basic elements of humanity are present in all our strivings." You might ask students to explore how "Tears of Autumn" can serve as a transition from Uchida's concern with Japanese culture to that of Japanese-American culture.

"You are Takeda San?" she asked again. He looked older than thirty-one.

"I am afraid I no longer resemble the early photo my parents gave you. I am sorry."

Hana had not meant to begin like this. It was not going well.

"No, no," she said quickly. "It is just that I . . . that is, I am terribly nervous. . . . " Hana stopped abruptly, too flustered to go on.

"I understand," Taro said gently. "You will feel better when you meet my friends and have some tea. Mr. and Mrs. Toda are expecting you in Oakland. You will be staying with them until . . . " He couldn't bring himself to mention the marriage just yet and Hana was grateful he hadn't.

He quickly made arrangements to have her baggage sent to Oakland, then led her carefully along the rain-slick pier toward the streetcar that would take them to the ferry.

Hana shuddered at the sight of another boat, and as they climbed to its upper deck she felt a queasy tightening of her stomach.

"I hope it will not rock too much," she said anxiously. "Is it many hours to your city?"

Taro laughed for the first time since their meeting, revealing the gold fillings of his teeth. "Oakland is just across the bay," he explained. "We will be there in twenty minutes."

Raising a hand to cover her mouth, Hana laughed with him and suddenly felt better. I am in America now, she thought, and this is the man I came to marry. Then she sat down carefully beside Taro, so no part of their clothing touched.

**Visualize:** *I can see them behaving as if they were at a business meeting.*

**Respond:** *Hana seems to be a little more at ease, though still self-conscious. I think that things are going to turn out all right.*

13

---

Yoshiko Uchida (1921–1992) experienced firsthand the discrimination to which many Japanese Americans were subjected during World War II. She spent a year with her family in a concentration camp for Japanese Americans in Topaz, Utah. Since then, she has been a student of Japanese American history and Japanese folklore. Her twenty-seven children's books include *Picture Bride, Journey to Topaz,* and *Desert Exile.* She said of her writing, "I hope to give young Asian Americans a sense of their past and to reinforce their self-esteem and self-knowledge."

*Tears of Autumn* 9

---

---

(Answers begin on p. 9.)

## Applying

8. Discussion might center on the idea that when children reach the age at which they seek independence, they must often assume risks as part of the maturation process.

## ANSWERS TO ANALYZING LITERATURE

1. Hana's uncle wishes to please Taro's father and to ease Taro's loneliness.
2. Hana wishes to avoid the oppressive life in her village and the encirclement of her family as well as the bleak marriage options available to her in Japan.

## ANSWERS TO CRITICAL THINKING AND READING

1. Students who predicted that Hana would be pleased may cite the positive references to Taro's success, affluence, and good family. Those who predicted her disappointment may cite the carefully worded letters and the formality and courtesy that could cover up her disappointment.
2. Students who think Hana and Taro will be happy may cite the fact that each wants this marriage to establish a better life for himself or herself. Students who think they will be unhappy may refer to the impersonal letters and to Hana's initial disappointment.

## THINKING AND WRITING

**Alternative Assessment** *Protocol:* Ask your students to assess their own work on the Thinking and Writing Assignment by responding to the following questions:

What experiences have you envisioned for Hana?

What are Hana's feelings about each experience?

What details from the story helped you imagine Hana's experiences and feelings during the first week of her new life?

What made this assignment difficult for you?

What new understanding of Hana did you gain in creating her diary?

# RESPONDING TO THE SELECTION

## Your Response

1. Hana hopes to be happy in a land she has never seen, with a man she has never met. Do you think these risks are worth taking?
2. Imagine that you, like Hana, were about to meet a person you knew would play a major role in your life. Compare your feelings to Hana's.

## Recalling

3. Why is Hana attracted to the idea of marrying a man in America?
4. Why does Hana's mother change her mind about the marriage?

## Interpreting

5. The writer uses these phrases at the opening of the story: "the small ship that shuddered," "her dark eyes shadowed in her pale face," and "the relentless smell of fish." How do they reflect Hana's feelings?
6. What does Taro's behavior toward Hana suggest about his personality?
7. Reread the last sentence of the story. Why does Hana avoid contact with Taro?

## Applying

8. Hana chooses between the security of home and the independence of a new life. Is the need to make such a choice universal? Why or why not?

# ANALYZING LITERATURE

## Understanding Motivation

A character's **motivation** is the reason or reasons behind his or her thoughts and actions. When an author makes clear *why* a character does what he or she does, the character comes alive for us.

1. What motivates Hana's uncle to arrange the marriage?
2. Why does Hana want to marry Taro?

# CRITICAL THINKING AND READING

## Making Predictions

An active reader makes **predictions,** or intelligent guesses, about what will happen in a story. Predictions are based on evidence from the story and on the reader's general knowledge of people and literature.

1. Did you think Hana would be disappointed or pleased when she first met Taro? On what evidence was your prediction based?
2. Do you think Hana and Taro will be happy as man and wife? Why or why not?

# THINKING AND WRITING

## Writing an Extension of the Story

"Tears of Autumn" is open-ended—it leaves us wondering what will happen next. Continue the story in the form of a diary Hana starts after her arrival in Oakland. As Hana, tell your experiences and feelings during the first week of your new life.

# LEARNING OPTIONS

1. **Art.** Review the third paragraph of the story. Draw or paint Oka Village as you picture it, based on the author's vivid description.
2. **Writing.** Hana is disappointed by Taro's letters, which are brief and formal. Yet she would also have disliked letters that revealed too much about his feelings. Imagine that you are Taro. Write a letter that would please and impress Hana.

You may have your students use the information gained from their protocols as a guide for revising their versions of Hana's diary.

**Software** If your students have access to computers, you might have them use the publishing portion of **Bank Street Writer** to generate a "diary" with representative entries from students.

Have your students use the product as a basis for discussing plausibility of the entries.

## LEARNING OPTIONS

Option 1 will appeal to visual and kinesthetic learners as well as to art students. You might suggest that students work together to make a mural.

Option 2 will appeal to students who are more comfortable

identifying with Taro rather than Hana. You may want these students to discuss how they think Taro may feel before they write.

**Teaching to Ability Levels** You might ask your **more advanced** students to plan, write, and perform a skit that extends the story for a week or a month. Ask **less advanced** students to respond to the characterizations.

# Plot

**JAMES FOLLY GENERAL STORE AND POST OFFICE**
*Winfield Scott Clime*

## Humanities Note

Fine art, *James Folly General Store and Post Office,* by Winfield Scott Clime. Winfield Scott Clime (1881–1958), an American painter and watercolorist, was born in Philadelphia. He studied art at the Corcoran Art School in Washington, D.C., and at the Art Students League of New York. His paintings are represented in the collections of several American museums.

*James Folly General Store and Post Office* is American genre painting at its finest. Painted with humor and skillful realism, it shows a small-town scene of early twentieth-century America. This painting is a charming reminder of the General Store that has all but disappeared.

**Speaking and Listening** Have pairs of students role-play short vignettes from the story. Suggested pairs: Hana and her mother discussing prospective husbands, Hana's mother and uncle talking about Takeda's family, Hana and Taro on the boat to Oakland. Other pairs, in real or extended situations: mother and older daughter(s), mother and son(s)-in-law, uncle and Taro's father, Hana and sister(s), Hana and brother(s)-in-law.

## Preparation

**More About the Author** Isaac Asimov derived his interest in writing science fiction from reading the many magazines stocked in his father's candy store in Brooklyn. He nurtured that interest and began to write at eighteen while majoring in biochemistry at Columbia College and earning his Ph.D. Ask students to discuss the relationship between science and science fiction. In what ways does having a science background help a science-fiction writer?

**Literary Focus** Suggest that there may be many conflicts in a plot. Can, for example, curiosity cause conflict? What types of conflicts can develop between people? With other forces? How can one person have a conflict within him or her?

**Prereading Focus** Remind students of some science-fiction stories they might have read or seen, such as the *Star Wars* trilogy, the *Star Trek* films and television series, or *Fahrenheit 451*. Allow them to contribute their favorite titles. Have students share with the class some realistic (or unrealistic) details they remember and their effect on the story.

**Vocabulary** Have your less advanced students read the words aloud so that you can be sure they can pronounce them.

**Electronic Handbook** If they have access to the Language Master 6000, suggest that your less advanced students listen to the pronunciations of the vocabulary words.

---

# GUIDE FOR READING

**Isaac Asimov**

(1920–1992), born in the Soviet Union, came to the United States when he was three. Asimov once remarked, "I imagine there must be such a thing as a born writer; at least, I can't remember when I wasn't on fire to write." Asimov had the ability to combine science with fiction to create astounding science-fiction and fantasy stories. He won a Locus Award, a National Science Fiction Writers Award, a Nebula Award, and a Hugo Award. In "Rain, Rain, Go Away," Asimov gives a new twist to an old song.

## Rain, Rain, Go Away

### Plot

**Plot** is the series of related actions or events in a short story. This sequence of events centers on a **conflict,** which is a struggle between opposing forces, or on a problem that must be solved. The plot includes exposition, in which the situation is revealed. The events build toward a **climax,** the point of highest interest. They continue toward a **resolution,** in which the story comes to a close.

### Focus

"Rain, Rain, Go Away" is an amusing story about a very strange family. Although the story is a blend of science fiction and fantasy, the dialogue and characterization are realistic. It is important for an author to include realistic elements in such stories in order to make the fantastic turns of events seem believable. Recall a work of science fiction that you have read or seen on television or in film. Was the story realistic, up to a point? If so, did the realism contribute to or detract from the overall story? As you read "Rain, Rain, Go Away," notice how real the characters seem. How does the believability of the characters set you up for the surprise at the end?

### Vocabulary

Knowing the following words will help you as you read "Rain, Rain, Go Away."

**forestall** (fôr stôl′) *v.*: Prevent (p. 13)

**meticulous** (mə tik′ yoo ləs) *adj.*: Extremely careful about details (p. 15)

**affectation** (af′ ek tā′ shən) *n.*: Artificial behavior intended to impress others (p. 15)

**semblance** (sem′ bləns) *n.*: Outward appearance (p. 16)

**centrifugal** (sen trif′ yə gəl) *adj.*: Tending to move away from the center (p. 16)

**celestial** (səl es′ chəl) *adj.*: Of the sky (p. 18)

---

## Objectives

1 To understand the elements of a short story's plot
2 To understand sequence of events
3 To write a short story
4 To express individual interests and abilities through an optional activity

## Support Material

**Teaching Portfolio**
Teacher Backup, p. 25
Grammar in Action Worksheet, *Understanding Dialogue,* p. 28
Usage and Mechanics Worksheet, p. 30
Vocabulary Check, p. 31
Analyzing Literature Worksheet, *Understanding Plot,* p. 32

Critical Thinking and Reading Worksheet, *Understanding Sequence of Events,* p. 33
Selection Test, p. 34

**Prentice Hall Literature Writing Studio**

# Rain, Rain, Go Away

### Isaac Asimov

"There she is again," said Lillian Wright as she adjusted the venetian blinds carefully. "There she is, George."

"There who is?" asked her husband, trying to get satisfactory contrast on the TV so that he might settle down to the ball game.

**1** "Mrs. Sakkaro," she said, and then, to forestall her husband's inevitable "Who's that?" added hastily, "The new neighbors, for goodness sake."

"Oh."

"Sunbathing. Always sunbathing. I wonder where her boy is. He's usually out on a nice day like this, standing in that tremendous yard of theirs and throwing the ball against the house. Did you ever see him, George?"

"I've heard him. It's a version of the Chinese water torture.[1] Bang on the wall, biff on the ground, smack in the hand. Bang, biff, smack, bang, biff—"

"He's a *nice* boy, quiet and well-behaved. I wish Tommie would make friends with him. He's the right age, too, just about ten, I should say."

"I didn't know Tommie was backward about making friends."

"Well, it's hard with the Sakkaros. They keep so to themselves. I don't even know what Mr. Sakkaro does."

"Why should you? It's not really anyone's business what he does."

"It's odd that I never see him go to work."

"No one ever sees me go to work."

"You stay home and write. What does *he* do?"

"I dare say Mrs. Sakkaro knows what Mr. Sakkaro does and is all upset because she doesn't know what *I* do."

"Oh, George." Lillian retreated from the window and glanced with distaste at the television. (Schoendienst was at bat.) "I think we should make an effort; the neighborhood should."

"What kind of an effort?" George was comfortable on the couch now.

"To get to know them."

"Well, didn't you, when she first moved in? You said you called."

"I said hello but, well, she'd just moved in and the house was still upset, so that's all it could be, just hello. It's been two months now and it's still nothing more than hello, sometimes.—She's so odd."

"Is she?"

**2** "She's always looking at the sky; I've seen her do it a hundred times and she's never been out when it's the least bit cloudy. Once, when the boy was out playing, she called to him to come in, shouting that it was going to rain. I happened to hear her

---

**1. Chinese water torture:** A form of torture in which the slow, steady drip of water on the victim's head can drive him or her mad.

**Presentation**

**Motivation/Prior Knowledge** To heighten the suspense of this story, it is best to have students read it with very little introduction. Ask them to imagine that new neighbors have just moved in next door. What would be some things they would want to know about these new neighbors?

**Purpose-Setting Question** Does Mrs. Sakkaro seem like a real person, someone you might know?

**1 Discussion** What does the name "Sakkaro" sound like? Point out that Karo is a brand name for a corn syrup. You might also point out that the name sounds like the first syllable in "saccharin." Why do you think the author chose this name for this family?

**2 Discussion** Why does Mrs. Wright think Mrs. Sakkaro is odd?

**Making Connections** Two other selections that contain fantasy are "A Canary's Ideas" (page 10) and "The Smallest Dragonboy" (page 159). You might want to have students consider similarities and differences.

**Thematic Focus** Exploring the unknown fascinates most of us and in this story has unexpected consequences. Ask students to discuss some consequences of learning about unknown persons and places.

**3 Discussion** What type of climate is Arizona known for?

**4 Discussion** Why do you think Mrs. Sakkaro is so preoccupied with the weather?

**5 Critical Thinking and Reading** Explain that sometimes an author gives clues about events that will happen later in the plot. This technique is called foreshadowing. Ask the students what they think the author is hinting at. What other references to water or rain have there been since the beginning of the story?

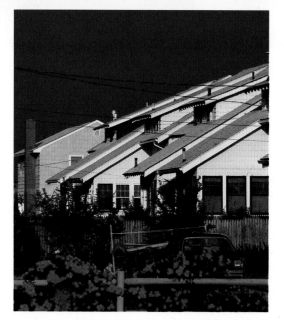

and I thought, Oh no, wouldn't you know and me with a wash on the line, so I hurried out and, you know, it was broad sunlight. Oh, there were some clouds, but nothing, really."

"Did it rain, eventually?"

"Of course not. I just had to run out in the yard for nothing."

George was lost amid a couple of base hits and a most embarrassing bobble that meant a run. When the excitement was over and the pitcher was trying to regain his composure, George called out after Lillian, who was vanishing into the kitchen, "Well, since they're from Arizona, I dare say they don't know rainclouds from any other kind."

Lillian came back into the living room. "From where?"

"From Arizona, according to Tommie."

"How did Tommie know?"

"He talked to their boy, in between ball chucks, I guess, and he told Tommie they came from Arizona and then the boy was called in. At least, Tommie says it might have been Arizona, or maybe Alabama or some place like that. You know Tommie and his nontotal recall. But if they're that nervous about the weather, I guess it's Arizona and they don't know what to make of a good rainy climate like ours."

"But why didn't you ever tell me?"

"Because Tommie only told me this morning and because I thought he must have told you already and, to tell the absolute truth, because I thought you could just manage to drag out a normal existence even if you never found out. Wow—"

The ball went sailing into the right field stands and that was that for the pitcher.

Lillian went back to the venetian blinds and said, "I'll simply just have to make her acquaintance. She looks *very* nice.—Oh, look at that, George."

George was looking at nothing but the TV.

Lillian said, "I know she's staring at that cloud. And now she'll be going in. Honestly."

George was out two days later on a reference search in the library and came home with a load of books. Lillian greeted him jubilantly.

She said, "Now, you're not doing anything tomorrow."

"That sounds like a statement, not a question."

"It *is* a statement. We're going out with the Sakkaros to Murphy's Park."

"With—"

"With the next-door neighbors, George. *How* can you never remember the name?"

"I'm gifted. How did it happen?"

## Grammar in Action

**Dialogue** is conversation between characters. By beginning a new paragraph for each speaker, the writer makes it easy for the reader to follow a conversation. When a writer wants the reader to move through dialogue in a rapid, realistic manner, he or she will omit the introductory, concluding, and interrupting expressions and begin new paragraphs.

In the following excerpt, notice the lack of explanatory expressions. However, the reader knows the change in speaker because each time Lillian and George speak, there is a new paragraph:

She said, "Now, you're not doing anything tomorrow."

"That sounds like a statement, not a question."

"It *is* a statement. We're going out with the Sakkaros to Murphy's Park."

"With—"

"With the next-door neighbors, George. *How* can you never remember the name?"

"I'm gifted. How did it happen?"

"I just went up to their house this morning and rang the bell."

"I just went up to their house this morning and rang the bell."

"That easy?"

"It wasn't easy. It was hard. I stood there, jittering, with my finger on the doorbell, till I thought that ringing the bell would be easier than having the door open and being caught standing there like a fool."

"And she didn't kick you out?"

"No. She was sweet as she could be. Invited me in, knew who I was, said she was so glad I had come to visit. *You* know."

"And you suggested we go to Murphy's Park."

"Yes. I thought if I suggested something that would let the children have fun, it would be easier for her to go along with it. She wouldn't want to spoil a chance for her boy."

"A mother's psychology."

"But you should see her home."

"Ah. You had a reason for all this. It comes out. You wanted the Cook's tour.[2] But, please, spare me the color-scheme details. I'm not interested in the bedspreads, and the size of the closets is a topic with which I can dispense."

It was the secret of their happy marriage that Lillian paid no attention to George. She went into the color-scheme details, was most meticulous about the bedspreads, and gave him an inch-by-inch description of closet-size.

"And *clean?* I have never seen any place so spotless."

"If you get to know her, then, she'll be setting you impossible standards and you'll have to drop her in self-defense."

---

2. **Cook's tour:** A brief, well-organized tour named after a British travel agent.

---

"Her kitchen," said Lillian, ignoring him, "was so spanking clean you just couldn't believe she ever used it. I asked for a drink of water and she held the glass underneath the tap and poured slowly so that not one drop fell in the sink itself. It wasn't affectation. She did it so casually that I just knew she always did it that way. And when she gave me the glass she held it with a clean napkin. Just hospital-sanitary."

"She must be a lot of trouble to herself. Did she agree to come with us right off?"

"Well—not right off. She called to her husband about what the weather forecast was, and he said that the newspapers all said it would be fair tomorrow but that he was waiting for the latest report on the radio."

"*All* the newspapers said so, eh?"

"Of course, they all just print the official weather forecast, so they would all agree. But I think they do subscribe to all the newspapers. At least I've watched the bundle the newsboy leaves—"

"There isn't much you miss, is there?"

"Anyway," said Lillian severely, "she called up the weather bureau and had them tell her the latest and she called it out to her husband and they said they'd go, except they said they'd phone us if there were any unexpected changes in the weather."

"All right. Then we'll go."

The Sakkaros were young and pleasant, dark and handsome. In fact, as they came down the long walk from their home to where the Wright automobile was parked, George leaned toward his wife and breathed into her ear, "So *he's* the reason."

"I wish he were," said Lillian. "Is that a handbag he's carrying?"

*Rain, Rain, Go Away* 15

---

6 **Discussion** Why do you think the kitchen looks as though it was never used? Do you think it was never used? Why do you think Mrs. Sakkaro was so careful getting the glass of water?

7 **Discussion** Does Mr. Sakkaro appear to be as interested in the weather as his wife? How can you tell?

8 **Reading Strategy** Have students summarize the events that have occurred so far in the story and predict what will happen at Murphy's Park.

**Electronic Handbook** You may want students to review how to write dialogue before completing the Grammar in Action activities. If students have access to the Language Master 6000, have them enter the access word *quotation* and press the GRAMMAR key to get information on dialogue.

---

"That easy?"

"It wasn't easy. It was hard. I stood there, jittering, with my finger on the doorbell, till I thought that ringing the bell would be easier than having the door open and being caught standing there like a fool."

"And she didn't kick you out?"

Asimov places the only explanatory phrase at the beginning of the dialogue, but he skillfully leads the reader through the conversation in a rapid and realistic manner. Beginning a new paragraph each time the speaker changes makes it easy to follow the conversation.

**Student Activity.** Make up your own dialogue between two people but do not use any explanatory phrases. Each person should speak at least five times. You might make up an imaginary conversation between a boy asking a girl out to a movie or between you and one of your parents on the day you show them your report card.

9 **Discussion** Why would the boy bring an aneroid barometer?

10 **Discussion** What does a "student of human nature" do?

"Pocket-radio. To listen to weather forecasts, I bet."

9 ⎡ The Sakkaro boy came running after them, waving something which turned out to be an aneroid barometer,[3] and all three got into the back seat. Conversation was turned on and lasted, with neat give-and-take on impersonal subjects, to Murphy's Park.

The Sakkaro boy was so polite and reasonable that even Tommie Wright, wedged between his parents in the front seat, was subdued by example into a semblance of civilization. Lillian couldn't recall when she had spent so serenely pleasant a drive.

She was not the least disturbed by the fact that, barely to be heard under the flow of the conversation, Mr. Sakkaro's small radio was on, and she never actually saw him put it occasionally to his ear.

It was a beautiful day at Murphy's Park; hot and dry without being too hot; and with a cheerfully bright sun in a blue, blue sky. Even Mr. Sakkaro, though he inspected every quarter of the heavens with a careful eye and then stared piercingly at the barometer, seemed to have no fault to find.

Lillian ushered the two boys to the amusement section and bought enough tickets to allow one ride for each on every variety of centrifugal thrill that the park offered.

"Please," she had said to a protesting Mrs. Sakkaro, "let this be my treat. I'll let you have your turn next time."

When she returned, George was alone. "Where—" she began.

"Just down there at the refreshment stand. I told them I'd wait here for you and we would join them." He sounded gloomy.

3. **aneroid** (an' ər oid) **barometer:** An instrument that registers air pressure changes on a dial and is used to predict weather changes. A "falling barometer" indicates an increase in air pressure and the likelihood of rain.

"Anything wrong?"

"No, not really, except that I think he must be independently wealthy."

"What?"

"I don't know what he does for a living. I hinted—"

"Now who's curious?"

"I was doing it for you. He said he's just a student of human nature." ⎤ 10

He looked so surprised, it was obvious he didn't. Then he laughed and asked if he had an Arizona accent.''

Lillian said thoughtfully, ''He has some kind of accent, you know. There are lots of Spanish-ancestry people in the Southwest so he could still be from Arizona. Sakkaro could be a Spanish name.''

''Sounds Japanese to me.—Come on, they're waving. Oh, look what they've bought.''

The Sakkaros were each holding three sticks of cotton candy, huge swirls of pink foam consisting of threads of sugar dried out of frothy syrup that had been whipped about in a warm vessel. It melted sweetly in the mouth and left one feeling sticky.

The Sakkaros held one out to each Wright, and out of politeness the Wrights accepted. 11

They went down the midway, tried their hand at darts, at the kind of poker game where balls were rolled into holes, at knocking wooden cylinders off pedestals. They took pictures of themselves and recorded their voices and tested the strength of their handgrips.

Eventually they collected the youngsters, who had been reduced to a satisfactorily breathless state of roiled-up[4] insides, and the Sakkaros ushered theirs off instantly to the refreshment stand. Tommie hinted the extent of his pleasure at the possible purchase of a hot-dog and George tossed him a quarter. He ran off, too.

''How philosophical. That would explain all those newspapers.''

''Yes, but with a handsome, wealthy man next door, it looks as though I'll have impossible standards set for me, too.''

''Don't be silly.''

''And he doesn't come from Arizona.''

''He doesn't?''

''I said I heard he was from Arizona.

''Frankly,'' said George, ''I prefer to stay here. If I see them biting away at another cotton candy stick I'll turn green and sicken on the spot. If they haven't had a dozen apiece, I'll eat a dozen myself.'' 12

''I know, and they're buying a handful for the child now.''

---

4. **roiled-up** *adj.*: Stirred up, agitated, unsettled.

**Discussion** Have you ever eaten two sticks of cotton candy at one sitting? Do you think you could? Did the Wrights really want their stick?

**12 Discussion** How does Mr. Wright feel about the Sakkaros' consumption of cotton candy?

**Multicultural Focus** Cotton candy, which plays a prominent role in this story, has long been a typical American confectionary delight, associated with circuses, carnivals, and amusement parks. Tell students that candy is a part of most cultures. A ''sweet tooth'' seems to be a universal attribute of humans. The Egyptians offered their candy, made of honey, to the gods. People in Asia were the first to use licorice and ginger to make candies. The Native American Algonquins tapped maple trees for sugar syrup.

Ask students to name their favorite kind of sweet. Many will probably say chocolate. Ask if they know where chocolate comes from. It comes from the beans of the cacao tree. Indians of Latin America were the first to cultivate cacao beans and process them into chocolate.

Point out that certain kinds of sweets are associated with special occasions in some countries. In India, on the holiday of Makara Sankranti, Brahmans serve family and visiting friends sugared sesame seeds and say, ''Eat sweetly, speak sweetly.'' On the Jewish holiday of Purim, many sweets made only at this time are served. On Ashura, Moslems celebrate the safe landing of Noah's Ark by making a pudding of dates, raisins, figs, nuts, and currants; legend says that Noah's wife made such a pudding to celebrate the joy of being on dry land again.

Have students choose a country and find out what its most popular sweets are. Are these sweets associated with a special place or time? Students can give oral reports to the class and perhaps bring in samples to share.

**13 Discussion** How do the Wrights feel about the Sakkaros' reaction to the offer of a hamburger and an orange drink? Point out that they think it was odd, but not abnormal.

**14 Discussion** How does Mrs. Wright react to Mrs. Sakkaro's insistence that George drive faster?

**15 Discussion** How do you think Helen was going to finish the sentence?

**16 Discussion** Which character from *The Wizard of Oz* reminds you of this description? Discuss the scene where the Wicked Witch of the West shriveled up and died.

**17 Discussion** Is the story's conclusion expected or unexpected? Why?

**Enrichment** Have students imagine that the Sakkaros were able to reach their home safely before it began to rain. Ask students if they think the Wrights would have still wanted to be friends with their mysterious neighbors. Would the Sakkaros ever reveal their secret to the Wrights and explain their true origin? Have your **more advanced** students write a new ending for Asimov's story in which they tell what happens after the Sakkaros reach home safely. Have the students make sure that their new endings deal with both the Sakkaros and the Wrights.

**Enrichment** Ask students if the ending was predictable and satisfying. Could the story have been eerier and more mysterious if the Sakkaros' meltability had been brought out in other ways—perhaps by a series of events rather than one? Have the students write another version of the story, preferably as a television script. Ask if any student has seen a *Twilight Zone* program. How would this story fit into the show's format?

18

"I offered to stand Sakkaro a hamburger and he just looked grim and shook his head. Not that a hamburger's much, but after enough cotton candy, it ought to be a feast."

"I know. I offered her an orange drink and the way she jumped when she said no, you'd think I'd thrown it in her face.—Still, I suppose they've never been to a place like this before and they'll need time to adjust to the novelty. They'll fill up on cotton candy and then never eat it again for ten years."

"Well, maybe." They strolled toward the Sakkaros. "You know, Lil, it's clouding up."

Mr. Sakkaro had the radio to his ear and was looking anxiously toward the west.

"Uh-oh," said George, "he's seen it. One gets you fifty, he'll want to go home."

All three Sakkaros were upon him, polite but insistent. They were sorry, they had had a wonderful time, a marvelous time, the Wrights would have to be their guests as soon as it could be managed, but now, really, they had to go home. It looked stormy. Mrs. Sakkaro wailed that all the forecasts had been for fair weather.

George tried to console them. "It's hard to predict a local thunderstorm, but even if it were to come, and it mightn't, it wouldn't last more than half an hour on the outside."

At which comment, the Sakkaro youngster seemed on the verge of tears, and Mrs. Sakkaro's hand, holding a handkerchief, trembled visibly.

"Let's go home," said George in resignation.

The drive back seemed to stretch interminably. There was no conversation to speak of. Mr. Sakkaro's radio was quite loud now as he switched from station to station, catching a weather report every time. They were mentioning "local thundershowers" now.

The Sakkaro youngster piped up that the barometer was falling, and Mrs. Sakkaro, chin in the palm of her hand, stared dolefully at the sky and asked if George could not drive faster, please.

"It does look rather threatening, doesn't it?" said Lillian in a polite attempt to share their guests' attitude. But then George heard her mutter, "Honestly!" under her breath.

A wind had sprung up, driving the dust of the weeks-dry road before it, when they entered the street on which they lived, and the leaves rustled ominously. Lightning flickered.

George said, "You'll be indoors in two minutes, friends. We'll make it."

He pulled up at the gate that opened onto the Sakkaro's spacious front yard and got out of the car to open the back door. He thought he felt a drop. They were *just* in time.

The Sakkaros tumbled out, faces drawn with tension, muttering thanks, and started off toward their long front walk at a dead run.

"Honestly," began Lillian, "you would think they were—"

The heavens opened and the rain came down in giant drops as though some celestial dam had suddenly burst. The top of their car was pounded with a hundred drum sticks, and halfway to their front door the Sakkaros stopped and looked despairingly upward.

Their faces blurred as the rain hit; blurred and shrank and ran together. All three shriveled, collapsing within their clothes, which sank down into three sticky-wet heaps.

And while the Wrights sat there, transfixed with horror, Lillian found herself unable to stop the completion of her remark: "—made of sugar and afraid they would melt."

18    *Short Stories*

**Reader's Response** Mr. Sakkaro calls himself a "student of human nature." What does "Rain, Rain, Go Away" tell you about human nature?

**Thematic Response** Curiosity impels many people to explore the unknown. Why do you think the Sakkaros, seemingly against their better judgment, agreed to go with the Wrights to the park?

## Closure and Extension

### ANSWERS TO RESPONDING TO THE SELECTION
#### Your Response

1. Encourage students to think about which of the Sakkaros' traits they find appealing and which they find disturbing. You could ask volunteers to share their responses with the class.

### Recalling

2. Mrs. Wright notes the Sakkaros' seemingly excessive fear of rain and the overly cautious manner in which Mrs. Sakkaro handles a glass of water.

3. Mr. Sakkaro brings a pocket radio for monitoring weather forecasts. The son carries a barometer. The family warily inspects the sky for signs of clouds.

# RESPONDING TO THE SELECTION

## Your Response

1. How would you have felt about having the Sakkaros as your neighbors? Explain.

## Recalling

2. Name two events involving the Sakkaros that make the Wrights curious about them, even before the outing to Murphy's Park.
3. How do the Sakkaros show their nervousness about the weather on their trip?

## Interpreting

4. Why does Mrs. Sakkaro fill the glass of water for Mrs. Wright so carefully?
5. What is unusual about what the Sakkaros eat at the park? Why do they refuse other food?
6. What does Mr. Sakkaro probably mean when he says he is a student of human nature?
7. Where do you think the Sakkaros are from? Find evidence to support your answer.
8. How is Mrs. Wright's statement at the end of the story truer than even she expects?

## Applying

9. Mrs. Wright's last sentence describes people who are behaving almost too carefully. A similar common saying is, "He looks as if he is walking on eggs." What other expressions describe especially careful behavior?

# ANALYZING LITERATURE

## Understanding Plot

**Plot** is a sequence of events or related actions. Usually, a **conflict** or a problem, such as Mrs. Wright's desire to know about the Sakkaros, is presented. Next, the action builds up to the high point, or **climax,** of the story. Finally, the action moves to a **resolution,** or final outcome.

1. Name two events that move the plot toward the climax of the story.
2. What is the climax of the story?
3. How is the conflict resolved?

# CRITICAL THINKING AND READING

## Understanding the Sequence of Events

Authors carefully plan the **sequence,** or order, of events in stories. Often they arrange events in **chronological order,** which shows how one event follows another in time. For example, Lillian first invites the Sakkaros to Murphy's Park; then the families go there.

On a piece of paper, write the numbers of the following events in chronological order:

1. The Wrights discuss their new neighbors.
2. The adults play games on the midway.
3. The Wrights and the Sakkaros go to the park.
4. The Sakkaros move to the neighborhood.
5. The Sakkaros race for their front door.

# THINKING AND WRITING

## Writing a Short Story

Sometimes a story starts by an author wondering "What if?" Use your imagination to complete this question: What if the people next door really were _____? Then imagine an outing with your neighbors. Write the first draft of a short story telling about the consequences of their true identity. Include dialogue between the characters. When you revise, be sure to start a new paragraph when you change speakers. Share your stories with your classmates when you are finished.

# LEARNING OPTION

**Writing.** Imagine that you are a member of the Wright family, and you have noticed that your new neighbors, the Sakkaros, are a little odd. You decide to record your observations of their habits and behavior in a journal. Write enough entries to cover a week's worth of activity. You may wish to follow the plot of "Rain, Rain, Go Away" closely in your journal or create your own story about the Sakkaros. When you are finished, share your journal entries with the class.

*Rain, Rain, Go Away*   19

3. The Sakkaros dissolve, and the Wrights finally understand the motivation underlying their neighbors' strange behavior.

## ANSWERS TO CRITICAL THINKING AND READING

4, 1, 3, 2, 5

**Challenge** Explain that Asimov's story is a fantasy—that is, it deals with events that could not possibly happen in real life. Even though the story is fantastic, Asimov gives his characters logical motivation for their actions. Have students choose specific actions in the story and tell the motivation for each.

## THINKING AND WRITING

For a review of and practice with the short story, have students do the Writing a Short Story activity sheet in the Writing Process Activities section of the Teaching Portfolio, Volume II.

**Writing Transparency** Your students may find it helpful to use the Series of Events graphic organizer in **Transparencies for Writing** to help them plan the plot for their short stories.

**Alternative Assessment** For Alternate Composition Assignment to assess your students' learning, see page 26 in the Teaching Portfolio.

**Publishing Student Writing** You might want to publish a ''What if?'' class magazine. Type some of the better stories and duplicate enough copies for your students.

## LEARNING OPTION

This activity is appropriate for students who are imaginative. You may wish to have students present their journal entries to their class.

## Interpreting

4. Mrs. Sakkaro is afraid of spilling water on herself, knowing how destructive water can be to her.
5. The Sakkaros eat only cotton candy, that is, sugar. Normal food and drink, which contain water, would dissolve them.
6. Answers will differ. Suggested Response: Mr. Sakkaro probably means that he himself is not human and must, therefore, observe human nature in order to act as if he

were a human being.
7. Answers will differ. Suggested Response: The Sakkaros are definitely not from Arizona. They are probably alien creatures who have come to Earth to study human nature. Their financial independence, strange diet, and unearthly physical composition suggests extraterrestrial origins.
8. The Sakkaros are indeed composed entirely of sugar and do melt.

## Applying

9. Answers will differ. Suggested Response: Another expression is ''handle with kid gloves.''

## ANSWERS TO ANALYZING LITERATURE

1. The two most crucial events are the outing in the park and the hurried drive home as the rainstorm approaches.
2. The climax occurs when the rain begins.

**More About the Author** Pearl S. Buck was not highly regarded by critics. She was faulted, before winning a Pulitzer Prize, for having written too few books and, after winning, for writing too many. Despite lack of strong critical support, Buck, along with Mark Twain, is today the most frequently translated author in Europe and the Orient. Ask students to discuss the relationship between popular success and literary merit. In what ways can popular success be a drawback for a serious writer?

**Literary Focus** If students have read "Rain, Rain, Go Away," ask them to explain how Asimov used chronology to organize his story. How might he have used flashback if he had used a narrator, such as Mrs. Wright, who, in her old age, wanted to tell about a good deed that turned out bad? How might such an arrangement have led to a tale with an obvious moral?

**Prereading Focus** You might direct students' responses by asking them to remember giving a gift they made themselves or a loving gift of work for a special person. Ask volunteers to share some of these recollections with the class.

**Spelling Tip** Point out the different spellings of the *s* sound in these two words. In *placidly,* the *s* sound is spelled *c,* and in *acquiescent,* the *s* sound is spelled *sc.*

**Electronic Handbook** If they have access to the Language Master 6000, suggest that your students find an antonym for *placidly,* which helps them better understand its meaning.

# GUIDE FOR READING

**Pearl S. Buck**

(1892–1973) grew up in China where her parents were missionaries. After teaching in China and the United States, she became a full-time writer of nonfiction and fiction. Her most famous novel, *The Good Earth,* earned her a Pulitzer Prize, and in 1938 she won the Nobel Prize for Literature. Buck was active throughout her life in child welfare work. Her caring about people is clearly seen in "Christmas Day in the Morning," where Buck shows that the greatest gift we have to give one another is love.

## Christmas Day in the Morning

### Flashback

A **flashback** is a scene inserted into a story showing events that occurred in the past. Usually the events in a story are arranged **chronologically;** that is, the order in which the events occurred in time is the order in which they appear in the story. Sometimes, however, an author might want to show something that happened at an earlier time than the events of the story. To do so, the author uses a flashback. In "Christmas Day in the Morning," the author uses a flashback to show why Robert, now an aging grandfather, has had special feelings about Christmas since he was fifteen.

### Focus

The narrator of "Christmas Day in the Morning" tells of a memorable Christmas in which he gave his father a special gift. The gift was not bought in a store. It was a gift of self in the form of work—done so that his father would not have to do it. Perhaps you have given a present that was not bought in a store. You may have made the gift yourself or done a special favor for the person. In what ways can such a gift be more meaningful than one that is store-bought? Now read the story to see how doing a chore for someone can be an unforgettable expression of love.

### Vocabulary

Knowing the following words will help you as you read "Christmas Day in the Morning."

**placidly** (plas′ id lē) *adv.*: Calmly; quietly (p. 22)

**acquiescent** (ak′ wē es′ ənt) *adj.*: Agreeing without protest (p. 22)

### Objectives

1 To understand the use of flashback in a short story
2 To understand time order in a story containing a flashback
3 To write an extended definition
4 To express individual interests and abilities through an optional activity

### Support Material

**Teaching Portfolio**
Teacher Backup, p. 37
Grammar in Action Worksheet, *Understanding Compound-Complex Sentences,* p. 40
Usage and Mechanics Worksheet, p. 42
Vocabulary Check, p. 43
Analyzing Literature Worksheet, *Understanding a Flashback,* p. 44

Language Worksheet, *Using Context Clues,* p. 45
Selection Test, p. 46

**Prentice Hall Literature Writing Studio**

# Christmas Day in the Morning

Pearl S. Buck

He woke suddenly and completely. It was four o'clock, the hour at which his father had always called him to get up and help with the milking. Strange how the habits of his youth clung to him still! Fifty years ago, and his father had been dead for thirty years, and yet he waked at four o'clock in the morning. He had trained himself to turn over and go to sleep, but this morning, because it was Christmas, he did not try to sleep.

Yet what was the magic of Christmas now? His childhood and youth were long past, and his own children had grown up and gone. Some of them lived only a few miles away but they had their own families, and though they would come in as usual toward the end of the day, they had explained with infinite gentleness that they wanted their children to build Christmas memories about *their* houses, not his. He was left alone with his wife.

Yesterday she had said, "It isn't worthwhile, perhaps—"

And he had said, "Oh, yes, Alice, even if there are only the two of us, let's have a Christmas of our own."

Then she had said, "Let's not trim the tree until tomorrow, Robert—just so it's ready when the children come. I'm tired."

He had agreed, and the tree was still out in the back entry.

Why did he feel so awake tonight? For it was still night, a clear and starry night. No moon, of course, but the stars were extraordinary! Now that he thought of it, the stars seemed always large and clear before the dawn of Christmas Day. There was one star now that was certainly larger and brighter than any of the others. He could even imagine it moving, as it had seemed to him to move one night long ago.

He slipped back in time, as he did so easily nowadays. He was fifteen years old and still on his father's farm. He loved his father. He had not known it until one day a few days before Christmas, when he had overheard what his father was saying to his mother.

"Mary, I hate to call Rob in the mornings. He's growing so fast and he needs his sleep. If you could see how he sleeps when I go in to wake him up! I wish I could manage alone."

"Well, you can't, Adam." His mother's voice was brisk. "Besides, he isn't a child anymore. It's time he took his turn."

"Yes," his father said slowly. "But I sure do hate to wake him."

When he heard these words, something in him woke: his father loved him! He had never thought of it before, taking for granted the tie of their blood. Neither his father nor his mother talked about loving their

*Christmas Day in the Morning* 21

---

**Thematic Focus** Often persons closely related do not realize how much they appreciate one another. The main character in this story suddenly comes to realize that his father truly appreciates and loves him. Ask students to think about someone they have come to appreciate.

**Alternative Assessment** To promote active reading, have your students create a reader's response journal as they read "Christmas Day in the Morning." Ask them to focus their observations on the details that reveal Robert's growing realization that his father loves him and on the change in Robert's behavior that results. Encourage students to respond personally to the insecurity Robert feels about his father's love for him and the importance to them of feeling loved.

You may use your students' response journals to assess their understanding of the concepts and issues in Buck's story.

## Presentation

**Motivation/Prior Knowledge** Discuss with students the spirit of love that Christmas symbolizes for Christians—the birth of a child, the joy and love of that birth, and the giving of gifts to celebrate the love. Ask what the most precious gift is that could be given to them. Steer the discussion away from material gifts. Ask students what gifts were precious to them.

**Purpose-Setting Question** What role does love play in this story?

**Making Connections** Another selection that deals with giving a gift of oneself is the excerpt from "I Know Why the Caged Bird Sings" (page 403), in which Mrs. Flowers gives Marguerite personal attention.

**1 Discussion** Do you agree with his children? How does the grandfather in the story feel about spending Christmas alone with his wife? How does his wife feel?

**2 Discussion** What star is Robert referring to?

**3 Literary Focus** Discuss how the author is inserting a flashback to tell what happened to Robert when he was fifteen. Discuss other stories where the authors used flashbacks.

**4 Discussion** In what ways did the simple fact of knowing that his father loved him make a difference in Robert's life? Could he have gone on without knowing this?

**5 Master Teacher Note** Discuss the idea that it is difficult for some parents to tell children that they love them. Why might this be? Is it easier to show love than to tell it? Is it more meaningful?

**Discussion** Have you ever done a chore around the house as a gift for one of your parents? Why did you choose this way of giving a gift? How did it make you feel?

**Multicultural Focus** All over the world, holidays are a time when people show their love and affection for one another. Tell students that this is often done through the giving and receiving of gifts that are more important for their symbolic value than for their monetary worth, as in this story. Mention, for example, how Mother's Day, Father's Day, and Valentine's Day are celebrated in this country.

Tell students that in China, children bow to their elders at the first stroke of the New Year and receive little red envelopes full of coins in return. On the second day of the New Year, the Chinese visit friends to offer New Year's cards and sometimes baskets of fruit.

Among Greek Orthodox people, Easter is celebrated by visiting friends and exchanging gifts of brightly colored eggs. On Durga Puja, the Feast of the Divine Mother, Hindu children in India honor their mothers with gifts.

Have students choose a country to research. Ask them to find the answers to these questions:

What are the most important holidays in that country?

Do people give gifts on these holidays?

What kinds of gifts do they give and to whom?

What is the purpose of the gifts?

Have students share their findings with the class.

---

children—they had no time for such things. There was always so much to do on a farm.

Now that he knew his father loved him, there would be no more loitering in the mornings and having to be called again. He got up after that, stumbling blind with sleep, and pulled on his clothes, his eyes tight shut, but he got up.

And then on the night before Christmas, that year when he was fifteen, he lay for a few minutes thinking about the next day. They were poor, and most of the excitement was in the turkey they had raised themselves and in the mince pies his mother made. His sisters sewed presents and his mother and father always bought something he needed, not only a warm jacket, maybe, but something more, such as a book. And he saved and bought them each something, too.

He wished, that Christmas he was fifteen, he had a better present for his father. As usual he had gone to the ten-cent store and bought a tie. It had seemed nice enough until he lay thinking the night before Christmas, and then he wished that he had heard his father and mother talking in time for him to save for something better.

He lay on his side, his head supported by his elbow, and looked out of his attic window. The stars were bright, much brighter than he ever remembered seeing them, and one star in particular was so bright that he wondered if it were really the Star of Bethlehem.

"Dad," he had once asked when he was a little boy, "what is a stable?"

"It's just a barn," his father had replied, "like ours."

Then Jesus had been born in a barn, and to a barn the shepherds and the Wise Men had come, bringing their Christmas gifts!

The thought struck him like a silver dagger. Why should he not give his father a

*22   Short Stories*

---

special gift too, out there in the barn? He could get up early, earlier than four o'clock, and he could creep into the barn and get all the milking done. He'd do it alone, milk and clean up, and then when his father went in to start the milking, he'd see it all done. And he would know who had done it.

He laughed to himself as he gazed at the stars. It was what he would do, and he mustn't sleep too sound.

He must have waked twenty times, scratching a match each time to look at his old watch—midnight, and half past one, and then two o'clock.

At a quarter to three he got up and put on his clothes. He crept downstairs, careful of the creaky boards, and let himself out. The big star hung lower over the barn roof, a reddish gold. The cows looked at him, sleepy and surprised. It was early for them too.

"So, boss," he whispered. They accepted him placidly and he fetched some hay for each cow and then got the milking pail and the big milk cans.

He had never milked all alone before, but it seemed almost easy. He kept thinking about his father's surprise. His father would come in and call him, saying that he would get things started while Rob was getting dressed. He'd go to the barn, open the door, and then he'd go to get the two big empty milk cans. But they wouldn't be waiting or empty; they'd be standing in the milkhouse, filled.

"What the—" he could hear his father exclaiming.

He smiled and milked steadily, two strong streams rushing into the pail, frothing and fragrant. The cows were still surprised but acquiescent. For once they were behaving well, as though they knew it was Christmas.

The task went more easily than he had ever known it to before. Milking for once was not a chore. It was something else, a gift to

---

## Grammar in Action

**Compound-complex sentences** indicate a mature style of writing. A compound-complex sentence consists of two or more independent clauses and one or more subordinate clauses.

Reread these sentences from "Christmas Day in the Morning":

It had seemed nice enough until he lay thinking the night before Christmas, and then he wished that he had heard his father and mother talking in time for him to save for something better.

The stars were bright, much brighter than he ever remembered seeing them, and one star in particular was so bright that he wondered if it were really the Star of Bethlehem.

He'd do it alone, milk and clean up, and then when his father went in to start the milking, he'd see it all done.

Each of these sentences is compound: Each has two independent clauses joined with a comma and the conjunction *and*. Notice that

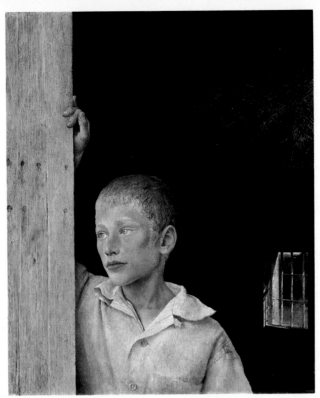

ALBERT'S SON
*Andrew Wyeth*
Nasjonalgalleriet, Oslo

7 **Discussion** How does Robert feel about his gift?

**Humanities Note**

Fine art, *Albert's Son,* 1959, by Andrew Wyeth. Andrew Wyeth (1917–    ), an American, is best known for his realistic and thoughtful pictures of people and places in rural Pennsylvania and Maine. All his figures are portraits of real people, especially his family and neighbors.

Tell students that this is a tempera painting. The word *tempera* refers to a technique in which egg yolk is added to paint. Tempera dries quickly, so the brushstrokes do not blend easily. In a tempera painting, most shapes are sharp and clear. Tones are bright and details are exact and strong. Elicit from your students how Wyeth's skill in using a tempera brush has brought forth the remarkable precision of the hairs —countless numbers of them, each finely drawn—on the boy's head and of the hay in the loft.

You might ask students the following questions:
1. What feeling do you see in the boy's face?
2. How has Wyeth created this feeling?
3. Is the painting an appropriate illustration for this story? Why?

his father who loved him. He finished, the two milk cans were full, and he covered them and closed the milkhouse door carefully, making sure of the latch. He put the stool in its place by the door and hung up the clean milk pail. Then he went out of the barn and barred the door behind him.

Back in his room he had only a minute to pull off his clothes in the darkness and jump into bed, for he heard his father up. He put the covers over his head to silence his quick breathing. The door opened.

"Rob!" his father called. "We have to get up, son, even if it is Christmas."

"Aw-right," he said sleepily.

"I'll go on out," his father said. "I'll get things started."

The door closed and he lay still, laughing to himself. In just a few minutes his father would know. His dancing heart was ready to jump from his body.

The minutes were endless—ten, fifteen, he did not know how many—and he heard his father's footsteps again. The door opened and he lay still.

"Rob!"

"Yes, Dad—"

"You son of a—" His father was laughing, a queer sobbing sort of a laugh. "Thought you'd fool me, did you?" His father was standing beside his bed, feeling for him, pulling away the cover.

"It's for Christmas, Dad!"

He found his father and clutched him in a great hug. He felt his father's arms go

*Christmas Day in the Morning* **23**

there is a complete sentence on each side of the conjunction. The comma and conjunction could be replaced by a period and a capital letter.

Each of these sentences is also complex: Each contains at least one subordinate clause beginning with a relative pronoun *(that)* or a subordinating conjunction *(until, when).*

**Student Activity 1.** Copy the example sentences. Underline the independent clauses, put parentheses around the subordinate clauses, and circle the comma and conjunction.

**Student Activity 2.** Write three compound-complex sentences of your own. You might try to follow the pattern of the example sentences.

**Electronic Handbook** You may want students to review how to build sentences before completing the Grammar in Action activities. If students have access to the Language Master 6000, have them enter the access words *complex, clause,* and *conjunction* and the symbol ; and press the GRAMMAR key to get information on clauses and compound-complex sentences.

**8 Discussion** How did Robert's father feel about receiving the gift? Ask students to explain the change that occurred in the relationship between the father and son that Christmas Day.

**9 Literary Focus** As the flashback scene ends, ask why the author used this technique. Discuss how the author used flashback to create the meaning on this Christmas day. Be sure the students are aware of how the chronological sequence of events differs from the order of events when the flashback device is used.

**10 Discussion** Is the true joy of life the ability to love? Are there people who are genuinely unable to love anyone?

**11 Enrichment** Have students make a list of the things they could do to show their love to someone. What could others do to show love to them?

**Reader's Response** What is the best gift you've ever given or received? Why?

**Thematic Response** Robert realizes that he appreciates and loves his father after overhearing his parents' conversation. Find evidence in the story that the memory of this incident that happened when he was fifteen can still change his feelings fifty years later.

**Teaching to the Ability Levels** Many writers over the centuries have offered their definitions and descriptions of love. Have your **more advanced** students use *Bartlett's Familiar Quotations* or another quotation book to locate definitions or descriptions of love with which they strongly agree or disagree. Then have them write a paragraph in which they present a quotation and explain why they agree or disagree with it.

24

around him. It was dark and they could not see each other's faces.

"Son, I thank you. Nobody ever did a nicer thing—"

"Oh, Dad, I want you to know—I do want to be good!" The words broke from him of their own will. He did not know what to say. His heart was bursting with love.

"Well, I reckon I can go back to bed and sleep," his father said after a moment. "No, hark—the little ones are waked up. Come to think of it, son, I've never seen you children when you first saw the Christmas tree. I was always in the barn. Come on!"

He got up and pulled on his clothes again and they went down to the Christmas tree, and soon the sun was creeping up to where the star had been. Oh, what a Christmas, and how his heart had nearly burst again with shyness and pride as his father told his mother and made the younger children listen about how he, Rob, had got up all by himself.

**8**
**9** "The best Christmas gift I ever had, and I'll remember it, son, every year on Christmas morning, so long as I live."

They had both remembered it, and now that his father was dead he remembered it alone: that blessed Christmas dawn when, alone with the cows in the barn, he had made his first gift of true love.

Outside the window now the great star slowly sank. He got up out of bed and put on his slippers and bathrobe and went softly upstairs to the attic and found the box of Christmas-tree decorations. He took them downstairs into the living room. Then he brought in the tree. It was a little one— they had not had a big tree since the children went away—but he set it in the holder and put it in the middle of the long table under the window. Then carefully he began to trim it.

*24  Short Stories*

It was done very soon, the time passing as quickly as it had that morning long ago in the barn. He went to his library and fetched the little box that contained his special gift to his wife, a star of diamonds, not large but dainty in design. He had written the card for it the day before. He tied the gift on the tree and then stood back. It was pretty, very pretty, and she would be surprised.

But he was not satisfied. He wanted to tell her—to tell her how much he loved her. It had been a long time since he had really told her, although he loved her in a very special way, much more than he ever had when they were young.

**10** He had been fortunate that she had loved him—and how fortunate that he had been able to love! Ah, that was the true joy of life, the ability to love! For he was quite sure that some people were genuinely unable to love anyone. But love was alive in him, it still was.

**11** It occurred to him suddenly that it was alive because long ago it had been born in him when he knew his father loved him. That was it: love alone could waken love.

And he could give the gift again and again. This morning, this blessed Christmas morning, he would give it to his beloved wife. He could write it down in a letter for her to read and keep forever. He went to his desk and began his love letter to his wife: *My dearest love . . .*

When it was finished he sealed it and tied it on the tree where she would see it the first thing when she came into the room. She would read it, surprised and then moved, and realize how very much he loved her.

He put out the light and went tiptoeing up the stairs. The star in the sky was gone, and the first rays of the sun were gleaming in the sky. Such a happy, happy Christmas!

**Closure and Extension**

**ANSWERS TO RESPONDING TO THE SELECTION**
*Your Response*

1. Have volunteers share their remembered feelings with the class.
2. Suggest that students debate the truth of this statement and give examples of their position from their experience or from literature.

*Recalling*

3. Rob was awakened to help his father milk the cows.
4. When Rob overhears his father say that he regrets having to wake his son each morning, the boy realizes that his father loves him. This realization makes Rob aware of his own love for his father.
5. Rob had planned to give his father an inexpensive tie. Knowing that his father truly loves him, he decides to give his father a special

## RESPONDING TO THE SELECTION

### Your Response

1. What feelings or memories does this story evoke in you? Explain.
2. Do you agree with the statement "Love alone could waken love"? Why or why not?

### Recalling

3. Why did young Rob's father wake him every morning at 4:00 A.M.?
4. How did Rob learn that he loved his father?
5. What gift did young Rob plan to give his father? Why does he alter his plan?
6. How did Rob's father show his gratitude for Rob's gift?

### Interpreting

7. Why is the gift young Rob gives his father special? How does giving it make Rob feel?
8. Explain the significance of the two gifts the adult Robert gives his wife.
9. When Robert first awakens at the beginning of the story, he wonders where the magic of Christmas is now. How do his feelings change by the end of the story? What has brought about the change?

### Applying

10. Do you agree with Robert that people who can love are fortunate? Explain your answer.

## ANALYZING LITERATURE

### Understanding a Flashback

A **flashback** presents events of the past in the midst of a story in the present. Pearl Buck uses a flashback to relate a Christmas in Robert's youth to a Christmas today. As a reader, you need to be able to tell when a flashback begins and when it ends.

1. When does the flashback begin in "Christmas Day in the Morning"?

2. How does the reader know when it is over?
3. What is the effect of the flashback?
4. How does the flashback prove Robert's statement: "Love alone could waken love"?

## CRITICAL THINKING AND READING

### Understanding Time Order

When an author uses flashbacks, events in the plot are not all in time or chronological order. To understand the story, you must mentally put the events in chronological order as you read.

Tell whether each event happens in the past as part of the flashback or in the present.

1. Robert overhears his father talking about him.
2. Robert writes a love letter to his wife.
3. Rob gets up at quarter to three to milk cows.

## THINKING AND WRITING

### Writing an Extended Definition

An **extended definition** includes examples of what you are defining and points out important aspects that cannot be explained in a brief definition. Brainstorm about what the word *love* means to you. Make a list of examples of the kinds of love with which you are familiar. Then write an extended definition of the word *love*. Use specific examples from your list to illustrate your definition. Check carefully to see that you have covered as many types of love as you can.

## LEARNING OPTION

**Writing.** At the end of "Christmas Day in the Morning," the narrator begins a love letter to his wife. Finish the letter for him, writing what you think he might have said. Before you begin writing, review the story, focusing on the narrator's character and tone. Try to keep in character and maintain a similar tone as you write.

*Christmas Day in the Morning* 25

---

## The Adventure of the Speckled Band

**More About the Author** Sir Arthur Conan Doyle refused to believe his Sherlock Holmes stories were as important as his many other works. The public loudly disagreed. In fact, Doyle wrote a story in 1893 in which Holmes was killed. But public demand forced Doyle to bring Holmes back to life in another story. Ask students what may motivate a practicing physician to want to write stories.

**Literary Focus** Ask students to recall the conflicts in Buck's and Asimov's stories. Ask if they would expect a conflict in a mystery or detective story to be different. How would it differ?

**Prereading Focus** Ask volunteers to name an aspect of the job description of detective they would like and one they would not like and give reasons. Write them on the chalkboard. Have students refer to them as they make their own lists.

**Vocabulary** It would be helpful for students to also know the following words: *agitation* (p. 28), *perpetrated* (p. 30), *avert* (p. 30), *fortnight* (p. 31), *impending* (p. 32), *averse* (p. 34), *insolence* (p. 36), and *cunning* (p. 37).

**Electronic Handbook** If students have access to the Language Master 6000, suggest that they listen to the pronunciations of these multisyllabic words to help them spell the words.

**Spelling Tip** Point out that the vocabulary words in the Guide for Reading are all multisyllabic. Emphasize that careful pronunciation of the syllables will help in spelling these words.

### Sir Arthur Conan Doyle

(1859–1930) was born in Edinburgh, Scotland. He began to study medicine and took up writing mystery stories in his early twenties. According to one of his professors, Doyle was often more accurate in guessing the occupation of patients than in diagnosing their illnesses. By 1886 Doyle had published his first Sherlock Holmes mystery, "A Study in Scarlet." In "The Adventure of the Speckled Band," you will see that Holmes, like Doyle himself, displays extraordinary powers of observation.

### Conflict

A **conflict** is a struggle between opposing forces or characters. Often a conflict occurs between two characters or between a character and the forces of nature. Conflict adds interest to a story, since it makes us wonder who will win.

### Focus

In the story you are about to read, Sherlock Holmes's client offers to pay him, and Holmes replies, "As to my reward, my profession is its own reward." Do you think you would enjoy being a detective as much as Sherlock Holmes does? If so, list the aspects of the profession that you would like and your reasons. If not, list the aspects of the profession that you would not like and your reasons. Then read "The Adventure of the Speckled Band" and notice how Holmes's extraordinary skills make him well suited for his profession.

### Vocabulary

Knowing the following words will help you as you read "The Adventure of the Speckled Band."

**defray** (di frā') v.: Pay the money for the cost of (p. 29)
**manifold** (man' ə fōld') adj.: Many and varied (p. 29)
**dissolute** (dis' ə lōōt') adj.: Unrestrained (p. 30)
**morose** (mə rōs') adj.: Gloomy; ill-tempered; sullen (p. 30)
**convulsed** (kən vulst') v.: Suffered a violent, involuntary spasm (p. 32)

**imperturbably** (im' pər tur' bə blē) adv.: Unexcitedly; calmly (p. 35)
**reverie** (rev' ər ē) n.: Daydreaming (p. 40)
**tangible** (tan' jə b'l) adj.: Having form and substance; that can be touched or felt by touch (p. 40)

### Objectives

1. To examine conflict in a short story
2. To understand logical reasoning
3. To write about deductive reasoning

### Support Material

**Teaching Portfolio**
Teacher Backup, p. 49
Grammar in Action Worksheets, *Using Who and Whom*, p. 54; *Understanding Adjective Clauses*, p. 55; *Understanding Compound Sentences*, p. 57; *Understanding Passive Voice*, p. 59
Usage and Mechanics Worksheet, p. 61
Vocabulary Check, p. 62

Critical Thinking and Reading Worksheet, *Understanding Logical Reasoning*, p. 63
Language Worksheet, *Choosing the Meaning That Fits the Context*, p. 64
Selection Test, p. 65

**The Library of Video Classics**
"The Speckled Band"

**Prentice Hall Literature Writing Studio**

# The Adventure of the Speckled Band

## Sir Arthur Conan Doyle

On glancing over my notes of the seventy odd cases in which I have during the last eight years studied the methods of my friend Sherlock Holmes, I find many tragic, some comic, a large number merely strange, but none commonplace; for, working as he did rather for the love of his art than for the acquirement of wealth, he refused to associate himself with any investigation which did not tend towards the unusual, and even the fantastic. Of all these varied cases, however, I cannot recall any which presented more singular features than that which was associated with the well-known Surrey family of the Roylotts of Stoke Moran. The events in question occurred in the early days of my association with Holmes when we were sharing rooms as bachelors in Baker Street. It is possible that I might have placed them upon record before but a promise of secrecy was made at the time, from which I have only been freed during the last month by the untimely death of the lady to whom the pledge was given. It is perhaps as well that the facts should now come to light, for I have reasons to know that there are widespread rumors as to the death of Dr. Grimesby Roylott which tend to make the matter even more terrible than the truth.

It was early in April in the year 1883 that I woke one morning to find Sherlock Holmes standing, fully dressed, by the side of my bed. He was a late riser, as a rule, and as the clock on the mantelpiece showed me that it was only a quarter past seven, I blinked up at him in some surprise, and perhaps just a little resentment, for I was myself regular in my habits.

"Very sorry to wake you up, Watson," said he, "but it's the common lot this morning. Mrs. Hudson has been awakened, she retorted upon me, and I on you."

"What is it, then—a fire?"

"No; a client. It seems that a young lady has arrived in a considerable state of excitement who insists upon seeing me. She is waiting now in the sitting room. Now, when young ladies wander about the metropolis at this hour of the morning, and get sleepy people up out of their beds, I presume that it is something very pressing which they have to communicate. Should it prove to be an interesting case, you would, I am sure, wish to follow it from the outset. I thought, at any rate, that I should call you and give you the chance."

"My dear fellow, I would not miss it for anything."

I had no keener pleasure than in following Holmes in his professional investigations, and in admiring the rapid deductions, as swift as intuitions, and yet always found-

---

**Thematic Focus** Much of the fascination and excitement of this story comes from the clever way the detective Sherlock Holmes unravels a mystery. Ask students to discuss methods their favorite detective, real or fictional, uses to solve a crime.

**Alternative Assessment** To promote active reading, have your students create a reader's response journal as they read "The Adventure of the Speckled Band." Ask them to focus their observations on the facts and clues Holmes uses to determine the identity of the murderer, the murder weapon, and the motive. Encourage them to respond personally to Holmes's powers of ob-servation and logical reasoning.

You may use your students' response journals to assess their understanding of the concepts and issues in Doyle's story.

## Presentation

**Motivation/Prior Knowledge** Tell students that this story is about the famous detective Sherlock Holmes and his assistant, Dr. Watson. The often-heard phrase "Elementary, my dear Watson" is associated with the stories by Sir Arthur Conan Doyle. Ask students what they think a mystery about a speckled band might be.

**Purpose-Setting Question** How is the conflict resolved between Sherlock Holmes and Dr. Roylott?

**1 Teaching to Ability Levels** Have your **more advanced** students note the length of the first sentence and all of the sentences in the first paragraph. Have them take the first sentence apart grammatically—phrases, clauses, and punctuation marks. Note that the story's complexity is reflected in the sentence structure.

**2 Discussion** Who is the narrator?

**3 Literary Focus** Discuss first-person point of view. Explain that it is the position from which the story is told. In the first-person point of view, the narrator is a character in the story who uses the pronoun *I* while narrating.

**4 Discussion** How does Sherlock Holmes treat Dr. Watson?

**5 Discussion** What does Dr. Watson think of Holmes? What qualities of an investigator does Watson attribute to Holmes.

**6 Master Teacher Note** Explain the differences between inductive and deductive reasoning. Present two reasoning exercises—inductive from the specific to the general; deductive from the general to the specific. Have students identify each. Explain that Holmes is known for his ability to solve baffling crimes through clever observation and deduction.

**7 Discussion** What does this tell you about Sherlock Holmes?

**Making Connections** Two other stories that involve criminals and detectives are "A Retrieved Reformation" (page 61) and "Crime on Mars" (page 137). Your students might enjoy comparing and contrasting the detectives' methods in these stories.

ed on a logical basis, with which he unraveled the problems which were submitted to him. I rapidly threw on my clothes and was ready in a few minutes to accompany my friend down to the sitting room. A lady dressed in black and heavily veiled, who had been sitting in the window, rose as we entered.

"Good morning, madam," said Holmes cheerily. "My name is Sherlock Holmes. This is my intimate friend and associate, Dr. Watson, before whom you can speak as freely as before myself. Ha! I am glad to see that Mrs. Hudson has had the good sense to light the fire. Pray draw up to it, and I shall order you a cup of hot coffee, for I observe that you are shivering."

"It is not cold which makes me shiver," said the woman in a low voice, changing her seat as requested.

"What, then?"

"It is fear, Mr. Holmes. It is terror." She raised her veil as she spoke, and we could see that she was indeed in a pitiable state of agitation, her face all drawn and gray, with restless, frightened eyes, like those of some hunted animal. Her features and figure were those of a woman of thirty, but her hair was shot with premature gray, and her expression was weary and haggard. Sherlock Holmes ran her over with one of his quick, all-comprehensive glances.

"You must not fear," said he soothingly, bending forward and patting her forearm. "We shall soon set matters right, I have no doubt. You have come in by train this morning, I see."

"You know me, then?"

"No, but I observe the second half of a return ticket in the palm of your left glove. You must have started early, and yet you had a good drive in a dogcart[1] along heavy roads, before you reached the station."

---

**1. dogcart:** Small horse-drawn carriage with seats arranged back-to-back.

28  *Short Stories*

## Grammar in Action

**Who** and **whom** are personal pronouns that indicate case; *who* is nominative, and *whom* is objective. The nominative case, *who,* is used as a subject. Often, *who* is the subject of a question, such as "Who is Sherlock Holmes?" *Who* can also begin a subordinate clause in a complex sentence. For example, *who* is the subject of a subordinate clause when Helen Stoner says that she is living with her stepfather, "who is the last survivor of the oldest Saxon families . . ."

The objective case, *whom,* is used as the direct object of a verb and the object of a preposition. In the following sentence from the story, *whom* is the direct object of a verb:

"I have heard of you, Mr. Holmes, I have heard of you from Mrs. Farintosh, whom you helped in the hour of her sore need."

Doyle uses *whom* as the object of a preposition as Helen Stoner says,

". . . that even he to whom of all others I have a right to look for help and advice looks upon all that I tell him about it as fancy."

The lady gave a violent start and stared in bewilderment at my companion.

"There is no mystery, my dear madam," said he, smiling. "The left arm of your jacket is spattered with mud in no less than seven places. The marks are perfectly fresh. There is no vehicle save a dogcart which throws up mud in that way, and then only when you sit on the left-hand side of the driver."

"Whatever your reasons may be, you are perfectly correct," said she. "I started from home before six, reached Leatherhead at twenty past, and came in by the first train to Waterloo. Sir, I can stand this strain no longer; I shall go mad if it continues. I have no one to turn to—none, save only one, who cares for me, and he, poor fellow, can be of little aid. I have heard of you, Mr. Holmes, I

have heard of you from Mrs. Farintosh, whom you helped in the hour of her sore need. It was from her that I had your address. Oh, sir, do you not think that you could help me, too, and at least throw a little light through the dense darkness which surrounds me? At present it is out of my power to reward you for your service, but in a month or six weeks I shall be married, with the control of my own income, and then at least you shall not find me ungrateful."

Holmes turned to his desk and, unlocking it, drew out a small case book, which he consulted.

"Farintosh," said he. "Ah yes, I recall the case; it was concerned with an opal tiara. I think it was before your time, Watson. I can only say, madam, that I shall be happy to devote the same care to your case as I did to that of your friend. As to reward, my profession is its own reward; but you are at liberty to defray whatever expenses I may be put to, at the time which suits you best. And now I beg that you will lay before us everything that may help us in forming an opinion upon the matter." **8**

"Alas!" replied our visitor, "the very horror of my situation lies in the fact that my fears are so vague, and my suspicions depend so entirely upon small points, which might seem trivial to another, that even he to whom of all others I have a right to look for help and advice looks upon all that I tell him about it as fancy. He does not say so, but I can read it from his soothing answers and averted eyes. But I have heard, Mr. Holmes, that you can see deeply into the manifold wickedness of the human heart. You may advise me how to walk amid the dangers which encompass me."

"I am all attention, madam."

"My name is Helen Stoner, and I am living with my stepfather, who is the last survivor of one of the oldest Saxon families **9**

*The Speckled Band* 29

**8 Discussion** How does Holmes feel about his job? Does his attitude sound practical? How do you suppose he can support himself with this type of attitude about payment for his services?

**9 Enrichment** Tell students that this story is set in London and the English countryside in the 1880's. Set the period for this story by bringing in pictures of Victorian London, especially those showing horsedrawn carriages and steam-driven trains. To help students visualize the manor house at Stoke Moran, show them pictures of typical English great houses.

Whenever *whom* follows a preposition, it is the object of the preposition.

**Student Activity 1.** Identify the case and purpose of the pronouns *who* and *whom* in the following sentences from the story:

"This is my intimate friend and associate, Dr. Watson, before whom you can speak as freely as before myself."

"I have no one to turn to—none, save only one, who cares for me, and he, poor fellow, can be of little aid."

**Student Activity 2.** Write a paragraph in which you summarize the important details in the story at this point, correctly using the pronouns *who* and *whom*.

**Electronic Handbook** You may want students to review pronoun case before completing the Grammar in Action activities. If students have access to the Language Master 6000, have them enter the access word *case* and press the GRAMMAR key to get information on the case of the pronouns *who* and *whom*.

10 **Clarification** An income of £250 was worth, at the time, about $1,250. The total income, once amounting to about $5,000, had fallen to about $3,750.

11 **Discussion** What do you learn about Helen's stepfather?

in England; the Roylotts of Stoke Moran, on the western border of Surrey."

Holmes nodded his head. "The name is familiar to me," said he.

"The family was at one time among the richest in England, and the estates extended over the borders into Berkshire in the north, and Hampshire in the west. In the last century, however, four successive heirs were of a dissolute and wasteful disposition, and the family ruin was eventually completed by a gambler in the days of the Regency. Nothing was left save a few acres of ground, and the two-hundred-year-old house, which is itself crushed under a heavy mortgage. The last squire dragged out his existence there, living the horrible life of an aristocratic pauper; but his only son, my stepfather, seeing that he must adapt himself to the new conditions, obtained an advance from a relative, which enabled him to take a medical degree and went out to Calcutta, where, by his professional skill and his force of character, he established a large practice. In a fit of anger, however, caused by some robberies which had been perpetrated in the house, he beat his native butler to death and narrowly escaped a capital sentence. As it was, he suffered a long term of imprisonment and afterwards returned to England a morose and disappointed man.

"When Dr. Roylott was in India he married my mother, Mrs. Stoner, the young widow of Major-General Stoner, of the Bengal Artillery. My sister Julia and I were twins, and we were only two years old at the time of my mother's remarriage. She had a 10 | considerable sum of money—not less than £1000 a year[2]—and this she bequeathed to Dr. Roylott entirely while we resided with him, with a provision that a certain annual

_____

**2. £1000:** One thousand pounds. £ is the symbol for pound or pounds, the British unit of money.

sum should be allowed to each of us in the event of our marriage. Shortly after our return to England my mother died—she was killed eight years ago in a railway accident near Crewe. Dr. Roylott then abandoned his attempts to establish himself in practice in London and took us to live with him in the old ancestral house at Stoke Moran. The money which my mother had left was enough for all our wants, and there seemed to be no obstacle to our happiness.

"But a terrible change came over our stepfather about this time. Instead of making friends and exchanging visits with our neighbors, who had at first been overjoyed to see a Roylott of Stoke Moran back in the old family seat, he shut himself up in his house and seldom came out save to indulge in ferocious quarrels with whoever might cross his path. Violence of temper approaching to mania has been hereditary in the men of the family, and in my stepfather's case it had, I believe, been intensified by his long residence in the tropics. A series of disgraceful brawls took place, two of which ended in the police court, until at last he became the terror of the village, and the folks would fly at his approach, for he is a man of immense strength, and absolutely uncontrollable in his anger.

"Last week he hurled the local blacksmith over a parapet into a stream, and it was only by paying over all the money which I could gather together that I was able to avert another public exposure. He had no friends at all save the wandering gypsies, and he would give these vagabonds leave to encamp upon the few acres of bramble-covered land which represent the family estate, and would accept in return the hospitality of their tents, wandering away with them sometimes for weeks on end. He has a passion also for Indian animals, which are sent over to him by a correspondent, and he

11

## Grammar in Action

**Adjective clauses** enable a writer to include information that is important but not important enough to stand as a separate sentence. Adjective clauses are easy to recognize because they begin with one of five words called relative pronouns—*that, which, who, whom,* and *whose,* or with the relative adverbs *where* or *when.* Adjective clauses are subordinate clauses: Although they contain a subject and a verb, they cannot stand alone as a sentence. They are attached to and modify a word in an independent clause.

Adjective clauses can help a writer vary sentence length. Instead of writing two short choppy sentences, a writer can combine them, making one into an adjective clause.

The following sentences or excerpts by Sir Arthur Conan Doyle contain adjective clauses:

Nothing was left save a few acres of ground, and the two-hundred-year-old house, which is itself crushed under a heavy mortgage.

In a fit of anger, however, caused by some robberies which had been perpetrated in the house . . .

has at this moment a cheetah and a baboon, which wander freely over his grounds and are feared by the villagers almost as much as is their master.

"You can imagine from what I say that my poor sister Julia and I had no great pleasure in our lives. No servant would stay with us, and for a long time we did all the work of the house. She was but thirty at the time of her death, and yet her hair had already begun to whiten, even as mine has."

"Your sister is dead, then?"

"She died just two years ago, and it is of her death that I wish to speak to you. You can understand that, living the life which I have described, we were little likely to see anyone of our own age and position. We had, however, an aunt, my mother's maiden sister, Miss Honoria Westphail, who lives near Harrow, and we were occasionally allowed to pay short visits at this lady's house. Julia went there at Christmas two years ago, and met there a major in the Marines, to whom she became engaged. My stepfather learned of the engagement when my sister returned and offered no objection to the marriage; but within a fortnight of the day which had been fixed for the wedding, the terrible event occurred which has deprived me of my only companion."

Sherlock Holmes had been leaning back in his chair with his eyes closed and his head sunk in a cushion, but he half opened his lids now and glanced across at his visitor.

"Pray be precise as to details," said he.

"It is easy for me to be so, for every event of that dreadful time is seared into my memory. The manor house is, as I have already said, very old, and only one wing is now inhabited. The bedrooms in this wing are on the ground floor, the sitting rooms being in the central block of the buildings. Of these bedrooms the first is Dr. Roylott's, the second my sister's, and the third my own. There is no communication between them, but they all open out into the same corridor. Do I make myself plain?"

"Perfectly so."

"The windows of the three rooms open out upon the lawn. That fatal night Dr. Roylott had gone to his room early, though we knew that he had not retired to rest, for my sister was troubled by the smell of the strong Indian cigars which it was his custom to smoke. She left her room, therefore, and came into mine, where she sat for some time, chatting about her approaching wedding. At eleven o'clock she rose to leave me, but she paused at the door and looked back.

" 'Tell me, Helen,' said she, 'have you ever heard anyone whistle in the dead of the night?'

" 'Never,' said I.

" 'I suppose that you could not possibly whistle, yourself, in your sleep?'

" 'Certainly not. But why?'

" 'Because during the last few nights I have always, about three in the morning, heard a low, clear whistle. I am a light sleeper, and it has awakened me. I cannot tell where it came from—perhaps from the next room, perhaps from the lawn. I thought that I would just ask you whether you had heard it.'

" 'No, I have not. It must be the gypsies in the plantation.'

" 'Very likely. And yet if it were on the lawn, I wonder that you did not hear it also.'

" 'Ah, but I sleep more heavily than you.'

" 'Well, it is of no great consequence, at any rate.' She smiled back at me, closed my door, and a few moments later I heard her key turn in the lock."

"Indeed," said Holmes. "Was it your custom always to lock yourselves in at night?"

"Always."

*The Speckled Band* 31

12 **Discussion** If Helen's sister Julia had married, what would she have received?

**Electronic Handbook** You may want students to review adjective clauses before completing the Grammar in Action activities. If students have access to the Language Master 6000, have them enter the access word *clause* and press the GRAMMAR key to get information on adjective clauses and the words that introduce them.

The money which my mother had left was enough for all our wants . . .

Instead of making friends and exchanging visits with our neighbors, who had at first been overjoyed to see a Roylott of Stoke Moran back in the old family seat, he shut himself up in his old house and seldom came out . . .

. . . and he would give these vagabonds leave to encamp upon the few acres of bramble-covered land which represent the family estate . . .

**Student Activity 1.** Write out the adjective clauses in the example sentences and excerpts.

**Student Activity 2.** Write five of your own sentences with adjective clauses. Try to use a different relative pronoun in each. to get information on adjective clauses and the words that introduce them.

"And why?"

"I think that I mentioned to you that the doctor kept a cheetah and a baboon. We had no feeling of security unless our doors were locked."

"Quite so. Pray proceed with your statement."

"I could not sleep that night. A vague feeling of impending misfortune impressed me. My sister and I, you will recollect, were twins, and you know how subtle are the links which bind two souls which are so closely allied. It was a wild night. The wind was howling outside, and the rain was beating and splashing against the windows. Suddenly, amid all the hubbub of the gale, there burst forth the wild scream of a terrified woman. I knew that it was my sister's voice. I sprang from my bed, wrapped a shawl round me, and rushed into the corridor. As I opened my door I seemed to hear a low whistle, such as my sister described, and a few moments later a clanging sound, as if a mass of metal had fallen. As I ran down the passage, my sister's door was unlocked, and revolved slowly upon its hinges. I stared at it horror-stricken, not knowing what was about to issue from it. By the light of the corridor lamp I saw my sister appear at the opening, her face blanched with terror, her hands groping for help, her whole figure swaying to and fro like that of a drunkard. I ran to her and threw my arms round her, but at that moment her knees seemed to give way and she fell to the ground. She writhed as one who is in terrible pain, and her limbs were dreadfully convulsed. At first I thought that she had not recognized me, but as I bent over her she suddenly shrieked out in a voice which I shall never forget, 'Oh, Helen! It was the band! The speckled band!' There was something else which she would fain have said, and she stabbed with her finger into the air in the direction of the doctor's room, but a fresh convulsion seized her and choked her words. I rushed out, calling loudly for my stepfather, and I met him hastening from his room in his dressing gown. When he reached my sister's side she was unconscious, and though he poured brandy down her throat and sent for medical aid from the village, all efforts were in vain, for she slowly sank and died without having recovered her consciousness. Such was the dreadful end of my beloved sister."

"One moment," said Holmes; "are you sure about this whistle and metallic sound? Could you swear to it?"

"That was what the county coroner asked me at the inquiry. It is my strong impression that I heard it, and yet, among the crash of the gale and the creaking of an old house, I may possibly have been deceived."

"Was your sister dressed?"

"No, she was in her nightdress. In her right hand was found the charred stump of a match, and in her left a matchbox."

"Showing that she had struck a light and looked about her when the alarm took place. That is important. And what conclusions did the coroner come to?"

"He investigated the case with great care, for Dr. Roylott's conduct had long been notorious in the county, but he was unable to find any satisfactory cause of death. My evidence showed that the door had been fastened upon the inner side, and the windows were blocked by old-fashioned shutters with broad iron bars, which were secured every night. The walls were carefully sounded, and were shown to be quite solid all round, and the flooring was also thoroughly examined, with the same result. The chimney is wide, but is barred up by four large staples. It is certain, therefore, that my sister was quite alone when she met her

## Grammar in Action

Writers join closely related ideas of equal importance in **compound sentences.** By joining several ideas in one sentence, the writer shows the logical relationship between the ideas and eliminates choppy sentences.

A compound sentence consists of two or more independent clauses joined with a comma and one of the coordinating conjunctions: *and, but, for, nor, or, so, yet.* The following sentences from "The Adventure of the Speckled Band" are compound:

The wind was howling outside, and the rain was beating and splashing against the windows.

I ran to her and threw my arms around her, but at that moment her knees seemed to give way and she fell to the ground.

I rushed out, calling loudly for my stepfather, and I met him hastening from his room in his dressing gown.

end. Besides, there were no marks of any violence upon her."

"How about poison?"

"The doctors examined her for it, but without success."

"What do you think that this unfortunate lady died of, then?"

"It is my belief that she died of pure fear and nervous shock, though what it was that frightened her I cannot imagine."

"Were there gypsies in the plantation at the time?"

"Yes, there are nearly always some there."

"Ah, and what did you gather from this allusion to a band—a speckled band?"

"Sometimes I have thought that it was merely the wild talk of delirium, sometimes that it may have referred to some band of people, perhaps to these very gypsies in the plantation. I do not know whether the spotted handkerchiefs which so many of them wear over their heads might have suggested the strange adjective which she used."

Holmes shook his head like a man who is far from being satisfied.

"These are very deep waters," said he; "pray go on with your narrative."

"Two years have passed since then, and my life has been until lately lonelier than ever. A month ago, however, a dear friend, whom I have known for many years, has done me the honor to ask my hand in marriage. His name is Armitage—Percy Armitage—the second son of Mr. Armitage, of Crane Water, near Reading. My stepfather has offered no opposition to the match, and we are to be married in the course of the spring. Two days ago some repairs were started in the west wing of the building, and my bedroom wall has been pierced, so that I have had to move into the chamber in which my sister died, and to sleep in the very bed in which she slept. Imagine, then, my thrill of terror when last night, as I lay awake, thinking over her terrible fate, I suddenly heard in the silence of the night the low whistle which had been the herald of her own death. I sprang up and lit the lamp, but nothing was to be seen in the room. I was too shaken to go to bed again, however, so I dressed, and as soon as it was daylight I slipped down, got a dogcart at the Crown Inn, which is opposite, and drove to Leatherhead, from whence I have come on this morning with the one object of seeing you and asking your advice."

"You have done wisely," said my friend. "But have you told me all?"

"Yes, all."

"Miss Roylott, you have not. You are screening your stepfather."

"Why, what do you mean?"

For answer Holmes pushed back the frill of black lace which fringed the hand that lay upon our visitor's knee. Five little livid spots, the marks of four fingers and a thumb, were printed upon the white wrist.

"You have been cruelly used," said Holmes.

The lady colored deeply and covered over her injured wrist. "He is a hard man," she said, "and perhaps he hardly knows his own strength."

There was a long silence, during which Holmes leaned his chin upon his hands and stared into the crackling fire.

"This is a very deep business," he said at last. "There are a thousand details which I should desire to know before I decide upon our course of action. Yet we have not a moment to lose. If we were to come to Stoke Moran today, would it be possible for us to look over these rooms without the knowledge of your stepfather?"

"As it happens, he spoke of coming into town today upon some most important business. It is probable that he will be away all

---

He investigated the case with great care, for Dr. Roylott's conduct had long been notorious in the county, but he was unable to find any satisfactory cause of death.

**Student Activity 1.** Reread the example sentences substituting a period for the comma and the coordinating conjunction. What difference do you notice?

**Student Activity 2.** Write five sets of two simple but related sentences. Exchange papers with a partner, and write the shorter sentences as one compound sentence. Be sure to use a comma before the coordinating conjunction that joins the two sentences.

**Electronic Handbook** You may want students to review compound sentences before completing the Grammar in Action activities. If students have access to the Language Master 6000, have them enter the access words *clause* and *conjunction* and press the GRAMMAR key to get information on independent clauses and the words that join them to make compound sentences.

<br>

<br>

**13 Reading Strategy** Have students summarize the events that have occurred so far in the story. Ask them if they have any ideas as to the cause of Julia's death.

day, and that there would be nothing to disturb you. We have a housekeeper now, but I could easily get her out of the way."

"Excellent. You are not averse to this trip, Watson?"

"By no means."

"Then we shall both come. What are you going to do yourself?"

"I have one or two things which I would wish to do now that I am in town. But I shall return by the twelve o'clock train, so as to be there in time for your coming."

"And you may expect us early in the afternoon. I have myself some small business matters to attend to. Will you not wait and breakfast?"

"No, I must go. My heart is lightened already since I have confided my trouble to you. I shall look forward to seeing you again this afternoon." She dropped her thick black veil over her face and glided from the room.

**13** "And what do you think of it all, Watson?" asked Sherlock Holmes, leaning back in his chair.

"It seems to me to be a most dark and sinister business."

"Dark enough and sinister enough."

"Yet if the lady is correct in saying that the flooring and walls are sound, and that the door, window, and chimney are impassable, then her sister must have been undoubtedly alone when she met her mysterious end."

"What becomes, then, of these nocturnal whistles, and what of the very peculiar words of the dying woman?"

"I cannot think."

"When you combine the ideas of whistles at night, the presence of a band of gypsies who are on intimate terms with this old doctor, the fact that we have every reason to believe that the doctor has an interest in preventing his stepdaughter's marriage,

the dying allusion to a band, and, finally, the fact that Miss Helen Stoner heard a metallic clang, which might have been caused by one of those metal bars that secured the shutters, falling back into its place, I think that there is good ground to think that the mystery may be cleared along those lines."

"But what, then, did the gypsies do?"

"I cannot imagine."

"I see many objections to any such theory."

"And so do I. It is precisely for that reason that we are going to Stoke Moran this day. I want to see whether the objections are fatal, or if they may be explained away. But what in the name of the devil!"

The ejaculation had been drawn from my companion by the fact that our door had been suddenly dashed open, and that a huge man had framed himself in the aperture. His costume was a peculiar mixture of the professional and of the agricultural, having a black top hat, a long frock coat, and a pair of high gaiters,[3] with a hunting crop swinging in his hand. So tall was he that his hat actually brushed the crossbar of the doorway, and his breadth seemed to span it across from side to side. A large face, seared with a thousand wrinkles, burned yellow with the sun, and marked with every evil passion, was turned from one to the other of us, while his deep-set, bile-shot eyes, and his high, thin, fleshless nose, gave him somewhat the resemblance to a fierce old bird of prey.

"Which of you is Holmes?" asked this apparition.

"My name, sir; but you have the advantage of me," said my companion quietly.

---

**3. gaiters** (gāt′ ərz) *n.*: A high overshoe with a cloth upper.

"I am Dr. Grimesby Roylott, of Stoke Moran."

"Indeed, Doctor," said Holmes blandly. "Pray take a seat."

"I will do nothing of the kind. My stepdaughter has been here. I have traced her. What has she been saying to you?"

"It is a little cold for the time of the year," said Holmes.

"What has she been saying to you?" screamed the old man furiously.

"But I have heard that the crocuses promise well," continued my companion imperturbably.

"Ha! You put me off, do you?" said our new visitor, taking a step forward and shaking his hunting crop. "I know you, you scoundrel! I have heard of you before. You are Holmes, the meddler."

My friend smiled.

"Holmes, the busybody!"

His smile broadened.

"Holmes, the Scotland Yard Jack-in-office!"

Holmes chuckled heartily. "Your conversation is most entertaining," said he. "When you go out close the door, for there is a decided draft."

"I will go when I have said my say. Don't you dare to meddle with my affairs. I know that Miss Stoner has been here. I traced her! I am a dangerous man to fall foul of! See here." He stepped swiftly forward, seized the poker, and bent it into a curve with his huge brown hands.

"See that you keep yourself out of my grip," he snarled, and hurling the twisted poker into the fireplace he strode out of the room.

"He seems a very amiable person," said Holmes, laughing. "I am not quite so bulky, but if he had remained I might have shown him that my grip was not much more feeble than his own." As he spoke he picked up the steel poker and, with a sudden effort, straightened it out again.

14

14 **Discussion** How does Holmes's physical strength compare with Dr. Roylott's? How does his physical appearance compare with the doctor's?

15 **Discussion** How does Holmes feel about Dr. Roylott thinking he is a member of Scotland Yard?

16 **Clarification** A trap was a one-horse, two-wheeled carriage on springs.

15 "Fancy his having the insolence to confound me with[4] the official detective force! This incident gives zest to our investigation, however, and I only trust that our little friend will not suffer from her imprudence in allowing this brute to trace her. And now, Watson, we shall order breakfast, and afterwards I shall walk down to Doctors' Commons, where I hope to get some data which may help us in this matter.''

It was nearly one o'clock when Sherlock Holmes returned from his excursion. He held in his hand a sheet of blue paper, scrawled over with notes and figures.

"I have seen the will of the deceased wife,'' said he. "To determine its exact meaning I have been obliged to work out the present prices of the investments with which it is concerned. The total income, which at the time of the wife's death was little short of £1100, is now, through the fall in agricultural prices, not more than £750. Each daughter can claim an income of £250, in case of marriage. It is evident, therefore, that if both girls had married, this beauty would have had a mere pittance,[5] while even one of them would cripple him to a very serious extent. My morning's work has not been wasted, since it has proved that he has the very strongest motives for standing in the way of anything of the sort. And now, Watson, this is too serious for dawdling, especially as the old man is aware that we are interesting ourselves in his affairs; so if you are ready, we shall call a cab and drive to Waterloo. I should be very much obliged if you would slip your revolver into your pocket. An Eley's No. 2 is an excellent argument with gentlemen who can twist steel pokers

---

4. **confound . . . with:** Mistake me for.
5. **pittance** (pit′ 'ns) *n.*: A small or barely sufficient allowance of money.

into knots. That and a toothbrush are, I think, all that we need.''

At Waterloo we were fortunate in catching a train for Leatherhead, where we hired a trap at the station inn and drove for four or 16 five miles through the lovely Surrey lanes. It was a perfect day, with a bright sun and a few fleecy clouds in the heavens. The trees and wayside hedges were just throwing out their first green shoots, and the air was full of the pleasant smell of the moist earth. To me at least there was a strange contrast between the sweet promise of the spring and this sinister quest upon which we were engaged. My companion sat in the front of the trap, his arms folded, his hat pulled down over his eyes, and his chin sunk upon his breast, buried in the deepest thought. Suddenly, however, he started, tapped me on the shoulder, and pointed over the meadows.

"Look there!'' said he.

A heavily timbered park stretched up in a gentle slope, thickening into a grove at the highest point. From amid the branches there jutted out the gray gables and high rooftop of a very old mansion.

"Stoke Moran?'' said he.

"Yes, sir, that be the house of Dr. Grimesby Roylott,'' remarked the driver.

"There is some building going on there,'' said Holmes; "that is where we are going.''

"There's the village,'' said the driver, pointing to a cluster of roofs some distance to the left; "but if you want to get to the house, you'll find it shorter to get over this stile, and so by the footpath over the fields. There it is, where the lady is walking.''

"And the lady, I fancy, is Miss Stoner,'' observed Holmes, shading his eyes. "Yes, I think we had better do as you suggest.''

We got off, paid our fare, and the trap rattled back on its way to Leatherhead.

"I thought it as well,'' said Holmes as we

climbed the stile, "that this fellow should think we had come here as architects, or on some definite business. It may stop his gossip. Good afternoon, Miss Stoner. You see that we have been as good as our word."

Our client of the morning had hurried forward to meet us with a face which spoke her joy. "I have been waiting so eagerly for you," she cried, shaking hands with us warmly. "All has turned out splendidly. Dr. Roylott has gone to town, and it is unlikely that he will be back before evening."

"We have had the pleasure of making the doctor's acquaintance," said Holmes, and in a few words he sketched out what had occurred. Miss Stoner turned white to the lips as she listened.

"Good heavens!" she cried, "he has followed me, then."

"So it appears."

"He is so cunning that I never know when I am safe from him. What will he say when he returns?"

"He must guard himself, for he may find that there is someone more cunning than himself upon his track. You must lock yourself up from him tonight. If he is violent, we shall take you away to your aunt's at Harrow. Now, we must make the best use of our time, so kindly take us at once to the rooms which we are to examine."

The building was of gray, lichen-blotched[6] stone, with a high central portion and two curving wings, like the claws of a crab, thrown out on each side. In one of these wings the windows were broken and blocked with wooden boards, while the roof was partly caved in, a picture of ruin. The central portion was in little better repair, but the right-hand block was comparatively modern, and the blinds in the windows,

---

**6. lichen-blotched** (lī′ kən blächt) *adj.*: Covered with patches of fungus.

with the blue smoke curling up from the chimneys, showed that this was where the family resided. Some scaffolding had been erected against the end wall, and the stonework had been broken into, but there were no signs of any workmen at the moment of our visit. Holmes walked slowly up and down the ill-trimmed lawn and examined with deep attention the outsides of the windows.

"This, I take it, belongs to the room in which you used to sleep, the center one to your sister's, and the one next to the main building to Dr. Roylott's chamber?"

"Exactly so. But I am now sleeping in the middle one."

"Pending the alterations, as I understand. By the way, there does not seem to be any very pressing need for repairs at that end wall."

"There were none. I believe that it was an excuse to move me from my room."

"Ah! that is suggestive. Now, on the other side of this narrow wing runs the corridor from which these three rooms open. There are windows in it, of course?"

"Yes, but very small ones. Too narrow for anyone to pass through."

"As you both locked your doors at night, your rooms were unapproachable from that side. Now, would you have the kindness to go into your room and bar your shutters?"

Miss Stoner did so, and Holmes, after a careful examination through the open window, endeavored in every way to force the shutter open, but without success. There was no slit through which a knife could be passed to raise the bar. Then with his lens he tested the hinges, but they were of solid iron, built firmly into the massive masonry. "Hum!" said he, scratching his chin in some perplexity, "My theory certainly presents some difficulties. No one could pass through these shutters if they were bolted. Well, we

17 **Discussion** Note Holmes's careful screening of the room. Ask students if they can think of some conclusions about Miss Stoner's death.

shall see if the inside throws any light upon the matter."

A small side door led into the white-washed corridor from which the three bedrooms opened. Holmes refused to examine the third chamber, so we passed at once to the second, that in which Miss Stoner was now sleeping, and in which her sister had met with her fate. It was a homely little room, with a low ceiling and a gaping fireplace, after the fashion of old country houses. A brown chest of drawers stood in one corner, a narrow white-counterpaned bed in another, and a dressing table on the left-hand side of the window. These articles, with two small wickerwork chairs, made up all the furniture in the room save for a square of Wilton carpet in the center. The boards round and the paneling of the walls were of brown, worm-eaten oak, so old and discolored that it may have dated from the original building of the house. Holmes drew one of the chairs into a corner and sat silent, while his eyes traveled round and round and up and down, taking in every detail of the apartment.

"Where does that bell communicate with?" he asked at last, pointing to a thick bell-rope which hung down beside the bed, the tassel actually lying upon the pillow.

"It goes to the housekeeper's room."

"It looks newer than the other things?"

17 "Yes, it was only put there a couple of years ago."

"Your sister asked for it, I suppose?"

"No, I never heard of her using it. We used always to get what we wanted for ourselves."

"Indeed, it seemed unnecessary to put so nice a bell-pull there. You will excuse me for a few minutes while I satisfy myself as to this floor." He threw himself down upon his face with his lens in his hand and crawled swiftly backward and forward, examining

minutely the cracks between the boards. Then he did the same with the woodwork with which the chamber was paneled. Finally he walked over to the bed and spent some time in staring at it and in running his eye up and down the wall. Finally he took the bell-rope in his hand and gave it a brisk tug.

"Why, it's a dummy," said he.

"Won't it ring?"

"No, it is not even attached to a wire. This is very interesting. You can see now that it is fastened to a hook just above where the little opening for the ventilator is.''

"How very absurd! I never noticed that before!''

"Very strange!'' muttered Holmes, pulling at the rope. "There are one or two very singular points about this room. For example, what a fool a builder must be to open a ventilator into another room, when, with the same trouble, he might have communicated with the outside air!''

"That is also quite modern,'' said the lady.

"Done about the same time as the bell-rope?'' remarked Holmes.

"Yes, there were several little changes carried out about that time.''

"They seem to have been of a most interesting character—dummy bell-ropes, and ventilators which do not ventilate. With your permission, Miss Stoner, we shall now carry our researches into the inner apartment.''

Dr. Grimesby Roylott's chamber was larger than that of his stepdaughter, but was as plainly furnished. A camp bed, a small wooden shelf full of books, mostly of a technical character, an armchair beside the bed, a plain wooden chair against the wall, a round table, and a large iron safe were the principal things which met the eye. Holmes walked slowly round and examined each and all of them with the keenest interest.

"What's in here?'' he asked, tapping the safe.

"My stepfather's business papers.''

"Oh! you have seen inside, then?''

"Only once, some years ago. I remember that it was full of papers.''

"There isn't a cat in it, for example?''

"No. What a strange idea!''

"Well, look at this!'' He took up a small saucer of milk which stood on the top of it.

"No; we don't keep a cat. But there is a cheetah and a baboon.''

"Ah, yes, of course! Well, a cheetah is just a big cat, and yet a saucer of milk does not go very far in satisfying its wants, I daresay. There is one point which I should wish to determine.'' He squatted down in front of the wooden chair and examined the seat of it with the greatest attention.

"Thank you. That is quite settled,'' said he, rising and putting his lens in his pocket. "Hello! Here is something interesting!''

The object which had caught his eye was a small dog lash hung on one corner of the

*The Speckled Band*  39

**Speaking and Listening** Allow volunteers to select a short scene from the story to dramatize. Have them prepare a script and choose actors for the characters. Suggest that they bring appropriate costumes and props when they perform the scene for their class.

bed. The lash, however, was curled upon itself and tied so as to make a loop of whip-cord.

"What do you make of that, Watson?"

"It's a common enough lash. But I don't know why it should be tied."

"That is not quite so common, is it? Ah, me! it's a wicked world, and when a clever man turns his brains to crime it is the worst of all. I think that I have seen enough now, Miss Stoner, and with your permission we shall walk out upon the lawn."

I had never seen my friend's face so grim or his brow so dark as it was when we turned from the scene of this investigation. We had walked several times up and down the lawn, neither Miss Stoner nor myself liking to break in upon his thoughts before he roused himself from his reverie.

"It is very essential, Miss Stoner," said he, "that you should absolutely follow my advice in every respect."

"I shall most certainly do so."

"The matter is too serious for any hesitation. Your life may depend upon your compliance."[7]

"I assure you that I am in your hands."

"In the first place, both my friend and I must spend the night in your room."

Both Miss Stoner and I gazed at him in astonishment.

"Yes, it must be so. Let me explain. I believe that that is the village inn over there?"

"Yes, that is the Crown."

"Very good. Your windows would be visible from there?"

"Certainly."

"You must confine yourself to your room, on pretense of a headache, when your stepfather comes back. Then when you hear

him retire for the night, you must open the shutters of your window, undo the hasp,[8] put your lamp there as a signal to us, and then withdraw quietly with everything which you are likely to want into the room which you used to occupy. I have no doubt that, in spite of the repairs, you could manage there for one night."

"Oh, yes, easily."

"The rest you will leave in our hands."

"But what will you do?"

"We shall spend the night in your room, and we shall investigate the cause of this noise which has disturbed you."

"I believe, Mr. Holmes, that you have already made up your mind," said Miss Stoner, laying her hand upon my companion's sleeve.

"Perhaps I have."

"Then, for pity's sake, tell me what was the cause of my sister's death."

"I should prefer to have clearer proofs before I speak."

"You can at least tell me whether my own thought is correct, and if she died from some sudden fright."

"No, I do not think so. I think that there was probably some more tangible cause. And now, Miss Stoner, we must leave you, for if Dr. Roylott returned and saw us our journey would be in vain. Goodbye, and be brave, for if you will do what I have told you, you may rest assured that we shall soon drive away the dangers that threaten you."

Sherlock Holmes and I had no difficulty in engaging a bedroom and sitting room at the Crown Inn. They were on the upper floor, and from our window we could command a view of the avenue gate, and of the inhabited wing of Stoke Moran Manor House. At dusk we saw Dr. Grimesby Roylott drive past, his huge form looming up beside

---

7. **compliance** (kəm plī′ əns) *n.*: Agreeing to a request.

8. **hasp** *n.*: Hinged metal fastening of a window.

## Grammar in Action

Action verbs can be either active or passive. When a verb is active, the subject of the verb performs the action. By contrast, in the **passive voice,** the subject of a verb receives the action. In general, passive voice is to be avoided because it is not specific and weakens your writing by making it less interesting. However, passive voice is useful when you don't know who performed the action. For example, Doyle uses the passive voice as Watson narrates: "The trap drove on, and a few minutes later we saw a sudden light spring up among the trees as the lamp was *lit* in one of the sitting rooms." In addition passive voice can be used when you know who performed the action but don't wish to specify the individual.

Passive voice is recognizable because a passive verb has two parts: a form of the verb "to be" and a past participle. Remarking on Miss Stoner's sister's bed, Sherlock Holmes says, "It *was clamped* to the floor." Here is the conjugation of passive forms of the verb *clamp* with the pronoun *it:*

| Tense | Passive Form |
| --- | --- |
| Present | it is clamped |

the little figure of the lad who drove him. The boy had some slight difficulty in undoing the heavy iron gates, and we heard the hoarse roar of the doctor's voice and saw the fury with which he shook his clinched fists at him. The trap drove on, and a few minutes later we saw a sudden light spring up among the trees as the lamp was lit in one of the sitting rooms.

"Do you know, Watson," said Holmes as we sat together in the gathering darkness, "I have really some scruples as to taking you tonight. There is a distinct element of danger."

"Can I be of assistance?"

"Your presence might be invaluable."

"Then I shall certainly come."

"It is very kind of you."

"You speak of danger. You have evidently seen more in these rooms than was visible to me."

"No, but I fancy that I may have deduced a little more. I imagine that you saw all that I did."

"I saw nothing remarkable save the bell-rope, and what purpose that could answer I confess is more than I can imagine."

"You saw the ventilator, too?"

"Yes, but I do not think that it is such a very unusual thing to have a small opening between two rooms. It was so small that a rat could hardly pass through."

"I knew that we should find a ventilator before ever we came to Stoke Moran."

"My dear Holmes!"

"Oh, yes, I did. You remember in her statement she said that her sister could smell Dr. Roylott's cigar. Now, of course that suggested at once that there must be a communication between the two rooms. It could only be a small one, or it would have been remarked upon at the coroner's inquiry. I deduced a ventilator."

"But what harm can there be in that?"

"Well, there is at least a curious coincidence of dates. A ventilator is made, a cord is hung, and a lady who sleeps in the bed dies. Does not that strike you?"

"I cannot as yet see any connection."

"Did you observe anything very peculiar about that bed?"

"No."

"It was clamped to the floor. Did you ever see a bed fastened like that before?"

"I cannot say that I have."

"The lady could not move her bed. It must always be in the same relative position to the ventilator and to the rope—or so we may call it, since it was clearly never meant for a bell-pull."

"Holmes," I cried, "I seem to see dimly what you are hinting at. We are only just in time to prevent some subtle and horrible crime."

"Subtle enough and horrible enough. When a doctor does go wrong he is the first of criminals. He has nerve and he has knowledge. Palmer and Pritchard were among the heads of their profession. This man strikes even deeper, but I think, Watson, that we shall be able to strike deeper still. But we shall have horrors enough before the night is over; for goodness' sake let us have a quiet pipe and turn our minds for a few hours to something more cheerful."

About nine o'clock the light among the trees was extinguished, and all was dark in the direction of the Manor House. Two hours passed slowly away, and then, suddenly, just at the stroke of eleven, a single bright light shone out right in front of us.

"That is our signal," said Holmes, springing to his feet; "it comes from the middle window."

As we passed out he exchanged a few words with the landlord, explaining that we were going on a late visit to an acquaint-

*The Speckled Band* 41

18 **Discussion** By now Watson has an idea of the cause of death. Ask students again if they have any ideas.

19 **Literary Focus** Point out how the author is building toward the climax and resolution. Little by little clues are being given to the reader.

20 **Clarification** William Palmer was executed in 1856 for the murder of a friend by poison. Edward Pritchard, a Glasgow practitioner, was hanged in 1865 for poisoning his wife and mother-in-law.

| Past | it was clamped |
|---|---|
| Future | it will be clamped |
| Present Perfect | it has been clamped |
| Past Perfect | it had been clamped |
| Future Perfect | it will have been clamped |

**Student Activity 1.** Locate three more examples of passive voice on pages 41–42. Why is the use of passive voice appropriate in the examples you found?

**Student Activity 2.** Compose five sentences in which you use the passive voice, and briefly explain why passive voice is appropriate in each sentence.

**Electronic Handbook** You may want students to review verbs in the passive voice before completing the Grammar in Action activities. If students have access to the Language Master 6000, have them enter the access word *active* and press the GRAMMAR key to get information on when it is appropriate to use the passive rather than the active voice.

ance, and that it was possible that we might spend the night there. A moment later we were out on the dark road, a chill wind blowing in our faces, and one yellow light twinkling in front of us through the gloom to guide us on our somber errand.

There was little difficulty in entering the grounds; for unrepaired breaches gaped in the old park wall. Making our way among the trees, we reached the lawn, crossed it, and were about to enter through the window when out from a clump of laurel bushes there darted what seemed to be a hideous and distorted child, who threw itself upon the grass with writhing limbs and then ran swiftly across the lawn into the darkness.

"My God!" I whispered; "did you see it?"

Holmes was for the moment as startled as I. His hand closed like a vise upon my wrist in his agitation. Then he broke into a low laugh and put his lips to my ear.

"It is a nice household," he murmured. "That is the baboon."

I had forgotten the strange pets which the doctor affected. There was a cheetah, too; perhaps we might find it upon our shoulders at any moment. I confess that I felt easier in my mind when, after following Holmes's example and slipping off my shoes, I found myself inside the bedroom. My companion noiselessly closed the shutters, moved the lamp onto the table, and cast his eyes round the room. All was as we had seen it in the daytime. Then creeping up to me and making a trumpet of his hand, he whispered into my ear again so gently that it was all that I could do to distinguish the words:

"The least sound would be fatal to our plans."

I nodded to show that I had heard.

"We must sit without light. He would see it through the ventilator."

I nodded again.

"Do not go asleep; your very life may depend upon it. Have your pistol ready in case we should need it. I will sit on the side of the bed, and you in that chair."

I took out my revolver and laid it on the corner of the table.

Holmes had brought up a long thin cane, and this he placed upon the bed beside him. By it he laid the box of matches and the stump of a candle. Then he turned down the lamp, and we were left in darkness.

How shall I ever forget that dreadful vigil? I could not hear a sound, not even the drawing of a breath, and yet I knew that my companion sat open-eyed, within a few feet of me, in the same state of nervous tension in which I was myself. The shutters cut off the least ray of light, and we waited in absolute darkness. From outside came the occasional cry of a night bird, and once at our very window a long-drawn catlike whine, which told us that the cheetah was indeed at liberty. Far away we could hear the deep tones of the parish clock, which boomed out every quarter of an hour. How long they seemed, those quarters! Twelve struck, and one and two and three, and still we sat waiting silently for whatever might befall.

Suddenly there was the momentary gleam of a light up in the direction of the ventilator, which vanished immediately, but was succeeded by a strong smell of burning oil and heated metal. Someone in the next room had lit a dark lantern.[9] I heard a gentle sound of movement, and then all was silent once more, though the smell grew stronger. For half an hour I sat with straining ears.

---

**9. dark lantern:** A lantern with a shutter that can hide the light.

Then suddenly another sound became audible—a very gentle, soothing sound, like that of a small jet of steam escaping continually from a kettle. The instant that we heard it, Holmes sprang from the bed, struck a match, and lashed furiously with his cane at the bell-pull.

"You see it, Watson?" he yelled. "You see it?"

But I saw nothing. At the moment when Holmes struck the light I heard a low, clear whistle, but the sudden glare flashing into my weary eyes made it impossible for me to tell what it was at which my friend lashed so savagely. I could, however, see that his face was deadly pale and filled with horror and loathing.

He had ceased to strike and was gazing up at the ventilator when suddenly there broke from the silence of the night the most horrible cry to which I have ever listened. It swelled up louder and louder, a hoarse yell of pain and fear and anger all mingled in the one dreadful shriek. They say that away down in the village, and even in the distant parsonage, that cry raised the sleepers from their beds. It struck cold to our hearts, and I stood gazing at Holmes, and he at me, until the last echoes of it had died away into the silence from which it rose.

"What can it mean?" I gasped.

"It means that it is all over," Holmes answered. "And perhaps, after all, it is for the best. Take your pistol, and we will enter Dr. Roylott's room."

With a grave face he lit the lamp and led the way down the corridor. Twice he struck at the chamber door without any reply from within. Then he turned the handle and entered, I at his heels, with the cocked pistol in my hand.

It was a singular sight which met our eyes. On the table stood a dark lantern with the shutter half open, throwing a brilliant beam of light upon the iron safe, the door of which was ajar. Beside this table, on the wooden chair, sat Dr. Grimesby Roylott, clad in a long gray dressing gown, his bare ankles protruding beneath, and his feet thrust into red heelless Turkish slippers. Across his lap lay the short stock with the long lash which we had noticed during the day. His chin was cocked upward and his eyes were fixed in a dreadful, rigid stare at the corner of the ceiling. Round his brow he had a peculiar yellow band, with brownish speckles, which seemed to be bound tightly round his head. As we entered he made neither sound nor motion.

"The band! the speckled band!" whispered Holmes.

I took a step forward. In an instant his strange headgear began to move, and there reared itself from among his hair the squat diamond-shaped head and puffed neck of a loathsome serpent.

"It is a swamp adder!" cried Holmes; "the deadliest snake in India. He has died within ten seconds of being bitten. Violence does, in truth, recoil upon the violent, and the schemer falls into the pit which he digs for another. Let us thrust this creature back into its den, and we can then remove Miss Stoner to some place of shelter and let the county police know what has happened."

As he spoke he drew the dog whip swiftly from the dead man's lap, and throwing the noose round the reptile's neck he drew it from its horrid perch and, carrying it at arm's length, threw it into the iron safe, which he closed upon it.

Such are the true facts of the death of Dr. Grimesby Roylott, of Stoke Moran. It is not necessary that I should prolong a narrative which has already run to too great a

21

22

**21 Teaching to Ability Levels** You might have your **more advanced** students research poisonous snakes. Is there a real snake that fits the description of the one in this story? If so, what is the identity of the snake?

**22 Clarification** There are certain statements made about the snake in the story that are not true of any snake. You might wish to point these out to your class.
1. No snake bite would kill "within ten seconds."
2. Snakes are deaf. It could not hear the doctor's whistle.
3. No snake drinks milk by choice unless water is not available.

**Multicultural Focus** The speckled band turned out to be a poisonous snake, a swamp adder, according to Sherlock Holmes. Tell students that more than 2,400 species of snakes are known to exist. They are found all over the world, except where the ground is permanently frozen, but are most abundant in tropical regions. Cobras, for example, are indigenous to Africa and southern Asia. Anacondas and boa constrictors are large snakes that inhabit South America.

Mention that Asia is home to many of the world's poisonous snakes, not only the cobra, which is especially common in India, but the krait and the viper as well. Even snakes that are not poisonous can be killers. In Africa the largest nonpoisonous snake is the rock python, a huge snake that wraps itself around its prey and can grow to be 25 feet long.

People of various cultures have different attitudes toward snakes. In some places they are hated and feared; in others they are honored. Have students research the folklore of countries where snakes are common, looking for stories about snakes. Ask them to prepare a bulletin board display about what they have learned.

**Discussion** How surprised were you by the ending? Had you any ideas as to the cause of Miss Stoner's death?

**Reader's Response** Holmes believes it is dangerous to reason from insufficient data. Support his belief with an example from your own experience.

**Thematic Response** Why is the detective story so enormously popular? Have students give examples from this story as a basis for their answers.

**Enrichment** Encourage your students to read other stories by Sir Arthur Conan Doyle. Discuss the observation powers of Sherlock Holmes. How is he different from private investigators on television or in the movies?

## Closure and Extension

### ANSWERS TO RESPONDING TO THE SELECTION
#### Your Response
1. Have students think about how Holmes treats Watson before they respond. Ask two volunteers to share their responses and reasons—one who would like to be Holmes's partner and one who would not.

#### Recalling
2. Fearing for her life, she has come to ask Holmes, as she says, to "advise me how to walk amid the dangers which encompass me."
3. From the return ticket in her hand, Holmes notes that Helen has come to London by train. From the mud on her left sleeve, he deduces that she traveled to the train station in a dogcart. From the fingerprint bruises on her wrist, he deduces that she has been "cruelly used" by her stepfather.
4. Soon after his wife's death, Dr. Roylott abandons his practice in London and moves with his stepdaughters to his ancestral home at Stoke Moran.

   Helen's mother bequeathed her annual income of £1,000 entirely to her husband for as long as her daughters resided with him.

length by telling how we broke the sad news to the terrified girl, how we conveyed her by the morning train to the care of her good aunt at Harrow, of how the slow process of official inquiry came to the conclusion that the doctor met his fate while indiscreetly playing with a dangerous pet. The little which I had yet to learn of the case was told me by Sherlock Holmes as we traveled back next day.

"I had," said he, "come to an entirely erroneous conclusion which shows, my dear Watson, how dangerous it always is to reason from insufficient data. The presence of the gypsies, and the use of the word *band,* which was used by the poor girl, no doubt to explain the appearance which she had caught a hurried glimpse of by the light of her match, were sufficient to put me upon an entirely wrong scent. I can only claim the merit that I instantly reconsidered my position when, however, it became clear to me that whatever danger threatened an occupant of the room could not come either from the window or the door. My attention was speedily drawn, as I have already remarked to you, to this ventilator, and to the bell-rope which hung down to the bed. The discovery that this was a dummy, and that the bed was clamped to the floor, instantly gave rise to the suspicion that the rope was there as a bridge for something passing through the hole and coming to the bed. The idea of a snake instantly occurred to me, and when I coupled it with my knowledge that the doctor was furnished with a supply of creatures from India, I felt that I was probably on the right track. The idea of using a form of poison which could not possibly be discovered by any chemical test was just such a one as would occur to a clever and ruthless man who had had an Eastern training. The rapidity with which such a poison would take effect would also, from his point of

view, be an advantage. It would be a sharp-eyed coroner, indeed, who could distinguish the two little dark punctures which would show where the poison fangs had done their work. Then I thought of the whistle. Of course he must recall the snake before the morning light revealed it to the victim. He had trained it, probably by the use of the milk which we saw, to return to him when summoned. He would put it through this ventilator at the hour that he thought best, with the certainty that it would crawl down the rope and land on the bed. It might or might not bite the occupant, perhaps she might escape every night for a week, but sooner or later she must fall a victim.

"I had come to these conclusions before ever I had entered his room. An inspection of his chair showed me that he had been in the habit of standing on it, which of course would be necessary in order that he should reach the ventilator. The sight of the safe, the saucer of milk, and the loop of whipcord were enough to finally dispel any doubts which may have remained. The metallic clang heard by Miss Stoner was obviously caused by her stepfather hastily closing the door of his safe upon its terrible occupant. Having once made up my mind, you know the steps which I took in order to put the matter to the proof. I heard the creature hiss as I have no doubt that you did also, and I instantly lit the light and attacked it."

"With the result of driving it through the ventilator."

"And also with the result of causing it to turn upon its master at the other side. Some of the blows of my cane came home and roused its snakish temper, so that it flew upon the first person it saw. In this way I am no doubt indirectly responsible for Dr. Grimesby Roylott's death, and I cannot say that it is likely to weigh very heavily upon my conscience."

Upon marrying, each daughter was to be provided with "a certain annual sum."
5. Helen reports having heard a low whistle followed a few moments later by a clanging sound. Her sister's last words were: "Oh Helen! It was the band! The speckled band!"
6. Having followed Helen, Dr. Roylott warns Holmes not to meddle in his private affairs and threatens Holmes with violence if he does.
7. They spend the night in Helen's

room in total darkness, waiting for Dr. Roylott to make his move against Helen, whom Holmes has safely sent to her old room.
8. The speckled band is a swamp adder, a poisonous snake resembling a yellow band with brownish speckles.

#### Interpreting
9. Holmes had thought that Julia's last words referred to the band of gypsies encamped on Dr. Roylott's estate and to the spotted

handkerchiefs that they customarily wore on their heads.
10. Like Julia, Helen is planning to marry. Helen now sleeps in the bed that Julia occupied on the night of her death. Furthermore, Helen has heard the low whistle that Julia had heard.
11. These items provide the avenue for the snake to travel from Dr. Roylott's room to his victim's bed. The snake traveled through the ventilator, down the rope, and onto the bed anchored beneath it.

## RESPONDING TO THE SELECTION

### Your Response

1. Would you like to be Sherlock Holmes's partner? Why or why not?

### Recalling

2. Why has Helen Stoner come to see Holmes?
3. What does Holmes learn about Helen by observing her?
4. What does Dr. Roylott do shortly after his wife's death? What are the terms of her will?
5. What two sounds did Helen hear after she was awakened by her sister's scream?
6. Why does Dr. Roylott pay a visit to Holmes?
7. How do Holmes and Watson spend the night at Stoke Moran?
8. What is the speckled band?

### Interpreting

9. What had Holmes thought was the significance of Julia's last words?
10. Name three ways in which Helen's situation now is similar to Julia's just before Julia's death.
11. Explain the significance of the dummy bell rope, the ventilator leading to Dr. Roylott's room, and the bed anchored to the floor in Julia's room.
12. Explain the significance of each of the four clues Holmes finds in Roylott's room.
13. What is Roylott's motive for the crimes?
14. How does Roylott's plan backfire?

### Applying

15. Sherlock Holmes uses his powers of observation well. Name three ways to improve your own powers of observation.

## ANALYZING LITERATURE

### Examining Conflict

**Conflict** is a struggle between opposing forces or characters. One type of conflict involves a struggle of one character with another. Often the characters are fairly evenly matched.

1. How does Roylott prove his physical strength? How does Holmes prove to be his match?
2. In what way does Holmes's nerve, or courage, help him win the conflict?
3. How does his superior intellect help him win?
4. What does Holmes say that indicates he recognizes nerve and intellect in Dr. Roylott?

## CRITICAL THINKING AND READING

### Understanding Logical Reasoning

A detective reasons in a logical way to solve a crime. Holmes uses a process of elimination. First he gathers all the information he can about Julia's death. Then he tests each piece of information to see if it leads to the truth. If not, Holmes eliminates it from his thinking. For example, when Holmes realizes that gypsies could not have gotten into Julia's room, he stops thinking they might be responsible for her death. In this way, he can focus his skills on fewer and fewer facts or clues, fitting them together in a sequence of events that will lead to the solution.

1. What early clues suggest that Dr. Roylott has something to hide from the authorities?
2. How did you know Dr. Roylott would make an attempt on Helen's life that very night?

## THINKING AND WRITING

### Understanding Your Thinking

Holmes uses deductive reasoning to solve problems. For example, after observing Helen, he concludes that she drove in a dogcart along heavy roads before reaching the train station. He bases his conclusion on evidence: Her jacket is splattered with fresh mud, and the only vehicle that throws up mud that way is a dogcart.

Write the first draft of a composition explaining how you have solved a problem through deductive reasoning, such as solving a television mystery. Revise your composition to make sure your reasoning is clear. Prepare a final draft.

*The Speckled Band* 45

3. His superior intellect allows him to deduce the facts surrounding the first murder, note the similarities between that murder and Helen's present predicament, and predict Dr. Roylott's next move.
4. He says, "When a doctor does go wrong, he is the first of criminals. He has nerve and he has knowledge."

### ANSWERS TO CRITICAL THINKING AND READING

1. Dr. Roylott's murdering of his butler and subsequent imprisonment are bits of personal history he might want to hide from the authorities in England. However, the unexplained death of his wife in a train accident, his hasty departure from London, and his subsequent antisocial behavior suggest that he might have killed his wife to control her money.
2. Julia had heard a low whistle on several nights just before her death, and now Helen has heard that whistle, too. Holmes realizes that Dr. Roylott has been trying to murder Helen ever since she moved into Julia's room and will try again that night.

### THINKING AND WRITING

**Writing Transparency** Before your students begin writing, you might work with them on **Transparencies for Writing,** Model 5: *Essay.* The model will help them with their explanations of how they solved a problem.

**Alternative Assessment** *Peer Review:* Have students assess one another's work by responding to the following questions:

What problem does the writer discuss?

What explanation of the problem does the writer give?

What are the steps that led to the resolution of the problem?

What suggestions can you give to improve the logic of the reasoning the writer employs?

What concrete suggestions do you have to improve the language mechanics of the piece?

To validate the peer review, have students revise their work, incorporating those suggestions that will enhance their compositions.

12. Holmes shows a keen interest in Dr. Roylott's large iron safe, a saucer of milk atop the safe, the seat of the wooden chair, and a small dog lash tied into a loop.

    The safe is where Dr. Roylott keeps the snake. He uses the saucer of milk to lure the snake back when he whistles. He stands on the chair to coax the snake through the ventilator. He uses the dog lash as a noose to restrain the snake while handling it.
13. Dr. Roylott's motive is greed. By murdering his stepdaughters, he

hopes to maintain control over their mother's bequest to them.
14. Instead of Helen, Dr. Roylott becomes the snake's victim when Holmes lashes at it with a cane and chases it back through the ventilator toward Dr. Roylott.

### Applying

15. Answers will differ. They might suggest describing what you see to someone else who hasn't seen it, taking notes on what you see, and asking yourself questions about what you see.

### ANSWERS TO ANALYZING LITERATURE

1. Dr. Roylott bends Holmes's fireplace poker "into a curve with his huge brown hands." Holmes proves himself Roylott's equal by bending it back to normal.
2. Holmes had deduced that Dr. Roylott will use a snake to try to murder Helen. Nevertheless, he is willing to wait in the dark room for Dr. Roylott to make his move. Holmes displays additional nerve when he lashes out at the snake with his cane.

## Preparation

**More About the Author** Beryl Markham's father was a scholar, a horse breeder, an adventurer, and a farmer. With his four-year-old daughter, he left England to live in Africa "because it was new and you could feel the future of it under your feet." His daughter inherited from him his fierce independence and love of adventure. Once students have read the story, ask them whether they can see the influence of Markham's father in the story.

**Literary Focus** Ask students to think of suspenseful stories, novels, movies, or television shows they have enjoyed. Ask them to try to remember if the plots offered hints about events to come. How do such hints add to the suspense of a plot?

**Prereading Focus** Before students work in groups, have a brief class discussion on the meaning of loyalty. Note the major points from students' comments on the chalkboard for them to see while they work in groups. After the group discussions, have one member of each group summarize their discussion.

**Vocabulary** Some students may be unfamiliar with the following words: *benevolent* (p. 47), *frugality* (p. 48), *lavished* (p. 48), *futile* (p. 48), *counterpane* (p. 51), *flanking* (p. 51), *stealth* (p. 51), *tawny* (p. 52).

**Spelling Tip** The word *derisively* follows the general rule for adding the suffix *ly* to change an adjective to an adverb. The spelling of *euphemistically* is irregular in that *al* is added to the adjective *euphemistic* before the suffix.

# GUIDE FOR READING

### Beryl Markham

(1902–1986) was born in Leicester, England, and raised in Kenya, where she spent her days hunting with the Murani natives and helping her father breed horses. She was the first woman in Africa to obtain a racehorse trainer's license. She also had a passion for flying and obtained her pilot's license; in 1936 she made a historic solo flight across the Atlantic. "The Captain and His Horse," her first short story, is based on a true incident that took place in Njoro during World War I.

## The Captain and His Horse

### Suspense and Foreshadowing

**Suspense** is the quality of a story that makes the reader curious and excited about what will happen next. A suspenseful plot keeps the reader interested in how the story unravels and what the outcome will be. Beryl Markham creates suspense in the story by maintaining a sense of anticipation while the narrator and the Baron hunt kongoni.

Suspenseful plots often contain **foreshadowing,** clues that hint at later events in the story. In describing the Baron, the narrator calls him a soldier, preparing the reader for what happens to the Baron at the end of the story.

### Focus

The characters in "The Captain and His Horse" show loyalty of one kind or another: to their countrymen, to their fellow soldiers, to their principles. In small groups brainstorm to list stories from literature, television, film, or your own experience in which the characters or the people involved were motivated by loyalty. Then read the following story and see how the loyalty of an extraordinary horse inspires reciprocal devotion in his master.

### Vocabulary

Knowing the following words will help you as you read "The Captain and His Horse."

**static** (stat′ ik) *adj.*: Not changing or progressing (p. 47)
**euphemistically** (yōō′ fə mis′ ti kə lē) *adv.*: As a less direct term that substitutes for an offensive word or phrase (p. 47)
**nebulous** (neb′ yə ləs) *adj.*: Vague; unclear (p. 47)
**indiscretion** (in′ dis kresh′ ən)

*n.*: Lack of judgment (p. 49)
**plebeian** (plē bē′ ən) *adj.*: Common; ordinary (p. 50)
**derisively** (di rī′ siv lē) *adv.*: As if to ridicule (p. 50)
**wistful** (wist′ fəl) *adj.*: Expressing vague yearnings (p. 50)
**atones** (ə tōnz′) *v.*: Makes amends for wrongdoing (p. 55)

## Objectives

1 To investigate suspense in a short story
2 To make predictions about the events in a short story
3 To write about suspense
4 To express individual interests and abilities through an optional activity

## Support Material

**Teaching Portfolio**
Teacher Backup, p. 67
Grammar in Action Worksheet, *Using Demonstrative Pronouns,* p. 71
Usage and Mechanics Worksheet, p. 73
Vocabulary Check, p. 74
Analyzing Literature Worksheet, *Understanding Suspense and Foreshadowing,* p. 75

Critical Thinking and Reading Worksheet, *Making Predictions,* p. 76
Selection Test, p. 77

**Prentice Hall Literature Writing Studio**

# The Captain and His Horse

### Beryl Markham

The world is full of perfectly well-meaning people who are sentimental about the horse. They believe that God in His wisdom charged the horse tribe with two duties; the first being to serve man generally, and the second being to eat lump sugar from the palms of kindly strangers. For centuries the horse has fulfilled these obligations with little complaint, and as a result his reputation has become static, like that of a benevolent mountain, or of an ancient book whose sterling[1] qualities most people accept without either reservation or investigation. The horse is "kind," the horse is "noble." His virtues are so emphasized that his character is lost.

The personalities of many horses have remained in my mind from early East African days. Horses peopled my life then and, in a measure, they still people my memory. Names like these—Cambrian, the Baron, Wee MacGregor—are to me bright threads in a tapestry of remembrance hardly tarnished after all these years.

Now there is war, and it is hard to say a thing or think a thing into which that small but most tyrannical of words does not insert itself. I suppose it is because of this that the name of the Baron comes most often to me—because of this and, of course, because, among other things, the Baron was himself a warrior. There was a war, too, when I was a girl of thirteen living on what was euphemistically called a Kenya farm, but which was in fact a handful of cedar huts crouching on alien earth and embraced by wilderness. That was the old war, the nearly forgotten war, but it had the elements of all wars: it bred sorrow and darkness, it bred hope, and it threw strong lights on the souls of men, so that you could see, sometimes, courage that you never knew was there.

Like all wars—like this one—it produced strange things. It brought people together who had never before had a common cause or a common word. One day it brought to my father's farm at Njoro[2] a small company of sick and tired men—mounted on horses that were tired, too—who had the scars of bullets in their flesh.

It goes without saying that the men were cast of heroic stuff. I remember them. A man who has fought for six months in blinding desert heat and stinging desert cold and lives only to fight again has no respect for the word "heroic." It is a dead word, a verbal medal[3] too nebulous to conceal even the smallest wound. Still, you can utter it—you can write it for what it is worth.

---

**2. Njoro** (ny ŏr′ ō) *n.*: Place in Kenya, Africa.
**3. verbal medal:** A word that acts as an award for distinguished action.

---

**1. sterling** (stŭr′ lĭŋ) *adj.*: Of high quality; excellent.

*The Captain and His Horse* 47

**9 Clarification** Explain to students that in this context, the word *husbands* means saves or uses carefully.

**10 Clarification** Explain that a mud-and-daub house is made of dried mud covered with a material such as plaster.

**11 Discussion** Ask students why the narrator calls Africa a "gentle land." Would you describe the part of the world in which you live as gentle? How would you describe it?

**Master Teacher Note** You might arrange for the class to view Public Broadcasting System's (PBS) documentary *World Without Walls: Beryl Markham's African Memoir*. Your local public library or public broadcasting station may provide information on how to obtain the video.

But these men came on horses. Each man rode a horse, each was carried to the restful safety of our farm not by an animal, but by his companion, by his battle friend.

"Who are they?" I asked my father.

**9** He is a tall man, my father, a lean man, and he husbands his words. It is a kind of frugality, a hatred of waste, I think. Through all his garnered[4] store of years, he has regarded wasted emotion as if it were strength lavished on futile things. "Save strength for work," he used to say, "and tears for sorrow, and space it all with laughter."

**10** We stood that morning on the little porch of our mud-and-daub house, and I asked my father who these men were with torn clothes and bearded faces and harsh guns in such a gentle land. It is true that leopards came at night and that there were lions to be met with on the plains and in the valleys not far away. But we had learned to live with these and other beasts—or at least they had learned to live with us—and it seems to me now that it was a land gentle beyond all others. **11**

"They are soldiers of the British army," my father said, "and they are called Wilson's Scouts. It is very simple. They have never seen you before, but they have been fighting for your right to grow up, and now they have come here to rest. Be kind to

---

**4. garnered** (gär′ nərd) *adj.*: Collected.

48

them—and above all, see to it that their horses want nothing. In their way, they are soldiers, too.''

''I see,'' I said. But I was a child and I saw very little. In the days that followed, the tired men grew strong again and most of their wounds healed, and they would talk in the evening as they sat around our broad table. The men would sit under hurricane lamps whose flames danced when a joke was made, or grew steady again when there was silence. Sometimes the flames would falter, and I could stand in the room for long minutes nursing a failing lamp and hearing what there was to hear.

12

13

I heard of a German, General von Lettow-Vorbeck, who, with his Prussian-officered troops based in German East Africa, was striking north to take our country. It seemed that these troops were well-enough trained, that they responded to orders without question, like marionettes responding to strings. But they were lost men; they were fighting British settlers, they were trying to throw Englishmen out of their homes—an undertaking in which I sensed, even then, the elements of flamboyant ambition, and not a small measure of indiscretion.

They were well-enough trained, these Germans, but, among other things, they had Wilson's Scouts to consider; hard-riding volunteer colonials whose minds were unhampered with military knowledge, but whose hearts were bitter and strong—and free. No, it seemed to me, as I listened to them, that the enemy they fought was close to his grave. And as things developed, he was, when I met the Baron, already anticipating its depth.

There was a captain in our small group of cavalrymen, and he would sometimes talk about the Baron—short snatches of talk of the kind that indicated that everybody everywhere must, of course, have heard of him. The captain would say things like this. He would say, ''It looked difficult to me. There was a *donga*[5] six feet across and

14

15

16

17

---

5. *donga* (dän′ gə) *n.*: In South Africa, a channel of water in a large, treeless, grassy area.

*The Captain and His Horse* 49

deep with wait-a-bit thorns, and three of the enemy on the other side, but the Baron wasn't worried and so I couldn't be. We cleaned them out after a little skirmish —though the Baron caught one in the shoulder. He holds it still." And the other men would shake their heads and drink their drinks, which I knew was just a quiet way of paying tribute to the Baron.

He was the pride of the regiment, of course, but when I first saw him in the stable my father had given him near our thoroughbreds, I was disappointed. I couldn't have helped that; I was used to sensitive, symmetrical, highly strung horses, clean-bred and jealous of their breeding.

But the Baron was not like this. He was crude to look at. Surrounded by the aristocrats of his species, the Baron seemed a common animal, plebeian. It was almost as if he had been named derisively. At our first meeting he stood motionless and thoughtful —a dark brown gelding[6] with a boxlike head. There was thick hair around his pasterns and fetlock joints, and he wore his rough coat indifferently, the way a man without vanity, used to war, will wear his tattered tunic.

It is a strange thing to say of a horse, but when I went into the Baron's stable I felt at once both at ease and a little inferior. I think it was his eyes more than anything—they were dark, larger than the eyes of most horses, and they showed no white. It wasn't a matter of their being kind eyes—they were eyes that had seen many things, understanding most of them and fearing none. They held no fire, but they were alive with a glow of wisdom, neither quiet nor fiercely burning. You could see in his eyes that his soul had struck a balance.

He turned to me, not wanting to smell my hair or to beg for food, but only to present

———

**6. gelding** (gel′ diŋ) *n.*: A castrated male horse.

himself. His breathing was smooth and unhurried, his manner that of an old friend, and I stroked his thick hard neck that was like a stallion's, because I could think of nothing else to do. And then I left quietly, though there was no need for silence, and walked through one of our pastures and beyond the farm into the edge of the Mau forest, where, if you were a child, it was easier to think.

I thought for a long time, concluding nothing, answering nothing, because there was nothing I could answer.

The war, the wounded men, the big thoughts, the broad purposes—all were still questions to me, beyond my answering. Yet I could not help but think that the dark brown gelding standing there in his stable was superior, at least to me, because he made it evident that he had no questions and needed no answers. He was, in his way, as my father had said, a soldier, too.

It is easy enough to say such a thing, but as one day nudged another through that particular little corridor of time the Baron proved himself a soldier—and it seems to me now, something more.

I don't think I ever learned the full name of the young captain who owned him, but that was not my fault. There was little formality about Wilson's Scouts. The men at our farm were part of a regiment, but more than that they were a brotherhood. They called their captain "Captain Dennis" or just Dennis. Wilson himself, the settler of Machakos who had first brought them together was simply "F.O.B." because those were his initials.

Captain Dennis took the Baron out of his stable one morning, and two of the other men got their horses, and when they were all saddled and bridled—while I leaned against the stable door watching the Baron with what must have been wistful eyes— Captain Dennis led the big gelding over to

## Grammar in Action

Sometimes demonstrative words—words that specify—are used as pronouns. *This, that, these,* and *those* can be used as **demonstrative pronouns.** A demonstrative pronoun may refer to a whole thought rather than to just one or more nouns. As with any pronoun, the writer must be careful that the antecedent (the word or words to which the pronoun refers) is clear to the reader. The antecedent usually precedes the pronoun; however, the pronoun should be close enough to its antecedent so that the reference is clear.

The demonstrative pronoun *this* appears at the end of the following passage from "The Captain and His Horse." As you read over the passage, note to what the word *this* refers.

The days were clear and many-colored. You could sit in your saddle and look at the huge mountains and at the river valleys, green, and aimless as fallen threads on a counterpane—and you could not count the colors or know them, because some were nameless. Some colors you never saw again, because each day the light was different, and often the colors you saw yesterday never came back. But none of *this* meant much to me that morning.

To what does *this* refer?

**25** me and handed me the reins. The captain was a lanky man with fierce gray eyes and a warm smile that laughed at their fierceness —and I think at me as well.

**26** He said, "You've been watching the Baron like that for weeks and I can't stand it. We're going to shoot kongonis[7] with revolvers from horseback, and you're coming along."

I had a currycomb[8] in my hand and I turned without saying anything and hung the comb on its peg in the stable. When I came out again my father was standing next to the captain with a revolver in his hand. It **27** was a big revolver, and when my father gave it to me he said:

"It's a little heavy, Beryl, but then you never had much fun with toys. What the captain can't teach you, the Baron will. It doesn't matter if you don't hit a kongoni, but don't come back without having learned something—even if it's the knowledge that you can't shoot from horseback."

The captain smiled, and so did my father. Then he kissed me and I mounted the Baron and we rode away from the farm—the captain, two cavalrymen, and myself— through some low hills and down into the Rongai Valley, where the kongonis were.

To say that it was a clear day is to say almost nothing of that country. Most of its days were clear as the voices of the birds that unfailingly coaxed each dawn away from the night. The days were clear and many-colored. You could sit in your saddle and look at the huge mountains and at the river valleys, green, and aimless as fallen **28** threads on a counterpane—and you could not count the colors or know them, because some were nameless. Some colors you never saw again, because each day the light was different, and often the colors you saw yesterday never came back.

But none of this meant much to me that morning. The revolver slung at my waist in a rawhide holster, the broad, straight backs of the cavalrymen riding ahead, the confident pace of the Baron—all these made me feel very proud, but conscious of my youth, smaller, even, than I was.

We hit the bowl of the valley, and in a little while the captain raised his hand, and we looked east into the sun and saw a herd of game about a mile away, feeding in the yellow grass. I had hunted enough on foot to know the tricks: move upwind toward your **29** quarry;[9] keep the light behind you if you can; fan out; be quiet; if there is cover, use it. The captain nodded to me and I waved a hand to show that I would be all right by myself, and then we began to circle, each drifting away from the others, but still joined in the flanking maneuver.

The grass in the Rongai Valley is waist-high and it does not take much of a rise in the plain to hide a man and his horse. In a moment the Baron and I were hidden, and so were the men hidden from us, but the herd of game was just there toward the sun, gathered in a broad clearing—perhaps five thousand head of kongonis, zebras, wildebeests, and oryxes[10] grazing together.

I rode loose-reined, giving the brown gelding his head, watching his small alert ears, his great bowed neck, feeling the strength of his forthright stride—and I felt that he was hunting with me. He moved with stealth, in easy silence, and I dropped my hand to the revolver, self-consciously, and realized that it was really I who was **30** hunting with him.

He was not an excitable horse, yet he

---

**7. kongonis** (kŏŋ′ gə nēz) n.: Large African antelopes.
**8. currycomb** (kŭr′ ē kŏm′) n.: A circular comb used to groom a horse's coat.

**9. quarry** (kwôr′ ē) n.: An animal being hunted.
**10. wildebeests** (wil′ də bēsts′) **and oryxes** (or′ iks əs) n.: Large African antelopes.

*The Captain and His Horse* 51

---

**25 Reading Strategy** The narrator uses a physical description to characterize Captain Dennis. What can students tell about his personality from the description?

**26 Clarification** Explain that kongoni are large African antelopes armed with curved, spear-sharp horns that may exceed 5 feet in length.

**27 Discussion** Do you find it unusual that a father would give a young girl a revolver and allow her to hunt? How do you account for his actions?

**28 Enrichment** Markham's description brings to mind the series paintings by Claude Monet (*Rouen Cathedral, Water Lilies, Haystacks*), in which the same scene is depicted in different lights. Showing students reproductions of these paintings will make the description more concrete.

**29 Literary Focus** What parts of this paragraph heighten the suspense of the story?

**30 Discussion** What does the narrator mean?

---

**Student Activity 1.** Rewrite the sentence "But none of this meant much to me that morning" substituting a specific phrase for the demonstrative pronoun *this*. How does the use of the pronoun enhance the reading of the passage?

**Student Activity 2.** Write as Beryl Markham does about a beautiful place you have seen. You might describe a natural scene such as a view from a mountaintop or a quiet place in the woods, or you might choose the interior of a beautiful building you have visited. Use demonstrative pronouns in your description, but be careful not to overuse them, and make sure they are placed correctly.

**Electronic Handbook** You may wish to have students review pronouns in general before they complete the Grammar in Action activities. If they have access to the Language Master 6000, have them enter the access word *pronoun* and press the GRAMMAR key for a review of pronouns.

52

31 **Discussion** What does this passage tell you about the character of the narrator at the time of the story?

32 **Literary Focus** Ask students how the author creates suspense in these two paragraphs.

33 **Critical Thinking and Reading** Ask students to predict whether the narrator will kill the kongoni. Ask them on what they base their predictions.

34 **Literary Focus** Ask students how the author builds suspense in this paragraph.

35 **Literary Focus** Ask students to specify what tense the author has been using. Why do they think she shifts to the present? Ask students to watch for the point at which the author switches back to the past.

36 **Discussion** What is the narrator's state of mind? Have you ever been so excited that you have forgotten everything around you?

37 **Clarification** Explain that the men are angry because the narrator has frightened away the herd of animals they were hunting.

seemed to become even more calm as the distance between the game and ourselves narrowed, while I grew more tense. I sat more rigidly upon the back of the Baron than anyone should ever sit upon the back of any horse, but I had the vanity of youth; I was not to be outdone—not even by soldiers.

By the time the identity of the game had become clear—the horns of oryxes reflecting sunlight like drawn rapiers,[11] the ungainly bulk of wildebeests, zebras flaunting their elaborate camouflage, eland[12] and kongonis in the hundreds—by the time the outlines of their bodies had become distinct to my eyes, I was so on fire with anticipation that I had forgotten my companions.

The Baron and I took advantage of what cover there was and crept up on the outer fringe of the herd until we could smell the dust they stirred to motion with their hooves. Then the Baron stopped and I leaned forward in the saddle. I was breathing unevenly, but the Baron scarcely breathed at all.

Not a hundred yards away, a kongoni stood in long grass, half buried in it. The sun was on him, playing over his sleek fawn coat, and he looked like a beast carved from teakwood and polished by age. He was motionless, he was still, he was alert. High in the shoulders, the line that ran sloping to his hips was scarcely curved, and it forewarned us of his strength and his speed.

It didn't occur to me that I might have been wiser in choosing a smaller animal. One half as big would have been faster than most horses, with perhaps more endurance, but this one was a challenge I could not resist. In a quick instant of apprehension I peered in all directions, but there was no

11. **rapiers** (rā′ pē ərz) n.: Slender, two-edged swords.
12. **eland** (ē′ lənd) n.: Oxlike African antelopes with spirally twisted horns.

52  *Short Stories*

one near. There were only the Baron, the kongoni, and myself, none of us moving, none of us breathing. Not even the grass moved, and if there were birds they were motionless too.

Leaning low over the Baron's crest, I begin to whisper, smothering my excitement in broken phrases. I ease the reins forward, giving him full head, pressing my hands upon his neck, talking to him, telling him things he already knows: "He's big! He's the biggest of all. He's out of the herd, he's alone, he's ours! Careful, careful!"

The Baron is careful. He sees what I see, he knows more than I know. He tilts his ears, his nostrils distend[13] ever so slightly, the muscles of his shoulders tighten under his skin like leather straps. The tension is so great that it communicates itself to the kongoni. His head comes up and he trembles, he smells the air, he is about to plunge.

"Now!"

The word bursts from my lips because I can no longer contain it; it shatters the stillness. Frightened birds dart into the air, the kongoni leaps high and whirls, but we are off—we are onto him, we are in full gallop, and as the tawny rump of our prey fades into the tawny dust that springs from his heels, I am no longer a girl riding a horse; I am part of the dust, part of the wind in my face, part of the roar of the Baron's hooves, part of his courage, and part of the fear in the kongoni's heart. I am part of everything and it seems that nothing in the world can ever change it.

We run, we race. The kongoni streaks for the open plain. Somewhere to the left there is the drumming of a thousand hooves and the voices of men—angry men with a right to be angry. I have committed the unpardonable; I have bolted their game, but I can't help it.

13. **distend** (di stend′) v.: Stretch; expand.

We're on our own now—the Baron and I—and no sense of guilt can stop us.

We gain, we lose, we hold it even. I grope for the revolver at my thigh and pull it from its sheath. I have used one before, but not like this. Always before it has been heavy in my hand, but now it is weightless; now it fits my hand. Now, I think, I cannot miss.

Rocks, anthills, leleshwa bush, thorn trees—all rush past my eyes, but I do not see them; they are swift streaks of color, unreal and evanescent.[14] And time does not move. Time is a marble moment. Only the Baron moves, his long muscles responding to his will, surging in steady, driving rhythm.

Closer, closer. Without guidance the Baron veers to the left, avoiding the dust that envelops the racing kongoni, exposing him to my aim—and I do aim. I raise the gun to shoulder height, my arm sways, I lower it. No. Too far, I can't get a bead. Faster! It's no good just shooting. I've got to hit his heart. Faster! I do not speak the word; I only frame it on my lips, because the Baron knows. His head drops ever so slightly and he stretches his neck a bit more. Faster? There, you have it—this is faster!

And it is. I raise my arm again and fire twice and the kongoni stumbles. I think he stumbles. He seems to sway, but I am not sure. Perhaps it is imagination, perhaps it is hope. At least he swerves. He swerves to the right, but the Baron outgenerals him; the Baron is on his right flank before I can shift my weight in the saddle.

Then something happens. I want to shoot again, but I can't—there's nothing to shoot at. He's gone—our kongoni's gone. He's disappeared as if his particular god had that moment given him wings. The Baron slows, my hand drops to my side and I mumble my frustration, staring ahead.

It's a *donga,* of course—a pit in the plain, deeper than most, crowded with high grass, its sides steep as walls. Our prize has plunged into it, been swallowed in it, and there is nothing to do except to follow.

That's my impulse, but not the Baron's. He looks from side to side, sudden suspicion in his manner, tension in his body. He slows his pace to scarcely more than a canter[15] and will not be urged. At the rim of the *donga* he almost stops. It is steep, but in the high grass that clothes it I can see the wake of the kongoni, and I am impatient.

"There! Get onto him!"

For the first time I slap the Baron with the flat of my hand, coaxing him forward. He hesitates, and there is so little time to waste. Why is he failing me? Why stop now? I am disappointed, angry. I can't return empty-handed. I won't.

"Now then!"

My heels rap sharply against his ribs, my hand is firmer on the reins, my revolver is ready—and the Baron is a soldier. He no longer questions me; surefooted and strong, half walking, half sliding, he plunges over the rim of the *donga* at such an angle that I brace myself in my stirrups and shut my eyes against the plumes of dust we raise. When it is gone, we are on level ground again, deep in grass still studded with morning dew—and the path of the kongoni is clear before us, easy to see, easy to follow.

We have lost time, but this is no place for speed. Our prey is hiding, must be hiding. Now, once more, we stalk; now we hunt. Careful. Quiet. Look sharply, watch every moving thing; gun ready, hands ready.

I'm ready, but not the Baron. His manner has changed. He is not with me. I can feel it. He responds, but he does not anticipate my will. Something concerns him, and

---

14. **evanescent** (ev′ ə nes′ ənt) *adj.*: Tending to fade from sight.

15. **canter** (kant′ ər) *n.*: A smooth, moderate gallop.

*The Captain and His Horse* 53

38 **Reading Strategy** Ask students how the tone of the story changes in this passage. How does the author achieve this change in tone?

39 **Critical Thinking and Reading** Ask students how the Baron's behavior has changed. Why might he be hesitating? What do students predict will happen next?

40 **Discussion** How would you describe the narrator's actions? Is she being brave or foolish? What would you advise her to do now?

41 **Discussion** What does the narrator mean by "the Baron is a soldier"? What are the qualities of a good soldier?

**42 Critical Thinking and Reading**
Ask students what the narrator is catching from the Baron. What does their nervousness foreshadow?

**43 Literary Focus** Ask students how the author builds suspense in this paragraph. What question do students ask themselves at this point in the story?

**44 Reading Strategy** Ask students whether this interruption in the action increases or decreases the suspense.

**42** I'm getting nervous too—I'm catching it from him. It won't do. It's silly.

I look around. On three sides we are surrounded by steep banks easier to get down than up—and just ahead there's nothing but bush and high grass that you can't see into. Even so there's a way out —straight ahead through the bush. That's where the kongoni went—it's where we'll go.

"Come on!"

**43** I jab the Baron's ribs once more and he takes a step forward—a single step—and freezes. He does not tremble. With his ears and his eyes and by the sheer power of his will, he forces me into silence, into rigidity, into consciousness of danger.

I feel and see it at the same moment. Wreathed in leaves of shining grass, framed in the soft green garland of the foliage, there is an immense black head into which are sunk two slowly burning eyes. Upon the head, extending from it like lances[16] fixed for battle, are the two horns of a buffalo. I am young, but I am still a child of Africa—and I know that these, without any question, are

---

16. **lances** (lans' əz) *n.*: Long wooden weapons with sharp metal spearheads.

Africa's most dreaded weapon.

Nor is our challenger alone. I see that not one but a dozen buffalo heads are emerging from the bush, across our path like links in an indestructible chain—and behind us the walls of the *donga* are remote and steep and friendless. Instinctively I raise my revolver, but as I raise it I realize that it won't help. I know that even a rifle wouldn't help. I feel my meager store of courage dwindle, my youthful bravado[17] becomes a whisper less audible than my pounding heart. I do not move, I cannot. Still grasping the reins, but unaware of them, the fingers of my left hand grope for the Baron's mane and cling there. I do not utter them, but the words are in my heart. I am afraid. I can do nothing. I depend on you!

Now, as I remember that moment and write it down, I am three times older than I was that day in the *donga*, and I can humor my ego, upon occasion, by saying to myself that I am three times wiser. But even then I knew what African buffaloes were. I knew that it was less dangerous to come upon a family of lions in the open plain than to

**44**

---

17. **bravado** (brə vä' dō) *n.*: Pretended courage; false confidence.

**Multicultural Focus** The Baron was trained as a war horse. Tell students that horses have been bred throughout the world for various purposes. The Arabian, the world's oldest pure horse breed, was developed on the Arabian Peninsula more than 1,000 years ago. From just three Arabian horses, the British at the turn of the eighteenth century developed thoroughbreds to use as racehorses. The Appaloosa, a spotted horse used in the American West as a cow pony, is descended from horses from central Asia. Draft horses like the Belgian (in Belgium), the Clydesdale (in Scotland), and the Percheron (in France) were bred to do heavy work. Wales and the Shetland Islands produced the Welsh Pony and the Shetland Pony, respectively.

The largest number of horses in the world today are in Brazil. The United States, the countries of the former Soviet Union, China, Mexico, and Argentina also have many horses. One of the few wild breeds of horses, known as Przhevalsky's horse, used to roam the plains of Mongolia but may already be extinct.

Have students work together in groups to research these various breeds of horses and discover in more detail the different purposes for which each has been bred. They may put the results of their research into a chart, complete with pictures of the various breeds, to display on a bulletin board.

come upon a herd of buffaloes, or to come upon a single buffalo; everyone knew it—everyone except amateur hunters who liked to roll the word "lion" on their lips. Few lions will attack men unless they are goaded into it; most buffaloes will. A lion's charge is swift and often fatal, but if it is not, he bears no grudge. He will not stalk you, but a buffalo will. A buffalo is capable of mean cunning that will match the mean cunning of the men who hunt him, and every time he kills a man he atones for the death at men's hands of many of his species. He will gore you, and when you are down, he will kneel upon you and grind you into the earth.

I remember that as I sat on the Baron's back the things I had heard about buffaloes swept swiftly into my mind. I remember fingering the big revolver, suddenly becoming heavy in my hand, while the buffaloes moved closer in strategic[18] order.

---

**18. strategic** (strə tē′ jik) *adj.*: Having to do with advantageous results.

45

45 **Clarification** The African buffalo weighs about 1,800 pounds and carries 5-foot-long curved horns. It is reputed to be Africa's most dangerous animal. Although it is normally peaceful unless provoked, a buffalo may stalk and charge a human, even without provocation.

46 **Literary Focus** Although the narrator's situation seems hopeless, we know that she will escape, simply because she lives to tell the story. What, then, is the source of suspense? What questions does the author leave unanswered?

47 **Critical Thinking and Reading** The author gives readers a clue as to what will happen next by reminding us of the Baron. How do students predict the narrator will escape?

48 **Discussion** Do you believe that animals can reason? Can you think of any stories from your own experience or from fiction in which an animal acted intelligently?

49 **Discussion** What thoughts might go through your mind if you were in a similarly dangerous situation?

They stood in an almost mathematical semicircle across the only avenue of escape from the *donga*. They did not gather together for the charge, they did not hurry. They did not have to. They saw to it that every loophole was blocked with their horns, and it seemed that even the spaces between their bodies were barred to us by the spears of light that bristled from their bright, black hides. Their eyes were round and small and they burned with a carnelian[19] fire. They moved upon us with slow leisurely steps, and the intensity of their fury was hypnotic. I could not move.

I would not think, because to think was to realize that behind us there was only a wall of earth impossible to climb in time.

As the nearest bull raised his head, preliminary to the final charge, I raised my revolver and with strange detachment, watched my own hand tremble. It wasn't any good. Thinking of my father, fear changed to guilt and then back to fear again, and then to resignation. All right—come on, then. Let's get it over. It's happened to lots of others and now it's going to happen to me. But I had forgotten my companion. All this time the Baron had not moved. Yet neither had he trembled, nor made a sound.

You can find many easy explanations for the things that animals do. You can say that they act out of fear, out of panic, that they cannot think or reason. But I know that this is wrong; I know now that the Baron reasoned, though what he did at the precise instant of our greatest danger seemed born more of terror than of sense.

He whirled, striking a flame of dust from his heels; he reared high into the air until all his weight lay upon his great haunches, until his muscles were tightened like

springs. Then he sprang toward the farthest, steepest wall—while behind us came the drumming, swelling thunder of the herd.

For perhaps a hundred yards the *donga* was broad and flat, and then it ended. I remember that the wall of earth loomed so closely in front of my eyes that they were blinded by it. I saw nothing, but just behind us I could hear the low, the almost soothing undertones of destruction. There was a confident, an all-but-casual quality in the sound; not hurried, hardly in crescendo,[20] not even terrifying, just steady—and inescapable.

Another minute, I thought—a whole minute at least. It's a lot of time, it's sixty seconds. You can do a lot of living in sixty seconds.

And then the Baron turned. I do not know how he turned—I do not know how, running at such speed, he could have turned so swiftly and so cleanly—and I do not know how it was that I stayed in the saddle. I do know that when, at a distance of less than a hundred feet, we faced the onrushing buffaloes once more, they had been beaten, outgeneraled, frustrated, they had lost their battle. An instant ago they had presented an impassable barrier, but now their ranks were spread; now their line was staggered and there were spaces between their beautiful, embracing horns that not one but two horses might have galloped through.

The Baron chose the widest breach and sprinted. He moved toward the open end of the *donga* in great exultant[21] leaps, springing like a reedbuck,[22] laughing in his heart. And when the *donga* was far behind us and the sun was hot on our backs and sweat

---

19. **carnelian** (kär nēl′ yən) *adj.*: Having the color of red quartz.

20. **crescendo** (kri shen′ dō) *adj.*: In music, a gradual increase in loudness and intensity.
21. **exultant** (eg zult′ ′nt) *adj.*: Triumphant.
22. **reedbuck** (rēd′ buk′) *n.*: A small African antelope with widely spread hooves and ringed horns.

50 stood on the Baron's flanks, we came slowly up the wagon track that led to the farm.

I remember that my father and Captain Dennis were talking near the doorway of our house when I rode by, and it may have been that they were smiling; I am not sure. But at least I said nothing and they said nothing, and in a few days all the soldiers left, and it 51

# MULTICULTURAL CONNECTION

## The Role of the Horse

Beryl Markham writes that horses "people" her "memory." She might also have said that horses people the memory of the human race.

**The origin of the horse.** The horse is an ancient animal that, according to one theory, evolved in North America about 60 million years ago. At some point, horses crossed over to Asia on the land bridge that once connected Alaska to Siberia. From there, they spread to the rest of Asia, Europe, and Africa, evolving into different breeds in all of those places. By the time the ancestors of Native Americans began migrating to America from Asia, the horse had mysteriously disappeared from the Americas.

**The horse in history.** In the rest of the world, however, the horse was playing an important role. As horse-riding nomads swooped into the Mediterranean basin in 3000 B.C., simple Greek shepherds were startled; they had never seen the creatures before. Soon horses were helping the great Middle Eastern and Mediterranean empires to conquer their enemies. The Greeks, Persians, Babylonians, and Egyptians excelled in the art of warfare with armed cavalries. Somewhat later, barbarian tribes used their superior numbers of horses to overthrow mighty Rome. In addition, the Arabs' use of horses in the seventh century A.D. helped them to build an empire and spread Islam throughout the Middle East and North Africa, as well as Spain. There they crossed their own horses with a local breed to produce a highly valued breed of Spanish horse.

**Horses in the New World.** Columbus took Spanish-bred horses with him to the Americas when he sailed there for the second time in 1493. Later, these horses enabled Spanish explorers to conquer whole populations of Native Americans.

**The horse and Native Americans.** Almost 100 years passed before the Native Americans began to ride horses. The Apache nation of the Southwest became the first group to use them. Riding on horses, they were able to join other regional groups, including the Navajo, to revolt against the Spanish in New Mexico in 1680. As a result of this action, the Apaches and Navajos gained an additional 5,000 horses. The era of the horse had begun for Native Americans.

The use of horses by Native Americans spread throughout the continent. The Great Plains peoples, in particular, became skilled riders. Their traditional way of life—farming and buffalo hunting—was not radically changed by the horse. What changed was their ability to fight the Spanish and the encroaching English colonists from the East Coast. The horse became the Native Americans' most valued possession.

### Exploring on Your Own

Research the use of the horse by other cultures and share your information with the class.

*The Captain and His Horse* 57

50 **Literary Focus** Now that the narrator is safe, how does the author continue to keep the reader in suspense? What does the reader still want to know about the final outcome?

51 **Discussion** Why do you think the narrator's father says nothing? Do you think he is satisfied that she has learned something? What might he suspect she has learned?

**Multicultural Connection** Engage students in a discussion about their knowledge and possible experiences with horses. You might share with them the information in the Multicultural Focus note on page 54. Ask these questions:
1. What uses have humans made of horses through the centuries?
2. How have horses furthered the advancement of civilization?
3. How are horses used by humans today?

After students have researched the use of horses by other cultures, provide time for them to share their findings in class.

**Cooperative Learning** Viewed in one way, "The Captain and His Horse" is a growing-up story. A group of students may want to compile a list of titles, authors, and brief summaries of other stories they have read in which a character has an experience that results in learning and growth. Post the suggested reading list in your classroom for other students who would like to read more stories with this theme.

Another group may want to compile a similar suggested reading list of stories in which an animal saves a person's life.

57

**52 Clarification** Tell students that World War I ended in 1918.

**53 Critical Thinking and Reading** Ask students what emotion the colonel's facial expressions reveal. Do they predict that Captain Dennis survived, or not?

**54 Clarification** Tell students that the letters CO stand for commissioned officer.

**55 Clarification** Explain that Kilimanjaro is a mountain in Kenya. Kibo, one of its two peaks, is the highest point in Africa. Kibo peak is always covered with snow and ice about 200 feet deep.

**56 Discussion** Why did Captain Dennis disobey orders? Do you think he did the right thing? Do you agree that he was a fool?

**57 Reading Strategy** Ask students to identify the narrator's father's tone. Do they think he believes what he is saying?

**58 Literary Focus** Ask students what effect this long silence has on the reader.

**59 Discussion** How were Captain Dennis, the Baron, and the colonel different from the Prussian soldiers mentioned earlier?

**60 Discussion** What is the reason for the colonel's anger?

**Reader's Response** Most of the action of this story takes place when the narrator is thirteen years old, but her experiences and ideas are probably very different from yours. Does this affect your enjoyment of the story? In what ways are you able to relate to the character in spite of the differences?

**Thematic Response** What other situations do you know of in which a horse or another animal meets and overcomes a life-threatening challenge?

58

was not until five years had passed that I heard the Baron's name again.

My father spoke it first. We sat at our table one night, and with us sat the colonel of the East African Mounted Rifles. He was not an imposing man; he was red-faced and he looked a little like the colonels in the cartoons you used to see, though of course he was out of uniform.

**52** ⎾ The war was over and the men had returned to their farms—or some men had. Only a handful of Wilson's Scouts survived, and the colonel and my father talked about that, and then my father asked about Captain Dennis, and the colonel's face got redder. At least he made a grimace with his lips that could only have meant displeasure.

**53** ⎿

"Dennis," he said, "ah, yes. We had a lot of confidence in him, but he proved a fool. Went dotty²³ over some horse."

My father and I looked at each other. "The Baron," my father said.

The colonel nodded. "That was it. The Baron—big brute with a head like a cartridge case. I remember him."

"What happened?" said my father.

The colonel coughed. He flipped a large hand over on the table and shrugged. "One of those things. CO sent Dennis through von Lettow's lines one night to pick up a spot of news. It was south of Kilimanjaro. Not nice country, but he got through on that clumsy half-breed of his—or almost got through, that is."

**54** ⎾

**55** ⎾

"They got him, did they?" said my father.

"Got him in the face with grenade shrapnel,"²⁴ said the colonel. "Not fatal though. With a little sense he would have made it. He clung to that horse and the horse brought him almost all the way back.

---

**23. dotty** (dät′ ē) *adj.*: Crazy.
**24. shrapnel** (shrap′ nəl) *n.*: Fragments of an exploded bomb.

*58   Short Stories*

Then Dennis went off his chump.²⁵ Disobeyed orders. Had to be rescued. Blasted fool."

My father nodded but said nothing.

"Blasted fool," repeated the colonel. "He was within a mile of our lines with all the information we wanted—then he quit."

"It seems hard to believe," I said.

"Not at all," said the colonel, looking at me with stern eyes. "It was that horse. The brute suddenly went under. Dennis found he'd been shot in the lung. The Baron went down and Dennis wouldn't leave him—sat there the whole night with his face half shot away, trying first aid, holding the brute's head in his lap." The colonel looked at my father with sudden anger. "He'd disobeyed orders. You see that, don't you?"

My father let a smile, half gay, half sad, twist his lips. "Oh clearly! Orders are orders. No room for sentiment in war. You had Captain Dennis court-martialed,²⁶ of course?"

A hurricane lamp makes almost no sound, but for a long time after my father's question there was no sound but the sound of our hurricane lamp. It gave a voice to silence—the colonel's silence. He looked at both of us. He looked at the table. Then he stared at the wrinkled palms of his clumsy hands until we thought he would never utter another word, but he did.

He stood up. "It took a little time," he said, "but finally Dennis recovered—the Baron died with his head toward our guns. In the end I had them both decorated for bravery beyond the call of duty—the captain and his horse. You see," the colonel added angrily, "I'm afraid I'm a blasted fool myself."

**56**
**57**
**58**
**59**
**60**

---

**25. chump** (chump) *n.*: British slang expression meaning insane or crazy.
**26. court-martialed** (kôrt′ mär′ shəld) *v.*: Tried or convicted in military court for breaking military law.

## Closure and Extension

### ANSWERS TO RESPONDING TO THE SELECTION
**Your Response**

1. Some students will cite examples in which an animal, perhaps a pet, appears to have demonstrated the ability to reason. Urge students to explain their answers.

### Recalling

2. War brings people together who

otherwise would have nothing in common.

3. She loses her courage, becomes terrified, feels totally dependent upon the Baron, loses the ability to think, and gives up hope.

### Interpreting

4. She means that the soldiers have earned the right to be called heroic by their courageous actions.

5. She trusts the Baron because she feels he is braver, wiser, and more experienced than she is.

6. He means that, in war, giving in to one's feelings rather than simply following orders may be dangerous. However, he is being facetious; his facial expression reveals that he suspects the colonel of acting on his feelings.

7. They are both courageous and daring, and they share feelings of love and respect for the Baron, who saved both their lives.

8. The narrator learns to think before she acts, to respect the wisdom and experience of others, and to stay calm in the face of

## RESPONDING TO THE SELECTION

### Your Response

1. Do you agree with the author that some animals have the ability to reason? Explain.

### Recalling

2. According to the narrator, what strange things does the war produce?
3. What happens to the narrator as she and the Baron are challenged by the buffalo?

### Interpreting

4. The narrator calls the word *heroic* "a verbal medal." What does she mean?
5. Why does the narrator trust the Baron?
6. Interpret what the narrator's father means by saying "No room for sentiment in war" when he discusses Captain Dennis's loyalty to the wounded Baron.
7. What do the narrator and Captain Dennis have in common?
8. The narrator's father tells her not to come back without learning something. Explain what she learns.

### Applying

9. Put yourself in Captain Dennis's shoes. When the Baron went down, would you have left him or stayed with him? Explain. If you were the colonel, would you have had Captain Dennis court-martialed or decorated? Explain.

## ANALYZING LITERATURE

### Investigating Suspense

When you read this story, did you find yourself sitting on the edge of your seat? Were you excited to find out what would happen next? **Suspense** is the quality of a story that keeps you wondering about the outcome. Sometimes a writer **foreshadows** the outcome by hinting at upcoming events.

1. When does the suspense in this story reach its greatest intensity?

2. Find the hint that foreshadows Captain Dennis's disobedience.
3. List two other examples of foreshadowing.
4. Why do you think people enjoy reading suspenseful stories?

## CRITICAL THINKING AND READING

### Making Predictions

As you read, you make **predictions,** intelligent guesses about what will happen next based on evidence. For example, you can predict the approaching danger as you notice the Baron becoming nervous.

1. What helped you predict that the narrator had had an extraordinary experience with the Baron?
2. What did you predict when the Baron refused to move toward the kongoni?

## THINKING AND WRITING

### Writing About Suspense

The writer Max Lerner has said: "The turning point in the process of growing up is when you discover the core strength within you . . ." Discuss this quotation with your classmates. Was there ever a time when you discovered the strength within yourself? Write a composition about an incident that marks your passage from childhood. Revise your composition, making sure you have explained how the incident made you aware that you were growing up.

## LEARNING OPTION

**Cross-curricular Connection.** Look in an encyclopedia or other reference materials for more information about the African wildlife mentioned in the story. For example, what features distinguish the kongonis from the wildebeests and the oryxes? Briefly report the information you find to your classmates.

### THINKING AND WRITING

◆ **Software** If students have access to computers, have them use **Bank Street Writer** to complete all stages of the assignment. Using the program's cut-and-paste features, students will easily be able to draft and revise their work.

**Alternative Assessment** *Protocol:* Ask students to assess their own work by responding to the following questions:

About what experience have you written?

What strength within yourself was revealed through this experience?

What details do you include to explain how it marks your passage from childhood?

What is the turning point in your story, the moment during which you became aware of the significance of the experience?

What made this assignment difficult for you?

What new understanding of yourself did you come to as a result of writing about this experience?

You may have students use the information they have gained from their protocols as a guide for revising their compositions.

**Writing Across the Curriculum** Many animals native to Africa are unknown in this part of the world. Have students research animals of Africa. You might inform the social studies and biology departments of this assignment.

### LEARNING OPTION

Students might work in pairs or small groups, each group learning about a different animal. Those students who enjoy visual expression might include pictures in their reports.

danger. In other words she learns to act as an adult rather than as a child.

*Applying*

9. Answers will differ.

### ANSWERS TO ANALYZING LITERATURE

1. Suspense is most intense as the narrator and the Baron are charged by the buffalo.
2. The colonel says that Captain Dennis "proved a fool. Went dotty over some horse."
3. Students might cite the passage in which Captain Dennis describes how the Baron had once before gotten out of a difficult situation in a donga, or the passage in which the narrator's father tells her, "It doesn't matter if you don't hit a kongoni, but don't come back without having learned something."
4. Students might answer that because suspense stories are so engrossing, they offer an escape

from everyday life; or that they allow us to feel the excitement of danger and adventure absent from most of our lives.

### ANSWERS TO CRITICAL THINKING AND READING

1. The narrator says, ". . . the Baron proved himself a soldier—and it seems to me now, something more."
2. Students may answer that they thought the Baron sensed danger.

**More About the Author** O. Henry's early interest in writing was a result of his education by Evelina, his maiden sister and surrogate mother, after his mother's death. She would begin stories and have her brother add incidents to continue and conclude them. This interest also resulted in his stealing money from the First National Bank in order to continue publishing *Rolling Stone,* a humor magazine he began in 1891. Ask students in what ways prison life might lead to contemplation and writing.

**Literary Focus** Ask students whether Asimov's "Rain, Rain, Go Away" had a surprise ending. How did Asimov prepare readers for that surprise? Do all surprise endings have to be happy?

**Prereading Focus** Have a person from each group share the group's interpretation of the title. You might put their suggestions on the chalkboard for students to see as they are reading.

**Vocabulary** The following words may give your **less advanced** students some difficulty: *compulsory* (p. 55), *chronicled* (p. 55), *genially* (p. 56), *clemency* (p. 56), *sauntered* (p. 59), and *implements* (p. 60).

# GUIDE FOR READING

## O. Henry

(1862–1910) was born William Sidney Porter in North Carolina. In his youth he worked as a reporter, a bank teller, and a draftsman. He lived in Austin, Texas, in the country of Honduras, in Pittsburgh, and in New York City. He even spent three years in an Ohio penitentiary. It was there that he wrote his first short stories. It was also there that he learned about a bank robber and a safecracker who became models for Jimmy Valentine, the hero of "A Retrieved Reformation."

## A Retrieved Reformation

### The Surprise Ending

Sometimes writers surprise you at the ending of a story. A **surprise ending** is an unexpected twist at the end of a story that you did not predict. Even though an ending is a surprise, it must be believable. Writers make surprise endings believable by giving you a few hints about the ending without giving it away. O. Henry is known for startling his readers with surprise endings.

### Focus

This story is titled "A Retrieved Reformation." In small groups look up the words *retrieve* and *reformation* in a dictionary and write down their definitions. Brainstorm together to figure out what the title might mean. Continue working together to predict what this story is about, based on the meaning you have derived from the title. Then read the story to see whether your predictions were correct.

### Vocabulary

Knowing the following words will help you as you read "A Retrieved Reformation."

**assiduously** (ə sij′ oo əs lē) *adv.:* Carefully and busily (p. 61)
**eminent** (em′ ə nənt) *adj.:* Well-known; of high achievement (p. 62)
**retribution** (re′ trə byoo′ shən) *n.:* A punishment deserved for a wrong done (p. 62)
**specious** (spē′ shəs) *adj.:* Seeming to be true without really being so (p. 63)
**guile** (gīl) *n.:* Craftiness (p. 63)
**alterative** (ôl′ tə rāt′ iv) *adj.:* Causing a change (p. 63)
**unobtrusively** (un əb troo′ siv lē) *adv.:* Without calling attention to oneself (p. 64)

## Objectives

1 To understand the surprise ending of a short story
2 To recognize allusions
3 To write about a surprise ending of a short story
4 To express individual interests and abilities through optional activities

## Support Material

**Teaching Portfolio**
Teacher Backup, p. 79
Grammar in Action Worksheets, *Using Dashes,* p. 82; *Understanding Pronoun/Antecedent Agreement,* p. 84
Usage and Mechanics Worksheet, p. 86
Vocabulary Check, P. 87
Analyzing Literature Worksheet, *Understanding the Surprise Ending,* p. 88

Language Worksheet, *Finding Meanings to Fit the Context,* p. 89
Selection Test, p. 90

**Literature Videodisc**
*O. Henry's "Jimmy Valentine"*

**Prentice Hall Literature Writing Studio**

# A Retrieved Reformation

## O. Henry

A guard came to the prison shoe-shop, where Jimmy Valentine was assiduously stitching uppers, and escorted him to the front office. There the warden handed Jimmy his pardon, which had been signed that morning by the governor. Jimmy took it in a tired kind of way. He had served nearly ten months of a four-year sentence. He had expected to stay only about three months, at the longest. When a man with as many friends on the outside as Jimmy Valentine had is received in the "stir" it is hardly worthwhile to cut his hair.

"Now, Valentine," said the warden, "you'll go out in the morning. Brace up, and make a man of yourself. You're not a bad fellow at heart. Stop cracking safes, and live straight."

"Me?" said Jimmy, in surprise. "Why, I never cracked a safe in my life."

"Oh, no," laughed the warden. "Of course not. Let's see, now. How was it you happened to get sent up on that Springfield job? Was it because you wouldn't prove an alibi for fear of compromising somebody in extremely high-toned society? Or was it simply a case of a mean old jury that had it in for you? It's always one or the other with you innocent victims."

"Me?" said Jimmy, still blankly virtuous. "Why, warden, I never was in Springfield in my life!"

"Take him back, Cronin," smiled the warden, "and fix him up with outgoing clothes. Unlock him at seven in the morning, and let him come to the bullpen.[1] Better think over my advice, Valentine."

At a quarter past seven on the next morning Jimmy stood in the warden's outer office. He had on a suit of the villainously fitting, ready-made clothes and a pair of the stiff, squeaky shoes that the state furnishes to its discharged compulsory guests.

The clerk handed him a railroad ticket and the five-dollar bill with which the law expected him to rehabilitate himself into good citizenship and prosperity. The warden gave him a cigar, and shook hands. Valentine, 9762, was chronicled on the books "Pardoned by Governor," and Mr. James Valentine walked out into the sunshine.

Disregarding the song of the birds, the waving green trees, and the smell of the flowers, Jimmy headed straight for a restaurant. There he tasted the first sweet joys of liberty in the shape of a chicken dinner. From there he proceeded leisurely to the depot and boarded his train. Three hours set him down in a little town near the state line. He went to the café of one Mike Dolan and shook hands with Mike, who was alone behind the bar.

"Sorry we couldn't make it sooner, Jimmy, me boy," said Mike. "But we had

---

**1. bullpen** *n.*: A barred room in a jail, where prisoners are kept temporarily.

**Presentation**

**Motivation/Prior Knowledge**
Tell students that O. Henry's stories are known for their surprise endings. In this story the main character is a bank robber. Ask them to try to predict the "twist" at the end of this story.

**Purpose-Setting Question** What role does love play in this story?

**1 Discussion** How would having "friends on the outside" help Jimmy shorten his prison stay?

**2 Discussion** According to the warden, what type of friends does Jimmy have?

**3 Literary Focus** Discuss how O. Henry uses irony in his stories. Calling a prisoner a "compulsory guest" is one example. Have students read the next paragraph to find another example of irony.

**Making Connections** Both "The Adventure of the Speckled Band" (page 27) and "Crime on Mars" (page 137) involve criminals and detectives. "Thank you M'am" (page 179) also deals with a reformation. You might wish to use these selections together and have students note similarities and differences.

**Thematic Focus** The main character in this story, Jimmy Valentine, has lived a life of crime, but he chooses to "go straight." Yet he finds himself in a situation in which he must make another difficult choice and accept its consequences. What choice does he make?

**Videodisc** To provide students with additional background information about O. Henry, you might want to play the segment of the **Literature Videodisc** *O. Henry's "Jimmy Valentine"* in which O. Henry's life and works are discussed. Have students respond to the information provided in the segment and discuss how it shapes their expectations of the story.

Frames 2700 to 3728

61

**4 Discussion** What is Mike Dolan really asking Jimmy?

**5 Literary Focus** Point out that ''a scant eight hundred dollars'' is ironic again since this story was written in the early 1900's and eight hundred dollars would hardly have been considered ''scant.''

 **Videodisc** After students have been introduced to Jimmy Valentine and read about his release from prison, you might want to show them how the opening of the story is adapted to film in the **Literature Videodisc** *O. Henry's ''Jimmy Valentine.''* Have students compare and contrast the depiction of Jimmy Valentine in the film with the way they envisioned him as they read the opening of the story.

Frames 6178 to 13229

that protest from Springfield to buck against, and the governor nearly balked. Feeling all right?''

''Fine,'' said Jimmy. ''Got my key?''

He got his key and went upstairs, unlocking the door of a room at the rear. Everything was just as he had left it. There on the floor was still Ben Price's collar-button that had been torn from that eminent detective's shirt-band when they had overpowered Jimmy to arrest him.

Pulling out from the wall a folding-bed, Jimmy slid back a panel in the wall and dragged out a dust-covered suitcase. He opened this and gazed fondly at the finest set of burglar's tools in the East. It was a complete set, made of specially tempered steel, the latest designs in drills, punches, braces and bits, jimmies, clamps, and augers,[2] with two or three novelties invented by Jimmy himself, in which he took pride. Over nine hundred dollars they had cost him to have made at—, a place where they make such things for the profession.

In half an hour Jimmy went downstairs and through the café. He was now dressed in tasteful and well-fitting clothes, and carried his dusted and cleaned suitcase in his hand.

**4** ''Got anything on?'' asked Mike Dolan, genially.

''Me?'' said Jimmy, in a puzzled tone. ''I don't understand. I'm representing the New York Amalgamated Short Snap Biscuit Cracker and Frazzled Wheat Company.''

This statement delighted Mike to such an extent that Jimmy had to take a seltzer-and-milk on the spot. He never touched ''hard'' drinks.

A week after the release of Valentine, 9762, there was a neat job of safe-burglary done in Richmond, Indiana, with no clue to

----

**2. drills . . . augers** (ô′ gərz): Tools used in metalwork.

the author. A scant eight hundred dollars was all that was secured. Two weeks after that a patented, improved, burglar-proof safe in Logansport was opened like a cheese to the tune of fifteen hundred dollars, currency; securities and silver untouched. That began to interest the rogue-catchers.[3] Then an old-fashioned bank-safe in Jefferson City became active and threw out of its crater an eruption of bank-notes amounting to five thousand dollars. The losses were now high enough to bring the matter up into Ben Price's class of work. By comparing notes, a remarkable similarity in the methods of the burglaries was noticed. Ben Price investigated the scenes of the robberies, and was heard to remark:

''That's Dandy Jim Valentine's autograph. He's resumed business. Look at that combination knob—jerked out as easy as pulling up a radish in wet weather. He's got the only clamps that can do it. And look how clean those tumblers were punched out! Jimmy never has to drill but one hole. Yes, I guess I want Mr. Valentine. He'll do his bit next time without any short-time or clemency foolishness.''

Ben Price knew Jimmy's habits. He had learned them while working up the Springfield case. Long jumps, quick getaways, no confederates,[4] and a taste for good society —these ways had helped Mr. Valentine to become noted as a successful dodger of retribution. It was given out that Ben Price had taken up the trail of the elusive cracksman, and other people with burglar-proof safes felt more at ease.

One afternoon, Jimmy Valentine and his suitcase climbed out of the mail hack[5] in

----

**3. rogue-catchers** *n*.: The police.
**4. confederates** (kən fed′ər its) *n*.: Accomplices; partners in crime.
**5. mail hack:** A horse and carriage used to deliver mail to surrounding towns.

**5**

## Grammar in Action

**Dashes** are helpful tools for skillful writers. They are used to set off information that is loosely related to the rest of the sentence—not essential, but desired by the writer to make the meaning clearer. Explanations, examples, and interrupting comments can be added to sentences with dashes. Note O. Henry's use of dashes:

Ben Price had learned Jimmy's habits. He had learned them while working up the Springfield case. Long jumps, quick getaways, no confederates, and a taste for good society—these ways had helped Mr. Valentine to become noted as a successful dodger of retribution.

Mr. Ralph Spencer, the phoenix that arose from Jimmy Valentine's ashes—ashes left by the flame of a sudden and alternative attack of love—remained in Elmore, and prospered.

In the first example, the explanation of Jimmy's ways comes at the

Elmore, a little town five miles off the railroad down in the blackjack country of Arkansas. Jimmy, looking like an athletic young senior just home from college, went down the board sidewalk toward the hotel.

A young lady crossed the street, passed him at the corner and entered a door over which was the sign "The Elmore Bank." Jimmy Valentine looked into her eyes, forgot what he was, and became another man. She lowered her eyes and colored slightly. Young men of Jimmy's style and looks were scarce in Elmore.

6 | Jimmy collared a boy that was loafing on the steps of the bank as if he were one of the stockholders, and began to ask him questions about the town, feeding him dimes at intervals. By and by the young lady came out, looking royally unconscious of the young man with the suitcase, and went her way.

"Isn't that young lady Miss Polly Simpson?" asked Jimmy, with specious guile.

"Naw," said the boy. "She's Annabel Adams. Her pa owns this bank. What'd you come to Elmore for? Is that a gold watch chain? I'm going to get a bulldog. Got any more dimes?"

Jimmy went to the Planters' Hotel, registered as Ralph D. Spencer, and engaged a room. He leaned on the desk and declared his platform[6] to the clerk. He said he had come to Elmore to look for a location to go into business. How was the shoe business,
7 | now, in the town? He had thought of the shoe business. Was there an opening?

The clerk was impressed by the clothes and manner of Jimmy. He, himself, was something of a pattern of fashion to the thinly gilded[7] youth of Elmore, but he now perceived his shortcomings. While trying to figure out Jimmy's manner of tying his four-in-hand,[8] he cordially gave information.

Yes, there ought to be a good opening in the shoe line. There wasn't an exclusive shoe store in the place. The dry-goods and general stores handled them. Business in all lines was fairly good. Hoped Mr. Spencer would decide to locate in Elmore. He would find it a pleasant town to live in, and the people very sociable.

Mr. Spencer thought he would stop over in the town a few days and look over the situation. No, the clerk needn't call the boy. He would carry up his suitcase, himself; it was rather heavy.

Mr. Ralph Spencer, the phoenix[9] that arose from Jimmy Valentine's ashes— ashes left by the flame of a sudden and alterative attack of love—remained in Elmore, and prospered. He opened a shoe store and secured a good run of trade. | 8

Socially he was also a success, and made many friends. And he accomplished the wish of his heart. He met Miss Annabel Adams, and became more and more captivated by her charms.

At the end of a year the situation of Mr. Ralph Spencer was this: he had won the respect of the community, his shoe store was flourishing, and he and Annabel were engaged to be married in two weeks. Mr. Adams, the typical, plodding, country banker, approved of Spencer. Annabel's pride in him almost equalled her affection. He was as much at home in the family of Mr. Adams and that of Annabel's married sister as if he were already a member. | 9

---

6. **platform** n.: Here, statement of intention.
7. **thinly gilded** adj.: Coated with a thin layer of gold: here, appearing well-dressed.

8. **four-in-hand** n.: A necktie.
9. **phoenix** (fē'niks), n.: In Egyptian mythology, a beautiful bird that lived for about 600 years and then burst into flames; a new bird arose from its ashes.

6 **Discussion** What happens to Jimmy Valentine when he sees the young lady?

7 **Discussion** Where did Jimmy learn about the shoe business?

8 **Discussion** Do you think love has the power to reform people? Do you believe this new character?

9 **Reading Strategy** Have your students summarize the events that have occurred so far in the story and predict what will happen to Ralph Spencer.

---

end of the sentence; therefore, only one dash is used to separate it from the rest of the sentence. In the second example, the explanation of the ashes is in the middle of the sentence; a dash is needed before and after the nonessential material.

If you are typing or using a word processor, use two hyphens to indicate a dash. When you are writing by hand, make the dash a little longer than a hyphen.

**Student Activity 1.** Find four other places where O. Henry uses dashes. Discuss the effective use of the dashes. Do you think other punctuation marks would have been better? Do dashes seem to emphasize meaning differently than commas do? If so, how?

**Student Activity 2.** Write a paragraph describing Jimmy Valentine. Use dashes to set off information that is loosely related to the rest of the sentence.

**10 Discussion** How do you think Ben Price found Jimmy after more than a year had gone by?

**11 Discussion** What do you think Ben is planning to do?

**12 Discussion** Why did Jimmy bring his tools into the bank? Do you think he is planning to rob a bank again?

One day Jimmy sat down in his room and wrote this letter, which he mailed to the safe address of one of his old friends in St. Louis:

Dear Old Pal:

I want you to be at Sullivan's place, in Little Rock, next Wednesday night, at nine o'clock. I want you to wind up some little matters for me. And, also, I want to make you a present of my kit of tools. I know you'll be glad to get them—you couldn't duplicate the lot for a thousand dollars. Say, Billy, I've quit the old business—a year ago. I've got a nice store. I'm making an honest living, and I'm going to marry the finest girl on earth two weeks from now. It's the only life, Billy—the straight one. I wouldn't touch a dollar of another man's money now for a million. After I get married I'm going to sell out and go West, where there won't be so much danger of having old scores brought up against me. I tell you, Billy, she's an angel. She believes in me; and I wouldn't do another crooked thing for the whole world. Be sure to be at Sully's, for I must see you. I'll bring along the tools with me.

Your old friend,

Jimmy.

On the Monday night after Jimmy wrote this letter, Ben Price jogged unobtrusively into Elmore in a livery buggy.[10] He lounged about town in his quiet way until he found out what he wanted to know. From the drugstore across the street from Spencer's shoe store he got a good look at Ralph D. Spencer.

"Going to marry the banker's daughter are you, Jimmy?" said Ben to himself, softly. "Well, I don't know!"

The next morning Jimmy took breakfast at the Adamses. He was going to Little Rock that day to order his wedding suit and buy something nice for Annabel. That would be the first time he had left town since he came to Elmore. It had been more than a year now since those last professional "jobs," and he thought he could safely venture out.

After breakfast quite a family party went downtown together—Mr. Adams, Annabel, Jimmy, and Annabel's married sister with her two little girls, aged five and nine. They came by the hotel where Jimmy still boarded, and he ran up to his room and brought along his suitcase. Then they went on to the bank. There stood Jimmy's horse and buggy and Dolph Gibson, who was going to drive him over to the railroad station.

All went inside the high, carved oak railings into the banking-room—Jimmy included, for Mr. Adam's future son-in-law was welcome anywhere. The clerks were pleased to be greeted by the good-looking, agreeable young man who was going to marry Miss Annabel. Jimmy set his suitcase down. Annabel, whose heart was bubbling with happiness and lively youth, put on Jimmy's hat, and picked up the suitcase. "Wouldn't I make a nice drummer?[11] said Annabel. "My! Ralph, how heavy it is! Feels like it was full of gold bricks."

"Lot of nickel-plated shoehorns in there," said Jimmy, coolly, "that I'm going to return. Thought I'd save express charges by taking them up. I'm getting awfully economical."

---

**10. livery buggy:** A horse and carriage for hire.

**11. drummer** *n.*: A traveling salesman.

## Grammar In Action

To maintain clarity in your writing, make sure **pronouns** and **antecedents agree.** An antecedent is the noun for which a pronoun stands. Personal pronouns, those that refer to the person speaking, the person spoken to, or the person, place, or thing spoken about, must agree with antecedents in person and number. Person indicates whether a pronoun refers to an individual in the first person, second person, or third person. Number indicates whether a pronoun is singular or plural.

A common agreement error occurs when a pronoun does not have the same person as its antecedent. In the following sentence, a second-person pronoun, you, refers to a third-person antecedent: "*Jimmy* has decided to take the straight road, the only road *you* can take if you're honest." The sentence should read, "*Jimmy* has decided to take the straight road, the only road *he* can take if he's honest."

Singular antecedents must have singular pronouns, and plural antecedents must have plural pronouns. Notice how O. Henry's pronouns and antecedents agree in number.

The Elmore Bank had just put in a new safe and vault. Mr. Adams was very proud of it, and insisted on an inspection by everyone. The vault was a small one, but it had a new, patented door. It fastened with three solid steel bolts thrown simultaneously with a single handle, and had a time lock. Mr. Adams beamingly explained its workings to Mr. Spencer, who showed a courteous but not too intelligent interest. The two children, May and Agatha, were delighted by the shining metal and funny clock and knobs.

While they were thus engaged Ben Price sauntered in and leaned on his elbow, looking casually inside between the railings. He

13

**13 Reading Strategy** What do you think will happen next?

**Multicultural Focus** Ask students where they keep their money. Many will say, "In a bank." Although people have not always kept their money in banks, banking services are surprisingly ancient. Countries with flourishing trade and commerce, like ancient Lydia, Phoenicia, China, and Greece, all had modern banking services. The Ancient Greeks often allowed their worshipers to use temples as safe-deposit vaults.

Have students write reports on the history of banks in the Eastern and Western Hemispheres. They should find answers to the following questions:

What were the first banks like?

What kinds of services did banks come to provide?

What are some of the major banks in the world today?

Have students present their papers to the class.

"After breakfast quite a family party went downtown together—Mr. Adams, Annabel, Jimmy, and Annabel's married sister with *her* two little girls, aged five and nine. *They* came by the hotel where Jimmy still boarded, and *he* ran up to *his* room and brought along *his* suitcase."

In your writing make sure pronouns agree with antecedents in person and number. In addition be sure to place pronouns close to antecedents to avoid vague pronoun references.

**Student Activity 1.** Each of the following pronouns appears in Jimmy's letter on page 64: *them, I, some, another, she.* Identify the antecedent of each pronoun.

**Student Activity 2.** Locate five more pronouns on pages 64–65, identify their antecedents, and explain how they agree in person and number.

**Electronic Handbook** You may wish to have students review pronouns before they complete the Grammar in Action activities. If they have access to the Language Master 6000, have them enter the access words *pronoun* and *each,* pressing the GRAMMAR key with each access word to get information about pronoun usage.

**Enrichment** Suggest to students that they create their own story about a "bad" person who goes "good." Allow time for classroom discussion and brainstorming. Perhaps this could even be a group-effort story.

**Master Teacher Note** Although Ben Price permits Valentine to keep his new identity, Ralph still needs to explain to his fiancée and to her father why he happened to have his burglar tools with him. Will Ralph be able to maintain his reputation as a successful shoe merchant, or will his real identity have to be revealed? Have your students write a final scene to "A Retrieved Reformation" in which Ralph explains why he was able to free little Agatha from the bank vault.

**Reader's Response** From the surprise ending, we can infer that Ben Price thinks Jimmy has changed his ways. Do you think Jimmy is a reformed citizen? Explain.

**Thematic Response** What do you think were the consequences of Jimmy's choice?

---

told the teller that he didn't want anything; he was just waiting for a man he knew.

Suddenly there was a scream or two from the women, and a commotion. Unperceived by the elders, May, the nine-year-old girl, in a spirit of play, had shut Agatha in the vault. She had then shot the bolts and turned the knob of the combination as she had seen Mr. Adams do.

The old banker sprang to the handle and tugged at it for a moment. "The door can't be opened," he groaned. "The clock hasn't been wound nor the combination set."

Agatha's mother screamed again, hysterically.

"Hush!" said Mr. Adams, raising his trembling hand. "All be quiet for a moment. Agatha!" he called as loudly as he could. "Listen to me." During the following silence they could just hear the faint sound of the child wildly shrieking in the dark vault in a panic of terror.

"My precious darling!" wailed the mother. "She will die of fright! Open the door! Oh, break it open! Can't you men do something?"

"There isn't a man nearer than Little Rock who can open that door," said Mr. Adams, in a shaky voice. "My God! Spencer, what shall we do? That child—she can't stand it long in there. There isn't enough air, and, besides, she'll go into convulsions from fright."

Agatha's mother, frantic now, beat the door of the vault with her hands. Somebody wildly suggested dynamite. Annabel turned to Jimmy, her large eyes full of anguish, but not yet despairing. To a woman nothing seems quite impossible to the powers of the man she worships.

"Can't you do something, Ralph—*try*, won't you?"

14 He looked at her with a queer, soft smile on his lips and in his keen eyes.

"Annabel," he said, "give me that rose you are wearing, will you?"

Hardly believing that she heard him aright, she unpinned the bud from the bosom of her dress, and placed it in his hand. Jimmy stuffed it into his vest pocket, threw off his coat and pulled up his shirt sleeves. With that act Ralph D. Spencer passed away and Jimmy Valentine took his place.

"Get away from the door, all of you," he commanded, shortly.

He set his suitcase on the table, and opened it out flat. From that time on he seemed to be unconscious of the presence of anyone else. He laid out the shining, queer implements swiftly and orderly, whistling softly to himself as he always did when at work. In a deep silence and immovable, the others watched him as if under a spell.

In a minute Jimmy's pet drill was biting smoothly into the steel door. In ten minutes —breaking his own burglarious record—he threw back the bolts and opened the door.

Agatha, almost collapsed, but safe, was gathered into her mother's arms.

Jimmy Valentine put on his coat, and walked outside the railings toward the front door. As he went he thought he heard a far-away voice that he once knew call 15 "Ralph!" But he never hesitated.

At the door a big man stood somewhat in his way.

"Hello, Ben!" said Jimmy, still with his strange smile. "Got around at last, have you? Well, let's go. I don't know that it makes much difference, now."

And then Ben Price acted rather strangely.

"Guess you're mistaken, Mr. Spencer," 16 he said. "Don't believe I recognize you. Your buggy's waiting for you, ain't it?"

And Ben Price turned and strolled down the street.

66   *Short Stories*

---

## Closure and Extension

### ANSWERS TO RESPONDING TO THE SELECTION
#### Your Response
1. Students should give reasons for their answer.

#### Recalling
2. Valentine was convicted for "cracking safes." The governor grants Valentine clemency because he has "many friends on the outside."
3. He resumes his life of crime as a safecracker.
4. From the pattern of robberies, Ben deduces that the perpetrator must be Valentine and sets out to bring him to justice.
5. Valentine becomes another man when he looks into the banker's daughter's eyes. The change is caused by a "sudden and alterative attack of love."
6. When his fiancée's niece is accidentally locked in a vault, Valentine risks his new way of life to free her.

#### Interpreting
7. Valentine abandons his plans to rob the bank in Elmore. He remains in town and opens a successful shoe store. He writes a letter to an old friend in which he admits to a change and arranges to give away his burglary tools. For the sake of love, he is willing to risk exposure to save his fiancée's niece.

## RESPONDING TO THE SELECTION

### Your Response

1. If you were Ben Price, what would you have done when you confronted Jimmy?

### Recalling

2. Why is Valentine in prison? Why is he pardoned?
3. Out of prison, how does Valentine support himself?
4. Why does Ben start looking for Jimmy again?
5. At what point in the story does Valentine become another man? What causes this change?
6. Why does Valentine use his old talents once again?

### Interpreting

7. Find three details in the story that support the idea that Valentine really has changed.
8. Why does Ben pretend not to know Jimmy?
9. Explain the meaning of the story's title.

### Applying

10. People speak of turning points in their lives, when they seem to change greatly. Can people really change? Support your answer.

## ANALYZING LITERATURE

### Understanding the Surprise Ending

A **surprise ending** depends on an unexpected resolution of the main conflict. To make the surprise ending believable, authors include hints in the story that point toward the ending.

1. How did you think this story would end? Which clues led you to expect this ending?
2. How did the story really end? What clues did the author plant leading to this ending?

## CRITICAL THINKING AND READING

### Recognizing Allusions

An **allusion** is a reference in a work of literature to a person, place, or thing in another work, such as literature, art, music, history, painting, mythology. For example, O. Henry writes, "Mr. Ralph Spencer, the phoenix that arose from Jimmy Valentine's ashes—ashes left by the flame of a sudden and alterative attack of love—remained in Elmore, and prospered." The phoenix is a mythical bird that lived in the Arabian wilderness. Every 500 or 600 years it would burn itself up and rise from its ashes anew.

1. In what way is Valentine like a phoenix?
2. How does this allusion help you predict that Valentine is now truly Ralph Spencer?

## THINKING AND WRITING

### Writing About a Surprise Ending

Stephen Leacock, a writer and critic, once wrote about O. Henry: "No one better than he can hold the reader in suspense. Nay, more than that, the reader scarcely knows that he is 'suspended,' until at the very close of the story, O. Henry, so to speak, turns on the lights, and the whole tale is revealed as an entirety." Discuss Leacock's statement with your classmates. Then write a paper using examples from the story to agree or disagree with this opinion. Revise your paper to make sure you have organized your support in a logical order. Proofread for correct sentence structure, spelling, and punctuation.

## LEARNING OPTIONS

1. **Art.** In a small group, tell the story of Jimmy Valentine in comic-strip form. Work together to draw cartoons and write captions that recreate the most important events from the story. Share your finished comic strip with the class.
2. **Writing.** Write a new ending for "A Retrieved Reformation." In your version have Ben Price recognize Jimmy Valentine. What would happen next? Would Jimmy go to prison? How would Annabel Adams react? Would she forgive her fiancé for his former life as a criminal?

*A Retrieved Reformation* 67

---

**More About the Author** Paul Laurence Dunbar, who died at the age of thirty-three, was physically weak since early childhood. He suffered from frequent colds and often missed school due to illness. During his adult years, he contracted pneumonia, which developed into tuberculosis, and his doctors insisted that he live in a place where the air was dry and brisk. In 1899 he moved to the mountains of Colorado. There he went horseback riding as often as his health would allow. (He grew to love his favorite horse so much that he wrote a poem about her.) In that same year, ''The Finish of Patsy Barnes'' appeared in *The Saturday Evening Post.* How might Dunbar's love of horses and his familiarity with the suffering of pneumonia be reflected in this story?

**Literary Focus** Ask students to give examples of the climax, or turning point, of stories they have enjoyed. Have them consider how an author might heighten a reader's interest in and anticipation of the story's climax. Lead students to see that the more the tension builds before the climax, the more powerful and exciting it is.

**Prereading Focus** Have students brainstorm to list a variety of coincidences. They might look for the following qualities that coincidences may share: mystery, simultaneity, irony, an element of surprise, an element of accident, and a suggestion of inevitability, among others. Ask students to consider why an author would decide to build a story around a coincidence.

**Vocabulary** Have students work with a partner to write a story using all the vocabulary words.

**Electronic Handbook** You may suggest that students use the Language Master 6000 to listen to the pronunciation of the vocabulary words.

68

# GUIDE FOR READING

## The Finish of Patsy Barnes

## Climax

The **climax** is the turning point of a story. During the rising action, the part of the story that precedes the climax, the main character faces a problem and tries to overcome it. Sometimes, as in "The Finish of Patsy Barnes," the problem intensifies, making it seem impossible for the character to solve. The tension builds to such an extent that the climax is greatly anticipated; when it unfolds, it has a powerful effect.

## Focus

The plot of "The Finish of Patsy Barnes" centers on a strange coincidence. In small groups discuss coincidences found in literature, film, television, or your own experience. What do these examples have in common? Answer this question by filling in a diagram like the one below.

## Vocabulary

Knowing the following words will help you as you read "The Finish of Patsy Barnes."

**incorrigible** (in kôr′ ə jə bəl) *adj.*: Incapable of being reformed (p. 69)
**compulsory** (kəm pul′ sə rē) *adj.*: Enforced by law (p. 69)
**sonorous** (sə nôr′ əs) *adj.*: Having a powerful, impressive sound (p. 69)
**meager** (mē′ gər) *adj.*: Lacking in some way (p. 71)

**obdurate** (äb′ dōōr it) *adj.*: Stubbornly persistent (p. 71)
**diplomatic** (dip′ lə mat′ ik) *adj.*: Tactful (p. 74)
**inordinately** (in ôr′ də nit lē) *adv.*: Extremely (p. 74)
**derision** (di rizh′ ən) *n.*: Ridicule or scorn (p. 75)

### Paul Laurence Dunbar

(1872–1906) was considered by Frederick Douglass to be "the most promising black man of his time." The son of former slaves, Dunbar was the first African American to support himself through his writing. He wrote short stories and novels, but he is best remembered for his poetry and has been called the "poet laureate of the Negro race." (A poet laureate is the official or most respected poet of a nation or people.) Concerned about racial injustice, Dunbar weaves social comment throughout his work gracefully and subtly.

### Objectives

1 To understand climax in plot
2 To examine details important to plot
3 To write about the story's climax
4 To express individual interests and abilities through optional activities

### Support Material

**Teaching Portfolio**
Art Transparency 6: *The Banjo Lesson,* 1893, by Henry Ossawa Tanner
Teacher Backup, p. 93
Grammar in Action Worksheet, *Varying Sentence Length,* p. 97
Usage and Mechanics Worksheet, p. 99
Vocabulary Check, p. 100

Analyzing Literature Worksheet, *Understanding Climax in Plot,* p. 101
Critical Thinking and Reading Worksheet, *Examining Details Important to Plot,* p. 102
Selection Test, p. 103

**Prentice Hall Literature Writing Studio**

# The Finish of Patsy Barnes

## Paul Laurence Dunbar

His name was Patsy Barnes, and he was a denizen of Little Africa.[1] In fact, he lived on Douglass Street. By all the laws governing the relations between people and their names, he should have been Irish—but he was not. He was colored, and very much so. That was the reason he lived on Douglass Street. The Negro has very strong within him the instinct of colonization and it was in accordance with this that Patsy's mother had found her way to Little Africa when she had come North from Kentucky.

Patsy was incorrigible. Even into the confines of Little Africa had penetrated the truant officer and the terrible penalty of the compulsory education law. Time and time again had poor Eliza Barnes been brought up on account of the shortcomings of that son of hers. She was a hard-working, honest woman, and day by day bent over her tub, scrubbing away to keep Patsy in shoes and jackets, that would wear out so much faster than they could be bought. But she never murmured, for she loved the boy with a deep affection, though his misdeeds were a sore thorn in her side.

She wanted him to go to school. She wanted him to learn. She had the notion that he might become something better, something higher than she had been. But for him school had no charms; his school was the cool stalls in the big livery stable[2] near at hand; the arena of his pursuits its sawdust floor; the height of his ambition, to be a horseman. Either here or in the racing stables at the Fair-grounds he spent his truant hours. It was a school that taught much, and Patsy was as apt a pupil as he was a constant attendant. He learned strange things about horses, and fine, sonorous oaths that sounded eerie on his young lips, for he had only turned into his fourteenth year.

A man goes where he is appreciated; then could this slim black boy be blamed for doing the same thing? He was a great favorite with the horsemen, and picked up many a dime or nickel for dancing or singing, or even a quarter for warming up a horse for its owner. He was not to be blamed for this, for, first of all, he was born in Kentucky, and had spent the very days of his infancy about the paddocks[3] near Lexington, where his father had sacrificed his life on account of his love for horses. The little fellow had shed no tears when he looked at his father's bleeding body, bruised and broken by the fiery young two-year-old he was trying to subdue. Patsy did not sob or whimper, though his heart ached, for over all the feeling of his grief was a mad, burning desire to ride that horse.

His tears were shed, however, when, actuated by the idea that times would be easier up North, they moved to Dalesford. Then, when he learned that he must leave

---

1. **denizen of Little Africa:** Someone who lives in an area heavily populated by African Americans.
2. **livery** (liv′ ər ē) **stable** adj.: Place where horses are kept and fed.

---

3. **paddocks** (pad′ əks) n.: An enclosed area near a stable, in which horses are exercised.

---

## Presentation

### Motivation/Prior Knowledge
Have students discuss some things that parents want for their children. When these things are not what the children want for themselves, what problems may arise? Tell students that the story they are about to read is about an independent boy who, despite his devotion to his mother, follows his own dreams instead of the ones she has for him.

**Purpose-Setting Question** How do Patsy's hopes for himself differ from his mother's hopes for him?

1 **Discussion** Why do you think Dunbar gave the main character of the story an Irish name?

2 **Enrichment** Douglass Street was probably named in honor of Frederick Douglass, the famous abolitionist whom Dunbar knew personally.

3 **Clarification** At the time that this story was written—the end of the nineteenth century—the terms *colored* and *Negro* were used to refer to people of African descent and did not have the negative connotations they carry today.

4 **Reading Strategy** Based on these descriptions, what kind of relationship do you predict Patsy and his mother will have?

5 **Discussion** Other than his love for horses, why might Patsy prefer this school to the one his mother wanted him to attend?

6 **Clarification** Kentucky is the horse-breeding capital of the United States.

7 **Discussion** What is unusual about Patsy's reaction to his father's death? What does it tell you about Patsy's character?

8 **Enrichment** Dalesford is a town in southern Ohio that Dunbar used as the setting for several short stories. Dunbar usually referred to Dalesford as "Little Africa."

**Thematic Focus** Conflicts between parents and children and between racial groups are frequent themes in literature. Ask students to consider what kinds of challenges might arise from such conflicts.

**Making Connections** Dunbar was also a poet. The last line of his poem "Sympathy" is the title of the book *I Know Why the Caged Bird Sings,* by Maya Angelou, an excerpt of which begins on page 403. This autobiographical piece is also about a young African American person searching for a way to follow personal dreams.

**Master Teacher Note** Art Transparency 6: *The Banjo Lesson,* 1893, by Henry Ossawa Tanner was painted just six years before "The Finish of Patsy Barnes" was published. Have students compare the painting to the story. What similarities in content and theme do they see? What emotions do the painting and the story evoke? How are the painting and the story different? Interested students may wish to write an essay relating to these two works.

## Humanities Note

Fine art, *Farm Boy,* 1941, by Charles Alston. The African American artist Charles Henry Alston was born in Charlotte, North Carolina, in 1907. He began his career as a painter and teacher after studying art and education at Columbia University and New York University, both in New York City. He taught at the Harlem Art Center and the Harlem Art Workshop in the 1930's and later at City College of New York.

At the time at which *Farm Boy* was painted, African American artists were continuing to explore their ethnic roots and celebrate their cultural heritage through their art. This portrait is executed in the "primitive" style that Alston favored. The serious and somewhat melancholy expression of the boy may reflect the many injustices his people had endured in the almost feudal atmosphere of the rural South. Through Alston's sensitive and expressive portrayal, the boy comes to symbolize the total experience of his culture and assumes a significance beyond the painted canvas.

The work of Charles Alston carried the message to all Americans that the African American experience was a rich subject, worthy of artistic expression. In his career as an educator, he influenced the work of celebrated artists such as Romare Bearden and Jacob Lawrence. His importance to American art is recognized today, and his works are exhibited in major museums, including the Metropolitan Museum of Art.

You might use the following questions for discussion:

1. What does the boy in the painting have in common with Patsy Barnes?
2. If you were to paint a portrait of Patsy, how would his pose and expression differ from those of the boy in this painting? Why?

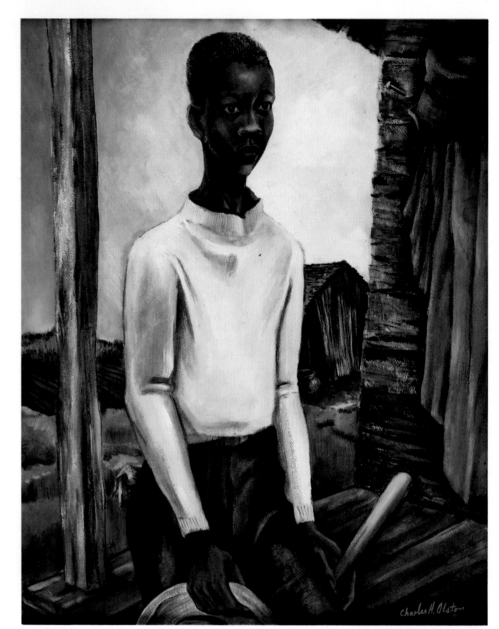

**FARM BOY, 1941**
*Charles Alston*
*Courtesy of Clark Atlanta University*

*70 Short Stories*

his old friends, the horses and their masters, whom he had known, he wept. The comparatively meager appointments of the Fair-grounds at Dalesford proved a poor compensation for all these. For the first few weeks Patsy had dreams of running away—back to Kentucky and the horses and stables. Then after a while he settled himself with heroic resolution to make the best of what he had, and with a mighty effort took up the burden of life away from his beloved home.

Eliza Barnes, older and more experienced though she was, took up her burden with a less cheerful philosophy than her son. She worked hard, and made a scanty livelihood, it is true, but she did not make the best of what she had. Her complainings were loud in the land, and her wailings for her old home smote the ears of any who would listen to her.

They had been living in Dalesford for a year nearly, when hard work and exposure brought the woman down to bed with pneumonia.[4] They were very poor—too poor even to call in a doctor, so there was nothing to do but to call in the city physician. Now this medical man had too frequent calls into Little Africa, and he did not like to go there. So he was very gruff when any of its denizens called him, and it was even said that he was careless of his patients.

Patsy's heart bled as he heard the doctor talking to his mother:

"Now, there can't be any foolishness about this," he said. "You've got to stay in bed and not get yourself damp."

"How long you think I got to lay hyeah, doctah?" she asked.

"I'm a doctor, not a fortune-teller," was the reply. "You'll lie there as long as the disease holds you."

---

4. **pneumonia** ($n\overline{oo}$ mōn′ yə) n.: Inflammation of the lungs.

"But I can't lay hyeah long, doctah, case I ain't got nuffin' to go on."

"Well, take your choice: the bed or the boneyard."

Eliza began to cry.

"You needn't sniffle," said the doctor; "I don't see what you people want to come up here for anyhow. Why don't you stay down South where you belong? You come up here and you're just a burden and a trouble to the city. The South deals with all of you better, both in poverty and crime." He knew that these people did not understand him, but he wanted an outlet for the heat within him.

There was another angry being in the room, and that was Patsy. His eyes were full of tears that scorched him and would not fall. The memory of many beautiful and appropriate oaths came to him; but he dared not let his mother hear him swear. Oh! to have a stone—to be across the street from that man!

When the physician walked out, Patsy went to the bed, took his mother's hand, and bent over shamefacedly to kiss her. The little mark of affection comforted Eliza unspeakably. The mother-feeling overwhelmed her in one burst of tears. Then she dried her eyes and smiled at him.

"Honey," she said; "mammy ain' gwine lay hyeah long. She be all right putty soon."

"Nevah you min'," said Patsy with a choke in his voice. "I can do somep'n', an' we'll have anothah doctah."

"La, listen at de chile; what kin you do?"

"I'm goin' down to McCarthy's stable and see if I kin git some horses to exercise."

A sad look came into Eliza's eyes as she said: "You'd bettah not go, Patsy; dem hosses'll kill you yit, des lak dey did yo' pappy."

But the boy, used to doing pretty much as he pleased, was obdurate, and even while she was talking, put on his ragged jacket and left the room.

**Alternative Assessment** To promote active reading, have students create a reader's response journal as they read "The Finish of Patsy Barnes." Ask them to focus their observations on the events of the plot that make Patsy's problem seem impossible to solve. Encourage them to respond personally to the obstacles of circumstance, poverty, age, and racial prejudice that Patsy must overcome to resolve the conflict.

You may use students' response journals to assess their understanding of the concepts and issues in Dunbar's story.

9 **Reading Strategy** In what ways is Patsy a complex character?

10 **Discussion** Would Eliza Barnes be an easy person to get along with? Explain.

11 **Reading Strategy** Dunbar was known for his skill in using dialect. How does he use dialect to differentiate his characters?

12 **Reading Strategy** What "heat" did the doctor have within him?

13 **Critical Thinking and Reading** What possible turn of events does Eliza's comment suggest to the reader? How does this detail help to build tension and suspense?

## Humanities Note

Fine art, *Backstretch Morning,* by Ernie Barnes. Ernie Barnes, born in 1939 in Durham, North Carolina, began formally studying art at North Carolina Central University. His paintings of ordinary twentieth-century subjects, ranging from pool halls to baseball stadiums, are executed with skill and humor. His many works are featured in collections and exhibits across the United States.

In his painting *Backstretch Morning,* the subject is the racetrack, whose denizens are depicted with affectionate amusement. The figures of horses and riders, presented against a dazzling expanse of yellow sky, are captured in the casual poses of warming up in the backstretch. Barnes has distorted the figures of horses and riders slightly by elongating their legs, which serves to emphasize their grace and delicacy. At the same time, the rounded, heavily muscled bodies of the horses suggest great physical power. These figures are familiar and accessible, as are most of Ernie Barnes's subjects. His wry observations of ordinary life have earned Barnes the title "Premier Twentieth-Century Genre Painter."

You might use these questions for discussion:

1. How does the atmosphere of this painting relate to "The Finish of Patsy Barnes"?
2. The horses in this painting are depicted in a way that emphasizes their grace and power. Would you portray Black Boy similarly or differently? Why?

72   *Short Stories*

## Grammar in Action

Writers use a variety of sentence lengths to achieve emphasis through contrast and to keep their writing from sounding choppy or wordy. Notice how Paul Laurence Dunbar uses sentences of different lengths in this paragraph:

As Patsy saw his mother growing worse, saw her gasping for breath, heard the rattling as she drew in the little air that kept going her clogged lungs, felt the heat of her burning hands, and saw the pitiful appeal in her poor eyes, he became convinced that the city doctor was not helping her. She must have another. But the money?

The first sentence in this paragraph is a complex sentence introduced by a long series of sensory images. The second sentence is a short, emphatic, declarative sentence. The last is a fragment.

Writers sometimes break rules of grammar to achieve a desired effect. The fragment could have been combined with the preceding sentence in this way:

She must have another doctor, but where would we get the money?

Although this sentence is grammatically correct, the emphasis achieved by the abrupt change in rhythm and the introduction of the fragment is lost.

BACKSTRETCH MORNING (detail)
*Ernie Barnes*
*Courtesy of the Artist*

**Student Activity 1.** Find two other paragraphs in the story that contain sentences of varying lengths. Tell why Dunbar varied the length of his sentences in the examples you found.

**Student Activity 2.** The following paragraph has been broken into four sections. Copy the paragraph, combining sentences and fragments where necessary to make the passage read smoothly. Retain some short sentences for emphasis. When you have finished, compare your version with Dunbar's.

1. Patsy's heart was beating beneath his jacket. His heart was beating very wildly.
2. That horse. He knew that glossy coat.
3. He knew that raw-boned frame. He knew those flashing nostrils.
4. That black horse there. He owed something to the orphan he had made.

**Student Activity 3.** Write a paragraph modeled on Student Activity 2 in which you describe your reactions to something unexpected. Use sentences of different lengths for emphasis.

**Electronic Handbook** You may want students to review sentence types and fragments before completing the Grammar in Action activities. If students have access to the Language Master 6000, have them enter the access words *declarative* and *fragment* and press the GRAMMAR key to review types of sentences and fragments.

73

**14 Reading Strategy** What is McCarthy's attitude toward Patsy, at first?

**15 Reading Strategy** What do you predict will happen to Eliza Barnes? Why?

**16 Discussion** What is the significance of the horse's name?

**17 Reading Strategy** How does the mention of Boone's paddock establish Patsy's credentials?

**18 Discussion** Why was Patsy's heart beating wildly?

**19 Clarification** Racing jockeys wear jackets and caps of bright, recognizable colors to identify the horse's owner.

**20 Discussion** What was curious about the combination of this particular horse and rider?

**Multicultural Focus** Be sensitive to students' possible reactions to the story—for example, to the city doctor's offensive manner. Explain that African Americans moving North shared an immigrant experience often including prejudice, low economic status, and limited opportunities for education and advancement.

Believing that "these people" are "just a burden and a trouble [and do not] understand him," the city doctor reveals that he is the one who has failed to comprehend others.

Patsy was not wise enough to be diplomatic. He went right to the point with McCarthy, the liveryman.

The big red-faced fellow slapped him until he spun round and round. Then he said, "Ye little devil, ye, I've a mind to knock the whole head off o' ye. Ye want harses to exercise, do ye? Well git on that 'un, an' see what ye kin do with him."

The boy's honest desire to be helpful had tickled the big, generous Irishman's peculiar sense of humor, and from now on, instead of giving Patsy a horse to ride now and then as he had formerly done, he put into his charge all the animals that needed exercise.

It was with a king's pride that Patsy marched home with his first considerable earnings.

They were small yet, and would go for food rather than a doctor, but Eliza was inordinately proud, and it was this pride that gave her strength and the desire of life to carry her through the days approaching the crisis of her disease.

As Patsy saw his mother growing worse, saw her gasping for breath, heard the rattling as she drew in the little air that kept going her clogged lungs, felt the heat of her burning hands, and saw the pitiful appeal in her poor eyes, he became convinced that the city doctor was not helping her. She must have another. But the money?

That afternoon, after his work with McCarthy, found him at the Fair-grounds. The spring races were on, and he thought he might get a job warming up the horse of some independent jockey. He hung around the stables, listening to the talk of men he knew and some he had never seen before. Among the latter was a tall, lanky man, holding forth to a group of men.

"No, suh," he was saying to them generally, "I'm goin' to withdraw my hoss, because thaih ain't nobody to ride him as he ought to be rode. I haven't brought a jockey along with me, so I've got to depend on pick-ups. Now, the talent's set again my hoss, Black Boy, because he's been losin' regular, but that hoss has lost for the want of ridin', that's all."

The crowd looked in at the slim-legged, raw-boned horse, and walked away laughing.

"The fools!" muttered the stranger. "If I could ride myself I'd show 'em!"

Patsy was gazing into the stall at the horse.

"What are you doing thaih?" called the owner to him.

"Look hyeah, mistah," said Patsy, "ain't that a bluegrass hoss?"

"Of co'se it is, an' one o' the fastest that evah grazed."

"I'll ride that hoss, mistah."

"What do you know 'bout ridin'?"

"I used to gin'ally be' roun' Mistah Boone's paddock in Lexington, an'—"

"Aroun' Boone's paddock—what! Look here, if you can ride that hoss to a winnin' I'll give you more money than you ever seen before."

"I'll ride him."

Patsy's heart was beating very wildly beneath his jacket. That horse. He knew that glossy coat. He knew that raw-boned frame and those flashing nostrils. That black horse there owed something to the orphan he had made.

The horse was to ride in the race before the last. Somehow out of odds and ends, his owner scraped together a suit and colors for Patsy. The colors were maroon and green, a curious combination. But then it was a curious horse, a curious rider, and a more curious combination that brought the two together.

Long before the time for the race Patsy went into the stall to become better ac-

## Primary Source

In April of 1895, Dunbar began corresponding with another talented African American writer, Alice Ruth Moore, whom he married three years later. In his first letter to his future wife, Dunbar introduced himself and raised a question about the kinds of stories they should be writing.

I suppose I must present my credentials, with as little egotism as possible. In the first place I am a writer, one trying to struggle up the thorny path of literature, with the summit of Parnassus not yet in sight. My chief work has been done on the Chicago Record and News, some on the Detroit Free Press. . . . But my regular work is done on the Chicago News for whom I furnish three to four short stories a month. I am hopeful at present both for myself and the future of our race in literature.

I want to know whether or not you believe in preserving by Afro-American—I don't like the word—writers those quaint old tales and songs of our fathers which have made the fame of Joel Chandler Harris, Thomas Nelson Page, Ruth McEnery Stuart and others! Or whether you like so many others think we should ignore the past and all its capital literary materials.

quainted with his horse. The animal turned its wild eyes upon him and neighed. He patted the long, slender head, and grinned as the horse stepped aside as gently as a lady.

"He sholy is full o' ginger," he said to the owner, whose name he had found to be Brackett.

"He'll show 'em a thing or two," laughed Brackett.

"His dam[5] was a fast one," said Patsy, unconsciously.

Brackett whirled on him in a flash. "What do you know about his dam?" he asked.

The boy would have retracted, but it was too late. Stammeringly he told the story of his father's death and the horse's connection therewith.

"Well," said Bracket, "if you don't turn out a hoodoo,[6] you're a winner, sure. But I'll be blessed if this don't sound like a story! But I've heard that story before. The man I got Black Boy from, no matter how I got him, you're too young to understand the ins and outs of poker, told it to me."

When the bell sounded and Patsy went out to warm up, he felt as if he were riding on air. Some of the jockeys laughed at his get-up, but there was something in him—or under him, maybe—that made him scorn their derision. He saw a sea of faces about him, then saw no more. Only a shining white track loomed ahead of him, and a restless steed[7] was cantering with him around the curve. Then the bell called him back to the stand.

They did not get away at first, and back

---

5. **dam** (dam) *n.*: Female parent of a four-legged animal.
6. **hoodoo** (hoo′ doo′) *n.*: Someone or something that causes bad luck.
7. **steed** (stēd) *n.*: High-spirited riding horse.

they trooped. A second trial was a failure. But at the third they were off in a line as straight as a chalk-mark. There were Essex and Firefly, Queen Bess and Mosquito, galloping away side by side, and Black Boy a neck ahead. Patsy knew the family reputation of his horse for endurance as well as fire, and began riding the race from the first. Black Boy came of blood that would not be passed, and to this his rider trusted. At the eighth the line was hardly broken, but as the quarter was reached Black Boy had forged a length ahead, and Mosquito was at his flank. Then, like a flash, Essex shot out ahead under whip and spur, his jockey standing straight in the stirrups.

The crowd in the stand screamed; but Patsy smiled as he lay low over his horse's neck. He saw that Essex had made his best spurt. His only fear was for Mosquito, who hugged and hugged his flank. They were nearing the three-quarter post, and he was tightening his grip on the black. Essex fell back; his spurt was over. The whip fell unheeded on his sides. The spurs dug him in vain.

Black Boy's breath touches the leader's ear. They are neck and neck—nose to nose. The black stallion passes him.

Another cheer from the stand, and again Patsy smiles as they turn into the stretch. Mosquito has gained a head. The colored boy flashes one glance at the horse and rider who are so surely gaining upon him, and his lips close in a grim line. They are half-way down the stretch, and Mosquito's head is at the stallion's neck.

For a single moment Patsy thinks of the sick woman at home and what that race will mean to her, and then his knees close against the horse's sides with a firmer dig. The spurs shoot deeper into the steaming flanks. Black Boy shall win; he must win. The horse that has taken away his father

**21 Discussion** Why does Brackett respond to Patsy's comment in this way?

**22 Clarification** When a horse canters, it runs faster than when it trots but slower than when it gallops.

**23 Reading Strategy** Try to visualize the race as you read.

**24 Literary Focus: Climax** Is the climax of this story believable? Why or why not?

I should like to exchange opinions and work with you if you will agree. The counsel and encouragement of one who is striving toward the same end that I am would, I know, greatly help.

**Reader's Response** How did your feelings about the characters in this story change as you read? Explain.

**Thematic Response** What is the most important conflict Patsy had to resolve? What challenge grew out of this conflict?

## Closure and Extension

### ANSWERS TO RESPONDING TO THE SELECTION
*Your Response*

1. Some students will say that Patsy is admirable because he works hard to save his mother's life. However, others may feel that his defiance of his mother by not attending school was less than admirable.

2. Suggested Response: The story would not be as interesting if Patsy rode another horse. The challenge Patsy faced by riding the very horse that killed his father gives the race—and the story— its special tension.

shall give him back his mother. The stallion leaps away like a flash, and goes under the wire—a length ahead.

Then the band thundered, and Patsy was off his horse, very warm and very happy, following his mount to the stable. There, a little later, Brackett found him. He rushed to him, and flung his arms around him.

25 ''You little devil,'' he cried, ''you rode like you were kin to that hoss! We've won! We've won!'' And he began sticking banknotes[8] at the boy. At first Patsy's eyes bulged, and

---

**8. banknotes** (baŋk' nōts) *n.*: A form of paper money.

then he seized the money and got into his clothes.

''Goin' out to spend it?'' asked Brackett.

''I'm goin' for a doctah fu' my mother,'' said Patsy, ''she's sick.''

''Don't let me lose sight of you.''

''Oh, I'll see you again. So long,'' said the boy.

An hour later he walked into his mother's room with a very big doctor, the greatest the druggist could direct him to. The doctor left his medicines and his orders, but, when Patsy told his story, it was Eliza's pride that started her on the road to recovery. Patsy did not tell his horse's name. 26

### RESPONDING TO THE SELECTION
**Your Response**

1. Do you think Patsy is an admirable character? Why or why not?
2. Do you think the story would be as interesting if Patsy were to ride a horse other than Black Boy in the race? Why or why not?

**Recalling**

3. Instead of going to school, as his mother would like, how does Patsy spend most of his time?
4. What circumstances brought Patsy and Black Boy together once before?
5. How does Patsy spend the prize money he wins?

**Interpreting**

6. Name three details from the story that illustrate Patsy's love for horses.
7. Why does the city physician treat his patients from Little Africa so rudely and carelessly? How does Patsy's anger toward him affect the story's plot?

8. Explain the meaning of this statement: "That black horse there owed something to the orphan he had made."
9. Patsy's father "sacrificed his life on account of his love of horses." How is Patsy's triumph a victory for his father as well as for himself?
10. Why doesn't Patsy tell his mother the name of the horse he rode?

**Applying**

11. Patsy pursues his passion for horses despite his father's fatal accident, his mother's discouragement, and barriers of age and race. Because of this passion of his, Patsy is able to save his mother's life. What comment might the story be making about following your dreams in life? Explain.

### ANALYZING LITERATURE
**Understanding Climax in Plot**

As the action of the plot rises in "The Finish of Patsy Barnes," the problem becomes more serious and complicated. Patsy loses his father and

*Recalling*

3. Patsy spends his time caring for horses at the livery and racing stables.
4. Patsy witnessed his father's death as his father tried to break Black Boy when the horse was a two-year-old.
5. Patsy uses the money to pay for the best doctor he can find to care for his mother.

*Interpreting*

6. Students may cite any three of the

following details: Patsy's burning desire to ride Black Boy after witnessing his father's death, his preference for being with horses over going to school, his eagerness to learn everything about horses, his willingness to hang around horsemen, his tears when he left the horses behind in Kentucky, his decision to get a job exercising horses, his clear memories about Black Boy's background and temperament, his gentle attention to Black Boy be-

fore the race, and his joy when racing.

7. Suggested Response: The doctor is overworked and prejudiced. Patsy's anger toward the doctor fuels his determination to earn enough money to pay for a good doctor.
8. Suggested Response: The horse owed Patsy his mother's life for the life he had taken (his father's).
9. Suggested Response: Patsy's father wanted to break Black Boy, and he died trying. Patsy suc-

is forced to adjust to life away from the Kentucky home he loves. Then he finds that his mother has become seriously ill with pneumonia. The events continue to build toward the **climax,** the turning point of the story, which occurs as Patsy rides Black Boy to victory across the finish line.

1. What further complication in the plot drives Patsy to seek work at McCarthy's stable?
2. How does Patsy's victory resolve the problem of his mother's much-needed medical care?
3. How does Patsy's victory help to settle an old score with a certain horse? What is the significance of Patsy's settling this score?

## CRITICAL THINKING AND READING

### Examining Details Important to Plot

Details are important to the plot of a story when they affect its outcome. How do each of the following details affect the outcome of "The Finish of Patsy Barnes"?

1. Patsy lives in Little Africa.
2. Patsy's father is killed trying to subdue a horse named Black Boy.
3. Patsy's mother contracts pneumonia.
4. Patsy recognizes Black Boy.

## THINKING AND WRITING

### Writing About the Story's Climax

Suppose that Patsy succeeded in mastering Black Boy but did not win the race. How would

this change in the climax affect the story's resolution? Do you think the story would be as satisfying? Why or why not? Write a brief essay responding to these questions.

## LEARNING OPTIONS

1. **Writing.** Write a new ending for "The Finish of Patsy Barnes" based on the changes in the story's climax described in the Thinking and Writing section. Would Patsy feel proud about having mastered the horse that killed his father even though he did not win the race? How would Patsy get the money for a doctor without his winnings? Would Black Boy's owner give Patsy another chance to race? Think about these questions as you develop your story ending.
2. **Speaking and Listening.** Review the part of the story in which the horse race is described (pages 75–76). Imagine that you are a sportscaster who is reporting the events of the race as they happen. Write a script for a "live" report of Patsy's race that you will "broadcast" to your classmates. Make your report as exciting as possible by using the information provided in the story and adding other descriptive details. Deliver your finished report to the class.

2. After witnessing his father's death, Patsy is left with a burning desire to ride the horse that killed him.
3. Eliza's illness forces Patsy to look for work.
4. The recognition rekindles Patsy's desire to ride the horse and to have the horse pay him back for killing his father. It also enables Patsy to convince Black Boy's owner to let him ride in the race.

### THINKING AND WRITING

**Writing Transparency**
Models are good tools for showing the elements and structure of different forms of writing. Before students write their essays, have them use Model 5: *Essay* in **Transparencies for Writing.**

**Software** If students are working on computers, have them use the **Writer's Helper** activity *Crazy Contrasts* to generate ideas for their essays.

**Publishing Student Writing**
Have students form small groups for the purpose of reading their essays aloud, commenting on one another's conclusions, and suggesting improvements.

**Writing Across the Curriculum**
You may want to coordinate your study of "The Finish of Patsy Barnes" with a history unit on the years following the Civil War. The social studies teacher could assign an essay on African American life in northern cities after the Civil War.

### LEARNING OPTIONS

1. Extend the Writing option to appeal to visual learners by having them locate photographs of horses, jockeys, and races and then showing them to their class.
2. The Speaking and Listening option will appeal to students who have a flair for public speaking. Help them prepare for this activity by playing recordings of actual horse races. Extend this activity for auditory and kinesthetic learners by recording the final "broadcast."

---

ceeded in subduing Black Boy, thus accomplishing the task that his father set out to do.
10. Suggested Response: Knowing that her son had ridden the same horse that had killed her husband might have upset Patsy's mother enough to interfere with her recovery.

### Applying

11. Suggested Response: The story suggests that you should follow your dreams in spite of obstacles.

Encourage students to share their explanations.

### ANSWERS TO ANALYZING LITERATURE

1. Suggested Response: The doctor's cruelty to Patsy's mother drives Patsy to seek work so that he might pay for a better doctor.
2. Black Boy's owner pays Patsy handsomely for winning the race. Patsy uses the money to pay for a good doctor.

3. Black Boy killed Patsy's father; now the horse that killed his father helps save his mother. The father's failure to subdue the horse is redeemed by the son's victory.

### ANSWERS TO CRITICAL THINKING AND READING

1. This detail informs readers that Patsy is an African American and prepares them for the prejudice that Patsy and his mother face.

## Preparation

**More About the Author** Shirley Jackson first knew fame when, in 1948, the *New Yorker* printed her short story "The Lottery." Now widely anthologized, the piece brought the magazine its greatest reader response: 450 letters from twenty-five states, two territories, and six foreign countries. Point out that the character Laurie in this story was modeled directly on Jackson's real son. Discuss the importance of a writer's experience in creating fiction and ways of enlarging and making an actual happening into a made-up story.

**Literary Focus** Have your students glance back at the short stories they have read thus far to decide which one is told from a first-person point of view. Point out that only "The Adventure of the Speckled Band" has a first-person narrator—Watson.

**Prereading Focus** You might have students work in small groups on this activity for five or ten minutes. You might also have students brainstorm about the positive and negative aspects of a vivid imagination. Have a representative from each group share the group's findings.

**Vocabulary** Have your less advanced students read the words aloud so that you can be sure they can pronounce them.

**Spelling Tip** Point out that four of these words are adverbs ending in *-ly*. In each of these cases, there is no change in the spelling of the adjective to which the *-ly* is added when forming the adverb.

# GUIDE FOR READING

## Charles

### Point of View

An author often chooses to write a story as though the events were being seen through the eyes of one of the characters. The vantage point from which an author chooses to tell a story is called **point of view.** One point of view an author may use is first-person narrative. In a **first-person narrative,** a character tells the story, referring to himself or herself as "I," and presenting only what he or she knows about events.

"Charles" is a first-person narrative, told by Laurie's mother. You learn at the same time as she does about the events in Laurie's kindergarten class.

### Focus

A young child with an active imagination can tell you something he or she has just made up as though it were a fact. This can lead to misconceptions in the minds of adults, who cannot always distinguish a child's fantasies from his or her statements of fact. Think of a story from literature, film, television, or your own experience in which an adult mistakenly believes what an imaginative child says. What happens as a result of this misconception? Then read the story "Charles" and see just how inventive one little boy can be.

### Vocabulary

Knowing the following words will help you as you read "Charles."

**renounced** (ri nounst′) *v.:* Gave up (p. 79)

**swaggering** (swag′ ər iŋ) *v.:* Strutting; walking with a bold step (p. 79)

**insolently** (in′ sə lənt lē) *adv.:* Boldly disrespectful in speech or behavior (p. 79)

**simultaneously** (sī′ məl tā′ nē əs lē) *adv.:* At the same time (p. 80)

**elaborately** (i lab′ ər it lē) *adv.:* Painstakingly (p. 80)

**incredulously** (in krej′ oo ləs lē) *adv.:* With doubt or disbelief (p. 81)

**haggard** (hag′ ərd) *adj.:* Having a tired look (p. 81)

### Shirley Jackson

(1919–1965) was born in San Francisco and was graduated from Syracuse University. Jackson was married and had four children. As a writer, she produced mainly two types of stories—spine-tingling tales of supernatural events and hilarious stories about family life. She once said that she wrote because "It's the only chance I get to sit down" and because it gave her an excuse not to clean her closets. The main character in "Charles" is patterned after Jackson's own son Laurie.

78 *Short Stories*

### Objectives
1 To understand first-person point of view in a short story
2 To make inferences about the plot
3 To extend the story by writing from a different point of view

### Support Material

**Teaching Portfolio**
Teacher Backup, p. 105
Grammar in Action Worksheet, *Using Dialogue,* p. 108
Usage and Mechanics Worksheet, p. 110
Vocabulary Check, p. 111
Analyzing Literature Worksheet, *Investigating Point of View,* p. 112

Language Worksheet, *Using the Suffix -ly to Form Adverbs,* p. 113
Selection Test, p. 114

**Literature Videodisc**
*The Storyteller/Charles*

**Prentice Hall Literature Writing Studio**

# Charles

## Shirley Jackson

The day my son Laurie started kindergarten he renounced corduroy overalls with bibs and began wearing blue jeans with a belt; I watched him go off the first morning with the older girl next door, seeing clearly that an era of my life was ended, my sweet-voiced nursery-school tot replaced by a long-trousered, swaggering character who forgot to stop at the corner and wave goodbye to me.

He came home the same way, the front door slamming open, his cap on the floor, and the voice suddenly become raucous[1] shouting, "Isn't anybody *here?*"

At lunch he spoke insolently to his father, spilled his baby sister's milk, and remarked that his teacher said we were not to take the name of the Lord in vain.

"How *was* school today?" I asked, elaborately casual.

"All right," he said.

"Did you learn anything?" his father asked.

Laurie regarded his father coldly. "I didn't learn nothing," he said.

"Anything," I said. "Didn't learn anything."

"The teacher spanked a boy, though," Laurie said, addressing his bread and butter. "For being fresh," he added, with his mouth full.

"What did he do?" I asked. "Who was it?"

---

1. **raucous** (rô' kəs) *adj.*: Boisterous; disorderly.

Laurie thought. "It was Charles," he said. "He was fresh. The teacher spanked him and made him stand in a corner. He was awfully fresh."

"What did he do?" I asked again, but Laurie slid off his chair, took a cookie, and left, while his father was still saying, "See here, young man."

The next day Laurie remarked at lunch, as soon as he sat down, "Well, Charles was bad again today." He grinned enormously and said, "Today Charles hit the teacher."

"Good heavens," I said, mindful of the Lord's name, "I suppose he got spanked again?"

"He sure did," Laurie said. "Look up," he said to his father.

"What?" his father said, looking up.

"Look down," Laurie said. "Look at my thumb. Gee, you're dumb." He began to laugh insanely.

"Why did Charles hit the teacher?" I asked quickly.

"Because she tried to make him color with red crayons," Laurie said. "Charles wanted to color with green crayons so he hit the teacher and she spanked him and said nobody play with Charles but everybody did."

The third day—it was Wednesday of the first week—Charles bounced a see-saw on to the head of a little girl and made her bleed, and the teacher made him stay inside all during recess. Thursday Charles had to stand in a corner during story-time because he kept pounding his feet on the

*Charles* 79

**3 Discussion** Why do you think Laurie stayed after school with Charles?

**4 Discussion** How do you think Charles's teacher will handle him? Will she punish him? Suspend him? Would the school suspend a kindergartener? How would you deal with Charles if you were his teacher?

**5 Discussion** How is Charles affecting Laurie's family?

 **Videodisc** After students read about how Charles was kept after school, you may want to have them watch the corresponding segment of the film adaptation of the story on the **Literature Videodisc.** Have them discuss how the depiction of the events in the film compares with the way in which they envisioned them as they read. Does the film enhance their understanding of the story? Why or why not?

Frames 33053 to 35309

floor. Friday Charles was deprived of blackboard privileges because he threw chalk.

On Saturday I remarked to my husband, "Do you think kindergarten is too unsettling for Laurie? All this toughness, and bad grammar, and this Charles boy sounds like such a bad influence."

"It'll be all right," my husband said reassuringly. "Bound to be people like Charles in the world. Might as well meet them now as later."

On Monday Laurie came home late, full of news. "Charles," he shouted as he came up the hill; I was waiting anxiously on the front steps. "Charles," Laurie yelled all the way up the hill, "Charles was bad again."

"Come right in," I said, as soon as he came close enough. "Lunch is waiting."

3 "You know what Charles did?" he demanded, following me through the door. "Charles yelled so in school they sent a boy in from first grade to tell the teacher she had to make Charles keep quiet, and so Charles had to stay after school. And so all the children stayed to watch him."

"What did he do?" I asked.

"He just sat there," Laurie said, climbing into his chair at the table. "Hi, Pop, y'old dust mop."

"Charles had to stay after school today," I told my husband. "Everyone stayed with him."

"What does this Charles look like?" my husband asked Laurie. "What's his other name?"

"He's bigger than me," Laurie said. "And he doesn't have any rubbers and he doesn't ever wear a jacket."

Monday night was the first Parent-Teachers meeting, and only the fact that the baby had a cold kept me from going; I wanted passionately to meet Charles's mother. On Tuesday Laurie remarked suddenly, "Our teacher had a friend come to see her in school today."

"Charles's mother?" my husband and I asked simultaneously.

"Naaah," Laurie said scornfully. "It was a man who came and made us do exercises, we had to touch our toes. Look." He climbed down from his chair and squatted down and touched his toes. "Like this," he said. He got solemnly back into his chair and said, picking up his fork, "Charles didn't even *do* exercises."

"That's fine," I said heartily. "Didn't Charles want to do exercises?"

"Naaah," Laurie said. "Charles was so fresh to the teacher's friend he wasn't *let* do exercises."

"Fresh again?" I said.

"He kicked the teacher's friend," Laurie said. "The teacher's friend told Charles to touch his toes like I just did and Charles kicked him."

"What are they going to do about Charles, do you suppose?" Laurie's father asked him. 4

Laurie shrugged elaborately. "Throw him out of school, I guess," he said.

Wednesday and Thursday were routine; Charles yelled during story hour and hit a boy in the stomach and made him cry. On Friday Charles stayed after school again and so did all the other children.

With the third week of kindergarten Charles was an institution in our family; the baby was being a Charles when she cried all afternoon; Laurie did a Charles when he filled his wagon full of mud and pulled it through the kitchen; even my husband, when he caught his elbow in the telephone cord and pulled the telephone and a bowl of flowers off the table, said, after the first minute, "Looks like Charles." 5

During the third and fourth weeks it looked like a reformation in Charles; Laurie reported grimly at lunch on Thursday of the third week, "Charles was so good today the teacher gave him an apple."

## Grammar in Action

Grammatical rules for **dialogue** require exact positioning of other punctuation marks with quotation marks. Quotation marks separate dialogue from the narration of the story. Commas are most commonly used to separate the spoken words from the explanatory phrase; however, when the spoken words are in question form, a question mark must be used.

Notice the punctuation that Shirley Jackson uses in the following excerpt:

"Charles's mother?" my husband and I asked simultaneously.

"Naaah," Laurie said scornfully. "It was a man who came and made us do exercises, we had to touch our toes. Look." He climbed down from his chair and squatted down and touched his toes, "Like this," he said. He got solemnly back into his chair and said, picking up his fork, "Charles didn't even *do* the exercises."

"That's fine," I said heartily. "Didn't Charles want to do exercises?"

"What?" I said, and my husband added warily, "You mean Charles?"

"Charles," Laurie said. "He gave the crayons around and he picked up the books afterward and the teacher said he was her helper."

"What happened?" I asked incredulously.

"He was her helper, that's all," Laurie said, and shrugged.

"Can this be true, about Charles?" I asked my husband that night. "Can something like this happen?"

"Wait and see," my husband said cynically.[2] "When you've got a Charles to deal with, this may mean he's only plotting." He seemed to be wrong. For over a week Charles was the teacher's helper; each day he handed things out and he picked things up; no one had to stay after school.

"The PTA meeting's next week again," I told my husband one evening. "I'm going to find Charles's mother there."

"Ask her what happened to Charles," my husband said. "I'd like to know."

"I'd like to know myself," I said.

On Friday of that week things were back to normal. "You know what Charles did today?" Laurie demanded at the lunch table, in a voice slightly awed. "He told a little girl to say a word and she said it and the teacher washed her mouth out with soap and Charles laughed."

"What word?" his father asked unwisely, and Laurie said, "I'll have to whisper it to you, it's so bad." He got down off his chair and went around to his father. His father bent his head down and Laurie whispered joyfully. His father's eyes widened.

"Did Charles tell the little girl to say *that?*" he asked respectfully.

---

**2. cynically** (sin′ i k′l ē) *adv.*: With disbelief as to the sincerity of people's intentions or actions.

"She said it *twice*," Laurie said. "Charles told her to say it *twice*."

"What happened to Charles?" my husband asked.

"Nothing," Laurie said. "He was passing out the crayons."

Monday morning Charles abandoned the little girl and said the evil word himself three or four times, getting his mouth washed out with soap each time. He also threw chalk.

My husband came to the door with me that evening as I set out for the PTA meeting. "Invite her over for a cup of tea after the meeting," he said. "I want to get a look at her."

"If only she's there," I said prayerfully.

"She'll be there," my husband said. "I don't see how they could hold a PTA meeting without Charles's mother."

At the meeting I sat restlessly, scanning each comfortable matronly face, trying to determine which one hid the secret of Charles. None of them looked to me haggard enough. No one stood up in the meeting and apologized for the way her son had been acting. No one mentioned Charles.

After the meeting I identified and sought out Laurie's kindergarten teacher. She had a plate with a cup of tea and a piece of chocolate cake; I had a plate with a cup of tea and a piece of marshmallow cake. We maneuvered[3] up to one another cautiously, and smiled.

"I've been so anxious to meet you," I said. "I'm Laurie's mother."

"We're all so interested in Laurie," she said.

"Well, he certainly likes kindergarten," I said. "He talks about it all the time."

"We had a little trouble adjusting, the

---

**3. maneuvered** (mə n$\overline{oo}$′ vərd) *v.*: Moved in a planned way.

---

In the first paragraph, the quoted material is a question; therefore, a question mark to end the quotation is placed inside the last quotation mark. There is a period at the end of the entire statement.

In the second paragraph, Laurie's first statement is an interjection. It is followed by a comma and then the quotation mark. A period follows the explanatory phrase. Notice that when Laurie begins speaking again, a new set of quotation marks is needed, and the dialogue continues in the same paragraph.

Notice the repetition of this pattern in the third paragraph.

**Student Activity.** Write your own dialogue in which you use commas, periods, and question marks with quotation marks. Make up a dialogue similar to Laurie's in which you relate a school experience. You might begin with: "Guess what! You'll never believe what _____ did in school today!" I exclaimed as I roared through the door.

**Electronic Handbook** If students have access to the Language Master 6000, have them enter the access word *quotation* or the quotation mark symbol (") and press the GRAMMAR key for a review of punctuation for dialogue.

**6 Discussion** Were you surprised by the ending? When did you first suspect that Charles and Laurie were the same person?

**Reader's Response** Why do you think children Laurie's age have active imaginations? Were you especially imaginative when you were five? Explain.

**Thematic Response** How do you think Laurie's parents should treat his behavior? Should they take it lightly or seriously?

## Closure and Extension

### ANSWERS TO RESPONDING TO THE SELECTION
**Your Response**

1. Urge students to point out clues that led them to their response.
2. Encourage students to imagine the situations Laurie describes from the teacher's point of view as they respond.

*Recalling*

3. Examples of Charles's poor behavior include being "awfully fresh," hitting the teacher, bouncing the seesaw on the head of a classmate, throwing chalk, yelling in class, kicking the gym instructor, hitting a classmate in the stomach, and using profanity.
4. Examples of Laurie's poor behavior at home include slamming the door, speaking insolently to his father, and pulling his mud-filled wagon through the kitchen.

*Interpreting*

5. Answers will differ. Laurie was probably testing the limits of his teacher's endurance.
6. Laurie's behavior at home is essentially the same as Charles's behavior in school.
7. Answers will differ. Laurie probably invented Charles because he has mixed feelings about his behavior. He knows his parents would disapprove if they knew the truth. Nevertheless, he is pleased that Charles is able to get so much attention.

*Applying*

8. Answers will differ. Some may opt for Laurie's teacher's methods. Others may suggest confronting Laurie and admonishing him.

82

first week or so," she said primly, "but now he's a fine little helper. With occasional lapses, of course."

"Laurie usually adjusts very quickly," I said. "I suppose this time it's Charles's influence."

## RESPONDING TO THE SELECTION
### Your Response
1. Were you surprised to learn that Charles and Laurie were the same person? Why or why not?
2. If you were Laurie's teacher, how would you have reacted to his behavior?

### Recalling
3. Give three examples of Charles's poor behavior in school.
4. Give three examples of Laurie's poor behavior at home.

### Interpreting
5. Why did Laurie act the way he did in school?
6. What clues to Laurie's behavior in school can you find in his behavior at home?
7. Why do you think Laurie invented Charles?

### Applying
8. Imagine that you were Laurie's parent. What would you do about Laurie's behavior?

## ANALYZING LITERATURE
### Investigating Point of View
"Charles" is a **first-person narrative.** A character, Laurie's mother, tells the story. As the narrator, she uses language such as "my son" and "I said." The plot reveals information only as Laurie's mother learns it. The story's ending is as much of a surprise to her as it is to you.

1. Before the PTA meeting, how does Laurie's mother learn about incidents in school?

82 *Short Stories*

"Charles?"

"Yes," I said, laughing, "you must have your hands full in that kindergarten, with Charles."

"Charles?" she said. "We don't have any Charles in the kindergarten."

2. Why is a first-person point of view effective for developing the plot of "Charles"?

## CRITICAL THINKING AND READING
### Making Inferences About the Plot
An **inference** is a conclusion based on evidence. Sometimes an author does not state directly everything that is happening. The reader must make inferences based on the clues given. For example, the author does not tell you directly that Laurie's behavior at home changes after he starts kindergarten, but you infer it.

Find and list four clues from which you can make the inference that Charles is Laurie.

## THINKING AND WRITING
### Writing From Another Point of View
Make a list of several questions you might want to ask Laurie's parents if you were his kindergarten teacher. Use the questions to write a new scene at the PTA meeting between Laurie's mother and his teacher. Instead of writing the episode from the point of view of Laurie's mother, write your episode from the point of view of Laurie's teacher. The pronouns "I" and "me" will refer to the teacher in your scene. Remember that she knows only about what has happened at school.

Revise your story to make sure you have maintained a consistent point of view throughout. Finally, proofread your story and share it with your classmates.

### ANSWERS TO ANALYZING LITERATURE

1. She gets her information only from Laurie.
2. It gives the plot the illusion of truth, as if the events described actually happened to the "I" of the story. As a result, the fictional story seems to be nonfiction.

### ANSWERS TO CRITICAL THINKING AND READING

When his mother first learns of Charles and asks what he did that was fresh, Laurie is reluctant to answer, as if he has something to hide. When his father asks about Charles's appearance and last name, Laurie is evasive and responds vaguely. When Charles's behavior temporarily improves, so do Laurie's table manners. We never actually "see" Charles. The only evidence that he exists is hearsay.

### THINKING AND WRITING

**Publishing Student Writing** As students read aloud their new scene, have the rest of the class consider these questions:

1. Does the scene shift the first-person point of view from Laurie's mother to the teacher?
2. Is the new point of view consistent with the teacher's limited knowledge of Laurie?

# Character

**WOMAN WITH PARASOL**
*Claude Monet*
Scala/Art Resource

**Humanities Note**

Fine art, *Woman with Parasol*, 1875, by Claude Monet. Claude Monet (1840–1926) was one of the most prominent of the French Impressionist painters. Impressionism was a movement in painting characterized by the breaking down of form and light into flecks of color. Monet is often considered the purest of the Impressionist painters. The title of one of his paintings, *Impression: Sunrise,* inspired the name of the entire movement, Impressionism. Monet's belief in painting out of doors, directly onto the canvas, did much to redefine the fixed concepts of painting at the end of the nineteenth century.

In *Women with Parasol,* the models were Monet's wife and their son Jean. The painting is not a portrait so much as a study of the effects of strong sunlight on figures and landscape. The features and outlines of the figures are blurred by the intensity of the light. Yet a portrayal of character comes through. The variety of colors used in the grassy bank is apparent upon close examination but is blended by the eye into a more homogeneous hue when viewed from a distance. The artist painted with frantic speed to try to record the light before it changed. The resulting directness and spontaneity truly capture the essence of a bright and breezy summer scene.

**Master Teacher Note** To introduce the element of character in stories, show Art Transparency 2, *Farewell to Lincoln Square* by Raphael Soyer, from the Teaching Portfolio. Have students look at the people in this painting. Ask by what means the artist made each person individual. What might be the character of the girl in the center of the painting, as revealed by her functional clothing, downcast expression, and dispirited posture? How do the expressions of the other characters reveal what they are thinking or feeling? What is the effect of the artist's use of color on the mood of the painting? You might then ask how writers, without visual means, create characters in stories.

# Preparation

**More About the Author** Gish Jen, who grew up apart from the Chinese community, has said, "The conscious impulse of my family was to assimilate. We were almost the only Asian American family in town. In Yonkers people threw things at us and called us names. We thought it was normal —it was only much later that I realized it had been hard." What influence might the urge to assimilate and the difficulties faced by her family have had on Jen's fiction?

**Literary Focus** Lead students to see that characters are revealed by what they do and say as well as by what they don't do and don't say. Suggest that students compare the character traits of the two sisters as they read the story. How do the differences in their personalities help to point out each sister's traits?

**Prereading Focus** After students have finished brainstorming and making their list, have them discuss how they came to associate these things with the particular qualities they listed. Encourage students to share their feelings about whether these things actually possessed the special powers they had attributed to them.

**Vocabulary** Have students work with a partner to use all the vocabulary words in a paragraph.

**Electronic Handbook** You may suggest that your students use the Language Master 6000 to listen to the pronunciation of the vocabulary words.

# GUIDE FOR READING

## The White Umbrella

### Character Traits

**Character traits** are the qualities that make up a character's personality. For example, a character may be headstrong, witty, or sentimental. You can discover these traits through a character's actions and words and through the writer's description of the character. Some characters may show only one major character trait, whereas others, like real people, show a number of different traits.

### Focus

Have you ever yearned for something so much that the object became almost sacred or magical in your mind? Did you feel that once you possessed this thing you would be a better, more powerful, or more interesting person? With your classmates, brainstorm to list things that you have wanted so badly that you came to attribute special powers to them. On a chart like the one following, write these things and what you felt these things would do for you.

| Things | What the Things Would Do |
|---|---|
| pair of sneakers with air pockets in the soles | would make me able to run faster than anyone in my gym class |

In this short story, the narrator longs for an umbrella that belongs to someone else. As you read "The White Umbrella," think about what the object might represent for the narrator.

### Vocabulary

Knowing the following words will help you as you read "The White Umbrella."

**discreet** (di skrēt′) *adj.*: Careful about what one says or does; prudent (p. 85)

**credibility** (kred′ ə bil′ ə tē) *n.*: Believability (p. 85)

**constellation** (kän′ stə lā′ shən) *n.*: A group of stars named after and thought to re-semble an object, an animal, or a mythological character in outline (p. 87)

**revelation** (rev′ ə lā′ shən) *n.*: Something revealed; a disclosure of something not previously known or realized (p. 90)

### Gish Jen

(1956–  ) is the daughter of Chinese immigrants. She grew up in Yonkers and Scarsdale, New York, where her family were the only Asian Americans. Jen began writing fiction as an undergraduate at Harvard but did not stay to finish her degree. After teaching English in China, she entered the University of Iowa writing program, where she wrote the story "The White Umbrella." Her first novel, *Typical American,* was published in 1991.

*84   Short Stories*

## Objectives

1  To understand character traits
2  To understand figurative language
3  To write from a different point of view
4  To express individual interests and abilities through an optional activity

## Support Material

**Teaching Portfolio**
Teacher Backup, p. 117
Grammar in Action Worksheet, *Using Complex Sentences,* p. 121
Usage and Mechanics Worksheet, p. 123
Vocabulary Check, p. 124
Analyzing Literature Worksheet, *Understanding Character Traits,* p. 125

Critical Thinking and Reading Worksheet, *Understanding Figurative Language,* p. 126
Selection Test, p. 127

**Audio Prose Library**
Maxine Hong Kingston: Interview

**Prentice Hall Literature Writing Studio**

# The White Umbrella

## Gish Jen

When I was twelve, my mother went to work without telling me or my little sister.

"Not that we need the second income." The lilt of her accent drifted from the kitchen up to the top of the stairs, where Mona and I were listening.

"No," said my father, in a barely audible voice. "Not like the Lee family."

The Lees were the only other Chinese family in town. I remembered how sorry my parents had felt for Mrs. Lee when she started waitressing downtown the year before; and so when my mother began coming home late, I didn't say anything, and tried to keep Mona from saying anything either.

"But why shouldn't I?" she argued. "Lots of people's mothers work."

"Those are American people," I said.

"So what do you think we are? I can do the pledge of allegiance with my eyes closed."

Nevertheless, she tried to be discreet; and if my mother wasn't home by 5:30, we would start cooking by ourselves, to make sure dinner would be on time. Mona would wash the vegetables and put on the rice; I would chop.

For weeks we wondered what kind of work she was doing. I imagined that she was selling perfume, testing dessert recipes for the local newspaper. Or maybe she was working for the florist. Now that she had learned to drive, she might be delivering boxes of roses to people.

"I don't think so," said Mona as we walked to our piano lesson after school. "She would've hit something by now."

A gust of wind littered the street with leaves.

"Maybe we better hurry up," she went on, looking at the sky. "It's going to pour."

"But we're too early." Her lesson didn't begin until 4:00, mine until 4:30, so we usually tried to walk as slowly as we could. "And anyway, those aren't the kind of clouds that rain. Those are cumulus clouds."[1]

We arrived out of breath and wet.

"Oh, you poor, poor dears," said old Miss Crosman. "Why don't you call me the next time it's like this out? If your mother won't drive you, I can come pick you up."

"No, that's okay," I answered. Mona wrung her hair out on Miss Crosman's rug. "We just couldn't get the roof of our car to close, is all. We took it to the beach last summer and got sand in the mechanism." I pronounced this last word carefully, as if the credibility of my lie depended on its middle syllable. "It's never been the same." I thought for a second. "It's a convertible."

"Well then make yourselves at home." She exchanged looks with Eugenie Roberts, whose lesson we were interrupting. Eugenie smiled good-naturedly. "The towels are in the closet across from the bathroom."

Huddling at the end of Miss Crosman's

---

1. **cumulus** (kyōō′ myōō ləs) **clouds** n.: Fluffy, white clouds that usually indicate fair weather.

*The White Umbrella*  85

**Presentation**

**Motivation/Prior Knowledge** What impact might a mother's decision to take a job outside the home have on her children? What determines whether they would be pleased or upset by her decision? Tell students that they are about to read a story about a young girl who has difficulty accepting her mother's decision to go to work.

**Purpose-Setting Question** How do the narrator's feelings toward her mother change during the course of the story?

1 **Discussion** Do you think the narrator's mother and father really needed the money? If so, why do they pretend otherwise?

2 **Discussion** Why does the narrator question her family's identity as American?

3 **Discussion** Why doesn't the mother tell her daughters what her job is?

4 **Literary Focus: Character Traits** What is your first impression of Miss Crosman?

5 **Literary Focus: Character Traits** Why does the narrator feel it necessary to make up a story? What does this reveal about her? Why doesn't Mona contradict her sister?

**Thematic Focus** Why is it that young people sometimes have difficulty appreciating the members of their own family?

**Making Connections** Another selection that deals with the importance of family and the meeting of different cultures is the story "The Medicine Bag," by Virginia Driving Hawk Sneve, on page 225. You may want to have your students read and discuss these selections as a pair.

**ESL Teaching Strategy** You may wish to pair your ESL students with other students from the class as reading partners. As they read the story, the partners can help ESL students understand difficult words and concepts.

**6 Reading Strategy** How does the author make it clear that the narrator envies Eugenie?

**7 Reading Strategy** Contrast Eugenie's departure with the narrator's arrival. Predict what will happen to the umbrella.

## Humanities Note

Fine art, *Chinese-American Girl*, by painter Violet Chew-MacLean. This watercolor portrait is rendered with a great deal of sensitivity toward its subject. The artist has captured the strength and willful nature of this young girl but allows her gentle side to show through. The severe geometric background offsets the soft, curving shapes of the girl's features, hair, and shoulders. Violet Chew-MacLean has caught the dramatic play of light on the girl's face with the skill of a consummate watercolor painter.

You might use these questions for discussion:

1. Do you think this portrait is more representative of the narrator or Mona? Why?

2. What aspects of the appearance of the girl in the painting are more American than Chinese? Give reasons for your answers.

**6** nine-foot leatherette couch, Mona and I watched Eugenie play. She was a grade ahead of me and, according to school rumor, had a boyfriend in high school. I believed it. . . . She had auburn hair, blue eyes, and, I noted with a particular pang, a pure white folding umbrella.

"I can't see," whispered Mona.

"So clean your glasses."

"My glasses *are* clean. You're in the way."

I looked at her. "They look dirty to me."

"That's because *your* glasses are dirty."

Eugenie came bouncing to the end of her piece.

"Oh! Just stupendous!" Miss Crosman hugged her, then looked up as Eugenie's mother walked in. "Stupendous!" she said again. "Oh! Mrs. Roberts! Your daughter has a gift, a real gift. It's an honor to teach her."

**7** Mrs. Roberts, radiant with pride, swept her daughter out of the room as if she were royalty, born to the piano bench. Watching the way Eugenie carried herself, I sat up, and concentrated so hard on sucking in my stomach that I did not realize until the Robertses were gone that Eugenie had left her umbrella. As Mona began to play, I jumped up and ran to the window, meaning to call to them—only to see their brake lights flash then fade at the stop sign at the corner. As if to allow them passage, the rain had let up; a quivering sun lit their way.

The umbrella glowed like a scepter on the blue carpet while Mona, slumping over the keyboard, managed to eke out[2] a fair rendition of a catfight. At the end of the piece, Miss Crosman asked her to stand up.

"Stay right there," she said, then came back a minute later with a towel to cover the bench. "You must be cold," she continued. "Shall I call your mother and have her bring over some dry clothes?"

"No," answered Mona. "She won't come because she . . . "

"She's too busy," I broke in from the back of the room.

"I see." Miss Crosman sighed and shook her head a little. "Your glasses are filthy, honey," she said to Mona. "Shall I clean them for you?"

Sisterly embarrassment seized me. Why hadn't Mona wiped her lenses when I told her to? As she resumed abuse of the piano, I

---

**2. eke** (ēk) **out:** Barely manage to play.

**CHINESE-AMERICAN GIRL**
*Violet Chew-MacLean*
*Courtesy of the Artist*

## Grammar in Action

A **complex sentence** contains an independent clause and one or more dependent clauses. Both types of clause contain a subject and a verb, but only an independent clause can stand by itself as a sentence. A dependent clause cannot stand alone because it is introduced by a subordinating conjunction such as *when, before, if, although,* and *as.*

Notice how Gish Jen uses complex sentences to show the relationship between ideas in this passage from "The White Umbrella." The dependent clauses have been italicized.

"Why hadn't Mona wiped her lenses *when I told her to? As she resumed abuse of the piano,* I stared at the umbrella."

The dependent clause can appear at the beginning or at the end of the complex sentence. If it comes at the beginning, it is set off from the independent clause with a comma. No comma is necessary when the dependent clause comes at the end of a complex sentence.

If you read the independent clauses by themselves, you will see that they can stand alone as complete sentences. When you try the same thing with the dependent clauses, you will see that they cannot stand alone.

stared at the umbrella. I wanted to open it, twirl it around by its slender silver handle; I wanted to dangle it from my wrist on the way to school the way the other girls did. I wondered what Miss Crosman would say if I offered to bring it to Eugenie at school tomorrow. She would be impressed with my consideration for others; Eugenie would be pleased to have it back; and I would have possession of the umbrella for an entire night. I looked at it again, toying with the idea of asking for one for Christmas. I knew, however, how my mother would react.

"Things," she would say. "What's the matter with a raincoat? All you want is things, just like an American."

Sitting down for my lesson, I was careful to keep the towel under me and sit up straight.

"I'll bet you can't see a thing either," said Miss Crosman, reaching for my glasses. "And you can relax, you poor dear." She touched my chest, in an area where she never would have touched Eugenie Roberts. "This isn't a boot camp."[3]

When Miss Crosman finally allowed me to start playing I played extra well, as well as I possibly could. See, I told her with my fingers. You don't have to feel sorry for me.

"That was wonderful," said Miss Crosman. "Oh! Just wonderful."

An entire constellation rose in my heart.

"And guess what," I announced proudly. "I have a surprise for you."

Then I played a second piece for her, a much more difficult one that she had not assigned.

"Oh! That was stupendous," she said without hugging me. "Stupendous! You are a genius, young lady. If your mother had started you younger, you'd be playing like Eugenie Roberts by now!"

---

3. **boot camp:** Place where soldiers receive basic training and are treated roughly.

I looked at the keyboard, wishing that I had still a third, even more difficult piece to play for her. I wanted to tell her that I was the school spelling bee champion, that I wasn't ticklish, that I could do karate.

"My mother is a concert pianist," I said.

She looked at me for a long moment, then finally, without saying anything, hugged me. I didn't say anything about bringing the umbrella to Eugenie at school.

The steps were dry when Mona and I sat down to wait for my mother.

"Do you want to wait inside?" Miss Crosman looked anxiously at the sky.

"No," I said. "Our mother will be here any minute."

"In a while," said Mona.

"Any minute," I said again, even though my mother had been at least twenty minutes late every week since she started working.

According to the church clock across the street we had been waiting twenty-five minutes when Miss Crosman came out again.

"Shall I give you ladies a ride home?"

"No," I said. "Our mother is coming any minute."

"Shall I at least give her a call and remind her you're here? Maybe she forgot about you."

"I don't think she *forgot*," said Mona.

"Shall I give her a call anyway? Just to be safe?"

"I bet she already left," I said. "How could she forget about us?"

Miss Crosman went in to call.

"There's no answer," she said, coming back out.

"See, she's on her way," I said.

"Are you sure you wouldn't like to come in?"

"No," said Mona.

"Yes," I said. I pointed at my sister. "She meant yes too. She meant no, she wouldn't like to go in."

*The White Umbrella* 87

8 **Discussion** Why might it be important for the narrator to be like the other girls at school?

9 **Reading Strategy** What attitude toward Americans does the mother's comment reveal?

10 **Literary Focus: Character Traits** How is Miss Crosman's attitude toward the girls different from her attitude toward Eugenie? How do you think the narrator feels about this discrepancy?

11 **Critical Thinking and Reading** The author is using a metaphor in this sentence. What kind of emotion is described by a constellation rising in one's heart?

12 **Reading Strategy** Why does the narrator mention that Miss Crosman did not hug her?

13 **Literary Focus: Character Traits** This is the second time the narrator has made up a story for Miss Crosman. What compels her to do this? Does Miss Crosman believe her? How do you know?

14 **Literary Focus: Character Traits** How does the author use characterization to create tension in this scene?

---

**Student Activity 1.** Identify the dependent clause in each complex sentence from the story and indicate where commas are necessary.

1. "Now that she had learned to drive she might be delivering boxes of roses to people."
2. "If your mother won't drive you I can come pick you up."
3. "I wondered what Miss Crosman would say if I offered to bring it to Eugenie at school tomorrow."
4. "As we entered the downtown area Mona started leaning hard against me every time the car turned right. . . ."

**Student Activity 2.** Write a paragraph about one of your own memorable lessons in music, art, or a sport. Use complex sentences to connect related ideas. Check to see that you have punctuated your complex sentences correctly.

**Electronic Handbook** You may want students to review complex sentences before completing the Grammar in Action activities. If students have access to the Language Master 6000, have them enter the access word *complex* and press the GRAMMAR key to review the structure of complex sentences.

15 **Discussion** Why does the narrator fantasize that her mother has an unusual job?

16 **Critical Thinking and Reading** What two things are being compared in this sentence? How does this comparison make the description come to life?

17 **Literary Focus: Character Traits** In what ways is Mona a perfect foil for the narrator?

18 **Literary Focus: Character Traits** What does the narrator's refusal to go inside reveal about her character?

19 **Discussion** How does the narrator feel about Miss Crosman's sympathy? Explain your response.

**Cooperative Learning** Have students form small groups to write a dialogue that the girls might have had with their mother when they arrived home. Have students begin by referring to the story and listing the traits of the sisters and their mother. These lists will serve as guides to help students write dialogue that is in character. After the first draft has been completed, have students read their dialogue aloud to determine whether the characters sound true to the story. Students can revise the dialogue based on their critique of the first draft. Finally, have each group present its dialogue to the class.

Miss Crosman looked at her watch. "It's 5:30 now, ladies. My pot roast will be coming out in fifteen minutes. Maybe you'd like to come in and have some then?"

"My mother's almost here," I said. "She's on her way."

We watched and watched the street. I tried to imagine what my mother was doing; I tried to imagine her writing messages in the sky, even though I knew she was afraid of planes. I watched as the branches of Miss Crosman's big willow tree started to sway; they had all been trimmed to exactly the same height off the ground, so that they looked beautiful, like hair in the wind.

It started to rain.

"Miss Crosman is coming out again," said Mona.

"Don't let her talk you into going inside," I whispered.

"Why not?"

"Because that would mean Mom isn't really coming any minute."

"But she isn't," said Mona. "She's *working.*"

"Shhh! Miss Crosman is going to hear you."

"She's working! She's working! She's working!"

I put my hand over her mouth, but she licked it, and so I was wiping my hand on my wet dress when the front door opened.

"We're getting even *wetter,*" said Mona right away. "Wetter and wetter."

"Shall we all go in?" Miss Crosman pulled Mona to her feet. "Before you young ladies catch pneumonia? You've been out here an hour already."

"We're *freezing.*" Mona looked up at Miss Crosman. "Do you have any hot chocolate? We're going to catch *pneumonia.*"

"I'm not going in," I said. "My mother's coming any minute."

"Come on," said Mona. "Use your *noggin.*"[4]

"Any minute."

"Come on, Mona," Miss Crosman opened the door. "Shall we get you inside first?"

"See you in the hospital," said Mona as she went in. "See you in the hospital with *pneumonia.*"

I stared out into the empty street. The rain was pricking me all over; I was cold; I wanted to go inside. I wanted to be able to let myself go inside. If Miss Crosman came out again, I decided, I would go in.

She came out with a blanket and the white umbrella.

I could not believe that I was actually holding the umbrella, opening it. It sprang up by itself as if it were alive, as if that were what it wanted to do—as if it belonged in my hands, above my head. I stared up at the network of silver spokes, then spun the umbrella around and around and around. It was so clean and white that it seemed to glow, to illuminate everything around it.

"It's beautiful," I said.

Miss Crosman sat down next to me, on one end of the blanket. I moved the umbrella over so that it covered that too. I could feel the rain on my left shoulder and shivered. She put her arm around me.

"You poor, poor dear."

I knew that I was in store for another bolt of sympathy, and braced myself by staring up into the umbrella.

"You know, I very much wanted to have children when I was younger," she continued.

"You did?"

She stared at me a minute. Her face looked dry and crusty, like day-old frosting.

---

4. **Use your *noggin*** (näg' in): Colloquial expression for "use your head" or "think."

**Multicultural Focus** Some children internalize negative attitudes about their native culture and become ashamed of their own ethnic background. Signs of this problem appear in various ways. Children may make self-deprecating remarks about themselves and people of their culture. They may assume people of other groups are better, smarter, or more attractive. Others may affect a grandiose, bragging manner.

Begin a discussion by asking students what a person can do to feel more pride in his or her own cultural background. Suggest that studying the lives of admirable men and women of this person's culture can have a powerful effect. Have a volunteer write down students' suggestions for later implementation.

"I did. But then I never got married."

I twirled the umbrella around again.

"This is the most beautiful umbrella I have ever seen," I said. "Ever, in my whole life."

"Do you have an umbrella?"

"No. But my mother's going to get me one just like this for Christmas."

"Is she? I tell you what. You don't have to wait until Christmas. You can have this one."

"But this one belongs to Eugenie Roberts," I protested. "I have to give it back to her tomorrow in school."

"Who told you it belongs to Eugenie? It's not Eugenie's. It's mine. And now I'm giving it to you, so it's yours."

"It is?"

She hugged me tighter. "That's right. It's all yours."

"It's mine?" I didn't know what to say. "Mine?" Suddenly I was jumping up and down in the rain. "It's beautiful! Oh! It's beautiful!" I laughed.

Miss Crosman laughed too, even though she was getting all wet.

"Thank you, Miss Crosman. Thank you very much. Thanks a zillion. It's beautiful. It's *stupendous*!"

"You're quite welcome," she said.

"Thank you," I said again, but that didn't seem like enough. Suddenly I knew just what she wanted to hear. "I wish you were my mother."

Right away I felt bad.

"You shouldn't say that," she said, but her face was opening into a huge smile as the lights of my mother's car cautiously turned the corner. I quickly collapsed the umbrella and put it up my skirt, holding onto it from the outside, through the material.

"Mona!" I shouted into the house. "Mona! Hurry up! Mom's here! I told you she was coming!"

Then I ran away from Miss Crosman, down to the curb. Mona came tearing up to my side as my mother neared the house. We

**RAINY DAY, 1991**
*Kenneth Kaye*
*The Mulberry Gallery*

20 **Reading Strategy** Why does the narrator change the subject?

21 **Reading Strategy** What is significant about the narrator's use of the word *stupendous* to describe the umbrella?

22 **Literary Focus: Character Traits** What do the narrator's repeated attempts to please Miss Crosman reveal about her character?

23 **Discussion** Why does the narrator feel bad about what she said to Miss Crosman?

24 **Discussion** Why does the narrator hide the umbrella?

## Humanities Note

Fine art, *Rainy Day,* 1991, by Kenneth Kaye. Kaye was born in 1951 in New York City and grew up on Long Island. After studying drawing and design at Arizona State University, he attended CCNY School of Environmental Design to study architecture. The influence of his architectural training can be seen in his work. Notice how the skyscrapers in the background— perpendicular to the slick street— provide an architectural framework for the composition of *Rainy Day.* Kaye's work also shows the influence of the Impressionists, capturing fleeting moments and the temporary play of sunlight. He has developed his own style of painting, in which he uses palette knife and brush to create bold strokes and exciting textures. Kaye's work has been shown in group exhibits and one-man shows all over the United States.

You might use the following questions for discussion:

1. Which of the umbrellas in the painting reflects the sunlight most strikingly?

2. Notice how the gaiety of the bright umbrellas livens up this rainy scene. What effect does the white umbrella have on the narrator of the story?

**Audiocassette** You may wish to use the **Audio Prose Library** interview with Maxine Hong Kingston, another Chinese American writer. Students may compare Gish Jen with Maxine Hong Kingston.

25 **Discussion** Why does the mother choose this moment to tell the girls about her job?

26 **Discussion** What does this saying mean?

27 **Discussion** What kinds of prejudice does the narrator's family face?

28 **Literary Focus: Character Traits** Why does the mother think the narrator is sick? What is the real reason for her behavior?

**Reader's Response** The two sisters are clearly differentiated in the story. Can you identify with both girls? With which girl do you identify more? Explain your response.

**Thematic Response** Do you think the narrator will continue to appreciate her mother after this crisis passes? Or will she lapse into her earlier attitude and behavior?

both backed up a few feet, so that in case she went onto the curb, she wouldn't run us over.

"But why didn't you go inside with Mona?" my mother asked on the way home. She had taken off her own coat to put over me, and had the heat on high.

"She wasn't using her noggin," said Mona, next to me in the back seat.

"I should call next time," said my mother. "I just don't like to say where I am."

**25** That was when she finally told us that she was working as a check-out clerk in the A&P. She was supposed to be on the day shift, but the other employees were unreliable, and her boss had promised her a promotion if she would stay until the evening shift filled in.

For a moment no one said anything. Even Mona seemed to find the revelation disappointing.

"A promotion already!" she said, finally.

I listened to the windshield wipers.

"You're so quiet." My mother looked at me in the rear view mirror. "What's the matter?"

"I wish you would quit," I said after a moment.

**26** She sighed. "The Chinese have a saying: one beam cannot hold the roof up."

"But Eugenie Roberts's father supports their family."

She sighed once more. "Eugenie Roberts's father is Eugenie Roberts's father," she said.

As we entered the downtown area, Mona started leaning hard against me every time the car turned right, trying to push me over. Remembering what I had said to Miss Crosman, I tried to maneuver the umbrella under my leg so she wouldn't feel it.

"What's under your skirt?" Mona wanted to know as we came to a traffic light. My mother, watching us in the rear view mirror again, rolled slowly to a stop.

"What's the matter?" she asked.

"There's something under her skirt!" said Mona, pulling at me.

"Under her skirt?"

Meanwhile, a man crossing the street started to yell at us. "Who do you think you are, lady?" he said. "You're blocking the whole crosswalk."

We all froze. Other people walking by stopped to watch.

**27** "Didn't you hear me?" he went on, starting to thump on the hood with his fist. "Don't you speak English?"

My mother began to back up, but the car behind us honked. Luckily, the light turned green right after that. She sighed in relief.

"What were you saying, Mona?" she asked.

We wouldn't have hit the car behind us that hard if he hadn't been moving too, but as it was our car bucked violently, throwing us all first back and then forward.

"Uh oh," said Mona when we stopped. "*Another* accident."

I was relieved to have attention diverted from the umbrella. Then I noticed my mother's head, tilted back onto the seat. Her eyes were closed.

"Mom!" I screamed. "Mom! Wake up!"

She opened her eyes. "Please don't yell," she said. "Enough people are going to yell already."

**28** "I thought you were dead," I said, starting to cry. "I thought you were dead."

She turned around, looked at me intently, then put her hand to my forehead.

"Sick," she confirmed. "Some kind of sick is giving you crazy ideas."

As the man from the car behind us started tapping on the window, I moved the umbrella away from my leg. Then Mona and my mother were getting out of the car. I got out after them; and while everyone else was inspecting the damage we'd done, I threw the umbrella down a sewer.

*90    Short Stories*

## Closure and Extension

### ANSWERS TO RESPONDING TO THE SELECTION
#### Your Response
1. Answers will differ. Encourage students to share their responses to the ending of the story.

#### Recalling
2. The narrator told Miss Crosman that they weren't able to close the roof of their convertible.
3. She works as a check-out clerk in a supermarket and is often detained.

#### Interpreting
4. The narrator's mother is embarrassed about the kind of job she has.
5. The white umbrella represents everything that seems to be just out of the narrator's grasp, especially being just like the "American" girls at school.
6. Suggested Response: The narrator, in realizing how much she cares for her mother, becomes more accepting of her mother and herself. She no longer needs what the umbrella represents: acceptance from others.

#### Applying
7. Answers will differ. Ask students to define the terms *generalization* and

# RESPONDING TO THE SELECTION

## Your Response

1. Were you surprised when the narrator threw away the umbrella at the end of the story? Why or why not?

## Recalling

2. What excuse does the narrator give for arriving at the piano lesson soaking wet?
3. Why is the narrator's mother always late?

## Interpreting

4. Why doesn't the narrator's mother tell her daughters what job she has taken?
5. What does the white umbrella represent to the narrator?
6. Why does the narrator throw the umbrella away at the end of the story?

## Applying

7. The narrator believes that her mother's response to her desire for an umbrella will be "All you want is things, just like an American." Discuss your response to this generalization about American materialism.

# ANALYZING LITERATURE

## Understanding Character Traits

**Character traits** are the qualities of a character's personality. They are revealed through a character's actions and words and through description. For example, Jen suggests that Mona is not a particularly motivated piano student by describing her this way: ". . . Mona, slumping over the keyboard, managed to eke out a fair rendition of a catfight."

What traits about the character indicated are shown by the following lines from the story?

1. Mrs. Roberts: "Mrs. Roberts, radiant with pride, swept her daughter out of the room as if she were royalty, born to the piano bench." (page 86)
2. The narrator: "I wanted to tell her that I was the school spelling bee champion, that I wasn't ticklish, that I could do karate." (page 87)

# CRITICAL THINKING AND READING

## Understanding Figurative Language

When a writer compares one thing to something apparently very different in order to create a vivid image, he or she is using **figurative language**. For example, Jen compares the noise produced by Mona's piano playing to that of a catfight. In the context of the story, this comparison serves to emphasize, by contrast, the fine piano playing of Eugenie and the narrator.

Identify what is being compared in these comparisons, and explain the significance of each in the story's context.

1. "The umbrella glowed like a scepter. . . ."
2. "Her face looked dry and crusty, like day-old frosting."

# THINKING AND WRITING

## Exploring Point of View

Unlike her sister, Mona does not see any reason to pretend to be other than she is. Rewrite a segment of the story from Mona's point of view. Keep in mind that because Mona's character is so different from her sister's, her account of the same events will be quite different.

# LEARNING OPTION

**Writing.** Imagine that you are the narrator of "The White Umbrella." Write a diary entry in which you discuss how you could have thrown away something that had been so important to you.

*The White Umbrella* 91

**Alternative Assessment** *Protocol:* Ask students to assess their own work by responding to the following questions:

What segment of the story have you chosen to retell from Mona's point of view?

What changes in telling the event have you had to make because you are looking at the event through Mona's eyes?

In what ways have your feelings or attitudes toward the girls been affected as a result of looking at the events from a different perspective?

What new understanding of the effect of point of view have you gained as a result of this assignment?

You may have students use the information they have gained from their protocols as a guide for revising their stories.

**Publishing Student Writing**
Have students form small groups for the purpose of discussing Mona's character, reading their stories aloud, commenting on one another's work, and suggesting improvements. When the stories have been completed, compile them in a book and display it in your classroom library for others to read and enjoy.

## LEARNING OPTION

Extend the Writing activity to appeal to kinesthetic learners by having them make decorative covers for their diaries. Students who wish to share their diaries with their class could put them on display.

---

*materialism.* Then encourage them to share their responses.

## ANSWERS TO ANALYZING LITERATURE

1. Mrs. Roberts is a haughty woman who takes great pride in her daughter's accomplishments.
2. The narrator feels insignificant; she wants Miss Crosman to notice her, to understand that she is special.

## ANSWERS TO CRITICAL THINKING AND READING

1. The umbrella is likened to a symbol of royal authority, which reveals the importance the narrator has attached to the umbrella and the qualities she imagines its owner would possess.
2. The comparison of Miss Crosman's face to day-old frosting reveals that the narrator is suddenly seeing the woman whose approval she had desperately wanted as old and unwanted.

## THINKING AND WRITING

**Writing Transparency**
Graphic Organizers are good tools for making clear what may at first seem confusing. Before students write Mona's version of the story, have them use the *Venn Diagram* in **Transparencies for Writing** to differentiate between the narrator's version of the story and Mona's.

## Preparation

**More About the Author** Juan A. A. Sedillo is from New Mexico. The magazine *New Mexico* each month carries evidence that many people within the United States do not recognize New Mexico as part of the nation. They reprint letters and notices by people labeling the state as part of Mexico. Have students locate New Mexico on a map and name its capital. Have them find out how and why the United States acquired the land. The information will provide background for the cultural differences described in the story.

**Literary Focus** This story is primarily a two-character piece, with a major and a minor character. Who are the major and minor characters in other stories students have read? How can students tell?

**Prereading Focus** Ask students to think of someone they believe to be a true gentleman. Have them name some characteristics that make him worthy of that label. Write them on the chalkboard. Then have students brainstorm in small groups for other qualities to list on their character wheel.

**Vocabulary** Have your **less advanced** students read the words aloud so that you can be sure they can pronounce them.

**Spelling Tip** Point out the silent *g* at the beginning of *gnarled* and the double *n* in *innumerable*.

**Electronic Handbook** Two of the vocabulary words have silent letters. If your students have access to the Language Master 6000, suggest that they listen to the pronunciations of *gnarled* and *broached*.

### Juan A. A. Sedillo

(1902–1982) was born in New Mexico and lived in the Southwest. He was a lawyer and public servant, as well as a writer. "Gentleman of Río en Medio" is based on an actual legal case that arose over a conflict about the ownership of some property. In this story, Sedillo makes use of his legal background and his understanding of people.

## Gentleman of Río en Medio

### Major and Minor Characters

A story usually has both major and minor characters. A **major character** is the most important person in the story. You learn the most information about this character when you read the story. A **minor character** is a person of less importance in the story, but who is necessary for the story to develop. You learn only a little about each minor character in the story.

### Focus

The major character in the story you are about to read is Don Anselmo, who is the "*gentleman* of Río en Medio." What are the qualities that make someone a gentleman? In small groups, brainstorm to list qualities that a gentleman possesses. Copy the following character wheel on a separate sheet of paper and fill it in as you brainstorm. Then read the story and see how many of the qualities you listed are found in the character Don Anselmo.

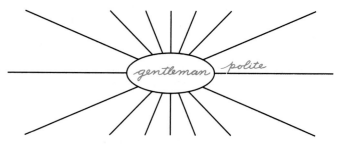

### Vocabulary

Knowing the following words will help you as you read "Gentleman of Río en Medio."

**negotiation** (ni gō′ shē ā′ shən) *n.*: Bargaining or discussing to reach an agreement (p. 93)

**gnarled** (närld) *adj.*: Knotty and twisted (p. 93)

**innumerable** (i nōō′ mər ə bəl) *adj.*: Too many to be counted (p. 93)

**broached** (brōcht) *v.*: Started a discussion about a topic (p. 94)

---

### Objectives

1 To understand the differences between major and minor characters in a short story

2 To compare and contrast cultural celebrations

### Support Material

**Teaching Portfolio**
Teacher Backup, p. 129
Usage and Mechanics Worksheet, p. 132
Vocabulary Check, p. 133
Critical Thinking and Reading Worksheet, *Comparing and Contrasting Attitudes*, p. 134
Language Worksheet, *Understanding Words From Spanish*, p. 135
Selection Test, p. 136

**Prentice Hall Literature Writing Studio**

# Gentleman
of Río en Medio

### Juan A. A. Sedillo

It took months of negotiation to come to an understanding with the old man. He was in no hurry. What he had the most of was time. He lived up in Río en Medio,[1] where his people had been for hundreds of years. He tilled the same land they had tilled. His house was small and wretched, but quaint. The little creek ran through his land. His orchard was gnarled and beautiful.

The day of the sale he came into the office. His coat was old, green and faded. I thought of Senator Catron,[2] who had been such a power with these people up there in the mountains. Perhaps it was one of his old Prince Alberts.[3] He also wore gloves. They were old and torn and his finger tips showed through them. He carried a cane, but it was only the skeleton of a worn-out umbrella. Behind him walked one of his innumerable kin—a dark young man with eyes like a gazelle.

The old man bowed to all of us in the room. Then he removed his hat and gloves, slowly and carefully. Chaplin[4] once did that in a picture, in a bank—he was the janitor. Then he handed his things to the boy, who stood obediently behind the old man's chair.

**THE SACRISTAN OF TRAMPAS (detail)**
*Paul Burlin*
Museum of New Mexico

There was a great deal of conversation, about rain and about his family. He was very proud of his large family. Finally we got down to business. Yes, he would sell, as he had agreed, for twelve hundred dollars, in cash. We would buy, and the money was ready. "Don[5] Anselmo," I said to him in Spanish, "We have made a discovery. You remember that we sent that surveyor, that

---

**1. Río en Medio** (rē′ ō en mä′ dē ō)
**2. Senator Catron** (kaˈtrən): Thomas Benton Catron, senator from New Mexico, 1912–1917.
**3. Prince Alberts:** Long, double-breasted coats.
**4. Chaplin:** Charlie Chaplin (1889–1977), actor and producer of silent films in the United States.

**5. don:** A Spanish title of respect, similar to *Sir* in English.

*Gentleman of Río en Medio* 93

---

**Thematic Focus** The major and minor characters in this story feel that the land of Río en Medio has great significance and value. Discuss why people become extremely attached to a particular plot of land.

**Making Connections** Other selections that deal with the theme of the importance of personal dignity are "Thank You, M'am" (page 179) and *The Diary of Anne Frank* (page 303). You might help students to see the similarities in the value of personal dignity in these selections.

---

## Closure and Extension

### ANSWERS TO RESPONDING TO THE SELECTION
#### Your Response

1. Encourage students to support their opinions with illustrations from the story. Have them think carefully of the consequences of refusing the extra money.

#### Recalling

2. It took months because Don Anselmo was in no hurry to sell his house and land. His people had lived in Río en Medio for hundreds of years.

engineer, up there to survey your land so as to make the deed. Well, he finds that you own more than eight acres. He tells us that your land extends across the river and that you own almost twice as much as you thought." He didn't know that. "And now, Don Anselmo," I added, "These Americans are *buena gente*,[6] they are good people, and they are willing to pay you for the additional land as well, at the same rate per acre, so that instead of twelve hundred dollars you will get almost twice as much, and the money is here for you."

The old man hung his head for a moment in thought. Then he stood up and stared at me. "Friend," he said, "I do not like to have you speak to me in that manner." I kept still and let him have his say. "I know these Americans are good people, and that is why I have agreed to sell to them. But I do not care to be insulted. I have agreed to sell my house and land for twelve hundred dollars and that is the price."

I argued with him but it was useless. Finally he signed the deed and took the money but refused to take more than the amount agreed upon. Then he shook hands all around, put on his ragged gloves, took his stick and walked out with the boy behind him.

A month later my friends had moved into Río en Medio. They had replastered the old adobe house, pruned the trees, patched the fence, and moved in for the summer. One day they came back to the office to complain. The children of the village were overrunning their property. They came every day and played under the trees, built little play fences around them, and took blossoms. When they were spoken to they only laughed and talked back good-naturedly in Spanish.

---

6. *buena gente* (bwā′ nä hen′ tā)

I sent a messenger up to the mountains for Don Anselmo. It took a week to arrange another meeting. When he arrived he repeated his previous preliminary performance. He wore the same faded cutaway,[7] carried the same stick and was accompanied by the boy again. He shook hands all around, sat down with the boy behind his chair, and talked about the weather. Finally I broached the subject. "Don Anselmo, about the ranch you sold to these people. They are good people and want to be your friends and neighbors always. When you sold to them you signed a document, a deed, and in that deed you agreed to several things. One thing was that they were to have the complete possession of the property. Now, Don Anselmo, it seems that every day the children of the village overrun the orchard and spend most of their time there. We would like to know if you, as the most respected man in the village, could not stop them from doing so in order that these people may enjoy their new home more in peace."

Don Anselmo stood up. "We have all learned to love these Americans," he said, "Because they are good people and good neighbors. I sold them my property because I knew they were good people, but I did not sell them the trees in the orchard."

This was bad. "Don Anselmo," I pleaded, "When one signs a deed and sells real property one sells also everything that grows on the land, and those trees, every one of them, are on the land and inside the boundaries of what you sold."

"Yes, I admit that," he said. "You know," he added, "I am the oldest man in the village. Almost everyone there is my relative and all the children of Río en Medio

---

7. **cutaway** (kut′ ə wā′) n.: A coat worn by men for formal daytime occasions.

3. They offered additional money because they discovered that he owned twice as much land as they originally thought. He reacts to the offer by refusing the additional money.

4. They complain that the children of the village overrun the orchard and spend most of their time there. Don Anselmo tells the Americans that the trees in the orchard belong to the children of the village.

5. The Americans buy the trees from the children.

6. He was formally dressed, with a faded coat, torn gloves, and the skeleton of an umbrella for a cane. When he entered the room, he bowed to everyone. It suggests that he is poor, yet proud.

#### Interpreting

7. It suggests that he is a man of his word. He makes sure the Ameri-cans understand that he does not own the trees in the orchard. They belong to the children in the village.

8. The Americans make an effort to understand and tolerate the customs of Don Anselmo. They also show a willingness to compromise. They buy back the trees from the children.

9. He is a gentleman because he is courteous and has a strong sense of honor.

are my *sobrinos* and *nietos*,[8] my descendants. Every time a child has been born in Río en Medio since I took possession of that house from my mother I have planted a tree for that child. The trees in that orchard are not mine, *Señor*, they belong to the children of the village. Every person in Río en Medio

---

**8. sobrinos** (sō brē′ nōs) and **nietos** (nyä′ tōs): Spanish for "nieces and nephews" and "grandchildren."

born since the railroad came to Santa Fé owns a tree in that orchard. I did not sell the trees because I could not. They are not mine."

There was nothing we could do. Legally we owned the trees but the old man had been so generous, refusing what amounted to a fortune for him. It took most of the following winter to buy the trees, individually, from the descendants of Don Anselmo in the valley of Río en Medio.

7

## RESPONDING TO THE SELECTION

### Your Response

1. Why do you think Don Anselmo refused the extra money? Would you have done the same? Why or why not?

### Recalling

2. Why does it take months to reach the first agreement with Don Anselmo?
3. Why do the Americans offer additional money for the property? How does Don Anselmo react to the offer?
4. What complaint do the Americans have after they have bought the property? What is Don Anselmo's response to their complaint?
5. How do the Americans solve their problem?
6. Describe how Don Anselmo acts when he comes into the office to finalize the sale. What does his behavior suggest about him?

### Interpreting

7. What does Don Anselmo's refusal of more money for the land suggest about him? Find one other detail that supports this impression.
8. What does the Americans' solution to the problem suggest about them? Find one other detail that supports this impression.
9. What makes Don Anselmo the "Gentleman of Río en Medio"?

### Applying

10. Put yourself in the Americans' place. Explain how you would have solved their problem.

## ANALYZING LITERATURE

### Identifying Major and Minor Characters

In a work of literature, the **major** character is the person the story is about—the one about whom you learn the most and who plays the largest role in the tale. The **minor** characters play less essential roles.

1. What role does Don Anselmo play in this story?
2. What do you learn about him as the story progresses?
3. What role do the Americans play in the story?
4. What role does the narrator play?

## THINKING AND WRITING

### Comparing and Contrasting Cultures

Imagine that you have just received a letter from a pen pal in Mexico. Your pen pal has described his or her birthday celebration and has asked you how you celebrate your birthday. Write a letter to your pen pal explaining how you celebrate birthdays. Include not only what you do but your attitude about birthdays. After you have drafted your letter, revise it to make sure that your explanation is clear. Then prepare a final draft.

*Gentleman of Río en Medio* 95

"Raymond's Run" appeared in a 1971 anthology edited by Toni Cade Bambara called *Tales and Stories for Black Folks.* In the preface she urged her readers to take the contents "seriously as valuable lessons in human behavior and examples of living history." Students should note the critic's quote carefully. What "new awareness" allows black women to "create their own choices about the kinds of women they will be"? How does the quote apply to women of all colors?

**Literary Focus** Have students consider other stories for examples of round and flat characters. Which of the two main characters is more fully developed? Which reveals only admirable character traits? Point out that often round characters exhibit at least two traits at odds with each other with a resulting inner conflict. Direct students to look for evidence of this struggle within Squeaky and for the way she resolves the conflict.

**Prereading Focus** Write several of the casual, everyday expressions that students name on the chalkboard. Ask them to watch for additional expressions as they read. Help them discover other techniques besides Squeaky's speech that make her a memorable character.

**Vocabulary** Have your less advanced students use each word in a sentence orally before reading the story.

**Electronic Handbook** If your students have access to the Language Master 6000, have them find the etymology of *glockenspiel* and listen to its pronunciation.

---

# GUIDE FOR READING

### Toni Cade Bambara

(1939–    ) was born in New York City and educated in the United States and Europe. She has studied mime and dance and has taught students of all ages, from preschoolers to college students. A critic has said that Bambara writes of "black women at the edge of a new awareness, who create their own choices about the kinds of women they will be." In "Raymond's Run," Squeaky reaches that point and makes a clear choice about the kind of person she intends to be.

## Raymond's Run

### Round and Flat Characters

Characters are sometimes described as being round or flat. **Round** characters are like real people. They are complex, revealing several sides to their personality and growing and changing as the story progresses. **Flat** characters are one-dimensional, often revealing a single personal quality and staying the same throughout the story.

### Focus

The narrator and the main character of "Raymond's Run" is Squeaky—events in the story are told in Squeaky's voice and from Squeaky's point of view. Bambara makes Squeaky seem real to us by having her narrate the story in a casual voice, as though she were telling the story to a friend. Squeaky uses expressions such as "on account of" and "Oh, brother," which help to make her sound like a real person. What expressions do you use? With your classmates, brainstorm to list expressions that you use and hear every day in casual conversation. Then read the story and see what other techniques Bambara uses to make Squeaky come to life.

### Vocabulary

Knowing the following words will help you as you read "Raymond's Run."

**prodigy** (präd′ ə jē) *n.*: A child of extraordinary genius (p. 99)
**glockenspiels** (gläk′ ən spēlz′) *n.*: Musical instruments, like xylophones, that are carried upright and often used in marching bands (p. 100)

**periscope** (per′ ə skōp) *n.*: An instrument containing mirrors and lenses to see objects not in a direct line from the viewer; often used in submarines to see objects above the water (p. 101)

---

### Objectives

1 To understand the differences between round and flat characters
2 To identify the reasons that motivate a character
3 To write an extension of the story
4 To express individual interests and abilities through optional activities

### Support Material

**Teaching Portfolio**
Teacher Backup, p. 139
Grammar in Action Worksheets, *Understanding Parallelism*, p. 143; *Using Consistent Verb Tense*, p. 145
Usage and Mechanics Worksheet, p. 147
Vocabulary Check, p. 148
Analyzing Literature Worksheet,

*Recognizing Flat and Round Characters*, p. 149
Language Worksheet, *Understanding Idioms*, p. 150
Selection Test, p. 151

**Prentice Hall Literature Writing Studio**

**Audio Prose Library**
Toni Cade Bambara: Reading

**Presentation**

**Motivation/Prior Knowledge**
This is a story told humorously by a very strong character. Have students note the humorous phrases she uses. Most students will have no difficulty recognizing the humor in this story.

**Making Connections** Another selection that deals with an older sister helping a younger sibling is ''For My Sister Molly Who in the Fifties,'' by Alice Walker, on page 560.

**Thematic Focus** This story reveals the narrator's deep appreciation for an older brother whom she must look after. Discuss problems that may arise when a family member requires help to get through a day's activities.

**Purpose-Setting Question** What role does humor play in this story?

1 **Discussion** What have you learned about the main character from the first two paragraphs? How do you feel about her?

# Raymond's Run

## Toni Cade Bambara

I don't have much work to do around the house like some girls. My mother does that. And I don't have to earn my pocket money by hustling; George runs errands for the big boys and sells Christmas cards. And anything else that's got to get done, my father does. All I have to do in life is mind my brother Raymond, which is enough.

Sometimes I slip and say my little brother Raymond. But as any fool can see he's much bigger and he's older too. But a lot of people call him my little brother cause he needs looking after cause he's not quite right. And a lot of smart mouths got lots to say about that too, especially when George was minding him. But now, if anybody has anything to say to Raymond, anything to say about his big head, they have to come by me. And I don't play the dozens[1] or believe in standing around with somebody in my face doing a lot of talking. I much rather just knock you down and take my chances even if I am a little girl with skinny arms and a squeaky voice, which is how I got the name Squeaky. And if things get too rough, I run. And as anybody can tell you, I'm the fastest thing on two feet.

There is no track meet that I don't win the first place medal. I use to win the twenty-yard dash when I was a little kid in kindergarten. Nowadays it's the fifty-yard dash. And tomorrow I'm subject to run the quarter-meter relay all by myself and come in first, second, and third. The big kids call me Mercury[2] cause I'm the swiftest thing in the neighborhood. Everybody knows that —except two people who know better, my father and me.

---

**2. Mercury** *n.*: In Roman mythology, the messenger of the gods, known for great speed.

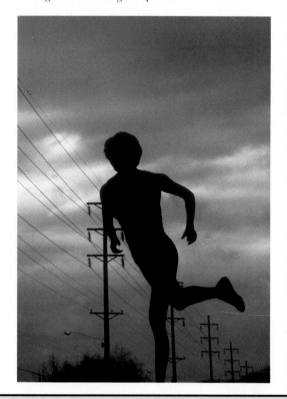

---

**1. the dozens:** A game in which the players insult one another; the first to show anger loses.

**2 Critical Reading** Have students compare and contrast the different approach to excellence each girl takes.

**3 Master Teacher Note** Squeaky's directness makes her angry with girls who are not direct, but evasive—Cynthia, for example. Ask your students which character traits they find least tolerable. For those who have read J. D. Salinger's *The Catcher in the Rye,* have them explain why the book's hero, Holden Caulfield, was also angry with the world's phonies. Have students contrast how he and Squeaky dealt with this anger. Bring out how Holden would pump gas, pretending he was mute, to escape communicating with people. Squeaky would fight them.

He can beat me to Amsterdam Avenue with me having a two fire-hydrant headstart and him running with his hands in his pockets and whistling. But that's private information. Cause can you imagine some thirty-five-year-old man stuffing himself into PAL[3] shorts to race little kids? So as far as everyone's concerned, I'm the fastest and that goes for Gretchen, too, who has put out the tale that she is going to win the first place medal this year. Ridiculous. In the second place, she's got short legs. In the third place, she's got freckles. In the first place, no one can beat me and that's all there is to it.

I'm standing on the corner admiring the weather and about to take a stroll down Broadway so I can practice my breathing exercises, and I've got Raymond walking on the inside close to the buildings cause he's subject to fits of fantasy and starts thinking he's a circus performer and that the curb is a tight-rope strung high in the air. And sometimes after a rain, he likes to step down off his tightrope right into the gutter and slosh around getting his shoes and cuffs wet. Or sometimes if you don't watch him, he'll dash across traffic to the island in the middle of Broadway and give the pigeons a fit. Then I have to go behind him apologizing to all the old people sitting around trying to get some sun and getting all upset with the pigeons fluttering around them, scattering their newspapers and upsetting the wax-paper lunches in their laps. So I keep Raymond on the inside of me, and he plays like he's driving a stagecoach, which is O.K. by me so long as he doesn't run me over or interrupt my breathing exercises, which I have to do on account of I'm serious about my running and don't care who knows it.

Now some people like to act like things come easy to them, won't let on that they practice. Not me. I'll high prance down 34th Street like a rodeo pony to keep my knees strong even if it does get my mother uptight so that she walks ahead like she's not with me, don't know me, is all by herself on a shopping trip, and I am somebody else's crazy child.

Now you take Cynthia Procter for instance. She's just the opposite. If there's a test tomorrow, she'll say something like, "Oh I guess I'll play handball this afternoon and watch television tonight," just to let you know she ain't thinking about the test. Or like last week when she won the spelling bee for the millionth time, "A good thing you got 'receive,' Squeaky, cause I would have got it wrong. I completely forgot about the spelling bee." And she'll clutch the lace on her blouse like it was a narrow escape. Oh, brother.

But of course when I pass her house on my early morning trots around the block, she is practicing the scales on the piano over and over and over and over. Then in music class, she always lets herself get bumped around so she falls accidently on purpose onto the piano stool and is so surprised to find herself sitting there, and so decides just for fun to try out the ole keys and

**3. PAL** *adj.*: Police Athletic League.

## Grammar in Action

When ideas within a sentence are of equal weight or importance, effective writers put them in the same grammatical form. This technique, called **parallelism,** gives rhythm and balance to writing.

Look at the following sentence from "Raymond's Run." Read the sentence aloud. Notice how smoothly it flows from your tongue. This smoothness is a result of parallel structure.

Then I have to go behind him apologizing to all the old people sitting around trying to get some sun and getting upset with the pigeons fluttering around them, scattering their newspapers and upsetting the wax-paper lunches in their laps.

The old people are doing two things. They are "sitting around trying to get some sun" and they are "getting upset with the pigeons." Notice that both these activities are given equal weight since they are placed in the same grammatical form. Both begin with a participle, an *-ing* form of the verb used as an adjective. Notice how much less effective the following passage is:

what do you know—Chopin's[4] waltzes just spring out of her fingertips and she's the most surprised thing in the world. A regular prodigy. I could kill people like that.

I stay up all night studying the words for the spelling bee. And you can see me anytime of day practicing running. I never walk if I can trot and shame on Raymond if he can't keep up. But of course he does, cause if he hangs back someone's liable to walk up to him and get smart, or take his allowance from him, or ask him where he got that great big pumpkin head. People are so stupid sometimes.

So I'm strolling down Broadway breathing out and breathing in on counts of seven, which is my lucky number, and here comes Gretchen and her sidekicks—Mary Louise who used to be a friend of mine when she first moved to Harlem from Baltimore and got beat up by everybody till I took up for her on account of her mother and my mother used to sing in the same choir when they were young girls, but people ain't grateful, so now she hangs out with the new girl Gretchen and talks about me like a dog; and Rosie who is as fat as I am skinny and has a big mouth where Raymond is concerned and is too stupid to know that there is not a big deal of difference between herself and Raymond and that she can't afford to throw stones. So they are steady coming up Broadway and I see right away that it's going to be one of those Dodge City[5] scenes cause the street ain't that big and they're close to the buildings just as we are. First I think I'll step into the candy store and look over the new comics and let them pass. But that's chicken and I've got a reputation to consider. So

---

4. **Chopin** (shō pan'): Frédéric François Chopin (1810–1849), Polish composer and pianist.
5. **Dodge City:** The location of the television program "Gunsmoke," which often presented a gunfight between the sheriff and an outlaw.

then I think I'll just walk straight on through them or over them if necessary. But as they get to me, they slow down. I'm ready to fight, cause like I said I don't feature a whole lot of chit-chat, I much prefer to just knock you down right from the jump and save everybody a lotta precious time.

"You signing up for the May Day races?" smiles Mary Louise, only it's not a smile at all.

A dumb question like that doesn't deserve an answer. Besides, there's just me and Gretchen standing there really, so no use wasting my breath talking to shadows.

"I don't think you're going to win this time," says Rosie, trying to signify with her hands on her hips all salty, completely forgetting that I have whupped her many times for less salt than that.

"I always win cause I'm the best," I say straight at Gretchen who is, as far as I'm concerned, the only one talking in this ventriloquist-dummy routine.

Gretchen smiles but it's not a smile and I'm thinking that girls never really smile at each other because they don't know how and don't want to know how and there's probably no one to teach us how cause grown-up girls don't know either. Then they all look at Raymond who has just brought his mule team to a standstill. And they're about to see what trouble they can get into through him.

"What grade you in now, Raymond?"

"You got anything to say to my brother, you say it to me, Mary Louise Williams of Raggedy Town, Baltimore."

"What are you, his mother?" sasses Rosie.

"That's right, Fatso. And the next word out of anybody and I'll be *their* mother too." So they just stand there and Gretchen shifts from one leg to the other and so do they. Then Gretchen puts her hands on her hips

4 **Literary Focus** Point out the length of the first sentence in this paragraph. Explain that this story is told from a first-person point of view where the narrator is a character in the story. All events are described from Squeaky's viewpoint, which may or may not be slanted. Here we are inside Squeaky's mind.

---

Then I have to go behind him apologizing to all the old people sitting around trying to get some sun. These people got upset with the pigeons. . . .

**Student Activity 1.** Read the sample sentence again. Which three groups of words describe what the pigeons were doing? What grammatical form begins each of these groups of words? Do you think the use of parallelism makes this part of the sentence more or less effective? Explain.

**Student Activity 2.** Using the second part of Toni Cade Bambara's sentence as a pattern, complete each of the following sentences:

1. They were getting upset with the dogs. . . .
2. They were getting annoyed by the children. . . .
3. They were getting bothered by the mosquitoes. . . .
4. They were getting angry at the peddlers. . . .

**Electronic Handbook** You may want students to review parallelism before completing the Grammar in Action activities. If students have access to the Language Master 6000, have them enter the access word *parallel* and press the GRAMMAR key to get information on understanding parallelism and on lack of parallel structure.

and is about to say something with her freckle-face self but doesn't. Then she walks around me looking me up and down but keeps walking up Broadway, and her sidekicks follow her. So me and Raymond smile at each other and he says, "Gidyap" to his team and I continue with my breathing exercises, strolling down Broadway toward the ice man on 145th with not a care in the world cause I am Miss Quicksilver herself.

I take my time getting to the park on May Day because the track meet is the last thing on the program. The biggest thing on the program is the May Pole dancing, which I can do without, thank you, even if my mother thinks it's a shame I don't take part and act like a girl for a change. You'd think my mother'd be grateful not to have to make me a white organdy dress with a big satin sash and buy me new white baby-doll shoes that can't be taken out of the box till the big day. You'd think she'd be glad her daughter ain't out there prancing around a May Pole getting the new clothes all dirty and sweaty and trying to act like a fairy or a flower or whatever you're supposed to be when you should

**5**   be trying to be yourself, whatever that is, which is, as far as I am concerned, a poor black girl who really can't afford to buy shoes and a new dress you only wear once a lifetime cause it won't fit next year.

I was once a strawberry in a Hansel and Gretel pageant when I was in nursery school and didn't have no better sense than to dance on tiptoe with my arms in a circle over my head doing umbrella steps and being a perfect fool just so my mother and father could come dressed up and clap. You'd think they'd know better than to encourage that kind of nonsense. I am not a strawberry. I do not dance on my toes. I run. That is what I am all about. So I always come late to the May Day program, just in time to get my

number pinned on and lay in the grass till they announce the fifty-yard dash.

I put Raymond in the little swings, which is a tight squeeze this year and will be impossible next year. Then I look around for Mr. Pearson, who pins the numbers on. I'm really looking for Gretchen if you want to know the truth, but she's not around. The park is jam-packed. Parents in hats and corsages and breast-pocket handkerchiefs peeking up. Kids in white dresses and light-blue suits. The parkees unfolding chairs and chasing the rowdy kids from Lenox as if they had no right to be there. The big guys with their caps on backwards, leaning against the fence swirling the basketballs on the tips of their fingers, waiting for all these crazy people to clear out the park so they can play. Most of the kids in my class are carrying bass drums and glockenspiels and flutes. You'd think they'd put in a few bongos or something for real like that.

Then here comes Mr. Pearson with his clipboard and his cards and pencils and whistles and safety pins and fifty million other things he's always dropping all over the place with his clumsy self. He sticks out in a crowd cause he's on stilts. We used to call him Jack and the Beanstalk to get him mad. But I'm the only one that can outrun him and get away, and I'm too grown for that silliness now.

"Well, Squeaky," he says checking my name off the list and handing me number seven and two pins. And I'm thinking he's got no right to call me Squeaky, if I can't call him Beanstalk.

"Hazel Elizabeth Deborah Parker," I correct him and tell him to write it down on his board.

"Well, Hazel Elizabeth Deborah Parker, going to give someone else a break this year?" I squint at him real hard to see if he is

## Grammar In Action

**Consistent verb tense** is an important quality of good writing. Just as clauses within a sentence should be parallel in structure, the verb tense in which a writer chooses to tell a story should be consistently past or present. For example, a writer who is describing events that already happened using past tense should maintain past tense throughout the story.

Occasionally, writers shift tenses when necessary. For example, in "Raymond's Run" Toni Cade Bambara writes predomi-

nantly in the present tense. She shifts to past tense when she depicts Squeaky reflecting on incidents that happened outside the boundaries of her story. For most of the story, however, Squeaky uses present tense to narrate events that happened in the past. Through present-tense narration, Squeaky paints a picture of the May Day program so that we can see the events as they happen, through the eyes of Squeaky's memory. Relating past events in present tense as Bambara does makes the story more immediate to the reader.

Notice how Bambara shifts to past tense in the paragraph that begins "I was once a strawberry." Squeaky's attention drifts temporarily away from the action of the May Day races as she

**Multicultural Focus** Female runners like Squeaky are making their mark in the athletic world. Remind students that in the Olympic Games, women from all over the world gather to compete in track and field events. Every year, in contests like the Boston and New York marathons, women runners demonstrate their skill. Florence Joyner and Jackie Joyner-Kersey are two African American women runners who have made their mark in international competitions.

Explain that for many years women were not allowed to run in long-distance races, or marathons. In 1983, however, the first international women's marathon was run in Helsinki, Finland. Women from fourteen different nations —including Norway, Russia, Portugal, Japan, and the United States—took part.

Have students research women runners from each of the countries that participated in recent Olympic Games or in marathons. How do these women train? Who are the leading female runners? What inspired them to begin running? Students can compile the information they gather, along with photographs, for a bulletin board display called "Women Runners of the World."

seriously thinking I should lose the race on purpose just to give someone else a break.

"Only six girls running this time," he continues, shaking his head sadly like it's my fault all of New York didn't turn out in sneakers. "That new girl should give you a run for your money." He looks around the park for Gretchen like a periscope in a submarine movie. "Wouldn't it be a nice gesture if you were . . . to ahhh . . ."

I give him such a look he couldn't finish putting that idea into words. Grownups got a lot of nerve sometimes. I pin number seven to myself and stomp away—I'm so burnt. And I go straight for the track and stretch out on the grass while the band winds up with "Oh the Monkey Wrapped His Tail Around the Flag Pole," which my teacher calls by some other name. The man on the loudspeaker is calling everyone over to the track and I'm on my back looking at the sky trying to pretend I'm in the country, but I can't, because even grass in the city feels hard as sidewalk and there's just no pretending you are anywhere but in a "concrete jungle" as my grandfather says.

The twenty-yard dash takes all of two minutes cause most of the little kids don't know no better than to run off the track or run the wrong way or run smack into the fence and fall down and cry. One little kid, though, has got the good sense to run straight for the white ribbon up ahead, so he wins. Then the second-graders line up for the thirty-yard dash and I don't even bother to turn my head to watch cause Raphael Perez always wins. He wins before he even begins by psyching the runners,

remembers an early childhood scene. Then toward the end of the paragraph, Squeaky shifts back to present tense and announces:

"I am not a strawberry. I do not dance on my toes. I run. That is what I am all about. So I always come late to the May Day program, just in time to get my number pinned on and lay in the grass till they announce the fifty-yard dash."

Bambara carefully maintains present tense throughout the story, except for occasional, intentional shifts to past tense.

**Student Activity 1.** As you read the rest of the story, record examples of shifts in verb tenses. Explain why it is necessary for Bambara to shift tenses.

**Student Activity 2.** Imitate Bambara's writing style by writing an original paragraph about an experience in your past that you narrate in the present tense.

**Electronic Handbook** You may want students to review consistent verb tense before completing the Grammar in Action activities. If students have access to the Language Master 6000, have them enter the access word *tense* and press the GRAMMAR key to get information on verb tenses.

telling them they're going to trip on their shoelaces and fall on their faces or lose their shorts or something, which he doesn't really have to do since he is very fast, almost as fast as I am. After that is the forty-yard dash, which I use to run when I was in first grade. Raymond is hollering from the swings cause he knows I'm about to do my thing cause the man on the loudspeaker has just announced the fifty-yard dash, although he might just as well be giving a recipe for angel food cake cause you can hardly make out what he's saying for the static. I get up and slip off my sweat pants and then I see Gretchen standing at the starting line kicking her legs out like a pro. Then as I get into place I see that ole Raymond is in line on the other side of the fence, bending down with his fingers on the ground just like he knew what he was doing. I was going to yell at him but then I didn't. It burns up your energy to holler.

Every time, just before I take off in a race, I always feel like I'm in a dream, the kind of dream you have when you're sick with fever and feel all hot and weightless. I dream I'm flying over a sandy beach in the early morning sun, kissing the leaves of the trees as I fly by. And there's always the smell of apples, just like in the country when I was little and use to think I was a choo-choo train, running through the fields of corn and chugging up the hill to the orchard. And all the time I'm dreaming this, I get lighter and lighter until I'm flying over the beach again, getting blown through the sky like a feather that weighs nothing at all. But once I spread my fingers in the dirt and crouch over for the Get on Your Mark, the dream goes and I am solid again and am telling myself, Squeaky you must win, you must win, you are the fastest thing in the world, you can even beat your father up Amsterdam if you really try. And then I feel my weight coming back just behind my knees then down to my feet then into the earth and the pistol shot explodes in my blood and I am off and weightless again, flying past the other runners, my arms pumping up and down and the whole world is quiet except for the crunch as I zoom over the gravel in the track. I glance to my left and there is no one. To the right a blurred Gretchen, who's got her chin jutting out as if it would win the race all by itself. And on the other side of the fence is Raymond with his arms down to his side and the palms tucked up behind him, running in his very own style and the first time I ever saw that and I almost stop to watch my brother Raymond on his first run. But the white ribbon is bouncing toward me and I tear past it racing into the distance till my feet with a mind of their own start digging up footfuls of dirt and brake me short. Then all the kids standing on the side pile on me, banging me on the back and slapping my head with their May Day programs, for I have won again and everybody on 151st Street can walk tall for another year.

"In first place . . ." the man on the loudspeaker is clear as a bell now. But then he pauses and the loudspeaker starts to whine. Then static. And I lean down to catch my breath and here comes Gretchen walking back for she's overshot the finish line too, huffing and puffing with her hands on her hips taking it slow, breathing in steady time like a real pro and I sort of like her a little for the first time. "In first place . . ." and then three or four voices get all mixed up on the loudspeaker and I dig my sneaker into the grass and stare at Gretchen who's staring back, we both wondering just who did win. I can hear old Beanstalk arguing with the man on the loudspeaker and then a few others running their mouths about what the stop watches say.

Then I hear Raymond yanking at the fence to call me and I wave to shush him, but he keeps rattling the fence like a gorilla in a cage like in them gorilla movies, but then like a dancer or something he starts climbing up nice and easy but very fast. And it occurs to me, watching how smoothly he climbs hand over hand and remembering how he looked running with his arms down to his side and with the wind pulling his mouth back and his teeth showing and all, it occurred to me that Raymond would make a very fine runner. Doesn't he always keep up with me on my trots? And he surely knows how to breathe in counts of seven cause he's always doing it at the dinner table, which drives my brother George up the wall. And I'm smiling to beat the band cause if I've lost this race, or if me and Gretchen tied, or even if I've won, I can always retire as a runner and begin a whole new career as a coach with Raymond as my champion. After all, with a little more study I can beat Cynthia and her phony self at the spelling bee. And if I bugged my mother, I could get piano lessons and become a star. And I have a big rep as the baddest thing around. And I've got a roomful of ribbons and medals and awards. But what has Raymond got to call his own?

So I stand there with my new plan, laughing out loud by this time as Raymond

Raymond's Run    103

**7 Discussion** Discuss what kind of growth this smile of respect shows. Ask the students how this scene represents an important aspect of growing up. Have students recount any instances in which they came to recognize an opponent's true worth. Why was doing so a way of maturing?

**Enrichment** Discuss students' feelings about competition and competitors. Is athletic competition a good preparation for dealing with life? Explain.

**Reader's Response** In your eyes what is Squeaky's most outstanding quality? In what way or ways do you find her most admirable?

**Thematic Response** Discuss with students how the love and appreciation Squeaky feels for Raymond affects her life. What attitudes and values does she learn from taking care of him?

## Closure and Extension

### ANSWERS TO RESPONDING TO THE SELECTION
*Your Response*
1. Encourage students to think carefully and include reasons to support their answers.
2. Have students think about which of Squeaky's characteristics they find appealing and which are not appealing. Ask two volunteers to share their responses—one who would like to be Squeaky's friend and one who would not.

*Recalling*
3. She got her name because she has a squeaky voice. She is sometimes called Mercury because she runs very fast. She refers to herself as "Miss Quicksilver" because she runs so fast.
4. Her mother wants her to participate in the May Pole dance. Squeaky doesn't want her mother to buy her a white organdy dress and white baby-doll shoes that she would wear only once. She feels her mother can't afford them.
5. Mr. Pearson asks Squeaky to let someone else win the race. Squeaky gives him "such a look that he couldn't finish putting that

jumps down from the fence and runs over with his teeth showing and his arms down to the side, which no one before him has quite mastered as a running style. And by the time he comes over I'm jumping up and down so glad to see him—my brother Raymond, a great runner in the family tradition. But of course everyone thinks I'm jumping up and down because the men on the loudspeaker have finally gotten themselves together and compared notes and are announcing "In first place—Miss Hazel Elizabeth Deborah Parker." (Dig that.) "In second place—Miss Gretchen P. Lewis." And I look over at Gretchen wondering what the P stands for. And I smile. Cause she's good, no doubt about it. Maybe she'd like to help me coach Raymond; she obviously is serious about running, as any fool can see. And she nods to congratulate me and then she smiles. And I smile. We stand there with this big smile of respect between us. It's about as real a smile as girls can do for each other, considering we don't practice real smiling every day you know, cause maybe we too busy being flowers or fairies or strawberries instead of something honest and worthy of respect . . . you know . . . like being people.

---

### RESPONDING TO THE SELECTION

**Your Response**
1. If you were Squeaky, how would you have felt if you had *not* won the race? Why?
2. Do you think you would like to be a friend of Squeaky's? Why or why not?

**Recalling**
3. How did Squeaky gain her name? Why is she also called Mercury? Why does she refer to herself as "Miss Quicksilver"?
4. What would Squeaky's mother like her to do in the May Day program? Why doesn't Squeaky do this?
5. What does Mr. Pearson want her to do during the race? How does she react even before he can finish putting this idea into words?
6. How does Squeaky feel before each race? How does she "psych herself up," or encourage herself, to win?
7. What does Squeaky realize about herself at the end of the race? What does she realize about Raymond?

**Interpreting**
8. Squeaky's main responsibility is taking care of Raymond. How does she feel about this responsibility? Find evidence to support your answer.
9. How does Squeaky act toward people who talk smart to her? What does this behavior suggest about her?
10. When Squeaky runs into Gretchen, Mary Louise, and Rosie, she thinks, "Besides, there's just me and Gretchen standing there really. . . ." What does this thought indicate about her feelings toward the other girls? Why does she feel this way about them?
11. Early in the story, how did Squeaky feel about girls smiling at each other? Why do she and Gretchen smile at each other at the end of the race? What does this change suggest that Squeaky has learned?
12. Why is this story called "Raymond's Run" instead of "Squeaky's Run"?

**Applying**
13. What makes you respect other people?
14. Squeaky suggests that it is difficult for girls in our society to be "something honest and worthy of respect." Explain why you agree or disagree with her opinion.

idea into words."
6. Before each race Squeaky dreams she is flying over a sandy beach in the early morning sun. Then she tells herself that she must win, that she is the fastest thing in the world, and that she could even beat her father if she tried.
7. At the end of the race, she decides to coach Raymond in running. She realizes that while she has always loved her brother, she is now going to give him a greater gift, something of his own. She

realizes that Raymond would make a fine runner.

*Interpreting*
8. Squeaky loves her brother and doesn't mind taking care of him. When taking Raymond outdoors, she makes sure he walks close to buildings so that he won't step off the curb and run into traffic.
9. Squeaky would "knock you down" if you talk smart to her. It suggests that she is aggressive, direct, and immature.
10. It indicates that she doesn't feel

Mary Louise and Rosie are important enough even to acknowledge. She feels this way because Mary Louise used to be her friend when Mary Louise first moved to Harlem. Squeaky had befriended her, but she wasn't grateful and now hangs out with Gretchen. Squeaky doesn't like Rosie because she talks against Raymond.
11. She feels that girls don't know how to smile at one another. At the end of the race, Squeaky and Gretchen smile because they respect each other. It suggests that

## Recognizing Round and Flat Characters

Writers often people their stories with both round and flat characters. The **round** characters grow and change as the story progresses. The **flat** characters generally reveal only one side of their personality and may serve to highlight the positive qualities of the round characters.

1. Describe how Squeaky grows and changes as the story progresses.
2. In what way does Cynthia Procter serve as a foil to Squeaky? That is, how does she serve to point up Squeaky's positive characteristics?
3. In what way do Mary Louise and Rosie serve as a foil to Squeaky? In what way do they also serve as a foil to Gretchen?

## CRITICAL THINKING AND READING

### Identifying Reasons

A **reason** is the information that explains or justifies a condition, an action, or a decision. A reason may be a fact, an opinion, a situation, or an occurrence. In "Raymond's Run," for example, the reason for Squeaky's nickname is that she has a squeaky voice.

Give the reasons for the following situations in "Raymond's Run."

1. Squeaky changes her view of Gretchen.
2. At the end Squeaky feels that winning the race does not matter.

## THINKING AND WRITING

### Writing an Extension of the Story

Imagine Squeaky in a different situation—for example, during Raymond's first race after she has coached him. Write about the race from Squeaky's point of view, speaking as "I." First make an outline of what you will write. Think about what advice Squeaky will give Raymond: how she will feel and think before, during, and after the race; and how the race will end. Then write a first draft. Revise your story, making sure you have told it consistently from Squeaky's point of view. Finally, proofread your story and share it with your classmates.

## LEARNING OPTIONS

1. **Writing.** Raymond does not say anything at all in the story. If he could, what do you think he might say? In a short paragraph, have Raymond comment on what it is like to have Squeaky for a sister.
2. **Language.** An idiom is an expression with a meaning that is different from the literal meaning of the words. For example, *to catch one's eye* is an idiom that means "to get one's attention." What is the meaning of each of the following italicized idioms?
   a. "Rosie is too stupid to know that there is not a big deal of difference between herself and Raymond and that she can't afford *to throw stones.*"
   b. "Grown-ups got a lot of nerve sometimes. I pin number seven to myself and stomp away, I'm so *burnt.*"

   Review the story and see what other idioms you can find.
3. **Cross-curricular Connection.** In a small group, brainstorm to list the important events of the story, in the order in which they occurred. Work together to create a map showing where each event happened. Remember that the story takes place in New York City. You may wish to consult a map of New York and add details not mentioned in the story. Label your map clearly, and add color illustrations if you like. Share your finished work with your class.

*Raymond's Run* 105

grows and matures, accepting Squeaky at the end of the story.

### ANSWERS TO CRITICAL THINKING AND READING

1. Squeaky sees that Gretchen is a serious runner. Gretchen acknowledges Squeaky's win by nodding her congratulations.
2. Squeaky realizes that she can give more than love to Raymond. She can help him win his own races.

### THINKING AND WRITING

**Writing Transparency** A graphic organizer may help students. Use the Outline graphic in **Transparencies for Writing.**

**Alternative Assessment** *Peer Review:* In pairs or groups of four, have students assess one another's stories by responding to the following questions:

What situation does the writer tell about from Squeaky's point of view? How does the writer connect this situation with the original story to make a logical extension?

What specific details of the situation does the writer include to develop it?

What would you suggest the writer add to make his or her ending more interesting and believable?

What, if anything, would you suggest the writer delete to clarify Squeaky's point of view?

What concrete suggestions do you have to improve the language mechanics of the story?

To validate the peer review, have students revise their work, incorporating those suggestions they believe will enhance their stories.

### LEARNING OPTIONS

1. Option 1 is appropriate for students who are verbally skilled. Before they write you may want these students to discuss what they think Raymond might say.
2. Option 2 is appropriate for ESL students. Many of them may be unfamiliar with the idiomatic expressions Squeaky uses.
3. Option 3 will appeal to visual and kinesthetic learners as well as to art students. Provide time for these students to present to the class their map and narrate the events they included.

Squeaky has matured and now accepts Gretchen as a worthy competitor.
12. It's called "Raymond's Run" because Raymond runs the race on the other side of the fence. Seeing him run "in his very own style," Squeaky resolves to forgo running to coach him.

### Applying

13. Answers will differ. Students might respect people who are honest, friendly, sincere, and good friends.

14. Answers will differ. Students who agree might say that girls are catty and competitive. Those who disagree could argue that girls like Squeaky are honest and worthy of respect.

### ANSWERS TO ANALYZING LITERATURE

1. At first Squeaky is defensive and immature in her relationships with the other girls. If anyone says something she disagrees with, Squeaky responds by starting a fight. By the end of the story, she realizes her opponent's worth and wants her help in coaching Raymond.
2. Cynthia is not honest about the efforts she exerts in order to excel. Squeaky prides herself on her honesty and lets everyone see how much she practices for the race.
3. Mary Louise used to be Squeaky's friend. Now she talks against Squeaky. Rosie is fat and talks against Raymond. The two girls serve as a foil to Gretchen because Gretchen is the only one of the three with positive qualities. She

## A Canary's Ideas

### Direct and Indirect Characterization

**Characterization** refers to a character's personality or the method by which the writer reveals this personality. A writer using **direct characterization** tells you directly about the character. For example, the writer might state, "Dorothy is a stubborn woman." A writer using **indirect characterization** lets you learn about the character through the dialogue and action. For example, the writer might describe an incident in which Dorothy shows her stubbornness. The writer may also use the character's own words or those of other characters to reveal indirectly what the character is like.

### Focus

What if your view of the world were limited to what you could see from inside a bird cage? Draw a bird cage similar to the one that follows. On each bar write a word or phrase that describes your impression of the world from within the cage.

spacious

My View of the World

After you have read "A Canary's Ideas," think about how each impression you've listed would change after you left the cage.

### Vocabulary

Knowing the following words will help you as you read "A Canary's Ideas."

**austere** (ô stir′) *adj.*: Bare; stark (p. 107)

**inherent** (in hir′ ənt) *adj.*: Existing in something as a natural quality (p. 107)

**banal** (bā′ nəl) *adj.*: Commonplace (p. 107)

**desolation** (des′ ə lā′ shən) *n.*: Loneliness (p. 107)

**indignation** (in′ dig nā′ shən) *n.*: Anger in reaction to injustice or unfairness (p. 108)

**treatise** (trēt′ is) *n.*: A long scholarly article (p. 110)

**cursory** (kʉr′ sə rē) *adj.*: Hastily done (p. 110)

### Preparation

**More About the Author** Joaquim Maria Machado de Assis (zhō ə kēm′ mə rē′ə mə shä′ thoo jē ə sēzh′) was born in Rio de Janeiro, Brazil. His mother was Portuguese and his father was of African descent, the son of former slaves. He was taught to read and write by his mother, who died when he was ten. His father, a poor house painter, died two years later. By the age of fifteen, Machado de Assis had already become a professional writer. In addition to hundreds of short stories, he wrote novels, poetry, plays, opera librettos, and news articles. What do the untimely deaths of his parents and his precocious display of talent and responsibility suggest about Machado de Assis's early years? What does the variety of literature he produced tell you about him?

**Literary Focus** Lead a discussion about the differences between direct and indirect characterization. Elicit examples of both types of characterization from familiar literature, films, or television shows. Ask students why a writer might prefer one type of characterization to the other.

**Prereading Focus** Before students write their impressions, ask them to imagine what it would be like to be caged and then consider what effect, if any, this would have on their perception of the outside world.

**Vocabulary** Have students work in small groups to write a dialogue using all the vocabulary words.

**Electronic Handbook** You may suggest that your students use the Language Master 6000 to listen to the pronunciation of the vocabulary words.

### Joaquim Maria Machado de Assis

(1838–1908), recently recognized in the English-speaking world, has been widely read and enjoyed in his native Brazil for more than a century. Far ahead of his time, Machado de Assis is best known for innovative fiction that investigates the psychological motivations behind human behavior. His novel *Dom Casmurro* ("Mr. Pigheaded"), a study of the effects of jealousy, is regarded by many as his masterpiece. Much of his work, including the story "A Canary's Ideas," explores the nature of reality, addressing the question, "What is 'real' and what is not?"

### Objectives

1  To understand characterization
2  To make inferences about characters
3  To write a journal entry
4  To express individual interests and abilities through an optional activity

### Support Material

**Teaching Portfolio**

Art Transparency 15: *La Chiave dei Campi (The Key of the Fields)*, 1936, by René Magritte
Teacher Backup, p. 153
Usage and Mechanics Worksheet, p. 156
Vocabulary Check, p. 157
Analyzing Literature Worksheet, *Understanding Characterization*, p. 158

Critical Thinking and Reading Worksheet, *Making Inferences About Characters*, p. 159
Selection Test, p. 160

**Prentice Hall Literature Writing Studio**

# A Canary's Ideas

### Joaquim Maria Machado de Assis

### translated by Lorie Ishimatsu and Jack Schmitt

1    A man by the name of Macedo, who had a fancy for ornithology,[1] related to some friends an incident so extraordinary that no one took him seriously. Some came to believe he had lost his mind. Here is a summary of his narration.

2    At the beginning of last month, as I was walking down the street, a carriage darted past me and nearly knocked me to the ground. I escaped by quickly side-stepping into a secondhand shop. Neither the racket of the horse and carriage nor my entrance stirred the proprietor, dozing in a folding chair at the back of the shop. He was a man of shabby appearance: his beard was the color of dirty straw, and his head was covered by a tattered cap which probably had not found a buyer. One could not guess that there was any story behind him, as there could have been behind some of the objects he sold, nor could one sense in him that austere, disillusioned sadness inherent in 3 the objects which were remnants of past lives.

4    The shop was dark and crowded with the sort of old, bent, broken, tarnished, rusted articles ordinarily found in secondhand shops, and everything was in that state of semidisorder befitting such an establishment. This assortment of articles, though banal, was interesting. Pots without lids, lids without pots, buttons, shoes, locks, a black skirt, straw hats, fur hats, picture frames, binoculars, dress coats, a fencing foil, a stuffed dog, a pair of slippers, gloves, nondescript vases, epaulets,[2] a velvet satchel, two hatracks, a slingshot, a thermometer, chairs, a lithographed portrait by the late Sisson, a backgammon board, two wire masks for some future Carnival[3]—all this and more, which I either did not see or do not remember, filled the shop in the area around the door, propped up, hung, or displayed in glass cases as old as the objects inside them. Further inside the shop were many objects of similar appearance. Predominant were the large objects—chests of drawers, chairs, and beds—some of which were stacked on top of others which were lost in the darkness.

   I was about to leave, when I saw a cage hanging in the doorway. It was as old as everything else in the shop, and I expected it to be empty so it would fit in with the general appearance of desolation. However, it wasn't empty. Inside, a canary was hopping about. The bird's color, liveliness, and charm added a note of life and youth to that heap of wreckage. It was the last passenger 5 of some wrecked ship, who had arrived in the shop as complete and happy as it had

---

1. **ornithology** (ôr′nə thäl′ə jē) *n.*: The scientific study of birds.

2. **epaulets** (ep′ə lets′) *n.*: Shoulder ornaments, as on military uniforms.

3. **Carnival:** A period of feasting and merrymaking.

*A Canary's Ideas*   107

## Presentation

**Motivation/Prior Knowledge**
What kinds of things would you expect to find in a secondhand shop? How would the collection of objects in such a shop provide a good springboard for a story?

**Purpose-Setting Question** The canary's perception of the world changes repeatedly as the story progresses. Have students monitor these changes as they read, explaining the circumstances in the story that cause each change.

**Thematic Focus** Ask students to define *creative spirit*. Can the creative spirit appear in many forms?

1 **Discussion** Why does the author preface his story with this paragraph? What important information do you learn about Macedo?

2 **Reading Strategy** How has the point of view changed? Who is the ''I'' in this paragraph?

3 **Critical Thinking and Reading** What does his manner of describing the owner and the objects in the shop suggest about Macedo?

4 **Reading Strategy** Try to visualize the interior of the secondhand shop as you read this paragraph. What methods does the author use to convey the images clearly and vividly?

5 **Discussion** What is your first impression of the canary?

**Making Connections** The difference between perception and reality is also a theme in Shirley Jackson's story ''Charles,'' which begins on page 79. Have students compare the discoveries made at the ends of the stories by Macedo and Charles's mother.

**ESL Teaching Strategy** Explain to ESL students that this story was written in Portuguese and then translated into English. Ask them to discuss difficulties that arise when they have to translate something from their native language into English. Then pair ESL students with other students in the class as reading partners. As they read the story together, they can discuss difficult words and concepts.

**Master Teacher Note** Have students look at Art Transparency 15: *La Chiave dei Campi (The Key of the Fields),* 1936, by René Magritte. Ask them in what ways this painting might be interpreted as a representation of what happens to the canary's view of the world in the story.

6 **Reading Strategy** What are the bird and the shop being compared to in this sentence? What does this comparison reveal about Macedo's attitudes toward the canary and the shop?

7 **Reading Strategy** What assumptions is Macedo making about the canary's feelings and experiences?

8 **Discussion** About what does the canary feel that Macedo is deluded?

9 **Reading Strategy** In what ways is the canary's view of his situation the opposite of Macedo's? How might it have developed such a point of view?

10 **Literary Focus: Characterization** This is the canary's first definition of the world. Compare the tone and content of the bird's speech to the tone and content of Macedo's discourse. Is the canary a good conversational match for Macedo? Why or why not?

**Multicultural Focus** Ask students how much they know about canaries. If any students keep canaries as pets, have them describe what the birds look and sound like. Explain that canaries are native to the Canary Islands, the Azores, and Madeira, all islands in the Atlantic. Over the years canaries have been selectively bred for both their color and song. They are popular all over the world as songbirds and pets. Ask students to think of other birds people keep as pets. Are they valued for their color, their song, or something else?

Invite students to imagine a plot in which a bird talks to them. Where would their story take place? What kind of bird would it be? Would other people be able to understand the bird as well? Have students think of surprise endings for their stories.

originally been. As soon as I looked at the bird, it began to hop up and down, from perch to perch, as if it meant to tell me that a ray of sunshine was frolicking in the midst of that cemetery. I'm using this image to describe the canary only because I'm speaking to rhetorical[4] people, but the truth is that the canary thought about neither cemetery nor sun, according to what it told me later. Along with the pleasure the sight of the bird brought me, I felt indignation regarding its destiny and softly murmured these bitter words:

"What detestable owner had the nerve to rid himself of this bird for a few cents? Or what indifferent soul, not wishing to keep his late master's pet, gave it away to some child, who sold it so he could make a bet on a soccer game?"

The canary, sitting on top of its perch, trilled this reply:

"Whoever you may be, you're certainly not in your right mind. I had no detestable owner, nor was I given to any child to sell. Those are the delusions of a sick person. Go and get yourself cured, my friend . . ."

"What?" I interrupted, not having had time to become astonished. "So your master didn't sell you to this shop? It wasn't misery or laziness that brought you, like a ray of sunshine, to this cemetery?"

"I don't know what you mean by 'sunshine' or 'cemetery.' If the canaries you've seen use the first of those names, so much the better, because it sounds pretty, but really, I'm sure you're confused."

"Excuse me, but you couldn't have come here by chance, all alone. Has your master always been that man sitting over there?"

"What master? That man over there is my servant. He gives me food and water

---

4. **rhetorical** (ri tôr′ i kəl) *adj.*: Here, able to use and appreciate vividly expressive language.

every day, so regularly that if I were to pay him for his services, it would be no small sum, but canaries don't pay their servants. In fact, since the world belongs to canaries, it would be extravagant for them to pay for what is already in the world."

Astonished by these answers, I didn't know what to marvel at more—the language or the ideas. The language, even though it entered my ears as human speech, was uttered by the bird in the form of charming trills. I looked all around me so I could determine if I were awake and saw that the street was the same, and the shop was the same dark, sad, musty place. The canary, moving from side to side, was waiting for me to speak. I then asked if it were lonely for the infinite blue space . . .

"But, my dear man," trilled the canary, "what does 'infinite blue space' mean?"

"But, pardon me, what do you think of this world? What is the world to you?"

"The world," retorted the canary, with a certain professorial air, "is a secondhand shop with a small rectangular bamboo cage hanging from a nail. The canary is lord of the cage it lives in and the shop that surrounds it. Beyond that, everything is illusion and deception."

With this, the old man woke up and approached me, dragging his feet. He asked me if I wanted to buy the canary. I asked if he had acquired it in the same way he had acquired the rest of the objects he sold and learned that he had bought it from a barber, along with a set of razors.

"The razors are in very good condition," he said.

"I only want the canary."

I paid for it, ordered a huge, circular cage of wood and wire, and had it placed on the veranda of my house so the bird could see the garden, the fountain, and a bit of blue sky.

## Primary Source

As a writer, Machado de Assis was intrigued with the creation of characters. In the preface to his novel *Hand and Glove,* he discusses this interest:

> The portrayal of these characters . . . has been my principal, if not my only, object, the action serving as no more than a canvas on which I daubed the outlines of the figures in broad strokes. They are incomplete but have they, by chance, come out natural and true?

Apply his question to the characters in "A Canary's Ideas." Are they natural and true?

SPANISH BIRD, 1983
*Max Papart*
Nahan Galleries

## 11

It was my intention to do a lengthy study of this phenomenon, without saying anything to anyone until I could astound the world with my extraordinary discovery. I began by alphabetizing the canary's language in order to study its structure, its relation to music, the bird's appreciation of aesthetics,[5] its ideas and recollections. When this philological[6] and psychological analysis was done, I entered specifically into the study of canaries: their origin, their early history, the geology and flora[7] of the Canary Islands, the bird's knowledge of navigation, and so forth. We conversed for hours while I took notes, and it waited, hopped about, and trilled.

5. **aesthetics** (es thet' iks) *n.*: The study of beauty in art.
6. **philological** (fil' ō läj' i kəl) *adj.*: Relating to the scientific investigation of language.
7. **flora** (flôr' ə) *n.*: The plants of a specified region.

As I have no family other than two servants, I ordered them not to interrupt me, even to deliver a letter or an urgent telegram or to inform me of an important visitor. Since they both knew about my scientific pursuits, they found my orders perfectly natural and did not suspect that the canary and I understood each other.

Needless to say, I slept little, woke up two or three times each night, wandered about aimlessly, and felt feverish. Finally, I returned to my work in order to reread, add, and emend. I corrected more than one observation, either because I had misunderstood something or because the bird had not expressed it clearly. The definition of the world was one of these. Three weeks after the canary's entrance into my home, I asked it to repeat to me its definition of the world.

"The world," it answered, "is a sufficiently broad garden with a fountain in the

## 12

*A Canary's Ideas* 109

**Humanities Note**

Fine art, *Spanish Bird,* 1983, by Max Papart. The painter and printmaker Max Papart (born in 1911) is a native of Marseilles, France. His work is greatly influenced by the early Cubist paintings of Picasso and Braque. This influence is evident in Papart's painting *Spanish Bird.* The subject is depicted by means of an abstract arrangement of geometric shapes, each of which represents a feature of the bird. The result is a brightly colored patchwork of different textures suggestive of feathers and other features, assembled into the shape of a bird.

The bird is a recurring subject in the work of this popular artist. Papart now resides in New Orleans, Louisiana, where he devotes much of his time to printmaking.

You might use these questions for discussion:
1. What makes this bird an appropriate representation of the unusual canary in the story?
2. The shape of the bird in the painting is defined by the space around it. How is the point of view of the canary in the story similarly defined by the world around it?

**11** **Critical Thinking and Reading** What do his plans for the scientific study of the bird reveal about Macedo's character?

**12** **Reading Strategy** This is the canary's second definition of the world. How is it different from the first? What is the same?

**Speaking and Listening** A group of three students may enjoy reading this short story aloud to the class. Ask one student to read the introductory paragraph, a second to read Macedo's narration and dialogue, and a third to read the canary's dialogue. Suggest that students make photocopies of the story and use highlighting pens to mark the words they will read. Then have them rehearse until they can read the story fluently. As they rehearse, instruct them to mark pauses and words that need special emphasis on their copies of the story. When they are ready, have them assemble the class for a reading.

**13 Clarification** Macedo is an advocate of the scientific method, which requires that all hypotheses be verified by testing.

**14 Literary Focus: Characterization** Macedo says that the canary was "everything" to him. In what ways is his view of the world as limited as the bird's?

**15 Discussion** Is Macedo likely to find the bird this way? What does this suggest about his state of mind?

**16 Literary Focus: Characterization** Why did the canary think Macedo had disappeared? Is this consistent with the bird's character?

**17 Literary Focus: Characterization** What "annoying professorial habits" does Macedo have?

**18 Reading Strategy** Compare the canary's third definition of the world with the first two definitions.

**19 Discussion** Why does the canary doubt the existence of the secondhand shop?

**Reader's Response** How do *you* define the world?

**Thematic Response** In which is the creative spirit best reflected: Macedo's scientific observations? The canary's philosophy? The author's humorous short story? Explain your response.

**Challenge** What do you think will happen to the narrator and the canary after the end of the story? Will either of them be changed by the events in the story? Explain your response.

middle, flowers, shrubbery, some grass, clear air, and a bit of blue up above. The canary, lord of the world, lives in a spacious cage, white and circular, from which it looks out on the rest of the world. Everything else is illusion and deception."

The language of my treatise also suffered some modifications, and I saw that certain conclusions which had seemed simple were actually presumptuous. I still could not write the paper I was to send to the National Museum, the Historical Institute, and the German universities, not due to a lack of material but because I first had to put together all my observations and test their validity. During the last few days, I neither left the house, answered letters, nor wanted to hear from friends or relatives. The canary was everything to me. One of the servants had the job of cleaning the bird's cage and giving it food and water every morning. The bird said nothing to him, as if it knew the man was completely lacking in scientific background. Besides, the service was no more than cursory, as the servant was not a bird lover.

On Saturday I awoke ill, my head and back aching. The doctor ordered complete rest. I was suffering from an excess of studying and was not to read or even think, nor was I even to know what was going on in the city or the rest of the outside world. I remained in this condition for five days. On the sixth day I got up, and only then did I find out that the canary, while under the servant's care, had flown out of its cage. My first impulse was to strangle the servant—I was choking with indignation and collapsed into my chair, speechless and bewildered. The guilty man defended himself, swearing he had been careful, but the wily bird had nevertheless managed to escape.

"But didn't you search for it?"

"Yes, I did, sir. First it flew up to the roof, and I followed it. It flew to a tree, and then

who knows where it hid itself? I've been asking around since yesterday. I asked the neighbors and the local farmers, but no one has seen the bird."

I suffered immensely. Fortunately, the fatigue left me within a few hours, and I was soon able to go out to the veranda and the garden. There was no sign of the canary. I ran everywhere, making inquiries and posting announcements, all to no avail. I had already gathered my notes together to write my paper, even though it would be disjointed and incomplete, when I happened to visit a friend who had one of the largest and most beautiful estates on the outskirts of town. We were taking a stroll before dinner when this question was trilled to me:

"Greetings, Senhor[8] Macedo, where have you been since you disappeared?"

It was the canary, perched on the branch of a tree. You can imagine how I reacted and what I said to the bird. My friend presumed I was mad, but the opinions of friends are of no importance to me. I spoke tenderly to the canary and asked it to come home and continue our conversations in that world of ours, composed of a garden, a fountain, a veranda, and a white circular cage.

"What garden? What fountain?"

"The world, my dear bird."

"What world? I see you haven't lost any of your annoying professorial habits. The world," it solemnly concluded, "is an infinite blue space, with the sun up above."

Indignant, I replied that if I were to believe what it said, the world could be anything—it had even been a secondhand shop . . .

"A secondhand shop?" it trilled to its heart's content. "But is there really such a thing as a secondhand shop?"

---

**8. Senhor** (si nyôr') *n.*: Portuguese title equivalent to *Mr.* or *Sir.*

## Closure and Extension

### ANSWERS TO RESPONDING TO THE SELECTION
#### Your Response
1. Encourage students to support their opinions with reasons.

#### Recalling
2. Macedo plans to study the canary.
3. The canary's definition of the world exactly corresponds to its own situation of the moment. (a) When it is confined in a small cage in a secondhand shop, the canary defines the world as a secondhand shop in which the canary is lord of the cage it lives in and of the shop that surrounds it. (b) When it is confined in a large cage on Macedo's veranda overlooking a garden, the canary defines the world as a garden in which the canary is lord of the large cage it lives in and of everything it can see. (c) When it is perched in the tree after its escape, the canary defines the world as

infinite blue space with the sun up above.

#### Interpreting
4. Suggested Response: Macedo is struck by the incongruity of the canary's lively presence in such depressing surroundings. He assumes that the bird has been abandoned by a careless owner and is in desperate need of rescue, whereas the canary is actually quite content.
5. Suggested Response: Macedo's initial assumptions about the ca-

## Your Response

1. Do you agree or disagree with the canary's assertion that anything beyond one's own personal experience of the world is "illusion and deception"? Explain.

## Recalling

2. What does Macedo intend to do with the canary he buys?
3. The canary defines the world three times in the course of the story. Give each definition and describe the canary's circumstances at the time.

## Interpreting

4. Why is the narrator first attracted to the canary? In what ways are his perceptions of the bird inaccurate?
5. What is the narrator's attitude toward the canary and its ideas?
6. With each change in its immediate surroundings, the canary changes its definition of the world. What might the author be saying about the limitations of one's perceptions?
7. How are the narrator and the canary alike? How is this significant?

## Applying

8. Human perception of the world changes over time. For example, long ago people "knew" that the Earth was flat. Discuss whether you think our current perceptions of the world will seem ridiculous in the future.

# ANALYZING LITERATURE

## Understanding Characterization

When writers state what characters are like, they are using **direct characterization.** When writers show you what the characters are like through what the characters say and do, they are using **indirect characterization.** In "A Canary's Ideas," most of the characterization is achieved indirectly.

The following are statements about the characters in "A Canary's Ideas." Find an example—in the character's actions, circumstances, thoughts, or words—that shows the character trait indirectly.

1. The narrator is sentimental.
2. The narrator is a lonely man.
3. The canary is void of feeling.
4. The narrator is devoted to his work.

# CRITICAL THINKING AND READING

## Making Inferences About Characters

When writers use indirect characterization, you must make **inferences** about the character's personality. Inferences are the guesses you make based on the information given. What inferences can you make about Macedo from the following statements he makes?

1. "What detestable owner had the nerve to rid himself of this bird for a few cents?"
2. "I began by alphabetizing the canary's language in order to study its structure, its relation to music, the bird's appreciation of aesthetics, its ideas. . . ."

# THINKING AND WRITING

## Writing a Journal Entry

Write a journal entry from the point of view of an animal such as an ant, a bird, or a fish. As you write, keep in mind that an animal's perspective of the world is limited by where it lives and how it moves.

# LEARNING OPTION

**Art.** Create a series of illustrations to show the canary's changing view of the world. Write captions explaining how the canary's circumstances at the time influenced its perceptions.

*A Canary's Ideas* 111

scientific studies at the cost of all other aspects of life. He works so long and hard that he becomes ill.

## ANSWERS TO CRITICAL THINKING AND READING

1. Macedo is sentimental; he sympathizes with the bird and romanticizes its situation.
2. Macedo is a dedicated and methodical scholar.

## THINKING AND WRITING

**Writing Transparency** Before students write their journal entries, have them use the *Series of Events Chain* in **Transparencies for Writing.** Remind them to keep the point of view in mind as they organize the events they will record in their journals.

**Software** If students are working on computers, have them use the **Writer's Helper** activity *Questioner* to help them find ideas for their journal entries.

### Publishing Student Writing

Have volunteers read their journal entries aloud. Then display the finished work on a bulletin board for others to read and enjoy.

### Writing Across the Curriculum

Before assigning "A Canary's Ideas," ask the science teacher to explain the scientific method to your students. When they have finished reading the story, ask students to write a paragraph evaluating whether the narrator's plan for studying the canary followed accepted scientific procedures.

### LEARNING OPTION

Extend the Art activity to appeal to auditory learners by having them locate recordings of music to accompany each illustration. Invite them to play the music when showing their illustrations to the class.

---

nary reveal a sentimental yet condescending attitude. When the canary speaks, however, Macedo begins to see the bird as a fascinating object of scientific study that will bring him fame and recognition.
6. Suggested Response: Machado de Assis is saying that our perceptions of the world, like the canary's, are faulty and limited by our experience.
7. Suggested Response: Both Macedo and the canary are isolated and limited by their own personal views of the world.

## Applying

8. Answers will differ. Encourage students to be creative in their predictions of future scientific discoveries that will make currently accepted ideas appear quaint or ridiculous.

## ANSWERS TO ANALYZING LITERATURE

Suggested Responses:

1. Macedo romanticizes the canary's situation by assuming that it has been abandoned and is in need of rescuing.
2. Macedo has no family, he devotes his life to scientific pursuits at the expense of a social life, and the canary—who does not seem to care about him—is "everything" to him.
3. The canary's answers to Macedo's questions—spoken with a certain professorial air—lack any emotional content. The bird feels no gratitude to Macedo for giving it more space or more pleasant surroundings.
4. The narrator devotes his life to his

**More About the Author** Almost all of Isaac Singer's work appeared first in the *Jewish Daily Forward,* a Yiddish newspaper in New York City. Point out that Singer lectures in perfect, though highly accented, English. Why might he choose to write in Yiddish although he has lived most of his life in New York?

**Literary Focus** Remind the class that a first-person narrator does not necessarily indicate the author is speaking of his or her own life. It means you are getting one character's viewpoint, which may or may not be slanted.

**Prereading Focus** Ask students to name some ways that a person who has forgotten his address can find his way home. List several suggested strategies on the chalkboard. Then have students brainstorm in small groups for additional strategies, eliminating those that require the use of memory.

**Vocabulary** Most students will have no difficulty with these words. You might have them use each word in a sentence orally before reading the story.

**Electronic Handbook** If students have access to the Language Master 6000, suggest that they locate synonyms for *pandemonium.* Have them think about why Singer chose that word instead of one of its synonyms.

# GUIDE FOR READING

## Isaac Bashevis Singer

(1904–1991) was born in Poland, where he received a traditional Jewish education. In 1935 he settled in New York City, where he became a United States citizen. Singer wrote in Yiddish, a language of some East European Jews and their descendants. In 1978 he was awarded the Nobel Prize for Literature. Many of his stories involve people with exaggerated traits. In "The Day I Got Lost," the professor typifies a *schlemiel,* a Yiddish word for a bungler or unlucky person.

## The Day I Got Lost

### Narrator

A **narrator** is the person who tells a story. In this story the narrator speaks in the first person as "I." He tells the story as he experiences it, presenting only his own thoughts, feelings, observations, and interpretations of events.

In "The Day I Got Lost," the way the narrator tells the story adds to its humor. Professor Shlemiel tells his story matter-of-factly; he does not realize how utterly ridiculous it is.

### Focus

Think of some facts about yourself that you never forget. For example, when was the last time you forgot your own age or your address? You are about to read a humorous story about a professor who is so absent-minded that he cannot remember where he lives, and winds up lost in his own hometown. In a small group, brainstorm to list strategies that this professor might use to get himself home. Remember that none of the methods you list can rely in any way on the professor's memory. Then, as you read the story, compare the strategies you've listed with those that our forgetful hero actually uses. How many of your predictions were correct?

### Vocabulary

Knowing the following words will help you as you read "The Day I Got Lost."

**eternal** (ē tʉr' nəl) *adj.*: Everlasting (p. 114)

**destined** (des' tind) *v.*: Determined by fate (p. 114)

**forsaken** (fər sā' kən) *adj.*: Abandoned; desolate (p. 115)

**pandemonium** (pan' də mō' nē əm) *n.*: A scene of wild disorder (p. 115)

### Objectives

1 To understand the character of the narrator in a short story
2 To understand how caricature can create a humorous effect
3 To write a humorous sequel to the story
4 To express individual interests and abilities through an optional activity

## Support Material

**Teaching Portfolio**
Teacher Backup, p. 163
Grammar in Action Worksheet, *Understanding Verb Tense,* p. 166
Usage and Mechanics Worksheet, p. 168
Vocabulary Check, p. 169
Analyzing Literature Worksheet, *Understanding the Narrator,* p. 170

Language Worksheet, *Understanding Synonyms and Antonyms,* p. 171
Selection Test, p. 172

**Prentice Hall Literature Writing Studio**

# The Day I Got Lost

### Isaac Bashevis Singer

It is easy to recognize me. See a man in the street wearing a too long coat, too large shoes, a crumpled hat with a wide brim, spectacles with one lens missing, and carrying an umbrella though the sun is shining, and that man will be me, Professor Shlemiel.[1] There are other unmistakable clues to my identity. My pockets are always bulging with newspapers, magazines, and just papers. I carry an overstuffed briefcase, and I'm forever making mistakes. I've been living in New York City for over forty years, yet whenever I want to go uptown, I find myself walking downtown, and when I want to go east, I go west. I'm always late and I never recognize anybody.

I'm always misplacing things. A hundred times a day I ask myself, Where is my pen? Where is my money? Where is my handkerchief? Where is my address book? I am what is known as an absentminded professor.

For many years I have been teaching philosophy in the same university, and I still have difficulty in locating my classrooms. Elevators play strange tricks on me. I want to go to the top floor and I land in the basement. Hardly a day passes when an elevator door doesn't close on me. Elevator doors are my worst enemies.

In addition to my constant blundering and losing things, I'm forgetful. I enter a coffee shop, hang up my coat, and leave without it. By the time I remember to go back for it, I've forgotten where I've been. I lose hats, books, umbrellas, rubbers, and above all manuscripts. Sometimes I even forget my own address. One evening I took a taxi because I was in a hurry to get home. The taxi driver said, "Where to?" And I could not remember where I lived.

"Home!" I said.

"Where is home?" he asked in astonishment.

"I don't remember," I replied.

"What is your name?"

"Professor Shlemiel."

"Professor," the driver said, "I'll get you

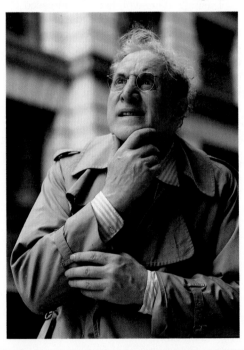

---

**1. Shlemiel** (shlə mēl'): Version of the slang word *schlemiel*, an ineffectual, bungling person.

**Multicultural Focus** Professors in many different cultures are often stereotyped as absent-minded or unable to perform simple, every-day functions. Perhaps the most famous absent-minded professor of the twentieth century was the German-born American physicist Albert Einstein, who, it is said, often forgot to put on his socks and shoes in the morning. Students may have heard of another famous, although fictional, absent-minded professor—the one in Jerry Lewis's movie *The Nutty Professor*. In the movie a bumbling, inarticulate professor drinks a potion he concocts and turns into a debonair bachelor.

Discuss the idea of stereotypes with students. Invite them to suggest other stereotypes that exist of professionals, such as the dumb athlete or the haughty waiter. Discuss why these untrue stereotypes can often be harmful.

to a telephone booth. Look in the telephone book and you'll find your address."

He drove me to the nearest drugstore with a telephone booth in it, but he refused to wait. I was about to enter the store when I realized I had left my briefcase behind. I ran after the taxi, shouting, "My briefcase, my briefcase!" But the taxi was already out of earshot.

In the drugstore, I found a telephone book, but when I looked under S, I saw to my horror that though there were a number of Shlemiels listed, I was not among them. At that moment I recalled that several months before, Mrs. Shlemiel had decided that we should have an unlisted telephone number. The reason was that my students thought nothing of calling me in the middle of the night and waking me up. It also happened quite frequently that someone wanted to call another Shlemiel and got me by mistake. That was all very well—but how was I going to get home?

I usually had some letters addressed to me in my breast pocket. But just that day I had decided to clean out my pockets. It was my birthday and my wife had invited friends in for the evening. She had baked a huge cake and decorated it with birthday candles. I could see my friends sitting in our living room, waiting to wish me a happy birthday. And here I stood in some drugstore, for the life of me not able to remember where I lived.

Then I recalled the telephone number of a friend of mine, Dr. Motherhead, and I decided to call him for help. I dialed and a young girl's voice answered.

"Is Dr. Motherhead at home?"

"No," she replied.

"Is his wife at home?"

"They're both out," the girl said.

"Perhaps you can tell me where they can be reached?" I said.

"I'm only the babysitter, but I think they went to a party at Professor Shlemiel's.

Would you like to leave a message?" she said. "Who shall I say called, please?"

"Professor Shlemiel," I said.

"They left for your house about an hour ago," the girl said.

"Can you tell me where they went?" I asked.

"I've just told you," she said. "They went to your house."

"But where do I live?"

"You must be kidding!" the girl said, and hung up.

I tried to call a number of friends (those whose telephone numbers I happened to think of), but wherever I called, I got the same reply: "They've gone to a party at Professor Shlemiel's."

As I stood in the street wondering what to do, it began to rain. "Where's my umbrella?" I said to myself. And I knew the answer at once. I'd left it—somewhere. I got under a nearby canopy. It was now raining cats and dogs. It lightninged and thundered. All day it had been sunny and warm, but now that I was lost and my umbrella was lost, it had to storm. And it looked as if it would go on for the rest of the night.

To distract myself, I began to ponder the ancient philosophical problem. A mother chicken lays an egg, I thought to myself, and when it hatches, there is a chicken. That's how it has always been. Every chicken comes from an egg and every egg comes from a chicken. But was there a chicken first? Or an egg first? No philosopher has ever been able to solve this eternal question. Just the same, there must be an answer. Perhaps I, Shlemiel, am destined to stumble on it.

It continued to pour buckets. My feet were getting wet and I was chilled. I began to sneeze and I wanted to wipe my nose, but my handkerchief, too, was gone.

At that moment I saw a big black dog. He was standing in the rain getting soaked and

## Grammar in Action

In composing a story, the writer selects the time in which it will be told: the present, the past, or the future. The writer then uses the appropriate **verb tense** consistently in the story. Notice the verbs in the following passages from "The Day I Got Lost":

In the drugstore, I found a telephone book, but when I looked under S, I saw to my horror that though there were a number of Shlemiels listed, I was not among them.

I usually had some letters addressed to me in my breast pocket. But just that day I had decided to clean out my pockets. It was my birthday and my wife had invited friends in for the evening.

Then I recalled the number of a friend of mine . . .

The verbs are in the past tense or the past perfect tense: *was, had, had decided, was, had invited, recalled*. The two past perfect looking at me with sad eyes. I knew immediately what the trouble was. The dog was lost. He, too, had forgotten his address. I felt a great love for that innocent animal. I called to him and he came running to me. I talked to him as if he were human. "Fellow, we're in the same boat," I said. "I'm a man shlemiel and you're a dog shlemiel. Perhaps it's also your birthday, and there's a party for you, too. And here you stand shivering and forsaken in the rain, while your loving master is searching for you everywhere. You're probably just as hungry as I am."

I patted the dog on his wet head and he wagged his tail. "Whatever happens to me will happen to you," I said. "I'll keep you with me until we both find our homes. If we don't find your master, you'll stay with me. Give me your paw," I said. The dog lifted his right paw. There was no question that he understood.

A taxi drove by and splattered us both. Suddenly it stopped and I heard someone shouting, "Shlemiel! Shlemiel!" I looked up and saw the taxi door open, and the head of a friend of mine appeared. "Shlemiel," he called. "What are you doing here? Who are you waiting for?"

"Where are you going?" I asked.

"To your house, of course. I'm sorry I'm late, but I was detained. Anyhow, better late than never. But why aren't you at home? And whose dog is that?"

"Only God could have sent you!" I exclaimed. "What a night! I've forgotten my address, I've left my briefcase in a taxi, I've lost my umbrella, and I don't know where my rubbers are."

"Shlemiel," my friend said, "if there was ever an absentminded professor, you're it!"

When I rang the bell of my apartment, my wife opened the door. "Shlemiel!" she shrieked. "Everybody is waiting for you. Where have you been? Where is your brief-

case? Your umbrella? Your rubbers? And who is this dog?"

Our friends surrounded me. "Where have you been?" they cried. "We were so worried. We thought surely something had happened to you!"

"Who is this dog?" my wife kept repeating.

"I don't know," I said finally. "I found him in the street. Let's just call him Bow Wow for the time being."

"Bow Wow, indeed!" my wife scolded. "You know our cat hates dogs. And what about the parakeets? He'll scare them to death."

"He's a quiet dog," I said. "He'll make friends with the cat. I'm sure he loves parakeets. I could not leave him shivering in the rain. He's a good soul."

The moment I said this the dog let out a bloodcurdling howl. The cat ran into the room. When she saw the dog, she arched her back and spat at him, ready to scratch out his eyes. The parakeets in their cage began flapping their wings and screeching. Everybody started talking at once. There was pandemonium.

Would you like to know how it all ended? | 8

Bow Wow still lives with us. He and the cat are great friends. The parakeets have learned to ride on his back as if he were a horse. As for my wife, she loves Bow Wow even more than I do. Whenever I take the dog out, she says, "Now, don't forget your address, both of you."

I never did find my briefcase, or my umbrella, or my rubbers. Like many philosophers before me, I've given up trying to solve the riddle of which came first, the chicken or the egg. Instead, I've started writing a book called *The Memoirs of Shlemiel*. If I don't | 9 forget the manuscript in a taxi, or a restaurant, or on a bench in the park, you may read them someday. In the meantime, here is a sample chapter.

*The Day I Got Lost* 115

7

7 **Discussion** Note the use of the word *shlemiel* not as the professor's name. Why does he call the dog "a dog shlemiel"?

8 **Reading Strategy** Have your students predict the end of the story.

9 **Discussion** Do you think he'll ever finish his book? Why? Would you read his memoirs? Why?

**Enrichment** For students who enjoyed reading this story, suggest they read some short stories by another famous Yiddish writer, Sholom Aleichem. He wrote humorous stories about Jewish life in Russia and Jewish immigration to the United States.

**Master Teacher Note** Explain that Singer's brand of exaggeration differs from Twain's. Twain exaggerates individual details by stretching them out of proportion to reality. Singer exaggerates by piling one realistic detail on top of another until the sum defies belief. In a sense Singer's technique is deadpan. Can students think of any stand-up comics who use this kind of delivery?

**Reader's Response** Choose an aspect of your personality or the personality of a friend and describe how it could be exaggerated for a humorous effect in a caricature.

**Thematic Response** Have students discuss how humor is created in this story. How do the realistic details of time and place enhance the effectiveness of a greatly exaggerated situation?

verbs (*had decided, had invited*) indicate an action that was completed earlier. (Past perfect verbs are formed by using *had* with the past form of the verb.)

**Student Activity 1.** Find ten more verbs in the story that are in the past tense and three verbs in the past perfect tense.

**Student Activity 2.** Write a paragraph in which you tell about something that happened to you in the past few days. Underline all of the verbs you use. Check over your writing or have a partner check it to make sure that you used the past tense throughout.

**Electronic Handbook** You may want students to review the use of appropriate verb tense before completing the Grammar in Action activities. If students have access to the Language Master 6000, have them enter the access word *tense* and press the GRAMMAR key to get information on verb tenses.

# Closure and Extension

## ANSWERS TO RESPONDING TO THE SELECTION

### Your Response

1. Ask students to name specific traits of Professor Shlemiel's that would influence their feelings about him if he were their teacher.

### Recalling

2. His most outstanding trait is his forgetfulness.
3. First he looks up his address in a telephone book. Then he tries to telephone a friend.
4. Everybody is at Shlemiel's house for his birthday party.
5. He met a friend who was taking a taxi to his birthday party.
6. He feels sorry for the dog who was wet and hungry.

### Interpreting

7. They were both wet from the rain and hungry. The dog appeared lost, as was Professor Shlemiel.
8. He is constantly losing or misplacing things. He can't remember addresses and phone numbers. He gets splattered by cars and almost misses his own birthday party.
9. The end of Professor Shlemiel's day was ridiculous because he brought a dog home who he claimed was very quiet. But the dog ran after the cat and scared the parakeet and everyone at his party started talking at once. There was pandemonium.

### Applying

10. Answers will differ. Examples include any of the super heroes, such as Superman.

## ANSWERS TO ANALYZING LITERATURE

1. He tells you what he looks like, that he is always late, and that he never recognizes anybody. He also says he always misplaces things and is absent-minded.
2. His wife and friends view him as absent-minded and careless. His wife says, "Now, don't forget your address, both of you." His friends query, "Where have you been? . . . We were so worried. We thought surely something had happened to you!"

116

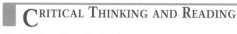

## RESPONDING TO THE SELECTION

### Your Response

1. How would you feel about Professor Shlemiel if he were your teacher?

### Recalling

2. What is Shlemiel's most outstanding trait?
3. In what two ways does Professor Shlemiel try to find out his own address?
4. Why can't he get in touch with anybody?
5. How does Professor Shlemiel get home?
6. Why does he bring the dog home with him?

### Interpreting

7. In what ways are Shlemiel and the dog alike?
8. In what ways is the professor a true *schlemiel,* or bungler?
9. Explain what is ridiculous about the outcome of Professor Shlemiel's day.

### Applying

10. Describe a character from books, movies, or television whose traits are exaggerated to be funny. An example is the classic comic strip character Popeye the Sailor Man, whose strength is exaggerated to create humor.

## ANALYZING LITERATURE

### Understanding Narrator

The **narrator,** or person who tells the story, is Professor Shlemiel, who speaks in the first person as "I." You experience the story through his eyes, knowing only his thoughts and feelings; you do not learn the views of anyone else, such as his wife or his friend in the taxi. However, as an active reader, you read between the lines, and see humor where Shlemiel does not.

1. What does Shlemiel tell you about himself?
2. How do you think Professor Shlemiel's wife views him? How do you think his friends view him? Find evidence to support your answer.
3. How do you think this story would have been different if Mrs. Shlemiel had told it?

## CRITICAL THINKING AND READING

### Understanding Caricature

**Caricature** is the distortion or exaggeration of the peculiarities in a character's personality. Often a writer will use caricature to create a humorous effect. The exaggerated traits can be amusing or ridiculous in themselves, or they can cause preposterous situations.

1. A *schlemiel* is a bungler. How is Shlemiel a perfect example of this type of person?
2. In what way is he a perfect example of an absent-minded professor?
3. The author reveals only one side of the professor's personality and blows this side out of proportion. Would this story have been as amusing if the author had presented the professor as a well-rounded individual? Explain.

## THINKING AND WRITING

### Writing a Story

Write a story telling of another day in the life of Shlemiel. First freewrite for three minutes about what an absent-minded professor might do. Imagine as many ridiculous incidents as you can. Using this freewriting, write in the first person. Make your tone serious as you describe the humorous events. Revise, making sure you have used exaggeration.

## LEARNING OPTION

**Multicultural Activity.** Singer wrote in Yiddish, a language of some East European Jews and their descendants. Many Yiddish words, such as *schlemiel,* have entered the English language and are used and understood widely. Define the following Yiddish words. (You should be able to find them in a good dictionary.)

| | |
|---|---|
| *nebbish* | *schmo* |
| *schlep* | *schmooze* |
| *schmaltz* | *schnook* |

3. Answers will differ. Students may say the story wouldn't be as funny if Mrs. Shlemiel told it. It's funnier because Professor Shlemiel sees these traits in himself. If Mrs. Shlemiel told the story, it could be interpreted as a wife's opinion of her husband.

## ANSWERS TO CRITICAL THINKING AND READING

1. He loses his rubbers and umbrella and then it starts to rain. Elevator doors close on him. He gets splashed by a taxi in the rain.
2. He is an absent-minded professor in that he always misplaces things. He misplaces his pen, his money, his handkerchief, or his address book. He loses hats, books, and manuscripts. He even forgets his own address and phone number.
3. Answers will differ. Most students will probably say no. The idea that he is so absent minded should be the main focus of the story. If Professor Shlemiel were more well-rounded, he wouldn't be as funny.

## THINKING AND WRITING

**Writing Transparency** Your students may find it helpful to use the Story Map graphic organizer in **Transparencies for Writing.**

**Alternative Assessment** You may vary the Thinking and Writing

# Setting

**LAVENDER AND OLD LACE**
*Charles Burchfield*
*From the collection of the New Britain Museum of American Art*

## Humanities Note

Fine art, *Lavender and Old Lace,* by Charles Burchfield. The American artist Charles Burchfield (1893–1967) was schooled in painting at the Cleveland Institute of Art. His teacher there, Henry Keller, encouraged Burchfield to develop an individualistic style of painting. To finance his painting career, Charles Burchfield worked at many things, including designing wallpaper, illustrating, and teaching art classes. He eventually gained fame for his intense and imaginative paintings of nature and his moody, psychological studies of buildings.

The painting *Lavender and Old Lace* is a watercolor painted between 1939 and 1947. This brooding study of a Victorian house is filled with gloom and mystery. Burchfield has made the building come alive as if its awareness grew on the emotions of those that dwelled there. The melancholy air is nurtured by the overshadowing tree and the gingerbread trim, which hangs from the house like a malevolent growth. Burchfield referred to this painting as "an elegy." He used the twilight time of evening and the crowding vegetation to instill a sense of mystery into this painting. Burchfield's ability to give life to inanimate objects and plant forms is apparent in this work.

**Master Teacher Note** To Introduce the element of setting, have students look at Art Transparency 4, *Diner* by Richard Estes, in the Teaching Portfolio. Explain that a writer uses words to create a setting that expresses time, place, and mood. Ask students what they think is the time and place of the painting. What details of the diner's style and appearance give them this impression? Does the use of lighting, shadow, and color produce any particular mood? What might take place in this diner?

Assignment as follows: Have your students complete the Responding to the Selection and Analyzing Literature activities. Then ask them to write a character sketch of Professor Shlemiel in which they take his outstanding trait and discuss it, using specific incidents from the story to explain how the author caricatures the Professor.

## LEARNING OPTION

This activity will appeal to students with an interest in languages. Encourage students to add words from their own language that have recently entered the English language.

**More About the Author** Though Shirley Ann Grau has written some travel essays, she is essentially a regionalist, preferring to write mainly about New Orleans and the coast, terrain, and bayous of Louisiana. At the same time, she is often able, as she is in this story, to make her setting so universal that the story could occur in New England, California, or almost anywhere there is a coast. How might her writings reflect her love of solitude and dislike of travel?

**Literary Focus** After students have read the definition of setting, have them consider the settings of some of the stories they have read. Why, for example, are specific settings needed in some stories and not in others?

**Prereading Focus** Put the chart on the chalkboard. Have students volunteer naming a few of the ocean's qualities and their responses to them. Briefly discuss their ideas. Then have students refer to these ideas as they brainstorm for others in small groups.

**Vocabulary** You might have students use each word in a sentence orally before reading the story.

**Electronic Handbook**
You may suggest that your students use the Language Master 6000 to hear the pronunciations of *luminous, spume,* and *impenetrable.*

# GUIDE FOR READING

## Shirley Ann Grau

(1929–    ) has lived in New Orleans most of her life. She attended Tulane University and raised four children while writing novels, short stories, and journal articles. *Black Prince and Other Stories* is a collection of stories Grau has written especially for teenagers. "The Land and the Water," like many of her other short stories, is set in Louisiana. This story is an example of the importance of nature and its forces in stories Grau creates.

## The Land and the Water

### Setting

The **setting** of a story is the time and place of the action. In a short story the setting is usually presented through detailed descriptions. In some stories the setting plays a very important role. It affects what happens to the characters and what they learn about life.

### Focus

Many a writer and artist has been inspired to great feats of creativity by the might and mystery of the ocean. What thoughts and feelings does the ocean evoke in you? In a small group, brainstorm to list your responses to the ocean's many qualities. Organize your thoughts in a chart similar to the one below. Then read "The Land and the Water" to see how the ocean can play a crucial role in some people's lives.

| The Ocean's Qualities | Thoughts and Feelings |
|---|---|
| It's huge — looks like it goes on forever. | Its size amazes me — fills me with wonder |

### Vocabulary

Knowing the following words will help you as you read "The Land and the Water."

**stifled** (stī′ f'ld) *adj.*: Muffled; suppressed (p. 119)

**luminous** (lo͞o′ mə nəs) *adj.*: Glowing in the dark (p. 122)

**scuttling** (skut′ 'liŋ) *v.*: Running or moving quickly (p. 122)

**lee** (lē) *n.*: Sheltered place; the side away from the wind (p.122)

**spume** (spyo͞om) *n.*: Foam; froth (p. 122)

**swamped** (swämpt) *v.*: Sank by filling with water (p. 123)

**tousled-looking** (tou′ z'ld lo͞ok′ iŋ) *adj.*: Rumpled or mussed (p. 123)

**impenetrable** (im pen′ i trə b'l) *adj.*: Not able to be passed through (p. 126)

1  To understand the setting of a short story
2  To make inferences about a story's setting
3  To write a description of a setting
4  To express individual interests and abilities through optional activities

## Support Material

**Teaching Portfolio**
Teacher Backup, p. 175
Grammar in Action Worksheets, *Using Semicolons,* p. 178, *Understanding Sentence Fragments,* p. 180
Usage and Mechanics Worksheet, p. 182
Vocabulary Check, p. 183
Analyzing Literature Worksheet, *Understanding Setting,* p. 184

Language Worksheet, *Choosing Meaning to Fit the Context,* p. 185
Selection Test, p. 186

**Prentice Hall Literature Writing Studio**

# The Land and the Water

## Shirley Ann Grau

From the open Atlantic beyond Timbalier Head a few scattered foghorns grunted, muffled and faint. That bank[1] had been hanging offshore for days. We'd been watching the big draggers[2] chug up to it, get dimmer and dimmer, and finally disappear in its grayness, leaving only the stifled sounds of their horns behind. It had been there so long we got used to it, and came to think of it as always being there, like another piece of land, maybe.

The particular day I'm thinking about started out clear and hot with a tiny breeze —a perfect day for a Snipe or a Sailfish.[3] There were a few of them moving on the big bay, not many. And they stayed close to shore, for the barometer was drifting slowly down in its tube and the wind was shifting slowly backward around the compass.[4]

Larger sailboats never came into the bay—it was too shallow for them—and these small ones, motorless, moving with the smallest stir of air, could sail for home, if the fog came in, by following the shore—or if there was really no wind at all, they could be paddled in and beached. Then their crews could walk to the nearest phone and call to be picked up. You had to do it that way, because the fog always came in so quick. As it did that morning.

My sister and I were working by our dock, scraping and painting the little dinghy.[5] Because the spring tides washed over this stretch, there were no trees, no bushes even, just snail grass and beach lettuce and pink flowering sea lavender, things that liked salt. All morning it had been bright and blue and shining. Then all at once it turned gray and wet, like an unfalling rain, moveless and still. We went right on sanding and from being sweaty hot we turned sweaty cold, the fog chilling and dripping off our faces.

"It isn't worth the money," my sister said. She is ten and that is her favorite sentence. This time it wasn't even true. She was the one who'd talked my father into giving us the job.

I wouldn't give her the satisfaction of an answer, though I didn't like the wet any more than she did. It was sure to make my hair roll up in tight little curls all over my

---

1. **bank** *n*.: Mass of fog.
2. **draggers** *n*.: Fishing boats that use large nets to catch fish.
3. **Snipe . . . Sailfish:** names of sailboats.
4. **barometer . . . compass:** The decrease in barometric pressure and change in wind direction indicate that a storm is approaching.

5. **dinghy** (diŋ′ gē) *n*.: Small rowboat.

*The Land and the Water* 119

**Presentation**

**Motivation/Prior Knowledge**
On the board paraphrase Louise Gossett's quotation about Shirley Grau: "People are not free agents protected by their environment but, rather, stoics reconciled to the violence of nature that assails them." Ask students to explain the meaning of the quotation. They will probably need help with the vocabulary. Ask them to decide, after finishing the story, whether or not the story illustrates the critic's quotation.

**Purpose-Setting Question** What role does nature play in this story?

1 **Clarification** Timbalier Head is south of New Orleans, Louisiana. It is on the Gulf of Mexico.

2 **Discussion** What does a falling barometer mean?

3 **Discussion** Who is the narrator of the story? What is her relationship to the ten-year-old girl?

**Making Connections** Another selection in which the ocean is a powerful force is "Tears of the Sea" (page 129).

**Thematic Focus** Ask students to reflect on their relationship with the world around them. Have volunteers share experiences in which elements of nature, such as the sea and weather, determined what happened.

## Humanities Note

*Perkins Cove*, by Jane Betts. Those students who have enjoyed summer visits to the Maine coast will recognize the fishing village shown here. Point out the tidy design of the houses near the dock. A customer is seen stopping at the small snack bar. A gangway goes from the land's edge to a floating dock, and to complete this ordered hamlet, there is a mountain in the background. The portrait of a rational way of life is meant to be deceiving. Those who know the Maine coast know how menacing the water can become and how dangerous it is to go out on it once the fog comes in. Tragedy has come to many fishermen. Parts of boats have been found floating miles from shore or washed up on the beach.

1. Why was this picture of a peaceful scene chosen to accompany a story of a drowning?
2. Do you agree with using this painting to accompany the story? Why or why not?
3. Would you have chosen another one instead? Explain.

**4 Discussion** What does the phrase "The land and the water all looked the same . . ." mean?

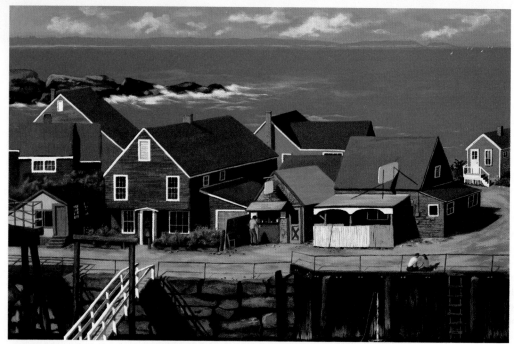

**PERKINS COVE**
*Jane Betts*
*Collection of Wendy Betts*

head and I would have to wash it again and sleep on the hard metal curlers to get it back in shape.

Finally my sister said, "Let's go get something to drink."

When we turned around to go back up to the house, we found that it had disappeared. It was only a couple of hundred yards away, right behind us and up a little grade, a long slope of beach plum and poison ivy, salt burned and scrubby. You couldn't see a thing now, except gray. The land and the water all looked the same; the fog was that thick.

There wasn't anything to drink. Just a lot of empty bottles waiting in cases on the back porch. "Well," my sister said, "let's go tell her."

She meant my mother of course, and we didn't have to look for her very hard. The house wasn't big, and being a summer house, it had very thin walls: we could hear her playing cards with my father in the living room.

They were sitting by the front window. On a clear day there was really something to see out there: the sweep of the bay and the pattern of the inlets and, beyond it all, the dark blue of the Atlantic. Today there was nothing, not even a bird, if you didn't count the occasional yelp of a seagull off high overhead somewhere.

"There's nothing to drink," my sister said. "Not a single thing."

"Tomorrow's grocery day," my mother said. "Go make a lemonade."

120    *Short Stories*

## Grammar in Action

**Semicolons** are used to join independent clauses in certain instances. If the meaning of the two clauses is closely related, and a coordinating conjunction is either unnecessary or unwanted because it would change the meaning, writers use semicolons.

In the following example from "The Land and the Water," a period would be too much of a break, and a comma with a conjunction wouldn't sound right. Therefore, the writer chooses a semicolon; it is the correct punctuation mark for this instance.

The land and the water all looked the same; the fog was just that thick.

If two independent clauses are joined with either a conjunctive adverb (*also, besides, furthermore, consequently, however, indeed, instead, moreover, nevertheless, otherwise, therefore, thus*) or a transitional expression (*as a result, at this time, for instance, in fact, on the other hand, that is*), a semicolon goes before the conjunctive adverb or the transitional expression, and a comma follows it.

A semicolon is also used to separate independent clauses if there are two or more commas within any of the independent

"Look," my father said, "why not go back to work on the dinghy? You'll get your money faster."

So we went, only stopping first to get our oilskin hats. And pretty soon, fog was dripping from the brims like a kind of very gentle rain.

But we didn't go back to work on the dinghy. For a while we sat on the edge of the dock and looked at the minnow-flecked water, and then we got out the crab nets and went over to the tumbled heap of rocks to see if we could catch anything. We spent a couple of hours out there, skinning our knees against the rough barnacled[6] surfaces. Once a seagull swooped down so low he practically touched the tops of our hats. Almost but not quite. I don't think we even saw a crab, though we dragged our nets around in the water just for the fun of it. Finally we dug a dozen or so clams, ate them, and tried to skip the shells along the water. That was how the afternoon passed, with one thing or the other, and us not hurrying, not having anything we'd rather be doing.

We didn't have a watch with us, but it must have been late afternoon when they all came down from the house. We heard them before we saw them, heard the brush of their feet on the grass path.

It was my mother and my father and Robert, my biggest brother, the one who is eighteen. My father had the round black compass and a coil of new line. Robert had a couple of gas lanterns and a big battery one. My mother had the life jackets and a little wicker basket and a thermos bottle. They all went out along the narrow rickety dock and began to load the gear into my father's *Sea*

*Skiff*. It wasn't a big boat and my father had to take a couple of minutes to pack it, stowing the basket way up forward under the cowling[7] and wedging the thermos bottle on top of that. Robert, who'd left his lanterns on the ground to help him, came back to fetch them.

"I thought you were at the McKays," I said. "How'd you get over here?"

"Dad called me." He lifted one eyebrow. "Remember about something called the telephone?" And he picked up his gear and walked away.

"Well," my sister said.

They cast off, the big outboard sputtered gently, throttled way down. They would have to move very slowly in the fog. As they swung away, Robert at the tiller, we saw my father set out his compass and take a bearing off it.

My mother watched them out of sight, which didn't take more than a half minute. Then she stood watching the fog for a while and, I guess, following the sound of the steady put-put. It seemed to me, listening to it move off and blend with the sounds of the bay—the sounds of a lot of water, of tiny waves and fish feeding—that I could pick out two or three other motors.

Finally my mother got tired of standing on the end of the dock and she turned around and walked up to us. I expected her to pass right by and go on up to the house. But she didn't. We could hear her stop and stand looking at us. My sister and I just scraped a little harder, pretending we hadn't noticed.

"I guess you're wondering what that was all about?" she said finally.

"I don't care," my sister said. She was lying. She was just as curious as I was.

---

6. **barnacled** (bär′ nə k'ld) *adj.*: Covered with small shellfish that attach themselves to rocks, ships, wood, and whales.

7. **cowling** *n.*: A removable metal covering for an engine.

*The Land and the Water* 121

5 **Literary Focus**. How has the author established the setting and the tempo of life of summer vacationers in a seaside resort? In reviewing the story with the class, explain how the reference to getting pocket money for painting the dinghy is a note of normalcy, not preparing the reader for future developments.

6 **Discussion** In your own words, describe how the sisters spent the afternoon.

clauses or when another comma might result in confusion. Look at the following example:

The story was touching, sensitive, and humorous; but the movie version was soapy and slapstick.

**Student Activity.** Write three sentences in which you demonstrate each of the uses of the semicolon. Be sure that each of the independent clauses is closely related in meaning.

**Electronic Handbook** You might want students to review semicolons before completing the Grammar in Action activities. If students have access to the Language Master 6000, have them enter the access symbol ; (the semicolon symbol) and press the GRAMMAR key to get information on semicolons.

**7 Discussion** What is the girl's reaction to the people in the sailboat? Contrast her mother's reaction to hers.

**8 Language** Note the use of descriptive language here. What is the fog compared to? Explain that a simile is a comparison of two unlike things using *like* or *as.* You might have your **more advanced** students write their own similes about fog.

My mother didn't seem to have heard her. "It's Linda Holloway and Stan Mitchell and Butch Rodgers."

We knew them. They were sailing people, a little older than I, a little younger than my brother Robert. They lived in three houses lined up one by the other on the north shore of Marshall's Inlet. They were all right kids, nothing special either way, sort of a gang, living as close as they did. This year they had turned up with a new sailboat, a twelve-foot fiberglass job that somebody had designed and built for Stan Mitchell as a birthday present.

"What about them?" my sister asked, forgetting that she wasn't interested.

"They haven't come home."

"Oh," I said.

"They were sailing," my mother said. "The Brewers think they saw them off their place just before the fog. They were sort of far out."

"You mean Dad's gone to look for them?"

She nodded.

"Is that all?" my sister said. "Just somebody going to have to sit in their boat and wait until the fog lifts."

My mother looked at us. Her curly red hair was dripping with the damp of the fog and her face was smeared with dust. "The Lord save me from children," she said quietly. "The glass is twenty-nine eighty and it's still going down fast."

We went back up to the house with her, to help fix supper—a quiet nervous kind of supper. The thick luminous fish-colored fog turned into deep solid night fog. Just after supper, while we were drying the dishes, the wind sprang up. It shook the whole line of windows in the kitchen and knocked over every single pot of geraniums on the back porch.

"Well," my mother said, "it's square into the east now."

A low barometer and a wind that had gone backwards into the east—there wasn't one of us didn't know what that meant. And it wasn't more than half an hour before there was a grumble of approaching thunder and the fog began to swirl around the windows, streaming like torn cotton as the wind increased.

"Dad'll come back now, huh?" my sister asked.

"Yes," my mother said. "All the boats'll have to come back now."

We settled down to television, half watching it and half listening to the storm outside. In a little while, an hour or so, my mother said, "Turn off that thing."

"What?"

"Turn it off, quick." She hurried on the porch, saying over her shoulder: "I hear something."

The boards of the wide platform were wet and slippery under our feet, and the eaves of the house poured water in steady small streams that the wind grabbed and tore away. Between the crashes of thunder, we heard it too. There was a boat coming into our cove. By the sound of it, it would be my father and Robert.

"Is that the motor?" my mother asked.

"Sure," I said. It had a little tick and it was higher pitched than any of the others. You couldn't miss it.

Without another word to us she went scuttling across the porch and down the stairs toward the cove. We followed and stood close by, off the path and a little to one side. It was tide marsh there, and salt mud oozed over the tops of our sneakers. The cove itself was sheltered—it was in the lee of Cedar Tree Neck—but even so it was pretty choppy. Whitecaps were beginning to run high and broken, wind against tide, and the spume from them stung as it hit your face and your eyes. You could hear the real stuff blowing overhead, with the

**CLOUDS AND WATER. 1930**
*Arthur Dove*
Metropolitan Museum of Art, The Alfred Stieglitz Collection,
1949 © 1979 by the Metropolitan Museum of Art

peculiar sound wind has when it gets past half a gale.

My father's boat was sidling up to the dock now, pitching and rolling in the broken water. Its motor sputtered into reverse and then the hull rubbed gently against the pilings. They had had a bad time. In the quick lightning flashes you could see every scupper[8] pouring water. You could see the slow weary way they made the lines fast.

"There wasn't anything else to do," my father was saying as they came up the path, beating their arms for warmth, "with it blowing straight out the east, we had to come in."

Robert stopped a moment to pull off his

oilskins. Under them his shirt was as drenched as if he hadn't had any protection at all.

"We came the long way around," my father said, "hugging the lee as much as we could."

"We almost swamped," Robert said.

Then we were at the house and they went off to dry their clothes, and that was that. They told us later that everybody had come in, except only for the big Coast Guard launch. And with only one boat it was no wonder they didn't find them.

The next morning was bright and clear and a lot cooler. The big stretch of bay was still shaken and tousled-looking, spotted with whitecaps. Soon as it was light, my father went to the front porch and looked

---

**8. scupper** *n.*: An opening in a ship's side that allows water to run off the deck.

*The Land and the Water*   123

9

**Humanities Note**

Fine art, *Clouds and Water,* 1930, by Arthur Dove. Dove was a man who loved the water. Born in 1880, in 1920 he began living on a houseboat on the Harlem River, which runs east of Manhattan in New York City. In 1923 he and another artist bought a yawl on which they lived, cruising the waters of Long Island Sound for seven years. The environment of the rivers, bay, and sound in and around New York City gave Dove the inspiration and the subjects to paint.

1. Ask students to describe both the colors and shapes of this painting. Of what are they suggestive?
2. Guide students into an awareness of the twisting, dark lines that define the clouds, hills, and water. In what ways do these lines speak of the gathering, and virtual imminence, of a giant storm?
3. Is Dove saying that these tiny sailboats will be engulfed and overwhelmed by the storm? Or will they survive it?
4. Is this work of art appropriate to illustrate this story? Explain your answer.

**9 Reading Strategy** Have students summarize the story up to this point and predict what has happened to the three people in the sailboat.

and looked with his glasses. He checked the anemometer[9] dial, and shook his head. "It's still too rough for us." In a bit the Coast Guard boats—two of them—appeared, and a helicopter began its chopping noisy circling.

It was marketing day too, so my mother, my sister, and I went off, as we always did. We stopped at the laundromat and the hardware, and then my mother had to get some pine trees for the slope behind the house. It was maybe four o'clock before we got home.

---

9. **anemometer** (an′ ə mäm′ ə tər) **dial:** The dial on an instrument that determines wind speed and sometimes direction.

The wind had dropped, the bay was almost quiet again. Robert and my father were gone, and so was the boat. "I thought they'd go out again," my mother said. She got a cup of coffee and the three of us sat watching the fleet of boats work their way back and forth across the bay, searching.

Just before dark—just when the sky was beginning to take its twilight color—my father and Robert appeared. They were burned lobster red with great white circles around their eyes where their glasses had been.

"Did you find anything?" my sister asked.

My father looked at my mother.

# MULTICULTURAL CONNECTION

### Fishing Customs

It is not surprising that fishing is part of the background of Shirley Ann Grau's story "The Land and the Water." Louisiana, the story's setting, is the nation's leading state for fishing. In many other parts of the world, too, fishing is a good livelihood and a way of life. Fishing customs and techniques, however, differ from country to country.

**In Russia and Japan.** In industrial Russia and Japan, large fishing fleets travel offshore ocean waters. They are equipped not only to catch fish but also to clean, process, and store them. Fishing crews can number as many as a hundred, and often include women as well as men.

**In the South Pacific.** In other places, such as the South Pacific islands, fishers combine modern technology with the traditional methods of their forebears. For example, they often use outboard motors to power traditional outrigger canoes.

In the Philippines, fishers observe the traditional practice of fishing at night with a light or lantern hung on the prow of their boat or held on a pole. The fish attracted by the light are then caught in small nets. When many boats are on the water, this kind of night fishing creates a beautiful, if somewhat eerie, scene for spectators on the shore.

**The angry sea.** As seen in Shirley Ann Grau's story, the sea can also have a dark and frightening side. In many languages the sea is called a "widowmaker" because it has claimed the lives of large numbers of fishers and sailors.

### Exploring on Your Own

Research a fishing custom of a culture other than your own and report on this custom to the class.

124   *Short Stories*

# Grammar in Action

Accomplished writers sometimes break grammatical rules. However, when they break a rule, they usually do so for a specific purpose. Students learn that sentences must have a subject and a verb. If one or both is missing, the result is a **sentence fragment.** Sentence fragments are generally considered unacceptable. However, notice how skillfully fragments have been used in the following paragraph:

But not to sleep. We played cards for an hour or so, until we couldn't stand that any more. Then we did a couple of crossword puzzles together. Finally we just sat in our beds, in the chilly night, and listened. There were the usual sounds from outside the open window, sounds of the land and the water. Deer moving about in the brush on their way to eat the wild watercress and wild lettuce that grew around the spring. The deep pumping sounds of an owl's wings in the air. Little splashes from the bay—the fishes and the muskrats and the otters.

"You might as well tell them," she said. "They'll know anyway."

"Well," my father said, "they found the boat."

"That's what they were expecting to find, wasn't it?" my mother asked quietly.

He nodded. "It's kind of hard to say what happened. But it looks like they got blown on East Shoal with the tide going down and the chop tearing the keel out."[10]

"Oh," my mother said.

"Oh," my sister said.

"They found the boat around noon."

My mother said: "Have they found them?"

"Not that I heard."

"You think," my mother said, "they could have got to shore way out on Gull Point or some place like that?"

"No place is more than a four-hour walk," my father said. "They'd have turned up by now."

And it was later still, after dark, ten o'clock or so, that Mr. Robinson, who lived next door, stopped by the porch on his way home. "Found one," he said wearily. "The Mitchell boy."

"Oh," my mother said, "oh, oh."

"Where?" my father asked.

"Just off the shoal,[11] they said, curled up in the eel grass."

"My God," my mother said softly.

Mr. Robinson moved off without so much as a good-by. And after a while my sister and I went to bed.

But not to sleep. We played cards for an hour or so, until we couldn't stand that any more. Then we did a couple of crossword puzzles together. Finally we just sat in our

---

10. **the chop tearing the keel out:** The choppy waves tearing out the beam supporting the boat frame.

11. **shoal** (shōl) *n.*: Sand bar.

beds, in the chilly night, and listened. There were the usual sounds from outside the open windows, sounds of the land and the water. Deer moving about in the brush on their way to eat the wild watercress and wild lettuce that grew around the spring. The deep pumping sounds of an owl's wings in the air. Little splashes from the bay—the fishes and the muskrats and the otters.

"I didn't know there'd be so many things moving at night," my sister said.

"You just weren't ever awake."

"What do you reckon it's like," she said, "being on the bottom in the eel grass?"

"Shut up," I told her.

"Well," she said, "I just asked. Because I was wondering."

"Don't."

Her talking had started a funny shaking quivering feeling from my navel right straight back to my backbone. The tips of my fingers hurt too, the way they always did.

"I thought the dogs would howl," she said.

"They can't smell anything from the water," I told her. "Now quit."

She fell asleep then and maybe I did too, because the night seemed awful short. Or maybe the summer dawns really come that quick. Not dawn, no. The quiet deep dark that means dawn is just about to come. The birds started whistling and the gulls started shrieking. I got up and looked out at the dripping beach plum bushes and the twisted, salt-burned jack pines, then I slipped out the window. I'd done it before. You lifted the screen, and lowered yourself down. It wasn't anything of a drop—all you had to watch was the patch of poison ivy. I circled around the house and took the old deer trail down to the bay. It was chilly, and I began to wish I had brought my robe or a coat. With just cotton pajamas my teeth would begin chattering very soon.

I don't know what I expected to see. And

---

*The Land and the Water* 125

**Student Activity 1.** Find the four sentence fragments in the example paragraph. Explain why you think each is effective in this passage.

**Student Activity 2.** Write your own paragraph in which you describe a similar situation: You and a sister or brother or friend cannot for some reason fall asleep right away. Model your paragraph after the example—and this time you get to use sentence fragments, provided that you use them effectively.

**Electronic Handbook** You might want students to review sentence fragments before completing the Grammar in Action activities. If students have access to the Language Master 6000, have them enter the access word *fragment* and press the GRAMMAR key to get information on sentence fragments.

**Reader's Response** Have you ever had an experience similar to the narrator's in which you were "spooked" by something that probably wasn't real? Explain the circumstances of your experience and describe your reaction at the time. If you have not had such an experience, what do you think caused the narrator's fear at the end of the story?

**Thematic Response** Ask students to discuss how this story reveals the relationship between people and the world around them. To what extent do elements of nature determine what happens to the characters?

**Alternative Assessment** You may vary the Thinking and Writing assignment as follows: Have your students reread the ending of the story on page 126. Then, writing in the persona of the narrator, re-create her thoughts and feelings as she reacts to the drowning of the Mitchell boy by imagining what it would be like to be dead and as she runs away from her fear of the water, barely escaping the "something that had reached out for me and missed."

I didn't see anything at all. Just some morning fog in the hollows and around the spring. And the dock, with my father's boat bobbing in the run of the tide.

The day was getting close now. The sky overhead turned a sort of luminous dark blue. As it did, the water darkened to a lead-colored gray. It looked heavy and oily and impenetrable. I tried to imagine what would be under it. I always thought I knew. There would be horsehoe crabs and hermit crabs and blue crabs, and scallops squirting their way along, and there'd be all the different kinds of fish, and the eels. I kept telling myself that that was all.

But this time I couldn't seem to keep my thoughts straight. I kept wondering what it must be like to be dead and cold and down in the sand and mud with the eel grass brushing you and the crabs bumping you and the fish—I had felt their little sucking mouths sometimes when I swam.

The water was thick and heavy and the color of a mirror in a dark room. Minnows broke the surface right under the wharf. I jumped. I couldn't help it.

10 And I got to thinking that something might come out of the water. It didn't have a name or a shape. But it was there.

I stood where I was for a while, trying to fight down the idea. When I found I couldn't do that, I decided to walk slowly back to the house. At least I thought I was going to walk, but the way the boards of the wharf shook under my feet I know that I must have been running. On the path up to the house my bare feet hit some of the sharp cut-off stubs of the rosa rugosa bushes, but I didn't stop. I went crashing into the kitchen because that was the closest door.

The room was thick with the odor of frying bacon, the softness of steam: my mother had gotten up early. She turned around when I came in, not seeming surprised—as if it was the most usual thing in the world for me to be wandering around before daylight in my pajamas.

"Go take those things off, honey," she said. "You're drenched."

"Yes ma'am," I told her.

11 I stripped off the clothes and saw that they really were soaking. I knew it was just the dew and the fog. But I couldn't help thinking it was something else. Something that had reached for me, and missed. Something that was wet, that had come from the water, something that had splashed me as it went past.

---

## RESPONDING TO THE SELECTION

### Your Response

1. In what ways does the mood of the story change as the weather changes? Explain your answer.

### Recalling

2. What are the two girls doing at the beginning of the story?
3. Why do the girls' father and brother go out in the boat?

4. Why do they return when they do?
5. What happens to the three lost people?

### Interpreting

6. How does the girl react to the boy's death? Why does she slip out of her house just before dawn?
7. What comparison is the author suggesting when the girl's clothing gets wet at the end of the story? What is the "something else" the girl feels has reached for her and missed?
8. What does the girl learn about life?

---

## Closure and Extension

### ANSWERS TO RESPONDING TO THE SELECTION

#### Your Response

1. Encourage students to support their ideas with specific details from the story that illustrate the changes.

#### Recalling

2. They were scraping and painting their little dinghy.

3. They went out searching for three people in a sailboat.
4. They returned because it started to thunder, the wind increased, and the fog got thicker.
5. They were killed in the storm.

#### Interpreting

6. She is very upset with the news and can't sleep. She leaves her house to go down to the dock in search of something she cannot define.
7. The author suggests that the

something that reached for her was her own death. She has become aware of her own mortality.
8. She learns to question her own mortality. She has also learned that although the surface of nature can look calm and peaceful, it can change all too quickly, without much warning and without reason.
9. The land in the title might refer to the people living on it and life in general. The water might represent death. The title stands for life and death.

9. What do you think the land represents to the girl? What do you think the water represents? Why is this story called "The Land and the Water"?

### Applying

10. The author Joseph Conrad wrote, ". . . for all the celebration it has been the object of . . . , the sea has never been friendly to man." Explain the meaning of these words. How do they relate to this story?

## ANALYZING LITERATURE

### Understanding Setting

Setting is the time and place of a story. Sometimes the setting is so important it affects what the characters do and what they feel. In "The Land and the Water," for example, the ocean almost becomes a character in the story.

1. At what time of year does "The Land and the Water" take place? How do you know this?
2. Describe the weather during the course of this story.
3. In what way does the setting affect what the characters do and what they feel?
4. In what way can the setting be thought of as almost a character in this story?

## CRITICAL THINKING AND READING

### Making Inferences About Setting

An **inference** is a judgment or conclusion based on evidence. Not all information about the setting of a story is stated directly by the author. You must also make inferences about the setting from the clues given by the author just as you do about the other elements of a story.

1. What evidence helped you make the inference that this is not the family's first summer here?

2. What clues indicate that the land and sea are unaffected by what has happened?

## THINKING AND WRITING

### Describing a Setting

Choose one of the pieces of art used to illustrate "The Land and the Water." List descriptive details about it. Include details about the way the picture makes you feel—or your mood. Use your list to write a description of the art. Use vivid, specific words so that a friend who has not seen the picture will be able to envision it. When you are finished, read over your paper to be sure your friend will be able to visualize the illustration you described.

## LEARNING OPTIONS

1. **Art.** Suppose this story were being distributed as a small book. Design a cover for this book. Review the story, the accompanying fine art, and other book covers for ideas. You may wish to illustrate a key scene on your cover or just generally convey an idea from the story, such as the power of the ocean. Include a brief summary of the story on the inside flap of the jacket and information about the author on the other. For the back of your book jacket, pretend that you are a critic and write a sentence or two praising the story.
2. **Writing.** Imagine that you are a reporter from a local newspaper covering the events in the narrator's hometown in Louisiana. Write a news story about the storm and the sailing accident. Use the information provided in "The Land and the Water," adding facts and descriptive details of your own to make your news article as thorough and informative as possible. Include quotes (actual or invented) from characters in the story to give your news article an authentic feeling.

*The Land and the Water* 127

---

### Applying

10. The sea is unpredictable and has caused many accidents and deaths. In this story it caused the deaths of three young people.

### ANSWERS TO ANALYZING LITERATURE

1. It takes place during the summer. The author describes the day as "clear and hot with a tiny breeze."

Also there were many sailboats out in the bay.
2. The story starts out on a beautiful, clear day. It suddenly becomes very foggy, with a falling barometer and shifting wind. It begins to thunder and the fog thickens. The wind starts blowing at gale force. The next day is "bright and clear and a lot cooler."
3. When the weather gets stormy, the story becomes grim. The characters worry about the people out at

sea, and the girl contemplates "what it must be like to be dead."
4. The setting is almost a character because it affects everyone's thoughts and actions. People react to the storm as they might to another character in the story.

### ANSWERS TO CRITICAL THINKING AND READING

1. The family knew the area well and reacted quickly when told of the three young people lost at sea.

2. The sea went back to normal height and the storm subsided.

**Challenge** The narrator in "The Land and the Water" is deeply moved when she learns that Stan Mitchell has drowned. Considering her feelings about the ocean at the end of the story, as well as what she has learned about life, ask students what they think she would have to say to the dead boy's parents.

### THINKING AND WRITING

**Software** If your students are working on computers, you may wish to have them use the *Lists* feature of **Writer's Helper** to help them generate details for their description.

**Writing Transparency** A graphic organizer may help your students with their listing of descriptive details. Use the Sensory Language Chart in **Transparencies for Writing**.

**Writing Across the Curriculum** Artists have long found the ocean an interesting and challenging subject to paint. Have students look through art books to find paintings by artists who specialize in seascapes. Students might specifically look for works by Winslow Homer or J.M.W. Turner. Have students choose one painting that especially appeals to them and write what precisely they like about it—its mood, its colors, or the ideas it suggests about life. You might want to inform the art department of this writing assignment. Art teachers might provide guidance for students.

### LEARNING OPTIONS

Option 1 will appeal to artistic students. Display their book covers for all students to enjoy.

Option 2 will appeal to students who are verbally skilled. To help less advanced students, develop a chronological list of important events with the class.

# Preparation

**More About the Author** Olive Senior grew up in rural villages on the Caribbean island of Jamaica and attended high school in the town of Montego Bay. Although Senior has traveled to Canada and the United Kingdom, all her stories are set in Jamaica. What influence do you think Senior's background has had on her stories?

**Literary Focus** Setting can be a major element in a story or it can be relatively insignificant. Ask students to consider what facts determine the importance of setting in a story: Then have students discuss the role that descriptive details play in making a setting come alive for the reader, especially when the setting is vital to the story's plot.

**Prereading Focus** How do you define a friend? Do all your friends have the same qualities? What things do they have in common? How are they different?

**Electronic Handbook** You may suggest that your students use the Language Master 6000 to listen to the pronunciation of the vocabulary words.

## Olive Senior

(1941–    ) grew up on the island of Jamaica in the West Indies. After graduating from high school, Senior traveled to Ottawa, Canada, where she earned a degree in journalism at Carleton University. She then returned to Jamaica and became a successful journalist. In addition to her journalistic work, she has published a reference book about Jamaica, a book on Caribbean women, a volume of poetry, and two collections of short stories. "Tears of the Sea" comes from the second of these collections, *Arrival of the Snake-Woman and Other Stories*.

# GUIDE FOR READING

## Tears of the Sea

### Descriptive Details

A writer can make a story come alive by using vivid details to describe the setting, a character's appearance, or the actions of the characters in the story. **Descriptive details** are words specifically chosen to appeal to your senses, allowing you to experience as fully as possible what the writer is relating. Notice Olive Senior's masterful use of descriptive details in the following excerpt from "Tears of the Sea": ". . . this little shell was new and inviting, its deep interior shading to a salmon color luster with a touch of mother-of-pearl, its outside ranging from the most delicate pink to gleaming white."

### Focus

"Tears of the Sea" is about a girl who uses her imagination to combat her loneliness. If you could invent the perfect friend, what qualities would he or she have? With your classmates, brainstorm to list the qualities you would find in a friend of your own invention. Write these qualities on a diagram similar to the one below. Then read "Tears of the Sea" to see what kind of friend the main character imagines for herself.

### Vocabulary

Knowing the following words will help you as you read "Tears of the Sea."

**surge** (sʉrj) *v.*: Rise and fall (p. 129)

**amends** (ə mendz′) *n.*: Something given or done to make up for injury or loss that one has caused (p. 133)

**crestfallen** (krest′ fôl′ ən) *adj.*: Saddened or humbled (p. 133)

**conspired** (kən spīrd′) *v.*: Combined or worked together for a purpose (p. 133)

**concoction** (kən käk′ shən) *n.*: A preparation made up of a combination of ingredients (p. 133)

**repertoire** (rep′ ər twär′) *n.*: The stock of songs that a singer knows and is ready to perform (p. 134)

**tremulous** (trem′ yo͞o ləs) *adj.*: Trembling; quivering (p. 134)

128   Short Stories

## Objectives

1 To understand descriptive details
2 To analyze the effect of setting on plot
3 To write using descriptive details
4 To express individual interests and abilities through optional activities

## Support Material

**Teaching Portfolio**
Teacher Backup, p. 189
Grammar in Action Worksheet, *Punctuating Items in a Series*, p. 192
Usage and Mechanics Worksheet, p. 194
Vocabulary Check, p. 195
Analyzing Literature Worksheet, *Understanding Descriptive Details*, p. 196

Critical Thinking and Reading Worksheet, *Analyzing the Effect of Setting on Plot*, p. 197
Selection Test, p. 198

**Prentice Hall Literature Writing Studio**

# Tears of the Sea

## Olive Senior

She never knew why the load of sand with the shells had been brought there in the first place, all she could remember was the excitement of its arrival: the truck huffing over the hill and belching smoke, the rush to open the gate, the backing up and to-and-froing, the revving of the engine, everyone gathered round for the moment when the back of the truck was finally in line with the top barbecue,[1] the gate opened and the gleaming load of sand was shoveled out. Even before the sand stopped falling from the truck she found herself in it and everyone laughed; she was laughing herself, jumping up and down in the sand, fully dressed, believing that it had been brought all the way from the seashore especially for her.

Usually the barbecues had no space for anything as frivolous as sand. The barbecues were constantly in use for drying things—pimento[2] and corn, cocoa and coffee and ginger. But now perhaps everything was out of season for the barbecues were empty except for the one truckload of sand. And this sand was white and gleaming and different from the black river sand which was all she was used to, for she had never been to the seashore.

But she had often seen the sea as the car rounded a bend in the hill which overlooked the town, for a moment glimpsed from afar as part of a world split in three—the sky, the land, and the sea. The sea was always changeable, always surprising: sometimes indigo,[3] sometimes pale green, sometimes emerald, sometimes indistinguishable from the sky itself when it was gray and threatening. And where the sea hit the shore there was a constant band of gleaming white which, Grandma said, were beaches. The sea in her imagination was something that was constantly alive, constantly changing and, though she could hear no sounds from afar, constantly roaring. But the sea she had never seen up close for once they got off the hill and into the town which was hot and sticky and crowded and noisy, they could no longer see anything but the streets, the houses, could no longer imagine even that something as remarkable as the sea was a living, breathing thing so close to them just beyond the tops of the houses. More than anything else she yearned to see the sea real close, to walk on the beach, to watch the breakers surge. But Grandma had instantly dismissed her wish to go to the seaside as something impossible. "Do you imagine we are tourists?" she said, and though she didn't explain what those were, they were not, she implied, good solid people like themselves. But that didn't stifle her yearning,

---

1. **barbecue** (bär′ bə kyoo′) *n.*: Raised framework for broiling foods and meats.
2. **pimento** (pə men′ tō) *n.*: A sweet variety of pepper, or its red, bell-shaped fruit, used as a relish.

---

3. **indigo** (in′ di gō′) *n.*: A deep violet blue.

*Tears of the Sea* 129

**Presentation**

**Motivation/Prior Knowledge** Discuss why we all need friends. What could happen to someone who loses the only friend he or she has?

**Master Teacher Note** Tell students that the story they are about to read is rich in sensory details. As they read, have students list details that refer to the five senses.

**Purpose-Setting Question** The main character of this story is never named. How does this fact contribute to your understanding of the story?

1 **Discussion** Why do you think the main character is so excited by this event?

2 **Critical Thinking and Reading** What do these details tell you about the setting of the story?

3 **Clarification** Jamaica, the third-largest island in the Caribbean, has a ridge of mountains that extends across the island from east to west. The northern coast, with its beautiful beaches, is the center of the island's tourist industry.

4 **Literary Focus: Descriptive Details** What impression of the sea do you get from the details in this passage?

5 **Reading Strategy** What does Grandma think of tourists? Do you agree with her? Why or why not?

**Thematic Focus** Ask students to think about a place that is special to them. Have them imagine how they would feel if this place were very close to their home, but they could never visit it.

**Making Connections** Shirley Ann Grau's "The Land and the Water," on page 119, is another story in which the sea is an important element of the setting. Have students compare the ways in which the setting affects the plot in these two very different stories.

## Humanities Note

Fine art, *Splash, Splash, Splash,* by Raymond Lark. Lark (born in 1939) began drawing as a young child, and by the age of nine was formally enrolled in the Philadelphia Museum's School of Art. He later attended Temple University and worked in several administrative positions before devoting himself to painting.

Lark's seascape *Splash, Splash, Splash* reveals a celebratory enjoyment of the beauty of the sea. Though the surf is crashing against the rocks, this image of the sea is not threatening. These waves splash playfully, sparkling in the sunlight.

Lark's personal and artistic achievements are catalogued in more than 700 periodicals, directories, and history books. In 1966 Lark became the youngest and only African American artist whose works were included in the 200 Years of American Masters Bicentennial Exhibit. He received an honorary doctorate from the University of Colorado in 1985.

You might use the following questions for discussion:

1. How might Lark's seascape represent the main character's idealized vision of the sea?
2. What sensory details from the story could be used to describe the image in this painting?

**6 Reading Strategy** How is the sand personified in this sentence? What does this tell you about the girl's feelings about the sea?

**7 Discussion** What do these details suggest about the main character's loneliness?

SPLASH, SPLASH, SPLASH
*Raymond Lark*
*The Collection of Dr. Wilbur L. Lewis*

only smoldered her desire to see the sea, walk on the sands, even once, although she never voiced the desire again. And now here was sand from that sea, white and gleaming, full, she discovered almost immediately, of tiny shells.

Now she spent all her time in the sand pile on the barbecue, pushing deeper and deeper down to watch the sand grains fall, lying down and completely covering herself in the hot sand which rocked her in its cradle until she almost fell asleep. Sometimes when she was lying in the sand and was perfectly relaxed she would feel softly at first, then stronger, a breeze which she knew was coming directly from the sea and she heard in its wake the faint roar, the sound of the sea coming all the way from the coast to where she lay on a barbecue on a mountaintop.

And she played games with the shells. She lined them up on the ledge of the barbecue according to shape, to color, then in order of size. She became a general and they her army, a schoolteacher and they her pupils, a mother and they her numerous children. Each day she found more and more shells as if they were as endless as the sand grains, bits and pieces of shell, of coral and seafans.[4] And one day she found *the* shell. It

---

4. **coral and seafans** *n.*: Structures found in the sea made from the hard, stony skeletons of marine-life.

130   *Short Stories*

## Grammar in Action

Words, phrases, or clauses in a series can be punctuated in a number of ways. In this sentence notice how Olive Senior punctuates phrases in a series with commas:

"More than anything else she yearned to see the sea real close, to walk on the beach, to watch the breakers surge."

Sometimes a series of items is separated by conjunctions, as in this series of adjectives:

". . . this sand was white and gleaming and different from the black river sand. . . ."

A writer may occasionally present a series of items as separate sentences:

"Don't laugh. Don't talk. Don't skylark."

The advantage of having different methods for presenting items in a series is that it allows a writer to change sentence structure for variety and emphasis.

**Student Activity 1.** Rewrite the following sentences, adding commas if necessary:

1. "The sea was . . . always surprising: sometimes indigo some-

was the only one of its kind in the sand pile, in the whole world, she thought, almost a replica of the giant conch shells[5] in the garden, but so tiny that it fitted in the palm of her hand and unlike the big conch shells that were bleached white and looked old and worn, this little shell was new and inviting, its deep interior shading to a salmon color luster with a touch of mother-of-pearl, its outside ranging from the most delicate pink to gleaming white. It was the most beautiful thing she had ever seen. She immediately knew that it was a magic shell sent specially to her as a gift from the sea, and so she was not surprised one day when she held it to her ear to hear first the faint but familiar roar of the ocean and then coming scratchily at first, like the radio, a voice from afar. "Hello," it said. "Hello. Hello." And she finally answered breathless and timid, "Hello."

But after their initial shyness the shell and she became good friends. They held long conversations on many subjects but mostly about the sea and the creatures that lived there, of seashells and seaweed, for she had an intense curiosity about the sea. "Why don't you go and see for yourself," the shell had asked her.

"Because I have nobody to take me," she replied. So the seashell told her as much as she could about the sea.

"We seashells," the seashell said, "are the tears of the sea."

"But why does the sea cry so much?" she couldn't help asking.

"Because it needs a lot of water. Otherwise it would run dry."

"Oh." The seashell seemed so wise.

"Oh yes. You see, once the sea was everything. The whole earth, everything was covered by the sea. But the earth has been fighting the sea all these years, ever since the beginning of time, pushing the sea back and back. So now, there isn't that much sea left. And you can see how crumpled the earth is. From pushing and pushing the sea."

She said nothing for the sea still seemed very vast to her.

"So the sea cries and cries all the time so it can grow and cover the whole earth once again. And we are its tears, its children."

She was both confused by this and frightened at the idea of the sea covering everything, even the barbecues on the mountaintop. So she hurriedly moved the shell from her ear so that she wouldn't have to hear any more. She always did this when the shell spoke of things that felt threatening. Or else she changed the subject to inconsequential things. Such as the bad behavior of all the little shells lined up on the barbecue and how to control them.

But more and more when she went into the house she missed the seashell terribly, and one day when she was about to leave the barbecue she finally screwed up her courage and asked her if she could take her home.

"Oh no no no," the shell cried in horror. "I do not wish to be separated from the other shells. For then I would be as lonely as you are. With nobody to talk to and nobody to play with."

She quickly moved the shell from her ear so she wouldn't have to hear any more. For although what the shell said was true, she thought it was a shameful thing and certainly didn't want anyone to know. The shell could be so cruel though for another time she said, "*My* mother is the sea, *my* father is the sky. Where are *your* mother and father?" That time she got so angry with the shell that she flung it into the sand and stomped off, vowing never to return again to talk to a creature so rude.

---

5. **conch** (käŋk) **shells:** The large, spiral shells of marine animals.

*Tears of the Sea* 131

---

8 **Enrichment** There are conchs, such as the West Indian Fighting Conch, that are only 2 inches long.

9 **Literary Focus: Descriptive Details** How do these details help you to visualize the shell?

10 **Discussion** What could the seashell's explanation of the struggle between the sea and the land be saying about the main character?

11 **Discussion** How does the seashell know that the girl is lonely?

12 **Discussion** What does the seashell's cruel remark and the girl's response to it tell you about the girl's home life?

---

times pale green sometimes emerald sometimes indistinguishable from the sky itself. . . ."

2. ". . . the town . . . was hot and sticky and crowded and noisy. . . ."

3. "She lined them up on the ledge of the barbecue according to shape to color then in order of size."

**Student Activity 2.** Write a paragraph describing a memorable place. You may want to model your paragraph on the third paragraph of "Tears of the Sea." Be sure to include items in a series and punctuate them correctly.

**Electronic Handbook** You may want students to review commas and conjunctions before completing the Grammar in Action activities. If students have access to the Language Master 6000, have them enter the comma symbol and the access word *conjunction* and press the GRAMMAR key.

So she tried to stay away but it was very hard for what the shell said was true: she really was very lonely and had no one to play with. Except for the shells. So she went back and hung her head and picked up the shell and apologized.

"Please forgive me," she said as her grandmother had taught her to say, "I am most dreadfully sorry."

After a pause the shell said, "Oh that's all right. I am sorry too. It is excessively ill mannered to introduce into polite conversation subjects that are painful."

But after that they found that they were still embarrassed and could find nothing to say to each other and the shell cleared her throat several times and each was thinking hard of something nice to say until the shell,

**ILLUMINATIONS, 1987**
*Mira Hocking*
*Courtesy of the Artist*

wanting to make amends burst out with, "You know what? *I* shall take you to the sea."

"You?"

"Of course. I came here from the sea didn't I? So I can find my way back."

And she said, "Of course. What better person to go to sea with than a seashell. You really would take me?" she breathed, not quite believing.

"Oh yes. I never fail to do anything that I promise to do," the shell said huffily. "We shall go on Sunday. Sunday is the best day for that is when the beach is full of children. There will be lots of people for you to play with. Come on Sunday morning very early and we will set out for the sea."

The sea! She could hardly believe it. She was going to the sea.

I *shall* take you to the sea, she sang as she ran home.

I *will* take you to the sea.

I *can* take you to the sea.

When she got home she felt so excited that she had to tell someone. So that evening she whispered to Cherry who was helping to get her ready for bed:

"Cherry, guess what?"

"What?"

"Can you keep a secret?"

"Keep it to me 'eart. Don't laugh. Don't talk. Don't skylark,"[6] Cherry laughed. "What?"

"Tomorrow-I-am-going-to-the-sea," she whispered.

"Liard!"[7] said Cherry who was very direct and knew everything that went on in the house and knew that nobody was going to the sea tomorrow or any other day. "Yu love mek-up story too much. Who tekking you to sea?"

---

**6. skylark** (skī′ lärk) *v*.: Play in a noisy, lively way.
**7. Liard** (lī′ ərd) *n*.: Dialect term for "liar."

"A friend," she whispered, already crestfallen and sorry that she had shared her secret with Cherry for whenever she tried to share her secrets the same thing happened.

"A friend?" Cherry said scornfully. "Which friend? You don't have no friend."

She wanted to say, well you are my friend. Sometimes. Instead she tossed her head and stuck out her mouth and cut her eyes at Cherry and got into bed without speaking to her again. She would show her! But her heart began to beat so fast that she could hardly sleep and she tossed and turned all night in feverish dreams with a roaring in her ears as loud as an angry sea.

In the morning she woke up feeling wracked with pain and really ill and instead of getting better in the days that followed she got worse and worse until the doctor was sent for. And among other things she heard the doctor say that she needed plenty of bed rest and absolutely no excitement, it was bad for her heart, for she had had rheumatic fever.[8] And so for weeks on end she stayed in bed, first in a haze of sleep and medicines. Then as she got better it was as if the entire household conspired to be nice to her, to coddle and entertain her.

Grandma moved her sewing machine into her room so she could talk to her as she sewed. Maud was in and out of the room all day with some new concoction from the kitchen and unbent enough to tell her Anansi stories.[9] Grandpa taught her to play draughts[10] and checkers in the time before supper. Even Marse George the penman[11]

---

**8. rheumatic** (rōō mat′ ik) **fever** *n*.: A disease in young people that affects the joints and the heart.
**9. Anansi** (ə năn′ sē) **stories:** Folk tales of African origin that tell how a spider, Anansi, fools bigger and stronger animals.
**10. draughts** (drafts) *n*.: British version of checkers.
**11. penman** *n*.: A stockyard worker who drives hogs to and from weighing pens.

*Tears of the Sea* 133

---

**13 Enrichment** Although the official language of Jamaica is English—most Jamaicans speak creole English—a regional dialect that is different from the English spoken by Americans or the British.

**14 Discussion** How is the main character repeatedly disappointed by the people she tries to befriend?

**15 Reading Strategy** Predict what the main character's feverish dreams might foreshadow.

**16 Discussion** Who are Cherry, Maud, and Marse George? Why do you think the author is not more explicit about their relationships to the main character?

---

**Multicultural Focus** Point out to students that many cultures have their own myths and stories about the sea. In much of this literature, the sea is characterized as harsh, mysterious, and powerful. In the mythology of the Ancient Greeks, the god Poseidon was called upon to rule the tempestuous sea. In other societies the sea is commonly seen as either a giver or taker of life. It provides food and livelihood, but it also presents the possibility of death by drowning or shipwreck.

Ask students to choose a country that has a coastline and research sea stories from that country. How is the sea portrayed in these stories? Is it warm and welcoming or harsh and mysterious? Have students give reports on their stories to their class.

**17 Discussion** Why doesn't the main character think about the shell while she is ill?

**18 Reading Strategy** On what other occasion did the girl sing this song? Summarize what happened between the first time she sang the song and now.

**19 Discussion** Why does the author refer to the pimentos as a "sea" of berries?

**20 Discussion** What do you think the "great wave" represents? Why?

**Reader's Response** Was the seashell a good friend to the girl? Explain your response.

**Thematic Response** The main character's family seemed to be content staying near home. What made the main character different? Why did she so desperately want to visit the sea?

## Closure and Extension

### ANSWERS TO RESPONDING TO THE SELECTION
#### Your Response
1. Encourage students to discuss the reasons for their answers.

### Recalling

2. She is too young to go by herself, and no one in her family will take her.
3. She is lonely because she does not have any friends and her family does not seem to have much time for her.
4. During her illness her family is very attentive: They keep her company, play games with her, cook special treats for her, sing to her, and teach her riddles and rhymes.

134

---

who was very shy would sometimes come in the evenings and sit in the doorway of her bedroom, singing hymns softly. Best of all she had Cherry around her night and day, Cherry to teach her riddles and rhymes, fill her head with songs and nonsense verses of which she had an endless repertoire:

> Wapsie kaisie cum pindar shell
> Wapsie kaisie cum pindar shell.

**17** The shell! She hadn't thought of the seashells for a long long time, first because she had been too ill, then because she had been so engrossed in the life of the household with everyone trying to please, trying to make her well again. But now she started thinking of the shells again, for as she got back to normal so the household too seemed to resume its normal course in which nobody had much time for her. Grandma wheeled her sewing machine back into her own room saying now she was out of bed she did not need her any more. Maud ceased to bring her delicacies and had no more time for Anansi stories. Cherry had found or been given back all her household chores and had little time for what she now called foolishness and Grandpa found it less and less convenient to play draughts and Chinese checkers. It was as if time had speeded up for a while but was slowing back down again to a pace of such boredom and emptiness the days actually seemed to falter.

She became acutely conscious again of her loneliness. She began to spend more and more of her time thinking of the shells, yearning for the day when she would finally be well enough to be left to wander off on her own, to walk over to the barbecues where the shells would all be anxiously waiting to hear what had happened to her. And her friend would tell her all the news and they would plan another trip to the sea. She would inquire if the little shells had been behaving and whether the sea was rough or smooth today (for the seashell said that all who came from the sea, no matter where they ended up, whether whole or in little fragments, continued to carry a part of the sea with them forever and ever). And she felt happy knowing that the shells were there, waiting.

Finally one day the doctor, Grandma, everyone, seemed to agree that she was completely well (but no excitement, mind, the doctor kept telling Grandma and she wondered each time exactly what he meant). So she headed for the barbecues and sang the seasong which popped into her head and as she neared them, she could almost hear the seashells, tremulous, waiting to answer her in chorus: **18**

> I *shall* take you to the sea
> I *will* take you to the sea
> I *can* take you to the sea

But as she got within sight of the barbecues she saw in a blinding flash that the entire barbecue, all the barbecues were covered totally with pimento berries, a sea of them, **19** and that nowhere in a corner of the top barbecue or anywhere else was there a truckload of gleaming sand or even the slightest hint that it had ever been there, until falling on her hands and knees and searching in the grass she found beneath the blades traces of sand and, finally, a glint of mother-of-pearl, a tiny fragment of a shell and nothing else. Bewildered, her heart beating so hard she could hardly breathe, she held it to her ear just as a great wave came tumbling over the mountains from the sea. **20**

134    Short Stories

---

### Interpreting
5. Suggested Response: The main character wants to visit the sea because she wants to witness its beauty and its excitement up close. She thinks she will find something there that will make her feel happy and less lonely.
6. Suggested Response: The shell is important because it is beautiful, because it comes from the sea, and because it befriends her in her loneliness.
7. Suggested Response: "Tears of the Sea" refers to several aspects of the story: the seashells; the sea itself, crying because it needs water; and the tears of loneliness shed by the main character.
8. Answers will differ. Because the conclusion lends itself to several interpretations, this is an excellent opportunity for a discussion. Some students may say that the wave represents the main character's own tears of grief at losing her friend. Others may say that the wave represents the shell's (or the sea's) sympathetic response to the girl's grief.

### Applying
9. Answers will differ. Encourage students to give examples to support their answers.

### ANSWERS TO ANALYZING LITERATURE
1. Suggested Response: The sea is described as changeable and surprising. Its colors vary from indigo to pale green, to emerald, and to gray. The main character sees it in her imagination as something alive and roaring. The town, on the other

# RESPONDING TO THE SELECTION

## Your Response

1. Would you want to be friends with the main character of this story? Why or why not?

## Recalling

2. Why hasn't the main character visited the sea before in her life?
3. Why is the main character lonely?
4. How does the main character's family treat her when she is ill with rheumatic fever?

## Interpreting

5. Why does the main character want so badly to visit the sea? What does she think she will find there?
6. Why is the shell she finds important to the main character?
7. What is the significance of the story's title?
8. What do you think is happening in the last sentence of the story? Explain.

## Applying

9. The main character has special needs due to her exceptionally sensitive nature. Do you think such people should receive extra attention to meet their special needs? Explain.

# ANALYZING LITERATURE

## Understanding Descriptive Details

**Descriptive details** create a picture of an event, a character, or a place and often reveal clues to main ideas in the story. Notice the details that Olive Senior uses in this passage: "And this sand was white and gleaming and different from the black river sand which was all she was used to, for she had never been to the seashore." The sand is described throughout the story as "white and gleaming," which reveals how the main character idealizes the seashore.

1. Review the story to find three details that describe the sea. How do these details contrast with those that describe the town? How does

this contrast reveal the main character's feelings of deprivation?
2. What details in the final scene of the story help to reveal the main character's feelings of desperation?

# CRITICAL THINKING AND READING

## Analyzing the Effect of Setting on Plot

The girl in "Tears of the Sea" lives near the sea and desires more than anything to see it, but has never seen it up close.

1. How does the fact that the sea is nearby, often glimpsed from afar, affect the main character's desire to see it? What effect does the nearness to the sea have on the plot?
2. The main character's grandmother does not indulge her granddaughter's wish to see the sea, saying, "Do you imagine we are tourists?" How does the fact that the story is set in a place that attracts tourists affect the plot?

# THINKING AND WRITING

## Using Descriptive Details

Write a letter to a friend describing a place you love. In your letter use descriptive details so that your friend will experience your favorite place as he or she reads. Before you begin writing, list the details that make this place special. Use details that appeal to as many senses as possible.

# LEARNING OPTIONS

1. **Cross-curricular Connection.** With a partner find out more information about seashells. Select five shells and draw them on a poster board. Beneath each drawing write their names and two important characteristics of the shells.
2. **Writing.** Change the story ending so that the main character does go to the sea. How does she respond to finally seeing the sea up close? What happens to her feelings of loneliness?

*Tears of the Sea* 135

## THINKING AND WRITING

  **Writing Transparency**
Graphic Organizers are good tools for making clear what may at first seem confusing. Before students write their letters, have them use the *Sensory Language Chart* in **Transparencies for Writing.**

**Software** If students are working on computers, have them use the **Writer's Helper** activity *Brainstorm* to help them find ideas for their letters.

**Publishing Student Writing** Exchange letters with a partner. Read each other's letters and make specific suggestions for adding or improving descriptive details.

**Alternative Assessment** You may vary the Thinking and Writing Assignment as follows: Ask students to consider the title of Olive Senior's story "Tears of the Sea." What do they think the title reveals about the main character and her feelings of deprivation and desperation? Have students discuss their thoughts in a short composition in which they explain the meaning of the title by referring to specific details of the story.

**Writing Across the Curriculum** For a science project, students could research marine snails and bivalves of the Caribbean and report on their frequency and distribution.

## LEARNING OPTIONS

1. The cross-curricular option will appeal to visual learners. Extend this activity by locating seashells, bringing them to class, and allowing the students to identify them using reference books.
2. Extend this writing option for auditory learners by having them collect tapes of Jamaican music and playing them for their class.

hand, is described as hot, sticky, crowded, and noisy. The disparity between the descriptions of these two places—one an alluring place where the girl is never taken and the other a harsh, unappealing place where the girl is often taken —reveals the acute deprivation that she feels.
2. Suggested Response: The following details help to reveal the girl's desperation: the "blinding flash" she experiences when she sees that the sand is gone, her search-

ing for traces of shells on her hands and knees, her picking out a tiny shell fragment from beneath blades of grass, the beating of her heart, her holding the tiny shell fragment to her ear. (Some students may cite the great wave tumbling over the mountain as well.)

### ANSWERS TO CRITICAL THINKING AND READING

1. Suggested Response: The main character's proximity to the sea

and the glimpses she catches of it feed her passionate desire to see it. The plot of this story is dependent on the setting: If the girl did not live near the sea, she probably would not have a burning desire to see it and would not respond to the sand and the shell as she does.
2. The grandmother's attitude toward tourists, combined with a setting that attracts these "undesirable" people, guarantees that the family will never take the girl to the beach.

**More About the Author** Arthur C. Clarke is also active in promoting space travel and communication and in underwater exploration and photography. For a year he had the only television set in Sri Lanka and a special dish antenna, a loan from India and the United States as a reward for originating the concept of satellite communication. Have your students discuss the advantages and disadvantages for a writer, such as Clarke, who lives apart from the Western world. What recent problems in Sri Lanka may have upset the author's routine?

**Literary Focus** Point out that most science fiction is set in the future, but that some is also set in the present or past. Explain that some fiction, such as *1984*, is set so little ahead of publication that that time is already past. What might be the purpose of such settings?

**Prereading Focus** Have students volunteer details of different things they planned to see and do on a tourist trip they have taken. Write them on the chalkboard. Let students refer to them as they prepare their group chart on a tourist trip to a Martian colony.

**Vocabulary** Have your less advanced students read the words aloud so that you can be sure they can pronounce them.

**Spelling Tip** Point out the exceptional spelling, *cean,* of the ending sound in *crustacean.*

**Electronic Handbook** Students may find many of the vocabulary words difficult to pronounce. If you have access to the Language Master 6000, suggest that students listen to their pronunciations.

136

# GUIDE FOR READING

## Arthur C. Clarke

(1917–    ) grew up in England. Now he lives in Sri Lanka, a small island country off the coast of India. Because he lives in a remote area, Clarke keeps up with world events by subscribing to twenty scientific journals, by listening to the news on his shortwave radio, and by using a modem with his computer. Author of countless science-fiction novels and short stories, Clarke also wrote the screenplay of *2001: A Space Odyssey.* "Crime on Mars" is not only a science-fiction story but also a mystery story.

## Crime on Mars

### Time as an Element of Setting

Setting includes the time as well as the location of a story. In some stories the time period is important, and it is therefore reflected in the characters' dress, customs, actions, and beliefs. The time of a story can be any time in the past, present, or future. Science-fiction stories, like "Crime on Mars," are usually set in the future.

### Focus

Imagine that you are a tourist visiting a human colony on Mars. Naturally you would take lots of pictures, visit museums and historic sites, eat Martian food, and buy souvenirs to take home. With your classmates discuss what a trip to the Martian colony would be like. What would you see in the museums? What strange foods would you eat? What kinds of souvenirs would you bring home? Jot down your ideas on a group chart. Then read "Crime on Mars" to see Arthur C. Clarke's conception of a visit to a civilized Martian colony.

### Vocabulary

Knowing the following words will help you as you read "Crime on Mars."

**enigma** (ə nig′ mə) *n.*: An unexplainable matter or event (p. 138)

**sects** (sekts) *n.*: Small groups of people with the same leaders and beliefs (p. 138)

**crustaceans** (krus tā′ shənz) *n.*: Shellfish, such as lobsters, crabs, or shrimp (p. 138)

**aboriginal** (ab′ ə rij′ ə n'l) *adj.*: First; native (p. 138)

**reconnoitering** (rē′ kə nɔit′ ər iŋ) *v.*: Making an exploratory examination to get information about a place (p. 139)

**artifacts** (är′ tə fakts′) *n.*: Any objects made by human work, left behind by a civilization (p. 139)

**discreet surveillance** (dis krēt′ sər vā′ ləns): Careful, unobserved watch kept over a person, especially one who is a suspect or a prisoner (p. 142)

## Objectives

1 To understand that time is an important aspect of setting
2 To identify scientific details in a science-fiction setting
3 To write an extension of the short story
4 To express individual interests and abilities through optional activities

## Support Material

**Teaching Portfolio**
Teacher Backup, p. 201
Grammar in Action Worksheets, *Understanding Adverbs,* p. 205
Usage and Mechanics Worksheet, p. 207
Vocabulary Check, p. 208
Critical Thinking and Reading Worksheet, *Identifying Scientific Details,* p. 209

Language Worksheet, *Recognizing New Words,* p. 210
Selection Test, p. 211

**Prentice Hall Literature Writing Studio**

# Crime on Mars

## Arthur C. Clarke

"We don't have much crime on Mars," said Detective Inspector Rawlings, a little sadly. "In fact, that's the chief reason I'm going back to the Yard.[1] If I stayed here much longer, I'd get completely out of practice."

We were sitting in the main observation lounge of the Phobos Spaceport, looking out across the jagged, sun-drenched crags of the tiny moon. The ferry rocket that had brought us up from Mars had left ten minutes ago, and was now beginning the long fall back to the ocher-tinted[2] globe hanging there against the stars. In half an hour we would be boarding the liner for Earth—a world upon which most of the passengers had never set foot, but which they still called "home."

"At the same time," continued the Inspector, "now and then there's a case that makes life interesting. You're an art dealer, Mr. Maccar; I'm sure you heard about that spot of bother at Meridian City a couple of months ago."

"I don't think so," replied the plump, olive-skinned little man I'd taken for just another returning tourist. Presumably the Inspector had already checked through the passenger list; I wondered how much he knew about me, and tried to reassure myself that my conscience was—well—reasonably clear. After all, everybody took *something* out through Martian Customs—

"It's been rather well hushed up," said the Inspector, "but you can't keep these things quiet for long. Anyway, a jewel thief from Earth tried to steal Meridian Museum's greatest treasure—the Siren Goddess."

"But that's absurd!" I objected. "It's priceless, of course—but it's only a lump of sandstone. You couldn't sell it to anyone—you might just as well steal the Mona Lisa."[3]

The Inspector grinned, rather mirthlessly. *"That's* happened once," he said. "Maybe the motive was the same. There are collectors who would give a fortune for such an object, even if they could only look at it themselves. Don't you agree, Mr. Maccar?"

"That's perfectly true. In my business, you meet all sorts of crazy people."

"Well, this chappie—name's Danny Weaver—had been well paid by one of them. And if it hadn't been for a piece of fantastically bad luck, he might have brought it off."

The Spaceport P.A. system apologized for a further slight delay owing to final fuel checks, and asked a number of passengers to report to Information. While we were waiting for the announcement to finish, I

---

1. **Yard:** Scotland Yard, headquarters of the London police force.
2. **ocher** (ō′ kər)**-tinted** *adj.*: Yellow-colored.

3. **Mona Lisa:** Priceless portrait by Leonardo da Vinci (1452-1519), an Italian painter.

recalled what little I knew about the Siren Goddess. Though I'd never seen the original, like most other departing tourists I had a replica[4] in my baggage. It bore the certificate of the Mars Bureau of Antiquities, guaranteeing that "this full-scale reproduction is an exact copy of the so-called Siren Goddess, discovered in the Mare Sirenium by the Third Expedition, A.D. 2012 (A.M. 23)."

It's quite a tiny thing to have caused so much controversy. Only eight or nine inches high—you wouldn't look at it twice if you saw it in a museum on Earth. The head of a young woman, with slightly oriental features, elongated earlobes, hair curled in tight ringlets close to the scalp, lips half parted in an expression of pleasure or surprise—that's all. But it's an enigma so baffling that it's inspired a hundred religious sects, and driven quite a few archaeologists[5] round the bend. For a perfectly human head has no right whatsoever to be found on Mars, whose only intelligent inhabitants were crustaceans—"educated lobsters," as the newspapers are fond of calling them. The aboriginal Martians never came near to achieving space flight, and in any event their civilization died before men existed on Earth. No wonder the Goddess is

---

4. **replica** (rep′ li kə) *n.*: A copy of a work of art.

5. **archaeologists** (är′ kē äl′ ə jistz) *n.*: Scientists who study the life and culture of ancient peoples.

138  *Short Stories*

## Grammar in Action

**Adverbs** make sentence meaning more specific. They answer one of these questions: *Where? When? In what manner? To what extent?* Notice the adverbs (in italics) and the questions they answer in the following sentences from "Crime on Mars":

*Where?:* He stayed *there* until about midnight, just in case there were any enthusiastic researchers still in the building.

*When?:* Danny was counting on this, when he checked into the hotel in Meridian West, *late* Friday afternoon.

*In what manner?:* "Danny's plan was *beautifully* simple," continued the Inspector.

*To what extent?:* Beyond those electronic shields is the *utterly* hostile emptiness of the Martian Outback, where a man will die in seconds without protection.

In addition to making meaning precise, adverbs enable writers to expand sentences and to vary sentence patterns.

the solar system's number-one mystery; I don't suppose we'll find the answer in my lifetime—if we ever do.

"Danny's plan was beautifully simple," continued the Inspector. "You know how absolutely dead a Martian city gets on Sunday, when everything closes down and the colonists stay home to watch the TV from Earth. Danny was counting on this, when he checked into the hotel in Meridian West, late Friday afternoon. He'd have Saturday for reconnoitering the Museum, an undisturbed Sunday for the job itself, and on Monday morning he'd be just another tourist leaving town. . . .

"Early Saturday he strolled through the little park and crossed over into Meridian East, where the Museum stands. In case you don't know, the city gets its name because it's exactly on longitude one hundred and eighty degrees; there's a big stone slab in the park with the prime meridian engraved on it, so that visitors can get themselves photographed standing in two hemispheres at once. Amazing what simple things amuse some people.

"Danny spent the day going over the Museum, exactly like any other tourist determined to get his money's worth. But at closing time he didn't leave; he'd holed up in one of the galleries not open to the public, where the Museum had been arranging a Late Canal Period reconstruction but had run out of money before the job could be finished. He stayed there until about midnight, just in case there were any enthusiastic researchers still in the building. Then he emerged and got to work."

"Just a minute," I interrupted. "What about the night watchman?"

The Inspector laughed.

"My dear chap! They don't have such luxuries on Mars. There weren't even any alarms, for who would bother to steal lumps of stone? True, the Goddess was sealed up neatly in a strong glass-and-metal cabinet, just in case some souvenir hunter took a fancy to her. But even if she were stolen, there was nowhere the thief could hide, and of course all outgoing traffic would be searched as soon as the statue was missed."

That was true enough. I'd been thinking in terms of Earth, forgetting that every city on Mars is a closed little world of its own beneath the force-field that protects it from the freezing near-vacuum. Beyond those electronic shields is the utterly hostile emptiness of the Martian Outback, where a man will die in seconds without protection. That makes law enforcement very easy; no wonder there's so little crime on Mars. . . .

"Danny had a beautiful set of tools, as specialized as a watchmaker's. The main item was a microsaw no bigger than a soldering iron; it had a wafer-thin blade, driven at a million cycles a second by an ultrasonic power pack. It would go through glass or metal like butter—and left a cut only about as thick as a hair. Which was very important for Danny, since he had to leave no traces of his handiwork.

"I suppose you've guessed how he intended to operate. He was going to cut through the base of the cabinet, and substitute one of those souvenir replicas for the real Goddess. It might be a couple of years before some inquisitive expert discovered the awful truth; long before then the original would have traveled back to Earth, perfectly disguised as a copy of itself, with a genuine certificate of authenticity. Pretty neat, eh?

"It must have been a weird business, working in that darkened gallery with all those million-year-old carvings and unexplainable artifacts around him. A museum on Earth is bad enough at night, but at least it's—well—*human*. And Gallery Three,

*Crime on Mars* 139

**5 Discussion** What do you think everyone watches on television on Sundays?

**6 Discussion** What is the importance of the prime meridian? Why would visitors want a picture of themselves in two hemispheres?

**7 Enrichment** Artistic students might like to draw their conceptions of these Martian cities.

**8 Making Connections** In which other short story did the main character have a beautiful set of tools used to cut through metal? How are Danny and Jimmy Valentine from "A Retrieved Reformation" (page 61) alike? How are they different?

**Student Activity 1.** Find ten other examples of adverbs in the story.

**Student Activity 2.** Make up ten sentences in which you use adverbs. You might use as examples the model sentences given here or the other sentences on these pages in which you found adverbs.

**Electronic Handbook** You might want students to review adverbs before completing the Grammar in Action activities. If students have access to the Language Master 6000, have them enter the access word *adverb* and press the GRAMMAR key to get information on adverbs.

**9** **Reading Strategy** Have students summarize the story up to this point and tell why they think the museum opened up for the day.

which houses the Goddess, is particularly unsettling. It's full of bas-reliefs[6] showing quite incredible animals fighting each other; they look rather like giant beetles, and most paleontologists[7] flatly deny that they could ever have existed. But imaginary or not, they belonged to this world, and they didn't disturb Danny as much as the Goddess, staring at him across the ages and defying him to explain her presence here. She gave him the creeps. How do I know? He told me.

"Danny set to work on that cabinet as carefully as any diamond cutter preparing to cleave a gem. It took most of the night to slice out the trap door, and it was nearly dawn when he relaxed and put down the

---

**6. bas-reliefs** (bä′ rə lēfs′) *n.*: Sculpture in which figures are carved on a flat surface, such as a wall, so that they stand out from the background.
**7. paleontologists** (pā′ lē än täl′ ə jists) *n.*: Scientists who investigate prehistoric forms of life by studying plant and animal fossils.

saw. There was still a lot of work to do, but the hardest part was over. Putting the replica into the case, checking its appearance against the photos he'd thoughtfully brought with him, and covering up his traces might take most of Sunday but that didn't worry him in the least. He had another twenty-four hours, and would positively welcome Monday's first visitors so that he could mingle with them and make his inconspicuous exit.

"It was a perfectly horrible shock to his nervous system, therefore, when the main

**9**

**Multicultural Focus** Interest in a future life on other planets has long interested humans. Explain that people all over the world have been interested in astronomy and space travel since ancient times. For the Dogon people of West Africa, studying the stars is part of their spiritual tradition. The Indian Moghul emperor Jai Singh was so interested in astronomy that in 1728 he began building a giant observatory in Jaipur, India. In modern times much interest in astronomy has focused on space travel. The Russians were the first people to send a human into space. Today countries often work together to launch satellites and plan major unmanned voyages to the farther reaches of our solar system.

Invite students to do research about a planet, a star, black holes, or some other astronomical phenomenom that interests them. Have them present their findings to the class.

doors were noisily unbarred at eight-thirty and the museum staff—all six of them—started to open up for the day. Danny bolted for the emergency exit, leaving everything behind—tools, Goddesses, the lot. He had another big surprise when he found himself in the street; it should have been completely deserted at this time of day, with everyone at home reading the Sunday papers. But here were the citizens of Meridian East, as large as life, heading for plant or office on what was obviously a normal working day.

"By the time poor Danny got back to his hotel, we were waiting for him. We couldn't claim much credit for deducing that only a visitor from Earth—and a very recent one at that—could have overlooked Meridian City's chief claim to fame. And I presume you know what *that* is."

"Frankly, I don't," I answered. "You can't see much of Mars in six weeks, and I never went east of the Syrtis Major."

"Well, it's absurdly simple, but we shouldn't be too hard on Danny; even the locals occasionally fall into the same trap. It's something that doesn't bother us on Earth, where we've been able to dump the problem in the Pacific Ocean. But Mars, of course, is all dry land; and that means that *somebody* has to live with the International Date Line. . . .[8]

"Danny, you see, had worked from Meridian West. It was Sunday over there all right—and it was still Sunday when we picked him up back at the hotel. But over in Meridian East, half a mile away, it was only Saturday. That little trip across the park had made all the difference; I told you it was rotten luck."

---

**8. International Date Line:** Imaginary line drawn north and south that marks the beginning of different time zones. When it is Sunday on one side of the line, it is Saturday on the other.

There was a long moment of silent sympathy; then I asked, "What did he get?"

"Three years," said Inspector Rawlings.

"That doesn't seem very much."

"Mars years; that makes it almost six of ours. And a whacking fine which, by an odd coincidence, came to just the refund value of his return ticket to Earth. He isn't in jail, of course; Mars can't afford that kind of nonproductive luxury. Danny has to work for a living, under discreet surveillance. I told you that the Meridian Museum couldn't afford a night watchman. Well, it has one now. Guess who."

"All passengers prepare to board in ten minutes! Please collect your hand baggage!" ordered the loud-speakers.

As we started to move toward the air lock,[9] I couldn't help asking one more question.

"What about the people who put Danny up to it? There must have been a lot of money behind him. Did you get them?"

"Not yet; they'd covered their tracks pretty thoroughly, and I believe Danny was telling the truth when he said he couldn't give us any leads. Still, it's not my case; as I told you, I'm going back to my old job at the Yard. But a policeman always keeps his eyes open—like an art dealer, eh, Mr. Maccar? Why, you look a bit green about the gills. Have one of my space-sickness tablets."

"No, thank you," answered Mr. Maccar, "I'm quite all right."

His tone was distinctly unfriendly; the social temperature seemed to have dropped below zero in the last few minutes. I looked at Mr. Maccar, and I looked at the Inspector. And suddenly I realized that we were going to have a very interesting trip.

---

**9. air lock:** An airtight compartment between two places that have different air pressures.

## RESPONDING TO THE SELECTION

### Your Response

1. Would you like to visit a colony on Mars if it were like the one described in "Crime on Mars"? Why or why not?
2. Do you think that Clarke succeeds in making his fantastic story believable? Explain your answer.

### Recalling

3. About what crime does the Inspector tell the narrator and Mr. Maccar?
4. Why does the narrator consider such a crime absurd? What is the Inspector's explanation for the motive?
5. What goes wrong with Danny's plan? Why are the police able to find him so easily?

### Interpreting

6. Which detail at the beginning of the story indicates that the Inspector has checked through the passenger list?
7. For what two reasons does the Inspector tell this story?
8. What does the narrator mean when he says, "And suddenly I realized that we were going to have a very interesting trip"?

### Applying

9. Compare and contrast the life of the settlers on Mars as shown in this story with the life of settlers of the American frontier.

## ANALYZING LITERATURE

### Understanding Time as Part of Setting

The setting of a short story includes both its location and the time in which it takes place. Both are very important in "Crime on Mars."

1. Why is there so little crime on Mars?
2. Why is the city named Meridian City?
3. How does time foil Danny's plot?

## CRITICAL THINKING AND READING

### Identifying Scientific Details

In a science-fiction story such as "Crime on Mars," many of the details are based on scientific information. However, the author also includes imaginary characters and situations.

Are the following details based on science or imagination?

1. "The ferry rocket that had brought us up from Mars had left ten minutes ago, and was now beginning the long fall back to the ocher-tinted globe hanging there against the stars."
2. "For a perfectly human head has no right whatsoever to be found on Mars, whose only intelligent inhabitants were crustaceans— 'educated lobsters.' . . ."
3. "Beyond those electronic shields is the utterly hostile emptiness of the Martian Outback, where a man will die in seconds without protection."

## THINKING AND WRITING

### Continuing a Science-Fiction Story

Imagine that you are the person telling the story "Crime on Mars." Continue the story by writing a newspaper account of what happened between the Inspector and Mr. Maccar during their trip from Mars and after they landed on Earth. Make sure your account contains enough details to be clear and interesting.

## LEARNING OPTIONS

1. **Cross-curricular Connection.** In a reference book, look up the names of the four United States time zones and the time differences between them. Then work with a partner to make a map of the United States, showing where these zones are located.
2. **Art.** Create an illustrated map of Meridian City. Label relevant details on your map.

*Crime on Mars* 143

---

**More About the Author** In his short life, Edgar Allan Poe invented the detective story. His poetry —coolly received in this country, as was the rest of his output— inspired a school of poetry in France. He was so ignored by his generation that when, twenty-six years after his death, a stone was finally erected over his grave, the only American writer to attend the ceremony was Walt Whitman. Point out that, though Poe is an American author, most of his stories are not set in American locales. Ask why a writer of horror stories might choose to set a tale, for example, in an Italian wine cellar or on an island in a swampy pond.

**Literary Focus** Have your students recall the short story by Doyle. Which setting in "The Adventure of the Speckled Band" created the best atmosphere for terror? How would it be possible for a writer to create suspenseful terror in an old man's bedroom? In a person's mind?

**Prereading Focus** You might direct students' responses by asking them to remember details of an event that made them feel scared. Write these details on the chalkboard and have students refer to them as they complete the sensory detail chart.

**Vocabulary** Have your students use each word in a sentence orally before reading the story.

**Electronic Handbook** The vocabulary words contain many difficult vowel sounds. If your students have access to the Language Master 6000, have **less advanced** or ESL students listen to their pronunciations.

144

# GUIDE FOR READING

### Edgar Allan Poe

(1809–1849) was born in Boston. He wrote many short stories, poems, and essays before he died at the age of 40. During his life Poe endured personal tragedies, including the death of his mother, a difficult stay in a foster home, a college career shortened by debts and misconduct, the death of his wife at a young age, and years of poverty. These tragedies influenced Poe's writing so that his short stories were filled with horror. "The Tell-Tale Heart" is one of the best examples of Poe's tales of terror.

*144    Short Stories*

## The Tell-Tale Heart

### Atmosphere and Mood

The **atmosphere** or **mood** of a story is the overall emotional feeling created by the details the author uses: Sometimes you may be able to describe the atmosphere in a single word—sad, frightening, or mysterious, for example. Authors create atmosphere by their descriptions of settings, characters, and events. They choose their words carefully so that you will be affected by their writing in the way they want you to be.

### Focus

Descriptive details help to create the grim and terrifying atmosphere in "The Tell-Tale Heart." What words or descriptions would you use to create a mood or atmosphere of horror in a story? Make a sensory-detail chart modeled on the one below and fill it to create this mood. Then, as you read the story, notice Poe's details.

| Sights | Sounds | Smells | Tastes | Touch |
|--------|--------|--------|--------|-------|
|        |        |        |        |       |

### Vocabulary

Knowing the following words will help you as you read "The Tell-Tale Heart."

**acute** (ə kyoot′) *adj.*: Sensitive (p. 145)

**dissimulation** (di sim′ yə lā′ shən) *n.*: The hiding of one's feelings or purposes (p. 145)

**profound** (prō found′) *adj.*: Seeing beyond what is obvious (p. 145)

**sagacity** (sə gas′ ə tē) *n.*: High intelligence and sound judgment (p. 146)

**crevice** (krev′ is) *n.*: A narrow opening (p. 147)

**suavity** (swä′ və tē) *n.*: Graceful politeness (p. 148)

**gesticulations** (jes tik′ yoo lā′ shənz) *n.*: Energetic hand or arm gestures (p. 148)

**derision** (di rizh′ ən) *n.*: Contempt; ridicule (p. 148)

## Objectives

1 To describe the atmosphere or mood of a short story
2 To choose words that create a specific atmosphere
3 To write a scene that creates an atmosphere of horror

## Support Material

**Teaching Portfolio**
Teacher Backup, p. 213
Grammar in Action Worksheet, *Appreciating Connotations*, p. 216
Usage and Mechanics Worksheet, p. 218
Vocabulary Check, p. 219
Critical Thinking and Reading Worksheet, *Choosing Words to Create Atmosphere*, p. 220

Language Worksheet, *Choosing the Meaning that Fits the Context*, p. 221
Selection Test, p. 222

**Listening to Literature**
"The Tell-Tale Heart"

**Prentice Hall Literature Writing Studio**

# The Tell-Tale Heart

### Edgar Allan Poe

**1** True!—nervous—very, very dreadfully nervous I had been and am; but why *will* you say that I am mad? The disease had sharpened my senses—not destroyed—**2** not dulled them. Above all was the sense of hearing acute. I heard all things in the heaven and in the earth. I heard many things in hell. How, then, am I mad? Hearken![1] and observe how healthily—how calmly I can tell you the whole story.

It is impossible to say how first the idea entered my brain; but once conceived, it haunted me day and night. Object there was none. Passion there was none. I loved the old man. He had never wronged me. He had never given me insult. For his gold I had no desire. I think it was his eye! yes, it was this! One of his eyes resembled that of a vulture—a pale blue eye, with a film over it. Whenever it fell upon me, my blood ran cold; and so by degrees—very gradually—I made up my mind to take the life of the old man, and thus rid myself of the eye forever.

Now this is the point. You fancy me mad. Madmen know nothing. But you should have seen *me*. You should have seen how wisely I proceeded—with what caution—with what foresight—with what dissimulation I went to work! I was never kinder to the old man than during the whole week before I killed him. And every night, about midnight, I turned the latch of his door and opened it—oh, so gently! And then, when I had made an opening sufficient for my head, I put in a dark lantern, all closed, closed, so that no light shone out, and then I thrust in my head. Oh, you would have laughed to see how cunningly I thrust it in! I moved it slowly—very, very slowly, so that I might not disturb the old man's sleep. It took me an hour to place my whole head within the opening so far that I could see him as he lay upon his bed. Ha!—would a madman have been so wise as this? And then, when my head was well in the room, I undid the lantern cautiously—oh, so cautiously—cautiously (for the hinges creaked)—I undid it just so much that a **3** single thin ray fell upon the vulture eye. And this I did for seven long nights—every night just at midnight—but I found the eye always closed; and so it was impossible to do the work; for it was not the old man who vexed me, but his evil eye. And every morning, when the day broke, I went boldly into the chamber, and spoke courageously to him, calling him by name in a hearty tone, and inquiring how he had passed the night. So you see he would have been a very profound old man, indeed, to suspect that every night, just at twelve, I looked in upon him while he slept.

Upon the eighth night I was more than usually cautious in opening the door. A watch's minute hand moves more quickly

---

**1. Hearken** (här′ kən) *v.*: Listen.

*The Tell-Tale Heart* 145

## Presentation

**Motivation/Prior Knowledge** Discuss the idea of terror. Ask your students if they have ever been terrified or filled with horror. Discuss horror movies or stories they have read. Tell your class that Poe was a master of suspense and horror stories and that this is one of his most famous.

**Purpose-Setting Question** How might a disturbed person behave if forced to live in close contact with a man or woman whose appearance is in some way abhorrent?

**1 Discussion** What does the first sentence stress? How does it immediately suggest terror?

**2 Literary Focus** Who is telling the story? Discuss first-person point of view. Here the narrator is a character in the story. The ''I'' narrator tells us only his thoughts. He cannot enter the minds of the other characters.

**3 Discussion** What does the term ''vulture eye'' suggest? How does this add to the mood of the story? Bring out that it suggests a beast of prey, hunching over, waiting for its victim.

**Thematic Focus** The narrator in this story follows an inner voice that leads to horrifying consequences. What other choices did the narrator have after ''the idea first entered his brain''?

**Making Connections** Incidents of crime and discovery also occur in ''The Adventure of the Speckled Band,'' page 27, and ''Crime on Mars,'' page 137. Incidents of crime with unexpected outcomes occur in ''A Retrieved Reformation,'' page 61, and ''Thank You, M'am,'' page 179. You might have students compare and contrast the character' situations and motivations in these stories.

**Alternative Assessment** To promote active reading, have your students keep a reader's response journal as they read ''The Tell-Tale Heart.'' Ask them to focus their observations on the descriptive details that create the atmosphere of the story. Encourage them to respond personally to the details and suggest additional words or descriptions that could add to the story's mood of horror.

Students' observations and comments will enable you to assess their understanding and appreciation of Poe's technique.

4 **Visualization** Imagine the narrator being completely still for an hour. Have you ever kept this still? Under what circumstances? What mood or feeling is created by the narrator's behavior?

**Audiocassette** Some students have difficulty reading Poe's language. Have them listen to the reading of "The Tell-Tale Heart" in **Listening to Literature** Audiocassettes, Side 2. You might have them listen to the reading and follow along in their textbooks, or they might listen after they have read the story. Have students notice how the reader creates a mood of terror. How does the reader's voice show the narrator's state of mind?

than did mine. Never, before that night, had I *felt* the extent of my own powers—of my sagacity. I could scarcely contain my feelings of triumph. To think that there I was, opening the door, little by little, and he not even to dream of my secret deeds or thoughts. I fairly chuckled at the idea; and perhaps he heard me; for he moved on the bed suddenly, as if startled. Now you may think that I drew back—but no. His room was as black as pitch with the thick darkness (for the shutters were close fastened, through fear of robbers), and so I knew that he could not see the opening of the door, and I kept pushing it on steadily, steadily.

I had my head in, and was about to open the lantern, when my thumb slipped upon the tin fastening, and the old man sprang up in the bed, crying out—"Who's there?"

I kept quite still and said nothing. For a whole hour I did not move a muscle, and in the meantime I did not hear him lie down. He was still sitting up in the bed, listening;—just as I have done, night after night, hearkening to the deathwatches[2] in the wall.

Presently I heard a slight groan, and I knew it was the groan of mortal terror. It was not a groan of pain or of grief—oh, no!—it was the low stifled sound that arises from the bottom of the soul when overcharged with awe. I knew the sound well. Many a night, just at midnight, when all the world slept, it has welled up from my own bosom, deepening, with its dreadful echo, the terrors that distracted me. I say I knew it well. I knew what the old man felt, and pitied him, although I chuckled at heart. I knew that he had been lying

4

---

**2. deathwatches** (deth′ woch′ əz) *n.*: Wood-boring beetles that make a tapping noise in the wood they invade. They are thought to predict death.

## Grammar in Action

The **connotation** of a word is the feelings and associations it arouses. Through their choice of words, writers suggest meaning, mood, and atmosphere. Careful readers can pick up on this word connotation and can more accurately feel the writer's intended meaning. Since the purpose of writing is to convey a message or feeling to a reader, skillful writers are aware of word connotation and select words that bring the intended meaning to mind. For example, a writer describing a garden party on a summer day would probably choose bright, cheerful words such as *golden, glowing,* and *glittering* to describe the scene. On the other hand, a writer describing an eerie, deserted mansion would probably use words like *dreary, bleak,* and *ghostly.*

Edgar Allan Poe is a master at choosing words with connotations that fit his desired mood. Read the following paragraph from "The Tell-Tale Heart" and think about which words connote the evil, dark atmosphere and mood that he wants to create.

Presently I heard a slight groan, and I knew it was the groan of mortal terror. It was not a groan of pain or of grief—oh, awake ever since the first slight noise, when he had turned in the bed. His fears had been ever since growing upon him. He had been trying to fancy them causeless, but could not. He had been saying to himself—"It is nothing but the wind in the chimney—it is only a mouse crossing the floor," or "it is merely a cricket which has made a single chirp." Yes, he has been trying to comfort himself with these suppositions: but he had found all in vain. *All in vain*; because Death, in approaching him, had stalked with his black shadow before him, and enveloped the victim. And it was the mournful influence of the unperceived shadow that caused him to feel—although he neither saw nor heard—to *feel* the presence of my head within the room.

When I had waited a long time, very patiently, without hearing him lie down, I resolved to open a little—a very, very little crevice in the lantern. So I opened it—you cannot imagine how stealthily, stealthily —until, at length, a single dim ray, like the thread of the spider, shot from out the crevice and fell upon the vulture eye.

It was open—wide, wide open—and I grew furious as I gazed upon it. I saw it with perfect distinctness—all a dull blue, with a hideous veil over it that chilled the very marrow in my bones; but I could see nothing else of the old man's face or person for I had directed the ray as if by instinct, precisely upon the spot.

And now—have I not told you that what you mistake for madness is but over-acuteness of the senses?—now, I say, there came to my ears a low, dull, quick sound, such as a watch makes when enveloped in cotton. I knew *that* sound well, too. It was the beating of the old man's heart. It increased my fury, as the beating of a drum stimulates the soldier into courage.

But even yet I refrained and kept still. I scarcely breathed. I held the lantern motionless. I tried how steadily I could maintain the ray upon the eye. Meantime the hellish tattoo of the heart increased. It grew quicker and quicker, and louder and louder every instant. The old man's terror *must* have been extreme! It grew louder, I say, louder every moment!—do you mark me well? I have told you that I am nervous: so I am. And now at the dead hour of the night, amid the dreadful silence of that old house, so strange a noise as this excited me to uncontrollable terror. Yet, for some minutes longer I refrained and stood still. But the beating grew louder, louder! I thought the heart must burst. And now a new anxiety seized me—the sound would be heard by a neighbor! The old man's hour had come! With a loud yell, I threw open the lantern and leaped into the room. He shrieked once —once only. In an instant I dragged him to the floor, and pulled the heavy bed over him. I then smiled gaily, to find the deed so far done. But, for many minutes, the heart beat on with a muffled sound. This, however, did not vex me; it would not be heard through the wall. At length it ceased. The old man was dead. I removed the bed and examined the corpse. Yes, he was stone, stone dead. I placed my hand upon the heart and held it there many minutes. There was no pulsation. He was stone dead. His eye would trouble me no more.

If still you think me mad, you will think so no longer when I describe the wise precautions I took for the concealment of the body. The night waned, and I worked hastily, but in silence. First of all I dismembered the corpse. I cut off the head and the arms and the legs.

I then took up three planks from the flooring of the chamber, and deposited all

5 **Literary Focus** Discuss personification. In personification, something abstract is given human attributes. What is death personified as? How does this add to the mood of the story?

6 **Discussion** How does the narrator react to the sight of the old man's eye and the beating of his heart?

7 **Master Teacher Note** Poe's horror tales have often been adapted to film. One element of his style lends itself to movie editing techniques. He stretches or contracts time for psychological emphasis. Filmmakers do the same with images. Have your students find passages where time is suspensefully slowed or where lengthy but dull real-time events are encapsulated in a few words.

8 **Reading Strategy** Have students summarize the story up to this point and have them predict what will happen next. Will the narrator get away with his crime? Will the police catch him?

9 **Enrichment** Ask your **more advanced** students why they think some writers and artists gravitate to the macabre. What artistic fulfillments are possible through it? Elicit names of artists who deal with the macabre. You might also show paintings in Paul Haesart's book *James Ensor* (N.Y.: Harry N. Abrams, 1959). Ask your students which of the paintings they identify with Poe's stories.

no!—it was the low stifled sound that arises from the bottom of the soul when overcharged with awe. I knew the sound well. Many a night, just at midnight, when all the world slept, it has welled up from my own bosom, deepening, with its dreadful echo, the terrors that distracted me. . . . *All in vain*; because Death, in approaching him, had stalked with his black shadow before him, and enveloped the victim. And it was the mournful influence of the unperceived shadow that caused him to feel—although he neither saw nor heard—to *feel* the presence of my head within the room.

**Student Activity 1.** Which words in the example passage suggest the evil, perverse atmosphere that Poe wants to create?

**Student Activity 2.** With the class, brainstorm for a mood or feeling that you wish to convey to a reader. Then write a paragraph that suggests this mood or feeling. Without coming right out and telling the reader what the mood or feeling is, choose words and actions that suggest your intent.

**10 Discussion** How does the narrator at first react to the police?

**11 Discussion** What do you think is making the noise? Is it a real noise or just in the narrator's mind?

**12 Master Teacher Note** Poe's horror tales are exciting because they emphasize sensual experience. In describing sights and sounds he pulls our imaginations along, forcing us to "feel" the emotional events unfolding. Have your students point out passages where seeing and hearing are key elements in the ongoing narrative.

**13 Discussion** Why did he reveal the parts of the body to the officers?

**Reader's Response** Although the narrator's anxiety is brought on by the crime he knows he has committed, such anxiety plagues everyone at one time or another. Describe an experience you've had in which the normal circumstances of your surroundings (lights, sounds, temperature) seemed exaggerated and bothered you intensely. What was the real cause of your anxiety?

**Thematic Response** The narrator kills the old man to rid himself of the vulture eye. Ironically, the sound of the beating heart after he kills the old man is worse than the vulture eye. Have you ever made a choice and unexpectedly found the consequences to be far different from what you expected? Did you have a premonition regarding the consequence of your decision?

**Enrichment** Encourage your artistic students to draw or paint the scene with the old man in bed and the light shining on his eye. Ask them what colors they would use.

**Enrichment** Have your students imagine that they are one of the police officers in "The Tell-Tale Heart." You have just witnessed the narrator's nervous behavior

between the scantlings.[3] I then replaced the boards so cleverly, so cunningly, that no human eye—not even *his*—could have detected anything wrong. There was nothing to wash out—no stain of any kind—no blood-spot whatever. I had been too wary for that. A tub had caught all—ha! ha!

When I had made an end of these labors, it was four o'clock—still dark as midnight. As the bell sounded the hour, there came a knocking at the street door. I went down to open it with a light heart—for what had I *now* to fear? There entered three men, who introduced themselves, with perfect suavity, as officers of the police. A shriek had been heard by a neighbor during the night; suspicion of foul play had been aroused; information had been lodged at the police office, and they (the officers) had been deputed to search the premises.

I smiled—for *what* had I to fear? I bade the gentlemen welcome. The shriek, I said, was my own in a dream. The old man, I mentioned, was absent in the country. I took my visitors all over the house. I bade them search—search *well*. I led them, at length, to *his* chamber. I showed them his treasures, secure, undisturbed. In the enthusiasm of my confidence, I brought chairs into the room, and desired them *here* to rest from their fatigues, while I myself, in the wild audacity of my perfect triumph, placed my own seat upon the very spot beneath which reposed the corpse of the victim.

The officers were satisfied. My *manner* had convinced them. I was singularly at ease. They sat, and while I answered cheerily, they chatted of familiar things. But, ere long, I felt myself getting pale and wished them gone. My head ached, and I fancied a ringing in my ears: but still they sat and still chatted. The ringing became

more distinct:—it continued and became more distinct: I talked more freely to get rid of the feeling: but it continued and gained definitiveness—until, at length, I found that the noise was *not* within my ears.

No doubt I now grew *very* pale—but I talked more fluently, and with a heightened voice. Yet the sound increased—and what could I do? It was *a low, dull, quick sound—much such a sound as a watch makes when enveloped in cotton.* I gasped for breath—and yet the officers heard it not. I talked more quickly—more vehemently; but the noise steadily increased. I arose and argued about trifles, in a high key and with violent gesticulations; but the noise steadily increased. Why *would* they not be gone? I paced the floor to and fro with heavy strides, as if excited to fury by the observations of the men—but the noise steadily increased. Oh! what *could* I do? I foamed—I raved—I swore! I swung the chair upon which I had been sitting, and grated it upon the boards, but the noise arose over all, and continually increased. It grew louder—louder—*louder!* And still the men chatted pleasantly, and smiled. Was it possible they heard not?—no, no! They heard!—they suspected!—they *knew!*—they were making a mockery of my horror!—this I thought, and this I think. But anything was better than this agony! Anything was more tolerable than this derision! I could bear those hypocritical smiles no longer! I felt that I must scream or die!—and now again! hark! louder! louder! louder! *louder!*—

"Villains!" I shrieked, "dissemble[4] no more! I admit the deed!—tear up the planks!—here, here!—it is the beating of his hideous heart!"

---

**3. scantling** (skant' lin) *n.:* A small beam or timber.

**4. dissemble** (di sem' b'l) *v.:* To conceal under a false appearance; to conceal the truth of one's true feelings or motives.

and heard his startling admission of guilt. As the arresting officer you must write an official account of the circumstances leading to his arrest. How would you explain the narrator's strange behavior? What besides his confession proves his guilt? Write an official report.

**Multicultural Focus** Begin by telling students that horror tales exist in all cultures. Tales of zombies, the walking dead, are a part of Haitian folklore. Tales of vampires abound in Transylvania, a region in Romania, and helped provide the prototype for *Dracula*, the classic horror novel by English writer Bram Stoker, born two years before the death of Edgar Allan Poe. Even though in African cultures, ghosts are often

thought of as positive sources of family power, ghosts of people who have died a violent death are considered dangerous and are feared.

If you have students of different backgrounds, ask them to tell the class about what is feared in their cultures. Do they know any horror stories to share with their classmates?

## Your Response

1. What is your impression of the narrator? Why?

## Recalling

2. Why does the narrator kill the old man?
3. How long does it take him to accomplish his plan?
4. Why do the police arrive, even though the narrator planned the murder so carefully?

## Interpreting

5. How does the narrator reveal his cunning throughout the course of the crime? How does he reveal his powers of concentration?
6. When the police arrive, why does the narrator place his chair over the spot where the old man lies buried?
7. Do you think the police suspect the truth from the beginning? Explain your answer.
8. Do you think anyone but the narrator hears the beating of the old man's heart? Explain your answer. Why does he hear it so loudly?
9. What finally drives the narrator to confess?
10. To whom may he be recounting his tale?

## Applying

11. Why do people like to read tales of terror?

## A NALYZING LITERATURE

### Describing Atmosphere or Mood

**Atmosphere,** or **mood,** is the overall feeling created in a story. Poe builds the atmosphere by the use of words, details, and pictures that allow you to feel what the characters feel. In the scene where the old man awakens, for instance, Poe includes these details and pictures: ". . . he moved on the bed suddenly, as if startled," "His room was as black as pitch," and "I kept pushing it in, steadily, steadily." These details help you to feel the atmosphere of terror.

1. Look at the paragraph that begins "Presently I heard a slight groan" (page 146). List three details that help you to feel what the old man feels at this time.
2. Look at the paragraph that begins "I then took up three planks from the flooring" (page 147). List three details that create the mood of the narrator at this time.
3. Look at the paragraph that begins "No doubt I now grew *very* pale" (page 148). List three details that create the narrator's mood at this point.

## C RITICAL THINKING AND READING

### Choosing Words to Create Atmosphere

To create a particular atmosphere, you must choose words carefully. For example, notice the word *vulture* in the following sentence by Poe: "One of his eyes resembled that of a *vulture.*" To create a different atmosphere an author might say: "His eyes resembled those of a *puppy.*"

For each of the following words, a comparison is given that creates a mood. Create a different mood by writing another sentence comparing the item to something different.

1. *moon:* The golden globe of the moon lit up the road like a street lamp.
2. *store:* The tiny store displays so many jewels that it resembles a huge jewelry box.
3. *cat:* The eyes of the cat gleamed like stars.

## T HINKING AND WRITING

### Writing to Create Atmosphere

Imagine that Edgar Allan Poe were writing a story using the descriptions you wrote before you read this story. Write one scene as he might have written it. When you have finished, check your scene to make sure that you have used words and phrases that create a mood of horror.

*The Tell-Tale Heart* 149

8. No, the narrator is mad. The heart really isn't beating; he just imagines it. He hears it so loudly because the police are in the room and he suspects that they know of his crime.
9. He finally confesses because he thought the police suspected and were making a mockery of his horror. He was in agony and anything was better than the agony.
10. Answers will differ. He might be telling the story to his doctor or psychiatrist.

## Applying

11. Answers will differ. Students might say that they like being scared. It's a form of escapism, where their everyday cares and worries are left behind.

## ANSWERS TO ANALYZING LITERATURE

1. The three details might be "the groan of mortal terror"; "it was the low stifled sound that arises from the bottom of the soul when overcharged with awe"; and "it has welled up from my own bosom, deepening, with its dreadful echo the terrors that distracted me."
2. The three details might be "so cleverly, so cunningly"; "I had been too wary for that"; and "ha!ha!"
3. The three details might be "I gasped for breath"; "I foamed—I raved—I swore!"; and "I swung the chair upon which I had been sitting."

## ANSWERS TO CRITICAL THINKING AND READING

1 through 3. Answers will differ. Be sure students write sentences that include comparisons.

## THINKING AND WRITING
**Publishing Student Writing**
Have the better scenes read aloud in class. Have students note what words and phrases were used to create the mood of horror.

---

## Closure and Extension

### ANSWERS TO RESPONDING TO THE SELECTION
#### Your Response

1. Have students discuss their definitions of insanity and apply them to the narrator.

### Recalling

2. He decided to kill the old man because one of the old man's eyes resembled that of a vulture and made his blood run cold.

3. It took him eight nights to kill the old man.
4. The police came to the house because a neighbor had heard a shriek.

### Interpreting

5. He quietly entered the old man's room for seven nights before he found the old man's eye open on the eighth night. On the eighth night he waited for one hour without moving until he made his move to kill the old man.

6. He placed his seat over the corpse because he was so sure he committed the perfect crime and would not be found out.
7. Answers will differ. If students say yes, they should bring out that the police sat down and talked to the narrator long after he explained the reason for the shriek. If they say no, they could point out that the police never directly questioned the narrator about the old man. He confessed without them ever accusing him.

## Preparation

**More About the Author** Ray Bradbury has been a full-time author since 1943. He has published both long and short fiction, children's books, plays, and film scripts, including the one for *Moby-Dick*. The movie *Fahrenheit 451* was based on his novel of the same name. Point out to your students that Bradbury was not born until fifty-five years after the Civil War, the setting of "The Drummer Boy of Shiloh." How do students suppose Bradbury was able to re-create a period of which he had no firsthand experience?

**Literary Focus** After your students have read the explanation of historical setting, discuss what they know about the Civil War period. How was warfare then different from the way it is today? Consider such details as uniforms, weapons, and methods of fighting.

**Prereading Focus** Ask students to name and briefly discuss events that have made them feel apprehensive. Then have them brainstorm in small groups for words and phrases that describe a soldier's feelings on the eve of battle.

**Vocabulary** It would be helpful for students to know the following words also: *miraculously* (p. 151), *lunar* (p. 151), *legitimately* (p. 153), and *hindside* (p. 154).

**Electronic Handbook** If students have access to the Language Master 6000, you may suggest that they listen to the pronunciations of *askew* and *muted*.

### Ray Bradbury

(1920– ) was born in Waukegan, Illinois, and began his working life as a newsboy. Bradbury writes chiefly fantasy and science-fiction stories, such as his famous book *The Martian Chronicles*. The feelings and people that Bradbury writes about, however, could exist in any time or place. He writes stories of people—real, honest people—such as the Civil War drummer boy and the general in the "The Drummer Boy of Shiloh." This story is not science fiction, however; it is an example of historical fiction.

*150 Short Stories*

## The Drummer Boy of Shiloh

### Historical Setting

Stories may be set in a real place in a past time. If these stories are accurate in the way the places, times, and historical events are described, the stories are said to have a **historical setting.** Though the setting and some characters and events may be realistic, most of the characters and events are fictional. "The Drummer Boy of Shiloh," for example, has as its setting the battlefield at Shiloh, Tennessee, on the night before a famous Civil War battle. Although drummer boys and generals really were there, the ones you will meet in the story are creations of the author's imagination.

### Focus

Imagine that you are a soldier waiting to be called into battle. What would you be thinking about? How would you deal with the fears that would crowd out your more pleasant thoughts? How would you keep yourself from despairing? In small groups, brainstorm to list words and phrases that describe what a soldier experiences as he waits to fight. Use a diagram like the one below. Then read "The Drummer Boy of Shiloh" to learn what a young soldier in the Civil War might have been experiencing.

*soldier*

### Vocabulary

Knowing the following words will help you as you read "The Drummer Boy of Shiloh."

**askew** (ə skyo͞o′) *adv.*: Crookedly (p. 151)
**benediction** (ben′ ə dik′s hən) *n.*: A blessing (p. 151)
**riveted** (riv′ it əd) *adj.*: Fastened or made firm (p. 153)
**compounded** (käm pound′ əd) *adj.*: Mixed or combined (p. 153)

**remote** (ri mōt′) *adj.*: Distant (p. 153)
**resolute** (rez′ ə lo͞ot′) *adj.*: Showing a firm purpose; determined (p. 154)
**tremor** (trem′ ər) *n.*: Shaking or vibration (p. 155)
**muted** (myo͞ot′ id) *adj.*: Muffled; subdued (p. 155)

---

# The Drummer Boy of Shiloh

## Ray Bradbury

1 In the April night, more than once, blossoms fell from the orchard trees and lit with rustling taps on the drumskin. At midnight a peach stone left miraculously on a branch through winter, flicked by a bird, fell swift and unseen, struck once, like panic, which jerked the boy upright. In silence he listened to his own heart ruffle away, away—at last gone from his ears and back in his chest again.

2 After that, he turned the drum on its side, where its great lunar face peered at him whenever he opened his eyes.

His face, alert or at rest, was solemn. It was indeed a solemn time and a solemn night for a boy just turned fourteen in the peach field near the Owl Creek not far from the church at Shiloh.[1]

"... thirty-one, thirty-two, thirty-three ..."

Unable to see, he stopped counting.

Beyond the thirty-three familiar shadows, forty thousand men, exhausted by nervous expectation, unable to sleep for romantic dreams of battles yet unfought, lay crazily askew in their uniforms. A mile yet farther on, another army was strewn helter-skelter, turning slow, basting themselves[2] with the thought of what they would do when the time came: a leap, a yell, a blind plunge their strategy, raw youth their protection and benediction. 3

4 Now and again the boy heard a vast wind come up, that gently stirred the air. But he knew what it was—the army here, the army there, whispering to itself in the dark. Some men talking to others, others murmuring to themselves, and all so quiet it was like a natural element arisen from South or North with the motion of the earth toward dawn.

5 What the men whispered the boy could only guess, and he guessed that it was: "Me, I'm the one, I'm the one of all the rest who won't die. I'll live through it. I'll go home. The band will play. And I'll be there to hear it."

Yes, thought the boy, that's all very well for them, they can give as good as they get!

6 For with the careless bones of the young men harvested by night and bindled[3] around campfires were the similarly strewn steel bones of their rifles, with bayonets fixed like eternal lightning lost in the orchard grass.

---

**1. Shiloh** (shī′ lō): The site of a Civil War battle in 1862; now a national military park in southwest Tennessee.

**2. basting themselves:** Here, letting their thoughts pour over them as they turn in their sleep.
**3. bindled** (bin′ d′ ld) *adj.*: Bedded.

*The Drummer Boy of Shiloh* 151

**Making Connections** Another selection that deals with a teenager's response to war is *The Diary of Anne Frank* (page 303).
Students who want to further explore the issues of the Civil War from a young person's perspective can read *Shades of Gray,* by Carolyn Reeder, in the **Prentice Hall Literature Multicultural Library.**

**Thematic Focus** On the eve of the battle at Shiloh, a decisive battle that affected the outcome of the Civil War, the young drummer boy thinks fleetingly of remaining behind when the fighting begins. Ask students to discuss how just one person's behavior at a crucial time can influence American history.

## Presentation

**Motivation/Prior Knowledge**
Have your students discuss their ideas of fear. What are some common fears people have? What is the difference between irrational and rational fears? What are some ways people overcome their fears? Ask them to consider as they read whether Joby's fear is rational or irrational.

**Purpose-Setting Question** What role does fear play in this story?

1 **Discussion** What sounds do you hear in the first paragraph? From the boy's reaction to the falling pit, what do you know about his thoughts?

2 **Language** Note the use of figurative language in the second paragraph. Metaphors are used by writers to compare unlike objects in order to produce a startlingly real image in the mind of the reader. What is being compared in this paragraph? Have the students note the many other uses of metaphors in this story.

3 **Discussion** What does Bradbury mean by "raw youth their protection and benediction"?

4 **Language** Have your students say the word *murmur* aloud several times. How does it sound? The reproduction of a sound in the word itself is called onomatopoeia. Writers frequently use this device to heighten the sense of reality in a scene.

5 **Discussion** What is it about human nature that produces this thought instead of the negative one of imminent death?

6 **Discussion** Have your students reread this sentence and fix the image in their minds. What is being compared?

## Humanities Note

Fine art, *Drummer Boy*, by Julian Scott. Scott (1846–1901), is an American painter who was born in Vermont. After serving in the army during the Civil War, he decided to study fine art. He attended the school of the National Academy and studied with the painter Leutze until 1868.

Ask the class if this is the face of an innocent boy untouched by war or do we see in it the experience of having known and survived battle. Have your students explain their perceptions based on their findings in the canvas and reactions to the portrait. Have students study the face.

1. What character do you see in it?
2. Is this the face of an automaton, drumming out marching and fighting music mechanically, doing what he has been told to do? Or is there a sense of independence in the face: a young man, strong of spirit, aware of the importance of his drum in rallying the spirit of his fellow soldiers?
3. How else do you perceive this young man-boy?

**Master Teacher Note** Ask some students to interview soldiers who fought in wars. Have them ask about their thoughts on the subjects of survival, the night before an assault, and how well prepared they felt. What sounds did they hear? Did they have trust and faith in their commanding officers? If possible, have some war veterans come to class to be interviewed.

**DRUMMER BOY**
*Julian Scott*
N. S. Mayer

## Grammar in Action

Writers punctuate **dialogue** to separate it from the rest of the story. Direct speech by characters is set off within quotation marks. Explanatory words or phrases, such as *he said* or *whispered the boy,* are separated from the speaker's words with a comma.

Sometimes the explanatory phrase appears before the quotation. Look at how Bradbury punctuates this situation:

Then, after a moment, he said, "So there you are, that's it. Will you do that, boy? Do you know now you're general of the army when the general's left behind?"

Bradbury places a comma after the explanatory phrase and capitalizes the opening word in the quotation.

Often the explanatory phrase is at the end of the quotation:

"Fool question," said the general.

When the phrase appears at the end, the comma is placed inside the quotation mark, and the first letter of the explanatory phrase is a small letter.

Frequently, the explanatory phrase comes in the middle of a sentence in the quotation:

Me, thought the boy, I got only a drum, two sticks to beat it, and no shield.

**7** There wasn't a man-boy on this ground tonight who did not have a shield he cast, riveted or carved himself on his way to his first attack, compounded of remote but nonetheless firm and fiery family devotion, flag-blown patriotism and cocksure immortality strengthened by the touchstone of very real gunpowder, ramrod, Minié ball[4] and flint. But without these last, the boy felt his family move yet farther off away in the dark, as if one of those great prairie-burning trains had chanted them away never to **8** return—leaving him with this drum which was worse than a toy in the game to be played tomorrow or some day much too soon.

The boy turned on his side. A moth brushed his face, but it was a peach blossom. A peach blossom flicked him, but it was a moth. Nothing stayed put. Nothing had a name. Nothing was as it once was.

If he lay very still, when the dawn came up and the soldiers put on their bravery with their caps, perhaps they might go away, the **9** war with them, and not notice him lying small here, no more than a toy himself.

"Well, now," said a voice.

The boy shut up his eyes, to hide inside himself, but it was too late. Someone, walking by in the night, stood over him.

"Well," said the voice quietly, "here's a soldier crying *before* the fight. Good. Get it over. Won't be time once it all starts."

And the voice was about to move on when the boy, startled, touched the drum at his elbow. The man above, hearing this, stopped. The boy could feel his eyes, sense **10** him slowly bending near. A hand must have come down out of the night, for there was a

4. **Minié** (min' ē) **ball:** A cone-shaped rifle bullet that expands when fired.

little *rat-tat* as the fingernails brushed and the man's breath fanned his face.

"Why, it's the drummer boy, isn't it?"

The boy nodded, not knowing if his nod was seen. "Sir, is that *you?*" he said.

"I assume it is." The man's knees cracked as he bent still closer.

He smelled as all fathers should smell, of salt sweat, ginger tobacco, horse and boot leather, and the earth he walked upon. He **11** had many eyes. No, not eyes—brass buttons that watched the boy.

He could only be, and was, the general.

"What's your name, boy?" he asked.

"Joby," whispered the boy, starting to sit up.

"All right, Joby, don't stir." A hand pressed his chest gently, and the boy relaxed. "How long you been with us, Joby?"

"Three weeks, sir."

"Run off from home or joined legitimately, boy?"

Silence.

"Fool question," said the general. "Do you shave yet, boy? Even more of a fool. **12** There's your cheek, fell right off the tree overhead. And the others here not much older. Raw, raw, the lot of you. You ready for tomorrow or the next day, Joby?"

"I think so, sir."

"You want to cry some more, go on ahead. I did the same last night."

"*You*, sir?"

"It's the truth. Thinking of everything ahead. Both sides figuring the other side will just give up, and soon, and the war done in weeks, and us all home. Well, that's not how it's going to be. And maybe that's why I cried."

"Yes, sir," said Joby.

The general must have taken out a cigar now, for the dark was suddenly filled with the smell of tobacco unlit as yet, but chewed as the man thought what next to say.

*The Drummer Boy of Shiloh*  153

**7 Discussion** Why does Bradbury use the term "man-boy" here?

**8 Discussion** How does the boy feel about his family?

**9 Discussion** Do you think that thoughts of cowardice would be normal for a boy of fourteen under these circumstances? Explain.

**10 Language** Which word in this sentence is another example of onomatopoeia?

**11 Language** In this metaphor, to what does the author compare brass buttons?

**12 Discussion** What does comparing the boy's cheeks to peach blossoms suggest?

**Multicultural Focus** Explain that traditionally many armies around the world had a drummer boy or someone playing a musical instrument who led troops into battle. In Scotland bagpipes were played before fighting to inspire Scottish soldiers and give them courage. In many African societies, certain drum rhythms were used to declare war or inspire men before battle.

Invite students to choose countries or societies and do research on who traditionally led the armies of these countries into battle. Have them present their findings to the class.

"Well," said the voice quietly, "here's a soldier crying *before* the fight. Good. Get it over. Won't be time once it all starts."

In this situation a comma is placed inside the quotation mark before the explanatory phrase and another is placed immediately after the phrase and before the continuing quotation. Because the explanatory phrase interrupts a single sentence, the first word of the second part of the quotation is not capitalized.

**Student Activity.** Create a dialogue between two people. Place the explanatory phrases at the beginning, in the middle, and at the end of quotations. Include some lines of dialogue with no explanatory phrase.

**Electronic Handbook** You might want students to review punctuating dialogue before completing the Grammar in Action activity. If students have access to the Language Master 6000, have them enter the access word *quotation* and press the GRAMMAR key and the access symbol " (quotation mark) and press the GRAMMAR key to get information on dialogue.

**Master Teacher Note** Have your students reread the general's monologue. What is he saying about the upcoming battle? What do you think about what he is saying? Do you agree? Why or why not? This paragraph could produce a lively discussion about war. Ask why war touches even the strongest. Do you believe any soldier—firm-jawed, iron-willed—does not suffer the general's apprehension of the slaughter to come?

14 **Discussion** Why does the author suggest that the sun might not show its face here?

15 **Discussion** Why does the general compare the soldiers to wild horses?

16 **Discussion** Why does the general compare the army of soldiers to waves rolling in on a beach?

17 **Enrichment** Is this good advice for fighting men? Tell your **more advanced** students that this speech is based on Henry's advice to his troops in Shakespeare's *Henry V,* Act III, scene 1: "Then imitate the action of the tiger,/Stiffen the sinews, summon up the blood . . . /Now set the teeth and stretch the nostril wide." Ask your students why Bradbury made use of Henry's speech.

---

"It's going to be a crazy time," said the general. "Counting both sides, there's a hundred thousand men, give or take a few thousand out there tonight, not one as can spit a sparrow off a tree, or knows a horse clod from a Minié ball. Stand up, bare the breast, ask to be a target, thank them and sit down, that's us, that's them. We should turn tail and train four months, they should do the same. But here we are, taken with spring fever and thinking it blood lust, taking our sulfur with cannons instead of with molasses, as it should be, going to be a hero, going to live forever. And I can see all of them over there nodding agreement, save the other way around. It's wrong, boy, it's wrong as a head put on hindside front and a man marching backward through life. More innocents will get shot out of pure enthusiasm than ever got shot before. Owl Creek was full of boys splashing around in the noonday sun just a few hours ago. I fear it will be full of boys again, just floating, at sundown tomorrow, not caring where the tide takes them."

The general stopped and made a little pile of winter leaves and twigs in the darkness, as if he might at any moment strike fire to them to see his way through the coming days when the sun might not show its face because of what was happening here and just beyond.

The boy watched the hand stirring the leaves and opened his lips to say something, but did not say it. The general heard the boy's breath and spoke himself.

"Why am I telling you this? That's what you wanted to ask, eh? Well, when you got a bunch of wild horses on a loose rein somewhere, somehow you got to bring order, rein them in. These lads, fresh out of the milkshed, don't know what I know, and I can't tell them: men actually die, in war. So each is his own army. I got to make *one* army of them. And for that, boy, I need you."

"Me!" The boy's lips barely twitched.

"Now, boy," said the general quietly, "you are the heart of the army. Think of that. You're the heart of the army. Listen, now."

And, lying there, Joby listened. And the general spoke on.

If he, Joby, beat slow tomorrow, the heart would beat slow in the men. They would lag by the wayside. They would drowse in the fields on their muskets. They would sleep forever, after that, in those same fields—their hearts slowed by a drummer boy and stopped by enemy lead.

But if he beat a sure, steady, ever faster rhythm, then, then their knees would come up in a long line down over that hill, one knee after the other, like a wave on the ocean shore! Had he seen the ocean ever? Seen the waves rolling in like a well-ordered cavalry charge to the sand? Well, that was it, that's what he wanted, that's what was needed! Joby was his right hand and his left. He gave the orders, but Joby set the pace!

So bring the right knee up and the right foot out and the left knee up and the left foot out. One following the other in good time, in brisk time. Move the blood up the body and make the head proud and the spine stiff and the jaw resolute. Focus the eye and set the teeth, flare the nostrils and tighten the hands, put steel armor all over the men, for blood moving fast in them does indeed make men feel as if they'd put on steel. He must keep at it, at it! Long and steady, steady and long! Then, even though shot or torn, those wounds got in hot blood—in blood he'd helped stir—would feel less pain. If their blood was cold, it would be more than slaughter, it would be murderous nightmare and pain best not told and no one to guess.

The general spoke and stopped, letting his breath slack off. Then, after a moment,

---

## Grammar in Action

The voice of a verb shows whether or not the subject is performing the action. In **active voice** the subject performs the action of the verb. In "The Drummer Boy of Shiloh," the general uses active voice when he says ". . . men actually die, in war." The subject, "men," perform the action of the verb "die." In the passive voice, the sentence would read, ". . . men are actually killed, in war"; the subject receives rather than performs the action.

Active voice clearly expresses action while specifying who or what performs the action. Therefore, active voice strengthens your writing. Consider the active voice in the following paragraph:

"The *general stopped* and *made* a little pile of winter leaves and twigs in the darkness, as if *he might* at any moment *strike fire* to them to see his way through the coming days when the *sun might* not *show* its face because of what was happening here and just beyond."

How do the active verbs give the reader a specific impression of what is happening in the paragraph?

**THE BATTLE OF SHILOH, TENNESSEE (6–7 APRIL 1862), 1886**
*Kurz and Allison*
*The Granger Collection*

18

he said, "So there you are, that's it. Will you do that, boy? Do you know now you're general of the army when the general's left behind?"

The boy nodded mutely.

"You'll run them through for me then, boy?"

"Yes, sir."

"Good. And, maybe, many nights from tonight, many years from now, when you're as old or far much older than me, when they ask you what you did in this awful time, you will tell them—one part humble and one part proud—'I was the drummer boy at the battle of Owl Creek,' or the Tennessee River, or maybe they'll just name it after the church there. 'I was the drummer boy at Shiloh.' Good grief, that has a beat and sound to it fitting for Mr. Longfellow. 'I was the drummer boy at Shiloh.' Who will ever hear those words and not know you, boy, or what you thought this night, or what you'll think tomorrow or the next day when we must get up on our legs and *move!*"

The general stood up. "Well, then. Bless you, boy. Good night."

"Good night, sir." And tobacco, brass, boot polish, salt sweat and leather, the man moved away through the grass.

Joby lay for a moment, staring but unable to see where the man had gone. He swallowed. He wiped his eyes. He cleared his throat. He settled himself. Then, at last, very slowly and firmly, he turned the drum so that it faced up toward the sky.

He lay next to it, his arm around it, feeling the tremor, the touch, the muted thunder as, all the rest of the April night in the year 1862, near the Tennessee River, not far from the Owl Creek, very close to the church named Shiloh, the peach blossoms fell on the drum.

*The Drummer Boy of Shiloh*  155

---

**Student Activity 1.** Locate three more examples of active voice in "The Drummer Boy of Shiloh." Identify the active verbs and explain how active voice enhances the story.

**Student Activity 2.** Use active voice in a short paragraph on each of the following topics:
a. a summary of "The Drummer Boy of Shiloh"
b. a character sketch of the general
c. a character sketch of the drummer boy

**Electronic Handbook** You may want students to review verbs in the active and passive voice before completing the Grammar in Action activities. If students have access to the Language Master 6000, have them enter the access word *active* and press the GRAMMAR key to get information on when to use active and passive voice.

---

**18 Discussion** What kind of feeling do you have as you think about the peach blossoms falling on the drum during the night?

**Reader's Response** The general calls Joby "the heart of the army." How would you feel about having Joby's responsibility?

**Thematic Response** Discuss with students the drummer boy's possible influence on American history. Why does Joby turn the drum face up toward the sky after the general leaves?

## Humanities Note

Fine art, *The Battle of Shiloh, Tennessee* (6–7 April 1862), 1886. This is a lithograph produced by the Kurz and Allison Company. Artists, hired by magazines, newspapers, and printing companies were sent to the front to record, with drawings and watercolors, battles, skirmishes, and scenes of camp life. Ask the class how this lithograph relates to the fears of the young drummer boy. Question the class as to their understanding of the battle. Bring out that the infantry ranged along the river, facing one another, and the opposing artillery batteries are in the upper left and right of the print.

1. What is the purpose of the Union cavalry being grouped on the hill? What are these horse soldiers waiting for?
2. Does this seem to be a bona fide battle scene? Or is it a romanticized product of the artist's imagination of what war is like? Have your students justify their viewpoints.
3. Is this art appropriate to illustrate this story? As you answer, think about the characters, the feeling, and the details in both the art and the story.

**Enrichment** Your more advanced students could be encouraged to read *The Red Badge of Courage* by Stephen Crane and report to the class the feelings that the main character had about going to battle.

## Closure and Extension

### ANSWERS TO RESPONDING TO THE SELECTION
#### Your Response

1. Some students will say that the general is exaggerating, and others will disagree. Have them evaluate the general's argument that the general will give the orders but Joby will set the pace.

#### Recalling

2. The boy just turned fourteen.
3. He is thinking about the battle to be fought tomorrow morning.
4. The general cried thinking of everything ahead.
5. He needs Joby to lead the men into battle with a steady, fast beat of his drum.

#### Interpreting

6. Answers will differ. Joby might have run away from home because of an argument with his parents or because he didn't like school.
7. Answers will differ. The general might have stopped because he heard Joby crying.
8. Joby is the "heart of the army" because he sets the beat that the army moves by.
9. He means that Joby will be leading the men into battle, as a general would.
10. He felt calmer and stopped crying. The general had instilled a sense of duty and responsibility in the drummer boy.

#### Applying

11. The drummer boy never lost his fear, he was just able to master it. He was right to feel fear about tomorrow's battle, but after his talk with the general, he was able to face his fear.

### ANSWERS TO ANALYZING LITERATURE

1. The five details might be "Owl Creek was full of boys . . ."; "I was the drummer boy at the battle of Owl Creek, or the Tennessee River, or maybe they'll just name it after the church there"; "I was the drummer boy at Shiloh"; ". . . near the Tennessee River . . ."; and ". . . not far from the Owl Creek, very close to the church named Shiloh."

## R ESPONDING TO THE SELECTION
### Your Response

1. Do you think the role of the drummer boy is really as crucial as the general says it is, or is the general exaggerating in order to inspire the boy and improve morale? Explain.

### Recalling

2. How old is the drummer boy?
3. What is the boy thinking about as he lies in the orchard?
4. Why did the general cry the night before?
5. Why does the general say he needs Joby?

### Interpreting

6. Why do you think Joby joined the army?
7. Why do you think the general stops to talk to the boy?
8. In what way is Joby "the heart of the army"?
9. What does the general mean when he says, "Do you know now you're general of the army when the general's left behind?"
10. How do you think the boy felt after his talk with the general?

### Applying

11. Mark Twain once said, "Courage is resistance to fear, mastery of fear—not absence of fear." How does this quotation apply to "The Drummer Boy of Shiloh"?

## A NALYZING LITERATURE
### Recognizing Historical Details

To create a historical setting, an author includes details that help you recognize and visualize the setting of the story accurately. When Bradbury writes "in the peach field near the Owl Creek not far from the church at Shiloh," he introduces a setting where a historical event occurred. As the story continues, he includes other details that are historically accurate.

1. List at least five details in the story that place the setting geographically.
2. List at least five details in the story that place the setting in time.

## C RITICAL THINKING AND READING
### Identifying Appropriate Historical Details

Authors must be careful to include only details that describe a place and time accurately if they want their historical settings to be true.

Name the item in each of the following groups that does not belong in the same historical setting with the others.

1. battlefield at Shiloh; drummer boy; Jeep; general
2. Cape Canaveral; rocket; television crew; General Custer
3. George Washington; Benjamin Franklin; Douglas MacArthur; Patrick Henry

## T HINKING AND WRITING
### Writing About a Historical Setting

Suppose you were preparing a time capsule for someone to open one hundred years from now. List and write about the items you would include in it to give people of the future a clear picture of the place and time you live in today. Explain why you would include each item. Make sure your spelling, grammar, and punctuation are correct.

## L EARNING OPTION

**Cross-curricular Connection.** Look in your public or school library to find song books or records with Civil War songs. Working with some of your classmates, arrange and present a program of Civil War music for your class.

2. The five details might be "In the April night . . ."; "At midnight . . ."; ". . . at sundown tomorrow, not caring where the tide takes them"; ". . . pile of winter leaves and twigs in the darkness . . ."; and ". . . all the rest of the April night in the year 1862."

### ANSWERS TO CRITICAL THINKING AND READING

1. Jeep

2. General Custer
3. Douglas MacArthur

**Challenge** The calm and beauty of the peach orchard offers a sharp contrast to Joby's fears about the next day's battle. What do you think Bradbury was suggesting by creating this contrast?

### THINKING AND WRITING
**Alternative Assessment** You may vary the Thinking and Writ-

ing assignment as follows: Have your students complete the Responding to the Selection and reread the last two pages of the story. Then ask them to assume the persona of the boy and record his thoughts as he digests the encouragement of the general and dreams about his role in the battle the next day. You may also ask them to research the Battle of Shiloh and write The Ballad of the Drummer Boy, cele-

# Theme

ROOMS BY THE SEA
*Edward Hopper*
*Yale University Art Gallery*

Fine art, *Rooms by the Sea,* 1951, by Edward Hopper. The American artist Edward Hopper (1882–1967) was born in Nyack, New York. At the age of seventeen, he enrolled in the art class of New York artist Robert Henri. He gained technical training from this class but was not influenced by Henri's style. Later, he went to Paris to continue his studies. While there, he kept to himself, avoiding fellow Americans. Such reserved behavior was a lifelong characteristic. Strongly individualistic, Hopper quietly pursued his own style of art and painted the lonely rooms, houses, and urban scenes for which he is best remembered.

In this painting, *Rooms by the Sea,* the sunlight cuts into an open doorway, creating a sharp diagonal shape on the wall and floor. This diagonal of light is repeated in another room glimpsed on the left. The simple, spare colors and clean bareness of the canvas create an almost abstract geometrical effect. The rooms seem still, lonely, and isolated. The sea, right outside the door, seems an almost surreal presence. To Edward Hopper this painting was simply a study of sunlight. He felt that any psychological interpretations were left to the viewer.

**Master Teacher Note** Use the overhead projector to show Fine Art Transparency 20, *The Trapper,* by Rockwell Kent, in the Teaching Portfolio. Ask students what themes the art calls to mind.

brating his role in that battle and including details they learned from their research.

**Writing Across the Curriculum**
Though the general in Bradbury's story is not identified, the historical details provide clues that Bradbury probably had General W. T. Sherman in mind. Have students find a history book that describes the Battle of Shiloh. What similarities support the notion that

Bradbury's fictional general was modeled after Sherman? What might disprove the theory? Have your students write a short paper either proving or disproving that Bradbury's general was Sherman. You might inform the history department of this assignment.

### LEARNING OPTION

This activity is particularly appropriate for auditory and kinesthetic

learners. Encourage them to use a variety of instruments and media. If possible, tape-record their presentation.

## Preparation

**More About the Author** Anne McCaffrey is best known for her novels about the dragonriders of Pern. Pern, a lost colony of Earth, is a "fully conceived and complex civilization whose politics, social structure, and traditions are based on a recurring ecological battle." Why might a science-fiction writer have chosen an ecological battle as the basis for many of her novels?

**Literary Focus** Lead students to see that the theme of a short story, whether it is stated directly or is implied, underlies the structure and influences the meaning of the entire story.

**Prereading Focus** After you have brainstormed to list things Keevan could do, discuss which would be most effective for proving himself to his peers.

**Vocabulary** Have students use all the vocabulary words in a paragraph or story about life on another planet.

**Electronic Handbook** You may suggest that your students use the Language Master 6000 to listen to the pronunciation of the vocabulary words.

# GUIDE FOR READING

### Anne McCaffrey

(1926–    ) has gained a reputation as science fiction's "Dragon Lady" as a result of her many novels about the dragonriders of Pern. McCaffrey, who has studied physics, bases her fantasy world on sound scientific principles. Born in the United States, she has lived for many years in Ireland in a home she calls Dragonhold. She has won numerous awards for her "Dragonriders of Pern" books, which, according to one reviewer, "must now rank as the most enduring serial in the history of science fantasy."

## The Smallest Dragonboy

### Theme

A **theme** is the central idea that is conveyed by a story. An author can state a theme directly or only suggest it. When an author suggests a theme, you must consider what the story seems to say about the nature of people or about life. Although "The Smallest Dragonboy" takes place in a strange world, the suggested, or implied, theme relates to a struggle that many people experience.

### Focus

"The Smallest Dragonboy" is about Keevan, a boy who is brave, good, and patient, but small in stature. Bullied and teased relentlessly by the other boys, Keevan desperately wants to prove himself, to show everyone that being small doesn't mean you don't count. What advice would you give Keevan about dealing with the other boys? With your classmates, brainstorm to list things Keevan could do to earn the respect of his peers. Then read the story to see how the smallest dragonboy makes his mark.

### Vocabulary

Knowing the following words will help you as you read "The Smallest Dragonboy."

**sloth** (slôth) *n.*: Laziness (p. 159)

**reprehensible** (rep' ri hen' sə bəl) *adj.*: Deserving of blame (p. 159)

**imminent** (im' ə nənt) *adj.*: About to happen (p. 161)

**deigned** (dānd) *v.*: Lowered oneself (p. 162)

**gingerly** (jin' jər lē) *adv.*: Carefully; cautiously (p. 167)

**plaintive** (plān' tiv) *adj.*: Mournful (p. 168)

**ignominious** (ig' nə min' ē əs) *adj.*: Dishonorable (p. 168)

**consternation** (kän' stər nā' shən) *n.*: Dismay (p. 168)

*158    Short Stories*

### Objectives

1  To understand theme
2  To identify realistic details
3  To write about rites of passage
4  To express individual interests and abilities through an optional activity

### Support Material

**Teaching Portfolio**
Teacher Backup, p. 239
Grammar in Action Worksheets, *Recognizing Degrees of Comparison*, p. 243; *Using Transitional Words and Phrases*, p. 245
Usage and Mechanics Worksheet, p. 247
Vocabulary Check, p. 248
Analyzing Literature Worksheet, *Understanding Theme*, p. 249

Selection Test, p. 250

**Prentice Hall Literature Writing Studio**

# The Smallest Dragonboy

## Anne McCaffrey

Although Keevan lengthened his walking stride as far as his legs would stretch, he couldn't quite keep up with the other candidates. He knew he would be teased again.

[1] Just as he knew many other things that his foster mother told him he ought not to know, Keevan knew that Beterli, the most senior of the boys, set that spanking pace just to embarrass him, the smallest dragonboy. Keevan would arrive, tail fork-end of the group, breathless, chest heaving, and maybe get a stern look from the instructing [2] wingsecond.

Dragonriders, even if they were still only hopeful candidates for the glowing eggs which were hardening on the hot sands of the Hatching Ground cavern, were expected to be punctual and prepared. Sloth was not [3] tolerated by the Weyrleader of Benden Weyr. A good record was especially important now. It was very near hatching time, when the baby dragons would crack their mottled shells, and stagger forth to choose their lifetime companions. The very thought of that glorious moment made Keevan's breath catch in his throat. To be chosen—to be a dragonrider! To sit astride the neck of a winged beast with jeweled eyes: to be his friend, in telepathic communion[1] with him for life; to be his companion in good times

and fighting extremes; to fly effortlessly over the lands of Pern! Or, thrillingly, *between* to any point anywhere on the world! Flying [4] *between* was done on dragonback or not at all, and it was dangerous.

Keevan glanced upward, past the black mouths of the Weyr caves in which grown dragons and their chosen riders lived, toward the Star Stones that crowned the ridge of the old volcano that was Benden Weyr. On the height, the blue watch dragon, his rider mounted on his neck, stretched the great transparent pinions[2] that carried him on the winds of Pern to fight the evil Thread [5] that fell at certain times from the skies. The many-faceted rainbow jewels of his eyes glistened fleetingly in the greeny sun. He folded his great wings to his back, and the watch pair resumed their statuelike pose of alertness.

Then the enticing view was obscured as Keevan passed into the Hatching Ground cavern. The sands underfoot were hot, even through heavy wherhide boots. How the bootmaker had protested having to sew so small! Keevan was forced to wonder why being small was reprehensible. People were always calling him "babe" and shooing him [6] away as being "too small" or "too young" for this or that. Keevan was constantly working, twice as hard as any other boy his

---

1. **telepathic communion:** The sharing of thoughts and emotions between minds, without the use of normal means of communication.

2. **pinions** (pin'yənz) *n.*: Wings.

*The Smallest Dragonboy*   159

## Presentation

**Motivation/Prior Knowledge**
What dragon stories or legends do you know? Are the dragons usually good or bad? Tell students that the dragons in the science-fiction story they are going to read were so named because of their resemblance to the dragons of Earth's legends.

**Purpose-Setting Question** How does McCaffrey blend science and fiction to create a believable world?

1 **Discussion** How does this detail set Keevan apart as someone special?

2 **Clarification** A wingsecond is an officer of the dragonriders; he or she is second in command to the wingleader.

3 **Clarification** A Weyr is a dragon stronghold located on a mountain-top. A Weyrleader is the male dragonrider in charge of the fighting units of the Weyr; he is responsible for training all riders.

4 **Clarification** These dragons have the ability to telepathically transport themselves and their riders, called going *between*.

5 **Clarification** Thread is the name the settlers of Pern gave to the deadly organisms that fall to their planet every time its orbit coincides with that of the Red Star.

6 **Discussion** How would you feel if you were in Keevan's place?

**Thematic Focus** A rite of passage is a ceremony or ritual associated with an event in a person's life that marks an important transition, such as the transition from adolescence to adulthood. Ask students to consider what problems might be associated with rites of passage.

**Making Connections** In this selection both Keevan and the dragon have to make important decisions. "The Road Not Taken" by Robert Frost, which appears on page 600, is a poem about making decisions. You may suggest that your students read Frost's poem before reading "The Smallest Dragonboy."

**7 Discussion** What is your first impression of Beterli?

**8 Clarification** Harpers are very important on Pern. They function as storytellers, historians, teachers, and entertainers.

**9 Reading Strategy** What do you learn about the hierarchy of dragons in this paragraph?

## Humanities Note

Fine art, *Untitled Illustration,* by Michael Whelan. Whelan (born in 1950) is an eminent illustrator of science fiction and fantasy. His work has appeared on the covers of works by many famous writers of the genre, including Isaac Asimov, Arthur C. Clarke, and Anne McCaffrey. In 1988 Michael Whelan was awarded the prestigious Hugo award for illustration.

The style Whelan uses in his work has been called hyperrealism, which is characterized by fantastic subjects painted in brilliant color and meticulously rendered detail. This untitled illustration is a prime example of this style. Every detail of the dragon, from the bat-like wings to the reptilian scales on its body, reflects a basis in realism. However, the unearthly color scheme and the dramatic lighting create an aura of fantasy and fear. The realistic and fantastic elements of this illustration work together to create a believable world.

You might use these questions for discussion:

1. How does the dragon in this illustration compare with your conception of the dragons of Pern? Explain the similarities and differences.

2. In what ways does Anne McCaffrey use hyperrealism in her writing?

age, to prove himself capable. What if his muscles weren't as big as Beterli's? They were just as hard. And if he couldn't overpower anyone in a wrestling match, he could outdistance everyone in a footrace.

"Maybe if you run fast enough," Beterli had jeered on the occasion when Keevan had been goaded to boast of his swiftness, "you could catch a dragon. That's the only way you'll make a dragonrider!"

"You just wait and see, Beterli, you just wait," Keevan had replied. He would have liked to wipe the contemptuous smile from Beterli's face, but the guy didn't fight fair even when a wingsecond was watching. "No one knows what Impresses a dragon!"

"They've got to be able to *find* you first, babe!"

Yes, being the smallest candidate was not an enviable position. It was therefore imperative that Keevan Impress a dragon in his first Hatching. That would wipe the smile off every face in the cavern and accord him the respect due any dragonrider, even the smallest one.

Besides, no one knew exactly what Impressed the baby dragons as they struggled from their shells in search of their lifetime partners.

"I like to believe that dragons see into a man's heart," Keevan's foster mother, Mende, told him. "If they find goodness, honesty, a flexible mind, patience, courage —and you've got that in quantity, dear Keevan—that's what dragons look for. I've seen many a well-grown lad left standing on the sands, Hatching Day, in favor of someone not so strong or tall or handsome. And if my memory serves me"—which it usually did: Mende knew every word of every Harper's tale worth telling, although Keevan did not interrupt her to say so—"I don't believe that F'lar, our Weyrleader, was all that tall when bronze Mnementh chose him. And

Mnementh was the only bronze dragon of that Hatching."

Dreams of Impressing a bronze were beyond Keevan's boldest reflections, although that goal dominated the thoughts of every other hopeful candidate. Green dragons were small and fast and more numerous. There was more prestige to Impressing a blue or brown than a green. Being practical, Keevan seldom dreamed as high as a big fighting brown, like Canth, F'nor's fine fellow, the biggest brown on all Pern. But to fly

**UNTITLED ILLUSTRATION**
*Michael Whelan*
*Courtesy of the Artist*

a bronze? Bronzes were almost as big as the queen, and only they took the air when a queen flew at mating time. A bronze rider could aspire to become Weyrleader! Well, Keevan would console himself, brown riders could aspire to become wingseconds, and that wasn't bad. He'd even settle for a green dragon: they were small, but so was he. No matter! He simply had to Impress a dragon his first time in the Hatching Ground. Then no one in the Weyr would taunt him anymore for being so small.

Shells, Keevan thought now, but the sands are hot!

"Impression time is imminent, candidates," the wingsecond was saying as everyone crowded respectfully close to him. "See the extent of the striations[3] on this promising egg." The stretch marks *were* larger than yesterday.

**10** Everyone leaned forward and nodded thoughtfully. That particular egg was the one Beterli had marked as his own, and no other candidate dared, on pain of being beaten by Beterli at his first opportunity, to approach it. The egg was marked by a large yellowish splotch in the shape of a dragon backwinging to land, talons outstretched to grasp rock. Everyone knew that bronze eggs bore distinctive markings. And naturally, Beterli, who'd been presented at eight Impressions already and was the biggest of the candidates, had chosen it.

"I'd say that the great opening day is almost upon us," the wingsecond went on, and then his face assumed a grave expression. "As we well know, there are only forty **11** eggs and seventy-two candidates. Some of you may be disappointed on the great day. That doesn't necessarily mean you aren't dragonrider material, just that *the* dragon

---

**3. striations** (strī ā'shənz) *n.*: Stripes.

for you hasn't been shelled. You'll have other Hatchings, and it's no disgrace to be left behind an Impression or two. Or more."

Keevan was positive that the wingsecond's eyes rested on Beterli, who'd been stood off at so many Impressions already. Keevan tried to squinch down so the wingsecond wouldn't notice him. Keevan had been reminded too often that he was eligible to be a candidate by one day only. He, of all the hopefuls, was most likely to be left standing on the great day. One more reason why he simply had to Impress at his first Hatching.

"Now move about among the eggs," the wingsecond said. "Touch them. We don't know that it does any good, but it certainly doesn't do any harm."

Some of the boys laughed nervously, but everyone immediately began to circulate among the eggs. Beterli stepped up officiously to "his" egg, daring anyone to come near it. Keevan smiled, because he had already touched it—every inspection day, when the others were leaving the Hatching Ground **12** and no one could see him crouch to stroke it.

Keevan had an egg he concentrated on, too, one drawn slightly to the far side of the others. The shell had a soft greenish-blue tinge with a faint creamy swirl design. The consensus was that this egg contained a mere green, so Keevan was rarely bothered by rivals. He was somewhat perturbed then to see Beterli wandering over to him.

"I don't know why you're allowed in this Impression, Keevan. There are enough of us without a babe," Beterli said, shaking his head.

"I'm of age." Keevan kept his voice level, **13** telling himself not to be bothered by mere words.

"Yah!" Beterli made a show of standing on his toetips. "You can't even see over an egg; Hatching Day, you better get in front or

---

The Smallest Dragonboy  161

**10 Discussion** Does Beterli's behavior here confirm or contradict your first impression of him? Why?

**11 Discussion** How do you think Beterli feels as he hears the wingsecond's speech? Why?

**12 Discussion** Why does secretly touching "Beterli's egg" give Keevan pleasure?

**13 Discussion** What do Keevan's response and behavior reveal about his character?

## Primary Source

In the following excerpt from the introduction to her novel *The Renegades of Pern*, Anne McCaffrey provides information about the planet Pern:

When Mankind first discovered Pern, third planet of the sun Rukbat in the Sagittarian Sector, they paid little attention to the eccentric orbit of the Red Star, another satellite in the system.

Settling the new planet, adjusting to its differences, the colonists spread out across the southern, more hospitable continent. Then disaster struck in the form of a rain of mycorrhizoid organisms, which voraciously devoured all but stone, metal, and water. The initial losses were staggering. But fortunately for the young colony, "Thread," as the settlers called the devastating showers, was not entirely invincible: Both water and fire would destroy the menace on contact.

162

**14 Clarification** Glows are sources of light that are carried in hand baskets. Firestone is rock containing phosphorus that the dragons are fed to enable them to breathe a flame that destroys Thread.

**15 Reading Strategy** Pern was settled by people from Earth. What do you think black rock is?

**16 Reading Strategy** What do you think a Turn is? Why?

**17 Critical Thinking and Reading** In what sense are the details describing the dragonriders' topics of conversation realistic?

## Humanities Note

Fine art, *Untitled Illustration*, by Michael Whelan. Whelan is an award-winning science-fiction illustrator. This untitled illustration was created for the book jacket of a novel by Anne McCaffrey. Typical of the style Whelan uses in much of his work, this illustration depicts a mysterious alien landscape whose denizens are painstakingly rendered mythical creatures. Whelan's technical proficiency and flair for surrealistic coloring are well suited to his choice of subject: McCaffrey's dragons and their riders.

You might use these questions for discussion:

1. In what ways does this illustration convey the sense of fear and danger that dragonriders must feel during Thread attack?

2. Do you feel that Keevan will be able to ride a dragon such as the ones in this illustration? Why or why not?

the dragons won't see you at all. 'Course, you could get run down that way in the mad scramble. Oh, I forget, you can run fast, can't you?"

"You'd better make sure a dragon sees *you*, this time, Beterli," Keevan replied. "You're almost overage, aren't you?"

Beterli flushed and took a step forward, hand half-raised. Keevan stood his ground, but if Beterli advanced one more step, he would call the wingsecond. No one fought on the Hatching Ground. Surely Beterli knew that much.

Fortunately, at that moment, the wingsecond called the boys together and led them from the Hatching Ground to start on evening chores. There were "glows" to be replenished in the main kitchen caverns and sleeping cubicles, the major hallways, and the queen's apartment. Firestone sacks had to be filled against Thread attack, and black rock brought to the kitchen hearths. The boys fell to their chores, tantalized by the odors of roasting meat. The population of the Weyr began to assemble for the evening meal, and the dragonriders came in from the Feeding Ground on their sweep checks.

It was the time of day Keevan liked best: once the chores were done but before dinner was served, a fellow could often get close enough to the dragonriders to hear their talk. Tonight, Keevan's father, K'last, was at the main dragonrider table. It puzzled Keevan how his father, a brown rider and a tall man, could *be* his father—because he, Keevan, was so small. It obviously puzzled K'last, too, when he deigned to notice his small son: "In a few more Turns, you'll be as tall as I am—or taller!"

K'last was pouring Benden wine all around the table. The dragonriders were relaxing. There'd be no Thread attack for three more days, and they'd be in the mood to tell tall tales, better than Harper yarns,

about impossible maneuvers they'd done a-dragonback. When Thread attack was closer, their talk would change to a discussion of tactics of evasion, of going *between*, how long to suspend there until the burning but fragile Thread would freeze and crack and fall harmlessly off dragon and man. They would dispute the exact moment to feed firestone to the dragon so he'd have the

**UNTITLED ILLUSTRATION**
*Michael Whelan*
*Courtesy of the Artist*

best flame ready to sear Thread midair and render it harmless to ground—and man—below. There was such a lot to know and understand about being a dragonrider that sometimes Keevan was overwhelmed. How would he ever be able to remember everything he ought to know at the right moment? He couldn't dare ask such a question; this would only have given additional weight to the notion that he was too young yet to be a dragonrider.

"Having older candidates makes good sense," L'vel was saying, as Keevan settled down near the table. "Why waste four to five years of a dragon's fighting prime until his rider grows up enough to stand the rigors?" L'vel had Impressed a blue of Ramoth's first clutch. Most of the candidates thought L'vel was marvelous because he spoke up in front of the older riders, who awed them. "That was well enough in the Interval when you didn't need to mount the full Weyr complement to fight Thread. But not now. Not with more eligible candidates than ever. Let the babes wait."

"Any boy who is over twelve Turns has the right to stand in the Hatching Ground," K'last replied, a slight smile on his face. He never argued or got angry. Keevan wished he were more like his father. And oh, how he wished he were a brown rider! "Only a dragon—each particular dragon—knows what he wants in a rider. We certainly can't tell. Time and again the theorists," K'last's smile deepened as his eyes swept those at the table, "are surprised by dragon choice. *They* never seem to make mistakes, however."

"Now, K'last, just look at the roster this Impression. Seventy-two boys and only forty eggs. Drop off the twelve youngest, and there's still a good field for the hatchlings to choose from. Shells! There are a couple of weyrlings unable to see over a wher egg much less a dragon! And years before they can ride Thread."

"True enough, but the Weyr is scarcely under fighting strength, and if the youngest Impress, they'll be old enough to fight when the oldest of our current dragons go *between* from senility."

"Half the Weyr-bred lads have already been through several Impressions," one of

**18** **Clarification** Ramoth is the queen dragon of Benden Weyr and the largest dragon on the planet Pern. A clutch is composed of the eggs that are laid at one time.

**19** **Clarification** An Interval is the period of time between Threadfalls, approximately 200 Turns.

**20** **Discussion** In what ways is Keevan more like his father than he realizes?

**21** **Reading Strategy** What do you predict might surprise the theorists about dragon choice in the upcoming Impression? Give reasons to support your prediction.

**22** **Reading Strategy** Which candidate would be excluded according to this plan?

**23** **Reading Strategy** Which candidate would be excluded according to the second plan?

*The Smallest Dragonboy* 163

24 **Clarification** The Weyrwoman shares the leadership of the Weyr with the Weyrleader. Lessa rides the queen dragon, Ramoth. Because all dragons obey the queen, the Weyrwoman is the most powerful person on Pern.

25 **Discussion** Do you agree with Lessa's decision? Why or why not?

26 **Reading Strategy** What does Keevan's clumsiness indicate about his state of mind?

27 **Critical Thinking and Reading** How do Mende's words and behavior in this paragraph realistically express the concerns of a mother?

the bronze riders said then. "I'd say drop some of *them* off this time. Give the untried a chance."

"There's nothing wrong in presenting a clutch with as wide a choice as possible," said the Weyrleader, who had joined the table with Lessa, the Weyrwoman.

"Has there ever been a case," she said, smiling in her odd way at the riders, "where a hatchling didn't choose?"

Her suggestion was almost heretical[4] and drew astonished gasps from everyone, including the boys.

F'lar laughed. "You say the most outrageous things, Lessa."

"Well, *has* there ever been a case where a dragon didn't choose?"

"Can't say as I recall one," K'last replied.

"Then we continue in this tradition," Lessa said firmly, as if that ended the matter.

But it didn't. The argument ranged from one table to the other all through dinner, with some favoring a weeding out of the candidates to the most likely, lopping off those who were very young or who had had multiple opportunities to Impress. All the candidates were in a swivet,[5] though such a departure from tradition would be to the advantage of many. As the evening progressed, more riders were favoring eliminating the youngest and those who'd passed four or more Impressions unchosen. Keevan felt he could bear such a dictum[6] only if Beterli were also eliminated. But this seemed less likely than that Keevan would

---

**4. heretical** (hə ret'i kəl) *adj.*: Opposing the accepted views or beliefs.
**5. swivet** (swiv'it) *n.*: A state of irritation or annoyance.
**6. dictum** (dik'təm) *n.*: A formal statement or pronouncement.

be turfed out, since the Weyr's need was for fighting dragons and riders.

By the time the evening meal was over, no decision had been reached, although the Weyrleader had promised to give the matter due consideration.

He might have slept on the problem, but few of the candidates did. Tempers were uncertain in the sleeping caverns next morning as the boys were routed out of their beds to carry water and black rock and cover the "glows." Twice Mende had to call Keevan to order for clumsiness.

"Whatever is the matter with you, boy?" she demanded in exasperation when he tipped black rock short of the bin and sooted up the hearth.

"They're going to keep me from this Impression."

"What?" Mende stared at him. "Who?"

"You heard them talking at dinner last night. They're going to turf the babes from the hatching."

Mende regarded him a moment longer before touching his arm gently. "There's lots of talk around a supper table, Keevan. And it cools as soon as the supper. I've heard the same nonsense before every Hatching, but nothing is ever changed."

"There's always a first time," Keevan answered, copying one of her own phrases.

"That'll be enough of that, Keevan. Finish your job. If the clutch does hatch today, we'll need full rock bins for the feast, and you won't be around to do the filling. All my fosterlings make dragonriders."

"The first time?" Keevan was bold enough to ask as he scooted off with the rockbarrow.

Perhaps, Keevan thought later, if he hadn't been on that chore just when Beterli was also fetching black rock, things might have turned out differently. But he had dutifully trundled the barrow to the outdoor

---

## Grammar in Action

The **comparative** and **superlative** degrees of adjectives and adverbs are used to make comparisons. The comparative is used to compare one thing with another. The superlative is used to compare one thing with all the others in a group.

Use *-er*, *more*, or *less* to form the comparative degree and *-est*, *most*, or *least* to form the superlative degree of most one- and two-syllable modifiers: *smaller, smallest; more capable, most capable*. The comparative and superlative forms of irregular modifiers such as *good, bad, much*, and *little* must be memorized.

Notice how effectively McCaffrey uses a series of adjectives in the superlative degree in this sentence from the story:

"... Keevan staggered forward and threw his arms around the dragon's neck ... wordlessly assuring the hatchling over and over again that he was the *most perfect, most beautiful, most beloved* dragon in the Weyr...."

Why was the word *most* used to form the superlative degree of each adjective in the sentence above?

**Student Activity 1.** Identify the comparative and superlative degrees of the modifiers in these sentences from the story. Then tell whether each is comparative or superlative:

bunker for another load just as Beterli arrived on a similar errand.

"Heard the news, babe?" Beterli asked. He was grinning from ear to ear, and he put an unnecessary emphasis on the final insulting word.

"The eggs are cracking?" Keevan all but dropped the loaded shovel. Several anxieties flicked through his mind then: he was black with rock dust—would he have time to wash before donning the white tunic of candidacy? And if the eggs were hatching, why hadn't the candidates been recalled by the wingsecond?

"Naw! Guess again!" Beterli was much too pleased with himself.

With a sinking heart, Keevan knew what the news must be, and he could only stare with intense desolation at the older boy.

"C'mon! Guess, babe!"

"I've no time for guessing games," Keevan managed to say with indifference. He began to shovel black rock into the barrow as fast as he could.

"I said, guess." Beterli grabbed the shovel.

"And I said I have no time for guessing games."

Beterli wrenched the shovel from Keevan's hands. "Guess!"

"I'll have that shovel back, Beterli." Keevan straightened up, but he didn't come to Beterli's bulky shoulder. From somewhere, other boys appeared, some with barrows, some mysteriously alerted to the prospect of a confrontation among their numbers.

"Babes don't give orders to candidates around here, babe!"

Someone sniggered and Keevan, incredulous, knew that he must've been dropped from the candidacy.

He yanked the shovel from Beterli's loosened grasp. Snarling, the older boy tried to regain possession, but Keevan clung with all his strength to the handle, and was dragged back and forth as the stronger boy jerked the shovel about.

With a sudden, unexpected movement, Beterli rammed the handle into Keevan's chest, knocking him over the barrow handles. Keevan felt a sharp, painful jab behind his left ear, an unbearable pain in his left shin, and then a painless nothingness.

Mende's angry voice roused him, and, startled, he tried to throw back the covers, thinking he'd overslept. But he couldn't move, so firmly was he tucked into his bed. And then the constriction of a bandage on his head and the dull sickishness in his leg brought back recent occurrences.

"Hatching?" he cried.

"No, lovey," Mende said in a kind voice. Her hand was cool and gentle on his forehead. "Though there's some as won't be at any Hatching again." Her voice took on a stern edge.

Keevan looked beyond her to see the Weyrwoman, who was frowning with irritation.

"Keevan, will you tell me what occurred at the black-rock bunker?" asked Lessa in an even voice.

He remembered Beterli now and the quarrel over the shovel and . . . what had Mende said about some not being at any Hatching? Much as he hated Beterli, he couldn't bring himself to tattle on Beterli and force him out of candidacy.

"Come, lad," and a note of impatience crept into the Weyrwoman's voice. "I merely want to know what happened from you, too. Mende said she sent you for black rock. Beterli—and every weyrling in the cavern —seems to have been on the same errand. What happened?"

"Beterli took my shovel. I hadn't finished with it."

*The Smallest Dragonboy* 165

28 **Enrichment** The word *candidate* comes from the Latin word *candidatus,* which means "clothed in white." In ancient Rome candidates for public office wore white togas. The use of the term and the wearing of white tunics remind the reader that the distant ancestors of Pern's inhabitants were from Earth.

29 **Discussion** Why don't the other boys stop the fight? What would you have done if you had been one of the other candidates?

30 **Discussion** To whom do you think Mende is referring? Why?

31 **Literary Focus: Theme** What does Keevan's behavior toward Beterli indicate about his level of maturity?

1. "Yes, being the smallest candidate was not an enviable position."
2. "Dreams of Impressing a bronze were beyond Keevan's boldest reflections. . . ."
3. ". . . they'd be in the mood to tell tall tales, better than Harper yarns. . . ."
4. "When Thread attack was closer, their talk would change to a discussion of tactics of evasion. . . ."
5. "You say the most outrageous things, Lessa."

**Student Activity 2.** Write a paragraph about training an animal or about your favorite pet. Use comparative and superlative modifiers in your paragraph.

**Electronic Handbook** You may want students to review the degrees of comparison before completing these Grammar in Action activities. If students have access to the Language Master 6000, have them enter the access word *comparative* and press the GRAMMAR key to review the comparison of adjectives. For additional practice students may play the comparison of adjectives game, which can be accessed from the grammar lesson by hitting the GAMES key.

**32 Reading Strategy** Predict why the other candidates are avoiding Keevan. Give reasons to support your ideas.

**ESL Teaching Strategy** Because ESL students may experience difficulty reading and understanding terms that refer to the planet Pern, you may wish to pair them with other students from the class as reading partners. As they read the story, the partners can help ESL students understand vocabulary and difficult concepts.

**Cooperative Learning** Students may enjoy forming small groups to read and discuss some of the author's novels about the dragon-riders of Pern. Suggest that the groups take notes on characters and places that appear in this story.

"There's more than one shovel. What did he *say* to you?"

"He'd heard the news."

"What news?" The Weyrwoman was suddenly amused.

"That . . . that . . . there'd been changes."

"Is that what he said?"

"Not exactly."

"What did he say? C'mon, lad, I've heard from everyone else, you know."

"He said for me to guess the news."

"And you fell for that old gag?" The Weyrwoman's irritation returned.

"Consider all the talk last night at supper, Lessa," Mende said. "Of course the boy would think he'd been eliminated."

"In effect, he is, with a broken skull and leg." Lessa touched his arm in a rare gesture of sympathy. "Be that as it may, Keevan, you'll have other Impressions. Beterli will not. There are certain rules that must be observed by all candidates, and his conduct proves him unacceptable to the Weyr."

She smiled at Mende and then left.

"I'm still a candidate?" Keevan asked urgently.

"Well, you are and you aren't, lovey," his foster mother said. "Is the numbweed working?" she asked, and when he nodded, she said, "You just rest. I'll bring you some nice broth."

At any other time in his life, Keevan would have relished such cosseting,[7] but now he just lay there worrying. Beterli had been dismissed. Would the others think it was his fault? But everyone was there! Beterli provoked that fight. His worry increased, because although he heard excited comings and goings in the passageway, no one tweaked back the curtain across the sleeping alcove he shared with five other boys. Surely one of them would have to come

7. **cosseting** (käs'it iŋ) *n.*: Pampering.

*166  Short Stories*

in sometime. No, they were all avoiding him. And something else was wrong. Only he didn't know what.

Mende returned with broth and beach-berry bread.

"Why doesn't anyone come see me, Mende? I haven't done anything wrong, have I? I didn't ask to have Beterli turfed out."

Mende soothed him, saying everyone was busy with noontime chores and no one was angry with him. They were giving him a chance to rest in quiet. The numbweed made him drowsy, and her words were fair enough. He permitted his fears to dissipate. Until he heard a hum. Actually, he felt it first, in the broken shin bone and his sore head. The hum began to grow. Two things registered suddenly in Keevan's groggy mind: the only white candidate's robe still on the pegs in the chamber was his; and the dragons hummed when a clutch was being laid or being hatched. Impression! And he was flat abed.

Bitter, bitter disappointment turned the warm broth sour in his belly. Even the small voice telling him that he'd have other opportunities failed to alleviate his crushing depression. *This* was the Impression that mattered! This was his chance to show *everyone*, from Mende to K'last to L'vel and even the Weyrleader that he, Keevan, was worthy of being a dragonrider.

He twisted in bed, fighting against the tears that threatened to choke him. Dragon-men don't cry! Dragonmen learn to live with pain.

Pain? The leg didn't actually pain him as he rolled about on his bedding. His head felt sort of stiff from the tightness of the bandage. He sat up, an effort in itself since the numbweed made exertion difficult. He touched the splinted leg; the knee was unhampered. He had no feeling in his bone, really. He swung himself carefully to the side of his bed and stood slowly. The room

## Grammar in Action

Writers use **transitional words** and **phrases** to link ideas, to help organize events, and to make writing flow smoothly. This sentence begins with a transitional word:

"Although Keevan lengthened his walking stride as far as his legs would stretch, he couldn't quite keep up with the other candidates."

Anne McCaffrey uses the transitional word *although* to signal a contrast between Keevan and the other candidates.

The next sentence contains a transitional phrase:

"On the height, the blue watch dragon . . . stretched the great transparent pinions that carried him on the winds of Pern to fight the evil Thread. . . ."

Here, McCaffrey uses the transitional phrase *on the height* to indicate the spatial relationship between the watch dragon and the inhabitants of the Weyr.

In addition to showing contrast and spatial relationships, transitions can also link cause and effect, show time order, indicate additional details, and add emphasis.

**Student Activity 1.** Identify the transitional word or phrase in each of the following sentences from the story. Tell the purpose of each transition.

wanted to swim about him. He closed his eyes, which made the dizziness worse, and he had to clutch the wall.

Gingerly, he took a step. The broken leg dragged. It hurt in spite of the numbweed, but what was pain to a dragonman?

No one had said he couldn't go to the Impression. "You are and you aren't," were Mende's exact words.

Clinging to the wall, he jerked off his bedshirt. Stretching his arm to the utmost, he jerked his white candidate's tunic from the peg. Jamming first one arm and then the other into the holes, he pulled it over his head. Too bad about the belt. He couldn't wait. He hobbled to the door, hung on to the curtain to steady himself. The weight on his leg was unwieldy. He wouldn't get very far without something to lean on. Down by the bathing pool was one of the long crook-necked poles used to retrieve clothes from the hot washing troughs. But it was down there, and he was on the level above. And there was no one nearby to come to his aid: everyone would be in the Hatching Ground right now, eagerly waiting for the first egg to crack.

The humming increased in volume and tempo, an urgency to which Keevan responded, knowing that his time was all too limited if he was to join the ranks of the hopeful boys standing around the cracking eggs. But if he hurried down the ramp, he'd fall flat on his face.

He could, of course, go flat on his rear end, the way crawling children did. He sat down, sending a jarring stab of pain through his leg and up to the wound on the back of his head. Gritting his teeth and blinking away tears, Keevan scrambled down the ramp. He had to wait a moment at the bottom to catch his breath. He got to one knee, the injured leg straight out in front of him. Somehow, he managed to push himself erect, though the room seemed about to tip

over his ears. It wasn't far to the crooked stick, but it seemed an age before he had it in his hand.

Then the humming stopped!

Keevan cried out and began to hobble frantically across the cavern, out to the bowl of the Weyr. Never had the distance between living caverns and the Hatching Ground seemed so great. Never had the Weyr been so breathlessly silent. It was as if the multitude of people and dragons watching the Hatching held every breath in suspense. Not even the wind muttered down the steep sides of the bowl. The only sounds to break the stillness were Keevan's ragged gasps and the thump-thud of his stick on the hard-packed ground. Sometimes he had to hop twice on his good leg to maintain his balance. Twice he fell into the sand and had to pull himself up on the stick, his white tunic no longer spotless. Once he jarred himself so badly he couldn't get up immediately.

Then he heard the first exhalation of the crowd, the oohs, the muted cheer, the susurrus[8] of excited whispers. An egg had cracked, and the dragon had chosen his rider. Desperation increased Keevan's hobble. Would he never reach the arching mouth of the Hatching Ground?

Another cheer and an excited spate of applause spurred Keevan to greater effort. If he didn't get there in moments, there'd be no unpaired hatchling left. Then he was actually staggering into the Hatching Ground, the sands hot on his bare feet.

No one noticed his entrance or his halting progress. And Keevan could see nothing but the backs of the white-robed candidates, seventy of them ringing the area around the eggs. Then one side would surge forward or back and there'd be a cheer. Another dragon had been Impressed. Suddenly a large gap

---

8. **susurrus** (sə sûr'əs) *n.*: A murmuring or rustling sound.

*The Smallest Dragonboy* 167

34

**33 Critical Thinking and Reading** List the details that make this scene realistic.

**34 Reading Strategy** What is the effect of this single-sentence paragraph?

**Multicultural Focus** Point out that the dragon has historically been a symbol of both good and evil all over the world. In early Christianity these mythical creatures represented evil, such as the one slain by Saint George. In China and Japan, however, dragons are considered good and are endowed with special powers. In fact the dragon is the Chinese national symbol. Help students understand that the dragons in these cultures are symbolic. The only "real" dragons in the world are the giant lizards of Komodo Island in Indonesia. Because of their size, these lizards are popularly called Komodo Dragons.

Ask students to research information and stories about dragons. Have them present their findings in class.

---

1. "'Now move about among the eggs,' the wingsecond said."
2. "Fortunately, at that moment, the wingsecond called the boys together and led them from the Hatching Ground to start on evening chores."
3. "Tonight, Keevan's father, K'last, was at the main dragonrider table."
4. "From somewhere, other boys appeared, some with barrows, some mysteriously alerted to the prospect of a confrontation among their numbers."

**Student Activity 2.** Combine each pair of sentences with a transitional word or phrase.
1. The watch dragon stretched his wings. He was perched on the mountaintop.

2. The candidates touched the eggs. They went to do their evening chores.
3. The dragonriders debated restricting the number of candidates. The candidates listened intently.
4. Keevan struggled with Beterli. The other candidates watched.

**Student Activity 3.** Write a paragraph about traveling to an unusual place. Use transitional words and phrases in your paragraph. Then proofread to be sure that you have used transitions correctly.

## Humanities Note

Fine art, *Untitled Illustration,* by Michael Whelan. The American artist Michael Whelan has made the illustration of fantasy and science-fiction literature his lifework. This untitled illustration was created for the cover of a novel by Anne McCaffrey. The dragons and riders in this painting are captured in a moment of calm. The soft pastel tones and the whites of the clouds and the dragon in the foreground help to establish a restful atmosphere, yet the eerie yellow light striking the subject from a source on the right adds a note of drama and suggests the possibility of action. Whelan maintains a consistency in his rendering of dragons, having illustrated several of Anne McCaffrey's works about the dragonriders of Pern. His conceptualization is based on both a knowledge of and respect for the literature he illustrates, as well as a natural flair for dramatic realism. Whelan's technically pristine illustrations have given a fascinating visual dimension to literature in the genre.

You might use these questions for discussion:

1. What about the landscape tells you that this is not the planet Earth?
2. Compare these dragons with those in the other two illustrations accompanying this story. Describe the similarities and differences you see.

**35 Discussion** Throughout the story the size and power of the dragons have been emphasized. How does this description of the newly hatched dragons change your feelings about them?

appeared in the white human wall, and Keevan had his first sight of the eggs. There didn't seem to be *any* left uncracked, and he could see the lucky boys standing beside wobble-legged dragons. He could hear the unmistakable plaintive crooning of hatchlings and their squawks of protest as they'd fall awkwardly in the sand.

Suddenly he wished that he hadn't left his bed, that he'd stayed away from the Hatching Ground. Now everyone would see his ignominious failure. So he scrambled as desperately to reach the shadowy walls of the Hatching Ground as he had struggled to cross the bowl. He mustn't be seen.

He didn't notice, therefore, that the shifting group of boys remaining had begun to drift in his direction. The hard pace he had set himself and his cruel disappointment took their double toll of Keevan. He tripped and collapsed sobbing to the warm sands. He didn't see the consternation in the watching Weyrfolk above the Hatching Ground, nor did he hear the excited whispers of speculation. He didn't know that the Weyrleader and Weyrwoman had dropped to the arena and were making their way toward the knot of boys slowly moving in the direction of the entrance.

"Never seen anything like it," the Weyr-

**UNTITLED ILLUSTRATION**
*Michael Whelan*
*Courtesy of the Artist*

168   *Short Stories*

leader was saying. "Only thirty-nine riders chosen. And the bronze trying to leave the Hatching Ground without making Impression."

"A case in point of what I said last night," the Weyrwoman replied, "where a hatchling makes no choice because the right boy isn't there."

"There's only Beterli and K'last's young one missing. And there's a full wing of likely boys to choose from . . ."

"None acceptable, apparently. Where is the creature going? He's not heading for the entrance after all. Oh, what have we there, in the shadows?"

Keevan heard with dismay the sound of voices nearing him. He tried to burrow into the sand. The mere thought of how he would be teased and taunted now was unbearable.

*Don't worry! Please don't worry!* The thought was urgent, but not his own.

Someone kicked sand over Keevan and butted roughly against him.

"Go away. Leave me alone!" he cried.

*Why?* was the injured-sounding question inserted into his mind. There was no voice, no tone, but the question was there, perfectly clear, in his head.

Incredulous, Keevan lifted his head and stared into the glowing jeweled eyes of a small bronze dragon. His wings were wet, the tips drooping in the sand. And he sagged in the middle on his unsteady legs, although he was making a great effort to keep erect.

Keevan dragged himself to his knees, oblivious of the pain in his leg. He wasn't even aware that he was ringed by the boys passed over, while thirty-one pairs of resentful eyes watched him Impress the dragon. The Weyrmen looked on, amused and surprised at the draconic[9] choice, which could

---

9. **draconic** (drə kăn'ik) *adj.*: Made by a dragon.

not be forced. Could not be questioned. Could not be changed.

*Why?* asked the dragon again. *Don't you like me?* His eyes whirled with anxiety, and his tone was so piteous that Keevan staggered forward and threw his arms around the dragon's neck, stroking his eye ridges, patting the damp, soft hide, opening the fragile-looking wings to dry them, and wordlessly assuring the hatchling over and over again that he was the most perfect, most beautiful, most beloved dragon in the Weyr, in all the Weyrs of Pern.

"What's his name, K'van?" asked Lessa, smiling warmly at the new dragonrider. K'van stared up at her for a long moment. Lessa would know as soon as he did. Lessa was the only person who could "receive" from all dragons, not only her own Ramoth. Then he gave her a radiant smile, recognizing the traditional shortening of his name that raised him forever to the rank of dragonrider.

*My name is Heth,* the dragon thought mildly, then hiccuped in sudden urgency. *I'm hungry.*

"Dragons are born hungry," said Lessa, laughing. "F'lar, give the boy a hand. He can barely manage his own legs, much less a dragon's."

K'van remembered his stick and drew himself up. "We'll be just fine, thank you."

"You may be the smallest dragonrider ever, young K'van," F'lar said, "but you're one of the bravest!"

And Heth agreed! Pride and joy so leaped in both chests that K'van wondered if his heart would burst right out of his body. He looped an arm around Heth's neck and the pair, the smallest dragonboy and the hatchling who wouldn't choose anybody else, walked out of the Hatching Ground together forever.

*The Smallest Dragonboy* 169

---

36 **Discussion** Where do you think the bronze is going?

37 **Reading Strategy** What does the use of italics signify?

38 **Literary Focus: Theme** How and why has Keevan's name changed?

39 **Reading Strategy** How do you know that Heth agreed?

**Reader's Response** How did you feel when Keevan was struggling to reach the Hatching Ground?

**Thematic Response** Would Keevan's rite of passage have made as interesting a story if he had Impressed a green, blue, or brown dragon? Why or why not?

---

## Closure and Extension

### ANSWERS TO RESPONDING TO THE SELECTION
#### Your Response

1. Encourage students to support their opinions with reasons.
2. Divide the class into two teams: those who favor limiting the number of candidates and those who favor including all eligible candidates. Provide class time for the two teams to debate the issue.

### Recalling

3. Mende says that dragons look for goodness, honesty, a flexible mind, patience, and courage.
4. Because there are so many more candidates than eggs, the dragonriders always debate whether or not the field of candidates should be limited to the older candidates, to the untried candidates, or not limited at all. Each time, tradition wins out and all candidates are allowed to stand.

### Interpreting

5. Suggested Response: As the smallest of the candidates, Keevan needs to be chosen by a dragon in order to restore his self-confidence and win the respect due a dragonrider.
6. Suggested Response: Lessa is saying that the issue of the number of candidates present is irrelevant; each dragon will choose only the rider that is right for it.

7. Suggested Response: Keevan has all the qualities that Mende says the dragons look for, especially courage. It takes courage to stand up to Beterli, to refuse to tattle on Beterli, to drag himself to the Hatching Ground, and to Impress a bronze dragon.

## Applying

8. Lead students to understand that Beterli, like most bullies, probably picks on Keevan to compensate for his feelings of inadequacy.

## ANSWERS TO ANALYZING LITERATURE

1. Suggested Response: When provoked by Beterli's taunting, Keevan refuses to let Beterli see how upset he is. During the fight over the shovel, Keevan holds on, refusing to relinquish it. Later, when Lessa asks Keevan about the fight, he cannot bring himself to tattle on Beterli.
2. Suggested Response: Keevan lives with the emotional pain of being taunted by Beterli and with the physical pain in his head and leg.

## ANSWERS TO CRITICAL THINKING AND READING

Suggested Response: Teenagers may face any of the following problems presented in the story: being teased about size, being picked on by older teenagers, being afraid of being excluded from some activity, having to stand up to a bully, wanting to live up to parents' expectations, having to do chores when you'd rather be doing something else, having to decide whether or not to tattle on a classmate.

**Challenge** What do you think will happen to K'van and Heth after the end of the story? What will happen to Beterli?

## THINKING AND WRITING

**Writing Transparency** Paragraph exercises are good tools for reviewing paragraph structure. Before students describe a rite of passage, assign *Transitions* in **Transparencies for Writing.**

**Software** If students are working on computers, have them use the **Writer's Helper** activity *Transitions* to help them revise their descriptions of a rite of passage.

---

# RESPONDING TO THE SELECTION

## Your Response

1. Anne McCaffrey creates a whole world in her story. Would you like to live in the lands of Pern? Why or why not?
2. If you were a dragonrider debating which boys should take part in the Impression, what would your decision have been?

## Recalling

3. According to Keevan's mother, what qualities do the dragons look for?
4. What issue is debated around the supper table before every Hatching? What is the decision each time?

## Interpreting

5. Why is it so important to Keevan to be chosen by a dragon?
6. What point is Lessa the Weyrwoman making when she asks whether a dragon had ever refused to choose a rider?
7. What qualities make Keevan a good candidate to be a dragonrider? How does he show these qualities?

## Applying

8. Beterli taunts Keevan for reasons beyond just the difference in their sizes. Discuss reasons why bullies pick on people.

# ANALYZING LITERATURE

## Understanding Theme

The **theme,** or central idea, in "The Smallest Dragonboy" is suggested, not stated directly. You can uncover the theme by analyzing the story and considering what it seems to say about the nature of people or about life. At the end of the story, Keevan earns the status of dragonrider, but first he has to prove himself worthy. Keevan goes through certain experiences that test his courage

and strength of character, just as we all go through "rites of passage" as we achieve adulthood in real life.

1. How does Keevan show courage and strength of character in his confrontation with Beterli?
2. Keevan thinks to himself, ". . . Dragonmen learn to live with pain." How does he prove that he, too, can live with pain?

# CRITICAL THINKING AND READING

## Identifying Realistic Details

Many of the details of both the setting and the plot of this story could be found only in a work of fantasy or science fiction. Yet the details describing Keevan's feelings and struggles with other characters realistically describe experiences many teenagers go through.

Review the selection to find problems real teenagers might face. Then list these problems.

# THINKING AND WRITING

## Writing About Rites of Passage

Many cultures celebrate the passage from adolescence into adulthood in a formal way. A bar mitzvah, celebrated in the Jewish religion, is an example of such a ceremony.

Write a description of a rite of passage that you or someone you know has experienced. It may be about a formal celebration or a personal experience that resulted in new-found growth and understanding.

# LEARNING OPTION

**Writing.** Imagine that you are a dragon seeking a rider. Make up an advertisement to aid your search. Include a description of the qualities you look for in a dragonrider.

---

**Publishing Student Writing** Have students exchange their first drafts with a partner to read and suggest improvements. Have volunteers read their final drafts to their class. Then lead a discussion about the similarities and differences in the various rites of passage.

**Alternative Assessment** You may vary the Thinking and Writing Assignment as follows: Ask your students to tell the story of a time they or someone they know has had to deal with a bully. As Anne McCaffrey does in "The Smallest Dragonboy," have them show the feelings of the main character and realistically describe his or her struggles to overcome a bully.

**LEARNING OPTION**

Extend the writing activity to appeal to auditory learners by having them collect stories and legends of dragons and read them to their class.

# ONE WRITER'S PROCESS

## Anne McCaffrey and "The Smallest Dragonboy"

### PREWRITING

**Lucky False Start** Anne McCaffrey was trying to write a short story about a completely different character when, as she puts it, "The story plain wouldn't *write.* So I abandoned that project and wrote about Keevan, 'The Smallest Dragonboy.'"

**The Trigger to Write** Getting started on a writing project is not a problem for McCaffrey. She says, "Early in my writing career, when my children were small, I would think about what I would write when I got a chance to sit down at the 'keyboard.' That was always the trigger for me to write."

### DRAFTING

**Picturing the Scene** Although McCaffrey writes about places that don't exist, her imagination is precise and concrete. She visualizes each scene as she writes: "I know where everyone is in a particular scene, and if I don't, I make sure I visualize the stage at some point so I know where I am."

**Solidly Grounded in Science** As she writes, she also makes sure that her imagined places are based on scientific knowledge. That is why she considers her work to be science fiction rather than fantasy.

### REVISING

**Tightening, Reducing, and Ordering** McCaffrey revises as she writes, and again at the end of the project. "Mostly," she says, "I revise dialogue, and tighten scenes, reduce the use of adjectives and adverbs, and make sure phrases are in the proper order."

Following is an example of how she revised a sentence in her new novel:

---

**First Draft:**

Now everything Bunny cared about and counted on was changing, coming apart the way the ice, **usually as much to be depended upon as the ground** this time of year, had broken away beneath her.

**Revision:**

All of a sudden, everything Bunny cared about and counted on was changing: coming apart the way the ice, **usually as dependable as the solid ground** this time of year, had broken away beneath her.

---

McCaffrey says, "Sometimes just rereading shows you where you've used one word too often in a paragraph, so that it falls uneasily upon the ear of the mind."

### PUBLISHING

**High Praise** The author says, "I'm always of two minds about being included in any school program because sometimes the books you *have* to read can turn you off to other books by the same author. However, I was somewhat reassured on this point . . . when three youngsters said they'd had to read 'The Smallest Dragonboy' in school and 'it really wasn't bad.'" That, says McCaffrey, was "high praise indeed."

### THINKING ABOUT THE PROCESS

1. Does the "ear" of your mind help you revise your writing? Explain.
2. **Writing** Get together with a small group of classmates and design a planet that could serve as the setting for a science-fiction tale.

*One Writer's Process* **171**

**More About the Author** Toshio Mori's first collection of stories included twenty-two about the Japanese communities in Oakland and San Leandro, California. The stories received mixed reviews because of their unconventional style of language. One critic noted about Mori, ''His is the language of a writer dependent on the dictionary rather than on an extensive knowledge of connotations, and for this very reason often wonderfully fresh and spontaneous.'' Ask students to comment on this review. What advantages and disadvantages are there in being ''dependent on the dictionary''? Why might a writer be unfamiliar with the connotations of the English language? Why might this unfamiliarity result in good, clear writing?

**Literary Focus** Even in everyday conversation, note key statements in people's speech that alert you to the main point they are making.

**Prereading Focus** Put the chart on the chalkboard. Ask volunteers to name a few responsibilities and what they could learn from them. Have students refer to them as they fill in their charts.

**Vocabulary** Most students will have no difficulty with these words. You might have them use each word in a sentence orally before reading the story.

**Spelling Tip** You might point out that *lagged* is an example of a word whose final consonant is doubled when an inflectional ending beginning with a vowel is added.

**Electronic Handbook** If students have access to the Language Master 6000, suggest that they find a synonym with a different connotation for *anxious*.

172

# GUIDE FOR READING

## Toshio Mori

(1910–1980) wrote short stories and novels about the Japanese Americans of northern California. Mori was born in Oakland, California; his parents were Japanese immigrants. Mori's collection of stories, *Yokohama, California,* was published in 1949. The stories—including "The Six Rows of Pompons"—take place in the years before World War II. This story shows the qualities that the author William Saroyan has identified in Mori's writing: "understanding sympathy, generosity and kindliness."

## The Six Rows of Pompons

### Key Statements

Theme is the central idea of a story, or the general idea about life that is revealed through a story. Sometimes the theme is implied, or suggested. A **key statement** in the story is a sentence that may point to the implied theme or help you see what the theme is. A key statement may be made directly by a character.

### Focus

This story is about responsibility and the lessons it teaches. Fill in a chart like the one that follows to indicate some new responsibilities you would like to take on and what you might learn from them.

| New Responsibility | Lesson to Be Learned |
|---|---|
| 1. | |
| 2. | |
| 3. | |
| 4. | |

Then, as you read "The Six Rows of Pompons," think about what Nephew Tatsuo is learning from his new responsibilities.

### Vocabulary

Knowing the following words will help you as you read "The Six Rows of Pompons."

**rampage** (ram′ pāj) *n.*: An outbreak of violent behavior (p. 173)
**enthusiasm** (en thoo′ zē az′ əm) *n.*: Intense or eager interest (p. 175)

**lagged** (lagd) *v.*: Fell behind (p. 175)
**anxious** (aŋk′ shəs) *adj.*: Eagerly wishing (p. 175)

*172   Short Stories*

# The Six Rows of Pompons
## Toshio Mori

When little Nephew Tatsuo[1] came to live with us he liked to do everything the adults were doing on the nursery, and although his little mind did not know it, everything he did was the opposite of adult conduct, unknowingly destructive and disturbing. So Uncle Hiroshi[2] after witnessing several weeks of rampage said, "This has got to stop, this sawing the side of a barn and nailing the doors to see if it would open. But we must not whip him. We must not crush his curiosity by any means."

And when Nephew Tatsuo, who was seven and in high second grade, got used to the place and began coming out into the fields and pestering us with difficult questions as "What are the plants here for? What is water? Why are the bugs made for? What are the birds and why do the birds sing?" and so on, I said to Uncle Hiroshi, "We must do something about this. We cannot answer questions all the time and we cannot be correct all the time and so we will do harm. But something must be done about this beyond a doubt."

"Let us take him in our hands," Uncle Hiroshi said.

So Uncle Hiroshi took little Nephew Tatsuo aside, and brought him out in the fields and showed him the many rows of pompons[3] growing. "Do you know what these are?" Uncle Hiroshi said. "These things here?"

"Yes. Very valuable," Nephew Tatsuo said. "Plants."

"Do you know when these plants grow up and flower, we eat?" Uncle Hiroshi said.

Nephew Tatsuo nodded. "Yes," he said, "I knew that."

"All right. Uncle Hiroshi will give you six rows of pompons," Uncle Hiroshi said. "You own these six rows. You take care of them. Make them grow and flower like your uncle's."

"Gee!" Nephew Tatsuo said.

"Do you want to do it?" Uncle Hiroshi said.

"Sure!" he said.

"Then jump right in and start working," Uncle Hiroshi said. "But first, let me tell you something. You cannot quit once you start. You must not let it die, you must make it grow and flower like your uncles'."

"All right," little Nephew Tatsuo said, "I will."

"Every day you must tend to your plants. Even after the school opens, rain or shine," Uncle Hiroshi said.

"All right," Nephew Tatsuo said. "You'll see!"

---

1. **Tatsuo** (tăt sōō' ō)
2. **Hiroshi** (hěr ō' shē)

3. **pompons** (păm' pănz') n.: Flowers that have small, rounded heads, such as chrysanthemums.

174   *Short Stories*

So the old folks once more began to work
peacefully, undisturbed, and Nephew Tatsuo began to work on his plot. However,
every now and then Nephew Tatsuo would
run to Uncle Hiroshi with much excitement.

"Uncle Hiroshi, come!" he said.
"There's bugs on my plants! Big bugs,
green bugs with black dots and some
brown bugs. What shall I do?"

"They're bad bugs," Uncle Hiroshi said.
"Spray them."

"I have no spray," Nephew Tatsuo said
excitedly.

"All right. I will spray them for you
today," Uncle Hiroshi said. "Tomorrow I will
get you a small hand spray. Then you must
spray your own plants."

Several tall grasses shot above the pompons and Uncle Hiroshi noticed this. Also,
he saw the beds beginning to fill with
young weeds.

"Those grasses attract the bugs," he
said. "Take them away. Keep the place
clean."

It took Nephew Tatsuo days to pick the
weeds out of the six beds. And since the
weeds were not picked cleanly, several
weeks later it looked as if it was not
touched at all. Uncle Hiroshi came around
sometimes to feel the moisture in the
soil. "Tatsuo," he said, "your plants need
water. Give it plenty, it is summer. Soon
it will be too late."

Nephew Tatsuo began watering his
plants with the three-quarter hose.

"Don't hold the hose long in one place
and short in another," Uncle Hiroshi said.
"Keep it even and wash the leaves often."

In October Uncle Hiroshi's plants stood
tall and straight and the buds began to
appear. Nephew Tatsuo kept at it through
summer and autumn, although at times he
looked wearied and indifferent. And each

time Nephew Tatsuo's enthusiasm lagged Uncle Hiroshi took him over to the six rows of pompons and appeared greatly surprised.

"Gosh," he said, "your plants are coming up! It is growing rapidly; pretty soon the flowers will come."

"Do you think so?" Nephew Tatsuo said.

"Sure, can't you see it coming?" Uncle Hiroshi said. "You will have lots of flowers. When you have enough to make a bunch I will sell it for you at the flower market."

"Really?" Nephew Tatsuo said. "In the flower market?"

Uncle Hiroshi laughed. "Sure," he said. "That's where the plant business goes on, isn't it?"

One day Nephew Tatsuo wanted an awful lot to have us play catch with him with a tennis ball. It was at the time when the nursery was the busiest and even Sundays were all work.

"Nephew Tatsuo, don't you realize we are all men with responsibilities?" Uncle Hiroshi said. "Uncle Hiroshi has lots of work to do today. Now is the busiest time. You also have lots of work to do in your beds. And this should be your busiest time. Do you know whether your pompons are dry or wet?"

"No, Uncle Hiroshi," he said. "I don't quite remember."

"Then attend to it. Attend to it," Uncle Hiroshi said.

Nephew Tatsuo ran to the six rows of pompons to see if it was dry or wet. He came running back. "Uncle Hiroshi, it is still wet," he said.

"All right," Uncle Hiroshi said, "but did you see those holes in the ground with the piled-up mounds of earth?"

"Yes. They're gopher holes," Nephew Tatsuo said.

"Right," Uncle Hiroshi said. "Did you catch the gopher?"

"No," said Nephew Tatsuo.

"Then attend to it, attend to it right away," Uncle Hiroshi said.

One day in late October Uncle Hiroshi's pompons began to bloom. He began to cut and bunch and take them early in the morning to the flower market in Oakland.[4] And by this time Nephew Tatsuo was anxious to see his pompons bloom. He was anxious to see how it feels to cut the flowers of his plants. And by this time Nephew Tatsuo's six beds of pompons looked like a patch of tall weeds left uncut through the summer. Very few pompon buds stood out above the tangle.

Few plants survived out of the six rows. In some parts of the beds where the pompons had plenty of water and freedom, the stems grew strong and tall and the buds were big and round. Then there were parts where the plants looked shriveled and the leaves were wilted and brown. The majority of the plants were dead before the cool weather arrived. Some died by dryness, some by gophers or moles, and some were dwarfed by the great big grasses which covered the pompons altogether.

When Uncle Hiroshi's pompons began to flower everywhere the older folks became worried.

"We must do something with Tatsuo's six beds. It is worthless and his bugs are coming over to our beds," Tatsuo's father said. "Let's cut it down and burn them today."

"No," said Uncle Hiroshi. "That will be a very bad thing to do. It will kill Nephew Tatsuo. Let the plants stay."

So the six beds of Nephew Tatsuo remained intact, the grasses, the gophers, the bugs, the buds and the plants and all. Soon

---

**4. Oakland** (ōk′ lənd): A port city in western California, on San Francisco Bay.

6 **Critical Thinking and Reading** What is Uncle Hiroshi's technique for encouraging Tatsuo?

7 **Literary Focus** What is the key statement here? Explain your answer.

8 **Discussion** Why didn't Tatsuo's rows flourish like his uncle's? Was it his fault? What might Tatsuo have learned from this?

9 **Discussion** Why does Tatsuo's father want to burn Tatsuo's flower beds? Why does Uncle Hiroshi disagree?

176

**10** Critical Thinking and Reading
What is Uncle Hiroshi trying to teach Tatsuo by selling his pompons?

**11** Discussion  How does Tatsuo react when his pompons are sold?

**12** Discussion  Why does Uncle Hiroshi feel that Tatsuo should spend the money he earned?

**13** Discussion  What has Uncle Hiroshi learned about Tatsuo? What kind of person might Tatsuo grow up to be?

**14** Critical Thinking and Reading
What does Uncle Hiroshi mean by this? How does he expect Tatsuo to change?

**15** Critical Thinking and Reading
What is Tatsuo's "unfinished work"? What are the men talking about?

**Reader's Response**  What has helped you to learn responsibility? What do you take pride in the way Tatsuo takes pride in his pompons?

**Thematic Response**  In addition to a chance to make some money growing flowers, what more important opportunity does Uncle Hiroshi give Tatsuo that will help him in becoming an adult?

after, the buds began to flower and Nephew Tatsuo began to run around calling Uncle Hiroshi. He said the flowers are coming. Big ones, good ones. He wanted to know when can he cut them.

**10** "Today," Uncle Hiroshi said. "Cut it today and I will sell it for you at the market tomorrow."

Next day at the flower market Uncle Hiroshi sold the bunch of Nephew Tatsuo's pompons for twenty-five cents. When he came home Nephew Tatsuo ran to the car.

"Did you sell it, Uncle Hiroshi?" Nephew Tatsuo said.

"Sure. Why would it not sell?" Uncle Hiroshi said. "They are healthy, carefully cultured pompons."

**11** Nephew Tatsuo ran around excitedly. First, he went to his father. "Papa!" he said, "someone bought my pompons!" Then he ran over to my side and said, "The bunch was sold! Uncle Hiroshi sold my pompons!"

At noontime, after the lunch was over, Uncle Hiroshi handed over the quarter to Nephew Tatsuo.

"What shall I do with this money?" asked Nephew Tatsuo, addressing all of us, with shining eyes.

"Put it in your toy bank," said Tatsuo's father.

**12** "No," said Uncle Hiroshi. "Let him do what he wants. Let him spend and have a taste of his money."

"Do you want to spend your quarter, Nephew Tatsuo?" I said.

"Yes," he said.

"Then do anything you wish with it," Uncle Hiroshi said. "Buy anything you want. Go and have a good time. It is your money."

On the following Sunday we did not see Nephew Tatsuo all day. When he came back late in the afternoon Uncle Hiroshi said, "Nephew Tatsuo, what did you do today?"

"I went to a show, then I bought an ice cream cone and then on my way home I watched the baseball game at the school, and then I bought a popcorn from the candy man. I have five cents left," Nephew Tatsuo said.

"Good," Uncle Hiroshi said. "That shows a good spirit."

Uncle Hiroshi, Tatsuo's father, and I sat in the shade. It was still hot in the late afternoon that day. We sat and watched Nephew Tatsuo riding around and around the yard on his red tricycle, making a furious dust.

"Next year he will forget what he is doing this year and will become a wild animal and go on a rampage again," the father of Tatsuo said.

"Next year is not yet here," said Uncle Hiroshi.

"Do you think he will be interested to raise pompons again?" the father said.

**13** "He enjoys praise," replied Uncle Hiroshi, "and he takes pride in good work well done. We will see."

"He is beyond a doubt the worst gardener in the country," I said. "Probably he is the worst in the world."

"Probably," said Uncle Hiroshi.

"Tomorrow he will forget how he enjoyed spending his year's income," the father of Tatsuo said.

**14** "Let him forget," Uncle Hiroshi said. "One year is nothing. We will keep this six rows of pompon business up till he comes to his senses."

**15** We sat that night the whole family of us, Uncle Hiroshi, Nephew Tatsuo's father, I, Nephew Tatsuo, and the rest, at the table and ate, and talked about the year and the prospect of the flower business, about Uncle Hiroshi's pompon crop, and about Nephew Tatsuo's work and, also, his unfinished work in this world.

## Closure and Extension

### ANSWERS TO RESPONDING TO THE SELECTION
*Your Response*

1. When formulating their answers, have students think about some effective ways to change a child's rambunctious behavior.

### Recalling

2. Uncle Hiroshi tells Tatsuo that he must care for his plants every day, rain or shine.

3. Tatsuo's pompons have bugs, weeds, and gophers.
4. Tatsuo's father suggests this because the bugs from Tatsuo's beds are attacking the men's flowers.
5. Hiroshi encourages Tatsuo to spend his money.

### Interpreting

6. Tatsuo's questions are bothersome to people who are trying to work, and many of the questions are unanswerable. Tatsuo is a child.
7. Hiroshi gives Tatsuo the pompons to keep him busy in a productive way and to teach him a sense of responsibility.
8. Hiroshi wants Tatsuo to identify with the men and take his responsibilities seriously.
9. At the beginning of the story, Tatsuo doesn't know what it means to work hard. He pesters the

# RESPONDING TO THE SELECTION

## Your Response

1. Do you feel that giving Nephew Tatsuo six rows of pompons was a good idea? Explain.

## Recalling

2. What instructions does Uncle Hiroshi give Tatsuo about growing pompons?
3. What problems does Tatsuo have with his pompons?
4. Why does Tatsuo's father suggest cutting Tatsuo's flowers down and burning them?
5. What does Hiroshi encourage Tatsuo to do with the money he got for his flowers?

## Interpreting

6. Why do the older folks dislike Tatsuo's questions? How is Hiroshi different from them?
7. Why does Hiroshi give Tatsuo the pompons?
8. Why does Hiroshi ask Tatsuo, "Don't you realize we are all men with responsibilities"?
9. Compare and contrast Tatsuo at the beginning and the end of the story. Will he remember the lesson next spring? Explain.

## Applying

10. How can someone be taught responsibility?

# ANALYZING LITERATURE

## Understanding Key Statements

**Key statements** help you understand the theme of a story, especially a story whose theme is implied, or suggested. In "The Six Rows of Pompons," for example, Uncle Hiroshi says, "You cannot quit once you start." This key statement says that staying with a project to the end is part of being responsible. It points to the theme that responsibility can be taught through experience rather than through punishment.

Explain how the following key statements lead you to understand the implied theme.

1. "That will be a very bad thing to do. It will kill Nephew Tatsuo."

2. "One year is nothing. We will keep this six rows of pompons business up till he comes to his senses."

# CRITICAL THINKING AND READING

## Comparing and Contrasting Attitudes

When you look at similarities, you **compare.** When you look at differences, you **contrast.** Comparing and contrasting characters' attitudes can help you understand the implied theme. Tatsuo's father and Uncle Hiroshi both want to teach Tatsuo responsibility, but their attitudes differ on how to teach it.

Contrast their attitudes on the following, and explain what this suggests about theme.

1. Bugs from Tatsuo's bed start going over to the other beds.
2. Tatsuo earns money for his flowers.

# THINKING AND WRITING

## Writing a Letter About Theme

Imagine that you are Tatsuo recalling this experience several years after the event. First freewrite about your pompon-growing experience. Then use these ideas to draft a letter to Uncle Hiroshi describing what the experience taught you about responsibility. Proofread your letter and prepare a final draft.

# LEARNING OPTIONS

1. **Writing.** Caring for a garden, as you have seen in "The Six Rows of Pompons," is hard work. In a small group, create a manual for growing flowers, taking your information from what is written in the story. Present your instructions in the order in which they should be carried out. Illustrate your manual if you like.

2. **Art.** Use magazines, catalogs, paint, markers, and other materials to create a colorful flower collage. You may wish to label the different types of flowers.

*The Six Rows of Pompons* 177

---

Langston Hughes began to be published, he was criticized for his extensive use of African American colloquialisms. Hughes responded that although his characters were not people "whose shoes were always shined," they were good people, too. Now that his works have been translated into German, French, Spanish, Russian, Yiddish, and Czech, do you think the criticism was valid? Ask students to discuss how people of such diverse backgrounds can appreciate African American colloquial dialogue. Why does it speak to all people?

**Literary Focus** Character and theme are often inextricably bound. The way the characters act and react exemplify the theme of a story. Suggest that students ask themselves, "What is this story about?" and the characters will tell them.

**Prereading Focus** Have volunteers offer suggestions as to how the article might end. Discuss these briefly. Then encourage students to think creatively as they work in small groups to finish the article.

**Vocabulary** Most students will have no difficulty with these words. You might have them use each word in a sentence orally before reading the story.

**Electronic Handbook** If students have access to the Language Master 6000, suggest that they find an antonym for *presentable*.

178

# GUIDE FOR READING

## Langston Hughes

(1902–1967) was born in Joplin, Missouri. He attended Columbia University for a year and held a number of odd jobs before the publication of his first collection of poetry in 1926. Hughes published many volumes of poetry and fiction, as well as essays, histories, and dramas. He was awarded numerous prizes and grants and is often called the "Poet Laureate of Harlem," which is a section of New York City in northern Manhattan. "Thank You, M'am" is one of Hughes's many stories about city life for African Americans.

## Thank You, M'am

### Key to Theme: Character

The way that a character in a story changes and grows often can be a key to theme. Sometimes a character may grow through being affected by others. In "Thank You, M'am," Mrs. Jones's treatment of Roger brings about a change in him. By thinking about how Mrs. Jones treats Roger, you can understand the implied theme of the story.

### Focus

Imagine that you came across an article in the newspaper that began as follows: "Last night at about eleven o'clock, a large woman walking alone on Main Street caught a boy attempting to steal her purse." How do you think the article might end? Work together with a small group of classmates to finish the article, telling what happens to the woman and the boy. As you read "Thank You, M'am," notice how a similar situation is resolved.

### Vocabulary

Knowing the following words will help you as you read "Thank You, M'am."

**willow-wild** (wil′ ō wild′) *adj.*: Slender and pliant, like a reed blowing in the wind (p. 179)
**kitchenette-furnished** (kich ə net′ fʉr′ nisht) *n.*: Having a small, compact kitchen (p. 181)
**presentable** (pri zen′ tə b'l) *adj.*: Suitable to be seen by others (p. 181)

## Objectives

1 To understand an implied theme through a story's characters
2 To identify generalizations about the characters
3 To write a letter from the point of view of a story's character
4 To express individual interests and abilities through an optional activity

## Support Material

**Teaching Portfolio**
Teacher Backup, p. 263
Grammar in Action Worksheet, *Understanding Compound Predicates*, p. 266
Usage and Mechanics Worksheet, p. 268
Vocabulary Check, p. 269
Critical Thinking and Reading Worksheet, *Identifying Generalizations*, p. 270

Language Worksheet, *Understanding Compound Words*, p. 271
Selection Test, p. 272

**Prentice Hall Literature Writing Studio**

# Thank You, M'am

### Langston Hughes

She was a large woman with a large purse that had everything in it but hammer and nails. It had a long strap and she carried it slung across her shoulder. It was about eleven o'clock at night, and she was walking alone, when a boy ran up behind her and tried to snatch her purse. The strap broke with the single tug the boy gave it from behind. But the boy's weight, and the weight of the purse combined caused him to lose his balance so, instead of taking off full blast as he had hoped, the boy fell on his back on the sidewalk, and his legs flew up. The large woman simply turned around and kicked him right square in his blue-jeaned sitter. Then she reached down, picked the boy up by his shirt front, and shook him until his teeth rattled.

After that the woman said, "Pick up my pocketbook, boy, and give it here."

She still held him. But she bent down enough to permit him to stoop and pick up her purse. Then she said, "Now ain't you ashamed of yourself?"

Firmly gripped by his shirt front, the boy said, "Yes'm."

The woman said, "What did you want to do it for?"

The boy said, "I didn't aim to."

She said, "You a lie!"

By that time two or three people passed, stopped, turned to look, and some stood watching.

"If I turn you loose, will you run?" asked the woman.

"Yes'm," said the boy.

"Then I won't turn you loose," said the woman. She did not release him.

"I'm very sorry, lady, I'm sorry," whispered the boy.

"Um-hum! And your face is dirty. I got a great mind to wash your face for you. Ain't you got nobody home to tell you to wash your face?"

"No'm," said the boy.

"Then it will get washed this evening," said the large woman starting up the street, dragging the frightened boy behind her.

He looked as if he were fourteen or fifteen, frail and willow-wild, in tennis shoes and blue jeans.

The woman said, "You ought to be my son. I would teach you right from wrong. Least I can do right now is to wash your face. Are you hungry?"

"No'm," said the being-dragged boy. "I just want you to turn me loose."

"Was I bothering *you* when I turned that corner?" asked the woman.

"No'm."

*Thank You, M'am   179*

**Presentation**

**Motivation/Prior Knowledge** Have students imagine that they have been surprised by someone's act of kindness and concern for them. Perhaps it came at a particularly significant point in their lives and made a profound difference in the way they view the world. Would they always remember this person? Would they try to perform an act of kindness toward someone else? Have students explore how a brief encounter with someone can change a life.

**Master Teacher Note** Point out to students that purse snatching is a major urban crime problem. Hughes set many of his stories in Harlem, which, because of its socioeconomic problems, is plagued with various types of street crime. Harlem was once the black jazz capital of the world, however, and many people are striving to restore Harlem's dignity through urban renewal programs. Bring in photographs of Harlem jazz clubs of the 1920's and contrast them with photographs of Harlem tenements and urban renewal projects today.

**Making Connections** Another selection that deals with lessons in living is "The Six Rows of Pompons" (page 173).

**Purpose-Setting Question** What role does compassion play in this story?

**1 Discussion** How experienced at purse snatching do you think this boy is? How can you tell?

**2 Literary Focus** How does Hughes use colloquial language to provide information on the characters and setting of the story?

**3 Critical Thinking and Reading** Does the woman regard the boy as a criminal? How does she treat him? Why is she getting involved with him?

**Thematic Focus** Discuss with students whether a person can be accurately evaluated during a brief observation. Ask students to discuss characteristics of a person whom they later came to appreciate after closer acquaintance.

**Alternative Assessment** To promote active reading, have students create a reader's response journal as they read "Thank You, M'am." Ask them to focus on the details that reveal Mrs. Jones's personality, those that indicate Roger's fear of what she will do, and those that reveal the effect on him of her kindness and understanding. Encourage students to respond personally to

the characters and events in this story. Have them discuss a person who has had a major impact on their lives.

## Humanities Note

Fine Art, *Mother Courage,* by Charles White. The African American painter, graphic artist, and educator Charles White was born in poverty in Chicago, Illinois. From age seven he drew and painted constantly. Through the support of his mother and the numerous awards his talent earned him, White received his education at the Chicago Art Institute, the Art Students League of New York, and the Taeler de la Grafica in Mexico. His powerful, articulate style extols the dignity, history, and strength of African American people.

*Mother Courage,* a linoleum cut print, was done in 1974 as a magazine illustration. The graceful solidity of this solitary figure illustrates Charles White's skill as a draftsman. He brings us face to face with his subject, a strong African American woman, aptly named "Mother Courage." White's works are exhibited in major collections nationwide.

You might want to ask students the following questions about the art:

1. Why do you think White entitled this piece *Mother Courage?*
2. What are other possible titles for this piece?

**4 Critical Thinking and Reading**
What do you think Mrs. Jones is going to do to the boy? How do you think the boy is feeling?

**MOTHER COURAGE, 1974**
*Charles White*
National Academy of Design

"But you put yourself in contact with *me,*" said the woman. "If you think that that contact is not going to last awhile, you got another thought coming. When I get through with you, sir, you are going to remember Mrs. Luella Bates Washington Jones."

Sweat popped out on the boy's face and he began to struggle. Mrs. Jones stopped, jerked him around in front of her, put a half

180    *Short Stories*

## Grammar In Action

A good way to combine sentences when writing is to use **compound predicates.** A compound predicate is two or more verbs that have the same subject and are joined by a conjunction such as *and, but,* and *or.* Writers who wish to vary their sentence structure and combine related phrases use compound verbs. The result is a sequence of actions performed by one subject in one sentence.

Using compound predicates allows a writer to illustrate a series of actions more effectively. One simple sentence after another can interrupt the flow of actions, whereas compound predicates capture the actions to give the reader a sense of timing. Notice how Langston Hughes uses compound predicates in the following two sentences:

> Mrs. Jones stopped, jerked him around in front of her, put a half nelson about his neck, and continued to drag him up the street. When she got to her door, she dragged the boy inside, down a hall, and into a large kitchenette–furnished room at the rear of the house.

Consider how drawn out the first series of events would read if Hughes had separated each action:

nelson[1] about his neck, and continued to drag him up the street. When she got to her door, she dragged the boy inside, down a hall, and into a large kitchenette-furnished room at the rear of the house. She switched on the light and left the door open. The boy could hear other roomers laughing and talking in the large house. Some of their doors were open, too, so he knew he and the woman were not alone. The woman still had him by the neck in the middle of her room.

She said, "What is your name?"

"Roger," answered the boy.

**5** "Then, Roger, you go to that sink and wash your face," said the woman, whereupon she turned him loose—at last. Roger looked at the door—looked at the woman—looked at the door—*and went to the sink.*

"Let the water run until it gets warm," she said. "Here's a clean towel."

"You gonna take me to jail?" asked the boy, bending over the sink.

"Not with that face, I would not take you nowhere," said the woman. "Here I am trying to get home to cook me a bite to eat and you snatch my pocketbook! Maybe you ain't been to your supper either, late as it be. Have you?"

**6** "There's nobody home at my house," said the boy.

"Then we'll eat," said the woman. "I believe you're hungry—or been hungry—to try to snatch my pocketbook."

"I wanted a pair of blue suede shoes," said the boy.

**7** "Well, you didn't have to snatch *my* pocketbook to get some suede shoes," said Mrs. Luella Bates Washington Jones. "You could of asked me."

"M'am?"

———————
**1. half nelson:** A wrestling hold using one arm.

The water dripping from his face, the boy looked at her. There was a long pause. A very long pause. After he had dried his face and not knowing what else to do dried it again, the boy turned around, wondering what next. The door was open. He could make a dash for it down the hall. He could run, run, run, run, *run!*

The woman was sitting on the day bed. After awhile she said, "I were young once and I wanted things I could not get."

There was another long pause. The boy's mouth opened. Then he frowned, but not knowing he frowned.

**8** The woman said, "Um-hum! You thought I was going to say *but,* didn't you? You thought I was going to say, *but I didn't snatch people's pocketbooks.* Well, I wasn't going to say that." Pause. Silence. "I have done things, too, which I would not tell you, son—neither tell God, if He didn't already know. So you set down while I fix us something to eat. You might run that comb through your hair so you will look presentable."

In another corner of the room behind a screen was a gas plate and an icebox. Mrs. Jones got up and went behind the screen. The woman did not watch the boy to see if he was going to run now, nor did she watch her purse which she left behind her on the day bed. But the boy took care to sit on the far side of the room where he thought she could easily see him out of the corner of her eye, if she wanted to. He did not trust the woman *not* to trust him. And he did not want to be mistrusted now.

**9** "Do you need somebody to go to the store," asked the boy, "maybe to get some milk or something?"

"Don't believe I do," said the woman, "unless you just want sweet milk yourself. I was going to make cocoa out of this canned milk I got here."

*Thank You, M'am* 181

**5 Discussion** Why does Roger cooperate when he could run?

**6 Discussion** What does this suggest about Roger's home life?

**7 Critical Thinking and Reading** What kind of person is Mrs. Jones?

**8 Discussion** Do you think Mrs. Jones's past makes her more sympathetic to Roger? Why or why not?

**9 Critical Thinking and Reading** Why does Roger make this offer? Do you think it's genuine?

**Multicultural Focus** Explain that matriarchal societies are those in which lineage descends through the mother. Certain African societies are matriarchal: A man pays a "bride price" when he gets married and goes to live with his wife's family; their children identify with the mother's clan or ethnic group. Help students understand that, traditionally, African American culture has had a strong matriarchal element; mothers or grandmothers are often the focus of the family. Discuss the idea that, with the increase of single-parent families in the United States, more and more women are becoming the dominant force in their families.

Ask students to think of or find a story in which a woman plays an important family role. Invite students to discuss how the stories would be different if the major characters were men.

After Mrs. Jones stopped, she jerked him around in front of her. Then she put a half nelson about his neck. Next, she continued to drag him up the street.

Although each sentence in the paragraph above is grammatically correct, the paragraph does not read as smoothly as Hughes's version nor is it as interesting.

Study another sentence in which Hughes uses a compound predicate:

Roger looked at the door—looked at the woman—looked at the door—and went to the sink.

In the sentence above, Hughes uses dashes rather than commas to set the actions apart from one another while combining them.

**Student Activity 1.** Write a series of simple sentences that illustrate a series of actions. Exchange papers with classmates and rewrite the sentences using compound predicates.

**Student Activity 2.** Using sentences with compound predicates, describe an exciting event you have witnessed or seen on television or at the movies.

**Electronic Handbook** If students have access to the Language Master 6000, have them enter the access word *subject* and press the GRAMMAR key to get information on compound subjects and compound predicates.

**10 Literary Focus** Discuss Mrs. Jones's character. What qualities does she have? Why does she show Roger kindness instead of calling the police? What can you infer about her past from the way she treats Roger?

**11 Discussion** What effect do you think this gift has on Roger? Do you think he has learned a lesson from Mrs. Jones?

**12 Critical Thinking and Reading** What else do you think Roger wanted to say to Mrs. Jones? Are you surprised that Roger never saw her again? Do you think Roger will ever forget her?

## Humanities Note

Fine art, *Sunny Side of the Street,* by Philip Evergood. The American artist Philip Evergood (1901–1973) was a social-realist painter. He obtained his education at many fine art schools in Europe, England, and New York City. His striking, bright canvases are powerful comments on American life and social tragedy.

*Sunny Side of the Street* was painted in 1950. The crowded exuberance of this street scene is typical of Evergood and exemplifies his devotion to painting his personal response to life experience. His technique of laying one flat color field next to another is an expressive device used to evoke an emotional response in the viewer. The odd perspective and proportion of the painting were used for the same result.

The paintings of Philip Evergood are lively and rich with the symbols of American life. The poor and underprivileged people were his favorite subject.

You might want to ask the following questions about the art:
1. What associations do you make with this scene?
2. What is your emotional response to this scene?

**Reader's Response** Mrs. Jones trusts Roger even though he has proven himself untrustworthy. In

182

**SUNNY SIDE OF THE STREET**
*Philip Evergood*

"That will be fine," said the boy.

She heated some lima beans and ham she had in the icebox, made the cocoa, and set the table. The woman did not ask the boy anything about where he lived, or his folks, or anything else that would embarrass him. Instead, as they ate, she told him about her job in a hotel beauty shop that stayed open late, what the work was like, and how all kinds of women came in and out, blondes, redheads, and brunettes. Then she cut him a half of her ten-cent cake.

"Eat some more, son," she said.

When they were finished eating she got up and said, "Now, here, take this ten dollars and buy yourself some blue suede shoes. And next time, do not make the mistake of latching onto *my* pocketbook *nor nobody else's*—because shoes come by devilish like that will burn your feet. I got to get my rest now. But I wish you would behave yourself, son, from here on in."

She led him down the hall to the front door and opened it. "Goodnight! Behave yourself, boy!" she said, looking out into the street.

The boy wanted to say something else other than, "Thank you, m'am," to Mrs. Luella Bates Washington Jones, but he couldn't do so as he turned at the barren stoop and looked back at the large woman in the door. He barely managed to say, "Thank you," before she shut the door. And he never saw her again.

182   *Short Stories*

other words, she gives him a chance to prove that he can be trusted. Describe a situation in which you were given a chance to prove yourself when the odds were against you.

**Thematic Response** Roger finally comes to appreciate Mrs. Luella Bates Washington Jones. What feelings does he have about her during their encounter? What changes his mind?

## Closure and Extension

### ANSWERS TO RESPONDING TO THE SELECTION
*Your Response*

1. Suggest that students discuss this very important issue and think about the possible consequences of trusting and of not trusting the boy.

2. Encourage students to support their opinions with specific details from the story about Mrs. Jones's past.

*Recalling*

3. Mrs. Jones kicks him and then picks him up and drags him to her house.

4. She says she would teach him right from wrong.

5. Roger tried to steal her purse to buy blue suede shoes. Mrs. Jones responds that Roger could simply have asked her for the money.

6. Mrs. Jones gives Roger the money so that he won't steal anymore and because she says that shoes

# RESPONDING TO THE SELECTION

## Your Response

1. Do you feel that Mrs. Jones is wise or foolish in trusting Roger? Why?
2. Why do you think Mrs. Jones chooses not to punish Roger? Explain.

## Recalling

3. What does Mrs. Jones do when Roger tries to steal her purse?
4. What does she say she would teach Roger if he were her son?
5. What reason does Roger give for trying to steal her purse? How does Mrs. Jones respond to this reason?
6. Why does Mrs. Jones give Roger ten dollars?

## Interpreting

7. Why doesn't Roger run away from Mrs. Jones's apartment at the first opportunity?
8. What does the following tell about Roger: "He did not trust the woman *not* to trust him. And he did not want to be mistrusted now."
9. Early in the story, Mrs. Jones says, "When I get through with you, sir, you are going to remember Mrs. Luella Bates Washington Jones." How do her words turn out to be true?
10. At the end of the story, why does Roger want to say more than just "Thank you, m'am"?

## Applying

11. Can you change people's behavior through kindness and understanding? Explain.

# ANALYZING LITERATURE

## Using Character to Understand Theme

The way that a character changes is often a clue to the theme of a story. In this story Mrs. Jones's treatment of Roger brings about a change in him that points to the theme.

1. How does Mrs. Jones show that she respects Roger? In what ways does she treat him with understanding and kindness?

2. Explain how you think Mrs. Jones's treatment makes Roger feel about himself.
3. How does Roger change?
4. What do you think is the theme of this story?

# CRITICAL THINKING AND READING

## Identifying Generalizations

A **generalization** is a conclusion you draw from similarities among a large number of cases. A **hasty generalization** is a conclusion that is based on too few cases. For example, if the pizza is good the first time you eat at a new pizza parlor, you might conclude that the pizza there is *always* good. This would be a hasty generalization, because the number of cases is too small.

1. What generalization had Roger made about older women walking alone at night?
2. What did Roger learn about applying this generalization to this particular case?

# THINKING AND WRITING

## Writing About a Character

Imagine that you are Roger twenty years after the story. You decide to write a letter to Mrs. Jones describing why the event in the story was so important to you. In your letter include a statement about how the event helped shape your future decisions and actions. Revise your letter, making sure that your reasoning is clear.

# LEARNING OPTION

**Speaking and Listening.** In Readers Theater two or more speakers give a dramatic reading of a literature selection. The words and the way they are spoken are more important than the gestures used. With classmates, prepare and present a Readers Theater version of "Thank You, M'am." Decide how the characters will speak or present themselves. Then write a script and practice reading, putting emphasis on oral interpretation of the characters and their actions.

*Thank You, M'am* 183

---

bought with stolen money would "burn" his feet.

## Interpreting

7. Answers will differ. Suggested Response: Roger is curious and has nowhere to go anyway.
8. Answers will differ. Suggested Response: He knew the woman had reason to mistrust him, but he wanted her to trust him now that she was being so kind to him.
9. Answers will differ. Suggested Response: Mrs. Jones's words are even truer than she expected be-

cause she makes Roger's dream come true.
10. Answers will differ. Suggested Response: Roger wants to say more because he is moved and grateful for her kindness and generosity.

## Applying

11. Answers will differ. Suggested Response: Kindness and understanding can change a person's behavior, especially if the person is unaccustomed to being treated well. Being treated with dignity

can give a person a feeling of self-worth so that he or she wants to improve.

## ANSWERS TO ANALYZING LITERATURE

1. Mrs. Jones shares her dinner with Roger, doesn't ask him any personal questions that might embarrass him, and gives him ten dollars for the shoes he wants.
2. Answers will differ. Suggested Response: Roger probably felt ashamed of himself for trying to

steal Mrs. Jones's purse. He probably also felt that he was a human deserving of kindness and respect.
3. Answers will differ. Suggested Response: Roger relaxes, becomes more trusting, and grateful for human kindness.
4. Answers will differ. Students should see that experiencing a little kindness and generosity of spirit can make a big difference in someone's life.

### ANSWERS TO CRITICAL THINKING AND READING

1. Roger probably thought that all older women walking alone at night were vulnerable and helpless.
2. Roger learned that some older people are strong and fearless despite their age.

**Challenge** Discuss how the story makes a universal statement about people through only two characters. Describe both Mrs. Jones's background and Roger's home life, as they are suggested in the story. How do these characters represent larger segments of society?

### THINKING AND WRITING

**Writing Transparency** A graphic organizer may help your students with their listing of future decisions and actions. Use the *Series of Events Chain* in Transparencies for Writing.

**Alternative Assessment** You may vary the Thinking and Writing assignment as follows: Have your students write a dialogue between Roger (several years after the incident described in this story) and Tatsuo (from "The Six Rows of Pompons") in which both young men recall how their lives were changed by an early experience with a wise and understanding adult.

### LEARNING OPTION

Kinesthetic learners and students with a flair for drama will enjoy this activity. Tape-record their presentation, if possible.

---

## Preparation

**More About the Author** Edward Everett Hale was the grandnephew of the Revolutionary War hero Nathan Hale whose last words, "I only regret that I have but one life to give for my country," have become famous. Nathan Hale was hanged as a spy by the British in New York City in 1776 when he was only twenty-one years old. Ask students to discuss if having a famous ancestor could influence a writer. Would Edward Hale have been more likely than another writer to write from a historical or military perspective, for example?

**Literary Focus** Many objects that you see every day are symbolic. Some of these are so common that you don't even realize that what you're looking at is a symbol. For example, a swirling, striped pole is the symbol for a barber shop.

**Prereading Focus** Introduce the concept of how important it is to think before speaking by asking students to remember an instance when they spoke rashly and then regretted it. Then have them brainstorm for other examples in small groups.

**Vocabulary** These words may also give students some difficulty: *catastrophe, court-martials* (p. 186); *frenzy, plantation, adjourned, etiquette* (p. 187); *insignia, minstrel* (p. 189); *beggarly, farce* (p. 190); *rammer, cockpit* (p. 191); *dispatches* (p. 192); *midshipman, schooner* (p. 193); *volubly, liberality* (p. 194); *accumulated* (p. 197); *manifold,* and *transgressions* (p. 198).

**Electronic Handbook** If students have access to the Language Master 6000, suggest that they locate a list of synonyms for *blunders.* Have them think about instances when a writer might choose the word *blunders* instead of a synonym with a similar meaning.

### Edward Everett Hale

(1822–1909), the grandnephew of American Revolutionary War hero Nathan Hale, began writing stories when he was a boy. He later published his own small newspaper. After graduating from Harvard University, Hale became a Unitarian minister and a journalist, but continued writing short stories, essays, and novels. His well-known story "The Man Without a Country" seemed so realistic that many people who read it in *The Atlantic Monthly* in 1863 believed it was true.

## The Man Without a Country

### Symbols

A **symbol** is an object, an action, or an idea that stands for something other than itself. For example, a lion is an animal that lives in Africa and Asia, but it is also a symbol of courage and strength. In a story, a writer may use symbols that are familiar to most readers or symbols that occur only in that story. Recognizing and understanding symbols can help you understand a story's theme, or central idea.

### Focus

It is always a good idea to think before you speak. At times, however, we have probably all been guilty of carelessly blurting out our feelings. This can cause misunderstandings and sometimes leads to problems. With your classmates, brainstorm to list instances from life, literature, film, or television in which someone says or does something without thinking and then regrets it. What happens as a result of the rash statement or action? How would things be different if the person had thought before speaking or acting? What does the person learn from the experience?

In the following story, a man's life is changed forever by a careless statement. As you read, think of how things might have been different for Philip Nolan if he had thought before he spoke.

### Vocabulary

Knowing the following words will help you as you read "The Man Without a Country."

**obscure** (äb skyoor´) *adj.*: Hidden; not obvious (p. 185)

**availed** (ə vāld´) *v.*: Made use of (p. 185)

**stilted** (stil´ təd) *adj.*: Unnatural; very formal (p. 185)

**swagger** (swag´ ər) *n.*: Arrogance or boastfulness (p. 187)

**intercourse** (int´ ər kôrs) *n.*: Communication between people (p. 188)

**blunders** (blun´ dərz) *n.*: Foolish or stupid mistakes (p. 191)

### Objectives

1 To recognize symbols in a short story
2 To paraphrase the theme of a short story
3 To write about the theme of a short story

### Support Material

**Teaching Portfolio**
Teacher Backup, p. 275
Grammar In Action Worksheets, *Using Colons,* p. 278; *Understanding Action Verbs,* pp. 280–281; *Using Sentence Variety,* p. 282
Usage and Mechanics Worksheet, p. 284
Vocabulary Check, p. 285
Critical Thinking and Reading Worksheet, *Paraphrasing,* p. 286
Language Worksheet, *Choosing the Meaning That Fits the Context,* p. 287
Selection Test, p. 288

**Prentice Hall Literature Writing Studio**

# The Man Without a Country

### Edward Everett Hale

I suppose that very few casual readers of the *New York Herald* of August 13, 1863, observed, in an obscure corner, among the "Deaths," the announcement:

NOLAN. Died, on board U.S. Corvette *Levant,* Lat. 2° 11′ S., Long. 131° W., on the 11th of May, PHILIP NOLAN.

Hundreds of readers would have paused at the announcement had it read thus: "Died, May 11, THE MAN WITHOUT A COUNTRY." For it was as "The Man Without a Country" that poor Philip Nolan had generally been known by the officers who had him in charge during some fifty years, as, indeed, by all the men who sailed under them.

There can now be no possible harm in telling this poor creature's story. Reason enough there has been till now for very strict secrecy, the secrecy of honor itself, among the gentlemen of the Navy who have had Nolan in charge. And certainly it speaks well for the profession and the personal honor of its members that to the press this man's story has been wholly unknown —and, I think, to the country at large also. This I do know, that no naval officer has mentioned Nolan in his report of a cruise.

But there is no need for secrecy any longer. Now the poor creature is dead, it seems to me worthwhile to tell a little of his story, by way of showing young Americans of today what it is to be "A Man Without a Country."

Philip Nolan was as fine a young officer as there was in the "Legion of the West," as the Western division of our army was then called. When Aaron Burr[1] made his first dashing expedition down to New Orleans in 1805, he met this gay, dashing, bright young fellow. Burr marked[2] him, talked to him, walked with him, took him a day or two's voyage in his flatboat,[3] and, in short, fascinated him. For the next year, barrack life was very tame to poor Nolan. He occasionally availed himself of the permission the great man had given him to write to him. Long, stilted letters the poor boy wrote and rewrote and copied. But never a line did he have in reply. The other boys in the garrison[4] sneered at him, because he lost the fun which they found in shooting or rowing while he was working away on these grand letters to his grand friend. But before long the young fellow had his revenge. For this

1. **Aaron Burr:** American political leader (1756–1836). Burr was U.S. Vice-President from 1801 to 1805. He was believed to have plotted to build an empire in the Southwest.
2. **marked** *v.*: Here, paid attention to.
3. **flatboat** *n.*: Boat with a flat bottom.
4. **garrison** (gar′ ə s′n) *n.*: Military post or station.

*The Man Without a Country* 185

Fine art, *Officer of the Watch on the Horseblock,* 1851, from *Heck's Iconographic Encyclopedia.* Before photographs, etchings were used to represent people, places, and things realistically. This nineteenth-century engraving shows a typical naval scene. Before the advent of elaborate navigational and tracking equipment, men had to take turns on a ship watching for changes in weather conditions, for other ships, and for enemy attacks.

1. How is this engraving like a photograph?
2. What do you learn about life aboard a nineteenth-century ship from this picture?

5 **Discussion** Why did Burr pursue Nolan?

6 **Critical Thinking and Reading** What had Burr accomplished with Nolan? Why was Nolan loyal to Burr?

**OFFICER OF THE WATCH ON THE HORSEBLOCK**
*Heck's Iconographic Encyclopedia, 1851*
New York Public Library

time His Excellency, the Honorable Aaron Burr, appeared again under a very different aspect. There were rumors that he had an army behind him and an empire before him. At that time the youngsters all envied him. Burr had not been talking twenty minutes with the commander before he asked him to send for Lieutenant Nolan. Then, after a little talk, he asked Nolan if he could show him something of the great river and the plans for the new post. He asked Nolan to take him out in his skiff to show him a canebrake[5] or a cottonwood tree, as he said —really to win him over; and by the time the sail was over, Nolan was enlisted body and soul. From that time, though he did not yet know it, he lived as a man without a country.

What Burr meant to do I know no more than you. It is none of our business just now. Only, when the grand catastrophe came —Burr's great treason trial at Richmond —some of the lesser fry at Fort Adams[6] got up a string of court-martials on the officers there. One and another of the colonels and majors were tried, and, to fill out the list, little Nolan, against whom there was evidence enough that he was sick of the service, had been willing to be false to it, and would have obeyed any order to march anywhere had the order been signed "By command of His Exc. A. Burr." The courts dragged on. The big flies[7] escaped—rightly, for all I know. Nolan was proved guilty enough, yet you and I would never have heard of him but that, when the president

_____
**5. canebrake** (kān′ brāk′) *n.*: A dense area of cane plants.

_____
**6. Fort Adams:** The fort at which Nolan was stationed.
**7. big flies:** Burr and the other important men who may have been involved in his scheme.

## Grammar in Action

The **colon** is used to direct attention to the information following it. One of the most important uses of the colon is to introduce a list of miscellaneous items that follow an independent clause. (Never use a colon to introduce a list that does not follow an independent clause.) As an introductory device, the colon precedes quotations. When you want to quote something you heard someone say or something you read, use a colon to introduce the quotation. Notice how the colon is used to introduce what Nolan said in "The Man Without a Country."

". . . when the president of the court asked him at the close whether he wished to say anything to show that he had always been faithful to the United States, he cried out, in a fit of frenzy:

"'Damn the United States! I wish I may never hear of the United States again!'"

An especially important function of the colon is to signal important ideas or information. You may have seen the colon on medication labels or labels on toxic products such as cleaners. For instance, "Warning: If taken internally, consult a physician immediately."

of the court asked him at the close whether he wished to say anything to show that he had always been faithful to the United States, he cried out, in a fit of frenzy:

7 "Damn the United States! I wish I may never hear of the United States again!"

I suppose he did not know how the words shocked old Colonel Morgan, who was holding the court. Half the officers who sat in it had served through the Revolution, and their lives had been risked for the very idea which he cursed in his madness. He, on his part, had grown up in the West of those days. He had been educated on a plantation where the finest company was a Spanish officer or a French merchant from Orleans.
8 His education had been perfected in commercial expeditions to Vera Cruz, and I think he told me his father once hired an Englishman to be a private tutor for a winter on the plantation. He had spent half his youth with an older brother, hunting horses in Texas; and to him "United States" was scarcely a reality. I do not excuse Nolan; I only explain to the reader why he cursed his country and wished he might never hear her name again.

From that moment, September 23, 1807, till the day he died, May 11, 1863, he never heard her name again. For that half-century and more he was a man without a country.

Old Morgan, as I said, was terribly shocked. If Nolan had compared George Washington to Benedict Arnold, or had cried, "God save King George," Morgan would not have felt worse. He called the court into his private room, and returned in fifteen minutes, with a face like a sheet, to say: "Prisoner, hear the sentence of the
9 Court! The Court decides, subject to the approval of the President, that you never hear the name of the United States again."

Nolan laughed. But nobody else laughed. Old Morgan was too solemn, and the whole room was hushed dead as night for a minute. Even Nolan lost his swagger in a moment. Then Morgan added: "Mr. Marshal, take the prisoner to Orleans in an armed boat, and deliver him to the naval commander there."

The marshal gave his orders and the prisoner was taken out of court.

"Mr. Marshal," continued old Morgan, "see that no one mentions the United States to the prisoner. Mr. Marshal, make my repects to Lieutenant Mitchell at Orleans, and request him to order that no one shall mention the United States to the prisoner while he is on board ship. You will receive your written orders from the officer on duty here this evening. The court is adjourned."

Before the *Nautilus*[8] got round from New Orleans to the Northern Atlantic coast with the prisoner on board, the sentence had
10 been approved, and he was a man without a country.

The plan then adopted was substantially the same which was necessarily followed ever after. The Secretary of the Navy was requested to put Nolan on board a government vessel bound on a long cruise, and to direct that he should be only so far confined there as to make it certain that he never saw or heard of the country. We had few long cruises then, and I do not know certainly what his first cruise was. But the commander to whom he was entrusted regulated the etiquette and the precautions of the affair, and according to his scheme they were carried out till Nolan died.

When I was second officer of the *Intrepid,* some thirty years after, I saw the original paper of instructions. I have been sorry ever since that I did not copy the whole of it. It ran, however, much in this way:

---

**8. Nautilus:** The naval ship to which Nolan was assigned.

*The Man Without a Country* 187

7 **Discussion** Do you think Nolan meant that? Why did he say it?

8 **Critical Thinking and Reading** What is the difference between the way Colonel Morgan and the other officers perceived the United States and the way Nolan perceived it? Could Nolan's background have led to his involvement with Burr? Explain your answer.

9 **Discussion** How serious does Nolan's sentence sound? What are its ramifications?

10 **Critical Thinking and Reading** What does it mean to be without a country? What are the disadvantages?

**Student Activity 1.** Locate three other sentences in which the colon is used. How is it used in each sentence?

**Student Activity 2.** Compose three sentences in which you use the colon to signal items in a list, quotations, and important information you wish to emphasize.

**Electronic Handbook** You might want students to review the use of colons before completing the Grammar in Action activities. If students have access to the Language Master 6000, have them enter the access symbol (:) and press the GRAMMAR key to get information on colons.

**11 Discussion** Explain the relevance of the following saying, "Be careful of what you wish for because you may get it." How does this apply to Nolan?

**12 Discussion** Why didn't the men like to eat with Nolan? Identify other problems Nolan might have had with his shipmates by being the man without a country.

Washington (with a date, which must have been late in 1807).

Sir:

You will receive from Lieutenant Neale the person of Philip Nolan, late a lieutenant in the United States Army.

This person on his trial by court-martial expressed, with an oath, the wish that he might "never hear of the United States again."

The court sentenced him to have his wish fulfilled.

For the present, the execution of the order is entrusted by the President to this department.

You will take the prisoner on board your ship, and keep him there with such precautions as shall prevent his escape.

You will provide him with such quarters, rations, and clothing as would be proper for an officer of his late rank, if he were a passenger on your vessel on the business of his government.

The gentlemen on board will make any arrangements agreeable to themselves regarding his society. He is to be exposed to no indignity of any kind, nor is he ever unnecessarily to be reminded that he is a prisoner.

But under no circumstances is he ever to hear of his country or to see any information regarding it; and you will especially caution all the officers under your command to take care that this rule, in which his punishment is involved, shall not be broken.

It is the intention of the government that he shall never again see the country which he has disowned. Before the end of your cruise you will receive orders which will give effect to this intention.

Respectfully yours,

W. SOUTHARD,
for the Secretary of the Navy.

The rule adopted on board the ships on which I have met "the man without a country" was, I think, transmitted from the beginning. No mess[9] liked to have him permanently, because his presence cut off all talk of home or of the prospect of return, of politics or letters, of peace or of war—cut off more than half the talk men liked to have at sea. But it was always thought too hard that he should never meet the rest of us, except to touch hats, and we finally sank into one system. He was not permitted to talk with the men, unless an officer was by. With officers he had unrestrained intercourse, as far as they and he chose. But he grew shy, though he had favorites: I was one. Then the captain always asked him to dinner on Monday. Every mess in succession took up the invitation in its turn. According to the size of the ship, you had him at your mess more or less often at dinner. His breakfast he ate in his own stateroom. Whatever else he ate or drank, he ate or drank alone. Sometimes, when the marines or sailors had any special jollification,[10] they were permitted to invite "Plain Buttons," as they called him. Then Nolan was sent with some officer, and the men were forbidden to speak of home while he was there. I believe the theory was that the sight of his punishment did them good. They called him "Plain But-

---

**9. mess** *n.*: Here, a group of people who routinely have their meals together.
**10. jollification** (jäl′ ə fi kā′ shən) *n.*: Merry-making.

tons," because, while he always chose to wear a regulation army uniform, he was not permitted to wear the army button, for the reason that it bore either the initials or the insignia of the country he had disowned.

I remember, soon after I joined the Navy, I was on shore with some of the older officers from our ship and some of the gentlemen fell to talking about Nolan. Someone told of the system which was adopted from the first about his books and other reading. As he was almost never permitted to go on shore, even though the vessel lay in port for months, his time at the best hung heavy. Everybody was permitted to lend him books, if they were not published in America and made no allusion to it. These were common enough in the old days. He had almost all the foreign papers that came into the ship, sooner or later; only somebody must go over them first, and cut out any advertisement or stray paragraph that referred to America. This was a little cruel sometimes, when the back of what was cut out might be innocent. Right in the midst of one of Napoleon's battles poor Nolan would find a great hole, because on the back of the page of that paper there had been an advertisement of a packet[11] for New York, or a scrap from the President's message. This was the first time I ever heard of this plan. I remember it, because poor Phillips, who was of the party, told a story of something which happened at the Cape of Good Hope on Nolan's first voyage. They had touched at the Cape, paid their respects to the English Admiral and the fleet, and then Phillips had borrowed a lot of English books from an officer. Among them was *The Lay of the Last Minstrel*,[12] which they had all of them heard of, but which most of them had never seen. I think it could not have been published long. Well, nobody thought there could be any risk of anything national in that. So Nolan was permitted to join the circle one afternoon when a lot of them sat on deck reading aloud. In his turn, Nolan took the book and read to the others; and he read very well. Nobody in the circle knew a line of the poem, only it was all magic and chivalry, and was ten thousand years ago. Poor Nolan read steadily through the fifth canto,[13] stopped a minute and drank something, and then began, without a thought of what was coming:

> Breathes there the man, with soul so
>   dead
> Who never to himself hath said,—

It seems impossible to us that anybody ever heard this for the first time; but all these fellows did then, and poor Nolan himself went on, still unconsciously or mechanically:

> This is my own, my native land!

Then they all saw that something was to pay; but he expected to get through, I suppose, turned a little pale, but plunged on:

> Whose heart hath ne'er within him
>   burned,
> As home his footsteps he hath
>   turned
> From wandering on a foreign
>   strand?—
> If such there breathe, go, mark him
>   well,—

---

**11. packet** *n.*: A boat that carries passengers, freight, and mail along a regular route.
**12. *The Lay of the Last Minstrel*:** Narrative poem by Sir Walter Scott, Scottish poet and novelist (1771–1832).

---

**13. canto** (kan′ tō) *n.*: A main division of certain long poems.

*The Man Without a Country* 189

**13 Critical Thinking and Reading** What effect do you think Nolan's nickname had on him?

**14 Discussion** Why is this line so significant to Nolan?

**Multicultural Focus** Remind students of the poem "The Lay of the Last Minstrel," which Nolan reads, and discuss patriotism, or the love of one's country. Explain that many people throughout history have been punished by being sent into exile, unable to return to their own country. Perhaps the most famous of these was Napoleon, who was exiled to Elba, a small island in the Mediterranean. Other famous patriots have fought for the independence of their native lands, such as Gandhi in India, Nasser in Egypt, and Kenyatta in Kenya. Point out that although patriotism is something to be admired, it must always be tempered by a respect for other people's native lands.

Ask students to write their definition of a good patriot. What qualities should a patriot have? Does being a patriot mean always agreeing with the policies of your country? Have students name patriots they admire and tell why.

15 **Discussion** Why was reading the poem so devastating for Nolan?

16 **Critical Thinking and Reading** How do you think Nolan felt every time he got close to his home shore?

By this time the men were all beside themselves, wishing there was any way to make him turn over two pages; but he had not quite presence of mind for that; he gagged a little, colored crimson, and staggered on:

> For him no minstrel raptures swell;
> High though his titles, proud his
> name,
> Boundless his wealth as wish can
> claim,
> Despite these titles, power, and
> pelf,[14]
> The wretch, concentered all in
> self,—

15 and here the poor fellow choked, could not go on, but started up, swung the book into the sea, vanished into his stateroom, "And by Jove," said Phillips, "we did not see him for two months again. And I had to make up some beggarly story to that English surgeon why I did not return his Walter Scott to him."

That story shows about the time when Nolan's braggadocio[15] must have broken down. At first, they said, he took a very high tone, considered his imprisonment a mere farce, affected to enjoy the voyage, and all that; but Phillips said that after he came out of his stateroom he never was the same man again. He never read aloud again, unless it was the Bible or Shakespeare, or something else he was sure of. But it was not that merely. He never entered in with the other young men exactly as a companion again. He was always shy afterwards, when I knew him—very seldom spoke unless he was spoken to, except to a

---

14. **pelf** *n.*: Ill-gotten wealth.
15. **braggadocio** (brag′ ə dō′ shē ō) *n.*: Here, pretense of bravery; Nolan acts as if he does not mind his imprisonment.

---

very few friends. Generally he had the nervous, tired look of a heart-wounded man.

When Captain Shaw was coming home, rather to the surprise of everybody they made one of the Windward Islands, and lay off and on for nearly a week. The boys said the officers were sick of salt-junk,[16] and meant to have turtle-soup before they came home. But after several days the *Warren* came to the same rendezvous;[17] they exchanged signals; she told them she was outward bound, perhaps to the Mediterranean, and took poor Nolan and his traps[18] on the boat to try his second cruise. He looked very blank when he was told to get ready to join her. He had known enough of the signs of the sky to know that till that moment he was going "home." But this was a distinct evidence of something he had not thought of, perhaps—that there was no going home for him, even to a prison. And this was the first of some twenty such transfers, which brought him sooner or later into half our best vessels, but which kept him all his life at least some hundred miles from the country he had hoped he might never hear of again.

16

It may have been on that second cruise —it was once when he was up the Mediterranean—that Mrs. Graff, the celebrated Southern beauty of those days, danced with him. The ship had been lying a long time in the Bay of Naples, and the officers were very intimate in the English fleet, and there had been great festivities, and our men thought they must give a great ball on board the ship. They wanted to use Nolan's stateroom for something, and they hated to do it without asking him to the ball; so the captain said they might ask

---

16. **salt-junk** *n.*: Hard salted meat.
17. **rendezvous** (rän′ dā voo) *n.*: Meeting place.
18. **traps** *n.*: Here, bags or luggage.

---

---

## Grammar in Action

**Action verbs** show the action in sentences. An action verb is **intransitive** if the receiver of the action is not named in the sentence. Since there is no person or object receiving the action of the verb, the emphasis is placed on the subject. For example,

he gagged     he staggered

Writers use intransitive action verbs to heighten the action of their subject. Notice how vividly Nolan's actions are described:

. . . but he had not quite presence of mind for that; he *gagged* a little, *colored* crimson, and *staggered* on: . . .

. . . and here the poor fellow *choked, could* not *go* on, but *started* up, swung the book into the sea, *vanished* into his stateroom . . .

The verbs show what Nolan is doing; they place the emphasis of the sentence on the subject.

him, if they would be responsible that he did not talk with the wrong people, "who would give him intelligence."[19] So the dance went on. For ladies they had the family of the American consul, one or two travelers who had adventured so far, and a nice bevy of English girls and matrons.

Well, different officers relieved each other in standing and talking with Nolan in a friendly way, so as to be sure that nobody else spoke to him. The dancing went on with spirit, and after a while even the fellows who took this honorary guard of Nolan ceased to fear any trouble.

As the dancing went on, Nolan and our fellows all got at ease—so much so, that it seemed quite natural for him to bow to that splendid Mrs. Graff, and say, "I hope you have not forgotten me, Miss Rutledge. Shall I have the honor of dancing?"

He did it so quickly, that Fellows, who was with him, could not hinder him. She laughed and said, "I am not Miss Rutledge any longer, Mr. Nolan; but I will dance all the same." She nodded to Fellows, as if to say he must leave Mr. Nolan to her, and led him off to the place where the dance was forming.

Nolan thought he had got his chance. He had known her at Philadelphia, and at other places had met her. He began with her travels, and Europe, and then he said boldly—a little pale, she said, as she told me the story years after—"And what do you hear from home, Mrs. Graff?"

And that splendid creature looked through him. How she must have looked through him!

"Home! Mr. Nolan! I thought you were the man who never wanted to hear of home again!"—and she walked directly up the deck to her husband, and left poor Nolan alone. He did not dance again.

A happier story than either of these I have told is of the war.[20] That came along soon after. I have heard this affair told in three or four ways—and, indeed, it may have happened more than once. In one of the great frigate[21] duels with the English, in which the navy was really baptized, it happened that a round-shot[22] from the enemy entered one of our ports[23] square, and took right down the officer of the gun himself, and almost every man of the gun's crew. Now you may say what you choose about courage, but that is not a nice thing to see. But, as the men who were not killed picked themselves up, and as they and the surgeon's people were carrying off the bodies, there appeared Nolan in his shirt sleeves, with the rammer in his hand, and, just as if he had been the officer, told them off with authority—who should go to the cockpit with the wounded men, who should stay with him—perfectly cheery, and with that way which makes men feel sure all is right and is going to be right. And he finished loading the gun with his own hands, aimed it, and bade the men fire. And there he stayed, captain of that gun, keeping those fellows in spirits, till the enemy struck[24] —sitting on the carriage while the gun was cooling, though he was exposed all the time —showing them easier ways to handle heavy shot—making the raw hands laugh at their own blunders—and when the gun cooled again, getting it loaded and fired

---

19. **intelligence** *n.*: Here, news about his country.

20. **the war:** The War of 1812 between the United States and Great Britain.
21. **frigate** (frig' it) *n.*: A fast-sailing warship equipped with guns.
22. **round-shot:** A cannonball.
23. **ports** *n.*: Here, portholes or openings for cannonballs.
24. **struck,** (struk) *v.*: Lowered their flag to admit defeat.

*The Man Without a Country* 191

**17 Reading Strategy** Predict what Nolan will ask Mrs. Graff and what her response will be.

**18 Discussion** How did Nolan act in the War of 1812? What did he do to save his ship? Why did he do it?

**Student Activity.** Write several sentences in which you use vivid action verbs to describe what someone is doing. You might describe an embarrassed classmate who has forgotten his lines in a play, or describe a child learning how to ride a bicycle. A thesaurus may be helpful for finding vivid words.

**Electronic Handbook** You may want students to review action verbs that are intransitive before completing the Grammar in Action activity. If students have access to the Language Master 6000, have them enter the access word *transitivity* and press the GRAMMAR key to get information on intransitive action verbs.

Fine art, *U.S.S. Constitution and H.M.S. Guerriere (Aug. 19, 1812)*, by Thomas Birch. Thomas Birch (1779–1851) emigrated to the United States from England in 1793. A boat trip down the Delaware River sparked Birch's interest in the sea and ships.

During the War of 1812, Thomas Birch painted a series of historical views of American naval victories. The painting *U.S.S. Constitution and H.M.S. Guerriere (Aug. 19, 1812)* is from this series. The painting is a glorified impression of the encounter of the two ships.

1. Evaluate Nolan's act of bravery in view of how a typical sea battle looked.
2. Study the painting and identify the features that made these ships so vulnerable.
3. Which side is winning? How can you tell?

**19 Discussion** Do you think Nolan has a reason to hope that he'll be pardoned now? Is this why he acted courageously?

**20 Reading Strategy** Summarize the story to this point and predict what will happen to Nolan.

USS CONSTITUTION AND HMS GUERRIERE (Aug. 19, 1812)
*Thomas Birch*
U.S. Naval Academy Museum

twice as often as any other gun on the ship. The captain walked forward by way of encouraging the men, and Nolan touched his hat and said, "I am showing them how we do this in the artillery, sir."

19 And this is the part of the story where all the legends agree; the commodore said, "I see you do, and I thank you, sir; and I shall never forget this day, sir, and you never shall, sir."

And after the whole thing was over, and the commodore had the Englishman's sword[25] in the midst of the state and ceremony of the quarter-deck, he said, "Where is Mr. Nolan? Ask Mr. Nolan to come here."

And when Nolan came, he said, "Mr. Nolan, we are all very grateful to you today; you are one of us today; you will be named in the dispatches." 20

---

25. **the Englishman's sword:** A defeated commander would turn over his sword to the victor.

## Grammar in Action

**Sentence variety** within a paragraph produces a more interesting passage and reflects a careful molding of the sentences by the writer to form exact meaning and emphasis. The overuse of short, simple sentences as well as the overuse of complex, convoluted sentences can create either monotonous or confusing paragraphs. Sentence variety is essential to good writing.

Notice the sentence variety Hale uses in the following passage:

All that was nearly fifty years ago. If Nolan was thirty then, he must have been near eighty when he died. He looked sixty when he was forty. But he never seemed to me to change a hair afterwards. As I imagine his life, from what I have seen and heard of it, he must have been in every sea, and yet almost never on land. Till he grew very old, he went aloft a great deal. He always kept up his exercise, and I never heard that he was ill. If any other man was ill, he was the kindest nurse in the world; and he knew more than half the surgeons do. Then if anybody was sick or died, or if the captain wanted him to, on any other occasion, he was always ready to read prayers. I have said that he read beautifully.

And then the old man took off his own sword of ceremony, gave it to Nolan, and made him put it on. The man told me this who saw it. Nolan cried like a baby, and well he might. He had not worn a sword since that infernal day at Fort Adams. But always afterwards on occasions of ceremony, he wore that quaint old French sword of the commodore's.

The captain did mention him in the dispatches. It was always said he asked that Nolan might be pardoned. He wrote a special letter to the Secretary of War, but nothing ever came of it.

All that was nearly fifty years ago. If Nolan was thirty then, he must have been near eighty when he died. He looked sixty when he was forty. But he never seemed to me to change a hair afterwards. As I imagine his life, from what I have seen and heard of it, he must have been in every sea, and yet almost never on land. Till he grew very old, he went aloft a great deal. He always kept up his exercise, and I never heard that he was ill. If any other man was ill, he was the kindest nurse in the world; and he knew more than half the surgeons do. Then if anybody was sick or died, or if the captain wanted him to, on any other occasion, he was always ready to read prayers. I have said that he read beautifully.

My own acquaintance with Philip Nolan began six or eight years after the English war, on my first voyage after I was appointed a midshipman. From the time I joined, I thought Nolan was a sort of lay chaplain—a chaplain with a blue coat. I never asked about him. Everything in the ship was strange to me. I knew it was green to ask questions, and I suppose I thought there was a "Plain Buttons" on every ship. We had him to dine in our mess once a week, and the caution was given that on that day nothing was to be said about home. But if they had told us not to say anything about the planet Mars or the Book of Deuteronomy,[26] I should not have asked why; there were a great many things which seemed to me to have as little reason. I first came to understand anything about "The Man Without a Country" one day when we overhauled a dirty little schooner which had slaves[27] on board. An officer named Vaughan was sent to take charge of her, and after a few minutes, he sent back his boat to ask that someone might be sent to him who could speak Portuguese. None of the officers did; and just as the captain was sending forward to ask if any of the people could, Nolan stepped out and said he should be glad to interpret, if the captain wished, as he understood the language. The captain thanked him, fitted out another boat with him, and in this boat it was my luck to go.

When we got there, it was such a scene as you seldom see, and never want to. Nastiness beyond account, and chaos run loose in the midst of the nastiness. There were not a great many of the Negroes; but by way of making what there were understand that they were free, Vaughan had had their handcuffs and anklecuffs knocked off. The Negroes were, most of them, out of the hold and swarming all round the dirty deck, with a central throng surrounding Vaughan and addressing him in every dialect.

As we came on deck, Vaughan looked down from a hogshead,[28] which he had mounted in desperation, and said, "Is there anybody who can make these people understand something?"

---

**26. Book of Deuteronomy** (do͞ot′ ər än′ ə mē): The fifth book of the Bible.
**27. slaves:** In 1808 it became illegal to bring slaves into the United States. In 1842 the U.S. and Great Britain agreed to use ships to patrol the African coast, to prevent slaves being taken.
**28. hogshead** (hôgz′ hed′) n.: A large barrel or cask.

*The Man Without a Country* 193

**21 Discussion** Is it surprising that Nolan isn't pardoned? Do you think he should be?

**22 Critical Thinking and Reading** Why did Nolan always go aloft, or up to the crow's nest? What was he hoping to see?

**23 Discussion** Why would the narrator of this story have thought at first that Nolan was a chaplain? What kind of man had Nolan become?

**24 Critical Thinking and Reading** Why do you think Aaron Burr had been interested in Nolan? Does he seem like a typical seaman? Explain your answer.

Hale uses both simple and complex sentences in order to produce a smooth, readable style of writing.

**Student Activity.** Write a paragraph in which you describe someone as Hale did in the example. Strive to vary your sentences by using both simple sentences and complex ones.

**Electronic Handbook** You may want students to review sentence variety before completing the Grammar in Action activity. If students have access to the Language Master 6000, have them enter the access word *complex* and press the GRAMMAR key to get information on how to vary sentence structure.

25 **Discussion** Why is this speech so difficult for Nolan? What statement is the author making about slavery? As this story was written during the Civil War, which side would you say the author was on?

26 **Critical Thinking and Reading** Contrast the Nolan at the beginning of the story with the Nolan who makes this speech. What makes this speech so unexpected and meaningful?

Nolan said he could speak Portuguese, and one or two fine-looking Kroomen who had worked for the Portuguese on the coast were dragged out.

"Tell them they are free," said Vaughan.

Nolan explained it in such Portuguese as the Kroomen could understand, and they in turn to such of the Negroes as could understand them. Then there was a yell of delight, clenching of fists, and leaping and dancing by way of celebration.

"Tell them," said Vaughan, well pleased, "that I will take them all to Cape Palmas."

This did not answer so well. Cape Palmas was practically as far from the homes of most of them as New Orleans or Rio de Janeiro was; that is, they would be eternally separated from home there. And their interpreters, as we could understand, instantly said, "*Ah, non Palmas,*" and began to protest volubly. Vaughan was rather disappointed at this result of his liberality, and asked Nolan eagerly what they said. The drops stood on poor Nolan's white forehead, as he hushed the men down, and said, "He says, 'Not Palmas.' He says, 'Take us home; take us to our own country; take us to our own house; take us to our own children and our own women.' He says he has an old father and mother who will die if they do not see him. And this one says he left his people all sick, and paddled down to Fernando to beg the white doctor to come and help them, and that these devils caught him in the bay just in sight of home, and that he has never seen anybody from home since then. And this one says," choked out Nolan, "that he has not heard a word from his home in six months."

Vaughan always said he grew gray himself while Nolan struggled through this interpretation. I, who did not understand anything of the passion involved in it, saw that the very elements were melting with

fervent heat and that something was to pay somewhere. Even the Negroes themselves stopped howling, as they saw Nolan's agony and Vaughan's almost equal agony of sympathy. As quick as he could get words, Vaughan said, "Tell them yes, yes, yes; tell them they shall go to the Mountains of the Moon, if they will. If I sail the schooner through the Great White Desert, they shall go home!"

And after some fashion Nolan said so. And then they all fell to kissing him again.

But he could not stand it long; and getting Vaughan to say he might go back, he beckoned me down into our boat. As we started back he said to me, "Youngster, let that show you what it is to be without a family, without a home, and without a country. And if you are ever tempted to say a word or to do a thing that shall put a bar between you and your family, your home, and your country, pray God in His mercy to take you that instant home to His own heaven. Think of your home, boy; write and send, and talk about it. Let it be nearer and nearer to your thought the farther you have to travel from it, and rush back to it when you are free, as that poor slave is doing now. And for your country, boy" and the words rattled in his throat, "and for that flag," and he pointed to the ship, "never dream a dream but of serving her as she bids you, though the service carry you through a thousand hells. No matter what happens to you, no matter who flatters you or who abuses you, never look at another flag, never let a night pass but you pray God to bless that flag. Remember, boy, that behind all these men you have to do with, behind officers, and government, and people even, there is the Country herself, your Country, and that you belong to her as you belong to your own mother. Stand by her, boy, as you would stand by your mother!"

I was frightened to death by his calm, hard passion; but I blundered out that I would, by all that was holy, and that I had never thought of doing anything else. He hardly seemed to hear me; but he did, almost in a whisper, say, "Oh, if anybody had said so to me when I was of your age!"

I think it was this half-confidence of his, which I never abused, that afterward made us great friends. He was very kind to me. Often he sat up, or even got up, at night, to walk the deck with me, when it was my watch. He explained to me a great deal of my mathematics, and I owe to him my taste for mathematics. He lent me books and helped me about my reading. He never referred so directly to his story again; but from one and another officer I have learned, in thirty years, what I am telling.

After that cruise I never saw Nolan again. The other men tell me that in those fifteen years he aged very fast, but he was still the same gentle, uncomplaining, silent sufferer that he ever was, bearing as best he could his self-appointed punishment. And now it seems the dear old fellow is dead. He has found a home at last, and a country.

Since writing this, and while considering whether or not I would print it, as a warning to the young Nolans of today of what it is to throw away a country, I have received from Danforth, who is on board the *Levant,* a letter which gives an account of Nolan's last hours. It removes all my doubts about telling this story.

Here is the letter:

Dear Fred,

I try to find heart and life to tell you that it is all over with dear old

**WARRANT OFFICERS' MESS**
*Heck's Iconographic Encyclopedia, 1851*
New York Public Library

*The Man Without a Country*   195

**27** **Critical Thinking and Reading** Might Nolan's life have been different if someone had taught him what it means to belong to a country? How did Nolan learn this lesson?

**28** **Discussion** What does the author mean by this?

## Humanities Note

This nineteenth-century engraving shows an officers' mess. The artist strove to depict the scene as realistically and in as much detail as possible.
1. Judging from the engraving, what was life like aboard these ships? What is the dominant feeling of the men?
2. What must Nolan's life have been like if this shows a typical moment of rest for the seamen?
3. Identify the details that make the engraving realistic and photographic.

**29 Literary Focus** What symbols decorate Nolan's room? What do they stand for? How meaningful have they become for Nolan? Why?

**30 Critical Thinking and Reading** According to Nolan, what had Burr's plan been?

Nolan. I have been with him on this voyage more than I ever was, and I can understand wholly now the way in which you used to speak of the dear old fellow. I could see that he was not strong, but I had no idea the end was so near. The doctor has been watching him very carefully, and yesterday morning came to me and told me that Nolan was not so well, and had not left his stateroom —a thing I never remember before. He had let the doctor come and see him as he lay there—the first time the doctor had been in the stateroom —and he said he should like to see me. Do you remember the mysteries we boys used to invent about his room in the old *Intrepid* days? Well, I went in, and there, to be sure, the poor fellow lay in his berth, smiling pleasantly as he gave me his hand, but looking very frail. I could not help a glance round, which showed me what a little shrine he had made of the box he was lying in. The Stars and Stripes were draped up above and around a picture of Washington and he had painted a majestic eagle, with lightning blazing from his beak and his foot just clasping the whole globe, which his wings overshadowed. The dear old boy saw my glance, and said, with a sad smile, "Here, you see I have a country!" And then he pointed to the foot of his bed, where I had not seen before a great map of the United States, as he had drawn it from memory, and which he had there to look upon as he lay. Quaint, queer old names were on it, in large letters: "Indiana Territory," "Mississippi Territory," and "Louisiana Territory," as I suppose our fathers learned such things: but the old fellow had patched in Texas, too: he had carried his western boundary all the way to the Pacific, but on that shore he had defined nothing.

"O Captain," he said, "I know I am dying. I cannot get home. Surely you will tell me something now? —Stop! stop! Do not speak till I say what I am sure you know, that there is not in this ship, that there is not in America a more loyal man than I. There cannot be a man who loves the old flag as I do, or prays for it as I do, or hopes for it as I do. There are thirty-four stars in it now, Danforth, though I do not know what their names are. There has never been one taken away. I know by that that there has never been any successful Burr. O Danforth, Danforth," he sighed out, "how like a wretched night's dream a boy's idea of personal fame or of separate sovereignty seems, when one looks back on it after such a life as mine! But tell me—tell me something—tell me everything, Danforth, before I die!"

I swear to you that I felt like a monster that I had not told him everything before. "Mr. Nolan," said I, "I will tell you everything you ask about. Only, where shall I begin?"

Oh, the blessed smile that crept over his white face! He pressed my hand and said, "Bless you! Tell me their names," and he pointed to the stars on the flag. "The last I know is Ohio. My father lived in Kentucky. But I have guessed Michigan and Indiana and Mississippi—that was where Fort Adams was—they make twenty. But where are your other fourteen? You have not cut up any of the old ones, I hope?''

Well, that was not a bad text, and I told him the names in as good order as I could, and he bade me take down his beautiful map and draw them in as I best could with my pencil. He was wild with delight about Texas, told me how his cousin died there; he had marked a gold cross near where he supposed his grave was; and he had guessed at Texas. Then he was delighted as he saw California and Oregon;—that, he said, he had suspected partly, because he had never been permitted to land on that shore, though the ships were there so much. Then he asked whether Burr ever tried again—and he ground his teeth with the only passion he showed. But in a moment that was over. He asked about the old war —told me the story of his serving the gun the day we took the *Java*. Then he settled down more quietly, and very happily, to hear me tell in an hour the history of fifty years.

How I wished it had been somebody who knew something! But I did as well as I could. I told him of the English war. I told him about Fulton[29] and the steamboat beginning. I told him about old Scott,[30] and Jackson:[31] told him all I could think of about the Mississippi, and New Orleans, and Texas, and his own old Kentucky.

---

**29. Fulton:** Robert Fulton (1765–1815), who invented the steamboat.
**30. Scott:** General Winfield Scott (1786–1866), who served in the War of 1812 and the Mexican War.
**31. Jackson:** Andrew Jackson (1767–1845), seventh President of the United States (1829–1837) and a general in the War of 1812.

I tell you, it was a hard thing to condense the history of half a century into that talk with a sick man. And I do not now know what I told him—of emigration, and the means of it—of steamboats, and railroads, and telegraphs—of inventions, and books, and literature—of the colleges, and West Point, and the Naval School—but with the queerest interruptions that ever you heard. You see it was Robinson Crusoe asking all the accumulated questions of fifty-six years!

I remember he asked, all of a sudden, who was President now; and when I told him, he asked if Old Abe was General Benjamin Lincoln's son. He said he met old General Lincoln, when he was quite a boy himself, at some Indian treaty. I said no, that Old Abe was a Kentuckian like himself, but I could not tell him of what family; he had worked up from the ranks. ''Good for him!'' cried Nolan; ''I am glad of that.'' Then I got talking about my visit to Washington. I told him about the Smithsonian, and the Capitol. I told him everything I could think of that would show the grandeur of his country and its prosperity.

And he drank it in and enjoyed it as I cannot tell you. He grew more and more silent, yet I never thought he was tired or faint. I gave him a glass of water, but he just wet his lips, and told me not to go away. Then he asked me to bring the Presbyterian Book of Public Prayer which lay there, and said, with a smile, that it would open at the right place —and so it did. There was his double red mark down the page; and I knelt

*The Man Without a Country* 197

**31** **Critical Thinking and Reading** What does Nolan think of Burr now?

**32** **Clarification** Robinson Crusoe was a character created by Daniel Defoe in 1719. Crusoe was marooned on a desert island, removed from news of the world, for twenty-eight years.

**33** **Critical Thinking and Reading** Describe how Nolan must have felt while hearing about the ''grandeur of his country.''

34 **Critical Thinking and Reading**
How have these prayers acted as Nolan's penance for his crime? Do you think his punishment was appropriate or overly harsh? Explain your answer.

35 **Discussion** Discuss the meaning of the Biblical quotation. Why was it appropriate for Nolan?

36 **Critical Thinking and Reading**
Why does Nolan want a tombstone even though he will be buried at sea? Based on the epitaph he wrote for himself, how did Nolan judge himself? Did he think he had been too severely punished for his crime?

**Reader's Response** In your opinion, was Nolan's punishment fair? Explain.

**Thematic Response** At his trial Nolan thoughtlessly wishes never to hear of the United States again. Do you think he later gains a sense of belonging to his home and country? Explain.

down and read, and he repeated with me:

> For ourselves and our country, O gracious God, we thank Thee, that, notwithstanding our manifold transgressions of Thy holy laws, Thou hast continued to us Thy marvelous kindness . . .

and so to the end of that thanksgiving. Then he turned to the end of the same book, and I read the words more familiar to me:

> Most heartily we beseech Thee with Thy favor to behold and bless Thy servant, the President of the United States, and all others in authority.

34 "Danforth," said he, "I have repeated those prayers night and morning—it is now fifty-five years." And then he said he would go to sleep. He bent me down over him and kissed me; and he said, "Look in my Bible, Captain, when I am gone." And I went away.

But I had no thought it was the end. I thought he was tired and would sleep. I knew he was happy, and I wanted him to be alone.

But in an hour, when the doctor went in gently, he found Nolan had breathed his life away with a smile.

We looked in his Bible, and there was a slip of paper at the place where he had marked the text:

> They desire a country, even a heavenly: where God is not ashamed to be called their God: for He hath prepared for them a city.[32]

35

On this slip of paper he had written:

> Bury me in the sea; it has been my home, and I love it. But will not someone set up a stone for my memory at Fort Adams or at Orleans, that my disgrace may not be more than I ought to bear? Say on it:
>
> In Memory of
> PHILIP NOLAN,
> Lieutenant in the Army of the United States.
> He loved his country as no other man has loved her; but no man deserved less at her hands.

36

**32. They desire . . . a city:** A passage from Hebrews 11:16.

## MULTICULTURAL CONNECTION

*Patriotism and Cultural Loyalties*

**Patriotism.** "The Man Without a Country" stresses the importance of patriotism. For many Americans, the notion of patriotism is tied to symbols and often associated with the past. In a society as culturally diverse as ours, however, patriotism often coexists with other loyalties.

**Cultural symbols.** For many Americans, cultural symbols are at least as meaningful as patriotic ones. One such symbol is kente cloth, a traditional African fabric worn by African Americans to show pride in their heritage. Members of religious groups, such as Hasidic Jews, Sikhs, and the Amish, also wear distinctive styles of dress. Even "the wearing o' the green" on St. Patrick's Day was originally a statement of ethnic pride.

**Exploring and Sharing**

Conduct interviews with classmates, family, or friends. Ask what patriotism means to them and what cultural and patriotic symbols are important to them. Present your findings to the class.

*198 Short Stories*

**Closure and Extension**

**ANSWERS TO RESPONDING TO THE SELECTION**
*Your Response*

1. Urge students to focus on Nolan's personal characteristics and how he changed over the decades.
2. Encourage students to give reasons for the punishment they choose.

*Recalling*

3. The narrator is a man who served with Nolan on a ship. He tells the story to show young Americans what it means to be without a country.
4. Nolan is tried for his participation in subversive activities with Aaron Burr.
5. Nolan says, "Damn the United States! I wish I may never hear of the United States again!" The judge is shocked and grants Nolan his wish as a punishment.

6. Nolan's sentence is to "never hear the name of the United States again." The sentence will be carried out by assigning Nolan to different ships for the rest of his life. The men on each ship are instructed not to mention home to Nolan, and his reading material is censored.
7. Nolan places symbols of the United States all over his room and a map, which he filled in himself.
8. Nolan's last wish is that he be buried at sea but that a tombstone be erected for him on land.

*Interpreting*

9. Burr impresses Nolan and courts him. Burr singles him out to show him different sights so that ordinary barracks life seems boring to Nolan by comparison.
10. The poem affects Nolan because it is about the feeling most people get about seeing their native land after traveling and about the wretchedness of those who don't experience this feeling. Nolan

# RESPONDING TO THE SELECTION

## Your Response

1. Did you feel sympathy for Philip Nolan as you read the story? Why or why not?
2. If you were the judge, what punishment would you have given Philip Nolan?

## Recalling

3. Who is the narrator of this story? What is the narrator's purpose in telling the story?
4. Why is Nolan brought to trial?
5. What rash words does Nolan utter when the judge asks him if he wishes to say anything? What effect do these words have on the judge?
6. What is Nolan's sentence? Explain the plan to carry out the sentence.
7. How does Nolan create a country for himself in his stateroom?
8. What is Nolan's last wish?

## Interpreting

9. How is it that Aaron Burr is able to win over the young Nolan so easily?
10. Why does the poem *The Lay of the Last Minstrel* have such an effect on Nolan? Why does Nolan cry when he receives the sword of the commodore?
11. After interpreting for the slaves to be sent home, why does Nolan advise the narrator to love and serve his country?
12. How has Nolan changed during the course of the story?

## Applying

13. What epitaph would you write for Nolan?
14. Do you think Nolan's punishment fit his crime? Explain your answer.

# ANALYZING LITERATURE

## Recognizing Symbols

A **symbol** can be a word, an object, or an action in a story that represents, or stands for, some-thing else. For example, a snake is a reptile, but it can also symbolize evil.

The writer usually emphasizes or repeats a symbol, or places it in a particular place in the story. The symbol's meaning depends on its context. A story may have more than one symbol.

1. What do Nolan's plain buttons symbolize?
2. What symbol of honor does the commodore of Philip Nolan's ship give him for bravery in the battle with a British frigate?
3. What do the Stars and Stripes draped in Philip Nolan's stateroom symbolize?
4. What do these symbols suggest about the importance of one's country?

# CRITICAL THINKING AND READING

## Paraphrasing

**Paraphrasing** is restating in your own words something you read or hear; you do not repeat the words *exactly*. Paraphrasing may help you understand better what you read or hear. To paraphrase the theme, or central idea, of a story, read and consider what the story is about. Then state its main points in your own words.

1. Paraphrase the story's theme: "And for your country . . . never dream a dream but of serving her as she bids you, though the service carry you through a thousand hells."
2. Paraphrase Nolan's epitaph: "He loved his country as no other man has loved her; but no man deserved less at her hands."

# THINKING AND WRITING

## Writing About Theme

Suppose Fred read the obituary in *The New York Herald* and wanted to set the record straight about Philip Nolan's true feelings about his country. List examples from the story of how Nolan felt about the United States. Then, as Fred, write a letter to the editor describing Nolan's patriotism and giving the examples to support your points.

*The Man Without a Country* 199

## Preparation

**More About the Author** Daniel Keyes was a teacher of high school English for many years before he became a university professor of English. "Flowers for Algernon" reflects his firsthand knowledge of teaching and learning. Ask students to discuss the relationship between teaching literature and writing it. Would a deep appreciation for literature motivate someone to become a writer?

**Literary Focus** Although the narrator of "Flowers for Algernon" is the main character, you see events from other characters' points of view as well as Charlie's. In fact, because of Charlie's limitations, the reader understands the events better than does the main character.

**Prereading Focus** Discuss with students their understanding of what the word *intelligence* means. Get several definitions. Name different kinds of intelligence. Then put the diagram on the chalkboard. Have volunteers name some advantages and disadvantages of superintelligence. Let students refer to them as they fill in their diagrams in small groups.

**Vocabulary** These words also may give students some difficulty: *plateau* (p. 209); *conscious, unconscious, psychology* (p. 210); *coattails* (p. 212); *specialization* (p. 213); *calculus, variations, psychoexperimentalist, invariably* (p. 214); *infuriated* (p. 215); *sensational, applicability* (p. 217); *regressed, impaired, glandular, progressive, amnesia, deterioration, syndromes,* and *proportional* (p. 218).

**Electronic Handbook/ESL Teaching Strategy** If students have access to the Language Master 6000, suggest that your ESL students listen to the pronunciations of the words.

### Daniel Keyes

(1927–    ), raised in Brooklyn, New York, is an English professor. He has worked at many jobs, including that of photographer, merchant seaman, and editor. His many works of fiction include the novels *The Touch* (1968) and *The Fifth Sally* (1980). Keyes's best-known story, "Flowers for Algernon," won the Hugo Award of the Science Fiction Writers of America in 1959. It was later adapted for the movie *Charly* and the Broadway musical *Charlie and Algernon*.

# Flowers for Algernon

## Point of View and Theme

**Theme** is the central insight into life communicated by the events in the story. Sometimes we see the events unfold from one character's point of view. It is as though we stand in this character's shoes and see with this character's eyes. In a story that unfolds this way, we come to understand the theme gradually, as we see what this character sees and sometimes even more than what he or she sees.

## Focus

The main character in "Flowers for Algernon" takes part in an experiment that triples his intelligence level. Think about the consequences of such a change. With your classmates fill in a diagram like the one that follows to indicate the advantages and disadvantages of this experiment.

| Superintelligence | |
|---|---|
| Advantages | Disadvantages |
| Could work on an exciting science project. | Might be very lonely. |

## Vocabulary

Knowing the following words will help you as you read "Flowers for Algernon."

**tangible** (tan′ jə bəl) *adj.*: Observable; understandable (p. 213)

**specter** (spek′ tər) *n.*: A disturbing thought (p. 213)

**refute** (ri fyoot′) *v.*: Disprove (p. 214)

**vacuous** (vak′ yōō əs) *adj.*: Empty; shallow (p. 215)

**obscure** (äb skyoor′) *v.*: Hide (p. 217)

**convolutions** (kän′ və lū′ shənz) *n.*: Uneven ridges on the brain's surface (p. 218)

**fissures** (fish′ ərz) *n.*: Narrow openings (p. 218)

**introspective** (in′ trə spek′ tiv) *adj.*: Looking into one's own thoughts and feelings (p. 218)

## Objectives

1  To use point of view to understand theme
2  To compare and contrast views
3  To write about theme
4  To express individual interests and abilities through optional activities

## Support Material

**Teaching Portfolio**
Teacher Backup, p. 291
Grammar in Action Worksheets, *Understanding First-Person Narration,* p. 294; *Understanding Adverb Clauses,* p. 296; *Understanding Second-Person Point of View,* p. 298; *Using Participles and Participial Phrases,* p. 300
Usage and Mechanics Worksheet, p. 302

Vocabulary Check, p. 303
Analyzing Literature Worksheet, *Understanding Point of View and Theme,* p. 304
Language Worksheet, *Understanding Synonyms and Antonyms,* p. 305
Selection Test, p. 306

**Prentice Hall Literature Writing Studio**

# Flowers for Algernon

## Daniel Keyes

*progris riport 1—martch 5 1965*

Dr. Strauss says I shud rite down what I think and evrey thing that happins to me from now on. I dont know why but he says its importint so they will see if they will use me. I hope they use me. Miss Kinnian says maybe they can make me smart. I want to be smart. My name is Charlie Gordon. I am 37 years old and 2 weeks ago was my brithday. I have nuthing more to rite now so I will close for today.

*progris riport 2—martch 6*

I had a test today. I think I faled it. and I think that maybe now they wont use me. What happind is a nice young man was in the room and he had some white cards with ink spillled all over them. He sed Charlie what do you see on this card. I was very skared even tho I had my rabits foot in my pockit because when I was a kid I always faled tests in school and I spillled ink to.

I told him I saw a inkblot. He said yes and it made me feel good. I thot that was all but when I got up to go he stopped me. He said now sit down Charlie we are not thru yet. Then I dont remember so good but he wantid me to say what was in the ink. I dint see nuthing in the ink but he said there was picturs there other pepul saw some picturs. I coudnt see any picturs. I reely tryed to

Edited for this edition.

see. I held the card close up and then far away. Then I said if I had my glases I coud see better I usally only ware my glases in the movies or TV but I said they are in the closit in the hall. I got them. Then I said let me see that card agen I bet Ill find it now.

I tryed hard but I still coudnt find the picturs I only saw the ink. I told him maybe I need new glases. He rote somthing down on a paper and I got skared of faling the test. I told him it was a very nice inkblot with littel points all around the eges. He looked very sad so that wasnt it. I said please let me try agen. Ill get it in a few minits becaus Im not so fast somtimes. Im a slow reeder too in Miss Kinnians class for slow adults but I'm trying very hard.

He gave me a chance with another card that had 2 kinds of ink spilled on it red and blue.

He was very nice and talked slow like Miss Kinnian does and he explained it to me that it was a *raw shok*.[1] He said pepul see things in the ink. I said show me where. He said think. I told him I think a inkblot but that wasnt rite eather. He said what does it remind you—pretend somthing. I closd my eyes for a long time to pretend. I told him I pretned a fowntan pen with ink leeking all over a table cloth. Then he got up and went out.

I dont think I passd the *raw shok* test.

1. **raw shok:** A misspelling of Rorschach (rôr′ s·häk) test, a psychological test involving inkblots that the subject describes.

*Flowers for Algernon* 201

**4 Reading Strategy** What do you think Charlie is referring to here? Predict what will happen to Charlie.

**5 Discussion** What are the doctors asking Charlie to do now?

**6 Discussion** Are mice that smart? What do you suspect about Algernon?

**Multicultural Focus** Discuss with students how people often treat a person with a mental disability, such as Charlie Gordon. Elicit the idea that making fun of or looking down on people with mental disabilities is insensitive and harmful. Explain that society's perception of how to treat people with mental disabilities has changed in the past thirty years. Instead of being taken care of at home or in an institution, many people with mental disabilities are now taught to be as self-sufficient as possible. They hold a variety of jobs. Some actors with mental disabilities star in television series.

Invite students to call or write their local mental health agencies for more information on persons with mental disabilities.

*progris report 3—martch 7*

Dr Strauss and Dr Nemur say it dont matter about the inkblots. I told them I dint spill the ink on the cards and I coudnt see anything in the ink. They said that maybe they will still use me. I said Miss Kinnian never gave me tests like that one only spelling and reading. They said Miss Kinnian told that I was her bestist pupil in the adult nite scool becaus I tryed the hardist and I reely wantid to lern. They said how come you went to the adult nite scool all by yourself Charlie. How did you find it. I said I askd pepul and sumbody told me where I shud go to lern to read and spell good. They said why did you want to. I told them becaus all my life I wantid to be smart and not dumb. But its very hard to be smart. They said you know it will probly be tempirery. I said yes. Miss Kinnian told me. I dont care if it herts.

Later I had more crazy tests today. The nice lady who gave it me told me the name and I asked her how do you spellit so I can rite it in my progris riport. THEMATIC AP-PERCEPTION TEST.[2] I dont know the frist 2 words but I know what *test* means. You got to pass it or you get bad marks. This test lookd easy becaus I coud see the picturs. Only this time she dint want me to tell her the picturs. That mixd me up. I said the man yesterday said I shoud tell him what I saw in the ink she said that dont make no difrence. She said make up storys about the pepul in the picturs.

I told her how can you tell storys about pepul you never met. I said why shud I make up lies. I never tell lies any more becaus I always get caut.

She told me this test and the other one the raw-shok was for getting personalty. I laffed so hard. I said how can you get that thing from inkblots and fotos. She got sore and put her picturs away. I dont care. It was sily. I gess I faled that test too.

Later some men in white coats took me to a difernt part of the hospitil and gave me a game to play. It was like a race with a white mouse. They called the mouse Algernon. Algernon was in a box with a lot of twists and turns like all kinds of walls and they gave me a pencil and a paper with lines and lots of boxes. On one side it said START and on the other end it said FINISH. They said it was *amazed*[3] and that Algernon and me had the same *amazed* to do. I dint see how we could have the same *amazed* if Algernon had a box and I had a paper but I dint say nothing. Anyway there wasnt time because the race started.

One of the men had a watch he was trying to hide so I woudnt see it so I tryed not to look and that made me nervus.

Anyway that test made me feel worser than all the others because they did it over 10 times with difernt *amazeds* and Algernon won every time. I dint know that mice were so smart. Maybe thats because Algernon is a white mouse. Maybe white mice are smarter than other mice.

*progris riport 4—Mar 8*

Their going to use me! Im so exited I can hardly write. Dr Nemur and Dr Strauss had a argament about it first. Dr Nemur was in the office when Dr Strauss brot me in. Dr Nemur was worryed about using me but Dr Strauss told him Miss Kinnian rekem-

---

**2. THEMATIC** (*th*ē mat′ ik) **APPERCEPTION** (ap′ ər sep′ s**ʂ**ən) **TEST:** A personality test in which the subject makes up stories about a series of pictures.

**3. amazed:** A maze, or confusing series of paths. Often, the intelligence of animals is assessed by how fast they go through a maze.

**7** **Critical Thinking and Reading**
How does Miss Kinnian feel about Charlie? Why did she recommend him for this experiment?

**8** **Enrichment** Intelligence quotient, or IQ, is based on a comparison of a person's score on an intelligence test with the scores of others on the same test. Average adult IQ ranges from 90 to 110.

**9** **Critical Thinking and Reading**
What is Charlie's motivation?

**ESL Strategy** Students who are not native English speakers may have difficulty understanding the early progress reports because of the misspellings. Pair your ESL students with a native English-speaking partner to give help as needed.

mended me the best from all the pepul who she was teaching. I like Miss Kinnian becaus shes a very smart teacher. And she said Charlie your going to have a second chance. If you volenteer for this experment you mite get smart. They dont know if it will be perminint but theirs a chance. Thats why I said ok even when I was scared because she said it was an operashun. She said dont be scared Charlie you done so much with so little I think you deserv it most of all.

So I got scaird when Dr Nemur and Dr Strauss argud about it. Dr Strauss said I had something that was very good. He said I had a good *motor-vation*.[4] I never even knew I had that. I felt proud when he said that not every body with an *eye-q*[5] of 68 had that thing. I dont know what it is or where I got it but he said Algernon had it too. Algernons *motor-vation* is the cheese they put in his box. But it cant be that because I didnt eat any cheese this week.

---

**4. motor-vation:** Motivation, or desire to work hard and achieve a goal.
**5. eye-q:** I.Q., intelligence quotient, a way of measuring human intelligence.

*Flowers for Algernon* 203

Why are the doctors arguing? Why does Dr. Nemur think Charlie will be a good subject for the experiment? What is their goal?

11 **Discussion** Is it possible to make a conscious effort to think? How is Charlie's way of thinking different from the nondisabled person's?

Then he told Dr Nemur something I dint understand so while they were talking I wrote down some of the words.

He said Dr Nemur I know Charlie is not what you had in mind as the first of your new brede of intelek** (coudnt get the word) superman. But most people of his low ment** are host** and uncoop** they are usualy dull apath** and hard to reach. He has a good natcher hes intristed and eager to please.

Dr Nemur said remember he will be the first human beeng ever to have his intelijence trippled by surgicle meens.

Dr Strauss said exakly. Look at how well hes lerned to read and write for his low mentel age its as grate an acheve** as you and I lerning einstines therey of **vity without help. That shows the intenss motorvation. Its comparat** a tremen** achev** I say we use Charlie.

I dint get all the words and they were talking to fast but it sounded like Dr Strauss was on my side and like the other one wasnt.

Then Dr Nemur nodded he said all right maybe your right. We will use Charlie. When he said that I got so exited I jumped up and shook his hand for being so good to me. I told him thank you doc you wont be sorry for giving me a second chance. And I mean it like I told him. After the operashun Im gonna try to be smart. Im gonna try awful hard.

*progris ript 5—Mar 10*

Im skared. Lots of people who work here and the nurses and the people who gave me the tests came to bring me candy and wish me luck. I hope I have luck. I got my rabits foot and my lucky penny and my horse shoe. Only a black cat crossed me when I was comming to the hospitil. Dr Strauss says dont be supersitis Charlie this is sience. Anyway Im keeping my rabits foot with me.

I asked Dr Strauss if Ill beat Algernon in the race after the operashun and he said maybe. If the operashun works Ill show that mouse I can be as smart as he is. Maybe smarter. Then Ill be abel to read better and spell the words good and know lots of things and be like other people. I want to be smart like other people. If it works perminint they will make everybody smart all over the wurld.

They dint give me anything to eat this morning. I dont know what that eating has to do with getting smart. Im very hungry and Dr Nemur took away my box of candy. That Dr Nemur is a grouch. Dr Strauss says I can have it back after the operashun. You cant eat befor a operashun . . .

*Progress Report 6—Mar 15*

The operashun dint hurt. He did it while I was sleeping. They took off the bandijis from my eyes and my head today so I can make a PROGRESS REPORT. Dr Nemur who looked at some of my other ones says I spell PROGRESS wrong and he told me how to spell it and REPORT too. I got to try and remember that.

I have a very bad memary for spelling. Dr Strauss says its ok to tell about all the things that happin to me but he says I shoud tell more about what I feel and what I think. When I told him I dont know how to think he said try. All the time when the bandijis were on my eyes I tryed to think. Nothing happened. I dont know what to think about. Maybe if I ask him he will tell me how I can think now that Im suppose to get smart. What do smart people think about. Fancy things I suppose. I wish I knew some fancy things alredy.

*Progress Report 7—mar 19*

Nothing is happining. I had lots of tests and different kinds of races with Algernon. I

## Grammar in Action

In **first-person narration,** the story is told from the narrator's point of view ("I"). As a character in the story, the narrator relates the events of the story from his or her unique perspective. We learn about the events of the story as well as other characters in the story through the narrator's impressions. Therefore, in some cases, the truth or accuracy of the information may be questionable. When reading a story written from the first-person point of view, it is always a good idea to think about the reliability of the narrator.

In first-person narration, we are likely to learn the most about the narrator and his or her innermost thoughts and feelings, as is certainly the case with Charlie Gordon in "Flowers for Algernon." Charlie Gordon's narration reveals essential information about his character, as well as the other characters. His unique spelling and punctuation alert the reader to his mental handicap, whereas his observations indicate the keenly perceptive quality of his character. Consider the following excerpt:

"Sometimes somebody will say hey look at Joe or Frank or George he really pulled a Charlie Gordon. I don't know why they say that but they always laff."

With its lack of punctuation and misspelling, this passage and hate that mouse. He always beats me. Dr Strauss said I got to play those games. And he said some time I got to take those tests over again. Thse inkblots are stupid. And those pictures are stupid too. I like to draw a picture of a man and a woman but I wont make up lies about people.

I got a headache from trying to think so much. I thot Dr Strauss was my frend but he dont help me. He dont tell me what to think or when Ill get smart. Miss Kinnian dint come to see me. I think writing these progress reports are stupid too.

### Progress Report 8—Mar 23

Im going back to work at the factery. They said it was better I shud go back to work but I cant tell anyone what the operashun was for and I have to come to the hospitil for an hour evry night after work. They are gonna pay me mony every month for lerning to be smart.

Im glad Im going back to work because I miss my job and all my frends and all the fun we have there.

Dr Strauss says I shud keep writing things down but I dont have to do it every day just when I think of something or something speshul happins. He says dont get discoridged because it takes time and it happins slow. He says it took a long time with Algernon before he got 3 times smarter then he was before. Thats why Algernon beats me all the time because he had that operashun too. That makes me feel better. I coud probly do that *amazed* faster than a reglar mouse. Maybe some day Ill beat Algernon. Boy that would be something. So far Algernon looks like he mite be smart perminent.

*Mar 25* (I dont have to write PROGRESS REPORT on top any more just when I hand it in once a week for Dr Nemur to read. I just have to put the date on. That saves time)

We had a lot of fun at the factery today. Joe Carp said hey look where Charlie had his operashun what did they do Charlie put some brains in. I was going to tell him but I remembered Dr Strauss said no. Then Frank Reilly said what did you do Charlie forget your key and open your door the hard way. That made me laff. Their really my friends and they like me.

Sometimes somebody will say hey look at Joe or Frank or George he really pulled a Charlie Gordon. I dont know why they say that but they always laff. This morning Amos Borg who is the 4 man at Donnegans used my name when he shouted at Ernie the office boy. Ernie lost a packige. He said Ernie what are you trying to be a Charlie Gordon. I dont understand why he said that. I never lost any packiges.

*Mar 28* Dr Straus came to my room tonight to see why I dint come in like I was suppose to. I told him I dont like to race with Algernon any more. He said I dont have to for a while but I shud come in. He had a present for me only it wasnt a present but just for lend. I thot it was a little television but it wasnt. He said I got to turn it on when I go to sleep. I said your kidding why shud I turn it on when Im going to sleep. Who ever herd of a thing like that. But he said if I want to get smart I got to do what he says. I told him I dint think I was going to get smart and he put his hand on my sholder and said Charlie you dont know it yet but your getting smarter all the time. You wont notice for a while. I think he was just being nice to make me feel good because I dont look any smarter.

Oh yes I almost forgot. I asked him when I can go back to the class at Miss Kinnians school. He said I wont go their. He said that soon Miss Kinnian will come to the hospitil

205

**12 Discussion** Do you see any evidence of a change in Charlie yet?

**13 Discussion** Are Joe Carp and Frank Reilly really Charlie's friends? Why does Charlie think they are?

others like it tells us that Charlie has a low level of intelligence, but at the same time, we learn that he is observant and sensitive. Narration from another character's point of view might not have revealed Charlie's awareness that he is being ridiculed.

**Student Activity 1.** Choose another passage from the story in which first-person narration reveals important information to the reader.

**Student Activity 2.** Using first-person narration, write a few short paragraphs about an event that would not have the same meaning if it were narrated by someone other than you.

**14 Discussion** Notice how Charlie spells ''don't'' two different ways here. What do you think is happening to him?

**15 Literary Focus** Although Charlie is narrating this story from his point of view, what do you know about Joe Carp and Frank Reilly that Charlie doesn't know? Do you think it's better that Charlie doesn't know?

**Cooperative Learning** Have volunteers work in small groups to dramatize the scene of the party at Muggsy's Saloon. Encourage them to prepare a script from the point of view of Joe Carp or Frank Reilly. Let the group present the skit to their class. Provide time to discuss how different the party seems from the point of view of other characters rather than from Charlie's.

to start and teach me speshul. I was mad at her for not comming to see me when I got the operashun but I like her so maybe we will be frends again.

*Mar 29* That crazy TV kept me up all night. How can I sleep with something yelling crazy things all night in my ears. And the nutty pictures. Wow. I dont know what it says when Im up so how am I going to know when Im sleeping.

Dr Strauss says its ok. He says my brains are lerning when I sleep and that will help me when Miss Kinnian starts my lessons in the hospitl only I found out it isnt a hospitil its a labatory. I think its all crazy. If you can get smart when your sleeping why do people go to school. That thing I dont think will work. I use to watch the late show and the late late show on TV all the time and it never made me smart. Maybe you have to sleep while you watch it.

*PROGRESS REPORT 9—April 3*

**14** Dr Strauss showed me how to keep the TV turned low so now I can sleep. I don't hear a thing. And I still dont understand what it says. A few times I play it over in the morning to find out what I lerned when I was sleeping and I dont think so. Miss Kinnian says Maybe its another langwidge or something. But most times it sounds american. It talks so fast faster then even Miss Gold who was my teacher in 6 grade and I remember she talked so fast I coudnt understand her.

I told Dr Strauss what good is it to get smart in my sleep. I want to be smart when Im awake. He says its the same thing and I have two minds. Theres the *subconscious* and the *conscious* (thats how you spell it). And one dont tell the other one what its doing. They dont even talk to each other.

Thats why I dream. And boy have I been having crazy dreams. Wow. Ever since that night TV. The late late late late late show.

I forgot to ask him if it was only me or if everybody had those two minds.

(I just looked up the word in the dictionary Dr Strauss gave me. The word is *subconscious. adj. Of the nature of mental operations yet not present in consciousness; as, subconscious conflict of desires.*) There's more but I still dont know what it means. This isnt a very good dictionary for dumb people like me.

Anyway the headache is from the party. My frends from the factery Joe Carp and Frank Reilly invited me to go with them to Muggsys Saloon for some drinks. I dont like to drink but they said we will have lots of fun. I had a good time.

Joe Carp said I shoud show the girls how I mop out the toilet in the factory and he got me a mop. I showed them and everyone laffed when I told that Mr Donnegan said I was the best janiter he ever had because I like my job and do it good and never come late or miss a day except for my operashun.

I said Miss Kinnian always said Charlie be proud of your job because you do it good.

Everybody laffed and we had a good time and they gave me lots of drinks and Joe said Charlie is a card when hes potted. I **15** dont know what that means but everybody likes me and we have fun. I cant wait to be smart like my best frends Joe Carp and Frank Reilly.

I dont remember how the party was over but I think I went out to buy a newspaper and coffe for Joe and Frank and when I came back there was no one their. I looked for them all over till late. Then I dont remember so good but I think I got sleepy or sick. A nice cop brot me back home. Thats what my landlady Mrs Flynn says.

But I got a headache and a big lump on my head and black and blue all over. I think maybe I fell. Anyway I got a bad headache and Im sick and hurt all over. I dont think Ill drink anymore.

*April 6*   I beat Algernon! I dint even know I beat him until Burt the tester told me. Then the second time I lost because I got so exited I fell off the chair before I finished. But after that I beat him 8 more times. I must be getting smart to beat a smart mouse like Algernon. But I dont *feel* smarter.

I wanted to race Algernon some more but Burt said thats enough for one day. They let me hold him for a minit. Hes not so bad. Hes soft like a ball of cotton. He blinks and when he opens his eyes their black and pink on the eges.

I said can I feed him because I felt bad to beat him and I wanted to be nice and make frends. Burt said no Algernon is a very specshul mouse with an operashun like mine, and he was the first of all the animals to stay smart so long. He told me Algernon is so smart that every day he has to solve a test to get his food. Its a thing like a lock on a door that changes every time Algernon goes in to eat so he has to lern something new to get his food. That made me sad because if he coudnt lern he woud be hungry.

I dont think its right to make you pass a test to eat. How woud Dr Nemur like it to have to pass a test every time he wants to eat. I think Ill be frends with Algernon.

*April 9*   Tonight after work Miss Kinnian was at the laboratory. She looked like she was glad to see me but scared. I told her dont worry Miss Kinnian Im not smart yet and she laffed. She said I have confidence in you Charlie the way you struggled so hard to read and right better than all the others. At werst you will have it for a littel wile and your doing something for sience.

We are reading a very hard book. I never read such a hard book before. Its called *Robinson Crusoe*[6] about a man who gets merooned on a dessert Iland. Hes smart and figers out all kinds of things so he can have a house and food and hes a good swimmer. Only I feel sorry because hes all alone and has no frends. But I think their must be somebody else on the iland because theres a picture with his funny umbrella looking at footprints. I hope he gets a frend and not be lonly.

*April 10*   Miss Kinnian teaches me to spell better. She says look at a word and close your eyes and say it over and over until you remember. I have lots of truble with *through* that you say *threw* and *enough* and *tough* that you dont say *enew* and *tew*. You got to say *enuff* and *tuff*. Thats how I use to write it before I started to get smart. Im confused but Miss Kinnian says theres no reason in spelling.

*Apr 14*   Finished Robinson Crusoe. I want to find out more about what happens to him but Miss Kinnian says thats all there is. *Why*

*Apr 15*   Miss Kinnian says Im lerning fast. She read some of the Progress Reports and she looked at me kind of funny. She says Im a fine person and Ill show them all. I asked her why. She said never mind but I shoudnt feel bad if I find out that everybody isnt nice like I think. She said for a person who god gave so little to you done more then

---

6. *Robinson Crusoe* (kr$\overline{oo}'$ sō): Novel written in 1719 by Daniel Defoe, a British author.

16 **Discussion** Does it appear that the operation was successful?

17 **Discussion** Why does Charlie decide to be friends with Algernon? What do they have in common?

18 **Critical Thinking and Reading** What is Charlie doing for science?

19 **Discussion** How significant is the conclusion that Charlie draws from looking at the picture of Robinson Crusoe? Compare this conclusion with some of Charlie's earlier conclusions. How are they different?

20 **Discussion** Why is Miss Kinnian worried about Charlie?

a lot of people with brains they never even used. I said all my frends are smart people but there good. They like me and they never did anything that wasnt nice. Then she got something in her eye and she had to run out to the ladys room.

21     *Apr 16*  Today, I lerned, the *comma,* this is a comma (,) a period, with a tail, Miss Kinnian, says its important, because, it makes writing, better, she said, sombeody, coud lose, a lot of money, if a comma, isnt, in the, right place, I dont have, any money, and I dont see, how a comma, keeps you, from losing it,

    But she says, everybody, uses commas, so Ill use, them too,

    *Apr 17*  I used the comma wrong. Its punctuation. Miss Kinnian told me to look up long words in the dictionary to lern to spell them. I said whats the difference if you can read it anyway. She said its part of your education so now on Ill look up all the words Im not sure how to spell. It takes a long time to write that way but I think Im remembering. I only have to look up once and after that I get it right. Anyway thats how come I got the word *punctuation* right. (Its that way in the dictionary). Miss Kinnian says a period is punctuation too, and there are lots of other marks to lern. I told her I thot all the periods had to have tails but she said no.

You got to mix them up, she showed? me" how. to mix! them( up,. and now; I can! mix up all kinds" of punctuation, in! my writing? There, are lots! of rules? to lern; but Im gettin'g them in my head.

One thing I? like about, Dear Miss Kinnian: (thats the way it goes in a business letter if I ever go into business) is she, always gives me' a reason" when—I ask. She's a gen'ius! I wish! I cou'd be smart" like, her;

(Punctuation, is; fun!)

*April 18*  What a dope I am! I didn't even understand what she was talking about. I read the grammar book last night and it explanes the whole thing. Then I saw it was the same way as Miss Kinnian was trying to tell me, but I didn't get it. I got up in the middle of the night, and the whole thing straightened out in my mind.

Miss Kinnian said that the TV working in my sleep helped out. She said I reached a plateau. Thats like the flat top of a hill.

After I figgered out how punctuation worked, I read over all my old Progress Reports from the beginning. Boy, did I have crazy spelling and punctuation! I told Miss Kinnian I ought to go over the pages and fix all the mistakes but she said, "No, Charlie, Dr. Nemur wants them just as they are. That's why he let you keep them after they were photostated, to see your own progress. You're coming along fast, Charlie."

That made me feel good. After the lesson I went down and played with Algernon. We don't race any more.

*April 20*  I feel sick inside. Not sick like for a doctor, but inside my chest it feels empty like getting punched and a heartburn at the same time.

I wasn't going to write about it, but I guess I got to, because its important. Today was the first time I ever stayed home from work.

Last night Joe Carp and Frank Reilly invited me to a party. There were lots of girls and some men from the factory. I remembered how sick I got last time I drank too much, so I told Joe I didn't want anything to drink. He gave me a plain coke instead. It tasted funny, but I thought it was just a bad taste in my mouth.

We had a lot of fun for a while. Joe said I should dance with Ellen and she would teach me the steps. I fell a few times and I couldn't understand why because no one else was dancing besides Ellen and me. And all the time I was tripping because somebody's foot was always sticking out.

Then when I got up I saw the look on Joe's face and it gave me a funny feeling in my stomack. "He's a scream," one of the girls said. Everybody was laughing.

Frank said, "I ain't laughed so much since we sent him off for the newspaper that night at Muggsy's and ditched him."

"Look at him. His face is red."

"He's blushing. Charlie is blushing."

"Hey, Ellen, what'd you do to Charlie? I never saw him act like that before."

I didn't know what to do or where to turn. Everyone was looking at me and laughing and I felt naked. I wanted to hide myself. I ran out into the street and I threw up. Then I walked home. It's a funny thing I never knew that Joe and Frank and the others liked to have me around all the time to make fun of me.

Now I know what it means when they say "to pull a Charlie Gordon."

I'm ashamed.

22 **Discussion** What are some of the signs that Charlie is getting smarter?

23 **Critical Thinking and Reading** How can you tell that Charlie is not learning in traditional ways?

24 **Discussion** What does Charlie realize here? Why is he ashamed?

**25 Critical Thinking and Reading** What insights does Charlie's analysis give you on persons with physical and mental disabilities?

**26 Discussion** Has Charlie's point of view matured yet? How can you tell?

**27 Clarification** An IQ of 200 would be very high. It would indicate that a person was very intelligent.

*April 21* Still didn't go into the factory. I told Mrs. Flynn my landlady to call and tell Mr. Donnegan I was sick. Mrs. Flynn looks at me very funny lately like she's scared of me.

I think it's a good thing about finding out how everybody laughs at me. I thought about it a lot. It's because I'm so dumb and I don't even know when I'm doing something dumb. **25** People think it's funny when a dumb person can't do things the same way they can.

Anyway, now I know I'm getting smarter every day. I know punctuation and I can spell good. I like to look up all the hard words in the dictionary and I remember them. I'm reading a lot now, and Miss Kinnian says I read very fast. Sometimes I even understand what I'm reading about, and it stays in my mind. There are times when I can close my eyes and think of a page and it all comes back like a picture.

Besides history, geography and arithmetic, Miss Kinnian said I should start to learn a few foreign languages. Dr. Strauss gave me some more tapes to play while I sleep. I still don't understand how that conscious and unconscious mind works, but Dr. Strauss says not to worry yet. He asked me to promise that when I start learning college subjects next week I wouldn't read any books on psychology—that is, until he gives me permission.

I feel a lot better today, but I guess I'm still a little angry that all the time people were laughing and making fun of me because I wasn't so smart. **26** When I become intelligent like Dr. Strauss says, with three times my I.Q. of 68, then maybe I'll be like everyone else and people will like me and be friendly.

I'm not sure what an *I.Q.* is. Dr. Nemur said it was something that measured how intelligent you were—like a scale in the drugstore weighs pounds. But Dr. Strauss had a big arguement with him and said an I.Q. didn't weigh intelligence at all. He said an I.Q. showed how much intelligence you could get, like the numbers on the outside of a measuring cup. You still had to fill the cup up with stuff.

Then when I asked Burt, who gives me my intelligence tests and works with Algernon, he said that both of them were wrong (only I had to promise not to tell them he said so). Burt says that the I.Q. measures a lot of different things including some of the things you learned already, and it really isn't any good at all.

So I still don't know what I.Q. is except that mine is going to be over 200 soon. **27** I didn't want to say anything, but I don't see how if they don't know *what* it is, or *where* it is—I don't see how they know *how much* of it you've got.

Dr. Nemur says I have to take a *Rorshach Test* tomorrow. I wonder what *that* is.

*April 22* I found out what a *Rorshach* is. It's the test I took before the operation—the one with the inkblots on the pieces of cardboard. The man who gave me the test was the same one.

I was scared to death of those inkblots. I knew he was going to ask me to find the pictures and I knew I wouldn't be able to. I was thinking to myself, if only there was some way of knowing what kind of pictures were hidden there. Maybe there weren't any pictures at all. Maybe it was just a trick to see if I was dumb enough too look for something that wasn't there. Just thinking about that made me sore at him.

"All right, Charlie," he said, "you've seen these cards before, remember?"

"Of course I remember."

The way I said it, he knew I was angry,

## Grammar in Action

When writers want to express one idea in relation to another within one sentence, they frequently use **adverb clauses.** An adverb clause begins with a subordinating conjunction (words like *after, although, as, because, since,* and others) and contains a subject and a verb. It expresses an idea that is less important than the idea expressed in the main clause. Adverb clauses cannot stand alone as a sentence.

The following sentences contain adverb clauses:

People think it's funny *when a dumb person can't do things the same way they can.*

Dr. Strauss gave me some more tapes to play *while I sleep.*

*When I become intelligent like Dr. Strauss says, with three times my I.Q. of 68,* then maybe I'll be like everyone else and people will like me and be friendly.

*While he was making his notes,* I peeked out of the corner of my eye to read it.

and he looked surprised. "Yes, of course. Now I want you to look at this one. What might this be? What do you see on this card? People see all sorts of things in these inkblots. Tell me what it might be for you—what it makes you think of."

I was shocked. That wasn't what I had expected him to say at all. "You mean there are no pictures hidden in those inkblots?"

He frowned and took off his glasses. "What?"

"Pictures. Hidden in the inkblots. Last time you told me that everyone could see them and you wanted me to find them too."

**28** He explained to me that the last time he had used almost the exact same words he was using now. I didn't believe it, and I still have the suspicion that he misled me at the time just for the fun of it. Unless—I don't know any more—could I have been *that* feeble-minded?

We went through the cards slowly. One of them looked like a pair of bats tugging at some thing. Another one looked like two men fencing with swords. I imagined all sorts of things. I guess I got carried away. But I didn't trust him any more, and I kept turning them around and even looking on the back to see if there was anything there I was supposed to catch. While he was making his notes, I peeked out of the corner of my eye to read it. But it was all in code that looked like this:

$$WF + A \quad DdF\text{-}Ad \text{ orig.} \quad WF\text{-}A$$
$$SF + obj$$

The test still doesn't make sense to me. It seems to me that anyone could make up lies about things that they didn't really see. How could he know I wasn't making a fool of him by mentioning things that I didn't really imagine? Maybe I'll understand it when Dr. Strauss lets me read up on psychology.

*April 25* I figured out a new way to line up the machines in the factory, and Mr. Donnegan says it will save him ten thousand dollars a year in labor and increased production. He gave me a $25 bonus.

I wanted to take Joe Carp and Frank Reilly out to lunch to celebrate, but Joe said he had to buy some things for his wife, and Frank said he was meeting his cousin for lunch. I guess it'll take a little time for them to get used to the changes in me. Everybody seems to be frightened of me. When I went over to Amos Borg and tapped him on the shoulder, he jumped up in the air.

People don't talk to me much any more or kid around the way they used to. It makes the job kind of lonely.

**29**

*April 27* I got up the nerve today to ask Miss Kinnian to have dinner with me tomorrow night to celebrate my bonus.

At first she wasn't sure it was right, but I asked Dr. Strauss and he said it was okay. Dr. Strauss and Dr. Nemur don't seem to be getting along so well. They're arguing all the time. This evening when I came in to ask Dr. Strauss about having dinner with Miss Kinnian, I heard them shouting. Dr. Nemur was saying that it was *his* experiment and *his* research, and Dr. Strauss was shouting back that he contributed just as much, because he found me through Miss Kinnian and he performed the operation. Dr. Strauss said that someday thousands of neurosurgeons[7] might be using his technique all over the world.

Dr. Nemur wanted to publish the results of the experiment at the end of this month. Dr. Strauss wanted to wait a while longer to be sure. Dr. Strauss said that Dr. Nemur

---

**7. neurosurgeons** (noor′ ō sur′ jənz) *n.*: Doctors who operate on the nervous system, including the brain and spine.

*Flowers for Algernon* 211

**28 Discussion** How is Charlie's current performance on the Rorschach test different from his first?

**29 Discussion** As Charlie becomes more intelligent, how do his co-workers respond to him?

---

Notice the punctuation of adverb clauses in the examples. If the adverb clause is at the end of the sentence, usually there is no comma before it. If the adverb clause is at the beginning of the sentence, it must be followed by a comma.

**Student Activity 1.** Look at each of the sample sentences. What two ideas are expressed in each sentence? Which idea is more important?

**Student Activity 2.** Write four of your own sentences in which you include an adverb clause. Two of the sentences should have

the adverb clause before the main clause, and two should have the adverb clause after the main clause.

**Electronic Handbook** You may want students to review adverb clauses before completing the Grammar in Action activities. If students have access to the Language Master 6000, have them enter the access word *clause* and press the GRAMMAR key to get information on subordinating ideas in adverb clauses.

**30 Discussion** What makes Charlie's speculation about the doctors so amazing?

**31 Critical Thinking and Reading** What is it that Charlie doesn't want to think of?

was more interested in the Chair[8] of Psychology at Princeton than he was in the experiment. Dr. Nemur said that Dr. Strauss was nothing but an opportunist who was trying to ride to glory on *his* coattails.

30 When I left afterwards, I found myself trembling. I don't know why for sure, but it was as if I'd seen both men clearly for the first time. I remember hearing Burt say that Dr. Nemur had a shrew of a wife who was pushing him all the time to get things published so that he could become famous. Burt said that the dream of her life was to have a big shot husband.

Was Dr. Strauss really trying to ride on his coattails?

*April 28* I don't understand why I never noticed how beautiful Miss Kinnian really is. She has brown eyes and feathery brown hair that comes to the top of her neck. She's only thirty-four! I think from the beginning I had the feeling that she was an unreachable genius—and very, very old. Now, every time I see her she grows younger and more lovely.

We had dinner and a long talk. When she said that I was coming along so fast that soon I'd be leaving her behind, I laughed.

"It's true, Charlie. You're already a better reader than I am. You can read a whole page at a glance while I can take in only a few lines at a time. And you remember every single thing you read. I'm lucky if I can recall the main thoughts and the general meaning."

"I don't feel intelligent. There are so many things I don't understand."

She took out a cigarette and I lit it for her.

"You've got to be a *little* patient. You're accomplishing in days and weeks what it takes normal people to do in half a lifetime.

---

**8. chair:** Professorship.

That's what makes it so amazing. You're like a giant sponge now, soaking things in. Facts, figures, general knowledge. And soon you'll begin to connect them, too. You'll see how the different branches of learning are related. There are many levels, Charlie, like steps on a giant ladder that take you up higher and higher to see more and more of the world around you.

"I can see only a little bit of that, Charlie, and I won't go much higher than I am now, but you'll keep climbing up and up, and see more and more, and each step will open new worlds that you never even knew existed." She frowned. "I hope . . . I just hope to God—"

"What?"

"Never mind, Charles. I just hope I wasn't wrong to advise you to go into this in the first place."

I laughed. "How could that be? It worked, didn't it? Even Algernon is still smart."

We sat there silently for a while and I knew what she was thinking about as she watched me toying with the chain of my rabbit's foot and my keys. I didn't want to think of that possibility any more than elderly people want to think of death. I *knew* that this was only the beginning. I knew what she meant about levels because I'd seen some of them already. The thought of leaving her behind made me sad.

31

I'm in love with Miss Kinnian.

PROGRESS REPORT 12

*April 30* I've quit my job with Donnegan's Plastic Box Company. Mr. Donnegan insisted that it would be better for all concerned if I left. What did I do to make them hate me so?

The first I knew of it was when Mr. Donnegan showed me the petition. Eight hundred and forty names, everyone con-

## Grammar in Action

Although stories are usually narrated from one point of view consistently, other points of view also provide important insight or commentary. For example, "Flowers for Algernon" is told from the first-person point of view, but in dialogue, **second-person** is also used. Although works of literature are rarely told from the second-person point of view, dialogue frequently uses second-person.

The sentence "I don't understand why I never noticed how beautiful Miss Kinnian really is" is an example of information we can learn only through first-person narration. However, second-person voice ("you") also provides important information from other characters' perspectives. The following excerpt illustrates the second-person point of view:

"You've got to be a *little* patient. You're accomplishing in days and weeks what it takes normal people to do in half a lifetime. That's what makes it so amazing. You're like a giant sponge now, soaking things in."

It is unlikely that Charlie would have made such an observation.

nected with the factory, except Fanny Girden. Scanning the list quickly, I saw at once that hers was the only missing name. All the rest demanded that I be fired.

Joe Carp and Frank Reilly wouldn't talk to me about it. No one else would either, except Fanny. She was one of the few people I'd known who set her mind to something and believed it no matter what the rest of the world proved, said or did—and Fanny did not believe that I should have been fired. She had been against the petition on principle and despite the pressure and threats she'd held out.

**32**
"Which don't mean to say," she remarked, "that I don't think there's something mighty strange about you, Charlie. Them changes. I don't know. You used to be a good, dependable, ordinary man—not too bright maybe, but honest. Who knows what you done to yourself to get so smart all of a sudden. Like everybody around here's been saying, Charlie, it's not right."

"But how can you say that, Fanny? What's wrong with a man becoming intelligent and wanting to acquire knowledge and understanding of the world around him?"

She stared down at her work, and I turned to leave. Without looking at me, she said: "It was evil when Eve listened to the snake and ate from the tree of knowledge. It was evil when she saw that she was naked. If not for that none of us would ever have to grow old and sick, and die."

Once again now I have the feeling of shame burning inside me. This intelligence has driven a wedge between me and all the people I once knew and loved. Before, they laughed at me and despised me for my ignorance and dullness; now, they hate me for my knowledge and understanding. What do they want of me?

They've driven me out of the factory. Now I'm more alone than ever before . . .

*May 15* Dr. Strauss is very angry at me for not having written any progress reports in two weeks. He's justified because the lab is now paying me a regular salary. I told him I was too busy thinking and reading. When I pointed out that writing was such a slow process that it made me impatient with my poor handwriting, he suggested that I learn to type. It's much easier to write now because I can type nearly seventy-five words a minute. Dr. Strauss continually reminds me of the need to speak and write simply so that people will be able to understand me.

**33**

I'll try to review all the things that happened to me during the last two weeks. Algernon and I were presented to the American Psychological Association sitting in convention with the World Psychological Association last Tuesday. We created quite a sensation. Dr. Nemur and Dr. Strauss were proud of us.

I suspect that Dr. Nemur, who is sixty—ten years older than Dr. Strauss—finds it necessary to see tangible results of his work. Undoubtedly the result of pressure by Mrs. Nemur.

Contrary to my earlier impressions of him, I realize that Dr. Nemur is not at all a genius. He has a very good mind, but it struggles under the specter of self-doubt. He wants people to take him for a genius. Therefore, it is important for him to feel that his work is accepted by the world. I believe that Dr. Nemur was afraid of further delay because he worried that someone else might make a discovery along these lines and take the credit from him.

**34**

Dr. Strauss on the other hand might be called a genius, although I feel that his areas of knowledge are too limited. He was educated in the tradition of narrow specialization; the broader aspects of background were neglected far more than necessary—even for a neurosurgeon.

*Flowers for Algernon*  213

**32 Discussion** Why have the people at the factory turned against Charlie?

**33 Discussion** Why hasn't Charlie written any progress reports in two weeks? What is Dr. Strauss's solution?

**34 Critical Thinking and Reading** What do you notice about Charlie's perception of the doctors?

**Student Activity 1.** After each sentence tell whether the sentence is in the first- or second-person voice:

1. I'm in love with Miss Kinnian.
2. I realize that Dr. Nemur is not at all a genius.
3. You remember everything you read.
4. But how can you say that, Fanny?
5. I've quit my job with Donnegan's plastic box company.

**Student Activity 2.** Compose a dialogue between Charlie and one of the other characters in the story in which you use first- and second-person point of view.

**35** **Discussion** Why is this humorous? Is knowing Latin, Greek, and Hebrew a small accomplishment?

**36** **Critical Thinking and Reading** What do you think the look on Dr. Strauss's face means?

**37** **Critical Thinking and Reading** How is Charlie handling his new intelligence? Is it making him happy? Why or why not?

**35** I was shocked to learn that the only ancient languages he could read were Latin, Greek and Hebrew, and that he knows almost nothing of mathematics beyond the elementary levels of the calculus of variations. When he admitted this to me, I found myself almost annoyed. It was as if he'd hidden this part of himself in order to deceive me, pretending—as do many people I've discovered—to be what he is not. No one I've ever known is what he appears to be on the surface.

Dr. Nemur appears to be uncomfortable around me. Sometimes when I try to talk to him, he just looks at me strangely and turns away. I was angry at first when Dr. Strauss told me I was giving Dr. Nemur an inferiority complex. I thought he was mocking me and I'm oversensitive at being made fun of.

How was I to know that a highly respected psychoexperimentalist like Nemur was unacquainted with Hindustani[9] and Chinese? It's absurd when you consider the work that is being done in India and China today in the very field of his study.

**36** I asked Dr. Strauss how Nemur could refute Rahajamati's attack on his method and results if Nemur couldn't even read them in the first place. That strange look on Dr. Strauss' face can mean only one of two things. Either he doesn't want to tell Nemur what they're saying in India, or else—and this worries me—Dr. Strauss doesn't know either. I must be careful to speak and write clearly and simply so that people won't laugh.

*May 18* I am very disturbed. I saw Miss Kinnian last night for the first time in over a week. I tried to avoid all discussions of intel-

---

**9. Hindustani** (hin′ d$\overline{oo}$ stan′ ē) *n.*: A language of northern India.

lectual concepts and to keep the conversation on a simple, everyday level, but she just stared at me blankly and asked me what I meant about the mathematical variance equivalent in Dorbermann's *Fifth Concerto.*

**37** When I tried to explain she stopped me and laughed. I guess I got angry, but I suspect I'm approaching her on the wrong level. No matter what I try to discuss with her, I am unable to communicate. I must review Vrostadt's equations on *Levels of Semantic Progression.* I find that I don't communicate with people much any more. Thank God for books and music and things I can think about. I am alone in my apartment at Mrs. Flynn's boarding house most of the time and seldom speak to anyone.

*May 20* I would not have noticed the new dishwasher, a boy of about sixteen, at the corner diner where I take my evening meals if not for the incident of the broken dishes.

They crashed to the floor, shattering and sending bits of white china under the tables. The boy stood there, dazed and frightened, holding the empty tray in his hand. The whistles and catcalls from the customers (the cries of "hey, there go the profits!" . . . "*Mazeltov!*" . . . and "well, *he* didn't work here very long . . ." which invariably seems to follow the breaking of glass or dishware in a public restaurant) all seemed to confuse him.

When the owner came to see what the excitement was about, the boy cowered as if he expected to be struck and threw up his arms as if to ward off the blow.

"All right! All right, you dope," shouted the owner, "don't just stand there! Get the broom and sweep that mess up. A broom . . . a broom, you idiot! It's in the kitchen. Sweep up all the pieces."

The boy saw that he was not going to be

## Grammar in Action

Skillful writers use participles in order to enhance the meaning of sentences. **Participles** are verb forms used as adjectives to describe a noun or pronoun. Present participles end in *-ing;* past participles usually end in *-ed* (irregular verbs form their past participle in various ways: *-t, -en* among others).

Participles along with their own modifiers and complements are called **participial phrases** and can also be used to describe nouns and pronouns in sentences.

Notice the use of participles and participial phrases in the following sentences from "Flowers for Algernon":

They crashed to the floor, *shattering and sending bits of white china under the tables.* The boy stood there, *dazed and frightened, holding the empty tray in his hand.*

His *frightened* expression disappeared and he smiled and hummed as he came back with the broom to sweep the floor.

As his vacant eyes moved across the crowd of *amused* onlookers, he slowly mirrored their smiles . . .

punished. His frightened expression disappeared and he smiled and hummed as he came back with the broom to sweep the floor. A few of the rowdier customers kept up the remarks, amusing themselves at his expense.

"Here, sonny, over here there's a nice piece behind you . . ."

"C'mon, do it again . . ."

"He's not so dumb. It's easier to break 'em than to wash 'em . . ."

As his vacant eyes moved across the crowd of amused onlookers, he slowly mirrored their smiles and finally broke into an uncertain grin at the joke which he obviously did not understand.

I felt sick inside as I looked at his dull, vacuous smile, the wide, bright eyes of a child, uncertain but eager to please. They were laughing at him because he was mentally retarded.

And I had been laughing at him too.

**38** Suddenly, I was furious at myself and all those who were smirking at him. I jumped up and shouted, "Shut up! Leave him alone! It's not his fault he can't understand! He can't help what he is! But . . . he's still a human being!"

The room grew silent. I cursed myself for losing control and creating a scene. I tried not to look at the boy as I paid my check and walked out without touching my food. I felt ashamed for both of us.

**39** How strange it is that people of honest feelings and sensibility, who would not take advantage of a man born without arms or legs or eyes—how such people think nothing of abusing a man born with low intelligence. It infuriated me to think that not too long ago I, like this boy, had foolishly played the clown.

And I had almost forgotten.

I'd hidden the picture of the old Charlie Gordon from myself because now that I was intelligent it was something that had to be pushed out of my mind. But today in looking at that boy, for the first time I saw what I had been. *I was just like him!*

Only a short time ago, I learned that people laughed at me. Now I can see that unknowingly I joined with them in laughing at myself. That hurts most of all.

**40** I have often reread my progress reports and seen the illiteracy, the childish naïveté,[10] the mind of low intelligence peering from a dark room, through the keyhole, at the dazzling light outside. I see that even in my dullness I knew that I was inferior, and that other people had something I lacked—something denied me. In my mental blindness, I thought that it was somehow connected with the ability to read and write, and I was sure that if I could get those skills I would automatically have intelligence too.

Even a feeble-minded man wants to be like other men.

A child may not know how to feed itself, or what to eat, yet it knows of hunger.

This then is what I was like. I never knew. Even with my gift of intellectual awareness, I never really knew.

**41** This day was good for me. Seeing the past more clearly, I have decided to use my knowledge and skills to work in the field of increasing human intelligence levels. Who is better equipped for this work? Who else has lived in both worlds? These are my people. Let me use my gift to do something for them.

Tomorrow, I will discuss with Dr. Strauss the manner in which I can work in this area. I may be able to help him work out the problems of widespread use of the technique which was used on me. I have several good ideas of my own.

---

10. **naïveté** (nä ēv′ tā) *n.*: Simplicity.

*Flowers for Algernon* 215

**38 Discussion** Why does Charlie react this way?

**39 Discussion** Do you think this is true? Why might people be less sensitive to persons with mental disabilities than to persons with physical disabilities.

**40 Reading Strategy** Summarize Charlie's evaluation of his mental condition as it was before the operation.

**41 Discussion** What does Charlie decide to work on? What can you tell about him from his decision?

---

*Seeing the past more clearly,* I have decided to use my knowledge and skills to work in the field of increasing human intelligence levels.

The participles and participial phrases describe the nouns and pronouns in the above sentences and make them more vivid. Like adjectives, participles act to intensify meaning.

**Student Activity 1.** Write four sentences about Charlie. Use a participle in each sentence.

**Student Activity 2.** Write four of your own sentences based on "Flowers for Algernon." Begin each sentence with a participial phrase.

**Electronic Handbook** You may want students to review participles and participial phrases before completing the Grammar in Action activities. If students have access to the Language Master 6000, have them enter the access word *participial* and press the GRAMMAR key to get information on how to make nouns and pronouns more vivid by using participles and participial phrases.

**42 Critical Thinking and Reading** Why is Algernon's behavior a bad sign for Charlie?

**43 Literary Focus** How has Charlie's point of view changed in the course of the story?

**44 Reading Strategy** Summarize Charlie's progress from the time when the bandages were removed to this point.

**Challenge** Explain that writers often use a device called foreshadowing to increase suspense and prepare readers for the outcome; that is, they give readers hints about coming events. Have students find examples of foreshadowing in the story that prepare them for what happens to Charlie.

There is so much that might be done with this technique. If I could be made into a genius, what about thousands of others like myself? What fantastic levels might be achieved by using this technique on normal people? On *geniuses*?

There are so many doors to open. I am impatient to begin.

PROGRESS REPORT 13

*May 23* It happened today. Algernon bit me. I visited the lab to see him as I do occasionally, and when I took him out of his cage, he snapped at my hand. I put him back and watched him for a while. He was unusually disturbed and vicious.

*May 24* Burt, who is in charge of the experimental animals, tells me that Algernon is changing. He is less cooperative; he refuses to run the maze any more; general motivation has decreased. And he hasn't been eating. Everyone is upset about what this may mean.

*May 25* They've been feeding Algernon, who now refuses to work the shifting-lock problem. Everyone identifies me with Algernon. In a way we're both the first of our kind. They're all pretending that Algernon's behavior is not necessarily significant for me. But it's hard to hide the fact that some of the other animals who were used in this experiment are showing strange behavior.

Dr. Strauss and Dr. Nemur have asked me not to come to the lab any more. I know what they're thinking but I can't accept it. I am going ahead with my plans to carry their research forward. With all due respect to both of these fine scientists, I am well aware of their limitations. If there is an answer, I'll have to find it out for myself. Suddenly, time has become very important to me.

*May 29* I have been given a lab of my own and permission to go ahead with the research. I'm on to something. Working day and night. I've had a cot moved into the lab. Most of my writing time is spent on the notes which I keep in a separate folder, but from time to time I feel it necessary to put down my moods and my thoughts out of sheer habit.

I find the *calculus of intelligence* to be a fascinating study. Here is the place for the application of all the knowledge I have acquired. In a sense it's the problem I've been concerned with all my life.

*May 31* Dr. Strauss thinks I'm working too hard. Dr. Nemur says I'm trying to cram a lifetime of research and thought into a few weeks. I know I should rest, but I'm driven on by something inside that won't let me stop. I've got to find the reason for the sharp regression in Algernon. I've got to know *if* and *when* it will happen to me.

June 4

LETTER TO DR. STRAUSS *(copy)*

Dear Dr. Strauss:

Under separate cover I am sending you a copy of my report entitled, "The Algernon-Gordon Effect: A Study of Structure and Function of Increased Intelligence," which I would like to have you read and have published.

As you see, my experiments are completed. I have included in my report all of my formulae, as well as mathematical analysis in the appendix. Of course, these should be verified.

Because of its importance to both you and Dr. Nemur (and need I say to

**45 Critical Thinking and Reading**
What had Dr. Strauss meant by
this? Is this how science works?
Explain your answer.

myself, too?) I have checked and re-
checked my results a dozen times in
the hope of finding an error. I am
sorry to say the results must stand.
Yet for the sake of science, I am
grateful for the little bit that I here
add to the knowledge of the function
of the human mind and of the laws
governing the artificial increase of
human intelligence.

**45**       I recall your once saying to me
that an experimental *failure* or the
*disproving* of a theory was as important to the advancement of learning
as a success would be. I know now
that this is true. I am sorry, however,

that my own contribution to the field
must rest upon the ashes of the work
of two men I regard so highly.

                Yours truly,

                Charles Gordon

encl.: rept.

   *June 5*   I must not become emotional.
The facts and the results of my experiments
are clear, and the more sensational aspects
of my own rapid climb cannot obscure the
fact that the tripling of intelligence by the
surgical technique developed by Drs.
Strauss and Nemur must be viewed as having little or no practical applicability (at the

*Flowers for Algernon*   217

**46 Reading Strategy** Paraphrase Charlie's experimental conclusion.

**47 Discussion** What are the signs that the experiment was not a success after all?

**48 Critical Thinking and Reading** How does Charlie's behavior parallel Algernon's?

**49 Discussion** Is Charlie worse off now than he was before the operation? Why?

present time) to the increase of human intelligence.

As I review the records and data on Algernon, I see that although he is still in his physical infancy, he has regressed mentally. Motor activity[11] is impaired; there is a general reduction of glandular activity; there is an accelerated loss of coordination.

There are also strong indications of progressive amnesia.

As will be seen by my report, these and other physical and mental deterioration syndromes can be predicted with statistically significant results by the application of my formula.

The surgical stimulus to which we were both subjected has resulted in an intensification and acceleration of all mental processes. The unforeseen development, which I have taken the liberty of calling the "Algernon-Gordon Effect," is the logical extension of the entire intelligence speedup. The hypothesis here proven may be described simply in the following terms: Artificially increased intelligence deteriorates at a rate of time directly proportional to the quantity of the increase.

I feel that this, in itself, is an important discovery.

As long as I am able to write, I will continue to record my thoughts in these progress reports. It is one of my few pleasures. However, by all indications, my own mental deterioration will be very rapid.

I have already begun to notice signs of emotional instability and forgetfulness, the first symptoms of the burnout.

*June 10* Deterioration progressing. I have become absent-minded. Algernon died two days ago. Dissection shows my predic-

---

11. **motor activity:** Movement, physical coordination.

tions were right. His brain had decreased in weight and there was a general smoothing out of cerebral convolutions as well as a deepening and broadening of brain fissures.

I guess the same thing is or will soon be happening to me. Now that it's definite, I don't want it to happen.

I put Algernon's body in a cheese box and buried him in the back yard. I cried.

*June 15* Dr. Strauss came to see me again. I wouldn't open the door and I told him to go away. I want to be left to myself. I have become touchy and irritable. I feel the darkness closing in. I keep telling myself how important this introspective journal will be.

It's a strange sensation to pick up a book that you've read and enjoyed just a few months ago and discover that you don't remember it. I remembered how great I thought John Milton[12] was, but when I picked up *Paradise Lost* I couldn't understand it at all. I got so angry I threw the book across the room.

I've got to try to hold on to some of it. Some of the things I've learned. Oh, God, please don't take it all away.

*June 19* Sometimes, at night, I go out for a walk. Last night I couldn't remember where I lived. A policeman took me home. I have the strange feeling that this has all happened to me before—a long time ago. I keep telling myself I'm the only person in the world who can describe what's happening to me.

*June 21* Why can't I remember? I've got to fight. I lie in bed for days and I don't know who or where I am. Then it all comes

---

12. **John Milton:** British poet (1608–1674).
13. **fugues** (fyo͞ogz) **of amnesia** (am nē′ zhə): Periods of loss of memory.

back to me in a flash. Fugues of amnesia.[13] Symptoms of senility—second childhood. I can watch them coming on. It's so cruelly logical. I learned so much and so fast. Now my mind is deteriorating rapidly. I won't let it happen. I'll fight it. I can't help thinking of the boy in the restaurant, the blank expression, the silly smile, the people laughing at him. No—please—not that again . . .

*June 22* I'm forgetting things that I learned recently. It seems to be following the classic pattern—the last things learned are the first things forgotten. Or is that the pattern? I'd better look it up again . . .

I reread my paper on the "Algernon-Gordon Effect" and I get the strange feeling that it was written by someone else. There are parts I don't even understand.

Motor activity impaired. I keep tripping over things, and it becomes increasingly difficult to type.

*June 23* I've given up using the typewriter completely. My coordination is bad. I feel that I'm moving slower and slower. Had a terrible shock today. I picked up a copy of an article I used in my research, Krueger's "Uber psychische Ganzheit," to see if it would help me understand what I had done. First I thought there was something wrong with my eyes. Then I realized I could no longer read German. I tested myself in other languages. All gone.

*June 30* A week since I dared to write again. It's slipping away like sand through my fingers. Most of the books I have are too hard for me now. I get angry with them because I know that I read and understood them just a few weeks ago.

I keep telling myself I must keep writing these reports so that somebody will know what is happening to me. But it gets harder to form the words and remember spellings. I have to look up even simple words in the dictionary now and it makes me impatient with myself.

Dr. Strauss comes around almost every day, but I told him I wouldn't see or speak to anybody. He feels guilty. They all do. But I don't blame anyone. I knew what might happen. But how it hurts.

*July 7* I don't know where the week went. Todays Sunday I know because I can see through my window people going to church. I think I stayed in bed all week but I remember Mrs. Flynn bringing food to me a few times. I keep saying over and over Ive got to do something but then I forget or maybe its just easier not to do what I say Im going to do.

I think of my mother and father a lot these days. I found a picture of them with me taken at a beach. My father has a big ball under his arm and my mother is holding me by the hand. I dont remember them the way they are in the picture. All I remember is my father arguing with mom about money.

He never shaved much and he used to scratch my face when he hugged me. He said he was going to take me to see cows on a farm once but he never did. He never kept his promises . . .

*July 10* My landlady Mrs Flynn is very worried about me. She said she doesnt like loafers. If Im sick its one thing, but if Im a loafer thats another thing and she wont have it. I told her I think Im sick.

I try to read a little bit every day, mostly stories, but sometimes I have to read the same thing over and over again because I dont know what it means. And its hard to write. I know I should look up all the words in the dictionary but its so hard and Im so tired all the time.

*Flowers for Algernon* 219

50 **Discussion** Why is Charlie's deterioration so rapid? Do you think it would have been better for him never to have been intelligent than to go through the agony of losing all his new skills?

51 **Critical Thinking and Reading** What does Charlie's writing indicate about his condition?

**52 Discussion** Why does Charlie put flowers on Algernon's grave? Why is ''Flowers for Algernon'' a good title for this story?

**53 Discussion** What new problem is Charlie going to have with people now?

**54 Critical Thinking and Reading** How do you think Miss Kinnian feels about the results of the experiment? How can you tell?

**55 Discussion** Why does Mr. Donnegan give Charlie his old job back?

**56 Literary Focus** Identify the latest change in Charlie's point of view.

**52** Then I got the idea that I would only use the easy words instead of the long hard ones. That saves time. I put flowers on Algernons grave about once a week. Mrs. Flynn thinks Im crazy to put flowers on a mouses grave but I told her that Algernon was special.

*July 14* Its sunday again. I dont have anything to do to keep me busy now because my television set is broke and I dont have any money to get it fixed. (I think I lost this months check from the lab. I dont remember)

I get awful headaches and asperin doesnt help me much. Mrs. Flynn knows Im really sick and she feels very sorry for me. Shes a wonderful woman whenever someone is sick.

*July 22* Mrs. Flynn called a strange doctor to see me. She was afraid I was going to die. I told the doctor I wasnt too sick and that I only forget sometimes. He asked me did I have any friends or relatives and I said no I dont have any. I told him I had a friend called Algernon once but he was a mouse and we used to run races together. He looked at me kind of funny like he thought I was crazy.

**53** He smiled when I told him I used to be a genius. He talked to me like I was a baby and he winked at Mrs Flynn. I got mad and chased him out because he was making fun of me the way they all used to.

*July 24* I have no more money and Mrs Flynn says I got to go to work somewhere and pay the rent because I havent paid for over two months. I dont know any work but the job I used to have at Donnegans Plastic Box Company. I dont want to go back there because they all knew me when I was smart and maybe they'll laugh at me. But I dont know what else to do to get money.

*July 25* I was looking at some of my old progress reports and its very funny but I cant read what I wrote. I can make out some of the words but they dont make sense.

**54** Miss Kinnian came to the door but I said go away I dont want to see you. She cried and I cried too but I wouldnt let her in because I didnt want her to laugh at me. I told her I didn't like her any more. I told her I didn't want to be smart any more. Thats not true. I still love her and I still want to be smart but I had to say that so shed go away. She gave Mrs. Flynn money to pay the rent. I dont want that. I got to get a job.

Please . . . please let me not forget how to read and write . . .

**55** *July 27* Mr. Donnegan was very nice when I came back and asked him for my old job of janitor. First he was very suspicious but I told him what happened to me then he looked very sad and put his hand on my shoulder and said Charlie Gordon you got guts.

**56** Everybody looked at me when I came downstairs and started working in the toilet sweeping it out like I used to. I told myself Charlie if they make fun of you dont get sore because you remember their not so smart as you once thot they were. And besides they were once your friends and if they laughed at you that doesnt mean anything because they liked you too.

One of the new men who came to work there after I went away made a nasty crack he said hey Charlie I hear your a very smart fella a real quiz kid. Say something intelligent. I felt bad but Joe Carp came over and grabbed him by the shirt and said leave him alone or Ill break your neck. I didnt expect

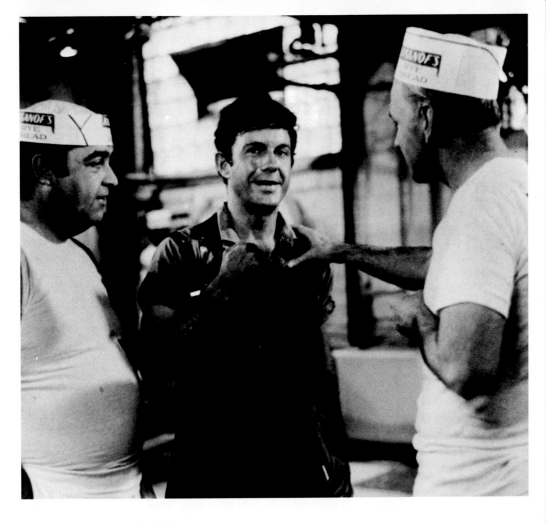

**57 Discussion** Why do Joe and Frank want to defend Charlie now? Could Charlie have been right about their friendship after all?

Joe to take my part so I guess hes really my friend.

**57** Later Frank Reilly came over and said Charlie if anybody bothers you or trys to take advantage you call me or Joe and we will set em straight. I said thanks Frank and I got choked up so I had to turn around and go into the supply room so he wouldnt see me cry. Its good to have friends.

*July 28* I did a dumb thing today I forgot I wasnt in Miss Kinnians class at the adult center any more like I use to be. I went in and sat down in my old seat in the back of the room and she looked at me funny and she said Charles. I dint remember she ever called me that before only Charlie so I said hello Miss Kinnian Im ready for my lesin today only I lost my reader that we was

*Flowers for Algernon* 221

using. She startid to cry and run out of the room and everybody looked at me and I saw they wasnt the same pepul who use to be in my class.

Then all of a suddin I rememberd some things about the operashun and me getting smart and I said holy smoke I reely pulled a Charlie Gordon that time. I went away before she come back to the room.

Thats why Im going away from New York for good. I dont want to do nothing like that agen. I dont want Miss Kinnian to feel sorry for me. Evry body feels sorry at the factery and I dont want that eather so Im going someplace where nobody knows that Charlie Gordon was once a genus and now he cant even reed a book or rite good.

Im taking a cuple of books along and even if I cant reed them Ill practise hard and maybe I wont forget every thing I lerned. If I try reel hard maybe Ill be a littel bit smarter then I was before the operashun. I got my rabits foot and my luky penny and maybe they will help me.

If you ever reed this Miss Kinnian dont be sorry for me Im glad I got a second chanse to be smart becaus I lerned a lot of things that I never even new were in this world and Im grateful that I saw it all for a littel bit. I

dont know why Im dumb agen or what I did wrong maybe its becaus I dint try hard enuff. But if I try and practis very hard maybe Ill get a littl smarter and know what all the words are. I remember a littel bit how nice I had a feeling with the blue book that has the torn cover when I red it. Thats why Im gonna keep trying to get smart so I can have that feeling agen. Its a good feeling to know things and be smart. I wish I had it rite now if I did I woud sit down and reed all the time. Anyway I bet Im the first dumb person in the world who ever found out somthing importent for sience. I remember I did somthing but I dont remember what. So I gess its like I did it for all the dumb pepul like me.

Goodbye Miss Kinnian and Dr Strauss and evreybody. And P.S. please tell Dr Nemur not to be such a grouch when pepul laff at him and he woud have more frends. Its easy to make frends if you let pepul laff at you. Im going to have lots of frends where I go.
P.P.S. Please if you get a chanse put some flowrs on Algernons grave in the bak yard . . .

---

■ **R**ESPONDING TO THE **S**ELECTION

### Your Response

1. Do you think being part of such an experiment was a good experience for Charlie, or would he have been better off if he hadn't participated? Explain.
2. If you were a friend of Charlie's, how would you have reacted to the changes he was undergoing? Why?

### Recalling

3. Why is Charlie keeping a journal?

4. Why does Miss Kinnian believe Charlie should take part in this experiment? Why does she also fear for him?
5. Why does Charlie believe he failed the Rorschach test? What does he come to learn about the Rorschach test?
6. Why does Dr. Strauss think that Charlie is a fit subject for the experiment? Why does Dr. Nemur disagree?
7. How do Charlie's co-workers treat him after he becomes smart? Why does he leave his job?

222   Short Stories

8. In his June 22 report, what feeling about his scientific paper does Charlie reveal?
9. Why does Charlie decide to leave New York?

### Interpreting

10. Explain how Charlie's development parallels Algernon's.
11. How do the spelling and punctuation in Charlie's reports contribute to your view of his progress? How do the books he reads contribute?
12. How is Charlie at the end of the story different from Charlie at the beginning?
13. Do you think "Flowers for Algernon" is a good title for this story? Explain your answer.

### Applying

14. As Charlie grows smarter, he asks questions. Explain why the ability to ask questions is an important part of intelligence.

## ANALYZING LITERATURE

### Understanding Point of View and Theme

When a story is told by a character in it, you see events through this character's eyes. What this character learns helps reveal the theme.

1. What kind of person is Charlie?
2. At the beginning of the story, Charlie views Miss Kinnian, Dr. Strauss, and Dr. Nemur as almost perfect human beings. How does he view them as he grows smarter? How does he view them at the end of the story?
3. Find three examples in the story of how Charlie's views of friendship change.
4. What is the theme of this story?

## CRITICAL THINKING AND READING

### Comparing and Contrasting Views

When you examine the similarities between two subjects, you **compare** them. When you examine the differences, you **contrast** them.

In "Flowers for Algernon," Charlie's perceptions change as he moves from unintelligence to genius and back again. The views of the people around him also change.

1. Contrast Charlie's reaction to the first party (page 206) with the second (page 209).
2. Compare Charlie's general attitude at the end when he visits the classroom by mistake (page 221) with his attitude at the beginning.
3. Contrast Miss Kinnian's attitude toward Charlie before his operation with that on April 28 (page 212).

## THINKING AND WRITING

### Writing About Theme

Assume that at the time of the June 10 progress report, Charlie learns that another retarded person has the opportunity to undergo the same operation. Freewrite for three minutes as Charlie about his feelings about the operation. Then write a letter in which Charlie gives the person advice on whether to have the operation. Revise your letter, making sure you have presented your case clearly. Proofread, checking for spelling, grammar, and punctuation.

## LEARNING OPTIONS

1. **Performance.** With a group of classmates, choose a scene from the story to perform dramatically. Work together to write dialogue and stage directions from the information in Charlie's journal. Once you have prepared your material and assigned roles, rehearse with simple props. Then perform your scene for the class.
2. **Writing.** Imagine that you are Miss Kinnian and you have been asked by a magazine to write about your experiences with Charlie. Tell how you came to know Charlie and describe what kind of person he is. Talk about the changes that you witnessed in Charlie during the time of the experiment. Finally, discuss whether you feel his taking part in the experiment was good or bad for him in the long run.

*Flowers for Algernon* 223

**Reading and Responding** Stu-
**Reading and Responding** Students have already studied each of the literary elements summarized on this page in the short story unit. The purpose of Reading and Responding is to emphasize the interrelationship of these elements. By reading actively students can study these elements, understand their effect on each other, and understand their contribution to the overall effect of the story.

The plot affects the other elements of a short story. The events of the story affect the actions and emotions of characters, as well as the time and place of the action. The theme is usually revealed through the outcome of the story as well as through the actions of the characters.

Remind students that the Reading and Responding process is part of reading actively. As they are reading the selection, they should not only consider the elements that make up the story, but they should also question, predict, visualize, clarify, and make connections. This interaction will increase their understanding and enjoyment of the story and help them to be better readers.

For further practice with these elements, use the selection in the Teaching Portfolio, "The Story of Keesh," pages 312–317, with which students can record their own annotations.

# READING AND RESPONDING

## The Short Story

As an active reader, you involve yourself in a story and derive meaning from it. You apply your active reading strategies to the plot, characters, setting, and theme, the elements that work together to create an effective whole. Your response is what you think and feel about the story and its elements.

**RESPONDING TO PLOT** The plot is what happens in a short story. Knowing how a plot is structured can help you make connections and predictions as you read. Involving yourself in the plot can enhance your response to the resolution of the conflict. The more involved you are, the more satisfaction you derive from a good ending.

**RESPONDING TO CHARACTERS** Characters are the people in a story. Like real people, characters have traits and personalities that determine the way they behave. When you read, let yourself identify with the characters: Share their emotions, and think about what you would do in their place.

**RESPONDING TO SETTING** Setting is the time and the place in which the events in a story occur. As you read actively, respond to the details of the setting. What kind of atmosphere or mood does the author create? How does the setting affect the plot and the characters? How does it affect you?

**RESPONDING TO THEME** Theme is the general idea about life presented in a story, or what the story means to you. As you read actively, you will notice how the author has constructed the story to reveal the theme. Does the main character learn something about life? Is the theme stated or implied? What does this story say to you?

On pages 225–234 is an example of active reading and responding by Dustin Brumbaugh of Marysville School in Marysville, Washington. The notes in the side column include Dustin's thoughts as he read "The Medicine Bag." Your own thoughts as you read may be different because you bring your own experiences to your reading.

*224   Short Stories*

## Objectives

1 To understand how different elements work together in a short story
2 To review a short story
3 To evaluate a story
4 To continue a story
5 To express individual interests and abilities through an optional activity

## Support Material

**Teaching Portfolio**
Teacher Backup, p. 309
Reading and Responding, "The Story of Keesh," p. 312
Grammar in Action Worksheets, *Using Descriptive Words,* p. 318; *Using Compound Sentences,* p. 320
Usage and Mechanics Worksheet, p. 322

Analyzing Literature Worksheet, *Reviewing the Short Story,* p. 323
Critical Thinking and Reading Worksheet, *Evaluating a Short Story,* p. 324
Selection Test, p. 325

**Prentice Hall Literature Writing Studio**

# MODEL

# The Medicine Bag

### Virginia Driving Hawk Sneve

**Plot:** *This story is going to be about a medicine bag. What is a medicine bag?*

My kid sister Cheryl and I always bragged about our Sioux[1] grandpa, Joe Iron Shell. Our friends, who had always lived in the city and only knew about Indians from movies and TV, were impressed by our stories. Maybe we exaggerated and made Grandpa and the reservation sound glamorous, but when we'd return home to Iowa after our yearly summer visit to Grandpa, we always had some exciting tale to tell.

**Character:** *The main character's desire to impress his friends shows that he has pride in his Sioux heritage, but also that he is a bit too concerned about what his friends think of him.*

We always had some authentic Sioux article to show our listeners. One year Cheryl had new moccasins[2] that Grandpa had made. On another visit he gave me a small, round, flat, rawhide drum that was decorated with a painting of a warrior riding a horse. He taught me a real Sioux chant to sing while I beat the drum with a leather-covered stick that had a feather on the end. Man, that really made an impression.

**Plot:** *The main character probably hopes that his friends will be satisfied hearing stories about his grandfather and not insist on seeing him. I think that he will try to prevent his friends from meeting his grandfather.*

We never showed our friends Grandpa's picture. Not that we were ashamed of him, but because we knew that the glamorous tales we told didn't go with the real thing. Our friends would have laughed at the picture because Grandpa wasn't tall and stately like TV Indians. His hair wasn't in braids but hung in stringy, gray strands on his neck, and he was old. He was our great-grandfather, and he didn't live in a tepee,[3] but all by himself in a part log, part tar-paper shack on the Rosebud Reservation[4] in South Dakota. So when Grandpa came to visit us, I was so ashamed and embarrassed I could've died.

There are a lot of yippy poodles and other fancy little dogs in our neighborhood, but they usually barked singly

---

**1. Sioux** (soō) *n.*: Native American tribes of the northern plains of the United States and nearby southern Canada.
**2. moccasins** (mäk′ ə s′nz) *n.*: Heelless slippers of soft flexible leather, originally worn by Native Americans.
**3. tepee** (tē′ pē) *n.*: A cone-shaped tent of animal skins, used by the Plains Indians.
**4. Rosebud Reservation:** A small Indian reservation in south-central South Dakota.

*The Medicine Bag* 225

## Presentation

**Motivation/Prior Knowledge** Have students discuss traditions that are passed along from one generation to the next, from father to son, mother to daughter, family to family, and generation to generation. What kinds of things can be passed along? Why are these traditions important?

**Master Teacher Note** Students might appreciate the story more if they had an idea of what life on an Indian reservation was like. You could show students pictures of some reservations. You could probably obtain pictures of Indian reservations from reference books in your school or local library.

**Making Connections** Another selection that deals with passing along something of importance to the next generation is "Taught Me Purple" (page 551).

**Purpose-Setting Question** How does Martin's attitude toward his grandfather and his Sioux heritage change during the story?

---

**Thematic Focus** In many cultures traditions are passed from generation to generation, especially when a young boy or girl passes into adulthood or when an elder senses that the end is near. Ask volunteers to describe significant traditions they know or have read about that are transferred.

**Alternative Assessment** To promote active reading, have your students create a reader's response journal as they read "The Medicine Bag." Ask them to focus their observations on the details that reveal Martin's changing attitude toward his Native American grandfather and on those that re-

veal the significance of the medicine bag and its transfer from the grandfather to Martin. Encourage them to respond personally to the characters and events in this story. Have them discuss what they learned about Native Americans from reading the story.

**Setting:** *This scene is easy to picture, especially "the yippy dogs . . . growling and nipping at the old man's baggy pant legs" and how "they put their tails between their legs and scattered."*

at the mailman from the safety of their own yards. Now it sounded as if a whole pack of mutts were barking together in one place.

I got up and walked to the curb to see what the commotion was. About a block away I saw a crowd of little kids yelling, with the dogs yipping and growling around someone who was walking down the middle of the street.

I watched the group as it slowly came closer and saw that in the center of the strange procession was a man wearing a tall black hat. He'd pause now and then to peer at something in his hand and then at the houses on either side of the street. I felt cold and hot at the same time as I recognized the man. "Oh, no!" I whispered. "It's Grandpa!"

I stood on the curb, unable to move even though I wanted to run and hide. Then I got mad when I saw how the yippy dogs were growling and nipping at the old man's baggy pant legs and how wearily he poked them away with his cane. "Stupid mutts," I said as I ran to rescue Grandpa.

When I kicked and hollered at the dogs to get away, they put their tails between their legs and scattered. The kids ran to the curb where they watched me and the old man.

"Grandpa," I said and felt pretty dumb when my voice cracked. I reached for his beat-up old tin suitcase, which was tied shut with a rope. But he set it down right in the street and shook my hand.

"*Hau, Takoza,* Grandchild," he greeted me formally in Sioux.

All I could do was stand there with the whole neighborhood watching and shake the hand of the leather-brown old man. I saw how his gray hair straggled from under his big black hat, which had a drooping feather in its crown. His rumpled black suit hung like a sack over his stooped frame. As he shook my hand, his coat fell open to expose a bright red satin shirt with a beaded bolo tie[5] under the collar. His get-up wasn't out of place on the reservation, but it sure was here, and I wanted to sink right through the pavement.

"Hi," I muttered with my head down. I tried to pull my hand away when I felt his bony hand trembling, and looked up to see fatigue in his face. I felt like crying. I couldn't think of

---

**5. bolo** (bō′ lō) **tie** *n.*: A man's string tie, held together with a decorated sliding device.

## Grammar in Action

Writers carefully select vivid, interesting **descriptive words** to enliven their writing and to create the desired image in the mind of the reader. They choose specific and precise words to communicate to the reader.

Carefully reread this description of Grandfather and notice the vividness of the picture you receive from the writer. Vivid words are italicized.

All I could do was stand there with the whole neighborhood watching and shake the hand of the *leather-brown* old man. I saw how his gray hair *straggled* from under his big black hat, which had a *drooping feather,* in its crown. His *rumpled* black suit hung *like a sack* over his *stooped* frame. As he shook my hand, his coat fell open to expose a bright *red satin* shirt with a *beaded* bolo tie under the collar. His get-up wasn't out of place on the reservation, but it sure was here, and I wanted to sink right through the pavement.

**Student Activity 1.** Find ten other vivid words in "The Medicine Bag." Discuss with your classmates your reasons for selecting each word.

anything to say so I picked up Grandpa's suitcase, took his arm, and guided him up the driveway to our house.

Mom was standing on the steps. I don't know how long she'd been watching, but her hand was over her mouth and she looked as if she couldn't believe what she saw. Then she ran to us.

"Grandpa," she gasped. "How in the world did you get here?"

She checked her move to embrace Grandpa and I remembered that such a display of affection is unseemly to the Sioux and would embarrass him.

"*Hau*, Marie," he said as he shook Mom's hand. She smiled and took his other arm.

As we supported him up the steps, the door banged open and Cheryl came bursting out of the house. She was all smiles and was so obviously glad to see Grandpa that I was ashamed of how I felt.

"Grandpa!" she yelled happily. "You came to see us!"

Grandpa smiled, and Mom and I let go of him as he stretched out his arms to my ten-year-old sister, who was still young enough to be hugged.

"*Wicincala*, little girl," he greeted her and then collapsed.

He had fainted. Mom and I carried him into her sewing room, where we had a spare bed.

After we had Grandpa on the bed, Mom stood there helplessly patting his shoulder.

"Shouldn't we call the doctor, Mom?" I suggested, since she didn't seem to know what to do.

"Yes," she agreed with a sigh. "You make Grandpa comfortable, Martin."

I reluctantly moved to the bed. I knew Grandpa wouldn't want to have Mom undress him, but I didn't want to, either. He was so skinny and frail that his coat slipped off easily. When I loosened his tie and opened his shirt collar, I felt a small leather pouch that hung from a thong[6] around his neck. I left it alone and moved to remove his boots. The scuffed old cowboy boots were tight, and he moaned as I put pressure on his legs to jerk them off.

I put the boots on the floor and saw why they fit so tight.

---

6. **thong** *n.*: A narrow strip of leather.

**Character:** *Cheryl's reaction to Grandpa is much warmer than the boy's. The boy is ashamed because he is not able to do what his younger sister can do: look past her grandfather's appearance and see what he is on the inside.*

**Plot:** *Grandpa seems to be ill. I think that this will affect the way Martin feels about him. Martin will probably realize that he took his grandfather for granted and that he owes his grandfather respect.*

**Enrichment** The Sioux Indians at one time lived throughout the northern plains of North America. Among the many divisions are the Santee Sioux, the Yankton Sioux, and the Teton Sioux.

Originally, the Sioux, as well as other Plains Indian groups, lived in villages along rivers and streams, where they farmed and hunted small game. However, the introduction of the horse by the Spanish in the 1600's changed their lives greatly. Daily life became centered on the great buffalo herds, and the tribes became mobile.

The Teton Sioux, the group that Grandpa is part of, agreed to settle on a reservation in 1868. They rebelled in 1876, and groups led by Crazy Horse and Sitting Bull were responsible for killing General Custer and all of his command at Little Big Horn in Montana. However, the superiority of the U.S. Army, in men and weapons, forced the Teton Sioux to eventually surrender in the autumn of 1876.

**Student Activity 2.** Write a description of someone who looks a little odd or out of place. Enhance it with vivid and precise words. Have a partner go over the first draft and circle words that could be improved.

**Electronic Handbook** You may want students to review adjectives and adverbs before completing the Grammar in Action activities. If students have access to the Language Master 6000, have them enter the access words *adjective* and *adverb* and press the GRAMMAR key to get information on selecting vivid descriptive words.

Each one was stuffed with money. I looked at the bills that lined the boots and started to ask about them, but Grandpa's eyes were closed again.

Mom came back with a basin of water. "The doctor thinks Grandpa is suffering from heat exhaustion," she explained as she bathed Grandpa's face. Mom gave a big sigh, *"Oh, hinh, Martin. How do you suppose he got here?"*

We found out after the doctor's visit. Grandpa was angrily sitting up in bed while Mom tried to feed him some soup.

"Tonight you let Marie feed you, Grandpa," spoke my dad, who had gotten home from work just as the doctor was leaving. "You're not really sick," he said as he gently pushed Grandpa back against the pillows. "The doctor said you just got too tired and hot after your long trip."

Grandpa relaxed, and between sips of soup, he told us of his journey. Soon after our visit to him, Grandpa decided that he would like to see where his only living descendants lived and what our home was like. Besides, he admitted sheepishly, he was lonesome after we left.

**Theme:** *Martin's family is removed from their Sioux heritage. Maybe Martin will be able to get back in touch with it.*

I knew that everybody felt as guilty as I did—especially Mom. Mom was all Grandpa had left. So even after she married my dad, who's a white man and teaches in the college in our city, and after Cheryl and I were born, Mom made sure that every summer we spent a week with Grandpa.

I never thought that Grandpa would be lonely after our visits, and none of us noticed how old and weak he had become. But Grandpa knew, and so he came to us. He had ridden on buses for two and a half days. When he arrived in the city, tired and stiff from sitting for so long, he set out, walking, to find us.

He had stopped to rest on the steps of some building downtown, and a policeman found him. The cop, according to Grandpa, was a good man who took him to the bus stop and waited until the bus came and told the driver to let Grandpa out at Bell View Drive. After Grandpa got off the bus, he started walking again. But he couldn't see the house numbers on the other side when he walked on the sidewalk, so he walked in the middle of the street. That's when all the little kids and dogs followed him.

**Character:** *Martin does not feel ashamed of his grandfather when he thinks about how courageous he was to travel so far alone.*

I knew everybody felt as bad as I did. Yet I was so proud of this eighty-six-year-old man, who had never been away from the reservation, having the courage to travel so far alone.

228    *Short Stories*

## Grammar in Action

**Transitions** are words or phrases used to link sentences and paragraphs to create coherence. Coherence involves ideas that follow each other logically and meaningfully. Transitions make connections between sentences and paragraphs read smoothly.

Transitions can show location (*beneath, over*) and time (*today, when*). They can be used to compare (*like, as*) or to contrast (*yet, but, however*). Transitions also serve to show emphasis (*again, indeed*), to conclude or summarize (*finally,*

*thus*), to add information (*also, in addition*), and to clarify (*that is, in other words*). Many transitions in "The Medicine Bag" serve to clarify or to show time. For example, the transition *finally* indicates an action that occurs last:

"Finally, one day after school, my friends came home with me because nothing I said stopped them."

It is usually a good idea to begin paragraphs with a transition the way the author does with the word *finally*.

Sometimes conjunctions serve as transitions: "But after they left," Mom said, "No more visitors for a while, Martin." Starting a sentence with a conjunction is a valid way to connect related sentences, but be careful not to rely too heavily on conjunctions

"You found the money in my boots?" he asked Mom.

"Martin did," she answered, and roused herself to scold. "Grandpa, you shouldn't have carried so much money. What if someone had stolen it from you?"

Grandpa laughed. "I would've known if anyone tried to take the boots off my feet. The money is what I've saved for a long time—a hundred dollars—for my funeral. But you take it now to buy groceries so that I won't be a burden to you while I am here."

"That won't be necessary, Grandpa," Dad said. "We are honored to have you with us, and you will never be a burden. I am only sorry that we never thought to bring you home with us this summer and spare you the discomfort of a long trip."

Grandpa was pleased. "Thank you," he answered. "But do not feel bad that you didn't bring me with you, for I would not have come then. It was not time." He said this in such a way that no one could argue with him. To Grandpa and the Sioux, he once told me, a thing would be done when it was the right time to do it, and that's the way it was.

"Also," Grandpa went on, looking at me, "I have come because it is soon time for Martin to have the medicine bag."

We all knew what that meant. Grandpa thought he was going to die, and he had to follow the tradition of his family to pass the medicine bag, along with its history, to the oldest male child.

**Theme:** *The last sentence in this paragraph seems important. I think it means that you should never rush things, that doing things at the right time gives you the best results.*

**Theme:** *For Martin the medicine bag will be a remembrance of Grandpa. In the end I think it will be as important to Martin as it is to Grandpa.*

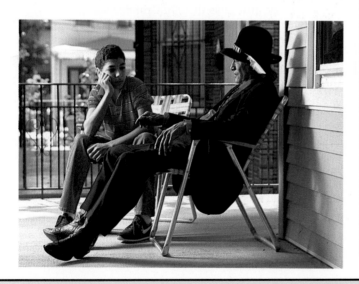

*The Medicine Bag* 229

as transitions. Overusing conjunctions as transitions weakens your writing.

**Student Activity 1.** Identify five more examples of transitions in "The Medicine Bag" and explain how each is used.

**Student Activity 2.** Write a brief review of one of your favorite stories in this unit. Strive for coherence by using transitions.

**Plot:** *Martin again feels a conflict regarding his grandfather. He will probably end up taking the medicine bag but will figure out a way not to have to wear it.*

"Even though the boy," he said still looking at me, "bears a white man's name, the medicine bag will be his."

I didn't know what to say. I had the same hot and cold feeling that I had when I first saw Grandpa in the street. The medicine bag was the dirty leather pouch I had found around his neck. "I could never wear such a thing," I almost said aloud. I thought of having my friends see it in gym class or at the swimming pool and could imagine the smart things they would say. But I just swallowed hard and took a step toward the bed. I knew I would have to take it.

But Grandpa was tired. "Not now, Martin," he said, waving his hand in dismissal. "It is not time. Now I will sleep."

So that's how Grandpa came to be with us for two months. My friends kept asking to come see the old man, but I put them off. I told myself that I didn't want them laughing at Grandpa. But even as I made excuses, I knew it wasn't Grandpa that I was afraid they'd laugh at.

Nothing bothered Cheryl about bringing her friends to see Grandpa. Every day after school started, there'd be a crew of giggling little girls or round-eyed little boys crowded around the old man on the patio, where he'd gotten in the habit of sitting every afternoon.

Grandpa would smile in his gentle way and patiently answer their questions, or he'd tell them stories of brave warriors, ghosts, animals; and the kids listened in awed silence. Those little guys thought Grandpa was great.

Finally, one day after school, my friends came home with me because nothing I said stopped them. "We're going to see the great Indian of Bell View Drive," said Hank, who was supposed to be my best friend. "My brother has seen him three times so he oughta be well enough to see us."

When we got to my house, Grandpa was sitting on the patio. He had on his red shirt, but today he also wore a fringed leather vest that was decorated with beads. Instead of his usual cowboy boots, he had solidly beaded moccasins on his feet that stuck out of his black trousers. Of course, he had his old black hat on—he was seldom without it. But it had been brushed, and the feather in the beaded headband was proudly erect, its tip a brighter white. His hair lay in silver strands over the red shirt collar.

I stared just as my friends did, and I heard one of them murmur, "Wow!"

Grandpa looked up, and, when his eyes met mine, they twinkled as if he were laughing inside. He nodded to me, and my face got all hot. I could tell that he had known all along I was afraid he'd embarrass me in front of my friends.

"*Hau, hoksilas,* boys," he greeted and held out his hand.

My buddies passed in a single file and shook his hand as I introduced them. They were so polite I almost laughed. "How, there, Grandpa," and even a "How-do-you-do, sir."

"You look fine, Grandpa," I said as the guys sat on the lawn chairs or on the patio floor.

"*Hanh,* yes," he agreed. "When I woke up this morning, it seemed the right time to dress in the good clothes. I knew that my grandson would be bringing his friends."

"You guys want some lemonade or something?" I offered. No one answered. They were listening to Grandpa as he started telling how he'd killed the deer from which his vest was made.

Grandpa did most of the talking while my friends were there. I was so proud of him and amazed at how respectfully quiet my buddies were. Mom had to chase them home at supper time. As they left, they shook Grandpa's hand again and said to me,

"Martin, he's really great!"

"Yeah, man! Don't blame you for keeping him to yourself."

"Can we come back?"

But after they left, Mom said, "No more visitors for a while, Martin. Grandpa won't admit it, but his strength hasn't returned. He likes having company, but it tires him."

That evening Grandpa called me to his room before he went to sleep. "Tomorrow," he said, "when you come home, it will be time to give you the medicine bag."

I felt a hard squeeze from where my heart is supposed to be and was scared, but I answered, "OK, Grandpa."

All night I had weird dreams about thunder and lightning on a high hill. From a distance I heard the slow beat of a drum. When I woke up in the morning, I felt as if I hadn't slept at all. At school it seemed as if the day would never end and, when it finally did, I ran home.

**Character:** *Martin learns in this scene that his grandfather loves and understands him and will go to trouble to save him embarrassment.*

**Plot:** *Martin's tension mounts before his confrontation with Grandpa.*

*The Medicine Bag* 231

**Cooperative Learning** Have students work in small groups to compile a collection of other significant Native American traditions. Encourage them to use various sources, including personal interviews, if appropriate. Allow the groups to share their findings with their classmates.

**Theme:** *Grandpa's story reveals how his Sioux father learned to live on the reservation, working with "the white man's iron." His vision quest showed him the way to live in harmony with white people.*

Grandpa was in his room, sitting on the bed. The shades were down, and the place was dim and cool. I sat on the floor in front of Grandpa, but he didn't even look at me. After what seemed a long time he spoke.

"I sent your mother and sister away. What you will hear today is only for a man's ears. What you will receive is only for a man's hands." He fell silent, and I felt shivers down my back.

"My father in his early manhood," Grandpa began, "made a vision quest[7] to find a spirit guide for his life. You cannot understand how it was in that time, when the great Teton Sioux were first made to stay on the reservation. There was a strong need for guidance from *Wakantanka,*[8] the Great Spirit. But too many of the young men were filled with despair and hatred. They thought it was hopeless to search for a vision when the glorious life was gone and only the hated confines of a reservation lay ahead. But my father held to the old ways.

"He carefully prepared for his quest with a purifying sweat bath, and then he went alone to a high butte top[9] to fast and pray. After three days he received his sacred dream—in which he found, after long searching, the white man's iron. He did not understand his vision of finding something belonging to the white people, for in that time they were the enemy. When he came down from the butte to cleanse himself at the stream below, he found the remains of a campfire and the broken shell of an iron kettle. This was a sign that reinforced his dream. He took a piece of the iron for his medicine bag, which he had made of elk skin years before, to prepare for his quest.

"He returned to his village, where he told his dream to the wise old men of the tribe. They gave him the name *Iron Shell,* but neither did they understand the meaning of the dream. The first Iron Shell kept the piece of iron with him at all times and believed it gave him protection from the evils of those unhappy days.

---

**7. vision quest:** A search for a revelation that would aid understanding.
**8. Wakantanka** (wä′ kən tank′ ə) *n.:* The Sioux religion's most important spirit—the creator of the world.
**9. butte** (byo͞ot) **top** *n.:* The top of a steep hill standing alone in a plain.

**Discussion** The author has also stated that she wished "to present an accurate portrayal of American Indian life as I have known it [and] to interpret Indian history from the viewpoint of the American Indian." What aspects of the story about the medicine bag are uniquely from an Indian perspective? How does learning about the Indians from this perspective change your ideas about them?

"Then a terrible thing happened to Iron Shell. He and several other young men were taken from their homes by the soldiers and sent far away to a white man's boarding school. He was angry and lonesome for his parents and the young girl he had wed before he was taken away. At first Iron Shell resisted the teacher's attempts to change him, and he did not try to learn. One day it was his turn to work in the school's blacksmith shop. As he walked into the place, he knew that his medicine had brought him there to learn and work with the white man's iron.

"Iron Shell became a blacksmith and worked at the trade when he returned to the reservation. All of his life he treasured the medicine bag. When he was old, and I was a man, he gave it to me, for no one made the vision quest any more."

Grandpa quit talking, and I stared in disbelief as he covered his face with his hands. His shoulders were shaking with quiet sobs, and I looked away until he began to speak again.

"I kept the bag until my son, your mother's father, was a man and had to leave us to fight in the war across the ocean. I gave him the bag, for I believed it would protect him in battle, but he did not take it with him. He was afraid that he would lose it. He died in a faraway place."

Again Grandpa was still, and I felt his grief around me.

"My son," he went on after clearing his throat, "had only a daughter, and it is not proper for her to know of these things."

*The Medicine Bag*   233

He unbuttoned his shirt, pulled out the leather pouch, and lifted it over his head. He held it in his hand, turning it over and over as if memorizing how it looked.

"In the bag," he said as he opened it and removed two objects, "is the broken shell of the iron kettle, a pebble from the butte, and a piece of the sacred sage."[10] He held the pouch upside down and dust drifted down.

"After the bag is yours you must put a piece of prairie sage within and never open it again until you pass it on to your son." He replaced the pebble and the piece of iron, and tied the bag.

I stood up, somehow knowing I should. Grandpa slowly rose from the bed and stood upright in front of me holding the bag before my face. I closed my eyes and waited for him to slip it over my head. But he spoke.

"No, you need not wear it." He placed the soft leather bag in my right hand and closed my other hand over it. "It would not be right to wear it in this time and place where no one will understand. Put it safely away until you are again on the reservation. Wear it then, when you replace the sacred sage."

Grandpa turned and sat again on the bed. Wearily he leaned his head against the pillow. "Go," he said. "I will sleep now."

"Thank you, Grandpa," I said softly and left with the bag in my hands.

That night Mom and Dad took Grandpa to the hospital. Two weeks later I stood alone on the lonely prairie of the reservation and put the sacred sage in my medicine bag.

_____

**10. sage** (sāj) *n.:* Plant belonging to the mint family.

**Virginia Driving Hawk Sneve** (1933–     ) grew up on the Sioux Reservation in South Dakota. This writer and teacher has won many awards for her fiction, including the Council on Interracial Books Award and the Western Writers of America award. In books such as *Jimmy Yellow Hawk, High Elk's Treasure,* and *When the Thunder Spoke,* she draws on her intimate knowledge of Sioux life. Her Sioux heritage also plays an important role in "The Medicine Bag."

*234    Short Stories*

## RESPONDING TO THE SELECTION

### Your Response

1. Do you think that you would have felt as Martin did when he kept his friends away from his grandfather? Why or why not?
2. What do you think Martin was feeling when he put the sacred sage in the medicine bag at the end of the story?

### Recalling

3. Why is Martin embarrassed when Grandpa comes to visit? How is Cheryl's reaction to Grandpa's visit different from Martin's?
4. What three reasons does Grandpa give for his visit?
5. What is the purpose of a vision quest? How did Grandpa's father receive the name Iron Shell?
6. What does Martin do at the end of the story?

### Interpreting

7. Compare the real Grandpa with the Grandpa Martin at first brags to his friends about.
8. How is the Sioux heritage Martin at first brags about different from the Sioux heritage he learns about from Grandpa?
9. What happens to Grandpa at the story's end?
10. Explain how Martin comes to stand alone on the lonely prairie.

### Applying

11. Why is it important for people to maintain their cultural heritage?

## ANALYZING LITERATURE

### Reviewing the Short Story

The elements of plot, character, setting, and theme all work together to create a total effect. Think of all of these elements and apply them to "The Medicine Bag."

1. Give a brief summary of the story, focusing on the conflict and the resolution.

2. Compare Martin and his grandfather.
3. How is setting important in this story?
4. How would you express the theme?

## CRITICAL THINKING AND READING

### Evaluating a Story

To evaluate a story means to judge how successfully it works. Using your knowledge of literary elements and how they work in short stories, comment on what you think works best in any story. Then prepare an answer to one of the following questions. Present your answer in a brief oral report to your classmates.

1. Do you think the characters in "The Medicine Bag" were well drawn?
2. Do you think the conflict was presented successfully?
3. What does the story say about the importance of a cultural heritage?

## THINKING AND WRITING

### Continuing a Story

Imagine you are Martin thirty years in the future. You now have a son of your own and want to pass on the medicine bag. Write a continuation of this story telling what you would say to your son. Revise your story, making sure you have clearly expressed the importance of the medicine bag to you.

## LEARNING OPTION

**Writing.** Grandpa gives Martin the medicine bag that his own father had passed down to him. In it are items that were meaningful to Grandpa's father (a scrap of iron and a pebble from the butte) and something that is sacred to the Sioux people (a piece of sage). Suppose that a relative of yours were to give you a group of important items. Write a brief description of these items and explain the meaning of each.

*The Medicine Bag*   235

---

---

## Preparation

**Motivation/Prior Knowledge**
Have student volunteers find and read aloud passages from stories in this unit that relate a humorous series of events. What makes these passages funny? Ask the students to identify the techniques each author uses to make us laugh. Does the author use irony, hyperbole, understatement, or some other technique?

**Focus** Emphasize the importance of style and tone in this assignment. Point out how the same events can be humorous or not, depending on how they are related.

## Presentation

**Prewriting** After students have completed their timelines, they can experiment with different techniques for telling the events in a humorous fashion. Have them try exaggerating the situation and the reactions of the people involved. Can they relate the events so that the result is different from what the reader expects? How do these techniques affect the humor of their story? You may wish to allow students to work in discussion groups for this portion of the prewriting exercise.

**Drafting** As students recount the events, they can include personal observations and comments. Suggest that students use colloquialisms and contractions to achieve an informal tone. Another effective technique is to use sentence fragments that allow the reader to imagine the completion of a thought or an action.

Instruct students to draft in chronological order, to ensure clarity and to help build suspense.

**Writing Transparency** You can use the paragraph exercise *Chronological Order* in **Transparencies for Writing** to model the organization of events for your students.

236

# YOUR WRITING PROCESS

*"As for style of writing, if one has anything to say, it drops from him simply and directly, as a stone falls to the ground."*
**Henry David Thoreau**

## WRITING A HUMOROUS ANECDOTE

Were you ever on the telephone with a friend and had the feeling that your mom or younger brother or sister might be listening in? Personal letters allow you the privacy and time to express ideas and feelings that you might feel uncomfortable discussing over the telephone. Imagine that your best friend has just moved to another city and is feeling lonely and homesick. What better way to cheer up your friend than by writing him or her a humorous letter? In your letter, bring a funny experience to life, just as some of the writers in this unit captured the humorous escapades of their characters.

---
**Focus**

**Assignment:** Write a humorous anecdote.
**Purpose:** To entertain.
**Audience:** A friend in another city.
---

### Prewriting

**1. Which events are really funny?** Look back at the stories in this unit and consider one that contained a series of humorous events. For example, you might select "The Day I Got Lost" by Isaac Bashevis Singer. How did the author present the events? Why were they funny?

**2. Sketch out the situation.** Remember that your friend won't be able to rely on you to answer questions he or she may have about the way things happened. Rather, your friend will expect you to convey the situation simply and in chronological order. Create a timeline, tracing the order in which the events occurred.

---
**Student Model**

| Mom serves meatloaf for dinner | I pick at it with my fork | Mom leaves the table to answer phone | I shove the meatloaf in my sock | Mom finds the sock in my drawer 2 weeks later |
---

*236   Short Stories*

**Revising and Editing** As an alternative to peer editing, you may wish to allow students to take their anecdotes home and solicit comments from family members. Provide an "editor's checklist" to guide their families in focusing on the concepts you have taught in class. Family members may also identify portions of the anecdote that they found to be most humorous. Students may then incorporate the successful techniques into other parts of the anecdote.

**Writer's Hint** Encourage students to use a thesaurus to assist them in replacing ineffective adjectives and verbs.

**Software** If students have access to computers, have them complete their revisions on the **Bank Street Writer**. They can use the program's on-line thesaurus to explore alternatives to vague adjectives and passive verbs.

## Drafting

**1. Start with a bang.** A good way to get your friend's attention is to begin with a funny or thought-provoking statement or question.

> ### Student Model
>
> What's the best way to get rid of food you don't want to eat when you don't have a dog? Well, let me tell you about a foolproof solution . . . or at least I thought it was!

**2. Fill in the holes.** Include humorous dialogue, colorful descriptions, and imaginative language in the body of your letter. As details come to mind, think about how you can best describe them. Don't spend too much time on a specific word or sentence. Just let the ideas flow naturally. Remember that this is an informal anecdote, not a formal report.

**3. Build suspense.** An important part of relating a humorous story is the element of surprise. Since the purpose of your letter is to entertain your friend, you wouldn't want to spoil the ending or punchline by stating it in the beginning. Instead, lead up to the climactic moment and leave your friend suspended, waiting to hear more.

**4. Close the letter.** After you have presented the events in your story, ask your friend some questions. What did he or she think of it? What would he or she have done in a similar situation? By asking questions, you show an interest in your friend's opinions and reactions and a desire to keep the correspondence going.

## Revising and Editing

**1. Read your anecdote to yourself.** Don't read it right away, however. Instead, put the anecdote aside for a day or two. Then imagine that you have just received it in the mail. Do the opening sentences grab your attention? Are the events presented in a logical order? Do you find the details interesting and humorous?

**2. Proofread for clarity.** Unlike a formal essay, personal letters can include sentence fragments, contractions, and unconventional punctuation. However, spelling and grammatical errors can confuse your reader and detract from the story. Check to see that your letter contains no mistakes that would make its meaning unclear.

### Writer's Hint

Whenever possible, use vivid adjectives and active verbs to paint a clear picture of the experiences for your audience. For example, "I *shove* the meatloaf in my sock" is much funnier than "I *put* the meatloaf in my sock."

### Options for Publishing

- If you have a friend who lives in another city, send him or her the anecdote.
- Read the anecdote aloud to your classmates and ask for comments. How would they respond if they received it?

### Reviewing Your Writing Process

1. Did you find the timeline helpful? Why or why not?
2. How did you build suspense in your anecdote?
3. What was the most challenging part of this assignment? Explain.

## Closure and Extension

### Guidelines for Evaluation

The following questions may assist you in evaluating each student's humorous anecdote:

1. Does the writer make effective use of exaggeration, understatement, or surprise to give a humorous account of the events?
2. Does the anecdote begin with an attention-getting image or thought?
3. Are the events related in chronological order?
4. Are details provided to enhance the humor of the situation?
5. Does the writer use vivid adjectives and active verbs?
6. Is the anecdote free of errors in spelling and usage?

**Publishing** Students can use an audio recorder to create a tape of humorous anecdotes to be shared with another class.

**Student Portfolios** You may wish to have students include their anecdotes in their writing portfolios.

**Enrichment** Many stand-up comedians use anecdotal material in their monologues. Share with your students the work of a comedian that draws inspiration from the events in his or her life. Bill Cosby's recording "Why Is There Air?" provides good examples of humorous anecdotes that relate to the experiences of youth.

## Preparation

### Motivation/Prior Knowledge

Role-play a counseling situation. Take the role of a guidance counselor and invite a volunteer to play a student seeking advice. Have the student imagine that he or she wants to go to Hollywood to become an actor after high school, but an older relative wants him or her to go to college. Ask the student to describe this dilemma, before asking you for advice. Emphasize that the more clear the student makes the problem, the better you will be able to help. Work out the problem with the student by giving advice on how to talk to the relative, and how to negotiate a compromise (such as trying a year of college before making a final decision). Ask the class for feedback about how the problem was expressed and solved.

**Focus** Before students begin writing, emphasize that they will work cooperatively with a partner to write two letters: one to an advice columnist, and a second letter in which the columnist responds. Point out also that the first audience is the receiver of the letter—before the letter is published in the paper.

## Presentation

**Prewriting** Students do not have to stick to the actual problem of a particular story character; they can make up a problem that a character might face. Encourage students to let their imaginations loose when they are writing down problems in their chart or role-playing with their partners.

**Drafting** While one partner is at work drafting his or her letter, the other partner might want to get into a "problem-solving frame of mind" by adding more problems and solutions to the chart or starting a new list of interesting problems and solutions. Remind both partners that as they draft they should write freely and get their ideas down in rough form.

# YOUR WRITING PROCESS

## WRITING AN ADVICE COLUMN

Characters in short stories are often people with problems. If they could only get help, their stories might turn out differently. Imagine the kinds of letters that fictional characters might write to an advice columnist like Abby (Abigail Van Buren). Then imagine how she might respond.

---

### Focus

**Assignment:** Working with a partner, write a letter to an advice columnist and write the columnist's letter in response.
**Purpose:** To express a problem and offer a solution to it.
**Audience:** Readers of the column.

---

### Prewriting

**1. Study examples.** With your partner, read and discuss examples of advice columns in newspapers and magazines. What do the letters directed to these columnists have in common? What do the responses have in common?

**2. Explore the possibilities.** Consider several of the characters from stories in this unit as potential letter writers. Who would write the most dramatic letters? To whom could you give the best, or most humorous, advice? You and your partner might want to use a chart to organize your thoughts.

---

**Student Model**

| STORY/CHARACTER | PROBLEM | TONE | SOLUTION |
|---|---|---|---|
| "The Tell-Tale Heart" Narrator | wants to kill the old man | Nervous crazy | move away; seek help; find ways to relax |

---

**3. Role-play to try out the voices.** After you have chosen the character you will use, discuss the character's problem with your partner. One of you can pretend to be the character, while the other pretends to be the columnist. Jot down any ideas or phrases that could be used in the letters.

**4. Have fun inventing names.** When people write letters to advice columnists, they keep their identities secret by using a made-up name. This name usually sums up their dilemma in a catchy phrase, such as Dismayed in Detroit. Work with your partner to come up with a pseudonym that will express your character's dilemma. Then invent a good name for the advice columnist.

## Drafting

**1. Divide the work.** Decide which of you will write as the character and which as the columnist. Of course, the one who is writing the columnist's response cannot begin drafting a reply until the letter asking for advice is ready.

**2. Keep to the point.** Whether you write as the character or as the columnist, make sure that all your thoughts relate to your main purpose. If you are the character, begin by explaining your problem clearly. Then use specific details from the story to make your explanation more vivid. If you are the columnist, present your solution and demonstrate how it will relieve the problem.

---

**Student Model**

Dear Abby,
Call me crazy, but I'm haunted by one idea: an old man's eye. It is a horrible thing to behold, and I am unable to think of anything else. Every night I go to kill him, but his eye is closed, so I just retire to my bed. I'm afraid that it is just a matter of time before the dread deed is done. I love the old man, but I still want to murder him. Does that make any sense?

Nervous, Dreadfully Nervous

---

## Revising and Editing

**1. Get the character's voice right.** Work together with your partner to revise both letters. First, scan the story and look for details of style that can make the character's letter more vivid. For example, if it is written in the voice of Poe's narrator, you may want to include some of the dashes, exclamations, and repetitions that Poe uses to bring his character to life.

**2. Is the columnist's tone consistent?** The solution to the character's problem can be humorous or serious. However, make sure that the letter maintains the same tone.

**3. Use a variety of sentences.** If all your sentences are the same type and length, readers will become bored. Give them variety to keep their attention.

**4. Go for zero errors.** Proofread your letters carefully for errors in spelling, mechanics, and punctuation.

---

**Options for Publishing**
● Create a newspaper column with a title and the letters you have written with your partner. Display your column on the class bulletin board.
● Together with your partner, read your letters aloud to the class. Then have them imagine how the story might have turned out differently if the character had followed the columnist's advice.

**Reviewing Your Writing Process**
1. Were you able to capture the character's voice by including stylistic devices from the story? Explain.
2. What were the benefits and disadvantages of working with a partner?

**Enrichment** Students might wish to write another letter to an advice columnist. Have them scan newspapers and magazines to find a columnist whose advice they respect. Suggest they write a brief letter to the columnist that focuses on one problem, perhaps related to school, for which they would like to find a solution. Students may or may not choose to share their letter and the response with the class.

---

**Revising** As they edit their work, have students check that they have used the correct letter form.

Peer editors might use these questions as guidelines for evaluation:

Does the letter seeking advice bring the character and his or her problem to life by using vivid details?

Do both letters use a consistent, believable tone so that the character and the columnist always sound like themselves?

Is the problem clearly explained? Does the solution seem logical?

◆ **Software** If your students are working on computers, have them use the **Writer's Helper** activity *Peer Review,* which also poses questions that will help students evaluate classmates' work.

## Closure and Extension

**Guidelines for Evaluation** You might use the following criteria in evaluating pairs of student letters:
1. Do the letters make the role of each writer (character and columnist) clear?
2. Does the letter expressing a problem keep to its main point, express the problem clearly, and use specific details from the story or realistic imaginary details?
3. Does the letter from the columnist present a solution and demonstrate how it will relieve the problem?
4. Are the letters free of grammar, usage, and mechanics errors?

**FIRST ROW ORCHESTRA, 1951**
*Edward Hopper*
Hirshhorn Museum and Sculpture Garden, Smithsonian Institution

# DRAMA

What do you think of when you hear the word *drama*? Do you think of the theater with actors, a stage, costumes, sets, and a live audience? Do you think of the movies with action presented on a large screen? Do you think of the pleasure of sitting home and watching a drama unfold on television? Or do you think of hearing a play over the radio? The live theater, the movies, television, and radio—all are means by which drama comes to us.

A play is written to be performed. Therefore, when you read a play, you must visualize how it would appear and sound to an audience. By using your imagination, you can build a theater in your mind. Because a play is written to be performed, it uses certain conventions you do not encounter in short stories. It contains stage directions that tell the actors how to speak and how to move upon the stage. A screenplay for a movie also contains camera directions that tell the camera operator what to shoot and how to shoot it. Most of the story is presented through dialogue, the words the characters speak. In addition a typical play is divided into short units of action called "scenes" and larger ones called "acts."

In this unit you will encounter a film screenplay based on a novel and a stage play based on the diary of a young girl.

## Humanities Note

Fine art, *First Row Orchestra*, 1951, by Edward Hopper. Edward Hopper (1882–1967) was an American painter of sunlight on houses, lonely streets, and scenes that most Americans take for granted. His education in art consisted of a painting class in New York City and a trip to Paris to learn and paint. He was an introspective and dedicated artist who pursued his own realistic style. His paintings transform the ordinary into something unforgettable.

*First Row Orchestra*, a look at the front row of a theater before the curtain goes up, is typical of Hopper's detached way of observing people. He politely records their preshow anticipation without attempting to interpret their personalities. The architectural features of the theater are painted with a minimum of detail; anything that cannot be seen in a quick glance has been eliminated. It is a pure uncomplicated depiction, from an interesting point of view, of an audience preparing to experience drama on stage.

**Reading Actively** There are two plays presented in this unit. One is a screenplay and the other is a stage play. Both plays will give students a sense of how actors would move and speak in performing the play—either before a camera or on a stage. You might point out that some critics believe that a written script is not considered a play until it has been performed before an audience. Drama is, therefore, the most dynamic literary form.

## Drama

The word *drama* brings to mind the world of the theater. It is an exciting world—a curtain rising on a stage with sets, lights, and actors in costume. But drama includes more than the theater. Because drama is a story told in dialogue by performers before an audience, the definition includes television plays, radio plays, and even movies. In all these kinds of drama, actors make a world come alive before an audience.

Plays are meant to be performed, but it is possible just to read a play. When you read a play, you can make it come alive by staging it in your imagination. Tha play that you are reading is a script. It contains not only the words that the actors speak but also the stage directions the playwright provides to indicate how to put on the play. Stage directions tell what the stage should look like, what the characters wear, how they speak their lines, and where they move.

Stage directions use a particular vocabulary. *Right, left, up, down,* and *center* refer to areas of the stage as the actors see it. To help you visualize what is meant when a stage direction tells an actor to move down left, for example, picture the stage like this:

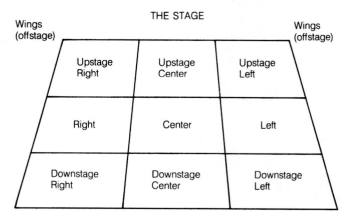

Unlike a play, a film screenplay contains camera directions that tell the camera operator how the movie is to be filmed. It is important to pay attention to the camera directions as you read so that you can visualize what each shot includes, how the camera is positioned, and so on.

Becoming an active reader of drama will increase your understanding and enjoyment of plays and screenplays. Reading actively includes seeing the play or movie in your mind while you continually question the meaning of what the characters are saying and doing.

Use the following strategies to help you read drama actively. These strategies will help you to enjoy and appreciate the selections in this unit.

VISUALIZE Use the directions and information supplied by the playwright or screenwriter to picture the story and the characters in action. Create the scene in your mind. Hear the characters' voices. See their gestures. Doing so will give meaning to their words.

QUESTION Question the meaning of each character's words and actions. What motives and traits do the words and actions reveal? What situation does each character face?

PREDICT Once you recognize the conflict and understand the characters' motives, predict what you think will happen. How will the conflict be resolved? What will become of each character?

CLARIFY If a character's words or actions are not clear to you, stop and try to make sense of them. You may need to look for clues in earlier words or actions. As you read, look also for answers to your questions, and check your predictions.

CONNECT Occasionally pause to review what has happened. What is the conflict? What is happening toward its resolution? Try to summarize how the characters' actions and words fit together. Use your own knowledge and experience to make connections between the drama and real life.

RESPOND Think about all the elements of the play or film. What does it mean? What does it say to you about life?

*Reading Actively 243*

**Reading Strategies** A feature that makes plays different from other forms of literature is the stage or screen directions. If students are unfamiliar with reading drama, they may initially find these insertions intrusive. On the contrary, these directions are integral to a successful rendition of the play. Be sure students understand what the directions mean and their purpose. To read the play actively, students must not overlook the stage directions, which will help them to visualize the action and characters.

Visualization is a particularly important strategy in reading drama. Encourage students to create each scene in their minds, using the stage or screen directions to help them see the characters, hear their voices, and understand their gestures. Doing this will make the plays come alive for students.

# Preparation

**More About the Author** Although most of Virginia Hamilton's work has been fiction for young adults, she has written nonfiction as well. In her words, "The nonfiction not only provides a rest from novels and stories, but satisfies a need to do ongoing research and to tell the factual, historical stories of our people." How is Hamilton's interest in researching and retelling history apparent in *The House of Dies Drear?*

**More About the Author** Richard Wesley's screenplay for *The House of Dies Drear* won the CEBA "TV Movie of the Year" award in 1984. In addition to his work for television, Wesley has written a number of screenplays for feature films, including *Native Son,* based on the novel by Richard Wright, and *Not Without Laughter,* based on the book by Langston Hughes.

**Literary Focus** Discuss with students the ways in which a screenplay differs from narrative fiction. Lead them to see that a screenplay is visually oriented. Instead of a narrator, a screenplay uses camera directions, dialogue, and a minimal amount of description to tell the story. In order to follow the story action, students must visualize what the camera is shooting and must read between the lines of dialogue.

**Prereading Focus** If possible, show several scenes from a movie and ask students to observe how the scenes were filmed. Have them watch what the camera does from scene to scene, pointing out noteworthy shots or effects as they do so. Ask students to consider why the director chose to film these shots in the manner he or she did. You may wish to have students who have access to a television try this exercise as a homework assignment.

**Virginia Hamilton**

(1936–    ) grew up in Ohio, where her grandfather settled after escaping from slavery. Hamilton's childhood wonder at the courage and cleverness of those who fled to freedom inspired her to write *The House of Dies Drear:* "Perhaps with this book I have at last touched them the way they first touched me so long ago."

**Richard Wesley**

(1945–    ) graduated from Howard University and the Black Theater Workshop. As a playwright and screenwriter, he deals with the lives of African Americans.

# GUIDE FOR READING

## The House of Dies Drear, Acts I and II

### Screenplay

A **screenplay** is the script from which a film is produced. Like a script for a stage play, a screenplay is divided into acts and includes dialogue, or lines that the characters speak, and stage directions that tell the characters how to speak and move. Unlike a play, however, a screenplay includes directions for the person working the camera. Camera directions establish the positions from which you will view the action. As you read *The House of Dies* (pronounced dīz) *Drear,* try to be aware of how these camera directions shape your experience of the story and influence your responses to it.

### Focus

From your film-going experience, you are probably already familiar with several camera directions, such as a *close-up* shot or a *blackout* at the end of a scene. With your classmates, brainstorm to list camera directions you have observed in movies. Don't worry about using the correct technical terms; just describe whatever you noticed. Then compare your list with the list of technical terms on page 245.

### Vocabulary

Knowing the following words will help you as you read Acts I and II of *The House of Dies Drear.*

**calamity** (kə lam' i tē) *n.:* A great misfortune or disaster (p. 246)

**ominous** (äm' ə nəs) *adj.:* Threatening; acting as an evil omen (p. 250)

**buffets** (buf' its) *v.:* Strikes against forcefully; batters (p. 250)

**apprehension** (ap' rē hen' shən) *n.:* Anxiety about the future (p. 252)

**emanate** (em' ə nāt') *v.:* To come forth; issue (p. 253)

**veranda** (və ran' də) *n.:* A porch or balcony, usually roofed, that extends along the outside of a building (p. 253)

**evasive** (ē vā' siv) *adj.:* Seeking to avoid answering directly (p. 257)

**incredulously** (in krej' oo ləs lē) *adv.:* In a way that shows doubt or disbelief (p. 259)

## Objectives

1  To understand the screenplay as a literary genre
2  To appreciate the importance of visualizing a screenplay
3  To write from a character's point of view
4  To express individual interests and abilities through an optional activity

## Support Material

**Teaching Portfolio**
Teacher Backup, p. 347
Grammar in Action Worksheet, *Using Informal Language in Dialogue,* p. 350
Usage and Mechanics Worksheet, p. 352
Vocabulary Check, p. 353
Analyzing Literature Worksheet, *Understanding a Screenplay,* p. 354

Critical Thinking and Reading Worksheet, *Visualizing a Screenplay,* p. 355
Selection Test, p. 356

**Prentice Hall Literature Writing Studio**

# The House of Dies Drear
## based on the novel by Virginia Hamilton
### Richard Wesley

## CHARACTERS

**Thomas Small,** a thirteen-year-old boy

**Walter Small,** Thomas's father

**Sheila Small,** Thomas's mother

**Kenneth Small,** Thomas's brother

**Great-grandmother Jeffers,** Walter's grandmother

**Pluto Skinner,** caretaker of the house of Dies Drear

**Mayhew Skinner,** Pluto's son

**River Lewis Darrow,** head of the Darrow family

**Pesty,** a twelve-year-old girl

**Mac Darrow,** the youngest Darrow boy

**Wilbur Darrow,** thirty-eight

**River Ross Darrow,** thirty-seven

**Russell Darrow,** late twenties

**Edgar Carr,** handyman

**Pastor, Two Young Pastors, Choir**

## TECHNICAL TERMS

**BLACKOUT:** End a scene by cutting and leaving the screen black.

**CLOSE-UP:** Move the camera in close to focus on a detail.

**CUT TO:** Change directly from one scene to the next.

**DISSOLVE** (also called "lap dissolve"): Change scenes by fading in a new image while the existing one fades out.

**DOLLY:** Move the camera on a wheeled platform (a "dolly") to change the view.

**EXT:** Exterior shot.

**FADE-IN:** Begin a scene by bringing it into focus gradually.

**FADE-OUT:** End a scene by darkening the image until it disappears.

**FREEZE FRAME:** Repeat a single frame of film many times so as to create the effect of a still photograph.

**INT:** Interior shot.

**MONTAGE** (män tazh′): Create a sequence of alternating scenes or images.

**OC:** Off camera.

**OS:** Off screen.

**POV:** A character's point of view.

**TWO-SHOT:** A medium-range camera shot of two persons.

**VO** (voice-over): Have a voice speaking or narrating off camera.

*The House of Dies Drear*   245

**Motivation/Prior Knowledge** To help prepare students for the screenplay, give them background information on the Underground Railroad. Explain that the Underground Railroad was a system by which slaves escaped to the North in the days before the Civil War. The story centers on an old house that once served as an Underground Railroad "station," where fugitives were provided with food, shelter, instructions, and a place to hide. In order to hide people effectively, "stations" were equipped with secret passageways and underground tunnels. How would students feel if their family were to move into such a house?

**Purpose-Setting Question** In what way does the atmosphere influence the behavior and reactions of the characters?

**Making Connections** Escaping slavery by way of the Underground Railroad is also the subject of Ann Petry's essay "Harriet Tubman: Guide to Freedom," on page 383, and Robert Hayden's poem "Runagate Runagate," on page 516. You may wish to present these selections as a group.

**Thematic Focus** The former home of the abolitionist Dies Drear is a huge, dark Victorian house, unnatural in appearance, bristling with secrets and mystery. In what ways does the house provide a perfect opportunity for an imaginative boy to explore the unknown?

**ESL Teaching Strategy** Students may not be aware that much of the dialogue in the screenplay is in colloquial English. Point this out, emphasizing that the screenwriter is using the true speech patterns of the characters in order to make them realistic. With students, analyze the nonstandard elements in the characters' speech.

**Alternative Assessment** To promote active reading, have your students create a reader's response journal as they read *The House of Dies Drear*. Ask them to focus their observations of what Thomas learns about Dies Drear and the Underground Railroad. Encourage them to respond personally to the bits of information they learn, speculating as to their significance to the story. You may use your students' response journals to assess their understanding of the concepts and issues in the screenplay.

1 **Critical Thinking and Reading**
What atmosphere is created in this scene?

2 **Enrichment** Tell students that chicory is a plant whose leaves are used for salads and whose roots are dried, ground, and roasted for use as a coffee substitute. Have students discuss Great-grandmother Jeffers's use of the plant. How does her roasting of the chicory help to create suspense in the story?

3 **Literary Focus: Screenplay**
What information do you get from this single camera shot?

## Act I

FADE IN TO INT: GREAT-GRANDMOTHER JEFFERS' KITCHEN—DAY

1 *Tight close-up of an old woman's strong, wrinkled hands carefully putting pieces of chicory in a smoking pan; the pan is on an ancient, wood-burning cast-iron stove. We can hear the woman humming a tune and muttering as she goes about her task. Her hands, the pan, and the stove are lit by the flames from the fire; the smoke and surrounding darkness give the scene an eerie atmosphere.*

**THOMAS.** (VO) Great-grandmother?

CUT TO INT: KITCHEN—ANOTHER ANGLE—DAY

*THOMAS SMALL, thirteen years old, stands by the door in the flickering light from the stove. He moves closer to his ninety-one-year-old great-grandmother, fascinated by her actions.*

**THOMAS.** What're you doin'?

2 **GREAT-GRANDMOTHER.** Fixin' to roast some chicory. 'Spect I'll roast it all night and all day tomorrow.

**THOMAS.** But why're you gonna do that, Great-grandmother?

**GREAT-GRANDMOTHER.** Because, boy . . . because!

**THOMAS.** Because what, Great-grandmother?

**GREAT-GRANDMOTHER.** Because no tellin' what fool thought took hold of your Daddy to leave these hills an' go live in some craven house. Roastin' chicory's the best way to ward off calamity.

**THOMAS.** Calamity?

*We hear the sound of a car horn.*

**GREAT-GRANDMOTHER.** C'mon, boy, best we go on outside. Your folks is waitin'.

*They start to move out of the kitchen.*

CUT TO EXT: FARMHOUSE—DAY

3 *The front gate of the home of GREAT-GRAND-MOTHER JEFFERS, in North Carolina. The small house is fronted by a yard filled with freshly grown vegetables. The picket fence has a broken gate. A dog sleeps lazily on the front porch. We see a car, laden with suitcases and packages stuffed in its trunk and tied to its roof, parked in front of the house. WALTER SMALL, thirty-eight, his wife SHEILA, thirty-seven, and KENNETH, five, are waiting by the car. GREAT-GRANDMOTHER and THOMAS emerge from the house. As they walk through the gate, THOMAS stops.*

**THOMAS.** Great-grandma, I was s'posed to fix your gate—and who gon' paint it each spring?

**GREAT-GRANDMOTHER.** You think you the only boy who can paint my gate?

**THOMAS.** I'm the only one who ever has.

**GREAT-GRANDMOTHER.** That's the truth for sure, right there.

**WALTER.** Grandma, I'll send him back in the spring during the Easter break. He can paint it then.

**GREAT-GRANDMOTHER.** [*quietly, somewhat sadly*] Spring. Hm. That's a long row to hoe, son. Don't see why you gotta go all the way to Ohio no way. Plenty-a colleges 'round here.

**WALTER.** Because they need a good history professor, Grandmother, an' they happen to think I fit the bill.

**GREAT-GRANDMOTHER.** Hear tell you bought yourself quite a house out there.

**WALTER.** I didn't buy it, Grandmother. I'm just renting it. Besides, the place is very historic.

**SHEILA.** Meanin' it's as old as the hills.

WALTER *looks at* SHEILA, *who stares right back at him.*

**GREAT-GRANDMOTHER.** Seems to me if you wanted an old house with some history you coulda found plenty of them 'round here. Ain't right y'all takin' these two fine little boys so far from they Great-grandmother now that she gettin' on in age. Come here, chirrun.[1]

THOMAS *and* KENNETH *move close to her.*

**THOMAS.** Will you sing me that ol' song you always sang when I was sad?

**GREAT-GRANDMOTHER.** You wanna hear that ol' thing?

**KENNETH.** Me, too.

_____

1. **chirrun** (chi' rən): Dialect term for "children."

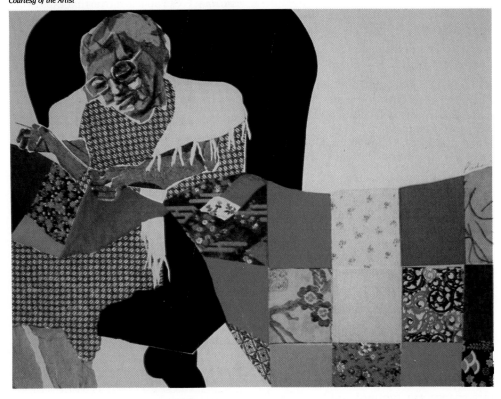

**HIS GRANDMOTHER'S QUILT, 1988**
*Phoebe Beasley*
*Courtesy of the Artist*

*The House of Dies Drear* 247

## Humanities Note

Fine art, *His Grandmother's Quilt,* 1988, by Phoebe Beasley. An African American artist born in Ohio, Beasley works often in the medium of collage. This collage, composed of oil paint, tissue paper, found objects, and Japanese block-print paper, depicts a woman sewing together the pieces of a patchwork quilt. The woman is typical of Beasley's subjects in that she is based on a real person who is frail and old and has stories to tell. This grandmother tells her stories through the quilt, which contains bits and pieces of her family's history. Traditionally, quilts were handed down from generation to generation, in a sense preserving the family's history.

You might use the following questions for discussion:
1. What parallels do you see between Great-grandmother Jeffers and the woman shown in the collage? Explain.
2. In what ways do both women preserve history? Compare their methods of preserving history with those of Walter Small.

4

**4 Reading Strategy** In what ways does Great-grandmother Jeffers's ragman song help to reinforce the importance of history and cultural background in the story?

**5 Literary Focus: Screenplay** What function does the montage, or the series of cuts, serve in this scene?

4

**GREAT-GRANDMOTHER.** [*She looks at both boys.*] Somethin' to remember me by, huh? Okay . . . [*sings*]
Any rags, any bones, any bottles today?
The big, black ragman's comin' your way.
Any rags, any rags,
Oh, any rags.
[*She repeats.*]

**THOMAS.** [*softly*] Great-grandmother, I'll write once we get settled in good.

**GREAT-GRANDMOTHER.** An' I'll read that letter, too, soon as I get to an eye doctor an' get my spectacles fixed.

*Everyone laughs, but the laughter gives way to an awkward silence.* THOMAS *looks at his great-grandmother for a long while, then embraces her. She holds him tightly and he, her. There is a tear in her eye.*

**GREAT-GRANDMOTHER.** Get along, now. An' take care of your baby brother.

*It is very hard for everyone to say goodbye. Everyone gives* GREAT-GRANDMOTHER *a hug and a gentle kiss.* THOMAS *moves away from his great-grandmother and goes with his father to the car. He gets in, waves to his great-grandmother as the car pulls away.*

CUT TO INT: THE CAR—DAY

THOMAS *sits in the back seat with his brother* KENNETH, *staring back at his* GREAT-GRANDMOTHER. *He watches her turn slowly and walk back toward the house and disappear inside. He turns in his seat, heaves a deep sigh, places his arm around* KENNETH, *and stares ahead.*

5

DISSOLVE TO EXT: DAY—A MONTAGE

*The* SMALLS' *car speeds down Interstate Highway 40 west. A sign indicates they are approaching the town of Asheville, North Carolina.*

CUT TO EXT: THE HIGHWAY AND CAR—DAY

*We are on a long shot of the* SMALLS' *car as it travels along. A sign indicates Knoxville, Tennessee.*

**THOMAS.** [VO] Papa, tell me again about Dies Drear and how he used our new house for the Underground Railroad.[2]

**WALTER.** [VO: BY ROTE] Dies Drear was a wealthy abolitionist, out of New England, who moved to Ohio and . . . Thomas, I've told you all this before.

CUT TO EXT: THE OUTSKIRTS OF CINCINNATI—DAY

*The* SMALLS' *car leaves Interstate 75 and makes the connection to Ohio Route 68.*

**THOMAS.** [VO] Papa, is it true that Dies Drear used to give escaped slaves money to go *back* into slavery?

**WALTER.** [VO] Yea, that's right, son.

**THOMAS.** [VO] But why?

CUT TO EXT: HIGHWAY—DAY

*The car passes through rolling hills and green fields. The sky is a clear blue.*

**WALTER.** [VO] Because after they were caught and went back, they passed the hidden money on to other slaves, who would attempt to escape.

**THOMAS.** [VO] But why would slaves need money?

**WALTER.** [VO] Well, even a fleeing slave needs maneuvering money. He would need food and shelter and the best and safest way for him to get it was to buy it from free black people.

CUT TO INT: THE CAR

**2. Underground Railroad:** A system set up by abolitionists, or opponents of slavery, before the Civil War to help slaves escape to free states and Canada. Dies Drear's house was used as an Underground Railroad "station."

248   Drama

## Commentary

Although a number of stories exist, it's not clear exactly when or how the Underground Railroad got its name. According to one story, a runaway slave was pursued by his master across the Ohio River. Once on shore, the master lost sight of the fugitive. Upon being questioned about the remarkable disappearance, the disappointed owner replied, "[He] must have gone off on an underground road."

**UNDERGROUND RAILROAD, 1982**
*Oberlin Seniors, Inc.*
Courtesy of the Artists

## Humanities Note

Quilt, *Underground Railroad,* 1982, by Oberlin Seniors, Inc. The making of this quilt was a communal effort in the traditional manner by the senior citizens of Oberlin, Ohio. Each member of the group prepared a quilted scene from the history of Oberlin's involvement in the Underground Railroad.

The story that the quilt tells unfolds as the viewer examines the different squares. For example, references are made to the proximity of Ohio, a free state, and to Kentucky, a state where slave keeping flourished. A boat is shown crossing the river that separates these two states, and in another square, a railroad track leads from the South to Ohio. An escaping slave is shown following an arrow marked "Oberlin," which, along with a square showing a map and one exhibiting the North Star, tells the viewer that the town was an organized destination and haven for fugitive slaves. Other squares refer to the philosophy that motivated the town to participate in the Underground Railroad. One explicitly states that the town was founded on the principles of human freedom, and another displays hands of all colors clasped in friendship.

The town of Oberlin is proud of its historic involvement in the Underground Railroad. This effort by the senior citizens glorifies the efforts of their founding fathers in America's greatest human rights struggle.

You might use the following questions for discussion:
1. Choose a square on the quilt and describe its significance to the class.
2. Why is a quilt a particularly appropriate medium for the Oberlin Seniors' purpose?

**6** **Reading Strategy** What is the effect of the approaching rainstorm? What reason might the author have had to include it at this point in the story?

**7** **Discussion** Why do you suppose Thomas hums his great-grandmother's song here?

**8** **Reading Strategy** Why is River Lewis Darrow's appearance so frightening?

SHEILA, *half-asleep, stirs.* KENNETH *and* THOMAS *are dozing.* WALTER *looks tired.*

**SHEILA.** How close are we?

**WALTER.** 'Bout another hour and a half, baby.

KENNETH *begins to stir.*

**SHEILA.** [*comforting* KENNETH] Whatsamatter, honey?

**KENNETH.** I'm scared.

**THOMAS.** Hey, look! That's what's botherin' Kenneth, I'll bet.

*His parents look ahead.*

CUT TO EXT: THE HIGHWAY—DAY

**6** *A huge rain-filled cloud, as dark as night, is approaching them head-on. The sky grows more and more ominous. The wind begins to howl, kicking up dust and buffeting the car. Traffic on the highway begins to slow as the storm rapidly approaches.*

CUT TO INT: THE CAR

KENNETH *begins to cry.*

CUT TO EXT: THE HIGHWAY—DAY

*Wind and rain slam into the car, causing it to swerve violently.*

CUT TO INT: THE CAR

*The family is shaken about and frightened.*

CUT TO EXT: THE HIGHWAY—DAY

*The car continues on through the storm and wind and driving rain. There is violent thunder and lightning.*

DISSOLVE TO EXT: A TWO-LANE BLACKTOP—DAY

*The storm continues unabated. We see the headlights of the* SMALLS' *car as it moves down the small road. The car turns off the road and proceeds down a dirt road.*

CUT TO INT: THE CAR

KENNETH *is now curled up asleep in the back.* THOMAS *is crouched behind the front seat, peering out through the front windshield.* WALTER *is hunched over the wheel, squinting because the driving rain has reduced visibility to a near impossibility.*

CUT TO EXT: DIRT ROAD—WALTER'S POV

*The car's headlights illuminate the road in front of them. The thick storm clouds have made it seem as if it were night. The wind buffets the leaves and bushes violently. Rain splatters against the windshield.*

CUT TO INT: THE CAR

**THOMAS.** Papa, we aren't lost, are we?

**WALTER.** No . . . not yet, anyway.

**THOMAS.** [*reassuringly*] Don't worry, you'll get us through, Papa.

**WALTER.** [*smiling*] How can I fail when I got a big man like you on my side?

**7** THOMAS *begins to hum* GREAT-GRAND-MOTHER's "Ragman" *song. There is only the humming for a while; then, suddenly:*

**SHEILA.** Walter, look out!

WALTER *quickly hits the brakes.*

CUT TO INT: THE CAR—WALTER'S POV OF THE ROAD—DUSK

**8** *As if out of nowhere, the figure of a man appears. He is* RIVER LEWIS DARROW, *a huge man, well over six feet tall and in excess of 200 pounds. He wears a black raincoat and a black rainhat.*

CUT TO EXT: SIDE OF ROAD—DUSK

*The man wears long black rubber boots. A snarling dog, rather large in size, stands drenched next to him. In one hand* DARROW *carries a large double-barreled rifle. In the other he holds the carcasses of several freshly killed rabbits. There is a scowl on the man's face as he glares at the car.*

CUT TO INT: THE CAR—DUSK

*The whole family stares at the man.*

**THOMAS.** Papa, where'd he come from?

**WALTER.** I don't know, son. Guess he was standin' there all the time.

**SHEILA.** Maybe he knows how to get to the house. Ask him, Walter.

**THOMAS.** But, Mama, he got a gun.

**SHEILA.** Oh, Thomas, he was just out huntin'. You've seen men hunt before.

**THOMAS.** I ain't never seen no man like him before, Mama.

WALTER *rolls down the window.*

CUT TO EXT: CAR—DUSK

*The man and the dog walk near. The dead rabbits are held in plain sight.* THOMAS *and* KENNETH *spend equal amounts of time looking at the rabbits and the dog, while* SHEILA *and* WALTER *stare intently at the man.*

**WALTER.** Excuse me, sir. I'm trying to find a house.

**DARROW.** [*sullen*] Plenty houses 'round here, mista. Which one you want?

**WALTER.** I'm lookin' for the house of Dies Drear.

DARROW'*s eyes flash for the briefest instant. His grip tightens on the gun.*

**DARROW.** Why you want that house? Ain't nobody lived in there for nigh on sixty years.

**WALTER.** Well, some do, now. We're moving in. We leased it.

WALTER'*s smile disappears when he sees that* DARROW'*s already hardened visage*[3] *has turned to a countenance of sheer hatred.*

**DARROW.** That so? Follow this road. It'll take you straight there. Not that it'll matter much. You won't be there long.

DARROW *steps back from the car.*

**WALTER.** Hey, what's that supposed to mean?

**DARROW.** [*firmly*] I'm tired of standin' in this rain.

WALTER *rolls up the window and puts the car in gear.* KENNETH *crawls over the front seat and curls in his mother's arms.* THOMAS *presses against the window and tries to get a better look at* DARROW, *the dog, and the dead rabbits. The dog snarls and barks vigorously as the car moves away.* DARROW *stands staring at them. There is a look of contempt and hatred etched on his face. He slings the rabbits over his shoulder and walks off into the rain and night, the dog at his side.*

CUT TO INT: THE CAR

THOMAS *stares out of the back window at* DARROW *and the dog. He is both fascinated and frightened. He sits back down and holds out his hand. It is trembling. He tucks it into his lap and tries to force himself to relax, but he cannot.*

**SHEILA.** He came out of nowhere! Frightened me to death.

**WALTER.** Well, relax. He's gone and we'll be there, soon.

---

**3. visage** (viz′ ij) *n.*: The face and the expression on it.

---

**9 Clarification** Explain to students that *nigh* is a dialect term for "nearly" or "almost."

**10 Reading Strategy** Based on his physical appearance and his behavior, predict the kind of role that River Lewis Darrow might play in the story.

**11 Discussion** How does the house of Dies Drear compare in appearance with haunted houses that you have read about or seen in films?

## Humanities Note

Fine art, *Landscape With Sun Setting*, 1930, by William H. Johnson. Johnson (1901–1970) was a leading Harlem Renaissance painter. Using a deliberately primitive painting style, he explored themes from his own African American heritage and his personal experience. Johnson painted this landscape in the South Carolina town where he was born. The entire painting seems to pulsate with hidden energy. The boldly delineated branches of the bare trees reach above the dark and gloomy landscape, in sharp contrast with the fiery sky, creating a striking linear rhythm. This emotionally charged work gives the viewer a glimpse of the strong feelings the artist had for his birthplace.

You might use the following questions for discussion:
1. What emotions might the artist have associated with this place?
2. Compare the way this painting makes you feel with how the Smalls felt as they first glimpsed the house of Dies Drear.

CUT TO INT: THE CAR—DUSK

SHEILA *holds* KENNETH *and glances over at* WALTER, *who concentrates on his driving. He is nervous but tries not to show it.* THOMAS *watches them both with growing apprehension.*

CUT TO EXT: THE ROAD—DUSK

**11** *The car proceeds through the woods and suddenly the trees give way to a clearing. There is a loud, shattering clap of thunder; then a searing flash of lightning hits a tree and fells it near the car.* WALTER *swerves to avoid it. Another flash of lightning, and they see it. A huge, monstrous-looking house, made more ominous by the storm. It is Victorian[4] in nature, yet seems formless and unnatural. It has a dark, isolated look about it. It stands on a hill.*

CUT TO INT: THE CAR—DUSK

KENNETH *looks at the house and begins to cry, burying his head against* SHEILA*'s*

---

**4. Victorian** (vik tôr′ ē ən): Of a style of architecture popular during Queen Victoria's reign (1837–1901), characterized by massiveness and ornate carving.

**LANDSCAPE WITH SUN SETTING, 1930**
*William H. Johnson*
*Howard University Gallery of Art, Washington, D.C.*

breast. THOMAS and SHEILA *simply stare in quiet disbelief.*

**SHEILA.** [*quietly, with apprehension*] Walter . . . ?

**THOMAS.** Papa, is that it?

**WALTER.** Yes, son . . . our new home. [*softly*] Our new home.

CUT TO EXT: THE HOUSE OF DIES DREAR—DUSK

*Lightning continues to illuminate the house against the sky. The howling wind mixes with* KENNETH's *crying to create an eerie sound that seems to emanate from the house itself.*

*The rainstorm continues as the* SMALL *family gets out of the car and runs onto the veranda of the house. The house itself sits on an outcropping on the side of a hill. The face of the outcropping is rock, from which mineral springs gush. These springs empty into a small nearby stream. Running down the face of the ledge, these springs paint the rocks in their path with red and yellow rust. As he stands on the veranda waiting for* WALTER *to open the door,* THOMAS *watches these springs.*

**THOMAS.** Hey, it looks just like the house is bleedin'. Like somebody cut this place open underneath and let all the blood run out.

**KENNETH.** Mama, I'm scared!

**SHEILA.** Enough of that kinda talk. Walter, you got that door, yet?

WALTER *grunts an answer, and the door swings open. Everyone enters.*

CUT TO INT: THE HOUSE OF DIES DREAR—FRONT HALLWAY—DUSK

*The heavy front doors through which they enter swing shut silently and effortlessly behind them. They enter a house that is* still and quiet, *and despite the fact that the electricity is working and a few lights are on, there is still an eerie quality about the place. The entrance is a long wide hall, one part of which is cut by stairs that rise in a curve and disappear into the darkness of the upper floors. In the distance in front of them is a wide doorway leading to the kitchen. On either side of the hall are large doors leading into sitting rooms. One door is closed, the other half opened. Something has stopped* WALTER *dead in his tracks.* THOMAS *looks up at him.* SHEILA *and* KENNETH *walk ahead into another room.*

**THOMAS.** Papa?

**WALTER.** Something's wrong. I had expected our furniture from the van to be piled up in this hall, Thomas.

**THOMAS.** Where is it?

**SHEILA.** [VO] Walter! Walter, come here, quick!

WALTER *heads for the sitting room.* THOMAS *lags behind his father just a bit. He passes by a grand, old, gilded mirror, on either side of which are two end tables.* THOMAS *catches his image in the mirror out of the side of his eye and is startled momentarily. He jumps and takes several steps back, sucking in his breath. When he realizes it is only a mirror, he relaxes, then notices the tables. He touches them, then heads inside the sitting room.*

INT: THE SITTING ROOM—TWILIGHT

WALTER *stands near* SHEILA. KENNETH *is holding onto his father's leg very tightly and standing a bit behind him.* THOMAS *comes in and is surprised by what he sees: Two oversized easy chairs are placed side by side with a mahogany lamp between them. The chairs sit like soldiers on their guard. A couch is across the room*

*The House of Dies Drear* 253

**12 Discussion** What does the image of the house bleeding suggest about its history?

## Primary Source

Virginia Hamilton admits, "I love setting up scenes, starting with a wide view and then gradually moving in for the close-up." Although Hamilton wrote the original novel and not the screenplay for *The House of Dies Drear,* it seems as though she had a "movie" in her mind as she did so. Have students point out several places in Acts I and II in which the screenwriter uses the technique that Hamilton describes above.

**13 Clarification** In Roman mythology Pluto was the god of the underworld, the ruler of the dead, and the giver of wealth.

**14 Discussion** Do you agree with Thomas's interpretation of Pluto's actions? Why or why not?

*from the chairs. Between two of the floor-to-ceiling windows stands the worktable from the kitchen in the* SMALLS' *old home. At the far end of the room is a massive fireplace. No fire has been lit, but wood is neatly piled nearby, and* KENNETH's *little rocking chair sits to one side of the hearth.*

**SHEILA.** Walter, our furniture. But, who could have done this?

**WALTER.** Pluto.

**THOMAS.** Who?

**WALTER.** Pluto. He's the caretaker for this house. Has been for years. I think he was brought in by the foundation that owns this place.

**THOMAS.** Pluto? Where'd he *get* that name?

**WALTER.** That's not his real name, Thomas. Sort of a nickname he's come to be known by around here.

**13** **THOMAS.** Papa, Pluto's another name for the Devil, right?

**WALTER.** Right.

**THOMAS.** Now, why on earth would somebody take a name like that?

**SHEILA.** Well, whoever this Mr. Pluto is, he sure knows how to decorate a home. This is just *beautiful!* How could he have known I was gonna want it like this?

SHEILA *walks over to the worktable.*

**SHEILA.** Look! My old worktable from the kitchen back home. He's sanded it and smoothed it over with linseed oil. Oh, it's just beautiful!

*At either end of the table are plants of ivy in white china tureens.*

**WALTER.** Pluto's a pretty old man. And he's got a bad leg. This must've been quite a chore for him. He could've hurt himself.

**SHEILA.** Well, I'm going to fix him the most delicious meal I can think of as a way of saying thanks.

THOMAS *looks around, frowning, as he holds* KENNETH's *hand.* KENNETH *has stopped crying, but he still seems a little frightened. Something is bothering* THOMAS.

**THOMAS.** Kenneth, go on with Mama a moment.

KENNETH *is hesitant.*

**SHEILA.** Look, Kenneth, there's your favorite little rockin' chair, right over here by the fireplace.

THOMAS *pushes* KENNETH *gently toward* SHEILA. KENNETH *goes, reluctantly, at first, but then is pulled by the curiosity provoked by* SHEILA's *statement.* THOMAS *comes nearer to his father.*

**THOMAS.** Papa, you notice somethin' about the way this furniture is set up?

**WALTER.** [*looks around*] No. Just arranged perfectly to fit this room. That's all I see.

**THOMAS.** That old Pluto, whoever he is, has arranged all the furniture in here so it's pointin' in one direction . . . right at those two large windows, there.

THOMAS *points toward the windows. When* WALTER *looks around the room again, he can see that* THOMAS *is right, but he hides his feelings behind an expressionless stare.*

**THOMAS.** See, Papa. It's a sign—a warning. We'd better not stay here. **14**

WALTER *says nothing.* SHEILA *comes near them again.*

**SHEILA.** I hope you two are whispering about dividing up the chores I have planned for you.

THOMAS *frowns.*

**SHEILA.** Thomas, what's wrong?

**THOMAS.** Who does this Mr. Pluto think he is, workin' out the cuts on Mama's table? He's sure taken a lot on himself. He's got no business in here! This is our house!

THOMAS's *outburst surprises everyone.* WALTER *speaks, finally, as* KENNETH *now moves to* THOMAS's *side and stands behind him.*

**WALTER.** You have no business talking like that, Thomas. It was very decent of him, puttin' the house in order. No one expected him to, and you don't speak ill of kindness.

THOMAS *stares at his father a moment, but* WALTER *does not meet his gaze.*

**SHEILA.** Uh, oh. Cranky people means everybody is tired. Let's go on upstairs and get ready for bed.

SHEILA *starts out and* WALTER *follows.* KENNETH *takes* THOMAS's *hand.*

**THOMAS.** You see the look on Papa's face when I said that? He didn't like all this any more than I did. I *know* he didn't.

KENNETH *says nothing. He pulls* THOMAS *along in an attempt to catch up to their parents. As the boys exit the room, the camera swings back across the room and settles on the large windows. Camera moves toward the windows. Outside the rain has stopped. Only water dripping from the eaves on the veranda and from the leaves in the nearby trees can be seen. A mist is quite visible outside. But, there is something else there . . . barely visible. An outline, or shadow, something man-like, large and powerfully built, standing near a tree, motionless, dressed in black. We cannot get a good view of the shadow. It backs away into the darkness and is gone. From a distance we hear a mysterious sound: Ahhhhh. Ahhhhhh. Ahhhhhh.*

## Act II

EXT: HOUSE—MORNING

*The sun is bright and shining. We see the House of Dies Drear, the surrounding hills, the dirt road, the nearby stream with an old wooden bridge going across it. There is green everywhere and the sky is a clear blue.*

CUT TO INT: KITCHEN—DAY

*The boys are finishing breakfast and* SHEILA *is searching a fully stocked refrigerator for choices for that night's dinner.*

**THOMAS.** Sorry I missed Papa. I was gonna talk to him.

**SHEILA.** [*at the refrigerator*] No, he left early, Thomas. My, I can't get over this. That old Pluto even stocked this refrigerator. There's all kindsa goodies in here.

**THOMAS.** Mama, me an' Kenneth finished eatin'. We're gonna go on out.

**SHEILA.** Okay, but don't stray far. You still don't know this land that well.

**THOMAS.** Okay, c'mon, Kenneth.

THOMAS *and* KENNETH *clear the kitchen table and go out of the kitchen down the long hall toward the front of the house.*

CUT TO EXT: VERANDA—DAY

KENNETH *exits the front door, which is oak and trimmed with carved quatrefoils.[5] He stands before the door, staring. He seems frightened by something.* THOMAS *comes onto the veranda and stands beside* KENNETH.

**THOMAS.** Kenneth, what's wrong with you?

---

**5. quatrefoils** (kat′ər foilz) *n.*: Designs resembling flowers with four petals.

*The House of Dies Drear* 255

15

**Reading Strategy** Lead students to apply what they know about the history of the house to Thomas's discovery of the hole under the steps. What function might the hole have had in Dies Drear's day?

**17 Discussion** Based on her physical description, in what ways is Pesty unusual? Would you be interested in getting to know her if you were Thomas? Why or why not?

---

**KENNETH.** I don't like that door!

**THOMAS.** Aw, c'mon, Kenneth. It's just a door. Look.

THOMAS *moves closer to the door to get a better look, but can see nothing. He backs away and stands near the weathered front steps, painted white to match the rest of the house, then comes back toward the door.* KENNETH *says nothing—but starts to whimper.*

**THOMAS.** What are you staring at?

*Now, he sees something; the quatrefoils are shaped like petals. One has a tiny wooden button in the center.* THOMAS *cautiously waves his hand over the button—he can feel and we can hear a stream of cold air emanating from around it. His trembling finger presses the button, but nothing happens.* THOMAS *jerks it, pulls it, and presses it again. Suddenly,* KENNETH *screams and runs back into the house.*

**THOMAS.** Hey, Kenneth, come back here! What's wrong with you?

KENNETH *does not return.* THOMAS *stands puzzled for a moment. He looks around, turns and goes to the edge of the veranda.* 16 *He looks down and is surprised to find that the steps have shifted over about four feet. And where they once were is a gaping black hole about three feet around. Quickly he looks back at the quatrefoil and realizes that the steps were moved by the button he pushed. He is about to go down the hole when a sound from around the side of the house draws his attention. He backs away from the hole and follows the veranda around the side to investigate. He can hardly believe what greets him.*

CUT TO EXT: THE HOUSE AND ITS GROUNDS—DAY

*Out of the trees on the right side of the house, a huge black horse appears. It is the largest horse* THOMAS *has ever seen. Astride its back is* PESTY, *a girl with jet black skin and flashing, almost dancing, eyes. Her head is wrapped in a white silk scarf that has lace at the edges and she wears red flannel pajamas with lace at the neck and sleeves. She is about twelve* 17 *years old. She wears no shoes and sits well forward near the horse's shoulders. Her arms are folded across her chest and she is staring into the distance, serene and happy. She seems to take no notice of* THOMAS *on the veranda. Following behind, on foot, is* MAC DARROW, *a big fourteen-year-old black youth, rather husky and well-muscled for his age. He is clutching the big horse's tail. [These children and other locals will speak with an Ohio accent, similar to southern but not quite the same. It will be noticeably different from that of* THOMAS *and his family.]*

**MAC.** Whoa, you mean old devil horse! Whoa, I said!

*The horse continues to walk with* PESTY *astride its back. It's plain that* PESTY *is in control.*

**MAC.** Pesty, get down off that horse and let's go! I got things I want to do!

PESTY *only laughs and turns the horse with just her legs and toes.* MAC *throws the horse's tail aside in disgust.*

**MAC.** Well, go 'head on, then. It's your behind that get whipped. Not mine.

PESTY *laughs again and she and the horse seem to head right for* THOMAS *and the veranda. She seems not to notice him at all.* MAC *follows behind, walking casually, his hands thrust in the pockets of his jeans. He glances at* THOMAS *but says nothing.*

---

## Primary Source

The protagonists of Virginia Hamilton's novels are usually African American adolescents who face problems relevant to all young people, reflecting her belief that "the experience of a people must come to mean the experience of humankind." Ask students to comment on how relevant Thomas's experiences are to their own experiences.

THOMAS *follows them both around the side of the house back to the front steps and the hole. There the horse comes to a halt.* PESTY *and* MAC *look down at the hole.* THOMAS *remains silent, however, as he moves near the button, his eyes on* MAC *and* PESTY.

**MAC.** Pesty, tell that horse to hold it! You want to walk him clear down that hole, there, or you want to walk him right through the front door of this house?

PESTY *says nothing. She laughs and peers down at the hole. Then she looks up at* THOMAS *for the first time and grins. Just as quickly she looks away and back down the hole.* THOMAS *is affected by the sweet smile and a faint smile crosses his lips before he catches sight of* MAC *moving close to the hole and peering down into it.*

**MAC.** Oooweee, Pesty. Anybody go foolin' around down there might get themselves lost forever. Lost in one of Dies Drear's old tunnels, never to be found again.

**PESTY.** Shoot, ain't true, atall.

**MAC.** Now, how do you know that?

**PESTY.** [*evasive*] 'Cause I *know*, that's how.

**MAC.** [*finally turns to Thomas*] Hey? You goin' down there?

**THOMAS.** Maybe.

THOMAS *glares at* MAC. *He feels they are making fun of him.*

**MAC.** [*laughing*] Good luck.

**PESTY.** You quit laughin' at him, you ol' laughin' high-eena.

**MEMORIES OF THE MEADOW**
*John Holyfield*
*Courtesy of Essence Art*

## Humanities Note

Fine art, *Memories of the Meadow*, by John Holyfield. Born in 1969, Holyfield was raised by his grandmothers in Clarksburg, West Virginia. He attributes his "Southern, folksy" style to his rural upbringing, and works to capture on canvas the normal, everyday situations he remembers from childhood.

You might use the following questions for discussion:
1. How is the casual, everyday scene depicted in the painting similar to Thomas's chance encounter with Pesty and Mac?
2. In what ways is Thomas's experience more unusual than the scene captured in the painting?

**18** **Reading Strategy** What previous clues in the screenplay support Thomas's statement that Kenneth may be psychic?

**19** **Reading Strategy** Summarize the factual information about Pluto that Pesty and Mac give Thomas. How does this information reinforce the suspicions that Thomas already harbors about Pluto?

**MAC.** You got any smartmouth little people like this in your family?

**18**

**THOMAS.** I got a kid brother, but he ain't no smartmouth. My family been told that he might be psychic. He feels things before they happen.

**PESTY.** Psycho?[6] Like in that old movie? Wow!

**THOMAS.** No . . . oh, never mind. Forget it.

**MAC.** Well, if you go down there, look out for the ghost of Dies Drear.

**PESTY.** Ain't no need to worry, though. Mr. Pluto is his earthly friend. An' if the ghost mess with you, you call Mr. Pluto. If Mr. Pluto takes a likin' to you he'll save you, if he don't, well . . . too bad for you.

PESTY *laughs.*

**THOMAS.** Pluto may scare you, but he don't scare me.

**PESTY.** That's cause you don't know him. Everybody 'round here knows he's a demon. You cross him, an' that's it. You could be walkin' down the street an' the next thing you know, both your arms can fall right off. An' you'll say, "Aaa, my arms." An' that's when you'll know ol' demon Pluto done gotcha.

**19**

PESTY *looks at* THOMAS *and* THOMAS *looks back at her. Suddenly, she breaks out into a wide grin.*

**MAC.** Girl, you better go 'head on, tellin' them stories.

**PESTY.** So? Daddy sho' nuff believes 'em. I heard him call Mr. Pluto a demon plenty of times.

**MAC.** Daddy just talkin', that's all.

---

**6. Psycho** (sī' kō): Famous movie directed by Alfred Hitchcock, released in 1960.

**PESTY.** Wanna bet? [*to* THOMAS] Listen, don't nobody mess around this property less Mr. Pluto wants 'em to. An' if he don't like you, he'll come up out the ground like the devil an' grab you. So you just go on an' climb down that hole an' see if what I say ain't true.

**MAC.** Guess you plannin' on findin' out just how quick you can get scared in the dark.

MAC *chuckles, and* PESTY *maintains her sweet smile as she looks at* THOMAS. THOMAS *is a little angry at both, by now.*

**THOMAS.** Who are you?

*He moves closer to the edge of the veranda, just above the gaping hole.*

**THOMAS.** Y'all from around here?

*A very polite smile crosses* MAC's *face as he looks up from the hole again. He addresses* THOMAS *almost as though seeing him for the first time.*

**MAC.** Well, how you been an' how you feelin'? We the Darrow's children. I'm Mac, the youngest son.

**PESTY.** And I'm Pesty. I live with them, too.

**MAC.** Pesty's a name I give her 'cause she likes to bother me so. You know, like a pest. My Daddy calls her Sarah, an' my Mama calls her Sooky. That ol' Mr. Pluto calls her Little Miss Bee, and . . .

**PESTY.** [*interrupting*] An' I guess you can make up a name, too. It won't matter to me 'cause I'm *always* gonna know who *I* am.

**THOMAS.** You live with him, but you ain't his sister?

**PESTY.** All he got is brothers. I was left on their doorstep in a new tin tub when he was just three years old an' 'sleep in bed. [*pointing to* MAC] His mama brought me in the house, showed me to his daddy an' I been livin' there ever since.

## Grammar in Action

In order to make dialogue realistic, writers often bend the rules of grammar and usage. Conversations among characters may contain slang, run-on sentences, sentence fragments, and incorrect verb forms just to illustrate a unique personality or to reveal the nuances in speech of a particular part of the country. For example, in the following passage, what could be a serious warning to Thomas is presented lightheartedly by Pesty:

Ain't no need to worry, though. Mr. Pluto is his earthly friend. An' if the ghost mess with you, you call Mr. Pluto. If Mr. Pluto takes a likin' to you he'll save you, if he don't, well . . . too bad for you.

Notice how Pesty's characteristic voice changes when the grammar and usage is corrected to standard English. Without the idiomatic phrases, the hesitations in speech, and the contractions, Pesty sounds formal and unlike herself:

There is no need to worry, however. Mr. Pluto is his earthly friend. If the ghost interferes with you, call Mr. Pluto. If Mr. Pluto likes you, he will save you. If he does not, it will be too bad for you.

MAC *and* PESTY *laugh.*

**THOMAS.** Adopted.

**PESTY.** Hey, whatchu doin' on Mr. Pluto's porch? He'll snatch you baldheaded if he finds you.

**MAC.** What's worse, he'll turn Pesty loose on you, then you'll really be in a mess.

**THOMAS.** [*angry*] First off, Mr. Pluto just works here, cause this is my father's house now, and second off, y'all ain't got no business on private property.

MAC *and* PESTY *convulse in derisive laughter.* THOMAS *jumps down off the veranda and lands near the hole. He peers down inside.*

**THOMAS.** Y'all better go 'head on. Nobody wants to be bothered with you.

**MAC.** Where you think you goin'?

**THOMAS.** Part of the Underground Railroad must be down this hole. I aim to find it.

MAC *and* PESTY *look at one another.*

**PESTY.** Underground Railroad? Boy, ain't no railroad tracks down there.

THOMAS *looks at her incredulously, then prepares to jump down into the hole.*

**MAC.** You really fixin' to go down that hole?

THOMAS *simply looks at him without saying a word.*

**MAC.** Want some company?

**THOMAS.** I don't need any help.

**MAC.** Yea, say that now. But 'spect you'll be needin' me later on.

PESTY *begins to laugh, so does* MAC.

**PESTY.** If you get scared, just holler!

**MAC.** Come on, girl. I know Mama must got breakfast ready by now. Come on!

*They start off.* MAC *turns.*

**MAC.** What's your name?

**THOMAS.** Thomas Small.

**MAC.** Reckon I'll be seein' you around. Come on, Pesty!

THOMAS *watches as* MAC *walks away.* PESTY *looks down from her horse.*

**PESTY.** Hey, Thomas Small, the new boy. How you like these new red night clothes? Ain't they pretty? I like red. Mr. Pluto said red was the best color.

**MAC.** It's the color of fire. Pluto keeps fire.

**THOMAS.** Like the Devil.

**PESTY.** What? You sure strange, new boy Thomas Small. Well, I'm Mr. Pluto's helper around here. You ever get in some trouble, you call me 'cause I can getchu outa it. Hear?

THOMAS *does not answer.* PESTY *smiles her sweet smile.*

**PESTY.** Bye. Gidap, hoss!

*The horse trots away with the girl clutching its mane. They move past* MAC, *who saunters along leisurely, his hands thrust into his pockets.* THOMAS *watches them a moment, then turns his gaze toward the hole. He picks up a small stone and drops it to gauge the depth. The sound indicates that it is not too deep. He takes a deep breath, looks around, and jumps down into the hole.*

CUT TO INT: THE HOLE UNDER THE HOUSE AND TUNNEL

*The hole is almost pitch black. The only light showing emanates from above. The drop of five feet has momentarily stunned* THOMAS *and he has to wait to catch his breath. The ground is damp and smells like mildew. When he gets to his feet,* THOMAS *fumbles in his pocket and finds a small*

*The House of Dies Drear*   259

20 **Discussion** In what ways is Mac different from River Lewis Darrow?

---

**Student Activity 1.** Select a short passage of dialogue spoken by Pesty or Mac, and rewrite it in standard English. Be prepared to discuss the changes you made, why you made them, and how they affect the realism of the dialogue.

**Student Activity 2.** Write a brief dialogue that realistically captures the way two people speak. Try to reveal the personality of the characters through their words. Remember to set off direct quotations with quotation marks and to begin a new paragraph with each change of speaker.

**Electronic Handbook** You might want students to review informal language and idioms before completing the Grammar in Action activities. If students have access to the Language Master 6000, have them enter the access words *informal* and *idiom* and press the GRAMMAR key to get information about these special kinds of language.

**21 Discussion** What does Thomas's response to seeing the places where fugitive slaves hid reveal about his character?

**22 Literary Focus: Screenplay** Why do you think the screenwriter ended the act at this point in the action? How does the blackout add to the drama?

**Challenge** In these first two acts, what has Thomas learned about the Dies Drear house and its caretaker?

**Reader's Response** How would you have reacted to moving into the house of Dies Drear?

**Thematic Response** Why are people typically hesitant about exploring the unknown?

## Closure and Extension

### ANSWERS TO RESPONDING TO THE SELECTION
*Your Response*

1. Have students share their feelings about moving and discuss how these feelings compare with Thomas's.
2. Encourage students to discuss the conflict between the desire to explore and the fear of the unknown.

*Recalling*

3. The Smalls are moving because Walter has taken a job as a history professor at a university in Ohio.
4. Dies Drear was an abolitionist whose house was used as a "station" on the Underground Railroad in the days before the Civil War.

*pencil-thin flashlight, which he uses to light his way. He spies a steep stairway leading downward not too far from where he has fallen. He is surrounded on all sides by brick—a wall of some sort. The boy makes his way down the steps and into the darkness—down, down, down, deep inside the ground. He is below the foundation of the house. The pathway is cramped and tiny. As he presses more deeply into the passageway, he is aware that his feet are becoming wet. Some distance away he can hear the sound of one of the brooks. His sneakered feet are now in a few inches of water, which flows along the passageway floor. The place is strangely silent. His breathing is the only other sound he can hear now. For effect, he grunts aloud. The sound has a full resonance to it, the likes of which he has never heard before. It is almost as though he was speaking through a speaker system that had the bass turned up full blast. He continues until he comes to a place where the path widens. The walls are now four feet away on either side. Long slabs are along each wall.*

**THOMAS.** [*whispering*] Places for the runaway slaves to sit.

THOMAS *sits on the slab and touches it.*

**THOMAS.** They musta been so scared. Alone. How could they see down here? How could they stand it?

THOMAS *sits in silence for a brief second, then rises and continues on. The path narrows again. Somewhere in the distance, he hears the faint sound of movement. He shines the light ahead, but can see nothing. He continues on, but slips on the wet floor and drops the light. It rolls behind him into the darkness. We can barely see THOMAS, but we can hear his breathing and his voice.*

*260    Drama*

**THOMAS.** The light's gotta be here someplace. All I gotta do is get on my knees and feel . . .

*He feels around, but without luck.*

**THOMAS.** I couldn'a kicked it that far. Where is it? Where . . . ?

*We hear his scrambling about, but we can tell now that it will get him nowhere.*

**THOMAS.** All I gotta do is crawl along this path. It's leadin' up, now. I'll just follow it right on outa here.

*He begins to whistle* GREAT-GRANDMOTHER*'s song as he crawls along. Then:*

**THOMAS.** What's that?

THOMAS *is silent. We can hear his heavy breathing. We can also hear a strange sound—something forlorn and lost and cold.*

*We hear: AHHHHH, AHHHHH, AHHHHH.*

*We can hear* THOMAS *begin to scramble frightfully. The sound seems to be drawing nearer and nearer as* THOMAS *continues to scramble, feeling along the walls. We can hear his palms slapping and sliding along the rock and his feet slipping and splashing in the trickling water.*

**THOMAS.** No! No! Keep it away!

*Louder and louder, closer and closer, the sound comes.*

**THOMAS.** Papa! Mama! Papa! Papa! Come get me, Papa!

*Frantically he scrambles along as the sound seems to come closer and closer. Suddenly, the boy slams into a wall and falls to the ground, screaming and pounding his fists against the rocks. From somewhere, we hear a woman scream.*

BLACKOUT

*Interpreting*

5. Suggested Response: Walter is a good-natured family man who teaches history and is especially interested in African American history. Sheila, though supportive of her husband's work, is more concerned with her family's well-being. Thomas is an intelligent, imaginative, and thoughtful boy who is intensely curious about the history of the Dies Drear house and the mysteries that surround it. Kenneth is a sensitive boy who may be psychic.

6. Answers will differ but ought to include Pesty's comment about everyone knowing that Pluto is a demon. Some students may feel this is true, citing the fact that "Pluto" is another name for the devil. Thomas's belief that Pluto's arrangement of the furniture was a warning for them to leave supports the idea that Pluto is evil. Other students may feel, as Sheila does, that Pluto's actions were a sign of friendship and welcome.

7. Answers will differ. Students may cite the scene in which River Lewis Darrow suddenly appears on the road and makes cryptic remarks to Walter. They may interpret this action as an attempt to warn Walter of future trouble or to frighten him away from the Dies Drear house. Students may also cite the appearance of the shadowy figure at the window. Some may think that this figure is Pluto,

# RESPONDING TO THE SELECTION

## Your Response

1. How would you feel if your family moved to a different part of the country, leaving friends and relatives behind? Explain.
2. If you were Thomas, would you have explored the hole under the house? Give reasons for your answer.

## Recalling

3. Why do the Smalls move to Ohio?
4. Who was Dies Drear? What was his house used for?

## Interpreting

5. In your own words, briefly describe the personality of each member of the Small family.
6. Review all the comments made about Pluto. Which of them do you think are true? Explain your answer.
7. Describe an unexplained event that occurs in the screenplay. What do you think it means?
8. What do you predict will happen to Thomas in the next act? Explain.

## Applying

9. Walter tells Thomas about the Underground Railroad. What do you know about this "railroad"? Where could you find out more about it?

# ANALYZING LITERATURE

## Understanding a Screenplay

A **screenplay** is much like a stage play, except that it includes camera directions. Camera directions tell the camera operator what to shoot and how to shoot it. Each camera direction creates an intended effect. For example, the *close-up* shot of Great-grandmother Jeffers's hands at the beginning of the screenplay emphasizes her age and her strength of character. However, "the smoke and surrounding darkness" create "an eerie atmosphere" in keeping with the strange events that follow.

1. At the end of Act I, the camera moves to the windows and focuses on a figure in the shadows. What is the effect of this shot?
2. What is the effect of the blackout at the end of Act II?

# CRITICAL THINKING AND READING

## Visualizing a Screenplay

When you read a screenplay, you must use your imagination to visualize what the camera would be showing you. You can do this by paying close attention to the camera directions and creating a film in your mind as you read.

Review the series of scenes that make up the Smalls' car trip to Ohio (pages 248–253). Then imagine that you are watching several of these scenes in a film. In your own words, describe what you would see on the screen.

# THINKING AND WRITING

## Taking a Character's Point of View

Imagine that you are Thomas, and write a letter to your great-grandmother describing your initial reactions to your new house. Describe all the mysterious events that have occurred and the new people you have met and heard about. Also, try to re-create the atmosphere of the house. Revise your letter to make your descriptions as clear and vivid as possible.

# LEARNING OPTION

**Performance.** With several classmates, perform any part of the screenplay for your class. Treat the screenplay as a stage play, ignoring the camera directions. Then share your performance with the class.

*The House of Dies Drear* 261

## THINKING AND WRITING

**Software** If students have access to a computer, have them use the **Writer's Helper** activity *Five W's* to explore ideas for their letter.

**Writing Transparency** Students may need some guidance in organizing the impressions they want to convey in their letter. Once they have collected their details, suggest that they practice chronological order, developmental order, or order of importance with the Paragraph Exercises in **Transparencies for Writing**.

**Alternative Assessment** *Peer Review:* In pairs or groups of four, have your students assess one another's work by responding to the following questions:

> What is Thomas's general reaction to his new house?
>
> What specific details and events does Thomas share with his great-grandmother?
>
> What does he tell her about the new people he has met and heard about?
>
> What suggestions can you offer the writer to improve the letter?

**Publishing Student Writing** Students may enjoy creating a piece of art to accompany their letter. Display the letters and accompanying drawings on a bulletin board in your classroom or in your school library.

## LEARNING OPTION

This activity will appeal to auditory learners as well as those students who enjoy acting. Students may want to discuss the differences they observe between the characters' vocabulary, grammar, and pronunciation and their own. Point out to students that dialect in literature adds realism, giving a vivid portrait of people in a particular section of the country.

whereas others may believe it to be River Lewis Darrow or the ghost of Dies Drear.

8. Answers will differ, but students should include examples to support their predictions.

## Applying

9. Answers will differ, but students should include the fact that they could find out more about the Underground Railroad by consulting encyclopedias or other reference books.

## ANSWERS TO ANALYZING LITERATURE

1. Suggested Response: The shot of the shadowy figure through the window creates suspense and dramatic irony for the viewer.
2. Suggested Response: The blackout adds drama and suspense to the cliffhanger ending of Act II.

## ANSWERS TO CRITICAL THINKING AND READING

To help students visualize the montage, suggest that they draw a series of frames in which they sketch what is seen on the screen in each shot.

# Preparation

**Literary Focus** Before students read Acts III–V of the screenplay, review with them the ways in which suspense is created in Acts I and II. Ask them to comment on how the atmosphere contributes to the building of tension. What mysterious aspects of conflict and character have been introduced? What foreshadowing techniques has the screenwriter used?

**Prereading Focus** Suggest that students identify the mystery they are trying to solve before they begin gathering clues. To help them formulate their predictions, suggest that they analyze the clues to see whether they are related in any way. Can students identify any patterns or trends?

You may wish to have students repeat this activity at the end of Act V.

**Vocabulary** Have students work in pairs to create a two-character dialogue using the vocabulary words. Explain that they can use the words as part of the characters' speeches, or they can incorporate them into character tags, such as, "Sean replied in a dejected tone."

**Spelling Tip** Explain that students may see *specter* spelled elsewhere as *spectre*. Point out that this is a variant spelling that is chiefly British.

# GUIDE FOR READING

## The House of Dies Drear, Acts III–V

### Suspense and Foreshadowing

**Suspense** is the quality in a film that makes you keep watching in order to find out how the action is resolved. One way of creating suspense is through **foreshadowing,** hinting at events to come. The hints provide just enough information to make you wonder where they will lead. An example of foreshadowing in *The House of Dies Drear* is River Lewis Darrow's appearance on the road just as the Smalls approach their new home in Act I. This scene suggests that the Smalls are going to find trouble in the Dies Drear house and that Darrow may be part of it.

### Focus

*The House of Dies Drear* is a mystery. To create and maintain interest in a mystery, an author needs to provide clues to the mystery's solution. With your classmates, brainstorm to list the clues that the author has given in Acts I and II of the screenplay. Next to each clue, make a prediction about the resolution of the mystery. Later, compare your predictions to the actual resolution of the screenplay.

| Clues | Predictions |
|---|---|
|  |  |

### Vocabulary

Knowing the following words will help you as you read Acts III–V of *The House of Dies Drear*.

**dejected** (dē jek′ tid) *adj.:* In low spirits; depressed (p. 263)
**meander** (mē an′ dər) *v.:* Follow a winding course (p. 264)
**ascends** (a sendz′) *v.:* Moves upward (p. 265)
**specter** (spek′ tər) *n.:* Object of fear or dread (p. 267)
**agitated** (aj′ i tāt′ id) *adj.:* Upset; disturbed (p. 268)

**engulfed** (en gulft′) *v.:* Surrounded and enclosed completely; swallowed up (p. 269)
**quaint** (kwānt) *adj.:* Unusual or old-fashioned in a pleasing way (p. 270)
**baleful** (bāl′ fəl) *adj.:* Threatening harm or evil; sinister (p. 270)

*262    Drama*

## Objectives

1 To understand the development of suspense
2 To appreciate how the screenwriter creates atmosphere
3 To write a report about the pattern of clues and to draw conclusions
4 To express individual interests and abilities through an optional activity

## Support Material

**Teaching Portfolio**
Teacher Backup, p. 359
Grammar in Action Worksheet, *Recognizing Participial Phrases*, p. 362
Usage and Mechanics Worksheet, p. 364
Vocabulary Check, p. 365
Analyzing Literature Worksheet, *Understanding Suspense*, p. 366

Critical Thinking and Reading Worksheet, Making Inferences, p. 367
Selection Test, p. 368

**Prentice Hall Literature Writing Studio**

# Act III

FADE IN TO INT: THE TUNNEL

THOMAS *pounds on the wall, screaming for help. He hears* SHEILA's *voice.*

**SHEILA.** [VO] Thomas!

*Suddenly, a wall slides up and* THOMAS *is face to face with* SHEILA, *who is standing in the kitchen, just as surprised as* THOMAS. THOMAS, *out of breath, stumbles out of the tunnel, frightened and trembling.*

CUT TO INT: THE KITCHEN—DAY

SHEILA *embraces* THOMAS *as* KENNETH *comes near, looking on with curiosity.*

**SHEILA.** Thomas! Are you all right, chile?

**THOMAS.** [*finally catching his breath*] Somethin's in there, Mama. It . . . it tried to kill me.

SHEILA *embraces him again, soothing him and trying to calm him down. Finally* THOMAS *is calmed and* SHEILA *helps him to his feet. Regaining his breath,* THOMAS *begins to speak.*

**THOMAS.** Mama, it kept comin' at me. It was gonna jump up an' kill me. I know it!

**SHEILA.** [*soothingly*] Shhh. Hush now. Nothin's after you an' nothin's gonna kill you.

**THOMAS.** But—

**SHEILA.** It's just an old passageway.

WALTER *comes running into the kitchen.*

**WALTER.** What happened? I heard shoutin' down here.

WALTER *looks toward the raised wall panel. He smiles slightly.*

**WALTER.** Well, son, I see you found yourself a secret passage. Didn't figure you'd find that front door button so soon.

**THOMAS.** [*somewhat disappointed*] You mean you knew?

**WALTER.** If any unexpected guests came to the front door, the slaves could hide in this tunnel till whoever it was had gone. Or, if someone searched the house the slaves could escape through here or by way of the front steps.

**THOMAS.** [*dejected*] You shoulda told me y'all knew about that tunnel, Papa.

**SHEILA.** [*embraces* THOMAS] Almost every room in this house has some kind of secret this or hidden that, Thomas.

**THOMAS.** [*insistent*] Mama, I heard somethin' in there. Like sighin'. It kept comin' closer. An' Mama? It wasn't human. It wasn't alive.

SHEILA *looks at* THOMAS *for a moment, then down into the dark of the passageway. The look in her eyes shows that she just might believe some of what her son has to say.*

**SHEILA.** Walter, maybe you better take a look.

*Walter goes to a cabinet and takes a flashlight from one of the drawers. He moves toward the passageway.* THOMAS *is about to follow.*

**WALTER.** Stay here. I'll be right back.

**THOMAS.** But—

**WALTER.** Oh, I'll be all right. I just wanna see what it was in here that *really* frightened you. That's all.

*He checks the light to make sure it is working, then proceeds into the passageway.* SHEILA, THOMAS, *and* KENNETH *peer into it after him. The light from the kitchen spills a few feet into the passageway, then gives way to complete darkness.* WALTER's *flashlight can be seen darting from here to there along the ceiling of the tunnel, then*

*The House of Dies Drear* 263

---

## Presentation

**Motivation/Prior Knowledge**
Ask students to discuss some of the characteristics of mystery stories that they enjoy. Students may mention plot twists, surprise endings, larger-than-life heroes, menacing villains, and chase scenes. They also may talk about the unsettling effects of suspense, the escapist enjoyment of vicariously experiencing events outside their own lives, and the challenge of figuring out "whodunit" before the author reveals the solution. Ask students to discuss the presence of these elements in the first two acts of the screenplay.

**Purpose-Setting Question** According to mystery novelist William Hallahan, a writer needs to prepare readers for an event in the plot in order to create the maximum amount of suspense. In what ways are you prepared for the situations that occur in Acts III–V?

**1 Discussion** Who or what do you think was following Thomas?

**2 Clarification** A great deal of ingenuity was used to secure the safety of runaway slaves. They found hiding places in the secret cellars of barns, in attics and belfries, and in specially constructed woodpiles. As Eli F. Brown of Amesville, Ohio, wrote in a letter, "I built an addition to my house in which I had a room with its partition in panels. One panel could be raised about a half inch and then slid back, so as to permit a man to enter the room. When the panel was in place it appeared like its fellows."

**3 Reading Strategy** Who or what does Thomas think was following him?

4 **Literary Focus: Suspense** In what ways does this scene between Thomas and his father contribute to the building of suspense in the screenplay?

5 **Reading Strategy** Thomas is providing a summary of the mysterious events that have occurred thus far. What relationship, if any, is there between these events?

*disappearing.* SHEILA *holds the two boys close, all of them facing the tunnel opening.*

**KENNETH.** [*frightened*] Can't see nothin', Mama. Can't see nothin'.

**SHEILA.** Sssh, baby. It'll be all right. Papa's just fine.

THOMAS *looks at* KENNETH *and* SHEILA, *then back into the tunnel. There is no sound and all is deathly silent for a few beats, when suddenly a door slams.* SHEILA *and the boys jump with fright. They spin around and see* WALTER *emerging from the hallway. His feet are muddy from the passageway and he tracks dirt all over the floor. Otherwise he is none the worse for wear.* SHEILA *looks displeased as she studies the muddy tracks on the floor.*

**WALTER.** I put the stairs back in place.

**SHEILA.** Did you find anything?

WALTER *shakes his head.* SHEILA *gets a mop.* WALTER *goes over to a control lever by the cabinet and pulls it. The tunnel door shuts.*

**WALTER.** I'll take this whole thing apart tonight. Seal that tunnel up once and for all. Fix the other entrance by the stairs, too.

**THOMAS.** There was some kids, too.

**SHEILA.** Kids? What kids? In the tunnel?

**THOMAS.** No, not in the tunnels, Mama. Out by the side of the house. Their names was Mac and Pesty, who is Mac's sister but not his sister. See, it's like this—

**SHEILA.** Look, you can tell me all about it while you and Kenneth help me clean all this mud up off this floor. C'mon, now.

THOMAS *and* KENNETH *do as they are told. Sheila turns and stares at the wall. She heaves a sigh and goes over to* WALTER.

**SHEILA.** [*quietly*] Walter, just what *is* going on around here?

*264 Drama*

DISSOLVE TO EXT: THE HILLS IN BACK OF THE HOUSE—LATE AFTERNOON

THOMAS *and his father are walking. In the distance we can see the town and the college.*

**WALTER.** Those tunnels meander like a maze. A person could get lost forever if they don't know the way they're laid out.

**THOMAS.** Then how did the slaves know?

**WALTER.** Well, they must've had a code.

*A pause.*

**THOMAS.** Papa?

**WALTER.** Yes, son?

**THOMAS.** You ever think that maybe that ol' house down there *is* haunted?

WALTER *laughs and hugs his son.*

**WALTER.** No. There's no such thing as hauntin', boy. Everything has a logical explanation.

**THOMAS.** I keep rememberin' what that foundation report said about that house. It said that three slaves who were escaping and had hid out with Dies Drear were captured. Two were killed by some bounty hunters,[1] and then Dies Drear himself got killed that same week. Right there in our house. But what happened to that third slave?

**WALTER.** No one knows, son.

**THOMAS.** And it said that no one's lived in that house since Dies Drear got killed, except for a caretaker or two.

**WALTER.** That's all true, son. But that has very little to do with any ghosts.

**THOMAS.** But, what about that furniture business in the house, then that noise in the

---

**1. bounty hunters:** People who captured fugitive slaves for a reward of money, called "bounty."

**Cooperative Learning** Ask students to work together in small groups to chart the action of Acts I and II. Have them compare the acts in terms of structure. Students should notice that the acts are structured in a similar way—characters are introduced, conflict is established and augmented, and both acts end with a mini-crisis that adds to the suspense and builds toward the climax.

Once students have completed their charts, they might discuss with their classmates the similarities they discovered.

tunnel . . . and that man on the road when we first came. How come he didn't greet us friendly? What did Pesty mean when she said old Pluto would come up outa the ground an' grab you if you made him mad? What's all that?

**WALTER.** Boy, you so fulla questions, it's hard to know which one to answer first. But I will tell you this. Your mamma an' I love you very much. An' I'll shake heaven and earth before I let any harm come to one hair on top of your inquisitive little head. Okay?

WALTER *extends his hand, and* THOMAS *takes it and shakes.*

**THOMAS.** Okay.

THOMAS *looks down the hill at the house once again.*

**THOMAS.** Papa, can I stay up here just a little bit? I wanna see if I can tell by the shape of the house where the secret rooms are.

**WALTER.** I don't know, son. Dinner'll be ready soon.

**THOMAS.** Please, Papa . . .

**WALTER.** [*thinks a moment*] I guess it'll be all right. You just try to stay out of trouble. It gets dark pretty quick up here in Ohio—not like in the South. Okay?

**THOMAS.** Okay.

**WALTER.** See you at dinner time, son.

WALTER *goes down the hill.* THOMAS *stands watching him.* THOMAS *walks over to a tree and seats himself in front of it. He stares up at the leaves blowing gently in the breeze, then looks west toward the sun lowering itself toward the horizon. He leans back against the tree and relaxes.*

**THOMAS.** Papa, someone *was* chasin' me.

THOMAS *sits relaxed and looks out over the valley.*

DISSOLVE TO EXT: THE HILL—DUSK

*The sky darkens rapidly.* THOMAS *starts and awakes. He jumps to his feet. He is stiff and cold. A light wind blows, rustling the leaves. He looks down the hill and can see the lights on in his home. He begins walking home. As he is about to descend, he stops. He hears a noise, the same sound he heard in the tunnel. He turns and ascends the hill, moving in the direction of the sound.*

QUICK DISSOLVE TO EXT: THE HILL—DUSK

*The eerie sound is almost hypnotic as it draws the boy to it. He ascends the hill, arriving at its summit. Now the sound seems to be coming from somewhere on the other side of the hill. He goes to investigate.*

QUICK DISSOLVE TO EXT: THE OTHER SIDE OF THE HILL—DUSK

THOMAS *moves as quietly as possible on a bed of dead leaves, listening carefully as he descends the hill.*

QUICK DISSOLVE TO EXT: THE HILL—DUSK

THOMAS *reaches a point near the bottom of the hill when he suddenly realizes he is no longer on a bed of leaves but what sounds and feels like a wooden platform. He gasps. Suddenly, the platform begins to rise.* THOMAS *quickly jumps to the ground, crouching down to see what is going on. He can see a bright light emanating from below the platform. The "aaaaaahhhhhhing" sound continues. The bright light is an eerie orange and red, tinting the trees above.*

*Suddenly, rising out of the light and smoke is a huge head with a large mane of hair tinted red and orange by the light of the fire below. The head is fully bearded and the eyes are piercing. The huge head sits atop massive shoulders and* THOMAS

*The House of Dies Drear* 265

6 **Discussion** Would you be satisfied and reassured by this response to your questions about the meaning of these events? Why or why not?

7 **Reading Strategy** Which details in this scene reinforce Thomas's notion that Pluto is demonic?

Fine art, *Wisdom,* by Joseph Hol-ston. The composition and color scheme of this portrait are impor-tant to its overall effect. The mas-sive triangular or pyramid shape of the figure is suggestive of great physical strength. The limit-ed amount of detail and the limit-ed color scheme focus our atten-tion on the subject's face, which wears an expression of serious-ness. This expression, the direct confrontational stare, and the glasses perched on the subject's forehead all suggest command-ing intellectual powers.

You might use the following questions for discussion:
1. How do the man's expression and gaze make you feel?
2. Compare and contrast the subject of this painting with the different sides of Pluto that you have seen.
3. If you were to create a portrait of Pluto, how would it differ from this painting?

8 **Reading Strategy** In Act I we learn that Pluto is a "pretty old man" with a "bad leg." In what ways is this description of Pluto not in keeping with his actions here?

**WISDOM**
*Joseph Holston*
*Vargas and Associates*

*can see two huge thickly muscled arms.* THOMAS *does not know it, but he is face to face with* PLUTO.

**PLUTO.** [*bellowing*] What demon walks on Pluto's house?

**THOMAS.** Aaaaiiiieeeee!!

THOMAS *leaps to his feet and begins to run, with the huge man hot on his trail. As he* *breaks through the thick underbrush, the boy falls and* PLUTO *is upon him, lifting him high into the air with one strong arm. As* THOMAS, *held high in the air, struggles to break free, the huge man laughs with a snarl.*

**PLUTO.** You little kids think you can scare ol' Pluto outa his wits with your sneakin' around, eh? Well, who's scared, now?!

8

266  *Drama*

## Grammar in Action

One of the ways writers achieve variety in sentence structure is by using **participial phrases.** A participial phrase begins with the basic form of the verb with an *-ing* or an *-ed* ending and includes all the words immediately related to it. Used as an adjective that modifies a noun or a pronoun, it adds further detail to the main part of the sentence. Participial phrases are used to combine ideas in a sentence, particularly when events occur at the same time. Notice how choppy and repetitive the following sentences are:

Sheila and Walter turn and are greeted by the huge specter of Pluto.
Pluto stood by the damaged screen door. His huge frame blotted out the night.

In contrast, the following sentence from the screenplay combines the three simultaneous actions into one sentence by using two participial phrases:

Sheila and Walter turn and are greeted by the huge specter of Pluto, *standing by the damaged screen door,* his huge frame *blotting out the night.*

Who's scared now?! You wanna see Pluto's hole in the ground? I'm gonna give you a real close look!

**THOMAS.** No! No! You the Devil! The Devilllll!!!!

PLUTO *laughs uproariously, which frightens* THOMAS *even more.* PLUTO *drapes a huge arm around the boy and holds him close as he attempts to carry him back.* THOMAS *quickly gives him an elbow to the solar plexus[2]—when he hears the loud grunt and feels himself dropped to the ground, he scrambles to his feet and flees toward home. Behind him he can hear the loud breathing and heavy footsteps of* PLUTO *gaining on him. Half-screaming and half-crying, he runs as hard and as fast as he can, moving ever closer to his home.*

CUT TO INT: THE KITCHEN—DUSK

SHEILA *has just finished preparing dinner and* KENNETH *and* WALTER *are seating themselves at the table.*

**SHEILA.** Walter, call that boy one more time, please. I don't want him missin' his meals.

**WALTER.** Relax, I'm sure he'll get here.

*Just then,* THOMAS *crashes through the rear screen door, breaking the lock, trips over the threshold, slides across the linoleum on his stomach, and crashes into the kitchen table, knocking dishes to the floor and smashing them. He lies under the table, trying to get his breath. The entire family is momentarily shocked, but Walter quickly pulls* THOMAS *to his feet and looks into the boy's face.* THOMAS, *breathing hard, says nothing, but looks wide-eyed toward the door.* KENNETH *begins crying.* SHEILA *runs to* THOMAS.

---

**2. solar plexus** (sō′ lər pleks′ əs) *n.*: The area of the belly just below the breastbone.

**WALTER.** Thomas? Thomas, speak to me. What is it?

*Suddenly,* KENNETH *screams and* THOMAS *points to the door.* SHEILA *and* WALTER *turn and are greeted by the huge specter of* PLUTO, *standing by the damaged screen door, his huge frame blotting out the night.*

## Act IV

FADE IN TO INT: THE KITCHEN—NIGHT

*The* SMALL *family stares at* PLUTO. *He looks at them a moment, then steps over the threshold in a cold but courteous manner as* SHEILA *moves forward to greet him, her hand outstretched.* WALTER *is just behind her, studying* PLUTO *intently. There is something "uncountry" about him. His manner seems too polished, even as he stands saying absolutely nothing. He is a very large man with dark brown skin framed by white hair and a beard. His large green eyes contrast sharply with the brown of his skin and the white of his hair. On his hands are a pair of new, heavy hide gloves, which he never removes while in their presence.* PLUTO *looks past* MRS. SMALL *to* WALTER. *Their eyes meet and hold.*

**PLUTO.** Mr. Small.

**WALTER.** Mr. Pluto.

*His eyes again fall on* SHEILA, *who extends her hand again.*

**SHEILA.** I'm Sheila Small.

*He shakes her hand, then retreats back to the threshold of the door, where there is the least light.* SHEILA *turns toward* THOMAS.

**SHEILA.** . . . and this is Thomas, our son.

PLUTO *lets his gaze fall on* THOMAS, *sending a shudder through the boy's entire body.*

*The House of Dies Drear* 267

**9 Reading Strategy** What is suggested by Pluto's avoiding being seen in the light?

---

The first participial phrase modifies the noun *Pluto* whereas the second modifies the noun *frame*.

**Student Activity 1.** Find five other examples of participial phrases in Acts III–V of *The House of Dies Drear*. For each example identify the participial phrase and indicate which noun or pronoun it modifies in the sentence.

**Student Activity 2.** Combine the following pairs of short sentences into a single sentence using a participial phrase:
1. a. Pluto could see that the Smalls were staring at him.
   b. He shifted his weight nervously.
2. a. Pesty wears an old-fashioned dress and high-button shoes.
   b. She rides beside Pluto in a horse-drawn buggy.

**Electronic Handbook** You may want students to review punctuation with participial phrases before they complete the Grammar in Action activities. If students have access to the Language Master 6000, have them enter the access word *participial* and press the GRAMMAR key to get information about using commas with participial phrases.

**PLUTO.** I'm sorry. . . . Guess I mistook your boy. . . . Strangers always pokin' aroun', up to no good. . . . I thought your boy was one, so I gave chase.

WALTER *moves to a different angle, trying to get a better look at* PLUTO. PLUTO *stares at him, but avoids* SMALL's *gaze whenever it appears that they will make eye contact.*

**WALTER.** I want to thank you for takin' care of things. Saved me a lot of time and energy fixin' the furniture and rooms the way you did.

**SHEILA.** Yes, it must've been a little difficult for a man your age alone.

**PLUTO.** I did just fine, Ma'am. The van came with the furniture at the start of the week, so I just took my time. Hope everything was all right.

**SHEILA.** Couldn'a been better. Thank you.

PLUTO *smiles a thank you.* WALTER *moves a little closer to* PLUTO. PLUTO *steps further back into the darkness, so that he is almost outside the house. He stands in the door-way clenching and unclenching his gloved hands, nervously. Suddenly,* WALTER *changes the subject, catching* PLUTO *totally off guard.*

**WALTER.** How're those horses of yours doin'? The black and the bay?

*The question startles* PLUTO. THOMAS *and* SHEILA *are also surprised when they hear the question.*

**THOMAS.** [*thinking of* PESTY *and* MAC *and the black horse*] Horses?

WALTER *gives him a stare and* THOMAS *again falls silent.*

**PLUTO.** Uh . . . er . . . they're fine. I'm work-in' on their shoes.

WALTER *takes a step toward* PLUTO. PLUTO, *a bit agitated, begins talking fast.*

**PLUTO.** The bay's all right, but I had to hobble that black. He's got the chill, but he won't stay still. Tries to run all night to get away from it, so I got to hobble him; tie his feet to keep him from burstin' his heart wide open.

THOMAS *listens much more closely now.*

**WALTER.** That's kinda odd, isn't it, Mr. Plu-to? I mean, the black horse havin' simple fever like that? That's a disease I thought peculiar only to horses with lighter coats, like grays or whites.

PLUTO *tightens his jaw a little nervously.*

**PLUTO.** [*evasive*] Yea, well. . . .

*Now he can see that the eyes of the entire* SMALL *family are on him and he shifts his weight nervously.*

**PLUTO.** . . . see, if it was just a heat problem, say like the kinda heat they have in India, it wouldna hurt the black, but see, it wasn't the heat. It was nervous shock.

WALTER *is incredulous. He succeeds in hid-ing it from everyone but* THOMAS, *who is watching him intently.*

**WALTER.** Never knew nervousness could act on a horse's heat centers, Mr. Pluto.

PLUTO *becomes quite agitated now.*

**PLUTO.** Ain't *nervousness.* I said, "nervous *shock.*" By haunted things no livin' thing oughta have the unhappiness to set eyes on.

**THOMAS.** [*whispering*] Papa, ghosts! He's talkin' 'bout ghosts!

*A stern glare from* WALTER *silences* THOMAS. *When the boy looks toward* PLUTO, *he sees a faint trace of amusement cross the old man's face, then fade away.* WALTER *does not notice it.*

**WALTER.** Thomas, here, told my wife 'bout meetin' two children, one of 'em a girl named Pesty, who was ridin' a black horse. Since she said she was your helper, I got the impression the horse belonged to you. And that horse had no limp. It was in good health.

*There is a long silence as* PLUTO *studies the entire family and they, him. Everyone in the room is aware that* WALTER *is trying to trap* PLUTO *in a lie, but* PLUTO *maintains his composure, seeming not to even consider that* MR. SMALL *had raised the possibility he might be lying.*

**PLUTO.** [*fondly*] Pesty . . . yes . . . she can do more with a wild animal than any child her age ought to be able to do with anything.

**WALTER.** [*becoming angry*] You mean to say a young girl like that could unhobble a horse—a *full-grown* quarter horse[3] suffering from simple fever?

PLUTO *studies him a moment.*

**PLUTO.** No. I mean to say Pesty can ride that black anytime. Anytime at all, so long as it's day. But once it gets night, that horse gets the fever of nervous shock. So I haveta hobble him so he won't burst his heart with runnin'.

WALTER *comes as close to* PLUTO *as he dares.* PLUTO *stands his ground, clenching and unclenching his fists.* WALTER *studies the man, seeming to look for something.*

**WALTER.** What you say makes no sense, atall!

**PLUTO.** [*angrily*] Sense?! [*then, much more sadly*] Sense. . . .

*His eyes fall on* SHEILA *and the boys. A gentleness comes over his face, then that look of amusement. His eyes drift upward toward the ceiling, and he speaks in a kind*

---

**3. quarter horse:** A lightweight, muscular horse, usually of a dark color, known for its quick reactions.

of chant that sounds old and worn, like history.*

**PLUTO.** When hoot owl screeching,
Westward flies,
Gauge the sun . . .
Look to Dies,
And *run.* . . .

MR. SMALL *steps forward, but now the old man is backing out the door, away from the kitchen light and into the darkness outside. His footsteps are not heard on the veranda. The darkness seems to have engulfed him. He is gone. There is a pause before* THOMAS *speaks.*

**THOMAS.** Papa, I couldn't even hear his footsteps. It's like he just disappeared. Poof! Jus' like that.

**WALTER.** Thomas, you know that's impossible. I taught you much better than that.

**THOMAS.** Yes, sir.

**SHEILA.** Well . . . he seems nice enough, but he's so *strange.*

**WALTER.** Yes, a little too strange. India! India! Now, whoever heard of anything so ridiculous!

**SHEILA.** I guess he didn't realize we come from farm country, too. Must've thought we were from the city.

**WALTER.** There's somethin' about that man that's not right. I just can't figure it, but somethin's not right.

**SHEILA.** Well, you try and figure it out while I get Kenneth ready for bed.

**KENNETH.** Aw, Mama, I'm not sleepy.

**SHEILA.** I don't want to hear it, Kenneth. Upstairs, right now, and Thomas, you hit the sack in one half hour. We have to get up early if we're going to get to church tomorrow. One half hour, young man.

*The House of Dies Drear* 269

**12 Discussion** Why is Walter trying to catch Pluto in a lie? What does he think Pluto is lying about?

**13 Discussion** Why does Pluto recite this poem?

**14 Discussion** What does Walter mean when he says that Pluto is tied to the land? How is Pluto "caught between the past and the present"?

**THOMAS.** Yes, Ma'am.

KENNETH *whines a bit, but* SHEILA *ushers him out.* WALTER *begins repairing the broken door hinges made unserviceable when* THOMAS *crashed through the door.*

**WALTER.** I'll just have to fix it so it'll hold till I can get into town and buy a new lock . . . hmph . . . maybe two or *three* locks, judgin' from the goin's on around here.

**THOMAS.** That sure was a scary little poem he recited. An' all that talk about his horse seein' things too awful to think about.

**WALTER.** An' that's all it was, too. Talk!

**THOMAS.** Him comin' up outa the ground the way he did, just the way Pesty said he would; an' talkin' the way he does, makes me a little scared of him, Papa.

**WALTER.** It's all right, Thomas. But keep in mind that he's just a quaint ol' man. He's no one to be scared of.

**THOMAS.** Papa, how come he kept his gloves on?

**WALTER.** I guess he did it 'cause he mighta burned his hand, or somethin' an' didn't want us to see the wound.

**THOMAS.** Back when we was ridin' in the car . . .

SHEILA *enters the room.*

**SHEILA.** [*correcting*] When we *were* riding in the car. . . .

**THOMAS.** Yes, ma'am . . . well, anyway, Papa, you said he had a limp, and I didn't see him limping.

**WALTER.** To tell you the truth, I didn't even notice. Maybe his leg felt better, or somethin', I don't know. But I do know he has a limp.

**SHEILA.** He seemed a little sad . . . lonely, even.

**WALTER.** Well, that old man is history. He's as tied to this land as those slaves were in the days of Dies Drear, and he chooses to stay here, caught between the past and the present.

**THOMAS.** But why, Papa? Why?

WALTER *says nothing as he stands at the screen door peering out into the night.* THOMAS *moves beside his father and stares out into the darkness. In the distance we can hear the baleful howling of a dog.* SHEILA *shivers and moves near* WALTER *and* THOMAS.

DISSOLVE TO INT: THOMAS AND KENNETH'S BEDROOM—NIGHT

KENNETH *lies in bed asleep, but* THOMAS *is wide awake in his bed staring at the ceiling. After a moment, some shadows appear on the ceiling.* THOMAS *rises and goes to check the huge closets in the room. No one is hiding there. He shudders a bit. The shadows seem to come from trees outside.* THOMAS *takes his pillow, blanket, and sheet and crosses to* KENNETH.

**THOMAS.** Kenneth, I'm goin' downstairs to the parlor. That way, if anybody tries to sneak into the house I'll see them an' I can run upstairs an' warn the family. Okay?

KENNETH *does not answer. The boy is sound asleep and breathing very heavily. He turns toward the wall at the sound of* THOMAS's *voice.* THOMAS *goes out of the bedroom.*

CUT TO INT: UPSTAIRS HALLWAY—NIGHT

THOMAS *moves from his bedroom and down a flight of stairs.*

CUT TO INT: DOWNSTAIRS HALLWAY—NIGHT

*A dim light has been left on in the hall and*

it illuminates THOMAS's way. At the entrance to the parlor, just beyond the oak door, is a large and ornate mirror. THOMAS poses in front of the mirror, studying his grave demeanor, and silently praising himself for his courageous bearing. He strikes a few brave poses. He moves from the mirror, through the oak door, and into the parlor.

CUT TO INT: THE PARLOR—NIGHT

Once inside, THOMAS makes his way to the sofa. He makes his bed. As he stares through the large bay windows into the night, his eyes become heavy. He lies down, and soon is sound asleep. In the distance we can hear water dripping in the kitchen, but other than that there is no sound. The camera dollies from THOMAS across the parlor to the entrance and through the door into the hall.

CUT TO INT: THE HALL—NIGHT

*Camera moves from the oak door to the mirror. The mirror opens silently and a shadowy, shrouded figure emerges. The mirror closes soundlessly behind it. The figure moves like a cat in the darkness and ascends the stairs.*

**15**

CUT TO INT: TOP OF THE STAIRS—NIGHT

**THE BACK ROOMS**
*Gilbert Fletcher*
*Collection of Joyce Johnson*

**15 Discussion** This is the second appearance of a shadowy figure. Do you think the two incidents are related? Why or why not?

## Humanities Note

Fine art, *The Back Rooms,* by Gilbert Fletcher. African American artist and illustrator Gilbert Fletcher was born in 1948 in New Orleans, Louisiana. He left his hometown in 1970 to pursue his career in New York. By 1977 he gained notice for his illustrations for a series of children's books in which the characters are of different races. Fletcher now holds the position of art director for *Library Journal* magazine, in which his reviews and articles frequently appear.

Fletcher's painting *The Back Rooms* is provocative in both its subject and title. Despite the emptiness of the room, there is the suggestion of a presence of someone or something in it. The partially opened door at the back of the room makes the viewer wonder who or what is behind it. The widely opened door on the right poses the same question. The dramatic lighting suggests an almost supernatural presence —it seems to emanate from within the back room as well as come from a source in front. Fletcher's ability to create a mysteriously charged atmosphere in a painting has added to his success as an artist.

You might use the following questions for discussion:
1. In what ways does this painting capture the atmosphere of *The House of Dies Drear?*
2. What do you think Thomas would see in this painting? Why?

At the top of the stairs, the figure pauses and studies the hall and bedrooms that lie before it. Now it moves to the boys' bedroom and enters.

CUT TO INT: BOYS' BEDROOM—NIGHT

The shape moves to where KENNETH lies asleep. Light from the moon outside shines through the windows, and we can see that the shape holds some metallic things in its hand. Turning, it exits the room, still holding the sharp objects.

CUT TO INT: UPSTAIRS HALLWAY—NIGHT

The figure moves across the hallway, then turns again and heads silently back down the stairs.

CUT TO INT: THE PARLOR—NIGHT

The figure comes into the parlor and creeps up to THOMAS. The boy turns in his sleep and the shadow moves away.

CUT TO INT: DOWNSTAIRS HALLWAY—NIGHT

The figure comes back to the mirror, listens intently, opens the mirror, and disappears behind it. The mirror closes.

CUT TO INT: THE PARLOR—NIGHT

Suddenly, THOMAS awakes with a start. He looks about, anxious and confused, but all he can hear is the water dripping in the kitchen, and all he can see outside is the misty darkness. He lies back down, his eyes wide and searching.

BLACKOUT

## Act V

FADE INTO INT: THE PARLOR—DAY

The early morning sun breaks through the

windows and falls on THOMAS's face, forcing him to wake involuntarily.

He sits up, rubs his eyes, and yawns. He squints into the sun then stands, stretching once more. He notices fresh underwear and his new Sunday suit lying across the foot of the couch. A note from his mother is pinned to the dress shirt. It reads, "You are to wear these clothes to church today." THOMAS smiles, gathers up the shirt, suit, and his shoes, and wanders toward the stairs leading to the second floor.

CUT TO INT: THE STAIRS—DAY

As he looks up the stairs, he can see his family, dressed for church, at the top of the landing. They seem to be studying some things in WALTER's hand very closely. From the bottom of the stairs, they appear to be metallic. WALTER is sitting on the top step with SHEILA next to him and KENNETH stands behind them. THOMAS climbs the stairs.

**THOMAS.** Morning.

The family is so engrossed in what they are doing that they can only mumble a reply. THOMAS finally joins them.

**THOMAS.** Say, what's those?

**SHEILA.** Oh, this chile's English is so bad. What are those?

**WALTER.** They're triangles, son.

WALTER places three metal triangles on the floor. THOMAS's eyes grow wide with curiosity and amazement.

**SHEILA.** Each one exactly alike. See here, the two legs that make up the right angles on each of them are made of wood.

**WALTER.** A hard wood, like oak. The surface between the legs looks like tin.

**SHEILA.** What's it all mean?

**WALTER.** We'll find out in a minute.

272  Drama

WALTER *begins to fit the triangles together, trying to see if he can find a pattern.*

**WALTER.** If this is supposed to be a square, then there's one triangle missing. Why? Where is it?

**SHEILA.** Walter, look . . .

SHEILA *traces her finger along the edges of a wooden area where the triangles are joined together.*

**SHEILA.** . . . see, it's a cross.

**16** **WALTER.** A Greek cross[4] . . . but, why?

**SHEILA.** One thing's certain, Walter. If there *is* to be a fourth triangle, it'll turn up . . . the same way as these three. But I hope it doesn't.

**THOMAS.** How'd these turn up, Mama?

**SHEILA.** We found them stuck in the door frames of our bedrooms when we got up this morning.

**THOMAS.** What? Then that means . . .

**SHEILA.** [*tense*] It means someone slipped in to this house last night while we were asleep.

**THOMAS.** But all the doors were locked, Mama.

**WALTER.** We know.

*They all look at one another.*

**17** **THOMAS.** [*quietly*] Old Pluto's second warning.

**WALTER.** Thomas . . .

**THOMAS.** Papa, doncha see? First was the way he fixed the furniture downstairs in the parlor, so it was all pointin' out toward those big bay windows. Telling us to go! To get out! Now this!

---

**4. Greek cross:** A cross with four equal arms at right angles.

**WALTER.** Boy, you lettin' your imagination get the best of you.

**THOMAS.** Papa, Old Man Pluto means for us to run from here. Run, while there's still time.

**KENNETH.** [*frightened*] Noooooooooooooo!

KENNETH *flees into his bedroom and slams the door behind him.*

**SHEILA.** Now you've gone an' done it.

*She gets up and runs after* KENNETH. WALTER *looks at his son.*

**WALTER.** Thomas?

**THOMAS.** Sir?

**WALTER.** Can I trust you with somethin' and have you keep quiet about it? I don't want your mother to haveta worry.

*A chill runs down* THOMAS*'s spine.*

**THOMAS.** You can trust me, Papa.

**WALTER.** Good. All these events prob'ly don't mean much at all. But then again, maybe they do. It looks like someone really is trying to drive us out. Things get worse, we may haveta call the police. **18**

**THOMAS.** The police—?!

**WALTER.** Sssshh! You an' me gon' set up watch. Midnight to five A.M. I'll take three hours, and you take the two from midnight to two A.M.

**THOMAS.** I can stay awake the three hours, Papa. I'm strong. I can do it.

**WALTER.** If I can figure things out soon enough, we may not have to do anything at all.

**SHEILA.** [OC] Hey, you two ready for church?

WALTER *gathers up the triangles and gets to his feet. He walks down the stairs as*

*The House of Dies Drear* 273

**16** **Clarification** Explain to students that the Greek cross, also called Saint George's cross, is the shape used on the flag of Great Britain. It differs from the Calvary, or Christian cross, in that it forms four equal triangles.

**17** **Reading Strategy** Why does Thomas interpret the appearance of the triangles as a warning? What do you suppose they are used for?

**18** **Discussion** Who do you think is trying to drive out the Smalls? Why?

**19 Critical Thinking and Reading**
How does Pluto's old-fashioned appearance in this scene reinforce the thematic association of Pluto with history?

## Humanities Note

Fine art, *Attending Church,* 1989, by Arthur Dawson. Dawson was born in 1963 in Wakulla, Florida. He is a self-taught painter and the son of a minister. Dawson claims that *Attending Church,* like much of his work, is an "extension of [his] experiences growing up . . . [which] many can relate to, no matter what their ethnic background."

You might use the following questions for discussion:
1. In what ways does this painting capture the mood of the scene outside the church in *The House of Dies Drear?*
2. How does this painting reveal the sense of community that going to a house of worship together creates?
3. Would the Darrows be out of place in this painting? Why or why not?

THOMAS *watches him. A shiver comes over* THOMAS *as he gazes about the house.*

**THOMAS.** Old house, I won't let you or that old man scare us away. We'll beatcha. You can count on that.

DISSOLVE TO EXT: MT. CALVARY CHURCH—DAY

*A white frame structure, one story tall and about one hundred years old. Parishioners, dressed in their Sunday finery, file inside as the* SMALLS *drive up in their car. The family gets out of the car and is walking toward the church when* THOMAS *spies something.*

**THOMAS.** Papa, look!

*The family looks in the direction* THOMAS *points. Coming up the road toward the church is a nineteenth-century vintage buggy drawn by two horses—one black and one bay. The black horse is the one on which* PESTY *rode earlier.* PLUTO, *wearing an old stovepipe hat[5] and a huge, though worn, black cape, drives the horses. He also wears a white shirt and a black string tie.* PESTY *rides beside him, wearing a pink tulle[6] dress and a blue polka-dot bonnet.*

**5. stovepipe hat:** A man's tall silk hat.
**6. tulle** (tool) *n.*: A thin, fine netting of silk or other fabric.

ATTENDING CHURCH, 1989
*Arthur Dawson*
Courtesy of the Artist

*Below pink stockings she wears white, high-button shoes. Unlike* PLUTO, *who is an exact replica of a nineteenth-century man,* PESTY *has accented her attire with some concessions to twentieth-century tastes, so that her combined costume has a unique other-worldly look to it.*

**THOMAS.** Mama, Papa, those horses—

**WALTER.** I know, son. I know. . . .

SHEILA *draws* KENNETH *close to her as the buggy comes near.* PLUTO *looks different. He is cheerful enough, but looks stooped and older.*

**WALTER.** [*in a low voice*] Where'd he put his gloves? I thought sure he had burned his hands.

**SHEILA.** [*to* WALTER] Those clothes! A bonnet, no less. Where'd she find *that*?

*The buggy comes to a halt. The* SMALL *family approaches the buggy. They are tense.* PLUTO *smiles broadly.*

**PLUTO.** Morning, folks!

*The pleasant manner catches the* SMALL *family totally by surprise.*

**WALTER.** [*quietly*] Good mornin', Mr. Pluto.

**PLUTO.** Nice to see you all out this fine Sunday.

**SHEILA.** [*pointedly*] And we're glad to be here so you could see us, Mr. Pluto.

**PLUTO.** That so? I hope you all slept well last night?

THOMAS *studies the old man closely. There seems to be no sinister intent in his voice. The boy turns his gaze to his father to measure his reply.*

**WALTER.** Yep. Slept just fine.

**PLUTO.** Well, y'all enjoy. Hear?

PLUTO *starts up the team.* PESTY *waves to* THOMAS.

**PESTY.** [*teasingly*] Hi, Thomas Small, the new boy. How ya like my new dress?

**THOMAS.** It's nice. Where'd ya get it?

**PESTY.** Oh, I got it . . .

*Her answer is drowned out in the sound of the buggy and horses hurrying off to park around the rear entrance of the church.*

**SHEILA.** Now, that has to be just about the most unusual sight that I've seen in a long time.

**WALTER.** [*half to himself*] Like a vision straight out of the time of Dies Drear himself.

**THOMAS.** Say what, Papa?

**WALTER.** Oh . . . uh . . . nothin'. C'mon, let's get inside.

*The* SMALL *family goes into the church.*

LAP DISSOLVE TO INT: THE CHURCH—DAY

*The* PASTOR, *flanked by* TWO YOUNG PASTORS, *sits on the church platform. In back of him is the* CHOIR. *The lead singer is* PESTY. *She has a voice like an angel and is singing the gospel hymn "There Must Be a God Somewhere."* THOMAS *is shocked to see* PESTY *singing, but even more surprised to see* MAC *playing the organ, and playing it well.*

**PESTY.** [*singing*] "Over my head, I hear
  music in the air
Up above my head, I see trouble in the air
I know
There must be a God somewhere . . ."

*As the hymn continues,* THOMAS *begins to study the faces of the congregation. The faces seem gentle enough; average, just like in North Carolina. The boy stiffens. His eyes have fallen upon those of old* PLUTO.

**20** **Reading Strategy** Contrast Pluto's physical appearance and behavior on Sunday morning with his appearance and behavior on Saturday night. What do you think caused the change?

*The House of Dies Drear* 275

21 **Reading Strategy** To whom are the Darrows referring here? Why might they be angry that the Smalls are living in the Dies Drear house?

22 **Reading Strategy** What do you predict the Darrows might try to do to the Smalls?

**Reader's Response** Do you think Thomas is foolish to think that the house of Dies Drear is haunted? Why or why not?

**Thematic Response** If you were Thomas, how would you go about meeting the challenge of solving the mystery of the Dies Drear house?

CUT TO INT: THE CHURCH—DAY.
CLOSE-UP ON PLUTO

PLUTO *sits staring at the* SMALL *family, then turns away.*

CUT TO INT: THE CHURCH—DAY.
CLOSE-UP ON THOMAS

THOMAS *swallows hard, then looks elsewhere as* PESTY's *singing continues.*

CUT TO INT: THE CHURCH—THOMAS'S POV. FOUR-SHOT—THE DARROWS—DAY

*Four huge men with caramel-colored skin and scowls on their faces sit in a pew toward the rear. They stare with hatred in their eyes at* THOMAS *and his family. They are* RIVER LEWIS, *the father, in his early sixties;* WILBUR, *the eldest son, about the same age as* WALTER SMALL; RIVER ROSS, *about a year younger; and* RUSSELL, *in his late twenties.*

CUT TO INT: THE CHURCH—DAY.
TWO-SHOT—THOMAS AND WALTER

**WALTER.** Thomas, turn around.

**THOMAS.** But, Papa . . .

**WALTER.** I know. I saw them.

THOMAS *turns around. He can still see* PLUTO *staring and he can feel the eyes of the* DARROWS.

**PESTY.** [*singing*] "I know there must be a God somewhere . . ."

DISSOLVE TO EXT: CHURCHYARD—DAY

*The* SMALLS *walk toward their car.*

**THOMAS.** One of them was that man on the road, Papa.

**WALTER.** Shhh. Their name's Darrow. The pastor told me about them.

**THOMAS.** They're Mac's people?

*276   Drama*

**SHEILA.** It looks that way, Thomas.

**THOMAS.** Why were they starin' at us so hard?

*The* SMALLS *get into their car and ride away.*

CUT TO EXT: THE CHURCHYARD—THOMAS'S POV—DAY

*The car passes near a large tree in front of the church. The* DARROWS, *now including* MAC, *still in his choir robes, move around in front of the tree and watch the disappearing car.*

**RIVER LEWIS.** So that's them, huh?

**MAC.** Yes, Daddy. They're nice folks, too.

**RIVER LEWIS.** I ain't asked you that.

**WILBUR.** Whatcha think, Daddy?

**RIVER LEWIS.** They prob'ly in with that old fool. That's prob'ly how they got that house.

**RIVER ROSS.** What we gon' do?

**RIVER LEWIS.** Never you mind. I'm gonna handle that end of it personally. Mac, whatchu found out from Pesty 'bout old Pluto?

**MAC.** Daddy, you know she won't tell me a thing. Never has. She so closed-mouth about it all.

**RIVER LEWIS.** Well, you just keep your eye on her. Hear?

**MAC.** Daddy, I don't like this spyin' on my own sister, an' besides, those folks down there seem nice enough. They even got a boy my age and—

RIVER LEWIS *slaps him.*

**RIVER LEWIS.** Just do like I tells ya, an' stop runnin' off at the mouth. As for that family there, I'll make them sorry they ever set foot in the House of Dies Drear.

BLACKOUT

## Closure and Extension

### ANSWERS TO RESPONDING TO THE SELECTION
*Your Response*

1. Answers will differ. Students who feel that Pluto is evil may cite his curious behavior and the fact that people believe him to be a demon. Students who feel that Pluto is not evil may cite his cordiality at church and the fact that Pesty is not afraid of him.

2. Answers will differ. Students who believe the figure to be a ghost may cite the many references to ghosts and haunting in the story. Students who believe the figure to be a person may cite the fact that the figure opens and closes the mirror, whereas a ghost would presumably be able to pass right through it.

*Recalling*

3. No one knows what became of one of the slaves who was captured near the time when Dies Drear was killed, from which Thomas infers that the slave might be haunting the house.

4. Pluto's first "warning" was to arrange the furniture so that it faced the windows. The second was the appearance of the triangles in the door frames.

*Interpreting*

5. Suggested Response: Pluto seems to be aware that Walter notices something different about

## RESPONDING TO THE SELECTION

### Your Response

1. Do you think that Pluto is evil? Give reasons for your answer.
2. Is the shrouded figure that emerges from the mirror a ghost or a person dressed up as a ghost? Explain.

### Recalling

3. What fact about Dies Drear's death supports Thomas's belief that the house is haunted?
4. What, according to Thomas, are Pluto's two warnings to the Smalls? What does Thomas think Pluto's warnings are telling them?

### Interpreting

5. When Pluto first meets the Smalls, why does he move out of the light and away from Walter? What does Walter's behavior toward Pluto indicate?
6. What do you think is the meaning of the poem that Pluto recites?
7. How do you know that the Darrows are probably not on friendly terms with Pluto?
8. Why do you think that River Lewis resents the Smalls?

### Applying

9. Do you agree with Walter that "Everything has a logical explanation"? Give reasons for your answer.

## ANALYZING LITERATURE

### Understanding Suspense

**Suspense** is the quality in a film that keeps you on the edge of your seat and makes you curious about the outcome. Through the screenwriter's use of **foreshadowing**, you get hints about what is going to happen. You don't know when or how the foreshadowed event will take place, however, until you see the end of the film.

Find details in Acts I and II that foreshadow the following events in Acts III–V, and explain your choices.

1. Pluto's fiery emergence from under the platform (Act III)
2. The shadowy figure coming through the mirror (Act IV)

## CRITICAL THINKING AND READING

### Appreciating Atmosphere

The atmosphere of *The House of Dies Drear* is one of eeriness and mystery. The screenwriter creates this atmosphere by using details that affect our senses of sight and hearing.

Explain how the sights and sounds on pages 265–266 suggest an atmosphere of mystery and fear.

## THINKING AND WRITING

### Writing a Report

Imagine that you are a detective called in to investigate the mysterious events at the Dies Drear house. Write a report to your superior summarizing what you have learned and explaining how you will go about solving the mystery. Remember that the tone of the report should be objective and businesslike. Also, you might want to include drawings and diagrams to illustrate your points. Revise to make your report as clear and crisp as possible. Then share your report with the class.

## LEARNING OPTION

**Cross-curricular Connection.** With several classmates, choose two scenes from the screenplay and select pieces of music to serve as background for them. Try to find musical pieces that express the mood of each scene. Notice how effective music can be in establishing mood and atmosphere. You may wish to play the musical selections for your class as you read your scenes aloud.

*The House of Dies Drear* 277

window foreshadow the scene in which a figure emerges from behind the mirror.

## Preparation

**Literary Focus** Point out to students that the setting of *The House of Dies Drear* is not an incidental element of the story. It plays an active role, providing the focus of and the background for the story's action. The setting —the house itself—also is largely responsible for the atmosphere, tone, and mood of the screenplay. Ask students to comment on the role that setting has played in Acts I–V. Could this story have taken place anywhere, or is the plot dependent on the location?

**Prereading Focus** Before students begin filling in their charts, have them discuss the traits of each character in the screenplay. Remind students that casting a film or a play involves matching not only the physical characteristics of the actors with those of the character roles, but matching the character traits as well.

**Vocabulary** Ask students to write a sentence for each vocabulary word that provides a hint, or a context clue, to its meaning.

▨ **Electronic Handbook**
Suggest that students use the Language Master 6000 to find synonyms with different connotations for *guffaw*. They can then write sentences illustrating the range of meaning for such verbs as *titter, giggle, chuckle, cackle,* and *snicker.*

# GUIDE FOR READING

## The House of Dies Drear, Acts VI and VII

### Setting

**Setting** is the time and place of a screenplay's action. In *The House of Dies Drear*, the house itself is a vital part of the setting. Having served as an Underground Railroad "station," where fleeing slaves could find food, shelter, directions, and a safe hiding place, the house is filled with history. With its tunnels and secret passageways, it is also filled with mystery, especially from the point of view of an imaginative boy. The sequence of events is so bound up with the house that the story could not take place anywhere else.

### Focus

Think about the characters in the story that you've met so far. If you were casting the movie, which actors would you like to see play the different characters? With your classmates brainstorm to list actors who would be right for each part. Next to each choice, write the traits that qualify the person for the role. Use a chart similar to the one that follows. When you are finished, read the concluding acts of *The House of Dies Drear.*

| Character | Actor | Traits |
|---|---|---|
|  |  |  |

### Vocabulary

Knowing the following words will help you as you read Acts VI and VII of *The House of Dies Drear.*

**douses** (dous′ iz) *v.*: Puts out; extinguishes (p. 284)
**menacing** (men′ əs iŋ) *adj.*: Threatening (p. 288)
**gossamer** (gäs′ ə mər) *adj.*: Delicate, light, or flimsy (p. 292)
**connote** (kə nōt′) *v.*: Suggest or imply (p. 292)
**guffaws** (gu fôz′) *n.*: Hearty bursts of laughter (p. 294)
**stealthily** (stel′ thə lē) *adv.*: In a secretive manner (p. 296)
**apparition** (ap′ ə rish′ ən) *n.*: Ghostly figure (p. 296)
**defilers** (dē fīl′ ərz) *n.*: Those who corrupt or make unclean (p. 296)

*278  Drama*

## Objectives

1 To understand the role of setting in this screenplay
2 To analyze the effect of setting on plot
3 To write a story
4 To express individual interests and abilities through optional activities

## Support Material

**Teaching Portfolio**
Teacher Backup, p. 371
Grammar in Action Worksheet, *Using Prepositions and Prepositional Phrases,* p. 375
Usage and Mechanics Worksheet, p. 377
Vocabulary Check, p. 378
Analyzing Literature Worksheet, *Understanding Setting,* p. 379

Critical Thinking and Reading Worksheet, *Understanding Setting and Plot,* p. 380
Selection Test, p. 381

**Prentice Hall Literature Writing Studio**

# Act VI

FADE INTO EXT: THE COLLEGE CAMPUS—DAY

*The main campus is a quadrangle¹ about one quarter of a mile long, bordered on all sides by a combination of new and old buildings and oak trees. At the eastern end of the quadrangle is the oldest and tallest building on the campus, a six-story structure. It is characterized by six towers, each with a turret² at the top. The* SMALL *family's car enters the campus and comes to a halt in front of the main building. The family gets out.*

**SHEILA.** Looks kinda like North Carolina A & T, back home, Walter.

**WALTER.** Hmm . . . yea . . . kind of. This is the main building. My office is in that left tower, right up there.

KENNETH *shades his eyes from the sun and looks upward.*

**KENNETH.** Oooo, that's way up there.

WALTER *looks at* THOMAS *a moment.* THOMAS *is looking at the ground, kicking the dirt with his shoe.*

**WALTER.** Thomas, why don't you come on upstairs an' let me show you my office.

**THOMAS.** [*shrugging*] I don't care.

**WALTER.** Sheila, how 'bout you an' Kenneth?

**SHEILA.** Is there an elevator?

**WALTER.** It's bein' repaired. We'll haveta walk.

**SHEILA.** No, thank you. Kenneth and I'll stay

---

1. **quadrangle** (kwä′ draŋ′ gəl) *n.*: An area, as of a college campus, surrounded on its four sides by buildings.
2. **turret** (tɜr′ it) *n.*: A small tower on top of a larger tower.

---

down here and enjoy the shade of one of these trees.

**WALTER.** Okay. But I'll getcha up there soon.

**SHEILA.** Only when they got that elevator workin', honey.

THOMAS *and* WALTER *walk to the entrance of the building.* THOMAS *has his head bowed and his hands thrust deeply into his pockets.* WALTER *puts his arm around his son.*

CUT TO INT: THE OFFICE—DAY

WALTER'S *office is a cramped circular space lit by an overhead fluorescent light. In the background are filing cabinets, a typewriter, a bookshelf crammed with books, and various papers scattered about. The office looks well used, even though* WALTER *has only been in it two days.* WALTER *opens the door with a key.*

**WALTER.** This is a pretty cool place in the summer. The ivy covers up the windows, keeping the moisture close and the sunlight out. But come winter I expect I'll freeze.

**THOMAS.** Papa, you mean there's no heat?

**WALTER.** Not in these towers.

**THOMAS.** Shoot, these northern colleges are somethin'! No heat.

**WALTER.** Whatchu haveta understand, son, is that this buildin' is history. It's much the same as it was a hundred years ago. Nothin' much changes in places like these. They give a man time to think and study.　｜1

**THOMAS.** Aw, Papa, sometimes I wish history would just die! How come you always haveta have history clutter up everything?! How is it you always know to go someplace where you don't ever haveta change?　｜2

THOMAS *goes and slumps down into a chair.* WALTER *looks at him.*

*The House of Dies Drear* 279

## Presentation

**Motivation/Prior Knowledge**
Robert Louis Stevenson makes clear the power of atmospheric setting in the following passage: "There is a fitness in events and places. One place suggests work, another idleness, a third early rising and long rambles in the dew. The effect of night, of any flowing water, of lighted cities, of the peep of day, of ships, of the open ocean, calls up in the mind an army of anonymous desires and pleasures. . . . Some places speak distinctly. Certain dank gardens cry aloud for a murder; certain old houses demand to be haunted; certain coasts are set apart for shipwreck." Ask students to comment on how the screenwriter has used setting and atmosphere in Acts I–V to suggest the plot of the story.

**Purpose-Setting Question** How does the setting affect Thomas and his choice of action?

**1 Critical Thinking and Reading** In what way does the description of Walter's office reinforce the development of his character?

**2 Discussion** Do you agree with Thomas that history just clutters up everything? Explain.

**Master Teacher Note** Explain to students that historically there were three requirements for dramatic unity: unity of action (every incident in a play should be logically connected to those before and after it); unity of time (all the incidents must occur within, or almost within, the time it takes to perform them); and unity of place (the incidents must take place close to one another). Ask students to comment on whether the screenwriter followed these dramatic unities.

**Thematic Focus** In what way does Thomas gain new insight about the history of his people? What does he learn during the course of the screenplay about justice and injustice?

**Making Connections** Another selection in which ghosts from the days of slavery haunt the present is the poem "Southern Mansion," by Arna Bontemps, on page 550.

For students who enjoy Virginia Hamilton's work, you might wish to recommend her novel *M. C. Higgins, the Great* in the **Prentice Hall Literature Multicultural Library.** In this novel a young boy comes to terms with his heritage and his identity.

**Discussion** What multiple purposes does this scene in Walter's office serve?

**Speaking and Listening** Ask students to work in pairs to create a dialogue between Thomas and his father about finding the fourth triangle. Students can then perform their dialogues for their class. Have the class evaluate the dialogues for realistic tone and content.

**WALTER.** [*watches him a moment*] What is it, Thomas? What've I done that's made you so mad?

**THOMAS.** Papa, I want to go home to Great-grandmother!

**WALTER.** Oh, I see . . . you miss her a lot, don't you?

**THOMAS.** At least I knew I belonged there.

**WALTER.** I'm sorry she wouldn't come with us, Thomas. But . . . well, she has the right to end where she began.

**THOMAS.** Everything was warm and good with her. Here in this North, we ain't had but one bad time after another. That old man don't like us. Those Darrows hate us. We hardly see anybody or talk to anybody. Even that house hates us. I wanna go home! I wanna go back to Great-grandmother and North Carolina!

WALTER *comes near and puts his arms around him.*

**WALTER.** Thomas, listen to me. Trust me. There are good people here, an' we'll meet them. Just give the town time.

**THOMAS.** Yea, but will the town give *me* time?

THOMAS *rises and moves toward the door. Something catches his eye. He moves to the bookcase and bends down to get a better look.*

**THOMAS.** [*softly*] Papa? They got in here too.

THOMAS *stands up and faces* WALTER. *He is holding another triangle in his hand. It is identical to the others that were found that morning.*

CUT TO EXT: XENIA AVENUE IN YELLOW SPRINGS—DAY

*The* SMALL *family sits in a car looking toward the locksmith's store. There is a*

"*Closed on Sunday*" *sign visible. Next door is a drugstore. We can see* WALTER *inside talking to the druggist. He is pointing down the street.* WALTER *is nodding his head and looking in the direction the man is pointing. He smiles, says thank you, and rushes out. He jumps into the car.*

CUT TO INT: THE CAR—DAY

*The car speeds off;* THOMAS *and* KENNETH *are in the back seat.* KENNETH *is watching the scenery and* THOMAS *is listening to the conversation between* WALTER *and* SHEILA.

**WALTER.** He said there's a fella named Carr, who owns a gas station out here on Highway 68, who's a kind of handyman, an' he might be able to help us out with some locks for that kitchen door.

**SHEILA.** Thank heavens. I'll sleep a lot better tonight knowin' that door has a lock on it.

**THOMAS.** Better make that two or *three* locks, Papa.

**WALTER.** You said it, son. This time we'll be ready for them.

CUT TO EXT: XENIA AVENUE AND HIGHWAY 68—DAY

*The car comes to a halt at the Carr gas station. It is big, modern, and very clean.* EDGAR CARR, *a big, athletic-looking white man of about forty, approaches. He has a kind, soft face that breaks into an easy grin. His long hair is all over the place and he is starting to grow a beard, which he scratches with regularity. He wears coveralls over a white T-shirt and a wristwatch.*

**WALTER.** Afternoon. Walter Small's the name. We just moved up to the old Dies Drear place. I need some locks installed. The druggist told me you might be able to help.

**CARR.** I sure can. But I won't be able to put 'em in till Monday. Will Monday do?

**BOY THINKING**
*Oliver Johnson*
*Courtesy of the Artist*

*The House of Dies Drear* 281

Fine art, *Boy Thinking,* by Oliver Johnson. This sensitive study was rendered in ink on paper with pen and brush by African American artist Oliver B. Johnson. The boy is shown in a relaxed posture, yet his head resting on his hand gives him a pensive air. Johnson's pen-and-ink treatment of the subject captures the vulnerability of the boy and the poignancy of the moment with an immediacy that might be lost if more detail were included.

This versatile artist is known for his intuitive portraits, especially of musicians. In addition to being a successful painter and illustrator, Oliver Johnson is a celebrated jazz musician.

You might use these questions for discussion:

1. Which of Thomas Small's qualities do you see in the subject of this pen-and-ink sketch?
2. At which points in the story does Thomas's mood most resemble that of the boy in this work?

**Alternative Assessment** Have your students continue their reader's response journals, focusing on the concluding events of the story and the solution to the mysteries of the house of Dies Drear. Encourage students to respond personally to the revelations about Pluto, Mayhew, the Darrows, and the treasure of Dies Drear.

4 **Reading Strategy** What important information do the Smalls learn from Edgar Carr?

*The entire* SMALL *family is dejected at this news.*

**WALTER.** It'll haveta do, I guess.

CARR *extends his hand.*

**CARR.** By the way. The name's Edgar Carr.

WALTER *shakes his hand.* CARR *looks into the car and waves to* SHEILA *and the boys. They smile a hello.*

**WALTER.** Think you can make it *early* Monday morning?

**CARR.** [*curious, intent*] You have some trouble out there, or somethin'?

**WALTER.** No, nothin' like that. My son, here, had a little accident. That's all.

**CARR.** The old Dies Drear place, huh? Been years since anybody lived up that way, you know . . . I mean, except for old Pluto.

**WALTER.** [*evasive*] Well, I wanted a place with plenty of space for my boys, an' I thought I might do a little farmin'.

**CARR.** Real fertile land up there. I should know. My dad's farm is next to the same stream that runs on your place.

**WALTER.** [*impatient to leave*] Is that a fact?

**CARR.** [*to* THOMAS] Say, young fella, you like berries?

**THOMAS.** Sure.

**CARR.** In that case, come on out to my dad's anytime an' pick all you want. We get plenty of 'em.

WALTER *looks to* SHEILA, *tries to start the engine to ease away.*

**CARR.** Then there's the Darrow spread nearby.

WALTER *shuts off the engine.* THOMAS *leans forward. Walter gets out of the car.*

**WALTER.** Did you say Darrow?

**CARR.** Oh, you know them?

**WALTER.** Kind of.

**CARR.** Except for my dad's place, they own all the property that surrounds yours. Right mean bunch when they want to be. Keep botherin' that old Pluto somethin' awful.

**WALTER.** Pluto never said anythin' to me 'bout it.

**CARR.** Always been bad blood between old Pluto an' the Darrows. Goes back to the Darrows' grandaddy, River Swift, who died years ago. He an' old Pluto used to be friends, but they had a fallin' out. Over what, I don't know.

**WALTER.** Well, I don't expect I'll be seein' that much of the Darrows, anyway.

4

**CARR.** I reckon not. They can stay out on that farm of theirs for six, seven months at a time without folks seein' 'em. Always diggin' up trees an' puttin' 'em back.

**WALTER.** Trees?

**CARR.** Heck, an' that ain't all. When old River Swift Darrow was alive, he an' his kin moved their whole house a few feet to one side and spent a week lookin' under it for somethin', then moved it back to where it was in the first place.

EDGAR CARR *chuckles at the thought and wipes the perspiration from his face.*

**WALTER.** Thank you for the information.

**CARR.** You're welcome. Just watch yourself with them Darrows. They don't like folks hangin' around. The youngest boy, Mac, don't seem too much like 'em, though. He's about your boy's age. Maybe they're changin'.

WALTER *has gotten back in the car and has*

282 *Drama*

*started up the engine.* CARR *chuckles again and wipes away the sweat.*

**CARR.** Still in all, watch 'em close. They got somethin' in for that old Pluto. You take care.

CARR *backs away and* WALTER *drives off.* THOMAS *watches him from the back window, and smiles and waves.* CARR *waves back.*

CUT TO INT: THE CAR—DAY

**SHEILA.** I wonder what the Darrows were looking for with so much digging?

**THOMAS.** They're prob'ly people who just like to tear stuff up just to be tearing it up.

**WALTER.** I'm sure there's more to it than that, Thomas.

**SHEILA.** There must be some kind of feud going on. Why else would those Darrows keep after that poor old man so much?

**THOMAS.** And now they're after us.

**WALTER.** Is that what you think, Thomas, or what you know?

**THOMAS.** Papa, the only thing I know is that Mr. Carr is one of the best things that's happened since we got here.

THOMAS *looks out the rear window back at the quickly disappearing gas station and smiles.*

CUT TO INT: THE KITCHEN—THE HOUSE OF DIES DREAR—DUSK

*The entire family stands at the entrance of the kitchen agape at what they see.* SHEILA *screams.* THOMAS *goes to her.* KENNETH *takes hold of her dress.* SHEILA *sways and leans against* THOMAS. WALTER *walks ahead to survey a kitchen in shambles. The large sack of flour* PLUTO *brought them has been emptied all over the floor in an even layer.*

*Over the floor, water and apple juice have been poured. The whole mess has been mixed into a sticky brown paste that has been spread over the kitchen table, stove, chairs, and cabinets. The door of the refrigerator hangs open, and all of the food inside has been removed; some of it is dumped on the floor. All of the dishes have been smashed in the sink and covered with goo. Rotting food is visible everywhere.* THOMAS *steps forward.* WALTER *stops him.*

**WALTER.** No. [SHEILA *comes to his side.*] They mean to make us run. That's why they did this.

**SHEILA.** Oh, Walter—we could move into town, where it's safe. . . .

**WALTER.** Is that all we're made of? We won't be runnin'. We're better than that. This is *our* home . . . our *life.* No one is gonna *scare* us outa it, an' no one is gonna take it from us, either. I've had enough! [*He turns to* THOMAS.] Thomas, I want you to come with me. Sheila, take Kenneth upstairs, turn on the lights, and lock yourself in with him. Stay here till we get back.

CUT TO EXT: THE HOUSE—DUSK

WALTER *and* THOMAS *exit the house and begin walking up the hill in back of the house, armed with clubs and a flashlight.*

CUT TO INT: THE BOYS' BEDROOM—DUSK

*Close-up on* SHEILA *as she sits still and determined, watching over the sleeping form of her son* KENNETH. *She stares out of the window at the flashlight that signals the progress of* WALTER *and* THOMAS, *with a baseball bat resting delicately in her lap.*

CUT TO EXT: HILL BEHIND THE HOUSE OF DIES DREAR—NIGHT

*The flashlight lighting their way,* WALTER *and* THOMAS *reach the base of the hill.*

*The House of Dies Drear* 283

5 **Discussion** Do you think Thomas's conclusion is reasonable? Why or why not?

6 **Reading Strategy** Who do you think is responsible for this mess? What makes you think so?

**7 Literary Focus: Setting** What is significant about this description of the cave entrance? What effect does it create?

**WALTER.** We'll go around. I don't want to take a chance on walking on top of that platform like you did the other night.

*They move around the base of the hill from left to right. They move silently through the darkness,* WALTER *in front and* THOMAS *behind. Presently, they come to a point in the thick underbrush where a light can be discerned, glowing somewhere in the distance. It seems near.* WALTER *douses his flashlight and signals* THOMAS *to remain silent. They keep forward.* THOMAS *falls and rolls down a gully.*[3] WALTER *helps him to his feet.* THOMAS *whispers that he is all right and they move forward toward the dim light. Finally, they come to a clearing where the pale glowing light shines brightest. They can see a bed of flat rock, rectangular in shape, at the end of which is a cave. The cave mouth has heavy plank doors with sconces on either side, which contain burning torches. These torches flare violently, sending smoke and a yellow glow up into the surrounding trees.*

*In the midst of it all, pacing back and forth, is* PLUTO. *He now seems younger, healthier than before. His gloves are on again, and he smokes a cigarette. He is not aware that they are watching him.* THOMAS *watches him intently with a mixture of fear and curiosity. Suddenly, his father bursts forward from the bush and approaches* PLUTO.

**WALTER.** Hold it right there, Pluto!

PLUTO *swings around and spies* THOMAS *and* WALTER. *His face is partially shadowed because the torches are directly above him. He backs toward the cave.*

**WALTER.** Wait!

---

**3. gully** (gul′ ē) *n.*: A channel or hollow worn in the ground by running water.

*284 Drama*

PLUTO *quickly disappears into the cave in a flash.* WALTER *and* THOMAS *rush to the cave,* WALTER *taking one of the torches.*

CUT TO INT: THE CAVE—NIGHT

HARRIET TUBMAN SERIES NO. 11, 1939–40
*Jacob Lawrence*
Hampton University Museum, Hampton, Virginia

*With the torch lighting their way, they enter a dark tunnel, similar to the one in which* THOMAS *became temporarily lost. As they move forward,* THOMAS *catches up to his father, trying to get his attention.*

**THOMAS.** He's got his gloves on again an' he was smokin' a cigarette.

**WALTER.** [*a hard edge in his voice*] I know, son. I saw . . . I saw, all right.

*The House of Dies Drear* 285

## Humanities Note

Fine art, *Harriet Tubman Series, No. 11,* 1939–40, by Jacob Lawrence. Born in 1917, African American artist and educator Jacob Armstead Lawrence is recognized as one of America's most important painters. From age fifteen he studied art in Harlem workshops sponsored by the Works Progress Administration and later won a scholarship to the American Artists School.

Lawrence's art celebrates the history, struggles, and aspirations of African Americans. *Harriet Tubman Series: No.11* is one of the forty paintings produced as part of Lawrence's Harriet Tubman series. The original caption chosen by Jacob Lawrence for this painting was the actual published reward notice for the return of Tubman, an escaped slave who led other slaves to freedom via the Underground Railroad. There is no human form in this painting, only a cold and lonely stretch of dark woods beneath the stars. The night sky was important to Tubman and her courageous followers. They traveled by the light of the moon and stars, using the North Star as their guide to the land of freedom.

You might use these questions for discussion:
1. What do you think the light-colored shape sweeping across the sky represents?
2. Imagine that you were a fugitive slave traveling night after night through cold and desolate places such as the one shown in this painting. You would have no food, no shelter from the rain, no place to rest, and no place to hide. How would you feel when you got to an Underground Railroad "station" such as the house of Dies Drear?

8 **Reading Strategy** Visualize the action in this shot. What two mysteries are solved here?

9 **Reading Strategy** Why do you suppose Pluto has disappeared?

CUT TO INT: FURTHER IN THE CAVE—NIGHT

*They keep moving forward. Thirty feet inside, they come to a room that is already lit.* WALTER *puts the torch aside and they move around in the room. A forge, where horseshoes are made, is visible. There is a bed, a radio, a hot stove, food in cans, and other amenities. Another tunnel entrance can be seen. The cave is some 25 feet wide, 30 feet long, and 15 feet high. A portion of the room is carpeted, with a large worn armchair and a kitchen set for eating. There are photographs on the wall nearest the table, and many yellowed calendars. A pair of slippers is placed neatly beside the bed, and a robe is flung across it. The light in the*

8 *room comes from the forge, which has a fire burning. Bellows rest on a tree stump next to the forge.* WALTER *and* THOMAS *approach the bellows and forge.* WALTER *walks over to the bellows and operates them.* THOMAS *immediately recognizes the sound. He nods his head and a knowing smile comes across his face. It is the sound he heard before in the tunnel.*

**WALTER.** [*He looks to a wall, then upward.*] See, look.

*He points to a ladder that leads up a wall to the underside of a platform.*

**WALTER.** That's the platform you stumbled on.

**THOMAS.** He came up through it and grabbed me. He's so strong for an old man.

9 **WALTER.** Yes . . . but where is he? He didn't come out the way we came in. He's gotta be in here someplace.

WALTER *climbs the ladder and checks the platform. It is locked.*

**WALTER.** Well, he didn't go through here, that's for sure.

THOMAS *points to the other tunnel.*

**THOMAS.** How 'bout through there?

THOMAS *runs into the tunnel and disappears into the darkness.*

CUT TO INT: THE SECOND TUNNEL

*The area is pitch black, except for a small circle of light that emanates from the main cave.* THOMAS *feels his way into the tunnel, when suddenly the heads of two horses— the black and the bay—appear in the circle of light, their eyes wide with excitement at the presence of a stranger, their loud whinnies echoing through the tunnel.* THOMAS *yells, turns, and runs.*

CUT TO INT: PLUTO'S CAVE

THOMAS *rushes out of the tunnel, catching his breath, smiling sheepishly, and shaking his head.*

**THOMAS.** Just horses in there, so I figured I'd better hurry back out here. You shouldn't be alone.

**WALTER.** We'll wait for him. He's gotta come back sooner or later.

**THOMAS.** But, Mama . . .

**WALTER.** You're right—if anything happens to her or Kenneth because of—

THOMAS *has walked over to one of the walls. His attention has been drawn to a strange-looking rope. It is looped loosely around a clothes hook.*

**WALTER.** What the heck . . . ?

WALTER *gets the ladder and climbs to a point where his eye is level with the hook. Just above the hook is a small hole. The rope comes out of this hole.* WALTER *climbs down the ladder. He smiles confidently at* THOMAS, *secure that he has found a clue to* PLUTO's *mysterious disappearance. He puts*

## Grammar in Action

**Prepositions** are connecting words that clarify the relationship between a noun or a pronoun and another word in the sentence. In the following sentence, notice how the prepositions indicate where things are located and what people are doing.

Walter and Thomas walk *down* a ramp *to* a huge chamber, lit *by* torches, where Pluto sits *behind* a huge desk, which is dark and elaborately veneered *with* fine woods.

Without the prepositions we would not know where Walter and Thomas walk or where Pluto sits.

Prepositions always connect a noun, a pronoun, or a word group functioning as a noun to another word in the sentence. The noun, pronoun, or word group is called the **object of the preposition.** The preposition plus its object and any modifiers is called a **prepositional phrase.** Prepositional phrases function as adjectives modifying nouns or as adverbs modifying verbs, adjectives, or other adverbs.

the ladder back, then takes the rope and pulls it down like a bell rope. When he lets go of it, it returns to its original position. The wall begins to slide with a loud, grating sound, and in a moment, stops. Before them is a huge cavern with stalagmites[4] and stalactites[5] clearly visible from the light of the forge. They can see a slippery, wet ramp of chalk-white limestone leading downward. Camera closes on WALTER and THOMAS's faces.*

**WALTER.** My Lord in heaven! Look at it! Just *look* at it!

## Act VII

FADE IN TO INT: THE CAVE—A RAMP
LEADING TO A LARGE CAVERN—NIGHT

*WALTER and THOMAS walk down a ramp to a huge chamber, lit by torches, where PLUTO sits behind a huge desk, which is dark and elaborately veneered[6] with fine woods. The desk is decorated with seventeenth-century ornamentation of a most superior quality. It is probably French Renaissance.[7] PLUTO sits behind the desk with his profile toward WALTER and THOMAS as they approach from the ramp. He has one elbow propped on the desk with his hand under his chin, index finger extended. A brown woolen cloak covers his shoulders. He seems to await THOMAS and WALTER's arrival with a certain sense of dread. PESTY*

---

4. **stalagmites** (stə lag' mīts) *n.*: Cone-shaped mineral deposits built up on a cave floor by water dripping from above.
5. **stalactites** (stə lak' tīts) *n.*: Icicle-shaped mineral deposits that hang from the roof of a cave.
6. **veneered** (və nērd') *adj.*: Covered with a thin layer of wood of finer quality.
7. **French Renaissance** (ren'ə säns): Of a style of furniture developed in France during the Renaissance, a period dating from about 1400 to 1600.

*stands near the chair, more protective of the old man than anything else.*
CUT TO INT: THE CAVE—WALTER AND THOMAS'S POV

*The more WALTER and THOMAS survey the room, the more awestruck they become. Hanging on all sides of the enormous barrel-shaped cavern are tapestries and Persian carpets of all colors and designs. Between the rows of hanging carpets are 40-foot canoes and whole, richly painted and crafted totem poles. Here and there are Indian-crafted chests of wood, and piled atop them are blankets of similar design. There are barrels of silks and embroidered materials, some of which spill out onto the floor. There are shoes, jewelry, watches, and chains of gold. One section of one huge wall is covered with glassware. It is like a prism, ranging in colors from aqua to deep brown and black.*

**THOMAS.** Papa, what *is* all this?

**WALTER.** The treasure of Dies Drear, son.

**THOMAS.** [*bewildered*] But everything looks so new.

**WALTER.** These chambers are so far underground that the temperature remains constant. There's no such thing as dust and erosion down here. It's as though time can stand still.

**PESTY.** That's not always true, Mr. Small. Sometimes I have to go up there and do a little polishing up. Like this.

*PESTY leaves PLUTO's side and goes to a ladder. She moves it to a place near the huge stacks of glass and begins to climb. Her reflection appears in the glass a thousand times over, creating an almost dream-like vision.*

**WALTER.** Be careful!

*The House of Dies Drear* 287

10 **Discussion** Why is this a good place to end Act VI?

11 **Literary Focus: Setting** How does the setting of this hidden cavern contrast with the description of Pluto's cave?

12 **Discussion** How does the concept of time standing still relate to other themes in *The House of Dies Drear*?

---

**Student Activity 1.** Identify the prepositional phrases in the following sentences. Indicate whether each phrase functions as an adjective or an adverb, and write the word that the phrase modifies.
1. Pluto sits behind the desk with his profile toward Walter and Thomas as they approach from the ramp.
2. Pesty moves the ladder to a place near the huge stacks of glass.
3. Thomas sits on the floor looking up at the second Pluto as he removes the rest of his stage makeup from his face.

**Student Activity 2.** Write a brief descriptive paragraph about your favorite place. Provide vivid details, using prepositional phrases to indicate physical relationships between the items you are describing.

**Electronic Handbook** You may want students to review prepositions before they complete the Grammar in Action activities. If students have access to the Language Master, have them enter the access word *preposition* and press the GRAMMAR key to get information about this part of speech.

288

**13 Discussion** Why might Dies Drear have acquired the old ledgers? Why do you think Pluto wants to preserve them?

**14 Reading Strategy** Which mysteries have been solved so far? How do these solutions compare or contrast with students' earlier predictions?

PESTY *moves deftly, smiles over her shoulder.*

**PESTY.** No need to worry, Mr. Small. This is my job. I been doin' this since I was six years old.

PLUTO *turns to face* THOMAS *and* WALTER *directly. His hands are atop a set of yellowing books.* WALTER *notices these old ledgers. He looks reassuringly at* PLUTO, *then at* PESTY, *then removes one of the ledgers from beneath the old man's hands.* WALTER *studies them.*

**PLUTO.** An accountin'.

PLUTO *seems old and tired now. He is not the spry man* THOMAS *and* WALTER *chased into the cave.* THOMAS *studies* PLUTO, PESTY, *and his father closely. His eyes move quickly from one to another.*

**13** **PLUTO.** The day-by-day sale of our people. They aren't Mr. Drear's. Don't know how he come by them. But they tell a tale or two.

**THOMAS.** That's about slavery, Papa?

**WALTER.** A list of slaves bought and sold.

**PLUTO.** Y'all found us out. I kinda figgered you would sooner or later when you first came over to the house. . . . All these years no one. . . . And then Pesty. My Little Old Miss Bee.

PESTY *looks at him and smiles and he smiles back.*

**PESTY.** I followed him here one day. He didn't know. I guess I musta been about five. He was scared I'd tell my stepfather, but I never did. He and my older brothers would've come here an' cleaned Mr. Pluto out. I decided this would be my little secret. Mr. Pluto's always been kind to me.

**PLUTO.** [*to* THOMAS *and* WALTER] Had to trick you, at first. I thought you'd be like the Darrows an' try an' steal all this. . . .

*288  Drama*

**WALTER.** I don't understand.

**PLUTO.** Some nights the Darrows like to try an' pretend they're ghosts and scare ol' Pluto off the land. But they don't know, do they, Miss Bee?

PESTY *smiles, but there is a sound, very faint, off screen. She hears it and sits up alert.*

**PLUTO.** We shouldn't have fooled you, like that. Nope. It wasn't the proper thing to do. We had no right. No business.

**VOICE.** [OS] [*booming, menacing*] Then again, maybe we had every right in the world!

WALTER *stands rigidly, as does* THOMAS. *Then* WALTER *spins and turns, a look of intense anger on his face. When* THOMAS *turns, the sight before him is so astonishing he sinks to his knees in disbelief. For there is another* PLUTO, *younger, more massive, but with the same flowing beard and piercing eyes. And this one wears the new hide gloves.*

**14**

**WALTER.** I knew it! I knew there had to be two of you!

THOMAS *looks back at the old* PLUTO, *then forward at the young one. He still doesn't comprehend totally what is happening. The younger* PLUTO *begins to laugh.*

**THOMAS.** [*to the younger* PLUTO] You *are* the Devil. You can make yourself into two people! Devil! Devil! Devil!

THOMAS *leaps to his feet and attacks the second* PLUTO *by jumping high and catching the man about the neck. He wraps his legs around the man's torso and entwines his fingers in the second* PLUTO's *long, flowing beard. The younger* PLUTO *shakes him off with little effort, but the boy still has hold of the beard, which peels off the man's face. There is gold and orange dye covering the*

**Primary Source**

Students may be curious about where the treasure actually came from. Explain to them that neither the screenplay nor the novel ever fully answers this question; however, in the novel, Mayhew says, "Father, do you have any idea how close you and Drear have become? He collected all this perhaps as a whim and he put it here, again perhaps, to save for slaves a portion of life which had been denied them." Ask students to discuss what the treasure might symbolize or represent.

*false beard and* THOMAS's *hands. Now the boy is totally stunned. He sits on the floor looking up at the second* PLUTO *as he removes the rest of his stage makeup from his face.*

**MAYHEW.** [*peeling away the mask*] "We wear the mask that grins and lies, It hides our cheeks and shades our eyes . . . With torn and bleeding hearts we smile . . . We wear the mask!"[8]

**THOMAS.** You're *not* a devil.

**MAYHEW.** [*the younger* PLUTO] No. I'm Mayhew Skinner. I'm my father's only son.

MAYHEW *removes a half mask with the rest of the beard attached, then the white wig and a dyed, plastic substance that looks like skin.*

**WALTER.** Why? Why all this?

**PLUTO.** Because of what you see in here. Me and that River Swift Darrow usedta be real close, an' when we was young we hunted for this treasure in here together. . . .[*angrily*] Funny how folks can turn on you.

**THOMAS.** Turn, Mr. Pluto?

**PLUTO.** Wasn't long before I come to realize that this here treasure was more than just a collection of riches; it was a legacy, boy. One I was bound to protect. A monument to the history of our people. All River Swift wanted was the money.

**THOMAS.** Does he know where this treasure is?

**PLUTO.** No. Once we split up, we searched for it separate. I found it, he didn't, but I never let on that I did. An' he got about as much

---

8. **"We wear the mask . . .":** These four lines are from the poem "We Wear the Mask," by American poet Paul Laurence Dunbar (1872–1906).

chance of findin' it as a leopard got of changin' his spots.

**MAYHEW.** That hasn't kept the Darrows from trying.

**PLUTO.** Yea, slinkin' around like snakes, that's what they been doin'.

**THOMAS.** But how did you keep them off this land for so long?

**WALTER.** Thomas, stop askin' so many questions. [*to* PLUTO] How *did* you?

**PLUTO.** I figured if they could act like the devil, then I'd act the devil, *for real.* I snuck in an' outa these tunnels, makin' it seem like I could appear an' disappear. Had 'em fooled for years. Other folks, too. People got to callin' me a demon. Can you imagine that. Here I was protectin' our heritage, an' my own people callin' *me* a demon. How's that for gratitude. I had me a good time, though. That is, till I got sick back in January.

**WALTER.** Why did you think *we* were your enemies?

**MAYHEW.** People in this town have been treatin' my father bad for years. That's one of the reasons I left an' went East to work. Couldn't stand it. 'Specially after my mother passed on.

**THOMAS.** But now you're back.

**MAYHEW.** Thanks to Edgar Carr.

**WALTER.** Yes, the man at the gas station.

**MAYHEW.** And one of the few friends I had in this town when I was growin' up. He called me when my father's illness turned worse three weeks ago.

PESTY *comes over to* THOMAS *and stands beside him. She smiles.*

**WALTER.** Then Carr knows about this cavern, too?

*The House of Dies Drear* 289

15 **Reading Strategy** What double meaning might these lines of poetry have? Who, besides an actor, might have to wear a mask?

16 **Discussion** What does Pluto mean when he calls the treasure "a legacy . . . [he] was bound to protect"?

17 **Discussion** How has Pluto's name turned out to be a misnomer?

## Primary Source

In Virginia Hamilton's novel, Walter Small explains his motive for preserving and passing on the history of slavery in the South. He says, "I mean not to glorify it. . . . I simply want people to know about it. It's a part of our history, and yet no one tells the truth about it." Ask students to comment on Walter's point of view.

**MAYHEW.** No. No one does. Carr only knew that strangers were moving into the house, and that my father had been trying to keep something secret from the Darrows and if it was that important, it should probably be kept from you, too.

**WALTER.** He was afraid we'd be like the Darrows.

**MAYHEW.** So was I. I was the one who arranged your furniture.

**PLUTO.** Scarin' innocent folks, like that. Ain't no need, I tell ya. Dies Drear *lives.* When he wants to be seen, he will be. No need to pretend he is. He *is.* Why, Dies Drear taught the slaves in this very room; how to read, how to follow the crosses, how to escape. . . .

**THOMAS.** [*to* MAYHEW] Did you know about this cavern, too?

**MAYHEW.** Not until a week ago, when my father decided he was mortal, like all of us, and thought it time to tell me.

**PLUTO.** [*sadly*] Do you blame me, son?

**MAYHEW.** [*quietly*] We were so poor, Father. All those years, and there was all this wealth. . . .

**PLUTO.** [*interrupting*] It wasn't mine to take! It wasn't mine!

18 **MAYHEW.** Dies Drear's been dead a hundred years. He had no family! You call this our heritage? The legacy of our people? Well, we couldn't eat heritage, Father. Legacy couldn't put clothes on our back. You and the memory of that dead abolitionist have become so close till sometimes you can't tell what's real and what's not!

*There is a long pause. Then:*

**THOMAS.** Papa, does that mean you're gonna tell the foundation about all this? Will you let them take it?

WALTER *looks at* THOMAS *a moment, then at* MAYHEW *and* PLUTO.

**MAYHEW.** Pesty, come on. It's gettin' late. Time you were home.

**WALTER.** Mayhew, we could talk about the answer to his question. That is, if you want to let me be a part of that decision.

MAYHEW *nods his head.*

**MAYHEW.** Pesty, you ready?

**PESTY.** [*rises*] I'm ready.

*She goes to* PLUTO *and throws her arms around his neck and gives him a kiss.*

**PESTY.** See you tomorrow, Mr. Pluto.

**PLUTO.** This still our secret. Right?

**PESTY.** I kept this place a secret six years an' I'll keep it sixty if I have to. G'night.

PLUTO *attempts to rise out of his seat, trembles, and nearly falls;* MAYHEW *rushes to his side, catching him.*

**MAYHEW.** Father, you're sick! Quick, let's get him up to his bed.

WALTER *and* MAYHEW *assist* PLUTO *up the ramp as* PESTY *and* THOMAS *follow.*

CUT TO INT: PLUTO'S LIVING QUARTERS

*They help* PLUTO *as he lies heavily upon his bed.*

**PLUTO.** I'm tired, son, so tired. . . .

**MAYHEW.** Father, I'll be back as soon as I can.

**PLUTO.** I'll be all right, son. I feel better, so much better; now that I know a man like Mr. Small is here. He understands what this place means. He's a keeper of history, just like me. He knows. He knows. . . .

PLUTO *drifts off to sleep and the others quietly exit.*

CUT TO EXT: THE CAVE—NIGHT

*They begin to walk away from the cave.*

**WALTER.** Mayhew, if neither you nor your father ransacked our kitchen, do you think the Darrows did it?

**PESTY.** They sure did. They was scared because they thought you'd find the treasure before they did, your bein' a historical man, an' all.

**THOMAS.** Was Mac in on it?

**PESTY.** No. He got slapped down 'cause he said Thomas was a good friend, and he wouldn't go along with nothin' that would hurt Thomas or his family. They been hittin' him a lot, lately. It was Daddy and my grown brothers, River Ross, Wilbur, and Russell.

**MAYHEW.** They'll have to be dealt with, actin' so stupid. Like a bunch of vandals on Halloween.

**WALTER.** I'll get the police to put an end to their games once and for all. After all, they've been trespassin' on foundation property.

**MAYHEW.** Nothing would give me greater pleasure, but first *I* want to exact the revenge myself, and I know just the way. I told you I worked back East, didn't I? Well, I'm an actor.

**THOMAS.** [*holding up the fake mask he has clutched since being in the cave*] You coulda fooled me.

*Laughter.*

**MAYHEW.** Let me see Pesty safely home. Then, Mr. Small, I'm gonna swing by your place tonight and fill you in on a little something I have in mind for the big, bad Darrow boys.

**PESTY.** What about me? I want to be in on it, too. I'm tired of them beatin' up on Mac.

**MAYHEW.** Don't worry, you'll be in on it, too. Folks, we're all about to become a company of actors!

PESTY *is led off by* MAYHEW, *as* THOMAS *and* WALTER *stand and watch them a moment.*

**THOMAS.** Papa, what on earth is he talkin' about?

**WALTER.** I don't know, son. But if I read Mayhew right, I wouldn't want to be in the Darrows' shoes for all the treasure stored in this cave.

**THOMAS.** Papa, we gotta get home! Mama and Kenneth still locked in there by themselves!

*They quickly rush off into the night.*

CUT TO INT: THE KITCHEN—NIGHT

THOMAS *is fighting to stay awake as he sits at the kitchen table with his parents and* MAYHEW. KENNETH *is asleep in his mother's lap.*

**MAYHEW.** What we're about to do is going to involve deception, danger, and the utmost timing in order to be successful. But, once it works, we will have no more trouble from the Darrows.

**SHEILA.** Danger? We're not going to break the law, are we?

**MAYHEW.** Not a chance. But we *are* going to break some spirits.

THOMAS *sits up straight.*

**MAYHEW.** Here's a list of things I want you to buy at the store in town. . . .

*He hands* WALTER *the list.* WALTER *reads it as* THOMAS *peers over his shoulder.*

**MAYHEW.** It's absolutely imperative that the

*The House of Dies Drear* 291

19 **Reading Strategy** How do you predict that Mayhew and the Smalls will get revenge on the Darrows?

19

Darrows get wind of the fact that my father is very ill and may be hospitalized.

**THOMAS.** Really?

**MAYHEW.** No, not really, but it's important that the Darrows believe what Pesty and you are going to tell them. And here's why.

*The family leans forward to hear the plan.*

CUT TO EXT: HIGHWAY 68—DAY

*We see the* SMALLS' *car speeding along.*

CUT TO INT: THE CAR—DAY

**WALTER.** Thomas, we figured out the riddle of the triangles last night while you were asleep.

**THOMAS.** You did?

**SHEILA.** Mayhew explained it to us as his father had explained it to him.

**WALTER.** The Darrows stuck those old triangles around but didn't even know how the slaves and Dies Drear really used 'em.

**THOMAS.** Then they weren't meant as warnings?

**SHEILA.** Not in the old days. They were actually signposts, or beacons, honey. Designed to lead slaves on a route to safety.

**THOMAS.** Wow.

**WALTER.** The only way to read them is if they are separate—not put together. Also, you can't read them if they are lying flat. They had to be stuck upright into somethin' like a tree, or a wall, or a riverbank.

**SHEILA.** Then, the slaves stood a certain way in front of the triangle and the points told 'em which way to run.

**THOMAS.** Man, that Dies Drear was somethin', wasn't he?

**WALTER.** That's right. And very soon now,

the Darrows are gonna find out just *how much* he was somethin' else.

THOMAS *looks at his parents as the car continues on to town.*

CUT TO EXT: A STREET IN TOWN—DAY

*The* SMALLS' *car moves slowly down a main street in town.*

CUT TO INT: THE CAR—DAY

*The whole family seems to be looking for one place in particular.*

**WALTER.** Okay, keep your eyes open. Mayhew said we'd find it along here, someplace.

**THOMAS.** Hey, there it is!

CUT TO EXT: STREET—DAY

*The car comes to a halt in front of a theater supply store. The* SMALL *family gets out and goes inside.*

DISSOLVE TO: CUT TO EXT: THEATER SUPPLY STORE—DAY

*The* SMALL *family exits with armloads of shopping bags.* WALTER *opens the trunk of the car and places them inside. They also place a pair of gossamer wings in the trunk.* WALTER *closes the trunk.*

**THOMAS.** [*looking down the street*] Papa!

THOMAS *nods in the direction he is looking and we see the adult* DARROW *men approaching them. The looks on their faces connote curiosity, anger, and hatred. The* SMALL *family freezes in place.*

**WALTER.** [*quietly*] Just remain calm. Don't let on to anything.

**RIVER LEWIS.** You be Mr. Small?

**WALTER.** That's right. Don't believe I know your name.

**RIVER LEWIS.** That's right.

**AFTERNOON CHECKERS**
*William Tolliver*
*Courtesy of the Artist*

*The House of Dies Drear* 293

## Humanities Note

Fine art, *Afternoon Checkers,* by William Tolliver. Tolliver was born in 1952 in Vicksburg, Missouri, and has been painting since the age of seven. Although he has had no formal art training, he has spent years reading books on the subject and studying the artwork of Chagall, Monet, Van Gogh, and Picasso. In his studio in Atlanta, Georgia, Tolliver paints figure studies, portraits, and human-interest scenes in a style that is somewhat abstract. He believes that the work of African American artists has brought new life to contemporary art over the last ten years.

You might use the following questions for discussion:

1. How do the blue and violet colors of the painting contribute to the peacefulness of the scene? What colors might the artist use to depict a moment of conflict between the Darrow brothers and the Small family?
2. Notice the curved and rounded shapes used to portray the figures in this painting. How might these shapes change if the figures were engaged in more aggressive behavior?

21 **Reading Strategy** To what excitement is River Ross referring?

22 **Reading Strategy** What is the effect of including a close-up shot of Thomas at this point in the screenplay? Why might the screenwriter then choose to show the cave entrance from a young boy's point of view?

23 **Literary Focus: Setting** How is the setting of the darkened cave entrance particularly suited to the trick that the Smalls, Pluto, Pesty, and Mayhew play on the Darrows?

*He notices the cans of paint and the paint brushes that are sitting in the back seat of the car.*

**RIVER LEWIS.** Gettin' ready for some paintin', huh?

**THOMAS.** [*broad grin*] Yes sir, the whole house.

WALTER *glares at him and* THOMAS *demurely steps back.*

21 **RIVER ROSS.** Hear tell you folks had a little excitement over there in that house of yours?

RIVER LEWIS *gives his young son a sharp look, but it is too late, for the statement has given* WALTER *just the opening he needs.*

**WALTER.** Oh, you mean old Pluto.

**RIVER LEWIS.** Old Pluto?

**WALTER.** Yea. He took real sick last night. We brought him here to the hospital.

**RIVER LEWIS.** How sick is he?

**WALTER.** Can't say. They don't allow visitors. He's gettin' a thorough examination, though, and I expect he'll be comin' back home tomorrow.

WALTER *looks away.* RIVER LEWIS *suspects he is hiding something.*

**WILBUR.** [*eyeing* WALTER] That all?

**WALTER.** [*innocently*] What more could there be? Well, we gotta be goin'. Got a lotta work in the house needs to be done.

WALTER *and his family bid them good day.* THOMAS *looks back at them. The* DARROWS *stand in the middle of the sidewalk pondering what they've just heard and gawking at the* SMALLS. THOMAS *turns his head forward and stifles several guffaws.*

**SHEILA.** [*at the car*] Walter, what if the Darrows go to the hospital checkin' on our story?

**WALTER.** Mayhew called Edgar Carr, and Carr took care of the alibi.

*The family gets into the car and drives away, as the* DARROWS *stand watching them.*

CUT TO EXT: STREET—DAY

**WILBUR.** I guess that note about Pesty runnin' over here to find ol' Pluto was the truth, Daddy.

**RIVER LEWIS.** Truth or not, I'm still gonna whup her butt good for runnin' away from her chores.

**RUSSELL.** Daddy, this is as good a chance as we're gonna get to search that old man's place.

**RIVER LEWIS.** I know that. Whatchu think, I'm some kinda fool?

**RIVER ROSS.** Then we go tonight? It's the only chance we got.

**RIVER LEWIS.** It'll be tonight. We gon' find that treasure, if it's the last thing we do.

CUT TO EXT: WOODS NEAR THE CAVE—NIGHT. CLOSE-UP ON THOMAS

22 THOMAS *lies quietly in the grass. We can barely see the rough clothes he wears. His eyes dart everywhere. He's frightened and breathes heavily. He hears footsteps.*

CUT TO EXT: THE ENTRANCE TO THE CAVE—THOMAS'S POV—NIGHT

23 *The torches out front are not lit. The entire area is quiet, dark, and eerie.*

CUT TO EXT: THE WOODS—NIGHT

*The* DARROWS, *flashlights in hand, make their way through the woods to the cave, passing dangerously close to* THOMAS. *When they come to the clearing in front of the cave they stop.*

**WILBUR.** I don't like it—why ain't his torches burnin' on the cave?

**RIVER LEWIS.** 'Cause he's gone, like they said, an' he ain't here to light them, fool!

**RIVER ROSS.** Well, let's quit arguin' an' get on in there before somebody comes.

CUT TO EXT: THE CAVE—NIGHT

**INTO BONDAGE, 1936**
*Aaron Douglas*
*Evans-Tibbs Collection, Washington, D.C.*

*The House of Dies Drear* 295

## Humanities Note

Fine art, *Into Bondage,* 1936, by Aaron Douglas. Douglas (1899–1979) is the best-known African American painter, illustrator, and educator of the Harlem Renaissance. Douglas painted the murals in the 137th Street branch of the New York City Public Library and created numerous paintings, posters, and illustrations for African American theater and literary works. As part of his extensive education, Douglas traveled around the world on art grants and fellowships.

The subjects of Douglas's work come from African American history, religion, or myths. *Into Bondage* is his interpretation of Africans being taken into slavery. It is painted in the flat, stylized method that is Douglas's own invention. The silhouettes of the figures shown against the blisteringly bright sky as they are led away creates a powerful and thought-provoking scene.

Aaron Douglas painted at a time when it was not popular to glorify African American heritage. He refused to compromise his ideals and his conviction that African Americans were a proud and majestic people worthy of the glory and dignity of his art.

You might use the following questions for discussion:
1. How does this artist indicate that these men are being led into bondage?
2. What is the significance of the star in this painting?
3. Which elements of this painting can you find in the scene in which Pluto, Mayhew, Pesty, and the Smalls trick the Darrows?

**Challenge** In Virginia Hamilton's novel, Mayhew explains Dies Drear's last will and testament to Walter Small: "And he willed this cavern and whatever was found in it to the first son of slaves that was able to find it. He knew . . . the one who found it would have to have been cut off from his past, his history, as were the slaves. He would have to find that past in order to find himself." To whom does this description apply? Which characters had to find their past in order to find themselves?

The DARROWS *move stealthily across the clearing and creep inside the cave entrance.* RUSSELL *takes one of the torches and lights it. All of the* DARROWS *are now inside. We hear a gasp, or scream, and the torch goes out.*

CUT TO INT: THE CAVE—NIGHT

*The* DARROWS *are cowered near the entrance and a flashlight is shining upward toward the most grotesque and chilling sight they could imagine.* PLUTO *has covered his entire body, save his head, with a giant cape that makes him look like a winged bat.*

**PLUTO.** Ooooooohhhhh! Come, my winged bird! My Glory! Nightbird! Come, allll ye demonnnnnnnnssssssss!!! Aaaaiiiieeee! Come all ye demons three who walk with me forever. Come parade awhile with Pluto, who has missed you so.

**RIVER LEWIS.** [*stunned*] What the—?

*The sight is so unexpected that he drops his flashlight and it breaks. The four men begin to back away from the seeming apparition, when another spectacle in the trees above the cave catches their sight.*

CUT TO EXT: CAVE—NIGHT

*On a ledge above the cave entrance* PESTY *is astride the bay horse, hidden from view behind a black canvas. She drops the canvas and creates the following vision: A huge white horse with glowing wings suddenly appears in the night. This scene is even more chilling than the last. The* DARROWS *tremble with fear at the sight of the winged creature.* WILBUR *sinks down to one knee as one of his brothers tries to hold onto him. They do not know that* PESTY *is crouched behind the wings and flapping them, for the wings hide her perfectly.*

**WILBUR.** Oooooooohhhhhhhhhhhhh. . . .

CUT TO EXT: LEDGE ABOVE CAVE—NIGHT

PESTY *is flapping the glowing wings with all she's got.*

CUT TO EXT: CAVE—ANOTHER ANGLE—NIGHT

*A rustling sound directly behind the* DARROWS *causes them to turn and face the edge of the clearing, where they come face to face with the spirits of Dies Drear and the three escaped slaves of legend, arms reaching out to them, chains clanking.*

**MAYHEW.** [*as Dies Drear*] Defilers! Come! Come to Dies Drear and meet your fate!

**RIVER LEWIS.** Oh, no! It's Dies Drear and the dead slaves!

*The* DARROWS *let go of* WILBUR.

**RIVER ROSS.** The legend's true! Aaaiiiieeeee!!

*The specter of Dies Drear begins to laugh hideously and stretches out its hands as the three slaves clank their chains and moan and groan.* PLUTO *screams from inside the cave and the glowing demon horse continues to flap its gossamer wings. The* DARROWS *are completely surrounded, confused, and frightened to death.*

**MAYHEW.** Defilers! Come! Come to Dies Drear! Come to Drear and die!

**RUSSELL.** That old Pluto wasn't kiddin'. He is a demon. Dies Drear is alive! Aaaa!!!

*The* DARROWS *nearly fall over each other trying to get away.*

**WILBUR.** Don't let 'em get us! No! No!

CUT TO EXT: THE CAVE—NIGHT

WILBUR *scrambles to his feet and leads the rest of the* DARROWS *in beating a hasty retreat through the woods.*

CUT TO EXT: THE CAVE—ANOTHER ANGLE—NIGHT

*The howling and moaning ghosts begin to laugh in their own natural voices once the* DARROWS *have disappeared.* PESTY *sits up from her crouched position behind the gossamer wings and laughs.*

CUT TO INT: THE CAVE

PLUTO *unhitches himself from the harness that held him suspended from the platform doors in the ceiling and comes down the ladder, laughing.*

CUT TO EXT: THE CAVE

WALTER, THOMAS, *and* SHEILA *begin peeling off their makeup, laughing, as well. And* MAYHEW, *as Dies Drear, begins to peel away his false face amid more laughter.*

**MAYHEW.** They'll figure it out sooner or later. The point is that for a good half a minute, we scared them half to death.

**PLUTO.** Serves 'em right—them fool Darrows'll never live it down.

**MAYHEW.** And tomorrow they'll hear from the police!

**WALTER.** Well, Thomas, how do you feel now?

**THOMAS.** [*serious*] I was lyin' on that cold ground so long, I began to think we *were* slaves, for real. Like to 've scared me to death!

*There is a moment when everyone looks at* THOMAS *with mixed emotions.*

24 **THOMAS.** I sure learned one thing. I never wanna be an actor, no sir, not a day in my life!

*Everyone laughs.*

CUT TO INT: THE CAVERN—FOLLOWING DAY—DAY

PLUTO, MAYHEW, WALTER, SHEILA, THOMAS, *and* PESTY *are viewing the treasure of Dies Drear.*

**SHEILA.** Mr. Skinner, how long did you look for this place?

**PLUTO.** Twenty years, but I always knew it was here.

**THOMAS.** Shucks, they gonna start talkin' about history in another minute.

**PESTY.** Let's go outside. You know how borin' grownups can get.

**THOMAS.** Good idea.

*They creep out as the conversation continues.*

**MAYHEW.** You see, Father's great-great-grandfather was that third slave in the legend.

**WALTER.** The one who got away from the bounty hunters?

**MAYHEW.** That's right. And he passed the story of the treasure down.

25 **WALTER.** I knew when I first read that foundation report that the house of Dies Drear was a wellspring of important history, but I didn't realize how much.

**PLUTO.** [*sadly*] Now it's all gonna be taken away.

**WALTER.** [*smiling*] Tell me, did Dies Drear ever catalog all of this property here?

**PLUTO.** No, sir.

**WALTER.** That would have to be done before it could be turned over to the foundation.

**PLUTO.** [*smiling*] Yes . . . that's a big job. Could take as long as the rest of an old man's life.

**WALTER.** [*smiling*] You don't say?

*The House of Dies Drear*  297

**24 Discussion** What else has Thomas learned? Explain.

**25 Discussion** In what way is the Dies Drear house a wellspring of important history?

**Enrichment** Students who enjoyed reading *The House of Dies Drear* may wish to know that Virginia Hamilton wrote a sequel, *The Mystery of Drear House*.

Reader's Response What was the most interesting historical fact that you learned from reading *The House of Dies Drear*? Why?

Thematic Response In what ways is justice served in this story?

WALTER *and* PLUTO *laugh.*

**MAYHEW.** Say, where's Thomas and Pesty?

CUT TO EXT: THE HILL—DAY

PESTY *and* THOMAS *are together on the hill overlooking the House of Dies Drear.*

**PESTY.** So, Thomas Small, the new boy, you gonna stop bein' so snooty like you was when we first met you the other day?

PESTY *laughs.*

**THOMAS.** Tell ya what. I won't be snooty if you stop callin' me "new boy." Okay?

**PESTY.** Okay.

*They shake hands on it.*

**PESTY.** Do you think we'll ever have as much excitement in our lives again?

**THOMAS.** I dunno. . . . Life is such a long time. . . . But I do know I've had enough adventure to last me the rest of my life.

**BOTH.** Aaaaaaaaaa-*men!*

*The kids laugh together as the camera pulls away; then we hear a sudden, ominous, rustling noise behind* PESTY *and* THOMAS *as they laugh. The children turn toward the camera and, frightened, they scream.*

CUT TO EXT: HILLSIDE, PESTY AND THOMAS'S POV—DAY

*A monster, covered head to toe with leaves, looms over the kids. The "Leaf Monster" begins to crumble toward the ground, revealing* MAC, *holding* KENNETH *on his shoulders. From under the pile of branches and leaves crawl* MAC *and* KENNETH, *both giggling and laughing. Angry at first,* PESTY *and* THOMAS *soon chase and catch them. All four youngsters wrap their arms around each other and tumble to the ground, laughing.*

FREEZE FRAME

FADE OUT

## R ESPONDING TO THE SELECTION

### Your Response

1. Do you think that Pluto was right to preserve the Dies Drear treasure intact, or should he, a poor man, have used some of it to help raise his family? Explain your answer.

2. Is the outcome of events in this screenplay satisfying? Explain.

### Recalling

3. Explain the solutions to the following mysteries: the sounds Thomas heard in the tunnel, the ransacking of the Smalls' kitchen, and the meaning of the triangles.

4. What is going to happen to the treasure of Dies Drear?

### Interpreting

5. What is the central conflict, or struggle, in this screenplay? How are the various characters involved in this struggle?

6. How is Pluto's interest in the Dies Drear treasure different from River Swift Darrow's? What is similar about Pluto's and Walter's attitudes toward the treasure?

7. Do you think the "punishment" given to the Darrows was equal to the wrongs they committed? Explain your answer.

### Applying

8. Walter calls the house of Dies Drear "a wellspring of important history." What does this screenplay suggest about the relationship between history and mystery?

## Closure and Extension

### ANSWERS TO RESPONDING TO THE SELECTION
#### Your Response
1. Some students may feel that Pluto was justified in not using what was not his to help himself or his family. Others may feel that Pluto's dedication to preserving the treasure caused him to neglect his family's needs.
2. Encourage students to give reasons to support their opinions.

#### Recalling
3. The bellows from Pluto's forge caused the sounds. The Darrows ransacked the Smalls' kitchen and

stuck the triangles in the door frames to frighten them out of the house. The triangles were actually markers that Dies Drear used to let fleeing slaves know in which direction the next "station" could be found.
4. Pluto and Walter plan to work together to catalog the treasure and turn it over to the foundation.

#### Interpreting
5. Suggested Response: Both the Darrows and the Skinners are

afraid that the Smalls are after the Dies Drear treasure, so they independently attempt to frighten the Smalls off the property. The Smalls, however, know nothing about the treasure and are interested only in the house's historical significance.
6. Suggested Response: The Darrows want to find the Dies Drear treasure and use it for selfish purposes. Pluto wants to keep the treasure hidden, to preserve it and its history.

7. Answers will differ. Some students may feel that the punishment was not adequate for the Darrows' many years of abuse. Others may feel that the punishment accomplished its main goal: to frighten the Darrows away for good.

#### Applying
8. Answers will differ. Lead students to see that what appears to be a mystery can sometimes be solved by researching the past.

## ANALYZING LITERATURE

### Understanding Setting

The most important element of the **setting,** or time and place of the action, in this screenplay is the house itself. With its distinctive appearance, atmosphere, and history, the house is such an integral part of the story that it almost takes on the role of a character.

1. When the Smalls first see the Dies Drear place, it is described as "a huge, monstrous-looking house, made more ominous by the storm. It is Victorian in nature, yet seems formless and unnatural" (page 252). What does this description suggest about the house?
2. Thomas, observing the rust-stained rocks at the base of the house, says, "It looks like the house is bleedin'. Like somebody cut this place open and let all the blood run out." How does this image affect your perception of the house?

## CRITICAL THINKING AND READING

### Understanding Setting and Plot

*The House of Dies Drear* is a story in which the setting greatly affects the plot. The whole story centers on the house. For example, Walter moves there because of its history, and Thomas tries to solve its mysteries, fearing it might be haunted.

1. Explain how the house is involved in the central conflict of the screenplay.
2. How is the "treasure" that the house once offered to runaway slaves related to the treasures it offers today?

## THINKING AND WRITING

### Writing a Story

Write a story about a place that is so mysterious that the characters fear it might be haunted. Give your place an interesting history that the characters can learn about by piecing together a series of clues. Combine history and mystery so that your readers will learn while they are being entertained. Then share your story with your class.

## LEARNING OPTIONS

1. **Art.** Imagine that you must design an advertising poster for a screening of the film *The House of Dies Drear.* Create a poster that conveys the spirit of the story and entices people to view it.
2. **Cross-curricular Connection.** Find out more information about the Underground Railroad. What states did the escaped slaves travel through? How did they know where to go? Who helped them? Prepare a report, either oral or written, and share it with your class.
3. **Community Connections.** Do some research to locate a house that has been preserved as a museum in your area or in a neighboring town or city. If possible, visit the house with a classmate. Try to imagine what it would have been like to live in the house, and think about the mysteries that it may still hold. If it is not possible for you to visit the museum, you may wish to send for brochures or other information.

*The House of Dies Drear*   299

299

## World War II and the Holocaust

**Preparation**

**Motivation/Prior Knowledge**
Ask students to share what they know about Hitler, the Holocaust, and World War II. Ask them to identify the source of their information as well. Is the knowledge drawn from a book, a movie, a television program, research for another class, a personal account by a relative? Record key words and phrases that illustrate common perceptions the students may have about these topics. Encourage students to compare and contrast their current knowledge and ideas with what they learn as they read the selection.

**Presentation**

**Discussion Questions**
1. Ask students to try to imagine what their lives would be like if they lived in Nazi Germany. How would their lives be different? What would they find most frightening?
2. Why do you think Britain and France declared war on Germany after Hitler invaded Poland?
3. Why do you think Hitler's invasion of the Soviet Union contributed to his downfall?
4. Why do you think the diary of a thirteen-year-old girl has become more well known than any report by a military or political leader? Why do you think people still read Anne's diary and produce this play?

**Enrichment** Ask students to interview grandparents or other relatives who were living during World War II. What effects did the war have on life in the United States? What were the different reasons people had for supporting or opposing American involvement?

**Hitler and the Nazis.** In 1933 Adolf Hitler and the National Socialist (Nazi) Party took power in Germany. According to the Nazis, Germans were superior to non-Germans, especially those of Jewish origin. Jews and other minorities were blamed for all Germany's troubles, from its defeat in World War I to the severe economic depression of the 1920's. To punish Jews for these imagined sins, the Nazis denied them the right to own property, attend schools, and serve in the professions.

**The start of World War II.** In foreign affairs, Hitler worked for a "Greater Germany" by seizing part of Czechoslovakia and occupying Austria. Then, after signing a secret treaty with the Soviet Union, he invaded Poland on September 1, 1939. Two days later, Britain and France declared war on Germany. However, they could not prevent Hitler's forces from conquering much of Europe, including Belgium and France.

**The defeat of Hitler.** Two events in 1941 foreshadowed Hitler's downfall. In June of that year, Hitler staged a surprise invasion of the Soviet Union, his former ally. Eventually, however, German troops would suffer great losses in this campaign. The second key development of that year was the entry of the United States into the war. American military and industrial might was important in defeating Germany. It was not until May 1945, however, that Germany surrendered to the Allies.

**The Holocaust.** Meanwhile, during the War, everywhere the German army went, Jews and other peoples were persecuted. The name that has been given to these events is the Holocaust, which comes from a Greek word meaning "burnt whole."

Jews were made to wear yellow stars on their clothing and were sent to ghettos—crowded, closed-off neighborhoods in cities. There many died of starvation and disease. Those that survived were eventually transported in freight cars to special prisons known as concentration camps, where most died within a few months. Then the Nazis thought of an even more efficient way to destroy the Jews: camps where people were gassed to death in special rooms almost as soon as they arrived.

The number of people killed by the Nazis is staggering. An estimated three million Jews died in concentration camps. Another three million were either shot or died in the ghettos of starvation and disease. By the end of the war, some six million Jews had perished, three quarters of Europe's Jewish population.

**Persecution of other peoples.** Another group that nearly disappeared during the Holocaust was Europe's Gypsies. Many Gypsies had lived for centuries in Germany, but along with the Jews, they were targeted for destruction as a so-called foreign race. It is estimated that during the Holocaust half a million Gypsies died, eighty percent of the European Gypsy population.

Millions of other people died as well, especially in Eastern Europe. In addition to losing three million Jews, Poland lost another three million citizens through slave labor, starvation, and murder. The Soviet Union lost at least seven million people, not counting the millions of prisoners of war who never returned home.

**The Story behind the play.** *The Diary of Anne Frank* is based on a real diary written by a young girl during the Holocaust.

*300 Drama*

**Clarification** Assist students in comprehending the magnitude of the destruction of human life during the Holocaust by comparing the numbers to the populations of American cities. Hitler exterminated enough Jewish people alone to annihilate almost the entire population of New York City, at 7,322,564 in 1992. The combined populations of Los Angeles, at 3,485,398, Chicago, at 2,783,726, and Dallas at 1,006,877 could similarly have been destroyed. Using the population of their hometown or city, ask students to compute how many towns or cities of that size would have been destroyed when Hitler killed more than 6 million Jewish people. Remind students that the conditions imposed by the Nazis were responsible for many millions of other deaths—of Jews and non-Jews.

**Enrichment** You may wish to point out that "Aryan race," the name for the ideal established by the Nazis, purported the superiority of certain physical characteristics, notably blond hair and Nordic features. Ironically, Hitler did not meet these criteria.

*People being rounded up to be sent to concentration camps by the Nazis*

Anne Frank was born to a Jewish family in Frankfurt, Germany, on June 12, 1929. She had a normal, happy childhood until the Nazis took power in 1933.

That year, Anne's family left their home in Germany to escape persecution, moving to the Netherlands. In Amsterdam Mr. Frank reestablished his business, and Mrs. Frank set up their new household. Anne and her older sister, Margot, attended school and made new friends.

Even as late as 1942, the Frank family and many other European Jews were unaware of the dangers they faced. Most simply thought they would be temporarily imprisoned by the Nazis. To avoid this fate, the Frank family hid in the attic of a warehouse and office building that had been part of Mr. Frank's business in Amsterdam.

On her thirteenth birthday, Anne had received a diary as a gift. When her family went into hiding, she began to write regularly in this diary. The play you are about to read is based on this diary, which Mr. Frank recovered when he returned to the secret attic after the war.

**Further Reading**

Read one of the following books, or another book on the Holocaust, and report on it to your class.

Frank, Anne. *The Diary of a Young Girl* (New York: Random House, 1978). This is the diary on which the play was based.

Wiesel, Elie. *Night* (New York: Avon, 1960). A famous author tells about his experiences as a teenager in a concentration camp.

Ziemian, Joseph. *The Cigarette Sellers of Three Crosses Square* (Minneapolis: Lerner Publications, 1975). This is the true story of how a group of Jewish children escaped from the Warsaw ghetto.

*Multicultural Connection* **301**

**Closure and Extension**

You may wish to have your students write their emotional and intellectual responses to the selection in their journals. Some students may wish to meet in groups and discuss what they have learned.

**Enrichment** If you wish to conduct a more in-depth study of the Holocaust with your students, you may find some of the following resources helpful:

*The Holocaust Years: Society on Trial* edited by Roselle Chartock and Jack Spender. Bantam, 1978. This collection of eighty-eight brief selections includes eyewitness accounts and memoirs.

*Image Before My Eyes: A Photographic History of Jewish Life in Poland, 1864–1939* by Lucjan Dobroszycki and Barbara Kirshenblatt-Gimblett. Schocken Books, 1977. More than 300 photographs show all aspects of Polish Jewish life.

*Atlas of the Holocaust* by Martin Gilbert. MacMillan Publishing Co., 1982. More than 300 maps give geographic perspective to Hitler's war against the Jews and people of other cultures.

For additional information you can contact:
Office of Education
U.S. Holocaust Memorial Council
Suite 588
2000 L Street, N.W.
Washington, DC 20036

## Preparation

**More About the Authors**
Frances Goodrich and Albert Hackett began working together in 1927, were married in 1931, and ended their writing careers in 1962 with a script for the screenplay based on their drama, *The Diary of Anne Frank.* Both had been actors. Hackett had started acting at age six and worked in both vaudeville and silent films. After Goodrich graduated from Vassar, she took to the road as an actor and in 1913 first appeared on Broadway. Ask students to discuss in what ways being a former actor can help in writing a play.

**Literary Focus** Explain that in this play all but the first and last scenes occur in flashback and dramatize events described in Anne's actual diary. The two "envelope" scenes depict Mr. Frank's state of mind before and after he has read his daughter's words. Tell students to look for the change in Mr. Frank by the end.

**Prereading Focus** You may wish to address the Focus activity to several learning styles. After a short period of individual contemplation, allow students to interact in discussion groups before completing their independent lists. Some students may prefer to express their choices through collages or drawings.

**Vocabulary** The following words may not be known by your **less advanced** students: *aggravating* (p. 322), *rebellious* (p. 323), *finicky* (p. 326), *improvised* (p. 336), *precious* (p. 337), *jubilation* (p. 339).

**Teaching to Ability Levels** Suggest to your **more advanced** students that they read *A Tribute to Anne Frank,* edited by Anna Steenmeijer. The book contains letters and photographs representing the most poignant and meaningful responses to Anne Frank's diary.

302

**Frances Goodrich**
(1890–1984) and
**Albert Hackett**
(1900–   ) spent two years writing *The Diary of Anne Frank,* which is based on *The Diary of a Young Girl* by Anne Frank. As part of their background work, Goodrich and Hackett visited with Anne's father, Otto Frank. Goodrich and Hackett's play won a Pulitzer Prize, the Drama Critics Circle Award, and the Tony Award for best play of the 1955–1956 season. *The Diary of Anne Frank* shows the unconquerable spirit of a young girl.

302 Drama

## The Diary of Anne Frank, Act I

### Flashback

Most of this play is presented as a flashback. A **flashback** is a technique that writers use to present events that happened at an earlier time. The writer inserts a scene that presents the earlier action as though it were taking place in the present. *The Diary of Anne Frank* begins in 1945 as Mr. Frank returns to the warehouse where he and his family hid from the Nazis. When Mr. Frank starts to read Anne's diary, however, the time changes back to 1942. The events of 1942 are presented as though they were taking place in the present. Using a flashback lets the authors show you how Mr. Frank is affected now by what has happened in the past.

### Focus

Anne, the main character in this story, is a young girl whose family was forced into hiding by Nazi invaders. In her diary she writes about many things that she misses. Make a list of at least five things you would miss if you had to leave your home for a long time. After you read the first act of *The Diary of Anne Frank,* review your list and compare it to what Anne says she misses.

### Vocabulary

Knowing the following words will help you as you read *The Diary of Anne Frank,* Act I.

**conspicuous** (kən spik′ yōō wəs) *adj.*: Noticeable (p. 307)
**mercurial** (mər kyoor′ ē əl) *adj.*: Quick or changeable in behavior (p. 307)
**unabashed** (un ə basht′) *adj.*: Unashamed (p. 311)
**insufferable** (in suf′ ər ə b′l) *adj.*: Unbearable (p. 317)

**meticulous** (mə tik′ yōō ləs) *adj.*: Extremely careful about details (p. 326)
**fatalist** (fā′ tə list) *n.*: One who believes that all events are determined by fate and cannot be changed (p. 334)
**ostentatiously** (äs′ tən tā′ shəs lē) *adv.*: Showily (p. 339)

---

## Objectives

1 To understand the use of flashback in a play
2 To make predictions about the outcome of a play
3 To write a letter as a character in a play

## Support Material

**Teaching Portfolio**
Teacher Backup, pp. 383–386
Grammar in Action Worksheets, *Using Simple Sentences,* pp. 387–388; *Connecting Ideas of Equal Weight,* pp. 389–390; *Understanding Infinitive Verbs,* pp. 391–392; *Understanding Imperative Sentences,* pp. 392–393
Usage and Mechanics Work-

sheet, p. 395
Vocabulary Check, p. 396
Critical Thinking and Reading Worksheet, *Predicting Outcomes,* p. 397
Language Worksheet, *Recognizing Words From German,* p. 398
Selection Test, pp. 399–400

**Library of Video Classics,**
*The Diary of Anne Frank*

**Prentice Hall Literature Writing Studio**

# The Diary of Anne Frank

### Frances Goodrich and Albert Hackett

---

**CHARACTERS**

| | | | |
|---|---|---|---|
| **Mr. Frank** | **Mr. Van Daan** | **Margot Frank** | **Mr. Kraler** |
| **Miep** | **Peter Van Daan** | **Anne Frank** | **Mr. Dussel** |
| **Mrs. Van Daan** | **Mrs. Frank** | | |

---

## ACT I

### Scene 1

[*The scene remains the same throughout the play. It is the top floor of a warehouse and office building in Amsterdam, Holland. The sharply peaked roof of the building is outlined against a sea of other rooftops, stretching away into the distance. Nearby is the belfry[1] of a church tower, the Westertoren, whose carillon[2] rings out the hours. Occasionally faint sounds float up from below: the voices of children playing in the street, the tramp of marching feet, a boat whistle from the canal.*

*The three rooms of the top floor and a small attic space above are exposed to our view. The largest of the rooms is in the center, with two small rooms, slightly raised, on either side. On the right is a bathroom, out of sight. A narrow steep flight of stairs at the back leads up to the attic. The rooms are sparsely furnished with a few chairs, cots, a table or two. The windows are painted over, or covered with makeshift blackout curtains.[3] In the main room there is a sink, a gas ring for cooking and a woodburning stove for warmth.*

*The room on the left is hardly more than a closet. There is a skylight in the sloping ceiling. Directly under this room is a small steep stairwell, with steps leading down to a door. This is the only entrance from the building below. When the door is opened we see that it has been concealed on the outer side by a bookcase attached to it.*

*The curtain rises on an empty stage. It is late afternoon November, 1945.*

*The rooms are dusty, the curtains in rags. Chairs and tables are overturned.*

*The door at the foot of the small stairwell swings open.* MR. FRANK *comes up the steps into view. He is a gentle, cultured European in his middle years. There is still a trace of a German accent in his speech.*

*He stands looking slowly around, making a supreme effort at self-control. He is weak, ill. His clothes are threadbare.*

---

**1. belfry** (bel′ frē) *n.*: The part of a tower that holds the bells.
**2. carillon** (kar′ ə län′) *n.*: A set of stationary bells, each producing one note of the scale.

**3. blackout curtains:** Draperies that conceal all lights that might otherwise be visible to enemy air raiders at night.

*The Diary of Anne Frank* 303

## Presentation

**Motivation/Prior Knowledge**
Explain to students that this play is based on a diary kept by Anne Frank while she and her family were in hiding from the Nazis in Amsterdam, the Netherlands, during World War II. Discuss the Holocaust and the extermination of 11 million people, including 6 million Jews. Mention that Holland was an occupied country and that there was an underground resistance, which, in addition to trying to undermine the Nazi occupation, also gave assistance to Jews.

**Making Connections** Other selections that deal with a teenager's response to war are "The Drummer Boy of Shiloh" (page 151) and "Fathers and Daughters" (page 421); with the need for acceptance is "Flowers for Algernon" (page 201); with courage is "Harriet Tubman: Guide to Freedom" (page 383).

**Thematic Focus** You can use a word web to explore the different perceptions students have of "finding a place." As your students read Act I, ask them to consider how these perceptions compare and contrast with Anne Frank's experience.

**Purpose-Setting Question** How does Anne relate to the different people in the play?

1 **Discussion** Discuss when the play takes place. Point out that the play opens about six months after the end of World War II.

(translation)
"This is a photo as I would wish myself to look all the time. Then I would maybe have a chance to come to Hollywood."
    Anne Frank, 10 Oct. 1942

*Anne Frank and her opinion of this photo*

After a second he drops his rucksack[4] on the couch and moves slowly about. He opens the door to one of the smaller rooms, and then abruptly closes it again, turning away. He goes to the window at the back, looking off at the Westertoren as its carillon strikes the hour of six, then he moves restlessly on.

2 From the street below we hear the sound of a barrel organ[5] and children's voices at play. There is a many-colored scarf hanging from a nail. MR. FRANK takes it, putting it around his neck. As he starts back for his rucksack, his eye is caught by something lying on the floor. It is a woman's white glove. He holds it in his hand and suddenly all of his self-control is gone. He breaks down, crying.

3

We hear footsteps on the stairs. MIEP GIES comes up, looking for MR. FRANK. MIEP is a Dutch girl of about twenty-two. She wears a coat and hat, ready to go home. She is

**4. rucksack** (ruk' sak') *n.*: A knapsack.
**5. barrel organ** *n.*: A mechanical musical instrument played by turning a crank.

304 *Drama*

*pregnant. Her attitude toward* MR. FRANK *is protective, compassionate.]*

**MIEP.** Are you all right, Mr. Frank?

**MR. FRANK.** [*Quickly controlling himself*] Yes, Miep, yes.

**MIEP.** Everyone in the office has gone home . . . It's after six. [*Then pleading*] Don't stay up here, Mr. Frank. What's the use of torturing yourself like this?

**MR. FRANK.** I've come to say good-bye . . . I'm leaving here, Miep.

**MIEP.** What do you mean? Where are you going? Where?

**MR. FRANK.** I don't know yet. I haven't decided.

**MIEP.** Mr. Frank, you can't leave here! This is your home! Amsterdam is your home. Your business is here, waiting for you . . . You're needed here . . . Now that the war is over, there are things that . . .

**MR. FRANK.** I can't stay in Amsterdam, Miep. It has too many memories for me. Everywhere there's something . . . the house we lived in . . . the school . . . that street organ playing out there . . . I'm not the person you used to know, Miep. I'm a bitter old man. [*Breaking off*] Forgive me. I shouldn't speak to you like this . . . after all that you did for us . . . the suffering . . .

**MIEP.** No. No. It wasn't suffering. You can't say we suffered. [*As she speaks, she straightens a chair which is overturned.*]

**MR. FRANK.** I know what you went through, you and Mr. Kraler. I'll remember it as long as I live. [*He gives one last look around.*] Come, Miep. [*He starts for the steps, then remembers his rucksack, going back to get it.*]

**MIEP.** [*Hurrying up to a cupboard*] Mr. Frank, did you see? There are some of your papers here. [*She brings a bundle of papers to him.*] We found them in a heap of rubbish on the floor after . . . after you left.

**MR. FRANK.** Burn them. [*He opens his rucksack to put the glove in it.*]

**MIEP.** But, Mr. Frank, there are letters, notes . . .

**MR. FRANK.** Burn them. All of them.

**MIEP.** Burn *this*? [*She hands him a paper-bound notebook.*]

**MR. FRANK.** [*Quietly*] Anne's diary. [*He opens the diary and begins to read.*] "Monday, the sixth of July, nineteen forty-two." [*To* MIEP] Nineteen forty-two. Is it possible, Miep? . . . Only three years ago. [*As he continues his reading, he sits down on the couch.*] "Dear Diary, since you and I are going to be great friends, I will start by telling you about myself. My name is Anne Frank. I am thirteen years old. I was born in Germany the twelfth of June, nineteen twenty-nine. As my family is Jewish, we emigrated to Holland when Hitler came to power."

[*As* MR. FRANK *reads on, another voice joins his, as if coming from the air. It is* ANNE'S VOICE.]

**MR. FRANK AND ANNE.** "My father started a business, importing spice and herbs. Things went well for us until nineteen forty. Then the war came, and the Dutch capitulation,[6] followed by the arrival of the Germans. Then things got very bad for the Jews."

[MR. FRANK'S VOICE *dies out.* ANNE'S VOICE *continues alone. The lights dim slowly to darkness. The curtain falls on the scene.*]

_____

**6. capitulation** (kə pich′ ə lā′ shən) *n.:* Surrender.

*The Diary of Anne Frank* 305

**4 Literary Focus: Flashback** Discuss the playwrights' technique for getting into the flashback. Point out that as Mr. Frank starts to read Anne's diary, the time goes back three years and Anne starts to tell the story.

**5 Discussion** What does the diary mean to Anne?

**6 Literary Focus: Point of View** Explain that the diary was considered by Anne as a confidante, an imaginary friend to whom she could confess her most private thoughts and emotions. There is no attempt by the author to control the content of her entries. This fact is important to the reader, whose perspective must be adjusted accordingly.

**7 Enrichment** Have students look at the picture of Anne on the preceding page. What does her inscription on the photo tell you about Anne?

**ANNE'S VOICE.** You could not do this and you could not do that. They forced Father out of his business. We had to wear yellow stars.[7] I had to turn in my bike. I couldn't go to a Dutch school any more. I couldn't go to the movies, or ride in an automobile, or even on a streetcar, and a million other things. But somehow we children still managed to have fun. Yesterday Father told me we were going into hiding. Where, he wouldn't say.

---

**7. yellow stars:** Stars of David, which are six-pointed stars that are symbols of Judaism. The Nazis ordered all Jews to wear them sewn to their clothing so that Jews could be easily identified.

At five o'clock this morning Mother woke me and told me to hurry and get dressed. I was to put on as many clothes as I could. It would look too suspicious if we walked along carrying suitcases. It wasn't until we were on our way that I learned where we were going. Our hiding place was to be upstairs in the building where Father used to have his business. Three other people were coming in with us . . . the Van Daans and their son Peter . . . Father knew the Van Daans but we had never met them . . .

[*During the last lines the curtain rises on the scene. The lights dim on.* ANNE'S VOICE *fades out.*]

*Front view and rear view of the building where the Franks and their friends hid*

## Grammar in Action

Usually writers vary their sentence patterns in order to achieve a lively and interesting style. However, sometimes a writer may purposely choose to use several short, **simple sentences** in succession in order to emphasize the content of each sentence; then each detail or event is treated as equally important.

Notice the style of writing in the following passage from *The Diary of Anne Frank:*

**ANNE'S VOICE.** You could not do this and you could not do that. They forced Father out of his business. We had to wear yellow stars. I had to turn in my bike. I couldn't go to a Dutch school any more. I couldn't go to the movies, or ride in an automobile, or even on a streetcar, and a million other things. But somehow we children still managed to have fun.

The short, precise sentences, void of detail, emphasize each action and create a vivid impression of the starkness of her life.

## Scene 2

[*It is early morning, July, 1942. The rooms are bare, as before, but they are now clean and orderly.*

MR. VAN DAAN, *a tall, portly*[8] *man in his late forties, is in the main room, pacing up and down, nervously smoking a cigarette. His clothes and overcoat are expensive and well cut.*

MRS. VAN DAAN *sits on the couch, clutching her possessions, a hatbox, bags, etc. She is a pretty woman in her early forties. She wears a fur coat over her other clothes.*

PETER VAN DAAN *is standing at the window of the room on the right, looking down at the street below. He is a shy, awkward boy of sixteen. He wears a cap, a raincoat, and long Dutch trousers, like "plus fours."*[9] *At his feet is a black case, a carrier for his cat.*

*The yellow Star of David is conspicuous on all of their clothes.*]

MRS. VAN DAAN. [*Rising, nervous, excited*] Something's happened to them! I know it!

MR. VAN DAAN. Now, Kerli!

MRS. VAN DAAN. Mr. Frank said they'd be here at seven o'clock. He said . . .

MR. VAN DAAN. They have two miles to walk. You can't expect . . .

MRS. VAN DAAN. They've been picked up. That's what's happened. They've been taken . . .

[MR. VAN DAAN *indicates that he hears someone coming.*]

MR. VAN DAAN. You see?

[PETER *takes up his carrier and his schoolbag, etc., and goes into the main room as* MR. FRANK *comes up the stairwell from below.* MR. FRANK *looks much younger now. His movements are brisk, his manner confident. He wears an overcoat and carries his hat and a small cardboard box. He crosses to the* VAN DAANS. *shaking hands with each of them.*]

MR. FRANK. Mrs. Van Daan, Mr. Van Daan, Peter. [*Then, in explanation of their lateness*] There were too many of the Green Police[10] on the streets . . . we had to take the long way around.

[*Up the steps come* MARGOT FRANK, MRS. FRANK, MIEP (*not pregnant now*) *and* MR. KRALER. *All of them carry bags, packages, and so forth. The Star of David is conspicuous on all of the* FRANKS' *clothing.* MARGOT *is eighteen, beautiful, quiet, shy.* MRS. FRANK *is a young mother, gently bred, reserved. She, like* MR. FRANK, *has a slight German accent.* MR. KRALER *is a Dutchman, dependable, kindly.*

*As* MR. KRALER *and* MIEP *go upstage to put down their parcels,* MRS. FRANK *turns back to call* ANNE.]

MRS. FRANK. Anne?

[ANNE *comes running up the stairs. She is thirteen, quick in her movements, interested in everything, mercurial in her emotions. She wears a cape, long wool socks and carries a schoolbag.*]

MR. FRANK. [*Introducing them*] My wife, Edith. Mr. and Mrs. Van Daan . . . their son, Peter . . . my daughters, Margot and Anne.

[MRS. FRANK *hurries over, shaking hands with them.*]

[ANNE *gives a polite little curtsy as she shakes* MR. VAN DAAN's *hand. Then she imme-*

---

**8. portly** (pôrt' lē) *adj.*: Large, heavy, and dignified.
**9. plus fours** *n.*: Loose knickers.

**10. Green Police:** The Nazi police who wore green uniforms.

---

*The Diary of Anne Frank* 307

**10 Reading Strategy** What can you infer from this exchange about the characters of Mr. and Mrs. Van Daan?

**11 Discussion** You may wish to emphasize this vocabulary word by having the students look up Mercury the god and mercury the element in a dictionary. Encourage students to make their own connections between these nouns and the connotations of the adjective. After students have agreed on reasons for the definition, help them internalize it by discussing situations in which they might have felt mercurial in their emotions. Do they know anyone who is mercurial? How does it feel to be mercurial? How does it feel to interact with someone who is mercurial?

**Student Activity.** Write a paragraph describing a highly dramatic situation. You would like to emphasize each action or event that takes place. An example of such a situation might be tryouts for a school play or athletic team or a particularly rigid structure at a summer camp. Try to pattern your sentences after those of Anne Frank in the example. Use several short, simple sentences to emphasize the importance of each.

**Electronic Handbook** You may wish to review creating simple sentences with your students before they complete the Grammar in Action activity. If your students are using the Language Master 6000, have them enter the access word *subject* and press the GRAMMAR key to get information about the parts of a simple sentence.

**12 Clarification** Explain the necessity of rationing here and abroad. During the war there was a world-wide shortage of consumer products. This was caused by the diversion of many raw materials into war goods. It was also caused by the impossibility of transporting materials through customary land, sea, and air channels blocked by hostile forces. As supplies were limited, governments (including that of the United States) issued to their citizens ration books containing coupons for different types of commodities. Ration books were intended to limit the quantity of available supplies and to provide equal distribution among the people. However, it was possible in some instances to get extra ration books by illegal means.

**13 Reading Strategy** How does Mrs. Van Daan's reaction fit in with your original evaluation of her character? Is this anxiety consistent with her previous behavior? How?

Mr. and Mrs. Van Daan and Victor Kraler in happier times

*diately starts off on a tour of investigation of her new home, going upstairs to the attic room.*

MIEP *and* MR. KRALER *are putting the various things they have brought on the shelves.*]

**MR. KRALER.** I'm sorry there is still so much confusion.

**MR. FRANK.** Please. Don't think of it. After all, we'll have plenty of leisure to arrange everything ourselves.

**MIEP.** [*To* MRS. FRANK] We put the stores of food you sent in here. Your drugs are here . . . soap, linen here.

**MRS. FRANK.** Thank you, Miep.

**MIEP.** I made up the beds . . . the way Mr. Frank and Mr. Kraler said. [*She starts out.*] Forgive me. I have to hurry. I've got to go to the other side of town to get some ration books[11] for you. 12

**MRS. VAN DAAN.** Ration books? If they see our names on ration books, they'll know we're here. 13

**MR. KRALER.** There isn't anything . . .

**MIEP.** Don't worry. Your names won't be on them. [*As she hurries out*] I'll be up later.

---

**11. ration books** (rash′ ən books′) *n.*: Books of stamps given to ensure even distribution of scarce items, especially in wartime. Stamps as well as money must be given to obtain an item that is scarce.

308 Drama

**Cooperative Learning** You may wish to allow time for students to work in groups of three or four to make a chart of the different characters in relationship to Anne. Names of characters should be connected with arrows pointing in both directions on which students may write concrete and abstract information about the relationship. For instance, on the arrow pointing from Mrs. Frank to Anne, students can write "mother" and a prediction or inference about her feelings toward Anne, such as "loving but disapproving." Encourage students to refer to and modify these charts throughout their reading of the play.

**MR. FRANK.** Thank you, Miep.

**MRS. FRANK.** [*To* MR. KRALER] It's illegal, then, the ration books? We've never done anything illegal.

**MR. FRANK.** We won't be living here exactly according to regulations.

[*As* MR. KRALER *reassures* MRS. FRANK, *he takes various small things, such as matches, soap, etc., from his pockets, handing them to her.*]

**MR. KRALER.** This isn't the black market,[12] Mrs. Frank. This is what we call the white market . . . helping all of the hundreds and hundreds who are hiding out in Amsterdam.

[*The carillon is heard playing the quarter-hour before eight.* MR. KRALER *looks at his watch.* ANNE *stops at the window as she comes down the stairs.*]

**ANNE.** It's the Westertoren!

**MR. KRALER.** I must go. I must be out of here and downstairs in the office before the workmen get here. [*He starts for the stairs leading out.*] Miep or I, or both of us, will be up each day to bring you food and news and find out what your needs are. Tomorrow I'll get you a better bolt for the door at the foot of the stairs. It needs a bolt that you can throw yourself and open only at our signal. [*To* MR. FRANK] Oh . . . You'll tell them about the **14** noise?

**MR. FRANK.** I'll tell them.

**MR. KRALER.** Good-bye then for the moment. I'll come up again, after the workmen leave.

**MR. FRANK.** Good-bye, Mr. Kraler.

**MRS. FRANK.** [*Shaking his hand*] How can we thank you?

---

12. **black market:** An illegal way of buying scarce items without ration stamps.

[*The others murmur their good-byes.*]

**MR. KRALER.** I never thought I'd live to see the day when a man like Mr. Frank would have **15** to go into hiding. When you think—

[*He breaks off, going out.* MR. FRANK *follows him down the steps, bolting the door after him. In the interval before he returns,* PETER *goes over to* MARGOT, *shaking hands with her. As* MR. FRANK *comes back up the steps,* MRS. FRANK *questions him anxiously.*]

**MRS. FRANK.** What did he mean, about the noise?

**MR. FRANK.** First let us take off some of these clothes.

[*They all start to take off garment after garment. On each of their coats, sweaters, blouses, suits, dresses, is another yellow Star of David.* MR. *and* MRS. FRANK *are under-dressed quite simply. The others wear several things, sweaters, extra dresses, bath-robes, aprons, nightgowns, etc.*]

**MR. VAN DAAN.** It's a wonder we weren't arrested, walking along the streets . . . Petronella with a fur coat in July . . . and that cat of Peter's crying all the way.

**ANNE.** [*As she is removing a pair of panties*] A cat?

**MRS. FRANK.** [*Shocked*] Anne, please!

**ANNE.** It's all right. I've got on three more—

[*She pulls off two more. Finally, as they have all removed their surplus clothes, they look to* MR. FRANK, *waiting for him to speak.*]

**MR. FRANK.** Now. About the noise. While the men are in the building below, we must have complete quiet. Every sound can be heard **16** down there, not only in the workrooms, but in the offices too. The men come at about eight-thirty, and leave at about five-thirty.

---

**14 Reading Strategy** Predict what Mr. Kraler means about the noise.

**15 Discussion** From Mr. Kraler's brief appearance, what conclusions can you draw about his personality?

**16 Discussion** Were your predictions correct? Discuss the conditions under which the Franks and the Van Daans must live. Ask students how they would feel living under such conditions.

**ESL Teaching Strategy** Students who are learning English as a second language will be confused by words for which they may know the literal definition but are used here in a colloquial manner. For instance, you might need to pause and explain the meaning of "black" market and Kraler's reference to a "white market." Expressions like "throwing the bolt," "put this off," "you didn't close your eyes last night," and "straighten things up" should also be clarified. Encourage ESL students to point out other words and expressions that cause confusion.

17 **Discussion** Why does the sound of marching feet cause everyone to stop talking? What sounds make you react with fear?

18 **Discussion** What other actions in ordinary daily life might reveal the existence of the secret hiding place?

19 **Discussion** What does this reveal about Mr. Frank's character?

So, to be perfectly safe, from eight in the morning until six in the evening we must move only when it is necessary, and then in stockinged feet. We must not speak above a whisper. We must not run any water. We cannot use the sink, or even, forgive me, the w.c.[13] The pipes go down through the workrooms. It would be heard. No trash . . .

17 [MR. FRANK *stops abruptly as he hears the sound of marching feet from the street below. Everyone is motionless, paralyzed with fear.* MR. FRANK *goes quietly into the room on the right to look down out of the window.* ANNE *runs after him, peering out with him. The tramping feet pass without stopping. The tension is relieved.* MR. FRANK, *followed by* ANNE, *returns to the main room and resumes his instructions to the group.*]

18 . . . No trash must ever be thrown out which might reveal that someone is living up here . . . not even a potato paring. We must burn everything in the stove at night. This is the way we must live until it is over, if we are to survive.

[*There is silence for a second.*]

**MRS. FRANK.** Until it is over.

**MR. FRANK.** [*Reassuringly*] After six we can move about . . . we can talk and laugh and have our supper and read and play games . . . just as we would at home. [*He looks at his watch.*] And now I think it would be wise if we all went to our rooms, and were settled before eight o'clock. Mrs. Van Daan, you and your husband will be upstairs. I regret that there's no place up there for Peter. But he will be here, near us. This will be our common room, where we'll meet to talk and eat and read, like one family.

**MR. VAN DAAN.** And where do you and Mrs. Frank sleep?

13. **w.c.:** water closet; bathroom.

**MR. FRANK.** This room is also our bedroom.

**MRS. VAN DAAN.** That isn't right. We'll sleep here and you take the room upstairs.

**MR. VAN DAAN.** It's your place.

} [*Together*]

**MR. FRANK.** Please. I've thought this out for weeks. It's the best arrangement. The only arrangement.

19

**MRS. VAN DAAN.** [*To* MR. FRANK] Never, never can we thank you. [*Then to* MRS. FRANK] I don't know what would have happened to us, if it hadn't been for Mr. Frank.

**MR. FRANK.** You don't know how your husband helped me when I came to this country . . . knowing no one . . . not able to speak the language. I can never repay him for that. [*Going to* VAN DAAN] May I help you with your things?

**MR. VAN DAAN.** No. No. [*To* MRS. VAN DAAN] Come along, *liefje.*[14]

**MRS. VAN DAAN.** You'll be all right, Peter? You're not afraid?

**PETER.** [*Embarrassed*] Please, Mother.

[*They start up the stairs to the attic room above.* MR. FRANK *turns to* MRS. FRANK.]

**MR. FRANK.** You too must have some rest, Edith. You didn't close your eyes last night. Nor you, Margot.

**ANNE.** I slept, Father. Wasn't that funny? I knew it was the last night in my own bed, and yet I slept soundly.

**MR. FRANK.** I'm glad, Anne. Now you'll be able to help me straighten things in here. [*To* MRS. FRANK *and* MARGOT] Come with me . . . You and Margot rest in this room for the time being.

14. *liefje* (lēf′ hyə): Dutch for "little love."

## Primary Source

On June 8, 1989 *The New York Times* reported that the Dutch government had proven the authenticity of Anne Frank's diary.

"One of the main reasons why we used scientific evidence to unravel all the facts about the diary was to expose the falsehoods of neo-Nazi and rightist groups in Europe and the United States," said David Barnouw, the co-editor of *The Diary of Anne Frank: The Critical Edition,* who is a researcher at the Netherlands State Institute for War Docu-

mentation. "Ever since her book first came out after the war, individuals and groups have made statements and issued anti-Semitic pamphlets claiming it was a hoax."

. . . Miss Frank's handwriting was closely analyzed by experts, as were specimens of her writing and those by 78 of her classmates. The experts took into account that sometimes Miss Frank used normal cursive lettering and sometimes a disconnected printing style. This is a common characteristic "applicable to the writing of young people," the experts said. Samples of her writing are included in the book to support their conclusion that the diary was indeed written by Anne Frank alone.

[*He picks up their clothes, starting for the room on the right.*]

**MRS. FRANK.** You're sure . . . ? I could help . . . And Anne hasn't had her milk . . .

**MR. FRANK.** I'll give it to her. [*To* ANNE *and* PETER] Anne, Peter . . . it's best that you take off your shoes now, before you forget.

[*He leads the way to the room, followed by* MARGOT.]

**MRS. FRANK.** You're sure you're not tired, Anne?

**ANNE.** I feel fine. I'm going to help Father.

**MRS. FRANK.** Peter, I'm glad you are to be with us.

**PETER.** Yes, Mrs. Frank.

[MRS. FRANK *goes to join* MR. FRANK *and* MARGOT.]

[*During the following scene* MR. FRANK *helps* MARGOT *and* MRS. FRANK *to hang up their clothes. Then he persuades them both to lie down and rest. The* VAN DAANS *in their room above settle themselves. In the main room* ANNE *and* PETER *remove their shoes.* PETER *takes his cat out of the carrier.*]

**ANNE.** What's your cat's name?

**PETER.** Mouschi.

**ANNE.** Mouschi! Mouschi! Mouschi! [*She picks up the cat, walking away with it. To* PETER] I love cats. I have one . . . a darling little cat. But they made me leave her behind. I left some food and a note for the neighbors to take care of her . . . I'm going to miss her terribly. What is yours? A him or a her?

**PETER.** He's a tom. He doesn't like strangers. [*He takes the cat from her, putting it back in its carrier.*]

**ANNE.** [*Unabashed*] Then I'll have to stop

Star of David patch that the Nazis forced Jews to wear

being a stranger, won't I? Is he fixed?

**PETER.** [*Startled*] Huh?

**ANNE.** Did you have him fixed?

**PETER.** No.

**ANNE.** Oh, you ought to have him fixed—to keep him from—you know, fighting. Where did you go to school?

**PETER.** Jewish Secondary.

**ANNE.** But that's where Margot and I go! I never saw you around.

**PETER.** I used to see you . . . sometimes . . .

**ANNE.** You did?

**PETER.** . . . In the school yard. You were always in the middle of a bunch of kids. [*He takes a penknife from his pocket.*]

**ANNE.** Why didn't you ever come over?

**PETER.** I'm sort of a lone wolf. [*He starts to rip off his Star of David.*]

**ANNE.** What are you doing?

*The Diary of Anne Frank*   311

311

---

**20 Literary Focus: Staging** Prompt students to read the stage directions carefully. Often in a play, the actions of the characters are as revealing as the words. When attending a play, the audience sees everything on the stage. When reading a play, we are dependent on the stage directions and our imaginations to get the whole picture. Some students may find it helpful at this point to make a rough sketch of the set to help them visualize the action.

**21 Critical Thinking and Reading** How do you think Anne feels about Peter? How do you think Peter feels about Anne? Ask your students if they have ever had a similarly awkward experience when trying to make friends. Possible responses include camp, distant relatives, or new neighbors. Based on the discussion, encourage students to make predictions about the likelihood of a friendship between Anne and Peter.

**22 Clarification** Explain that the Star of David is a symbol with both religious and political significance. It relates to the Jewish faith, and it appears on the flag of Israel. Have students look at the picture of the star on this page. Students may easily make their own stars by cutting two triangles of construction paper, overlapping them, and gluing them together. They can use the stars as bookmarks while reading this play.

---

The Forensic Science Laboratory report also points out that the paper, ink and glue in the diary and some of her accompanying loose sheets all existed in the early 1940's, before Miss Frank and her family were betrayed in their hiding place in Amsterdam and sent away to concentration camps.

The glue and fibers used in the binding of the diaries were analyzed by infrared spectrometry. Both were found in common use when Miss Frank wrote her diary. After 1950, a different kind of synthetic glue came into use. Similarly, the paper used in the diary was examined by X-ray fluorescence and found to have been manufactured between 1939 and 1942.

PETER. Taking it off.

ANNE. But you can't do that. They'll arrest you if you go out without your star.

[*He tosses his knife on the table.*]

PETER. Who's going out?

ANNE. Why, of course! You're right! Of course we don't need them any more. [*She picks up his knife and starts to take her star off.*] I wonder what our friends will think when we don't show up today?

PETER. I didn't have any dates with anyone.

ANNE. Oh, I did. I had a date with Jopie to go and play ping-pong at her house. Do you know Jopie de Waal?

PETER. No.

ANNE. Jopie's my best friend. I wonder what she'll think when she telephones and there's no answer? . . . Probably she'll go over to the house . . . I wonder what she'll think . . . we left everything as if we'd suddenly been called away . . . breakfast dishes in the sink . . . beds not made . . . [*As she pulls off her star, the cloth underneath shows clearly the color and form of the star.*] Look! It's still there!

[PETER *goes over to the stove with his star.*]

What're you going to do with yours?

PETER. Burn it.

ANNE. [*She starts to throw hers in, and cannot.*] It's funny, I can't throw mine away. I don't know why.

PETER. You can't throw . . . ? Something they branded you with . . . ? That they made you wear so they could spit on you?

ANNE. I know. I know. But after all, it *is* the Star of David, isn't it?

[*In the bedroom, right,* MARGOT *and* MRS. FRANK *are lying down.* MR. FRANK *starts quietly out.*]

PETER. Maybe it's different for a girl.

[MR. FRANK *comes into the main room.*]

MR. FRANK. Forgive me, Peter. Now let me see. We must find a bed for your cat. [*He goes to a cupboard.*] I'm glad you brought your cat. Anne was feeling so badly about hers. [*Getting a used small washtub*] Here we are. Will it be comfortable in that?

PETER. [*Gathering up his things*] Thanks.

MR. FRANK. [*Opening the door of the room on the left*] And here is your room. But I warn you, Peter, you can't grow any more. Not an inch, or you'll have to sleep with your feet out of the skylight. Are you hungry?

PETER. No.

MR. FRANK. We have some bread and butter.

PETER. No, thank you.

MR. FRANK. You can have it for luncheon then. And tonight we will have a real supper . . . our first supper together.

PETER. Thanks. Thanks. [*He goes into his room. During the following scene he arranges his possessions in his new room.*]

MR. FRANK. That's a nice boy, Peter.

ANNE. He's awfully shy, isn't he?

MR. FRANK. You'll like him, I know.

ANNE. I certainly hope so, since he's the only boy I'm likely to see for months and months.

[MR. FRANK *sits down, taking off his shoes.*]

MR. FRANK. Annele,[15] there's a box there. Will you open it?

_____

15. **Annele** (än′ ə lə): Nickname for *Anne.*

## Grammar in Action

Writers can emphasize ideas by putting them in the same grammatical form. By using the same grammatical form within a sentence or a series of sentences, writers connect ideas of equal weight for the reader.

For example, consider the following passage from *The Diary of Anne Frank:*

MR. FRANK. It'll be hard, I know. But always remember this, Anneke. There are no walls, there are no bolts, no locks that anyone can put on your mind. Miep will bring us books. We will read history, poetry, mythology.

What pattern do you find in the sentence "There are no walls, there are no books . . ."? What pattern do you see in the sentences "Miep will bring us books. We will read history, poetry, mythology"?

**Student Activity 1.** Rewrite each of the following sentences, connecting ideas by placing them in the same grammatical form.

[*He indicates a carton on the couch.* ANNE *brings it to the center table. In the street below there is the sound of children playing.*]

ANNE. [*As she opens the carton*] You know the way I'm going to think of it here? I'm going to think of it as a boarding house. A very peculiar summer boarding house, like the one that we—[*She breaks off as she pulls out some photographs.*] Father! My movie stars! I was wondering where they were! I was looking for them this morning . . . and Queen Wilhelmina![16] How wonderful!

MR. FRANK. There's something more. Go on. Look further. [*He goes over to the sink, pouring a glass of milk from a thermos bottle.*]

ANNE. [*Pulling out a pasteboard-bound book*] A diary! [*She throws her arms around her father.*] I've never had a diary. And I've always longed for one. [*She looks around the room.*] Pencil, pencil, pencil, pencil. [*She starts down the stairs.*] I'm going down to the office to get a pencil.

MR. FRANK. Anne! No! [*He goes after her, catching her by the arm and pulling her back.*]

ANNE. [*Startled*] But there's no one in the building now.

MR. FRANK. It doesn't matter. I don't want you ever to go beyond that door.

ANNE. [*Sobered*] Never . . . ? Not even at nighttime, when everyone is gone? Or on Sundays? Can't I go down to listen to the radio?

MR. FRANK. Never. I am sorry, Anneke.[17] It isn't safe. No, you must never go beyond that door.

[*For the first time* ANNE *realizes what "going into hiding" means.*]

ANNE. I see.

MR. FRANK. It'll be hard, I know. But always remember this, Anneke. There are no walls, there are no bolts, no locks that anyone can put on your mind. Miep will bring us books. We will read history, poetry, mythology. [*He gives her the glass of milk.*] Here's your milk. [*With his arm about her, they go over to the couch, sitting down side by side.*] As a matter of fact, between us, Anne, being here has certain advantages for you. For instance, you remember the battle you had with your mother the other day on the subject of overshoes? You said you'd rather die than wear overshoes? But in the end you had to wear them? Well now, you see, for as long as we are here you will never have to wear overshoes! Isn't that good? And the coat that you inherited from Margot, you won't have to wear that any more. And the piano! You won't have to practice on the piano. I tell you, this is going to be a fine life for you!

[ANNE'S *panic is gone.* PETER *appears in the doorway of his room, with a saucer in his hand. He is carrying his cat.*]

PETER. I . . . I . . . I thought I'd better get some water for Mouschi before . . .

MR. FRANK. Of course.

[*As he starts toward the sink the carillon begins to chime the hour of eight. He tiptoes to the window at the back and looks*

---

16. **Queen Wilhelmina** (kwēn′ wil′ hel mē′ nə): Queen of Holland from 1890 to 1948.

17. **Anneke** (ăn′ ə kə): Nickname for *Anne.*

*The Diary of Anne Frank* 313

24 **Discussion** What does this dialogue reveal about Anne?

25 **Critical Thinking and Reading** Based on what you know about Anne's character, what difficulties will she encounter with maintaining such a lifestyle?

26 **Discussion** In your own words, tell what Mr. Frank is saying.

---

1. There was no love, there wasn't any beauty either.
2. Some applauded, *bravo* was shouted by others.
3. Sharon will bring food. Records will be brought by Jack.
4. When my friend finds I'm gone, I wonder what she will think. What she will feel makes me wonder, too.

**Student Activity 2.** Write a paragraph in which you tell what things you think cannot be taken from a person's mind or spirit. Connect ideas of equal weight by placing them in the same grammatical form.

**Electronic Handbook** You may wish to review connecting ideas of equal weight with your students before they complete the Grammar in Action activities. If your students are using the Language Master 6000, have them enter the access word *conjunction* or *parallel* and press the GRAMMAR key to get information about using conjunctions and parallel structure when connecting ideas.

**27 Discussion** How long have the Franks been in hiding?

**28 Discussion** Elicit suggestions from students' own experiences of situations that might cause an exuberant burst of energy like Anne's.

■ **Videocassette** Play scenes 1 and 2 of *The Diary of Anne Frank* in the **Library of Video Classics.** How does the action in the film compare with the action described in the play? How do the characters compare with the way you envisioned them while reading? During discussion of similarities and differences between the film and the play, prompt students to record events from the play on their story map or in their reader's response journals. Their response to the visual stimulus of the film may also facilitate active discussions about character, theme, setting, and dramatic devices like the flashback.

*down at the street below. He turns to* PETER, *indicating in pantomime that it is too late.* PETER *starts back for his room. He steps on a creaking board. The three of them are frozen for a minute in fear. As* PETER *starts away again,* ANNE *tiptoes over to him and pours some of the milk from her glass into the saucer for the cat.* PETER *squats on the floor, putting the milk before the cat.* MR. FRANK *gives* ANNE *his fountain pen, and then goes into the room at the right. For a second* ANNE *watches the cat, then she goes over to the center table, and opens her diary.*

*In the room at the right,* MRS. FRANK *has sat up quickly at the sound of the carillon.* MR. FRANK *comes in and sits down beside her on the settee, his arm comfortingly around her.*

*Upstairs, in the attic room,* MR. *and* MRS. VAN DAAN *have hung their clothes in the closet and are now seated on the iron bed.* MRS. VAN DAAN *leans back exhausted.* MR. VAN DAAN *fans her with a newspaper.*

ANNE *starts to write in her diary. The lights dim out, the curtain falls.*

*In the darkness* ANNE'S VOICE *comes to us again, faintly at first, and then with growing strength.*]

**ANNE'S VOICE.** I expect I should be describing what it feels like to go into hiding. But I really don't know yet myself. I only know it's funny never to be able to go outdoors . . . never to breathe fresh air . . . never to run and shout and jump. It's the silence in the nights that frightens me most. Every time I hear a creak in the house, or a step on the street outside, I'm sure they're coming for us. The days aren't so bad. At least we know that Miep and Mr. Kraler are down there below us in the office. Our protectors, we call them. I asked Father what would happen to them if the Nazis found out they were hiding us. Pim said that they would suffer the same

fate that we would . . . Imagine! They know this, and yet when they come up here, they're always cheerful and gay as if there were nothing in the world to bother them . . . Friday, the twenty-first of August, nineteen forty-two. Today I'm going to tell you our general news. Mother is unbearable. She insists on treating me like a baby, which I loathe. Otherwise things are going better. The weather is . . .

[*As* ANNE'S VOICE *is fading out, the curtain rises on the scene.*]

### Scene 3

[*It is a little after six o'clock in the evening, two months later.*

MARGOT *is in the bedroom at the right, studying.* MR. VAN DAAN *is lying down in the attic room above.*

*The rest of the "family" is in the main room.* ANNE *and* PETER *sit opposite each other at the center table, where they have been doing their lessons.* MRS. FRANK *is on the couch.* MRS. VAN DAAN *is seated with her fur coat, on which she has been sewing, in her lap. None of them are wearing their shoes.*

*Their eyes are on* MR. FRANK, *waiting for him to give them the signal which will release them from their day-long quiet.* MR. FRANK, *his shoes in his hand, stands looking down out of the window at the back, watching to be sure that all of the workmen have left the building below.*

*After a few seconds of motionless silence,* MR. FRANK *turns from the window.*]

**MR. FRANK.** [*Quietly, to the group*] It's safe now. The last workman has left.

[*There is an immediate stir of relief.*]

**ANNE.** [*Her pent-up energy explodes.*] WHEE!

## 28

314 *Drama*

## Grammar in Action

An **infinitive** is the form of a verb that comes after the word *to;* it can act as a noun, an adjective, or an adverb. Infinitives are not to be confused with prepositional phrases beginning with *to.* Prepositional phrases beginning with *to* end with nouns (*to class*); infinitives begin with *to* and end with a verb (*to give*). An infinitive can be expanded to form an **infinitive phrase,** an infinitive with a modifier or complement, all acting together as a single part of speech. For example, on page 315, Margot says, "I

have to help with supper." "To help with supper" is an infinitive phrase.

The frequent use of infinitives in *The Diary of Anne Frank* enhances the poignancy of the story because of the limitations expressed in these verbs. Anne wants "to be able to go outdoors . . . to breathe fresh air . . . to run and shout and jump." Instead she has "to go into hiding . . . to be dignified."

**Student Activity 1.** In the following sentences from the play, identify whether the phrase is an infinitive or a prepositional phrase:

MRS. FRANK. [*Startled, amused*] Anne!

MRS. VAN DAAN. I'm first for the w.c.

[*She hurries off to the bathroom.* MRS. FRANK *puts on her shoes and starts up to the sink to prepare supper.* ANNE *sneaks* PETER'S *shoes from under the table and hides them behind her back.* MR. FRANK *goes in to* MARGOT'S *room.*]

MR. FRANK. [*To* MARGOT] Six o'clock. School's over.

[MARGOT *gets up, stretching.* MR. FRANK *sits down to put on his shoes. In the main room* PETER *tries to find his.*]

PETER. [*To* ANNE] Have you seen my shoes?

ANNE. [*Innocently*] Your shoes?

PETER. You've taken them, haven't you?

ANNE. I don't know what you're talking about.

PETER. You're going to be sorry!

ANNE. Am I?

[PETER *goes after her.* ANNE, *with his shoes in her hand, runs from him, dodging behind her mother.*]

MRS. FRANK. [*Protesting*] Anne, dear!

PETER. Wait till I get you!

ANNE. I'm waiting!

[PETER *makes a lunge for her. They both fall to the floor.* PETER *pins her down, wrestling with her to get the shoes.*]

Don't! Don't! Peter, stop it. Ouch!

MRS. FRANK. Anne! . . . Peter!

[*Suddenly* PETER *becomes self-conscious. He grabs his shoes roughly and starts for his room.*]

ANNE. [*Following him*] Peter, where are you going? Come dance with me.

PETER. I tell you I don't know how.

ANNE. I'll teach you.

PETER. I'm going to give Mouschi his dinner.

ANNE. Can I watch?

PETER. He doesn't like people around while he eats.

ANNE. Peter, please.

PETER. No! [*He goes into his room.* ANNE *slams his door after him.*]

MRS. FRANK. Anne, dear, I think you shouldn't play like that with Peter. It's not dignified.

ANNE. Who cares if it's dignified? I don't want to be dignified.

[MR. FRANK *and* MARGOT *come from the room on the right.* MARGOT *goes to help her mother.* MR. FRANK *starts for the center table to correct* MARGOT'S *school papers.*]

MRS. FRANK. [*To* ANNE] You complain that I don't treat you like a grownup. But when I do, you resent it.

ANNE. I only want some fun . . . someone to laugh and clown with . . . After you've sat still all day and hardly moved, you've got to have some fun. I don't know what's the matter with that boy.

MR. FRANK. He isn't used to girls. Give him a little time.

ANNE. Time? Isn't two months time? I could cry. [*Catching hold of* MARGOT] Come on, Margot . . . dance with me. Come on, please.

MARGOT. I have to help with supper.

*The Diary of Anne Frank* 315

29

30

29 **Discussion** How would you describe Anne's and Peter's feelings toward each other? Have they changed since they first met?

30 **Discussion** Ask students to share their thoughts and feelings about this exchange between Anne and her mother.

**Cooperative Learning** A role-playing activity may help students communicate their feelings and consider the discussion between Anne and Mrs. Frank from both viewpoints. Have students take turns acting as Mrs. Frank and Anne and continue the conversation further. Follow the group work with an independent response time. Students may write in their journals, express their responses in artwork, write poems, or make lists of songs and books that evoke similar responses in them.

1. He turns to Peter.
2. Anne starts to write in her diary.
3. For a second Anne watches the cat, then she goes over to the center table, and opens her diary.
4. Today I'm going to tell you our general news.
5. You're going to be sorry.

**Student Activity 2.** Write a diary entry of your own in which you discuss significant events of the day or of the past few days as well as your hopes for the future. Use infinitives in your entry.

**Electronic Handbook** You may wish to review the infinitive form of verbs with your students before they complete the Grammar in Action activities. If your students are using the Language Master 6000, have them enter the access word *verbal* and press the GRAMMAR key to get information about verb phrases and understanding infinitives.

**31 Discussion** Discuss Mr. Van Daan's emphasis on Peter's lessons. What does this reveal about Mr. Van Daan's attitude toward the future? How does this attitude compare with Anne's comment about not wanting to forget how to dance?

**32 Reading Strategy** Use this exchange of words to infer what Mr. Van Daan says.

**ESL Teaching Strategy** Use the passage of time in the play to reinforce words that express time for your students who are acquiring English proficiency. You may concretely show the passage of months by highlighting the diary dates and showing your students a calendar. Students who are proficient in English might help clarify the meaning of each month by illustrating some representative scene. Have students act out different activities for morning, afternoon, and evening. Help students become comfortable with abstract terms like "after a while," "soon," and "later" by using them to summarize the action of the play.

*Anne and her father, Otto Frank*

**ANNE.** You know we're going to forget how to dance . . . When we get out we won't remember a thing.

[*She starts to sing and dance by herself.* MR. FRANK *takes her in his arms, waltzing with her.* MRS. VAN DAAN *comes in from the bathroom.*]

**MRS. VAN DAAN.** Next? [*She looks around as she starts putting on her shoes.*] Where's Peter?

**ANNE.** [*As they are dancing*] Where would he be!

**31**

**MRS. VAN DAAN.** He hasn't finished his lessons, has he? His father'll kill him if he catches him in there with that cat and his work not done.

[MR. FRANK *and* ANNE *finish their dance. They bow to each other with extravagant formality.*]

Anne, get him out of there, will you?

**ANNE.** [*At* PETER'S *door*] Peter? Peter?

**PETER.** [*Opening the door a crack*] What is it?

**ANNE.** Your mother says to come out.

**PETER.** I'm giving Mouschi his dinner.

**MRS. VAN DAAN.** You know what your father says. [*She sits on the couch, sewing on the lining of her fur coat.*]

**32**

**PETER.** For heaven's sake, I haven't even looked at him since lunch.

**MRS. VAN DAAN.** I'm just telling you, that's all.

**ANNE.** I'll feed him.

**PETER.** I don't want you in there.

**MRS. VAN DAAN.** Peter!

**PETER.** [*To* ANNE] Then give him his dinner and come right out, you hear?

[*He comes back to the table.* ANNE *shuts the door of* PETER'S *room after her and disappears behind the curtain covering his closet.*]

**MRS. VAN DAAN.** [*To* PETER] Now is that any way to talk to your little girl friend?

**PETER.** Mother . . . for heaven's sake . . . will you please stop saying that?

**MRS. VAN DAAN.** Look at him blush! Look at him!

33 **PETER.** Please! I'm not . . . anyway . . . let me alone, will you?

**MRS. VAN DAAN.** He acts like it was something to be ashamed of. It's nothing to be ashamed of, to have a little girl friend.

**PETER.** You're crazy. She's only thirteen.

**MRS. VAN DAAN.** So what? And you're sixteen. Just perfect. Your father's ten years older than I am. [*To* MR. FRANK] I warn you, Mr. Frank, if this war lasts much longer, we're going to be related and then . . .

**MR. FRANK.** *Mazeltov!*[18]

34 **MRS. FRANK.** [*Deliberately changing the conversation*] I wonder where Miep is. She's usually so prompt.

[*Suddenly everything else is forgotten as they hear the sound of an automobile coming to a screeching stop in the street below.*

---

18. *mazeltov* (mä′ z'l tōv′): "Good luck" in Hebrew and Yiddish.

*They are tense, motionless in their terror. The car starts away. A wave of relief sweeps over them. They pick up their occupations again.* ANNE *flings open the door of* PETER'S *room, making a dramatic entrance. She is dressed in* PETER'S *clothes.* PETER *looks at her in fury. The others are amused.*]

35

**ANNE.** Good evening, everyone. Forgive me if I don't stay. [*She jumps up on a chair.*] I have a friend waiting for me in there. My friend Tom. Tom Cat. Some people say that we look alike. But Tom has the most beautiful whiskers, and I have only a little fuzz. I am hoping . . . in time . . .

**PETER.** All right, Mrs. Quack Quack!

**ANNE.** [*Outraged—jumping down*] Peter!

36 **PETER.** I heard about you . . . How you talked so much in class they called you Mrs. Quack Quack. How Mr. Smitter made you write a composition . . . "'Quack, quack,' said Mrs. Quack Quack."

**ANNE.** Well, go on. Tell them the rest. How it was so good he read it out loud to the class and then read it to all his other classes!

**PETER.** Quack! Quack! Quack . . . Quack . . . Quack . . .

[ANNE *pulls off the coat and trousers.*]

**ANNE.** You are the most intolerable, insufferable boy I've ever met!

[*She throws the clothes down the stairwell.* PETER *goes down after them.*]

**PETER.** Quack, quack, quack!

**MRS. VAN DAAN.** [*To* ANNE] That's right, Anneke! Give it to him!

**ANNE.** With all the boys in the world . . . Why I had to get locked up with one like you! . . .

*The Diary of Anne Frank* 317

**33 Critical Thinking and Reading** How do you think Peter feels about Anne? Why do you think he behaves the way he does?

**34 Reading Strategy** Why does Mrs. Frank change the subject? How is this consistent with what you know about her character?

**35 Reading Strategy** What is the emotional effect of juxtaposing the terror of hearing the car with the absurdity of seeing Anne dressed in Peter's clothes?

**36 Enrichment** As your students may already have inferred, Anne was very talkative in class and was often corrected for it. The incident to which Peter refers is actually recorded in Anne's diary. In fact she had to write three separate essays. The titles assigned by her teacher reflect a growing frustration with Anne's impulsive talking: "The Chatterbox," "The Incurable Chatterbox," and "'Quack, Quack, Quack,' Says Mrs. Natterbeak." It is also true that the teacher read an essay aloud and praised Anne's writing. More than one of Anne's teachers predicted she would have a future as a writer. Ask students to consider the different ways adults respond to Anne. Why do they think she inspires such varied reactions?

37 **Reading Strategy** What do Anne's actions say about her relationship with each of her parents?

38 **Clarification** You may wish to point out to your students that "w.c." stands for *water closet,* a term for lavatory or bathroom. How does this information add humor to Mrs. Van Daan's admonition to avoid giving pills to Anne? What might be the inconvenient result?

*Edith Frank, Anne's mother*

**PETER.** Quack, quack, quack, and from now on stay out of my room!

[*As* PETER *passes her,* ANNE *puts out her foot, tripping him. He picks himself up, and goes on into his room.*]

**MRS. FRANK.** [*Quietly*] Anne, dear . . . your hair. [*She feels* ANNE'S *forehead.*] You're warm. Are you feeling all right?

**ANNE.** Please, Mother. [*She goes over to the center table, slipping into her shoes.*]

**MRS. FRANK.** [*Following her*] You haven't a fever, have you?

**ANNE.** [*Pulling away*] No. No.

**MRS. FRANK.** You know we can't call a doctor here, ever. There's only one thing to do . . . watch carefully. Prevent an illness before it comes. Let me see your tongue.

**ANNE.** Mother, this is perfectly absurd.

**MRS. FRANK.** Anne, dear, don't be such a baby. Let me see your tongue. [*As* ANNE *refuses,* MRS. FRANK *appeals to* MR. FRANK.] Otto . . . ?

**MR. FRANK.** You hear your mother, Anne.

[ANNE *flicks out her tongue for a second, then turns away.*]

**MRS. FRANK.** Come on—open up! [*As* ANNE *opens her mouth very wide*] You seem all right . . . but perhaps an aspirin . . .

**MRS. VAN DAAN.** For heaven's sake, don't give that child any pills. I waited for fifteen minutes this morning for her to come out of the w.c.

**ANNE.** I was washing my hair!

318   *Drama*

**MR. FRANK.** I think there's nothing the matter with our Anne that a ride on her bike, or a visit with her friend Jopie de Waal wouldn't cure. Isn't that so, Anne?

[MR. VAN DAAN *comes down into the room. From outside we hear faint sounds of bombers going over and a burst of ack-ack.*][19]

**MR. VAN DAAN.** Miep not come yet?

**MRS. VAN DAAN.** The workmen just left, a little while ago.

**MR. VAN DAAN.** What's for dinner tonight?

**MRS. VAN DAAN.** Beans.

**MR. VAN DAAN.** Not again!

**MRS. VAN DAAN.** Poor Putti! I know. But what can we do? That's all that Miep brought us.

[MR. VAN DAAN *starts to pace, his hands behind his back.* ANNE *follows behind him, imitating him.*]

**ANNE.** We are now in what is known as the "bean cycle." Beans boiled, beans en casserole, beans with strings, beans without strings . . .

[PETER *has come out of his room. He slides into his place at the table, becoming immediately absorbed in his studies.*]

**MR. VAN DAAN.** [*To* PETER] I saw you . . . in there, playing with your cat.

**MRS. VAN DAAN.** He just went in for a second, putting his coat away. He's been out here all the time, doing his lessons.

**MR. FRANK.** [*Looking up from the papers*] Anne, you got an excellent in your history paper today . . . and very good in Latin.

**ANNE.** [*Sitting beside him*] How about algebra?

**MR. FRANK.** I'll have to make a confession. Up until now I've managed to stay ahead of you in algebra. Today you caught up with me. We'll leave it to Margot to correct.

**ANNE.** Isn't algebra *vile*, Pim!

**MR. FRANK.** Vile!

**MARGOT.** [*To* MR. FRANK] How did I do?

**ANNE.** [*Getting up*] Excellent, excellent, excellent, excellent!

**MR. FRANK.** [*To* MARGOT] You should have used the subjunctive[20] here . . .

**MARGOT.** Should I? . . . I thought . . . look here . . . I didn't use it here . . .

[*The two become absorbed in the papers.*]

**ANNE.** Mrs. Van Daan, may I try on your coat?

**MRS. FRANK.** No, Anne.

**MRS. VAN DAAN.** [*Giving it to* ANNE] It's all right . . . but careful with it.

[ANNE *puts it on and struts with it.*]

My father gave me that the year before he died. He always bought the best that money could buy.

**ANNE.** Mrs. Van Daan, did you have a lot of boy friends before you were married?

**MRS. FRANK.** Anne, that's a personal question. It's not courteous to ask personal questions.

**MRS. VAN DAAN.** Oh I don't mind. [*To* ANNE] Our house was always swarming with boys. When I was a girl we had . . .

---

**19. ack-ack** (ak′ ak′) *n.*: Slang for an antiaircraft gun's fire.

**20. subjunctive** (səb juŋk′ tiv) *n.*: A particular form of a verb.

*The Diary of Anne Frank* 319

**39 Discussion** Do you agree with Mr. Frank's statement? How would a bike ride or a visit with a friend help Anne?

**40 Reading Strategy** Contrast this attitude with how fortunate Mr. Van Daan felt at the beginning of the play. Why do you think his outlook has changed? What other changes in each character's attitudes and behaviors have you noticed?

**41 Literary Focus: Character** What do these responses reveal about each woman's ideas of good manners and appropriate behavior?

**Cooperative Learning** Divide the class into two groups, those who wish to explore Mrs. Van Daan's character and those who wish to explore Mrs. Frank's. Allow the groups to meet and discuss their thoughts on each character's feelings, motivations, beliefs, and attitudes. Encourage students to stretch their imaginations, using the text of the play as a basis for making inferences about the two women. They will then take turns to act as the character and field questions from the other group. Students might inquire how the character feels about each of the other characters, her response to the current situation, what her life was like prior to hiding, what she misses most in hiding, and how she feels about their chances for avoiding discovery.

**Reading Strategy** What can you infer from Mr. Van Daan's response to Mrs. Van Daan's story?

**Critical Thinking and Reading** Based on what you know about Mrs. Frank, how do you think she is responding to Mrs. Van Daan's actions? You may wish to have students role-play this part of the scene to allow them to express their responses with body language and facial expressions as well as descriptions.

**Discussion** Why do you think Mr. Frank suggests that they study in Peter's room instead of at the table as the girls do?

**42** **MR. VAN DAAN.** Oh, God. Not again!

**MRS. VAN DAAN.** [*Good-humored*] Shut up!

[*Without a pause, to* ANNE. MR. VAN DAAN *mimics* MRS. VAN DAAN. *speaking the first few words in unison with her.*]

One summer we had a big house in Hilversum. The boys came buzzing round like bees around a jam pot. And when I was sixteen! **43** . . . We were wearing our skirts very short those days and I had good-looking legs. [*She pulls up her skirt, going to* MR. FRANK.] I still have 'em. I may not be as pretty as I used to be, but I still have my legs. How about it, Mr. Frank?

**MR. VAN DAAN.** All right. All right. We see them.

**MRS. VAN DAAN.** I'm not asking you. I'm asking Mr. Frank.

**PETER.** Mother, for heaven's sake.

**MRS. VAN DAAN.** Oh, I embarrass you, do I? Well, I just hope the girl you marry has as good. [*Then to* ANNE] My father used to worry about me, with so many boys hanging round. He told me, if any of them gets fresh, you say to him . . . "Remember, Mr. So-and-So, remember I'm a lady."

**ANNE.** "Remember, Mr. So-and-So, remember I'm a lady." [*She gives* MRS. VAN DAAN *her coat.*]

**MR. VAN DAAN.** Look at you, talking that way in front of her! Don't you know she puts it all down in that diary?

**MRS. VAN DAAN.** So, if she does? I'm only telling the truth!

[ANNE *stretches out, putting her ear to the floor, listening to what is going on below. The sound of the bombers fades away.*]

**MRS. FRANK.** [*Setting the table*] Would you mind, Peter, if I moved you over to the couch?

**ANNE.** [*Listening*] Miep must have the radio on.

[PETER *picks up his papers, going over to the couch beside* MRS. VAN DAAN.]

**MR. VAN DAAN.** [*Accusingly, to* PETER] Haven't you finished yet?

**PETER.** No.

**MR. VAN DAAN.** You ought to be ashamed of yourself.

**PETER.** All right. All right. I'm a dunce. I'm a hopeless case. Why do I go on?

**MRS. VAN DAAN.** You're not hopeless. Don't talk that way. It's just that you haven't anyone to help you, like the girls have. [*To* MR. FRANK] Maybe you could help him, Mr. Frank?

**MR. FRANK.** I'm sure that his father . . . ?

**MR. VAN DAAN.** Not me. I can't do anything with him. He won't listen to me. You go ahead . . . if you want.

**MR. FRANK.** [*Going to* PETER] What about it, Peter? Shall we make our school coeducational?

**MRS. VAN DAAN.** [*Kissing* MR. FRANK] You're an angel, Mr. Frank. An angel. I don't know why I didn't meet you before I met that one there. Here, sit down, Mr. Frank . . . [*She forces him down on the couch beside* PETER.] Now, Peter, you listen to Mr. Frank.

**MR. FRANK.** It might be better for us to go into Peter's room.

**44**

[PETER *jumps up eagerly, leading the way.*]

**MRS. VAN DAAN.** That's right. You go in there, Peter. You listen to Mr. Frank. Mr. Frank is a highly educated man.

[*As* MR. FRANK *is about to follow* PETER *into his room,* MRS. FRANK *stops him and wipes the lipstick from his lips. Then she closes the door after them.*]

**ANNE.** [*On the floor, listening*] Shh! I can hear a man's voice talking.

**MR. VAN DAAN.** [*To* ANNE] Isn't it bad enough here without your sprawling all over the place?

[ANNE *sits up.*]

**MRS. VAN DAAN.** [*To* MR. VAN DAAN] If you didn't smoke so much, you wouldn't be so bad-tempered.

**MR. VAN DAAN.** Am I smoking? Do you see me smoking?

**45** **MRS. VAN DAAN.** Don't tell me you've used up all those cigarettes.

**MR. VAN DAAN.** One package. Miep only brought me one package.

**MRS. VAN DAAN.** It's a filthy habit anyway. It's a good time to break yourself.

**MR. VAN DAAN.** Oh, stop it, please.

**MRS. VAN DAAN.** You're smoking up all our money. You know that, don't you?

**MR. VAN DAAN.** Will you shut up?

[*During this,* MRS. FRANK *and* MARGOT *have studiously kept their eyes down. But* ANNE, *seated on the floor, has been following the discussion interestedly.* MR. VAN DAAN *turns to see her staring up at him.*]

And what are you staring at?

**ANNE.** I never heard grownups quarrel before. I thought only children quarreled.

**MR. VAN DAAN.** This isn't a quarrel! It's a discussion. And I never heard children so rude before.

**ANNE.** [*Rising, indignantly*] I, rude!

**MR. VAN DAAN.** Yes!

**MRS. FRANK.** [*Quickly*] Anne, will you get me my knitting?

[ANNE *goes to get it.*]

I must remember, when Miep comes, to ask her to bring me some more wool.

**MARGOT.** [*Going to her room*] I need some hairpins and some soap. I made a list. [*She goes into her bedroom to get the list.*]

**MRS. FRANK.** [*To* ANNE] Have you some library books for Miep when she comes?

**ANNE.** It's a wonder that Miep has a life of her own, the way we make her run errands for us. Please, Miep, get me some starch. Please take my hair out and have it cut. Tell me all the latest news, Miep. [*She goes over, kneeling on the couch beside* MRS. VAN DAAN] Did you know she was engaged? His name is Dirk, and Miep's afraid the Nazis will ship him off to Germany to work in one of their war plants. That's what they're doing with some of the young Dutchmen . . . they pick them up off the streets—

**MR. VAN DAAN.** [*Interrupting*] Don't you ever get tired of talking? Suppose you try keeping still for five minutes. Just five minutes.

[*He starts to pace again. Again* ANNE *follows him, mimicking him.* MRS. FRANK *jumps up and takes her by the arm up to the sink, and gives her a glass of milk.*]

**MRS. FRANK.** Come here, Anne. It's time for your glass of milk.

**MR. VAN DAAN.** Talk, talk, talk. I never heard such a child. Where is my . . . ? Every eve-

321

**45** **Discussion** What effect has living in hiding begun to have on the people?

**46** **Discussion** What effect does Mrs. Frank have on the quarrel?

**47** **Discussion** What points of Anne's assertions are valid? How do you think Miep feels about doing so much for these people? Why do you think she and Mr. Kraler do it?

**48** **Enrichment** People like Miep and Mr. Kraler were at work rescuing and protecting Jews in every country affected by the Holocaust. You will find accounts of these courageous individuals, including interviews, in *The Courage to Care,* edited by Carol Rittner, New York University Press, 1986.

**49 Discussion** How does Anne's present attitude differ from her attitude the first time she said these words? How did she seem to feel about Mrs. Van Daan's story then? How does she seem to feel about it now? Why do you think Anne is acting as she is?

**50 Discussion** Discuss how Anne is still able to fantasize and plan for the future. What does this show about her character?

**51 Critical Thinking and Reading** Point out to your students that including the fur coat in the conflict was probably a conscious choice by the playwrights. Why is it significant that the culmination of the argument is the accident with the fur coat? How did the fur coat function in Anne's and Mrs. Van Daan's relationship earlier in the play? How does it function now?

ning it's the same talk, talk, talk. [*He looks around.*] Where is my . . . ?

**MRS. VAN DAAN.** What're you looking for?

**MR. VAN DAAN.** My pipe. Have you seen my pipe?

**MRS. VAN DAAN.** What good's a pipe? You haven't got any tobacco.

**MR. VAN DAAN.** At least I'll have something to hold in my mouth! [*Opening* MARGOT'S *bedroom door*] Margot, have you seen my pipe?

**MARGOT.** It was on the table last night.

[ANNE *puts her glass of milk on the table and picks up his pipe, hiding it behind her back.*]

**MR. VAN DAAN.** I know. I know. Anne, did you see my pipe? . . . Anne!

**MRS. FRANK.** Anne, Mr. Van Daan is speaking to you.

**ANNE.** Am I allowed to talk now?

**MR. VAN DAAN.** You're the most aggravating . . . The trouble with you is, you've been spoiled. What you need is a good old-fashioned spanking.

**49** **ANNE.** [*Mimicking* MRS. VAN DAAN] "Remember, Mr. So-and-So, remember I'm a lady." [*She thrusts the pipe into his mouth, then picks up her glass of milk.*]

**MR. VAN DAAN.** [*Restraining himself with difficulty*] Why aren't you nice and quiet like your sister Margot? Why do you have to show off all the time? Let me give you a little advice, young lady. Men don't like that kind of thing in a girl. You know that? A man likes a girl who'll listen to him once in a while . . . a domestic girl, who'll keep her house shining for her husband . . . who loves to cook and sew and . . .

**ANNE.** I'd cut my throat first! I'd open my veins! I'm going to be remarkable! I'm going to Paris . . .

**MR. VAN DAAN.** [*Scoffingly*] Paris!

**ANNE.** . . . to study music and art.

**MR. VAN DAAN.** Yeah! Yeah!

**50** **ANNE.** I'm going to be a famous dancer or singer . . . or something wonderful.

[*She makes a wide gesture, spilling the glass of milk on the fur coat in* MRS. VAN DAAN'S *lap.* MARGOT *rushes quickly over with a towel.* ANNE *tries to brush the milk off with her skirt.*]

**MRS. VAN DAAN.** Now look what you've done . . . you clumsy little fool! My beautiful fur coat my father gave me . . .

**ANNE.** I'm so sorry.

**51** **MRS. VAN DAAN.** What do you care? It isn't yours . . . So go on, ruin it! Do you know what that coat cost? Do you? And now look at it! Look at it!

**ANNE.** I'm very, very sorry.

**MRS. VAN DAAN.** I could kill you for this. I could just kill you!

[MRS. VAN DAAN *goes up the stairs, clutching the coat.* MR. VAN DAAN *starts after her.*]

**MR. VAN DAAN.** Petronella . . . *liefje! Liefje!* . . . Come back . . . the supper . . . come back!

**MRS. FRANK.** Anne, you must not behave in that way.

**ANNE.** It was an accident. Anyone can have an accident.

**MRS. FRANK.** I don't mean that. I mean the answering back. You must not answer back. They are our guests. We must always show the greatest courtesy to them. We're all living under terrible tension.

[*She stops as* MARGOT *indicates that* VAN DAAN *can hear. When he is gone, she continues.*]

That's why we must control ourselves . . . You don't hear Margot getting into arguments with them, do you? Watch Margot. She's always courteous with them. Never familiar. She keeps her distance. And they respect her for it. Try to be like Margot.

**ANNE.** And have them walk all over me, the way they do her? No, thanks!

**MRS. FRANK.** I'm not afraid that anyone is going to walk all over you, Anne. I'm afraid for other people, that you'll walk on them. I don't know what happens to you, Anne. You are wild, self-willed. If I had ever talked to my mother as you talk to me . . .

**ANNE.** Things have changed. People aren't like that any more. "Yes, Mother." "No, Mother." "Anything you say, Mother." I've got to fight things out for myself! Make something of myself!

**MRS. FRANK.** It isn't necessary to fight to do it. Margot doesn't fight, and isn't she . . . ?

**ANNE.** [*Violently rebellious*] Margot! Margot! Margot! That's all I hear from everyone . . . how wonderful Margot is . . . "Why aren't you like Margot?"

**MARGOT.** [*Protesting*] Oh, come on, Anne, don't be so . . .

**ANNE.** [*Paying no attention*] Everything she does is right, and everything I do is wrong! I'm the goat around here! . . . You're all against me! . . . And you worst of all!

[*She rushes off into her room and throws herself down on the settee, stifling her sobs.* MRS. FRANK *sighs and starts toward the stove.*]

**MRS. FRANK.** [*To* MARGOT] Let's put the soup on the stove . . . if there's anyone who cares to eat. Margot, will you take the bread out?

[MARGOT *gets the bread from the cupboard.*]

I don't know how we can go on living this way . . . I can't say a word to Anne . . . she flies at me . . .

**MARGOT.** You know Anne. In half an hour she'll be out here, laughing and joking.

**MRS. FRANK.** And . . . [*She makes a motion upwards, indicating the* VAN DAANS.] . . . I told your father it wouldn't work . . . but no . . . no . . . he had to ask them, he said . . . he owed it to him, he said. Well, he knows now that I was right! These quarrels! . . . This bickering!

**MARGOT.** [*With a warning look*] Shush. Shush.

[*The buzzer for the door sounds.* MRS. FRANK *gasps, startled.*]

**MRS. FRANK.** Every time I hear that sound, my heart stops!

**MARGOT.** [*Starting for* PETER'S *door*] It's Miep. [*She knocks at the door.*] Father?

[MR. FRANK *comes quickly from* PETER'S *room.*]

**MR. FRANK.** Thank you, Margot. [*As he goes down the steps to open the outer door*] Has everyone his list?

**MARGOT.** I'll get my books. [*Giving her mother a list*] Here's your list.

[MARGOT *goes into her and* ANNE'S *bedroom on the right.* ANNE *sits up, hiding her tears, as* MARGOT *comes in.*]

Miep's here.

[MARGOT *picks up her books and goes back.* ANNE *hurries over to the mirror, smoothing her hair.*]

*The Diary of Anne Frank* 323

**52 Discussion** Compare and contrast how Mrs. Frank views each of her daughters.

**53 Discussion** How does Anne feel about Margot? How does she feel she compares with Margot?

**54 Literary Focus: Character** How accurate is Margot's assessment of Anne? Support your opinion with other examples of Anne's behavior.

**55 Reading Strategy** What is Margot's worry?

## Primary Source

Like many young people, Anne had some difficulty expressing her inner feelings, thoughts, fears, hopes, and dreams to adults. Sometimes her frustrations and confusion were expressed in outbursts such as the one in this scene. She often wrote in her diary how misunderstood she felt, a situation that was exacerbated by the constant confinement. Not only did the close quarters make everyone more irritable, it also gave Anne no chance to escape the scrutiny of those who would "improve" her. On the seventh of November in 1942, she wrote,

My treatment varies so much. One day Anne is sensible and is allowed to know everything; and the next day I hear that Anne is just a silly little goat who doesn't know anything at all and imagines that she's learned a wonderful lot from books. I'm not a baby or a spoiled darling any more, to be laughed at, . . . I have my own views, plans, and ideas, though I can't put them into words yet. Oh, so many things bubble up inside me as I lie in bed having to put up with people I'm fed up with, who always misinterpret my intentions. I too can reach the bursting point.

Have students write in their journals their responses to Anne's actions in the play and her words in the diary.

**56 Critical Thinking and Reading** Are you surprised that Mrs. Frank observes good manners even after such an argument? Why or why not?

*Aerial view of Amsterdam, Holland. The house where Anne Frank hid is tinted.*

**MR. VAN DAAN.** [*Coming down the stairs*] Is it Miep?

**MARGOT.** Yes. Father's gone down to let her in.

**MR. VAN DAAN.** At last I'll have some cigarettes!

**MRS. FRANK.** [*To* MR. VAN DAAN] I can't tell you how unhappy I am about Mrs. Van Daan's coat. Anne should never have touched it.

**MR. VAN DAAN.** She'll be all right.

**MRS. FRANK.** Is there anything I can do?

**MR. VAN DAAN.** Don't worry.

[*He turns to meet* MIEP. *But it is not* MIEP *who comes up the steps. It is* MR. KRALER, *followed by* MR. FRANK. *Their faces are* grave. ANNE *comes from the bedroom.* PETER *comes from his room.*]

**MRS. FRANK.** Mr. Kraler!

**MR. VAN DAAN.** How are you, Mr. Kraler?

**MARGOT.** This is a surprise.

**MRS. FRANK.** When Mr. Kraler comes, the sun begins to shine.

**MR. VAN DAAN.** Miep is coming?

**MR. KRALER.** Not tonight.

[KRALER *goes to* MARGOT *and* MRS. FRANK *and* ANNE, *shaking hands with them.*]

**MRS. FRANK.** Wouldn't you like a cup of coffee? . . . Or, better still, will you have supper with us?

56

324 *Drama*

**MR. FRANK.** Mr. Kraler has something to talk over with us. Something has happened, he says, which demands an immediate decision.

**MRS. FRANK.** [Fearful] What is it?

[MR. KRALER sits down on the couch. As he talks he takes bread, cabbages, milk, etc., from his briefcase, giving them to MARGOT and ANNE to put away.]

**MR. KRALER.** Usually, when I come up here, I try to bring you some bit of good news. What's the use of telling you the bad news when there's nothing that you can do about it? But today something has happened . . . Dirk . . . Miep's Dirk, you know, came to me just now. He tells me that he has a Jewish friend living near him. A dentist. He says he's in trouble. He begged me, could I do anything for this man? Could I find him a hiding place? . . . So I've come to you . . . I know it's a terrible thing to ask of you, living as you are, but would you take him in with you?

**MR. FRANK.** Of course we will.

**MR. KRALER.** [Rising] It'll be just for a night or two . . . until I find some other place. This happened so suddenly that I didn't know where to turn.

**MR. FRANK.** Where is he?

**MR. KRALER.** Downstairs in the office.

**MR. FRANK.** Good. Bring him up.

**MR. KRALER.** His name is Dussel . . . Jan Dussel.

**MR. FRANK.** Dussel . . . I think I know him.

**MR. KRALER.** I'll get him.

[He goes quickly down the steps and out. MR. FRANK suddenly becomes conscious of the others.]

**MR. FRANK.** Forgive me. I spoke without consulting you. But I knew you'd feel as I do.

**MR. VAN DAAN.** There's no reason for you to consult anyone. This is your place. You have a right to do exactly as you please. The only thing I feel . . . there's so little food as it is . . . and to take in another person . . .

[PETER turns away, ashamed of his father.]

**MR. FRANK.** We can stretch the food a little. It's only for a few days.

**MR. VAN DAAN.** You want to make a bet?

**MRS. FRANK.** I think it's fine to have him. But, Otto, where are you going to put him? Where?

**PETER.** He can have my bed. I can sleep on the floor. I wouldn't mind.

**MR. FRANK.** That's good of you, Peter. But your room's too small . . . even for *you.*

**ANNE.** I have a much better idea. I'll come in here with you and Mother, and Margot can take Peter's room and Peter can go in our room with Mr. Dussel.

**MARGOT.** That's right. We could do that.

**MR. FRANK.** No, Margot. You mustn't sleep in that room . . . neither you nor Anne. Mouschi has caught some rats in there. Peter's brave. He doesn't mind.

**ANNE.** Then how about *this?* I'll come in here with you and Mother, and Mr. Dussel can have my bed.

**MRS. FRANK.** No. No. *No!* Margot will come in here with us and he can have her bed. It's the only way. Margot, bring your things in here. Help her, Anne.

[MARGOT hurries into her room to get her things.]

**ANNE.** [To her mother] Why Margot? Why can't I come in here?

57 **Reading Strategy** Predict how each character will react to this new development. Which character's feelings do you identify with most strongly?

58 **Critical Thinking and Reading** What answer did Mr. Kraler expect? How do you know?

59 **Discussion** Contrast Mr. Frank's reaction to another person living with them to Mr. Van Daan's. How does Peter react to his father's reaction?

**ESL Teaching Strategy** Pair students with limited proficiency in English with students who have English proficiency. Have students sketch out the three rooms being discussed for the sleeping arrangements and use paper cutouts to demonstrate each of the possibilities mentioned. Ask English-proficient students to emphasize words and phrases that indicate movement and location like "come in here," "go in there," "on the floor," and "in there." Ask students with limited proficiency to try to create a new sleeping arrangement and use place words and phrases to describe what they have done.

*The Diary of Anne Frank* 325

**60 Discussion** What is Mr. Frank celebrating?

**61 Reading Strategy** Predict how you think Dussel will fit in with the group.

**62 Discussion** Why do you think Mr. Dussel clings to his medicine bag? What might it represent to him?

**63 Clarification** More than any other European country occupied by the Nazis, the Netherlands is remarkable for the resistance shown by her citizens. The Dutch were particularly resentful of the anti-Semitic legislation enacted by Hitler and sought at first to counteract it by open opposition, such as workers' strikes and violent propaganda in print. The sympathizers were finally forced underground where they secretly worked for the destruction of the occupational forces.

MRS. FRANK. Because it wouldn't be proper for Margot to sleep with a . . . Please, Anne. Don't argue. Please.

[ANNE *starts slowly away.*]

MR. FRANK. [*To* ANNE] You don't mind sharing your room with Mr. Dussel, do you, Anne?

ANNE. No. No, of course not.

MR. FRANK. Good.

[ANNE *goes off into her bedroom, helping* MARGOT. MR. FRANK *starts to search in the cupboards.*]

Where's the cognac?

MRS. FRANK. It's there. But, Otto, I was saving it in case of illness.

**60** MR. FRANK. I think we couldn't find a better time to use it. Peter, will you get five glasses for me?

[PETER *goes for the glasses.* MARGOT *comes out of her bedroom, carrying her possessions, which she hangs behind a curtain in the main room.* MR. FRANK *finds the cognac and pours it into the five glasses that* PETER *brings him.* MR. VAN DAAN *stands looking on sourly.* MRS. VAN DAAN *comes downstairs and looks around at all the bustle.*]

MRS. VAN DAAN. What's happening? What's going on?

MR. VAN DAAN. Someone's moving in with us.

MRS. VAN DAAN. In here? You're joking.

MARGOT. It's only for a night or two . . . until Mr. Kraler finds him another place.

MR. VAN DAAN. Yeah! Yeah!

**61** [MR. FRANK *hurries over as* MR. KRALER *and* DUSSEL *come up.* DUSSEL *is a man in his late fifties, meticulous, finicky . . . bewildered now. He wears a raincoat. He carries a*

briefcase, *stuffed full, and a small medicine case.*]

MR. FRANK. Come in, Mr. Dussel.

MR. KRALER. This is Mr. Frank.

DUSSEL. Mr. Otto Frank?

**62** MR. FRANK. Yes. Let me take your things. [*He takes the hat and briefcase, but* DUSSEL *clings to his medicine case.*] This is my wife Edith . . . Mr. and Mrs. Van Daan . . . their son, Peter . . . and my daughters, Margot and Anne.

[DUSSEL *shakes hands with everyone.*]

MR. KRALER. Thank you, Mr. Frank. Thank you all. Mr. Dussel, I leave you in good hands. Oh . . . Dirk's coat.

[DUSSEL *hurriedly takes off the raincoat, giving it to* MR. KRALER. *Underneath is his white dentist's jacket, with a yellow Star of David on it.*]

DUSSEL. [*To* MR. KRALER] What can I say to thank you . . . ?

MRS. FRANK. [*To* DUSSEL] Mr. Kraler and Miep . . . They're our life line. Without them we couldn't live.

MR. KRALER. Please. Please. You make us seem very heroic. It isn't that at all. We simply don't like the Nazis. [*To* MR. FRANK, *who offers him a drink*] No, thanks. [*Then going on*] We don't like their methods. We don't like . . .

**63** MR. FRANK. [*Smiling*] I know. I know. "No one's going to tell us Dutchmen what to do with our damn Jews!"

MR. KRALER. [*To* DUSSEL] Pay no attention to Mr. Frank. I'll be up tomorrow to see that they're treating you right. [*To* MR. FRANK] Don't trouble to come down again. Peter will bolt the door after me, won't you, Peter?

PETER. Yes, sir.

MR. FRANK. Thank you, Peter. I'll do it.

MR. KRALER. Good night. Good night.

GROUP. Good night, Mr. Kraler. We'll see you tomorrow, etc., etc.

[MR. KRALER *goes out with* MR. FRANK, MRS. FRANK *gives each one of the "grownups" a glass of cognac.*]

MRS. FRANK. Please, Mr. Dussel, sit down.

[MR. DUSSEL *sinks into a chair.* MRS. FRANK *gives him a glass of cognac.*]

DUSSEL. I'm dreaming. I know it. I can't believe my eyes. Mr. Otto Frank here! [*To* MRS. FRANK] You're not in Switzerland then? A woman told me . . . She said she'd gone to your house . . . the door was open, everything was in disorder, dishes in the sink. She said she found a piece of paper in the wastebasket with an address scribbled on it . . . an address in Zurich. She said you must have escaped to Zurich.

ANNE. Father put that there purposely . . . just so people would think that very thing!

DUSSEL. And you've been *here* all the time?

MRS. FRANK. All the time . . . ever since July.

[ANNE *speaks to her father as he comes back.*]

ANNE. It worked, Pim . . . the address you left! Mr. Dussel says that people believe we escaped to Switzerland.

MR. FRANK. I'm glad. . . . And now let's have a little drink to welcome Mr. Dussel.

[*Before they can drink,* MR. DUSSEL *bolts his drink.* MR. FRANK *smiles and raises his glass.*]

To Mr. Dussel. Welcome. We're very honored to have you with us.

MRS. FRANK. To Mr. Dussel, welcome.

[*The* VAN DAANS *murmur a welcome. The "grownups" drink.*]

MRS. VAN DAAN. Um. That was good.

MR. VAN DAAN. Did Mr. Kraler warn you that you won't get much to eat here? You can imagine . . . three ration books among the seven of us . . . and now you make eight.

[PETER *walks away, humiliated. Outside a street organ is heard dimly.*]

DUSSEL. [*Rising*] Mr. Van Daan, you don't realize what is happening outside that you should warn me of a thing like that. You don't realize what's going on . . .

[*As* MR. VAN DAAN *starts his characteristic pacing,* DUSSEL *turns to speak to the others.*]

Right here in Amsterdam every day hundreds of Jews disappear . . . They surround a block and search house by house. Children come home from school to find their parents gone. Hundreds are being deported . . . people that you and I know . . . the Hallensteins . . . the Wessels . . .

MRS. FRANK. [*In tears*] Oh, no. No!

DUSSEL. They get their call-up notice . . . come to the Jewish theater on such and such a day and hour . . . bring only what you can carry in a rucksack. And if you refuse the call-up notice, then they come and drag you from your home and ship you off to Mauthausen.[21] The death camp!

MRS. FRANK. We didn't know that things had got so much worse.

DUSSEL. Forgive me for speaking so.

---

21. **Mauthausen** (mou tou′ zən): A village in Austria that was the site of a Nazi concentration camp.

64 **Discussion** Why is Peter embarrassed?

65 **Discussion** How do the circumstances Dussel describes compare to the small portions of food and other difficulties faced by the group in hiding? You may wish to have students write their responses in their journals.

**66 Critical Thinking and Reading**
Why do you think Mr. Frank wants to change the subject?

**67 Critical Thinking and Reading**
Contrast Mr. Dussel's report of life in Holland to Mr. Kraler's.

*Dr. Albert Dussel*

**ANNE.** [*Coming to* DUSSEL] Do you know the de Waals? . . . What's become of them? Their daughter Jopie and I are in the same class. Jopie's my best friend.

**DUSSEL.** They are gone.

**ANNE.** Gone?

**DUSSEL.** With all the others.

**ANNE.** Oh, no. Not Jopie!

[*She turns away, in tears.* MRS. FRANK *motions to* MARGOT *to comfort her.* MARGOT *goes to* ANNE, *putting her arms comfortingly around her.*]

**MRS. VAN DAAN.** There were some people called Wagner. They lived near us . . . ?

**MR. FRANK.** [*Interrupting, with a glance at* ANNE] I think we should put this off until later. We all have many questions we want to ask . . . But I'm sure that Mr. Dussel would like to get settled before supper.

**DUSSEL.** Thank you. I would. I brought very little with me.

**MR. FRANK.** [*Giving him his hat and brief-case*] I'm sorry we can't give you a room alone. But I hope you won't be too uncomfortable. We've had to make strict rules here . . . a schedule of hours . . . We'll tell you after supper. Anne, would you like to take Mr. Dussel to his room?

**ANNE.** [*Controlling her tears*] If you'll come with me, Mr. Dussel? [*She starts for her room.*]

**DUSSEL.** [*Shaking hands with each in turn*] Forgive me if I haven't really expressed my gratitude to all of you. This has been such a shock to me. I'd always thought of myself as Dutch. I was born in Holland. My father was born in Holland, and my grandfather. And now . . . after all these years . . . [*He breaks off.*] If you'll excuse me.

[DUSSEL *gives a little bow and hurries off after* ANNE. MR. FRANK *and the others are subdued.*]

**ANNE.** [*Turning on the light*] Well, here we are.

[DUSSEL *looks around the room. In the main room* MARGOT *speaks to her mother.*]

**MARGOT.** The news sounds pretty bad, doesn't it? It's so different from what Mr. Kraler tells us. Mr. Kraler says things are improving.

**MR. VAN DAAN.** I like it better the way Kraler tells it.

328   Drama

---

## Primary Source

Hannah Pick-Goslar, a friend of Anne's who lived on the same street but did not go into hiding, described in an interview what was happening in the outside world.

When I came back to school after the summer, fewer children came to class every day. We stayed in Amsterdam almost a full year longer, until June 20, 1943, and all this time things were getting worse and worse. Jews had to wear a yellow star. We had an *Ausweis* (an identification card), with a large "J" on it—for Jew. People were stopped on the street. "May I see your *Ausweis?*" If you were Jewish, you were taken away and you never returned home. And a mother, waiting for her child would ask herself, Where is my child? Have they taken her away?

It became more dangerous every day. And day by day our classroom became emptier. We arrived in the morning and this boy would no longer be there and that girl wouldn't be there.

You may wish to allow time for silent reflection and then encourage the children to include their emotional and intellectual responses in their journals.

[*They resume their occupations, quietly.* PETER *goes off into his room. In* ANNE'S *room,* ANNE *turns to* DUSSEL.]

**ANNE.** You're going to share the room with me.

**DUSSEL.** I'm a man who's always lived alone. I haven't had to adjust myself to others. I hope you'll bear with me until I learn.

**ANNE.** Let me help you. [*She takes his briefcase.*] Do you always live all alone? Have you no family at all?

**DUSSEL.** No one. [*He opens his medicine case and spreads his bottles on the dressing table.*]

**ANNE.** How dreadful. You must be terribly lonely.

**DUSSEL.** I'm used to it.

**ANNE.** I don't think I could ever get used to it. Didn't you even have a pet? A cat, or a dog?

**DUSSEL.** I have an allergy for fur-bearing animals. They give me asthma.

**ANNE.** Oh, dear. Peter has a cat.

**DUSSEL.** Here? He has it here?

**ANNE.** Yes. But we hardly ever see it. He keeps it in his room all the time. I'm sure it will be all right.

**DUSSEL.** Let us hope so. [*He takes some pills to fortify himself.*]

**ANNE.** That's Margot's bed, where you're going to sleep. I sleep on the sofa there. [*Indicating the clothes hooks on the wall*] We cleared these off for your things. [*She goes over to the window.*] The best part about this room . . . you can look down and see a bit of the street and the canal. There's a houseboat . . . you can see the end of it . . . a bargeman lives there with his family . . . They have a baby and he's just beginning to walk and I'm so afraid he's going to fall into the canal some day. I watch him. . . .

**DUSSEL.** [*Interrupting*] Your father spoke of a schedule.

**ANNE.** [*Coming away from the window*] Oh, yes. It's mostly about the times we have to be quiet. And times for the w.c. You can use it now if you like.

**DUSSEL.** [*Stiffly*] No, thank you.

**ANNE.** I suppose you think it's awful, my talking about a thing like that. But you don't know how important it can get to be, especially when you're frightened . . . About this room, the way Margot and I did . . . she had it to herself in the afternoons for studying, reading . . . lessons, you know . . . and I took the mornings. Would that be all right with you?

**DUSSEL.** I'm not at my best in the morning.

**ANNE.** You stay here in the mornings then. I'll take the room in the afternoons.

**DUSSEL.** Tell me, when you're in here, what happens to me? Where am I spending my time? In there, with all the people?

**ANNE.** Yes.

**DUSSEL.** I see. I see.

**ANNE.** We have supper at half past six.

**DUSSEL.** [*Going over to the sofa*] Then, if you don't mind . . . I like to lie down quietly for ten minutes before eating. I find it helps the digestion.

**ANNE.** Of course. I hope I'm not going to be too much of a bother to you. I seem to be able to get everyone's back up.

68 **Discussion** How does Anne react to Mr. Dussel's statement about having no family?

69 **Discussion** Have students note how Anne can occupy herself with life outside the attic. What does this show about Anne's character?

70 **Critical Thinking and Reading** What can you infer about Dussel's personality from his conversation with Anne?

71 **Reading Strategy** How well does Anne assess her own character? What additional information would you include?

**Cooperative Learning** You may wish to allow time for story-map partners and character-chart groups to meet and evaluate the latest developments. The character of Dussel will need to be added to each group's character chart, and each group will need to determine a description for Dussel's relationship with Anne at this point in the story.

**Reading Strategy** Have students summarize the play up to this point and predict how Anne and Mr. Dussel will get along.

**Literary Focus: Point of View** Explain that the reader knows the thoughts and feelings of only Anne, the main character. The reader does not know what Mr. Dussel thinks or feels. Instead, the reader learns about Mr. Dussel only by what he says or does and by what Anne thinks of him. What do Anne's thoughts tell you about Mr. Dussel?

---

[DUSSEL *lies down on the sofa, curled up, his back to her.*]

**DUSSEL.** I always get along very well with children. My patients all bring their children to me, because they know I get on well with them. So don't you worry about that.

[ANNE *leans over him, taking his hand and shaking it gratefully.*]

**ANNE.** Thank you. Thank you, Mr. Dussel.

[*The lights dim to darkness. The curtain falls on the scene.* ANNE'S VOICE *comes to us faintly at first, and then with increasing power.*]

**ANNE'S VOICE.** . . . And yesterday I finished Cissy Van Marxvelt's latest book. I think she is a first-class writer. I shall definitely let my children read her. Monday the twenty-first of September, nineteen forty-two. Mr. Dussel and I had another battle yesterday. Yes, Mr. Dussel! According to him, nothing, I repeat . . . nothing, is right about me . . . my appearance, my character, my manners. While he was going on at me I thought . . . sometime I'll give you such a smack that you'll fly right up to the ceiling! Why is it that every grownup thinks he knows the way to bring up children? Particularly the grownups that never had any. I keep wishing that Peter was a girl instead of a boy. Then I would have someone to talk to. Margot's a darling, but she takes everything too seriously. To pause for a moment on the subject of Mrs. Van Daan. I must tell you that her attempts to flirt with father are getting her nowhere. Pim, thank goodness, won't play.

[*As she is saying the last lines, the curtain rises on the darkened scene.* ANNE'S VOICE *fades out.*]

*330 Drama*

---

**Scene 4**

[*It is the middle of the night, several months later. The stage is dark except for a little light which comes through the skylight in* PETER'S *room.*

*Everyone is in bed.* MR. *and* MRS. FRANK *lie on the couch in the main room, which has been pulled out to serve as a makeshift double bed.*

MARGOT *is sleeping on a mattress on the floor in the main room, behind a curtain stretched across for privacy. The others are all in their accustomed rooms.*

*From outside we hear two drunken soldiers singing "Lili Marlene." A girl's high giggle is heard. The sound of running feet is heard coming closer and then fading in the distance. Throughout the scene there is the distant sound of airplanes passing overhead.*

*A match suddenly flares up in the attic. We dimly see* MR. VAN DAAN. *He is getting his bearings. He comes quickly down the stairs, and goes to the cupboard where the food is stored. Again the match flares up, and is as quickly blown out. The dim figure is seen to steal back up the stairs.*

*There is quiet for a second or two, broken only by the sound of airplanes, and running feet on the street below.*

*Suddenly, out of the silence and the dark, we hear* ANNE *scream.*]

**ANNE.** [*Screaming*] No! No! Don't . . . don't take me!

[*She moans, tossing and crying in her sleep. The other people wake, terrified.* DUSSEL *sits up in bed, furious.*]

**DUSSEL.** Shush! Anne! Anne, for God's sake, shush!

**ANNE.** [*Still in her nightmare*] Save me! Save me!

---

## Grammar in Action

An **imperative sentence** gives an order or a direction and ends with either a period or an exclamation mark. Most imperative sentences begin with a verb. When imperative sentences begin with a verb and have no subject, the understood subject is *you*. However, sometimes imperative sentences have subjects. When they do, they sound like questions. Unlike questions, they end with a period or an exclamation mark instead of a question mark. The subject in the following imperative sentence is *somebody:* "Will somebody answer the phone!"

Imperative sentences in *The Diary of Anne Frank* reinforce the sense of urgency in the play. Notice that the understood subject of each of the following imperative sentences from the play is *you.* You should also see the sense of urgency in these lines.

ANNE. No! No! Don't . . . don't take me!
DUSSEL. Shush! Anne! Anne, for God's sake, shush!
ANNE. [Still in her nightmare] Save me! Save me!
DUSSEL. Quiet! Quiet! You want someone to hear?

Imperative sentences are recognizable because they give orders or directions.

[*She screams and screams.* DUSSEL *gets out of bed, going over to her, trying to wake her.*]

DUSSEL. For God's sake! Quiet! Quiet! You want someone to hear?

[*In the main room* MRS. FRANK *grabs a shawl and pulls it around her. She rushes in to* ANNE, *taking her in her arms.* MR. FRANK *hurriedly gets up, putting on his overcoat.* MARGOT *sits up, terrified.* PETER'S *light goes on in his room.*]

MRS. FRANK. [*To* ANNE, *in her room*] Hush, darling, hush. It's all right. It's all right. [*Over her shoulder to* DUSSEL] Will you be kind enough to turn on the light, Mr. Dussel? [*Back to* ANNE] It's nothing, my darling. It was just a dream.

[DUSSEL *turns on the light in the bedroom.* MRS. FRANK *holds* ANNE *in her arms. Gradually* ANNE *comes out of her nightmare still trembling with horror.* MR. FRANK *comes into the room, and goes quickly to the window, looking out to be sure that no one outside has heard* ANNE'S *screams.* MRS. FRANK *holds* ANNE, *talking softly to her. In the main room* MARGOT *stands on a chair, turning on the center hanging lamp. A light goes on in the* VAN DAANS' *room overhead.* PETER *puts his robe on, coming out of his room.*]

DUSSEL. [*To* MRS. FRANK, *blowing his nose*] Something must be done about that child, Mrs. Frank. Yelling like that! Who knows but there's somebody on the streets? She's endangering all our lives.

MRS. FRANK. Anne, darling.

DUSSEL. Every night she twists and turns. I don't sleep. I spend half my night shushing her. And now it's nightmares!

[MARGOT *comes to the door of* ANNE'S *room, followed by* PETER. MR. FRANK *goes to them, indicating that everything is all right.* PETER *takes* MARGOT *back.*]

MRS. FRANK. [*To* ANNE] You're here, safe, you see? Nothing has happened. [*To* DUSSEL] Please, Mr. Dussel, go back to bed. She'll be herself in a minute or two. Won't you, Anne?

DUSSEL. [*Picking up a book and a pillow*] Thank you, but I'm going to the w.c. The one place where there's peace!

[*He stalks out.* MR. VAN DAAN, *in underwear and trousers, comes down the stairs.*]

MR. VAN DAAN. [*To* DUSSEL] What is it? What happened?

DUSSEL. A nightmare. She was having a nightmare!

MR. VAN DAAN. I thought someone was murdering her.

DUSSEL. Unfortunately, no.

[*He goes into the bathroom.* MR. VAN DAAN *goes back up the stairs.* MR. FRANK, *in the main room, sends* PETER *back to his own bedroom.*]

MR. FRANK. Thank you, Peter. Go back to bed.

[PETER *goes back to his room.* MR. FRANK *follows him, turning out the light and looking out the window. Then he goes back to the main room, and gets up on a chair, turning out the center hanging lamp.*]

MRS. FRANK. [*To* ANNE] Would you like some water? [ANNE *shakes her head.*] Was it a very bad dream? Perhaps if you told me . . . ?

ANNE. I'd rather not talk about it.

MRS. FRANK. Poor darling. Try to sleep then. I'll sit right here beside you until you fall.

*The Diary of Anne Frank* 331

74

75

74 **Literary Focus: Point of View**
What do Mr. Dussel's speech and actions tell you about him? Is Anne's opinion of him justified? Point out that although we see the characters from Anne's point of view, the very revealing nature of the dialogue itself attests to the validity of the narrator's opinion.

75 **Discussion** How does Anne feel toward her mother? What is her mother's reaction toward Anne?

**Student Activity 1.** Find five more imperative sentences from the play. Explain what makes them imperative.

**Student Activity 2.** Imagine that you are directing a scene from *The Diary of Anne Frank*. Write stage directions and directions for characters. Use imperative sentences in your directions.

**Electronic Handbook** You may wish to review the use of imperative sentences with your students before having them complete the Grammar in Action activities. If your students are using the Language Master 6000, have them enter the access word *declarative* and press the GRAMMAR key to get information about imperative sentences.

76 **Literary Focus: Dialogue** Why do you think the playwrights have Mr. and Mrs. Frank speaking in German? What do you think about this choice?

**Cooperative Learning** Ask your students to mentally identify one of their great fears. Lead them to see how Anne's fear is so great that it is manifesting itself in vivid nightmares. Divide students into groups and ask them to discuss images and symbols that can represent fear in the general sense and the specific nature of Anne's fear. Allow time for the groups to work together on a visual-arts presentation that communicates these images and feelings. The project might be in a one-dimensional form such as a drawing or a painting, or it may be a three-dimensional project such as a sculpture from found objects or a mixed-media collage.

asleep. [*She brings a stool over, sitting there.*]

**ANNE.** You don't have to.

**MRS. FRANK.** But I'd like to stay with you . . . very much. Really.

**ANNE.** I'd rather you didn't.

**MRS. FRANK.** Good night, then.

[*She leans down to kiss* ANNE. ANNE *throws her arm up over her face, turning away.* MRS. FRANK, *hiding her hurt, kisses* ANNE'S *arm.*]

You'll be all right? There's nothing that you want?

**ANNE.** Will you please ask Father to come.

**MRS. FRANK.** [*After a second*] Of course, Anne dear.

[*She hurries out into the other room.* MR. FRANK *comes to her as she comes in.*]

*Sie verlangt nach Dir!*[22]

**MR. FRANK.** [*Sensing her hurt*] Edith, *Liebe, schau . . .*[23]

76 **MRS. FRANK.** *Es macht nichts! Ich danke dem lieben Herrgott, dass sie sich wenigstens an Dich wendet, wenn sie Trost braucht! Geh hinein, Otto, sie ist ganz hysterisch vor Angst.*[24] [*As* MR. FRANK *hesitates*] *Geh zu ihr.*[25]

---

**22. Sie verlangt nach Dir** (zē fer' laŋt' nak dir'): German for "She is asking for you."
**23. Liebe, schau** (lē' bə shou): German for "Dear, look."
**24. Es macht . . . vor Angst** (es makt nichts ich dan kə dəm lē' bən här' got das sē sich ven ig stəns an dish ven' dət ven sē trast broukt ge hē nin at tò sē ist ganz hi ste rik far aŋst): German for "It's all right. I thank dear God that at least she turns to you when she needs comfort. Go in, Otto, she is hysterical because of fear."
**25. Geh zu ihr** (gē tsoo ēr): German for "Go to her."

[*He looks at her for a second and then goes to get a cup of water for* ANNE. MRS. FRANK *sinks down on the bed, her face in her hands, trying to keep from sobbing aloud.* MARGOT *comes over to her, putting her arms around her.*]

She wants nothing of me. She pulled away when I leaned down to kiss her.

**MARGOT.** It's a phase . . . You heard Father . . . Most girls go through it . . . they turn to their fathers at this age . . . they give all their love to their fathers.

**MRS. FRANK.** You weren't like this. You didn't shut me out.

**MARGOT.** She'll get over it . . .

[*She smooths the bed for* MRS. FRANK *and sits beside her a moment as* MRS. FRANK *lies down. In* ANNE'S *room* MR. FRANK *comes in, sitting down by* ANNE. ANNE *flings her arms around him, clinging to him. In the distance we hear the sound of ack-ack.*]

**ANNE.** Oh, Pim. I dreamed that they came to get us! The Green Police! They broke down the door and grabbed me and started to drag me out the way they did Jopie.

**MR. FRANK.** I want you to take this pill.

**ANNE.** What is it?

**MR. FRANK.** Something to quiet you.

[*She takes it and drinks the water. In the main room* MARGOT *turns out the light and goes back to her bed.*]

**MR. FRANK.** [*To* ANNE] Do you want me to read to you for a while?

**ANNE.** No. Just sit with me for a minute. Was I awful? Did I yell terribly loud? Do you think anyone outside could have heard?

**MR. FRANK.** No. No. Lie quietly now. Try to sleep.

**ANNE.** I'm a terrible coward. I'm so disappointed in myself. I think I've conquered my fear . . . I think I'm really grown-up . . . and then something happens . . . and I run to you like a baby . . . I love you, Father. I don't love anyone but you.

**MR. FRANK.** [*Reproachfully*] Annele!

**ANNE.** It's true. I've been thinking about it for a long time. You're the only one I love.

**MR. FRANK.** It's fine to hear you tell me that you love me. But I'd be happier if you said you loved your mother as well . . . She needs your help so much . . . your love . . .

**ANNE.** We have nothing in common. She doesn't understand me. Whenever I try to explain my views on life to her she asks me if I'm constipated.

**MR. FRANK.** You hurt her very much just now. She's crying. She's in there crying.

**ANNE.** I can't help it. I only told the truth. I didn't want her here . . . [*Then, with sud-*

77

*Scene along a canal in Amsterdam after a bombing raid*

**77 Discussion** What does Mr. Frank feel is his role as a parent? How does Anne feel about showing her true self? How does she feel people will perceive her?

**Videocassette** Before beginning to read scene 5, you might want to view scenes 3 and 4 of the **Library of Video Classics** *The Diary of Anne Frank*. Ask students to look for differences in staging, action, and dialogue. They can also use the video to help them review their story maps for accuracy and completeness. You can use the questions on page 12 of the Viewing Guide for *The Diary of Anne Frank* to generate further discussion.

**78 Enrichment** Note the first thing that each person would want after the war. Ask students what would be the first thing they would want after being in hiding for four months.

**79 Clarifications** Explain the story of Hanukkah. The Hebrew word *hanukkah* means dedication. Hanukkah is a celebration of God's deliverance of the Jews in 165 B.C. That year the Jews won their first struggle for religious freedom by defeating the Syrians, who wanted them to give up Judaism. The Jews held festivities in the temple in Jerusalem and rededicated it to God. After cleaning the temple of Syrian idols, they found only one small container of oil with which to light their holy lamps. Miraculously, the container provided them with oil for eight days.

*den change]* Oh, Pim, I was horrible, wasn't I? And the worst of it is, I can stand off and look at myself doing it and know it's cruel and yet I can't stop doing it. What's the matter with me? Tell me. Don't say it's just a phase! Help me.

**MR. FRANK.** There is so little that we parents can do to help our children. We can only try to set a good example . . . point the way. The rest you must do yourself. You must build your own character.

**ANNE.** I'm trying. Really I am. Every night I think back over all of the things I did that day that were wrong . . . like putting the wet mop in Mr. Dussel's bed . . . and this thing now with Mother. I say to myself, that was wrong. I make up my mind, I'm never going to do that again. Never! Of course I may do something worse . . . but at least I'll never do *that* again! . . . I have a nicer side, Father . . . a sweeter, nicer side. But I'm scared to show it. I'm afraid that people are going to laugh at me if I'm serious. So the mean Anne comes to the outside and the good Anne stays on the inside, and I keep on trying to switch them around and have the good Anne outside and the bad Anne inside and be what I'd like to be . . . and might be . . . if only . . . only . . .

*[She is asleep.* MR. FRANK *watches her for a moment and then turns off the light, and starts out. The lights dim out. The curtain falls on the scene.* ANNE'S VOICE *is heard dimly at first, and then with growing strength.]*

**ANNE'S VOICE.** . . . The air raids are getting worse. They come over day and night. The noise is terrifying. Pim says it should be music to our ears. The more planes, the sooner will come the end of the war. Mrs. Van Daan pretends to be a fatalist. What will be, will be. But when the planes come over, who is the most frightened? No one else but Petronella! . . . Monday, the ninth of November, nineteen forty-two. Wonderful news! The Allies have landed in Africa. Pim says that we can look for an early finish to the war. Just for fun he asked each of us what was the first thing we wanted to do when we got out of here. Mrs. Van Daan longs to be home with her own things, her needle-point chairs, the Beckstein piano her father gave her . . . the best that money could buy. Peter would like to go to a movie. Mr. Dussel wants to get back to his dentist's drill. He's afraid he is losing his touch. For myself, there are so many things . . . to ride a bike again . . . to laugh till my belly aches . . . to have new clothes from the skin out . . . to have a hot tub filled to overflowing and wallow in it for hours . . . to be back in school with my friends . . .

*[As the last lines are being said, the curtain rises on the scene. The lights dim on as* ANNE'S VOICE *fades away.]*

### Scene 5

*[It is the first night of the Hanukkah[26] celebration.* MR. FRANK *is standing at the head of the table on which is the Menorah.[27] He lights the Shamos,[28] or servant candle, and holds it as he says the blessing. Seated*

---

26. **Hanukkah** (khä' noo kä') *n.:* A Jewish celebration that lasts eight days.
27. **menorah** (mə nô' rə) *n.:* A candle holder with nine candles, used during Hanukkah.
28. **shamos** (shä' məs) *n.:* The candle used to light the others in a menorah.

*listening is all of the "family," dressed in their best. The men wear hats,* PETER *wears his cap.*]

MR. FRANK. [*Reading from a prayer book*] "Praised be Thou, oh Lord our God, Ruler of the universe, who has sanctified us with Thy commandments and bidden us kindle the Hanukkah lights. Praised be Thou, oh Lord our God, Ruler of the universe, who has wrought wondrous deliverances for our fathers in days of old. Praised be Thou, oh Lord our God, Ruler of the universe, that Thou has given us life and sustenance and brought us to this happy season." [MR. FRANK *lights the one candle of the Menorah as he continues.*] "We kindle this Hanukkah light to celebrate the great and wonderful deeds wrought through the zeal with which God filled the hearts of the heroic Maccabees, two thousand years ago. They fought against indifference, against tyranny and oppression, and they restored our Temple to us. May these lights remind us that we should ever look to God, whence cometh our help." Amen.

ALL. Amen.

[MR. FRANK *hands* MRS. FRANK *the prayer book.*]

MRS. FRANK. [*Reading*] "I lift up mine eyes unto the mountains, from whence cometh my help. My help cometh from the Lord who made heaven and earth. He will not suffer thy foot to be moved. He that keepeth thee will not slumber. He that keepeth Israel doth neither slumber nor sleep. The Lord is thy keeper. The Lord is thy shade upon thy right hand. The sun shall not smite thee by day, nor the moon by night. The Lord shall keep thee from all evil. He shall keep thy soul. The Lord shall guard thy going out and thy com-

ing in, from this time forth and forevermore." Amen.

ALL. Amen.

[MRS. FRANK *puts down the prayer book and goes to get the food and wine.* MARGOT *helps her.* MR. FRANK *takes the men's hats and puts them aside.*]

DUSSEL. [*Rising*] That was very moving.

ANNE. [*Pulling him back*] It isn't over yet!

MRS. VAN DAAN. Sit down! Sit down!

ANNE. There's a lot more, songs and presents.

DUSSEL. Presents?

MRS. FRANK. Not this year, unfortunately.

MRS. VAN DAAN. But always on Hanukkah everyone gives presents . . . everyone!

DUSSEL. Like our St. Nicholas' Day.[29]

[*There is a chorus of "no's" from the group.*]

MRS. VAN DAAN. No! Not like St. Nicholas! What kind of a Jew are you that you don't know Hanukkah?

MRS. FRANK. [*As she brings the food*] I remember particularly the candles . . . First one, as we have tonight. Then the second night you light two candles, the next night three . . . and so on until you have eight candles burning. When there are eight candles it is truly beautiful.

MRS. VAN DAAN. And the potato pancakes.

MR. VAN DAAN. Don't talk about them!

MRS. VAN DAAN. I make the best *latkes* you ever tasted!

---

**29. St. Nicholas' Day:** December 6, the day Christian children in Holland receive gifts.

*The Diary of Anne Frank* 335

**Multicultural Focus** Holidays from many cultures are observed in December. Like Hanukkah, some of them are celebrated over the course of several days. In Latin America the nine days before Christmas are commemorated as the *posados,* the word for inns or lodgings. Processions honor the religious significance, reenacting Mary and Joseph's search for a place to stay. Celebrations include piñatas, brightly decorated paper or clay figures filled with toys and treats, for the children.

In some European countries, the Feast of Saint Nicholas is celebrated on December 6. On the Eve of Saint Nicholas, Dutch children fill their shoes with straw and carrots for Saint Nicholas's horse. In the morning they find that the straw has been replaced with candy, cookies, and little toys.

Although the significance is different, the ceremonies accompanying the African American holiday of Kwanzaa are similar to those of Hanukkah. The holiday begins on December 26 and lasts for seven days. On each evening of Kwanzaa, the family members light a candle and discuss one of the seven principles of their culture: unity, self-determination, collective work and responsibility, cooperative economics, purpose, creativity, and faith. Developed in 1966 by Professor Ron Karenga, the holiday is based on a traditional African festival that celebrates the harvest of the first crops. The word *Kwanzaa* means "first fruits" in the East African language of Swahili.

## 80

**MRS. FRANK.** Invite us all next year . . . in your own home.

**MR. FRANK.** God willing!

**MRS. VAN DAAN.** God willing.

**MARGOT.** What I remember best is the presents we used to get when we were little . . . eight days of presents . . . and each day they got better and better.

**MRS. FRANK.** [*Sitting down*] We are all here, alive. That is present enough.

**ANNE.** No, it isn't. I've got something . . .[*She rushes into her room, hurriedly puts on a little hat improvised from the lamp shade, grabs a satchel bulging with parcels and comes running back.*]

**MRS. FRANK.** What is it?

**ANNE.** Presents!

**MRS. VAN DAAN.** Presents!

**DUSSEL.** Look!

**MR. VAN DAAN.** What's she got on her head?

**PETER.** A lamp shade!

**ANNE.** [*She picks out one at random.*] This is for Margot. [*She hands it to* MARGOT. *pulling her to her feet.*] Read it out loud.

**MARGOT.** [*Reading*]
''You have never lost your temper.
You never will, I fear,
You are so good.
But if you should,
Put all your cross words here.''

[*She tears open the package.*] A new crossword puzzle book! Where did you get it?

**ANNE.** It isn't new. It's one that you've done. But I rubbed it all out, and if you wait a little and forget, you can do it all over again.

**MARGOT.** [*Sitting*] It's wonderful, Anne. Thank you. You'd never know it wasn't new.

[*From outside we hear the sound of a streetcar passing.*]

**ANNE.** [*With another gift*] Mrs. Van Daan.

**MRS. VAN DAAN.** [*Taking it*] This is awful . . . I haven't anything for anyone . . . I never thought . . .

**MR. FRANK.** This is all Anne's idea.

**MRS. VAN DAAN.** [*Holding up a bottle*] What is it?

**ANNE.** It's hair shampoo. I took all the odds and ends of soap and mixed them with the last of my toilet water.

**MRS. VAN DAAN.** Oh, Anneke!

**ANNE.** I wanted to write a poem for all of them, but I didn't have time. [*Offering a large box to* MR. VAN DAAN] Yours, Mr. Van Daan, is *really* something . . . something you want more than anything. [*As she waits for him to open it*] Look! Cigarettes!

**MR. VAN DAAN.** Cigarettes!

**ANNE.** Two of them! Pim found some old pipe tobacco in the pocket lining of his coat . . . and we made them . . . or rather, Pim did.

**MRS. VAN DAAN.** Let me see . . . Well, look at that! Light it, Putti! Light it.

[MR. VAN DAAN *hesitates.*]

**ANNE.** It's tobacco, really it is! There's a little fluff in it, but not much.

## 82

[*Everyone watches intently as* MR. VAN DAAN *cautiously lights it. The cigarette flares up. Everyone laughs.*]

**PETER.** It works!

**MRS. VAN DAAN.** Look at him.

**80 Reading Strategy** How do these words reflect the uncertainty of their situation? Do you think the group will be together next Hanukkah?

**81 Discussion** Why do you think it is so important to Anne to celebrate all the traditions, even if they are improvised?

**82 Critical Thinking and Reading** Why does Mr. Van Daan hesitate? What does he expect?

Margot and Anne Frank

83 **Reading Strategy** Why is it appropriate that Dussel expresses amazement and wants to buy the I.O.U.?

84 **Literary Focus: Flashback** What is the effect of our having seen the scarf in the first scene, when Mr. Frank was crying? What does this indicate about Anne's fate?

**ESL Teaching Strategy** Ask students from other countries about the holidays they celebrate. Do any of them have traditions or ceremonies similar to Hanukkah?

**MR. VAN DAAN.** [*Spluttering*] Thank you, Anne. Thank you.

[ANNE *rushes back to her satchel for another present.*]

**ANNE.** [*Handing her mother a piece of paper*] For Mother, Hanukkah greeting.

[*She pulls her mother to her feet.*]

**MRS. FRANK.** [*She reads*]
"Here's an I.O.U. that I promise to pay.
Ten hours of doing whatever you say.
Signed, Anne Frank." [MRS. FRANK. *touched, takes* ANNE *in her arms, holding her close.*]

**DUSSEL.** [*To* ANNE] Ten hours of doing what you're told? *Anything* you're told? |83

**ANNE.** That's right.

**DUSSEL.** You wouldn't want to sell that, Mrs. Frank?

**MRS. FRANK.** Never! This is the most precious gift I've ever had!

[*She sits, showing her present to the others.* ANNE *hurries back to the satchel and pulls out a scarf, the scarf that* MR. FRANK *found in the first scene.*] |84

*The Diary of Anne Frank*   337

ANNE. [*Offering it to her father*] For Pim.

MR. FRANK. Anneke . . . I wasn't supposed to have a present! [*He takes it, unfolding it and showing it to the others.*]

ANNE. It's a muffler . . . to put round your neck . . . like an ascot, you know. I made it myself out of odds and ends . . . I knitted it in the dark each night, after I'd gone to bed. I'm afraid it looks better in the dark!

MR. FRANK. [*Putting it on*] It's fine. It fits me perfectly. Thank you, Annele.

[ANNE *hands* PETER *a ball of paper; with a string attached to it.*]

ANNE. That's for Mouschi.

PETER. [*Rising to bow*] On behalf of Mouschi, I thank you.

ANNE. [*Hesitant, handing him a gift*] And . . . this is yours . . . from Mrs. Quack Quack. [*As he holds it gingerly in his hands*] Well . . . open it . . . Aren't you going to open it?

85 PETER. I'm scared to. I know something's going to jump out and hit me.

ANNE. No. It's nothing like that, really.

MRS. VAN DAAN. [*As he is opening it*] What is it, Peter? Go on. Show it.

ANNE. [*Excitedly*] It's a safety razor!

DUSSEL. A what?

ANNE. A razor!

MRS. VAN DAAN. [*Looking at it*] You didn't make that out of odds and ends.

ANNE. [*To* PETER] Miep got it for me. It's not new. It's second-hand. But you really do need a razor now.

DUSSEL. For what?

ANNE. Look on his upper lip . . . you can see the beginning of a mustache.

DUSSEL. He wants to get rid of that? Put a little milk on it and let the cat lick it off.

PETER. [*Starting for his room*] Think you're funny, don't you. 86

DUSSEL. Look! He can't wait! He's going in to try it!

PETER. I'm going to give Mouschi his present!

[*He goes into his room, slamming the door behind him.*]

MR. VAN DAAN. [*Disgustedly*] Mouschi, Mouschi, Mouschi.

[*In the distance we hear a dog persistently barking.* ANNE *brings a gift to* DUSSEL.]

ANNE. And last but never least, my room-mate, Mr. Dussel.

DUSSEL. For me? You have something for me? 87

[*He opens the small box she gives him.*]

ANNE. I made them myself.

DUSSEL. [*Puzzled*] Capsules! Two capsules!

ANNE. They're ear-plugs!

DUSSEL. Ear-plugs?

ANNE. To put in your ears so you won't hear me when I thrash around at night. I saw them advertised in a magazine. They're not real ones . . . I made them out of cotton and candle wax. Try them . . . See if they don't work . . . see if you can hear me talk . . .

DUSSEL. [*Putting them in his ears*] Wait now until I get them in . . . so.

ANNE. Are you ready?

DUSSEL. Huh?

ANNE. Are you ready?

*338 Drama*

**DUSSEL.** Good God! They've gone inside! I can't get them out! [*They laugh as* MR. DUSSEL *jumps about, trying to shake the plugs out of his ears. Finally he gets them out. Putting them away*] Thank you, Anne! Thank you!

**MR. VAN DAAN.** A real Hanukkah!

**MRS. VAN DAAN.** Wasn't it cute of her?

**MRS. FRANK.** I don't know when she did it.

**MARGOT.** I love my present.

[*Together*]

**ANNE.** [*Sitting at the table*] And now let's have the song, Father . . . please . . . [*To* DUSSEL] Have you heard the Hanukkah song, Mr. Dussel? The song is the whole thing! [*She sings.*] ''Oh, Hanukkah! Oh Hanukkah! The sweet celebration . . .''

**MR. FRANK.** [*Quieting her*] I'm afraid, Anne, we shouldn't sing that song tonight. [*To* DUSSEL] It's a song of jubilation, of rejoicing. One is apt to become too enthusiastic.

**ANNE.** Oh, please, please. Let's sing the song. I promise not to shout!

**MR. FRANK.** Very well. But quietly now . . . I'll keep an eye on you and when . . .

[*As* ANNE *starts to sing, she is interrupted by* DUSSEL, *who is snorting and wheezing.*]

**DUSSEL.** [*Pointing to* PETER] You . . . You!

[PETER *is coming from his bedroom, ostentatiously holding a bulge in his coat as if he were holding his cat, and dangling* ANNE'S *present before it.*]

How many times . . . I told you . . . Out! Out!

**MR. VAN DAAN.** [*Going to* PETER] What's the matter with you? Haven't you any sense? Get that cat out of here.

**PETER.** [*Innocently*] Cat?

**MR. VAN DAAN.** You heard me. Get it out of here!

**PETER.** I have no cat. [*Delighted with his joke, he opens his coat and pulls out a bath towel. The group at the table laugh, enjoying the joke.*]

**DUSSEL.** [*Still wheezing*] It doesn't need to be the cat . . . his clothes are enough . . . when he comes out of that room . . .

**MR. VAN DAAN.** Don't worry. You won't be bothered any more. We're getting rid of it.

**DUSSEL.** At last you listen to me. [*He goes off into his bedroom.*]

**MR. VAN DAAN.** [*Calling after him*] I'm not doing it for you. That's all in your mind . . . all of it! [*He starts back to his place at the table.*] I'm doing it because I'm sick of seeing that cat eat all our food.

**PETER.** That's not true! I only give him bones . . . scraps . . .

**MR. VAN DAAN.** Don't tell me! He gets fatter every day! Damn cat looks better than any of us. Out he goes tonight!

**PETER.** No! No!

**ANNE.** Mr. Van Daan, you can't do that! That's Peter's cat. Peter loves that cat.

**MRS. FRANK.** [*Quietly*] Anne.

**PETER.** [*To* MR. VAN DAAN] If he goes, I go.

**MR. VAN DAAN.** Go! Go!

**MRS. VAN DAAN.** You're not going and the cat's not going! Now please . . . this is Hanukkah . . . Hanukkah . . . this is the time to celebrate . . . What's the matter with all of you? Come on, Anne. Let's have the song.

*The Diary of Anne Frank* 339

**88 Discussion** Contrast the happy celebration of Hanukkah and the conditions under which the two families are living.

**89 Reading Strategy** What clues do you have that Peter is not really holding his cat under his coat?

**90 Discussion** At what other time did Mr. Van Daan voice his concern about the scarcity of food?

**91 Discussion** Note how quickly the scene goes from one of happiness to one of horror. Who or what do you think caused the crash downstairs?

**92 Critical Thinking and Reading** Compare and contrast the responses of Mr. Frank and Mrs. Van Daan. How is her behavior at this point consistent with her behavior at the opening of Act I?

**93 Discussion** How is Mr. Van Daan's behavior consistent with his actions in the rest of the play? Give examples of other times when he showed more concern for himself than for others. Explain the logic of Mr. Frank's response.

ANNE. [*Singing*]

"Oh, Hanukkah! Oh, Hanukkah!
The sweet celebration.''

MR. FRANK. [*Rising*] I think we should first blow out the candle . . . then we'll have something for tomorrow night.

MARGOT. But, Father, you're supposed to let it burn itself out.

MR. FRANK. I'm sure that God understands shortages. [*Before blowing it out*] "Praised be Thou, oh Lord our God, who hast sustained us and permitted us to celebrate this joyous festival.''

[*He is about to blow out the candle when suddenly there is a crash of something falling below. They all freeze in horror, motionless. For a few seconds there is complete silence.* MR. FRANK *slips off his shoes. The others noiselessly follow his example.* MR. FRANK *turns out a light near him. He motions to* PETER *to turn off the center lamp.* PETER *tries to reach it, realizes he cannot and gets up on a chair. Just as he is touching the lamp he loses his balance. The chair goes out from under him. He falls. The iron lamp shade crashes to the floor. There is a sound of feet below, running down the stairs.*]

MR. VAN DAAN. [*Under his breath*] God Almighty!

[*The only light left comes from the Hanukkah candle.* DUSSEL *comes from his room.* MR. FRANK *creeps over to the stairwell and stands listening. The dog is heard barking excitedly.*]

Do you hear anything?

MR. FRANK. [*In a whisper*] No. I think they've gone.

MRS. VAN DAAN. It's the Green Police. They've found us.

MR. FRANK. If they had, they wouldn't have left. They'd be up here by now.

MRS. VAN DAAN. I know it's the Green Police. They've gone to get help. That's all. They'll be back!

MR. VAN DAAN. Or it may have been the Gestapo,[30] looking for papers . . .

MR. FRANK. [*Interrupting*] Or a thief, looking for money.

MRS. VAN DAAN. We've got to do something . . . Quick! Quick! Before they come back.

MR. VAN DAAN. There isn't anything to do. Just wait.

[MR. FRANK *holds up his hand for them to be quiet. He is listening intently. There is complete silence as they all strain to hear any sound from below. Suddenly* ANNE *begins to sway. With a low cry she falls to the floor in a faint.* MRS. FRANK *goes to her quickly, sitting beside her on the floor and taking her in her arms.*]

MRS. FRANK. Get some water, please! Get some water!

[MARGOT *starts for the sink.*]

MR. VAN DAAN. [*Grabbing* MARGOT] No! No! No one's going to run water!

MR. FRANK. If they've found us, they've found us. Get the water. [MARGOT *starts again for the sink.* MR. FRANK, *getting a flashlight*] I'm going down.

[MARGOT *rushes to him, clinging to him.* ANNE *struggles to consciousness.*]

MARGOT. No, Father, no! There may be someone there, waiting . . . It may be a trap!

---

**30. Gestapo** (gə stä′ pō) *n.*: The secret police force of the German Nazi state, known for its terrorism and atrocities.

**MR. FRANK.** This is Saturday. There is no way for us to know what has happened until Miep or Mr. Kraler comes on Monday morning. We cannot live with this uncertainty.

**MARGOT.** Don't go, Father!

**MRS. FRANK.** Hush, darling, hush.

[MR. FRANK *slips quietly out, down the steps and out through the door below.*]

Margot! Stay close to me.

[MARGOT *goes to her mother.*]

**MR. VAN DAAN.** Shush! Shush!

[MRS. FRANK *whispers to* MARGOT *to get the water.* MARGOT *goes for it.*]

**MRS. VAN DAAN.** Putti, where's our money? Get our money. I hear you can buy the Green Police off, so much a head. Go upstairs quick! Get the money!

**MR. VAN DAAN.** Keep still!

**MRS. VAN DAAN.** [*Kneeling before him, pleading*] Do you want to be dragged off to a concentration camp? Are you going to stand there and wait for them to come up and get you? Do something, I tell you!

**MR. VAN DAAN.** [*Pushing her aside*] Will you keep still!

[*He goes over to the stairwell to listen.* PETER *goes to his mother, helping her up onto the sofa. There is a second of silence, then* ANNE *can stand it no longer.*]

**ANNE.** Someone go after Father! Make Father come back!

**PETER.** [*Starting for the door*] I'll go.

**MR. VAN DAAN.** Haven't you done enough?

[*He pushes* PETER *roughly away. In his anger against his father* PETER *grabs a chair as if to hit him with it, then puts it down,*

*burying his face in his hands.* MRS. FRANK *begins to pray softly.*]

**ANNE.** Please, please, Mr. Van Daan. Get Father.

**MR. VAN DAAN.** Quiet! Quiet!

[ANNE *is shocked into silence.* MRS. FRANK *pulls her closer, holding her protectively in her arms.*]

**MRS. FRANK.** [*Softly, praying*] "I lift up mine eyes unto the mountains, from whence cometh my help. My help cometh from the Lord who made heaven and earth. He will not suffer thy foot to be moved . . . He that keepeth thee will not slumber . . ."

[*She stops as she hears someone coming. They all watch the door tensely.* MR. FRANK *comes quietly in.* ANNE *rushes to him, holding him tight.*]

**MR. FRANK.** It was a thief. That noise must have scared him away.

**MRS. VAN DAAN.** Thank God!

**MR. FRANK.** He took the cash box. And the radio. He ran away in such a hurry that he didn't stop to shut the street door. It was swinging wide open. [*A breath of relief sweeps over them.*] I think it would be good to have some light.

**MARGOT.** Are you sure it's all right?

**MR. FRANK.** The danger has passed.

[MARGOT *goes to light the small lamp.*]

Don't be so terrified, Anne. We're safe.

**DUSSEL.** Who says the danger has passed? Don't you realize we are in greater danger than ever?

**MR. FRANK.** Mr. Dussel, will you be still!

[MR. FRANK *takes* ANNE *back to the table,*

*The Diary of Anne Frank* 341

341

---

**94 Reading Strategy** How would you describe Van Daan's response to his wife? Why do you think he reacts as he does?

**95 Reading Strategy** How would you describe Mr. Frank's response to Dussel? How is this different from his characteristic behavior? Why do you think he acts as he does?

**Cooperative Learning** Allow time for story-map partners to review their notes on Act I. Use the story maps to generate a class discussion on the significance of different events. How accurate were the students' predictions at various points? How well did they evaluate the importance of an event or a piece of dialogue? Students might use their story maps to guide them in writing a summary of Act I.

**Writing Transparency** You can use *Model 1: Writing a Summary* in **Transparencies for Writing** to demonstrate for your students the features of a well-written summary.

**Videocassette** You may wish to use the video *The Diary of Anne Frank* in the **Library of Video Classics** to emphasize the swift, dramatic change in mood that occurs when the thief is heard. You may wish to view the video through the end of Act I to review action to this point.

**Challenge** Why might Miep and Mr. Kraler hide news of the Jews' real situation in Amsterdam?

Reader's Response What traditions or celebrations do you feel strengthened by?

Thematic Response How does Anne feel about the place she and her family have found? Which of Anne's feelings about the hiding place do you identify with most strongly?

Master Teacher Note Ask the class if the play is more effective by limiting locale to the hideaway rather than allowing us to see Miep and Mr. Kraler functioning in the outside world. Why? How would the play change if we could see the office, the thief, the Nazis? What is the impact of our hearing but never seeing the Nazis?

Enrichment You might consider recommending that students see the French film *Peppermint Soda* if it is ever shown locally, or try to bring it into class for viewing. We urge you to preview the film in case there is any material in it to which individuals in your class might be sensitive. The film shows two Jewish teenagers in a girl's school where classmates are primarily Christian.

Enrichment Students may be encouraged to write poetry in tribute to Anne and those who died in concentration camps.

Closure and Extension

ANSWERS TO RESPONDING
TO THE SELECTION
Your Response
1. Responses will differ. Prompt students to explain why they feel as they do.

Recalling
2. At first Anne is unaffected and considers the hiding place "a

*making her sit down with him, trying to calm her.*]

DUSSEL. [*Pointing to* PETER] Thanks to this clumsy fool, there's someone now who knows we're up here! Someone now knows we're up here, hiding!

MRS. VAN DAAN. [*Going to* DUSSEL] Someone knows we're here, yes. But who is the someone? A thief! A thief! You think a thief is going to go to the Green Police and say . . . I was robbing a place the other night and I heard a noise up over my head? You think a thief is going to do that?

DUSSEL. Yes. I think he will.

MRS. VAN DAAN. [*Hysterically*] You're crazy!

[*She stumbles back to her seat at the table.* PETER *follows protectively, pushing* DUSSEL *aside.*]

DUSSEL. I think some day he'll be caught and then he'll make a bargain with the Green Police . . . if they'll let him off, he'll tell them where some Jews are hiding!

[*He goes off into the bedroom. There is a second of appalled silence.*]

MR. VAN DAAN. He's right.

ANNE. Father, let's get out of here! We can't stay here now . . . Let's go . . .

MR. VAN DAAN. Go! Where?

MRS. FRANK. [*Sinking into her chair at the table*] Yes. Where?

MR. FRANK. [*Rising, to them all*] Have we lost all faith? All courage? A moment ago we thought that they'd come for us. We were sure it was the end. But it wasn't the end. We're alive, safe.

[MR. VAN DAAN *goes to the table and sits.* MR. FRANK *prays.*]

"We thank Thee, oh Lord our God, that in Thy infinite mercy Thou hast again seen fit to spare us." [*He blows out the candle, then turns to* ANNE.] Come on, Anne. The song! Let's have the song!

[*He starts to sing.* ANNE *finally starts falteringly to sing, as* MR. FRANK *urges her on. Her voice is hardly audible at first.*]

ANNE. [*Singing*]
"Oh, Hanukkah! Oh, Hanukkah!
The sweet . . . celebration . . ."

[*As she goes on singing, the others gradually join in, their voices still shaking with fear.* MRS. VAN DAAN *sobs as she sings.*]

GROUP.
"Around the feast . . . we . . . gather
In complete . . . jubilation . . .
Happiest of sea . . . sons
Now is here.
Many are the reasons for good cheer."

[DUSSEL *comes from the bedroom. He comes over to the table, standing beside* MARGOT, *listening to them as they sing.*]

"Together
We'll weather
Whatever tomorrow may bring."

[*As they sing on with growing courage, the lights start to dim.*]

"So hear us rejoicing
And merrily voicing
The Hanukkah song that we sing.
Hoy!"

[*The lights are out. The curtain starts slowly to fall.*]

"Hear us rejoicing
And merrily voicing
The Hanukkah song that we sing."

[*They are still singing, as the curtain falls.*]

very peculiar summer boarding house."
3. Her father's command that she never go beyond the door of their hiding place makes Anne realize the severity of their confinement.
4. Margot, Anne, and Peter do school assignments under the guidance of Mr. Frank. Mrs. Frank and Mrs. Van Daan do sewing, embroidery, and prepare dinners. They all celebrate Hanukkah. The families cannot

make any noise for fear of people becoming aware that they are hiding upstairs. They are never allowed to leave the attic to go outside. When a thief enters the warehouse, his noise fills everyone with fear. They think the intruder is the Green Police.
5. Anne wants to be able to ride her bike, to laugh, to have new clothes. to have a hot bath, and to be back in school with her friends. Her nightmare was that

the Green Police broke down the door and grabbed her.
6. Hanukkah is a time of celebration, a way of renewing faith in God. Anne has surprised the group by finding appropriate Hanukkah presents for each one.

Interpreting
7. Peter is gentle and well-mannered. He is shy and at times withdrawn. Anne is intelligent, honest, and eager for perfection. However, at times she can be

## RESPONDING TO THE SELECTION

### Your Response

1. The families live by strict rules in order to prevent discovery. Which of these rules would be hardest for you to follow? Why?

### Recalling

2. How does going into hiding affect Anne at first?
3. When does Anne realize what going into hiding really means?
4. In what ways do the families try to live their lives normally? Which events intrude, showing that their lives are not normal?
5. What are Anne's dreams for her future? What fears are revealed through her nightmares?
6. What special meaning does Hanukkah have for the families? How does Anne make the celebration particularly special?

### Interpreting

7. Compare and contrast Peter and Anne. How do their differences account for the reaction of each to removing the yellow star?
8. Compare and contrast Margot and Anne. How does the difference between the two characters account for each's relationship with Mrs. Frank?
9. Mr. Frank tells Anne, "There are no walls, there are no bolts, no locks that anyone can put on your mind." Explain this statement. How does Anne prove its truth?
10. Describe the mood at the end of Act I. What event has caused this mood?

### Applying

11. Like the Franks and Van Daans, many people turn to traditions and celebrations to give them courage in times of trouble. How do such traditions help us through difficult times?
12. Does the fact that Anne Frank was a real person make this play more meaningful for you? Explain your answer.

## ANALYZING LITERATURE

### Appreciating the Use of Flashback

The play opens with Mr. Frank's returning to the warehouse apartment in 1945 after the war. Once he has begun reading the diary, the action flashes back to 1942.

1. From whose point of view are the events seen at the beginning of the play?
2. During the flashback, to what character does the point of view shift?
3. Why is using a flashback more effective than having Mr. Frank simply tell what had happened in 1942?

## CRITICAL THINKING AND READING

### Predicting Outcomes

As you read, you continually make predictions about what will happen next. You make predictions based on clues authors provide and on your own experiences and those about which you have read.

As you make the following predictions, give two clues from Act I on which you base your predictions.

1. Choose two characters from this play. How do you think being in hiding will affect the relationship of these characters?
2. What do you think will happen to Anne?

## THINKING AND WRITING

### Writing as a Character in the Play

Pretend you are either Anne or Peter. Write a letter to Jopie or to another friend about what life in hiding is like. Before you start writing, list several topics you want to include. The topics might be how you spend your day, how your relationships with people have changed, and so forth. When you have finished your letter, make sure your spelling and punctuation are correct.

*The Diary of Anne Frank* 343

---

difficult and temperamental. Peter impulsively rips the Star of David off his shirt and burns it. Anne has stronger feelings about what the star stands for and can't burn it.

8. Margot is quiet, courteous, and distant. Anne is boisterous, self-assertive, and engaging. Their mother prefers Margot's character to Anne's. Anne feels she is not understood and has nothing in common with her mother.

9. The statement means that even though they are virtually prisoners in the attic, they can go anywhere through books. Anne is eager for intellectual activity and Mr. Frank is a great source of intellectual stimulation for her.

10. Everyone is fearful that the intruder will go to the Green Police and tell of their hiding. Yet they try to renew their faith and courage by continuing to celebrate Hanukkah.

### Applying

11. Answers will differ. Suggested response: Traditions help us through difficult times by giving people a sense of security. Sharing long-established values prevents a sense of rootlessness.

12. Answers will differ. Students should note that Anne provides firsthand observations on the barbarism of the Nazis.

## Preparation

**Literary Focus** Point out that characters change as a result of conflicts, both external and internal. Review the conflicts that emerged in Act I, such as the Jews' conflict against Nazism, individual conflicts between characters, and Anne's internal conflict to overcome fear and have "the good Anne outside and the bad Anne inside."

**Prereading Focus** Help students to relate experiences they have had with being confined and quiet or anxious and fearful to stimulate ideas for strategies. Experiences students might use include a long car ride, a night when they had trouble falling asleep, or a hospital stay. Ask students to share how they coped with the tedium and/or anxiety of these situations and try to apply them to Anne's situation.

**Vocabulary** The following words may not be known by your **less advanced** students: *disgruntled* (p. 345), *foreboding* (p. 348), *animation* (p. 354), *pandemonium* (p. 362), *liberated* (p. 363), *remorse* (p. 364).

**Spelling Tip** When you add the suffix *-ly* to a word that ends in *l*, like *ineffectual*, the *l* is kept: *ineffectually*.

# GUIDE FOR READING

## The Diary of Anne Frank, Act II

### Characters and Theme

Act II begins a little more than a year after the end of Act I. The passage of time, along with the characters' living so closely together and always in fear, has changed the characters. Observing the changes in the characters can help you to understand the theme of the play.

When Anne Frank wrote the diary from which this play was created, she may not have set out to present a **theme,** or general observation about life. Nevertheless, the events in the play do point to a strong theme.

### Focus

The hardships apparent in Act I intensify in Act II, and the resulting tension builds accordingly. Anne removes herself mentally by daydreaming and writing in her diary. If you were in the same predicament as the characters in the play, how would you cope with the terrible strain of living in such close quarters and in constant fear? With your classmates, brainstorm to list strategies that you would use to find temporary relief from the pressures and discomforts of living in hiding. As you read Act II, notice how the characters cope with their terrible situation.

### Vocabulary

Knowing the following words will help you as you read *The Diary of Anne Frank,* Act II.

**inarticulate** (in' är tik' yə lit) *adj.*: Speechless or unable to express oneself (p. 347)

**apprehension** (ap' rə hen' shən) *n.*: A fearful feeling about the future; dread (p. 349)

**intuition** (in' too wish' ən) *n.*: Ability to know immediately, without reasoning (p. 354)

**sarcastic** (sär kas' tik) *adj.*: Speaking with sharp mockery intended to hurt another (p. 355)

**indignant** (in dig' nənt) *adj.*: Filled with anger over some meanness or injustice (p. 356)

**inferiority complex** (in fir' ē ôr' ə tē käm' pleks) *n.*: Tendency to belittle oneself (p. 356)

**stealthily** (stel' thi lē') *adv.*: In a secretive or sneaky manner (p. 359)

**ineffectually** (in' i fek' choo wə lē) *adv.*: Without producing the desired effect (p. 365)

*344    Drama*

---

### Objectives

1 To understand the relationship between characters and theme in a play
2 To find support for a character's opinion
3 To write a letter to the editor

### Support Material

**Teaching Portfolio**
Teacher Backup, pp. 401–403
Grammar in Action Worksheets, *Using Contractions,* pp. 404–405; *Understanding Ellipses,* p. 406–407
Usage and Mechanics Worksheet, p. 408
Vocabulary Check, p. 409

Analyzing Literature Worksheet, *Understanding Characters and Theme,* p. 410
Critical Thinking and Reading Worksheet, *Finding Support for Opinions,* p. 411
Selection Test, pp. 412–413

**Library of Video Classics**
*The Diary of Anne Frank*

**Prentice Hall Literature Writing Studio**

## ACT II

### Scene 1

[*In the darkness we hear* ANNE'S VOICE, *again reading from the diary.*]

ANNE'S VOICE. Saturday, the first of January, nineteen forty-four. Another new year has begun and we find ourselves still in our hiding place. We have been here now for one year, five months and twenty-five days. It seems that our life is at a standstill.

[*The curtain rises on the scene. It is late afternoon. Everyone is bundled up against the cold. In the main room* MRS. FRANK *is taking down the laundry which is hung across the back.* MR. FRANK *sits in the chair down left, reading.* MARGOT *is lying on the couch with a blanket over her and the many-colored knitted scarf around her throat.* ANNE *is seated at the center table, writing in her diary.* PETER, MR. *and* MRS. VAN DAAN *and* DUSSEL *are all in their own rooms, reading or lying down.*

*As the lights dim on,* ANNE'S VOICE *continues, without a break.*]

ANNE'S VOICE. We are all a little thinner. The Van Daans' "discussions" are as violent as ever. Mother still does not understand me. But then I don't understand her either. There is one great change, however. A change in myself. I read somewhere that girls of my age don't feel quite certain of themselves. That they become quiet within and begin to think of the miracle that is taking place in their bodies. I think that what is happening to me is so wonderful . . . not only what can be seen, but what is taking place inside. Each time it has happened I have a feeling that I have a sweet secret. [*We hear the chimes and then a hymn being played on the carillon outside.*] And in spite of any pain, I long for the time when I shall feel that secret within me again.

The Westertoren Church tower as seen through the window of the attic hiding place

[*The buzzer of the door below suddenly sounds. Everyone is startled,* MR. FRANK *tiptoes cautiously to the top of the steps and listens. Again the buzzer sounds, in* MIEP'S *V-for-Victory signal.*[1]]

MR. FRANK. It's Miep!

[*He goes quickly down the steps to unbolt the door.* MRS. FRANK *calls upstairs to the* VAN DAANS *and then to* PETER.]

MRS. FRANK. Wake up, everyone! Miep is here!

[ANNE *quickly puts her diary away.* MARGOT *sits up, pulling the blanket around her shoulders.* MR. DUSSEL *sits on the edge of his bed, listening, disgruntled.* MIEP *comes up the steps, followed by* MR. KRALER. *They bring flowers, books, newspapers, etc.* ANNE *rushes to* MIEP, *throwing her arms affectionately around her.*]

---

**1. V-for-Victory signal:** Three short rings and one long one (the letter *V* in Morse code).

*The Diary of Anne Frank* 345

## Presentation

**Motivation/Prior Knowledge**
Impress on students the fact that more than one year has elapsed between the end of Act I and the events of Act II. What do they think has happened to the various conflicts in that time? Do they think the characters have learned to control their bickering? Their fears? Is it likely that Anne succeeded in putting "the good Anne outside and the bad Anne inside"?

**Thematic Focus** Distribute several index cards to each student and instruct the students to write one example on each card of a circumstance or situation they consider to be just or unjust. Collect the cards and have student volunteers take turns reading them aloud. Have the class identify whether the writer has listed an example of justice or injustice. Discuss causes, solutions, and ways to replicate the positive examples in other areas.

**Purpose-Setting Question** What does Anne learn about herself as the play develops?

**1 Enrichment** In Act II readers will see significant areas of development in Anne's maturity. Not unique among people her age are the "growing pains" that signify the end of childhood and the beginning of adulthood. This uncomfortable period of adolescence is the subject of many articles and books. Have students discuss other books they have read dealing with the problems of adolescence. The works of Judy Blume would be a good starting point.

**2 Discussion** Explain and discuss the examples of irony in this scene: Colorful flowers and a band playing outside contrast with the life-threatening situation faced by all the characters.

**3 Reading Strategy** What do you think has happened to Mouschi? How long do you think Mouschi has been gone?

**4 Critical Thinking and Reading** What is Mrs. Van Daan's point? What do you think of her attitude?

**5 Critical Thinking and Reading** What reason does Van Daan give for not including Margot? Based on what you know about his character, what do you think is the real reason?

Miep . . . *and Mr. Kraler . . . What a delightful surprise!*

**MR. KRALER.** We came to bring you New Year's greetings.

**MRS. FRANK.** You shouldn't . . . you should have at least one day to yourselves. [*She goes quickly to the stove and brings down teacups and tea for all of them.*]

**ANNE.** Don't say that, it's so wonderful to see them! [*Sniffing at* MIEP'S *coat*] I can smell the wind and the cold on your clothes.

**MIEP.** [*Giving her the flowers*] There you are. [*Then to* MARGOT, *feeling her forehead*] How are you, Margot? . . . Feeling any better?

**MARGOT.** I'm all right.

**ANNE.** We filled her full of every kind of pill so she won't cough and make a noise.

2 [*She runs into her room to put the flowers in water.* MR. *and* MRS. VAN DAAN *come from upstairs. Outside there is the sound of a band playing.*]

**MRS. VAN DAAN.** Well, hello, Miep. Mr. Kraler.

**MR. KRALER.** [*Giving a bouquet of flowers to* MRS. VAN DAAN] With my hope for peace in the New Year.

3 **PETER.** [*Anxiously*] Miep, have you seen Mouschi? Have you seen him anywhere around?

**MIEP.** I'm sorry, Peter. I asked everyone in the neighborhood had they seen a gray cat. But they said no.

[MRS. FRANK *gives* MIEP *a cup of tea.* MR. FRANK *comes up the steps, carrying a small cake on a plate.*]

**MR. FRANK.** Look what Miep's brought for us!

**MRS. FRANK.** [*Taking it*] A cake!

**MR. VAN DAAN.** A cake! [*He pinches* MIEP'S *cheeks gaily and hurries up to the cupboard.*] I'll get some plates.

[DUSSEL, *in his room, hastily puts a coat on and starts out to join the others.*]

**MRS. FRANK.** Thank you, Miepia. You shouldn't have done it. You must have used all of your sugar ration for weeks. [*Giving it to* MRS. VAN DAAN] It's beautiful, isn't it?

4 **MRS. VAN DAAN.** It's been ages since I even saw a cake. Not since you brought us one last year. [*Without looking at the cake, to* MIEP] Remember? Don't you remember, you gave us one on New Year's Day? Just this time last year? I'll never forget it because you had "Peace in nineteen forty-three" on it. [*She looks at the cake and reads*] "Peace in nineteen forty-four!"

**MIEP.** Well, it has to come sometime, you know. [*As* DUSSEL *comes from his room*] Hello, Mr. Dussel.

**MR. KRALER.** How are you?

**MR. VAN DAAN.** [*Bringing plates and a knife*] Here's the knife, *liefje.* Now, how many of us are there?

**MIEP.** None for me, thank you.

**MR. FRANK.** Oh, please. You must.

**MIEP.** I couldn't.

**MR. VAN DAAN.** Good! That leaves one . . . two . . . three . . . seven of us.

**DUSSEL.** Eight! Eight! It's the same number as it always is!

5 **MR. VAN DAAN.** I left Margot out. I take it for granted Margot won't eat any.

**ANNE.** Why wouldn't she!

**MRS. FRANK.** I think it won't harm her.

**MR. VAN DAAN.** All right! All right! I just didn't want her to start coughing again, that's all.

**DUSSEL.** And please, Mrs. Frank should cut the cake.

**MR. VAN DAAN.** What's the difference? ⎫

**MRS. VAN DAAN.** It's not Mrs. Frank's cake, is it, Miep? It's for all of us. ⎬ [*Together*]

**DUSSEL.** Mrs. Frank divides things better.

**MRS. VAN DAAN.** [*Going to* DUSSEL] What are you trying to say? ⎫

**MR. VAN DAAN.** Oh, come on! Stop wasting time! ⎬ [*Together*]

**6**

**MRS. VAN DAAN.** [*To* DUSSEL] Don't I always give everybody exactly the same? Don't I?

**MR. VAN DAAN.** Forget it, Kerli.

**MRS. VAN DAAN.** No. I want an answer! Don't I?

**DUSSEL.** Yes. Yes. Everybody gets exactly the same . . . except Mr. Van Daan always gets a little bit more.

[VAN DAAN *advances on* DUSSEL, *the knife still in his hand.*]

**MR. VAN DAAN.** That's a lie!

[DUSSEL *retreats before the onslaught of the* VAN DAANS.]

**MR. FRANK.** Please, please! [*Then to* MIEP] You see what a little sugar cake does to us? It goes right to our heads!

**MR. VAN DAAN.** [*Handing* MRS. FRANK *the knife*] Here you are, Mrs. Frank.

**MRS. FRANK.** Thank you. [*Then to* MIEP *as she goes to the table to cut the cake*] Are you sure you won't have some?

**MIEP.** [*Drinking her tea*] No, really, I have to go in a minute.

[*The sound of the band fades out in the distance.*]

**PETER.** [*To* MIEP] Maybe Mouschi went back to our house . . . they say that cats . . . Do you ever get over there . . . ? I mean . . . do you suppose you could . . . ? **7**

**MIEP.** I'll try, Peter. The first minute I get I'll try. But I'm afraid, with him gone a week . . . **8**

**DUSSEL.** Make up your mind, already someone has had a nice big dinner from that cat! **9**

[PETER *is furious, inarticulate. He starts toward* DUSSEL *as if to hit him.* MR. FRANK *stops him.* MRS. FRANK *speaks quickly to ease the situation.*]

**MRS. FRANK.** [*To* MIEP] This is delicious, Miep!

**MRS. VAN DAAN.** [*Eating hers*] Delicious!

**MR. VAN DAAN.** [*Finishing it in one gulp*] Dirk's in luck to get a girl who can bake like this!

**MIEP.** [*Putting down her empty teacup*] I have to run. Dirk's taking me to a party tonight.

**ANNE.** How heavenly! Remember now what everyone is wearing, and what you have to eat and everything, so you can tell us tomorrow.

**MIEP.** I'll give you a full report! Good-bye, everyone!

**MR. VAN DAAN.** [*To* MIEP] Just a minute. There's something I'd like you to do for me.

[*He hurries off up the stairs to his room.*]

**MRS. VAN DAAN.** [*Sharply*] Putti, where are you going? [*She rushes up the stairs after him, calling hysterically.*] What do you want? Putti, what are you going to do?

**MIEP.** [*To* PETER] What's wrong?

**PETER.** [*His sympathy is with his mother.*] Father says he's going to sell her fur coat. She's crazy about that old fur coat.

*The Diary of Anne Frank*   347

**6 Discussion** What does this reveal about Mrs. Van Daan?

**7 Discussion** Why does Peter speak haltingly? How much hope does he have that the cat has returned to the house? Why does he ask Miep to check?

**8 Reading Strategy** Was your prediction correct?

**9 Critical Thinking and Reading** Why does Dussel say this? What does this reveal about him?

**ESL Teaching Strategy** You can use the argument between Dussel and the Van Daans as motivation for your students with limited proficiency in English to practice quantitative words and phrases such as *more than*, *less than*, *some*, *none*, *all*. Demonstrate each concept with manipulatives and verbally describe what you do, saying, for instance, "You have all the blue squares. I have none." Then ask students to use the words to identify a quantitive relationship that you show them. For instance, if you give yourself six counters and the student has four, he or she should respond, "You have more than I do."

10 **Discussion** What does this reveal about Mr. Van Daan's relationship with his wife? Why did he sell her coat?

**11** **Reading Strategy** What do you think is wrong with Mr. Kraler?

**12** **Critical Thinking and Reading** Why does Margot think something is wrong? What do you think the problem might be?

**DUSSEL.** Is it possible? Is it possible that anyone is so silly as to worry about a fur coat in times like this?

**PETER.** It's none of your darn business . . . and if you say one more thing . . . I'll, I'll take you and I'll . . . I mean it . . . I'll . . .

[*There is a piercing scream from* MRS. VAN DAAN *above. She grabs at the fur coat as* MR. VAN DAAN *is starting downstairs with it.*]

**MRS. VAN DAAN.** No! No! No! Don't you dare take that! You hear? It's mine!

[*Downstairs* PETER *turns away, embarrassed, miserable.*]

My father gave me that! You didn't give it to me. You have no right. Let go of it . . . you hear?

[MR. VAN DAAN *pulls the coat from her hands and hurries downstairs.* MRS. VAN DAAN *sinks to the floor, sobbing. As* MR. VAN DAAN *comes into the main room the others look away, embarrassed for him.*]

**MR. VAN DAAN.** [*To* MR. KRALER] Just a little —discussion over the advisability of selling this coat. As I have often reminded Mrs. Van Daan, it's very selfish of her to keep it when people outside are in such desperate need of clothing . . . [*He gives the coat to* MIEP.] So if you will please to sell it for us? It should fetch a good price. And by the way, will you get me cigarettes. I don't care what kind they are . . . get all you can.

**MIEP.** It's terribly difficult to get them, Mr. Van Daan. But I'll try. Good-bye.

[*She goes.* MR. FRANK *follows her down the steps to bolt the door after her.* MRS. FRANK *gives* MR. KRALER *a cup of tea.*]

**MRS. FRANK.** Are you sure you won't have some cake, Mr. Kraler?

**MR. KRALER.** I'd better not.

**MR. VAN DAAN.** You're still feeling badly? What does your doctor say?

**MR. KRALER.** I haven't been to him.

**MRS. FRANK.** Now, Mr. Kraler! . . .

**MR. KRALER.** [*Sitting at the table*] Oh, I tried. But you can't get near a doctor these days . . . they're so busy. After weeks I finally managed to get one on the telephone. I told him I'd like an appointment . . . I wasn't feeling very well. You know what he answers . . . over the telephone . . . Stick out your tongue! [*They laugh. He turns to* MR. FRANK *as* MR. FRANK *comes back.*] I have some contracts here . . . I wonder if you'd look over them with me . . .

**MR. FRANK.** [*Putting out his hand*] Of course.

**MR. KRALER.** [*He rises*] If we could go downstairs . . . [MR. FRANK *starts ahead;* MR. KRALER *speaks to the others.*] Will you forgive us? I won't keep him but a minute. [*He starts to follow* MR. FRANK *down the steps.*]

**MARGOT.** [*With sudden foreboding*] What's happened? Something's happened! Hasn't it, Mr. Kraler?

[MR. KRALER *stops and comes back, trying to reassure* MARGOT *with a pretense of casualness.*]

**MR. KRALER.** No, really. I want your father's advice . . .

**MARGOT.** Something's gone wrong! I know it!

**MR. FRANK.** [*Coming back, to* MR. KRALER] If it's something that concerns us here, it's better that we all hear it.

**MR. KRALER.** [*Turning to him, quietly*] But . . . the children . . . ?

## Primary Source

Co-editor of *The Diary of Anne Frank: Critical Edition* David Barnouw discusses the second version of Anne Frank's diary in a June 8, 1989 article of *The New York Times*.

To make her diary even more creative, she changed certain names in her second draft. For example, instead of calling her family Frank, she changed it to Robin; she became Anne Robin. And she attached other fictional names to people who were hiding from the Germans.

After her father returned from Auschwitz, he decided to publish the diary. He included some of the events that she had recorded in her "Tales." He restored the Frank family name that Anne had fictionalized, retained the fictional names that she had devised for other people, pared some of the criticism by Anne of her mother (who had also died in a concentration camp), and deleted some of the entries about her awakening sexual interest.

Some of Mr. Frank's deletions included minor entries on such things as French irregular verbs, washing her hair, hurting her little toe, breaking a vacuum cleaner. References to menstruation were omitted . . .

*The bookcase moved aside to show the stairs leading to the attic hiding place; the bookcase hiding the stairs*

13 **MR. FRANK.** What they'd imagine would be worse than any reality.

[*As* MR. KRALER *speaks, they all listen with intense apprehension.* MRS. VAN DAAN *comes down the stairs and sits on the bottom step.*]

**MR. KRALER.** It's a man in the storeroom . . . I don't know whether or not you remember him . . . Carl, about fifty, heavy-set, near-sighted . . . He came with us just before you left.

**MR. FRANK.** He was from Utrecht?

**MR. KRALER.** That's the man. A couple of weeks ago, when I was in the storeroom, he closed the door and asked me . . . how's Mr. Frank? What do you hear from Mr. Frank? I told him I only knew there was a rumor that you were in Switzerland. He said he'd heard that rumor too, but he thought I might know something more. I didn't pay any attention to it . . . but then a thing happened yesterday . . . He'd brought some invoices to the office for me to sign. As I was going through them, I looked up. He was standing staring at the bookcase . . . your bookcase. He said he thought he remembered a door there . . . Wasn't there a door there that used to go up to the loft? Then he told me he wanted more money. Twenty guilders[2] more a week.

14

---

**2. guilders** (gil' dərz) *n.*: The monetary unit of Holland.

*The Diary of Anne Frank* 349

13 **Discussion** What experiences have you had that support Mr. Frank's statement?

14 **Reading Strategy** Evaluate this information. Predict how it will affect the Franks' situation. Can you think of any possible actions that might be taken? How do you think each of the characters is reacting to this news?

**Cooperative Learning** You may wish to pause at this point to allow story-map partners to work collaboratively on evaluating this information while they record it on their story maps.

The critical edition discloses understandable motives behind Mr. Frank's deletions: his strong attachment to his dead daughter; his awareness that with publication of the diary he would be achieving her dearest wish—to become a famous writer one day; and his feelings of respect, first and foremost, toward his wife and others about whom Miss Frank had made unkind remarks during the occupation.

**15 Discussion** What would you do? Why?

**16 Discussion** What does Dussel fear?

**17 Reading Strategy** How do you feel about what Margot says? Do you think any of the other characters share her feelings?

MR. VAN DAAN. Blackmail!

MR. FRANK. Twenty guilders? Very modest blackmail.

MR. VAN DAAN. That's just the beginning.

DUSSEL. [*Coming to* MR. FRANK] You know what I think? He was the thief who was down there that night. That's how he knows we're here.

MR. FRANK. [*To* MR. KRALER] How was it left? What did you tell him?

15 MR. KRALER. I said I had to think about it. What shall I do? Pay him the money? . . . Take a chance on firing him . . . or what? I don't know.

16 DUSSEL. [*Frantic*] For God's sake don't fire him! Pay him what he asks . . . keep him here where you can have your eye on him.

MR. FRANK. Is it so much that he's asking? What are they paying nowadays?

MR. KRALER. He could get it in a war plant. But this isn't a war plant. Mind you. I don't know if he really knows . . . or if he doesn't know.

MR. FRANK. Offer him half. Then we'll soon find out if it's blackmail or not.

DUSSEL. And if it is? We've got to pay it, haven't we? Anything he asks we've got to pay!

MR. FRANK. Let's decide that when the time comes.

MR. KRALER. This may be all my imagination. You get to a point, these days, where you suspect everyone and everything. Again and again . . . on some simple look or word, I've found myself . . .

[*The telephone rings in the office below.*]

MRS. VAN DAAN. [*Hurrying to* MR. KRALER]

There's the telephone! What does that mean, the telephone ringing on a holiday?

MR. KRALER. That's my wife. I told her I had to go over some papers in my office . . . to call me there when she got out of church. [*He starts out.*] I'll offer him half then. Good-bye . . . we'll hope for the best!

[*The group calls their good-byes half-heartedly.* MR. FRANK *follows* MR. KRALER, *to bolt the door below. During the following scene,* MR. FRANK *comes back up and stands listening, disturbed.*]

DUSSEL. [*To* MR. VAN DAAN] You can thank your son for this . . . smashing the light! I tell you, it's just a question of time now.

[*He goes to the window at the back and stands looking out.*]

17 MARGOT. Sometimes I wish the end would come . . . whatever it is.

MRS. FRANK. [*Shocked*] Margot!

[ANNE *goes to* MARGOT, *sitting beside her on the couch with her arms around her.*]

MARGOT. Then at least we'd know where we were.

MRS. FRANK. You should be ashamed of yourself! Talking that way! Think how lucky we are! Think of the thousands dying in the war, every day. Think of the people in concentration camps.

ANNE. [*Interrupting*] What's the good of that? What's the good of thinking of misery when you're already miserable? That's stupid!

MRS. FRANK. Anne!

[*As* ANNE *goes on raging at her mother,* MRS. FRANK *tries to break in, in an effort to quiet her.*]

ANNE. We're young, Margot and Peter and I! You grownups have had your chance! But

## Grammar in Action

A **contraction** is a combination of two words in which one or more omitted letters is replaced by an apostrophe. Contractions are usually to be avoided in expository and formal types of writing. They are much more common in fiction, especially fiction that contains dialogue. Contractions create more realistic dialogue because people use contractions in speech. As shortened forms of words or phrases, contractions are used for convenience and to save time.

The use of contractions in the following excerpt gives strength and speed to Anne's outburst:

"What's the good of that? What's the good of thinking of misery when you're already miserable? That's stupid!"

Notice how different Anne's exclamations would have sounded had she said, "What is the good of that? What is the good of thinking of misery when you are already miserable? That is stupid!" The second version sounds flat and void of the emotional intensity of the original version.

look at us . . . If we begin thinking of all the horror in the world, we're lost! We're trying to hold onto some kind of ideals . . . when everything . . . ideals, hopes . . . everything, are being destroyed! It isn't our fault that the world is in such a mess! We weren't around when all this started! So don't try to take it out on us! [*She rushes off to her room, slamming the door after her. She picks up a brush from the chest and hurls it to the floor. Then she sits on the settee, trying to control her anger.*]

**MR. VAN DAAN.** She talks as if we started the war! Did we start the war?

[*He spots* ANNE'S *cake. As he starts to take it,* PETER *anticipates him.*]

**PETER.** She left her cake.

[*He starts for* ANNE'S *room with the cake. There is silence in the main room.* MRS. VAN DAAN *goes up to her room, followed by* VAN DAAN. DUSSEL *stays looking out the window.* MR. FRANK *brings* MRS. FRANK *her cake. She eats it slowly, without relish.* MR. FRANK *takes his cake to* MARGOT *and sits quietly on the sofa beside her.* PETER *stands in the doorway of* ANNE'S *darkened room, looking at her, then makes a little movement to let her know he is there.* ANNE *sits up, quickly, trying to hide the signs of her tears.* PETER *holds out the cake to her.*]

You left this.

**ANNE.** [*Dully*] Thanks.

[PETER *starts to go out, then comes back.*]

**PETER.** I thought you were fine just now. You know just how to talk to them. You know just how to say it. I'm no good . . . I never can think . . . especially when I'm mad . . . That Dussel . . . when he said that about Mouschi . . . someone eating him . . . all I could think is . . . I wanted to hit him. I wanted to give him such a . . . a . . . that he'd . . . That's what I used to do when there was an argument at school . . . That's the way I . . . but here . . . And an old man like that . . . it wouldn't be so good.

**ANNE.** You're making a big mistake about me. I do it all wrong. I say too much. I go too far. I hurt people's feelings . . . |19

[DUSSEL *leaves the window, going to his room.*]

**PETER.** I think you're just fine . . . What I want to say . . . if it wasn't for you around here, I don't know. What I mean . . . |20

[PETER *is interrupted by* DUSSEL'S *turning on the light.* DUSSEL *stands in the doorway, startled to see* PETER. PETER *advances toward him forbiddingly.* DUSSEL *backs out of the room.* PETER *closes the door on him.*]

**ANNE.** Do you mean it, Peter? Do you really mean it?

**PETER.** I said it, didn't I?

**ANNE.** Thank you, Peter!

[*In the main room* MR. *and* MRS. FRANK *collect the dishes and take them to the sink, washing them.* MARGOT *lies down again on the couch.* DUSSEL, *lost, wanders into* PETER'S *room and takes up a book, starting to read.*]

**PETER.** [*Looking at the photographs on the wall*] You've got quite a collection.

**ANNE.** Wouldn't you like some in your room? I could give you some. Heaven knows you spend enough time in there . . . doing heaven knows what . . .

**PETER.** It's easier. A fight starts, or an argument . . . I duck in there. |21

**ANNE.** You're lucky, having a room to go to. His lordship is always here . . . I hardly ever get a minute alone. When they start in on

*The Diary of Anne Frank* 351

18 **Discussion** Is Anne's attitude about the horrors happening in the world a typical attitude of youth? Do young people today feel the same way about their elders?

19 **Discussion** How does Anne characterize herself? How would you characterize Anne? What accounts for the difference?

20 **Reading Strategy** Compare Peter's words and actions to the way he behaved toward Anne at the beginning of the play. What clues have you noticed that make this new attitude believable?

21 **Discussion** Anne writes in her diary and Peter escapes to his room. What do you think the other characters do to escape?

**Student Activity 1.** Write out the full words of the following contractions:

1. weren't
2. isn't
3. we'd
4. would've
5. what's
6. that's
7. wouldn't
8. you've
9. you're
10. I'd

**Student Activity 2.** Rewrite Anne's speech that starts at the bottom of page 350 eliminating the contractions by writing out the words. How does this version of Anne's speech differ from the original version in terms of mood and tone?

**Electronic Handbook** You may wish to review contractions with your students before having them complete the Grammar in Action activities. If your students are using the Language Master 6000, have them key in the symbol for the apostrophe and press the GRAMMAR key to get information about using contractions.

22 **Reading Strategy** What unique problems do Anne and Peter have? What problems do they share with other young people?

23 **Discussion** Discuss Anne's changing attitude toward her father. What does this indicate about Anne?

24 **Discussion** What does this show about Anne's changing relationship with her father? Do you think she would have said this in Act I?

*Anne's bedroom wall in the hiding place and the photographs she hung there*

me, I can't duck away. I have to stand there and take it.

**PETER.** You gave some of it back just now.

22 **ANNE.** I get so mad. They've formed their opinions . . . about everything . . . but we . . . we're still trying to find out . . . We have problems here that no other people our age have ever had. And just as you think you've solved them, something comes along and bang! You have to start all over again.

**PETER.** At least you've got someone you can talk to.

23 **ANNE.** Not really. Mother . . . I never discuss anything serious with her. She doesn't understand. Father's all right. We can talk about everything . . . everything but one thing. Mother. He simply won't talk about her. I don't think you can be really intimate with anyone if he holds something back, do you?

**PETER.** I think your father's fine.

24 **ANNE.** Oh, he is, Peter! He is! He's the only one who's ever given me the feeling that I have any sense. But anyway, nothing can take the place of school and play and friends

352   *Drama*

## Primary Source

David Barnouw, co-editor of *The Diary of Anne Frank: The Critical Edition,* said the following about Anne Frank's diary in a June 8, 1989 article in *The New York Times:*

We decided to publish it all—her mistakes, additions and deletions. She rewrote her diary in 1944 so people can compare it with her original. Why? She heard a broadcast beamed from London by the Dutch Government-in-exile. The Education Minister advised people in German-occu-pied Holland to keep diaries as a record of what went on under the Nazis.

Anne took the words personally. So in the second version, she made improvements in content and language. She thought the diary could become a kind of detective story. She added "Tales From the Secret Annex" to her diary. In fact, the title of her diary in the original Dutch edition is "The Annex."

of your own age . . . or near your age . . . can it?

**PETER.** I suppose you miss your friends and all.

**ANNE.** It isn't just . . . [*She breaks off, staring up at him for a second.*] Isn't it funny, you and I? Here we've been seeing each other every minute for almost a year and a half, and this is the first time we've ever really talked. It helps a lot to have someone to talk to, don't you think? It helps you to let off steam.

**PETER.** [*Going to the door*] Well, any time you want to let off steam, you can come into my room.

**ANNE.** [*Following him*] I can get up an awful lot of steam. You'll have to be careful how you say that.

**PETER.** It's all right with me.

**ANNE.** Do you mean it?

**PETER.** I said it, didn't I?

[*He goes out.* ANNE *stands in her doorway looking after him. As* PETER *gets to his door he stands for a minute looking back at her. Then he goes into his room.* DUSSEL *rises as he comes in, and quickly passes him, going out. He starts across for his room.* ANNE *sees him coming, and pulls her door shut.* DUSSEL *turns back toward* PETER'S *room.* PETER *pulls his door shut.* DUSSEL *stands there, bewildered, forlorn.*

*The scene slowly dims out. The curtain falls on the scene.* ANNE'S VOICE *comes over in the darkness . . . faintly at first, and then with growing strength.*]

**ANNE'S VOICE.** We've had bad news. The people from whom Miep got our ration books have been arrested. So we have had to cut down on our food. Our stomachs are so empty that they rumble and make strange noises, all in different keys. Mr. Van Daan's is deep and low, like a bass fiddle. Mine is high, whistling like a flute. As we all sit around waiting for supper, it's like an orchestra tuning up. It only needs Toscanini[3] to raise his baton and we'd be off in the Ride of the Valkyries.[4] Monday, the sixth of March, nineteen forty-four. Mr. Kraler is in the hospital. It seems he has ulcers. Pim says we are his ulcers. Miep has to run the business and us too. The Americans have landed on the southern tip of Italy. Father looks for a quick finish to the war. Mr. Dussel is waiting every day for the warehouse man to demand more money. Have I been skipping too much from one subject to another? I can't help it. I feel that spring is coming. I feel it in my whole body and soul. I feel utterly confused. I am longing . . . so longing . . . for everything . . . for friends . . . for someone to talk to . . . someone who understands . . . someone young, who feels as I do . . .

[*As these last lines are being said, the curtain rises on the scene. The lights dim on.* ANNE'S VOICE *fades out.*]

## Scene 2

[*It is evening, after supper. From outside we hear the sound of children playing. The "grownups," with the exception of* MR. VAN DAAN, *are all in the main room.* MRS. FRANK *is doing some mending,* MRS. VAN DAAN *is reading a fashion magazine.* MR. FRANK *is going over business accounts.* DUSSEL, *in his dentist's jacket, is pacing up and down, impa-*

---

**3. Toscanini** (täs′ kə nē′ nē): Arturo Toscanini, a famous Italian orchestral conductor.
**4. Ride of the Valkyries** (val′ kir′ ēz): A stirring selection from an opera by Richard Wagner, a German composer.

25 **Enrichment** Discuss the use of similes in Anne's writing. Explain that a simile takes two essentially unlike things and draws an imaginative comparison between them using the word *like* or *as*. Anne compares the rumbling noises in their stomachs to musical instruments. Have students suggest other similes for the rest of the people in the Frank and Van Daan families.

26 **Reading Strategy** Were your predictions about Mr. Kraler correct? What does Mr. Frank mean when he says, ". . . we are his ulcers"?

27 **Master Teacher Note** Discuss the stage directions with students. Point out that stage directions in plays should be read carefully. They help the reader picture what the characters are doing. Question students on what each character is doing.

The American novelist Philip Roth became interested in the diary and those who have challenged it five years ago after a visit to the Anne Frank Foundation, which runs the museum at the house where Anne hid with her family for two years above a former office annex at 263 Prinsengracht, Amsterdam.

Discussing the changes Miss Frank made in her entries, Mr. Roth observed: "This brilliant young girl revised her diary because she discovered that she had become a much better writer. The fact that she rewrote it is one sign that, had she survived, she would have achieved an important literary career."

**Videocassette** You may wish to use *The Diary of Anne Frank* in the **Library of Video Classics** to help your students visualize the action of this portion of the scene. Begin with Mr. Dussel waiting to get into his room, play the video through Anne's walk across the common room, and then pause for discussion. Tell students to watch for how each person's activity demonstrates some aspect of his or her personality. You may also wish to allow time for character-chart groups to modify their charts to reflect the new relationship between Anne and Peter.

**28 Discussion** How is Margot's relationship with Anne changing?

**29 Critical Thinking and Reading** Based on what you know about Mrs. Frank's character, why do you think she is discouraging Anne from spending so much time with Peter?

**30 Reading Strategy** How accurate is Anne's assessment of Mrs. Van Daan's personality? Give examples of her behavior that support your opinion.

tient to get into his bedroom. MR. VAN DAAN *is upstairs working on a piece of embroidery in an embroidery frame.*

*In his room* PETER *is sitting before the mirror, smoothing his hair. As the scene goes on, he puts on his tie, brushes his coat and puts it on, preparing himself meticulously for a visit from* ANNE. *On his wall are now hung some of* ANNE'S *motion picture stars.*

*In her room* ANNE *too is getting dressed. She stands before the mirror in her slip, trying various ways of dressing her hair.* MARGOT *is seated on the sofa, hemming a skirt for* ANNE *to wear.*

*In the main room* DUSSEL *can stand it no longer. He comes over, rapping sharply on the door of his and* ANNE'S *bedroom.]*

ANNE. [*Calling to him*] No, no, Mr. Dussel! I am not dressed yet.

[DUSSEL *walks away, furious, sitting down and burying his head in his hands.* ANNE *turns to* MARGOT.]

How is that? How does that look?

MARGOT. [*Glancing at her briefly*] Fine.

ANNE. You didn't even look.

MARGOT. Of course I did. It's fine.

ANNE. Margot, tell me, am I terribly ugly?

MARGOT. Oh, stop fishing.

ANNE. No. No. Tell me.

MARGOT. Of course you're not. You've got nice eyes . . . and a lot of animation, and . . .

ANNE. A little vague, aren't you?

[*She reaches over and takes a brassiere out of* MARGOT'S *sewing basket. She holds it up to herself, studying the effect in the mirror. Outside,* MRS. FRANK, *feeling sorry for* DUSSEL, *comes over, knocking at the girls' door.]*

MRS. FRANK. [*Outside*] May I come in?

MARGOT. Come in, Mother.

MRS. FRANK. [*Shutting the door behind her*] Mr. Dussel's impatient to get in here.

ANNE. [*Still with the brassiere*] Heavens, he takes the room for himself the entire day.

MRS. FRANK. [*Gently*] Anne, dear, you're not going in again tonight to see Peter?

ANNE. [*Dignified*] That is my intention.

MRS. FRANK. But you've already spent a great deal of time in there today.

ANNE. I was in there exactly twice. Once to get the dictionary, and then three-quarters of an hour before supper.

MRS. FRANK. Aren't you afraid you're disturbing him?

ANNE. Mother, I have some intuition.

MRS. FRANK. Then may I ask you this much, Anne. Please don't shut the door when you go in.

ANNE. You sound like Mrs. Van Daan! [*She throws the brassiere back in* MARGOT'S *sewing basket and picks up her blouse, putting it on.]*

MRS. FRANK. No. No. I don't mean to suggest anything wrong. I only wish that you wouldn't expose yourself to criticism . . . that you wouldn't give Mrs. Van Daan the opportunity to be unpleasant.

ANNE. Mrs. Van Daan doesn't need an opportunity to be unpleasant!

MRS. FRANK. Everyone's on edge, worried about Mr. Kraler. This is one more thing . . .

ANNE. I'm sorry, Mother. I'm going to Peter's room. I'm not going to let Petronella Van Daan spoil our friendship.

[MRS. FRANK *hesitates for a second, then goes out, closing the door after her. She gets a pack of playing cards and sits at the center table, playing solitaire. In* ANNE'S *room* MARGOT *hands the finished skirt to* ANNE. *As* ANNE *is putting it on,* MARGOT *takes off her high-heeled shoes and stuffs paper in the toes so that* ANNE *can wear them.*]

**MARGOT.** [*To* ANNE] Why don't you two talk in the main room? It'd save a lot of trouble. It's hard on Mother, having to listen to those remarks from Mrs. Van Daan and not say a word.

**ANNE.** Why doesn't she say a word? I think it's ridiculous to take it and take it.

**31 MARGOT.** You don't understand Mother at all, do you? She can't talk back. She's not like you. It's just not in her nature to fight back.

**ANNE.** Anyway . . . the only one I worry about is you. I feel awfully guilty about you. [*She sits on the stool near* MARGOT, *putting on* MARGOT'S *high-heeled shoes.*]

**MARGOT.** What about?

**ANNE.** I mean, every time I go into Peter's room, I have a feeling I may be hurting you. [MARGOT *shakes her head.*] I know if it were me, I'd be wild. I'd be desperately jealous, if it were me.

**MARGOT.** Well, I'm not.

**32 ANNE.** You don't feel badly? Really? Truly? You're not jealous?

**MARGOT.** Of course I'm jealous . . . jealous that you've got something to get up in the morning for . . . But jealous of you and Peter? No.

[ANNE *goes back to the mirror.*]

**ANNE.** Maybe there's nothing to be jealous of. Maybe he doesn't really like me. Maybe I'm just taking the place of his cat . . . [*She picks up a pair of short white gloves, putting them on.*] Wouldn't you like to come in with us?

**MARGOT.** I have a book.

[*The sound of the children playing outside fades out. In the main room* DUSSEL *can stand it no longer. He jumps up, going to the bedroom door and knocking sharply.*]

**DUSSEL.** Will you please let me in my room!

**ANNE.** Just a minute, dear, dear Mr. Dussel. [*She picks up her mother's pink stole and adjusts it elegantly over her shoulders, then gives a last look in the mirror.*] Well, here I go . . . to run the gauntlet.[5]  **33**

[*She starts out, followed by* MARGOT.]

**DUSSEL.** [*As she appears—sarcastic*] Thank you so much.

[DUSSEL *goes into his room.* ANNE *goes toward* PETER'S *room, passing* MRS. VAN DAAN *and her parents at the center table.*]

**MRS. VAN DAAN.** My God, look at her!

[ANNE *pays no attention. She knocks at* PETER'S *door.*]

I don't know what good it is to have a son. I never see him. He wouldn't care if I killed myself.

[PETER *opens the door and stands aside for* ANNE *to come in.*]

Just a minute, Anne. [*She goes to them at the door.*] I'd like to say a few words to my son. Do you mind?

[PETER *and* ANNE *stand waiting.*]

---

**5. to run the gauntlet** (gônt' lit): Formerly, to pass between two rows of men who struck at the offender with clubs as he passed; here, a series of troubles or difficulties.

**31 Discussion** What do you learn about Mrs. Frank's character? Compare her character with that of Mrs. Van Daan.

**32 Discussion** How does Margot react to Peter and Anne's relationship?

**33 Discussion** Peter and Anne see each other in ordinary clothes almost constantly. Why do you think Anne dresses up to visit Peter's room?

**Critical Thinking and Reading**
Compare Mrs. Van Daan's reaction to Peter and Anne's relationship with that of Mrs. Frank. Which of the mothers' attitudes is more traditional?

**35 Discussion** How has Anne changed since the beginning of the play?

**Challenge** Use nonverbal communication to help your students think about a character's motivations and internal reactions. Assign a character to a student who is standing in front of the room. Members of the class take turns directing comments and questions from the play to the "character." The "character" must respond without speaking, by using facial expressions, gestures, or body language. After several students have had an opportunity to be a character, allow time for students to discuss what they think is being communicated and how accurate they find the interpretation of each character's feelings.

Peter, I don't want you staying up till all hours tonight. You've got to have your sleep. You're a growing boy. You hear?

**MRS. FRANK.** Anne won't stay late. She's going to bed promptly at nine. Aren't you, Anne?

**ANNE.** Yes, Mother . . . [*To* MRS. VAN DAAN] May we go now?

**MRS. VAN DAAN.** Are you asking me? I didn't know I had anything to say about it.

**MRS. FRANK.** Listen for the chimes, Anne dear.

[*The two young people go off into* PETER'S *room, shutting the door after them.*]

**MRS. VAN DAAN.** [*To* MRS. FRANK] In my day it was the boys who called on the girls. Not the girls on the boys.

**MRS. FRANK.** You know how young people like to feel that they have secrets. Peter's room is the only place where they can talk.

**MRS. VAN DAAN.** Talk! That's not what they called it when I was young.

[MRS. VAN DAAN *goes off to the bathroom.* MARGOT *settles down to read her book.* MR. FRANK *puts his papers away and brings a chess game to the center table. He and* MRS. FRANK *start to play. In* PETER'S *room,* ANNE *speaks to* PETER, *indignant, humiliated.*]

**ANNE.** Aren't they awful? Aren't they impossible? Treating us as if we were still in the nursery.

[*She sits on the cot.* PETER *gets a bottle of pop and two glasses.*]

**PETER.** Don't let it bother you. It doesn't bother me.

**ANNE.** I suppose you can't really blame them . . . they think back to what *they* were like at our age. They don't realize how much

more advanced we are . . . When you think what wonderful discussions we've had! . . . Oh, I forgot. I was going to bring you some more pictures.

**PETER.** Oh, these are fine, thanks.

**ANNE.** Don't you want some more? Miep just brought me some new ones.

**PETER.** Maybe later. [*He gives her a glass of pop and, taking some for himself, sits down facing her.*]

**ANNE.** [*Looking up at one of the photographs*] I remember when I got that . . . I won it. I bet Jopie that I could eat five ice-cream cones. We'd all been playing ping-pong . . . We used to have heavenly times . . . we'd finish up with ice cream at the Delphi, or the Oasis, where Jews were allowed . . . there'd always be a lot of boys . . . we'd laugh and joke . . . I'd like to go back to it for a few days or a week. But after that I know I'd be bored to death. I think more seriously about life now. I want to be a journalist . . . or something. I love to write. What do you want to do?

**PETER.** I thought I might go off some place . . . work on a farm or something . . . some job that doesn't take much brains.

**ANNE.** You shouldn't talk that way. You've got the most awful inferiority complex.

**PETER.** I know I'm not smart.

**ANNE.** That isn't true. You're much better than I am in dozens of things . . . arithmetic and algebra and . . . well, you're a million times better than I am in algebra. [*With sudden directness*] You like Margot, don't you? Right from the start you liked her, liked her much better than me.

**PETER.** [*Uncomfortably*] Oh, I don't know.

[*In the main room* MRS. VAN DAAN *comes from*

*the bathroom and goes over to the sink, polishing a coffee pot.*]

**ANNE.** It's all right. Everyone feels that way. Margot's so good. She's sweet and bright and beautiful and I'm not.

**PETER.** I wouldn't say that.

**ANNE.** Oh, no, I'm not. I know that. I know quite well that I'm not a beauty. I never have been and never shall be.

**PETER.** I don't agree at all. I think you're pretty.

**ANNE.** That's not true!

**PETER.** And another thing. You've changed . . . from at first, I mean.

**ANNE.** I have?

**PETER.** I used to think you were awful noisy.

**ANNE.** And what do you think now, Peter? How have I changed?

**PETER.** Well . . . er . . . you're . . . quieter.

[*In his room* DUSSEL *takes his pajamas and toilet articles and goes into the bathroom to change.*]

**ANNE.** I'm glad you don't just hate me.

**PETER.** I never said that.

**ANNE.** I bet when you get out of here you'll never think of me again.

**PETER.** That's crazy.

**ANNE.** When you get back with all of your friends, you're going to say . . . now what did I ever see in that Mrs. Quack Quack.

**PETER.** I haven't got any friends.

**ANNE.** Oh, Peter, of course you have. Everyone has friends.

**PETER.** Not me. I don't want any. I get along all right without them.

**ANNE.** Does that mean you can get along without me? I think of myself as your friend.

**PETER.** No. If they were all like you, it'd be different.

[*He takes the glasses and the bottle and puts them away. There is a second's silence and then* ANNE *speaks, hesitantly, shyly.*]

**ANNE.** Peter, did you ever kiss a girl?

**PETER.** Yes. Once.

**ANNE.** [*To cover her feelings*] That picture's crooked.

[PETER *goes over, straightening the photograph.*]

Was she pretty?

**PETER.** Huh?

**ANNE.** The girl that you kissed.

**PETER.** I don't know. I was blindfolded. [*He comes back and sits down again.*] It was at a party. One of those kissing games.

**ANNE.** [*Relieved*] Oh. I don't suppose that really counts, does it?

**PETER.** It didn't with me.

**ANNE.** I've been kissed twice. Once a man I'd never seen before kissed me on the cheek when he picked me up off the ice and I was crying. And the other was Mr. Koophuis, a friend of Father's who kissed my hand. You wouldn't say those counted, would you?

**PETER.** I wouldn't say so.

**ANNE.** I know almost for certain that Margot would never kiss anyone unless she was engaged to them. And I'm sure too that Mother never touched a man before Pim. But I don't know . . . things are so different now . . . What do you think? Do you think a girl shouldn't kiss anyone except if she's

36 **Discussion** Do you think Anne is being realistic about her looks or is she looking for Peter to disagree?

37 **Critical Thinking and Reading** How much do you think Anne has changed? How much do you think Peter has changed?

38 **Discussion** How does Anne's fear and uncertainty affect her relationship with Peter? How would you feel in the same circumstance?

**39 Discussion** Why do you think the playwrights have the nine o'clock bell ringing at precisely this moment?

**40 Reading Strategy** Why isn't Anne leaving?

**41 Discussion** Why does Anne suddenly kiss Mrs. Van Daan? Why does this kiss confirm Mrs. Van Daan's suspicions?

**42 Discussion** How well do you have to know someone to be able to finish a story for them? Ask students to suggest other statements that describe how familiar the group members have become with one another.

*Peter Van Daan*

engaged or something? It's so hard to try to think what to do, when here we are with the whole world falling around our ears and you think . . . well . . . you don't know what's going to happen tomorrow and . . . What do you think?

**PETER.** I suppose it'd depend on the girl. Some girls, anything they do's wrong. But others . . . well . . . it wouldn't necessarily be wrong with them.

**39** [*The carillon starts to strike nine o'clock.*]

I've always thought that when two people . . .

**ANNE.** Nine o'clock. I have to go.

**PETER.** That's right.

**40** **ANNE.** [*Without moving*] Good night.

[*There is a second's pause, then* PETER *gets up and moves toward the door.*]

**PETER.** You won't let them stop you coming?

**ANNE.** No. [*She rises and starts for the door.*] Sometimes I might bring my diary. There are so many things in it that I want to talk over with you. There's a lot about you.

**PETER.** What kind of thing?

**ANNE.** I wouldn't want you to see some of it. I thought you were a nothing, just the way you thought about me.

**PETER.** Did you change your mind, the way I changed my mind about you?

**ANNE.** Well . . . You'll see . . .

[*For a second* ANNE *stands looking up at* PETER, *longing for him to kiss her. As he makes no move she turns away. Then suddenly* PETER *grabs her awkwardly in his arms, kissing her on the cheek.* ANNE *walks out dazed. She stands for a minute, her back to the people in the main room. As she regains her poise she goes to her mother and father and* MARGOT, *silently kissing them. They murmur their good nights to her. As she is about to open her bedroom door, she catches sight of* MRS. VAN DAAN. *She goes quickly to her, taking her face in her hands and kissing her first on one cheek and then on the other. Then she hurries off into her room.* MRS. VAN DAAN *looks after her, and then looks over at* PETER'S *room. Her suspicions are confirmed.*] **41**

**MRS. VAN DAAN.** [*She knows.*] Ah hah!

[*The lights dim out. The curtain falls on the scene. In the darkness* ANNE'S VOICE *comes faintly at first and then with growing strength.*]

**ANNE'S VOICE.** By this time we all know each other so well that if anyone starts to tell a story, the rest can finish it for him. We're **42**

having to cut down still further on our meals. What makes it worse, the rats have been at work again. They've carried off some of our precious food. Even Mr. Dussel wishes now that Mouschi was here. Thursday, the twentieth of April, nineteen forty-four. Invasion fever is mounting every day. Miep tells us that people outside talk of nothing else. For myself, life has become much more pleasant. I often go to Peter's room after supper. Oh, don't think I'm in love, because I'm not. But it does make life more bearable to have someone with whom you can exchange views. No more tonight. P.S.... I must be honest. I must confess that I actually live for the next meeting. Is there anything lovelier than to sit under the skylight and feel the sun on your cheeks and have a darling boy in your arms? I admit now that I'm glad the Van Daans had a son and not a daughter. I've outgrown another dress. That's the third. I'm having to wear Margot's clothes after all. I'm working hard on my French and am now reading *La Belle Nivernaise*.[6]

[*As she is saying the last lines—the curtain rises on the scene. The lights dim on, as* ANNE'S VOICE *fades out.*]

### Scene 3

[*It is night, a few weeks later. Everyone is in bed. There is complete quiet. In the* VAN DAAN'S *room a match flares up for a moment and then is quickly put out.* MR. VAN DAAN, *in bare feet, dressed in underwear and trousers, is dimly seen coming stealthily down the stairs and into the main room, where* MR. *and* MRS. FRANK *and* MARGOT *are sleeping. He goes to the food safe and again*

---

6. *La Belle Nivernaise:* A story by Alphonse Daudet, a French author.

lights a match. Then he cautiously opens the safe, taking out a half-loaf of bread. As he closes the safe, it creaks. He stands rigid.* MRS. FRANK *sits up in bed. She sees him.*]

MRS. FRANK. [*Screaming*] Otto! Otto! *Komme schnell!*[7]

[*The rest of the people wake, hurriedly getting up.*]

MR. FRANK. *Was ist los? Was ist passiert?*[8]

[DUSSEL, *followed by* ANNE, *comes from his room.*]

MRS. FRANK. [*As she rushes over to* MR. VAN DAAN] *Er stiehlt das Essen!*[9]

DUSSEL. [*Grabbing* MR. VAN DAAN] You! You! Give me that.

MRS. VAN DAAN. [*Coming down the stairs*] Putti . . . Putti . . . what is it?

DUSSEL. [*His hands on* VAN DAAN'S *neck*] You dirty thief . . . stealing food . . . you good-for-nothing . . .

MR. FRANK. Mr. Dussel! For God's sake! Help me, Peter!

[PETER *comes over, trying, with* MR. FRANK, *to separate the two struggling men.*]

PETER. Let him go! Let go!

[DUSSEL *drops* MR. VAN DAAN, *pushing him away. He shows them the end of a loaf of bread that he has taken from* VAN DAAN.]

DUSSEL. You greedy, selfish . . . !

[MARGOT *turns on the lights.*]

MRS. VAN DAAN. Putti . . . what is it?

---

7. *Komme schnell* (käm′ ə sʰnel): German for "Come quick!"
8. *Was ist los? Was ist passiert?* (väs ist los väs ist päs′ ērt): German for "What's the matter? What happened?"
9. *Er stiehlt das Essen!* (er stēlt däs es′ ən): German for "He steals food!"

*The Diary of Anne Frank* 359

43 **Discussion** How does Anne really feel about Peter? Is she seriously in love with him? How does her relationship with Peter affect her daily life?

44 **Reading Strategy** Predict what Mr. Van Daan is doing.

45 **Reading Strategy** Was your prediction correct? What clues did you use to help you predict?

46 **Discussion** How has Mrs. Frank's attitude changed? Why is she angry at Mr. Van Daan? Make sure students realize her rage toward him is not just for stealing the bread, but for stealing what should have gone to the children.

47 **Discussion** Mrs. Van Daan was accused of giving Mr. Van Daan more than his fair share of food earlier in Act II. Judging from what she says here, do you think Mr. Dussel was correct in his accusation? How does Mrs. Frank's view of marriage differ from that of Mrs. Van Daan?

48 **Discussion** How would you define Mr. Frank's role in this argument? Is this role typical of him?

[*All of* MRS. FRANK's *gentleness, her self-control, is gone. She is outraged, in a frenzy of indignation.*]

**MRS. FRANK.** The bread! He was stealing the bread!

**DUSSEL.** It was you, and all the time we thought it was the rats!

**MR. FRANK.** Mr. Van Daan, how could you!

**MR. VAN DAAN.** I'm hungry.

46 **MRS. FRANK.** We're all of us hungry! I see the children getting thinner and thinner. Your own son Peter . . . I've heard him moan in his sleep, he's so hungry. And you come in the night and steal food that should go to them . . . to the children!

47 **MRS. VAN DAAN.** [*Going to* MR. VAN DAAN *protectively*] He needs more food than the rest of us. He's used to more. He's a big man.

[MR. VAN DAAN *breaks away, going over and sitting on the couch.*]

**MRS. FRANK.** [*Turning on* MRS. VAN DAAN] And you . . . you're worse than he is! You're a mother, and yet you sacrifice your child to this man . . . this . . . this . . .

**MR. FRANK.** Edith! Edith!

[MARGOT *picks up the pink woolen stole, putting it over her mother's shoulders.*]

**MRS. FRANK.** [*Paying no attention, going on to* MRS. VAN DAAN] Don't think I haven't seen you! Always saving the choicest bits for him! I've watched you day after day and I've held my tongue. But not any longer! Not after this! Now I want him to go! I want him to get out of here!

**MR. FRANK.** Edith!

**MR. VAN DAAN.** Get out of here?

**MRS. VAN DAAN.** What do you mean?

} *Together*

**MRS. FRANK.** Just that! Take your things and get out!

**MR. FRANK.** [*To* MRS. FRANK] You're speaking in anger. You cannot mean what you are saying.

**MRS. FRANK.** I mean exactly that!

[MRS. VAN DAAN *takes a cover from the* FRANKS' *bed, pulling it about her.*]

**MR. FRANK.** For two long years we have lived here, side by side. We have respected each other's rights . . . we have managed to live in peace. Are we now going to throw it all away? I know this will never happen again, will it, Mr. Van Daan?

**MR. VAN DAAN.** No. No.

**MRS. FRANK.** He steals once! He'll steal again!

[MR. VAN DAAN, *holding his stomach, starts for the bathroom.* ANNE *puts her arms around him, helping him up the step.*]

**MR. FRANK.** Edith, please. Let us be calm. We'll all go to our rooms . . . and afterwards we'll sit down quietly and talk this out . . . we'll find some way . . . 48

**MRS. FRANK.** No! No! No more talk! I want them to leave!

**MRS. VAN DAAN.** You'd put us out, on the streets?

**MRS. FRANK.** There are other hiding places.

**MRS. VAN DAAN.** A cellar . . . a closet. I know. And we have no money left even to pay for that.

**MRS. FRANK.** I'll give you money. Out of my own pocket I'll give it gladly. [*She gets her purse from a shelf and comes back with it.*]

**MRS. VAN DAAN.** Mr. Frank, you told Putti you'd never forget what he'd done for you

360 Drama

when you came to Amsterdam. You said you could never repay him, that you . . .

**MRS. FRANK.** [*Counting out money*] If my husband had any obligation to you, he's paid it, over and over.

**MR. FRANK.** Edith, I've never seen you like this before. I don't know you.

**MRS. FRANK.** I should have spoken out long ago.

**DUSSEL.** You can't be nice to some people.

**MRS. VAN DAAN.** [*Turning on* DUSSEL] There would have been plenty for all of us, if *you* hadn't come in here!

**49** **MR. FRANK.** We don't need the Nazis to destroy us. We're destroying ourselves.

[*He sits down, with his head in his hands.* MRS. FRANK *goes to* MRS. VAN DAAN.]

**MRS. FRANK.** [*Giving* MRS. VAN DAAN *some money*] Give this to Miep. She'll find you a place.

**ANNE.** Mother, you're not putting *Peter* out. Peter hasn't done anything.

**MRS. FRANK.** He'll stay, of course. When I say I must protect the children, I mean Peter too.

[PETER *rises from the steps where he has been sitting.*]

**50** **PETER.** I'd have to go if Father goes.

[MR. VAN DAAN *comes from the bathroom.* MRS. VAN DAAN *hurries to him and takes him to the couch. Then she gets water from the sink to bathe his face.*]

**MRS. FRANK.** [*While this is going on*] He's no father to you . . . that man! He doesn't know what it is to be a father!

**PETER.** [*Starting for his room*] I wouldn't feel right. I couldn't stay.

**MRS. FRANK.** Very well, then. I'm sorry.

**ANNE.** [*Rushing over to* PETER] No, Peter! No!

[PETER *goes into his room, closing the door after him.* ANNE *turns back to her mother, crying.*]

I don't care about the food. They can have mine! I don't want it! Only don't send them away. It'll be daylight soon. They'll be caught . . .

**MARGOT.** [*Putting her arms comfortingly around* ANNE] Please, Mother!

**MRS. FRANK.** They're not going now. They'll stay here until Miep finds them a place. [*To* MRS. VAN DAAN] But one thing I insist on! He must never come down here again! He must never come to this room where the food is stored! We'll divide what we have . . . an equal share for each!

[DUSSEL *hurries over to get a sack of potatoes from the food safe.* MRS. FRANK *goes on, to* MRS. VAN DAAN]

You can cook it here and take it up to him.

[DUSSEL *brings the sack of potatoes back to the center table.*]

**MARGOT.** Oh, no. No. We haven't sunk so far **51** that we're going to fight over a handful of rotten potatoes.

**DUSSEL.** [*Dividing the potatoes into piles*] Mrs. Frank, Mr. Frank, Margot, Anne, Peter, Mrs. Van Daan, Mr. Van Daan, myself . . . Mrs. Frank . . .

[*The buzzer sounds in* MIEP's *signal.*]

**MR. FRANK.** It's Miep! [*He hurries over, getting his overcoat and putting it on.*]

**MARGOT.** At this hour?

**MRS. FRANK.** It is trouble.

*The Diary of Anne Frank* 361

**49** **Discussion** What does Mr. Frank mean by this statement? Can Mrs. Frank's reaction and those of the others be blamed on their long confinement? Why?

**50** **Discussion** What do Peter's words and actions indicate about his character? How does his self-lessness compare with his father's behavior?

**51** **Discussion** Margot's dismayed response is similar to Mr. Frank's. Both are dismayed by the lack of unity in the group. Some students may identify with those feelings. Others may relate to Mrs. Frank's protective feelings, and still others may be disturbed by the injustice of Mr. Van Daan's actions. If time permits, you can hold a mock trial for Mr. Van Daan. An alternative for limited time is to lead a class discussion followed by a secret-ballot vote on whether Mr. Van Daan stays or goes. After the group interaction, allow time for students to respond to this incident in their reader's response journals.

**52** **Clarification** D-Day, under the command of General Dwight Eisenhower, took place on June 6, 1944. During the night about 176,000 soldiers crossed the English Channel. At dawn battleships opened fire on the beaches at Normandy, France. At 6:30 A.M., troops from the United States, Britain, Canada, and France stormed ashore on a sixty-mile (one hundred–kilometer) front in the largest seaborne invasion in history.

**53** **Discussion** Several times in the play there has been a sudden change in the mood and tone. Ask students to offer examples of other times this has happened in the play and to comment on the causes and effects of the change in this scene.

MR. FRANK. [*As he starts down to unbolt the door*] I beg you, don't let her see a thing like this!

MR. DUSSEL. [*Counting without stopping*] . . . Anne, Peter, Mrs. Van Daan, Mr. Van Daan, myself . . .

MARGOT. [*To* DUSSEL] Stop it! Stop it!

DUSSEL. . . . Mr. Frank, Margot, Anne, Peter, Mrs. Van Daan, Mr. Van Daan, myself, Mrs. Frank . . .

MRS. VAN DAAN. You're keeping the big ones for yourself! All the big ones . . . Look at the size of that! . . . And that! . . .

[DUSSEL *continues on with his dividing.* PETER, *with his shirt and trousers on, comes from his room.*]

MARGOT. Stop it! Stop it!

[*We hear* MIEP's *excited voice speaking to* MR. FRANK *below.*]

MIEP. Mr. Frank . . . the most wonderful news! . . . The invasion has begun!

MR. FRANK. Go on, tell them! Tell them!

[MIEP *comes running up the steps ahead of* MR. FRANK. *She has a man's raincoat on over her nightclothes and a bunch of orange-colored flowers in her hand.*]

**52** MIEP. Did you hear that, everybody? Did you hear what I said? The invasion has begun! The invasion!

[*They all stare at* MIEP, *unable to grasp what she is telling them.* PETER *is the first to recover his wits.*]

PETER. Where?

MRS. VAN DAAN. When? When, Miep?

MIEP. It began early this morning . . .

[*As she talks on, the realization of what she has said begins to dawn on them. Everyone goes crazy. A wild demonstration takes place.* MRS. FRANK *hugs* MR. VAN DAAN.]

MRS. FRANK. Oh, Mr. Van Daan, did you hear that?

[DUSSEL *embraces* MRS. VAN DAAN. PETER *grabs a frying pan and parades around the room, beating on it, singing the Dutch National Anthem.* ANNE *and* MARGOT *follow him, singing, weaving in and out among the excited grown-ups.* MARGOT *breaks away to take the flowers from* MIEP *and distribute them to everyone. While this pandemonium is going on* MRS. FRANK *tries to make herself heard above the excitement.*] **53**

MRS. FRANK. [*to* MIEP] How do you know?

MIEP. The radio . . . The B.B.C.![10] They said they landed on the coast of Normandy![11]

PETER. The British?

MIEP. British, Americans, French, Dutch, Poles, Norwegians . . . all of them! More than four thousand ships! Churchill spoke, and General Eisenhower! D-Day they call it!

MR. FRANK. Thank God, it's come!

MRS. VAN DAAN. At last!

MIEP. [*Starting out*] I'm going to tell Mr. Kraler. This'll be better than any blood transfusion.

MR. FRANK. [*Stopping her*] What part of Normandy did they land, did they say?

MIEP. Normandy . . . that's all I know now . . . I'll be up the minute I hear some more! [*She goes hurriedly out.*]

MR. FRANK. [*To* MRS. FRANK] What did I tell you? What did I tell you?

---

**10. B.B.C.:** British Broadcasting Corporation.
**11. Normandy** (nôr′ mən dē): A region in Northwest France, on the English channel.

*Postage stamp of Anne Frank issued in 1979*

**54 Discussion** Note how Mrs. Frank is forgiving Mr. Van Daan for stealing the bread. What made her change her attitude?

**Challenge** Have students look at the photograph of Anne on the postage stamp. Ask them to interpret her facial expression. How does it compare with the images of Anne they have been forming throughout their reading of the play? Your students may want to explore their perceptions of Anne using symbols. Ask them to try to design a stamp that does not show a literal representation of Anne's face, but rather symbols and images that convey the essence of her spirit. These might be displayed with the poems the students wrote at the end of Act I.

[MRS. FRANK *indicates that he has forgotten to bolt the door after* MIEP. *He hurries down the steps.* MR. VAN DAAN, *sitting on the couch, suddenly breaks into a convulsive*[12] *sob. Everybody looks at him, bewildered.*]

**MRS. VAN DAAN.** [*Hurrying to him*] Putti! Putti! What is it? What happened?

**MR. VAN DAAN.** Please, I'm so ashamed.

[MR. FRANK *comes back up the steps.*]

**DUSSEL.** Oh, for God's sake!

**MRS. VAN DAAN.** Don't, Putti.

---

12. **convulsive** (kən vul′ siv) *adj.*: Having an involuntary contraction or spasm of the muscles; shuddering.

**MARGOT.** It doesn't matter now!

**MR. FRANK.** [*Going to* MR. VAN DAAN] Didn't you hear what Miep said? The invasion has come! We're going to be liberated! This is a time to celebrate! [*He embraces* MRS. FRANK *and then hurries to the cupboard and gets the cognac and a glass.*]

**MR. VAN DAAN.** To steal bread from children!

**MRS. FRANK.** We've all done things that we're ashamed of.

**ANNE.** Look at me, the way I've treated Mother . . . so mean and horrid to her.

**MRS. FRANK.** No, Anneke, no.

[ANNE *runs to her mother, putting her arms around her.*]

*The Diary of Anne Frank* 363

**55** **Reading Strategy** How well did you predict the significance of Mr. Kraler's meeting with the warehouse man? How do you think the group found out the man doesn't know anything?

**56** **Discussion** Contrast the tone of this diary entry with the one immediately preceding it. Why do you think the playwrights included these two entries together? What can you infer about the group's emotional state from this pairing?

**57** **Discussion** Discuss Anne's desire to live on after her death. Was she able to do this? How does she live on?

**58** **Enrichment** Besides *The Diary of a Young Girl*, there is another book by Anne Frank titled *The Works of Anne Frank*. This is a collection of short stories, essays, and reminiscences that also includes her diary. All of the stories were written during her confinement in the attic. Students might wish to read some of her other works.

**Cooperative Learning** You may wish to pause at the end of scene 3 and allow story-map partners to meet and update their story maps. As they evaluate the progress of the invasion, encourage them to make predictions about the conclusion of the play. Point out that since they know the outcome of the war, the dramatic tension arises from the question of whether the group can remain successfully hidden until the Allied forces achieve victory.

**59** **Reading Strategy** What do you think is the cause of the tension in the room? What details help to create the sense of tension?

ANNE. Oh, Mother, I was. I was awful.

MR. VAN DAAN. Not like me. No one is as bad as me!

DUSSEL. [*To* MR. VAN DAAN] Stop it now! Let's be happy!

MR. FRANK. [*Giving* MR. VAN DAAN *a glass of cognac*] Here! Here! *Schnapps! L'chaim!*[13]

[VAN DAAN *takes the cognac. They all watch him. He gives them a feeble smile.* ANNE *puts up her fingers in a V-for-Victory sign. As* VAN DAAN *gives an answering V-sign, they are startled to hear a loud sob from behind them. It is* MRS. FRANK, *stricken with remorse. She is sitting on the other side of the room.*]

MRS. FRANK. [*Through her sobs*] When I think of the terrible things I said . . .

[MR. FRANK, ANNE *and* MARGOT *hurry to her, trying to comfort her.* MR. VAN DAAN *brings her his glass of cognac.*]

MR. VAN DAAN. No! No! You were right!

MRS. FRANK. That I should speak that way to you! . . . Our friends! . . . Our guests! [*She starts to cry again.*]

DUSSEL. Stop it, you're spoiling the whole invasion!

[*As they are comforting her, the lights dim out. The curtain falls.*]

ANNE'S VOICE. [*Faintly at first and then with growing strength*] We're all in much better spirits these days. There's still excellent news of the invasion. The best part about it is that I have a feeling that friends are coming. Who knows? Maybe I'll be back in school by fall. Ha, ha! The joke is on us! The warehouse man doesn't know a thing and we are paying him all that money! . . . Wednesday, the second of July, nineteen forty-four. The invasion seems temporarily to be bogged down. Mr. Kraler has to have an operation, which looks bad. The Gestapo have found the radio that was stolen. Mr. Dussel says they'll trace it back and back to the thief, and then, it's just a matter of time till they get to us. Everyone is low. Even poor Pim can't raise their spirits. I have often been downcast myself . . . but never in despair. I can shake off everything if I write. But . . . and that is the great question . . . will I ever be able to write well? I want to so much. I want to go on living even after my death. Another birthday has gone by, so now I am fifteen. Already I know what I want. I have a goal, an opinion.

[*As this is being said—the curtain rises on the scene, the lights dim on, and* ANNE'S VOICE *fades out.*]

---

13. *Schnapps! L'chaim!* (shnăps′ lə khä′ yim): German for "a drink" and a Hebrew toast meaning "To life."

## Scene 4

[*It is an afternoon a few weeks later . . . Everyone but Margot is in the main room. There is a sense of great tension.*

*Both* MRS. FRANK *and* MR. VAN DAAN *are nervously pacing back and forth,* DUSSEL *is standing at the window, looking down fixedly at the street below.* PETER *is at the center table, trying to do his lessons.* ANNE *sits opposite him, writing in her diary.* MRS. VAN DAAN *is seated on the couch, her eyes on* MR. FRANK *as he sits reading.*

*The sound of a telephone ringing comes from the office below. They all are rigid, listening tensely.* MR. DUSSEL *rushes down to* MR. FRANK.]

**DUSSEL.** There it goes again, the telephone! Mr. Frank, do you hear?

**MR. FRANK.** [*Quietly*] Yes. I hear.

**DUSSEL.** [*Pleading, insistent*] But this is the third time, Mr. Frank! The third time in quick succession! It's a signal! I tell you it's Miep, trying to get us! For some reason she can't come to us and she's trying to warn us of something!

**MR. FRANK.** Please. Please.

**MR. VAN DAAN.** [*To* DUSSEL] You're wasting your breath.

**DUSSEL.** Something has happened, Mr. Frank. For three days now Miep hasn't been to see us! And today not a man has come to work. There hasn't been a sound in the building!

**MRS. FRANK.** Perhaps it's Sunday. We may have lost track of the days.

**MR. VAN DAAN.** [*To* ANNE] You with the diary there. What day is it?

**DUSSEL.** [*Going to* MRS. FRANK] I don't lose track of the days! I know exactly what day it is! It's Friday, the fourth of August. Friday, and not a man at work. [*He rushes back to* MR. FRANK, *pleading with him, almost in tears.*] I tell you Mr. Kraler's dead. That's the only explanation. He's dead and they've closed down the building, and Miep's trying to tell us!

**MR. FRANK.** She'd never telephone us.

**DUSSEL.** [*Frantic*] Mr. Frank, answer that! I beg you, answer it!

**MR. FRANK.** No.

**MR. VAN DAAN.** Just pick it up and listen. You don't have to speak. Just listen and see if it's Miep.

**DUSSEL.** [*Speaking at the same time*] For God's sake . . . I ask you.

**MR. FRANK.** No. I've told you, no. I'll do nothing that might let anyone know we're in the building.

**PETER.** Mr. Frank's right.

**MR. VAN DAAN.** There's no need to tell us what side you're on.

**MR. FRANK.** If we wait patiently, quietly, I believe that help will come.

[*There is silence for a minute as they all listen to the telephone ringing.*]

**DUSSEL.** I'm going down.

[*He rushes down the steps.* MR. FRANK *tries ineffectually to hold him.* DUSSEL *runs to the tower door, unbolting it. The telephone stops ringing.* DUSSEL *bolts the door and comes slowly back up the steps.*]

Too late.

[MR. FRANK *goes to* MARGOT *in* ANNE'S *bedroom.*]

**MR. VAN DAAN.** So we just wait here until we die.

**MRS. VAN DAAN.** [*Hysterically*] I can't stand it! I'll kill myself! I'll kill myself!

**MR. VAN DAAN.** For God's sake, stop it!

[*In the distance, a German military band is heard playing a Viennese waltz.*]

**MRS. VAN DAAN.** I think you'd be glad if I did! I think you want me to die!

**MR. VAN DAAN.** Whose fault is it we're here?

[MRS. VAN DAAN *starts for her room. He follows, talking at her.*]

We could've been safe somewhere . . . in America or Switzerland. But no! No! You wouldn't leave when I wanted to. You couldn't leave your things. You couldn't leave your precious furniture.

*The Diary of Anne Frank*  365

**60 Reading Strategy** What do you think has happened? What do you think will happen next?

**61 Discussion** What would you do? Have you ever tried to ignore a ringing telephone? How did it make you feel? What effect do you think the persistent sound has on the tension of this scene?

**62 Discussion** How does Anne's imagination help her survive her confinement?

**63 Discussion** Contrast Anne's attitude toward religion with that of Peter's. Does suffering cause Anne to lose faith in God?

**64 Discussion** Does it seem possible for her to truly believe this? How do you think you would feel under the same circumstances?

**Enrichment** Encourage students to read *The Diary of a Young Girl.* Have them compare it to the play.

**Enrichment** *The Diary of Anne Frank* is a collaboration. With a partner have students write a continuation of Act II, scene 4. In it describe what happens immediately after the "mighty crash" when the Nazis break into the hideout.

**MRS. VAN DAAN.** Don't touch me!

[*She hurries up the stairs, followed by* MR. VAN DAAN. PETER, *unable to bear it, goes to his room.* ANNE *looks after him, deeply concerned.* DUSSEL *returns to his post at the window.* MR. FRANK *comes back into the main room and takes a book, trying to read.* MRS. FRANK *sits near the sink, starting to peel some potatoes.* ANNE *quietly goes to* PETER'S *room, closing the door after her.* PETER *is lying face down on the cot.* ANNE *leans over him, holding him in her arms, trying to bring him out of his despair.*]

**ANNE.** Look, Peter, the sky. [*She looks up through the skylight.*] What a lovely, lovely day! Aren't the clouds beautiful? You know what I do when it seems as if I couldn't stand being cooped up for one more minute? I *think* myself out. I think myself on a walk in the park where I used to go with Pim. Where the jonquils and the crocus and the violets grow down the slopes. You know the most wonderful part about *thinking* yourself out? You can have it any way you like. You can have roses and violets and chrysanthemums all blooming at the same time . . . It's funny . . . I used to take it all for granted . . . and now I've gone crazy about everything to do with nature. Haven't you?

**PETER.** I've just gone crazy. I think if something doesn't happen soon . . . if we don't get out of here . . . I can't stand much more of it!

**ANNE.** [*Softly*] I wish you had a religion, Peter.

**PETER.** No, thanks! Not me!

**ANNE.** Oh, I don't mean you have to be Orthodox[14] . . . or believe in heaven and hell and purgatory[15] and things . . . I just mean some religion . . . it doesn't matter what. Just to believe in something! When I think of all that's out there . . . the trees . . . and flowers . . . and seagulls . . . when I think of the dearness of you, Peter . . . and the goodness of the people we know . . . Mr. Kraler, Miep, Dirk, the vegetable man, all risking their lives for us every day . . . When I think of these good things, I'm not afraid any more . . . I find myself, and God, and I . . .

[PETER *interrupts, getting up and walking away.*]

**PETER.** That's fine! But when I begin to think, I get mad! Look at us, hiding out for two years. Not able to move! Caught here like . . . waiting for them to come and get us . . . and all for what?

**ANNE.** We're not the only people that've had to suffer. There've always been people that've had to . . . sometimes one race . . . sometimes another . . . and yet . . .

**PETER.** That doesn't make me feel any better!

**ANNE.** [*Going to him*] I know it's terrible, trying to have any faith . . . when people are doing such horrible . . . But you know what I sometimes think? I think the world may be going through a phase, the way I was with Mother. It'll pass, maybe not for hundreds of years, but some day . . . I still believe, in spite of everything, that people are really good at heart.

**PETER.** I want to see something now . . . Not a thousand years from now! [*He goes over, sitting down again on the cot.*]

**ANNE.** But, Peter, if you'd only look at it as

---

**14. Orthodox** (ôr′ thə däks′) *adj.*: Strictly observing the rites and traditions of Judaism.

**15. purgatory** (pur′ gə tôr′ ē) *n.*: A state or place of temporary punishment.

## Grammar in Action

Writers make use of a special punctuation mark known as an **ellipsis,** or three dots ( . . . ). The ellipsis indicates the omission of a word or words. It is used by writers for special effects: to show a character's forgetfulness, to show a character's mind jumping from one thought to another without completing the first, to show a voice trailing off, to indicate a pause between thoughts.

Notice the use of the ellipsis in the following passages from *The Diary of Anne Frank:*

ANNE. Oh, I don't mean you have to be Orthodox . . . or believe in heaven and hell and purgatory and things . . . I just mean some religion . . . it doesn't matter what. Just to believe in something! When I think of all that's out there . . . the trees . . . and flowers . . . and seagulls . . . when I think of the dearness of you, Peter . . . and the goodness of the people we know . . . Mr. Kraler, Miep, Dirk, the vegetable man, all risking their lives for us every day . . . When I think of these good things, I'm not afraid any more . . . I find myself, and God, and I . . .

PETER. That's fine! But when I begin to think, I get mad! Look at us, hiding out for two years. Not able to move!

part of a great pattern . . . that we're just a little minute in the life . . . [*She breaks off.*] Listen to us, going at each other like a couple of stupid grownups! Look at the sky now. Isn't it lovely?

[*She holds out her hand to him.* PETER *takes it and rises, standing with her at the window looking out, his arms around her.*]

Some day, when we're outside again, I'm going to . . .

[*She breaks off as she hears the sound of a car, its brakes squealing as it comes to a sudden stop. The people in the other rooms also become aware of the sound. They listen tensely. Another car roars up to a screeching stop.* ANNE *and* PETER *come from* PETER'S *room.* MR. *and* MRS. VAN DAAN *creep down the stairs.* DUSSEL *comes out from his room. Everyone is listening, hardly breathing. A doorbell clangs again and again in the building below.* MR. FRANK *starts quietly down the steps to the door.* DUSSEL *and* PETER *follow him. The others stand rigid, waiting, terrified.*

*In a few seconds* DUSSEL *comes stumbling back up the steps. He shakes off* PETER'S *help and goes to his room.* MR. FRANK *bolts the door below, and comes slowly back up the steps. Their eyes are all on him as he stands there for a minute. They realize that what they feared has happened.* MRS. VAN DAAN *starts to whimper.* MR. VAN DAAN *puts her gently in a chair, and then hurries off up the stairs to their room to collect their things.* PETER *goes to comfort his mother. There is a sound of violent pounding on a door below.*]

65

**MR. FRANK.** [*Quietly*] For the past two years we have lived in fear. Now we can live in hope.

[*The pounding below becomes more insistent. There are muffled sounds of voices, shouting commands.*]

**MEN'S VOICES.** *Auf machen! Da drinnen! Auf machen! Schnell! Schnell! Schnell!*[16] *etc., etc.*

[*The street door below is forced open. We hear the heavy tread of footsteps coming up.* MR. FRANK *gets two school bags from the shelves, and gives one to* ANNE *and the other to* MARGOT. *He goes to get a bag for* MRS. FRANK. *The sound of feet coming up grows louder.* PETER *comes to* ANNE, *kissing her good-bye, then he goes to his room to collect his things. The buzzer of their door starts to ring.* MR. FRANK *brings* MRS. FRANK *a bag. They stand together, waiting. We hear the thud of gun butts on the door, trying to break it down.*

ANNE *stands, holding her school satchel, looking over at her father and mother with a soft, reassuring smile. She is no longer a child, but a woman with courage to meet whatever lies ahead.*

*The lights dim out. The curtain falls on the scene. We hear a mighty crash as the door is shattered. After a second* ANNE'S *voice is heard.*]

**ANNE'S VOICE.** And so it seems our stay here is over. They are waiting for us now. They've allowed us five minutes to get our things. We can each take a bag and whatever it will hold of clothing. Nothing else. So, dear Diary, that means I must leave you behind. Good-bye for a while. P.S. Please, please, Miep, or Mr. Kraler, or anyone else. If you should find this diary, will you please keep it safe for me, because some day I hope . . .

---

16. **Auf machen! . . . Schnell!** (ɔuf mäk ən dä dri nən ɔuf mäk ən shnel shnel shnel): German for "Open up, you in there, open up, quick, quick, quick."

*The Diary of Anne Frank* 367

65 **Discussion** What does Mr. Frank mean by this statement?

**Multicultural Focus** The Holocaust is perhaps history's most infamous record of genocide. Hitler's mass extermination of Jewish people like Anne and her family introduced a new word into the English language. *Genocide* is a term coined after World War II, from the Greek, *genos,* meaning race, and the Latin, *cide,* meaning killing. It is used to describe the deliberate extermination of an entire people.

Even before the term was coined, however, people were persecuted in this way. At the beginning of World War I, large numbers of Armenians were massacred by Turks. Some political activists have charged that the near disappearance of certain Native American nations that resulted from the pressure of European settlers can be viewed as a form of genocide.

In modern times we have international laws and sanctions designed to combat attacks on any particular culture or race of people. Have interested students research these laws and their application to current international problems.

---

Caught here like . . . waiting for them to come and get us . . . and all for what?

ANNE. We're not the only people that've had to suffer. There've always been people that've had to . . . sometimes one race . . . sometimes another . . . and yet . . .

Writers use the ellipsis for a special purpose—to capture the flavor of conversation or thought. However, excessive use of the ellipsis could indicate a lack of understanding of its use, or it could indicate laziness on the part of the writer.

**Student Activity.** Make up an interior monologue (thoughts of a character) in which he or she jumps from one idea to another. Use the ellipsis to indicate incomplete thoughts, shifts from one thought to another, or forgotten ideas. A good topic might be a teenager thinking about what to wear to the next school dance or a student tardy to his or her class for the fifth time thinking about what to say to the teacher.

**Discussion** What does Mr. Frank mean by this statement?

**Enrichment** The movie *Shoah* (meaning *annihilation* in Hebrew) includes interviews with concentration camp survivors. The interviews are also in book form. You might read some of the passages to your students, if the film is unavailable for viewing.

Also, have the class assume that Anne survived. Ask members of the class to take on the role of Anne and perform a monologue in which she discusses her life in the camp and her views on fellow inmates and Nazi officials. Consider whether she will still declare that people are good at heart.

**Reader's Response** What do you find most admirable about Anne?

**Thematic Response** Which injustice that you learned about while reading this play affected you most deeply?

---

[*Her voice stops abruptly. There is silence. After a second the curtain rises.*]

### Scene 5

[*It is again the afternoon in November, 1945. The rooms are as we saw them in the first scene.* MR. KRALER *has joined* MIEP *and* MR. FRANK. *There are coffee cups on the table. We see a great change in* MR. FRANK. *He is calm now. His bitterness is gone. He slowly turns a few pages of the diary. They are blank.*]

**MR. FRANK.** No more. [*He closes the diary and puts it down on the couch beside him.*]

**MIEP.** I'd gone to the country to find food. When I got back the block was surrounded by police . . .

**MR. KRALER.** We made it our business to learn how they knew. It was the thief . . . the thief who told them.

[MIEP *goes up to the gas burner, bringing back a pot of coffee.*]

**MR. FRANK.** [*After a pause*] It seems strange to say this, that anyone could be happy in a concentration camp. But Anne was happy in the camp in Holland where they first took us. After two years of being shut up in these rooms, she could be out . . . out in the sunshine and the fresh air that she loved.

**MIEP.** [*Offering the coffee to* MR. FRANK] A little more?

**MR. FRANK.** [*Holding out his cup to her*] The news of the war was good. The British and Americans were sweeping through France.

We felt sure that they would get to us in time. In September we were told that we were to be shipped to Poland . . . The men to one camp. The women to another. I was sent to Auschwitz.[17] They went to Belsen.[18] In January we were freed, the few of us who were left. The war wasn't yet over, so it took us a long time to get home. We'd be sent here and there behind the lines where we'd be safe. Each time our train would stop . . . at a siding, or a crossing . . . we'd all get out and go from group to group . . . Where were you? Were you at Belsen? At Buchenwald?[19] At Mauthausen? Is it possible that you knew my wife? Did you ever see my husband? My son? My daughter? That's how I found out about my wife's death . . . of Margot, the Van Daans . . . Dussel. But Anne . . . I still hoped . . . Yesterday I went to Rotterdam. I'd heard of a woman there . . . She'd been in Belsen with Anne . . . I know now.

[*He picks up the diary again, and turns the pages back to find a certain passage. As he finds it we hear* ANNE'S VOICE.]

**ANNE'S VOICE.** In spite of everything, I still believe that people are really good at heart. [MR. FRANK *slowly closes the diary.*]

**MR. FRANK.** She puts me to shame.

[*They are silent.*]

---

17. **Auschwitz** (oush' vits): A Nazi concentration camp in Poland, notorious as an extermination center.
18. **Belsen** (bel' zən): A village in Germany that with the village of Bergen was the site of Bergen-Belsen, a Nazi concentration camp and extermination center.
19. **Buchenwald** (boo' k'n wôld'): A notorious Nazi concentration camp and extermination center in central Germany.

## Closure and Extension

### ANSWERS TO RESPONDING TO THE SELECTION
*Your Response*

1. Some students may be willing to share what they wrote in their reader's response journal.
2. Anne had the same desire for friendship, fun, and independence that many teenagers

have, yet Anne did not enjoy some of the freedoms that today we take for granted—meeting with friends in town, going to school, going to parties, riding a bike. For at least the last three years of her life, Anne could only dream of these things.

*Recalling*

3. The people from whom Miep had gotten the ration books have been arrested, and so the refugees are particularly hungry.

4. Some examples include Mr. Van Daan's attempt to sell his wife's fur coat, Peter's resentment over Dussel's remark about the boy's lost cat, news of the workman's blackmail of Mr. Kraler, Mrs. Van Daan's disapproval of her son's affection for Anne, and Mr. Van Daan's theft of food.
5. Mrs. Frank wants to turn out the Van Daans because she found Mr. Van Daan stealing bread that should have gone to the children. She has always been

shown to be concerned about the health and well-being of the children.
6. The Gestapo traces the stolen radio back to the thief, who reveals the location of the hideout to the Nazis.

*Interpreting*

7. Peter provides her with the security she craves, and now this confidence in his affection for her enables her to be less defensive with the other occupants.

## Your Response

1. Did you feel that Mrs. Frank was justified in telling the Van Daans to leave? Why or why not?
2. In what ways was Anne Frank an ordinary teenager? In what ways was she an extraordinary person? Explain.

## Recalling

3. Why is Miep's cake such a treat? How does it also reveal rising tensions?
4. Give two other indications that tensions in the hideout are rising.
5. Why does Mrs. Frank want to turn out the Van Daans? How has the playwright prepared you for this aspect of her character?
6. What role does the thief play in the events?

## Interpreting

7. How does Anne's friendship with Peter help her live through difficult times?
8. What does Mr. Frank mean when he says the people in hiding are Mr. Kraler's ulcers?
9. How does the families' behavior prove Mr. Frank's statement: "We don't need the Nazis to destroy us. We're destroying ourselves"?
10. How can Anne believe that "In spite of everything . . . people are really good at heart"?
11. Explain the meaning of Mr. Frank's last line: "She puts me to shame."

## Applying

12. How might Anne's speech on page 351, beginning "We're young . . . ," express the attitudes of young people today?
13. How is Anne's diary a portrait of courage?

# ANALYZING LITERATURE

## Understanding Characters and Theme

The **theme** is the insight into life revealed by a work of literature. Sometimes a theme is stated directly. At other times you may have to figure out the theme by analyzing what the characters do and say. In this play the way characters cope with adversity reveals something about life.

1. How does Anne change during the play?
2. What do the changes in the characters reveal about human beings in adversity?
3. What does the play reveal about hope?
4. What does it reveal about courage?

# CRITICAL THINKING AND READING

## Finding Support for Opinions

Opinions should be supported by reasons or evidence. For example, Anne tells Peter that he is wrong when he says she knows just how to talk to the adults. One piece of evidence that supports Anne's opinion is that she made her mother cry.

Anne wrote: "In spite of everything, I still believe that people are really good at heart."

1. Find three pieces of evidence in the play that support Anne's opinion about people.
2. Find three pieces of evidence in your own life that support Anne's opinion about people.

# THINKING AND WRITING

## Writing a Letter to the Editor

Imagine that it is the anniversary of Anne Frank's death. Write a letter to the editor of your local paper in which you explain why you feel it is good that the play based on her diary is read and performed regularly today.

First, make an outline of points you want to include. Explain what the theme of the play is and why it is still an important one to consider.

Write a first draft of your letter. Then read it carefully. Make any needed revisions.

Finally, write a final draft of your letter, being careful to follow the correct form for a business letter. When you finish, reread your letter to make sure the spelling and punctuation are correct.

*The Diary of Anne Frank* 369

---

2. The play suggests that humans need faith, hope, and courage, as well as compassion for others, in order to endure adversity.
3. Humans need hope in order to survive adversity.
4. Humans need courage in times of adversity.

## ANSWERS TO CRITICAL THINKING AND READING

1. Suggested Response: Evidence includes Miep's and Mr. Kraler's willingness to risk their lives for those in hiding; Mr. Frank's willingness to allow Dussel to join the group despite the inconvenience; Mr. Van Daan's realization that he was wrong to steal the bread; Mrs. Frank's admission that she was wrong to threaten the Van Daans with expulsion.
2. Answers will differ.

## THINKING AND WRITING

**Publishing Student Writing** Send some of the better-written letters to your school newspaper.

**Alternative Assessment** You may vary the Thinking and Writing assignment by asking your students to develop their responses to the Critical Thinking and Reading exercise. Have them write one full paragraph that explores their responses to Anne's opinions about people and another full paragraph that gives the evidence from their own lives that supports Anne's opinions. What hopeful statement can students make about people in general as a result of examining Anne's views and evidence from their own lives?

**Writing Across the Curriculum** Students might do a research report on D-Day. Have them prepare outlines and discuss them with you. Then have them write their reports. History teachers might provide guidance for students on conducting their research.

---

8. Ulcers can be caused by stress and aggravation. Mr. Frank feels that Mr. Kraler's ulcers were caused by constantly worrying about their safety.
9. Mr. Frank refers to the fact that living in confinement, compounded by the strain and tension of war, causes problems among people that might otherwise never occur.
10. Anne's successful struggle to achieve courage, hope, and compassion allows her to believe that people are really good at heart.
11. The implication is that Mr. Frank has lost his faith. Reading his daughter's entries restores his own faith in humanity.

## Applying

12. Suggested Response: Like Anne in this speech, some young people think they can ignore the world's evils and on the strength of their hopes and ideals make the world a better place.

13. Anne's diary is an enduring testimonial to the power of courage and hope to prevail over despair.

## ANSWERS TO ANALYZING LITERATURE

1. At first Anne is boisterous, mercurial, and self-assertive in ways that annoy others. By the play's end, Anne has learned to control her outbursts. She has established goals for herself, has found faith and courage, and displays a tolerance and concern for others.

## Preparation

**Motivation/Prior Knowledge**
Capture your students' interest in character analysis with a guessing game. Divide the class into two teams. Team A assigns a character to the leader of Team B. The leader, using one-word character trait clues, then tries to convey the identity of the character to his or her teammates. Points are awarded to the team that identifies the character using the least number of clues.

Have students assess which words are the most helpful in identifying a character. Students should discover that specific adjectives, like *generous,* are more enlightening than general ones, like *good.*

**Focus** Explain to students that an actor is familiar with the action of the play. The purpose of the character analysis is not to restate the plot, but to interpret what a character's actions indicate about his or her personality. Point out to students that they need to make inferences about a character's intentions and motives when evaluating his or her behavior.

## Presentation

**Prewriting** Guide students to use specific language in identifying character traits. You may wish to have students make lists of synonyms for the three traits that they choose as their focus. Students can choose the best word from each list to use in their thesis statements. The lists will also help students avoid repetition as they develop their character analyses.

**Drafting** During drafting some students may find themselves limited by thesis statements that are too narrow. Assist these students in adjusting their thesis statements to reflect three distinct characteristics. Instruct students to consider each character

---

370    Drama

> *"The discipline of the writer is to learn to be still and listen to what his subject has to tell him."*
> **Rachel Carson**

# YOUR WRITING PROCESS

## WRITING A CHARACTER ANALYSIS

As you read a play, the characters in it may become as familiar to you as old friends. By analyzing a specific character, you can get to know him or her even better. Then you can use your expertise to advise an actor how to play this role.

### Focus

**Assignment:** Write an analysis of a character in one of the plays you have read.
**Purpose:** To assist an actor who will play the part.
**Audience:** The actor.

### Prewriting

**1. What makes a character interesting?** Look back at the plays in the unit and choose a character you would like to analyze. What interests you about the character you chose?

**2. Gather more ideas.** To gather more ideas for your character analysis, create a cluster diagram. First, write the character's name in the middle of a sheet of paper and circle it. Then think of as many words as possible that describe that character's personality.

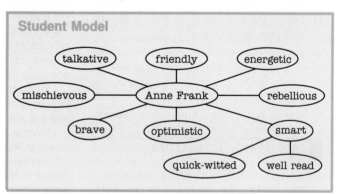

**Student Model**

**3. Find supporting details.** Choose three character traits from your cluster diagram that you would like to focus on. Write down these three traits across the top of another

---

trait as a controlling idea for a separate paragraph.

**Writing Transparency** You may wish to use the paragraph exercise *Transitions* in **Transparencies for Writing** to show your students how to maintain unity while changing from one character trait to the next.

**Revising and Editing** Encourage students to add modifying phrases and transitional expressions to clarify relationships between actions and character traits. Peer editors can help identify places where the connections are unclear.

**Software** Students can use the *Five Paragraph Theme* activity in **Writer's Helper** to improve the structure of their analyses.

sheet of paper. Under each, cite an example from the play that illustrates this trait.

**4. Write a thesis statement.** After you have listed your examples, summarize the character's traits in one sentence.

## Drafting

**1. Introduce the topic.** Begin with an introductory paragraph that clearly states what you are going to write about. This paragraph will include your thesis statement.

**2. Develop the topic.** In the next few paragraphs, develop your analysis. Support your statements with examples, using your chart as a guide. Finally, draw conclusions from your analysis about how certain scenes should be played.

## Revising and Editing

**1. Ask yourself questions.** Is your thesis statement clear and concise? Do your supporting paragraphs help to reveal the character's personality traits? Do you use examples from the play to illustrate these traits? Do you use your analysis to suggest how the character should behave in a few key scenes? Do you have a good conclusion?

**2. Have a classmate read your draft.** By letting a classmate read your draft, you will learn whether or not you have adequately analyzed your character. Have your classmate answer the same questions you asked yourself.

**3. Proofread your work.** Remember that the actor is counting on you for accurate information.

### Grammar Tip

When writing a character analysis, use the present, rather than the past, tense. The present tense suggests that the person is active and alive.

### Options for Publishing

• Share your character analysis with classmates. Ask for a volunteer to act out one of the key scenes involving the character you have chosen, using your character analysis to develop the role.

• Create an anthology of the character analyses completed by the class.

### Reviewing Your Writing Process

1. Did the diagram help you to generate ideas about your character? Explain.

2. What did this assignment help you to discover about the character you chose?

5. Does the writer explore how the character traits might affect the way some scenes might be played?

6. Does the concluding paragraph summarize the main points of the analysis?

7. Is the present tense used consistently throughout the analysis?

8. Does the writer use correct spelling, punctuation, and grammar?

**Alternative Assessment** *Collaborative Evaluation:* In groups of four, ask your students to evaluate one another's work by responding to the following questions:

What character from which play does the writer analyze?

Does the writer identify the personal qualities that make the character interesting?

Does the writer provide examples from the play that illustrate these traits?

Does the writer conclude with a general impression of the character?

Does the writer tell an actor the most important thing to keep in mind about the character?

Is the analysis free from errors in spelling and language usage?

What do you think is an appropriate grade for this analysis?

After the papers have been evaluated, you may ask each group to select a paper to share with the class.

**Student Portfolios** You might want students to include their analyses in their writing portfolios.

**Grammar Tip** Remind students to use the present tense consistently. Refer them to the Handbook of Grammar and Revising Strategies for information about and examples of consistent tense usage.

## Closure and Extension

**Guidelines for Evaluation** You may use the following questions to evaluate each student's analysis:

1. Is the thesis statement clearly expressed in the introductory paragraph?

2. Does the thesis statement include at least three key character traits?

3. Are examples of the character's actions used to illustrate the character traits?

4. Does the writer correctly organize the analysis into paragraphs?

**Enrichment** Actors frequently invent a history for their characters to help them understand the characters' attitudes and actions. Have students who analyzed the same character work in groups to create a past for the character. The past that they create should lay a logical foundation for the character's personality in the play.

## Preparation

**Motivation/Prior Knowledge** Allow time for students to look through magazines to find pictures of settings and locations that appeal to them. Display the pictures and ask student volunteers to describe the elements of each scene. Guide the students in describing the details of the scenes in spatial order.

**Focus** Describing a setting or location for a production challenges the students to communicate their creative visions as concrete realities. Remind students that their audience, the set designer or the location scout, can only meet the requirements as well as they are expressed. Students should focus on expressing every element of the setting, exactly as they envision it.

## Presentation

**Prewriting** Use the student model of a mansion to illustrate the different effects that can be achieved by changing the details described. Are the windows open, with freshly laundered curtains billowing in the breeze, or are the windows shut with the shades drawn? Instruct students to study the script and make notes on the mood or atmosphere that they wish to convey.

**Drafting** Help students move from the general to the specific with a visualization exercise. Ask them to close their eyes and imagine themselves standing at a distance from their scene. What do they see? Lead students further into the scene, pausing at intervals to have them formulate a descriptive sentence. Continue in this manner until students have had an opportunity to think of approximately ten increasingly specific sentences. Remind students to keep this process in mind as they draft their memos.

# YOUR WRITING PROCESS

## WRITING A DESCRIPTIVE MEMO

Weeks or months before a play is first performed or a film begins production, a set designer or location scout is hard at work finding or creating a setting for the action. If you were the director of a film or a play, what type of location or setting would you want for your production? What directions would you provide to make sure that the setting is suitable?

---

**Focus**

**Assignment:** Write a descriptive memo to the set designer or the location scout.
**Purpose:** To describe a setting for a play or film.
**Audience:** The set designer or the location scout.

---

### Prewriting

**1. What makes the setting important?** With a partner, look back at the two plays in this unit, paying close attention to the descriptions of the sets in the stage directions. Discuss how you envision the settings of the two plays.

**2. Gather ideas for your film or play.** Choose one of the plays from the unit, or think of an original idea for a film. Then explore possible settings. Select an environment that is appropriate for the action of the play or film.

**3. Focus on the details.** Develop a picture of the setting in your mind. If you have chosen a play from this unit, use the stage directions as a source for details. Create a list with general details at the top of the page and specific ones at the bottom.

---

**Student Model**

<u>Original Film Setting</u>
Time: Late 1800's, during the fall
Location: The southern United States
A white mansion with many rooms
   The dining room has an antique table, surrounded by chairs.
   There are two candles and a crystal bowl in the center of the table.

---

**Writing Transparency** You might want to use the paragraph exercise *Spatial Order* in **Transparencies for Writing** to show your students how to organize their descriptions.

**Grammar Tip** Call students' attention to the example on this page, pointing out how the specific language communicates more effectively than the nonspecific.

**Software** If your students have access to computers, you might have them draft on the **Bank Street Writer.** They can use the program's on-line thesaurus to find replacements for nonspecific words.

**4. Create a drawing of the setting.** Sketch out a drawing or a diagram of the setting. Label it with details from your list.

## Drafting

**1. Start with important general information.** Before offering specific details, you must make sure that the set designer or location scout has a clear general picture of the setting you envision. Indicate the time period in which your play or movie takes place. Then state the general characteristics of the location.

**2. Be clear and specific.** Create a vivid description that will enable the set designer or location scout to picture clearly what you have in mind. Arrange your details in spatial order so that the set designer or location scout can see how they fit together. If you are describing the set for a play from this unit, draw from the stage directions, but also make up suitable details.

---

**Student Model**

Set for "The Diary of Anne Frank"
The top floor of the house should have three rooms. The largest room is in the center. It is sparsely furnished: There are three straight-backed chairs, a small folding cot, and two wooden tables. One table is piled high with books. The other has a small vase with wilted flowers. The two small windows are covered with heavy, dark material.

---

## Revising and Editing

**1. Work with an editor.** Exchange memos with a classmate. Make editorial comments on each other's memos based on the following questions:
- Are the time period and general location of the setting made clear?
- Does the memo offer a detailed picture of the setting?
- Are the details presented in logical order?
- Which words could be more precise?
Use your editor's comments to guide your revision.

**2. Eliminate errors that may cause confusion.** Carefully proofread your memo. Errors in spelling, mechanics, and punctuation will make it more difficult to follow.

*Your Writing Process* 373

6. Is the memo free of errors in spelling, mechanics, and punctuation?

**Alternative Assessment** *Collaborative Evaluation:* In groups of four, ask your students to evaluate one another's work by responding to the following questions:

For what play or original idea has the writer developed a setting?

Does the writer create a vivid and detailed picture for the set designer?

Can you and your evaluation team see the same mental picture, based on the writer's description?

Are the details organized in a logical spatial order?

Is the description free from errors in spelling, mechanics, and punctuation?

What do you think is an appropriate grade for this memo?

After the memos have been evaluated, you may ask your students to write protocols summarizing what they learned about descriptive writing from writing the memos and evaluating one another's work.

**Student Portfolios** You might want to have students keep their memos in their writing portfolios.

**Cross-curricular Enrichment** Make it measure up! Team up with the math teacher to teach students how to use their math skills to render their set design to scale. Photocopy a list of symbols that set designers use to indicate the placement of furniture, doors, windows, and other set elements. Graph paper might aid the students in maintaining the accuracy of their scale. Remind students to label the dimensions of each set element. Advanced students might use their scale rendering to estimate how much lumber, fabric, and paint they will need to purchase.

---

**Revising and Editing** It may be helpful to the writer to have a peer editor render the setting, using the memo as a guide. The sketch can help the writer determine how well his or her vision is communicated to an objective party. Allow time for partners to discuss the drawings and the peer editors' questions listed on the student pages.

## Closure and Extension

**Guidelines for Evaluation** You might keep the following questions in mind as you evaluate each student's descriptive memo:
1. Is the setting that is described appropriate for the action of the play or film?
2. Does the writer indicate the time period in which the play or movie takes place?

3. Does the memo progress logically from generalities to details?
4. Does the writer use precise nouns and vivid adjectives to communicate his or her vision to the set designer or location scout?
5. Does the final draft reflect a constructive use of peer editors' and instructor's revision suggestions?

**MIRACLE OF NATURE**
*Thomas Moran*

# NONFICTION

Do you enjoy reading newspaper articles on sporting events? Do you take pleasure in reviews of performances you have seen? Do you particularly like stories of the lives of real people, both from the past and the present? Many people do. Newspaper articles, reviews, autobiographies, biographies—all are types of nonfiction.

Nonfiction deals with actual people, places, events, and topics based on real life. Autobiographies and biographies deal with the lives of real people, while essays provide a writer with room to express his or her thoughts and feelings on a particular subject. Nonfiction may inform, describe, persuade, or it may simply amuse.

In this unit you will encounter many types of nonfiction. The topics, too, will be varied; for example, a baseball player, a forest fire, shooting stars, and television.

## Humanities Note

Fine art, *Miracle of Nature,* Thomas Moran. Thomas Moran (1837–1926) was a British-born American landscape painter. Moran studied wood engraving as a young man and toured the museums of France and Germany. Upon arrival in the United States, he worked for a time as an illustrator in Philadelphia. Moran was asked to accompany the official geographical expedition to Yellowstone as the recording artist in 1871. He went on this and other expeditions to what were to become America's great national parks. Thomas Moran's visual records of the fantastic natural beauties of the American West were instrumental in the establishment of the National Parks Commission in 1916.

The deep appreciation Thomas Moran had for nature is reflected in his painting *Miracle of Nature.* He recognized the spiritual and uplifting qualities in nature and translated them visually to the viewer. This sensitivity to nature, coupled with Moran's supreme command of color and light, made him the right person to record the natural phenomena of the West for the news-eager American public. Paintings such as this not only made the tales of the sights of the western territories believable, but they were also an invaluable lobbying tool for the men who fought to preserve these beauties as national treasures.

**Alternative Assessment** *Portfolio Assignment:* To enable you and your students to assess their learning, ask them to create a portfolio of their written responses as they read selections in the Nonfiction unit. They may select the best pieces from among their written work on the nonfiction:

Reader's response journals
Learning Options assignments
Thinking and Writing assignments

Your Writing Process assignments
Alternative Composition assignments (in the Teaching Portfolio)
Essay question from the Unit Test (in the Teaching Portfolio)

Have your students then write a protocol for their portfolios in which they explain their reasons for selecting the pieces they chose to include in their portfolios and the learning that is reflected.

**Reading Actively** Based on research into the techniques of meaningful reading, the strategies outlined on this page will help students read nonfiction actively. Through this systematic approach, students interact with the text—questioning, predicting, and making connections with what they read. They also evaluate and respond personally to the text.

The strategies outlined here are similar to those on page 2 for reading short stories. One difference is the author's purpose. For nonfiction students should question the author's purpose, his or her reason for writing, instead of character's motives. The purpose is sometimes stated directly in a thesis statement and is supported through main ideas in the body of the essay.

For further practice with this process, you might have students use the selection in the Teaching Portfolio, "The Seeing See Little," by Helen Keller, pages 428–431, which they can annotate themselves. Also, encourage students to continue to use these strategies when reading the other nonfiction selections.

**Teaching to Ability Levels** If your less advanced students have trouble understanding any of these elements, you might have them review the instruction on the appropriate pages or look up the necessary terms in the Handbook of Literary Terms and Techniques on page 808.

# READING ACTIVELY

## Nonfiction

Nonfiction is a type of literature that gives information about real people, events, and ideas. Nonfiction may instruct you, entertain you, inform you, or satisfy your curiosity.

Reading nonfiction actively means interacting with and responding to the information the author presents. You do this by using the following strategies:

QUESTION  What questions come to mind as you preview the selection? What additional questions arise as you read it? For example, before you read, you may wonder what the title means. As you read, you might wish to know what the author's purpose is or why he or she includes certain information. Look for the answers to your questions as you continue to read.

PREDICT  Predict what the author will say about the topic. How will the author support his or her points? Make new predictions as you go.

CONNECT  Think of what you already know about the topic and make connections to what the author is saying. Take in new facts and ideas as you read and connect these to what you know. Doing so will help you to understand the information presented.

EVALUATE  What do you think of the author's conclusions? What have you learned?

RESPOND  Think about what the author has said. Allow yourself to respond personally. How do you feel about the topic? What will you do with this information?

Try to use these strategies as you read the selections in this unit. They will help you increase your enjoyment and understanding of nonfiction.

On pages 377–379 you can see an example of active reading by Danica Wilson of King School in Detroit, Michigan. The notes in the side column include Danica's thoughts and comments as she read the excerpt from *One Writer's Beginnings*. Your own thoughts as you read may be different because you bring your own experiences to your reading.

376   *Nonfiction*

### Objectives

1  To learn how to read nonfiction actively
2  To understand informal essays
3  To compare and contrast opinions
4  To write about the beginnings of a career
5  To express individual interests and abilities through an optional activity

### Support Material

**Teaching Portfolio**
Teacher Backup, p. 425
Reading Actively, "The Seeing See Little," p. 428
Grammar in Action Worksheet, *Understanding Complex Sentences,* p. 432
Usage and Mechanics Worksheet, p. 434
Critical Thinking and Reading Worksheet, *Comparing and Con-trasting Opinions,* p. 435
Language Worksheet, *Tracing Word Histories,* p. 436
Selection Test, p. 437

**Prentice Hall Literature Writing Studio**

# MODEL

## from One Writer's Beginnings

### Eudora Welty

Learning stamps you with its moments. Childhood's learning is made up of moments. It isn't steady. It's a pulse.

In a children's art class, we sat in a ring on kindergarten chairs and drew three daffodils that had just been picked out of the yard; and while I was drawing, my sharpened yellow pencil and the cup of the yellow daffodil gave off whiffs just alike. That the pencil doing the drawing should give off the same smell as the flower it drew seemed part of the art lesson—as shouldn't it be? Children, like animals, use all their senses to discover the world. Then artists come along and discover it the same way, all over again. Here and there, it's the same world. Or now and then we'll hear from an artist who's never lost it.

In my sensory[1] education I include my physical awareness of the *word*. Of a certain word, that is; the connection it has with what it stands for. At around age six, perhaps, I was standing by myself in our front yard waiting for supper, just at that hour in a late summer day when the sun is already below the horizon and the risen full moon in the visible sky stops being chalky and begins to take on light. There comes the moment, and I saw it then, when the moon goes from flat to round. For the first time it met my eyes as a globe. The word "moon" came into my mouth as though fed to me out of a silver spoon. Held in my mouth the moon became a word. It had the roundness of a Concord grape Grandpa took off his vine and gave me to suck out of its skin and swallow whole, in Ohio.

---

1. **sensory** (sen′ sər ē) *adj.*: Of receiving sense impressions.

**Predict:** *I think this selection is going to be about how the author got started in her writing career.*

**Connect:** *Life has its good times and its bad times. Sometimes you have to learn from bad experiences, which isn't pleasant.*

**Respond:** *As a child Welty noticed and appreciated the smell of sharpened pencils and daffodils. She probably knew then that she was going to be an artist of some kind some day.*

**Connect:** *The author has used her sensory education to remember her thoughts about the moon.*

*from One Writer's Beginnings*   377

## Presentation

**Motivation/Prior Knowledge**
You might lead the class in a discussion of memories. What are some of students' vivid memories? What things that they remember have had an impact on their lives? Are they big events, small events, or both? What are their first memories?

**Master Teacher Note** To give students the opportunity to share their questions and ideas with the rest of the class, consider having them read the selection aloud. Oral reading allows students to discuss the annotations more completely, leading to better understanding and comprehension.

**Making Connections** Other selections that deal with the impact of memories on the narrator's life are "Christmas Day in the Morning" (page 21) and "Fathers and Daughters" (page 421). You might have students consider these selections together and discuss the value of memories later in one's life.

**Thematic Focus** We often think of a person's creativity in terms of output or visible results. However, a creative mind or spirit sometimes manifests itself in a different view of the world. How does Welty's creative spirit show itself?

**Purpose-Setting Question** What influence do the memories described by the author have on her life?

**Multicultural Focus** Welty discusses words and what they stand for. Students may never have thought about the relationship between the words of a language and the things to which these words refer. Discussing pictographs can make these relationships more tangible. Many ancient civilizations used pictographs, including the Chinese, the Sumerians, and the Assyrians. Explain that a pictograph is a picture used to represent a particular object. A pictograph is not considered writing because it represents the object itself, not the word for the object.

Explain how pictographs slowly evolved into actual writing. First they stood for the object itself; then they were simplified so that they would be easier to draw. Finally, the simplified pictographs came to represent other words with the same sounds.

As an exercise, some students might want to design their own "alphabet" of pictographs, symbols used to represent various objects, actions, or feelings, which they can use to create simple messages that must be interpreted by the class.

378   *Nonfiction*

## Grammar in Action

**Complex sentences** signal mature, sophisticated writing. Writing complex sentences is a skill that can be learned through studying grammar, but it is best learned by reading complex sentences of writers and writing them ourselves.

A complex sentence is made up of one independent clause and one or more subordinate clauses. Study the following complex sentence taken from *One Writer's Beginnings:*

378

Though I was always waked for eclipses and indeed carried to the window as an infant in arms and shown Halley's Comet in my sleep, and though I'd been taught at our diningroom table about the solar system and knew the earth revolved around the sun, and our moon around us, I never found out the moon didn't come up in the west until I was a writer and Hershel Brickell, the literary critic, told me after I misplaced it in a story.

This complex sentence begins with two subordinate clauses, both beginning with the subordinating conjunction *though.* The independent clause (I never found out the moon didn't come up in the west) is followed by two more subordinate clauses, beginning with

This love did not prevent me from living for years in foolish error about the moon. The new moon just appearing in the west was the rising moon to me. The new should be rising. And in early childhood the sun and moon, those opposite reigning powers, I just as easily assumed rose in east and west respectively in their opposite sides of the sky, and like partners in a reel[2] they advanced, sun from the east, moon from the west, crossed over (when I wasn't looking) and went down on the other side. My father couldn't have known I believed that when bending behind me and guiding my shoulder, he positioned me at our telescope in the front yard and, with careful adjustment of the focus, brought the moon close to me.

The night sky over my childhood Jackson was velvety black. I could see the full constellations in it and call their names; when I could read, I knew their myths. Though I was always waked for eclipses and indeed carried to the window as an infant in arms and shown Halley's Comet[3] in my sleep, and though I'd been taught at our diningroom table about the solar system and knew the earth revolved around the sun, and our moon around us, I never found out the moon didn't come up in the west until I was a writer and Herschel Brickell, the literary critic, told me after I misplaced it in a story. He said valuable words to me about my new profession: "Always be sure you get your moon in the right part of the sky."

---

**2. reel** (rēl) *n.*: A lively Scottish dance.
**3. Halley's Comet:** A famous comet that reappears every 75 years.

**Question:** *What is the mistake that Welty made? How is she wrong about the position of the moon?*

**Connect:** *Welty carried her misconception about the moon with her even through her advanced education.*

**Evaluate:** *I agree with Brickell's comment. To be a good writer, you have to get your facts straight.*

**Respond:** *Because Welty was a deep thinker even as a child, this passage is full of ideas that you have to think about for a while.*

Eudora Welty (1909–      ) was born and raised in Jackson, Mississippi, and this environment has formed the backdrop for most of her writing. After college she returned to Mississippi, where her first full-time job for the Works Progress Administration took her all over the state, writing articles and taking photographs. Welty's first published short story appeared in 1936, and since then her reputation has grown steadily. In 1973 she was awarded a Pulitzer Prize for her novel *The Optimist's Daughter.*

*from One Writer's Beginnings* 379

the subordinating conjunctions *until* and *after*. The subject and verb in each clause is expanded with a number of prepositional phrases: *for eclipses, to the window, as an infant, in arms, in my sleep, at our diningroom table, about the solar system, around the sun, around us, in the west, in a story.*

**Student Activity.** Write a complex sentence in the pattern of Welty's example. Begin it with two subordinate clauses, each starting with the subordinating conjunction *although,* and end it with subordinate clauses beginning with *until* and *after*. A good way to start might be this: Although I am only an eighth grader at this school and indeed care about my education. . . . Compare your sentence with those of your classmates.

**Reader's Response** What does Welty's remark "Learning stamps you with its moments" mean to you? Describe an outstanding "learning moment" from your life.

**Thematic Response** In what creative ways do you see the world or express yourself?

**More About the Author** Eudora Welty has lived her entire life in the same house in Jackson, Mississippi. She has traveled widely in her lifetime, but her writing remains closely connected to the spirit and texture of the South.

## Closure and Extension

*(Questions begin on p. 380.)*

### ANSWERS TO RESPONDING TO THE SELECTION
*Your Response*

1. Students may agree and support their opinion with images such as the rising sun, indicating a new day, or a growing person, indicating a "new" person.

*Recalling*

2. Welty notices that the sharpened pencil is giving off the same odor as the daffodils she is drawing.
3. Children, animals, and artists are alike because they all discover the world through all of their senses.
4. Welty believed that the moon rose in the west. This seemed logical to her because she thought that the moon followed the sun's pattern, but in the opposite side of the sky.

*Interpreting*

5. Answers will differ. Suggested Response: She thinks that it is appropriate for the two objects to smell alike because, for it to be a part of art, one object used to record another object should have some sort of direct connection.
6. Answers will differ. Suggested Response: The meaning of the advice is that it is important not to have any misconceptions about life to be an effective writer. You cannot write about truth if you are inaccurate about the truth.

(Answers begin on p. 379.)

*Applying*

7. Answers will differ. Students who agree with the statement might support their answers by using the first paragraph from the essay and stating that by maintaining a child-like sense of wonder, an artist can record experiences from a fresh and untainted perspective. Students who disagree might support their answers by stating that artists are better able to record their perceptions accurately from the perspective of someone who has experienced things from many different vantage points.

8. Responses will differ. Encourage students to see this situation as an opportunity to learn.

## ANSWERS TO ANALYZING LITERATURE

1. The topic of the essay is the effect of certain memories of the author's life on her learning. Welty expresses the opinion that while these memories are important and lasting, they must nonetheless be free of misconceptions to be of any value in writing.

2. Suggested Response: The author is keenly aware of her natural surroundings and approaches her art with all of her senses aware. Students could use the first two paragraphs of the essay to support this particular impression.

## ANSWERS TO CRITICAL THINKING AND READING

1. Suggested Response: This statement contrasts sharply with Welty's feelings about words. Welty believes that words are closely linked with what they stand for while Glasow seems to view them with suspicion.

2. Suggested Response: This statement also contrasts with what Welty believes. Butler places no value at all on words while Welty sees them as inextricably linked with what they stand for.

3. Suggested Response: This statement reflects a sentiment about words that is the opposite of Welty's feelings. Hesse feels that words hide the meaning of what they stand for while Welty believes

## RESPONDING TO THE SELECTION

### Your Response

1. Do you agree with the author that "rising" is an appropriate image for "new" things, the new moon, for example? Explain your answer.

### Recalling

2. Explain the similarity Welty notices between the sharpened pencil and the daffodil.

3. According to Welty how are children, animals, and artists alike?

4. What error does Welty make about the moon? Why does this error seem logical to her?

### Interpreting

5. Why does Welty think it appropriate for the flower and the pencil to smell alike?

6. Explain the meaning of Herschel Brickell's advice.

### Applying

7. Do you think it necessary for an artist to see the world with a childlike sense of wonder? Explain your answer.

8. Has incomplete knowledge of a topic ever kept you from writing about it? What is the best thing to do in a situation like this?

## ANALYZING LITERATURE

### Understanding the Informal Essay

An essay is a brief work of nonfiction in which a writer explores a topic and expresses an opinion or a conclusion. It can be thought of as a kind of thinking aloud on paper. In an informal essay, writers use a conversational tone, injecting their personality into their observations.

1. What is the topic of this essay? What opinion does the writer express about this topic?

2. What impression do you form of Eudora Welty on the basis of this essay? Find evidence in the selection to support your answer.

## CRITICAL THINKING AND READING

### Comparing and Contrasting Opinions

An **opinion** is a personal view or a belief that rests on grounds insufficient to prove it true. People can consider the same topic and form different opinions. For example, Welty reached a special awareness of the meaning of words.

Compare and contrast Welty's understanding of words with those of the following writers.

1. Ellen Glasow: "I haven't much opinion of words . . . They're apt to set fire to a dry tongue, that's what I say."

2. Samuel Butler: "Words are like money; there is nothing so useless, unless in actual use."

3. Hermann Hesse: "Words are really a mask. They rarely express the true meaning; in fact they tend to hide it."

4. Aldous Huxley: "Words form the thread on which we string our experiences."

## THINKING AND WRITING

### Writing About Beginnings

Eudora Welty chose to write about a writer's beginnings. Think about another field—art, sports, teaching, medicine, or the like. Select a career. Then list the traits you think are necessary to be successful in that career. Using your list to guide you, write an essay entitled "A _____'s Beginnings." In your essay explain how you think a young person comes to realize these traits.

## LEARNING OPTION

**Language.** Design a poster that illustrates the idea that words have histories. An example that relates to "One Writer's Beginnings" might be a poster based on *luna,* the Latin word for moon. You may wish to include the words *lunar, lunatic,* and *lunate,* for example, and show how each word is derived from *luna.*

---

words are closely connected with what they stand for.

4. Suggested Response: Huxley's statement compares favorably to Welty's feelings about words. He also seems to feel that words are connected closely to experience.

### THINKING AND WRITING

To give students more help with their essays, have them use the Writing an Essay Practice activity in the Writing Process Activities section of the Teaching Portfolio, Volume II.

**Software** If your students are working on computers, have them use **Bank Street Writer** to complete all stages of this assignment.

**Publishing Student Writing** Ask for student volunteers to read their essays aloud. Have students in the audience compare the essays read with their own and record similar traits needed for different careers.

### LEARNING OPTION

Students who learn well visually will enjoy and excel at this activity.

# Biographies and Personal Accounts

**BASHFUL**
*Julie Lynette Johnson, Student,*
*Washougal, Washington*
Courtesy of the Artist

Fine art, *Bashful,* by Julie Johnson. Julie Johnson painted *Bashful* as a thirteen-year-old student at Jemtegaard School in Washougal, Washington. She comes from a family of artists, including a great-grandmother who studied art in Paris.

*Bashful* was inspired by a photograph in *National Geographic* magazine. It is a close-up view reminiscent of the Pop art portraits of Alex Katz. Not only does she skillfully capture the appearance of a shy child peering from behind a raised hand, but she also manages to capture the psychological essence of the human trait of shyness. When describing this painting, Julie Johnson states that she tried to "put a lot of feeling into it." With her expressive brushstrokes, sophisticated color palette, and intuition, she has achieved her goal. This glimpse into a personality provides a biographical insight just as the selections in this section do.

You might use these questions for discussion:
1. What comment do you have on the artist's choice of this close-up view?
2. Do you think this is a true representation of the feeling of shyness? Explain.

**More About the Author** Ann Petry believes that it is impossible to understand the present without a knowledge of the past. Ask students to discuss how knowledge of black history would be helpful to Petry, a black writer.

**Literary Focus** You might point out that biographies are often, but not always, written about people who are known for some achievement. Ask students to name biographies they have read about people who have well-known achievements.

**Prereading Focus** Before students try to imagine the hardships during the slaves' flights to freedom, help them to recall other historic journeys that were marked by hardship and danger. You might suggest the voyages of the explorers who discovered the New World or the colonists' voyages to America. Have students discuss what character traits helped people survive such difficult journeys. Ask what qualities the leaders of these trips might have had.

**Vocabulary** Point out that five of these words are adjectives. You might give students sentences with adjectives omitted and let them insert the appropriate adjectives from this list.

**Electronic Handbook** If your students have access to the Language Master 6000, suggest that they find antonyms for the adjectives *disheveled* and *fastidious*.

**Spelling Tip** Many adjectives like *fastidious* end in *dious*, including *studious*, *melodious*, and *invidious*.

382

# GUIDE FOR READING

## Ann Petry

(1912–    ) worked as a newspaper reporter in New York City after college. Her first book, *The Street,* was set in Harlem, in northern New York City. Her short stories have appeared in magazines. Growing up in Old Saybrook, Connecticut, Petry decided that Harriet Tubman stood for everything indomitable, or not easily discouraged, in the human spirit. The following selection is from *Harriet Tubman: Conductor of the Underground Railroad.*

## Harriet Tubman: Guide to Freedom

### Biography

A **biography** is an account of a person's life as written by another person. A biography tells you about events in the person's life, focusing on his or her achievements and the difficulties that the person had to overcome. The biographer must create a living, believable character and stick to the known facts about the person. Usually an author chooses as a subject of a biography someone who has achieved something significant.

### Focus

The Underground Railroad was an informal system of secret routes and safe houses that helped runaway slaves escape to free states and to Canada during the mid-1800's. The journey to freedom was not an easy one. Try to imagine what the journey was like. Write a journal entry describing the hardships and dangers you think the fugitives would have had to endure. As you read "Harriet Tubman: Guide to Freedom," compare the hardships and dangers Petry describes with the ones you wrote about.

### Vocabulary

Knowing the following words will help you as you read "Harriet Tubman: Guide to Freedom."

**incentive** (in sen' tiv) *n.*: Something that stirs up people or urges them on (p. 385)

**disheveled** (di shev' 'ld) *adj.*: Untidy; messy (p. 385)

**guttural** (gut' ər əl) *adj.*: Made in back of the throat (p. 386)

**mutinous** (myoot' 'n əs) *adj.*: Rebelling against authority (p. 387)

**cajoling** (kə jōl' iŋ) *v.*: Coaxing gently (p. 389)

**indomitable** (in däm' it ə b'l) *adj.*: Not easily discouraged (p. 389)

**fastidious** (fas tid' ē əs) *adj.*: Not easy to please (p. 390)

382    Nonfiction

---

# Harriet Tubman: Guide to Freedom

## Ann Petry

Along the Eastern Shore of Maryland, in Dorchester County, in Caroline County, the masters kept hearing whispers about the man named Moses, who was running off slaves. At first they did not believe in his existence. The stories about him were fantastic, unbelievable. Yet they watched for him. They offered rewards for his capture.

They never saw him. Now and then they heard whispered rumors to the effect that he was in the neighborhood. The woods were searched. The roads were watched. There was never anything to indicate his whereabouts. But a few days afterward, a goodly number of slaves would be gone from the plantation. Neither the master nor the overseer had heard or seen anything unusual in the quarter. Sometimes one or the other would vaguely remember having heard a whippoorwill call somewhere in the woods, close by, late at night. Though it was the wrong season for whippoorwills.

Sometimes the masters thought they had heard the cry of a hoot owl, repeated, and would remember having thought that the intervals between the low moaning cry were wrong, that it had been repeated four times in succession instead of three. There was never anything more than that to suggest that all was not well in the quarter. Yet when morning came, they invariably discovered that a group of the finest slaves had taken to their heels.

Unfortunately, the discovery was almost always made on a Sunday. Thus a whole day was lost before the machinery of pursuit could be set in motion. The posters offering rewards for the fugitives could not be printed until Monday. The men who made a living hunting for runaway slaves were out of reach, off in the woods with their dogs and their guns, in pursuit of four-footed game, or they were in camp meetings[1] saying their prayers with their wives and families beside them.

Harriet Tubman could have told them that there was far more involved in this matter of running off slaves than signaling the would-be runaways by imitating the call of a whippoorwill, or a hoot owl, far more involved than a matter of waiting for a clear night when the North Star was visible.

In December 1851, when she started out with the band of fugitives that she planned to take to Canada, she had been in the vicinity of the plantation for days, planning the trip, carefully selecting the slaves that she would take with her.

She had announced her arrival in the

---

**1. camp meetings** *n.*: Religious meetings held outdoors or in a tent.

*Harriet Tubman: Guide to Freedom*   383

**Thematic Focus** Young people often question issues of fairness and justice. As they mature, they realize that what happens is not always "fair." Have students discuss times when justice has not been served. They may begin with issues in their own lives, but encourage them to think of world events, historic as well as contemporary, that exemplify the complexity of the issue.

**Making Connections** Another selection that deals with humanity helping humanity is *The Diary of Anne Frank* (page 303). You can show the similarity between Tubman leading slaves to freedom and the Dutch hiding the Jews from the Gestapo during World War II.

Two other selections that touch on the topic of slaves escaping from bondage are *The* *House of Dies Drear* (p. 245) and "Runagate Runagate" (page 517).

## Presentation

**Motivation/Prior Knowledge** Have students imagine they are slaves in the old South who have an opportunity to escape. If caught, they would be whipped and sold further south, where they would be treated more harshly. What would they choose? Why?

**Master Teacher Note** Tubman would announce her arrival among the slaves by singing the spiritual "Go down, Moses." Find a recording of this spiritual (Paul Robeson, Vanguard Label, # 79193) and play it for the students.

**Purpose-Setting Question** Tubman is described as "indomitable"—not easily discouraged. What details make Tubman seem indomitable in spirit?

**1 Enrichment** Moses was the Biblical leader who brought the Israelites out of slavery in Egypt and led them to the Promised Land, received the Ten Commandments from God, and gave laws to the people.

**2 Clarification** The slave *quarter* was the section of the plantation where the slaves lived.

**3 Discussion** Have students discuss how these slave hunters were different from bounty hunters—men who pursued for money men on the "wanted list."

**4 Enrichment** Tell students that the North Star—Polaris—is a star almost directly above the northern end of the earth's axis. Tubman waited for the North Star in order to be guided by its bright light.

**HARRIET TUBMAN SERIES, #7**
*Jacob Lawrence*
Hampton University Museum

5 quarter by singing the forbidden spiritual [2]—"Go down, Moses, 'way down to Egypt Land"—singing it softly outside the door of a slave cabin, late at night. The husky voice was beautiful even when it was barely more than a murmur borne on the wind.

Once she had made her presence known, word of her coming spread from cabin to cabin. The slaves whispered to each other, ear to mouth, mouth to ear, "Moses is here." "Moses has come." "Get ready. Moses is back again." The ones who had

---

**2. forbidden spiritual:** In 1831 a slave named Nat Turner encouraged an unsuccessful slave uprising in Virginia, by talking about the Biblical story of the Israelites' escape from Egypt. Afterwards, the singing of certain spirituals was forbidden, for fear of encouraging more uprisings.

384 *Nonfiction*

agreed to go North with her put ashcake and salt herring in an old bandanna, hastily tied it into a bundle, and then waited patiently for the signal that meant it was time to start.

There were eleven in this party, including one of her brothers and his wife. It was the largest group that she had ever conducted, but she was determined that more and more slaves should know what freedom was like.

She had to take them all the way to Canada. The Fugitive Slave Law [3] was no longer a great many incomprehensible words written down on the country's lawbooks. The new law had become a reality. It was Thomas Sims, a boy, picked up on the streets of Boston at night and shipped back to Georgia. It was Jerry and Shadrach, arrested and jailed with no warning.

6 She had never been in Canada. The route beyond Philadelphia was strange to her. But she could not let the runaways who accompanied her know this. As they walked along she told them stories of her own first flight, she kept painting vivid word pictures of what it would be like to be free.

But there were so many of them this time. She knew moments of doubt when she was half-afraid, and kept looking back over her shoulder, imagining that she heard the sound of pursuit. They would certainly be pursued. Eleven of them. Eleven thousand dollars' worth of flesh and bone and muscle that belonged to Maryland planters. If they were caught, the eleven runaways would be whipped and sold South, but she—she would probably be hanged.

7 They tried to sleep during the day but they never could wholly relax into sleep. She

---

**3. Fugitive Slave Law:** This part of the Compromise of 1850 held that escaped slaves, even if found in free states, could be returned to their masters. As a result, fugitives were not safe until they were in Canada.

## Grammar in Action

**Subject-verb agreement** refers to the way subjects and verbs work together in sentences. A verb must agree with its subject in *number.* In terms of grammar, the *number* of a word can be either singular (one) or plural (more than one). Only nouns, pronouns, and verbs have number. Most nouns are made plural by adding *-s* or *-es* to the singular form. The plural of *moment,* for example, is *moments.* Verbs, on the hand, are singular when *-s* or *-es* is added to them.

A singular subject must have a singular verb; similarly, a plural subject must have a plural verb. In the following passage from could tell by the positions they assumed, by their restless movements. And they walked at night. Their progress was slow. It took them three nights of walking to reach the first stop. She had told them about the place where they would stay, promising warmth and good food, holding these things out to them as an incentive to keep going.

When she knocked on the door of a farmhouse, a place where she and her parties of runaways had always been welcome, always been given shelter and plenty to eat, there was no answer. She knocked again, softly. A voice from within said, "Who is it?" There was fear in the voice.

She knew instantly from the sound of the voice that there was something wrong. She said, "A friend with friends," the password on the Underground Railroad.

The door opened, slowly. The man who stood in the doorway looked at her coldly, looked with unconcealed astonishment and fear at the eleven disheveled runaways who were standing near her. Then he shouted, "Too many, too many. It's not safe. My place was searched last week. It's not safe!" and slammed the door in her face.

She turned away from the house, frowning. She had promised her passengers food and rest and warmth, and instead of that, there would be hunger and cold and more walking over the frozen ground. Somehow she would have to instill courage into these eleven people, most of them strangers, would have to feed them on hope and bright dreams of freedom instead of the fried pork and corn bread and milk she had promised them.

They stumbled along behind her, half-dead for sleep, and she urged them on, though she was as tired and as discouraged as they were. She had never been in Canada but she kept painting wondrous word pictures of what it would be like. She man-

aged to dispel their fear of pursuit, so that they would not become hysterical, panic-stricken. Then she had to bring some of the fear back, so that they would stay awake and keep walking though they drooped with sleep.

Yet during the day, when they lay down deep in a thicket, they never really slept, because if a twig snapped or the wind sighed in the branches of a pine tree, they jumped to their feet, afraid of their own shadows, shivering and shaking. It was very cold, but they dared not make fires because someone would see the smoke and wonder about it.

She kept thinking, eleven of them. Eleven thousand dollars' worth of slaves. And she had to take them all the way to Canada. Sometimes she told them about Thomas Garrett, in Wilmington. She said he was their friend even though he did not know them. He was the friend of all fugitives. He called them God's poor. He was a Quaker and his speech was a little different from that of other people. His clothing was different, too. He wore the wide-brimmed hat that the Quakers wear.

She said that he had thick white hair, soft, almost like a baby's, and the kindest eyes she had ever seen. He was a big man and strong, but he had never used his strength to harm anyone, always to help people. He would give all of them a new pair of shoes. Everybody. He always did. Once they reached his house in Wilmington, they would be safe. He would see to it that they were.

She described the house where he lived, told them about the store where he sold shoes. She said he kept a pail of milk and a loaf of bread in the drawer of his desk so that he would have food ready at hand for any of God's poor who should suddenly appear before him, fainting with hunger. There was a hidden room in the store. A whole wall

*Harriet Tubman: Guide to Freedom* 385

**8 Literary Focus** What challenge does Harriet Tubman face?

**9 Critical Thinking and Reading** Help students to see that this kind of detail, giving information about Tubman's feelings and thoughts, is a subjective detail. Such subjective details are interspersed with factual information.

**Alternative Assessment** To promote active reading, have students create a reader's response journal as they read "Harriet Tubman: Guide to Freedom." Ask them to focus their observations on the details that reveal Tubman's personality and show her as "the Moses" of her people. Have them note, too, the obstacles she and those she helped faced in their flight to freedom. Encouage students to respond personally to Harriet Tubman and the courage she displays. Ask them to tell what they learn from her example about the power of one person to make a difference. You may use their response journals to assess their understanding of this selection.

**Electronic Handbook** You might want students to review agreement of subjects and verbs before completing the Grammar in Action activities. If students have access to the Language Master 6000, have them enter the access word *number* and press the GRAMMAR key to get information on agreement of subjects and verbs.

"Harriet Tubman: Guide to Freedom," subjects and verbs agree; the subjects are underlined once, while verbs are underlined twice:

There <u>were</u> <u>eleven</u> in this party, including one of her brothers and his wife. <u>It</u> <u>was</u> the largest group that <u>she</u> <u>had</u> ever <u>conducted</u>, but <u>she</u> <u>was</u> determined that more and more <u>slaves</u> <u>should know</u> what <u>freedom</u> <u>was</u> like.

Had the passage begun "there was eleven in this party," and concluded "she were determined," subjects and verbs would not agree because *eleven* is plural and *was* is singular; similarly, *she* is singular and *were* is plural.

**Student Activity 1.** Locate two more examples of subject-verb agreement in the selection. Explain why the subjects and verbs agree.

**Student Activity 2.** Write three of your own sentences in which subjects and verbs agree in number.

Fine art, *Harriet Tubman Series, #16*, by Jacob Lawrence. Lawrence's paintings in the Tubman Series reflect a deep personal involvement in the ideals demonstrated in the life of Harriet Tubman and the plight of all African-Americans.

Point out that a strong element in the composition of this painting is repetition.
1. What part of the selection does this painting illustrate?
2. How does the artist show the element of repetition in this painting?
3. What repetitions would have been seen, heard, or felt by a slave fleeing on the Underground Railroad?

**HARRIET TUBMAN SERIES, #16**
*Jacob Lawrence*
*Hampton University Museum*

swung open, and behind it was a room where he could hide fugitives. On the wall there were shelves filled with small boxes —boxes of shoes—so that you would never guess that the wall actually opened.

While she talked, she kept watching them. They did not believe her. She could tell by their expressions. They were thinking. New shoes, Thomas Garrett, Quaker, Wilmington—what foolishness was this? Who knew if she told the truth? Where was she taking them anyway?

That night they reached the next stop—a farm that belonged to a German. She made the runaways take shelter behind trees at the edge of the fields before she knocked at the door. She hesitated before she approached the door, thinking, suppose that he, too, should refuse shelter, suppose—Then she thought, Lord, I'm going to hold steady on to You and You've got to see me through—and knocked softly.

She heard the familiar guttural voice say, "Who's there?"

She answered quickly, "A friend with friends."

He opened the door and greeted her warmly. "How many this time?" he asked.

"Eleven," she said and waited, doubting, wondering.

He said, "Good. Bring them in."

He and his wife fed them in the lamplit kitchen, their faces glowing, as they offered food and more food, urging them to eat,

## Grammar in Action

Writers vary their sentences by beginning some with subordinate clauses. A **subordinate clause** begins with a subordinating conjunction such as *after, because, as if, in order that, when, though,* and others. The subordinating conjunction is followed by a clause that contains a subject and a verb, but because the clause begins with a subordinating conjunction, it cannot stand alone as a sentence. It must be connected to an independent clause. When a subordinate clause appears at the beginning of the sentence, it must be followed by a comma. If a subordinate clause appears after the independent clause, usually there is no comma.

Read the following sentences beginning with subordinate clauses taken from "Harriet Tubman: Guide to Freedom":

*Once she had made her presence known,* word of her coming spread from cabin to cabin.

*If they were caught,* the eleven runaways would be whipped and sold South, but she—she would probably be hanged.

saying there was plenty for everybody, have more milk, have more bread, have more meat.

They spent the night in the warm kitchen. They really slept, all that night and until dusk the next day. When they left, it was with reluctance. They had all been warm and safe and well-fed. It was hard to exchange the security offered by that clean, warm kitchen for the darkness and the cold of a December night.

Harriet had found it hard to leave the warmth and friendliness, too. But she urged them on. For a while, as they walked, they seemed to carry in them a measure of contentment; some of the serenity and the cleanliness of that big warm kitchen lingered on inside them. But as they walked farther and farther away from the warmth and the light, the cold and the darkness entered into them. They fell silent, sullen, suspicious. She waited for the moment when some one of them would turn mutinous. It did not happen that night.

Two nights later she was aware that the feet behind her were moving slower and slower. She heard the irritability in their voices, knew that soon someone would refuse to go on.

She started talking about William Still and the Philadelphia Vigilance Committee.[4] No one commented. No one asked any questions. She told them the story of William and Ellen Craft and how they escaped from Georgia. Ellen was so fair that she looked as though she were white, and so she dressed up in a man's clothing and she looked like a wealthy young planter. Her husband, William, who was dark, played the role of her

---

4. **Philadelphia Vigilance Committee:** A group of citizens who helped escaped slaves. Its secretary was a free black man named William Still.

slave. Thus they traveled from Macon, Georgia, to Philadelphia, riding on the trains, staying at the finest hotels. Ellen pretended to be very ill—her right arm was in a sling, and her right hand was bandaged, because she was supposed to have rheumatism. Thus she avoided having to sign the register at the hotels for she could not read or write. They finally arrived safely in Philadelphia, and then went on to Boston.

No one said anything. Not one of them seemed to have heard her.

She told them about Frederick Douglass, the most famous of the escaped slaves, of his eloquence, of his magnificent appearance. Then she told them of her own first vain effort at running away, evoking the memory of that miserable life she had led as a child, reliving it for a moment in the telling.

But they had been tired too long, hungry too long, afraid too long, footsore too long. One of them suddenly cried out in despair, "Let me go back. It is better to be a slave than to suffer like this in order to be free."

She carried a gun with her on these trips. She had never used it—except as a threat. Now as she aimed it, she experienced a feeling of guilt, remembering that time, years ago, when she had prayed for the death of Edward Brodas, the Master, and then not too long afterward had heard that great wailing cry that came from the throats of the field hands, and knew from the sound that the Master was dead.

One of the runaways said, again, "Let me go back. Let me go back," and stood still, and then turned around and said, over his shoulder, "I am going back."

She lifted the gun, aimed it at the despairing slave. She said, "Go on with us or die." The husky low-pitched voice was grim.

He hesitated for a moment and then he joined the others. They started walking again. She tried to explain to them why none of them could go back to the plantation. If a

*Harriet Tubman: Guide to Freedom* 387

---

**10 Reading Strategy** Have students predict what Tubman will do now.

**11 Discussion** What might Tubman do if someone refuses to go on?

**12 Discussion** Tubman feels guilty about this childhood experience. What connection in her mind do you think she made as a child?

**Electronic Handbook** You might want students to review clauses before completing the Grammar in Action activities. If students have access to the Language Master 6000, have them enter the access word *clause* and press the GRAMMAR key to get information on clauses.

---

*When she knocked on the door of a farmhouse,* a place where she and her parties of runaways had always been welcome, always been given shelter and plenty to eat, there was no answer.

*Once they reached his house in Wilmington,* they would be safe.

*While she talked,* she kept watching them.

Notice in the above examples that each sentence begins with a subordinating conjunction *(once, if, when, while),* which is followed by a clause containing a subject and a verb. After each subordinate clause, there is a comma.

Subordinate clauses can be added to the beginning or end of a sentence in order to combine ideas and to make the sentences longer and more interesting.

**Student Activity 1.** Find four other subordinate clauses in "Harriet Tubman: Guide to Freedom."

**Student Activity 2.** Write four of your own sentences that begin with a subordinating clause. Be sure that you follow the clause with a comma.

---

Fine art, *Harriet Tubman Series, #10,* by Jacob Lawrence. In this painting Jacob Lawrence uses strong, hard-edged shapes of intense color in a unique, personal style. He often uses these dramatic elements to create symbols of oppression and protest.
1. What symbols can you find in this painting?
2. What message might the artist be communicating with these symbols?

**13 Discussion** What methods might have been used to force a captured runaway to turn traitor?

**14 Discussion** What does Tubman mean by these words?

**Multicultural Focus** Escaped slaves were not the only people who found their way north by the use of the North Star, referenced on page 383. Celestial navigation goes back to ancient times and has been used all over the world. Interested students may wish to research and present information on the North Star, or polestar. They will find that this highly visible star, almost directly over the North Pole, is of great use to navigators. However, exactly which star this is has changed over the centuries. At present the North Star is the star called Polaris.

**HARRIET TUBMAN SERIES, #10**
*Jacob Lawrence*
Hampton University Museum

**13** runaway returned, he would turn traitor, the master and the overseer would force him to turn traitor. The returned slave would disclose the stopping places, the hiding places, the cornstacks they had used with the full knowledge of the owner of the farm, the name of the German farmer who had fed them and sheltered them. These people who had risked their own security to help runaways would be ruined, fined, imprisoned.

**14** She said, "We got to go free or die. And freedom's not bought with dust."

This time she told them about the long agony of the Middle Passage on the old slave ships, about the black horror of the holds, about the chains and the whips. They too knew these stories. But she wanted to remind them of the long hard way they had come, about the long hard way they had yet to go. She told them about Thomas Sims, the boy picked up on the streets of Boston and sent back to Georgia. She said when they got him back to Savannah, got him in prison there, they whipped him until a

388   *Nonfiction*

doctor who was standing by watching said, "You will kill him if you strike him again!" His master said, "Let him die!"

Thus she forced them to go on. Sometimes she thought she had become nothing but a voice speaking in the darkness, cajoling, urging, threatening. Sometimes she told them things to make them laugh, sometimes she sang to them, and heard the eleven voices behind her blending softly with hers, and then she knew that for the moment all was well with them.

She gave the impression of being a short, muscular, indomitable woman who could never be defeated. Yet at any moment she was liable to be seized by one of those curious fits of sleep, which might last for a few minutes or for hours.[5]

Even on this trip, she suddenly fell asleep in the woods. The runaways, ragged, dirty, hungry, cold, did not steal the gun as they might have, and set off by themselves, or turn back. They sat on the ground near her and waited patiently until she awakened. They had come to trust her implicitly, totally. They, too, had come to believe her repeated statement, "We got to go free or die." She was leading them into freedom, and so they waited until she was ready to go on.

Finally, they reached Thomas Garrett's house in Wilmington, Delaware. Just as Harriet had promised, Garrett gave them all new shoes, and provided carriages to take them on to the next stop.

By slow stages they reached Philadelphia, where William Still hastily recorded their names, and the plantations whence they had come, and something of the life they had led in slavery. Then he carefully hid what he had written, for fear it might be discovered. In 1872 he published this record in book form and called it *The Underground Railroad.* In the foreword to his book he said: "While I knew the danger of keeping strict records, and while I did not then dream that in my day slavery would be blotted out, or that the time would come when I could publish these records, it used to afford me great satisfaction to take them down, fresh from the lips of fugitives on the way to freedom, and to preserve them as they had given them."

William Still, who was familiar with all the station stops on the Underground Railroad, supplied Harriet with money and sent her and her eleven fugitives on to Burlington, New Jersey.

Harriet felt safer now, though there were danger spots ahead. But the biggest part of her job was over. As they went farther and farther north, it grew colder; she was aware of the wind on the Jersey ferry and aware of the cold damp in New York. From New York they went on to Syracuse, where the temperature was even lower.

In Syracuse she met the Reverend J. W. Loguen, known as "Jarm" Loguen. This was the beginning of a lifelong friendship. Both Harriet and Jarm Loguen were to become friends and supporters of Old John Brown.[6]

From Syracuse they went north again, into a colder, snowier city—Rochester. Here they almost certainly stayed with Frederick Douglass, for he wrote in his autobiography:

"On one occasion I had eleven fugitives at the same time under my roof, and it was necessary for them to remain with me until

---

5. **sleep . . . hours:** When she was about 13, Harriet accidentally received a severe blow on the head. Afterwards, she often lost consciousness, and could not be woken until the episode was over.

---

6. **John Brown:** White abolitionist (1800–1859) who was hanged for leading a raid on the arsenal at Harpers Ferry, Virginia, as part of a slave uprising.

*Harriet Tubman: Guide to Freedom* 389

**19 Clarification** Point out that none of these rights was granted to slaves in the United States.

**Reader's Response** Tubman says that "freedom is not bought with dust." Substitute the word *freedom* with another appropriate noun.

**Thematic Response** From this selection students learn that Harriet Tubman worked throughout her life to lead as many slaves as possible to freedom. Ask students whether they think she was rewarded fairly. Is Harriet Tubman's life an example of justice being served? Considering the economic system of the South, were the slave owners and the slave hunters among the just or the unjust? Should they have been penalized for their actions?

I could collect sufficient money to get them to Canada. It was the largest number I ever had at any one time, and I had some difficulty in providing so many with food and shelter, but, as may well be imagined, they were not very fastidious in either direction, and were well content with very plain food, and a strip of carpet on the floor for a bed, or a place on the straw in the barnloft.''

Late in December, 1851, Harriet arrived in St. Catharines, Canada West (now Ontario), with the eleven fugitives. It had taken almost a month to complete this journey; most of the time had been spent getting out of Maryland.

That first winter in St. Catharines was a terrible one. Canada was a strange frozen land, snow everywhere, ice everywhere, and a bone-biting cold the like of which none of them had ever experienced before. Harriet rented a small frame house in the town and set to work to make a home. The fugitives boarded with her. They worked in the forests, felling trees, and so did she. Sometimes she took other jobs, cooking or cleaning house for people in the town. She cheered on these newly arrived fugitives, working herself, finding work for them, finding food for them, praying for them, sometimes begging for them.

Often she found herself thinking of the beauty of Maryland, the mellowness of the soil, the richness of the plant life there. The climate itself made for an ease of living that could never be duplicated in this bleak, barren countryside.

In spite of the severe cold, the hard work, she came to love St. Catharines, and the other towns and cities in Canada where black men lived. She discovered that freedom meant more than the right to change jobs at will, more than the right to keep the money that one earned. It was the right to vote and to sit on juries. It was the right to be elected to office. In Canada there were black men who were county officials and members of school boards. St. Catharines had a large colony of ex-slaves, and they owned their own homes, kept them neat and clean and in good repair. They lived in whatever part of town they chose and sent their children to the schools.

When spring came she decided that she would make this small Canadian city her home—as much as any place could be said to be home to a woman who traveled from Canada to the Eastern Shore of Maryland as often as she did.

In the spring of 1852, she went back to Cape May, New Jersey. She spent the summer there, cooking in a hotel. That fall she returned, as usual, to Dorchester County, and brought out nine more slaves, conducting them all the way to St. Catharines, in Canada West, to the bone-biting cold, the snow-covered forests—and freedom.

She continued to live in this fashion, spending the winter in Canada, and the spring and summer working in Cape May, New Jersey, or in Philadelphia. She made two trips a year into slave territory, one in the fall and another in the spring. She now had a definite crystallized purpose, and in carrying it out, her life fell into a pattern which remained unchanged for the next six years.

**Closure and Extension**

**ANSWERS TO RESPONDING TO THE SELECTION**
*Your Response*
1. Encourage students to speculate about what Harriet Tubman might be doing if she were alive today. Which of society's current issues might she be actively involved in?

*Recalling*
2. She announced her arrival by sing-

## RESPONDING TO THE SELECTION

### Your Response

1. Would you like to have met Harriet Tubman? Why or why not?

### Recalling

2. How did Harriet Tubman announce her arrival in the slave quarter?
3. Why was no fugitive allowed to turn back?

### Interpreting

4. Why was "Moses" an appropriate name for Harriet Tubman?
5. Why did Tubman never tell any of the fugitives that she was afraid?

### Applying

6. Like the Israelites escaping from Egypt, the African American slaves also escaped to freedom. What groups today have made similar escapes? What common qualities do these people have?

## ANALYZING LITERATURE

### Understanding Biography

A biography, or an account of a person's life written by another person, often focuses on the achievements of the person's life. The writer may tell you about the difficulties the person overcame.

1. How do you think the author wants you to feel about her subject—Harriet Tubman?
2. Find three details of Tubman's life that help create this feeling.
3. For what reasons do you think Tubman is a good subject for a biography?

## CRITICAL THINKING AND READING

### Recognizing Subjective Details

Writers often include both objective and subjective details in a biography. **Objective details**

are factual and true to life. For example, the writer says, "There were eleven in this party, including one of her brothers and his wife." This sentence does not reveal the author's beliefs or judgments.

**Subjective details,** on the other hand, do reveal the author's feelings, attitudes, or judgments. An example is, ". . . she was determined that more and more slaves should know what freedom was like."

Identify which of the following contain subjective and which contain objective details.

1. "She knew moments of doubt when she was half-afraid, and kept looking back over her shoulder, imagining that she heard the sound of pursuit."
2. "In December 1851, when she started out with the band of fugitives that she planned to take to Canada, she had been in the vicinity of the plantation for days. . . ."

## THINKING AND WRITING

### Writing a Biography

Choose a person whom you admire. Select one incident in the person's life that illustrates the qualities you most associate with that person. The incident may be one in which the person overcame an obstacle. Freewrite about this incident. Using the information from your freewriting, write a biographical sketch. Revise your sketch, making sure you have portrayed your subject vividly. Proofread your sketch.

## LEARNING OPTION

**Performance.** Prepare a radio news broadcast that describes one of the events in "Harriet Tubman: Guide to Freedom." Include as many details as you can. When you read the news bulletin to your classmates, speak dramatically and with excitement. You may wish to tape-record the broadcast to share it with other classes.

*Harriet Tubman: Guide to Freedom* 391

courageous citizens who were helping slaves to freedom.

3. Suggested Response: Tubman is a good subject for a biography because she risked danger and her life for an unselfish goal.

**Challenge** What aspects of this biography are factual and can be verified and which do you think the author developed as what *probably* happened in certain situations?

### ANSWERS TO CRITICAL THINKING AND READING

1. subjective detail
2. objective detail

### THINKING AND WRITING

🖥 Writing Transparency A model may help your students write their biographies. Use *Model 2, a Character Sketch,* in **Transparencies for Writing.**

◆ Software If your students have access to computers, have them use **Bank Street Writer** to complete the assignment. As students revise, they can use the program's on-line thesaurus to generate strong adjectives to vividly describe the people about whom they are writing.

### Publishing Student Writing

This is the kind of writing activity that can be shared—in groups, on a bulletin board, or in a booklet.

Students might enjoy reading one another's biographical sketches. Prepare a bulletin board display of their written sketches. Students might contribute pictures of their subjects to be displayed with their written sketches.

### LEARNING OPTION

Students with a flair for drama and who enjoy speaking and writing will choose to participate in this activity. Help them to imagine the event and to create as many sensory details as they can to make the event they describe become realistic.

---

ing the forbidden spiritual "Go down, Moses."

3. No fugitive was allowed to turn back because the master and overseer would force him or her to turn traitor, revealing hiding places and people who had helped him or her.

### Interpreting

4. "Moses" was an appropriate name for Tubman because in the Biblical story Moses led the enslaved Israelites out of Egypt to freedom.

5. Tubman never told the fugitives she was afraid because that would encourage their fear; she needed to instill courage in them to keep going.

### Applying

6. Answers will differ. Suggested Response: Groups who have made similar escapes are dissidents from the former Soviet Union, refugees from Vietnam and Cambodia. Such people probably possess courage, tenacity, endurance, and strong faith.

### ANSWERS TO ANALYZING LITERATURE

1. The author probably wants you to admire and respect Tubman for her courage and endurance.
2. Three details of Tubman's life that help create this feeling are that Tubman would not let the runaways know that the route beyond Philadelphia was strange to her, that she urged the runaways on even when she herself was tired and discouraged, and that she inspired them to go onward with her stories of other

## Preparation

**More About the Author** Izenberg has a Ph.D. from Harvard University, with postdoctoral education in psychoanalysis. Ask students what factors might motivate someone interested in the study of the human personality to write about a celebrated sports figure.

**Literary Focus** Point out that a memoir can be written by a close friend or relative of the subject without relying on interviews and anecdotes from other people. Usually, however, a memoir is supplemented with anecdotes from other people. Ask the students whom they think the writer would choose to interview about Roberto Clemente.

**Prereading Focus** Before students discuss the positive and negative characteristics of role models, have them list celebrities, politicians, and other famous people. Have students vote and then discuss briefly whether each name on the list is a person who commands respect and is a good example for young people to follow. Help students to see that personalities are complex and that well-known people are not simply "good" or "bad."

**Vocabulary** Point out to students that the vocabulary words *brace*, *banked*, and *prospect* are words with multiple meanings. Have students find in a dictionary the other common definitions for each of these words. You may wish to have them use each word in a sentence orally as they find the additional meanings.

**Electronic Handbook** If your students have access to the Language Master 6000, suggest that they find synonyms for *delineate* and *conjectured*. Have them find the two vocabulary words on pages 393 and 394 respectively and replace *delineate* and *conjectured* with the synonyms. Ask if the synonyms change the meaning of either of the original sentences.

**Spelling Tip** *Crypt* is one of a small group of words in which *y* sounds like a short *i*. Other words in this group include *myth*, *gyp*, *gypsy*, and *gypsum*.

---

# GUIDE FOR READING

## Roberto Clemente: A Bittersweet Memoir

### Jerry Izenberg

(1930–     ), a graduate of Rutgers University, is a sports-writer and reporter. He is a syndicated sports columnist based at the *Newark Star Ledger,* whose daily column appears in newspapers around the country. He has written seven books and written or directed thirty-one television specials. In the following selection from *Great Latin Sports Figures,* published in 1976, he portrays the inspiration of Roberto Clemente, the former All-Star right fielder and record-making hitter for the Pittsburgh Pirates.

### Memoir

A **memoir** is a biographical piece usually written by a relative or personal friend of the subject. The writer has based this memoir about Roberto Clemente on interviews and anecdotes.

An interview is a planned meeting at which writers obtain information about a topic from someone who is knowledgeable about it. Izenberg gathered firsthand information about Roberto Clemente through interviews with people who had known him well.

Answers to interview questions often provide anecdotes—brief stories about noteworthy incidents—that give information and show the person in a different light.

### Focus

You often hear people discussing whether a public figure is a positive role model. Make a word web similar to the one that follows. On it jot down the qualities and attributes you think a positive role model should possess. As you read the selection about Roberto Clemente, compare your ideas with the qualities that made Clemente a positive role model.

### Vocabulary

Knowing the following words will help you as you read "Roberto Clemente: A Bittersweet Memoir."

**delineate** (di lin′ ē āt′) *v.*: Describe in detail (p. 393)

**brace** (brās) *n.*: A pair of like things (p. 393)

**conjectured** (kən jek′ chərd) *v.*: Guessed from very little evidence (p. 394)

**banked** (baŋkt) *v.*: Tilted an airplane to the side when turning, making one wing higher than the other (p. 395)

**crypt** (kript) *n.*: An underground vault or room, used as a burial place (p. 397)

**prospect** (präs′ pekt) *n.*: A likely candidate (p. 399)

---

### Objectives

1  To understand the memoir
2  To identify primary and secondary sources
3  To write a memoir
4  To express individual interests and abilities through optional activities

### Support Material

**Teaching Portfolio**
Teacher Backup, p. 453
Grammar in Action Worksheet, *Using Dashes*, p. 456
Usage and Mechanics Worksheet, p. 458
Vocabulary Check, p. 459
Analyzing Literature Worksheet, *Understanding the Memoir*, p. 460

# Roberto Clemente:
# A Bittersweet Memoir

## Jerry Izenberg

**1** *I saw him play so often. I watched the grace of his movements and the artistry of his reflexes from who knows how many press boxes. None of us really appreciated how pure an athlete he was until he was gone. What follows is a personal retracing of the steps that took Roberto Clemente from the narrow, crowded streets of his native Carolina to the local ball parks in San Juan and on to the major leagues. But it is more. It is a remembrance formed as I stood at the water's edge in Puerto Rico and stared at daybreak into the waves that killed him. It is all the people I met in Puerto Rico who knew him and loved him. It is the way an entire island in the sun and a Pennsylvania city in the smog took his death. . . .*

The record book will tell you that Roberto Clemente collected 3,000 hits during his major-league career. It will say that he came to bat 9,454 times, that he drove in 1,305 runs, and played 2,433 games over an eighteen-year span.

But it won't tell you about Carolina, Puerto Rico; and the old square; and the narrow, twisting streets; and the roots that produced him. It won't tell you about the Julio Coronado School and a remarkable woman named María Isabella Casares,

whom he called "Teacher" until the day he died and who helped to shape his life in times of despair and depression. It won't tell you about a man named Pedron Zarrilla, who found him on a country softball team and put him in the uniform of the Santurce club and who nursed him from promising young athlete to major-league superstar.

**2** And most of all, those cold numbers won't begin to delineate the man Roberto Clemente was. To even begin to understand what this magnificent athlete was all about, you have to work backward. The search begins at the site of its ending.

The car moves easily through the pre-dawn streets of San Juan. A heavy all-night rain has now begun to drive, and there is that postrain sweetness in the air that holds the promise of a new, fresh, clear dawn. This is a journey to the site of one of Puerto Rico's deepest tragedies. This last says a lot. Tragedy is no stranger to the sensitive emotional people who make this island the human place it is.

Shortly before the first rays of sunlight, the car turns down a bumpy secondary road and moves past small shantytowns, where the sounds of the children stirring for the long walk toward school begin to drift out on the morning air. Then there is another turn, between a brace of trees and onto the hard-

*Roberto Clemente: A Bittersweet Memoir* 393

Language Worksheet, *Using Prefixes and Suffixes to Determine Meaning*, p. 461
Selection Test, p. 462

**Prentice Hall Literature Writing Studio**

**Making Connections** Another selection that pays tribute to a memorable person is "I Know Why the Caged Bird Sings," page 403. You might pair that selection with this one and have students compare the attitude of the writers toward their subjects.

**Motivation/Prior Knowledge**
Ask students to discuss what types of people will risk their own lives and put themselves in dangerous situations in order to help others.

**Thematic Focus** Adolescents, because of their need to separate emotionally from their parents, may not respond easily to the issues of "rootedness"—a person's family background, cultural attachments, the behaviors and values grounded in a person's history. Ask students to discuss how they are rooted to the place in which they live. Help them to think as broadly as they can about their immediate and extended families, their cultural heritages, and the influence of their community's values on their lives. Tell them that as they read, they will understand how Roberto Clemente was so greatly influenced by his Puerto Rican heritage.

**Purpose-Setting Question** Discuss the meaning of *bittersweet* —pleasant with overtones of sadness. Ask students why this is a "bittersweet memoir." What aspects of it are bitter, and what aspects of it are sweet?

**1 Literary Focus** What prompted Izenberg to write this memoir?

**2 Critical Thinking and Reading** What is the author's attitude about Clemente?

394

**3 Discussion** Ask students their opinion of this definition of friendship. What are their definitions of friendship?

**4 Discussion** Why did Vigereaux think a celebrity like Clemente would be more effective in getting help than, for example, he himself would?

**5 Discussion** What does this passage suggest about the economic status of the people who were donating?

**6 Clarification** The black market is a system for selling goods illegally, especially in violation of rationing. Products sold on the black market may not reach the people for whom they were intended and often are more expensive than they should be.

packed dirt and sand, and although the light has not yet quite begun to break, you can sense the nearness of the ocean. You can hear its waves, pounding harshly against the jagged rocks. You can smell its saltiness. The car noses to a stop, and the driver says, ''From here you must walk. There is no other way.'' The place is called Puente Maldonado and the dawn does not slip into this angry place. It explodes in a million lights and colors as the large fireball of the sun begins to nose above the horizon.

''This is the nearest place,'' the driver tells me. ''This is where they came by the thousands on that New Year's Eve and New Year's Day. Out there,'' he says, gesturing with his right hand, ''out there, perhaps a mile and a half from where we stand. That's where we think the plane went down.''

The final hours of Roberto Clemente were like this. Just a month or so before, he had agreed to take a junior-league baseball team to Nicaragua and manage it in an all-star game in Managua. He had met people and made friends there. He was not a **3** man who made friends casually. He had always said that the people you wanted to give your friendship to were the people for whom you had to be willing to give something in return—no matter what the price.

Two weeks after he returned from that trip, Managua, Nicaragua exploded into flames. The earth trembled and people died. It was the worst earthquake anywhere in the Western Hemisphere in a long, long time.

Back in Puerto Rico, a television personality named Luis Vigereaux heard the news and was moved to try to help the victims. He needed someone to whom the people would listen, someone who could say what **4** had to be said and get the work done that had to be done and help the people who had to be helped.

''I knew,'' Luis Vigereaux said, ''that Roberto was such a person, perhaps the only such person who would be willing to help.''

And so the mercy project, which would eventually claim Roberto's life, began. He appeared on television. But he needed a staging area. The city agreed to give him Sixto Escobar Stadium.

''Bring what you can,'' he told them. ''Bring medicine . . . bring clothes . . . bring food . . . bring shoes . . . bring yourself to help us load. We need so much. Whatever you bring, we will use.''

And the people of San Juan came. They walked through the heat and they drove old cars and battered little trucks, and the **5** mound of supplies grew and grew. Within two days, the first mercy planes left for Nicaragua.

Meanwhile, a ship had been chartered and loaded. And as it prepared to steam away, unhappy stories began to drift back from Nicaragua. Not all the supplies that had been flown in, it was rumored, were getting through. Puerto Ricans who had flown the planes had no passports, and Nicaragua was in a state of panic.

''We have people there who must be protected. We have black-market types who must not be allowed to get their hands on **6** these supplies,'' Clemente told Luis Vigereaux. ''Someone must make sure—particularly before the ship gets there. I'm going on the next plane.''

The plane they had rented was an old DC-7. It was scheduled to take off at 4 P.M. on December 31, 1972. Long before take-off time, it was apparent that the plane needed more work. It had even taxied onto the runway and then turned back. The trouble, a mechanic who was at the airstrip that day conjectured, ''had to do with both port [left side] engines. We worked on them most of the afternoon."

The departure time was delayed an hour, and then two, and then three. Across town, a man named Rudy Hernandez, who had been a teammate of Roberto's when they were rookies in the Puerto Rican League and who had later pitched for the Washington Senators, was trying to contact Roberto by telephone. He had just received a five-hundred-dollar donation, and he wanted to know where to send it. He called Roberto's wife, Vera, who told him that Roberto was going on a trip and that he might catch him at the airport. She had been there herself only moments before to pick up some friends who were coming in from the States, and she had left because she was fairly sure that the trouble had cleared and Roberto had probably left already.

"I caught him at the airport and I was surprised," Rudy Hernandez told me. "I said I had this money for Nicaraguan relief and I wanted to know what to do with it. Then I asked him where he was going."

"Nicaragua," Clemente told him.

"It's New Year's Eve, Roberto. Let it wait."

7 "Who else will go?" Roberto told him. "Someone has to do it."

At 9 P.M., even as the first stirrings of the annual New Year's Eve celebration were beginning in downtown San Juan, the DC-7 taxied onto the runway, received clearance, rumbled down the narrow concrete strip, and pulled away from the earth. It headed out over the Atlantic and banked toward Nicaragua, and its tiny lights disappeared on the horizon.

Just ninety seconds later, the tower at San Juan International Airport received this message from the pilot: "We are coming back around."

Just that.

Nothing more.

And then there was a great silence.

"It was almost midnight," recalls Rudy Hernandez, a former teammate of Roberto's. "We were having this party in my restaurant, and somebody turned on the radio and the announcer was saying that Roberto's plane was feared missing. And then, because my place is on the beach, we saw these giant floodlights crisscrossing the waves, and we heard the sound of the helicopters and the little search planes."

Drawn by a common sadness, the people of San Juan began to make their way toward the beach, toward Puente Maldonado. A cold rain had begun to fall. It washed their faces and blended with the tears.

They came by the thousands, and they watched for three days. Towering waves

*Roberto Clemente: A Bittersweet Memoir*   395

7 **Discussion** What does this response show about Roberto?

**Multicultural Focus** In 1866 skier Sondre Norheim amazed onlookers in a ski competition in Telemark, Norway, and became a legend in that country. At the 1936 Olympics in Berlin, Jesse Owens, son of an African American sharecropper, embarrassed Hitler's boasts of Aryan supremacy by winning four gold medals. Since early Greek times, athletes have served as models of courage, perseverance, and accomplishment. Often athletics has been the only vehicle by which a person could move from poverty and other limiting circumstances into a life of prominence and financial security. Ask students to research and report to the class on favorite athletes, focusing on their struggles to achieve success and explaining how their successes inspired others. Some students might be interested in researching the Special Olympics, which highlight the athletic performances of the physically challenged.

**8 Discussion** Why do some people react strangely during times of great sorrow or rejoicing?

**9 Critical Thinking and Reading** Point out that María Casares can give firsthand information about Clemente.

**10 Discussion** What is Izenberg's impression of María Casares as a teacher?

**11 Critical Thinking and Reading** Roberto comes to María Casares with a problem. What does this show about their relationship?

boiled up and made the search virtually impossible. The U.S. Navy sent a team of expert divers into the area, but the battering of the waves defeated them too. Midway through the week, the pilot's body was found in the swift-moving currents to the north. On Saturday bits of the cockpit were sighted.

And then—nothing else.

"I was born in the Dominican Republic," Rudy Hernandez said, "but I've lived on this island for more than twenty years. I have never seen a time or a sadness like that. The streets were empty, the radios silent, except for the constant bulletins about Roberto. Traffic? Forget it. All of us cried. All of us who knew him and even those who didn't, wept that week.

**8** "Manny Sanguillen, the Pittsburgh catcher, was down here playing winter ball, and when Manny heard the news he ran to the beach and he tried to jump into the ocean with skin-diving gear. I told him, man, there's sharks there. You can't help. Leave it to the experts. But he kept going back. All of us were a little crazy that week.

"There will never be another like Roberto."

Who was he . . . I mean really?

Well, nobody can put together all the pieces of another man's life. But there are so many who want the world to know that it is not as impossible a search as you might think.

He was born in Carolina, Puerto Rico. Today the town has about 125,000 people, but when Roberto was born there in 1934, it was roughly one sixth its current size.

**9** María Isabella Casares is a schoolteacher. She has taught the children of Carolina for thirty years. Most of her teaching has been done in tenth-grade history classes. Carolina is her home, and its children are her children. And among all of those whom she calls her own (who are all the children

she taught), Roberto Clemente was something even more special to her.

"His father was an overseer on a sugar plantation. He did not make much money," she explained in an empty classroom at Julio Coronado School. "But then, there are no rich children here. There never have been. Roberto was typical of them. I had known him when he was a small boy because my father had run a grocery store in Carolina, and Roberto's parents used to shop there.

**10** There is this thing that you have to know about María Isabella Casares before we hear more from her. What you have to know is that she is the model of what a teacher should be. Between her and her students even now, as back when Roberto attended her school, there is this common bond of mutual respect. Earlier in the day, I had watched her teach a class in the history of the Abolition Movement in Puerto Rico. I don't speak much Spanish, but even to me it was clear that this is how a class should be, this is the kind of person who should teach, and these are the kinds of students such a teacher will produce.

With this as a background, what she has to say about Roberto Clemente carries much more impact.

**11** "Each year," she said, "I let my students choose the seats they want to sit in. I remember the first time I saw Roberto. He was a very shy boy and he went straight to the back of the room and chose the very last seat. Most of the time he would sit with his eyes down. He was an average student. But there was something very special about him. We would talk after class for hours. He wanted to be an engineer, you know, and perhaps he could have been. But then he began to play softball, and one day he came to me and said, 'Teacher, I have a problem.'

"He told me that Pedron Zarrilla, who was one of our most prominent baseball

*396  Nonfiction*

## Grammar in Action

**Dashes** are punctuation marks that indicate an abrupt break in thought. Like commas, semicolons, and parentheses, dashes signal pause, but dashes signal a more striking, dramatic pause. Dashes are frequently used in punctuating fast-paced, dramatic sentences to capture the quick verbal exchange of the speakers. However, dashes do not necessarily indicate fast-paced dialogue. Dashes can also reflect the way we speak every day.

In "Roberto Clemente: A Bittersweet Memoir," Izenberg uses dashes both to emphasize important ideas and to capture the dramatic pauses used by the people he interviewed. Perhaps one of the most dramatic and effective uses of the dash in the selection occurs when Izenberg describes the disappointment of the search after Clemente's plane crashed: "And then—nothing else."

Another example of how Izenberg uses the dash occurs when he quotes María Isabella Casares. Casares emphasizes important information, which Izenberg sets off by dashes.

"He was like a son to me. This is why I want to tell you about him. This is why you must make people—particularly our people, our Puerto Rican children—understand what he was . . ."

people, had seen him play, and that Pedron wanted him to sign a professional contract with the Santurce Crabbers. He asked me what he should do.

"I have thought about that conversation many times. I believe Roberto could have been almost anything, but God gave him a gift that few have, and he chose to use that gift. I remember that on that day I told him, 'This is your chance, Roberto. We are poor people in this town. This is your chance to do something. But if in your heart you prefer not to try, then, Roberto, that will be your problem—and your decision.'"

There was and there always remained a closeness between this boy-soon-to-be-a-man and his favorite teacher.

"Once, a few years ago, I was sick with a very bad back. Roberto, not knowing this, had driven over from Rio Piedras, where his house was, to see me."

"Where is the teacher?" Roberto asked Mrs. Casares' stepdaughter that afternoon.

"Teacher is sick, Roberto. She is in bed."

"Teacher," Roberto said, pounding on the bedroom door "get up and put on your clothes. We are going to the doctor whether you want to or not."

"I got dressed," Mrs. Casares told me, "and he picked me up like a baby and carried me in his arms to the car. He came every day for fifteen days, and most days he had to carry me, but I went to the doctor and he treated me. Afterward, I said to the doctor that I wanted to pay the bill.

**12** "'Mrs. Casares', he told me, 'please don't start with that Clemente, or he will kill me. He has paid all your bills, and don't you dare tell him I have told you.'

"Well, Roberto was like that. We had been so close. You know, I think I was there the day he met Vera, the girl he later married. She was one of my students, too. I was working part-time in the pharmacy and he

was already a baseball player by then, and one day Vera came into the store.

"'Teacher,' Roberto asked me, 'who is that girl?'

"'That's one of my students,' I told him. 'Now don't you dare bother her. Go out and get someone to introduce you. Behave yourself.'

"He was so proper, you know. That's just what he did, and that's how he met her, and they were married here in Carolina in the big church on the square."

On the night Roberto Clemente's plane disappeared, Mrs. Casares was at home, and a delivery boy from the pharmacy stopped by and told her to turn on the radio and sit down. "I think something has happened to someone who is very close with you, Teacher, and I want to be here in case you need help."

María Isabella Casares heard the news. She is a brave woman, and months later, standing in front of the empty crypt in the cemetery at Carolina where Roberto Clemente was to have been buried, she said, "He was like a son to me. This is why I want to tell you about him. This is why you must make people—particularly our people, our Puerto Rican children—understand what he was. He was like my son, and he is all our sons in a way. We must make sure that the children never forget how beautiful a man he was."

**13** The next person to touch Roberto Clemente was Pedron Zarrilla, who owned the Santurce club. He was the man who discovered Clemente on the country softball team, and he was the man who signed him for a four-hundred-dollar bonus.

"He was a skinny kid," Pedron Zarrilla recalls, "but even then he had those large, powerful hands, which we all noticed right away. He joined us, and he was nervous. But I watched him, and I said to myself, 'this kid can throw and this kid can run, and this kid

*Roberto Clemente: A Bittersweet Memoir* **397**

**12 Literary Focus** What characteristics of Clemente does Mrs. Casares highlight in this anecdote?

**13 Literary Focus** Why do you think Izenberg chose to interview Zarrilla about Clemente?

In "Roberto Clemente: A Bittersweet Memoir," Izenberg captures the natural speech of the people he interviewed—what they said and how they said it—by using dashes.

**Student Activity 1.** Locate three more examples of the use of dashes in the selection. Explain why dashes work well in the examples you found.

**Student Activity 2.** Write a short description of someone you know who has made an important achievement. Use dashes in your description.

**Electronic Handbook** You may want students to review sentence fragments before completing the Grammar in Action activities. If students have access to the Language Master 6000, have them enter the access word *fragment* and press the GRAMMAR key to get information on sentence fragments.

**14 Clarification** Point out that because of the physical demands of
sports, an athlete usually retires
earlier than people in other fields
and takes up some other occupation.

**15 Discussion** What does Zarrilla
mean when he says he knew they
were going to lose Clemente?

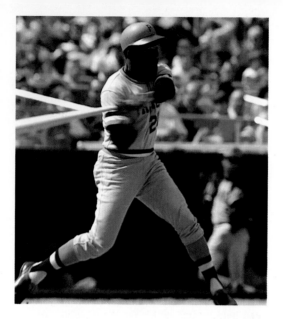

can hit. We will be patient with him.' The
season had been through several games before I finally sent him in to play.''

14 | Luis Olmo remembers that game. Luis
Olmo had been a major-league outfielder
with the Brooklyn Dodgers. He had been a
splendid ballplayer. Today he is in the insurance business in San Juan. He sat in his
office and recalled very well that first moment when Roberto Clemente stepped up to
bat.

"I was managing the other team. They
had a man on base and this skinny kid
comes out. Well, we had never seen him, so
we didn't really know how to pitch to him. I
decided to throw him a few bad balls and see
if he'd bite.

"He hit the first pitch. It was an outside
fast ball, and he never should have been
able to reach it. But he hit it down the
line for a double. He was the best bad-ball hitter I have ever seen, and if you ask major-
league pitchers who are pitching today,
they will tell you the same thing. After a
while it got so that I just told my pitchers

to throw the ball down the middle because
he was going to hit it no matter where
they put it, and at least if he decided not to
swing, we'd have a strike on him.

"I played in the big leagues. I know what
I am saying. He was the greatest we ever
had . . . maybe one of the greatest anyone
ever had. Why did he have to die?"

Once Pedron Zarrilla turned him loose,
there was no stopping Roberto Clemente. As
Clemente's confidence grew, he began to get
better and better. He was the one the crowds
came to see out at Sixto Escobar Stadium.

"You know, when Clemente was in the
lineup," Pedron Zarrilla says, "there was
always this undercurrent of excitement in
the ball park. You knew that if he was
coming to bat, he would do something spectacular. You knew that if he was on first
base, he was going to try to get to second
base. You knew that if he was playing right
field and there was a man on third base,
then that man on third base already knew
what a lot of men on third base in the majors
were going to find out—you don't try to get
home against Roberto Clemente's arm."

"I remember the year that Willie Mays
came down here to play in the same outfield
with him for the winter season. I remember
the wonderful things they did and I remember that Roberto still had the best of it.

"Sure I knew we were going to lose him. I
knew it was just a matter of time. But I was | 15
only grateful that we could have him if only
for that little time."

The major-league scouts began to make
their moves. Olmo was then scouting, and
he tried to sign him for the Giants. But it was
the Dodgers who won the bidding war. The
Dodgers had Clemente, but in having him,
they had a major problem. He had to be
hidden.

This part takes a little explaining. Under
the complicated draft rules that baseball
used at that time, if the Dodgers were not

prepared to bring Clemente up to their major-league team within a year (and because they were winning with proven players, they couldn't), then Clemente could be claimed by another team.

They sent him to Montreal with instructions to the manager to use him as little as possible, to hide him as much as possible, and to tell everyone he had a sore back, a sore arm, or any other excuse the manager could give. But how do you hide a diamond when he's in the middle of a field of broken soda bottles?

In the playoffs that year against Syracuse, they had to use Clemente. He hit two doubles and a home run and threw a man out at home the very first try.

The Pittsburgh Pirates had a man who saw it all. They drafted him at the season's end.

And so Roberto Clemente came to Pittsburgh. He was the finest prospect the club had had in a long, long time. But the Pirates of those days were spectacular losers, and even Roberto Clemente couldn't turn them around overnight.

"We were bad, all right," recalls Bob Friend, who later became a great Pirate pitcher. "We lost over a hundred games, and it certainly wasn't fun to go to the ball park under those conditions. You couldn't blame the fans for being noisy and impatient. Branch Rickey, our general manager, had promised a winner. He called it his five-year plan. Actually, it took ten."

When Clemente joined the club, it was Friend who made it his business to try to make him feel at home. Roberto was, in truth, a moody man, and the previous season hadn't helped him any.

"I will never forget how fast he became a superstar in this town," says Bob Friend. "Later he would have troubles because he was either hurt or thought he was hurt, and some people would say that he was loafing.

But I know he gave it his best shot and he helped make us winners."

The first winning year was 1960, when the Pirates won the pennant and went on to beat the Yankees in the seventh game of the World Series. Whitey Ford, who pitched against him twice in that Series, recalls that Roberto actually made himself look bad on an outside pitch to encourage Whitey to come back with it. "I did," Ford recalls, "and he unloaded. Another thing I remember is the way he ran out a routine ground ball in the last game, and when we were a little slow covering, he beat it out. It was something most people forget, but it made the Pirates' victory possible."

The season was over. Roberto Clemente had hit safely in every World Series game. He had batted over .300. He had been a superstar. But when they announced the Most Valuable Player Award voting, Roberto had finished a distant third.

"I really don't think he resented the fact that he didn't win it," Bob Friend says. "What hurt—and in this he was right—was how few votes he got. He felt that he simply wasn't being accepted. He brooded about that a lot. I think his attitude became one of 'Well, I'm going to show them from now on so that they will never forget.'

"And you know, he sure did."

Roberto Clemente went home and married Vera. He felt less alone. Now he could go on and prove what it was he had to prove. And he was determined to prove it.

"I know he was driven by thoughts like that," explains Buck Canel, a newspaper writer who covers all sports for most of the hemisphere's Spanish-language papers. "He would talk with me often about his feelings. You know, Clemente felt strongly about the fact that he was a Puerto Rican and that he was a black man. In each of these things he had pride.

"On the other hand, because of the early

*Roberto Clemente: A Bittersweet Memoir* 399

16 **Critical Thinking and Reading** Have students paraphrase this statement. What does it mean?

17 **Reading Strategy** Have students summarize the events leading up to Clemente's joining the Pittsburgh Pirates.

18 **Discussion** Discuss what this tells you about Clemente's character.

19 **Discussion** What kind of difficulties might Roberto face as a Puerto Rican and a black man in major league baseball in the United States?

21 **Reading Strategy** Have students summarize Clemente's major achievements as a baseball player.

22 **Discussion** An ideal in ancient Greece was for a young hero to die at the height of his powers. Why? Ask students their opinions about the ideal of dying before one's "powers" begin to fade. What other abilities in an older person can take the place of youthful powers?

23 **Discussion** Roberto Clemente was a national hero and role model for the people of Puerto Rico. What are other examples of national heroes?

**Reader's Response** In your eyes was Roberto Clemente a hero? Explain.

**Thematic Response** Ask students to consider how Roberto Clemente was influenced by his environment. Do they think he did what he did because of the people who had shaped his early life? Was he influenced by the values of the Puerto Rican culture? The island? How was he affected by being a celebrity baseball player? Have them conjecture what kind of person he might have been had he not become a star.

## Closure and Extension

### ANSWERS TO RESPONDING TO THE SELECTION
*Your Response*

1. Have students reflect on the different aspects of Clemente's personality that the author describes. They may comment on his generosity, his loyalty, his perseverance, his concern for the well-being of others. They may also remember that he is described as moody and that he was very selective about his friends. Some students may believe they would have been friends with him, and others may not.

400

language barriers, I am sure that there were times when he *thought* people were laughing at him when they were not. It is difficult for a Latin-American ballplayer to understand everything said around him when it is said at high speed, if he doesn't speak English that well. But, in any event, he wanted very much to prove to the world that he was a superstar and that he could do things that in his heart he felt he had already proven."

In later years, there would be people who would say that Roberto was a hypochondriac (someone who *imagined* he was sick or hurt when he was not). They could have been right, but if they were, it made the things he did even more remarkable. Because I can testify that I saw him throw his body into outfield fences, teeth first, to make remarkable plays. If he thought he was hurt at the time, then the act was even more courageous.

20

His moment finally came. It took eleven years for the Pirates to win a World Series berth again, and when they did in 1971, it was Roberto Clemente who led the way. I will never forget him as he was during that 1971 series with the Orioles, a Series that the Pirates figured to lose, and in which they, in fact, dropped the first two games down in Baltimore.

When they got back to Pittsburgh for the middle slice of the tournament, Roberto Clemente went to work and led this team. He was a superhero during the five games that followed. He was the big man in the Series. He was the MVP. He was everything he had ever dreamed of being on a ball field.

Most important of all, the entire country saw him do it on network television, and never again—even though nobody knew it would end so tragically soon—was anyone ever to doubt his ability.

The following year, Clemente ended the season by collecting his three thousandth

hit. Only ten other men had ever done that in the entire history of baseball.

"It was a funny thing about that hit," Willie Stargell, his closest friend on the Pirates, explains. "He had thought of taking himself out of the lineup and resting for the playoffs, but a couple of us convinced him that there had to be a time when a man had to do something for himself, so he went on and played and got it. I'm thankful that we convinced him, because, you know, as things turned out, that number three thousand was his last hit.

21

"When I think of Roberto now, I think of the kind of man he was. There was nothing phony about him. He had his own ideas about how life should be lived, and if you didn't see it that way, then he let you know in so many ways, without words, that it was best you each go your separate ways.

"He was a man who chose his friends carefully. His was a friendship worth having. I don't think many people took the time and the trouble to try to understand him, and I'll admit it wasn't easy. But he was worth it.

"The way he died, you know, I mean on that plane carrying supplies to Nicaraguans who'd been dying in that earthquake, well, I wasn't surprised he'd go out and do something like that. I wasn't surprised he'd go. I just never thought what happened could happen to him.

"But I know this. He lived a full life. And if he knew at that moment what the Lord had decided, well, I really believe he would have said, 'I'm ready.'"

22

He was thirty-eight years old when he died. He touched the hearts of Puerto Rico in a way that few people ever could. He touched a lot of other hearts, too. He touched hearts that beat inside people of all colors of skin.

23

He was one of the proudest of The Proud People.

*Recalling*

2. María Casares was Clemente's teacher and the person to whom he went for guidance. Pedron Zarrilla was the owner of the Santurce ball club who asked Clemente to join.
3. Luis Vigereaux enlisted Clemente's aid to encourage people to donate help to the Nicaraguans. Clemente was flying supplies to Nicaragua when he died.
4. Clemente's friends remember most that he was a man of principle, determination, pride, and true friendship.

*Interpreting*

5. Clemente revealed that he was a kind, generous, and caring friend.
6. This piece is called a "bittersweet memoir" because it highlights Clemente's giving personality and admirable achievements and also describes the tragedy of his death.

*Applying*

7. Answers will differ. Suggested Response: Clemente is a model or

inspiration to others in that he strove to achieve renown; once he achieved it, he was caring toward others and courageous.

### ANSWERS TO ANALYZING LITERATURE

1. The writer interviewed Luis Vigereaux, a television personality; Rudy Hernandez, a teammate; María Casares, a former teacher; Pedron Zarrilla, who discovered and signed up Clemente in the Santurce club;

# RESPONDING TO THE SELECTION

## Your Response

1. If you had met Roberto Clemente, do you think you would have been friends with him? Why or why not?

## Recalling

2. What roles did María Casares and Pedron Zarrilla play in Clemente's childhood?
3. Why did Luis Vigereaux try to enlist Clemente's aid? How was Clemente trying to help when he died?
4. What do Roberto Clemente's friends remember most about him?

## Interpreting

5. What did Clemente reveal about himself in the way that he treated Mrs. Casares when she was ill?
6. Why is this called a "bittersweet memoir"?

## Applying

7. How is Clemente a model for others?

# ANALYZING LITERATURE

## Understanding the Memoir

A **memoir,** or biographical piece often written by a relative or personal friend of the subject, can be about a well-known person or about someone important to the writer. A memoir can be one person's recollection or can be based on interviews with and anecdotes from several people.

An interview is a planned meeting at which writers obtain information about a topic from someone knowledgeable about it. Anecdotes are brief stories about noteworthy incidents.

1. List the people the writer interviewed.
2. What two anecdotes did María Casares tell about Roberto that no one else could tell?

# CRITICAL THINKING AND READING

## Identifying Primary Sources

A **primary source** is the original or direct source. For example, the wife of a famous ballplayer would be a primary source of information about him. A **secondary source** is one that is based on primary sources. For example, a writer who has interviewed the friends of a famous ballplayer would be a secondary source.

Which of the following could give you primary-source information about Clemente?

1. María Casares
2. Jerry Izenberg
3. Rudy Hernandez

# THINKING AND WRITING

## Writing a Memoir

Write a memoir of someone you know well, based on your own knowledge of him or her. First freewrite about that person, including details about his or her appearance or behavior. Include anecdotes that help reveal this person's character. Then use this information in your writing. Revise your memoir, making sure you have created a vivid portrait. Proofread your writing and share it with your classmates.

# LEARNING OPTIONS

1. **Speaking and Listening.** Interview one of your classmates to learn about a person he or she knows personally. Make a list of questions to ask your classmate that would help you get to know more about this person. Ask your classmate to tell you anecdotes he or she knows about the person's life.
2. **Cross-curricular Connection.** Select a sports figure who is known to have made a great contribution to society beyond the world of athletics. Research the athlete's life and report to your classmates the ways in which this person has become a positive role model.

*Roberto Clemente: A Bittersweet Memoir*   **401**

 **Writing Transparency**
Graphic organizers are helpful tools for organizing one's thoughts before writing. Have students brainstorm ideas for their memoirs using the Cluster Map in **Transparencies for Writing.**

**Alternative Assessment** *Peer Review:* In pairs or groups of four, have students assess one another's work by responding to the following questions:

    About whom does the writer choose to write a memoir?

    What traits and characteristics of the person does the writer present to show the special nature of the person?

    What specific details and anecdotes does the writer include to illustrate these traits and characteristics? What would you suggest the writer add to make the account more vivid for the reader?

    What concrete suggestions do you have to improve the organization and language mechanics of the memoir?

    To validate the peer review, have students revise their work, incorporating those suggestions they believe will enhance their final product.

**Publishing Student Writing**
Students might enjoy reading one another's memoirs. Consider breaking them into small groups in which they can read their essays aloud.

## LEARNING OPTIONS

1. This activity will appeal to students who enjoy social interaction and oral activities. Students may wish to record the interviews they conduct and to summarize on audiotape what they have learned from their interviews about the person.
2. Encourage students who like to do research to choose this activity. Remind them that they will find information not only in books, but also in newspapers and magazines. Such articles will have journalists' up-to-the-minute responses to the athletes the students are researching.

---

Luis Olmo, an outfielder with the Brooklyn Dodgers; Bob Friend, a Pittsburgh Pirates teammate; Whitey Ford, a Yankee baseball player; Buck Canel, a newspaper sportswriter; and Willie Stargell, Clemente's closest friend on the Pittsburgh Pirates.

2. María Casares told one anecdote about Clemente asking her for advice about joining the Santurce baseball club and one about Clemente getting proper care for her when she was sick.

### ANSWERS TO CRITICAL THINKING AND READING

Those who could give primary-source information about Clemente are María Casares, Manny Sanguillen, and Rudy Hernandez.

**Challenge** If Izenberg had used old newspaper stories for information on Clemente, would he have been using primary or secondary sources?

### THINKING AND WRITING

◆ **Software** If students are working on computers, have them write their memoirs using the word processor. Students who need additional help might use the **Bank Street Writer** activity *Describing a Real-Life Character* to help them write their memoirs.

**More About the Author** Maya Angelou writes about an experience from her own childhood. Discuss the pros and cons of writing about a childhood experience from the vantage point of an adult years later.

Angelou is also a teacher and a poet. In January 1993, she read her poem "On the Pulse of Morning" at the inauguration of President Bill Clinton. Have students consider how writing as a poet might affect one's view of personal events.

**Literary Focus** Have students discuss why a person might write his or her autobiography.

**Prereading Focus** To get students started, write the names of some sports stars, historical figures, and actors on the chalkboard. Have students select one person and write the main thing they would like to learn from this person. Then briefly discuss students' choices. Have students keep these ideas in mind as they read what young Maya learned from Mrs. Flowers.

**Vocabulary** Have your less advanced students use these words in sentences, so you can be sure they understand their meaning.

**Electronic Handbook** If you have access to the Language Master 6000, you may have students listen to the pronunciations of *taut, voile,* and *benign.*

**Spelling Tip** *Taut* is one of a group of words in which the *au* sounds like the *a* in ball. Other words in this group include *haul, maul, Paul,* and *Saul. Taut* should not be confused with its homophone *taught.*

# GUIDE FOR READING

### Maya Angelou

(1928–      ) was born Marguerite Johnson in St. Louis, Missouri. She and her older brother Bailey were raised by their grandmother, who owned a country store in Stamps, Arkansas. Angelou later became a journalist, a civil rights worker, and an author. In *I Know Why the Caged Bird Sings,* the first of four books of autobiography, she vividly recalls a woman from her childhood who influenced her life.

## *from* I Know Why the Caged Bird Sings

### Autobiography

An **autobiography** is a person's own account of his or her life. Usually in an autobiography, a writer uses the first-person pronoun "I" to write about his or her experiences. You experience the writer's story through his or her eyes—knowing not only what he or she observes and recalls, but also what he or she thinks and feels about the experience. Unlike biography, autobiography provides you with information about the subject from the subject.

### Focus

In this excerpt, Maya Angelou recalls the excitement of getting to know a person she admired. Imagine that you get to know someone you admire. Who would this person be? A sports star? A historical figure? A famous actor? Make a list of things that you would like to learn from this person. Then list the ways in which your life would change as a result of knowing him or her. As you read the selection, note how the narrator is changed by her encounter with Mrs. Flowers.

### Vocabulary

Knowing the following words will help you as you read this excerpt from *I Know Why the Caged Bird Sings.*

**fiscal** (fis′ kəl) *adj.*: Having to do with finances (p. 403)

**troubadours** (troo′ bə dôrz′) *n.*: Traveling singers, usually accompanying themselves on stringed instruments (p. 403)

**taut** (tôt) *adj.*: Tightly stretched (p. 405)

**voile** (voil) *n.*: A light cotton fabric (p. 405)

**benign** (bi nīn′) *adj.*: Kindly (p. 406)

**infuse** (in fyooz′) *v.*: To put into (p. 406)

**couched** (koucht) *v.*: Put into words; expressed (p. 407)

**wormwood** (wurm′ wood′) *n.*: A plant that produces a bitter oil (p. 408)

### Objectives

1  To understand autobiography
2  To infer the author's purpose
3  To write an autobiographical sketch
4  To express individual interests and abilities through optional activities

## Support Material

**Teaching Portfolio**
Teacher Backup, p. 465
Grammar in Action Worksheet, *Using Vivid Adjectives,* p. 468
Usage and Mechanics Worksheet, p. 470
Vocabulary Check, p. 471
Critical Thinking and Reading Worksheet, *Inferring the Author's Purpose,* p. 472

Language Worksheet, *Choosing the Meaning That Fits the Context,* p. 473
Selection Test, p. 474

**Library of Video Classics**
*I Know Why the Caged Bird Sings*

**Prentice Hall Literature Writing Studio**

# from I Know Why the Caged Bird Sings

## Maya Angelou

1 We lived with our grandmother and uncle in the rear of the Store (it was always spoken of with a capital s), which she had owned some twenty-five years.

Early in the century, Momma (we soon stopped calling her Grandmother) sold lunches to the sawmen in the lumberyard (east Stamps) and the seedmen at the cotton gin (west Stamps). Her crisp meat pies and cool lemonade, when joined to her miraculous ability to be in two places at the same time, assured her business success. From being a mobile lunch counter, she set up a stand between the two points of fiscal interest and supplied the workers' needs for a few years. Then she had the Store built in the heart of the Negro area. Over the years it became the lay center of activities in town. On Saturdays, barbers sat their customers in the shade on the porch of the Store, and troubadours on their ceaseless crawlings through the South leaned across its benches and sang their sad songs of The Brazos[1] while they played juice harps[2] and cigar-box guitars.

The formal name of the Store was the Wm. Johnson General Merchandise Store.

2 Customers could find food staples, a good variety of colored thread, mash[3] for hogs, corn for chickens, coal oil for lamps, light bulbs for the wealthy, shoestrings, hair dressing, balloons, and flower seeds. Anything not visible had only to be ordered.

Until we became familiar enough to belong to the Store and it to us, we were locked up in a Fun House of Things where the attendant had gone home for life. . . .

3 Weighing the half-pounds of flour, excluding the scoop, and depositing them dust-free into the thin paper sacks held a simple kind of adventure for me. I developed an eye for measuring how full a silver-looking ladle of flour, mash, meal, sugar or corn had to be to push the scale indicator over to eight ounces or one pound. When I was absolutely accurate our appreciative customers used to admire: "Sister Henderson sure got some smart grandchildrens." If I was off in the Store's favor, the eagle-eyed women would say, "Put some more in that sack, child. Don't you try to make your profit offa me."

---

1. **The Brazos** (brăz′ əs): An area in central Texas near the Brazos River.
2. **juice** (jew's) **harps:** Small musical instruments held between the teeth and played by plucking.

---

3. **mash** n.: A moist grain mixture fed to farm animals.

from *I Know Why the Caged Bird Sings* 403

## Presentation

**Motivation/Prior Knowledge** Ask students if they can think of a time when someone special to them did something nice for them. How did they feel? Maya Angelou writes about a similar incident in her life.

**Making Connections** Another selection that deals with the theme of a gift of personal attention is "Thank You, M'am" on page 179.

**Purpose-Setting Question** What effect does the kindness and attention of Mrs. Flowers have on Marguerite?

**Master Teacher Note** The title *I Know Why the Caged Bird Sings* is a line from the poem "Sympathy" by Paul Laurence Dunbar, who sympathizes with the caged bird who sings out of misery to be free. In this selection, the writer describes an experience that helped free her of her feelings of inferiority.

1 **Discussion** Why do you think the Store "was always spoken of with a capital s"?

2 **Discussion** How does "light bulbs for the wealthy" contrast with the other items mentioned? What do these items tell you about the lives of these customers?

3 **Literary Focus** A writer of an autobiography speaks in the first person. Angelou also uses "we" in the first paragraph. What effect does this have?

**Thematic Focus** Finding one's place in the world is a gradual process. Ask students to consider who has helped them to see who they are and how they fit into their community.

**4 Literary Focus** Throughout an autobiography, the writer describes thoughts and feelings as well as facts. What thoughts and feelings does Angelou express here?

**5 Discussion** The writer compares the Store to an unopened present. Why? She also compares it to a person who is tired. Why?

**ESL Strategy** Your ESL students may be unfamiliar with some of the foods mentioned in the selection. Students should use context clues to help determine meanings. "Silver-wrapped kisses" are defined as chocolate drops in the same sentence, for example. Have students find information in the context about how pineapple upside-down cakes are made as well.

Then I would quietly but persistently punish myself. For every bad judgment, the fine was no silver-wrapped kisses, the sweet chocolate drops that I loved more than anything in the world, except Bailey. And maybe canned pineapples. My obsession with pineapples nearly drove me mad. I dreamt of the days when I would be grown and able to buy a whole carton for myself alone.

Although the syrupy golden rings sat in their exotic cans on our shelves year round, we only tasted them during Christmas. Momma used the juice to make almost-black fruit cakes. Then she lined heavy soot-encrusted iron skillets with the pineapple rings for rich upside-down cakes. Bailey and I received one slice each, and I carried mine around for hours, shredding off the fruit until nothing was left except the perfume on my fingers. I'd like to think that my desire for pineapples was so sacred that I wouldn't allow myself to steal a can (which was possible) and eat it alone out in the garden, but I'm certain that I must have weighed the possibility of the scent exposing me and didn't have the nerve to attempt it.

Until I was thirteen and left Arkansas for good, the Store was my favorite place to be. Alone and empty in the mornings, it looked like an unopened present from a stranger. Opening the front doors was pulling the ribbon off the unexpected gift. The light would come in softly (we faced north), easing itself over the shelves of mackerel, salmon, tobacco, thread. It fell flat on the big vat of lard and by noontime during the summer the grease had softened to a thick soup. Whenever I walked into the Store in the afternoon, I sensed that it

## Grammar in Action

Sentences come alive when the writer uses **vivid adjectives** to enhance the meaning. Adjectives describe nouns and pronouns, and without them, language would be dull and uninteresting. The best writers use specific words to call an image to the reader's mind. Look at the following sentences from *I Know Why the Caged Bird Sings:*

Although the *syrupy golden* rings sat in their *exotic* cans on our shelves year round, we only tasted them during Christmas. Momma used the juice to make *almost-black* fruit cakes. Then she lined *heavy soot-encrusted* iron skillets with the pineapple rings for *rich* upside-down cakes.

. . . She was *thin* without the *taut* look of *wiry* people, and her *printed voile* dresses and *flowered* hats were as right for her as *denim* overalls for a farmer.

Her skin was a *rich black* that would have peeled like a plum if snagged, . . .

**SYMBOLS**
*Benny Andrew*
*Museum of Art, Wichita State University*

6

was tired. I alone could hear the slow pulse of its job half done. But just before bedtime, after numerous people had walked in and out, had argued over their bills, or joked about their neighbors, or just dropped in "to give Sister Henderson a 'Hi y'all,'" the promise of magic mornings returned to the Store and spread itself over the family in washed life waves. . . .

*When Maya was about ten years old, she returned to Stamps from a visit to St. Louis with her mother. She had become depressed and withdrawn.*

For nearly a year, I sopped around the house, the Store, the school and the church, like an old biscuit, dirty and inedible. Then I met, or rather got to know, the lady who threw me my first lifeline.

Mrs. Bertha Flowers was the aristocrat[4] of Black Stamps. She had the grace of control to appear warm in the coldest weather, and on the Arkansas summer days it seemed she had a private breeze which swirled around, cooling her. She was thin without the taut look of wiry people, and her printed voile dresses and flowered hats were as right for her as denim overalls for a farmer. She was our side's answer to the richest white woman in town.

Her skin was a rich black that would have peeled like a plum if snagged, but then no one would have thought of getting close enough to Mrs. Flowers to ruffle her dress, let alone snag her skin. She didn't encourage familiarity. She wore gloves too.

---
**4. aristocrat** (ə ris′ tə krat) *n.*: A person belonging to the upper class.

from *I Know Why the Caged Bird Sings*   405

**6 Clarification** "Sister" can mean any woman, often used colloquially as a familiar term of address.

## Humanities Note

Fine art, *Symbols,* by Benny Andrews. The African American artist and educator Benny Andrews was born in Georgia in 1930. From a very early age he knew he wanted to be an artist. Through hard work and a well-deserved scholarship, Andrews was able to attend the Art Institute of Chicago. His unique style is a combination of painting and collage.

*Symbols* (1971) is a monumental painting that measures thirty-six feet long. Andrews fills this canvas with symbols of the daily struggles of African Americans in our society. In creating this composition, Andrews drew upon his own life experience as well as the reality of our times. His insight and creativity make *Symbols* an important contribution to contemporary American art. The works of Benny Andrews are in many prestigious collections, including that of the Museum of Modern Art.

You might want to use the following questions to discuss the art:
1. Why do you think Andrews chose to make *Symbols* so large?
2. What do you suppose the tree in the center, filled with children, symbolizes?
3. Choose another symbol from this painting and discuss your ideas about it.

One *summer* afternoon, *sweet-milk* fresh in my memory, . . .

She smiled that *slow dragging* smile . . .

Notice how clear and precise each of the above adjectives is. It is quite easy to picture "syrupy golden rings," "almost-black fruitcakes," and "heavy soot-encrusted iron skillets."

**Student Activity 1.** Rewrite each of the example sentences substituting your own descriptive words. Try to keep your sentence structure as close to the writer's as possible, but you may change the meaning of each sentence.

**Student Activity 2.** Write a description of a person. Use vivid adjectives to make this person come alive for readers.

**Electronic Handbook** You might want students to review adjectives before completing the Grammar in Action activities. If students have access to the Language Master 6000, have them enter *adjectives* and press the GRAMMAR key.

**7 Literary Focus** What does this assessment of Mrs. Flowers tell you about her character?

**8 Discussion** Mrs. Flowers says that speaking words gives them deeper meaning. Do you agree with these statements about words?

**9 Discussion** What attitude is Mrs. Flowers trying to instill in Marguerite about property?

**10 Literary Focus** An autobiography includes a description of the writer's thoughts and feelings as well as facts.

I don't think I ever saw Mrs. Flowers laugh, but she smiled often. A slow widening of her thin black lips to show even, small white teeth, then the slow effortless closing. When she chose to smile on me, I always wanted to thank her. The action was so graceful and inclusively benign.

**7** She was one of the few gentlewomen I have ever known, and has remained throughout my life the measure of what a human being can be. . . .

One summer afternoon, sweet-milk fresh in my memory, she stopped at the Store to buy provisions. Another Negro woman of her health and age would have been expected to carry the paper sacks home in one hand, but Momma said, "Sister Flowers, I'll send Bailey up to your house with these things."

She smiled that slow dragging smile, "Thank you, Mrs. Henderson. I'd prefer Marguerite, though." My name was beautiful when she said it. "I've been meaning to talk to her, anyway." They gave each other age-group looks.

Momma said, "Well, that's all right then. Sister, go and change your dress. You going to Sister Flowers's. . . ."

There was a little path beside the rocky road, and Mrs. Flowers walked in front swinging her arms and picking her way over the stones.

She said, without turning her head, to me, "I hear you're doing very good school work, Marguerite, but that it's all written. The teachers report that they have trouble getting you to talk in class." We passed the triangular farm on our left and the path widened to allow us to walk together. I hung back in the separate unasked and unanswerable questions.

"Come and walk along with me, Marguerite." I couldn't have refused even if I wanted to. She pronounced my name so nicely. Or more correctly, she spoke each word with such clarity that I was certain a foreigner who didn't understand English could have understood her.

"Now no one is going to make you talk —possibly no one can. But bear in mind, language is man's way of communicating with his fellow man and it is language alone which separates him from the lower animals." That was a totally new idea to me, and I would need time to think about it.

"Your grandmother says you read a lot. Every chance you get. That's good, but not **8** good enough. Words mean more than what is set down on paper. It takes the human voice to infuse them with the shades of deeper meaning."

I memorized the part about the human voice infusing words. It seemed so valid and poetic.

She said she was going to give me some books and that I not only must read them, I must read them aloud. She suggested that I try to make a sentence sound in as many different ways as possible.

"I'll accept no excuse if you return a book to me that has been badly handled." **9** My imagination boggled at the punishment I would deserve if in fact I did abuse a book of Mrs. Flowers'. Death would be too kind and brief.

The odors in the house surprised me. **10** Somehow I had never connected Mrs. Flowers with food or eating or any other common experience of common people. There must have been an outhouse, too, but my mind never recorded it.

The sweet scent of vanilla had met us as she opened the door.

"I made tea cookies this morning. You

see, I had planned to invite you for cookies and lemonade so we could have this little chat. The lemonade is in the icebox.''

It followed that Mrs. Flowers would have ice on an ordinary day, when most families in our town bought ice late on Saturdays only a few times during the summer to be used in the wooden ice cream freezers.

She took the bags from me and disappeared through the kitchen door. I looked around the room that I had never in my wildest fantasies imagined I would see. Browned photographs leered or threatened from the walls and the white, freshly done curtains pushed against themselves and against the wind. I wanted to gobble up the room entire and take it to Bailey, who would help me analyze and enjoy it.

"Have a seat, Marguerite. Over there by the table." She carried a platter covered with a tea towel. Although she warned that she hadn't tried her hand at baking sweets for some time, I was certain that like everything else about her the cookies would be perfect.

They were flat round wafers, slightly browned on the edges and butter-yellow in the center. With the cold lemonade they were sufficient for childhood's lifelong diet. Remembering my manners, I took nice little ladylike bites off the edges. She said she had made them expressly for me and that she had a few in the kitchen that I could take home to my brother. So I jammed one whole cake in my mouth and the rough crumbs scratched the insides of my jaws, and if I hadn't had to swallow, it would have been a dream come true.

As I ate she began the first of what we later called "my lessons in living." She said that I must always be intolerant of ignorance but understanding of illiteracy. That some people, unable to go to school, were more educated and even more intelligent than college professors. She encouraged me to listen carefully to what country people called mother wit. That in those homely sayings was couched the collective wisdom of generations.

When I finished the cookies she brushed off the table and brought a thick, small book from the bookcase. I had read *A Tale of Two Cities* and found it up to my standards as a romantic novel. She opened the first page and I heard poetry for the first time in my life.

"It was the best of times and the worst of times . . ." Her voice slid in and curved down through and over the words. She was nearly singing. I wanted to look at the pages. Were they the same that I had read? Or were there notes, music, lined on the pages, as in a hymn book? Her sounds began cascading gently. I knew from listening to a thousand preachers that she was nearing the end of her reading, and I hadn't really heard, heard to understand, a single word.

"How do you like that?"

It occurred to me that she expected a response. The sweet vanilla flavor was still on my tongue and her reading was a wonder in my ears. I had to speak.

I said, "Yes, ma'am." It was the least I could do, but it was the most also.

"There's one more thing. Take this book of poems and memorize one for me. Next time you pay me a visit, I want you to recite."

I have tried often to search behind the sophistication of years for the enchantment I so easily found in those gifts. The essence escapes but its aura[5] remains. To be allowed, no, invited, into the private lives of strangers, and to share their joys and fears,

---

**5. aura** (ôr′ ə) *n*.: An atmosphere or quality.

11 **Discussion** The writer mentions an icebox instead of a refrigerator. What other examples can you find of life during this time period of the 1930's?

12 **Discussion** What advice does Mrs. Flowers give Marguerite? What do these statements tell you about the character of Mrs. Bertha Flowers? Do you agree with these statements?

**Videocassette** After students have read this excerpt, show the **Library of Video Classics** film *I Know Why the Caged Bird Sings*. Students will be familiar with the characters, the location, and one of the central incidents. They can compare and contrast the film rendering with the written text.

**Cooperative Learning** Food items related to the South appear throughout the selection. Have students work in small groups to compile a collection of Southern recipes. Each person in the group should find at least three recipes. All the recipes can be placed in a binder. Students in the group may try some of the recipes and share the foods with the class.

**Discussion** What do you think is the reason that Mrs. Flowers paid special attention to Marguerite?

**14** **Reading Strategy** Have students summarize the episode with Mrs. Flowers. Why was it so significant to Marguerite?

**Reader's Response** Angelou writes, "Childhood's logic never asks to be proved (all conclusions are absolute)." "Describe a "conclusion" from your childhood.

**Thematic Response** Through her friendship with Mrs. Flowers, the narrator comes to understand her own worth and develops a sense of belonging in her community. Ask students if any friendship has brought them a more positive sense of self? In what way did the friendship enrich their feeling of "fitting in"?

---

was a chance to exchange the Southern bitter wormwood for a cup of mead with Beowulf[6] or a hot cup of tea and milk with Oliver Twist. When I said aloud, "It is a far far better thing that I do, than I have ever done . . ."[7] tears of love filled my eyes at my selflessness.

On that first day, I ran down the hill and into the road (few cars ever came along it)

---

**6. Beowulf** (bā′ ə woolf′): The hero of an old Anglo-Saxon epic. People in this poem drink mead, (mĕd), a drink made with honey and water.

**7. "It is . . . than I have ever done"**: A speech from *A Tale of Two Cities* by Charles Dickens.

---

and had the good sense to stop running before I reached the Store.

I was liked, and what a difference it made. I was respected not as Mrs. Henderson's grandchild or Bailey's sister but for just being Marguerite Johnson.

Childhood's logic never asks to be proved (all conclusions are absolute). I didn't question why Mrs. Flowers had singled me out for attention, nor did it occur to me that Momma might have asked her to give me a little talking to. All I cared about was that she had made tea cookies for *me* and read to *me* from her favorite book. It was enough to prove that she liked me.

**13**

**14**

---

## RESPONDING TO THE SELECTION

### Your Response
1. Do you think that you would have liked helping out in the Store? Why or why not?
2. Does Mrs. Flowers remind you of anyone you know or have known? Explain your answer.

### Recalling
3. According to Mrs. Flowers, for what two reasons is language so important?
4. Although Marguerite reads a great deal, what does she *not* do? According to Mrs. Flowers, why is reading a great deal not enough?
5. What does Mrs. Flowers tell Marguerite as the first of her "lessons in living"?

6. What does Mrs. Flowers's making cookies and reading to Marguerite prove to Marguerite?

### Interpreting
7. The word *sopped* means "to have been wet, like a piece of bread soaked in gravy." What does the use of the word "sopped" tell you about how Marguerite feels about herself before meeting with Mrs. Flowers?
8. Why does Mrs. Flowers tell Marguerite to read aloud and in as many different ways as possible?
9. How do you think Marguerite changes as a result of her meetings with Mrs. Flowers?
10. Why has Mrs. Flowers remained "the measure of what a human being can be"?

---

## Closure and Extension

### ANSWERS TO RESPONDING TO THE SELECTION
*Your Response*
1. Urge students to focus on details, such as memorable items in the Store or the customers.
2. Have students point out the qualities of these people that remind them of Mrs. Flowers.

*Recalling*
3. Language is a person's way of communicating with other humans and language separates humans from the lower animals.

4. Marguerite does not speak much. Reading a great deal is not enough because "Words mean more than what is set down on paper. It takes the human voice to infuse them with the shades of deeper meaning."
5. As her first lesson in living, Mrs. Flowers tells Marguerite that she "must always be intolerant of ignorance but understanding of illiteracy. That some people, unable to go to school, were more

educated and even more intelligent than college professors," and that she should listen to "mother wit" for the "collective wisdom of generations."
6. It proves to Marguerite that Mrs. Flowers likes her.

*Interpreting*
7. The word *sopped,* implying soggy or used, tells you that Marguerite feels unhappy and negative about herself.

8. She wants Marguerite to read aloud to begin speaking more, and to read in as many different ways as possible to understand their deeper meaning.
9. Suggested Response: As a result of her meetings with Mrs. Flowers, Marguerite probably feels better about herself and speaks more.
10. Throughout Marguerite's life, Mrs. Flowers continued to be an example of graciousness and dignity in a human being.

11. Mrs. Flowers throws Marguerite a "lifeline" by inviting her to her house for lemonade and cookies and reading with her. In what other ways do people give others "lifelines"?

## ANALYZING LITERATURE

### Understanding Autobiography

An **autobiography** is the story of a person's life, written by that person. Through the writer's eyes, you see events unfold and come to understand his or her feelings and thoughts. The writer's view influences the telling of each incident. For example, Marguerite says, "I wanted to gobble up the room entire and take it to Bailey, who would help me analyze and enjoy it."

1. What does Marguerite tell you about the Store that only she could tell you?
2. What does Marguerite tell you about Mrs. Flowers that only she could tell you?

## CRITICAL THINKING AND READING

### Inferring the Author's Purpose

The autobiographer writes for a certain purpose, or reason. For example, authors may write autobiographies to entertain you, to preserve their memories, to inform you of their accomplishments, or for some other purpose. When you read, you usually infer, or draw conclusions about, the author's purpose. Of course, you can never get inside the author's mind, so your inference remains simply an intelligent guess.

Considering who the author is can help you infer his or her purpose. For example, a famous politician may want to emphasize in her autobiography that her policies improved people's lives.

Therefore she will emphasize those incidents from her career that highlight this favorable effect, rather than those incidents that point out her drawbacks.

1. Why do you think Maya Angelou wrote about Mrs. Flowers? Explain the reason for your answer.
2. How is the author's purpose evident? Explain the reason for your answer.

## THINKING AND WRITING

### Writing an Autobiographical Sketch

Choose an incident in your life that is important to you. First, freewrite about this incident. Then, using this information, write an autobiographical account of it. Use the first-person point of view. Revise your writing, making sure you have presented the information clearly. Proofread your autobiography and share it with your class.

## LEARNING OPTIONS

1. **Art.** Create a poster advertising the Wm. Johnson General Merchandise Store. Draw the Store as you think it might have looked. List the merchandise mentioned in the selection, with prices from the 1930's. You may need to do some research to find out the prices. Display your finished poster in the classroom.
2. **Speaking and Listening.** Mrs. Flowers says that the way in which words are spoken can help determine their meaning. Experiment with this idea by reading aloud a passage from the selection several times with a partner, changing the tone of your voice each time. See if you and your partner can detect different meanings in the same words spoken differently.

---

*Applying*

11. Answers will differ. Suggested Response: Other ways in which people can give others "lifelines" are spending time with them doing things that they like, making or giving them a present they like, or showing or telling them something helpful to them.

**ANSWERS TO ANALYZING LITERATURE**

1. Suggested Response: Marguerite

tells you that the Store was her favorite place to be; that the Store seemed tired in the afternoons; and that just before bedtime, the "promise of magic mornings" returned to the Store.
2. Marguerite tells you that when Mrs. Flowers smiled she wanted to thank her, since "the action was so graceful and inclusively benign," and that she was one of the few gentlewomen Marguerite has ever known.

**ANSWERS TO CRITICAL THINKING AND READING**

1. Suggested Response: Angelou probably wrote about Mrs. Flowers to explain a childhood experience that changed her life positively.
2. The author's purpose to explain is evident in the following passages:
a. the paragraph stating that she was depressed until she got to know "the lady who threw me my first lifeline." In this way you

expect that she is going to relate an incident to you.
b. the statement at the end of the incident saying "I was liked, and what a difference it made." In this way you know that the incident had a positive effect on Marguerite's life.

*THINKING AND WRITING*

**Software** If students are working on computers, have them use the **Writer's Helper** activity *Random Revelations* to generate ideas for their autobiographical sketch.

**Alternative Assessment** *Protocol:* Ask your students to assess their own work by responding to the following questions:

What is the specific incident about which you wrote?

What makes this incident important to you?

What specific details did you include? Why?

What made this assignment difficult for you?

What did you learn about yourself in writing about this important incident in your life?

You may have your students use the information gained from their protocols as a guide for revising their autobiographical sketches.

**Publishing Student Writing** You might prepare a class book of autobiographical sketches. Ask for volunteers to organize the sketches and put together the book.

*LEARNING OPTIONS*

Option 1 will appeal to artistic students. Reprints of department store catalogs, such as Sears and Roebuck, can be used as a source for 1930's prices.

Option 2 will appeal to kinesthetic learners who enjoy drama. You might expand this activity by having partners dramatize one passage of the selection for the class.

**More About the Author** Twain was strongly influenced by the Mississippi River while growing up. Discuss how the place in which an author lives can affect his or her writing.

**Literary Focus** Point out that, as in fiction, conflict in autobiography can be external or internal. Ask students for examples of external and internal conflicts.

**Prereading Focus** Have students discuss in small groups the types of conflicts that occur as part of school life. Remind students to consider internal as well as external conflicts and to keep in mind that the internal battles are often the most difficult to resolve. Have the groups share their lists. Then have the class make a chart that groups the types of conflicts and different strategies for resolving them. For example, students might say that honest, open communication is the best way to address interpersonal conflicts between peers or between parents and children or between teachers and students. They might say that making a decision chart is the best way to resolve an internal conflict about whether a student wants to take a very challenging course.

**Vocabulary** Students will benefit from hearing each of these words used in context. Include each word in a sentence and have students guess its meaning.

**Electronic Handbook** You may suggest that your students use the Language Master 6000 to hear the pronunciations of *furtive,* *intimation,* and *indulgent.*

# GUIDE FOR READING

## Cub Pilot on the Mississippi

### Conflict in Autobiography

In autobiographical accounts, writers often describe how they have dealt with **conflicts,** or struggles. The conflicts they describe may be external or internal. An **external conflict** is one that takes place between the writer and a person or a natural force. An **internal conflict** is one that exists in the writer's mind, such as the struggle to make a difficult decision or to overcome an overwhelming fear. The outcome of a conflict is called its resolution. In "Cub Pilot on the Mississippi," Twain tells of the conflicts he faced as an apprentice—a person learning a trade while working for a master craftsman.

### Focus

Sometimes a person with whom you must interact is so contrary and abusive that it is difficult, if not impossible, to accomplish your goals. What can you do when someone becomes impossible to deal with? Write a paragraph telling what strategies you would use to improve the situation. Mark Twain comes up against such a person in "Cub Pilot on the Mississippi." When you have finished writing your paragraph, compare your strategies with those of your classmates. As you read the selection, notice how Twain deals with his problems with Pilot Brown.

### Vocabulary

Knowing the following words will help you as you read "Cub Pilot on the Mississippi."

**furtive** (fər′ tiv) *adj.*: Sly or done in secret (p. 412)

**pretext** (prē′ tekst) *n.*: A false reason or motive given to hide a real intention (p. 413)

**intimation** (in′ tə mā′ shən) *n.*: Hint or suggestion (p. 415)

**indulgent** (in dul′ jənt) *adj.*: Very mild and tolerant; not strict or critical (p. 416)

**emancipated** (i man′ sə pā′ təd) *v.*: Freed from the control or power of another (p. 418)

### Mark Twain

(1835–1910) was the pen name of Samuel Langhorne Clemens. A phrase used by boatmen in taking river soundings, *mark twain* means "two fathoms deep." Twain was known for his humorous writing, including his novels about growing up, such as *The Adventures of Tom Sawyer.* Born in Florida, Missouri, he grew up in Hannibal on the Mississippi River. The influence of the river on Twain is evident in the following excerpt from *Life on the Mississippi,* published in 1883. In this excerpt, Twain tells of his experience steamboating.

*410 Nonfiction*

---

## Objectives

1 To understand conflict in autobiography
2 To separate fact from opinion
3 To write about conflict
4 To express individual interests and abilities through optional activities

## Support Material

**Teaching Portfolio**
Teacher Backup, p. 477
Grammar in Action Worksheets, *Appreciating Dialect,* p. 481; *Using Precise, Carefully Selected Verbs,* p. 483
Usage and Mechanics Worksheet, p. 485
Vocabulary Check, p. 486
Analyzing Literature Worksheet,

*Understanding Conflicts,* p. 487
Language Worksheet, *Using Contrast Clues,* p. 488
Selection Test, p. 489

**Prentice Hall Literature Writing Studio**

# Cub Pilot on the Mississippi

Mark Twain

THE GREAT MISSISSIPPI STEAMBOAT RACE, 1870
*Currier & Ives*

During the two or two and a half years of my apprenticeship[1] I served under many pilots, and had experience of many kinds of steamboatmen and many varieties of steamboats. I am to this day profiting somewhat by that experience; for in that brief, sharp schooling, I got personally and familiarly acquainted with about all the different types of human nature that are to be found in fiction, biography, or history.

The fact is daily borne in upon me that the average shore-employment requires as

1. **apprenticeship** (ə prenʹ tis ship) *n.*: The time spent by a person working for a master craftsman in a craft or trade in return for instruction and. formerly. support.

*Cub Pilot on the Mississippi*   411

**Thematic Focus** It is easy to understand that the type of conflict Mark Twain had to resolve with Mr. Brown created a memorable growth experience, a true rite of passage from carefree youthfulness to the responsibilities of adulthood. Ask students to consider what experiences they have had that have given them the first tastes of maturing from childhood to adulthood. Help them to define the transition as including taking responsibility for one's own actions.

## Presentation

### Humanities Note

Fine art, *The Great Mississippi Steamboat Race,* 1870, by Currier and Ives. Nathaniel Currier (1813–1888) and James Merritt Ives (1824–1895) built an enormously successful printmaking business, satisfying a demand for affordable, popular prints. With their own stable of artists, they created a pictorial record of the post–Civil War days.

Accompanying this print is the following information: " . . . from New Orleans to St. Louis, July 1870. Between the *R.E. Lee,* Capt. John W. Cann and the *Natchez,* Capt. Leathers. Won by the *R.E. Lee.* Time: 3 days, 18 hours, and 30 min., Distance: 1210 mi."

Explain to students that although Currier and Ives prints are not usually considered great artistic work, they did capture the feeling, the tempo, and the look of the Mississippi.
1. What information about steamboats can you get from this print?
2. Describe what you might see if you were standing on the upper deck of one of the steamboats in this picture.

### Motivation/Prior Knowledge
Have students imagine that they worked for a difficult boss. What would they do about it?

### Purpose-Setting Question How
might the conflict be different if it had been described by Brown, the cub pilot's boss, or the Captain?

1 **Enrichment** At the time Twain wrote this, the river was an important means of transportation, used to ship not only cargo but also passengers. Transportation took much longer at that time, although the pace of life in general was much slower than it is today.

**2 Discussion** Where in today's society would you be likely to meet a varied assortment of people to enjoy "people watching"?

**3 Discussion** Point out that Twain frequently uses exaggeration to provide humor. What details might be exaggerated in this description?

**4 Enrichment** A century ago an apprentice had to tolerate almost any action of his master, since he was under a legal agreement to him. In medieval times organizations called guilds gave the master powerful control over the lives of his apprentices. Today *apprentice* is a more informal term. More than 90 trades offer apprenticeship training in about 300 skilled occupations; conditions of the work often are regulated by agreements between unions and employers.

much as forty years to equip a man with this sort of an education. When I say I am still profiting by this thing, I do not mean that it has constituted me a judge of men—no, it has not done that, for judges of men are born, not made. My profit is various in kind and degree, but the feature of it which I value most is the zest which that early experience has given to my later reading. When I find a well-drawn character in fiction or biography I generally take a warm personal interest in him, for the reason that I have known him before—met him on the river.

The figure that comes before me oftenest, out of the shadows of that vanished time, is that of Brown, of the steamer *Pennsylvania.* He was a middle-aged, long, slim, bony, smooth-shaven, horse-faced, ignorant, stingy, malicious, snarling, fault-hunting, mote[2]-magnifying tyrant. I early got the habit of coming on watch with dread at my heart. No matter how good a time I might have been having with the off-watch below, and no matter how high my spirits might be when I started aloft, my soul became lead in my body the moment I approached the pilot-house.

I still remember the first time I ever entered the presence of that man. The boat had backed out from St. Louis and was "straightening down." I ascended to the pilothouse in high feather, and very proud to be semiofficially a member of the executive family of so fast and famous a boat. Brown was at the wheel. I paused in the middle of the room, all fixed to make my bow, but Brown did not look around. I thought he took a furtive glance at me out of the corner of his eye, but as not even this notice was repeated, I judged I had been mistaken. By

this time he was picking his way among some dangerous "breaks" abreast the woodyards; therefore it would not be proper to interrupt him; so I stepped softly to the high bench and took a seat.

There was silence for ten minutes; then my new boss turned and inspected me deliberately and painstakingly from head to heel for about—as it seemed to me—a quarter of an hour. After which he removed his countenance[3] and I saw it no more for some seconds; then it came around once more, and this question greeted me: "Are you Horace Bigsby's cub?[4]"

"Yes, sir."

After this there was a pause and another inspection. Then: "What's your name?"

I told him. He repeated it after me. It was probably the only thing he ever forgot; for although I was with him many months he never addressed himself to me in any other way than "Here!" and then his command followed.

"Where was you born?"

"In Florida, Missouri."

A pause. Then: "Dern sight better stayed there!"

By means of a dozen or so of pretty direct questions, he pumped my family history out of me.

The leads[5] were going now in the first crossing. This interrupted the inquest.[6] When the leads had been laid in he resumed:

"How long you been on the river?"

I told him. After a pause:

"Where'd you get them shoes?"

---

2. **mote** (mōt) *n.*: A speck of dust or other tiny particle.

3. **countenance** (koun′ tə nəns) *n.*: Face.
4. **cub** (kub) *n.*: Beginner.
5. **leads** (lēdz) *n.*: Weights that were lowered to test the depth of the river.
6. **inquest** (in′ kwest) *n.*: Investigation.

## Grammar in Action

**Dialect** is the form of language peculiar to a particular region or social group. By using dialect writers can capture the flavor of a particular area.

Dialect may contain special vocabulary words or may violate standard rules of grammar. For example, look at the following dialect from "Cub Pilot on the Mississippi:"

Where was you born?

Dern sight better stayed there!

Where'd you get them shoes?

I'll learn you to swell yourself up and blow around here . . .

I'm deuced glad of it! Hark ye, never mention that I said that.

**Student Activity 1.** Rewrite each of the examples above following the rules of standard grammar. Which sentences seem more appropriate for this selection—the ones you have rewritten or the original ones? Why?

I gave him the information.

"Hold up your foot!"

I did so. He stepped back, examined the shoe minutely and contemptuously, scratching his head thoughtfully, tilting his high sugar-loaf hat well forward to facilitate the operation, then ejaculated, "Well, I'll be dod derned!" and returned to his wheel.

What occasion there was to be dod derned about it is a thing which is still as much of a mystery to me now as it was then. It must have been all of fifteen minutes —fifteen minutes of dull, homesick silence —before that long horse-face swung round upon me again—and then what a change! It was as red as fire, and every muscle in it was working. Now came this shriek: "Here! You going to set there all day?"

I lit in the middle of the floor, shot there by the electric suddenness of the surprise. As soon as I could get my voice I said apologetically: "I have had no orders, sir."

"You've had no *orders!* My, what a fine bird we are! We must have *orders!* Our father was a *gentleman*—and *we've* been to *school.* Yes, *we* are a gentleman, *too,* and got to have *orders!* ORDERS, is it? ORDERS is what you want! Dod dern my skin, *I'll* learn you to swell yourself up and blow around *here* about your dod-derned *orders!* G'way from the wheel!" (I had approached it without knowing it.)

I moved back a step or two and stood as in a dream, all my senses stupefied by this frantic assault.

"What you standing there for? Take that ice-pitcher down to the texas-tender![7] Come, move along, and don't you be all day about it!"

The moment I got back to the pilothouse Brown said: "Here! What was you doing down there all this time?"

"I couldn't find the texas-tender; I had to go all the way to the pantry."

"Derned likely story! Fill up the stove."

I proceeded to do so. He watched me like a cat. Presently he shouted: "Put down that shovel! Derndest numskull I ever saw —ain't even got sense enough to load up a stove."

All through the watch this sort of thing went on. Yes, and the subsequent watches were much like it during a stretch of months. As I have said, I soon got the habit of coming on duty with dread. The moment I was in the presence, even in the darkest night, I could feel those yellow eyes upon me, and knew their owner was watching for a pretext to spit out some venom on me. Preliminarily he would say: "Here! Take the wheel."

Two minutes later: "*Where* in the nation you going to? Pull her down! pull her down!"

After another moment: "Say! You going to hold her all day? Let her go—meet her! meet her!"

Then he would jump from the bench, snatch the wheel from me, and meet her himself, pouring out wrath upon me all the time.

George Ritchie was the other pilot's cub. He was having good times now; for his boss, George Ealer, was as kind-hearted as Brown wasn't. Ritchie had steered for Brown the season before; consequently, he knew exactly how to entertain himself and plague me, all by the one operation. Whenever I took the wheel for a moment on Ealer's watch, Ritchie would sit back on the bench and play Brown, with continual ejaculations

---

**7. texas tender:** The waiter in the officers' quarters. On Mississippi steamboats, rooms were named after the states. The officers' area, which was the largest, was named after what was then the largest state, Texas.

*Cub Pilot on the Mississippi* 413

**5 Discussion** Why is Brown so angry that Twain had formal schooling? Is he envious or is he insecure, fearing that Twain is better than he?

**6 Literary Focus** Have students paraphrase the conflict between Brown and Twain.

**7 Discussion** Ask students why a fault-finder might derive satisfaction from destructive criticism. How do they think this kind of personality should be handled— with sympathy or combativeness? Explain your answer.

**Student Activity 2.** Pick a particular area of the country. Using dialect, write a conversation between two people from this region. Read it aloud to your classmates.

**Electronic Handbook** If students have access to the Language Master 6000, you may want them to prepare for the Grammar in Action activities. Tell them to access the word *informal* to review colloquialisms, slang, and jargon and to access the word *idiom* to learn more about idiomatic language.

*Samuel Clemens as a Young Man, M. T. Papers*

of "Snatch her! Snatch her! Derndest mudcat I ever saw!" "Here! Where are you going *now?* Going to run over that snag?" "Pull her *down!* Don't you hear me? Pull her *down!*" "There she goes! *Just* as I expected! I *told* you not to cramp that reef. G'way from the wheel!"

So I always had a rough time of it, no matter whose watch it was; and sometimes it seemed to me that Ritchie's good-natured badgering was pretty nearly as aggravating as Brown's dead-earnest nagging.

8   I often wanted to kill Brown, but this would not answer. A cub had to take every-

thing his boss gave, in the way of vigorous comment and criticism; and we all believed that there was a United States law making it a penitentiary offense to strike or threaten a pilot who was on duty.

However, I could *imagine* myself killing Brown; there was no law against that; and that was the thing I used always to do the moment I was abed. Instead of going over my river in my mind, as was my duty, I threw business aside for pleasure, and killed Brown. I killed Brown every night for months; not in old, stale, commonplace ways, but in new and picturesque ones

414   *Nonfiction*

## Grammar in Action

Mark Twain's writing, like the man himself, is filled with energy. **Precise, carefully selected verbs** create that energy in his writing.

Look at his use of verbs in the following excerpt from "Cub Pilot on the Mississippi":

His face *turned* red with passion; he *made* one bound, *hurled* me across the house with a sweep of his arm, *spun* the wheel

down, and *began* to pour out a stream of vituperation upon me which *lasted* until he was out of breath.

In the above example, Twain uses the following verbs: *turned, made, hurled, spun, began,* and *lasted.* Of these verbs, *hurled* and *spun* are especially precise, creating a vivid picture of the action. Each of the verbs is followed by additional descriptive words that add to the action of the sentence.

—ways that were sometimes surprising for freshness of design and ghastliness of situation and environment.

Brown was *always* watching for a pretext to find fault; and if he could find no plausible pretext, he would invent one. He would scold you for shaving a shore, and for not shaving it; for hugging a bar, and for not hugging it; for "pulling down" when not invited, and for *not* pulling down when not invited; for firing up without orders, and for waiting *for* orders. In a word, it was his invariable rule to find fault with *everything* you did and another invariable rule of his was to throw all his remarks (to you) into the form of an insult.

One day we were approaching New Madrid, bound down and heavily laden. Brown was at one side of the wheel, steering; I was at the other, standing by to "pull down" or "shove up." He cast a furtive glance at me every now and then. I had long ago learned what that meant; viz., he was trying to invent a trap for me. I wondered what shape it was going to take. By and by he stepped back from the wheel and said in his usual snarly way:

"Here! See if you've got gumption enough to round her to."

This was simply *bound* to be a success; nothing could prevent it; for he had never allowed me to round the boat to before; consequently, no matter how I might do the thing, he could find free fault with it. He stood back there with his greedy eye on me, and the result was what might have been foreseen: I lost my head in a quarter of a minute, and didn't know what I was about; I started too early to bring the boat around, but detected a green gleam of joy in Brown's eye, and corrected my mistake. I started around once more while too high up, but corrected myself again in time. I made other false moves, and still managed to save my-self; but at last I grew so confused and anxious that I tumbled into the very worst blunder of all—I got too far *down* before beginning to fetch the boat around. Brown's chance was come.

His face turned red with passion; he made one bound, hurled me across the house with a sweep of his arm, spun the wheel down, and began to pour out a stream of vituperation[8] upon me which lasted till he was out of breath. In the course of this speech he called me all the different kinds of hard names he could think of, and once or twice I thought he was even going to swear —but he had never done that, and he didn't this time. "Dod dern" was the nearest he ventured to the luxury of swearing.

Two trips later I got into serious trouble. Brown was steering; I was "pulling down." My younger brother Henry appeared on the hurricane deck, and shouted to Brown to stop at some landing or other, a mile or so below. Brown gave no intimation that he had heard anything. But that was his way: he never condescended to take notice of an underclerk. The wind was blowing; Brown was deaf (although he always pretended he wasn't), and I very much doubted if he had heard the order. If I had had two heads, I would have spoken; but as I had only one, it seemed judicious to take care of it; so I kept still.

Presently, sure enough, we went sailing by that plantation. Captain Klinefelter appeared on the deck, and said: "Let her come around, sir, let her come around. Didn't Henry tell you to land here?"

"*No*, sir!"

"I sent him up to do it."

---

**8. vituperation** (vī tōō′ pə rā′ shən) *n.*: Abusive language.

9 **Clarification** New Madrid is a town along the Mississippi River.

10 **Clarification** *Viz.* is Latin for "namely."

11 **Discussion** What is the possibility that Brown yelled loudly because he couldn't hear?

**Student Activity 1.** Find ten other precise verbs in "Cub Pilot on the Mississippi." Tell why you selected each one.

**Student Activity 2.** Think of a time when someone was extremely angry with you. Using Twain's description of the enraged steamboat pilot, write a description of that person and what he or she did to show rage and anger.

**Electronic Handbook** You might want students to review verbs before completing the Grammar in Action activities. If students have access to the Language Master 6000, have them enter the access word *verb* and press the GRAMMAR key to get information on using precise, carefully selected verbs.

"He *did* come up; and that's all the good it done, the dod-derned fool. He never said anything."

"Didn't *you* hear him?" asked the captain of me.

Of course I didn't want to be mixed up in this business, but there was no way to avoid it; so I said: "Yes, sir."

I knew what Brown's next remark would be, before he uttered it. It was: "Shut your mouth! You never heard anything of the kind."

I closed my mouth, according to instructions. An hour later Henry entered the pilot-house, unaware of what had been going on. He was a thoroughly inoffensive boy, and I was sorry to see him come, for I knew Brown would have no pity on him. Brown began, straightway: "Here! Why didn't you tell me we'd got to land at that plantation?"

"I did tell you, Mr. Brown."

"It's a lie!"

I said: "You lie, yourself. He did tell you."

Brown glared at me in unaffected surprise; and for as much as a moment he was entirely speechless; then he shouted to me: "I'll attend to your case in a half a minute!" then to Henry, "And you leave the pilot-house; out with you!"

**12** It was pilot law, and must be obeyed. The boy started out, and even had his foot on the upper step outside the door, when Brown, with a sudden access of fury, picked up a ten-pound lump of coal and sprang after him; but I was between, with a heavy stool, and I hit Brown a good honest blow which stretched him out.

I had committed the crime of crimes—I had lifted my hand against a pilot on duty! I supposed I was booked for the penitentiary sure, and couldn't be booked any surer if I went on and squared my long account with this person while I had the chance; consequently I stuck to him and pounded him

with my fists a considerable time. I do not know how long, the pleasure of it probably made it seem longer than it really was; but in the end he struggled free and jumped up and sprang to the wheel: a very natural solicitude, for, all this time, here was this steamboat tearing down the river at the rate of fifteen miles an hour and nobody at the helm! However, Eagle Bend was two miles wide at this bank-full stage, and correspondingly long and deep: and the boat was steering herself straight down the middle and taking no chances. Still, that was only luck—a body *might* have found her charging into the woods.

Perceiving at a glance that the *Pennsylvania* was in no danger, Brown gathered up the big spyglass, war-club fashion, and ordered me out of the pilothouse with more than ordinary bluster. But I was not afraid of him now; so, instead of going, I tarried, and criticized his grammar. I reformed his ferocious speeches for him, and put them into good English, calling his attention to the advantage of pure English over the dialect of the collieries[9] whence he was extracted. He could have done his part to admiration in a crossfire of mere vituperation, of course; but he was not equipped for this species of controversy; so he presently laid aside his glass and took the wheel, muttering and shaking his head; and I retired to the bench. The racket had brought everybody to the hurricane deck, and I trembled when I saw the old captain looking up from amid the crowd. I said to myself, "Now I *am* done for!" for although, as a rule, he was so fatherly and indulgent toward the boat's family, and so patient of minor shortcomings, he could be stern enough when the fault was worth it.

**13**

---

**9. collieries** (käl′ yər ēz) *n.*: Coal mines.

THE CHAMPIONS OF THE MISSISSIPPI
*Currier & Ives*

**Humanities Note**

Fine art, *The Champions of the Mississippi,* by Currier and Ives. Point out to students that although Currier and Ives faithfully recorded the mood and many details of life on the Mississippi, they often fabricated scenes to convey a certain amount of pictorial information. This very atmospheric night scene would, no doubt, have been a steamboat pilot's nightmare.

1. What is the mood Currier and Ives create in this picture? How does this mood fit the story?
2. Why is this scene a probable fabrication? Consider the dangers of piloting a steamboat in a night race in the early 1800's.

I tried to imagine what he *would* do to a cub pilot who had been guilty of such a crime as mine, committed on a boat guard-deep[10] with costly freight and alive with passengers. Our watch was nearly ended. I thought I would go and hide somewhere till I got a chance to slide ashore. So I slipped out of the pilothouse, and down the steps, and around to the texas-door, and was in the act of gliding within, when the captain confronted me! I dropped my head, and he stood over me in silence a moment or two, then said impressively: "Follow me."

I dropped into his wake; he led the way to his parlor in the forward end of the texas.

We were alone now. He closed the afterdoor, then moved slowly to the forward one and closed that. He sat down; I stood before him. He looked at me some little time, then said: "So you have been fighting Mr. Brown?"

I answered meekly: "Yes, sir."

"Do you know that that is a very serious matter?"

"Yes, sir."

"Are you aware that this boat was plowing down the river fully five minutes with no one at the wheel?"

"Yes, sir."

"Did you strike him first?"

"Yes, sir."

"What with?"

"A stool, sir."

"Hard?"

---

10. **guard-deep:** Here, a wooden frame protecting the paddle wheel.

*Cub Pilot on the Mississippi* 417

14 **Discussion** Why does the Captain want Twain to thrash Brown on shore rather than on the boat?

15 **Discussion** Ask students if they are surprised at the Captain's reaction. Why?

16 **Discussion** Conflicts have resolutions. How is Twain's conflict with Brown resolved?

**Master Teacher Note** A group of your **more advanced** students might read *Life on the Mississippi,* from which this excerpt comes. They could report to the class on some of Twain's other experiences as a cub pilot.

**Reader's Response** What acquaints you with "the various types of human nature" the way the narrator was acquainted during his apprenticeship?

**Thematic Response** Could Mark Twain have had a comparable growth experience by dealing with Mr. Brown in some other way? Was it necessary for him to have a physical fight in order for this conflict to become a rite of passage for the author?

---

"Middling, sir."

"Did it knock him down?"

"He—he fell, sir."

"Did you follow it up? Did you do anything further?"

"Yes, sir."

"What did you do?"

"Pounded him, sir."

"Pounded him?"

"Yes, sir."

"Did you pound him much? that is, severely?"

"One might call it that, sir, maybe."

14 "I'm deuced glad of it! Hark ye, never mention that I said that. You have been guilty of a great crime; and don't you ever be guilty of it again, on this boat. *But*—lay for him ashore! Give him a good sound thrashing, do you hear? I'll pay the expenses. Now go—and mind you, not a word of this to anybody. Clear out with you! You've been guilty of a great crime, you whelp!"[11]

15 I slid out, happy with the sense of a close shave and a mighty deliverance; and I heard

11. **whelp** (hwelp) *n.*: A young dog or puppy; here, a disrespectful young man.

him laughing to himself and slapping his fat thighs after I had closed his door.

When Brown came off watch he went straight to the captain, who was talking with some passengers on the boiler deck, and demanded that I be put ashore in New Orleans—and added: "I'll never turn a wheel on this boat again while that cub stays."

The captain said: "But he needn't come round when you are on watch, Mr. Brown."

"I won't even stay on the same boat with him. *One* of us has got to go ashore."

"Very well," said the captain, "let it be yourself," and resumed his talk with the passengers.

16 During the brief remainder of the trip I knew how an emancipated slave feels, for I was an emancipated slave myself. While we lay at landings I listened to George Ealer's flute, or to his readings from his two Bibles, that is to say, Goldsmith and Shakespeare, or I played chess with him—and would have beaten him sometimes, only he always took back his last move and ran the game out differently.

---

## RESPONDING TO THE SELECTION

### Your Response

1. Do you think that Mark Twain could have improved his relationship with Mr. Brown by behaving differently from the way he did? If so, tell what else he could have done.

2. Would you like to have worked on a nineteenth-century Mississippi River steamboat? Why or why not?

### Recalling

3. How does knowing the various kinds of steamboatmen profit Twain as a writer?

4. Why does Twain feel like "an emancipated slave" at the end?

### Interpreting

5. In what ways was Brown's treatment of the young Twain unfair?

6. How does the Captain feel about Mr. Brown? What evidence supports your answer?

### Applying

7. John Locke wrote: "It is easier for a tutor to command than to teach." Explain the meaning of this quotation. How does it relate to this selection?

418 *Nonfiction*

---

## Closure and Extension

### ANSWERS TO RESPONDING TO THE SELECTION
**Your Response**

1. Encourage students to speculate on what Mark Twain's alternative behaviors could have been. Then they can evaluate if other responses might have improved the relationship between the two men. Most students will probably believe that Twain had no choice but to fight physically with the pilot. Some, however, might suggest that he could have requested a meeting with his boss.

2. Students' answers will differ.

### Recalling

3. It acquaints him with all the different types of human nature; he can use this knowledge to make his fiction true to life.

4. Twain feels like an emancipated slave because he is free of Brown's abuse.

### Interpreting

5. Brown's treatment of the young Twain was unfair in that he yelled at him for no cause—even when Twain did things correctly.

6. The Captain does not like Mr. Brown. Evidence that supports this is that he says he is glad that Twain pounded Brown and offers to pay Twain for thrashing Brown on shore, and that Twain hears the Captain chuckling after he closes the door.

## ANALYZING LITERATURE

### Understanding Conflicts

Conflicts may provide the main element of a plot, or sequence of action, in an autobiography. For example, "Cub Pilot on the Mississippi" is based on the conflict between Mark Twain as a cub pilot and Mr. Brown. The outcome of the conflict is its resolution; however, a conflict may not always be resolved.

1. Why are the cub pilot and Mr. Brown in conflict?
2. What conflict does the cub pilot experience in his mind?
3. How are both conflicts resolved?

## CRITICAL THINKING AND READING

### Separating Fact From Opinion

Autobiographies may contain both facts and opinions. **Facts** are statements that can be proved true with reliable sources, such as an encyclopedia or an expert. For example, the statement that cub pilots were apprentices on Mississippi River steamboats can be verified with historical records.

**Opinions** are beliefs or judgments. The writer's opinions are not subject to verification, because they are based on the writer's attitudes or beliefs. For example, it is Twain's opinion that Mr. Brown is a "mote-magnifying tyrant."

Identify which of the following is fact and which is opinion. Indicate what source you might use to verify each fact.

1. The cub pilot's brother Henry was a thoroughly inoffensive boy.
2. A cub pilot was required to obey a steamboat pilot on duty.
3. The cub pilot was born in Florida, Missouri.
4. George Ealer was as kind-hearted as Brown was mean-spirited.

## THINKING AND WRITING

### Writing About Conflict

In *Life on the Mississippi*, Mark Twain writes about a variety of conflicts. In this excerpt, he focuses on the conflict between the cub pilot and his boss. Write an essay explaining the conflicting feelings in the selection. Develop your essay, showing the conflict between Mark Twain and Mr. Brown. Revise your essay, making sure that you use examples to support your views. Proofread your essay and share it with your classmates.

## LEARNING OPTIONS

1. **Writing.** Mark Twain tells us his feelings about Pilot Brown, but we know nothing of Pilot Brown's feelings and motivations. Write a diary entry as if you were Pilot Brown. Reveal your reasons for constantly criticizing and abusing the young cub pilot. Be sure to include what you thought was noteworthy about Mark Twain's shoes.
2. **Cross-curricular Connection.** Conduct research on the lives of riverboat pilots. Find out what they did and what caused the steamboat era to come to an end. Explain the meaning of the terms that you read in the selection, such as *pull down, shove up,* and *hugging a bar.*

*Cub Pilot on the Mississippi* 419

---

**Alternative Assessment** You may vary the Thinking and Writing assignment by having your students complete one of the Alternate Composition Assignments on page 478 of the Teaching Portfolio.

**Writing Transparency** A model may be of great help to your students in writing their essays. Use Model 5, *Essay,* in **Transparencies for Writing.**

**Publishing Student Writing** You might want to put together a booklet of the students' essays or display them on the bulletin board.

**Writing Across the Curriculum** You may wish to have students report on different aspects of the Mississippi River. If you do, you might notify the social studies department. Social studies teachers can provide guidance for students on conducting their research or offer them extra credit.

### LEARNING OPTIONS

1. This activity will appeal to students who enjoy probing into human behavior and writing about people's motivations. These students might be encouraged to keep a personal journal outside school to allow them an opportunity to explore their own feelings and behaviors with regard to other people. They will be constantly practicing the art of expressive writing.
2. This option will be selected by students who have an interest in history and who like to do research. Remind them that they can report their findings in any of several ways: a tape-recorded news report; a "live" interview conducted with a riverboat pilot; a written newspaper article, and so on.

---

*Applying*

7. Answers will differ. Suggested Responses: To command is simply to order; to teach involves providing with knowledge and insight through explanation and example. A person can perform something as ordered without any insight into it. In this selection Brown simply orders and shouts commands; he does not explain or show how to do things to help the cub pilot gain any insight.

**ANSWERS TO ANALYZING LITERATURE**

1. The cub pilot and Mr. Brown are in conflict because Brown continually abuses and screams at the cub pilot, who does not like such abuse.
2. The conflict in the cub pilot's mind is that he wanted to thwart Brown, which was not permitted.
3. The conflicts are resolved when Twain fights and beats Brown, and the Captain privately condones Twain's behavior.

**ANSWERS TO CRITICAL THINKING AND READING**

1. Opinion
2. Fact; can be verified by the Captain or a record of the law
3. Fact; can be verified by birth records in Florida, Mo., or an encyclopedia
4. Opinion

## Preparation

**More About the Author** Phung Thi Le Ly Hayslip says she wrote her autobiography with the help of her three sons. James first put her spoken words on paper; Thomas served her "many bowls of rice, hot tea, and tissues" while she worked; Alan gave her "love and hugs when all I could offer in return were tears." To explain the many tears, a biographer wrote in the introduction to Hayslip's book, "As the government and Viet Cong troops fought in and around Ky La, both sides recruited children as spies and saboteurs. Le Ly was one of those children." Writing the book dredged up the horrors of her experiences: near-starvation, imprisonment, torture, . . . and the deaths of beloved family members—experiences she faced before age sixteen. What evidence do you find in "Fathers and Daughters" that suggests Hayslip would be able to survive such horrors?

**Literary Focus** To help students identify the narrator in an autobiography, direct them to freewrite about something that happened to them recently. Then ask students to underline each instance of the first-person pronouns *I, me, my,* or *mine* in the freewriting. When they finish, explain that they have written as a first-person narrator, sharing what they saw, felt, and thought. Then reveal that Le Ly Hayslip writes "Fathers and Daughters" using the same literary technique.

**Prereading Focus** Remind students that as they complete the graphic organizer, they are illustrating a good principle of writing: Show your audience what you mean; don't tell. Explain that Hayslip shows the behavior, and readers draw inferences about the values. Good writers make steady use of these techniques, and good readers learn to watch for clues and make inferences.

# GUIDE FOR READING

### Le Ly Hayslip

(1949–   ) was born in Central Vietnam, near Danang. A child of war, she was twelve years old when United States helicopters landed in her village. Caught up in the conflict, Hayslip was imprisoned by South Vietnamese soldiers, then sentenced to death by the Viet Cong. In 1970 she married an American and escaped to the United States. In her autobiography, *When Heaven and Earth Changed Places,* Hayslip recounts her experiences growing up in a a world turned upside down by war.

## Fathers and Daughters

### The Narrator in Autobiography

An autobiography is an example of a first-person narrative. In it the writer is the **narrator** of his or her own life story. Using the first-person pronoun "I," the writer shares significant life experiences with the reader. You see events through the writer's eyes and come to understand the writer's feelings and thoughts.

### Focus

In "Fathers and Daughters," the author creates a full portrait of her father. You get to know the author's father through her descriptions of him, through anecdotes about family life that the author relates, and especially through the memorable conversation between father and daughter that the author retells. Copy the graphic organizer that follows. As you read the selection and the father's character traits become evident, write a brief description of one of the father's behaviors in the left column. Then in the right column, tell which of his values is reflected in that behavior. With your classmates compare these values with the values transmitted to you by your families.

| Behavior | Values |
|----------|--------|
|          |        |

### Vocabulary

Knowing the following words will help you as you read "Fathers and Daughters."

**diligent** (dil′ ə jənt) *adj.*: Persevering; industrious (p. 421)
**empathy** (em′ pə thē) *n.*: Capacity for sharing another's feelings or ideas (p. 421)
**abstained** (əb stānd′) *v.*: Refrained voluntarily (p. 421)
**absurdity** (ab sur′ də tē) *n.*: Ridiculousness (p. 422)
**eloquent** (el′ ə kwənt) *adj:*

Very expressive (p. 422)
**contradicting** (kän trə dikt′ iŋ) *v.*: Saying the opposite of (p. 423)
**cultivate** (kul′ tə vāt) *v.*: Prepare and use for the raising of crops; till (p. 426)
**avenge** (ə venj′) *v.*: Take revenge for or on behalf of (p. 427)

*420   Nonfiction*

## Objectives

1  To understand the narrator in autobiography
2  To determine the effect of point of view
3  To write from another point of view
4  To express individual interests and abilities through optional activities

## Support Material

**Teaching Portfolio**
Teacher Backup, p. 491
Grammar in Action Worksheet, *Understanding Relationships Among Punctuation Marks in Dialogue,* p. 495
Usage and Mechanics Worksheet, p. 497
Vocabulary Check, p. 498

Analyzing Literature Worksheet, *Understanding the Narrator in Autobiography,* p. 499
Critical Thinking and Reading Worksheets, *Recognizing the Effect of Point of View,* p. 500; *Understanding a Filmmaker's Point of View,* p. 501
Selection Test, p. 502

**Prentice Hall Literature Writing Studio**

# Fathers and Daughters
*from* **When Heaven and Earth Changed Places**
Le Ly Hayslip

After my brother Bon went North, I began to pay more attention to my father.

He was built solidly—big-boned—for a Vietnamese man, which meant he probably had well-fed, noble ancestors. People said he had the body of a natural-born warrior. He was a year younger and an inch shorter than my mother, but just as good-looking. His face was round, like a Khmer or Thai,[1] and his complexion was brown as soy[2] from working all his life in the sun. He was very easygoing about everything and seldom in a hurry. Seldom, too, did he say no to a request—from his children or his neighbors. Although he took everything in stride, he was a hard and diligent worker. Even on holidays, he was always mending things or tending to our house and animals. He would not wait to be asked for help if he saw someone in trouble. Similarly, he always said what he thought, although he knew, like most honest men, when to keep silent. Because of his honesty, his empathy, and his openness to people, he understood life deeply. Perhaps that is why he was so easygoing. Only a half-trained mechanic thinks everything needs fixing.

He loved to smoke cigars and grew a little tobacco in our yard. My mother always wanted him to sell it, but there was hardly ever enough to take to market. I think for her it was the principle of the thing: smoking cigars was like burning money. Naturally, she had a song for such gentle vices—her own habit of chewing betel nuts included:

> Get rid of your tobacco,
> And you will get a water buffalo.
> Give away your betel,
> And you will get more paddy land.

Despite her own good advice, she never abstained from chewing betel, nor my father from smoking cigars. They were rare luxuries that life and the war allowed them.

My father also liked rice wine, which we made; and enjoyed an occasional beer, which he purchased when there was nothing else we needed. After he'd had a few sips, he would tell jokes and happy stories and the village kids would flock around. Because I was his youngest daughter, I was entitled to listen from his knee—the place of honor. Sometimes he would sing funny songs about whoever threatened the village and we would feel better. For example, when the French or Moroccan soldiers were near, he would sing:

> There are many kinds of vegetables,
> Why do you like spinach?

---

1. **Khmer** (kə mer′) or **Thai** (tī) *n.*: A native of Cambodia or Thailand.
2. **soy** (soi) *n.*: Soybean, a plant raised for food in parts of Asia and elsewhere.

*Fathers and Daughters* 421

**Presentation**

**Motivation/Prior Knowledge**
Not many of us have lived in a war zone where troops burst through our towns and villages and the ravages of war surrounded us. Imagine how it would feel to be a middle-school-aged youth dragged into the trauma. What family-taught values might you need in order to survive?

**Master Teacher Note** Ask students to bring articles, photographs, or other mementos from the Vietnam War. Prepare a bulletin board display of news items, perhaps photocopied from newspaper or magazine files, microfiche files like Newsbank, or CD ROM files. Use the materials to establish the setting for "Fathers and Daughters."

**Purpose-Setting Question**
What characteristics make a good father?

**1 Critical Thinking and Reading**
Since Bay Ly tells about her father from her point of view, readers must guess at how he felt. How do you think he felt about always working?

**2 Reading Strategy** What is the intended comparison?

**3 Clarification** Betel (bēt″l) nuts are the fruit of the betel palm, a tree that grows in Southeast Asia. It is chewed with lime and the leaves of the betel pepper, a tropical climbing plant in the pepper family. The combination is somewhat comparable to chewing gum.

**4 Reading Strategy** What does this say about the war?

**ESL Teaching Strategy** You may want to use the Summary from the Teaching Portfolio, page 491, as a prereading survey and use the Check Test as a directed-reading tool.

**Thematic Focus** Sometimes we appreciate parents or other authority figures only later in life. Do you think Le Ly Hayslip's feelings toward her father have changed since childhood?

**Making Connections** You may want students to compare Bay Ly's war experiences with those of Anne Frank in *The Diary of Anne Frank,* page 303.

**5 Discussion** Why does the father sing songs of which the mother disapproves?

**6 Critical Thinking and Reading** Since this information comes from Bay Ly, what questions would you like to ask the father about this passage? How do you think he might answer?

**Multicultural Focus** Have students notice the photographs of Hayslip's family throughout this selection. Point out that families in Southeast Asian cultures often contained several generations of family members. Organize a class discussion about the change in America from the multigenerational family to the nuclear family—composed of parents and children only. Up until World War II, it was common for extended families to remain in close contact with one another throughout life. Grandparents, unmarried aunts, and even grown-up married children sometimes remained in the same house or at least in the same town. However, changing family values, greater mobility, and job opportunities across the country have made the nuclear family the basis of American society.

In the multigenerational family, being able to relate to many relatives from several generations created variety and a sense of belonging. It also brought members in closer contact with their own culture and past. On the other hand, the nuclear family may offer more personal freedom.

Ask volunteers to tell the class about extended-family members, such as grandmothers, uncles, or cousins, who have influenced them. Then encourage a discussion about the advantages and disadvantages of both types of family lifestyle.

There are many kinds of wealth,
Why do you use Minh money?
There are many kinds of people,
Why do you love terrorists?

We laughed because these were all the things the French told us about the Viet Minh fighters whom we favored in the war. Years later, when the Viet Cong were near, he would sing:

There are many kinds of vegetables,
Why do you like spinach?
There are many kinds of money,
Why do you use Yankee dollars?
There are many kinds of people,
Why do you disobey your ancestors?

This was funny because the words were taken from the speeches the North Vietnamese cadres[3] delivered to shame us for helping the Republic. He used to have a song for when the Viet Minh were near too, which asked in the same way, "Why do you use francs?"[4] and "Why do you love French traitors?" Because he sang these songs with a comical voice, my mother never appreciated them. She couldn't see the absurdity of our situation as clearly as we children. To her, war and real life were different. To us, they were all the same.

Even as a parent, my father was more lenient than our mother, and we sometimes ran to him for help when she was angry. Most of the time, it didn't work and he would lovingly rub our heads as we were dragged off to be spanked. The village saying went: "A naughty child learns more from a whipping stick than a sweet stick." We children were never quite sure about that, but agreed the whipping stick was an eloquent teacher.

---

3. **cadres** (ka′ drēz′) *n.*: Communist leaders who tried to persuade others to adopt their beliefs.
4. **francs** (franks) *n.*: French money.

*Le Ly Hayslip's father, Phung Van Trong*

When he absolutely had to punish us himself, he didn't waste time. Wordlessly, he would find a long, supple bamboo stick and let us have it behind our thighs. It stung, but he could have whipped us harder. I think seeing the pain in his face hurt more than receiving his halfhearted blows. Because of that, we seldom did anything to merit a father's spanking—the highest penalty in our family. Violence in any form offended him. For this reason, I think, he grew old before his time.

One of the few times my father ever touched my mother in a way not consistent with love was during one of the yearly floods, when people came to our village for safety from the lower ground. We sheltered many in our house, which was nothing more than a two-room hut with woven mats for a floor. I came home one day in winter rain to see refugees and Republican soldiers milling around outside. They did not know I lived there so I had to elbow my way inside. It was nearly supper time and I knew my mother would be fixing as much food as we could spare.

In the part of the house we used as our kitchen, I discovered my mother crying. She and my father had gotten into an argument outside a few minutes before. He had assured the refugees he would find something to eat for everyone and she insisted there would not be enough for her children if everyone was fed. He repeated his order to her, this time loud enough for all to hear. Naturally, he thought this would end the argument. She persisted in contradicting him, so he had slapped her.

This show of male power—we called it *do danh vo*[5]—was usual behavior for Vietnamese husbands but unusual for my father. My mother could be as strict as she wished with his children and he would seldom interfere. Now, I discovered there were limits even to his great patience. I saw the glowing red mark on her cheek and asked if she was crying because it hurt. She said no. She said she was crying because her action had caused my father to lose face in front of strangers. She promised that if I ever did what she had done to a husband, I would have both cheeks glowing: one from his blow and one from hers.

Once, when I was the only child at home, my mother went to Danang[6] to visit Uncle Nhu, and my father had to take care of me. I woke up from my nap in the empty house and cried for my mother. My father came in from the yard and reassured me, but I was still cranky and continued crying. Finally, he gave me a rice cookie to shut me up.

5. *do danh vo* (dỗ zăŋ vỗ)
6. **Danang** (dă năŋ'): Seaport in central Vietnam.

Needless to say, this was a tactic my mother never used.

The next afternoon I woke up and although I was not feeling cranky, I thought a rice cookie might be nice. I cried a fake cry and my father came running in.

"What's this?" he asked, making a worried face. "Little Bay Ly doesn't want a cookie?"

I was confused again.

"Look under your pillow," he said with a smile.

I twisted around and saw that, while I was sleeping, he had placed a rice cookie under my pillow. We both laughed and he picked me up like a sack of rice and carried me outside while I gobbled the cookie.

In the yard, he plunked me down under a tree and told me some stories. After that, he got some scraps of wood and showed me how to make things: a doorstop for my mother and a toy duck for me. This was unheard of—a father doing these things with a child that was not a son! Where my mother would instruct me on cooking and cleaning and tell stories about brides, my father showed me the mystery of hammers and explained the customs of our people.

His knowledge of the Vietnamese went back to the Chinese Wars in ancient times. I learned how one of my distant ancestors, a woman named Phung Thi Chinh, led Vietnamese fighters against the Han.[7] In one battle, even though she was pregnant and surrounded by Chinese, she delivered the baby, tied it to her back, and cut her way to safety wielding a sword in each hand. I was amazed at this warrior's bravery and impressed that I was her descendant. Even

7. **Phung Thi Chinh** (foɔŋ ti chin) . . . **the Han** (hăn): The Vietnamese were fighting warriors of a dynasty known as the Han, which ruled China from 202 B.C. to A.D. 220.

*Fathers and Daughters* 423

7 **Enrichment** What inference can you draw from this passage about the Vietnamese culture?

8 **Reading Strategy** What does this passage tell readers about Bay Ly's father?

9 **Literary Focus: Autobiography** Why do you think Bay Ly includes this detail in an autobiography?

## Primary Source

In *When Heaven and Earth Changed Places*, the book in which "Fathers and Daughters" is a chapter, the prologue is titled "Dedication to Peace." In it Hayslip writes:

For my first twelve years of life, I was a peasant girl in Ky La, now called Xa Hoa Qui, a small village near Danang in Central Vietnam. My father taught me to love God, my family, our traditions, and the people we could not see: our ancestors. He taught me that to sacrifice one's self for freedom—like our ancient kings who fought bravely against invaders; or in the manner of our women warriors, including Miss Trung Nhi

Trung Trac who drowned herself rather than give in to foreign conquerors—was a very high honor. From my love of my ancestors and my native soil, he said, I must never retreat.

As the war enveloped her, Hayslip explains how she became involved. "Everything I knew about the war I learned as a teenaged girl from the North Vietnamese cadre leaders in the swamps outside Ky La. During these midnight meetings, we peasants assumed everything we heard was true because what the Viet Cong said matched, in one way or another, the beliefs we already had."

10 **Reading Strategy** What inference can you make about the role of women in Vietnamese culture?

11 **Discussion** What do you think he truly meant?

12 **Literary Focus: Autobiography** What point does this story make in Bay Ly's autobiography?

**Speaking and Listening** To emphasize the dialogue, assign readers for Bay Ly, Father, and a female narrator. Have them read aloud segments of "Fathers and Daughters," beginning perhaps in column 2 on this page with Bay Ly's dialogue and continuing to the end of the selection.

*Le Ly Hayslip with her sister (left) and mother*

10 more, I was amazed and impressed by my father's pride in her accomplishments (she was, after all, a humble female), and his belief that I was worthy of her example.

11 "*Con phai theo got chan co ta*"[8] (Follow in her footsteps), he said. Only later would I learn what he truly meant.

Never again did I cry after my nap. Phung Thi women were too strong for that. Besides, I was my father's daughter and we had many things to do together.

On the eve of my mother's return, my father cooked a feast of roast duck. When we sat down to eat it, I felt guilty and my feelings showed on my face. He asked why I acted so sad.

"You've killed one of mother's ducks," I said. "One of the fat kind she sells at the market. She says the money buys gold which she saves for her daughters' weddings. Without gold for a dowry—*con o gia*[9]—I will be an old maid!"

My father looked suitably concerned, then brightened and said, "Well, Bay Ly, if you can't get married, you will just have to live at home forever with me!"

I clapped my hands at the happy prospect.

My father cut into the rich, juicy bird and

12

---

8. *Con phai theo got chan co ta* (kô fĭ tou gôt chăn kŏ tä)

9. *con o gia* (kôn u ʒă)

## Grammar in Action

To make written dialogue clear, writers follow certain punctuation rules. These rules specify the order in which punctuation marks appear when more than one mark is needed at any given spot. The **relationships among punctuation marks in dialogue** are illustrated well in Hayslip's work. In general put all punctuation marks inside closing quotation marks except semicolons and question marks or exclamation marks not part of the quotation. Study these examples:

"A naughty child learns more from a whipping stick than a sweet stick."

"What's this?" he asked, making a worried face.

said, "Even so, we won't tell your mother about the duck, okay?"

I giggled and swore myself to secrecy.

The next day, I took some water out to him in the fields. My mother was due home any time and I used every opportunity to step outside and watch for her. My father stopped working, drank gratefully, then took my hand and led me to the top of a nearby hill. It had a good view of the village and the land beyond it, almost to the ocean. I thought he was going to show me my mother coming back, but he had something else in mind.

He said, "Bay Ly, you see all this here? This is the Vietnam we have been talking about. You understand that a country is more than a lot of dirt, rivers, and forests, don't you?"

I said, "Yes, I understand." After all, we had learned in school that one's country is as sacred as a father's grave.

"Good. You know, some of these lands are battlefields where your brothers and cousins are fighting. They may never come back. Even your sisters have all left home in search of a better life. You are the only one left in my house. If the enemy comes back, you must be both a daughter and a son. I told you how the Chinese used to rule our land. People in this village had to risk their lives diving in the ocean just to find pearls for the Chinese emperor's gown. They had to risk tigers and snakes in the jungle just to find herbs for his table. Their payment for this hardship was a bowl of rice and another day of life. That is why Le Loi, Gia Long,[10] the Trung Sisters, and Phung Thi Chinh fought so hard to expel the Chinese. When the French came, it was the same old story. Your mother and I were taken to Danang to build a runway for their airplanes. We labored

---

10. **Le Loi** (lā loi), **Gia Long** (zä lổŋ)

from sunup to sundown and well after dark. If we stopped to rest or have a smoke, a Moroccan would come up and whip our behinds. Our reward was a bowl of rice and another day of life. Freedom is never a gift, Bay Ly. It must be won and won again. Do you understand?"

I said that I did.

"Good." He moved his finger from the patchwork of brown dikes, silver water, and rippling stalks to our house at the edge of the village. "This land here belongs to me. Do you know how I got it?"

I thought a moment, trying to remember my mother's stories, then said honestly, "I can't remember."

He squeezed me lovingly. "I got it from your mother."

"What? That can't be true!" I said. Everyone in the family knew my mother was poor and my father's family was wealthy. Her parents were dead and she had to work like a slave for her mother-in-law to prove herself worthy. Such women don't have land to give away!

"It's true." My father's smile widened. "When I was a young man, my parents needed someone to look after their lands. They had to be very careful about who they chose as wives for their three sons. In the village, your mother had a reputation as the hardest worker of all. She raised herself and her brothers without parents. At the same time, I noticed a beautiful woman working in the fields. When my mother said she was going to talk to the matchmaker about this hard-working village girl she'd heard about, my heart sank. I was too attracted to this mysterious tall woman I had seen in the rice paddies. You can imagine my surprise when I found out the girl my mother heard about and the woman I admired were the same.

"Well, we were married and my mother tested your mother severely. She not only

13 **Discussion** What does this passage say about the Vietnamese culture? Do you agree with this point of view?

14 **Discussion** What do you think may be the significance of a Vietnamese father charging a daughter with being "both a daughter and a son"? What may be the implication of that charge?

15 **Reading Strategy** How does Bay Ly's father clarify these sentences?

16 **Reading Strategy** What prediction can you make at this point?

17 **Discussion** What impact does this story have on Bay Ly? Why?

---

**Student Activity 1.** The following sentences from "Fathers and Daughters" have been written without certain punctuation marks. The needed marks are noted within parentheses. Place them properly.

1. "Without gold for a dowry I will be an old maid" (exclamation mark)
2. He said, "You understand that a country is more than a lot of dirt, rivers, and forests, don't you" (question mark)
3. That's why I say the land came from her, because it did" (period)
4. "Look under your pillow" he said with a smile. (comma)
5. "What's this" he asked, making a worried face. (question mark)

**Student Activity 2.** Imagine that you talked briefly with Bay Ly. Write the dialogue that you had with her. Use punctuation marks in proper relationships.

**Electronic Handbook** You may want students to review quotation marks before completing the Grammar in Action activities. If students have access to the Language Master 6000, have them enter the access word *quotation* and the quotation marks symbol (") and press the GRAMMAR key with each entry for information on the correct punctuation of dialogue.

had to cook and clean and know everything about children, but she had to be able to manage several farms and know when and how to take the extra produce to the market. Of course, she was testing her other daughters-in-law as well. When my parents died, they divided their several farms among their sons, but you know what? They gave your mother and me the biggest share because they knew we would take care of it best. That's why I say the land came from her, because it did.''

I suddenly missed my mother very much and looked down the road to the south, hoping to see her. My father noticed my sad expression.

''Hey.'' He poked me in the ribs. ''Are you getting hungry for lunch?''

''No. I want to learn how to take care of the farm. What happens if the soldiers come back? What did you and Mother do when the soldiers came?''

*Le Ly Hayslip's mother, Tran Thi Huyen*

My father squatted on the dusty hilltop and wiped the sweat from his forehead. ''The first thing I did was to tell myself that it was my duty to survive—to take care of my family and my farm. That is a tricky job in wartime. It's as hard as being a soldier. The Moroccans were very savage. One day the rumor passed that they were coming to destroy the village. You may remember the night I sent you and your brothers and sisters away with your mother to Danang.''

''You didn't go with us!'' My voice still held the horror of the night I thought I had lost my father.

''Right! I stayed near the village—right on this hill—to keep an eye on the enemy and on our house. If they really wanted to destroy the village, I would save some of our things so that we could start over. Sure enough, that was their plan.

''The real problem was to keep things safe and avoid being captured. Their patrols were everywhere. Sometimes I went so deep in the forest that I worried about getting lost, but all I had to do was follow the smoke from the burning huts and I could find my way back.

''Once, I was trapped between two patrols that had camped on both sides of a river. I had to wait in the water for two days before one of them moved on. When I got out, my skin was shriveled like an old melon. I was so cold I could hardly move. From the waist down, my body was black with leeches. But it was worth all the pain. When your mother came back, we still had some furniture and tools to cultivate the earth. Many people lost everything. Yes, we were very lucky.''

My father put his arms around me. ''My brother Huong—your uncle Huong—had three sons and four daughters. Of his four daughters, only one is still alive. Of his three sons, two went north to Hanoi and one went

*426  Nonfiction*

---

## Commentary

Oliver Stone, the film director who won fame for the movies set in Vietnam *Platoon* and *Born on the Fourth of July,* announced in 1992 his plan to make *Heaven on Earth,* his own adaptation of Hayslip's two autobiographical works, *When Heaven and Earth Changed Places* and *Child of War, Woman of Peace.* Stone calls the movie the Vietnamese woman's ''personal odyssey from the 1950's through the 1980's, from peasant to guerrilla fighter to beggar and hustler, to her relocation to the United States and transformation into an American housewife.''

## Closure and Extension

**ANSWERS TO RESPONDING TO THE SELECTION**
*Your Response*

1. You may want to first discuss his characteristics. Then have students talk about how different cultures hold different characteristics in high esteem.

20 **Reading Strategy** Why does Bay Ly's father tell about each of her cousins' fate? What do Bay Ly's aunts and uncles have in common?

21 **Literary Focus: Autobiography** What impact will this concluding sentence likely have on Bay Ly? Why is it an appropriate way to end this segment of her autobiography?

**Reader's Response** Bay Ly seems to share a closer relationship with her father than with her mother. Do you think this is unusual for a Vietnamese girl? Why or why not?

**Thematic Response** What cultural inferences can you make from this selection about Vietnamese children appreciating and honoring their elders?

**Master Teacher Note** If possible, ask interested students to read *When Heaven and Earth Changed Places* (Doubleday, 1989). Though some students may be willing to read the entire book, you may have greater success asking individuals to read one of the fourteen chapters (ranging from twenty to almost forty pages) including Chapter 2, "Fathers and Daughters," from which this selection is excerpted. Readers could then present oral reports in the numerical order of the chapters.

*Le Ly Hayslip (right) and her sister at the family grave site*

south to Saigon.[11] Huong's house is very empty. My other brother, your uncle Luc, had only two sons. One went north to Hanoi, the other was killed in the fields. His daughter is deaf and dumb. No wonder he has taken to drink, eh? Who does he have to sing in his house and tend his shrine when he is gone? My sister Lien had three daughters and four sons. Three of the four sons went to Hanoi and the fourth went to Saigon to find his fortune. The girls all tend their in-laws and mourn slain husbands. Who will care for Lien when she is too feeble to care for herself? Finally, my baby sister Nhien lost her husband to French bombers. Of her two sons, one went to Hanoi and the other joined the Republic, then defected, then was mur-

dered in his house. Nobody knows which side killed him. It doesn't really matter."

My father drew me out to arm's length and looked me squarely in the eye. "Now, Bay Ly, do you understand what your job is?"

I squared my shoulders and put on a soldier's face. "My job is to avenge my family. To protect my farm by killing the enemy. I must become a woman warrior like Phung Thi Chinh!"

My father laughed and pulled me close. "No, little peach blossom. Your job is to stay alive—to keep an eye on things and keep the village safe. To find a husband and have babies and tell the story of what you've seen to your children and anyone else who'll listen. Most of all, it is to live in peace and tend the shrine of our ancestors. Do these things well, Bay Ly, and you will be worth more than any soldier who ever took up a sword."

---

**11. Hanoi** (hä nơi′) **. . . Saigon** (sĭ′ gän′): The capitals of North and South Vietnam, respectively, during the period 1954–1976.

*Fathers and Daughters* 427

---

mand to his daughter that her job is to stay alive. Those who support the argument for a willingness to die may cite the examples from legend and history about warriors willing to die rather than suffer injustices.

## ANSWERS TO ANALYZING LITERATURE

1. Students may suggest that Bay Ly tells about the incident by way of explanation of a woman's obedience to her husband. She offers no refutation but accepts the fact that she will "have both cheeks glowing."

2. Ask students to think about not only their genealogy but also their neighborhoods, their religious affiliations, and their state's contributions to the nation and the world.

### Recalling

3. War has brought separation, threat of death, and poverty to Bay Ly's personal family. It has brought death, loss of property, poverty,

and separation as well as heroism and victory to Bay Ly's extended family.

4. Her job is to stay alive and look after the property, her family, and the family shrine.

### Interpreting

5. Suggested Response: Usually such relationships are shared only by fathers and sons.

6. Suggested Response: She learns to cope with a war that is the same as life.

7. Suggested Response: Bay Ly is proud of Phung Thi Chinh because she sacrificed to gain victory, a virtuous attribute in Vietnamese culture. Her father is proud of the woman warrior because she is a distant ancestor.

### Applying

8. Those who support the argument for a determination to live may cite Bay Ly's father's actions during the invasion to stay alive and his com-

2. She claps her hands "at the happy prospect" of staying home with her father and enjoys the secret they share.

## ANSWERS TO CRITICAL THINKING AND READING

1. Suggested Response: She admits that her father's whippings were not as severe as they could have been but that the hurt in his eyes was worse than the sting of the switch.
2. Suggested Response: Because Bay Ly writes about her father with admiration, readers also admire him.

**Challenge** What evidence in this selection suggests the Vietnamese cultural importance of honoring one's elders, even one's early ancestors?

## THINKING AND WRITING

**Software** If your students are working at computers, suggest that they use the **Writer's Helper** tool *Three Ways of Seeing* to help them generate ideas for topics.

**Writing Transparency** Before students write you may want to use Model 1: *Personal Narrative* in **Transparencies for Writing** to model the first-person narrative for students.

**Alternative Assessment** *Peer Review:* In pairs or groups of four, have your students assess one another's work by responding to the following questions:

What does the writer say are the topics of the father's unspoken thoughts?

To what details from the conversation with Bay Ly does the father refer?

What would you suggest the writer add to make the father's thoughts more interesting and more believable?

What concrete suggestions can you offer to help the writer maintain first-person point of view and to improve the mechanics of the piece?

To validate the peer review, have your students revise their work, incorporating those suggestions they believe will enhance their final product.

### Publishing Student Writing
When students have completed their compositions, have them share their work in reader re-

## RESPONDING TO THE SELECTION

### Your Response
1. Do you admire Bay Ly's father? Why or why not?
2. Bay Ly is proud to be her father's daughter and the descendant of a woman warrior. What makes you proud of your heritage?

### Recalling
3. What changes does war bring to Bay Ly's immediate family? What changes does it bring to her extended family?
4. According to her father, what is Bay Ly's responsibility in time of war?

### Interpreting
5. What is unusual about Bay Ly's relationship with her father?
6. What do you think Bay Ly learns from her father's songs?
7. Why is Bay Ly proud of her ancestor Phung Thi Chinh? Why is her father proud of the woman warrior?

### Applying
8. What do you think would be more important to Bay Ly's father, a determination to live or a willingness to die? Explain your answer.

## ANALYZING LITERATURE

### Understanding the Narrator in Autobiography
Autobiography is usually written in the first person, using the pronoun "I." The narrator, or person telling the writer's life story, is, in fact, the writer. In an autobiography the writer relates experiences from his or her own perspective. For example, Bay Ly tells about her father from the perspective of a loving and dutiful Vietnamese daughter.

1. How does Bay Ly show her acceptance of Vietnamese tradition in her account of her parents' argument on page 423?

*428   Nonfiction*

2. How does Bay Ly show her love for her father in her account of the meal on pages 424–425?

## CRITICAL THINKING AND READING

### Recognizing the Effect of Point of View
The way you see people and events in an autobiography is limited to the way the writer sees and tells about them. As in all first-person narratives, you see through the eyes of the narrator. You know what Bay Ly thinks, says, and does. Like Bay Ly you can only guess the unspoken thoughts and feelings of her father.

1. What does Bay Ly say about being whipped that her father might only guess?
2. How does Bay Ly's description of her father affect the way you feel about him?

## THINKING AND WRITING

### Writing From Another Point of View
How might Bay Ly's father feel about the conversation with his daughter on the dusty hilltop? Review what you know about him from Bay Ly's description. Then, in a paragraph or two, write what he might be thinking after the conversation. Write from the first-person point of view, as if Bay Ly's father were speaking.

## LEARNING OPTIONS

1. **Cross-curricular Connection.** Hayslip's life is shaped by war in her homeland. Investigate the early history of Vietnam, starting with 100 B.C., the beginning of China's 1,000-year rule. Make a timeline of critical events up to the year 1965, when United States combat troops arrived.
2. **Art.** This selection is entitled "Fathers and Daughters." Make a collage that represents the relationship between Bay Ly and her father or between fathers and daughters in general.

sponse groups. Ask each group to pick two works that represent different reactions from Bay Ly's father. Share these with the entire class as a basis for discussion about his character.

### Writing Across the Curriculum
In conjunction with a social studies teacher, invite to class or suggest that students interview a Vietnam War veteran. As a class, have students brainstorm for a list

of questions based on references made and inferences drawn from "Fathers and Daughters." If possible, ask the guest veteran to read the selection before his or her visit with the class.

## LEARNING OPTIONS

1. Students who appreciate history will enjoy this Cross-curricular Connection.
2. Visual and kinesthetic learners will respond well to the art activity.

# Essays for Enjoyment

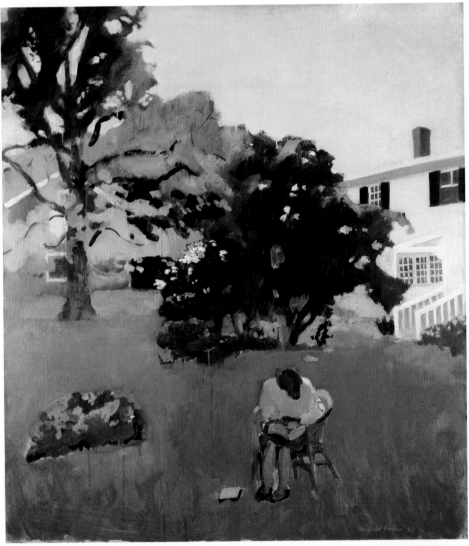

**GIRL READING OUTDOORS**
*Fairfield Porter*

**Humanities Note**

Fine art; *Girl Reading Outdoors,* by Fairfield Porter. Fairfield Porter (1907–1975), an American "Intimist" painter in the French style, was born in Winnetka, Illinois. He attended Harvard University for art history and studied painting at the Art Students' League in New York City. In addition to his prolific career as a painter, Porter has taught art at many prestigious schools and universities and has written noteworthy books and articles on the subject of American art and artists.

The subject of the painting *Girl Reading Outdoors* is typical of the pleasant and familiar scenes that Fairfield Porter preferred to paint. The girl in the painting is obviously enjoying her reading. Although the influence of the Impressionists is apparent in this work, Porter's interpretation of the style is direct, rough, and more typically American. He uses color rather than modeling to delineate the features of the girl, the shadows of the house, and the shade from the sunlight. Fine details are sacrificed in the effort to capture the essence of the scene. Like fellow American artists, Edward Hopper and Winslow Homer, Fairfield Porter concentrated on the study of color in the harsh northeastern light.

**More About the Author** Almost all of Frank Dobie's work has been on the history of Texas. Some critics see him as a folklorist, others as a historian of this cowboy state. Ask the class to consider the connection between folklore and history. How does one inform the other?

**Literary Focus** Ask students for examples of other narratives they have read—either fiction or nonfiction. Point out that a narrative essay contains the elements of a narrative but is true.

**Prereading Focus** You may wish to put the chart on the chalkboard and have the class begin by discussing the possibility of taking different stray newborn animals into their homes. The final chart will be more interesting because it will reflect the varied routines of different families. Finally, the class might discuss what was distinctly different about the Kerrs's adjustments to Sancho as a result of their being nineteenth-century cattle ranchers.

**Vocabulary** Students may also find it helpful to know these expressions: "paint bull calf" (p. 431), a young steer that is piebald, or covered with patches of two colors, or "drag drivers" (p. 433), the cowboys who rode at the back of a herd in a cattle drive.

**Electronic Handbook** If students have access to the Language Master 6000, suggest that they find the definition specific to ranching of each of these words also used in the selection. The words have other meanings, but students should find the meaning of each word as it is used in the context of this essay: *brush* (p. 431), *branded* (p. 433), and *steer* (p. 433).

# GUIDE FOR READING

## Sancho

### Narrative Essay

An essay is a short nonfiction composition exploring a topic. A **narrative essay** explores this topic by telling a true story. It discusses a topic of personal interest to the writer, giving the writer's view of the subject or personal experience with it. In "Sancho," the author, J. Frank Dobie, tells you about a Texas longhorn whose story he found unusual as well as interesting.

### Focus

Blending a stray animal into a family's routine is a difficult task. Often many adjustments must be made. Suppose you took a newborn stray animal into your home. Imagine what your family would have to do to accommodate to the needs of that animal. Copy the following chart into your notebook. On the left side of the chart, list the changes everyone would have to make to help the animal adjust to your family's routines. As you read "Sancho," list on the right side of the chart the problems and adjustments that Kerr and his wife, Maria, had to make to adopt Sancho into their lives. Compare your two lists.

| Your family's adjustments | The Kerrs' adjustments |
|---|---|
|  |  |
|  |  |
|  |  |

### Vocabulary

Knowing the following words will help you as you read "Sancho."

**dogie** (dō′ gē) **calves** *n*.: Motherless calves or strays in a range herd; used chiefly in the West (p. 431)

**vigorous** (vig′ ər əs) *adj*.: Strong and energetic (p. 431)

**yearling** (yir′ liŋ) *n*.: An animal that is between one and two years old (p. 433)

### J. Frank Dobie

(1888–1964) grew up in the southwest Texas brush country. He pursued a writing and teaching career devoted to the folklore and history of his native state. Over the years he became, in his words, "a historian of the longhorns, the mustangs, the coyote, and the other characters of the West." In his book *The Longhorns,* he tells of some memorable Texas steers. He included the story of Sancho, which he heard from John Rigby, a trail boss on the Texas Range.

*430    Nonfiction*

## Objectives

1 To understand a narrative essay
2 To put events in chronological order
3 To write a letter about Sancho
4 To express individual interests and abilities through an optional activity

## Support Material

**Teaching Portfolio**
Teacher Backup, p. 505
Grammar in Action Worksheet, *Understanding Prepositional Phrases,* p. 509–510
Usage and Mechanics Worksheet, p. 511
Vocabulary Check, p. 512
Analyzing Literature Worksheet,

*Understanding a Narrative Essay,* p. 513
Critical Thinking and Reading Worksheet, *Putting Events in Chronological Order,* p. 514
Selection Test, p. 515

**Prentice Hall Literature Writing Studio**

**Presentation**

**Motivation/Prior Knowledge**
Ask students to imagine that they worked on a cattle ranch in the late nineteenth century. Tell them to visualize what the ranch looked like and to describe it. Have them also try to imagine what life on the ranch was like and to describe that, too.

**Master Teacher Note** Bring in a map of the Southwest for students and trace the route of the cattle drive.

**Purpose-Setting Question** What is unusual about Sancho?

**1 Literary Focus** Point out that a narrative essay tells a *true* story.

**2 Enrichment** Sancho is suckled by another cow and is adopted as an orphan. Similarly, tell students about Romulus and Remus, founders of Rome, who were left as infants to die in the Tiber, and were suckled by a she-wolf.

**3 Discussion** Discuss whether animals are inclined to adopt young not their own. You might tell students that the United States government has done experiments encouraging adult birds of depleted species to hatch eggs not their own.

# Sancho

## J. Frank Dobie

A man by the name of Kerr had a little ranch on Esperanza Creek in Frio County, in the mesquite lands[1] south of San Antonio. He owned several good cow ponies, a few cattle, and a little bunch of goats that a dog guarded by day. At night they were shut up in a brush corral near the house. Three or four acres of land, fenced in with brush and poles, grew corn, watermelons and "kershaws"—except when the season was too drouthy.[2] A hand-dug well equipped with pulley wheel, rope and bucket furnished water for the establishment.

Kerr's wife was named María. They had no children. She was clean, thrifty, cheerful, always making pets of animals. She usually milked three or four cows and sometimes made cheese out of goat's milk.

Late in the winter of 1877, Kerr while riding over on the San Miguel found one of his cows dead in a bog-hole. Beside the cow was a mud-plastered little black-and-white paint bull calf less than a week old. It was too weak to run; perhaps other cattle had saved it from the coyotes. Kerr pitched his rope over its head, drew it up across the saddle in front of him, carried it home, and turned it over to María.

She had raised many dogie calves and numerous colts captured from mustang mares. The first thing she did now was to pour milk from a bottle down the orphan's throat. With warm water she washed the caked mud off its body. But hand-raising a calf is no end of trouble. The next day Kerr rode around until he found a thrifty brown cow with a young calf. He drove them to the pen. By tying this cow's head up close to a post and hobbling her hind legs, Kerr and María forced her to let the orphan suckle. She did not give a cup of milk at this first sucking. Her calf was kept in the pen next day, and the poor thing bawled herself hoarse. María began feeding her some prickly pear with the thorns singed off. After being tied up twice daily for a month, she adopted the orphan as a twin to her own offspring.

Now she was one of the household cows. Spring weeds came up plentifully and the guajilla brush put out in full leaf. When the brown cow came in about sundown and her two calves were released for their supper, it was a cheering sight to see them wiggle their tails while they guzzled milk.

The dogie was a vigorous little brute, and before long he was getting more milk than the brown cow's own calf. María called him Sancho, a Mexican name meaning "pet." She was especially fond of Sancho, and he grew to be especially fond of her.

---

**1. mesquite** (mes kēt') **lands** *n.:* Areas in which grow certain thorny trees and shrubs, common in the southwest U.S. and in Mexico.
**2. drouthy** (drouth' ē) *adj.:* Dried up due to drought—a lack of rain.

*Sancho* 431

**Making Connections** Another selection that deals with an animal displaying some human characteristics is "Debbie," by James Herriot, on page 439. "Debbie" also shows the human gift of love for animals. Ask students what special qualities such people have. Why are animals drawn to them?

**Thematic Focus** Ask students to consider whether animals, like humans, can have a sense of place. How do domesticated animals know what is "home"? Why is it that wild animals thrive in certain places and not in others? In this selection, why is Sancho drawn to a particular place?

## Humanities Note

Fine art, *In a Stampede,* 1888, by Frederic Remington. Frederic Remington (1861–1909) was born in Canton, New York. He attended the Yale School of Art and the Art Students' League. He worked primarily as an illustrator for magazines such as *Harper's Weekly* and *Outing.* Remington is best known for his small bronze sculptures of cowboys, Native Americans, and soldiers, and for his paintings of Western action.

In this illustration, the full front view of rampaging steer approaching with lowered horns and the cowboy trying to herd them with raised whip create strong dramatic tension.

1. What part of the story does this picture suggest?
2. What sounds might you hear in this scene?

**Enrichment** In this selection the author has created a vibrant setting, alive with the plants and animals of the Texas plains. Ask students to find and read aloud passages where descriptions of the setting are particularly detailed. Have students compare the setting of "Sancho" with the geographic setting of your region of the country. Are there any similarities? Could this essay have been written by a New Englander, an Alaskan, or a Puerto Rican, for example? Why or why not?

**IN A STAMPEDE**
*Illustration by Frederic Remington*

432 Nonfiction

She would give him the shucks wrapped around tamales. Then she began treating him to whole tamales, which are made of ground corn rolled around a core of chopped-up meat, this banana-shaped roll, done up in a shuck, then being steam-boiled. Sancho seemed not to mind the meat. As everybody who has eaten them knows, Mexican tamales are highly seasoned with pepper. Sancho seemed to like the seasoning.

In southern Texas the little chiltipiquin peppers, red when ripe, grow wild in low, shaded places. Cattle never eat them, leaving them for the wild turkeys, mockingbirds and blue quail to pick off. Sometimes in the early fall wild turkeys used to gorge on them so avidly that their flesh became too peppery for human consumption. By eating tamales Sancho developed a taste for the little red peppers growing in the thickets along Esperanza Creek. In fact, he became a kind of chiltipiquin addict. He would hunt for the peppers.

Furthermore, the tamales gave him a tooth for corn in the ear. The summer after he became a yearling he began breaking through the brush fence that enclosed Kerr's corn patch. A forked stick had to be tied around his neck to prevent his getting through the fence. He had been branded and turned into a steer, but he was as strong as any young bull. Like many other pets, he was something of a nuisance. When he could not steal corn or was not humored with tamales, he was enormously contented with grass, mixed in summertime with the sweet mesquite beans. Now and then María gave him a lump of the brown *piloncillo* sugar, from Mexico, that all the border country used.

Every night Sancho came to the ranch pen to sleep. His bed ground was near a certain mesquite tree just outside the gate. He spent hours every summer day in the shade of this mesquite. When it rained and other cattle drifted off, hunting fresh pasturage, Sancho stayed at home and drank at the well. He was strictly a home creature.

In the spring of 1880 Sancho was three years old and past, white of horn and as blocky of build as a long-legged Texas steer ever grew. Kerr's ranch lay in a big unfenced range grazed by the Shiner brothers. That spring they had a contract to deliver three herds of steers, each to number 2500 head, in Wyoming. Kerr was helping the Shiners gather cattle, and, along with various other ranchers, sold them what steers he had.

Sancho was included. One day late in March the Shiner men road-branded him *7 Z* and put him in the first herd headed north. The other herds were to follow two or three days apart.

It was late in the afternoon when the ''shaping up'' of the herd was completed. It was watered and thrown out on open prairie ground to be bedded down. But Sancho had no disposition to lie down—there. He wanted to go back to that mesquite just outside the pen gate at the Kerr place on the Esperanza where he had without variation slept every night since he had been weaned. Perhaps he had in mind an evening tamale. He stood and roamed about on the south side of the herd. A dozen times during the night the men on guard had to drive him back. As reliefs were changed, word passed to keep an eye on that paint steer on the lower side.

When the herd started on next morning, Sancho was at the tail end of it, often stopping and looking back. It took constant attention from one of the drag drivers to keep him moving. By the time the second night arrived, every hand in the outfit knew Sancho, by name and sight, as being the stubbornest and gentlest steer of the lot. About dark one of them pitched a loop over his

4 **Discussion** Explain that tamales are a native Mexican food of red peppers and minced meat rolled in cornmeal, wrapped in corn husks, and cooked by baking or steaming. Ask students who have had tamales to describe their taste.

5 **Clarification** Tell students that branding was burning a mark with a hot iron on the skin of cattle to show ownership. Different cattle brands were used to distinguish which steer belonged to which owner.

6 **Critical Thinking and Reading** What words in this paragraph indicate chronological order?

**Multicultural Focus** The American West is rich in history and culture. Stories of cowboys and cattle drives immediately come to mind, but the broad diversity of the population of that area should not be overlooked when considering the history of the West. Of all modern nations, the United States has perhaps the most diverse population. Point out that as the frontier pushed westward, several ethnic groups interacted to build the West. The pioneer experience involved four major ethnic groups: African Americans, Native Americans, Mexican Americans, and various European Americans.

Discuss the advantages and difficulties of close interaction among these ethnic groups. Touch on the fates of each group as a result of this interaction. You may wish to mention that Frederick Turner, a well-known historian of the West, saw the United States as composed of many population groups who were sometimes united and sometimes in conflict. This differed from older European cultures, which were more unified.

7 **Reading Strategy** Have students summarize the events so far. Ask them to predict what kinds of events could happen.

8 **Discussion** What does Sancho's mimicking of human behavior indicate about his intelligence?

horns and staked him to a bush. This saved bothering with his persistent efforts to walk off.

Daily when the herd was halted to graze, spreading out like a fan, the steers all eating their way northward, Sancho invariably pointed himself south. In his lazy way he grabbed many a mouthful of grass while the herd was moving. Finally, in some brush up on the Llano, after ten days of trailing, he dodged into freedom. On the second day following, one of the point men of the second Shiner herd saw him walking south, saw his *7 Z* road brand, rounded him in, and set him traveling north again. He became the chief drag animal of this herd. Somewhere north of the Colorado there was a run one night, and when morning came Sancho was missing. The other steers had held together; probably Sancho had not run at all. But he was picked up again, by the third Shiner herd coming on behind.

7 | He took his accustomed place in the drag and continued to require special driving. He picked up in weight. He chewed his cud peacefully and slept soundly, but whenever he looked southward, which was often, he raised his head as if memory and expectation were stirring. The boys were all personally acquainted with him, and every night one of them would stake him.

One day the cattle balked and milled at a bank-full river. "Rope Old Sancho and lead him in," the boss ordered, "and we'll point the other cattle after him." Sancho led like a horse. The herd followed. As soon as he was released, he dropped back to the rear. After this, however, he was always led to the front when there was high water to cross.

By the time the herd got into No Man's Land, beyond Red River, the sand-hill plums and the low-running possum grapes were 8 | turning ripe. Pausing now and then to pick a little of the fruit, Sancho's driver saw the pet steer following his example.

Meantime the cattle were trailing, trailing, always north. For five hundred miles across Texas, counting the windings to find water and keep out of breaks, they had come. After getting into the Indian Territory, they snailed on across the Wichita, the South Canadian, the North Canadian, and the Cimarron. On into Kansas they trailed and across the Arkansas, around Dodge City, cowboy capital of the world, out of Kansas into Nebraska, over the wide, wide Platte, past the roaring cow town of Ogalla-la, up the North Platte, under the Black Hills, and then against the Big Horn Mountains. For two thousand miles, making ten or twelve miles a day, the Shiner herds trailed. They "walked with the grass." Slow, slow, they moved. "Oh, it was a long and lonesome go"—as slow as the long drawn-out notes of "The Texas Lullaby," as slow as the night herder's song on a slow-walking horse:

> It's a whoop and a yea, get along
> my little dogies,
>     For camp is far away.
> It's a whoop and a yea and a-
> driving the dogies,
>     For Wyoming may be your new
> home.

When, finally, after listening for months, day and night, to the slow song of their motion, the "dogies" reached their "new home," Sancho was still halting every now and then to sniff southward for a whiff of the Mexican Gulf. The farther he got away from home, the less he seemed to like the change. He had never felt frost in September before. The Mexican peppers on the Esperanza were red ripe now.

The Wyoming outfit received the cattle. Then for a week the Texas men helped brand *C R* on their long sides before turning them loose on the new range. When San-

434  *Nonfiction*

## Grammar in Action

Writers effectively use **prepositional phrases** in order to construct vivid sentences with specific details. A prepositional phrase begins with a preposition (*in, on, around, near, through,* and others) and ends with a noun or pronoun that answers "who" or "what" of the preposition. Prepositional phrases modify nouns, pronouns, or verbs in the sentence. The prepositional phrase must appear close to the noun, pronoun, or verb that it describes.

Prepositional phrases provide description and show the relationship between a noun or a verb and the object of a preposition. Look at the following sentences that have been expanded with prepositional phrases:

After getting into the Indian Territory, they snailed on across the Wichita, the South Canadian, the North Canadian, and the Cimarron. On into Kansas they trailed and across the Arkansas, around Dodge City, cowboy capital of the world, out of Kansas into Nebraska, over the wide, wide Platte, past the roaring cow town of Ogalla-la, up the North Platte, under the Black Hills, and then against the Big Horn Mountains.

# MULTICULTURAL CONNECTION

## The Black Cowboy

When we think of cowboys like the ones in "Sancho," the faces we see are primarily white, although nearly a quarter of all the cowboys were black.

How did African Americans come to the West? Many of them were born and raised there, living as slaves on Texas ranches before the Civil War. Taught to rope and ride by their masters, many of these slaves became cowhands once they gained their freedom. After Emancipation other blacks headed west looking for new opportunities to work.

Although prejudice existed, black cowboys were mostly accepted on equal terms by white cowboys. Being a cowboy was a tough, hard life; anyone who could survive it was respected by his peers.

**Nat Love.** Probably the most famous black cowboy was Nat Love, nicknamed "Deadwood Dick" after winning a riding, roping, and shooting contest in the town of Deadwood, South Dakota.

Love was born a slave in Tennessee and left home at the age of fifteen to find work as a cowboy in legendary Dodge City, Kansas. For the next twenty years, Love worked cattle drives across the West, becoming famous for his riding skill and his uncanny ability to identify almost any cattle brand.

Love retired from the range in 1890 and years later wrote his autobiography, *The Life and Adventures of Nat Love, Better Known in Cattle Country as Deadwood Dick.* In this book Love described his exploits as a cowboy. Among the other Western legends who appear in his book are Bat Masterson, Billy the Kid, and Jesse James.

**Bill Pickett.** Another black cowboy was Bill Pickett, whose achievements were legendary. Pickett was an experienced cowhand on two continents—North and South America—when he invented the rodeo sport of bulldogging on an Oklahoma ranch. In bulldogging, the cowboy grips a steer's horns with his bare hands and wrestles it to the ground. His invention and promotion of bulldogging helped turn the Western rodeo into the popular sporting event it remains today.

Pickett traveled the country demonstrating his amazing skill at bulldogging. As he wrestled the steer to the ground, he was helped by his good friend, the cowboy humorist Will Rogers.

Unlike Love, who eventually became a Pullman porter for the railroad, Pickett remained a cowboy all his life.

Although black cowboys played an important role in taming the West and herding cattle, it was hard for them to find work when the cattle drives ended. Racial prejudice forced them to take a variety of menial jobs.

### Exploring on Your Own

Find out more about the contributions of black cowboys, or investigate the roles that other groups played in settling the West.

## Preparation

### Motivation/Prior Knowledge
Ask students to list characteristics of cowboys. What skills did cowboys have? What did they look like? What kind of lives did they lead? Who are well-known cowboys? Students may draw from the description in the essay "Sancho" and from any sources of prior knowledge. Lead them to think about cowboys from a variety of ethnic backgrounds.

## Presentation

Discussion Questions:
1. What skills distinguished Nat Love and Bill Pickett?
2. What happened to the black cowboys when the cattle drives ended?

## Closure and Extension

Encourage students to find out more about black cowboys as well as cowboys from other ethnic backgrounds. One source is *Reflections of a Black Cowboy* series by Robert Miller, published by Silver Burdett Press.

**Student Activity 1.** There are fourteen prepositional phrases in the example. Find each one.

**Student Activity 2.** Write your own description of a trip that you once took. Use a series of prepositional phrases in your description. Model your description after the example.

**Electronic Handbook** You may want students to review prepositions before completing the Grammar in Action activities. If students have access to the Language Master 6000, have them enter the access word *preposition* and press the GRAMMAR key to get information on prepositional phrases.

9 **Clarification** Tobacco juice would sting the eyes and keep the cowboys awake.

10 **Literary Focus** In a narrative essay, the writer gives his or her view of the subject or personal experience with it.

11 **Discussion** Discuss the strength of strong homing instincts in animals. Ask students for fictional and true-life examples of animals escaping from a new owner to return home.

12 **Discussion** What does Sancho's behavior tell you about his personality?

**Reader's Response** Describe an animal with which you are familiar who is part of a family the way Sancho was.

**Thematic Response** Students who have responded to the importance of the environment in this narrative will have a visual image of Sancho and the land surrounding the Kerr cabin on Esperanza Creek. Suggest that they sketch or paint pictures of the landscape that Sancho happily returned to. Display the student art on a classroom bulletin board. Some students may prefer to write a descriptive poem about Sancho and the land on which he lived.

cho's time came to be branded in the chute,[3] one of the Texans yelled out, "There goes my pet. Stamp that *C R* brand on him good and deep." Another one said, "The line riders had better watch for his tracks."

And now the Shiner men turned south, taking back with them their saddle horses and chuck wagons—and leaving Sancho behind. They made good time, but a blue norther was whistling at their backs when they turned the remuda[4] loose on the Frio River. After the "Cowboys' Christmas Ball" most of them settled down for a few weeks of winter sleep. They could rub tobacco juice in their eyes during the summer when they needed something in addition to night rides and runs to keep them awake.

Spring comes early down on the Esperanza. The mesquites were all in new leaf with that green so fresh and tender that the color seems to emanate into the sky. The bluebonnets and the pink phlox were sprinkling every hill and draw. The prickly pear was studded with waxy blossoms, and the glades were heavy with the perfume of white brush. It was a good season, and tallow weed and grass were coming together. It was time for the spring cow hunts and the putting up of herds for the annual drive north. The Shiners were at work.

"We were close to Kerr's cabin on Esperanza Creek," John Rigby told me, "when I looked across a pear flat and saw something that made me rub my eyes. I was riding with Joe Shiner, and we both stopped our horses."

"Do you see what I see?" John Rigby asked.

"Yes, but before I say, I'm going to read the brand," Joe Shiner answered.

They rode over. "You can hang me for a horse thief," John Rigby will tell, "if it wasn't that Sancho paint steer, four years old now, the Shiner *7 Z* road brand and the Wyoming *C R* range brand both showing on him as plain as boxcar letters."

The men rode on down to Kerr's.

"Yes," Kerr said, "Old Sancho got in about six weeks ago. His hoofs were worn mighty nigh down to the hair, but he wasn't lame. I thought Maria was going out of her senses, she was so glad to see him. She actually hugged him and she cried and then she begun feeding him hot tamales. She's made a batch of them nearly every day since, just to pet that steer. When she's not feeding him tamales, she's giving him *piloncillo*."

Sancho was slicking off and certainly did seem contented. He was coming up every night and sleeping at the gate, María said. She was nervous over the prospect of losing her pet, but Joe Shiner said that if that steer loved his home enough to walk back to it all the way from Wyoming, he wasn't going to drive him off again, even if he was putting up another herd for the *C R* owners.

As far as I can find out, Old Sancho lived right there on the Esperanza, now and then getting a tamale, tickling his palate with chili peppers in season, and generally staying fat on mesquite grass, until he died a natural death. He was one of the "walking Texas Longhorns."

---

**3. chute** (shoot) *n.*: A narrow, high-walled device used to restrain cattle.
**4. remuda** (rə moo′ də) *n.*: Group of extra saddle horses kept as a supply of remounts.

## Closure and Extension

### ANSWERS TO RESPONDING TO THE SELECTION
#### Your Response

1. Most students who love animals will respond positively because they will enjoy the idea of having a relationship with a pet who is as personable as Sancho.

2. Many students will relish the idea of having been a cowhand, working in the rough and tumble out-of-doors in an unstructured environment. Others will know why it would not have appealed to them and will be able to say what they would rather do.

# RESPONDING TO THE SELECTION

## Your Response

1. Do you think that you would have responded to Sancho as María did? Why or why not?
2. Would you have enjoyed working as a cowhand on a cattle drive? Explain your answer.

## Recalling

3. How does Sancho become María's pet?
4. Describe Sancho's behavior on the drive.
5. What finally happens to Sancho? Why does Joe Shiner agree to this decision?

## Interpreting

6. Dobie felt that Sancho was an animal worth remembering. Find three examples of Sancho's almost human personality.
7. Dobie said that Sancho's story was the best range story he had ever heard. Why do you think he liked the story so much?

## Applying

8. Think about where María lived and what her daily life must have been like. Why would a pet be so important to her?

# ANALYZING LITERATURE

## Understanding a Narrative Essay

A **narrative essay** is a nonfiction composition in which the writer explores the subject by telling a true story. People write essays to present their observations, views, or opinions about a topic. Dobie knew the section of Texas where Sancho lived, and he had written and studied about cattle drives like the one described in "Sancho." Dobie was able to include details that help make the events in the selection vivid to readers.

1. List three details about the section of Texas where Sancho lived that Dobie includes.
2. List three details about cattle drives that Dobie includes in the essay.

# CRITICAL THINKING AND READING

## Putting Events in Chronological Order

**Chronological order** is the order in which events happen in time. Authors use certain words and phrases to place events in time, such as "the first thing she did" and "the next day."

Write the numbers of the following events in the order in which they happened. Then list the phrases that signal the order in which they should appear.

1. When he was a yearling, Sancho broke into the corn patch.
2. Sancho lived on the ranch until he died.
3. Sancho at three years old was a handsome Texas steer.

# THINKING AND WRITING

## Writing a Letter

Look over the freewriting you did before you began this selection. Use ideas from it and from the selection as the basis for a letter to a friend telling about Sancho's return. Revise your letter, making sure you have presented the information from María's point of view. Proofread your letter and share it with your classmates.

# LEARNING OPTION

**Art.** Sancho was different in appearance from the other cattle on the Kerr ranch; the author describes him as a "paint." Find out what a paint looks like. Then draw or paint a picture of Sancho according to your research, according to Dobie's description, and according to how you see him based on his personality in the essay. Display your picture on the bulletin board with those of other students for all to enjoy.

*Sancho   437*

---

---

**Literary Focus** Ask students what they think would make "real" characters interesting to read about.

**Prereading Focus** Ask students to describe the veterinarians who have taken care of their sick pets. Elicit from students details about emergency events that led up to some of the veterinary visits—times when they were concerned about their pets' health, even worried that their pets might die. How did they feel about their veterinarians after the pets had been treated and were getting better?

**Vocabulary** For your less advanced students, you may also want to review these words: wheedling (p. 440), malignant (p. 441), irreverent (p. 442), incredulously (p. 442), and feline (p. 442).

**Electronic Handbook** If students have access to the Language Master 6000, suggest that they find a synonym with a different connotation for each of the following vocabulary words: *wafted, privations, ornate,* and *goading.*

**Spelling Tip** The final consonant of one-syllable words ending in consonant-vowel-consonant, like *fret,* is doubled before a consonant suffix. Thus
*fret* + *ed* = fretted
Other words following this pattern include
*big* + *er* = bigger
*wrap* + *ed* = wrapped

# GUIDE FOR READING

## Debbie

### Characters in a Narrative Essay

The characters in a narrative essay are real people. In fact, sometimes the author even appears as a character. You learn about these characters in the same way you learn about characters in a piece of fiction. You can read about their actions, listen to their words, share their thoughts, or read descriptive details about them. Finally, you can learn much about a character by reading what other characters say or think about him or her.

### Focus

People often have a concept of the kind of person who chooses to go into a certain field, such as acting, or teaching, or engineering. Make a word web like the one that follows, and use it to examine the kind of person who you think becomes a veterinarian. Expand the web with as many appropriate words as you can think of. As you read "Debbie," add other words and ideas that occur to you as you consider how James Herriot portrays himself in this essay.

### Vocabulary

Knowing the following words will help you as you read "Debbie."

**fretted** (fret' əd) *adj.*: Decoratively arranged (p. 440)

**sage** (sāj) *n.*: A plant used to flavor food (p. 440)

**wafted** (waf' təd) *v.*: Moved lightly through the air (p. 440)

**knell** (nel) *n.*: The sound of a bell slowly ringing, as for a funeral (p. 441)

**privations** (prī vā' shənz) *n.*: Lack of common comforts (p. 441)

**ornate** (ôr nāt') *adj.*: Having fancy decorations (p. 442)

**goading** (gōd' iŋ) *v.*: Urging to action (p. 442)

### James Herriot

(1916– ), who was born in Glasgow, Scotland, studied veterinary medicine. Since 1940 he has been a veterinarian in England, the setting for his true stories about being a "country vet." British veterinarians are not allowed to use any form of advertising. Since writing under his own name would be considered advertising, he chose James Herriot as his pen name. The incidents Herriot describes, such as the one in "Debbie," have filled more than ten books and have inspired a popular television series.

*438   Nonfiction*

## Objectives

1 To understand characters in a narrative essay
2 To compare and contrast characters
3 To write an article comparing and contrasting
4 To express individual interests and abilities through an optional activity

## Support Material

**Teaching Portfolio**
Teacher Backup, p. 517
Grammar in Action Worksheet, *Understanding Quotation Marks,* p. 520
Usage and Mechanics Worksheet, p. 522
Vocabulary Check, p. 523
Critical Thinking and Reading Worksheet, *Comparing and*

*Contrasting Characters,* p. 524
Language Worksheet, *Understanding Technical Words,* p. 525
Selection Test, p. 526

**Prentice Hall Literature Writing Studio**

# Debbie

## James Herriot

I first saw her one autumn day when I was called to see one of Mrs. Ainsworth's dogs, and I looked in some surprise at the furry black creature sitting before the fire.

"I didn't know you had a cat," I said.

The lady smiled. "We haven't, this is Debbie."

"Debbie?"

"Yes, at least that's what we call her. She's a stray. Comes here two or three times a week and we give her some food. I don't know where she lives but I believe she spends a lot of her time around one of the farms along the road."

"Do you ever get the feeling that she wants to stay with you?"

"No." Mrs. Ainsworth shook her head. "She's a timid little thing. Just creeps in, has some food then flits away. There's something so appealing about her but she doesn't seem to want to let me or anybody into her life."

I looked again at the little cat. "But she isn't just having food today."

"That's right. It's a funny thing but every now and again she slips through here into the lounge and sits by the fire for a few minutes. It's as though she was giving herself a treat."

**1** "Yes . . . I see what you mean." There was no doubt there was something unusual in the attitude of the little animal. She was sitting bolt upright on the thick rug which lay before the fireplace in which the coals glowed and flamed. She made no effort to curl up or wash herself or do anything other than gaze quietly ahead. And there was something in the dusty black of her coat, the half-wild scrawny look of her, that gave me a clue. This was a special event in her life, a rare and wonderful thing; she was lapping up a comfort undreamed of in her daily existence.

As I watched she turned, crept soundlessly from the room and was gone.

"That's always the way with Debbie," Mrs. Ainsworth laughed. "She never stays more than ten minutes or so, then she's off."

**2** Mrs. Ainsworth was a plumpish, pleasant-faced woman in her forties and the kind of client veterinary surgeons dream of; well off, generous, and the owner of three cosseted[1] Basset hounds. And it only needed the habitually mournful expression of one of the dogs to deepen a little and I was round there posthaste.[2] Today one of the Bassets had raised its paw and scratched its ear a couple of times and that was enough to send its mistress scurrying to the phone in great alarm.

**3** So my visits to the Ainsworth home were frequent but undemanding, and I had ample opportunity to look out for the little cat that had intrigued me. On one occasion I spotted her nibbling daintily from a saucer at the kitchen door. As I watched she turned and almost floated on light footsteps into the hall then through the lounge door.

---

**1. cosseted** (käs′ it əd) *adj.*: Pampered, indulged.
**2. posthaste** (pōst′ hāst′) *adv.*: With great quickness.

*Debbie*  439

440

**4 Literary Focus** What does Debbie's decision to roam free tell you about her? What are its advantages and disadvantages over a stable home?

**5 Discussion** Discuss the job of a veterinarian. What tasks and responsibilities are involved? What kind of person would make a good veterinarian? What kinds of inconvenience must a veterinarian accept?

**6 Reading Strategy** Have students predict what might be wrong.

**7 Enrichment** In several works by the English novelist Charles Dickens (1812–1870), some towns—especially on Christmas—are portrayed as quaint, picturesque, colorful, and having a festive feeling of townspeople preparing for bountiful celebrations.

---

The three Bassets were already in residence, draped snoring on the fireside rug, but they seemed to be used to Debbie because two of them sniffed her in a bored manner and the third merely cocked a sleepy eye at her before flopping back on the rich pile.

Debbie sat among them in her usual posture; upright, intent, gazing absorbedly into the glowing coals. This time I tried to make friends with her. I approached her carefully but she leaned away as I stretched out my hand. However, by patient wheedling and soft talk I managed to touch her and gently stroked her cheek with one finger. There was a moment when she responded by putting her head on one side and rubbing back against my hand but soon she was ready to leave. Once outside the house she darted quickly along the road then through a gap in a hedge and the last I saw was the little black figure flitting over the rain-swept grass of a field.

"I wonder where she goes," I murmured half to myself.

Mrs. Ainsworth appeared at my elbow. "That's something we've never been able to find out."

It must have been nearly three months before I heard from Mrs. Ainsworth, and in fact I had begun to wonder at the Bassets' long symptomless run when she came on the phone.

It was Christmas morning and she was apologetic. "Mr. Herriot, I'm so sorry to bother you today of all days. I should think you want a rest at Christmas like anybody else." But her natural politeness could not hide the distress in her voice.

"Please don't worry about that," I said. "Which one is it this time?"

"It's not one of the dogs. It's . . . Debbie."

"Debbie? She's at your house now?"

"Yes . . . but there's something wrong. Please come quickly."

Driving through the marketplace I thought again that Darrowby on Christmas Day was like Dickens come to life; the empty square with the snow thick on the cobbles and hanging from the eaves of the fretted lines of roofs; the shops closed and the colored lights of the Christmas trees winking at the windows of the clustering houses, warmly inviting against the cold white bulk of the fells[3] behind.

Mrs. Ainsworth's home was lavishly decorated with tinsel and holly, rows of drinks stood on the sideboard and the rich aroma of turkey and sage and onion stuffing wafted from the kitchen. But her eyes were full of pain as she led me through to the lounge.

Debbie was there all right, but this time everything was different. She wasn't sitting upright in her usual position; she was stretched quite motionless on her side, and huddled close to her lay a tiny black kitten.

I looked down in bewilderment. "What's happened here?"

"It's the strangest thing," Mrs. Ainsworth replied. "I haven't seen her for several weeks then she came in about two hours ago—sort of staggered into the kitchen, and she was carrying the kitten in her mouth. She took it through to the lounge and laid it on the rug and at first I was amused. But I could see all was not well because she sat as she usually does, but for a long time—over an hour—then she lay down like this and she hasn't moved."

I knelt on the rug and passed my hand over Debbie's neck and ribs. She was thinner than ever, her fur dirty and mudcaked. She did not resist as I gently opened her mouth. The tongue and mucous membranes

---

**3. fells** *n.*: Rocky or barren hills.

---

## Grammar in Action

**Quotation marks** enclose the exact words of a speaker. When an introductory expression identifying the speaker appears before the quoted words, place a comma after this expression:

Mrs. Ainsworth stated, "That's something we've never been able to find out."

When the expression identifying the speaker comes after the quoted words, place a comma, question mark, or exclamation mark before the final quotation mark.

"I've never had a cat before," she said.

"Oh, poor little thing!" she sobbed.

"Is she dying?" Mrs. Ainsworth asked.

When the expression identifying the speaker appears in the middle of a quoted sentence, end the first part of the quoted sentence with a comma placed before the quotation mark; then place a comma at the end of the expression identifying the speaker.

were abnormally pale and the lips ice-cold against my fingers. When I pulled down her eyelid and saw the dead white conjunctiva[4] a knell sounded in my mind.

I palpated[5] the abdomen with a grim certainty as to what I would find and there was no surprise, only a dull sadness as my fingers closed around a hard lobulated[6] mass deep among the viscera.[7] Massive lymphosarcoma. Terminal and hopeless. I put my stethoscope on her heart and listened to the increasingly faint, rapid beat then I straightened up and sat on the rug looking sightlessly into the fireplace, feeling the warmth of the flames on my face.

Mrs. Ainsworth's voice seemed to come from afar. "Is she ill, Mr. Herriot?"

I hesitated. "Yes . . . yes, I'm afraid so. She has a malignant growth." I stood up. "There's absolutely nothing I can do. I'm sorry."

"Oh!" Her hand went to her mouth and she looked at me wide-eyed. When at last she spoke her voice trembled. "Well, you must put her to sleep immediately. It's the only thing to do. We can't let her suffer."

"Mrs. Ainsworth," I said. "There's no need. She's dying now—in a coma—far beyond suffering."

She turned quickly away from me and was very still as she fought with her emotions. Then she gave up the struggle and dropped on her knees beside Debbie.

"Oh, poor little thing!" she sobbed and stroked the cat's head again and again as the tears fell unchecked on the matted fur. "What she must have come through. I feel I ought to have done more for her."

---

4. **conjunctiva** (kän′ jəŋk tī′ və) *n.*: Lining of the inner surface of the eyelids.
5. **palpated** (pal′ pāt ed) *v.*: Examined by touching.
6. **lobulated** (läb′ yōō lāt′ əd) *adj.*: Subdivided.
7. **viscera** (vis′ ər ə) *n.*: Internal organs.

For a few moments I was silent, feeling her sorrow, so discordant among the bright seasonal colors of this festive room. Then I spoke gently.

"Nobody could have done more than you," I said. "Nobody could have been kinder."

"But I'd have kept her here—in comfort. It must have been terrible out there in the cold when she was so desperately ill—I daren't think about it. And having kittens, too—I . . . I wonder how many she did have?"

I shrugged. "I don't suppose we'll ever know. Maybe just this one. It happens sometimes. And she brought it to you, didn't she?"

"Yes . . . that's right . . . she did . . . she did." Mrs. Ainsworth reached out and lifted the bedraggled black morsel. She smoothed her finger along the muddy fur and the tiny mouth opened in a soundless miaow. "Isn't it strange? She was dying and she brought her kitten here. And on Christmas Day."

I bent and put my hand on Debbie's heart. There was no beat.

I looked up. "I'm afraid she's gone." I lifted the small body, almost feather light, wrapped it in the sheet which had been spread on the rug and took it out to the car.

When I came back Mrs. Ainsworth was still stroking the kitten. The tears had dried on her cheeks and she was brighteyed as she looked at me.

"I've never had a cat before," she said.

I smiled. "Well, it looks as though you've got one now."

And she certainly had. That kitten grew rapidly into a sleek handsome cat with a boisterous nature which earned him the name of Buster. In every way he was the opposite to his timid little mother. Not for him the privations of the secret outdoor life; he stalked the rich carpets of the Ainsworth

*Debbie 441*

**Multicultural Focus** Students might enjoy investigating veterinary science in other cultures and at other times in history. Tell them that veterinarians have existed since earliest times. In fact, the term "horse doctor" originated with the ancient Greeks, and the Latin word *veterinarian* meant "pertaining to beasts of burden." The first schools for veterinary science in Europe began in the eighteenth century. Suggest that interested students research the care of animals and the maintenance of zoos in other countries today, including Latin America and the Far East.

---

"When the cat came into the kitchen," said Mrs. Ainsworth, "we could see she was not well."

**Student Activity 1.** Punctuate each of the following items.

1. Where does Debbie go asked the doctor.
2. Oh, what a delight she is cried Mrs. Ainsworth.
3. She is very ill said Dr. Herriot and we can't let her suffer.
4. Mrs. Ainsworth said I can't imagine a nicer cat.

**Student Activity 2.** Write a passage in which two people speak about a special pet. Be sure to punctuate the dialogue correctly.

**Electronic Handbook** You might want students to review the use of quotation marks before completing the Grammar in Action activities. If students have access to the Language Master 6000, have them enter the quotation marks symbol " and press the GRAMMAR key to access information on using quotation marks correctly.

8 **Discussion** What other jobs require one to work on some holidays? What do you think is a good attitude to have toward this requirement?

9 **Discussion** It is unusual for a cat to retrieve a ball. What other behaviors would be unusual in a cat or a dog?

**Reader's Response** Describe an animal you know who has humanlike characteristics like Debbie.

**Thematic Response** After reading this narrative essay, students will sense the level of appreciation that the client, Mrs. Ainsworth, and the doctor, Mr. Herriot, have for each other. Ask students to summarize what aspects of their personalities and their values created the bond between them.

---

home like a king and the ornate collar he always wore added something more to his presence.

On my visits I watched his development with delight but the occasion which stays in my mind was the following Christmas Day, a year from his arrival.

8  I was out on my rounds as usual. I can't remember when I haven't had to work on Christmas Day because the animals have never got round to recognizing it as a holiday; but with the passage of the years the vague resentment I used to feel has been replaced by philosophical acceptance. After all, as I tramped around the hillside barns in the frosty air I was working up a better appetite for my turkey than all the millions lying in bed or slumped by the fire.

I was on my way home, bathed in a rosy glow. I heard the cry as I was passing Mrs. Ainsworth's house.

"Merry Christmas, Mr. Herriot!" She was letting a visitor out of the front door and she waved at me gaily. "Come in and have a drink to warm you up."

I didn't need warming up but I pulled in to the curb without hesitation. In the house there was all the festive cheer of last year and the same glorious whiff of sage and onion which set my gastric juices surging. But there was not the sorrow; there was Buster.

He was darting up to each of the dogs in turn, ears pricked, eyes blazing with devilment, dabbing a paw at them then streaking away.

Mrs. Ainsworth laughed. "You know, he plagues the life out of them. Gives them no peace."

She was right. To the Bassets, Buster's arrival was rather like the intrusion of an irreverent outsider into an exclusive London club. For a long time they had led a life of measured grace; regular sedate walks with their mistress, superb food in ample quantities and long snoring sessions on the rugs and armchairs. Their days followed one upon another in unruffled calm. And then came Buster.

He was dancing up to the youngest dog again, sideways this time, head on one side, goading him. When he started boxing with both paws it was too much even for the Basset. He dropped his dignity and rolled over with the cat in a brief wrestling match.

"I want to show you something." Mrs. Ainsworth lifted a hard rubber ball from the sideboard and went out to the garden, followed by Buster. She threw the ball across the lawn and the cat bounded after it over the frosted grass, the muscles rippling under the black sheen of his coat. He seized the ball in his teeth, brought it back to his mistress, dropped it at her feet and waited expectantly. She threw it and he brought it   9 back again.

I gasped incredulously. A feline retriever!

The Bassets looked on disdainfully. Nothing would ever have induced them to chase a ball, but Buster did it again and again as though he would never tire of it.

Mrs. Ainsworth turned to me. "Have you ever seen anything like that?"

"No," I replied. "I never have. He is a most remarkable cat."

She snatched Buster from his play and we went back into the house where she held him close to her face, laughing as the big cat purred and arched himself ecstatically against her cheek.

Looking at him, a picture of health and contentment, my mind went back to his mother. Was it too much to think that that dying little creature with the last of her strength had carried her kitten to the only haven of comfort and warmth she had ever known in the hope that it would be cared for there? Maybe it was.

But it seemed I wasn't the only one with

---

## Closure and Extension

### ANSWERS TO RESPONDING TO THE SELECTION
#### Your Response

1. Students will have different responses to having a relationship with an animal that only visited their homes, but did not live with them. Many will say that if they came to love the animal, they would prefer that it live in their home; some may say that they would have fewer responsibilities if the stray animal only visited.

#### Recalling

2. Most students would be thrilled with a newborn kitten to raise, especially if they had come to love the mother cat as Mrs. Ainsworth had come to love Debbie.

3. She is a thin, black stray cat, muddy and bedraggled. She lives outdoors but occasionally visits Mrs. Ainsworth's home to be fed and simply to sit in front of the fire and enjoy its comforts; then she disappears again.

4. It is livelier and happier because Buster teases and plays with the dogs, runs about energetically, retrieves balls, and is affectionate with Mrs. Ainsworth.

#### Interpreting

5. Answers will differ. Suggested Response: Kindness, anxiety, responsibility, sympathy, playfulness, and appreciation.

such fancies. Mrs. Ainsworth turned to me and though she was smiling her eyes were wistful.

"Debbie would be pleased," she said.

I nodded. "Yes, she would . . . It was just a year ago today she brought him, wasn't it?"

"That's right." She hugged Buster to her again. "The best Christmas present I ever had."

## RESPONDING TO THE SELECTION

### Your Response

1. How would you like having a relationship with an animal that did not live at your home but visited regularly as Debbie did?
2. How would you react if Debbie had left her newborn kitten with you to raise?

### Recalling

3. Describe Debbie and her life.
4. How is the Ainsworth household different as a result of Buster?

### Interpreting

5. What qualities does Mrs. Ainsworth show in her treatment of animals?

### Applying

6. Mrs. Ainsworth receives an unexpected reward for her kindness to Debbie. She receives Buster. Why are unexpected rewards sometimes more valued than expected ones?

## ANALYZING LITERATURE

### Understanding Characters in an Essay

You can learn about characters by reading about their actions, by reading their words, by reading about their thoughts and feelings, by reading descriptive details about them, and by reading what other characters say or think about them. Skim the selection again and point out one example of information about Herriot that you found in each of the five ways listed above.

## CRITICAL THINKING AND READING

### Comparing and Contrasting Characters

When you **compare** characters, you discuss traits about each that are the same. When you **contrast** characters, you discuss traits that are different. Comparing and contrasting characters can help you to understand them better.

1. List traits that Debbie and Buster share.
2. List traits that differ between Debbie and Buster.
3. What is it about the presentation of Debbie that made her come alive for you?
4. What is it about the presentation of Buster that made him come alive for you?

## THINKING AND WRITING

### Comparing and Contrasting Cats

Using the lists of traits you wrote for Debbie and Buster, write an article for a pet journal comparing and contrasting the two cats. Describe one cat completely and follow that description with a complete description of the other cat. When you revise, check the organization of your article carefully. Finally, proofread your article and share it with your classmates.

## LEARNING OPTION

**Speaking and Listening.** Write a eulogy for Debbie, focusing on her personality strengths. Deliver your eulogy to your class.

*Debbie 443*

Christine McDonnell wrote in *The Horn Book Magazine* (March/April 1987), ''Brooks loves the difficult and the subtle because it requires more from a reader.'' Brooks says of himself, ''I have an affinity for independence, for loners, for smart people who are watchers.'' How does this affinity make itself apparent in ''Animal Craftsmen''?

**Literary Focus** To help students understand the concept of a reflective essay, ask them how they feel about a certain holiday or their birthday. Explain that if they wrote their thoughts about how they feel, they would be writing a reflective essay.

**Prereading Focus** To increase student participation, assign heterogeneous groups of three or four to complete the word web. To promote further ideas, have students complete the web on transparency film so that you can project and discuss each group's work with the class.

**Vocabulary** Use the Vocabulary Check in the Teaching Portfolio, p. 536, as the basis for a contest among cooperative groups. Also, you may want to ask **less advanced** students to create a list of any other unfamiliar words in the selection. Suggest that they work with one or two peers to derive meaning from context before turning to the dictionary.

 **Electronic Handbook**

Your **less advanced** students with access to the Language Master 6000 may listen to the pronunciation of the words, repeating them aloud as they listen.

**Spelling Tip** Review with the class the rule for adding suffixes to two-syllable words like *dispel:* Double the final consonant of a two-syllable word if the accent is on the second syllable.

444

# GUIDE FOR READING

## Bruce Brooks

(1950–    ) was born in Washington, D.C., and spent much of his childhood in North Carolina. A graduate of the University of North Carolina, Brooks has worked as a letterpress printer, a newspaper and magazine reporter, and a teacher. A versatile author, Brooks writes both fiction and nonfiction. His first novel, *The Moves Make the Man,* was named a Newbery Honor book; his first nonfiction book, *On the Wing,* was an American Library Association Best Book for Young Adults.

## Animal Craftsmen

### Reflective Essay

A **reflective essay** attempts to communicate a writer's thoughts about a topic of personal interest. Speaking directly to the reader, the writer often re-creates and evaluates his or her own experiences to make a point. In this essay Brooks expresses his appreciation of animal design, architecture, and engineering.

### Focus

What does the phrase "wonders of nature" bring to mind? Brainstorm with classmates. Free-associate and make a word web, like the one that follows, to record responses. As you read this reflective essay, think about how the writer reacts to the "strange wonder" that he discovers.

### Vocabulary

Knowing the following words will help you as you read "Animal Craftsmen."

**subtle** (sut′ ′l) *adj.:* Delicate; fine (p. 445)

**vigil** (vij′ əl) *n.:* Period of watching (p. 445)

**infusion** (in fyoo′ zhən) *n.:* The act of putting one thing into another (p. 446)

**habitable** (hab′ ə tə bəl) *adj.:* Fit to live in (p. 447)

**dispelled** (dis peld′) *v.:* Drove away (p. 447)

**attributing** (ə trib′ yoot iŋ) *v.:*

Thinking of as belonging to or appropriate to (p. 448)

**improvised** (im′ prə vīzd) *v.:* Done on the spur of the moment (p. 448)

**empathize** (em′ pə thīz) *v.:* Feel empathy for; share the feelings of (p. 448)

**adroitness** (ə droit′ nes) *n.:* Skill; dexterity (p. 448)

**replicated** (rep′ lə kāt id) *v.:* Duplicated; copied (p. 448)

444    Nonfiction

1 To understand a reflective essay
2 To analyze perspectives
3 To write about the wonder in nature
4 To express individual interests and abilities through optional activities

## Support Material

**Teaching Portfolio**
Teacher Backup, p. 529
Grammar in Action Worksheet, *Using Pronoun Case,* p. 533
Usage and Mechanics Worksheet, p. 535
Vocabulary Check, p. 536
Analyzing Literature Worksheet, *Understanding the Reflective Essay,* p. 537

Critical Thinking and Reading Worksheet, *Analyzing Perspectives,* p. 538
Selection Test, p. 539

**Prentice Hall Literature Writing Studio**

# Animal Craftsmen

## Bruce Brooks

One evening, when I was about five, I climbed up a ladder on the outside of a rickety old tobacco barn at sunset. The barn was part of a small farm near the home of a country relative my mother and I visited periodically; though we did not really know the farm's family, I was allowed to roam, poke around, and conduct sudden studies of anything small and harmless. On this evening, as on most of my jaunts, I was not looking for anything; I was simply climbing with an open mind. But as I balanced on the next-to-the-top rung and inhaled the spicy stink of the tobacco drying inside, I *did* find something under the eaves[1]—something very strange.

It appeared to be a kind of gray paper sphere, suspended from the dark planks by a thin stalk, like an apple made of ashes hanging on its stem. I studied it closely in the clear light. I saw that the bottom was a little ragged, and open. I could not tell if it had been torn, or if it had been made that way on purpose—for it was clear to me, as I studied it, that this thing had been *made*. This was no fruit or fungus.[2] Its shape, rough but trim; its intricately[3] colored surface with subtle swirls of gray and tan; and most of all the uncanny adhesiveness with

which the perfectly tapered stem stuck against the rotten old pine boards—all of these features gave evidence of some intentional design. The troubling thing was figuring out who had designed it, and why.

I assumed the designer was a human being: someone from the farm, someone wise and skilled in a craft that had so far escaped my curiosity. Even when I saw wasps entering and leaving the thing (during a vigil I kept every evening for two weeks), it did not occur to me that the wasps might have fashioned it for themselves. I assumed it was a man-made "wasp house" placed there expressly for the purpose of attracting a family of wasps, much as the "martin hotel," a giant birdhouse on a pole near the farmhouse, was maintained to shelter migrant[4] purple martins who returned every spring. I didn't ask myself why anyone would want to give wasps a bivouac;[5] it seemed no more odd than attracting birds.

As I grew less wary of the wasps (and they grew less wary of me), and as my confidence on the ladder improved, I moved to the upper rung and peered through the sphere's bottom. I could see that the paper swirled in layers around some secret center the wasps inhabited, and I marveled at the delicate hands of the craftsman who

---

**1. eaves** (ēvz) *n.*: Lower edges of a roof.
**2. fungus** (fuŋ′ gəs) *n.*: A growth caused by parasites on living organisms.
**3. intricately** (in′ tri kit lē) *adv.*: In a complex, highly detailed manner.

**4. migrant** (mī′ grənt) *adj.*: Moving from one region to another with the changing seasons.
**5. bivouac** (biv′ wak′) *n.*: Temporary shelter.

*Animal Craftsmen* 445

**Presentation**

**Motivation/Prior Knowledge** Some people think that we cannot appreciate what we do not understand. Do you agree? Does Brooks?

**Thematic Focus** Much of human behavior is similar to the behavior of other animals on our living earth. What parallels do you find in Brooks's essay between human and other animal architects?

**Purpose-Setting Question** Does Brooks think there is a difference between animals as craftsmen and humans as architects?

1 **Clarification** Tobacco barns, used for drying tobacco leaves prior to marketing, are usually wood and have numerous openings for ventilation. As a result of their structure, they become rickety more quickly than do other barns.

2 **Critical Thinking and Reading** What does this sentence show about Brooks as a youth?

3 **Critical Thinking and Reading** What does the comparison tell about Brooks's background?

4 **Literary Focus: Reflective Essay** As a youth, what did Brooks think about the wasp house?

5 **Critical Thinking and Reading** What does this sentence tell you about Brooks?

**ESL Teaching Strategy** Students from other cultures may be familiar with animals unknown to other members of the class. Ask them to share their experiences and to introduce these unfamiliar animals to the class or to their cooperative groups. Encourage students to use words and phrases from their first language to name and describe the animals.

**Making Connections** Have students read Robert Frost's poem "The Road Not Taken," on page 600. Ask them to consider how Frost's reflective poem is similar to Brooks's reflective essay.

To see how an author thinks and works in different forms, students may read Brooks's novel *The Moves Make the Man* in the **Prentice Hall Literature Multicultural Library**. They will find the work very different from "Animal Craftsmen."

**Alternative Assessment** To promote active reading, have students create a reader's response journal as they read "Animal Craftsmen." Ask them to focus their observations on the details of Brooks's discovery of the paper wasp nest and on his feelings, impressions, and opinions of his discovery. Encourage them to respond personally to Brooks's childhood experience, comparing similar experiences of their own.

They should describe what his reactions reveal about him.

You may use students' response journals to assess their understanding of this selection.

6 **Literary Focus: Reflective Essay** What part do you think the imagination plays in a reflective essay?

7 **Clarification** After the first hard freeze, wasps die, leaving the unprotected nest with its unhatched larvae for certain birds, which often shred the nest *in search of food.

8 **Literary Focus: Reflective Essay** What evidence do you find here that the experience was meaningful to Brooks?

9 **Critical Thinking and Reading** What example of personal perspective does this sentence give?

10 **Critical Thinking and Reading** What feelings does Brooks share with readers in this sentence?

11 **Clarification** This particular kind of wasp house is more commonly called a hornet's nest. Hornets, yellow and black striped wasps, are among the largest of the so-called social wasps.

12 **Critical Thinking and Reading** What does this parenthetical comment tell about Brooks's impression?

13 **Critical Thinking and Reading** What does this reminder tell about Brooks's perspective?

14 **Literary Focus: Reflective Essay** Why do you think Brooks tells about something he finds embarrassing?

had devised such tiny apertures[6] for their protection.

I left the area in the late summer, and in my imagination I took the strange structure with me. I envisioned unwrapping it, and in the middle finding—what? A tiny room full of bits of wool for sleeping, and countless manufactured pellets of scientifically determined wasp food? A glowing blue jewel that drew the wasps at twilight, and gave them a cool infusion of energy as they clung to it overnight? My most definite idea was that the wasps lived in a small block of fine cedar the craftsman had drilled full of holes, into which they slipped snugly, rather like the bunks aboard submarines in World War II movies.

As it turned out, I got the chance to discover that my idea of the cedar block had not been wrong by much. We visited our relative again in the winter. We arrived at night, but first thing in the morning I made straight for the farm and its barn. The shadows under the eaves were too dense to let me spot the sphere from far off. I stepped on the bottom rung of the ladder—slick with frost —and climbed carefully up. My hands and feet kept slipping, so my eyes stayed on the rung ahead, and it was not until I was secure at the top that I could look up. The sphere was gone.

I was crushed. That object had fascinated me like nothing I had come across in my life; I had even grown to love wasps because of it. I sagged on the ladder and watched my breath eddy[7] around the blank eaves. I'm afraid I pitied myself more than the apparently homeless wasps.

But then something snapped me out of

---

6. **apertures** (ap′ ər chərz) n.: Openings.
7. **eddy** (ed′ ē) v.: Move in a circular motion against the main current.

my sense of loss: I recalled that I had watched the farmer taking in the purple martin hotel every November, after the birds left. From its spruce appearance when he brought it out in March, it was clear he had cleaned it and repainted it and kept it out of the weather. Of course he would do the same thing for *this* house, which was even more fragile. I had never mentioned the wasp dwelling to anyone, but now I decided I would go to the farm, introduce myself, and inquire about it. Perhaps I would even be permitted to handle it, or, best of all, learn how to make one myself.

I scrambled down the ladder, leaping from the third rung and landing in the frosty salad of tobacco leaves and windswept grass that collected at the foot of the barn wall. I looked down and saw that my left boot had, by no more than an inch, just missed crushing the very thing I was rushing off to seek. There, lying dry and separate on the leaves, was the wasp house.

I looked up. Yes. I was standing directly beneath the spot where the sphere had hung—it was a straight fall. I picked up the wasp house, gave it a shake to see if any insects were inside, and, discovering none, took it home.

My awe of the craftsman grew as I unwrapped the layers of the nest. Such beautiful paper! It was much tougher than any I had encountered, and it held a curve (something my experimental paper airplanes never did), but it was very light, too. The secret at the center of the swirl turned out to be a neatly made fan of tiny cells, all of the same size and shape, reminding me of the heart of a sunflower that had lost its seeds to birds. The fan hung from the sphere's ceiling by a stem the thickness of a pencil lead.

The rest of the story is a little embarrassing. More impressed than ever, I decided to pay homage to the creator of this

## Grammar in Action

Writers and speakers use different forms of pronouns for different purposes. The form of the pronoun is called its **case**. How a pronoun is used in a sentence determines pronoun case. Pronouns used as subjects or predicate words are in the nominative case: *I, you, he, she, it, we, they.* Pronouns used as objects are in the objective case: *me, you, him, her, it, us, them.* Pronouns that show ownership are in the possessive case: *my, mine, your, yours, her, hers, his, its, our, ours, their, theirs.* Remember that possessive pronouns do not use an apostrophe.

**15 Reading Strategy** What inferences can you make about the farmer's wife?

**16 Reading Strategy** What purpose is served by Brooks's telling about the embarrassing incident?

**17 Critical Thinking and Reading** What feelings does Brooks share here?

habitable sculpture. I went boldly to the farmhouse. The farmer's wife answered my knock. I showed her the nest and asked to speak with the person in the house who had made it. She blinked and frowned. I had to repeat my question twice before she understood what I believed my mission to be; then, with a gentle laugh, she dispelled my illusion about an ingenious old papersmith fond of wasps. The nest, she explained, had been made entirely by the insects themselves, and wasn't that amazing?

Well, of course it was. It still is. I needn't have been so embarrassed—the structures that animals build, and the sense of design they display, *should* always astound us. On my way home from the farmhouse, in my own defense I kept thinking, "But *I* couldn't build anything like this! Nobody could!"

The most natural thing in the world for us to do, when we are confronted with a piece of animal architecture, is to figure out if we could possibly make it or live in it. Who hasn't peered into the dark end of a mys-

*Animal Craftsmen* 447

15

16

17

---

**Student Activity 1.** Identify the case of the pronouns in the following sentences from ''Animal Craftsmen.'' Some sentences include more than one pronoun.

1. I climbed up the ladder on the outside of a rickety old barn.
2. I studied it closely in the clear light.
3. Its shape was rough but trim.
4. They grew less wary of me.
5. I got the chance to discover that my idea of the cedar block had not been wrong by much.

**Student Activity 2.** Write five sentences of your own. Use at least one example of each of the three pronoun cases. You may wish to use the sentences above as models.

 **Electronic Handbook** You may want students to review pronouns before completing the Grammar in Action activities. If students have access to the Language Master 6000, have them enter *pronoun* and press the GRAMMAR key.

18 **Discussion** What similar examples can you cite?

19 **Discussion** What similar examples of creative wonder can you cite?

20 **Discussion** What similar examples of animal instinct and intelligence can you cite?

**Reader's Response** Who else do you think would enjoy this essay? Why?

**Thematic Response** Do the parallels Brooks draws between the wasp house and the martin house help you appreciate relationships among all things on our living earth? Why or why not?

terious hole in the woods and thought, "It must be pretty weird to live in there!" or looked up at a hawk's nest atop a huge sycamore and shuddered at the thought of waking up every morning with nothing but a few twigs preventing a hundred-foot fall. How, we wonder, do those twigs stay together, and withstand the wind so high?

18    It is a human tendency always to regard animals first in terms of ourselves. Seeing the defensive courage of a mother bear whose cubs are threatened, or the cooperative determination of a string of ants dismantling a stray chunk of cake, we naturally use our own behavior as reference for our empathy. We put ourselves in the same situation and express the animal's action in feelings—and words—that apply to the way people do things.

Sometimes this is useful. But sometimes it is misleading. Attributing human-like intentions to an animal can keep us from looking at the *animal's* sense of itself in its surroundings—its immediate and future needs, its physical and mental capabilities, its genetic[8] instincts. Most animals, for example, use their five senses in ways that human beings cannot possibly understand or express. How can a forty-two-year-old nearsighted biologist have any real idea what a two-week-old barn owl sees in the dark? How can a sixteen-year-old who lives in the Arizona desert identify with the muscular jumps improvised by a waterfall-leaping salmon in Alaska? There's nothing wrong with trying to empathize with an animal, but we shouldn't forget that ultimately animals live *animal* lives.

Animal structures let us have it both ways—we can be struck with a strange wonder, and we can empathize right away,

too. Seeing a vast spiderweb, taut and glistening between two bushes, it's easy to think, "I have no idea how that is done; the engineering is awesome." But it is just as easy to imagine climbing across the bright strands, springing from one to the next as if the web were a new Epcot attraction, the Invisible Flying Flexible Space Orb. That a clear artifact of an animal's wits and agility[9] stands right there in front of us—that we can touch it, look at it from different angles, sometimes take it home—inspires our imagination as only a strange reality can. We needn't move into a molehill to experience a life of darkness and digging; our creative wonder takes us down there in a second, without even getting our hands dirty.    19

But what if we discover some of the mechanics of how the web is made? Once we see how the spider works (or the hummingbird, or the bee), is the engineering no longer awesome? This would be too bad: we don't want to lose our sense of wonder just because we gain understanding.

And we certainly do *not* lose it. In fact, seeing how an animal makes its nest or egg case or food storage vaults has the effect of increasing our amazement. The builder's energy, concentration, and athletic adroitness are qualities we can readily admire and envy. Even more startling is the recognition that the animal is working from a precise design in its head, a design that is exactly replicated time after time. This knowledge of architecture—knowing where to build, what materials to use, how to put them together—remains one of the most intriguing mysteries of animal behavior. And the more *we* develop that same knowledge, the more we appreciate the instincts and intelligence of the animals.    20

---
**8. genetic** (jə net′ ik) *adj.*: Inherited biologically.

---
**9. agility** (ə jil′ ə tē) *n.*: Ability to move quickly and easily.

448    *Nonfiction*

---

## Primary Source

"Animal Craftsmen" is the opening segment of a nonfiction book that follows Bruce Brooks's earlier success as a young adult novelist. First honored for *The Moves Make the Man,* Brooks followed quickly with *Midnight Hour Encores.* Speaking of his reading audience, however, Brooks says, "I don't know what young adult means. I don't want to know the field. Nothing exists for me except the shape my books have. I need that freedom, that cockiness, to write my own books." Students may be interested in his reaction to his readership. In addition, you may want some students to read his fiction in order to draw comparisons with his nonfiction style, looking especially at the first-person narrator.

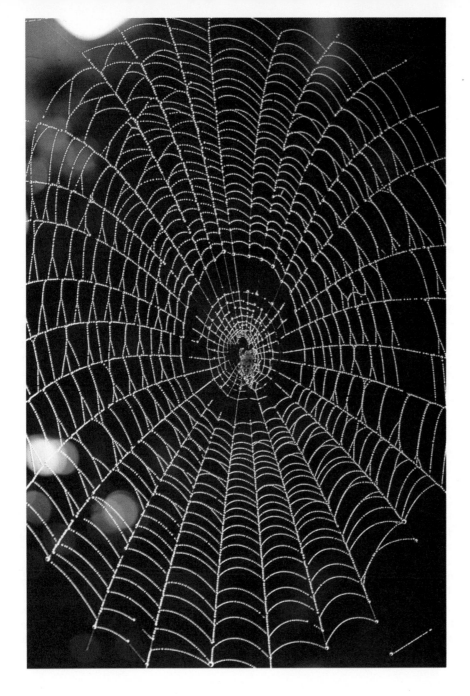

*Animal Craftsmen* 449

449

**Speaking and Listening** To help students identify with the narrator, ask them to think about their own experiences with some stinging insect and what they did to avoid being stung. They should plan their comments and then share them informally with a group of four or five peers, limiting their oral reports to one or two minutes. Then ask each group to choose two experiences to share with the class, but ask students to explain a peers' experiences, rather than their own.

**Master Teacher Note** Students who enjoy "Animal Craftsmen" or who show a particular interest in science may enjoy *Nature by Design,* the book from which this selection comes.

## Closure and Extension

### *ANSWERS TO RESPONDING TO THE SELECTION*
#### *Your Response*

1. To stimulate student response, ask the class to think about the word *awe* in nature in terms of *awesome* and *awful.*
2. Suggest that students think about what makes people interesting to know and apply these criteria to Brooks.

### *Recalling*

3. Brooks assumes the nest was made by a human the same way bird houses are.
4. Natural reactions include trying to figure out if we could make the animals' structures or live in them.

## Interpreting

5. Suggested Response: He thinks of the nest as a "wasp house" and in terms of who built it and who has taken it down.
6. Suggested Response: He is even more amazed because he knows he cannot make anything like it.
7. Suggested Response: The more we understand about animals' instincts and intelligence the more we appreciate them.

## Applying

8. Students' answers may include the ideas that Brooks as a child discovered natural mysteries that affect his adult life and that the wonders children pursue should remain a part of adult life.

## ANSWERS TO ANALYZING LITERATURE

1. Students may suggest that Brooks's remembering so many details about his experiences with the wasp house proves that he gave a lot of thought to his discovery.
2. Students may point out that Brooks applies the general ideas about the wasp nest to other animals and that he uses these examples to show how people react to the structures not in terms of themselves but in terms of the animals.

## ANSWERS TO CRITICAL THINKING AND READING

1. Students may cite various passages such as "I'm afraid I pitied myself more than the apparently homeless wasps" or "On my way home from the farmhouse, in my own defense I kept thinking, 'But I couldn't build anything like this! Nobody could!'"
2. Students may suggest that Brooks has been awed since childhood by animals' ability to know where, how, and by what means to build their nests. But until he reached adulthood, he measured other animals' abilities by human standards.

**Challenge** What do you think the farmer's wife told the farmer about Brooks's visit?

## THINKING AND WRITING

**Writing Transparency** Before students write, you may want

to use the Paragraph Exercise on chronological order in **Transparencies for Writing** to model for students the need for clear order in their writing.

**Software** For students working at computers, suggest that they use the **Writer's Helper** tool *Questioner* to help them generate ideas for topics.

---

# RESPONDING TO THE SELECTION

## Your Response

1. Do you share the writer's awe of nature? Describe your response.
2. Based on this essay, would you like to get to know the writer? Why or why not?

## Recalling

3. What assumptions does Brooks as a child make about the nest that he finds?
4. According to Brooks, what are two natural reactions to seeing animal structures?

## Interpreting

5. How does Brooks as a child show a tendency to regard animals in human terms?
6. How does learning that the nest he admires was made by wasps affect the way Brooks views it?
7. What is the theme, or central message, of the essay?

## Applying

8. Poet William Wordsworth wrote, "The Child is the father of the Man." Explain how this statement applies to Bruce Brooks.

# ANALYZING LITERATURE

## Understanding the Reflective Essay

The goal of a **reflective essay** is to impart a writer's personal view of a topic and the thinking behind it. The writer often relates a meaningful experience and discusses what he or she has learned from it. For example, Bruce Brooks begins this essay by recalling a childhood experience: his discovery of a paper wasp nest.

1. How does Brooks show that as a child he gave a lot of thought to his discovery?
2. After relating his experience with the nest, what does Brooks do in the essay?

# CRITICAL THINKING AND READING

## Analyzing Perspectives

A reflective essay is subjective. The writer does not present facts in an objective manner. Instead, from a first-person point of view, he or she shares feelings, impressions, and opinions. In so doing, the writer may reveal as much about himself or herself as about the topic.

1. Give two examples of statements in which Brooks shares feelings, impressions, or opinions.
2. What can you tell about Brooks from his choice of topic and the way he presents it?

# THINKING AND WRITING

## Writing About the Wonders in Nature

Brooks finds inspiration in a paper wasp nest, a hawk's nest, a spider web. What in nature inspires you? What wonders in nature would you want to write about? Skim "Animal Craftsmen" and use your brainstorming notes for ideas. You might write a brief reflective essay of your own, a photo essay, a poem, or a description.

# LEARNING OPTIONS

1. **Writing.** Welcome to the Invisible Flying Flexible Space Orb. Write a promotional piece or make a poster to advertise this new theme-park attraction. In deciding what to highlight, consider the features of the natural wonder on which the Orb is modeled, a vast intricate spider web.
2. **Cross-curricular Connection.** Are you intrigued by paper wasp nests, prairie dog burrows, or beaver lodges? Investigate an animal structure that interests you. Learn where it is built, how it is made, and what materials are used. Share your findings with classmates in a brief oral or written report.

---

## Publishing Student Writing

Share students' products with science classes, asking science students to respond with comments, shared observations, other illustrations, or questions.

## Writing Across the Curriculum

Ask a science teacher to read "Animal Craftsmen" and to share with you and the class any visuals that illustrate examples similar to

Brooks's. Use the illustrations as suggestions for topics for cross-curricular reports.

## LEARNING OPTIONS

1. Students who enjoy creative writing should be directed to the writing option.
2. Students who enjoy research or are animal lovers should be directed to the cross-curricular option.

# ONE WRITER'S PROCESS

## Bruce Brooks and "Animal Craftsmen"

### PREWRITING

**Begin at the Beginning** Bruce Brooks hadn't originally planned to introduce his book on animal architecture with "Animal Craftsmen." When he finished the book, however, he realized that he needed to tell the reader why he had chosen this topic in the first place. "It seemed that I had forgotten to begin with a beginning," he says. "So I went back to the incident that had started my interest, and I simply told that story, hoping my readers would get a similar sense of starting up." Does Brooks's essay give you that sense?

### REVISING

**Second Thoughts** When revising, a writer can make an earlier draft more poetic and accurate. Look at the following sentence from a draft of "Animal Craftsmen" along with Brooks's revisions. Do you see how replacing "center" with "heart" has made the image of the sunflower more vivid?

### PUBLISHING

**The Right Choice** Brooks says: "Many readers have commented on this essay by saying that the firsthand narrative draws

---

The secret at the center of the swirl turned out to be a neatly made fan of tiny cells, all of the same size and shape—reminding me of the ~~center~~ *heart* of a sunflower that had lost its seeds to birds—hanging ~~inside~~ from the sphere's ~~roof~~ *ceiling* by a stem the thickness of a pencil lead.

---

### DRAFTING

**More Than Just Facts** Writers need to remember that an essay is more than a simple presentation of information. Brooks suggests that essayists should put themselves in the reader's shoes. "Think about how your reader feels," says Brooks. "We have not done our job when we simply put the necessary information in front of the reader; we have to inspire the reader to feel certain ways about the material—curious, excited, at least partially satisfied, alert, and open-minded."

them into sharing my interest in animal-built structures. . . . I'm happy with the way it works."

### THINKING ABOUT THE PROCESS

1. Has Bruce Brooks made the topic of animal architecture more interesting by drawing on his own experiences? Why or why not?
2. **Rethinking.** Review an essay that you have written. List ways to enliven your work.

*One Writer's Process* 451

**More About the Author** Anais Nin has said that she wanted "to unmask the deeper self that lies hidden" [from the real world]. What does this statement tell you about the author? What are other reasons for writing?

**Literary Focus** Ask students what kinds of details they would include in describing a scene to someone who is blind.

**Prereading Focus** Discussions about values sometimes challenge young teenagers. Before they begin to commit their own values to the chart, you may wish to have the class list the kinds of values that they believe people in general live by. Most will mention such traits as honesty, perseverance, generosity, belief in God, friendship, and kindness. This list will help them reflect on their own personal values as they prioritize their possessions.

**Teaching to Ability Levels** for your **more advanced** students, you may want to review simile and metaphor. Explain that simile and metaphor are part of description. Students should look for them when reading this descriptive essay.

**Vocabulary** Have your **less advanced** students work with a partner to use each of these words in a sentence.

**Electronic Handbook** If students have access to the Language Master 6000, suggest that they locate synonyms for *pungent* and *tenacious*. Have them think about why Nin chose the words *pungent* and *tenacious* instead of one of their synonyms.

**Spelling Tip** When the last letter of the prefix *dis*, *mis*, or *un* is the same as the first letter of the stem, as in *dissolution*, the letter is doubled, in the new word. Other examples are *misspell*, *unnoticed*, *dissatisfaction*.

# GUIDE FOR READING

## Anaïs Nin

(1903–1977) was born in France but grew up in the United States. At age eleven she began the writing that continued her whole life. Although she wrote novels and short stories, Nin was best known for her six published diaries spanning sixty years. "Forest Fire," from the fifth diary, illustrates how Nin looked at life "as an adventure and a tale." The incident she wrote about in "Forest Fire" happened when she was living in Sierra Madre, California.

## Forest Fire

### Descriptive Essay

A **descriptive essay** is a short nonfiction composition in which an author describes or creates word pictures of a subject. Like most other kinds of essays, an author writes a descriptive essay to present his or her view of a subject. In descriptive essays, however, authors achieve their purpose mainly by including images and details that show us how things look, sound, smell, taste, or feel. Such details work to allow you to share the writer's experience fully.

### Focus

Suppose that your home were threatened by a spreading forest fire. Imagine that you had only a short time in which to rescue your most valued possessions from your house. On a chart like the one that follows, list on the left the possessions you would try to save. On the right side tell which of your values is represented by that item that you want to rescue. As you read "Forest Fire," notice what Anaïs Nin considered most valuable. What does saving this possession reveal about her?

| Possessions to save | My values |
| --- | --- |
| | |

### Vocabulary

Knowing the following words will help you as you read "Forest Fire."

**tinted** (tint′ əd) *v.*: Colored (p. 453)

**evacuees** (i vak′ yōō wēz′) *n.*: People who leave a place, especially because of danger (p. 453)

**pungent** (pun′ jənt) *adj.*: Sharp and stinging to the smell (p. 454)

**tenacious** (tə nā′ shəs) *adj.*: Holding on firmly (p. 454)

**dissolution** (dis′ə lōō′ shən) *n.*: The act of breaking down and crumbling (p. 454)

**ravaging** (rav′ ij iŋ) *adj.*: Severely damaging or destroying (p. 454)

# Forest Fire

## Anaïs Nin

A man rushed in to announce he had seen smoke on Monrovia Peak.[1] As I looked out of the window I saw the two mountains facing the house on fire. The entire rim burning wildly in the night. The flames, driven by hot Santa Ana winds[2] from the desert, were as tall as the tallest trees, the sky already tinted coral, and the crackling noise of burning trees, the ashes and the smoke were already increasing. The fire raced along, sometimes descending behind the mountain where I could only see the glow, sometimes descending toward us. I thought of the foresters in danger. I made coffee for the weary men who came down occasionally with horses they had led out, or with old people from the isolated cabins. They were covered with soot from their battle with the flames.

At six o'clock the fire was on our left side and rushing toward Mount Wilson. Evacuees from the cabins began to arrive and had to be given blankets and hot coffee. The streets were blocked with fire engines readying to fight the fire if it touched the houses. Policemen and firemen and guards turned away the sightseers. Some were relatives concerned over the fate of the foresters, or the pack station family. The policemen lighted flares, which gave the scene a theatrical, tragic air. The red lights on the police

cars twinkled alarmingly. More fire engines arrived. Ashes fell, and the roar of the fire was now like thunder.

We were told to ready ourselves for evacuation. I packed the diaries. The saddest spectacle, beside that of the men fighting the fire as they would a war, were the animals, rabbits, coyotes, mountain lions, deer, driven by the fire to the edge of the mountain, taking a look at the crowd of people and panicking, choosing rather to rush back into the fire.

The fire now was like a ring around Sierra Madre,[3] every mountain was burning. People living at the foot of the mountain were packing their cars. I rushed next door to the Campion children, who had been left with a baby-sitter, and got them into the car. It was impossible to save all the horses. We parked the car on the field below us. I called up the Campions, who were out for the evening, and reassured them. The baby-sitter dressed the children warmly. I made more coffee. I answered frantic telephone calls.

All night the fire engines sprayed water over the houses. But the fire grew immense, angry, and rushing at a speed I could not believe. It would rush along and suddenly leap over a road, a trail, like a monster, devouring all in its path. The firefighters cut breaks in the heavy brush, but when the wind was strong enough, the fire leaped

---

1. **Monrovia** (mɔn rō′ vē ə) **Peak:** Mountain in southwest California.
2. **Santa** (san′ tə) **Ana** (an′ ə) **winds:** Hot desert winds from the east or northeast in southern California.

---

3. **Sierra** (sē er′ ə) **Madre** (mä′ drā): Mountain range.

*Forest Fire*   453

**Presentation**

**Motivation/Prior Knowledge** Natural disasters can have a great impact on people's lives. Ask students for examples of any natural disaster they or their friends have lived through.

**Master Teacher Note** This essay derives some of its excitement from the race against time.
1. Discuss how quick thinking contributes to the excitement of the action.
2. Ask students to list three things they would do before making a "quick escape."

**Purpose-Setting Question** How is nature like a person or an animal?

**Thematic Focus** When we think of "our living earth," we generally envision the beauty of nature, the earth in its peaceful and comforting ways. In this essay, however, we experience the fury and the fearful danger that a natural disaster can bring—another view of the living earth. Discuss with students other types of natural disasters when the earth is similarly "furious," when human and animal life are also endangered.

**1 Discussion** What is it about natural disaster and human tragedy that excites curiosity?

**2 Discussion** What items would you take with you if you had to evacuate?

**3 Discussion** Why did the animals rush back into the fire to certain death rather than face the humans? What do you think was their previous experience with humans?

**4 Discussion** What other similarities can you think of between a fire and a monster?

**Multicultural Focus** Discuss some experiences, both positive and negative, that students have had with fire, such as campfires, fireworks, or home fires. Explain that the enormous energy in fire has inspired wonder and fear since prehistoric times. Fire has both helped people to survive, by warming them and by cooking their food, and has threatened their survival, by burning their homes or forests. Because of this,

almost all cultures have myths associated with fire. Recount some of these myths. For example, in Zaire, a hunting-and-gathering tribe called the Mbuti credit their god Tore with having stolen fire from the chimpanzees and giving it to humans. Have students research other fire myths including that of Prometheus. Then have them write their own myth about how fire came to exist on Earth.

**Making Connections** Other selections that deal with natural phenomena are "Animal Craftsmen," page 445, and "Shooting Stars," page 458. You might want to use these selections with "Forest Fire" and have students examine the different effects of natural phenomena.

454

**5 Clarification** *Backfiring* is starting a fire to stop an advancing forest fire by creating a burned area in its path.

**6 Discussion** Discuss how the reporter did not see the "human interest" in the writer saving her diaries.

**7 Clarification** People may stack sandbags around their homes to absorb water from the flood and prevent it from entering their homes.

**8 Critical Thinking and Reading** Ask students whether this is a fact or an opinion.

**9 Discussion** What are other examples of nature in its peaceful moments and in its furies?

**Reader's Response** Which image was the most vivid to you?

**Thematic Response** Direct students' attention to the two passages that relate to the wild animals, paragraph 3 on page 453 and paragraph 2 on page 454. Ask students to hypothesize why the laws of nature are such that the animals chose fire rather than facing human beings. Does this seem contrary to the ideas we hold about "our living earth"?

---

across them. At dawn one arm of the fire reached the back of our houses but was finally contained.

But high above and all around, the fire was burning, more vivid than the sun, throwing spirals of smoke in the air like the smoke from a volcano. Thirty-three cabins burned, and twelve thousand acres of forest still burning endangered countless homes below the fire. The fire was burning to the back of us now, and a rain of ashes began to fall and continued for days. The smell of the burn in the air, acid and pungent and tenacious. The dragon tongues of flames devouring, the flames leaping, the roar of destruction and dissolution, the eyes of the panicked animals, caught between fire and human beings, between two forms of death. They chose the fire. It was as if the fire had come from the bowels of the earth, like that of a fiery volcano, it was so powerful, so swift, and so ravaging. I saw trees become skeletons in one minute, I saw trees fall, I saw bushes turned to ashes in a second, I saw weary, ash-covered men, looking like men returned from war, some with burns, others overcome by smoke.

**5** The men were rushing from one spot to another watching for recrudescence.[4] Some started backfiring up the mountain so that the ascending flames could counteract the descending ones.

As the flames reached the cities below, hundreds of roofs burst into flame at once. There was no water pressure because all the fire hydrants were turned on at the same time, and the fire departments were helpless to save more than a few of the burning homes.

The blaring loudspeakers of passing police cars warned us to prepare to evacuate in

---

4. **recrudescence** (rē′ krōō des′ əns) *n*.: A fresh outbreak of something that has been inactive.

---

case the wind changed and drove the fire in our direction. What did I wish to save? I thought only of the diaries. I appeared on the porch carrying a huge stack of diary volumes, preparing to pack them in the car. A reporter for the Pasadena *Star News* was taking pictures of the evacuation. He came up, very annoyed with me. "Hey, lady, next time could you bring out something more important than all those old papers? Carry some clothes on the next trip. We gotta have human interest in these pictures!" **6**

A week later, the danger was over.

Gray ashy days.

In Sierra Madre, following the fire, the January rains brought floods. People are sandbagging their homes. At four A.M. the streets are covered with mud. The bare, burnt, naked mountains cannot hold the rains and slide down bringing rocks and mud. One of the rangers must now take photographs and movies of the disaster. He asks if I will help by holding an umbrella over the cameras. I put on my raincoat and he lends me hip boots which look to me like seven-league boots. **7**

We drive a little way up the road. At the third curve it is impassable. A river is rushing across the road. The ranger takes pictures while I hold the umbrella over the camera. It is terrifying to see the muddied waters and rocks, the mountain disintegrating. When we are ready to return, the road before us is covered by large rocks but the ranger pushes on as if the truck were a jeep and forces it through. The edge of the road is being carried away. **8**

I am laughing and scared too. The ranger is at ease in nature, and without fear. It is a wild moment of danger. It is easy to love nature in its peaceful and consoling moments, but one must love it in its furies too, in its despairs and wildness, especially when the damage is caused by us. **9**

454 *Nonfiction*

---

## Closure and Extension

### ANSWERS TO RESPONDING TO THE SELECTION
#### Your Response

1. Students will probably sense that Nin's vision of her life was largely as a writer. Elicit from students that

---

she first chose to help others in trouble, but when it was time to save her belongings, her diaries were the only belongings she chose to save.

2. Opinions will vary. Few students will have had real experiences by which to make such a judgment, so

---

their views will have been shaped by what they have seen in the movies and on television.

#### Recalling

3. The forest fire takes place in the Sierra Madre mountains. The writer begins reporting at night on the fire, which lasts for a week.

4. The forest fire has these effects: People were evacuated; at least twelve thousand acres of forest and countless homes were burned; and once the January floods came,

---

mudslides occurred down the mountains that were denuded of trees.

#### Interpreting

5. A fire is particularly dangerous in this setting because the mountains, bare of trees, "cannot hold the rains and slide down bringing rocks and mud."

#### Applying

6. Answers will differ. Suggested Response:

# RESPONDING TO THE SELECTION

## Your Response

1. Why do you think that Anaïs Nin valued her diaries so much?
2. Many people regard being in a forest fire as more frightening than being in any other natural disaster. What is your opinion?

## Recalling

3. Describe the setting—the time and place—of the forest fire.
4. What are the effects of the forest fire?

## Interpreting

5. Why is a fire so particularly dangerous in this setting?

## Applying

6. Imagine a natural disaster in your community. Develop a list of rules or guidelines for helping people survive the disaster.

# ANALYZING LITERATURE

## Understanding Descriptive Essays

Authors write descriptive essays to present their personal view of or experience with a subject. **Descriptive essays** usually contain two important elements: many specific details and figurative language—language that is not intended to be interpreted strictly or literally. For example, when Anaïs Nin describes the *angry fire,* she does not mean that the fire is really angry. She is saying that the fire has a wild, out-of-control quality that makes it like an angry person. Sometimes Nin uses the words *like* or *as, is* or *was.* At other times she gives the fire the qualities and movements of a living creature.

1. Find two examples of figurative language that contain the words *like* or *as* in the essay.
2. Find two examples of figurative language that describe something nonliving with the qualities of a living creature.

3. Find one descriptive detail you found especially effective. Explain the reasons for your choice.

# CRITICAL THINKING AND READING

## Separating Fact and Opinion

**Facts** are statements about things that have either happened or are happening. This information can always be proved true or false using reliable sources. **Opinions,** on the other hand, cannot be proved true or false because they are based on the writer's personal beliefs or attitudes. For example, the statement that the forest is a beautiful place is an opinion. This information cannot be proved true or false.

Which of the following are facts and which are opinions? Give reasons for your answers.

1. "I rushed next door to the Campion children . . . and got them into the car."
2. "The . . . lighted flares . . . gave the scene a theatrical, tragic air."
3. "It is easy to love nature in its peaceful and consoling moments, but one must love it in its furies too."

# THINKING AND WRITING

## Writing a Descriptive Essay

Write a descriptive essay that you could read as a radio news report. Write about the forest fire at Sierra Madre from a human-interest angle—that is, based on the feelings and reactions of the people the fire affected. When you finish your first draft, check to see that you included descriptive details and figurative language.

# LEARNING OPTION

**Writing.** Imagine that you are a newspaper reporter preparing to interview people who have just survived a forest fire. Write a list of questions about the fire and conduct interviews with your classmates. Then write a newspaper article that reports people's observations of the fire.

*Forest Fire   455*

**More About the Author** Bernard
DeVoto was an English professor
who wrote histories of the American West and who made Mark
Twain his major interest. What
kind of influence would you expect these factors to have on
DeVoto's writing?

**Literary Focus** An expository
essay is informative, as opposed
to a persuasive, descriptive, or
humorous essay. Ask students for
examples of topics that might be
discussed in an expository essay.

**Prereading Focus** Before students create their cluster maps,
you may wish to discuss the immigration patterns of many of the
major cultural groups in the United States. Knowing the reasons
and the timing for many groups to
leave their native countries to
come to the United States will
provide the background for students to consider the contributions these groups have made to
American life.

**Vocabulary** For your **less advanced** students, first give these
words in context to help them
guess their meaning.

**Electronic Handbook** You
may suggest that students use
the Language Master 6000 to hear
the pronunciations of *versatile* and
*tangible*.

# GUIDE FOR READING

## Bernard DeVoto

(1897–1955) was born in Og-
den, Utah, and became a respected critic, novelist, editor,
and magazine columnist during his varied literary career.
Above all, however, Bernard
DeVoto was a historian. His
book *Across the Wide Missouri,* one of a series of books
about America's westward
movement, received the
Pulitzer Prize for History in
1948. In his essay "The Indian
All Around Us," Bernard De-
Voto explains the history of
many Native American words
that are familiar to people of
the United States.

## The Indian All Around Us

### Expository Essay

An **expository essay** is a short nonfiction piece that explains or
gives information about a topic. The word *expository,* in fact, simply
means to give information about something or to explain what is difficult to understand. In expository essays writers not only explain information but may also express a particular point of view or opinion
about their topic.

### Focus

The language and customs of the United States reflect the diversity of its cultural groups. For example, people of Spanish origin
have contributed names of places like Los Angeles and San Antonio and foods such as *tacos* and *tortillas.* Working with a partner or
a small group of classmates, select a cultural group of people in the
United States. You may wish to consider your own family's cultural
heritage. Make a cluster map centered on the culture you have chosen. Cluster the words, foods, customs, games, and any other contributions of this group to the life or language of the United States.
As you read "The Indian All Around Us," make a similar cluster map
that shows the Native American contributions to the American language and life.

### Vocabulary

Knowing the following words will help you as you read "The
Indian All Around Us."

**versatile** (vʉr′ sə t'l) *adj.*: Having many uses (p. 457)
**tangible** (tan′ jə b'l) *adj.*: Capable of being perceived or
of being precisely identified
(p. 457)

**alkaloid** (al′ kə loid) *adj.*: Referring to certain bitter substances
found chiefly in plants (p. 458)
**gutturals** (gut′ ər əlz) *n.*:
Sounds produced in the throat
(p. 460)

## Objectives

1 To understand the expository essay
2 To identify the main idea
and supporting details
3 To write an expository
essay
4 To express individual interests and abilities through
an optional activity

## Support Material

**Teaching Portfolio**
Teacher Backup, p. 551
Grammar in Action Worksheet,
*Using Commas,* p. 555
Usage and Mechanics Work-
sheet, p. 557
Vocabulary Check, p. 558
Analyzing Literature Worksheet,
*Understanding an Expository
Essay,* p. 559

Critical Thinking and Reading
Worksheet, *Identifying Main
Idea,* p. 560
Selection Test, p. 561
Art Transparency 9, *The Indian
Trapper* by Frederic Remington

**Prentice Hall Literature Writing
Studio**

# The Indian All Around Us

## Bernard DeVoto

1 The Europeans who developed into the Americans took over from the Indians many things besides their continent. Look at a few: tobacco, corn, potatoes, beans (kidney, string and lima and therefore succotash), tomatoes, sweet potatoes, squash, popcorn and peanuts, chocolate, pineapples, hominy, Jerusalem artichokes, maple sugar. Moccasins, snowshoes, toboggans, hammocks, ipecac,[1] quinine, the crew haircut, goggles to prevent snow blindness—these are all Indian in origin. So is the versatile boat that helped the white man occupy the continent, the birch-bark canoe, and the custom canoeists have of painting designs on its bow.

A list of familiar but less important plants, foods and implements would run to several hundred items. Another long list would be needed to enumerate less tangible Indian contributions to our culture, such as arts, crafts, designs, ideas, beliefs, superstitions and even profanity. But there is something far more familiar, something that is always at hand and is used daily by every American and Canadian without awareness that it is Indian: a large vocabulary.

Glance back over the first paragraph. "Potato" is an Indian word, so is "tobacco," and if "corn" is not, the word "maize" is

**PAINTED BUFFALO HIDE SHIELD**
*Jémez, New Mexico*
*Museum of the American Indian*

and we used it for a long time, as the English do still. Some Indians chewed tobacco, some used snuff, nearly all smoked pipes or cigars or cigarettes, and the white man gladly adopted all forms of the habit. But he spoke of "drinking" tobacco, instead of smoking it, for a long time. Squash, hominy, ipecac, quinine, hammock, chocolate, canoe are all common nouns that have come into the English—or rather the American—language from Indian languages. Sometimes the word has changed on the way, perhaps only a little as with "potato," which was something like "batata" in the original, or sometimes a great deal, as with "cocoa,"

---

**1. ipecac** (ip′ ə kåk′) *n.*: A medicine made from certain dried roots.

*The Indian All Around Us* 457

## Humanities Note

Fine art, *Painted Buffalo Hide Shield,* Jémez, New Mexico. Of the art created by the Plains Indians, the best known is painting on animal hides. The Plains Indians used earth pigments, especially yellow, brown, and red. The color green was made from vegetable matter, and black from burned wood or bone. The Indians used a thin glue of boiled hide scrapings as a binder. Their tool for applying the paint was a semiresilient pointed object, such as the spongy part of a bone.

A warrior highly prized his shield, which was believed to have magical powers. A warrior painted his shield, say some historians, with a design received in a vision and whose meaning only he knew.

1. What kind of design would you create for a shield?
2. What examples can you suggest of other weapons or tools decorated with designs?

## Presentation

**Motivation/Prior Knowledge** Ask students to list all the geographical names from your state that reflect Native American language.

**Master Teacher Note** The English language has been influenced by the language of other cultures. Look at Art Transparency 8, *The Indian Trapper* by Frederic Remington in the Teaching Portfolio. Considering the way Indians lived and the help they gave some American settlers, what kinds of words would students expect to have come into common English use from Indian languages? In "The Indian All Around Us," the author discusses some of these words.

**Making Connections** Another selection about the effects of other cultures on American language is "A to Z in Foods as Metaphors" by Mimi Sheraton on page 491.

**Thematic Focus** Point out to students that DeVoto's essay touches on many aspects of our American heritage: the Native American contributions to our language, foods, tools, art, beliefs, and so on. It also mentions many different regions of the country, suggesting contributions from many Native American tribes in a variety of geographic locations. Ask students to discuss whether the Native American peoples have ever received appropriate recognition for their legacy to American culture.

**Purpose-Setting Question** How has the Native American culture affected our everyday lives?

1 **Enrichment** Early European settlers in America were those who established Spanish missions in California in the 1500's, those who founded Jamestown, Virginia in 1607, and Pilgrims who founded Plymouth Colony in Massachusetts in 1620.

**PAINTED BOWL: DEER FIGURE**
*Mimbres, New Mexico*
*Museum of the American Indian*

which began as, approximately, "cacahuatl."

Sometimes, too, we have changed the meaning. "Succotash" is a rendering of a Narraganset word that meant an ear of corn. The dish that the Indians ate was exactly what we call succotash today, though an Indian woman was likely to vary it as much as we do stew, by tossing in any leftovers she happened to have on hand. Similarly with "quinine." This is a modern word, made up by the scientists who first isolated the alkaloid substance from cinchona bark[2], but they derived it from the botanical name of the genus, which in turn was derived from the Indian name for it, "quinquina." The Indians, of course, used a decoction[3] made from the bark.

Put on your moccasins and take a walk in the country. If it is a cold day and you

---

**2. cinchona** (sin kō′ nə) **bark** n.: bark from certain tropical South American trees.
**3. decoction** (di käk′ shən) n.: An extract or flavor produced by boiling.

458 *Nonfiction*

wear a mackinaw, your jacket will be as Indian as your footwear, though "mackinaw" originally meant a heavy blanket of fine quality and, usually, bright colors. On your walk you may smell a skunk, see a raccoon or possum, hear the call of a moose. Depending on what part of the country you are in, you may see a chipmunk, muskrat, woodchuck or coyote. The names of all these animals are Indian words. (A moose is "he who eats off," that is, who browses on leaves. A raccoon is "he who scratches with his hands.") You may see hickory trees or catalpas,[4] pecans or mesquite,[5] and these too are Indian words. At the right season and place you may eat persimmons or pawpaws or scuppernongs.[6] All the breads and most of the puddings we make from cornmeal originated with the Indians but we haven't kept many of the original names, except "pone."

On a Cape Cod beach you may see clammers digging quahogs,[7] or as a Cape Codder would say, "coehoggin'." The Pilgrims learned the name and the method of getting at them from the Indians: they even learned the technique of steaming them with seaweed that we practice at clambakes. The muskellunge[8] and the terrapin[9] were named for us by Indians. Your children may build a wigwam to play in—it was a brush hut or a lodge covered with bark—or they may ask you to buy them a tepee, which was original-

2

---

**4. catalpas** (kə tal′ pəs) n.: American and Asiatic trees with large, heart-shaped leaves, trumpet-shaped flowers, and beanlike pods.
**5. mesquite** (mes kēt′) n.: Thorny trees or shrubs common in the southwest U.S. and in Mexico.
**6. pawpaws, scuppernongs** n.: Kinds of fruit.
**7. quahogs** (kwô′ hôgz) n.: Edible clams of the east coast of North America.
**8. muskellunge** (mus′ kə lunj) n.: A very large pike fish of the Great Lakes and upper Mississippi drainages.
**9. terrapin** (ter′ ə pin) n.: Several kinds of North American turtles.

---

ly made of buffalo hide but can be canvas now. They may chase one another with tomahawks. And we all go to barbecues.

The people earliest in contact with the Indians found all these words useful, but some Indian sounds they found hard to pronounce, such as the *tl* at the end of many words in Mexico and the Southwest. That is why "coyotl" became "coyote" and "tomatl" our tomato. Or accidental resemblances to English words might deceive them, as with "muskrat." The animal does look like a rat and has musk glands, but the Indian word was "musquash," which means "it is red."

Some words were simply too long. "Succotash" began as "musickwautash," "hominy" as "rockahominy," and "mackinaw" as "michilimackinac." (The last, of course, was the name given to the strait, the fort, the island, and ended as the name of a blanket and a jacket because the fort was a trading post.) At that, these are comparatively short; remember the lake in Massachusetts whose name is Chargoggagogg-manchaugagoggchaubunagungamaugg.[10]

Twenty-six of our states have Indian names, as have scores of cities, towns, lakes, rivers and mountains. In Maine are Kennebec, Penobscot, Androscoggin, Piscataqua, Wiscasset and many others, from Arowsic to Sytopilock by way of Mattawamkeag. California, noted for its Spanish names, still is well supplied with such native ones as Yosemite, Mojave, Sequoia, Truckee, Tahoe, Siskiyou. Washington has Yakima, Walla Walla, Spokane, Snoqualmie, Wenatchee; and Florida has Okeechobee, Seminole, Manitee, Ocala and as many

more as would fill a page. So with all the other states.

Consider such rivers as the Arkansas, Ohio, Mohawk, Wisconsin, Rappahannock, Minnesota, Merrimack, Mississippi, Missouri and Suwannee. Or such lakes as Ontario, Cayuga, Winnipesaukee, Memphremagog, Winnebago. Or such mountain ranges and peaks as Allegheny, Wichita, Wasatch, Shasta, Katahdin. Or cities: Milwaukee, Chattanooga, Sandusky.

The meaning of such names is not always clear. Tourist bureaus like to make up translations like bower-of-the-laughing-princess or land-of-the-sky-blue-water, but Indians were as practical-minded as anyone

**JAR WITH ANIMAL HEAD HANDLE**
*Socorro County, New Mexico*
*Museum of the American Indian*

10. **Char . . . maugg:** The translation is "You fish your side of the lake, we'll fish our side, and nobody fishes in the middle."

3 **Critical Thinking and Reading** What is the main idea in this paragraph? What are the supporting details?

4 **Discussion** Why might a tourist bureau like to make up such fanciful translations?

## Humanities Note

Fine art, *Jar with Animal Head Handle,* Socorro County, New Mexico. Native Americans, before the arrival of Europeans and the wheel, made pottery by the coil method. After building a vessel, the potter smoothed the surface by rubbing and scraping with a special paddle. Each village had its own subtly different set of pottery shapes, painted designs, and colors. Patterns and designs were handed down from generation to generation, sometimes for hundreds of years. Much of our knowledge of ancient Native Americans comes from the study of designs painted on jars such as this.
1. Considering the design and color of this jar, what do you think it was used for?
2. What kind of design and colors do you think would be used for a jar intended for use in a funeral or a burial?

"rockahominy," and "mackinaw" as "mickilimackinac."

Some Indians chewed tobacco, some used snuff, nearly all smoked pipes or cigars or cigarettes. . . .

**Student Activity.** American English has been enriched by words from many other languages. Think about the words from other languages you hear every day in the area where you live. Perhaps these words are from Spanish, from French, or from the American Indian languages. Write a paragraph telling about these words. Be sure to use commas to separate items in a series.

**Electronic Handbook** You might want students to review commas before completing the Grammar in Action activities. If students have access to the Language Master 6000, have them access the information on using commas correctly by entering the comma symbol, and then pressing the GRAMMAR key.

else and usually used a word that would identify the place. Our unpoetic pioneers christened dozens of streams Mud Creek or Muddy River—and that is about what Missouri means. The Sauk or Kickapoo word that gave Chicago its name had something to do with a strong smell. There may be some truth in the contention of rival cities that it meant "place of the skunks," but more likely it meant "place where wild onions grow." Kentucky does not mean "dark and bloody ground" as our sentimental legend says, but merely "place of meadows," which shows that the blue grass impressed Indians, too. Niagara means "point of land that is cut in two." Potomac means "something brought." Since the thing brought was probably tribute, perhaps in wampum,[11] we would not be far off if we were to render it "place where we pay taxes."

5 Quite apart from their meaning, such words as Kentucky, Niagara and Potomac are beautiful just as sounds. Though we usually take it for granted, the beauty of our Indian place names impresses foreign visitors. But since some Indian languages abounded with harsh sounds or gutturals, this beauty is unevenly distributed. In New England such names as Ogunquit, Megantic and Naugatuck are commoner than such more pleasing ones as Housatonic, Narragansett and Merrimack. The Pacific Northwest is overbalanced with harsh sounds like Nootka, Klamath, Klickitat and Clackamas, though it has its share of more agreeable ones—Tillamook, for instance, and Umatilla, Willamette, Multnomah. (Be sure to pronounce Willamette right: accent the second syllable.)

Open vowels were abundant in the languages spoken in the southeastern states,

---

**11. wampum** (wäm′ pəm) *n.*: Small beads made of shells and used by North American Indians as money and as ornaments.

so that portion of the map is thickly sown with delightful names. Alabama, Pensacola, Tuscaloosa, Savannah, Okefenokee, Chattahoochee, Sarasota, Ocala, Roanoke—they are charming words, pleasant to speak, pleasanter to hear. One could sing a child to sleep with a poem composed of just such names. In New York, if Skaneateles twists the tongue, Seneca glides smoothly from it and so do Tonawanda, Tuscarora, Oneonta, Saratoga, Genessee, Lackawanna, even Chautauqua and Canajoharie.

6 What is the most beautiful Indian place name? A surprising number of English writers have argued that question in travel books. No one's choice can be binding on anyone else. But there is a way of making a kind of answer: you can count the recorded votes. In what is written about the subject certain names appear repeatedly. Niagara and Tuscarora and Otsego are on nearly all the lists. So are Savannah and Potomac, Catawba, Wichita and Shenandoah.

But the five that are most often mentioned are all in Pennsylvania. That state has its Allegheny and Lackawanna, and many other musical names like Aliquippa, Towanda, Punxsutawney. But five others run away from them all. Wyoming (which moved a long way west and named a state)[12] and Conestoga and Monongahela seem to be less universally delightful than the two finalists, Juniata and Susquehanna. For 150 years, most of those who have written on the subject have ended with these two, and in the outcome Juniata usually takes second place. According to the write-in vote, then, the most beautiful place name in the United States is Susquehanna. It may be ungracious to remember that it first came into the language as "Saquesahannock."

---

**12. which . . . state:** The name Wyoming was originally given to a valley in Pennsylvania.

# RESPONDING TO THE SELECTION

## Your Response

1. Of all the Indian contributions that DeVoto mentions, which do you consider the most important? Explain.

## Recalling

2. Name two reasons why some Indian words were changed before becoming part of English.

## Interpreting

3. How would you interpret the title, "The Indian All Around Us"?
4. Why does the writer tell you to "put on your moccasins and take a walk in the country"?

## Applying

5. Do you think that you would enjoy a traditional Indian meal? What do you think the menu would include?
6. Based on what you learned in this essay, what criteria could you apply when you are naming something?

# ANALYZING LITERATURE

## Understanding an Expository Essay

**Expository essays** are usually written to inform or to explain. But many expository essays do both. For example, "The Indian All Around Us" not only informs us that the Indian word *coyotl* was changed to the American word *coyote,* but it also explains the reason why: because people found the *tl* sound hard to pronounce.

Give three examples of how this essay informs the reader.

# CRITICAL THINKING AND READING

## Identifying Main Ideas

In an expository essay, each paragraph usually has a main idea. In the fourth paragraph of "The Indian All Around Us," for example, the main idea is expressed in the first sentence: "Sometimes, too, we have changed the meaning." **Main ideas** are general statements that need supporting details, such as specific examples or reasons, to explain them. For example, DeVoto supports the main idea in the fourth paragraph with two specific examples—succotash and quinine.

Read the eleventh paragraph that begins "The meaning of such names."

1. What is the main idea of the paragraph?
2. List the supporting details that appear in the paragraph.

# THINKING AND WRITING

## Writing an Expository Essay

Write an expository essay about the contributions a particular culture has made to life in the United States. Before you write, be sure that you have narrowed your topic to fit what you can say in a short essay. For example, you may want to narrow your topic to foods, a sport, or place names. Revise your essay, making sure you have supported your main ideas. Then proofread your essay and share it with your classmates.

# LEARNING OPTION

**Multicultural Activity.** Trace an outline of the United States on a large sheet of drawing paper. With your classmates make a list of the many Indian place names that DeVoto mentions in his essay. Divide the list so that small groups of students can research where these places are. Have each group find the location of each place on its list and indicate it on your outline map. You may wish to research other American place names with origins in other languages, such as Spanish, French, and German, and show these places on your map as well.

*The Indian All Around Us*   461

## ANSWERS TO CRITICAL THINKING AND READING

1. The main idea of the paragraph is "For place names, Indians usually used a practical word that would identify the place."
2. The supporting details in this paragraph are that the Indians christened many streams Mud Creek or Muddy River, which is what Missouri means; that the Indian "word that gave Chicago its name had something to do with a strong smell"; that Kentucky means "place of meadows"; that Niagara means "point of land that is cut in two"; and that Potomac means "something brought."

**Challenge** Native Americans had the opportunity to name their natural surroundings. If you had been the first to see a river, mountain, or natural land formation in your area, what would you name it?

## THINKING AND WRITING

For practice for this assignment, students may do the practice activity *Writing an Expository Paragraph* in the Writing Process Activities section of the Teaching Portfolio, Volume II.

**Alternative Assessment** You may vary the Thinking and Writing Assignment as follows: Have students complete one of the Alternate Composition Assignments on page 552 of the Teaching Portfolio.

◆ **Software** If students have access to computers, you may wish to have them use the *Lists* feature of **Writer's Helper** to generate ideas for their essays.

## LEARNING OPTION

This activity will appeal to students who have an interest in maps and American geography. This is a fine opportunity for those students who like art projects to work together with those who like to do research or are interested in foreign languages.

## Interpreting

3. Answers will differ. Suggested Response: The title implies that there are many Native American influences, some of which we may not be aware, that affect our everyday lives.
4. Answers will differ. Suggested Response: The moccasins you would wear, along with some other clothing, and many of the things you would see have names that come from the Native American.

## Applying

5. Answers will differ. Suggested Response: The meal might include corn, potatoes, beans, tomatoes, squash, popcorn, hominy.
6. Answers will differ. Suggested Response: When naming something, you could apply the criteria that the name should be easy to pronounce and not long, the name should reflect the meaning of the thing, and the sound of the name should be beautiful.

## ANSWERS TO ANALYZING LITERATURE

Answers will differ. Suggested Responses:
a. Sometimes the original Native American word has changed over time.
b. Sometimes we have changed the meaning of the original Native American word.
c. "Twenty-six of our states have Indian names, as have scores of cities, towns, lakes, rivers and mountains."

## Preparation

**More About the Author** How does Robert MacNeil's experience as a co-host of an in-depth news program make him a good critic of television? How might it detract from his credibility?

**Literary Focus** Point out to students that we often use persuasive techniques—arguments or reasons to support our views, plus emotive language—in our everyday lives. Ask students for instances when they have used persuasion.

**Prereading Focus** Have students discuss different ways besides television in which they can be informed about current events and different ways in which they can be entertained. Have them also consider the amount of time they spend in those ways, as opposed to watching television.

**Electronic Handbook** If students have access to the Language Master 6000, suggest that they find a synonym with a different connotation for each of the following vocabulary words: *usurps* and *pervading.*

**Vocabulary** Have your **more advanced** students write single sentences in which they use each word with either an antonym or a group of words suggesting the opposite meaning. Example: The kaleidoscopic view seen from the window of the speeding train was more stimulating than the static view seen when the train was stopped.

### Robert MacNeil

(1931–    ) was born in Montreal, Canada. He is a radio and television journalist. He has worked for NBC radio and for the British Broadcasting Corporation. In the mid-1970's MacNeil came to public television station WNET to host his own news analysis program, which has grown into the highly regarded *MacNeil/Lehrer Newshour*. This differs from other news programs by offering more in-depth reports on important issues. In the following essay, MacNeil criticizes American television programming.

## The Trouble with Television

### Persuasive Essay

A **persuasive essay** is a short nonfiction composition in which a writer presents his or her views in order to convince you to accept the author's opinion or to act a certain way. Since you may not share the writer's opinion, the writer usually offers arguments, or reasons, to support the position. Because you may not care enough to take any action, the writer tries to stir your concern and emotions so that you will act.

### Focus

What did you watch on television this week? Make a list of the shows and commercials you watched and compare it with your classmates' lists. Then, in groups of four or five, choose the three shows and commercials that were watched most frequently, and jot down the group's critical comments about the intelligence level of those shows. As you read Robert MacNeil's article, "The Trouble with Television," note his criticisms of programs and commercials. In a class discussion, compare your overall comments about television with MacNeil's.

### Vocabulary

Knowing the following words will help you as you read "The Trouble with Television."

**gratification** (grat′ ə fi kā′ shən) *n.*: The act of pleasing or satisfying (p. 463)

**diverts** (də vʉrts′) *v.*: Distracts (p. 463)

**kaleidoscopic** (kə lī′ də skäp′ ik) *adj.*: Constantly changing (p. 463)

**usurps** (yo͞o sʉrps′) *v.*: Takes over (p. 463)

**medium** (mē′ dē əm) *n.*: Means of communication; television (p. 464)

**august** (ô gust′) *adj.*: Honored (p. 464)

**pervading** (pər vād′ iŋ) *v.*: Spreading throughout (p. 465)

**trivial** (triv′ ē əl) *adj.*: Of little importance (p. 465)

*462   Nonfiction*

### Objectives

1 To understand the persuasive essay
2 To recognize connotative language
3 To write a persuasive essay
4 To express individual interests and abilities through an optional activity

### Support Material

**Teaching Portfolio**
Teacher Backup, p. 563
Grammar in Action Worksheet, *Using Topic Sentences,* p. 566
Usage and Mechanics Worksheet, p. 568
Vocabulary Check, p. 569
Analyzing Literature Worksheet, *Understanding the Persuasive Essay,* p. 570

Language Worksheet, *Choosing the Meaning that Fits the Context,* p. 571.
Selection Test, p. 572

**Prentice Hall Literature Writing Studio**

# The Trouble with Television

## Robert MacNeil

It is difficult to escape the influence of television. If you fit the statistical averages, by the age of 20 you will have been exposed to at least 20,000 hours of television. You can add 10,000 hours for each decade you have lived after the age of 20. The only things Americans do more than watch television are work and sleep.

Calculate for a moment what could be done with even a part of those hours. Five thousand hours, I am told, are what a typical college undergraduate spends working on a bachelor's degree. In 10,000 hours you could have learned enough to become an astronomer or engineer. You could have learned several languages fluently. If it appealed to you, you could be reading Homer[1] in the original Greek or Dostoevski[2] in Russian. If it didn't, you could have walked around the world and written a book about it.

The trouble with television is that it discourages concentration. Almost anything interesting and rewarding in life requires some constructive, consistently applied effort. The dullest, the least gifted of us can achieve things that seem miraculous to those who never concentrate on anything. But television encourages us to apply no effort. It sells us instant gratification. It diverts us only to divert, to make the time pass without pain.

Television's variety becomes a narcotic,[3] not a stimulus.[4] Its serial, kaleidoscopic exposures force us to follow its lead. The viewer is on a perpetual guided tour: thirty minutes at the museum, thirty at the cathedral, then back on the bus to the next attraction —except on television, typically, the spans allotted are on the order of minutes or seconds, and the chosen delights are more often car crashes and people killing one another. In short, a lot of television usurps one of the most precious of all human gifts, the ability to focus your attention yourself, rather than just passively surrender it.

Capturing your attention—and holding it—is the prime motive of most television programming and enhances its role as a profitable advertising vehicle. Programmers live in constant fear of losing anyone's attention—anyone's. The surest way to

---

**1. Homer** (hō′ mər): Greek epic poet of the eighth century B.C.
**2. Dostoevski** (dôs′ tô yef′ skē): Fyodor (fyô′ dôr) Mikhailovich (mi khī′ lô vich) Dostoevski (1821–1881), Russian novelist.

**3. narcotic** (när kät′ ik) n.: Something that has a soothing effect.
**4. stimulus** (stim′ yə ləs) n.: Something that rouses to action.

*The Trouble with Television* 463

---

**Presentation**

**Motivation/Prior Knowledge** Ask students to think about the influence television has had in their lives. How would they describe its place and its impact?

**Master Teacher Note** You may want to bring and share with students any cartoons you find that show people being influenced by television.

**Thematic Focus** Many believe that television has been more destructive to the American creative spirit than any other cultural medium. Ask students to discuss the ways in which they believe television is a creative medium. Have them suggest the ways in which television has contributed positively to American cultural life.

**Purpose-Setting Question** What reasons does the writer give for questioning the value of television in our society?

**1 Discussion** Ask students how true this is for them. Consider that mini portable televisions can be taken virtually anywhere and that there is widespread use of cable television, video cassette recorders, and closed-circuit television.

**2 Literary Focus** Persuasive essays are often written in the third person, but can be written in the first person, with the writer speaking as "I."

**3 Discussion** What else could be accomplished within 20,000 hours?

**4 Discussion** Ask students if this is always true. What about the use of television for educational or business purposes?

**5 Clarification** The reasons they fear losing anyone's attention is that advertising pays for much of television, and advertisers want to know that they are reaching a large audience.

**Multicultural Focus** MacNeil's argument focuses so strongly on the faults of television that some students may feel compelled to defend it. To spark dialogue about the pros and cons of television, ask students to consider some ways in which television brings the world together. Explain the meaning of "global village," a world-wide community of people who share similar experiences through communications technology. Ask students to name some programs that provide them with information about world affairs about which they might not have otherwise learned. What new events, languages, art forms, or lifestyles have they been exposed to through television? Have students choose a television program they know and which they feel teaches them about people of other places, cultures, or religions. Ask them to watch that program and discuss it with the class.

**Making Connections** Another selection that deals with the disadvantages of technology is "Dial Versus Digital" on page 476.

Fine art, *Afternoon Television*, 1965, by Maxwell Hendler. Maxwell Hendler (1938– ) was born in St. Louis, Missouri. He studied at the University of California in Los Angeles and taught at California State University and the Art Center College of Design in Pasadena.

Hendler has exhibited his work, which has been labeled "realism," at the Ceeje Gallery in Los Angeles, the Metropolitan Museum of Art in New York, the Los Angeles County Museum of Art, and the Robert Miller Gallery in New York.

Although at first this picture seems to be an imitation of a camera image, the subject matter, attention to detail, and use of color and light seem to go beyond reality.

1. There are no people in this picture, except for the television image, and yet do you feel the presence of someone? Who might this person be?
2. What do you think the artist is saying about television in this painting?

**6 Clarification** David Sarnoff (1891–1971) was one of the first businessmen to see the full possibilities of using radio and television for entertainment. He was executive president of the Radio Corporation of America from 1930 to 1948 and was chairman of the board from 1947 to 1970.

**AFTERNOON TELEVISION**
*Maxwell Hendler*
The Metropolitan Museum of Art

avoid doing so is to keep everything brief, not to strain the attention of anyone but instead to provide constant stimulation through variety, novelty, action and movement. Quite simply, television operates on the appeal to the short attention span.

It is simply the easiest way out. But it has come to be regarded as a given, as inherent[5] in the medium itself: as an imperative, as though General Sarnoff, or one of the other august pioneers of video, had be-

6

_____
**5. inherent** (in hir′ ənt) *adj.*: Natural.

## Grammar in Action

Good writers begin every paragraph with a **topic sentence,** stating the main idea or topic of the paragraph. Although the topic sentence is not necessarily the first sentence of the paragraph, it should be somewhere in the beginning of the paragraph. The sentences in the paragraph should relate closely to the topic sentence. Otherwise, the paragraph will lack clarity, focus, and coherence.

Although it is always important to use topic sentences, it is especially important when writing to persuade, as MacNeil does in "The Trouble with Television." The more focused your writing, the more persuasive it is likely to be. Your audience must have a clear idea of what you are "selling" them before they will be convinced. For example, MacNeil believes that television news communicates inefficiently. Here is his topic sentence: "In the case of news, this practice, in my view, results in inefficient communication." In the sentences following his topic sentence he supports his assertion.

queathed to us tablets of stone commanding that nothing in television shall ever require more than a few moments' concentration.

In its place that is fine. Who can quarrel with a medium that so brilliantly packages escapist entertainment as a mass-marketing tool? But I see its values now pervading this nation and its life. It has become fashionable to think that, like fast food, fast ideas are the way to get to a fast-moving, impatient public.

In the case of news, this practice, in my view, results in inefficient communication. I question how much of television's nightly news effort is really absorbable and understandable. Much of it is what has been aptly described as ''machine gunning with scraps.'' I think its technique fights coherence.[6] I think it tends to make things ultimately boring and dismissable (unless they are accompanied by horrifying pictures) because almost anything is boring and dismissable if you know almost nothing about it.

I believe that TV's appeal to the short attention span is not only inefficient communication but decivilizing as well. Consider the casual assumptions that television tends to cultivate: that complexity must be avoided, that visual stimulation is a substitute for thought, that verbal precision is an anachronism.[7] It may be old-fashioned, but I was taught that thought is words, arranged in grammatically precise ways.

There is a crisis of literacy in this country. One study estimates that some 30 million adult Americans are ''functionally illiterate'' and cannot read or write well enough to answer a want ad or understand the instructions on a medicine bottle.

**6. coherence** (kō hir′ əns) n.: The quality of being connected in an intelligible way.
**7. anachronism** (ə nak′ rə niz'm) n.: Anything that seems to be out of its proper place in history.

Literacy may not be an inalienable human right, but it is one that the highly literate Founding Fathers might not have found unreasonable or even unattainable. We are not only not attaining it as a nation, statistically speaking, but we are falling further and further short of attaining it. And, while I would not be so simplistic as to suggest that television is the cause, I believe it contributes and is an influence.

Everything about this nation—the structure of the society, its forms of family organization, its economy, its place in the world—has become more complex, not less. Yet its dominating communications instrument, its principal form of national linkage, is one that sells neat resolutions to human problems that usually have no neat resolutions. It is all symbolized in my mind by the hugely successful art form that television has made central to the culture, the thirty-second commercial: the tiny drama of the earnest housewife who finds happiness in choosing the right toothpaste.

When before in human history has so much humanity collectively surrendered so much of its leisure to one toy, one mass diversion? When before has virtually an entire nation surrendered itself wholesale to a medium for selling?

Some years ago Yale University law professor Charles L. Black, Jr. wrote: ''. . . forced feeding on trivial fare is not itself a trivial matter.'' I think this society is being force fed with trivial fare, and I fear that the effects on our habits of mind, our language, our tolerance for effort, and our appetite for complexity are only dimly perceived. If I am wrong, we will have done no harm to look at the issue skeptically and critically, to consider how we should be resisting it. I hope you will join with me in doing so.

*The Trouble with Television* 465

**7 Discussion** What does this phrase mean?

**8 Discussion** Ask students for examples of television's lack of complexity. (One example is the use of the 10- to 90-second spot announcement by political candidates.)

**Reader's Response** What is your opinion of television? What advantages and disadvantages are there to television?

**Thematic Response** List some television shows that you think could win awards for creativity. Try to think of shows that fit different categories: educational, comedy, drama, science and nature, children's programs, and specials, for example. Tell why you think each of these shows is outstanding in its creativity and how each can enlarge our vision of the world.

activity it discourages concentration.

3. MacNeil's three assumptions that contribute to television's ''decivilizing'' are the following:
   a. complexity must be avoided;
   b. visual stimulation is a substitute for thought; and
   c. verbal precision is an anachronism.

*Interpreting*

4. MacNeil is trying to persuade you to view television critically and to cut down on the amount of time you spend watching television.
5. Answers will differ. Suggested Response: MacNeil might prefer people to pursue further education, to be more active in general, and to devote more concentration and attention to what is around them.

*Applying*

6. Answers will differ. Suggested Response: You might institute longer program times, a more complex approach to complicated issues, and greater verbal precision. These changes would make television a more valuable tool for society and would be changes that MacNeil would agree with.

465

**Student Activity 1.** Evaluate the success of each of MacNeil's topic sentences in "The Trouble with Television."

**Student Activity 2.** Write a reaction to MacNeil's essay. Be sure to use clear, focused, specific topic sentences.

## Closure and Extention

*(Questions begin on page 466.)*
**ANSWERS TO RESPONDING TO THE SELECTION**
*Your Response*

1. Many will think television is an excellent source of information and a good way to expand educational horizons. Others will prefer books and other print media.
2. MacNeil believes the major trouble with television is that as a passive

(Answers begin on p. 465.)

## ANSWERS TO ANALYZING LITERATURE

1. Answers will differ. Students may cite the following points: The only things Americans do more than watch television are work and sleep; television "discourages concentration"; and television "becomes a narcotic, not a stimulus."
2. Answers will differ. Some students may take exception to the point that programmers strive to "keep everything brief, not to strain the attention of anyone . . ." and that television "tends to make things ultimately boring and dismissable."
3. Answers will differ.

## ANSWERS TO CRITICAL THINKING AND READING

1. Answers will differ. Suggested Response: These words have a positive connotation and seem to suggest that studying for these professions would have been more beneficial than watching television.
2. Answers will differ. Suggested Response: This phrase has a negative connotation and seems to suggest that other activities—or even television programming—that require a longer attention span would be more beneficial.

**Challenge** You might want to ask students to research and report on what the effect of violence on television is on our society.

## THINKING AND WRITING

**Writing Transparency** The paragraph exercise *Order of Importance* in the **Transparencies for Writing** may help students be more persuasive in writing their suggestions to a television network or producer.

**Alternative Assessment** *Collaborative Assignment* You may vary the Thinking and Writing assignment as follows: Have students work in groups of three or four to write a response to Robert MacNeil in which they argue the virtues of television. Have them brainstorm the benefits they see

## RESPONDING TO THE SELECTION

### Your Response

1. How do you feel about television as a teaching tool or as a source of information?

### Recalling

2. According to MacNeil what is the major trouble with television?
3. MacNeil states that television's appeal is "decivilizing." What three assumptions does he give that contribute to this decivilization?

### Interpreting

4. What action is MacNeil trying to persuade you to take?
5. What do you think MacNeil would want people to do instead of watching television?

### Applying

6. If you were the president of a commercial television network, what changes in the programming would you make? Would these changes make television a more valuable tool for society? Are these changes that MacNeil would agree with?

## ANALYZING LITERATURE

### Understanding the Persuasive Essay

A **persuasive essay** is nonfiction in which writers strive to make readers accept a certain way of thinking about an issue. Whether or not they are successful depends on how strong their reasons are and what facts they use.

1. Write down three points MacNeil makes that caused you to think again about watching television. Explain why each was effective.
2. Write down any points in the essay that are not persuasive. Explain why you think each is not effective.
3. Explain why MacNeil is or is not successful in persuading you to think carefully about and possibly change your television viewing habits.

## CRITICAL THINKING AND REAI

### Recognizing Connotative Language

Persuasive writers often use words that provoke an emotional response in their readers. These words have certain **connotations,** or associated ideas and images, beyond their literal meanings. If the writer is supporting something, the words chosen will have positive connotations. If the writer opposes something, the words will be negative. For example, MacNeil states that television is a "narcotic," and that viewers "passively surrender" to it. Both of these words create negative images.

Explain what connotations the italicized words in the following sentences have for you.

1. "In 10,000 hours you could have learned enough to become an *astronomer* or *engineer.*"
2. "Quite simply, television operates on the appeal to the short attention span. It is simply the *easiest way out.*"

## THINKING AND WRITING

### Writing a Persuasive Essay

Make a list of suggestions about programming that would make television viewing a more worthwhile experience. Write the suggestions in a letter to a television network executive or producer. When you have finished, check to be sure you have used the correct form for a business letter. Proofread it and prepare a final draft. Mail your letter if you wish.

## LEARNING OPTION

**Art.** Work in a small group to create a cartoon about the importance of television in American life. Looking at political cartoons in a newspaper may help you figure out how to make fun of certain aspects of television. You may also wish to focus on some positive aspects of television.

---

in the programs they watch and discuss particular shows in some depth. Once the group has decided on the benefits they wish to discuss and the examples they will cite to support their argument, they can collaboratively write the introduction and conclusion of their essay and then divide the points they want to make in the body of the essay among the group's members.

**Writing Across the Curriculum** You might want to have students choose another aspect of modern technology and research it. They can report on how it affects our everyday lives and whether they think this effect is beneficial or not. Perhaps inform the social studies department of this assignment. Social studies teachers might provide guidance in conducting student research.

## LEARNING OPTION

Students who enjoy art and humor will be enthusiastic about this activity. It is not easy for students to create satire, but it would be worthwhile to show students good examples of cartoons that have serious messages delivered with satirical humor.

# Essays in the Content Areas

**STILL LIFE WITH SNEAKERS**
*Oliver Johnson*
*Courtesy of the Artist*

## Humanities Note

Fine art, *Still Life With Sneakers,* by Oliver Johnson. African American artist and musician Oliver Johnson ordinarily paints and illustrates in a sparse, dramatic style. However, *Still Life With Sneakers* was painted in his days as an art student. The paraphernalia of art study—art books and a canvas and stretcher—along with a pair of sneakers made a readily available still life for young Oliver Johnson. His developing skill is evident in the beautiful treatment of the book cover in the foreground as well as in the accuracy of his depiction of the shoes. His natural talent is evident in the repetition of rectangles in the composition and the interesting, warm colors of the work.

Oliver Johnson is known today for his skill as a jazz percussionist and for his insightful portraits of fellow musicians.

You might use these questions for discussion:

1. How does this still-life painting suggest study in a content area?
2. What story does this painting tell?

## Preparation

**More About the Author** Hal Borland spent a great deal of time in the Southwest, the homeland of the Ute Indians. As a young man, Borland knew many Utes and learned much about nature from them. One of his works, *When the Legends Die,* tells the story of a young Indian boy brought up in the wilderness. After attending school and becoming a famous bronco rider, the young man returns to the wilderness to find happiness. Ask students to discuss the relationship between nature and personal fulfillment. How did the natural world help Borland to fulfill his potential as a writer?

**Reading in the Content Areas** Observation is an important skill to cultivate in life. Careful observation results in scientific discoveries, crime solving, and lifesaving. Think about all the professions that require people to observe things closely and accurately.

**Prereading Focus** You may wish to display an array of books by noteworthy authors on space exploration, planets, meteors, and other related topics. Seymour Simon, Franklyn Branley, and Patricia Lauber are recommended science authors. Allow students time to browse among the books, to read, and to list questions they would like to have answered about space-related topics.

**Vocabulary** Most students will have no difficulty with these words. You might have them use each word in a sentence orally before reading the story.

 **Electronic Handbook** If students have access to the Language Master 6000, suggest that they find synonyms for the word *droves.* Discuss why the author chose to use *droves* rather than a synonym.

468

# GUIDE FOR READING

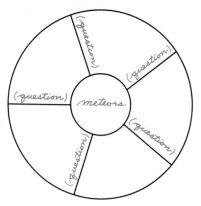

### Hal Borland

(1900–1978), born in Sterling, Nebraska, was a naturalist, a person who studies animals and plants. He worked as a reporter for the *Denver Post* and the *Brooklyn Times.* He was also a writer of documentary film scripts, radio scripts, and other nonfiction. Borland loved the outdoors. The National Audubon Society honored him by creating the Hal Borland Trail in Connecticut. Borland's essay "Shooting Stars" blends his fascination with nature and his ability to report facts in a clear, captivating manner.

*468 Nonfiction*

## Shooting Stars

### Observation

One of the skills required of a naturalist is acute observation. **Observation** is the act of looking at an object or event carefully and objectively. When you observe, you concentrate only on what you see, not on what you feel, think, or conclude about it. Observing allows you to report or describe clearly and factually what happens.

### Focus

Have you ever witnessed a real meteor shower? Were you impressed with the visuals of meteor showers in such films as *Star Trek* or *2001: A Space Odyssey*? Make a question wheel like the one that follows. Write the word *meteors* in the center and fill the wheel with questions that reflect everything you'd like to know about meteors. As you read "Shooting Stars," note answers to the questions that you have written in your wheel. You may also wish to add questions that puzzle you as you read.

### Vocabulary

Knowing the following words will help you as you read "Shooting Stars."

**horizon** (hə rī′ zən) *n.*: The line that forms the boundary between Earth and sky (p. 469)
**friction** (frik′ shən) *n.*: The rubbing of the surface of one body against another (p. 469)
**droves** (drōvz) *n.*: Large numbers; crowds (p. 470)

---

# Shooting Stars

## Hal Borland

Most clear, dark nights you can see a shooting star, as we call it, if you keep looking. Those shooting stars are meteors. They are points of light that suddenly appear in the sky, like distant stars, race across the darkness, usually toward the horizon, and disappear.

For a long time nobody knew what a meteor was. But finally those who study stars and the sky decided that a meteor is a piece of a comet that exploded long ago. Those pieces are still wandering about the universe in huge, looping paths that follow the original comet's orbit. There are uncounted pieces of such comets out there in the depths of space. Periodically clusters of them come close to the earth's orbit, or path around the sun. Most meteors are small, probably only a few inches in diameter, but when they enter the earth's atmosphere the friction makes them white-hot. Then they look big as stars streaking across the darkness.

There are half a dozen meteor showers

Shooting Stars    469

**3 Clarification** Constellations are groups of stars in which early peoples thought they saw imaginary figures of animals or people. Most of the constellations referred to today were named by the ancient Greeks after mythical heroes, heroines, and beasts such as Perseus, Andromeda, and Leo the lion.

**4 Critical Thinking and Reading** Evaluate Professor Olmstead's powers of observation. What do you think the relationship is between being a keen observer and being an astronomer?

**5 Discussion** Why do people watch for meteors? Why do the heavens fascinate people?

**6 Critical Thinking and Reading** What does this Indian legend probably refer to? Based on the author's background, how do you think he knows about the legend?

**7 Enrichment** A meteorite found recently in Antarctica appears to have come from the moon. It is made of materials very much like those brought back from the moon. Another meteorite found in Antarctica may have come from Mars. It is similar in composition to the Martian soil tested by *Viking I*.

**Reader's Response** Does "Shooting Stars" pique your interest in meteors? Explain.

**Thematic Response** Does this essay make you curious to find out more about space, about meteors and craters, about the planets and other bodies in space? Are there topics you want to know more about? Look at the list of questions you wrote in the Focus and add other questions to the list as they have occurred to you. Why do the many aspects of the solar system and outer space hold such fascination for human beings?

---

**3** each year. Each is named after the constellation from which it appears to come. The biggest of all, the Perseids, named for the constellation of Perseus, occurs on the 10th, 11th, and 12th of August. The next largest, the Leonids, named for the constellation of Leo, comes on the nights of November 14, 15, and 16. Another, the Andromedids, which is not quite so big, comes from November 17 through 23. There are other meteor showers in December, January, April, May, and July, but none of them is as big as those in August and November.

Most people watching meteors will be satisfied if they see ten or twenty in an hour of watching. On special occasions, however, the meteors seem to come in droves. The most remarkable meteor shower I ever heard of was seen by a distinguished astronomer, Professor Denison Olmstead, of New Haven, Connecticut, on the night of November 12, 1833. He was watching the Leonids, **4** which seem to come from directly overhead and race downward toward the horizon in all directions. He reported that meteors fell "like flakes of snow." He estimated that he saw 240,000 meteors in nine hours that night. He said they ranged in size from mere streaks of light to "globes of the moon's diameter." If he had not been a notable astronomer whose accuracy was beyond question, such statements would seem ridiculous. But there is no reason to doubt what he reported. He had seen one of the most unusual meteor showers ever reported. What he watched should be called a meteor storm rather than a shower.

I once watched the August Perseids with an astronomer on a hilltop in open country, and in two hours we counted almost a thousand meteors. That was the most I ever saw at one time. And we were bitten by one mosquito for every meteor we saw. After that I tried watching for meteors in November, when there were no mosquitoes. But the most I ever saw in November was about one hundred meteors in two hours of watching.

**5** The amazing thing about these meteor showers is that they come year after year. Professor Olmstead saw all those Leonids in November of 1833, but if you watch for meteors this year you almost certainly will see them on the same nights he saw them. They will come next year, the year after that, and for countless years more. Your grandfather saw them, and your grandchildren will see them if they look for them.

Occasionally a meteor reaches the earth. Then it is called a meteorite and it is valued as a sample of the vast mystery of the deep space in the sky. Scientists examine it, try to guess what it was to begin with, where it came from, what it is like out there. Nobody ever learned very much from the meteorites except that they often contain a great deal of nickel and iron.

Only a few large meteorites have struck the earth. The largest we know about fell in Arizona many centuries ago and made what is now called Meteor Crater, a hole about a mile across and 600 feet deep. **6** Some Indian legends of the Southwest tell of a big fire that fell from the sky and ate a huge hole in the earth, so this big meteorite may have fallen since man first arrived in America, perhaps twenty-five thousand years ago.

**7** Other big meteorites have fallen, in ancient times, in Texas, in Argentina, in northern Siberia, in South-West Africa, and in Greenland. A meteorite weighing more than thirty-six tons was found in Greenland and now can be seen in the Hayden Planetarium in New York City. Millions of meteors have flashed across the night sky, but only a few large meteorites have ever reached the earth. Never in all the centuries of written history has there been a report of anyone being struck by a meteorite.

470   Nonfiction

---

**Multicultural Focus** You can complement the scientific information in this essay by discussing different civilizations' imaginative interpretations of meteorites. Tell students that people in many countries have been amazed, frightened, or filled with religious awe at the sight of shooting stars. For example, in India some meteoric stones were worshiped as actual pieces of a god fallen from heaven. In some parts of China, meteors were thought to have come from thunderbolts and were considered evil omens.

Suggest that students imagine they are members of an early civilization without any scientific knowledge of meteors. Have them write a paragraph about what they might be thinking as they see a meteor fall through the sky.

**Closure and Extension**

**ANSWERS TO RESPONDING TO THE SELECTION**
*Your Response*

1. Encourage students to explain what makes an aspect of the sky beautiful to them.
2. Most students will say that they would like to observe a meteor shower.

## RESPONDING TO THE SELECTION

### Your Response

1. What do you think is the most beautiful part of the night sky?
2. Would you enjoy watching a real meteor shower? Why or why not?

### Recalling

3. What are meteors?
4. Why are meteorites valued so much?
5. What was the effect of the largest meteorite that fell to Earth?

### Interpreting

6. Why do you think scientists collect meteorites? Why do meteors stir the imagination?

### Applying

7. What is the difference between a scientific explanation and an explanation offered by a legend or myth? What can scientists learn from legends or myths?

## READING IN THE CONTENT AREAS

### Understanding Observation

**Observation,** or the act of looking at or noticing an object or event objectively, or factually, is a skill that scientists use to gain information. When observing, they try to concentrate only on the facts, not on their opinions.

You too can use observation to learn. By screening out your personal reactions, you can think only about the facts.

Take notes on one of the following situations, reporting the facts. Summarize what you observe.
a. the view outside your classroom window
b. students changing class

## CRITICAL THINKING AND READING

### Recognizing Observation and Inference

An **observation** is an act of noticing and recording facts and events. An **inference** is a rea-

sonable conclusion you can draw from given facts or clues. When you see storm clouds overhead and note that they are gray and gathering quickly, you are observing the facts. When you remark that it looks as though it will storm soon, you are inferring based on what you see and know about storm clouds.

State whether the following sentences from "Shooting Stars" are observations or inferences.

1. "I once watched the August Perseids with an astronomer on a hilltop in open country, and in two hours we counted almost a thousand meteors."
2. "Some Indian legends of the Southwest tell of a big fire that fell from the sky and ate a huge hole in the Earth, so this big meteorite may have fallen since man first arrived in America, perhaps twenty-five thousand years ago."

## THINKING AND WRITING

### Observing

Choose a common object such as a safety pin or a pencil sharpener. Observe it carefully, making notes. Then write a description of it, but do not name it. Revise to make sure you have described the object so precisely that someone reading it could guess what it is. Finally, read your description to your classmates and see if they can identify the object.

## LEARNING OPTION

**Writing.** Write a poem about shooting stars or some other element of the night sky. Close your eyes and visualize a spectacular event in the skies that you would love to observe. Create word images with figurative language—comparisons between unlike things—to represent the pictures that you see in your mind's eye. You may wish to make a painting around your poem that illustrates the beauty of this stunning phenomenon.

*Shooting Stars* 471

**Challenge** Discuss the importance of highly developed powers of observation in appreciating nature. Name some natural phenomena that require careful observation to be fully appreciated. What types of life might be missed altogether if people didn't observe carefully?

**Writing Across the Curriculum** You might have students research and report on the solar system. If you do, perhaps inform your school science department of this assignment. Science teachers might provide guidance for students in conducting their research.

### THINKING AND WRITING

**Writing Transparency** A graphic organizer may help your students write their descriptions. Use the *Sensory Language Chart* in **Transparencies for Writing.**

**Alternative Assessment** *Peer Review:* In pairs or groups of four, have students assess one another's work by responding to the following questions:

What common object does the writer describe?

What precise details of the object does the writer include to help you identify it?

What do you suggest the writer add or delete to help him or her present the object more vividly to the reader?

What concrete suggestions do you have to improve the organization and language mechanics of the description?

To validate the peer review, have your students revise their work, incorporating those suggestions they believe will enhance their descriptions.

### LEARNING OPTION

Students who enjoy writing, who enjoy self-expression and poetry, and who have an artistic flair will especially enjoy this activity.

Goodman writes about both famous people and her own friends and family. She portrays famous people with the same familiarity and warmth that characterize her more personal writing. Because she is a newspaper columnist, she tackles both controversial issues and amusing everyday-life experiences for a wide audience. Ask students to discuss how writing for a newspaper affects a writer's style. How is writing regularly for a widely read paper different from writing a book?

**Reading in the Content Areas** Every journalist has a purpose for writing every article. The purpose of a piece is particularly evident when it is nonfiction and biographical. However, you can apply the *who? what? when? where? why?* and *how?* formula to all your reading with enlightening results.

**Prereading Focus** You may wish to initiate a discussion with students about people who enjoy their work. Ask students to name adults who are visibly enthusiastic about the work they do. Ask students if they see any similarities among the jobs that people seem most to enjoy.

**Vocabulary** It would be helpful for students to know the following words also: *orchestrally, contagious* (p. 473); *intrigued, sustains,* and *spontaneously* (p. 474).

**Electronic Handbook** You may suggest that your students use the Language Master 6000 to hear the pronunciations of *esophagus, regimen,* and *legacy.*

# GUIDE FOR READING

## The Sounds of Richard Rodgers

### Ellen Goodman

(1941–    ) is a national columnist based at the *Boston Globe.* Her column is syndicated by the *Washington Post* Writers Groups and appears in more than 170 newspapers. Born in Newton, Massachusetts, Goodman graduated from Radcliffe College and is a former Nieman Fellow at Harvard University. In 1980 she received the Pulitzer Prize for Distinguished Commentary. "The Sounds of Richard Rodgers" shows her common-sense, realistic style of writing.

### Setting a Purpose for Reading

A **purpose** is a reason for doing something. If you set a purpose before you read, you will read more efficiently. One way of setting a purpose is to get a general idea of what the selection is about, first by looking at the title. Then ask yourself basic questions about the topic of the essay. You might use the journalistic formula *who? what? when? where? why?* and *how?* For example: Who was Richard Rodgers? For what is he best known? When and where did he live? How did he achieve success? Why do we remember him?

### Focus

Your work is to study and learn in school. Richard Rodgers's work was to write music for Broadway plays, movies, and television shows. What exactly is work? Many people have written definitions of *work.* Write a paragraph in which you define what work means to you and then give specific examples of it. When you read Ellen Goodman's portrait of Richard Rodgers and his definition of work, compare the attitudes expressed in his definition and yours.

### Vocabulary

Knowing the following words will help you as you read "The Sounds of Richard Rodgers."

**scores** (skôrz) *n.:* The music for a stage production or film, apart from the lyrics and dialogue (p. 473)

**esophagus** (i saf′ ə gəs) *n.:* The tube through which food passes to the stomach (p. 473)

**regimen** (rej′ ə mən) *n.:* A regulated system of diet and exercise (p. 474)

**legacy** (leg′ ə sē) *n.:* Anything handed down, as from an ancestor (p. 474)

## Objectives

1  To set a purpose for reading
2  To identify subjective and objective details
3  To write about an artistic person
4  To express individual interests and abilities through optional activities

## Support Material

**Teaching Portfolio**
Teacher Backup, p. 585
Usage and Mechanics Worksheet, p. 588
Vocabulary Check, p. 589
Critical Thinking and Reading Worksheet, *Recognizing Subjective Details,* p. 590
Language Worksheet, *Appreciating Music Terms,* p. 591
Selection Test, p. 592

**Prentice Hall Literature Writing Studio**

# The Sounds of Richard Rodgers[1]

## Ellen Goodman

He came into our house with the first Victrola[2] . . . and stayed. By the time I was ten I knew every song on our boxed and scratched[3] "78" records: songs from *Oklahoma!* and *Carousel* and *South Pacific.* They were, very simply, the earliest tunes in a house that was more alive with the sound of politics than the sound of music.

As I grew older, I knew he was no Beethoven[3] or Verdi,[4] or John Lennon[5] for that matter. By then his songs had been orchestrally overkilled into the sort of Muzak that kept you company in elevators or "on hold" at the insurance company line.

But the fact is that from the time I was a child, to the time I sat with my own child watching the Trapp family escape again over the mountains,[6] there has always been a Richard Rodgers song in the background.

His work has been, very simply, our musical common exchange—as familiar and contagious as the composer ever hoped.

By the time he died, he was that rare man, someone who accomplished what he set out to do: "All I really want to do is to provide a hard-working man in the blouse business with a method of expressing himself. If he likes a tune, he can whistle it and it will make his life happier."

And, at seventy-seven, he was something even rarer, a man who remained centered in his work over six decades.

The numbers were overwhelming: 1,500 songs, 43 stage musical scores, 9 film scores, 4 television scores. He wrote music when he had a heart attack and music when he had cancer and music when he was learning to talk through his esophagus. He wrote music when his plays were huge successes and music when they were not; music when he needed the money and music when he didn't.

At fourteen, he composed his first song and at sixty-seven he still wrote to a friend: "I have a strong need to write some more music, and I just hope nothing stands in the way."

Yet when he was praised, he said, "I admit with no modesty whatever that not

---

1. **Richard Rodgers** (1902–1979): U.S. composer of musicals.
2. **Victrola** (vik trō′ lə) *n.*: A trademark for a phonograph.
3. **Ludwig van Beethoven** (lōōt′ viH vän bā′ tō vən) (1770–1827): German composer.
4. **Giuseppe Verdi** (jōō zep′ pe ver′ dē) (1813–1901): Italian operatic composer.
5. **John Lennon** (1940–1980): Leader of the British rock music group The Beatles, which achieved world renown in the 1960's and 1970's.
6. **Trapp family . . . mountains:** An Austrian family who fled over mountains to escape Hitler, dictator of Germany during World War II. The musical *The Sound of Music* is about their experiences.

*The Sounds of Richard Rodgers* 473

**Making Connections** Another selection that deals with a creative personality is "Hokusai: The Old Man Mad About Drawing" on page 481.

**Thematic Focus** Composer Richard Rodgers is considered a central figure in the world of creative Americans. Have students define *creativity* and name notable people whose lives and spirits embody the traits delineated in the students' definitions.

**6 Discussion** How important to people are their jobs? What does a person's job tell you about that person? How does a person's feelings about a job influence that person's life?

**7 Clarification** It took Michelangelo four and a half years to complete the Sistine Chapel ceiling. He painted on the ceiling the history of the creation of the world, the fall of humanity, and the flood, according to the Bible.

**8 Discussion** Do you agree or disagree with Rodgers? Why?

**9 Discussion** What is the secret of Rodgers's success?

**10 Discussion** What does Goodman mean by this? What is Rodgers's legacy?

**Reader's Response** What does the word *work* mean to you?

**Thematic Response** Do you agree with the author's statement that Rodgers "knew something about the relationship between creativity and productivity"? If so, what was that relationship? In what ways did Rodgers's life epitomize that relationship? Do you respect Rodgers's creative energy?

**Multicultural Focus** In discussing Ellen Goodman's tone and point of view in this essay, point out that music not considered classical by educated people was an inspiration and sometimes even the basis for lasting works by the best classical composers. Debussy, Ravel, and Gershwin, as examples, borrowed heavily from jazz or popular melodies in their compositions. Many music historians believe that Dvořák used Czech folk music, in addition to Negro spirituals and Native American folk tunes, in his acclaimed Symphony no. 9 in E minor ("From the New World"). You might want to play some of these works for

many people can do it. But when they say, 'You're a genius,' I say, 'no, it's my job.' "

6 Music was his job. it is a curious phrase. Yet it seems to me, looking back over his career, how little attention we've paid recently to the relationship between a life and "a job." For the past several years we've been more intrigued by life styles than by work styles, more curious about how someone sustains a marriage or a health regimen than how someone sustains an interest in his work.

The magazines we read are more focused on how we play than how we produce. We assume now that work is what we do for a living and leisure is how we enjoy living. When we meet people who do not understand this split, we label them "workaholics."

But Richard Rodgers was never seen in *People* magazine wearing his jog-togs. His "job" was writing music and his hobby was listening to it.

7 Usually we think of creative work as either inspired or tortured. We remember both Handel[7] writing "The Messiah" in three weeks and Michelangelo mounting the scaffolding of the Sistine Chapel[8] year after year. Rodgers for his part once wrote a song in five minutes. But when asked about it, he said, "The song situation has probably been going around in my head for weeks. Sometimes it takes months. I don't believe that a writer does something wonderful spontane-

8 ously. I believe it's the result of years of

---

**7. George Frederick Handel** (han' d'l) (1685–1759): English composer, born in Germany.
**8. Michelangelo** (mī' k'l an' jə lō') . . . **Sistine Chapel:** Italian sculptor, painter, architect and poet (1475–1564) who painted the ceiling of the Sistine Chapel, the principal chapel in the Vatican at Rome.

---

living, or study, reading—his very personality and temperament."

The man knew something about the relationship between creativity and productivity. He knew something about the satisfactions of both, and managed to blend them. He could write music when handed the lyrics and write it before the lyrics. He could and would write a song to fit a scene. If Woody Allen is right in saying that "Eighty percent of life is showing up," well, Richard Rodgers showed up.

"Some Enchanted Evening" will never go into the annals of great classics. *The King and I* is not *Aida*.[9] Rodgers was a workaday artist and he knew it. But he also knew that for some people there is a fuzzy line between work and play, between what is hard and what is fun.

9 "I heard a very interesting definition of work from a lawyer. Work, he said, is any activity you'd rather not do. . . . I don't find it work to write music, because I enjoy it," said Rodgers. Yet he also said, "It isn't any easier than when I began, and by the same token it isn't any harder."

He was a man who was lucky in his work and lucky in his temperament. In an era when we tend to doubt the satisfactions that can come from work and tend to regard hard workers as a touch flawed in their capacity for pleasure, this composer showed what work can be: how it can sustain rather than drain, heighten rather than diminish, a full 10 life. He leaves us a legacy in the sound of his life as well as his music.

---

**9. The King . . . Aida:** *The King and I*, a musical by Rodgers and his partner Oscar Hammerstein (1895–1960), is not on the same level as *Aida*, an Italian opera by Verdi.

---

the students and then discuss the influence of popular or folk music on the compositions. Discuss with students the value of classical music versus popular music. Do students consider American musicals a special category of music, comparable to classical music?

## Closure and Extension

### ANSWERS TO RESPONDING TO THE SELECTION
*Your Response*

1. Have students discuss their responses, perhaps comparing writing music as "work" with other kinds of work.

### Recalling

2. Rodgers wanted to write music that would make people happy.

## RESPONDING TO THE SELECTION

### Your Response

1. Do you think that writing music is hard work? Why or why not?

### Recalling

2. What was Rodgers's goal in life?
3. What is Rodgers's special talent? Give examples of how he used his abilities.
4. On what, according to Rodgers, is writing music or performing an artistic task based?

### Interpreting

5. What is the difference between Muzak and music?
6. Why did Rodgers say that he wasn't a genius but simply someone doing his job?
7. The writer says that "we assume now that work is what we do for a living and leisure is how we enjoy living." What does this say about the way many people feel about their work? How were Rodgers's feelings about his work different?
8. How did Rodgers leave "a legacy in the sound of his life" as well as in his music?

### Applying

9. What do you think is the relationship between creativity and productivity?

## READING IN THE CONTENT AREAS

### Setting a Purpose for Reading

**Setting a purpose for reading** can help you read more efficiently. One way of setting a purpose for reading is imagining you are a journalist acquiring information for an article. Reading this essay should give you the answers to the questions you asked before reading.

1. Who was Richard Rodgers?
2. For what is he best known?
3. When and where did he live?
4. How did he achieve success?
5. Why do we remember him?

## CRITICAL THINKING AND READING

### Recognizing Subjective Details

Writers often include both objective and subjective details in their descriptions. **Objective details** are factual statements that are free from personal feelings. For example, Goodman gives this objective detail about Richard Rodgers's work, "The numbers were overwhelming: 1,500 songs, 43 stage musical scores, 9 film scores, 4 television scores." **Subjective details** are based on a person's feelings, interests, or opinions rather than on facts. For example, Goodman includes this subjective detail: "As I grew older, I knew he was no Beethoven or Verdi, or John Lennon for that matter."

Find two other objective details in the selection and two other subjective details.

## THINKING AND WRITING

### Writing About an Artistic Person

Think of someone skilled at singing, dancing, painting, or playing a musical instrument. First answer *who, what, when, where, why,* and *how* questions about this person. Then use this information in writing an article about this person for the cultural section of a newspaper.

## LEARNING OPTIONS

1. **Cross-curricular Connection.** Write a song about a significant experience in your life. First write the lyrics. If you do not feel comfortable writing music for your lyrics, see if one of your classmates will collaborate with you on it. Then perform your song for your classmates.
2. **Multicultural Activity.** Research a famous American musician whose African American, Hispanic, Native American, or other ethnic and cultural heritage has left its mark on American music. You may wish to give an oral report about the musician's life, accompanied by a recording of this person's music.

*The Sounds of Richard Rodgers* 475

---

3. Rodgers's special talent was enjoying his work. He used his abilities to write 1,500 songs, 43 stage musical scores, 9 film scores, and 4 television scores.
4. It is based on loving what you do.

### Interpreting

5. Music is creative and dynamic, whereas Muzak is overplayed and stale.
6. Rodgers said this because writing music to him was a job he loved.
7. Many people regard work as pure drudgery. Rodgers felt his work sustained and enriched him.
8. Rodgers left us a good example by his life.

### Applying

9. The more creative the job, the more people can produce in their own field.

### ANSWERS TO READING IN THE CONTENT AREAS

1. He was a composer.
2. He is best known for his songs from such musicals as *Oklahoma, Carousel, South Pacific,* and *The King and I.*
3. He lived from 1902 to 1979 in the United States.
4. He achieved success through hard work.
5. He is remembered because of his music and his satisfying life.

### ANSWERS TO CRITICAL THINKING AND READING

Answers will differ. Suggested Response: Two objective details are that Rodgers composed his first song at fourteen and at sixty-seven still had a need to write music.

Two subjective details are that the author, by the time she was ten, knew every song on their Richard Rodgers records, and that while she was growing up there was always a Richard Rodgers song in the background.

**Challenge** What can people do to make their jobs and their lives more rewarding? How can people fulfill themselves through their work?

### THINKING AND WRITING

◉ **Software** If students have access to computers, you may wish to have them use the *Five W's* activity in **Writer's Helper** to generate ideas for their articles.

**Alternative Assessment** You may vary the Thinking and Writing assignment as follows: Have your students complete one of the Alternate Composition Assignments on page 586 of the Teaching Portfolio.

**Writing Across the Curriculum** You might want to have students research and report on Richard Rodgers's musicals. If you do, perhaps inform your school music department of this assignment. Music teachers might provide guidance for students in conducting their research.

### LEARNING OPTIONS

Option 1 will appeal to students with an interest in music and poetry. Try to record the performances of students' groups.

Option 2 will appeal to students who enjoy doing research or whose interests pertain to sociocultural issues. Display the completed reports in your classroom where students can read them later.

476

## Preparation

**More About the Author** Isaac Asimov is well known for his science-fiction books and stories. But his nonfiction is noted for making scientific and technological material understandable to the general reader. He has also written on such nonscientific topics as the Bible and Shakespeare. Ask students to discuss how a writer can be so versatile. What do all kinds of writing have in common? What makes one kind of writing different from another?

**Reading in the Content Areas** In the course of your reading during the next week, note the kind of reading you are doing and the reason you are either scanning, skimming, or reading intensively. Note the reading rate you use most often.

**Prereading Focus** Before students use the graphic organizer, have them try to imagine life before the invention of television or the airplane. To many students that way of life was so long ago it might have been during the Age of the Dinosaurs. Help them to trace back to the lives their grandparents and great-grandparents lived, both the positive and negative features of slower lifestyles without high-speed travel and worldwide telecommunications.

**Vocabulary** Most students will have no difficulty with these words. You might have them use each word in a sentence orally before reading the story.

**Electronic Handbook** If students have access to the Language Master 6000, suggest that they find antonyms for *hovering* and *arbitrary*.

# GUIDE FOR READING

## Isaac Asimov

(1920–1992) was born in the Soviet Union and came to the United States with his family in 1923. Asimov wrote and edited more than four hundred books. His interests ranged from science to history, literature (especially science fiction), and humor—fields in which he did research, teaching, writing, or editing. "Dial Versus Digital" shows a fascination with time and how time is measured.

### Dial Versus Digital

### Varying Rates of Reading

When you read, you can use **varying rates of reading:** scanning, skimming, or reading intensively. You can vary your rate of reading depending on your purpose. You **scan** to find specific facts or details. You **skim,** or look through without reading carefully, to get a general idea of what is written. You **read intensively,** that is, you read slowly and carefully, to get a clear understanding of what is written.

### Focus

"Dial Versus Digital" discusses the replacement of dial clocks by digital clocks. Many other objects and day-to-day activities have been replaced by modern technologies. Consider, for example, how the microwave oven has replaced conventional ovens for certain purposes. Make a chart like the one that follows. Fill each rectangle with an object or activity that has dramatically changed because of new technologies. On the left side of each rectangle, write an advantage of the new product, and on the right side write a disadvantage. If you have difficulty seeing what has been lost with the new technology, reading the essay may give you another perspective.

### Vocabulary

Knowing the following words will help you as you read "Dial Versus Digital."

**digital** (dij′ i təl) *adj.*: Giving a reading in digits, which are the numerals from 0 to 9 (p. 477)

**hovering** (huv′ ər iŋ) *v.*: Staying suspended in the air (p. 478)

**arbitrary** (är′ bə trer′ ē) *adj.*: Based on one's preference or whim (p. 478)

## Objectives

1 To vary your rate of reading
2 To find main ideas and identify supporting details
3 To write about technology
4 To express individual interests and abilities through an optional activity

## Support Material

**Teaching Portfolio**
Teacher Backup, p. 595
Usage and Mechanics Worksheet, p. 598
Vocabulary Check, p. 599
Critical Thinking and Reading Worksheet, *Finding Main Ideas*, p. 600
Language Worksheet, *Using the Prefix Counter*, p. 601
Selection Test, p. 602

Art Transparency 8, *Study for Airport* by Theodore Roszak

**Prentice Hall Literature Writing Studio**

## Presentation

# Dial Versus Digital

## Isaac Asimov

There seems no question but that the clock dial, which has existed in its present form since the seventeenth century and in earlier forms since ancient times, is on its way out. More and more common are the digital clocks that mark off the hours, minutes, and seconds in ever-changing numbers. This certainly appears to be an advance in technology. You will no longer have to interpret the meaning of "the big hand on the eleven and the little hand on the five." Your digital clock wili tell you at once that it is 4:55. And yet there will be a loss in the conversion of dial to digital, and no one seems to be worrying about it.

When something turns, it can turn in just one of two ways, clockwise or counter-clockwise, and we all know which is which. Clockwise is the normal turning direction of the hands of a clock and counterclockwise is the opposite of that. Since we all stare at clocks (dial clocks, that is), we have no trouble following directions or descriptions that include those words. But if dial clocks disappear, so will the meaning of those words for anyone who has never stared at anything but digitals. There are no *good* substitutes for clockwise and counterclockwise. The nearest you can come is by a consideration of your hands. If you clench your fists with your thumbs pointing at your chest and

THE PERSISTENCE OF MEMORY 1931
*Salvador Dali*
*The Museum of Modern Art*

**Motivation/Prior Knowledge**
Give students some background on the history of clocks. The first mechanical clock was probably invented in China in the late 1000's. It is believed that the first mechanical clocks in Western civilization were developed in the late 1200's. By the mid-1300's, the dial and hour hand had been added. The pendulum was developed during the mid-1600's, when the minute and second hands became common. By the mid-1700's, most of the mechanisms in modern mechanical clocks had been invented. Digital clocks have been used only since the 1970's. How do students envision the clock of the future?

**Purpose-Setting Question** What comment is the author making on modern technology in this story?

1 **Critical Thinking and Reading** What is Asimov's opinion of the conversion of dial clocks to digital? How do you know?

## Humanities Note

Fine art, *The Persistence of Memory,* 1931, by Salvador Dali. Salvador Dali (1905–1989) was born in Spain but moved to the United States in 1940. He is best known as a leading member of the Surrealist movement, which developed after World War I. Surrealism is a kind of magic realism that explores the subconscious and shocks the viewer with impossible natural images.

In *The Persistence of Memory,* Dali has created a fantasy world. The painting leaves the viewer with the haunting feeling that there must be some sense in all the apparent madness.

1. If you had a dream similar to this painting, how would it make you feel?
2. In what ways does this painting illustrate the text?

**Master Teacher Note** Place Art Transparency 9, *Study for Airport* by Theodore Roszak in the Teaching Portfolio, on an overhead projector. Ask students what feeling this scene conveys, and why. How do they think the artist feels about technology?

In "Dial Versus Digital," the author expresses his views about one aspect of technology.

**Thematic Focus** Asimov demonstrates his creative thinking by addressing several "what-if's" related to the change from dial to digital clocks: What if people don't understand the concepts of *clockwise* and *counterclockwise*? What if people can no longer understand location by *o'clock*? What if people see time measured only as numbers, not as space? Have students discuss some oth-

er technological changes taking place in the world today and the "what-if's" that could occur, the ramifications of this change in technology. An example might be the development of the calculator-size computer.

2 **Discussion** What is the relationship between the traditional clock face and language?

3 **Discussion** Do you think digital clocks will eventually cause confusion in schools because they introduce an "irregularity into the number system"? Why or why not?

4 **Discussion** What is the "odd conservatism" referring to? How would most people feel about 100 minutes to the hour? What is the tone of this essay? How serious is Asimov?

5 **Critical Thinking and Reading** Do you agree with Asimov about the drawbacks of converting to digital or decimal clocks? Why or why not? How would the conversion affect our descendants?

**Reader's Response** Do you prefer dial or digital? Why?

**Thematic Response** Do you enjoy, as Asimov clearly does, the process of envisioning the future with certain changes? What is there in the process that captures your interest?

then look at your fingers, you will see that the fingers of your right hand curve counterclockwise from knuckles to tips while the fingers of your left hand curve clockwise. You could then talk about a "right-hand twist" and a "left-hand twist," but people don't stare at their hands the way they stare at a clock, and this will never be an adequate replacement.

Nor is this a minor matter. Astronomers define the north pole and south pole of any rotating body in such terms. If you are hovering above a pole of rotation and the body is rotating counterclockwise, it is the north pole; if the body is rotating clockwise, it is the south pole. Astronomers also speak of "direct motion" and "retrograde motion," by which they mean counterclockwise and clockwise, respectively.

2 Here is another example. Suppose you are looking through a microscope at some object on a slide or through a telescope at some view in the sky. In either case, you might wish to point out something to a colleague and ask him or her to look at it, too. "Notice that object at eleven o'clock," you might say—or five o'clock or two o'clock. Everyone knows exactly where two, five, or eleven—or any number from one to twelve—is located on the clock dial, and can immediately look exactly where he is told. (In combat, pilots may call attention to the approach of an enemy plane or the location of antiaircraft bursts or the target, for that matter, in the same way.)

Once the dial is gone, location by "o'clock" will also be gone, and we have nothing to take its place. Of course, you can use directions instead: "northeast," "southwest by south," and so on. However, you will have to know which direction is north to begin with. Or, if you are arbitrary and decide to let north be straight ahead or straight up, regardless of its real location, it still remains true that very few people are as familiar with a compass as with a clock face.

Here's still another thing. Children learn to count and once they learn the first few numbers, they quickly get the whole idea. You go from 0 to 9, and 0 to 9, over and over again. You go from 0 to 9, then from 10 to 19, then from 20 to 29, and so on till you reach 90 to 99, and then you pass on to 100. It is a very systematic thing and once you learn it, you never forget it. Time is different! The early Sumerians couldn't handle fractions very well, so they chose 60 as their base because it can be divided evenly in a number of ways. Ever since, we have continued to use the number 60 in certain applications, the chief one being the measurement of time. Thus, there are 60 minutes in an hour.

3 If you are using a dial, this doesn't matter. You simply note the position of the hands and they automatically become a measure of time: "half past five," "a quarter past three," "a quarter to ten," and so on. You see time as space and not as numbers. In a digital clock, however, time is measured *only* as numbers, so you go from 1:01 to 1:59 and then move directly to 2:00. It introduces an irregularity into the number system that is going to insert a stumbling block, and an unnecessary one, into education.

4 Just think: 5.50 is halfway between 5 and 6 if we are measuring length or weight or money or anything but time. In time, 5:50 is nearly 6, and it is 5:30 that is halfway between 5 and 6.

5 What shall we do about all this? I can think of nothing. There is an odd conservatism among people that will make them fight to the death against making time decimal and having a hundred minutes to the hour. And even if we do convert to decimal time, what will we do about "clockwise," "counterclockwise," and locating things at "eleven o'clock"? It will be a pretty problem for our descendants.

**Multicultural Focus** Time-keeping devices go back to 1400 B.C., when the Egyptians kept track of the hour by dripping water through a hole in the bottom of a bowl. The Chinese kept time by fire. They compressed slow-burning gunpowder into metal channels to make a kind of clock. Ask students to research the history of time-keeping instruments in other cultures, including hourglasses, sundials, and water clocks. They can write short descriptions of various time-keeping devices and make diagrams of them. Some students may want to describe and draw plans for their own time-keeping inventions.

## RESPONDING TO THE SELECTION

### Your Response

1. Were you surprised at the author's concerns about the changeover to digital clocks? Explain.

### Recalling

2. In addition to showing time, what are two uses of the dial clock?
3. In what two ways do you see time if you are using a dial clock? In what way do you see time if you are using a digital clock?

### Interpreting

4. Why do you think many directions say to turn clockwise or counterclockwise?
5. The digital clock is a replacement for the dial clock. What did the dial clock replace?

### Applying

6. Poll your classmates. How many have digital watches? How many have dial watches? How do you explain your findings?

## READING IN THE CONTENT AREAS

### Varying Your Rate of Reading

**Varying rates of reading** include reading intensively, or reading carefully to understand the meaning; scanning, or reading to locate specific information; and skimming, or looking over quickly without reading carefully.

Sometimes you **read intensively** for meaning, especially when reading a textbook. **Scanning** can be helpful when reading the newspaper or doing research to locate particular facts or details. **Skimming** is helpful for getting an idea of what a written work is about.

Indicate which rate of reading would be useful for the following tasks.

1. Looking through a magazine to find an article that interests you
2. Finding a fact in the encyclopedia
3. Reading a biography in preparation for an oral report on this person's life

## CRITICAL THINKING AND READING

### Finding Main Ideas

The **main idea** of each paragraph is the most important idea in it. Writers sometimes state the main idea directly in the topic sentence. However, when the main idea is not directly stated but is implied, you must discover it by making inferences from the **supporting details.**

1. Reread the second paragraph of the essay. What is the main idea?
2. What details support this main idea?

## THINKING AND WRITING

### Writing About Technology

Write an article for a magazine called *Contemporary Life* about an object or activity in our culture that has been replaced by technology. You can choose your subject from the list you made earlier, or you can choose another. Explain how the object was used or the activity was done in the past, how it changed, and what is done now. Revise your article, supporting your main ideas. Proofread your article.

## LEARNING OPTION

**Performance.** Imagine a lifestyle based on a 100-minute hour in a 24-hour day. Make a chart by dividing your paper into two columns. At the top of one column, draw a 60-minute clock face. At the top of the other column, draw a clock that is based on a 100-minute hour. List under the 60-minute clock your daily schedule in approximate time intervals. Then list under the 100-minute clock face what your daily schedule would be. Use your chart to create a science-fiction script about life in a world with new time measurements. You can make your play as humorous or as adventurous or as imaginative as you'd like. Perform the skit with a group of classmates.

*Dial Versus Digital* 479

**Reading in the Content Areas** Note taking is a valuable life skill. Journalists, doctors, and mechanics all must know how to take quick and accurate notes in order to do their jobs well. Students who learn to take good notes may find studying easier.

**Prereading Focus** To help students focus on people of talent, you may wish to gather a collection of biographies and autobiographies about famous people. Allow students to browse through the books and to gather impressions of how talent brought the subjects respect, fame, and perhaps fortune.

**Vocabulary** Most students will have no difficulty with these words. You might have them use each word in a sentence orally before reading the story.

**Electronic Handbook** If students have access to the Language Master 6000, suggest that they find a synonym with a different connotation for each of the following vocabulary words: *commissioned* and *engulfing*.

# GUIDE FOR READING

## Stephen Longstreet

(1907–    ) is a writer of movie screenplays, art criticism, novels, television scripts, and detective stories. An accomplished artist, Longstreet studied painting in Paris, Rome, London, and Berlin. While living in Europe in the 1920's, he became acquainted with such famous artists as Marc Chagall, Henri Matisse, and Pablo Picasso. "Hokusai: The Old Man Mad About Drawing" combines Longstreet's interests in both writing and art.

## Hokusai: The Old Man Mad About Drawing

### Note Taking

**Note taking** is an important tool for learning. It is the jotting down of the important points of what you read. Taking notes can help you understand what you read and how it is organized, and can be an aid to writing an essay or a research paper.

### Focus

Which of your talents could help you earn a living? Make a chart like the one that follows. At the top of the columns, write the talents that you think you have. Then in each column, list the ways in which you could use that talent to help you earn a living. Compare your chart with those of your classmates and consider how many different careers a person could have using one's talents and developing new ones during a lifetime. When you read Stephen Longstreet's short biography of Katsushika Hokusai, note the ways in which this artist used his talents as an artist to forge a brilliant career that lasted more than eighty years.

| Talents: | | | | |
|---|---|---|---|---|
| Ways to earn a living. | | | | |

### Vocabulary

Knowing the following words will help you as you read "Hokusai: The Old Man Mad About Drawing."

**apprenticed** (ə pren′ tist) *v.*: Contracted to learn a trade under a skilled worker (p. 481)

**commissioned** (kə mish′ ənd) *v.*: Ordered to make something (p. 481)

**engulfing** (in gulf′ iŋ) *v.*: Flowing over and swallowing (p. 481)

**mania** (mā′ nē ə) *n.*: Uncontrollable enthusiasm (p. 482)

### Objectives

1  To take notes
2  To find implied main ideas
3  To write about art
4  To express individual interests and abilities through an optional activity

### Support Material

**Teaching Portfolio**
Teacher Backup, p. 605
Usage and Mechanics Worksheet, p. 608
Vocabulary Check, p. 609
Reading in the Content Areas Worksheet, *Taking Notes,* p. 610
Language Worksheet, *Appreciating Art Terms,* p. 611
Selection Test, p. 612

**Prentice Hall Literature Writing Studio**

# Hokusai: The Old Man Mad About Drawing

### Stephen Longstreet

1 Of all the great artists of Japan, the one Westerners probably like and understand best is Katsushika Hokusai. He was a restless, unpredictable man who lived in as many as a hundred different houses and changed his name at least thirty times. For a very great artist, he acted at times like P.T. Barnum[1] or a Hollywood producer with his curiosity and drive for novelty.

2 Hokusai was born in 1760 outside the city of Edo[2] in the province of Shimofusa. He was apprenticed early in life to a mirror maker and then worked in a lending library, where he was fascinated by the woodcut illustrations of the piled-up books. At eighteen he became a pupil of Shunsho, a great artist known mainly for his prints of actors. Hokusai was soon signing his name as Shunro, and for the next fifteen years he, too, made actor prints, as well as illustrations for popular novels. By 1795 he was calling himself Sori and had begun working with the European copper etchings which had become popular in Japan. Every time Hokusai changed his name, he changed his style. He drew, he designed fine surimino (greeting prints), he experimented with pure landscape.

---

1. **P. T. Barnum:** Phineas Taylor Barnum (1810–1891). U.S. showman and circus operator.
2. **Edo** (ē′ dō): Now Tokyo.

Hokusai never stayed long with a period or style, but was always off and running to something new. A great show-off, he painted with his fingers, toothpicks, a bottle, an eggshell; he worked left-handed, from the bottom up, and from left to right. Once he painted two sparrows on a grain of rice. 3 Commissioned by a shogun (a military ruler in 18th century Japan) to decorate a door of the Temple of Dempo-ji, he tore it off its hinges, laid it in the courtyard, and painted wavy blue lines on it to represent running water, then dipped the feet of a live rooster in red seal ink and chased the bird over the painted door. When the shogun came to see the finished job, he at once saw the river Tatsuta and the falling red maple leaves of autumn. Another time Hokusai used a large broom dipped into a vat of ink to draw the full-length figure of a god, over a hundred feet long, on the floor of a courtyard.

When he was fifty-four, Hokusai began to issue books of his sketches, which he called *The Manga.* He found everything worth sketching: radish grinders, pancake women, street processions, jugglers, and wrestlers. And he was already over sixty 4 when he began his great series, *Thirty-six Views of Fuji,* a remarkable set of woodcut prints that tell the story of the countryside around Edo: people at play or work, great waves engulfing fishermen, silks drying in

*Hokusai: The Old Man Mad About Drawing* 481

**Presentation**

**Motivation/Prior Knowledge**
Katsushika Hokusai is not the only artist to ever use unconventional tools and painting techniques. In the United States in the 1940's, artists such as Jackson Pollack were called action painters because of the paintings they produced and the way in which they produced them. Pollack, for example, laid his canvas on the floor and splattered paint on the surface as he walked around it. Have students think of other unconventional ways to produce art.

**Master Teacher Note** Since this essay is about Hokusai and his different styles of painting, bring in some other examples of his work. An excellent example of his landscape painting is *Ono Waterfall,* painted in his characteristic colors of blue, brown, and green. Point out to students that it was not until after his death that some of his prints were shown in the West. Hokusai's work influenced such famous Western painters as Whistler, Gauguin, and van Gogh.

**Purpose-Setting Question** How are creativity and courage related in this essay?

1 **Discussion** What kind of man was Hokusai?

2 **Clarification** A woodcut is a picture made by carving an image into a block of wood. The uncut portions of the wood are coated with ink, and paper is pressed over the block to form the image on paper. The cutaway sections of the wood appear as white.

3 **Critical Thinking and Reading** Why might Hokusai be considered a man ahead of his time? How do you think he would fit into today's art world?

4 **Enrichment** It is thought that Hokusai's greatest work was done when he was past age sixty.

**Multicultural Focus** In the late nineteenth century, a flourishing exchange occurred between Asian and European artists. After the American commodore Matthew Perry forced the Japanese to open their ports to trade in 1853, Japanese color woodcuts began passing into the hands of European collectors. The flat planes, cameralike perspectives, and vivid colors of these prints intrigued European artists. The works of Utamaro, Hokusai, and Hiroshige had a strong influence on the paintings and posters of Monet, Manet, and Toulouse-Lautrec. They also influenced the craftspeople of the Art Nouveau movement. At the same time, the works of European masters began to influence Japanese art.

Have interested students find out more about this cultural exchange and report on it. You may wish to prepare a slide show to accompany student presentations.

**Making Connections** Another selection that deals with a creative personality is "The Sounds of Richard Rodgers" on page 473.

**Thematic Focus** So many aspects of Hokusai, the artist, exemplify his creative spirit. Which aspects of his life most impress you?

482

**THE GREAT WAVE OFF KANAGAWA**
*Katsushika Hokusai*
*The Metropolitan Museum of Art*

the sun, lightning playing on great mountains, and always, somewhere, the ash-tipped top of Fuji.

Hokusai did thirty thousand pictures during a full and long life. When he was seventy-five he wrote:

5

From the age of six I had a mania for drawing the shapes of things. When I was fifty I had published a universe of designs. But all I have done before the age of seventy is not worth bothering with. At seventy-five I have learned something of the pattern of nature, of animals, of plants, of trees, birds, fish, and insects. When I am eighty you will see

real progress. At ninety I shall have cut my way deeply into the mystery of life itself. At a hundred I shall be a marvelous artist. At a hundred and ten everything I create, a dot, a line, will jump to life as never before. To all of you who are going to live as long as I do, I promise to keep my word. I am writing this in my old age. I used to call myself Hokusai, but today I sign myself "The Old Man Mad About Drawing."

6

He didn't reach a hundred and ten, but he nearly reached ninety. On the day of his death, in 1849, he was cheerfully at work on a new drawing.

7

## RESPONDING TO THE SELECTION

### Your Response

1. What do you admire most about Hokusai? Explain.

### Recalling

2. Where and when was Hokusai born?
3. What jobs did he have early in his life?
4. What types of art did Hokusai create?

### Interpreting

5. What did Hokusai mean when he said, "At a hundred I shall be a marvelous artist"?
6. Hokusai called himself "The Old Man Mad About Drawing." Why is this name appropriate? Explain your answer.

### Applying

7. According to the author, Westerners like and understand Hokusai best of all Japan's great artists. Why do you think this is?

## READING IN THE CONTENT AREAS

### Taking Notes

**Note taking,** or jotting down the important points of what you read, can help you understand what is written and how it is organized.

To take notes you must be able to identify the main point, or important idea, of each paragraph. The writer may support the main point by giving details, examples, or quotes.

When you take notes, write in your own words, using words and phrases rather than complete sentences. Pay attention to words in italic, in boldface type, and in quotation marks. Notice words and phrases that may indicate main points; for example, *first, then, finally, most important, the reasons for, the result was.*

Reread the essay about Hokusai.

1. Take notes on the author's main points.
2. Compare your notes with your classmates'.

## CRITICAL THINKING AND READING

### Finding Implied Main Ideas

The **main idea** of each paragraph is the most important idea in it. Often the main idea is **implied** rather than stated. When this is the case, you must recognize it from the supporting details.

Look at the paragraph on page 481, beginning "When he was fifty-four." The implied main idea in this paragraph is that Hokusai continued to be a prolific painter throughout his life. The supporting details that tell you this are that Hokusai at age fifty-four issued books of numerous sketches.

Reread the paragraph on page 481, beginning "Hokusai never stayed long with a period."

1. What is the implied main idea?
2. What are the supporting details?

## THINKING AND WRITING

### Writing About Art

Look at Hokusai's print "Great Wave Off Kanagawa" on page 482. As you look at this work of art, freewrite about the thoughts and associations that come to mind. Then write several paragraphs describing the painting for someone who has never seen it. Include a description of its details, shapes, and colors.

## LEARNING OPTION

**Art.** Just as Hokusai was always trying a new medium for his work—his fingers, toothpicks, glass, eggshell, rooster feet—you, too, can paint in new and creative ways. Create a painting by experimenting with different ways to paint. First, decide what the subject of your painting will be: a still life, a portrait, a landscape, something realistic, or something abstract. Then decide what will be your "paintbrush." Be as imaginative in this project as you'd like to be.

**Challenge** Name some other artists who have undertaken major projects late in life and achieved success. You can name painters, sculptors, dancers, singers, writers, or actors. Identify the artist and his or her accomplishment.

### THINKING AND WRITING

**Alternative Assessment** *Protocol:* Ask students to assess their own work by responding to the following questions:

What thoughts and associations about the print *The Great Wave Off Kanagawa* do you discuss in your essay?

What specific details of the print do you include to make the picture come alive for the reader?

How do you use these details to support your thoughts and associations about the print?

What, if anything, made this assignment difficult for you?

What did you learn about responding to a print from completing this assignment?

You may have your students use the information they have gained from their protocols as a guide for revising their descriptions.

**Writing Across the Curriculum** You might want to have students research and report on Japanese art. If you do, perhaps inform your school art department of this assignment. Art teachers might provide guidance for students in conducting their research.

### LEARNING OPTION

Students who are particularly adventurous and curious or who enjoy the challenge of new art media will immediately choose to be involved in this activity. Be sure to display in your classroom the artwork produced by this project.

---

*Applying*

7. Answers will differ. Suggested Response: Hokusai's paintings have universal appeal because they are beautifully executed studies of everyday objects and nature, and they have great emotional impact for the viewer.

**ANSWERS TO READING IN THE CONTENT AREAS**

1. Answers will differ. Suggested Response: Born in 1760. Became interested in art while working in a library. Had many different styles over the years, and every time he changed his style, he changed his name. Used unconventional materials and techniques. When over sixty, began his greatest work: a series of woodcut prints that tell the story of country life. He felt that as he got older, he got better. He died drawing.

2. Students should note differences.

**ANSWERS TO CRITICAL THINKING AND READING**

1. The implied main idea is that Hokusai's experiments with his art worked, and he was a successful artist.
2. The supporting details are that the shogun recognized the river Tatsuta and falling red maple leaves on the temple door.

**More About the Author** Ursula K. Le Guin is a well-known writer of science fiction. In the introduction to one of her books, *The Left Hand of Darkness,* she says, ''In reading a novel, any novel, we have to know perfectly well that the whole thing is nonsense, and then, while reading, believe every word of it.'' Ask students to discuss the difficulty of making the fantastic believable. Do they ever forget when they are reading fiction that it is make-believe? Have they ever read a totally unbelievable work of fiction?

**Reading in the Content Areas** Point out to students that making an outline can help you to understand someone else's writing, and it can also help you to organize your own thoughts for a written composition. When writing a lengthy or complex paper, it is helpful to make an outline to order your thoughts and to be sure you are including all the important points that will make your work most effective.

**Prereading Focus** Have students discuss what traits are important in a person who wants to be a writer. What must a person do to become a writer?

**Vocabulary** It would be helpful for students to know the following words also: *stenographer, illegible* (p. 485); *immense* (p. 486); *intervals, dimensions, objective, superficial, collaboration* (p. 487); *installments, grudgingly, mutilate* (p. 488).

**Electronic Handbook** If students have access to the Language Master 6000, have them use it to hear the pronunciations of *prerequisite, vicarage,* and *premonition.*

# GUIDE FOR READING

**Ursula K. Le Guin**

(1929– ) was born in Berkeley, California, and grew up listening to Indian legends retold by her father, a scientist who worked with Native Americans. Le Guin's writing, which has been influenced also by Norwegian and Irish folk tales, includes imagined beings and invented places. Le Guin has won the Nebula Award of the Science Fiction Writers of America and the Hugo Award of the World Science Fiction Convention. In her speech "Talking About Writing," she expresses her love for writing.

## Talking About Writing

### Outlining

**Outlining** is the systematic listing of the most important points of a piece of writing. An outline lists the main points and supporting details in the order in which they occur.
I. First main topic
  A. First subtopic
    1. First supporting idea or detail
    2. Second supporting idea or detail
  B. Second subtopic
II. Second main topic (The outline continues in the same way.)

### Focus

In her speech "Talking About Writing," Ursula Le Guin talks about freedom, and she talks about rules. Think about freedom and rules in work situations. With a small group, make three lists: jobs in which people have many rules and policies to follow, jobs in which people have almost total freedom, and jobs in which people have rules and policies but are given room to express themselves and be creative. As you think about possible careers for yourself, consider where they fall on this continuum of freedom and constraint.

### Vocabulary

Knowing the following words will help you as you read "Talking About Writing."
**snide** (snīd) *adj.*: Intentionally mean (p. 485)
**fluctuating** (fluk′ chōō wāt′ iŋ) *adj.*: Constantly changing; wavering (p. 485)
**prerequisite** (pri rek′ wə zit) *n.*: An initial requirement (p. 486)
**vicarage** (vik′ ər ij) *n.*: A place where the clergy live (p. 486)

**premonition** (prē mə nish′ ən) *n.*: An omen; forewarning (p. 487)
**communal** (käm′ yōōn ′l) *adj.*: Shared by members of a group or a community (p. 487)
**axioms** (ak′ sē əmz) *n.*: Truths or principles that are widely accepted (p. 487)

### Objectives
1 To make an outline
2 To sequence events
3 To write advice about performing a skill
4 To express individual interests and abilities through an optional activity

### Support Material

**Teaching Portfolio**
Teacher Backup, p. 615
Usage and Mechanics Worksheet, p. 618
Vocabulary Check, p. 619
Reading in the Content Areas Worksheet, *Understanding Outlining,* p. 620
Language Worksheet, *Using Dictionary Terms,* p. 621
Selection Test, p. 622

**Prentice Hall Literature Writing Studio**

# Talking About Writing

Ursula K. Le Guin

Tonight we are supposed to be talking about writing. I think probably the last person who ought to be asked to talk about writing is a writer. Everybody else knows so much more about it than a writer does.

I'm not just being snide; it's only common sense. If you want to know all about the sea, you go and ask a sailor, or an oceanographer, or a marine biologist, and they can tell you a lot about the sea. But if you go and ask the sea itself, what does it say? Grumble grumble swish swish. It is too busy being itself to know anything about itself.

Anyway, meeting writers is always so disappointing. I got over wanting to meet live writers quite a long time ago. There is this terrific book that has changed your life, and then you meet the author, and he has shifty eyes and funny shoes and he won't talk about anything except the injustice of the United States income tax structure toward people with fluctuating income, or how to breed Black Angus cows, or something.

Well, anyhow, I am supposed to talk about writing, and the part I really like will come soon, when *you* get to talk to *me* about writing, but I will try to clear the floor for that by dealing with some of the most basic questions.

People come up to you if you're a writer, and they say, I want to be a writer. How do I become a writer?

I have a two-stage answer to that. Very often the first stage doesn't get off the ground, and we end up standing around the ruins on the launching pad, arguing.

The first-stage answer to the question, how do I become a writer, is this: You learn to type.

The only alternative to learning to type is to have an inherited income and hire a fulltime stenographer. If this seems unlikely, don't worry. Touch typing is easy to learn. My mother became a writer in her sixties, and realizing that editors will not read manuscripts written lefthanded in illegible squiggles, taught herself touch typing in a few weeks; and she is not only a very good writer but one of the most original, creative typists I have ever read.

Well, the person who asked, How do I become a writer, is a bit cross now, and he mumbles, but that isn't what I meant. (And I say, I know it wasn't.) I want to write short stories, what are the rules for writing short stories? I want to write a novel, what are the rules for writing novels?

Now I say Ah! and get really enthusiastic. You can find all the rules of writing in the book called Fowler's *Handbook of English Usage,* and a good dictionary. There are only a very few rules of writing not covered in those two volumes, and I can summarize them thus: Your story may begin in longhand on the backs of old shopping lists, but when it goes to an editor, it should be typed, double-spaced, on one side of the paper only, with generous margins—especially the left-

*Talking About Writing*   485

**Master Teacher Note** There are a number of essays and books that attempt to tell people how to become writers. Read to students excerpts from Alva Johnston's amusing essay "How to Become a Great Writer" in *A Subtreasury of American Humor.* Johnston relates how Edgar Rice Burroughs, who had failed in numerous endeavors, sought refuge from his problems in fantasizing. One of his fantasies became the *Tarzan of the Apes* series.

## Presentation

**Motivation/Prior Knowledge** Elicit from students the areas in which they excel. Then have them try to explain how someone else could excel in that area. Students should attempt to formulate rules that a person could follow to become a good history student, bowler, hiker, dancer, and so on. After certain students have attempted to formulate these rules, discuss the difficulty of making rules for someone who wants to succeed at something.

**Purpose-Setting Question** What roles do experience and self-knowledge play in someone's becoming a writer?

**Thematic Focus** Does creativity play a role in how Le Guin defines a successful writer? What aspects of this speech reveal the author's creative spirit?

**1 Discussion** Why, in Le Guin's opinion, is a writer the last person who should be asked to talk about writing?

**2 Critical Thinking and Reading** What is the distinction Le Guin is drawing between talking about writing and answering questions about her writing from the audience?

**3 Discussion** Is this the answer you expected? Why or why not?

**4 Discussion** Why might the person who asked the question be annoyed with Le Guin's first-stage answer?

**5 Discussion** Why does Le Guin's second-stage answer arouse resentment even among writers?

**6 Critical Thinking and Reading** What value does Le Guin place on experience for a would-be fiction writer? Why?

**7 Critical Thinking and Reading** What is the most valuable thing for a writer to know? What evidence does Le Guin provide to support her opinion?

hand one—and not too many really grotty corrections per page.

Your name and its name and the page number should be on the top of every single page; and when you mail it to the editor it should have enclosed with it a stamped, self-addressed envelope. And those are the Basic Rules of Writing.

I'm not being funny. Those are the basic requirements for a readable, therefore publishable, manuscript. And, beyond grammar and spelling, they are the only rules of writing I know.

All right, that is stage one of my answer. If the person listens to all that without hitting me, and still says All right all right, but how *do* you become a writer, then we've got off the ground, and I can deliver stage two. How do you become a writer? Answer: You write.

5 It's amazing how much resentment and disgust and evasion this answer can arouse. Even among writers, believe me. It is one of

those Horrible Truths one would rather not face.

The most frequent evasive tactic is for the would-be writer to say, But before I have anything to say, I must get *experience*.

Well, yes; if you want to be a journalist. But I don't know anything about journalism, I'm talking about fiction. And of course fiction is made out of the writer's experience, his whole life from infancy on, everything he's thought and done and seen and read and dreamed. But experience isn't something you go and *get*—it's a gift, and the only prerequisite for receiving it is that you be open to it. A closed soul can have the most immense adventures, go through a civil war or a trip to the moon, and have nothing to show for all that "experience"; whereas the open soul can do wonders with nothing. I invite you to meditate on a pair of sisters, Emily and Charlotte. Their life experience was an isolated vicarage in a small, dreary English village, a couple of bad years at a girls' school, another year or two in Brussels, which is surely the dullest city in all Europe, and a lot of housework. Out of that seething mass of raw, vital, brutal, gutsy Experience they made two of the greatest novels ever written: *Jane Eyre* and *Wuthering Heights*.

6

Now of course they were writing from experience; writing about what they knew, which is what people always tell you to do; but what was their experience? What was it they knew? Very little about "life." They knew their own souls, they knew their own minds and hearts; and it was not a knowledge lightly or easily gained. From the time they were seven or eight years old, they wrote, and thought, and learned the landscape of their own being, and how to describe it. They wrote with the imagination, which is the tool of the farmer, the plow you plow your own soul with. They wrote from

7

inside, from as deep inside as they could get by using all their strength and courage and intelligence. And that is where books come from. The novelist writes from inside. What happens to him outside, during most of his life, doesn't really matter.

I'm rather sensitive on this point, because I write science fiction, or fantasy, or about imaginary countries, mostly—stuff that, by definition, involves times, places, events that I could not possibly experience in my own life. So when I was young and would submit one of these things about space voyages to Orion or dragons or something, I was told, at extremely regular intervals, "You should try to write about things you know about." And I would say, But I do; I know about Orion, and dragons, and imaginary countries. Who do you think knows about my own imaginary countries, if I don't?

But they didn't listen, because they don't understand, they have it all backward. They think an artist is like a roll of photographic film, you expose it and develop it and there is a reproduction of Reality in two dimensions. But that's all wrong, and if any artist tells you "I am a camera," or "I am a mirror," distrust him instantly, he's fooling you, pulling a fast one. Artists are people who are not at all interested in the facts—only in the truth. You get the facts from outside. The truth you get from inside.

OK, how do you go about getting at that truth? You want to tell the truth. You want to be a writer. So what do you do?

You write.

Honestly, why do people ask that question? Does anybody ever come up to a musician and say, Tell me, tell me—How should I become a tuba player? No! it's too obvious. If you want to be a tuba player you get a tuba, and some tuba music. And you ask the neighbors to move away or put cotton in

their ears. And probably you get a tuba teacher, because there are quite a lot of objective rules and techniques both to written music and to tuba performance. And then you sit down and you play the tuba, every day, every week, every month, year after year, until you are good at playing the tuba; until you can—if you desire—play the truth on the tuba.

It is exactly the same with writing. You sit down and you do it, and you do it, and you do it, until you have learned how to do it.

Of course, there are differences. Writing makes no noise, except groans, and it can be done anywhere, and it is done alone.

It is the experience or premonition of that loneliness, perhaps, that drives a lot of young writers into this search for rules. I envy musicians very much, myself. They get to play together, their art is largely communal; and there are rules to it, an accepted body of axioms and techniques, which can be put into words or at least demonstrated, and so taught. Writing cannot be shared, nor can it be taught as a technique, except on the most superficial level. All a writer's real learning is done alone, thinking, reading other people's books, or writing—practicing. A really good writing class or workshop can give us some shadow of what musicians have all the time—the excitement of a group working together, so that each member outdoes himself—but what comes out of that is not a collaboration, a joint accomplishment, like a string quartet or a symphony performance, but a lot of totally separate, isolated works, expressions of individual souls. And therefore there are no rules, except those each individual makes up for himself.

I know. There are lots of rules. You find them in the books about The Craft of Fiction and The Art of the Short Story and so on. I know some of them. One of them says: Never

8 **Discussion** Why is Le Guin sensitive on this point? What early experiences could have ruined her career as a writer?

9 **Critical Thinking and Reading** What is the difference between facts and truth? How does a writer tell the truth?

10 **Discussion** How is learning to write like learning to do anything else?

11 **Discussion** Why do young writers search for rules? What is the rule for writing according to Le Guin? Explain why you agree or disagree with her.

**12 Critical Thinking and Reading**
What point is Le Guin making with her example of *War and Peace*?

**13 Discussion** What has a writer bought for his or her solitude? Why is it up to the individual writer to make up individual and unique rules?

**14 Critical Thinking and Reading**
What advice is Le Guin really giving to those who want to become writers?

**Reader's Response** Le Guin says of the sea, "It is too busy being itself to know anything about itself." How does this apply to your life or the life of someone you know well?

**Thematic Response** What do you feel is the relationship between a writer's freedom and a writer's creativity? What does Le Guin mean when she says, "It is up to you to make the maps, to build the cities"?

## Closure and Extension

### ANSWERS TO RESPONDING TO THE SELECTION
*Your Response*
1. Help students to think of careers that involve writing, as they respond to the question.

*Recalling*
2. The first stage is learning how to type and using Fowler's *Handbook of English Usage* and a dictionary. The second stage is writing.
3. She cannot encourage people to become writers, and yet she is glad

begin a story with dialogue! People won't read it; here is somebody talking and they don't know who and so they don't care, so—Never begin a story with dialogue.

Well, there is a story I know, it begins like this:

*"Eh bien, mon prince!* so Genoa and Lucca are now no more than private estates of the Bonaparte family!"

It's not only a dialogue opening, the first four words are in *French*, and it's not even a French novel. What a horrible way to begin a book! The title of the book is *War and Peace.*

There's another Rule I know: Introduce all the main characters early in the book. That sounds perfectly sensible, mostly I suppose it is sensible, but it's not a rule, or if it is somebody forgot to tell it to Charles Dickens. He didn't get Sam Weller into the Pickwick Papers for ten chapters—that's five months, since the book was coming out as a serial in installments.

Now you can say, all right, so Tolstoy can break the rules, so Dickens can break the rules, but they're geniuses; rules are made for geniuses to break, but for ordinary, talented, not-yet-professional writers to follow, as guidelines.

And I would accept this, but very very grudgingly, and with so many reservations that it amounts in the end to nonacceptance. Put it this way: if you feel you need rules and want rules, and you find a rule that appeals to you, or that works for you, then follow it. Use it. But if it doesn't appeal to you or doesn't work for you, then ignore it; in fact, if you want to and are able to, kick it in the teeth, break it, fold staple mutilate and destroy it.

See, the thing is, as a writer you are free. You are about the freest person that ever was. Your freedom is what you have bought with your solitude, your loneliness. You are

488 *Nonfiction*

in the country where *you* make up the rules, the laws. You are both dictator and obedient populace. It is a country nobody has ever explored before. It is up to you to make the maps, to build the cities. Nobody else in the world can do it, or ever could do it, or ever will be able to do it again.

Absolute freedom is absolute responsibility. The writer's job, as I see it, is to tell the truth. The writer's truth—nobody else's. It is not an easy job. One of the biggest implied lies going around at present is the one that hides in phrases like "self-expression" or "telling it like it is"—as if that were easy, anybody could do it if they just let the words pour out and didn't get fancy. The "I am a camera" business again. Well, it just doesn't work that way. You know how hard it is to say to somebody, just somebody you know, how you *really* feel, what you *really* think—with complete honesty? You have to trust them; and you have to *know yourself:* before you can say anything anywhere near the truth. And it's hard. It takes a lot out of you.

You multiply that by thousands; you remove the listener, the live flesh-and-blood friend you trust, and replace him with a faceless unknown audience of people who may possibly not even exist; and you try to write the truth to them, you try to draw them a map of your inmost mind and feelings, hiding nothing and trying to keep all the distances straight and the altitudes right and the emotions honest. . . . And you never succeed. The map is never complete, or even accurate. You read it over and it may be beautiful but you realize that you have fudged here, and smeared there, and left this out, and put in some stuff that isn't really there at all, and so on—and there is nothing to do then but say OK; that's done; now I come back and start a new map, and try to do it better, more truthfully. And all of

13

14

to know that she's not alone in wanting to write. She hopes would-be writers know the pitfalls of the process.

*Interpreting*
4. She means that a writer is too close to the process of writing to describe it clearly.
5. The facts are objective and verifiable, whereas the truth is subjective and based on the writer's personal observations and conclusions.

*Applying*
6. Answers will differ. Students may respond that experienced people are the best ones to ask because they know their professions so well that they have valuable advice to offer; or students may agree with Le Guin that experienced people are too close to their professions to describe them clearly. These people have become one with their careers and so cannot give sound, objective advice to anyone else.

### ANSWERS TO READING IN THE CONTENT AREAS

Answers will differ. The following is a sample outline of three paragraphs from the essay (p. 486, column 2).

*First Paragraph*
I. Experience is not of primary importance to fiction writers.
    A. It is what a person makes of experience that is important.

488

12

this, every time, you do alone—absolutely alone. The only questions that really matter are the ones you ask yourself.

15 | You may have gathered from all this that I am not encouraging people to try to be writers. Well, I can't. You hate to see a nice young person run up to the edge of a cliff and jump off, you know. On the other hand, it is awfully nice to know that some other people are just as nutty and just as determined to jump off the cliff as you are. You just hope they realize what they're in for.

## RESPONDING TO THE SELECTION

### Your Response
1. Based on what Le Guin says about writing, would you like to become a writer? Why or why not?

### Recalling
2. The speaker answers "How do I become a writer?" in two stages. What are they?
3. How does the speaker feel about encouraging people to be writers?

### Interpreting
4. What does the speaker mean by "I think probably the last person who ought to be asked to talk about writing is a writer"?
5. How is telling the truth different from telling the facts?

### Applying
6. Do you feel experienced people should not be asked about how to do their jobs? Explain.

## READING IN THE CONTENT AREAS

### Understanding Outlining

**Outlining** breaks down the most important points and their supporting details, following the order in which they are written. Begin an outline by listing the main point, or central idea, of each paragraph. Then note the supporting details of each main point. Supporting details may include facts, examples, or quotations.

Make an outline of three consecutive paragraphs from "Talking About Writing."

## CRITICAL THINKING AND READING

### Sequencing Events

**Sequencing** events is putting a series of events in a particular order. The events might be in chronological order—the order in which they happened. The events might be in order of the least important to the most important, or vice versa. Similar events may be grouped together.

1. What steps does the writer describe in answering the question "How do I become a writer?" How does she arrange these steps?
2. What steps does the writer identify in describing the process of becoming a tuba player? How does she arrange these steps?

## THINKING AND WRITING

### Writing Advice About Performing a Skill

Freewrite about how to accomplish a skill that you have. Then prepare a how-to list of steps for a younger relative. Revise your steps, arranging your details chronologically. Proofread your steps.

## LEARNING OPTION

**Community Connection.** Arrange to meet with someone in your community who has a job similar to one you think would interest you. Discuss with that person how he or she learned to do the work. Share your findings with your class.

*Talking About Writing* 489

---

**Reading and Responding** The information on this page summarizes how the ideas, techniques, and structure in nonfiction interrelate to produce the overall effect. By following the systematic approach shown in these sample annotations, students will increase their reading comprehension and literary appreciation. Students should read actively and form their own questions and opinions about the purpose, techniques, support, and organization of the selection.

Remind students that as they read actively, they should be able to see how the separate elements of nonfiction interrelate to produce an effective essay.

For further practice with these elements, use the selection "Manzanar, U.S.A.," by Jeanne Wakatsuki Houston and James D. Houston, pages 629–632, in the Teaching Portfolio, which students can annotate themselves. Encourage students to continue to use this strategy as they read other nonfiction selections.

# READING AND RESPONDING

## Nonfiction

Nonfiction deals with people, places, things, and events. The nonfiction writer usually keeps several things in mind while writing: an idea to present (the topic), a purpose for presenting the idea, and an audience. Responding to the elements of nonfiction and the writer's techniques will help you appreciate nonfiction more fully.

**RESPONDING TO PURPOSE**   The purpose is the reason for writing. A writer may have both a general and a specific purpose. The general purpose may be to explain, inform, describe, persuade, or entertain. The specific purpose may be to make a particular point about the topic. If the general purpose is to inform the reader about nutrition, for example, the specific purpose may be to persuade the reader to eat more fruits and vegetables and fewer fatty foods. Your understanding of the writer's purpose will affect your response to the work.

**RESPONDING TO IDEAS AND SUPPORT**   The main ideas are the most important points the writer is making. Main ideas can be facts or opinions. Support is the information the writer uses to develop or illustrate the main ideas. Support includes facts to back up opinions, reasons to explain events, examples to illustrate ideas, and descriptive details to give the reader a vivid picture of the topic. Your response to a selection is determined in part by your response to its main ideas and supporting information.

**RESPONDING TO ORGANIZATION**   The writer organizes the ideas and support in such a way as to achieve the purpose and move the reader's thinking in the intended direction. The information may be arranged in time order, order of importance, or any other order that serves the author's needs. How does the order help you grasp the writer's ideas?

**RESPONDING TO TECHNIQUES**   Writers may use a variety of techniques to achieve their purpose. They may use description, argumentation, or comparison and contrast. They may use emotional language to arouse your feelings, or they may use unexpected grammatical structures to create an effect. How do the author's techniques affect you as you read?

On pages 491–494 is an example of active reading and responding by Jennifer Dugliss of Yorktown School in Yorktown Heights, New York. The notes in the side column include Jennifer's thoughts as she read "A to Z in Foods as Metaphors." Your own thoughts as you read may be different because you bring your own experiences to your reading.

490   Nonfiction

---

## Objectives

1  To understand an essay's purpose
2  To interpret metaphorical language
3  To write about language arts
4  To express individual interests and abilities through an optional activity

## Support Material

**Teaching Portfolio**
Teacher Backup, p. 625
Grammar in Action Worksheet, *Understanding Parenthetical Expressions*, p. 633
Usage and Mechanics Worksheet, p. 635
Analyzing Literature Worksheet, *Understanding an Essay's Purpose*, p. 636
Critical Thinking and Reading

Worksheet, *Interpreting Metaphorical Language*, p. 637
Selection Test, p. 638

**Prentice Hall Literature Writing Studio**

# MODEL

## A to Z in Foods as Metaphors:
### Or, a Stew Is a Stew Is a Stew

Mimi Sheraton

Cooking styles may vary from one country to another, but certain foods inspire the same symbolism and human characteristics with remarkable consistency. The perception of food as metaphor is apparently more consistent than the perception of food as ingredient.

The inspiration for some of this imagery is easier to find than others. It is not too hard to understand, for example, why the big, compact, plebeian-tasting cabbage is widely regarded as being stupid, a role it shares with the starchy, inexpensive staple the potato. A cabbage head in this country is considered to be as dull-witted as a krautkopf in Germany, and a potato head indicates a similar, stodgy-brained individual, never mind that both are delicious and can be prepared in elegant ways.

Italians, on the other hand, consider the cucumber a symbol of ineptness, and to call a person a cetriolo is to cast him among the cabbages of the world.

Salt has been a highly regarded commodity throughout history, and so a valuable person is described as being the salt of the earth. Considering the bad press salt is getting these days, however, that remark may soon be taken as an insult.

It is difficult to understand why ham is the word for a bad actor who overacts. But no one has to explain why a pretty and delightful young woman is considered to be a peach, or why her adorable, accommodating brother is a lamb. With luck, he will not grow up to be a muttonhead, to be classified with the cabbage and potatoes. If he remains a lamb, he can

**Techniques:** *The title and subtitle catch your interest. They make you think that the article is going to have something to do with food and poetry.*

**Purpose:** *The purpose is to inform you about how foods are used metaphorically worldwide.*

**Organization:** *The author has organized the article according to what the foods refer to. These paragraphs are about the foods that refer to a stupid person: the cabbage, the potato, and the cucumber.*

**Ideas and Support:** *The main idea is that foods can represent similar ideas in different countries. For example, the cabbage head in our country means the same thing as the "krautkopf" in Germany.*

**Ideas and Support:** *The author uses a lot of food metaphors in this paragraph. This shows us that people use them all the time.*

*A to Z in Foods as Metaphors* 491

## Presentation

**Teaching to Ability Levels** If your **less advanced** students have difficulty understanding any of these elements, you might have them review the instruction on the appropriate pages or look up the necessary terms in the Handbook of Literary Terms and Techniques.

**Motivation/Prior Knowledge** You might lead your class in a discussion of the use of metaphor and simile to describe people. Ask students for examples of descriptions of people as animals or plants, such as "stubborn as a mule," "cunning as a fox," or expressions like "I'm in hot water." What do people really mean when they use these expressions? Why do people use expressions like these instead of saying exactly what they mean?

**Master Teacher Note** Have students read each annotation carefully and consider the questions raised as well as any questions of their own. Also, have them consider how each of the separate elements relates to the others.

**Thematic Focus** Humans express their creative spirits in many ways. One way is to see one thing in terms of another, that is, metaphorically. Ask students why food metaphors are so common and so readily understood.

**Purpose-Setting Question** What makes this topic interesting to people of all ages?

**Making Connections** Another selection that uses metaphors to describe people is the poem by Julio Noboa Polanco, "Identity," on page 598. You might have students compare the use of food as metaphors with Polanco's use of plants as metaphors. A selection that deals with the theme of another culture's effect on American language is "The Indian All Around Us," by Bernard DeVoto, on page 457.

Trading Cards, Courtesy of Kitchen Arts & Letters

492  Nonfiction

## Grammar in Action

A word or phrase that is not essential to the meaning of a sentence is called a **parenthetical expression.** Writers may place a parenthetical expression in the middle of a sentence. When they do this, they place a comma before and after the expression.

Look at the parenthetical expressions in the following sentences:

492

All things sweet, *especially sugar and honey,* inspire dozens of terms of endearment in every language. . . .

. . . the lemon, *despite its sunny and piquant flavor,* is best known for its sourness. . . .

Italians, *on the other hand,* consider the cucumber a symbol of ineptness. . . .

Considering the bad press salt is getting these days, *however,* that remark may soon be taken as an insult.

What effect is created by the use of parenthetical expressions in the above examples?

be counted on to bring home the bacon that is the bread and dough.

All things sweet, especially sugar and honey, inspire dozens of terms of endearment in every language; but the lemon, despite its sunny and piquant flavor, is best known for its sourness and so describes such things as an automobile always in need of repairs. In many countries the nut is, inexplicably, the metaphor for craziness, though it is easier to explain why someone who is sprightly and hot-tempered is said to be peppery.

Cooked foods or dishes also inspire such comparisons. To be in the soup (it's hot) is to be in trouble and to be in a stew indicates one is troubled. Stews and soups with many ingredients are the consistent metaphors in many languages for big, complicated events and procedures.

In New York the most commonly heard of such expressions is tsimmes,[1] referring to the Eastern European Jewish stew of carrots, sweet potatoes, prunes, onions and, often, beef. To make a whole tsimmes out of something is to create an event of endlessly involved complications. In English, a tsimmes is a hodgepodge, which in turn is named for the stew derived from the French hochepot, which became hotchpotch or hotpot.

But a tsimmes is no more complicated than the New Orleans gumbo, also an event of dazzling complexities derived from the soup that may include okra, onions, peppers, shrimp, oysters, ham, sausage, chicken and at least a dozen other possibilities. Similarly used in their own countries are bouillabaisse,[2] the French soup of many fishes, and the Rumanian ghivetch, a baked or simmered stew that can be made with more than a dozen vegetables plus meat.

In Spain, to make an olla podrida[3] out of something is to make it as complex as that mixed boil of meats, poultry and onions. And though some Italians refer to a big mess as a big minestrone, the more popular metaphor is a pasticci,[4] a mess derived from the complicated preparations of the pastry chef,

---

**1. tsimmes** (tsim′ əs)
**2. bouillabaisse** (bōō′ yä bes′)
**3. olla** (äl′ ə) **podrida** (pō drē′ də)
**4. pasticci** (päs tē′ chē)

*Techniques:* The author says that a lemon has a "sunny and piquant flavor" and a person is "peppery." These words are so descriptive that you can almost taste them.

*Organization:* Up to this point, the author has talked about food metaphors for people and things. In these paragraphs she talks about food metaphors for situations.

*Ideas and Support:* The author describes how cooked foods can be metaphors for similar things all over the world. This is supported with examples of stews and soups from different countries, which are all metaphors for complexity or confusion.

**Master Teacher Note** You might have students draw representations of some of the metaphors described in the essay. Using the illustrations on page 492 as examples, have students imagine what a "cabbage head" looks like and draw it. They could also devise their own metaphors and illustrate them. You could collect these drawings and put together a book or display them on the class bulletin board.

**Multicultural Focus** Ask students to offer examples from their own cultural backgrounds of foods used as metaphors or as parts of sayings. Students from different ethnic backgrounds can question parents, grandparents, or other relatives who may be familiar with languages other than English and who can explain the meaning of food metaphors in their culture. To stimulate research and discussion on the topic, offer some humorous or unusual examples: *Schmaltz*, which is the Yiddish word for rendered fat, also means something that is overly sentimental in both Yiddish and English. In French *assiette au beurre*, or butter dish, is a "cushy" job, something that Americans refer to as "the gravy train." People from Kenya say, "He who waits, drinks the milk of the calf," meaning that patience reaps its rewards.

Once students have given their own examples, discuss with them how a particular usage may have come into existence.

---

**Student Activity.** Write a paragraph about one category of common expressions—for example, common expressions from baseball or from football or from cooking. Use commas to set off parenthetical expressions.

**Electronic Handbook** To help students understand parenthetical expressions, a review of the uses of parentheses might be helpful. If students have access to the Language Master 6000, have them enter the access word *parentheses* and press the GRAMMAR key for a lesson on the use of parentheses. They may also enter the access word *interruption* and press the GRAMMAR key for a review of punctuating sentence interrupters like parenthetical expressions.

**Ideas and Support:** *The last sentence is loaded with as many food metaphors as possible, again showing how we use them in our language every day.*

or pasticcere.[5] In Denmark it is the sailor's hash or stew known as labskaus that signifies complications, and no wonder when you consider that such a dish contains meat and herring in the same pot.

Some foods inspire conflicting metaphors. Fish is brain food, but a cold and unemotional person is a cold fish. You can beef up a program and make it better, but don't beef about the work that it involves or you will be marked a complainer. Instead of being given a promotion that is a plum you will be paid peanuts, even though you know your onions and are the apple of your boss's eye.

_____

**5. pasticcere** (päs' tē cher' e)

**Mimi Sheraton** (1926–    ) was born in Brooklyn, New York. As a food critic for *The New York Times*, she traveled all over the world to do research on food and how it is prepared. One of her popular books is *Mimi Sheraton's Favorite New York Restaurants*. Sheraton traces her interest in food to her childhood in Brooklyn, where good food and family situations were important.

494    Nonfiction

## Closure and Extension

### ANSWERS TO RESPONDING TO THE SELECTION
*Your Response*

1. Encourage creative responses. Ask students to point out the similarities in qualities between themselves and what they compare themselves to metaphorically.

*Recalling*

2. Both the cabbage and the potato are used as metaphors for dull-witted people.
3. Valuable people are considered "the salt of the earth" because salt has been regarded as a valuable commodity throughout history.
4. The word *stew* expresses the idea of being troubled or a big, complicated event or procedure. Three words from other languages that express this idea are *tsimmes, olla podrida,* and *labskaus.*
5. Fish is a conflicting metaphor because it is used to represent brains and an unemotional person. Beef is conflicting as a metaphor because it is used to represent bolstering or strengthening, as well as complaining. In both cases the words represent two concepts whose meanings conflict.

*Interpreting*

6. Answers will differ. Suggested Response: You would call a promotion a plum because plums are sweet,

# RESPONDING TO THE SELECTION

## Your Response

1. How would you describe yourself in terms of a food metaphor? Why?

## Recalling

2. Explain what the cabbage and the potato have in common.
3. Why are valuable people considered "the salt of the earth"?
4. What idea is expressed by the word *stew*? Find three other words from other languages that express this same idea.
5. Explain the conflicting metaphors expressed by fish and beef.

## Interpreting

6. Why would you call a promotion a "plum"?
7. Why would knowledgeable people be said to "know their onions"?
8. Why might you call a loved one "the apple of my eye"?

## Applying

9. What foods would you use to describe someone with great physical strength? Explain.

# ANALYZING LITERATURE

## Understanding an Essay's Purpose

Sometimes writers will directly state their purpose for writing. At other times you must infer, or draw a conclusion from given facts or clues, what the writer's purpose is. The clues may be given in statements, quotes, examples, or tone.

For instance, a writer may use colorful, descriptive language and an emotional attitude to persuade; factual language and a serious attitude to inform; and humorous descriptions and a light attitude to entertain. In "A to Z in Foods as Metaphors," the writer sets the purpose directly.

1. What direct statement does the writer make that sets the purpose for writing?
2. List three quotations or examples the writer gives to support her purpose.

3. What tone does the writer use? Give examples.
4. Based on the writer's direct statement, examples, and tone, what is her purpose?

# CRITICAL THINKING AND READING

## Interpreting Metaphorical Language

A **metaphor** is a way of comparing two seemingly unlike objects to highlight a characteristic of one of the objects. Metaphors can produce images in your mind. Read the following metaphor to see the image created.

The wind-tossed field was an ocean of grain.

Explain the following metaphors.
1. She is the Rock of Gibraltar.
2. He is the guiding light of the department.
3. She is a wizard of the stock market.

# THINKING AND WRITING

## Writing About Language Arts

List five metaphors that are used to compare people or situations to animals. Working with a group of students, research the origins of these metaphors. Then write a brief explanation of each one. Turn these explanations into an essay on "Animals as Metaphors," patterning the style in "A to Z in Foods as Metaphors." Revise your essay, making sure you have adequately supported your main idea. Then proofread your essay and share it with your classmates.

# LEARNING OPTION

**Language.** With your classmates make an illustrated dictionary of food metaphors. Begin by listing as many food metaphors as you can think of. Divide the tasks as follows: One group can write the definitions, a second group can do the illustrations, and a third group can take care of the page layout and the binding of the dictionary. If possible, photocopy the dictionary so that each member of the class can have a copy.

*A to Z in Foods as Metaphors*  495

---

"All things sweet, especially sugar and honey, inspire dozens of terms of endearment in every language . . ." "But a tsimmes is no more complicated than the New Orleans gumbo, also an event of dazzling complexities . . ."

3. The tone is informal and conversational. Students can find examples to support this throughout the essay.
4. Her purpose is to informally convey the idea that people all over the world use foods to describe different things and situations.

## ANSWERS TO CRITICAL THINKING AND READING

1. This means that she has a steadfast character and is not given to extremes in emotion.
2. This means that he is the leader and source of inspiration for the department.
3. This means that she is very good at what she does and accomplishes things that others cannot.

**Challenge** Write down five other uses of metaphors and their meanings.

## THINKING AND WRITING

◆ **Software** If students are working on computers, have them use **Bank Street Writer** to complete all stages of the assignment. Using the program's cut-and-paste features, students will be able to easily incorporate ideas from their prewriting lists into their compositions.

**Publishing Student Writing** Have all the groups work together and combine the individual essays into one full-length essay on "Animals as Metaphors." Students can contribute artwork to illustrate the essay, which can be submitted to your school or your community newspaper.

## LEARNING OPTION

This activity will appeal to a variety of learning styles—both global and analytical learners, creative students who are artistically talented, and students who work well in a visual medium.

---

juicy, and delicious; a fruit that is desirable and enjoyable. A promotion is also desirable and enjoyable.

7. Answers will differ. Suggested Response: Knowledgeable people are said to "know their onions" because there are many different varieties of onions, which have similar tastes. So to "know your onions," you would have to be knowledgeable. Therefore, people who are knowledgeable in general are referred to this way.

8. Answers will differ. Suggested Response: A loved one might be referred to as the "apple of my eye" because of the universal appeal of the fruit. It is the favorite fruit of many people, so to be the "apple of one's eye" is also to be the favorite.

## Applying

9. Answers will differ. Students might choose words pertaining to strong animals such as "beefy" or "ox-like."

## ANSWERS TO ANALYZING LITERATURE

1. "Cooking styles may vary from one country to another, but certain foods inspire the same symbolism and human characteristics with remarkable consistency."
2. These quotations support her purpose: "A cabbage head in this country is considered to be as dull-witted as a krautkopf in Germany";

## Preparation

### Motivation/Prior Knowledge

Take advantage of this lesson's inherent esteem-building qualities! Have each student write one accomplishment of which he or she is proud. Read each accomplishment aloud and allow classmates to guess whose paper you are reading. In a class discussion about achievements, guide the students to recognize that worthwhile interests and achievements are not always spectacular events. In many biographical sketches, it is the subject's effort and perseverance that earn admiration.

**Focus** Explain to students that when we read about a famous person, we usually know his or her major accomplishments. We read to discover how the individual achieved his or her goals. What experiences, education, or personality traits contributed to his or her success? Students should keep this question in mind as they write the sketches about their own classmates.

**Writer's Hint** Caution students to review each sentence in which they replace a modifier to be sure that they have maintained agreement.

## Presentation

**Prewriting** Allow time for students to interview their subjects. Suggest that they use these questions: Which achievement makes you most proud? Why? Which accomplishment required the most effort? What motivated you to keep trying? Remind students to listen for an exceptionally interesting or inspiring thought from the subject that can be used as a quotation in the character sketch.

**Drafting** Assist students in reviewing their notes and determining the most appropriate method of organizing the information. Use

---

## WRITING A BIOGRAPHICAL SKETCH

*"The words! I collected them in all shapes and sizes and hung them like bangles in my mind."*

**Hortense Calisher**

Think about the biographies and autobiographies from this unit, especially Mark Twain's portrait of himself as a young man. Have you ever considered that your classmates may have unique personalities, just as famous people do? The interests and accomplishments of your peers might make fascinating reading in a school yearbook.

> ### Focus
>
> **Assignment:** Write a brief biographical sketch of a classmate or friend for the school yearbook.
> **Purpose:** Highlight this person's achievements and interests.
> **Audience:** Your school community.

### Prewriting

**1. What personal qualities are really intriguing?** Choose one of the biographies or autobiographies in this unit that really interests you. What is it about this subject that appeals to you most?

Think of other short character sketches you may have read, such as those written about authors on the dust jackets of hardcover books. What kind of information do you learn about a person from these sketches?

**2. Develop a character diagram.** Develop a character diagram for the subject of your sketch. List major personality traits and examples for each trait. Examples may include direct quotations, events or accomplishments in the subject's life, and descriptions of habits.

**Student Model**

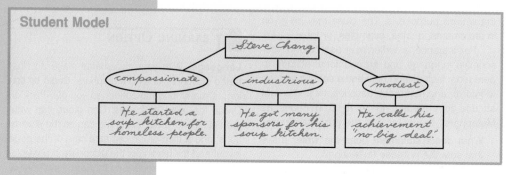

496   Nonfiction

---

the selections from the unit to demonstrate how different structures can be used to achieve the desired emphasis.

**Writing Transparency** Use the graphic organizer *Order of Importance* in **Transparencies for Writing** to demonstrate one method of organizing the structure of the biographical sketch.

**Revising and Editing** Instruct students to capture the reader's interest in the introductory paragraph by juxtaposing a success with an obstacle. Point out that curiosity about how the obstacle is overcome will induce the reader to read further.

Prompt students to consult their notes to verify dates, locations, statistical information, and direct quotations. Refer students

to the Handbook of Grammar and Revising Strategies for a review of the rules governing the punctuation of quotations.

**3. Find the key to your subject's character.** Open the door to your subject by discovering what you feel is most distinctive or important about that person. As you prepare to write, keep this question in mind: In what way is my subject unique?

## Drafting

**1. Captivate your readers in the opening.** Write an opening that will hook the readers' interest. Captivate your audience with concrete details about your subject's personality or experience.

> ### Student Model
> With arms circling like windmills and legs furiously kicking, Sara successfully gulps down the oxygen she needs to finish first in the women's junior all-state 1,500-meter freestyle competition. Who would have thought a shy, visually impaired child would have developed into an outgoing athlete, an Olympic hopeful right here in the Park Lane School District?

**2. Decide how to organize your information.** To help you decide, review selections from this unit. How was the material organized in each selection? By time-order? By the order of importance of events in the subject's life? By personality traits (beginning with the strongest or most important trait)?

## Revising and Editing

**1. Read your draft to a partner.** After you read your draft, have your partner respond to questions like the following: Does the beginning spark interest? Have I given you a vivid picture of the subject?

**2. Check for clear organization.** Have you organized your material in the best way possible? Is your organization consistent throughout your sketch?

**3. Use a tone appropriate for your audience.** Remember that members of your school community are the audience for your character sketch. Your writing may be friendly or even humorous in tone, but it should not include slang or improper grammar.

**4. Check for errors.** Finally, proofread your sketch carefully for errors in spelling and mechanics. Consult with a partner or your teacher if you are unsure of something.

**Options for Publishing**

- Submit your character sketch to the school yearbook, newspaper, or literary magazine.
- Prepare an oral presentation of your character sketch in which you include photographs or other visual aids.

**Reviewing Your Writing Process**

1. Did you refer to your character diagram as you wrote and revised your character sketch?

2. Was consultation with a partner during prewriting and revision helpful?

3. What was the most difficult part of this assignment? Explain.

## Closure and Extension

**Guidelines for Evaluation** The following questions can assist you in evaluating each student's biographical sketch:

1. Does the sketch describe some personality traits that may have helped the subject achieve success?
2. Is the organization consistent throughout the sketch?
3. Does the writer use precise modifiers to help create vivid pictures of the subject and the events?
4. Does the sketch include accurate details of time, date, and location?
5. Does the writer use quotations to bring the reader into direct contact with the subject?
6. Is the sketch free of errors in spelling, punctuation, and mechanics?

**Alternative Assessment** *Protocol:* Ask students to assess their own work by responding to the following questions:

About whom have you written a biographical sketch?

What do you say makes this person especially interesting or outstanding?

What concrete details of events, accomplishments, or character traits have you evaluated in your sketch?

How have you organized your material? By time order? By order of events? By personality traits?

What have you learned about the person you described as a result of doing this assignment?

**Publishing** You might make a photocopy of each sketch for the subject to take home and share with his or her family. Suggest that each student make a point of expressing appreciation to family members for any way in which they helped or supported the student in reaching his or her goals.

**Student Portfolios** You may wish to have students include their biographies in their writing portfolios.

**Enrichment** Have students read biographies or autobiographies of individuals who have overcome handicaps or discouraging setbacks to achieve their goals. Possible subjects include Dr. Charles Drew, Jim Abbot, Roberto Clemente, Mother Hale, Dr. Elizabeth Blackwell, and Dr. Jonas Salk. Have each student summarize the biography for the class, highlighting experiences and personality traits that contributed to the subject's ultimate success.

## Preparation

### Motivation/Prior Knowledge

Your students will probably be eager to share instances of times that they have been dissatisfied with a product. Prompt students to give specific reasons for their dissatisfaction. Was the product misrepresented in its advertising? Was the product defective? If so, in what way was it defective?

**Focus** Review the purpose of the assignment. Emphasize the importance of identifying the exact nature of the problem in order to determine the action that will solve the problem. For instance, if the complaint is that a product does not live up to its advertising claims, then a replacement will not solve the problem. A refund should be requested. If a piece of the product breaks under normal conditions, then a repair is a more realistic request than a refund.

**Revising and Editing** Tell students to review their prewriting notes to be sure they have included all the pertinent information. To check that all included information is relevant to the complaint, each sentence can be marked with a P or an S to indicate whether it relates to the problem or the solution. If a student is unsure about how to classify the sentence, it is probably unrelated. Have students consult you or their peer editors for assistance in determining if the sentence should be eliminated or revised.

## Presentation

**Prewriting** You might want to have students work in pairs, questioning each other from the company's point of view. This interaction will help each student organize his or her argument that the problem is the company's responsibility. Students should make notes of their responses to the "company" questions to prompt them in drafting.

Make sure each student has

# YOUR WRITING PROCESS

## WRITING A LETTER OF COMPLAINT

*"Getting even is one reason for writing."*
**William Gass**

Robert MacNeil's persuasive essay "The Trouble with Television" is a complaint about one branch of the mass media. Perhaps you have wanted to complain about something, too. For instance, did you ever buy a blouse that fell apart after the first washing, or a model airplane that failed to fly? By writing and sending a courteous and persuasive letter of complaint, you might be able to convince the company that sold you the defective product to either repair or replace it or to refund your money.

> **Focus**
>
> **Assignment:** Write a letter of complaint about a product you have bought.
> **Purpose:** To persuade a company to refund your money or to repair or replace the product.
> **Audience:** The complaint department of the company.

### Prewriting

**1. Choose the best strategy.** To begin with, understand your audience. Who is going to be reading your letter? What kind of letter would be appropriate and appealing to that audience? Remember also that good persuasive strategies include citing a precedent or an example from the past, anticipating and answering opposing views, calling for fairness, and predicting results.

**2. Examine the issue.** Ask yourself some questions: How do I feel about this issue? Which facts support my opinion? Try freewriting for several minutes to explore the issue.

> **Student Model**
>
> Ordered a red blouse from a catalog. After a few wearings, I washed it according to the instructions on the tag. Let it dry naturally. When I went to wear it again, noticed it was ruined. Lost its silky texture. Became stiff and shiny.

decided on the purpose of his or her letter. Explain that this purpose can be viewed as the thesis statement around which the letter is organized.

**Drafting** You may wish to instruct students to limit their letters to three paragraphs. Outline the structure of introduction, explanation, and conclusion to help them write a concise, well-organized letter.

**Software** If students have access to computers, they can use the *Business Structures* activity in **Writer's Helper** to guide them in using the correct format for a business letter.

**3. Establish your purpose.** Do you simply want to state your dissatisfaction with the product? Do you want your money back? Do you want the product replaced or repaired? Identifying your purpose will help you to write a clear, focused letter.

## Drafting

**1. Write the introduction.** Begin with a sentence or paragraph that identifies the purpose of your letter. Why are you writing to the company? What do you hope to accomplish in your letter?

---
**Student Model**

I am writing to you because a blouse I recently purchased from your company was defective, and I wish to request a replacement or a refund.

---

**2. Support your reason.** Avoid merely venting your emotions. It is better to explain the reasons why you think your money should be refunded or the product should be replaced rather than just stating how unfairly you have been treated.

**3. Provide a conclusion.** End with a brief statement that outlines your most important thought or recommendation.

---
**Student Model**

I am certain that upon consideration you will agree that the blouse should be replaced or the cost should be refunded.

---

**4. Use the correct format.** Your letter should conform to one of the three styles of business letters: block style, modified block style, or semiblock style.

## Revising and Editing

**1. Read and evaluate your letter.** Keep the following questions in mind: Is your opinion stated clearly and briefly? Do you support it with facts and examples? Do you make a reasonable recommendation?

**2. Have a peer editor review your letter.** Exchange letters with a classmate. Offer suggestions about how the letters could be made more convincing. Then revise your letter based on your peer editor's comments.

**3. Proofread your letter for grammar and spelling.** If your letter has errors in it, it won't be taken seriously.

### Writer's Hint

Look at how Robert MacNeil uses forceful language to highlight the urgency of his case in the following sentence from his essay "The Trouble with Television": "There is a crisis of literacy in this country."

### Options for Publishing

• If your letter reflects an actual complaint that you have with a product, mail it to the company that made it or sold it to you.

• Read your letter aloud to the class. Then, after hearing your classmates' letters, discuss the different persuasive strategies that you used and decide which were most effective.

### Reviewing Your Writing Process

1. Which persuasive strategies did you find most appropriate and effective for this assignment? Why?

2. How helpful was working with a peer editor during the revision process? Explain.

**Enrichment** Don't be fooled! You may wish to allow time for your class to explore the effects of advertising on their buying decisions. As a class, study examples of advertising and identify some of the subliminal messages used to influence consumers. Compare these messages to the actual facts about the products.

## Closure and Extension

**Guidelines for Evaluation** The following questions may provide a framework for evaluating each student's letter of complaint:

1. Are the cause for the complaint and the proposed solution clearly stated in the introductory paragraph?
2. Are the relevant supporting facts included in the explanation?
3. Is the argument summed up in the concluding paragraph?
4. Is the tone of the letter objective?
5. Is the assignment completed in correct business letter format?
6. Is the letter free of errors in spelling, punctuation, and grammar?

**Alternative Assessment** *Collaborative Evaluation:* In groups of four, ask students to evaluate one another's work by responding to the following questions:

What is the product and what is the complaint described in the letter?

Does the writer clearly state what his or her dissatisfaction is and what action he or she wants the company to take?

Does the writer explain his or her reasons for wanting a refund or a replacement product?

Does the writer conclude with a recommendation?

Is the letter written in correct business form?

Are the spelling and grammar correct?

What do you think is an appropriate grade for this letter?

After the letters have been evaluated, you may ask your students to write protocols summarizing what they learned about persuasive writing from writing their own letters and evaluating one another's work.

**Student Portfolios** You might want students to include this letter in their writing portfolios.

**ABOVE VITEBSK, 1922**
*Marc Chagall*

# POETRY

Short stories, essays, autobiographies—all are examples of prose, the language that you hear in your daily life. Poetry, unlike prose, consists of language with a strong musical quality in which the words are highly charged with meaning. Usually poetry is written in lines, and these lines are grouped into stanzas.

Poetry is one of the oldest forms of literature. Before literature was written down, people told stories. They used rhythm and rhyme to help them remember the stories better. Ballads were actually stories in poetic form that were sung. Many narrative poems still use rhythm and rhyme to tell stories.

In addition to using rhythm and rhyme, poets use language in other special ways to appeal to a reader's senses and emotions. Because many poems are short, poets choose each word and phrase with care to create vivid images, or pictures, in the reader's mind.

The poems in this unit include narrative poems and poems in which language is used in unusual and creative ways.

501

## Humanities Note

Fine art, *Above Vitebsk,* 1922, by Marc Chagall. The painter Marc Chagall (1887–1985) began his study of painting in his native Russia at schools in Vitebsk and St. Petersburg. His quest for knowledge and freedom in the arts took him to Berlin and then to Paris, where he was to spend most of his artistic life. In Paris he was exposed to all of the trends of modern art. These movements had little effect on Chagall's art. His fiercely independent style combines memories and dreams painted in a colorful, personal way.

Marc Chagall returned to Russia in 1914; the outbreak of World War I prevented him from leaving until 1922. During this period, Chagall looked to the Russian village life around him for subjects to express in his art. *Above Vitebsk* (1922) was one of the many paintings he produced in these years. This landscape is based on a view from a window of his rented room. Above the lanes of Vitebsk an image floats, cloudlike, defying gravity. The landscape in cool and pale colors is a sharp contrast to the bizarre image of the floating man. Chagall perhaps wanted to disrupt the placid order of the village with this fantastic shape above it. Chagall often introduced illogical images such as this into a composition for poetic emphasis.

## Preparation

**Reading Actively** The process outlined on this page will help students become more active readers of poetry.

You may want to explain to students that this process is similar to the one they have used in reading fiction. The special requirements of poetry, however, call for a few key differences in approach.

Since poetry tends to be more musical than prose, it is important to read a poem slowly and to read it several times—aloud as well as silently. You may also want to tell students that the music of a poem often reinforces its meaning. A poem about a cavalry charge, for instance, might have a galloping rhythm.

Another strategy that you might want to highlight for students is paraphrasing. In its intensity poetry can sometimes be intimidating. When students can put a poem in their own words, they will feel more at home with it. Caution them, however, that a paraphrase is not a substitute for a poem. Show them that although paraphrasing is a useful technique, it eliminates a poem's music.

After discussing each strategy with students, you may want to read "Drum Song" with them and show how these approaches work in action. Tell them that the annotations accompanying the poem are only one student's active-reading notes and that their own questions and responses might be different.

For further practice with the process, use the selection in the Teaching Portfolio, "Elizabeth Blackwell," page 664, which students can annotate themselves. Encourage them to continue using these strategies when reading other poems.

# READING ACTIVELY

## Poetry

The poet Wallace Stevens wrote: "In poetry, you must love the words, the ideas, and the images and rhythms with all your capacity to love anything at all." Using "all your capacity" means involving yourself actively as you read. The following active reading strategies will help you toward becoming a poetry lover:

**QUESTION** What is the poem saying? What questions come to mind as you are reading? Why does the poet include certain words and details? Look for answers to your questions as you read.

**USE YOUR SENSES** What images is the poet creating? How are these images created? Let your imagination see the pictures in your mind, and let your senses take in the poet's language.

**LISTEN** Much poetry is musical. Read the poem aloud so that you can hear the sound of it and feel its rhythm. Often the sound of the words and the rhythm they create suggest a mood or a feeling. How do the sound and the rhythm affect you?

**CONNECT** Bring your own experience and knowledge to the poem. What images and sounds are familiar? Which are new to you?

**PARAPHRASE** Put the poem in your own words. When you express a poem in your own words, you can better understand its meaning.

**RESPOND** Think about how the poem makes you feel as you read. What thoughts and emotions do the poet's words evoke in you? What does the poem say to you?

Try to use these strategies as you read the poems in this unit. They will help you increase your enjoyment and understanding of poetry.

On pages 503–504 you can see an example of active reading by Tham Dang of Horace Mann Middle School in San Francisco, California. The notes in the side column include Tham Dang's thoughts and comments as she read "Drum Song." Your thoughts as you read may differ because you bring your own experiences to your reading.

*502 Poetry*

# MODEL

# Drum Song
Wendy Rose

1     Listen. Turtle
       your flat round feet
       of four claws each
       go slow, go steady,
5      from rock to water
       to land to rock to
2    water.

    Listen. Woodpecker
       you lift your red head
10     on wind, perch
       on vertical earth
3        of tree bark and
    branch.

4    Listen. Snowhare[1]
15     your belly drags,
       your whiskers dance
       bush to burrow
       your eyes turn up
5      to where owls
20    hunt.

---

1. **Snowhare** (snō'her) *n.*: Snoeshoe hare, a large rabbitlike animal whose color changes from brown in summer to white in winter and whose broad feet resemble snowshoes.

**Connect:** *The poem's title makes me think that its rhythmic and musical qualities are going to be important.*

**Senses:** *The first word is listen, but what is being described doesn't seem to make much noise. I guess the speaker is addressing the turtle. I do see the turtle, walking slowly, carefully, back and forth between land and water.*

**Listen:** *I hear the quiet that occurs when a woodpecker stops its pecking for a moment to look at something.*

**Senses:** *I see a snowhare wrinkling its nose, sensing danger, and looking up to see whether an owl has spotted it.*

**Respond:** *The mood feels sort of calm and quiet.*

*Drum Song* 503

## Presentation

**Motivation/Prior Knowledge**
The title suggests a Native American message. How does the title fit the poem?

**Master Teacher Note** Before students read the poem, ask them to simply look at its shape and form on the page. Point out that each stanza begins with the word *listen*. Note that following "Listen" in each stanza is an animal's name. Then point out that each stanza ends with a key word. Set up the parallels on the board: turtle, water; woodpecker, branch; snowhare, hunt; women, hips. Ask students what message the visual pattern suggests even before a reader reads the entire poem. Students may want to speculate about why the poet uses singular nouns for all except women.

**Purpose-Setting Question** To whom is the command "Listen" given? What is the listener supposed to hear?

1 **Reading Strategy** Ask yourself who is supposed to listen.

2 **Discussion** Why does the poet place this word as she does?

3 **Reading Strategy** What does this description help you visualize?

4 **Discussion** After writing about a reptile and a bird, why does the poet choose to write about a rabbit?

5 **Clarification** Owls feed on small animals like rabbits.

**ESL Teaching Strategy** You might use the Check Test in the Teaching Portfolio, page 661, as a directed reading tool.

**Making Connections** "The Indian All Around Us," page 457, gives insight into Native American words now part of standard English, a literary approach of which Rose would approve.

**Thematic Focus** Many writers, especially poets, are traditionally in close touch with our living earth. What evidence do you find of that in this poem?

**6 Reading Actively** Why does the poet save writing about women for the last stanza?

**7 Reading Actively** What connection can you make with this description? Have you ever seen mountains that look like women with blankets on their hips?

**Reader's Response** Why do you think the poet chose the four animals she did? Would you choose different animals? Why or why not?

**Thematic Response** If you could ask the poet how she feels about the animals on our living earth, what do you think she would say?

## Humanities Note

Silk screen, *Medicine Wheel,* by L. White Eagle. Silk screen is a graphic technique in which a stencil is affixed to fine silk stretched on a frame. The frame is placed over paper or fabric, and colored ink is scraped across the silk. Different colors are achieved by using multiple screens.

The geometric design in *Medicine Wheel* is done in the earth colors common to Native American pottery. The mystical number five is repeated throughout the design as the five animal symbols, the five concentric square shapes that separate the animals, and the five mazelike symbols across the bottom. The central circle contains a stylized human face symbolizing the medicine man, or healer. Large medicine wheels like this were laid out in patterns of stone by Native American shamans as centers of healing power.

You might use these questions for discussion:
1. Which of the five animals shown in the medicine wheel are mentioned in the poem?
2. How does the artist achieve a rhythm or movement in this work? How does the poet achieve the same effect?

**Question:** *Why are women in the poem? What do they have to do with these other animals? I'm not sure what they are doing besides planting seeds.*

**Paraphrase:** *I think the poem is about different creatures going about their business. The drumbeat that goes through it could be something like a pulse or a heartbeat, daily rhythms of life.*

Listen. Women
    your tongues melt,
    your seeds are planted
    mesa[2] to mesa a shake
25    of gourds,
    a line of mountains
    with blankets
    on their
hips.

**2. mesa** (mā′sə) *n.*: A small, high plateau with steep sides.

**MEDICINE WHEEL**
*L. White Eagle*

Wendy Rose (1948–   ) believes that "For everything in this universe there is a song to accompany its existence; writing is another way of singing these songs." Rose sings songs in both words and pictures. A well-published poet, she also manages a museum bookstore, and she lectures at the University of California. As a visual artist, she designs postcards, posters, T-shirts, and bookbags. Rose is half Hopi, but she warns readers not to read her work as "Native American" but as human.

## RESPONDING TO THE SELECTION

### Your Response

1. Which of the four descriptions do you like the most? Why?
2. If you were asked to read the poem aloud, how would you read it? Why?

### Recalling

3. What is each of the animals in this poem doing?
4. What are the women in the last stanza doing?

### Interpreting

5. How are the women like the three animals described earlier in the poem?
6. Why do you think the women are described as "mountains"?
7. To whom is the word *listen* addressed? To what is the listener listening?
8. Why is "Drum Song" an apt title for this poem?

### Applying

9. This poem is about the everyday rhythms in the natural world. How could you adapt the poem so that it described the daily rhythms of your life?

## ANALYZING LITERATURE

### Appreciating Imagery

Poetry demands that we use our five senses to respond to it. When poets appeal to the senses with their words, they are using **imagery.** Study the imagery in "Drum Song." Notice how much sensation the poet packs into a relatively short poem.

1. To how many senses does "Drum Song" appeal? Support your answer with examples.
2. What kinds of sounds are described in the poem? What does the speaker want you to hear as you listen to these kinds of sounds?

## CRITICAL THINKING AND READING

### Understanding Repetition

The word *listen* is repeated at the beginning of each stanza of "Drum Song." In addition, the rhythm, sentence patterns, and visual format are the same in each stanza. Think about the effects these repetitions create and how these effects support the overall meaning of the poem.

1. How is the action described in each stanza similar? What relationship between the stanzas does this repetition set up?

*Drum Song*   505

---

### Interpreting

5. Suggested Response: The women are also going about their daily chores that allow them to survive.
6. Suggested Response: They are bent over in the fields, so their backs look like the humps of mountains.
7. Suggested Response: The word *listen* addresses the reader and asks him or her to pay attention to the song of life.
8. Suggested Response: The title suggests the rhythm of life, the song of life, the pattern that all living things follow to survive.

### Applying

9. Answers may include the idea that the rhythms of their own lives will include the routines of eating, sleeping, working, and relaxing.

**Challenge** Ask students to write the adaptation they describe in answering question 9.

### ANSWERS TO ANALYZING LITERATURE

1. Students should find all five senses: sight *(flat, round, red head),* sound *(woodpecker, shake of gourds),* smell *(whiskers dance),* taste *(tongues melt),* and touch *(claws, bark, belly drags).*
2. Students may recognize that turtles make sounds as they crawl up rocks and plop into water, that woodpeckers make sounds searching for food, that snowhares munch quietly and owls screech, and that women talk in the fields. The speaker probably wants the reader to hear the sounds of daily life.

### ANSWERS TO CRITICAL THINKING AND READING

1. Each stanza describes an action necessary for survival to each animal. The repetition sets up the idea that all animals, even humans, must follow life's rhythms to survive.
2. The repetition emphasizes the parallelism of all animal life.

---

**More About the Author** Poet **Wendy Rose** says, "There is a great deal of stereotyping of Indian poetry; we may be seen as 'nature children' tapping some great earth-nerve and producing poems like pulses. But all art is that way, not just Indian art." Ask students to respond to this comment.

## Closure and Extension

### ANSWERS TO RESPONDING TO THE SELECTION
### Your Response

1. Lead students to recognize what makes them respond positively to any description. Emphasize personal experiences and preferences as well as the writer's success in conveying a picture.

2. Lead students to understand that different inflections convey different meanings.

### Recalling

3. Each animal is going about its daily life.
4. The women are working in the fields, planting crops.

**Publishing Student Writing** Ask students to read aloud their poems or descriptive paragraphs in cooperative groups. As they do, others in the group should sketch the place described. Post the poems and sketches on the class bulletin board.

## LEARNING OPTIONS

1. Direct students who enjoy creative writing to this option.
2. Students who show a particular interest in animals will enjoy this cross-curricular option.

**Writing Across the Curriculum** Suggest that students interested in the cross-curricular learning option ask their science teacher for possible resources.

**Multicultural Connection** Discuss how a drum may function as more than a musical instrument in many cultures. Some ways include its use for coded communication, relaxation, theatrical sound effects, or ceremonial rites. Explain that, metaphorically, the "drum song" here may be thought of as a natural rhythm binding the land, animals, and humans together.

The Kodo drummers of Japan use drums in a celebratory, athletic, and sometimes meditative or ritualistic fashion. The aim of their concerts is to inspire emotions in the audience as well as to entertain. With a devotion like that of religious monks, the Kodo drum-

2. How does repetition help to express important themes in "Drum Song"?

# THINKING AND WRITING

### Using Imagery in Writing

Choose a place that you know well, for instance, a gymnasium, a shopping mall, or a meadow. As you visualize this place, list images that describe it, using as many of the five senses as possible. Use your list to write a poem or a descriptive paragraph about the place. Try to make your readers feel as though they are experiencing it the same way you did.

# MULTICULTURAL CONNECTION

### Drums Across Time and Cultures

The drum is probably the oldest of all instruments, valued not only by Native American peoples but also by others throughout the world. Drums have played important roles in many religious, military, and political ceremonies. Some societies have believed that the instrument is sacred.

**"Talking drums."** Drums that imitate the sounds and rhythms of the human voice are used for communication in parts of Africa and Asia. The Nigerian *kalengo* is a talking drum with an hourglass shape and cords stretching back and forth between the drumheads at each end. The drummer can raise the pitch of the drum by squeezing the cords. The talking drums of the Ashanti people of central Ghana are so powerful that they can be heard as far as twenty miles away.

**The bass drum.** Drums have evolved as they have passed from one culture to another. The bass drum used by today's sym-

# LEARNING OPTIONS

1. **Writing.** Choose an animal that you are familiar with and write a verse of poetry that would fit between the third and fourth stanzas of "Drum Song." Try to make the imagery, style, mood, and format consistent with the rest of the poem.
2. **Cross-curricular Connection.** Form a small group and have each member do some research on one of the animals in "Drum Song." Share your findings with one another. Then review the poem, applying the information you have found to your analysis of the poem's content. How does your knowledge add to your comprehension and appreciation of the poem?

phony orchestra was once a small drum with a rounded bottom, invented by the Arabs. A larger version used by Turkish military bands reached Western Europe in the 1400's, and it was further altered by European armies. However, the bass drum was not used by classical composers in the West until some 300 years later.

**A wide variety of drums.** Drums come in a surprising variety of shapes and sizes. Among them are drums that look like tubes, barrels, hourglasses, goblets, and picture frames. Not all drums are played by striking the drumhead with the hands or a drumstick. Some, like the rattle drums of Tibet, are shaken. Others rely on friction to produce sound—drummers pull their fingers across the surface.

### Exploring and Sharing

Find out about drums used in different cultures—for example, the goblet-shaped drum, *darabuka,* used in Egypt; the *tsuzumi,* a drum popular in Japan; or the oil drum traditionally used in the West Indies. Tell the class what you have learned.

mers live disciplined and secluded lives on Sado Island: They wake before dawn, endure rigorous exercise routines, meditate, practice on drums for hours, and repeat the regimen every day. In ancient, rural Japan, the farthest echo of a *taiko* (drum) beat is said to have marked the village limits. Touring with its ornate, 800-pound *o-daiko* drum carved from the trunk of a single tree and played

by two men, Kodo believes it may similarly extend all limits of the "global village."

Ask students to research the Kodo drummers, African or South American styles of drum-playing and design, or other uses of drums besides their use in popular musical entertainment. Perhaps include an interactive, group percussion session—even a few moments of drumming on desk-

tops—to enhance in a sensual way students' understanding of the poem's rhythm, subject, and title.

# Narrative Poetry

**HOLY MOUNTAIN III, 1945**
*Horace Pippin*
*Hirshhorn Museum and Sculpture Garden, Smithsonian Institution*

## Humanities Note

Fine art, *Holy Mountain III,* 1945, by Horace Pippin. The African American artist Horace Pippin (1888–1946) was born in West Chester, Pennsylvania. Pippin was a true primitive, or naive, painter; he had no formal art training. Wounded in World War I, he lost the use of his right arm. Unable to deny the urge to express himself through art, Pippin completed his first painting, at the age of forty-three, by guiding his lifeless arm with his left hand. His images of the people, fantasy scenes, and history are all painted from the heart.

Near the end of his life, Horace Pippin produced a series of four paintings entitled *The Holy Mountain.* They were inspired by the outbreak of World War II. His own memories of war were so vivid and horrible that he felt compelled to make an anti-war statement through his art. These paintings were a cry for world peace and love among mankind. *Holy Mountain III* shows a good shepherd in an idyllic, flower-studded field. Animals, wild and tame, and children are all together in harmony in this field. In the background is a line of trees under which are darkness, graves, and figures of war. A viewer can easily give a narrative interpretation to the painting.

## Preparation

**More About the Author** As a professor of romance languages, Henry Wadsworth Longfellow studied the cultures and tongues of Europe. But as a poet, he was drawn to write about the heroic figures in the American past —Paul Revere and Hiawatha among them. You might ask the class why, with a background in European languages, he chose to write about American subjects.

**Literary Focus** At this point, perhaps, you may want to review the narrative elements, including plot, character, setting, and point of view.

**Prereading Focus** Make a cluster map like the following on the chalkboard:

Have students volunteer one possible solution for each area. Then have them brainstorm for others in small groups.

**Vocabulary** Many of the words in the list help to set the mood of the poem. Your **more advanced** students might profit from writing sentences using the vocabulary words.

**Spelling Tip** The *ea* spelling of short *e* as in *tread* and *stealthy* is also found in *wealth, measure, read* (past tense).

---

**THEME:
OUR AMERICAN
HERITAGE**

### Henry Wadsworth Longfellow

(1807–1882) was born in Portland, in what is now the state of Maine. Longfellow published his first poem at the age of thirteen and two years later entered Bowdoin College, where he was a classmate of Nathaniel Hawthorne, who also became a famous writer. Longfellow's best-remembered works include the narrative poems "The Song of Hiawatha" and "Paul Revere's Ride." In "Paul Revere's Ride," he tells of a Revolutionary hero's historic ride.

---

# GUIDE FOR READING

## Paul Revere's Ride

### The Narrative Poem

A **narrative poem** is a poem that tells a story. Like short stories, narrative poems have plot, setting, characters, dialogue, and theme. "Paul Revere's Ride" is set around Boston on the eve of the American Revolution. The main action is Revere's legendary midnight ride, during which he warned his fellow colonists of the approaching British army. His bravery gave the colonists time to get ready so they could turn back the British that night. The main characters are Paul Revere and his friend.

However, a poem is not a short story. A narrative poem is in poetic form, not in prose. It relies on rhythm and rhyme. It is usually organized in **stanzas,** groups of lines that form units in a poem, just as paragraphs are the units of a story.

### Focus

In groups, brainstorm ways to solve the following problem: Only you and a few others know that a foreign army is about to attack a coastal area. You must warn people, but you don't know whether the attack is to be by land, sea, or air. What system would you set up to alert people? Whom would you contact first? How would you get your message out to the most people in the least amount of time? Make a list of solutions and share them with the class. Then read the poem to see how Paul Revere solved a similar problem long ago.

### Vocabulary

Knowing the following words will help you as you read "Paul Revere's Ride."

**phantom** (fan′ təm) *n.*: Ghost-like (p. 509)

**tread** (tred) *n.*: Step (p. 510)

**stealthy** (stel′thē) *adj.*: Secret; quiet (p. 510)

**somber** (säm′ bər) *adj.*: Dark; gloomy (p. 510)

**impetuous** (im pech′ o͞o əs) *adj.*: Impulsive (p. 511)

**spectral** (spek′ trəl) *adj.*: Ghostly (p. 511)

**aghast** (ə gast′) *adj.*: Horrified (p. 512)

---

### Objectives

1 To understand the elements of a narrative poem
2 To understand a sequence of events
3 To summarize the events in a narrative poem
4 To express individual interests and abilities through optional activities

### Support Material

**Teaching Portfolio**
Teacher Backup, p. 673
Usage and Mechanics Worksheet, p. 676
Vocabulary Check, p. 677
Critical Thinking and Reading Worksheet, *Sequencing Events,* p. 679
Language Worksheet, *Using a Thesaurus,* p. 680
Selection Test, p. 681

Art Transparency 10, *Paul Revere Gives the Alarm to the Countryside* by Charles Hoffbauer

**Listening to Literature**
"Paul Revere's Ride"

**Prentice Hall Literature Writing Studio**

# Paul Revere's Ride

## Henry Wadsworth Longfellow

Listen, my children, and you shall hear  1
Of the midnight ride of Paul Revere,
On the eighteenth of April, in Seventy-five;
Hardly a man is now alive
5   Who remembers that famous day and year. 2

He said to his friend, "If the British march 3
By land or sea from the town to-night,
Hang a lantern aloft in the belfry arch[1]
Of the North Church tower as a signal light,—
10  One, if by land, and two, if by sea;
And I on the opposite shore will be,
Ready to ride and spread the alarm
Through every Middlesex[2] village and farm,
For the country folk to be up and to arm."

15  Then he said, "Good night!" and with muffled oar
Silently rowed to the Charlestown[3] shore,
Just as the moon rose over the bay,
Where swinging wide at her moorings[4] lay
The Somerset, British man-of-war;[5]
20  A phantom ship, with each mast and spar[6]   4
Across the moon like a prison bar,
And a huge black hulk, that was magnified
By its own reflection in the tide.

---

1. **belfry arch** (bel′ frē ärch): The curved top of a tower or steeple that holds the bells.
2. **Middlesex** (mid′ ′l seks′): A county in Massachusetts.
3. **Charlestown** (chärlz′ toun′): Part of Boston on the harbor.
4. **moorings** (moor′ iŋz) n.: The lines, cables, or chains that hold a ship to the shore.
5. **man-of-war:** An armed naval vessel; warship.
6. **mast and spar:** Poles used to support sails.

Paul Revere's Ride   509

Meanwhile, his friend, through alley and street,
25 Wanders and watches with eager ears,
Till in the silence around him he hears
The muster[7] of men at the barrack door,
The sound of arms, and the tramp of feet,
And the measured tread of the grenadiers,[8]
30 Marching down to their boats on the shore.

Then he climbed the tower of the Old North Church,
By the wooden stairs, with stealthy tread,
To the belfry-chamber overhead,
And startled the pigeons from their perch
35 On the somber rafters,[9] that round him made
Masses and moving shapes of shade,—
By the trembling ladder, steep and tall,
To the highest window in the wall,
Where he paused to listen and look down
40 A moment on the roofs of the town,
And the moonlight flowing over all.

Beneath, in the churchyard, lay the dead,
In their night-encampment on the hill,
Wrapped in silence so deep and still
45 That he could hear, like a sentinel's[10] tread,
The watchful night-wind, as it went
Creeping along from tent to tent,
And seeming to whisper, "All is well!"
A moment only he feels the spell
50 Of the place and the hour, and the secret dread
Of the lonely belfry and the dead;
For suddenly all his thoughts are bent
On a shadowy something far away,
Where the river widens to meet the bay,—
55 A line of black that bends and floats
On the rising tide, like a bridge of boats.

---

**7. muster** *v.*: An assembly of troops summoned for inspection, roll call, or service.
**8. grenadiers** (gren' ə dirz') *n.*: Members of a special regiment or corps.
**9. rafters** *n.*: The beams that slope from the ridge of a roof to the eaves and serve to support the roof.
**10. sentinel** (sen' ti n'l) *n.*: A person who keeps guard.

Meanwhile, impatient to mount and ride,
Booted and spurred, with a heavy stride
On the opposite shore walked Paul Revere.
60  Now he patted his horse's side,
Now gazed at the landscape far and near,
Then, impetuous, stamped the earth,
And turned and tightened his saddle-girth;[11]
But mostly he watched with eager search
65  The belfry-tower of the Old North Church,
As it rose above the graves on the hill,
Lonely and spectral and somber and still.
And lo! as he looks, on the belfry's height
A glimmer, and then a gleam of light!
70  He springs to the saddle, the bridle[12] he turns,
But lingers and gazes, till full on his sight
A second lamp in the belfry burns!

A hurry of hoofs in a village street,
A shape in the moonlight, a bulk in the dark,
75  And beneath, from the pebbles, in passing, a spark
Struck out by a steed flying fearless and fleet:
That was all! And yet, through the gloom and the light,
The fate of a nation was riding that night;
And the spark struck out by that steed[13] in his flight,
80  Kindled the land into flame with its heat.

He has left the village and mounted the steep,[14]
And beneath him, tranquil and broad and deep,
Is the Mystic,[15] meeting the ocean tides;
And under the alders[16] that skirt its edge,
85  Now soft on the sand, now loud on the ledge,
Is heard the tramp of his steed as he rides.

7

8

---

11. **girth** (gɐrth) *n.*: A band put around the belly of a horse for holding a saddle.
12. **bridle** (brīd′ 'l) *n.*: A head harness for guiding a horse.
13. **steed** *n.*: A horse, especially a high-spirited riding horse.
14. **steep** *n.*: A slope or incline having a sharp rise.
15. **Mystic** (mis′ tik): A river in Massachusetts.
16. **alders** (ôl′ dərz) *n.*: Trees and shrubs of the birch family.

7 **Discussion** What details in this stanza create a feeling of eagerness and tension?

8 **Discussion** What was the "spark" struck by that steed in his flight?

**ESL Strategy** Many of the words in the first section on this page relate to horses and may be unfamiliar to ESL students. Have students brainstorm in small groups to decide the meaning of these words: *mount, booted, spurred, saddle girth, saddle,* and *bridle.* Students may use a dictionary or the Language Master 6000 to find the meanings.

**Writing Transparency/Cooperative Learning** Have students work in small groups to prepare a brief report on what actually happened on the night of April 18, 1775. They may then use a Venn diagram to compare and contrast what Longfellow wrote with the actual events. A Venn diagram can be found in the Graphic Organizers section of the **Transparencies for Writing.** Have the groups share their findings with the class.

**9 Critical Thinking and Reading**
What future events do these lines
foreshadow?

It was twelve by the village clock,
When he crossed the bridge into Medford[17] town.
He heard the crowing of the cock,
90  And the barking of the farmer's dog,
And felt the damp of the river fog,
That rises after the sun goes down.

It was one by the village clock,
When he galloped into Lexington.[18]
95  He saw the gilded weathercock[19]
Swim in the moonlight as he passed,
And the meeting-house windows, blank and bare,
Gaze at him with a spectral glare,
As if they already stood aghast
9 | 100  At the bloody work they would look upon.

---

**17. Medford** (med' fərd): A town outside of Boston.
**18. Lexington** (lek' siŋ tən): A town in eastern Massachusetts,
outside of Boston.
**19. weathercock** (wet͟h' ər kăk') *n*.: A weathervane in the form of a
rooster.

512  *Poetry*

It was two by the village clock,
When he came to the bridge in Concord[20] town.
He heard the bleating[21] of the flock,
And the twitter of birds among the trees,
105 And felt the breath of the morning breeze
Blowing over the meadows brown.
And one was safe and asleep in his bed
Who at the bridge would be first to fall,
Who that day would be lying dead,
110 Pierced by a British musket-ball.

You know the rest. In the books you have read,
How the British Regulars[22] fired and fled,—

10

---

**20. Concord** (kăn' kôrd): A town in eastern Massachusetts. The
first battles of the Revolutionary War (April 19, 1775) were fought in
Lexington and Concord.
**21. bleating** (blēt' ĭŋ) *n*.: The sound made by sheep.
**22. British Regulars:** Members of the army of Great Britain.

*Paul Revere's Ride* 513

513

---

**10 Discussion** The day after Revere's ride, colonists from Lexington and Concord fought the British troops. What details does the poet include about the tactics the colonists will use?

**Multicultural Focus** Point out to students that "the shot heard 'round the world" at Lexington and Concord was repeated in at least two other national revolutions after the American Revolution. The French Revolution began with the French people storming the king's prison, the Bastille, in 1789. The Russian Revolution reached its climax in 1917 with the taking of the Winter Palace in St. Petersburg by the Communists. Just as the American Revolution did, these two inspired revolutionary movements in many other countries.

Have students research and discuss revolutions in other lands. Did these movements live up to their promises?

Are there students in your class whose families came to the United States because of a revolution? Ask them to tell their classmates about it.

**Audiocassette** To emphasize the narrative aspects of this poem, play the recording of "Paul Revere's Ride" on Side 3 of the **Listening to Literature** Audiocassettes. Students may follow along in their textbooks, or they may listen for the regular rhythm and rhyme. Ask how the sound of the poem adds to its narrative effect.

**Speaking and Listening** Some social studies teachers might be interested in having a choral reading of the poem presented to a social studies class.

**11 Discussion** What was the mid-night message of Paul Revere?

**Reader's Response** You have probably read about Paul Revere in social studies class. How does reading about him in a poem affect your understanding of his role in history?

**Thematic Response** How important was Paul Revere's contribution to American history? What would you personally want your contribution to American history to be?

**Multicultural Connection** After students have read this feature, they might expand their investigations of the origins of American place names by finding the origins of the names of all the states and many of the major cities. They might classify their information in lists according to the nation of origin.

How the farmers gave them ball for ball,
From behind each fence and farm-yard wall,
115 Chasing the red-coats down the lane,
Then crossing the fields to emerge again
Under the trees at the turn of the road,
And only pausing to fire and load.

So through the night rode Paul Revere;
120 And so through the night went his cry of alarm
To every Middlesex village and farm,—
A cry of defiance and not of fear,
A voice in the darkness, a knock at the door,
And a word that shall echo forevermore!
125 For, borne on the night-wind of the Past,
Through all our history, to the last,
In the hour of darkness and peril and need,
The people will waken and listen to hear
The hurrying hoof-beats of that steed,
**11** 130 And the midnight message of Paul Revere.

# MULTICULTURAL CONNECTION

*Place Names in the United States—
A Multicultural Mosaic*

**British heritage.** The United States has always been made up of a mixture of cultures, and the names of many of our cities reflect this varied history. Some of the places mentioned in this poem—the county of Middlesex and the towns of Medford and Lexington—were named after places in England. These names reflect the British heritage of New England.

**Spanish names.** San Diego, Los Angeles (which means "the angels"), Santa Barbara, Monterey, San Jose, San Francisco—these names all attest to the Spanish settlement of California in the eighteenth century. Many of the cities have saints' names because they were founded as religious missions.

Spanish exploration and settlement can also be traced in other states. Albuquerque, New Mexico, was named after a city in Spain.

San Antonio, Texas, was originally a Spanish mission and fort.

**French names.** The French also left their mark on our cities' names. New Orleans was named after the French heir to the throne, the Duc d'Orléans, in 1718.

**Native American names.** Cities named after Native American groups or taken from their names and words can be found throughout the United States. Omaha, for example, was named after the local Omaha people. Cheyenne, in Wyoming, was named after the Cheyenne. Tallahassee, meaning "abandoned village," comes from the language of the Creek Indians.

**Dutch influence.** The Dutch, who settled New York before the English arrived, also left many names. For instance, Brooklyn was originally spelled Breuckelen and was named after a town in Holland.

**Exploring and Sharing**

Research the origin of your town's name in a book of local history.

514 *Poetry*

## Closure and Extension

### ANSWERS TO RESPONDING TO THE SELECTION
#### Your Response

1. In their answers, have students cite phrases from the poem that they feel capture the excitement.

#### Recalling

2. Paul Revere makes his ride on April 18, 1775, at midnight.
3. Revere and his friend agree that the friend would hang one lantern in the tower of North Church if the British marched by land and two lanterns if they came by sea. Revere, who would be waiting on the opposite shore, would ride throughout the countryside and spread the alarm so the people could arm themselves.
4. Revere sees two lamps.
5. He accomplished his purpose. The colonists were warned, were able to prepare themselves, and defeated the British the next day.

## RESPONDING TO THE SELECTION

### Your Response

1. Do you feel that this poem captures the excitement of that famous night? Explain.

### Recalling

2. When does Paul Revere make his ride? (lines 1–5)
3. What agreement does Revere make with his friend? (lines 6–14)
4. How many lamps does Paul Revere finally see in the belfry? (lines 70–72)
5. Explain whether or not Paul Revere accomplished his purpose.

### Interpreting

6. To what is the Somerset compared? (lines 15–23) What is the effect of this image?
7. From his position in the belfry-chamber, how does the friend feel at first? (lines 42–51)
8. What is the "shadowy something far away" that the friend suddenly sees? (lines 52–56)
9. How do lines 78 through 80 express the importance the poet places on the ride?

### Applying

10. Do you think Revere's friend is also a hero? Explain your answer.

## ANALYZING LITERATURE

### Understanding a Narrative Poem

Although it is a poem, "Paul Revere's Ride" resembles a short story in several important ways. First, the poem has a **plot,** a sequence of events that take place and that present a conflict. Characters are introduced, and the setting is established. Next, the poem builds suspense as Revere and his friend wait. The poet writes first of one and then of the other, and the tension mounts. At last the signal appears, and the climax of the poem—the ride—begins.

1. What is the conflict in this narrative poem?
2. Describe Paul Revere's character.

3. How does the poet create suspense in his description of the friend's climb to the belfry-chamber.
4. Cite two details that describe the setting effectively. Explain why you chose each.

## CRITICAL THINKING AND READING

### Sequencing Events

Narrative poems present a **sequence of events,** or arrangement of actions. In the first stanza, the poet tells about Revere's agreement with his friend. That information prepares you for events that follow. Every other stanza builds on the information in the first two stanzas.

1. What does the friend do even before he climbs the belfry-tower?
2. How does stanza 7 relate to stanza 2?
3. How do stanzas 6 and 7 help build suspense?

## THINKING AND WRITING

### Summarizing the Events in the Poem

Make a list of the main events in the poem. List them in the order in which they occur. Using this list as your guide, write a summary of the action. When you have finished, reread your summary, making sure you have covered all the important points. Proofread your summary.

## LEARNING OPTIONS

1. **Speaking and Listening.** As a class, perform a choral reading of "Paul Revere's Ride." Arrange yourselves in groups, and have each group recite a stanza in turn until the poem has been read. Try to match the tone of voice you use to the action and mood of the stanza you are reading.
2. **Cross-curricular Connection.** On a map of Boston and its suburbs, locate the rivers, towns, and other details mentioned in the poem. Then make a map of your own that illustrates the poem, showing the route Paul Revere used and key points along the way.

*Paul Revere's Ride* 515

masses and *moving shapes of shade* to describe the rafters.

4. Answers will differ. Suggested Response: Lines 44–47, 53, 67, 82, 97–98 all give effective details describing the setting. The details add to the mood of danger and suspense.

### ANSWERS TO CRITICAL THINKING AND READING

1. The friend wanders through Boston listening until he hears soldiers marching down to their boats.
2. Stanza 7 returns to describing Revere's actions, a continuation from stanza 2.
3. Stanzas 6 and 7 help build suspense by presenting the apprehensive friend making his way to the eerie belfry-tower and then switching to an impatient Revere on the shore waiting for his signal.

### THINKING AND WRITING

**Writing Transparency** A graphic organizer may help students with their listing of events. Use the Series of Events Chain graphic organizer in **Transparencies for Writing.**

### Writing Across the Curriculum

You may want to suggest that students share their summaries as well as the reports they prepare in the cooperative activity (on page 571) with their social studies teachers.

### LEARNING OPTIONS

Option 1 will appeal to students who excel in oral expression. If possible, provide tape recorders for practice so students can listen to their tone of voice.

Option 2 provides practical experience in spatial relationships.

---

### Interpreting

6. The poet compares the *Somerset* to a ghost and its masts and spars to prison bars. The effect is an ominous, eerie feeling of possible danger.
7. The friend feels dread at being in the lonely tower at midnight with the dead below in the church cemetery.
8. The "shadowy something far away" that the friend sees are the boats of the British soldiers.

9. The poet states directly that the fate of a nation rested on the outcome of the ride.

### Applying

10. Answers will differ. Suggested Response: Revere's friend was also a hero because he risked his life giving Revere information needed to give the alarm. If caught by the British, he would have been branded a traitor.

### ANSWERS TO ANALYZING LITERATURE

1. The conflict involves Paul Revere's riding into the countryside without the British knowing so that he could alert the colonists that the British were coming.
2. Paul Revere was brave, impatient, impetuous, and dependable.
3. The poet creates suspense by using words such as *stealthily* to describe the way the friend climbed and by using *somber* and

# GUIDE FOR READING

## Preparation

**More About the Author** Nationally acclaimed poet **Robert Earl Hayden,** was probably best honored when he was appointed as Consultant of Poetry to the Library of Congress, the first African American poet to hold that position. Thomas W. Ennis of *The New York Times* described that position as ''the American equivalent of the British poet laureate designation.''

**Literary Focus** Because allusions refer to things with which some students may not be familiar, this is a good time to introduce reference books such as biographical and cultural literacy dictionaries.

**Prereading Focus** Students might find it helpful to do this activity with a cluster map. You might use the Cluster Map in the **Transparencies for Writing.**

**Cooperative Learning** The prereading focus activity works well in heterogeneous cooperative groups.

**Vocabulary** Ask students to make sketches to represent each of the vocabulary words.

**Spelling Tip** Remind students of the spelling principle that the short vowel sound is usually followed by two consonants. Have them point out the words in the vocabulary list that illustrate this principle.

### Robert Hayden

(1913–1980), raised in a Detroit ghetto, became a student of the poet W. H. Auden. By the 1960's he had won an international poetry prize and gained widespread recognition. Though his eight volumes of poems cover a wide range of subjects, much of his work celebrates the history and achievements of African Americans. In "Runagate Runagate" Hayden pays tribute to the strength, intelligence, and bravery of Harriet Tubman and other abolitionists who devoted their lives to leading enslaved people to freedom.

## Runagate Runagate

### Allusion

An **allusion** is a reference to a well-known person, place, event, literary work, or work of art. Some of the allusions included in a narrative poem are directly related to the story being told. Other allusions are not part of the story itself but are related to the underlying ideas or themes the poet is expressing.

"Runagate Runagate" is a narrative poem about the Underground Railroad, a system by which slaves escaped to the North in the days before the Civil War. The poem includes allusions to Harriet Tubman and other abolitionists who organized and ran the Underground Railroad. It also includes Biblical allusions referring to experiences of the Israelites, who, like the slaves in the poem, were delivered out of bondage to freedom.

### Focus

"Runagate Runagate" explores the experiences of slaves escaping via the Underground Railroad. "Conductors" on the Underground Railroad would lead fugitive slaves by night to appointed "stations," where they would receive food, shelter, clothing, and directions. The most famous "conductor" was Harriet Tubman, who risked her life repeatedly in order to lead about 300 slaves to freedom.

For a moment suppose that you were a slave escaping to the North. What would you be thinking and feeling? Would the liberty you sought be worth the dangers and risks you would face? With your classmates, brainstorm to list answers to these questions.

### Vocabulary

Knowing the following words will help you as you read "Runagate Runagate."

**beckoning** (bek' ə niŋ) *v.*: Gesturing for someone to come, as by nodding or waving (p. 517)
**mulatto** (mə lat' ō) *n.*: A person who has one black parent and one white parent (p. 517)
**anguish** (an' gwish) *n.*: Great suffering (p. 518)

**shackles** (shak' əlz) *n.*: Cuffs and chains connecting the ankles of a slave (p. 517)
**summoning** (sum' ə niŋ) *n.*: A calling (p. 518)
**savanna** (sə van' ə) *n.*: A treeless plain or a grassland with scattered trees (p. 519)

*516  Poetry*

### Objectives

1  To understand allusions
2  To understand how allusions affect meaning
3  To write a response to a poem

### Support Material

**Teaching Portfolio**
Teacher Backup, p. 683
Usage and Mechanics Worksheet, p. 686
Vocabulary Check, p. 687
Analyzing Literature Worksheet, *Understanding Allusions,* p. 688
Critical Thinking and Reading Worksheet, *Understanding How Allusions Affect Meaning,* p. 689
Selection Test, p. 690

**Prentice Hall Literature Writing Studio**

# Runagate Runagate[1]

Robert Hayden

**I.**

Runs falls rises stumbles on from darkness into darkness

and the darkness thicketed with shapes of terror

and the hunters pursuing and the hounds pursuing

and the night cold and the night long and the river

5  to cross and the jack-muh-lanterns[2] beckoning beckoning

and blackness ahead and when shall I reach that
    somewhere

morning and keep on going and never turn back and keep
    on going

            Runagate

                  Runagate

                        Runagate

Many thousands rise and go

Many thousands crossing over

10                        O mythic North

                  O star-shaped yonder Bible city

Some go weeping and some rejoicing

some in coffins and some in carriages

some in silks and some in shackles

15            Rise and go or fare you well

No more auction block for me

no more driver's lash for me

      If you see my Pompey, 30 yrs of age,

      new breeches, plain stockings, negro shoes;

20      if you see my Anna, likely young mulatto

      branded E on the right cheek, R on the left,

      catch them if you can and notify subscriber.[3]

---

**1. Runagate** (run′ ə gāt′) *n.*: Runaway, fugitive.

**2. jack-muh-lanterns** (jak′ mə lant′ ərnz) *n.*: Jack-o'-
lanterns, shifting lights seen over a marsh at night.

**3. subscriber** (səb skrīb′ ər) *n.*: Here, the person
from whom the slave Pompey ran away.

*Runagate Runagate* 517

518

**6 Literary Focus: Allusion** Why do you think Hayden says the runaways go "underground"?

**7 Literary Focus: Allusion** What are the rest of the words for this song? How do they apply to the meaning of this poem?

**8 Discussion** Why do you think the poet refers to Harriet Tubman as rising "from their anguish and their power"?

**9 Reading Strategy** Why is Tubman a "woman of earth"? What caused her to be "whipscarred"? How is she "a summoning" or "a shining/Mean to be free"?

**10 Discussion** What does Tubman do to help the slaves journey "from Can't to Can," to help them make the long, difficult journey?

**11 Discussion** The slaves are saying "we'll never make it." Who responds, "Hush that now"?

**12 Discussion** Why would Tubman threaten to shoot her own people?

**13 Reading Strategy** Where would these words most likely appear?

## Humanities Note

Fine art, *No. 10: Forward,* Illustration for *Harriet and the Promised Land,* 1967, by Jacob Lawrence. Jacob Armstead Lawrence, born in Atlantic City, New Jersey, in 1917, learned art in the Works Progress Administration settlement-house programs and later at the Art Workshop in Harlem and the Harlem Art Center. He developed a primitive style that is forceful, straightforward, and human. One of the first African American artists to achieve public recognition, his work is an ongoing chronicle of the history and problems of black Americans.

*Forward* is the tenth work in a series of illustrations entitled *Harriet and the Promised Land,* painted in 1967. Here, Lawrence

**6**  25
Catch them if you can, but it won't be easy.
They'll dart underground when you try to catch them,
plunge into quicksand, whirlpools, mazes,
turn into scorpions when you try to catch them.

And before I'll be a slave
I'll be buried in my grave

**7**  30
North star and bonanza gold
I'm bound for the freedom, freedom-bound
and oh Susyanna don't you cry for me

Runagate

Runagate

**II.**

**8**
Rises from their anguish and their power,

Harriet Tubman,

**9**  35
woman of earth, whipscarred,
a summoning, a shining
Mean to be free

**10**
And this was the way of it, brethren brethren,
way we journeyed from Can't to Can.
40 Moon so bright and no place to hide,
the cry up and the patterollers[4] riding,
**11** hound dogs belling in bladed air.
And fear starts a-murbling. Never make it,
we'll never make it. *Hush that now,*
45 and she's turned upon us, leveled pistol
glinting in the moonlight:
**12** Dead folks can't jaybird-talk,[5] she says;
you keep on going now or die, she says.

**13**
Wanted    Harriet Tubman    alias The General
50 alias Moses    Stealer of Slaves
In league with Garrison    Alcott    Emerson
Garrett    Douglass    Thoreau    John Brown

Armed and known to be Dangerous

---

**4. patterollers** *n.*: Dialect term for "patrollers," those hunting for runaway slaves.
**5. jaybird-talk** *v.*: Dialect term meaning "to jabber."

**ILLUSTRATION FOR *HARRIET AND THE PROMISED LAND,* No. 10: FORWARD, 1967**
*Jacob Lawrence*

uses bright, flat areas of color to emphasize the stylized shapes of the landscape and the people fleeing from slavery. The powerful, linear motion of the painting leads to the distant star in the upper-right corner. Harriet Tubman, the figure in red at the right, accentuates this motion with the gesture of her arms. Harriet Tubman's bravery and strength were an inspiration to Jacob Lawrence and became a recurring theme in his work. His art led to a new conception of the African American artist in our society.

Use these questions for discussion:

1. What is the significance of the semihidden figures and animals in the trees?
2. Where was the "promised Land" to these people?
3. How does the artist convey a sense of urgency?

Wanted   Reward   Dead or Alive

55          Tell me, Ezekiel, oh tell me do you see
            mailed Jehovah coming to deliver me?          ⌐ 14

       Hoot-owl calling in the ghosted air,
       five times calling to the hants⁶ in the air.
       Shadow of a face in the scary leaves,
60     shadow of a voice in the talking leaves:

            Come ride-a my train

            *Oh that train, ghost-story train*                        ⌐
            *through swamp and savanna movering movering,*
            *over trestles of dew, through caves of the wish.*        ├ 15
65          *Midnight Special on a sabre track⁷ movering*
                *movering,*
            *first stop Mercy and the last Hallelujah.*   ⌐ 16

            Come ride-a my train

            Mean mean mean to be free.

---
**6. hants** (hants) *n.*: Dialect term for "ghosts."
**7. sabre track** *n.*: Track like a saber, a long sword.

## RESPONDING TO THE SELECTION

### Your Response

1. Which part or parts of the poem describe an experience or a feeling similar to one you have had? Explain the similarity.

### Recalling

2. In your own words, describe what is happening in lines 1–7.
3. Describe the ways in which Harriet Tubman helps others journey "from Can't to Can."

### Interpreting

4. In what way is "Runagate Runagate" a narrative poem?
5. How does the way the poem appears on the page relate to the story it tells?

### Applying

6. What does this poem say about the strength of the human spirit and the will to be free?

## ANALYZING LITERATURE

### Understanding Allusions

An **allusion** is a reference to a person, a place, an event, a literary work, or a work of art. To appreciate "Runagate Runagate" fully, you must understand the allusions in it. For example, you may know that "No more auction block for me" refers to the auction block at which slaves were sold, but you may not know that it is a line from a popular song about slavery. This knowledge helps you to appreciate the authenticity that such a line brings to the poem.

Look up "Moses" (line 50) in a reference book, and answer the questions that follow.

1. Why was Harriet Tubman called Moses?
2. In what ways did the slaves identify with the Biblical accounts of the Israelites in Egypt?

*Runagate Runagate*   519

---

---

## Preparation

**More About the Author** The name **Joaquin Miller** is the pen name of Cincinnatus Miller. At the age of seventeen, Miller ran away to the California gold fields. Later, he helped establish a pony express route between Washington Territory and Idaho. When he was in London, he wore a sombrero and cowboy boots and smoked three cigars at once, causing society people of London to accept him as representative of Americans of the West. Ask students why society people of London might have been eager to meet and talk with Joaquin Miller.

**Literary Focus** Lead students in a discussion of the ways that poetry differs from prose. Have them offer examples of rhythm (perhaps tapping it out on their desks), rhyme, and refrain.

**Prereading Focus** You might remind students to include any facts or opinions they possess about Columbus's background, his voyages across the Atlantic, and his actions once he reached the Americas.

**Vocabulary** Using the vocabulary words in sentences will help your **less advanced** students learn them.

**Teaching to Ability Levels** Ask your **less advanced** students what they know about Columbus's voyage. You might provide background information about the voyage to give the poem a context.

## Joaquin Miller

(1837–1913) was born near Liberty, Indiana, though he once claimed that his cradle was "a covered wagon pointed West." He lived in Oregon and California and worked as a teacher, lawyer, and journalist. Disappointed that poetry he had written was not well received, he left for England. In London both he and his poetry won admiration. In 1886 he returned to America to live near Oakland, California, until his death. "Columbus," Miller's best-known poem, recounts the famous voyage of this daring explorer.

# GUIDE FOR READING

## Columbus

### Elements of Poetry

Three basic elements of poetry are rhythm, rhyme, and refrain. **Rhythm** is the pattern of stressed and unstressed syllables in the lines of a poem. A poem's rhythm usually contributes to meaning. For example, the basic rhythm of "Columbus" is aggressive and forward-driving. It is a rhythm well suited to the poem's theme.

**Rhyme** is the repetition of sounds in words that appear close to one another in a poem. The commonest form of rhyme is **end rhyme,** which occurs at the end of two or more lines:

> This mad sea shows his teeth to-night.
> He curls his lip, he lies in wait,
> With lifted teeth as if to bite!

A **refrain** is a word, phrase, line, or group of lines that is repeated regularly in a poem. A refrain usually comes at the end of each stanza. Sometimes, as in "Columbus," the refrain recurs with small variations: "He said, 'Sail on! sail on! and on!'"

### Focus

Explore your knowledge of and feelings about the subject of this poem by making a group cluster diagram. With your classmates brainstorm to list facts and opinions about Christopher Columbus and his first voyage westward. Write the name "Columbus" in the center of the diagram and circle it. Then write the facts and opinions in circles, clustered by category. Use connecting lines to show relationships between bits of information.

### Vocabulary

Knowing the following words will help you as you read "Columbus."

**mutinous** (my$\overline{oo}$t′ 'n əs) *adj.*: Rebellious (p. 522)
**wan** (wän) *adj.*: Pale (p. 522)
**swarthy** (swôr′ *th*ē) *adj.*: Hav-

ing a dark complexion (p. 522)
**unfurled** (un fʉrld′) *adj.*: Unfolded (p. 522)

---

## Objectives

1 To understand the use of rhythm and refrain
2 To make inferences about theme
3 To write a poem about a historical figure
4 To express individual interests and abilities through an optional activity

## Support Material

**Teaching Portfolio**
Teacher Backup, p. 693
Usage and Mechanics Worksheet, p. 696
Vocabulary Check, p. 697
Critical Thinking and Reading Worksheet, *Making Inferences About Theme,* p. 698
Language Worksheet, *Appreciating Old-fashioned Words,* p. 699

Selection Test, p. 700

**Listening to Literature**
"Columbus"

**Prentice Hall Literature Writing Studio**

THE LANDING OF COLUMBUS, 1876
*Currier and Ives*
*Museum of the City of New York*

# Columbus

Joaquin Miller

> Behind him lay the gray Azores,[1]
> Behind the Gates of Hercules;[2]
> Before him not the ghost of shores;
> Before him only shoreless seas.
> 5   The good mate said: "Now must we pray,
> For lo! the very stars are gone.
> Brave Adm'r'l, speak; what shall I say?"
> "Why, say: 'Sail on! sail on! and on!'"

---

**1. Azores** (ā′ zōrz): A group of Portuguese islands in the North Atlantic west of Portugal.
**2. Gates of Hercules** (gāts uv hʉr′ kyə lēz′): Entrance to the Strait of Gibraltar, between Spain and Africa.

*Columbus*    521

**Presentation**

**Humanities Note**

Lithograph, *The Landing of Columbus,* by Currier & Ives. This illustration is a Currier and Ives lithograph. A lithograph is a print made with ink and stone or metal plates.

During the mid- and late-1800's, Currier and Ives published more than 4,000 scenes of American life and history. Their pictures have been used for illustration and for decoration ever since.
1. In what way does this lithograph symbolize Columbus's monumental deed?
2. What details in this print capture the spirit of Columbus's "Sail on!"
3. Could the message of the refrain have been visually stated by a symbol, rather than by the illustration? If so, what might the symbol have been?

**Motivation/Prior Knowledge** Lead students in a discussion of the dangers faced by early explorers. These dangers included environmental forces, such as storms, drought, and cold. Other dangers were encountering hostile inhabitants, losing their way, and running out of supplies. Remind students that when Columbus began his voyage, he did not know what challenges or dangers were in store for him.

**Thematic Focus** Miller's poem provides a heroic interpretation of one of the most cherished narratives in the nation's heritage—Columbus's voyage and "discovery" of America.

**Purpose-Setting Question** Why does Columbus continue in the face of his crew's fear?

1 **Clarification** You may want to explain that the Gates of Hercules were named for Hercules, hero of Greek and Roman mythology, who performed great feats of strength and courage.

**Master Teacher Note** Ask the class what comparable challenges twentieth-century people, undaunted by fear of the enormity of their undertaking, have faced. Who among these challengers have succeeded? Who have failed? What do they share with Columbus?

**Making Connections** Another selection in this book that depicts events in the establishment of the United States is "Paul Revere's Ride," page 509.

Courage and perseverance in the face of danger is a topic that recurs throughout this book. "The Captain and His Horse" (page 47), "The Drummer Boy of Shiloh" (page 151), *The Diary of Anne Frank* (page 303), "Harriet Tubman: Guide to Freedom" (page 383), "Paul Revere's Ride" (page 509), "Barbara Frietchie" (page 525), and "The Girl Who Hunted Rabbits" (page 635) involve courage in the face of danger.

**Reader's Response** Describe an occasion when perseverance brought success to you, and contrast that experience with one in which perseverance proved foolish.

**Thematic Response** Why do you think the story of Columbus's voyage is beloved by many Americans? Should Columbus be considered a great hero?

🎧 **Audiocassette** To help students appreciate this poem's rhythm and rhyme, have them listen to the recording of "Columbus" (Side 3) on the **Listening to Literature** Audiocassettes. As they listen, have students note the reader's treatment of Miller's strong, regular rhythms and end rhymes.

**Multicultural Focus** As a visual aid to understanding "Columbus" from a Native American perspective, ask students to look at the Currier and Ives lithograph on page 521. Have them note the figures of natives reacting to Columbus. Clearly the true discoverers of America were these natives, whose fires gave off "A light! A light!"

Ask students: "Imagine yourself as the natives on shore. What

2
10 "My men grow mutinous day by day;
My men grow ghastly wan and weak."
The stout mate thought of home; a spray
Of salt wave washed his swarthy cheek.
"What shall I say, brave Adm'r'l, say,
If we sight naught[3] but seas at dawn?"
15 "Why, you shall say at break of day:
'Sail on! sail on! sail on! and on!'"

They sailed and sailed, as winds might blow,
Until at last the blanched mate said:
"Why, now not even God would know
3  20 Should I and all my men fall dead.
These very winds forget their way,
For God from these dread seas is gone.
Now speak, brave Adm'r'l; speak and say—"
4  He said: "Sail on! sail on! and on!"

25 They sailed. They sailed. Then spake[4] the mate:
"This mad sea shows his teeth to-night.
He curls his lip, he lies in wait,
5  With lifted teeth, as if to bite!
Brave Adm'r'l, say but one good word:
30 What shall we do when hope is gone?"
The words leapt like a leaping sword:
"Sail on! sail on! sail on! and on!"

Then, pale and worn, he kept his deck,
And peered through darkness. Ah, that night
35 Of all dark nights! And then a speck—
A light! A light! A light! A light!
It grew, a starlit flag unfurled!
6  It grew to be Time's burst of dawn.
He gained a world; he gave that world
40 Its grandest lesson: "On! sail on!"

---

3. **naught** (nôt) *n*.: Nothing.
4. **spake** (spāk) *v*.: Old-fashioned word for "spoke."

522  *Poetry*

thoughts and feelings would you have about the men in the approaching boat?" Discuss how Columbus's era was characterized by violent conquest of lands and peoples by European explorers seeking gold and other riches. You might provide a map or globe on which students can trace Columbus's voyages.

**Closure and Extension**

**ANSWERS TO RESPONDING TO THE SELECTION**
*Your Response*

1. Encourage students to explain the challenges they faced and to describe their motivation or techniques for meeting them.

*Recalling*

2. The "Brave Adm'r'l" is Christopher Columbus. He responds each time

# RESPONDING TO THE SELECTION

## Your Response

1. Describe a time when you overcame difficulties in order to accomplish a goal. What made you keep going? Explain.

## Recalling

2. Who is the "Brave Adm'r'l"? What does he say each time in response to the mate?
3. What seems to frighten the mate in each of the first four stanzas?

## Interpreting

4. To what does the poet compare the sea in lines 26–28? What is the effect of this comparison?
5. What is the light sighted in the last stanza?
6. Interpret line 38.
7. What is the "grandest lesson"?
8. In what ways is this poem about the great value of determination and perseverance?

## Applying

9. What is the difference between perseverance and stubbornness? Explain why you do or do not think there is a point at which perseverance becomes foolish and dangerous.

# ANALYZING LITERATURE

## Understanding Rhythm and Refrain

A poem's **rhythm** is the pattern of stressed and unstressed syllables it contains. A **refrain** is a phrase or line or group of lines that is repeated several times in the poem. A refrain reinforces and helps express the meaning of the poem. The rhythm of "Columbus" creates a feeling of action; the refrain states the poet's main theme.

1. What general mood or feeling does the rhythm create?
2. What larger meaning does the refrain have?
3. How do the rhythm and refrain work together to convey the theme of the poem?

# CRITICAL THINKING AND READING

## Making Inferences About Theme

**Theme** is the main idea expressed in a literary work. Sometimes the theme is openly stated. More often it is implied, and you must **infer** it—you must draw a conclusion about it based on all the elements of the work. One way to infer the theme of a poem is to consider its refrain. In "Columbus" the simple refrain "sail on! and on!" expresses the theme of the poem.

1. How does the refrain apply to the actual events?
2. How does the refrain show what Columbus was like?
3. To what does the poet refer in his final use of the refrain?

# THINKING AND WRITING

## Writing a Poem About a Historical Figure

List historical people who interest you. Next to each name, note one key idea that you associate with that figure.

From your list select one historical figure, and write a line or two that expresses the main idea you noted about him or her. Using these lines as a refrain, write a narrative poem that tells about the person you have chosen. After you have written one draft of your poem, read it over and make any corrections and improvements you feel are necessary. When you have finished your second draft, proofread it and read your poem aloud to the class.

# LEARNING OPTION

**Cross-curricular Connection.** Do some research about Columbus's first voyage westward, and compare it with the information provided in the poem. Try to answer any questions that arose in your mind as you read the poem.

*Columbus* 523

# Preparation

**More About the Author** His Quaker upbringing led **John Greenleaf Whittier** to become heavily involved in matters of social conscience; he became an ardent abolitionist. You might want to ask students what abolitionists were seeking to abolish.

**Literary Focus** In discussing characters that stand for heroic qualities, you might want to have students list some qualities that authors could have characters represent, such as courage, honesty, loyalty, and so on.

**Prereading Focus** You might have students brainstorm as a group to identify various local or national figures who would make interesting subjects for this activity.

**Vocabulary** You may want to give **less advanced** students the vocabulary words in context. For example: As soon as the game was over, a *horde* of people left the stadium. As the soldier carrying the *banner* passed, the spectators all saluted.

**Alternative Assessment** To promote active reading, have students create a reader's response journal as they read the poem. Ask them to focus their observations on the words and phrases that reveal the characters of Frietchie and Jackson. Encourage students to respond personally to these two people and the human qualities they represent. Whom do they know who shows some of these same qualities?

You may use students' response logs to assess their understanding of this selection.

## John Greenleaf Whittier

(1807–1892) was born in Haverhill, Massachusetts. Whittier's poems are influenced by his Quaker upbringing and by his New England farm background. His most famous works express his political opinions, such as his opposition to slavery. Other works present the simple pleasures of country living. In the narrative poem "Barbara Frietchie," Whittier describes the courage and honor of people on both sides of the Civil War struggle.

*524    Poetry*

# GUIDE FOR READING

## Barbara Frietchie

### Characters in Narrative Poems

In narrative poems, **characters** often stand for certain ideas or heroic qualities that the poet wishes to celebrate. In order to understand a narrative poem, you must recognize the qualities that the characters in the poem represent. For example, in the poem about the Civil War that you are about to read, Barbara Frietchie, a Union supporter, is the subject, who represents human qualities that Whittier admires. To praise these qualities, he tells about her heroic action and Confederate General Stonewall Jackson's reaction to it.

### Focus

Imagine this situation: One person stands up against a group of people to defend what he or she believes is right. Then think of two specific examples of such an action: one that you've heard or read about and one that you've observed firsthand. Answer the following questions for both situations:

Describe the person.
Describe the group of people.
How do they disagree?
What does the person do?
How does the group react?
What is the final outcome?
In your opinion, who was right?

As you read, compare the situations you've just been thinking about with the one described in "Barbara Frietchie."

### Vocabulary

Knowing the following words will help you as you read "Barbara Frietchie."

**horde** (hôrd) *n.*: Large moving group (p. 525)

**banner** (ban′ ər) *n.*: Flag (p. 526)

## Objectives

1 To understand how authors create characters
2 To make inferences about characters
3 To write a definition of a hero
4 To express individual interests and abilities through an optional activity

## Support Material

**Teaching Portfolio**
Teacher Backup, p. 703
Grammar in Action Worksheet, *Understanding Verb Tense,* p. 706
Usage and Mechanics Worksheet, p. 708
Vocabulary Check, p. 709
Analyzing Literature Worksheet, *Creating Characters,* p. 711

Language Worksheet, *Choosing Meaning to Fit Context,* p. 712
Selection Test, p. 713

**Listening to Literature**
"Barbara Frietchie"

**Prentice Hall Literature Writing Studio**

# Barbara Frietchie

## John Greenleaf Whittier

Up from the meadows rich with corn,
Clear in the cool September morn,

The clustered spires of Frederick[1] stand
Green-walled by the hills of Maryland.

5  Round about them orchards sweep,
Apple and peach tree fruited deep,

Fair as the garden of the Lord
To the eyes of the famished rebel horde,

On that pleasant morn of the early fall
10  When Lee[2] marched over the mountain wall;

Over the mountains winding down,
Horse and foot, into Frederick town.

Forty flags with their silver stars,
Forty flags with their crimson bars,

15  Flapped in the morning wind: the sun
Of noon looked down, and saw not one.

Up rose old Barbara Frietchie then,
Bowed with her fourscore[3] years and ten;

Bravest of all in Frederick town,
20  She took up the flag the men hauled down

In her attic window the staff she set,
To show that one heart was loyal yet.

---

**1. Frederick** (fred′ rik): A town in Maryland.
**2. Lee** (lē): Robert E. Lee, commander in chief of the Confederate army in the Civil War.
**3. fourscore** (fôr′ skôr′) *adj.*: Four times twenty; eighty.

*Barbara Frietchie*  525

---

**Thematic Focus** In Whittier's poem a Civil War patriot demonstrates her pride in America's heritage by flying the Stars and Stripes from her window despite the challenge of Confederate troops.

**Multicultural Focus** Discuss the function of flags as symbols of nations or organizations. Often the elements of a flag are themselves symbolic: a ring of thirteen stars on the Stars and Stripes, for example, represented the American Colonies. Similarly, Israel's flag features a Jewish symbol, the Star of David; on New Zealand's flag, the four stars stand for the Southern Cross constellation, a blue field for the Pacific Ocean, and a Union Jack for the country's original British rule.

Have students research and report on various flags and the symbols used in their designs. Ask them also to identify flags that symbolize something other than a nation (for example, the United Nations or the Olympic Games).

525

## Humanities Note

Henri Cartier-Bresson was born in 1908 near Paris, France, and became a photographer in 1930. Cartier-Bresson usually photographs in black and white with a small hand-held camera. This Cartier-Bresson photograph is typical of his work, which captures the significance of events and characters by the arrangement of the people and objects.

You might ask students what details in this photograph make it look as though he could have taken it specifically to illustrate "Barbara Frietchie".

**5 Enrichment** In 1824 Thomas Jonathan Jackson was born in Clarksburg, Virginia, which is now in West Virginia. Although he was orphaned at an early age, he worked and studied hard and received an appointment to West Point. After his graduation Jackson served in the Mexican War. At the first Battle of Bull Run, he received his nickname Stonewall because he and his Confederate troops stood fast in the face of overwhelming odds. One of Robert E. Lee's most trusted generals, Jackson was accidentally shot by his own troops. He had gone out after dark to scout near Chancellorsville, Virginia, and some of his men mistook him for an enemy soldier. He died eight days later, on May 10, 1863.

© Henri Cartier-Bresson/Magnum

5   Up the street came the rebel tread,
    Stonewall Jackson[4] riding ahead.

25  Under his slouched hat left and right
    He glanced; the old flag met his sight.

    "Halt!"—the dust-brown ranks stood fast.
    "Fire!"—out blazed the rifle-blast.

    It shivered the window, pane and sash;[5]
30  It rent the banner with seam and gash.

    Quick, as it fell, from the broken staff
    Dame Barbara snatched the silken scarf.

---

**4. Stonewall Jackson** (stŏn′ wôl′ jak′ s'n): Nickname of Thomas Jonathan Jackson, Confederate general in the Civil War.
**5. sash** (sash) *n.*: The frame holding the glass panes of a window.

526   *Poetry*

## Grammar in Action

In both prose and poetry, a writer may begin a story in one time, change to the past, and return to the present. This may present a difficult problem for the reader. However, close attention to the **verb tense** makes reading and understanding a passage easier.

Whittier begins his poem in the present tense:

Up from the meadows rich with corn,
Clear in the cool September morn,

The clustered spires of Frederick *stand*
Green-walled by the hills of Maryland.

The spires stand—this is in the present tense. However, Whittier changes into the past tense as he describes the action on the day Lee marched into town:

Forty flags with their crimson bars,

*Flapped* in the morning wind: the sun
Of noon *looked* down, and *saw* not one.

The flags flapped, the noon sun looked and saw—the poem is now in the past tense.

She leaned far out on the window-sill,
And shook it forth with a royal will.　　6

35　"Shoot, if you must, this old gray head,
But spare your country's flag," she said.

A shade of sadness, a blush of shame,
Over the face of the leader came;

　　7

The nobler nature within him stirred
40　To life at that woman's deed and word;

"Who touches a hair of yon gray head
Dies like a dog! March on!" he said.　　8

All day long through Frederick street
Sounded the tread of marching feet:

45　All day long that free flag tost[6]
Over the heads of the rebel host.[7]

Ever its torn folds rose and fell
On the loyal winds that loved it well;

And through the hill-gaps sunset light
50　Shone over it with a warm good-night.

Barbara Frietchie's work is o'er,
And the Rebel rides on his raids no more.　　9

Honor to her! and let a tear
Fall, for her sake, on Stonewall's bier.[8]　　10

55　Over Barbara Frietchie's grave,
Flag of Freedom and Union, wave!

Peace and order and beauty draw
Round thy symbol of light and law;

And ever the stars above look down
60　On thy stars below in Frederick town!

---

**6. tost** (tŏst) *v.*: Old-fashioned form of *tossed*.
**7. host** (hōst) *n.*: An army; a multitude or great number.
**8. bier** (bir) *n.*: A coffin and its supporting platform.

*Barbara Frietchie*　527

**Student Activity 1.** Find the line where the poem again shifts to the present tense.

**Student Activity 2.** List ten other verbs in the poem. Identify them as either present or past tense.

**Student Activity 3.** Using the present tense, write a passage describing an event. Then rewrite the passage in the past tense.

**Electronic Handbook** You might want students to review the concept of verb tenses before completing the Grammar in Action activities. If students have access to the Language Master 6000, have them enter *verb*, *tense*, or *regular* and press the GRAMMAR key.

6 **Literary Focus** What words in these lines give clues about Barbara Frietchie's character?

7 **Literary Focus** What details in these lines show Stonewall Jackson's character?

8 **Literary Focus** Ask the class what is revealed about Jackson's respect for the woman through this order to his soldiers. Would Jackson have shot or arrested anyone else bold enough to display the Union flag on principle—say, a younger woman or a man?

9 **Literary Focus** You may want to have students realize that the poet seems to put into sharp focus the actions of admirable individuals, without regard to which side of the conflict they support.

10 **Critical Thinking and Reading** What do you learn about Stonewall Jackson from the poem? What other information might you want to know about him?

**Master Teacher Note** You might encourage students to do research on the life of Stonewall Jackson and his tragic death.

**Reader's Response** What do you admire most about Barbara Frietchie?

**Thematic Response** Why does Barbara Frietchie feel so strongly about the Stars and Stripes? How does Stonewall Jackson react to Frietchie's pride?

**Audiocassette** You might use the **Listening to Literature** Audiocassettes recording of "Barbara Frietchie" (Side 3) to enhance students' understanding of character in the poem. As they listen, have students note how the reader conveys Frietchie's dignity and strength.

# Closure and Extension

### Your Response

1. Have students give reasons for their actions.
2. Encourage students to cite the specific passages that inform their opinions.

### Recalling

3. The poem takes place during the Civil War in Frederick, Maryland.
4. The Confederate Army arrives in town. Before they arrive the men have taken down the Union flag and everyone has left the streets.
5. Stonewall Jackson has ordered the men to fire at the flag. Frietchie, grabbing the falling flag and shaking it out the window, says, "Shoot, if you must, this old gray head. But spare your country's flag."
6. Jackson feels sad and ashamed. His nobler nature stirs him to tell his men not to shoot Barbara Frietchie.

### Interpreting

7. Barbara Frietchie represents patriotism and courage.
8. Jackson represents understanding, compassion, and respect.
9. The last two lines express the hope that the qualities symbolized by Frietchie will be represented by Frederick and the United States.
10. The theme of this poem is that people's beliefs, patriotism, and courage deserve respect.

### Applying

11. Answers will differ. Suggested Response: Other patriotic themes that could be used in poetry might be responsibilities of citizens in a democratic republic, freedom of religion, freedom of speech, the right to assemble peaceably, the right to petition the government for a redress of grievances, the right to due process of law, and other Bill of Rights guarantees. The purpose of a poem with a patriotic theme is to inspire people to feel patriotic.

## ANSWERS TO ANALYZING LITERATURE

1. Whittier uses direct description.

528

## RESPONDING TO THE SELECTION

### Your Response

1. If you had been in Barbara Frietchie's place, would you have done what she did? Why or why not?
2. Who do you think is the more heroic character in this poem, General Stonewall Jackson or Barbara Frietchie? Why?

### Recalling

3. Describe the time and place of the poem.
4. Who arrives in the town? What has happened before their arrival?
5. Why do the soldiers fire their guns? What does Barbara Frietchie do after they fire?
6. What is Stonewall Jackson's reaction to what Barbara Frietchie does?

### Interpreting

7. What admirable human qualities does Barbara Frietchie represent?
8. What admirable human qualities does Stonewall Jackson represent?
9. Explain the last two lines of the poem.
10. What is the theme of this poem?

### Applying

11. This poem has a patriotic theme. What other patriotic themes might be suitable for poetry? What might be the purpose of a poem with a patriotic theme?

## ANALYZING LITERATURE

### Creating Characters

A writer can create a character in several ways. Whittier directly describes Barbara Frietchie as ninety years old, "bowed" with age, and "Bravest of all in Frederick town."

Whittier also uses other methods to develop the character of Barbara Frietchie. He recounts her actions and he quotes her speech. Finally, he shows the reactions of others to her and to her actions.

1. What method of developing a character does Whittier use in line 39?
2. What do Jackson's words in lines 41–42 tell you about his character?

## CRITICAL THINKING AND READING

### Making Inferences About Characters

To **infer** is to draw a conclusion based on available information. If a person always takes responsibility and completes given tasks, then it is reasonable to infer that this person is dependable.

1. List Barbara Frietchie's actions.
2. What does she say to Stonewall Jackson?
3. What does Stonewall Jackson's reaction to Barbara Frietchie tell you about *her*?
4. What inferences do you make about Stonewall Jackson?

## THINKING AND WRITING

### Writing a Definition of a Hero

Think about the admirable qualities that Barbara Frietchie has. Then make a list of other heroic qualities. Organize your list in order of increasing importance. Using your list as a guide, write an essay in which you define a true hero. Read your definition over after you have written it and make any changes you feel are needed. Proofread it and share it with your classmates.

## LEARNING OPTION

**Cross-curricular Connection.** Imagine that you were hired by a recording company to set the words of "Barbara Frietchie" to music. What type of music would you choose? Why? What singing style would you select to match the tone and theme of the poem? Why? If possible, work with a partner to find music, and record your song for others to hear.

---

2. Jackson's words in lines 41–42 show that he is used to giving orders and to being obeyed and that he respects Barbara Frietchie.

## ANSWERS TO CRITICAL THINKING AND READING

1. Barbara Frietchie takes up the flag and hangs it out her attic window. She grabs the flag as it falls and shakes it out the window.
2. She says to shoot her if he must but not to shoot his country's flag.

3. Jackson's reaction tells you that Frietchie is worthy of admiration because of her courage.
4. Inferences include that he is used to giving orders and having them obeyed and that he respects Frietchie's patriotism and courage.

## THINKING AND WRITING

Students could compare the heroic qualities they included in their compositions with those of their

classmates. You might compile a class list of heroic qualities against which heroes of other selections could be measured.

**Software** If your students are working on computers, they might begin the assignment by using the **Writer's Helper** activity *Lists*.

# Figurative Language and Imagery

THE BROOKLYN BRIDGE: VARIATION ON AN OLD THEME, 1939
*Joseph Stella*
*Collection of Whitney Museum of American Art*

## Humanities Note

Fine art, *Brooklyn Bridge: Variation on an Old Theme,* 1939, by Joseph Stella. Joseph Stella (1877–1946) was an Italian–American painter who immigrated to the United States in 1923. He had trained at the Art Students League and New York School of Art, both in New York City. His subsequent travels to Europe exposed him to the beginning movements of Cubism and Futurism. He saw the artistic possibilities of this new "modern" outlook in art and began to explore it.

*Brooklyn Bridge, Variation on an Old Theme* relates to the spirit, not to the actual details of the Brooklyn Bridge in New York City. Stella's imagery shows an assemblage of the dynamic motion, cable tension, shoreline views, sparkling lights, and low-pitched hum of this busy bridge. The painting becomes the symbol of the American urban experience—fast, tense, and neon-colored. Stella was influenced by the rapid technological changes of the twentieth century. He responded to this upheaval with his innovative and aggressive images of the urban experience.

## LEARNING OPTION

This activity will appeal to students interested in music. You might vary the activity by having students develop a dance interpretation of the poem.

## Preparation

**More About the Authors** Considered an original and talented poet, **José Garcia Villa** received the Shelley Memorial Award from the Poetry Society of America in 1959 and was elected Philippines National Artist in 1973. What might winning prizes for his poetry in two countries show about Villa's poetry?

The longest poem in *Leaves of Grass* is "Song of Myself," which is considered **Walt Whitman's** greatest poem. Whitman wrote essays as well as poetry. While his poetry is romantic, his essays are realistic. During the Civil War, Whitman volunteered to work in military hospitals in Washington, D.C. After the war, he held several government jobs until a stroke forced him to retire to Camden, New Jersey, where he continued to write. Which subjects might Whitman's varied jobs have given him for his poetry?

Although Japanese is his native language, **Naoshi Koriyama** has written poems in English because he is "interested to see how well one could write in a second language." You may want to point out some of the difficulties involved in writing poetry in a language other than your own. These difficulties include vocabulary, syntax, and especially differences in connotations and idioms.

## Lyric 17

**José Garcia Villa** (1914–    ) was born in Manila, Philippines, and emigrated to the United States in 1930. He attended the University of New Mexico and Columbia University in New York City. Villa has published several volumes of poetry as well as short stories. "Lyric 17" reflects the judgment of one critic, who said that Villa's poems come "straight from the poet's being, from his blood, from his spirit, as a fire breaks from wood, or as a flower grows from its soil."

## O Captain! My Captain!

**Walt Whitman** (1819–1892) was born in Long Island, New York, and grew up in Brooklyn. He worked as a printer and journalist in and around New York City. In 1848 he began working on *Leaves of Grass,* a long poem about America. Because of its unusual style, commercial publishers refused to publish it; therefore Whitman printed a first edition with his own money. Since then the style of Whitman's poetry has greatly influenced poets around the world. Whitman's most popular poem is "O Captain! My Captain!," which was inspired by the tragic death of President Lincoln.

## Jetliner

**Naoshi Koriyama** (1926–    ) was born on Kikai Island in the southern part of Japan. He studied at Kagoshima Normal School in Japan, at a foreign language school in Okinawa, and at the University of New Mexico and graduated from the State University of New York at Albany. A member of the Poetry Society of Japan, Koriyama now teaches courses in English and American literature at a Tokyo university. Although his native language is Japanese, he writes some poems, such as "Jetliner," in English.

530   Poetry

### Objectives

1 To understand similes
2 To write similes
3 To understand metaphors
4 To understand personification
5 To analyze a simile or metaphor in writing
6 To express individual interests and abilities through optional activities

### Support Material

**Teaching Portfolio**
Teacher Backup, p. 715
Usage and Mechanics Worksheet, p. 719
Vocabulary Check, p. 720
Analyzing Literature Worksheet, *Understanding Similes, Metaphors, and Personification,* p. 721

Language Worksheet, *Appreciating Diction,* p. 722
Selection Test, p. 723

**Listening to Literature**
"Lyric 17," "O Captain! My Captain!," and "Jetliner"

**Prentice Hall Literature Writing Studio**

## Figurative Language and Imagery

**Figurative language** is meant to be interpreted *imaginatively,* not literally. For example, if we write that the sun is like a golden eye, if we call a famous person an institution, or if we say that the summer night seems to whisper—then we are using figurative language.

In "Lyric 17," for example, the poet states that a poem must be "musical as a sea-gull." Poetry is compared to music; but it is beautiful music—music that darts, swoops, and soars. The comparison enables the poet to express this idea in an immediate, brief, and memorable way. This is an example of a particular form of figurative language called a simile. A **simile** is a comparison between two basically unlike things, using the words *like* or *as.*

Two other figures of speech are metaphor and personification. A **metaphor,** like a simile, is a comparison between two things. A metaphor, however, does not use the words *like* or *as* but simply identifies the two things. For example, according to "Lyric 17," a poem "must be a brightness moving." It must *shine,* and it must *move.* This radiance in motion is a metaphor for good poetry.

**Personification** is a figure of speech in which an animal, idea, or inanimate object is given human characteristics. In "Jetliner," a jet about to take off is personified as an athlete at the start of a race.

**Imagery** is the use of vivid language to describe people, places, things, and ideas. You must be able to picture in your mind what authors mean by their imagery in order for their writing to be effective.

## Focus

Below is a chart to help you understand the similes and metaphors in the poems in this section. As you read, complete the chart by listing the characteristics of each simile and metaphor you find.

| Simile or Metaphor | What Is Compared | Compared to | How They Are Similar |
|---|---|---|---|
| "musical as a sea-gull" | poem | sea-gull | Both dart, swoop, and soar like beautiful music. |

## Vocabulary

Knowing these words will help you as you read these poems.

**luminance** (lo͞o′ mə nəns) *n.:* Brightness; brilliance (p. 532)

**exulting** (ig zult′ iŋ) *v.:* Rejoicing (p. 534)

**tread** (tred) *n.:* Step (p. 534)

*Guide for Reading    531*

**Literary Focus** Your less advanced students could benefit from a class discussion of the three types of figurative language discussed. Elicit examples from the students of similes, metaphors, and personification and list them on the board.

**Prereading Focus** Introduce the concept of similes and metaphors by giving students several common examples, such as "She's as fresh as a daisy," or "My feet are like ice." Make a copy of the chart on the chalkboard. Have students volunteer additional similes or metaphors. Write these on the chart. Students should then be ready to proceed with the chart on their own as they read the poems.

**Vocabulary** Your less advanced students will benefit from pronouncing the vocabulary words and seeing them used in context. For example, "In the luminance of the moon, we could see the palm trees swaying," and "We were exulting over the team's victory in the tournament."

**Alternative Assessment** *Portfolio Assignment:* To enable you and your students to assess their learning, ask them to create a portfolio of their written responses to this group of poems, selecting the four best pieces from the following assignments:

Thinking and Writing assignment for "Lyric 17"

Alternative Assessment assignment, p. 535 in the Annotated Teacher's Edition

Thinking and Writing assignment for "Jetliner"

Alternative Assessment assignment for "Jetliner," p. 537 in the Annotated Teacher's Edition

Selection Test, Part A, p. 723 in the Teaching Portfolio

Selection Test Essay Question, p. 724 in the Teaching Portfolio

Reader's Response Question, p. 724 in the Teaching Portfolio

**Thematic Focus** Creativity is often the product of a unique point of view. Making new associations is one way of being creative. How can a new way of viewing something change your attitude toward it?

**Audiocassette** These three poems appear on Side 4 of the **Listening to Literature** Audiocassettes. Play the recordings for students either as they are reading the poems or after they have finished. You might have them focus on the references to sound in each poem.

# Lyric 17

José Garcia Villa

First, a poem must be magical,
Then musical as a sea-gull.
It must be a brightness moving
And hold secret a bird's flowering.
5   It must be slender as a bell,
And it must hold fire as well.
It must have the wisdom of bows
And it must kneel like a rose.
It must be able to hear
10  The luminance of dove and deer.
It must be able to hide
What it seeks, like a bride.
And over all I would like to hover
God, smiling from the poem's cover.

### Your Response

1. Do you agree with this poet's view of what a poem should be? Why or why not?

### Recalling

2. According to the poet, what qualities must a poem have?

### Interpreting

3. Look at the qualities the poet names. Which three do you consider the most important? Explain your answer.

### Applying

4. The poet Emily Dickinson defined poetry as follows: "If . . . it makes my whole body so cold no fire can warm me, I know that is poetry." Explain the meaning of Dickinson's definition. How would you define poetry?

## A NALYZING LITERATURE

### Understanding Similes

A **simile** is a comparison between two basically unlike things that uses the word *like* or *as.* For example, José Garcia Villa uses a simile when he writes that a poem must be "slender as a bell." The simile illustrates similarities between things we do not normally consider similar—a poem and a bell. But, through the simile, we see one way in which a poem and a bell *are* alike. The comparison connects the two things in a new way and extends our appreciation of *both.*

1. What simile occurs in line 2? What is the effect of this simile?

532   Poetry

---

## Presentation

**Motivation/Prior Knowledge**
You might discuss with the class what they think a poem should be. Put their ideas on the board. Note that "Lyric 17," the first poem they will read, is a poem about what a poem should be.

**Master Teacher Note** In Marianne Moore's poem "Poetry," she describes true poets as "literalists of the imagination" who can offer "imaginary gardens with real toads in them." Have the class discuss what she may have meant.

**Purpose-Setting Question** What does José García Villa think a poem should be?

1 **Discussion** Ask for views about whether a poem "must be able to hide what it seeks" or whether it should be direct in giving its insight.

**Discussion** Ask your students what quality they think every poet must have. Is it awareness of beauty? Sensitivity to the feelings of others? A love of words and phrasing?

**Reader's Response** What quality of poetry would you add to Garcia Villa's "Lyric 17"?

**Thematic Response** What do you think is the most creative image in this poem? Explain.

---

## Closure and Extension

### ANSWERS TO RESPONDING TO THE SELECTION
### Your Response

1. Have students support their answers. You might focus their discussion on the poet's criteria for a poem.

### Recalling

2. A poem must be magical and musical, be a moving brightness, hold secret a bird's flowering, be slender as a bell, hold fire, have the wisdom of bows, kneel like a rose, hear the luminance of dove and deer, be able to hide what it seeks, and have God hovering over it.

### Interpreting

3. Answers will differ. Suggested Response: The three most important qualities of a poem are to be magical, musical, and slender as a bell. It should be magical because its subject or descriptions should surprise and delight the reader. It should be musical to please the ear. Finally, a poem should be slender as a bell, so that it concentrates its message and presents only the essence.

### Applying

4. Answers will differ. Suggested Response: Emily Dickinson means that poetry touches her deepest feelings. Students might define poetry as appealing to their emo-

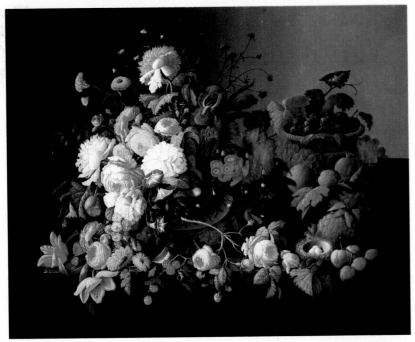

STILL LIFE: FLOWERS, 1855
*Severin Roesen*
*The Metropolitan Museum of Art*

2. Explain the simile in line 8. What is the effect of this simile?
3. Explain the simile in lines 11–12. What is the effect of this simile?

## THINKING AND WRITING

### Writing Similes

Think again of your definition of poetry. Following the pattern of Villa's poem, write your own poem explaining the qualities you think poetry must have. Be sure to use similes to help clarify your points. When you revise, check that you have expressed the qualities of poetry in a vivid way. Then proofread your poem and read it aloud to your classmates.

## LEARNING OPTIONS

1. **Speaking and Listening.** The poem, called a "lyric," states that a poem should be musical. In a small group, take turns reading the poem aloud. Then do the same with part of a magazine article. Of the two types of writing, which sounds more like a song? Why?
2. **Art.** Create a "visual poem" by selecting one or more images from the poem and representing them in a drawing, collage, diorama, or other piece of art. Present your work to the class, explaining how it relates to the imagery in the poem.

*Lyric 17    533*

tions by using original images and rhythm.

## ANSWERS TO ANALYZING LITERATURE

1. The simile in line 2 says a poem is as musical as a sea-gull. This simile makes one think about ways in which a sea-gull, with its raucous voice, is musical.
2. The simile in line 5 means that the poem's message must not waste

words but should be presented in a clear as a bell manner.
3. In lines 11–12, the poet says a poem "must be able to hide / What it seeks, like a bride." The effect of this simile is to help one understand why the meaning of a poem is not always obvious.

## THINKING AND WRITING

**Publishing Student Writing** Students can choose poems from the class to submit to the school newspaper or literary magazine.

**Writing Across the Curriculum** You might want to inform the art teacher about the poems written by your students. The art teacher might be interested in having stu-

dents illustrate their poems or in preparing illuminated manuscripts of them.

## LEARNING OPTIONS

Option 1 will appeal to students who enjoy oral expression. It will also provide practice for ESL students. To extend the activity, tape the oral readings. Play them back in class, using them to discuss the differences in writing styles.

Option 2 will appeal to artistic students. Display the visual poems under the heading "Lyric 17."

**Motivation/Prior Knowledge**
Show pictures of Abraham Lincoln and discuss with your class why people felt he was such a great man. Then you could ask your students to imagine how people might react when someone greatly admired dies unexpectedly.

**Master Teacher Note** You might tell your students that poets, artists, and other creative people sometimes cope with extreme circumstances, such as war, natural disaster, or the assassination of a leader, by using their creative talents. This poem was written by Walt Whitman as he grieved over President Lincoln's assassination.

**Purpose-Setting Question** How did Walt Whitman feel about Abraham Lincoln?

**1 Discussion** Ask students what is meant by the first four lines. Be sure they know that the "fearful trip" refers to the Civil War, the "ship" refers to the nation, and the "prize" and the "port" refer to peace. When does the poem take place? What is the mood of the people? What has happened?

**2 Discussion** The second stanza presents the first reaction of the poet. What was Whitman's first reaction to Lincoln's death?

**3 Literary Focus** What other metaphor is used for Lincoln in the second stanza?

**4 Discussion** How is the poet's reaction different in the last stanza? How might this poem illustrate the various reactions that people would experience when faced with any unexpected tragic event?

**Master Teacher Note** You might ask students what other "fearful" trips in U.S. history the ship of state has taken and which leaders

# O Captain! My Captain!

## Walt Whitman

**1**
O Captain! my Captain! our fearful trip is done,
The ship has weather'd every rack,[1] the prize we sought is won,
The port is near, the bells I hear, the people all exulting,
While follow eyes the steady keel,[2] the vessel grim and daring;
5    But O heart! heart! heart!
     O the bleeding drops of red,
      Where on the deck my Captain lies,
       Fallen cold and dead.

**2**
O Captain! my Captain! rise up and hear the bells;
10 Rise up—for you the flag is flung—for you the bugle trills,
For you bouquets and ribbon'd wreaths—for you the shores a-crowding,
For you they call, the swaying mass, their eager faces turning;
**3** Here Captain! dear father!
     This arm beneath your head!
15     It is some dream that on the deck,
      You've fallen cold and dead.

**4**
My Captain does not answer, his lips are pale and still,
My father does not feel my arm, he has no pulse nor will,
The ship is anchor'd safe and sound, its voyage closed and done,
20 From fearful trip the victor ship comes in with object won;
     Exult O shores, and ring O bells!
      But I with mournful tread,
       Walk the deck my Captain lies,
        Fallen cold and dead.

---

**1. rack** *n*.: A great stress.
**2. keel** *n*.: The chief structural beam extending along the entire length of the bottom of a boat or ship and supporting the frame.

have led the nation through to a safe harbor. A possible technique might be to have one student name a leader and other students provide the "fearful" trip.

**ESL Strategy** ESL students may not be familiar with many of the nautical words in the poem. If you have access to the Language Master 6000, have them look up the meanings of *port, keel, vessel, deck,* and *anchor.*

**Multicultural Focus** Tell students that fallen heroes such as the one in Whitman's poem are often an inspiration to the people of a nation or culture. Achilles was a great hero in ancient Greece, but had one weak spot —his heel. He was finally slain when an arrow struck him there. John Henry (see page 644) is a famous figure of African American folklore. A "steel-driving man" who worked on railroads,

Henry beat a new rail-laying machine in a contest, but then died of exhaustion.

Ask students why such fallen heroes as the ones discussed above are considered to be winners, even though they ultimately lost their lives. Have students tell about other fallen heroes or heroines whom they admire.

**ABRAHAM LINCOLN**
*William Willard*
*National Portrait Gallery, Smithsonian Institution*

## RESPONDING TO THE SELECTION

### Your Response

1. How did this poem make you feel?

### Recalling

2. What has happened to the Captain? Why is this event especially unfortunate?

3. What other name does the poet call the Captain?

### Interpreting

4. What pronoun does the poet use to modify the word *captain*? What is the significance of the pronoun?

5. What effect has the event described in this poem had on the poet? How would you describe the mood of the poem?

### Applying

6. Do you think the fate of a nation ever rests entirely on one person? Explain your answer.

## ANALYZING LITERATURE

### Understanding Metaphors

A **metaphor** is a direct comparison between two unlike things. Throughout "O Captain! My Captain!" Whitman compares President Lincoln to the captain of a ship. The metaphor conveys and reinforces the poet's feelings about President Lincoln—that he was a great leader of the country and a hero.

1. Walt Whitman wrote this poem in response to the assassination of President Lincoln in 1865. If the Captain is a metaphor for Lincoln, explain the metaphor of the ship.

2. What is the "fearful trip" that the ship has "weathered"?

3. Explain why you do or do not think that a ship's captain is an appropriate metaphor for any kind of leader.

*O Captain! My Captain!*   535

## ANSWERS TO ANALYZING LITERATURE

1. The ship is a metaphor for the United States. It has weathered every rack (the Civil War), has been led by the Captain (Lincoln), and is anchored safely (at peace).
2. The "fearful trip" that the ship has "weathered" is the Civil War.
3. Answers will differ. Suggested Response: A ship's captain is an appropriate metaphor for almost any leader. The captain can be a gently guiding force or a harsh authoritarian one as the occasion demands. You could not, however, use a ship's captain for a metaphor if the leader was actually a ship's captain.

**Challenge** You might have your more advanced students think of other metaphors that could effectively express the same feelings that Whitman's poem does.

**Alternative Assessment** Have your students select a person whom they admire and make a list of that person's admirable qualities. Help your students select a metaphor to convey their feelings about the person. Using "O Captain! My Captain!" as a model, have students write a poem in which they develop their metaphor to describe the person they admire.

You may assess their poems to determine their understanding of metaphor.

## Closure and Extension

### ANSWERS TO RESPONDING TO THE SELECTION
#### Your Response

1. Students will probably bring up feelings of sadness and loss. Have them point out words in the poem, such as the last line of each stanza—"fallen cold and dead"—that help create the feeling of despair.

### Recalling

2. The Captain is dead. It is extremely unfortunate because he has just brought the ship safely through and the people are exulting.

3. The poet calls the Captain father.

### Interpreting

4. The poet uses the pronoun *my* to refer to the Captain. This pronoun makes the Captain seem less distant and more personal.

5. At first the poet is unbelieving and then he is grief stricken. The mood of the poem is one of grief.

### Applying

6. Answers will differ. Suggested Response: The fate of a nation never rests entirely on one person because others will use their leadership abilities and take over.

# Jetliner

## Naoshi Koriyama

1
> now he takes his mark
> at the very farthest end of the runway
> looking straight ahead, eager, intense
> with his sharp eyes shining

2
> 5  he takes a deep, deep breath
> with his powerful lungs
> expanding his massive chest
> his burning heart beating like thunders

3
> then . . . after a few . . . tense moments . . . of pondering[1]
> 10  he roars at his utmost
> and slowly begins to jog
> kicking the dark earth hard
> and now he begins to run
> kicking the dark earth harder

4
> 15  then he dashes, dashes like mad, like mad
> howling, shouting, screaming, and roaring

5
> then with a most violent kick
> he shakes off the earth's pull
> softly lifting himself into the air
> 20  soaring higher and higher and higher still
> piercing the sea of clouds
> up into the chandelier[2] of stars

---

**1. pondering** (pän′ dər iŋ) *n.*: Thinking deeply; considering carefully.
**2. chandelier** (sḣan′ də lir′) *n.*: A lighting fixture hanging from a ceiling, with branches for several candles or electric bulbs.

## RESPONDING TO THE SELECTION

### Your Response

1. What images did this poem call up for you?

### Recalling

2. Where does "he" take his mark? Where does "he" wind up?

### Interpreting

3. Interpret lines 9–16. Describe what happened in this stanza. How is this poetic description different from a prose description?

### Applying

4. What is it about flight that stirs the imagination? Explain your answer.

## ANALYZING LITERATURE

### Understanding Personification

**Personification** is a figure of speech in which an animal, object, or idea is given human qualities. Personification gives us new ways of thinking about things.

Through personification, the poet provides us with a kind of "double vision." We see both a jetliner *and* a runner at the same time. We imagine a great machine in human terms.

1. What are the "sharp eyes shining" in line 4?
2. What are the "powerful lungs" in line 6? What is the "massive chest" in line 7?
3. Find three other examples of figurative language in this poem.

## THINKING AND WRITING

### Writing About Figurative Language

Review the definitions of figurative language: simile, metaphor, and personification. Be sure you understand the differences between these terms. Choose a simile or a metaphor from "Jetliner" and write an analysis of it. What two things are compared? How does the simile or metaphor add to your appreciation of both elements? Revise, making sure your analysis is clear. Then proofread your paper and share it with your classmates.

*Jetliner 537*

ends up in the sky, "piercing the sea of clouds up into the chandelier of stars."

**More About the Authors** For **William Carlos Williams,** a poem was an object that held a record of some direct worldly experience. In order to make his poems more available for his readers, Williams abandoned conventional methods of rhyme and meter. His poetic works varied from lyrics of fewer than a dozen words to his opus, *Paterson,* a book-length poem in five volumes. Williams also wrote short stories, essays, historical meditations, autobiographical works, and plays.

**Phyllis McGinley** praised the virtues of suburban living with humor. She also satirized the absurdities of life. She wrote two books of humorous essays, *The Province of the Heart* (1959) and *Sixpence in Her Shoe* (1964), as well as more than a dozen books for young people, including *The Horse Who Lived Upstairs* (1944) and *Sugar and Spice* (1960). McGinley once worked for an advertising agency. You might ask your students if they see any connection between writing advertising and writing poetry.

**Alfred, Lord Tennyson's** father was a clergyman in Lincolnshire, an area of England known for its lonely marshes. These marshes became the setting for many of Tennyson's poems. You might want to ask students how the message of poems written more than one hundred years ago can be as applicable today as when they were written.

# GUIDE FOR READING

## The Term

**William Carlos Williams** (1883–1963) was born in Rutherford, New Jersey. Williams spent most of his life in his hometown working as a pediatrician—a doctor who specializes in the care of children. Unlike traditional poets before him, Williams chose sights and incidents from his day-to-day life as the subjects for his poems. His language was also revolutionary in that it captured the essence of common speech. He avoided long, rhyming lines of poetry. His lines are short, Williams once suggested, "because of my nervous nature."

## Reflections Dental

**Phyllis McGinley** (1905–1978), born in Ontario, Oregon, began writing poetry when she was a schoolteacher in Utah. After several of her poems were accepted by New York magazines, she moved to New Rochelle, New York, to teach and to write. Her early poems were serious and even sad in tone. She turned to lighter subjects only after an editor urged her to avoid "the same sad song all . . . poets sing." *Times Three: Selected Verse From Three Decades, With Seventy New Poems* (1960) is the only book of light verse ever to be awarded a Pulitzer Prize.

## Ring Out, Wild Bells

**Alfred, Lord Tennyson** (1809–1892) was born in Somersby, Lincolnshire, England. Tennyson studied at Cambridge but never received a degree. He was an enthusiastic reader and worked hard to perfect his own craft as a poet. He composed short lyrics as well as longer works, such as *Idylls of the King* (a series of twelve narrative poems based on the King Arthur legends) and *In Memoriam* (a poem in memory of his closest friend, Arthur Henry Hallam). In 1850 Lord Tennyson was named poet laureate of England, serving in this capacity for more than forty years.

*538    Poetry*

## Objectives

1 To understand imagery that appeals to the senses
2 To understand how images create humor
3 To write a poem by following a pattern
4 To express individual interests and abilities through optional activities

## Support Material

**Teaching Portfolio**
Teacher Backup, p. 725
Usage and Mechanics Worksheet, p. 729
Vocabulary Check, p. 730
Analyzing Literature Worksheet, *Recognizing and Interpreting Imagery,* p. 732
Language Worksheet, *Recognizing Denotations and Connotations of Words,* p. 733

Selection Test, p. 734

**Listening to Literature**
"Reflections Dental"
"Ring Out, Wild Bells"

**Prentice Hall Literature Writing Studio**

## Imagery

**Imagery** is language that appeals to the senses. Imagery is the use of words and phrases to describe something so that a mental picture, or **image,** of it is created in your mind. Most images are visual, but often a writer may use language to suggest how something sounds, smells, tastes, or feels.

Images occur in all forms of writing, but they occur especially in poetry. For example, Phyllis McGinley portrays the teeth of television announcers as "rows of hybrid corn." Lord Tennyson evokes the *sound* of "wild bells" ringing "across the snow."

## Focus

Take a moment—right now—to observe the world around you. First, sit quietly for a few minutes and relax. Then answer the following questions:

What do you see? Describe it.
What do you hear? Describe it.
What do you smell? Describe it.
What do you taste? Describe it.
What can you touch? Describe it.

What you have written down are images, the building blocks of poetry. As you read the poems in this section, notice the different types of images that can be created.

## Vocabulary

Knowing the following words will help you as you read these poems.

**gleeful** (glē′ fəl) *adj.*: Merry (p. 542)

**hybrid** (hī′ brid) *adj.*: Here, grown from different varieties (p. 542)

**crooner** (krōōn′ ər) *n.*: Singer (p. 542)

**teem** (tēm) *v.*: Swarm (p. 542)

**strife** (strīf) *n.*: Conflict (p. 544)

**slander** (slan′ dər) *n.*: Lies (p. 544)

**Literary Focus** You can point out that the figures of speech (similes, metaphors, and personification) that students studied in the last three poems help to create vivid imagery.

**Prereading Focus** You might encourage students to observe the scene in their classroom and freewrite about images that come to mind. You might want students to share some of their best images with their classmates.

**Vocabulary** Your less advanced students will benefit from pronouncing and discussing the definitions of the vocabulary words together in class.

**Thematic Focus** In "The Term" Williams explores the mysterious nature of life itself by comparing a man's body to a large sheet of paper; in her rhyming lines about teeth, McGinley celebrates life's lighter side; and in "Ring Out, Wild Bells," Tennyson exhorts his readers to celebrate an important rite of passage, the ringing in of the new year. How does each of these poems illustrate that life involves continual movement and change?

**Audiocassettes** Use the **Listening to Literature** Audiocassette recordings of "Reflections Dental" and "Ring Out, Wild Bells" to enhance students' appreciation of imagery that appeals to the senses.

*Guide for Reading* 539

**Motivation/Prior Knowledge**
Have students list and explain why various objects are either animate or inanimate. Ask them if they have ever mistaken an inanimate object—such as a rock, a stump, or a scarecrow—for a real human. Tell students that in this lyric poem, the poet evokes the essential difference between animate and inanimate objects.

**Master Teacher Note** You might urge students to read and report on other Williams lyrics, such as "This Is Just to Say, "The Red Wheelbarrow," and "Flowers by the Sea."

**Purpose-Setting Question** What is the connection between a man and a rumpled sheet of paper?

1 **Discussion** What two things does the speaker compare?

2 **Critical Thinking and Reading** What can you infer about how a man would be affected by such an occurrence?

3 **Discussion** In what ways will it be "as it was before"?

**Reader's Response** What would you say to Williams if you could speak to him about the poem?

**Thematic Response** What mystery does Williams address in this poem? What makes the image of the car crushing the bulky brown form dramatic?

# The Term

## William Carlos Williams

1
A rumpled sheet
of brown paper
about the length

5  and apparent bulk
of a man was
rolling with the

wind slowly over
and over in
the street as

10  a car drove down
upon it and
crushed it to

2  the ground. Unlike
a man it rose
15  again rolling

3  with the wind over
and over to be as
it was before.

## RESPONDING TO THE SELECTION

### Your Response
1. What feelings or memories does this poem call up in you? Explain.

### Recalling
2. What happens in "The Term"?
3. What two things are being compared in the poem?

### Interpreting
4. What is significant about the fact that the brown paper rose again after the car crushed it? Explain your answer.
5. What phrase is repeated in the poem? What clue to the poem's meaning does this repetition provide?
6. What is the significance of the poem's title?

### Applying
7. Someone once called Williams "the master of the glimpse." What do you think this person meant?

540  Poetry

## Closure and Extension

### ANSWERS TO RESPONDING TO THE SELECTION

#### Your Response
1. Encourage students to share any personal associations or feelings that occur to them as they read the poem.

#### Recalling
2. A sheet of paper blows along a street in the wind; a car crushes it; it rolls through the street again.
3. Williams compares a sheet of paper and a man.

#### Interpreting
4. Suggested Response: The paper is not alive, so it cannot feel pain or die. A person would have been injured or killed by the car.
5. Suggested Response: The repetition of the phrase "rolling with the wind . . . over and over" underscores the idea that life contains natural cycles, changes, and movement.
6. Suggested Response: The title may refer to a lifetime or "the time for which something lasts."

#### Applying
7. Suggested Response: Williams was especially adept at evoking a momentary thought, feeling, or event in a poem.

**WINDY DAY IN ATCHISON, 1952**
*John Phillip Falter*
*University of Nebraska, Lincoln*

**Humanities Note**

Fine art, *Windy Day in Atcheson,* by John Falter. John Philip Falter (1910–1982) was an American illustrator and member of the prestigious Society of Illustrators. He received his art education at the Kansas City Art Institute and the Art Students League in New York City. Although this prolific artist produced hundreds of paintings and illustrations, he is best remembered for the 129 covers he created for the *Saturday Evening Post* magazine.

*Windy Day in Atcheson* is one of a series of paintings that recalls experiences from John Falter's early years in Nebraska. Here the tragicomic point of view that characterizes his work is seen in details such as the man's raising his car's convertible top while warily eyeing the sky, as well as the boy's racing to save a bundle of fresh wash.

As part of many leading museums' collections, Falter's work continues to delight the American public.

You may wish to use these questions to discuss the art:
1. Describe three things this artist uses to show the effect of the wind.
2. How does this artist's view of wind differ from the poet's?

## ANALYZING LITERATURE

### Understanding Imagery

The **imagery**—or language that appeals to the senses—in "The Term" is simple. There is one central image, that of a rumpled sheet of brown paper. It is crushed by a car, then bounces back to its original shape. The poem's meaning springs from the comparison of the brown paper to a man, which creates an image that is implied rather than stated directly.

1. In what ways is the rumpled sheet of brown paper like a man?

2. In what ways is the paper unlike a man?
3. What image is implied in the poem? Explain.

## LEARNING OPTION

**Writing.** Write a poem in the style of Williams, using simple, everyday language arranged in short lines. Choose your subject matter from your own experience. Share your poem with your classmates.

*The Term   541*

**ANSWERS TO ANALYZING LITERATURE**

1. It is approximately the same length and ''bulk'' of a man.
2. It resumes its original shape and movement after being crushed by a car.
3. The image of a man being crushed by a car is implied.

**LEARNING OPTION**

This activity will appeal to students interested in shaping a thought or an experience with language. You might extend the activity by having volunteers present poetry readings.

542

# Reflections Dental

## Phyllis McGinley

How pure, how beautiful, how fine
Do teeth on television shine!
No flutist flutes, no dancer twirls,
But comes equipped with matching pearls.
5  Gleeful announcers all are born
With sets like rows of hybrid corn.
Clowns, critics, clergy, commentators,
Ventriloquists and roller skaters,
M.C.s who beat their palms together,
10  The girl who diagrams the weather,
The crooner crooning for his supper—
All flash white treasures, lower and upper.
With miles of smiles the airwaves teem,
And each an orthodontist's[1] dream.
15  'Twould please my eye as gold a miser's—
One charmer with uncapped incisors.[2]

---

**1. orthodontist** (ôr' thə dän' tist) *n.*: A dentist who straightens teeth.
**2. incisors** (in sī' zərz) *n.*: The front teeth.

542  *Poetry*

**Reader's Response** Would a "charmer with uncapped incisors" be as charming? Why?

**Thematic Response** How would you describe this poem's tone? How do you know that the poet isn't expressing a serious theme?

**Multicultural Focus** Explain to students that notions of beauty may vary widely among different cultures. For example, it is thought stylish among the Masai of Kenya to display earlobes that have been stretched and elongated—sometimes down to the shoulder.

If fashions vary among places and cultures, so do some of the expressions, gestures, and signs used to communicate. An American asking for directions might be surprised to elicit only a frown from the Masai. However, the person may be using his or her lips to point the way rather than to convey unhappiness.

Have students give specific examples to illustrate that "beauty is in the eye of the beholder." Have them explain what they think a particular beholder finds beautiful about an object.

## RESPONDING TO THE SELECTION

### Your Response

1. Why do you think our society sets such a high value on having straight, white teeth? How important do you think it is? Why?

### Recalling

2. What has the poet observed about people on television?
3. Name three groups of people that the poet mentions.
4. What are two things to which she compares teeth?

### Interpreting

5. The poet uses alliteration, the repetition of initial consonant sounds, to help her poke fun at her topic. For example, look at the repetition of the *c* sound in line 7. Find two other examples of alliteration in the poem. Explain how each of these helps create a humorous effect.
6. A *reflection* is usually a serious thinking about or consideration of a topic. Why is the title of this poem humorous?

### Applying

7. Why do you think some viewers expect people on television to look perfect?

## ANALYZING LITERATURE

### Understanding Humorous Images

Images can be humorous in themselves if they are presented or put together in surprising ways. They can also be funny if they are exaggerated. Phyllis McGinley pictures an endless line of gleaming teeth: "miles of smiles." This is both a comical exaggeration and an unusual view of the behavior of television personalities.

1. List two other exaggerations the author uses.
2. What unusual image combinations occur in lines 3–6?

## LEARNING OPTION

**Writing.** Write a poem in the style of McGinley's about some other "perfect" aspect of television personalities, such as their hair or their clothes. Try to use vivid images to describe these perfect aspects. You may wish to imitate the rhyming pattern and humorous tone of "Reflections Dental." Share your poem with your classmates.

*Reflections Dental   543*

**Motivation/Prior Knowledge**
Most New Year's resolutions are personal goals. Have students imagine that someone was going to make a list of New Year's resolutions for the whole world. What are some of the resolutions or goals that a person might include on such a list?

**Master Teacher Note** Your more **advanced** students might benefit from a discussion of the meter and rhyme pattern of "Ring Out, Wild Bells." The poem is in iambic (one unaccented syllable followed by one accented one) tetrameter (four beats per line) and has a rhyme scheme of *a b b a*.

**Purpose-Setting Question** What does Tennyson hope the new year will bring?

1 **Discussion** To what does this line refer?

2 **Discussion** In this line what wish is expressed for the new year?

3 **Discussion** What three improvements are asked for in this stanza?

4 **Discussion** To what aspect of life do these lines refer?

5 **Discussion** What is meant by this line?

**Reader's Response** Did the poem involve your emotions? Which of Tennyson's images or topics touched a chord in you?

**Thematic Response** In what way is New Year's Day a rite of passage? How is it an opportunity to grow or change?

**Alternative Assessment** You may vary the Thinking and Writing assignment as follows: Have students complete one of the composition or Alternate Composition Assignments on pages 726, 727, and 728 of the Teaching Portfolio.

# Ring Out, Wild Bells

### Alfred, Lord Tennyson

Ring out, wild bells, to the wild sky,
   The flying cloud, the frosty light:
   The year is dying in the night;
Ring out, wild bells, and let him die.

5 Ring out the old, ring in the new,
   Ring, happy bells, across the snow:
   The year is going, let him go;
Ring out the false, ring in the true.

Ring out the grief that saps[1] the mind,
10    For those that here we see no more;
   Ring out the feud of rich and poor,
Ring in redress[2] to all mankind.

Ring out a slowly dying cause,
   And ancient forms of party strife;
15    Ring in the nobler modes[3] of life,
With sweeter manners, purer laws.

Ring out the want, the care, the sin,
   The faithless coldness of the times;
   Ring out, ring out thy mournful rhymes,
20 But ring the fuller minstrel[4] in.

Ring out false pride in place and blood,
   The civic[5] slander and the spite;
   Ring in the love of truth and right,
Ring in the common love of good.

25 Ring out old shapes of foul disease;
   Ring out the narrowing lust of gold;
   Ring out the thousand wars of old,
Ring in the thousand years of peace.

---

**1. saps** (saps) *v.*: Drains; exhausts.
**2. redress** (rē′ dres) *n.*: The righting of wrongs.
**3. modes** (mōdz) *n.*: Ways; forms.
**4. fuller minstrel** (min′ strəl) *n.*: A singer of the highest rank.
**5. civic** (siv′ ik) *adj.*: Of a city.

# RESPONDING TO THE SELECTION

## Your Response

1. Describe the emotions you feel on New Year's Eve.

## Recalling

2. This poem celebrates the new year. What does the poet wish to "ring out"? What does he wish to "ring in"?

## Interpreting

3. What does he hope for the future? Support your answer.
4. What is this poem about in addition to the passing of the old year? What is its theme?
5. Would you describe this poem as sad and pessimistic, or hopeful and optimistic? Find details to support your answer.

## Applying

6. Why does the start of a new year often make people feel hopeful?

# THINKING AND WRITING

## Writing a Patterned Poem

Write a poem that expresses your wishes for the new year. Begin by reviewing "Ring Out, Wild Bells." Take note of the *pattern* of the poem, especially the way every negative thing is balanced by something positive. Compose three stanzas following Tennyson's example. Tell what you would like to "ring out" and "ring in." Proofread your poem and share it with your classmates.

# LEARNING OPTION

**Multicultural Activity** Conduct an informal interview with someone from a different cultural background to find out about his or her New Year celebration. On what day do they mark the passing of an old year? What festivities take place? What qualities does the celebration share with your own?

*Ring Out, Wild Bells* 545

## Closure and Extension

### ANSWERS TO RESPONDING TO THE SELECTION

#### Your Response

1. Encourage students to respond as honestly as possible. They might mention sadness or worry as well as happiness or hopefulness.

#### Recalling

2. The poet wishes to ring out everything that is old and bad, such as the false, grief, the feud between rich and poor, a dying cause, party strife, want, care, sin, faithless coldness, mournful rhymes, false pride in station and family, civic slander, spite, disease, lust of gold, and the thousand wars of old. The poet wishes to ring in all that is good, such as the true, redress to all mankind, nobler modes of life, sweeter manners, purer laws, the fuller minstrel, love of truth and right, the common love of good, and the thousand years of peace.

#### Interpreting

3. The poet hopes only good for the future, including redress for all mankind, sweeter manners, purer laws, and so on.
4. Answers will differ. Suggested Response: This poem is about improving society. The theme of the poem seems to be that humans can improve their circumstances.
5. This poem is hopeful and optimistic because it implies that humans can rid the world of grief, the feud between the rich and poor, party strife, and so on.

#### Applying

6. Answers will differ. Suggested Response: The start of a new year often makes people feel hopeful because it seems to offer the opportunity to start anew.

#### THINKING AND WRITING

**Software** If students are working on computers, they might find it helpful to begin the assignment by using the **Writer's Helper** activities *Idea Wheel* and *Brainstorms.*

#### LEARNING OPTION

Students with interest in researching other cultures will enjoy this activity. You might vary the activity by having students interview grandparents or other elders about how their New Year's Day celebrations may have changed over the years.

## Preparation

**More About the Authors Ricardo Sánchez** has forged a distinguished career as a writer, an educator, and a social reformer. He has been a college professor in his native El Paso and at state universities in Wisconsin, Massachusetts, and Utah. Early in his career, he worked to improve health conditions for migrant families in Colorado. More recently he has developed both television programs and audio recordings to celebrate and promote Chicano culture.

After his graduation from college in California in 1923, **Arna Bontemps** traveled to New York City and soon became one of the most important writers of the Harlem Renaissance. His early poems appeared in leading magazines such as *The Crisis*. In later years Bontemps mostly wrote prose works and edited anthologies. His books include *Lonesome Boy, Frederick Douglass, 100 Years of Negro Freedom,* and *American Negro Poetry.*

**Evelyn Tooley Hunt** says, "I like to write from the inside of some culture other than my own." She has done this by writing "Man With a Word," which first appeared in the *Chicago Jewish Forum* (although she is not Jewish), by writing her own variation of haiku under the pen name of Tao-Li (although she is not Chinese), and by writing "Taught Me Purple," which first appeared in *Negro Digest* (although she is not black). You might ask your students if they think it is ever possible to adopt completely a culture not your own.

## Old Man

**Ricardo Sánchez** (1941–      ), born in a poor neighborhood of El Paso, Texas, has roots in both the Spanish-Mexican and North American cultures. This rich heritage is reflected in his poems, essays, and other writings. The overriding theme of most of his work is the attempt to build a firm sense of identity out of dual cultural roots. Sánchez combines English and Spanish in his writing, describing the experience as "flowing in and out of the linguistic worlds that I am able to inhabit simultaneously—creating thus a new world view that contains both."

## Southern Mansion

**Arna Bontemps** (1902–1973), born in Louisiana, was the son of a brick mason and a teacher. For more than twenty years, he served on the faculty of Fisk College in Nashville, Tennessee, while pursuing a brilliant career as an editor, a writer, a librarian, a literary critic, and a teacher. Bontemps described his vocation this way: ". . . to write something about the changes I have seen in my lifetime, and about the Negro's awakening and regeneration. That is my theme, and this is where the main action is."

## Taught Me Purple

**Evelyn Tooley Hunt** (1904–      ) was born in Hamburg, New York. In 1926 she graduated from William Smith College in Geneva, New York, where she had been an editor of the literary magazine. She received the Sidney Lanier Memorial Award for her first collection of poems, *Look Again, Adam,* published in 1961. Hunt's interest in different cultures is demonstrated in her writing. She is best known for her variations of haiku, a type of Asian poetry, which she writes under the pen name of Tao-Li. In "Taught Me Purple," Hunt writes of the lessons learned from a mother.

546   Poetry

## Objectives

1  To interpret symbols carefully
2  To write a poem about a symbol
3  To write an analysis of a symbol

## Support Material

**Teaching Portfolio**
Teacher Backup, pp. 737–740
Usage and Mechanics Worksheet, p. 741
Vocabulary Check, p. 742
Analyzing Literature Worksheet, *Interpreting Symbols Carefully,* p. 743
Language Worksheet, *Understanding Synonyms and Antonyms,* p. 744

Selection Test, pp. 745–746

**Listening to Literature**
"Taught Me Purple"

**Prentice Hall Literature Writing Process Guide**

## Symbols

A **symbol** is any person, place, or thing that has a meaning in itself and that also stands for something else. A symbol can be another living thing, an object, a situation, or an action. Usually symbols stand for ideas or qualities. You are probably familiar with certain common symbols: a flag symbolizing a nation; a dove symbolizing peace; the five interlocking rings (each ring symbolizing a continent) symbolizing the Olympic Games.

Symbols are a kind of figurative language. Like simile, metaphor, and personification, a symbol enables a writer to express a complicated idea or a deep feeling in few words, sometimes in a single image. For example, in "Old Man" the image of an old man's deeply wrinkled face is symbolic of the speaker's rich heritage.

## Focus

Choose one of the visual symbols below and freewrite for five minutes about what the symbol means to you. What does the symbol remind you of? Where would you expect to see it? Do you think it means the same thing for everyone? Why or why not?

## Vocabulary

Knowing the following words will help you as you read these poems.

**rivulets** (riv′ yōō lits) *n.*: Little streams (p. 548)

**furrows** (fur′ ōz) *n.*: Deep wrinkles (p. 548)

**stoic** (stō′ ik) *adj.*: Calm and unbothered in spite of suffering (p. 549)

**tenement** (ten′ ə mənt) *n.*: Here, a rundown apartment building (p. 551)

**molding** (mōl′ diŋ) *n.*: Ornamental woodwork that projects from the walls of a room (p. 551)

# Old Man

Ricardo Sánchez

*remembrance (smiles/hurts sweetly)*
October 8, 1972

old man
with brown skin
talking of past
    when being shepherd
    in utah, nevada, colorado and new mexico    5
was life lived freely;

old man,
    grandfather,
wise with time
running rivulets on face,    10

deep, rich furrows,
    each one a legacy,
deep, rich memories
of life . . .
    "you are indio,[1]    15
        among other things,"
    he would tell me
        during nights spent
so long ago
        amidst familial gatherings    20
    in albuquerque . . .

old man, loved and respected,
he would speak sometimes
of pueblos,[2]

---

**1. indio** (ēn' dyō) *n.*: Indian, Native American.
**2. pueblos** (pweb' lōz) *n.*: Here, Native American towns in central and northern New Mexico.

**PORTRAIT OF VULNERABILITY**
*Diogenes Ballester*
Courtesy of the Artist

san juan, santa clara,
  and even santo domingo,
and his family, he would say,
came from there:
  some of our blood was here,
  he would say,
  before the coming of coronado,[3]
other of our blood
  came with los españoles,[4]
and the mixture
was rich,
  though often painful . . .

old man,
who knew earth
  by its awesome aromas
and who felt                                          40
the heated sweetness
  of chile verde[5]
by his supple touch,
gone into dust is your body
  with its stoic look and resolution,        45
but your reality, old man, lives on
in a mindsoul touched by you . . .

Old Man . . .

_____
**3. coronado** (kŏ̂ rŏ̂ nă′ dŏ̂): Coronado was a Spaniard who, in the sixteenth century, explored what is today the American Southwest.
**4. los españoles** (lŏs es pä nyŏl′ es) *n.*: The Spaniards.

_____
**5. chile verde** (chĕ′ le vehr′ de) *n.*: Green pepper.

## RESPONDING TO THE SELECTION

### Your Response
1. Which of the old man's qualities do you admire most? Why?

### Recalling
2. Whom is the speaker of the poem addressing?
3. Name the two "bloods" that are mixed in the old man and the speaker.

### Interpreting
4. In your own words, explain the phrase "remembrance (smiles/hurts sweetly)."
5. In what ways is the mixture of blood "rich"? In what ways is it "painful"?
6. What type of knowledge did the old man have that the speaker especially admires?
7. What is the meaning of lines 46–47? How are these lines related to the theme of the poem?

### Applying
8. Whose "reality" lives on in your "mindsoul"? Why?

## ANALYZING LITERATURE

### Understanding Symbolism

A **symbol** is something that has meaning in itself and also stands for something else. A symbol may mean something particular to the poet but not to everyone. To understand what a symbol means, you must think about it in relation to the words and ideas that surround it. For example, the image of an old man whose skin is deeply wrinkled could stand for many things. In the poem "Old Man," however, the old man symbolizes the speaker's heritage.

1. What are the furrows on the old man's face referred to as?
2. What parallel relationship is created by the repetition of the phrase "deep, rich" in lines 11 and 13? What is the effect of this parallel relationship?
3. What else is described as rich? What is the effect of the repetition of the word *rich*?

*Old Man* 549

### 5 Literary Focus: Symbolism
How does the speaker's use of Spanish words and names affect the poem?

### 6 Critical Thinking and Reading
What contrast does the speaker draw in these lines? What comparison does the speaker imply?

**Reader's Response** What feelings do you have at the end of the poem? Do you find the character of the grandfather admirable? Why or why not?

**Thematic Response** What admirable traits does the speaker identify in his grandfather? Which of the old man's physical characteristics does the speaker appreciate?

_____
es the knowledge borne of years spent working and living close to nature.
7. Suggested Response: These lines indicate that some of the old man's sensibility or essence has been passed on to the speaker. The speaker's appreciation is such that he consciously carries on his grandfather's legacy.

### Applying
8. Answers will differ. Encourage students to share their responses with one or more classmates or to write them in a journal.

### ANSWERS TO ANALYZING LITERATURE

1. The speaker refers to them as "deep, rich memories of life" and legacies.
2. Suggested Response: The repetition creates a parallel relationship between "furrows" and "memories." It gives the furrows symbolic resonance: They are both furrows and representations of past experiences.
3. The mixture of bloods is described as "rich." It connects images of the past with those of the present.

_____
549

## Closure and Extension

### ANSWERS TO RESPONDING TO THE SELECTION
#### Your Response
1. Invite students to choose one quality and explain why they respond to it with admiration.

#### Recalling
2. The speaker is addressing his grandfather.
3. The two "bloods" are those from

the pueblos of northern New Mexico and from Spain.

#### Interpreting
4. Suggested Response: The speaker seems to be saying that memory can bring on feelings of both joy and pain.
5. Suggested Response: The mixture is rich because it traces an old and varied heritage; it could be painful because of the difficult lives of the speaker's forebears.
6. Suggested Response: He possess-

**Motivation/Prior Knowledge**
Have students think about a place or building they know that is filled with a sense of history. How would they describe the atmosphere of the place? What people lived or worked in the place in the past? How do they feel when they stand in or near the place? Tell students that this poem concerns a place in which the experiences of previous generations seem to linger in the air.

**Purpose-Setting Question** What happened years ago on the grounds of this mansion?

1 **Discussion** Who are these ghosts? What associations do you make with the image "marble steps"?

2 **Literary Focus: Symbol** What does this music represent? Who is it being played for?

3 **Literary Focus: Symbol** In what way does the contrast between these two sounds underscore the poem's theme?

4 **Discussion** Whose hand do you think this is? Why?

5 **Literary Focus: Symbol** What image does Bontemps use symbolically in this line? What meanings does the symbol suggest to you?

**Reader's Response** What emotions does the poem elicit in you? What are your thoughts about the ghosts of dead men and their ladies?

**Thematic Response** What injustices have been done on the grounds of this southern mansion? Who are the ghosts?

# Southern Mansion

## Arna Bontemps

**1**
Poplars[1] are standing there still as death
And ghosts of dead men
Meet their ladies walking
Two by two beneath the shade
5   And standing on the marble steps.

**2**
There is a sound of music echoing
Through the open door
And in the field there is

**3**
Another sound tinkling in the cotton:
10   Chains of bondmen[2] dragging on the ground.

**4**
The years go back with an iron clank,
A hand is on the gate,
A dry leaf trembles on the wall.
Ghosts are walking.

**5** 15   They have broken roses down
And poplars stand there still as death.

---

**1. Poplars** (păp′ lərz) *n.*: Trees of the willow family with soft wood and flowers.
**2. bondmen** (bănd′ men) *n.*: Slaves.

## RESPONDING TO THE SELECTION

### Your Response
1. Which image in the poem is the most powerful? Why?

### Recalling
2. What two sounds are heard in the poem?

### Interpreting
3. What do you think the "roses" in line 15 represent?
4. What is the effect of the repetition of line 1 at the end of the poem?
5. Explain the meaning of the poem in your own words.

550 *Poetry*

### Applying
6. How is a southern mansion an appropriate symbol for social conditions before the Civil War?

## THINKING AND WRITING

### Writing About a Symbol
Write a poem about a place that has symbolic significance for you. Use figurative language to describe the place and the feelings you have about it. Exchange first drafts with a partner and respond to each other's work. Then use your partner's suggestions as you revise.

## Closure and Extension

### ANSWERS TO RESPONDING TO THE SELECTION
*Your Response*
1. Insist that students be specific about a single image. Encourage them to explain what thoughts and feelings the image elicits in them.

*Recalling*
2. There is "a sound of music" and a "sound tinkling in the cotton."

*Interpreting*
3. Suggested Response: The roses represent beauty and right.
4. Suggested Response: The repetition creates an echo—a haunting effect that is an appropriate counterpart to images of ghosts and memories.
5. Suggested Response: The poem is a mournful meditation on the sins committed in a mansion in years past. For the speaker the pain and degradation of slavery remain in the air and grounds of the estate despite the passage of time.

*Applying*
6. Suggested Response: The southern mansion connotes the plantation system that thrived on slavery and dominated the South before the Civil War.

### THINKING AND WRITING
◆ **Software** If your students are working on computers, they might find it helpful to begin the assignment by using the **Writer's Helper** activities *Associations* and *Five W's*.

# Taught Me Purple

Evelyn Tooley Hunt

My mother taught me purple
    Although she never wore it.
Wash-gray was her circle,
    The tenement her orbit.

5  My mother taught me golden
    And held me up to see it,
Above the broken molding,
    Beyond the filthy street.

    My mother reached for beauty
10    And for its lack she died,
Who knew so much of duty
    She could not teach me pride.

1

2

3

4

5

6

SUMMER MILLINERY, 1915
*Charles W. Hawthorne*
*Chrysler Museum*

*Taught Me Purple* 551

## Humanities Note

Fine art, *Summer Millinery*, by Charles Webster Hawthorne (1872–1930). Hawthorne founded and directed the Cape Cod School of Art at Provincetown, Massachusetts. Although many of his paintings are of people engaged in commercial fishing off the Massachusetts coast, this particular painting shows a black woman making a hat. You might want to see how many of your students are familiar with the term *millinery*.

In what way does the illustration capture the message or theme of the poem?

Audiocassette To help students appreciate the tone of Hunt's poem, have them listen to the recording of "Taught Me Purple" (Side 4) on the **Listening to Literature** Audiocassettes. Have them notice how the reader conveys a note of sadness to the speaker's voice.

## Presentation

**Motivation/Prior Knowledge**
Discuss the different ways in which things can be taught. How is learning by following someone's example different from learning by listening to someone giving an explanation?

**Master Teacher Note** You might want to explain to students how purple became known as the color of royalty. In ancient times the purple dyes were extremely rare and costly, so only royalty could wear purple clothes.

**Purpose-Setting Question** What does the title of the poem mean?

1 **Literary Focus** How could the mother teach the child purple if she never wore it?

2 **Discussion** Where do the mother and child live?

3 **Literary Focus** To what do you think "golden" refers?

4 **Discussion** Where are the "broken molding" and "filthy street"?

5 **Literary Focus** For what does the mother yearn? Does she ever achieve what she wants?

6 **Discussion** Why is the mother unable to teach the child pride?

**Challenge** This poem presents a series of contrasting symbols. What are they, and to what do they refer?

**Challenge** You might want to have your more advanced students write poems using colors as symbols.

**Reader's Response** How is beauty beyond everyone's reach? How is it beyond your reach?

**Thematic Response** How does the mother bring beauty into the world for her daughter? What is the most important thing the mother creates?

## Your Response

1. If students are hesitant about answering, encourage them to determine what thing is important to teach a child. Then ask them if that lesson can be associated with a particular color.

### Recalling

2. The poet says her mother taught her purple and golden.
3. A lack of beauty causes the mother to die.

### Interpreting

4. The color purple symbolizes the beauty and wealth the world has to offer. The color gray symbolizes the lack of beauty and wealth and life as mere drab existence. Golden is another symbol of what was possible in life beyond the restrictions of poverty.
5. The mother's surroundings were drab and poor. The surroundings were rundown and filthy. The mother's goals were beauty and an interesting life without poverty.
6. The mother was so busy doing her duty in her difficult circumstances that she never developed pride. Therefore, she never taught the child pride.
7. The theme of this poem is that despite poverty people can find beauty even in unlikely places.

### Applying

8. The color red usually symbolizes the quality of courage. The red in the flag of the United States symbolizes courage. It is an effective symbol because its meaning is recognized by many people.

### THINKING AND WRITING

**Writing Transparency** A model may help students with their analytical essay. Use the Responding to Literature model in **Transparencies for Writing.**

**Publishing Student Writing** Your students' essays analyzing the use of symbols can be posted on the bulletin board or made avail-

# RESPONDING TO THE SELECTION

## Your Response

1. If you had to teach a child a color, what color would it be and why?

## Recalling

2. What two things does the poet say her mother taught her?
3. What lack causes the mother to die?

## Interpreting

4. What do the colors purple, gray, and golden symbolize?
5. Compare and contrast the mother's surroundings with her goals.
6. Why could the mother not teach the daughter pride?

7. What is the theme of this poem?

## Applying

8. We often use colors to symbolize qualities. What does the color red usually symbolize? Why is this symbol effective?

# THINKING AND WRITING

## Writing About Symbolism

Write an essay analyzing the use of symbols in "Taught Me Purple." First think of the meaning of the symbols. Then consider their effect on the theme. Write a first draft of your essay. When you revise, make sure your analysis is clear and well organized. Proofread your essay and share it with your classmates.

# MULTICULTURAL CONNECTION

## Color Symbolism and Cultural Attitudes

As you read "Taught Me Purple," think about the feelings that various colors evoke. Colors are often divided into "warm" and "cold" ones. Many Americans and Europeans think of red, orange, yellow, and brown hues as "warm," and the blues, greens, and grays as "cold."

In addition, you are probably familiar with the expressions in English that use colors metaphorically. When we're sad, we feel blue. When we're jealous, we go green with envy. When we're not sure of something, we say it occupies a gray area. When an issue is clear, we call it a black-and-white issue. In our daily lives, color enlivens our language and affects our feelings. Colors, however, mean different things in different parts of the world.

**Different cultural attitudes.** Often, the same color may have opposite meanings. For

example, black has become the color for mourning in the West, whereas in Ethiopia and other cultures, it signals good fortune. While white symbolizes innocence and purity in the West and is the traditional color worn by brides, it is the color used in funerals and mourning in countries like Japan, Korea, India, and China.

In different cultures, red has various meanings. In America, stop signs and police sirens are red to warn us of danger. In Russia, on the other hand, red symbolizes beauty, while in China and India, it is the color worn by brides and at New Year's festivals. It has still another meaning in Africa, where it is worn for funerals.

### Exploring On Your Own

Choose several colors and research what these colors symbolize in various cultures. Then create a "color wheel" to summarize your findings. This wheel should enable someone to select a color and learn what it symbolizes in different places.

able in a booklet. Students can then read others' papers to broaden their understanding of symbols.

If your students write the poems suggested in the Challenge activity, you might add them to booklets of creative writing they are collecting. Some of the better poems could also be submitted to your school newspaper or literary magazine.

**Multicultural Connection** Explain that various cultures may attribute different meanings to colors. In China, for example, bright gold, copper, orange, and red represent good luck and are abundant during the New Year.

Color combinations also vary in significance according to the culture. For Americans red, white, and blue may stir patriotic feelings; whereas for the citizens of the Republic of Ireland, green may inspire those feelings.

Remind students that colors are used to represent qualities or emotions ("feeling blue" or "seeing red"), as well as to categorize humans by race. Ask students to consider how the words *black, white, red,* and *yellow* have been used to characterize people racially.

Have students free-associate about various colors. Ask them why they endow a color with a particular significance.

# Lyric Poetry

**INVITATION TO THE SIDESHOW (LA PARADE)**
*Georges Pierre Seurat*
*The Metropolitan Museum of Art*

## Humanities Note

Fine art, *Invitation to the Side-show,* 1888, by Georges Seurat. Georges Seurat (1859–1891) was a French Post-Impressionist painter who invented Pointillism, a painting system of applying pure color in tiny dots that are visually blended when viewed from a distance. Seurat was educated in academic art at the École des Beaux-Arts in Paris. Although he admired the work of the Impressionists, he sought to establish his own, more ordered, style of painting. His Pointillist technique imbued his canvases with shimmering light and subtle, evocative atmosphere.

The painting *Invitation to the Sideshow* is clearly a forerunner of more modern styles of painting. The picture plane is organized into rigid geometric shapes that sacrifice warmth for precision. The colors are somber but rich in tone. The artificial light seems to scintillate in a light mist, creating a mood of mystery. The subtle shading of the faces and the formal composition show the intense planning that went into this work. Although circus entertainers are a favorite Impressionist theme, Seurat's lyrical handling of the subject sets his art apart from Impressionism.

**Master Teacher Note** To introduce lyric poetry, place Art Transparency 11, *Spring* by Ben Shahn, from the Teaching Portfolio, on the overhead projector. Explain that lyric poetry creates a mood, rather than tells a story. It expresses the poet's thoughts and feelings through descriptive words and musical rhythm. Discuss with students what mood this painting conveys. Discuss whether a painting, like this one, could be considered lyrical, and why.

**More About the Author** Tell students that **Lew Sarett** served as a woodsman, guide, and U.S. Ranger in the Northwest for several months each year over a long period of time. Ask them how such experience might be valuable for a nature poet.

**Langston Hughes** was involved in the Harlem Renaissance. Point out to students that Harlem became a cultural center for blacks who had come North during World War I (1914–1918) looking for jobs. Ask students to consider why a flowering of creativity might occur in a community of recently uprooted people living in a large city.

Tell students that **Robert Frost** lived in New England for most of his life, working as a farmer and schoolteacher until he became famous. Almost all of his poems have a New England setting. What advantages and disadvantages are there in getting to know and writing about one particular region?

**Alice Walker's** novel *The Color Purple* was made into a major motion picture. Ask students to consider what problems an author might face in adapting his or her novel for the movies.

# GUIDE FOR READING

## Four Little Foxes

**Lew Sarett** (1888–1954) first began working at age twelve to support his family in Chicago. It was then that he developed a love for nature, which is shown in poems like "Four Little Foxes." Some of Sarett's poems echo the rhythms of Native American music and folklore. "Much of whatever is joyous and significant in life, timeless, true, and peculiarly American," he wrote, "tends to be rooted in the wild earth of America."

## Harlem Night Song

**Langston Hughes** (1902–1967) was part of the Harlem Renaissance of the 1920's—a period of intense creativity among African American writers and artists living in the northern part of New York City. In his poems, short stories, and songs, Hughes wrote about the sorrows and joys of ordinary African Americans. "Harlem Night Song" shows how Hughes incorporated some aspects of African American music into his songs and poems.

## Blue-Butterfly Day

**Robert Frost** (1874–1963) was an unofficial poet laureate of the United States. Born in San Francisco, he moved to New England at age ten. He did not attend college but worked in a Massachusetts textile mill and began writing poetry. Frost's poetry was awarded the Pulitzer Prize four times. He read his poem "The Gift Outright" at the 1961 inauguration of President John F. Kennedy. In poems like "Blue-Butterfly Day," Frost deals with the relationship between people and nature.

## For My Sister Molly Who in the Fifties

**Alice Walker** (1944–     ), the youngest of eight children, grew up in Georgia, where her parents were sharecroppers. Her novel *The Color Purple* is based on true stories about her great-grandmother and on research Walker did at Spelman College. Many of Walker's works deal with her African American heritage. This interest can be seen in "For My Sister Molly Who in the Fifties," which is from *Revolutionary Petunias and Other Poems*.

554    Poetry

## Objectives

1 To understand the features of lyric poetry
2 To make inferences about the mood of a lyric poem
3 To write a lyric poem

## Support Material

**Teaching Portfolio**
Teacher Backup, p. 747
Usage and Mechanics Worksheet, p. 751
Vocabulary Check, p. 752
Critical Thinking and Reading Worksheet, *Making Inferences About Mood,* p. 753
Language Worksheet, *Recognizing Sensory Language,* p. 754
Selection Test, p. 755

## Listening to Literature

"Four Little Foxes," "Harlem Night Song," "Blue-Butterfly Day," "For My Sister Molly Who in the Fifties"

**Prentice Hall Literature Writing Studio**

## Lyric Poetry

Lyric poetry is poetry that expresses the poet's thoughts and feelings. It does not tell a story, as narrative poetry does, but creates a mood through vivid images—or pictures—descriptive words, and the musical quality of the lines. These means of creating mood help you remember the poet's thoughts and feelings, and "see" or "hear" the image the poet presents. Lyric poems may be made up of regular stanzas, like "Four Little Foxes," or they may have uneven stanzas, like "Harlem Night Song."

Originally, a lyric was a poem that was sung and accompanied by a lyre; today, lyric poetry reflects this musical heritage.

## Focus

Lyric poems are very much like songs. Working with several classmates, recall some of your favorite popular songs and write down their words. Then figure out what appeals to you about these song lyrics. Are the sounds of the words catchy? Do the words express emotions that you share? Do they present vivid images? Answer these questions by completing a chart like the one that follows, and then keep your ideas in mind as you read the lyric poems in this section.

| Song Lyrics | Appeal of Lyrics |
| --- | --- |
| | Emotions:<br>Ideas:<br>Images:<br>Sounds: |

## Vocabulary

Knowing the following words will help you as you read these poems.

**forbear** (fôr ber') *v.*: To refrain from (p. 556)

**suckled** (suk' 'ld) *v.*: Sucked at the breast (p. 556)

**rampant** (ram' pənt) *adj.*: Violent and uncontrollable (p. 556)

*Guide for Reading* 555

**Literary Focus** You may want to explain to students what is meant by the "musical quality" of lyric poetry. Poets no longer sing their songs to the accompaniment of a lyre, so they must create their own music from the sounds and stressed syllables of words. Read to students the following lines from Edgar Allan Poe's "Annabel Lee":

"It was many and many a year ago/In a kingdom by the sea./That a maiden there lived whom you may know/By the name of Annabel Lee;—/And this maiden she lived with no other thought/Than to love and be loved by me."

Poe creates the haunting music of these lines with end rhymes ("sea"-"Lee"-"me"; "ago"-"know"), repetitions ("many and many"; "a maiden there lived" and "this maiden she lived"), pleasing sounds (the long *a* sound in lines 2 and 3: ma*i*den-may-name), and a regular rhythmic pattern (lines of four beats and three beats alternating).

**Prereading Focus** Some students may work better in pairs than in larger groups. You might check to see if more than one student chooses the same song. These students might benefit from working together.

**Vocabulary** Ask **less advanced** students to read aloud the words and definitions.

Have **more advanced** students find five synonyms for *rampant* in a thesaurus. Also have them look up the word *forebear* and distinguish it from its homophone *forbear*.

🎧 **Audiocassettes** Use the **Listening to Literature** Audiocassette recordings of "Four Little Foxes," "Harlem Night Song," "Blue-Butterfly Day," and "For My Sister Molly Who in the Fifties" (Side 4) to illustrate the poems' musical qualities. Ask students to listen also for the mood established by each poem's reader.

**Thematic Focus** The speaker in "Four Little Foxes" celebrates nature and the wondrous creatures of the earth; in "Harlem Night Song," Hughes celebrates a person's appreciation of a city and a friend; in "Blue-Butterfly Day" Frost praises one of the planet's most delightful living things; and in "For My Sister Molly Who in the Fifties," Walker offers a host of vivid reasons why she appreciates her sibling. Ask students to compare the variety of people, situations, and things in nature they appreciate with those celebrated by the poets in this group of poems.

# Four Little Foxes

## Lew Sarett

**1**

Speak gently, Spring, and make no sudden sound;
For in my windy valley, yesterday I found
New-born foxes squirming on the ground—
    Speak gently.

**2**

5  Walk softly, March, forbear the bitter blow;
Her feet within a trap, her blood upon the snow,
The four little foxes saw their mother go—
    Walk softly.

Go lightly, Spring, oh, give them no alarm;
10  When I covered them with boughs to shelter them from harm,
The thin blue foxes suckled at my arm—
    Go lightly.

**3**

Step softly, March, with your rampant hurricane;
Nuzzling one another, and whimpering with pain,
15  The new little foxes are shivering in the rain—
    Step softly.

## RESPONDING TO THE SELECTION

### Your Response

1. What emotions does the poem make you feel toward the little foxes?
2. If you were one of the foxes, what would you be feeling?

### Recalling

3. What happened to the newborn foxes' mother?
4. What does the poet do to protect the foxes?

### Interpreting

5. To what two things does the phrase "bitter blow" in line 5 refer?

6. Why does the poet plead with nature rather than with people to protect the animals?
7. What two kinds of relationships between people and nature are presented in the poem?

### Applying

8. What is it about helpless creatures that makes us want to protect them? What other helpless creatures arouse strong protective feelings in people?

## ANALYZING LITERATURE

### Understanding Lyric Poetry

**Lyric poetry** expresses the poet's thoughts and feelings about a topic through vivid images and musical language.

In "Four Little Foxes," the phrase "The thin blue foxes suckled at my arm—" creates the vivid image of helpless creatures so hungry that they turn to a stranger's arm for milk.

1. What feeling does the image "Her feet within a trap, her blood upon the snow" suggest?
2. What is the effect of the repetition of such phrases as "Speak gently"?
3. What seems to be the poet's feelings or attitude about the foxes, who are "Nuzzling one another, and whimpering with pain"? What feelings do you think the poet wants to stir up in readers? Explain your answer.

## LEARNING OPTION

**Writing.** This poem addresses Spring and March as if they were living beings. Write a poem in response to the speaker, in which Spring or March replies to the requests presented in "Four Little Foxes." Will Spring or March be as concerned about the foxes' well-being as the speaker in this poem?

*Four Little Foxes 557*

---

say that humans have proved cruel —the trap that killed their mother is an example—and so the poet does not bother to plead with people.

7. Answers will differ. Suggested Response: People have both positive and negative relationships with nature. The poet helps the four little foxes, but someone else set a trap that killed their mother.

### Applying

8. Students' answers will differ. Suggested Response: Their helplessness seems to stir up a very deep-rooted desire to protect such creatures. This desire is probably not as strong with respect to animals that are more distantly related to us, like insects. The type of animals we would most want to protect are probably small children, puppies, kittens, baby birds, and so forth.

**Challenge** If you were setting this poem to music, what instruments would you use? Explain.

### ANALYZING LITERATURE

1. Answers will differ. Suggested Response: It suggests a feeling of sadness and even a touch of horror.
2. Answers will differ. Suggested Response: The repetition emphasizes the need to be gentle and reminds us of the dangers that these animals face. Especially insightful students will realize that it almost seems appropriate to whisper the repeated phrase.
3. Answers will differ. Suggested Response: The poet seems to feel a great sense of pity for them, as well as a wish to shelter them from harm. He urges "Spring" and "March" to be gentle with them, and he covers them "with boughs" to protect them. He seems to want to call up the same feeling in readers, because he describes the little foxes' pain and need so vividly.

### LEARNING OPTION

This activity will appeal to creative students. Consider allowing students to write their poem with a partner or a small group.

---

## Closure and Extension

### ANSWERS TO RESPONDING TO THE SELECTION
#### Your Response

1. Ask students to identify which words or details evoke their response.
2. Allow students to share imaginative responses, again citing details from the poem that evoke the response.

#### Recalling

3. She was caught in a trap and died.
4. He covers them with boughs.

#### Interpreting

5. It can refer to any shock or calamity in general or, more specifically, to a violent storm with blowing winds.
6. Answers will differ. Suggested Response: The poet may feel that the animals are in the natural world and therefore at the mercy of natural forces. Some students may also

**Master Teacher Note** For comparison and contrast, you may want to use "The City Is So Big," page 586. García also describes the city at night but sees the city as threatening.

**Purpose-Setting Question** Why do you think the poet used lines and stanzas of different lengths?

**1 Discussion** Whom do you think Hughes is addressing? Explain.

**2 Master Teacher Note** You may want to tell students that the Harlem Renaissance, in which Hughes participated, also involved music. Duke Ellington, jazz composer, band leader, and pianist, was known for his performances in Harlem in the late 1920's.

Play for students Ellington's famous jazz composition "Take the A Train" (on the record *Sophisticated Ellington,* RCA, CPL 2–4098, or the two-record set *Duke Ellington—Carnegie Hall Concerts,* Prestige, 24074). The A train is a subway line that stops in Harlem. Ask whether the mood of this piece is similar to that of the poem and how jazz might have influenced Hughes.

**Reader's Response** How would you describe Hughes's speaker? Have you ever felt the way the speaker does?

**Thematic Response** What makes the speaker so happy? Why is the "you" of the poem so important to its meaning?

# Harlem Night Song

**Langston Hughes**

1
Come,
Let us roam the night together
Singing.

I love you.

2
5   Across
The Harlem[1] roof-tops
Moon is shining.
Night sky is blue.
Stars are great drops
10  Of golden dew.

Down the street
A band is playing.

I love you.

Come,
15  Let us roam the night together
Singing.

---

**1. Harlem** (här′ ləm) *n.*: Section of New York City, in the northern part of Manhattan.

## ◼ RESPONDING TO THE SELECTION

**Your Response**
1. How would you describe the thrill of being alive that the speaker expresses?

**Recalling**
2. What invitation does the poet give the friend?

**Interpreting**
3. What feeling do short lines give the poem?
4. Why does the speaker feel full of life?

**Applying**
5. Elizabeth Bowen wrote: "When you love someone all your saved up wishes start coming out." Do you agree that love makes people feel generous? Explain your answer.

## ◼ CRITICAL THINKING AND READING

**Making Inferences About Mood**
An **inference about mood** is a reasonable conclusion you can draw about the overall feeling of a poem, based on clues. Find three details that suggest a joyful mood.

*558    Poetry*

## Closure and Extension

### ANSWERS TO RESPONDING TO THE SELECTION
*Your Response*
1. Encourage students to respond in terms of their own experience.

*Recalling*
2. "Let us roam the night together/ Singing."

*Interpreting*
3. Answers will differ. Suggested Response: The short lines make the poet's invitation seem urgent and direct and give a feeling of informality.
4. Answers will differ. Suggested Response: He feels full of life because the night is beautiful and he has the chance to be with someone he loves.

*Applying*
5. Answers will differ. Suggested Response: Love can make people feel generous because they are so happy that they want to share it.

### ANSWERS TO CRITICAL THINKING AND READING
Among the details that contribute to a mood of joyfulness are these: the poet's repeated assertion that he loves his friend; the beautiful description of the night sky; the band playing music; and the repetition of the invitation to "roam the night," like a refrain in a song.

# Blue-Butterfly Day

## Robert Frost

1
It is blue-butterfly day here in spring,
And with these sky-flakes down in flurry on flurry
There is more unmixed color on the wing
Than flowers will show for days unless they hurry.

2
5 But these are flowers that fly and all but sing:
And now from having ridden out desire
They lie closed over in the wind and cling
Where wheels have freshly sliced the April mire.[1]

———————
**1. mire** (mīr) *n.*: Deep mud.

---

## ▮ RESPONDING TO THE SELECTION

### Your Response

1. What images do you see as you read the poem? How do you feel about these images?

### Recalling

2. In what season does the poem take place?
3. What happens to the butterflies at the end of the poem?

### Interpreting

4. To what does the poet compare the butterflies in line 2? Why is this comparison especially appropriate for New England in the early part of this season?
5. In what way are the butterflies also like birds? In what way are they like flowers?
6. What is suggested by the last two lines of the poem? What contrast do you find between the beginning of the poem and the end?

### Applying

7. The poet describes the butterflies as "flowers that fly and all but sing." How else might you describe butterflies?

## ▮ THINKING AND WRITING

### Writing a Lyric Poem

"Blue-Butterfly Day" is a lyric poem about spring. The images of the color and movement of the butterflies, the descriptive language, and the musical quality suggest a mood of quiet, thoughtful delight.

Choose another season and write a lyric poem about it. Describe the mood you would like to create. Then freewrite about the season, including words and phrases that create the mood you have chosen and that express your thoughts and feelings. Use this information to write a lyric poem. When you revise, make sure you have maintained a consistent mood.

*Blue-Butterfly Day* 559

---

### Presentation

**Motivation/Prior Knowledge**
Ask students what qualities of butterflies make them seem so fascinating to many people. Have them describe butterflies they have seen. Then tell them that, in the poem they will read, Robert Frost describes butterflies in a magical way.

**Purpose-Setting Question** How does the poet make the butterflies seem magical and mysterious?

**1 Discussion** What rhyme scheme and rhythmic pattern does Frost use in this lyric poem? How do the regular rhymes and rhythms of the poem contribute to its mood?

**2 Master Teacher Note** This poem is set in New England during the early spring, when flowers have not yet blossomed and a last snowfall is still possible. Point out to students that the butterflies are a good symbol for this uncertain state, suggesting both snow and flowers. Also, they are delicate, as this time of year itself seems to be.

**Reader's Response** How do these butterflies make you feel? What kind of April does the poet portray?

**Thematic Response** Why are butterflies unique? How are they more wondrous than flowers?

---

### *THINKING AND WRITING*

**Alternative Assessment** *Peer Review:* In pairs or groups of four, have students assess one another's work by responding to the following questions:

What season does the writer select for the poem?

What mood does the writer create?

What words create the mood?

What can the writer add to help convey the mood more vividly?

What can you suggest to improve the poem's language mechanics?

To validate the peer review, have students revise their work, incorporating suggestions they feel will enhance their poems.

559

---

## Closure and Extension

### *ANSWERS TO RESPONDING TO THE SELECTION*
#### Your Response

1. Have students reread or listen to a reading of the poem to help them identify and analyze the images in their mind.

#### Recalling

2. It takes place in early spring.

3. They close up their wings and rest on the mud.

#### Interpreting

4. Answers will differ. Suggested Response: He compares them to snowflakes. Snow can still fall in New England at this time of year.
5. Answers will differ. Suggested Response: They are like birds in that they can fly, and like flowers in that they are colorful.
6. Answers will differ. Suggested Re-

sponse: The last two lines imply that the butterflies are tired of flying. They start by resembling flakes of snow, but end resembling flowers growing in the mud.

#### Applying

7. Answers will differ. Suggested Response: Encourage students to use their imaginations. Students might compare them to tiny kites or little circus aerialists with colorful capes.

You might ask students to think of an older sister, brother, or friend who has helped them. Have them describe what they learned from this person. Then tell them that the poem they are about to read is an expression of gratitude for an older sister's help.

**1 Master Teacher Note** You may want to tell students that some poems are patterned on lists. The items in such lists are often connected by means of repeated phrases and conjunctions like *and.*

In this poem the list is made up of the poet's memories of her sister. Ask students to look for the words and phrases that the poet uses to link these memories. Also, have them consider the way in which the individual memories contribute to a portrait of the sister.

**2 Clarification** Tell students that the first sentence in contemporary poems sometimes begins with the title rather than the first line.

**3 Discussion** Why do you think the poet chose to begin the poem with this image?

**4 Discussion** How do the children seem to respond to Molly?

# For My Sister Molly Who in the Fifties

## Alice Walker

Once made a fairy rooster from
Mashed potatoes
Whose eyes I forget
But green onions were his tail
5    And his two legs were carrot sticks
A tomato slice his crown.
Who came home on vacation
When the sun was hot
and cooked
10   and cleaned
And minded least of all
The children's questions
A million or more
Pouring in on her
15   Who had been to school
And knew (and told us too) that certain
Words were no longer good
And taught me not to say us for we
No matter what "Sonny said" up the
20   road.

FOR MY SISTER MOLLY WHO IN THE FIFTIES.
Knew Hamlet well and read into the night
And coached me in my songs of Africa
A continent I never knew
25   But learned to love
Because "they" she said could carry
A tune
And spoke in accents never heard
In Eatonton.[1]
30   Who read from *Prose and Poetry*
And loved to read "Sam McGee from Tennessee"
On nights the fire was burning low

————————
**1. Eatonton** (ēt'n tən): A town in Georgia.

**Alternative Assessment** Have students write a poem—modeled after Alice Walker's—in which they describe a person whom they appreciate. First have them make a list of the character traits, physical and behavioral characteristics, and actions that they appreciate about the person. Then have students "connect" the items in their lists, as Walker does, with repeated phrases and conjunctions.

And Christmas wrapped in angel hair[2]
And I for one prayed for snow.

5 | 35    WHO IN THE FIFTIES
             Knew all the written things that made
             Us laugh and stories by
             The hour      Waking up the story buds
             Like fruit. Who walked among the flowers
   40        And brought them inside the house
             And smelled as good as they
             And looked as bright.
             Who made dresses, braided
             Hair. Moved chairs about
   45        Hung things from walls
             Ordered baths
6            Frowned on wasp bites
             And seemed to know the endings
             Of all the tales
   50        I had forgot.

_____

**2. angel hair**: Fine, white, filmy Christmas tree decoration.

**5 Discussion** Why do you think the poet uses a different kind of type for lines 21 and 35? How do the words from the title serve as connecting links in the poem?

**6 Discussion** What picture of Molly emerges from this list of memories?

**Reader's Response** If you were to write a poem to someone influential, who would it be? Explain why.

**Thematic Response** What kind of person is Molly? How can you tell that the speaker appreciates her?

**Alternative Assessment** Have your students complete one of the Alternate Composition Assignments on page 749 in the Teaching Portfolio.

## ▌RESPONDING TO THE SELECTION

### Your Response

1. If you were to meet the speaker's sister Molly, do you think you would like her? Why or why not?

### Recalling

2. How does Molly act as a teacher to the children?
3. How does Molly take care of the house? How does she take care of the children?

### Interpreting

4. Explain the title of this poem.
5. How does Molly reveal her creative spirit? How does she awaken the creative spirit in the children?

6. How do you know that being away at school has not separated Molly from the children?
7. What adjectives would you use to describe Molly?
8. What do the last three lines of the poem suggest about Molly?
9. How do you think the speaker feels about her sister Molly?

### Applying

10. Think of a character in another work of literature who seems most like Molly. Explain how these characters are alike.
11. Think of an area in which you have expertise or experience. How might you interest a friend in this area?

*For My Sister Molly Who in the Fifties   561*

ative. Especially insightful students may see that she wakens their creative spirit by making them aware of the world beyond their home.
6. Answers will differ. Suggested Response: When she returns, she is still warm and generous toward them.
7. Answers will differ. Suggested Response: Creative, imaginative, generous, loving, capable, and intelligent.
8. Answers will differ. Suggested Response: These lines seem to indicate more than the fact that Molly remembered what the poet forgot. They symbolize Molly's role as family storyteller and leader.
9. Answers will differ. Suggested Response: She loves and admires her.

### Applying

10. Answers will differ. Suggested Response: Students should choose a character with the same qualities that Molly demonstrates—generosity, intelligence, creativity, and so forth.
11. Answers will differ. Suggested Response: You can show your friend how enjoyable and valuable this pursuit is.

## Closure and Extension

### ANSWERS TO RESPONDING TO THE SELECTION
#### Your Response

1. Encourage students to infer general characteristics of Molly from specific passages in the text.

#### Recalling

2. She answered their questions, told them that certain words were no longer "good," taught the poet

the correct way to speak, and coached the poet in singing.
3. She cooked, cleaned, brought flowers into the house, moved chairs, and hung things from walls. She took care of the children by making dresses, braiding their hair, ordering baths, and frowning on wasp bites.

#### Interpreting

4. Answers will differ. Suggested Response: The title means that the poem was written for the poet's

sister Molly, who did much to take care of her during the 1950's.
5. Answers will differ. Suggested Response: She reveals her creative spirit by making a "fairy rooster" from food, coaching her sister in singing, reading aloud in an entertaining way, bringing flowers into the house, making dresses, and hanging things from walls. She awakens the creative spirit in the children by reading to them, coaching them, and showing them by example how to be cre-

**Shel Silverstein** lives in a houseboat that is usually anchored off Sausalito, California. In this floating home, he keeps a saxophone, trombone, guitar, piano, and camera. Ask students what the advantages of such a living situation would be. Also, have them design other types of houses that would be ideal for a writer.

Tell students that some of **William Shakespeare's** lyric poems, like ''Blow, Blow, Thou Winter Wind,'' were written for plays. During the performance these lyrics would be sung to music. Many of the actors were skilled singers, and the theater companies kept a variety of musical instruments. Ask students why Shakespeare and other playwrights of the time might have included such lyric poems in their plays. Also ask them how the presentation of these poems was in keeping with the original meaning of lyric poetry.

# GUIDE FOR READING

## Silver

**Walter de la Mare** (1873–1956), British poet and novelist, attended St. Paul's Cathedral Choir School in London. After graduation, for eighteen years he worked as a clerk; later, a government grant allowed him to write full time. De la Mare believed that the world beyond human experience could best be understood through the imagination. His poems often stress the magical and the mysterious, as does "Silver," an enchanted look at a moonlit night.

## Forgotten Language

**Shel Silverstein** (1932–    ) is a writer of children's books, a cartoonist, a folk singer, a composer, and an author of a one-act play, "The Lady or the Tiger?" (1981). The critic William Cole has said that Silverstein's poems are "tender, funny, sentimental, philosophical, and ridiculous in turn, and they're for all ages." Youngsters delight in his poem's playful images, while older readers appreciate his observations about growing up. In "Forgotten Language" Silverstein vividly captures the magical moment called childhood.

## Blow, Blow, Thou Winter Wind

**William Shakespeare** (1564–1616) was born in Stratford-upon-Avon, England. At eighteen he married Anne Hathaway; they had three children. In London he joined the Lord Chamberlain's Company, which performed plays at the Globe Theatre. Shakespeare wrote plays and poems that are among the best in the English language. They endure through the years because of his insight into human nature, his ability to lighten the tragic with the humorous, and his portrayal of kings and scoundrels with equal understanding. "Blow, Blow, Thou Winter Wind" is from his play *As You Like It*.

*562    Poetry*

## Objectives

1 To understand alliteration
2 To understand parallel structure
3 To express individual interests and abilities through an optional activity

## Support Material

**Teaching Portfolio**
Teacher Backup, p. 757
Usage and Mechanics Worksheet, p. 761
Vocabulary Check, p. 762
Analyzing Literature Worksheet, *Understanding Alliteration,* p. 763
Language Worksheet, *Understanding Poetic Language,* p. 764

Selection Test, p. 765
Art Transparency 12, *Souvenir* by Marc Chagall

**Listening to Literature**
"Silver," "Blow, Blow, Thou Winter Wind"

**Prentice Hall Literature Writing Studio**

## Sound Devices

**Sound devices** contribute to the musical quality of a poem. Including alliteration and repetition, sound devices are most noticeable when a poem is read aloud.

**Alliteration** is the repetition of a consonant at the beginning of words. For example, in "Silver" the phrase "casements catch" repeats the *k* sound at the beginning of each word.

There are various types of **repetition** in poetry. Parallel structure is the repetition of a grammatical structure. In "Forgotten Language" several of the beginning phrases, such as "Once I spoke" and "Once I understood," are in parallel form. Like other sound devices, the repetition emphasizes the musical quality of the poem.

## Focus

Alliteration helps to make language catchy and memorable. This poetic technique is often used in the naming of commercial products, in hopes that the product name will stay on the tip of the consumer's tongue. The same principle is behind the naming of cartoon characters, such as Mickey Mouse, Donald Duck, and Roger Rabbit. In fact, much of the language in popular culture makes use of poetic sound devices. With your classmates, brainstorm to list examples of alliteration found in popular culture. Discuss whether the alliteration in each of the examples you list is effective.

## Vocabulary

Knowing the following words will help you as you read these poems.

**shoon** (shoon) *n.*: Old-fashioned word for *shoes* (p. 564)

**keen** (kēn) *adj.*: Having a sharp cutting edge (p. 566)

**feigning** (fān′ iŋ) *v.*: Making a false show of (p. 566)

**Literary Focus** You might point out to students that alliteration is a kind of rhyme. Many years ago poems written in an older version of English used patterns of alliteration rather than the end rhymes we are familiar with today.

The modern American poet Ezra Pound imitated these older patterns of alliteration in his poem "The Seafarer" (italics added): "*N*eareth *n*ightshade, *s*noweth from *n*orth,/*F*rost *f*roze the land, hail fell on earth then, . . .''

Tell students that poets' use of parallel structure in English has been strongly influenced by the King James Version of the Bible. To illustrate this point, you might want to read aloud the following passage from Ecclesiastes (3:1–2): "To every thing there is a season, and a time to every purpose under the heaven: A time to be born and a time to die; a time to plant; and a time to pluck up that which is planted . . .''

**Prereading Focus** Consider dividing the class into small groups to complete this assignment. Each group can then brainstorm to gather examples of alliteration.

**Vocabulary** Have less advanced students read aloud the words and definitions. Ask **more advanced** students to find other examples—besides *shoon*—of old-fashioned terms for clothes. One possible source for such words is the poem "The Highwayman," by Alfred Noyes.

**Spelling Tip** The *ei* spelling of long *a*, as in *feigning*, is also found in words like *weigh*, *neighbor*, *reign*, and *sleigh*.

**Thematic Focus** In "Silver" de la Mare describes the loveliness of the world by moonlight; in "Forgotten Language" Silverstein conveys the joy of communing with the earth and the melancholy of losing touch with it; in "Blow, Blow, Thou Winter Wind," Shakespeare compares nature's harshness with the even greater harshness of human beings. Each poem conveys a different aspect of "our living earth." Ask students which view they feel most strongly about.

**Motivation/Prior Knowledge**
Ask students to describe the effect of moonlight on different environments. Tell them that de la Mare captures the magical quality of moonlight in "Silver."

**Purpose-Setting Question** How does the repetition of the word *silver* contribute to the mood?

**Master Teacher Note** Play the first movement of Beethoven's "Moonlight Sonata" for students. Ask them what pictures the music brings to mind or what feelings it calls up in them. Have them compare its mood with that of the poem.

**1 Discussion** Why is the title fitting for a poem about the moon?

**2 Discussion** Do you think this poem should be read loudly or softly? Explain.

**3 Discussion** Why do you think the poet chose to describe the moon as if it were a person?

**Reader's Response** Do you ever gaze at the moon? Why is moonlight considered romantic?

**Thematic Response** How many living things does the poet describe?

**Closure and Extension**

**ANSWERS TO RESPONDING TO THE SELECTION**
*Your Response*
1. Encourage students to use imagery to describe scenes familiar to them.

*Recalling*
2. It is a country scene, with fruit trees, a cottage, a stream, and various animals.
3. A harvest mouse is the only animal that moves. The other animals are sleeping, or at least not moving.

*Interpreting*
4. Suggested Response: The effect of

# 1 Silver

## Walter de la Mare

2 Slowly, silently, now the moon
3 Walks the night in her silver shoon;[1]
This way, and that, she peers, and sees
Silver fruit upon silver trees;
5 One by one the casements catch
Her beams beneath the silvery thatch;
Couched in his kennel, like a log,
With paws of silver sleeps the dog;
From their shadowy coat the white breasts peep
10 Of doves in a silver-feathered sleep;
A harvest mouse goes scampering by,
With silver claws, and silver eye;
And moveless fish in the water gleam,
By silver reeds in a silver stream.

---

**1. shoon** (sho͞on) *n.*: Old-fashioned word for "shoes."

## RESPONDING TO THE SELECTION

### Your Response
1. How would you describe the effects of moonlight on a familiar scene?

### Recalling
2. Describe the "silver" scene.
3. What is the only animal that moves in the poem? What do the other animals do?

### Interpreting
4. Describe the effect of the moon's walk.
5. Find four details that create a picture of stillness. What mood is created by this?
6. In what way does the poem seem magical?

### Applying
7. Find three other examples of "magic" in nature. Explain the reason for your choices.

## ANALYZING LITERATURE

### Understanding Alliteration
**Alliteration,** the repetition of consonants at the beginning of words, is one sound device poets use to heighten the musical quality of their work. The repetition of the sounds is especially striking when the poem is recited aloud. Read "Silver" aloud before answering the following questions.

1. Find two examples of alliteration in lines 1–2.
2. Find three other examples in the poem of the repetition of the sound of *s*.
3. What effect is created by the repetition of the sound of *s*?

the moon's walk is to cast silver light on the earth.
5. Answers will differ. Suggested Response: Among the details that create a picture of stillness are the fruit hanging on "silver trees"; the dog sleeping "like a log"; the dove "in a silver-feathered sleep"; and the "moveless fish." A mood of hushed peacefulness is created.
6. Answers will differ. Suggested Response: The silence, stillness, and silver light make this seem like a magical fairy-tale world.

*Applying*
7. Answers will differ. Suggested Response: Examples of magic in nature are the poking of a bud through the earth; the pattern of veins in a leaf; a snowflake; and the reflection of sunlight in water.

**ANSWERS TO ANALYZING LITERATURE**
1. *s* sound—slowly, silently, silver; *n* sound—now, night
2. Lines 3–4, 8, 10, 12, and 14.
3. Suggested Response: It creates a hushed, whispering effect.

**Alternative Assessment** *Collaborative Assignment:* Have students work in small groups to create "poetry videos." One or two students might act out the poem as another reads it; another group might use a series of photographs or original illustrations to represent the moon's progress. Encourage them to select apt background music for a reading of the poem. Have students share and compare completed versions of the poem.

# Forgotten Language

Shel Silverstein

Once I spoke the language of the flowers,
Once I understood each word the caterpillar said,
Once I smiled in secret at the gossip of the starlings,[1]
And shared a conversation with the housefly
    in my bed.
5  Once I heard and answered all the questions
    of the crickets,
And joined the crying of each falling dying
    flake of snow,
Once I spoke the language of the flowers . . .
    How did it go?
    How did it go?

1      2

"FORGOTTEN LANGUAGE" (Text only)
from *Where the Sidewalk Ends: The Poems & Drawings of Shel Silverstein.*
Copyright © 1974 by Snake Eye Music, Inc. Reprinted by permission of Harper & Row, Publishers, Inc.

---

**1. starlings** (stär' liŋz) *n.*: Dark-colored birds with a short tail, long wings, and a sharp, pointed bill.

---

## RESPONDING TO THE SELECTION

### Your Response

1. Describe a time when something in nature "spoke" to you. How was that time special?

### Recalling

2. Name six languages from nature the poet once "understood."

### Interpreting

3. When do you think the events in the poem took place?
4. Explain the meaning of the lines "How did it go?" How would you answer this question?

### Applying

5. In "Forgotten Language" the poet says that once he understood the language of flowers and animals. What other things might people forget as they grow older?

## ANALYZING LITERATURE

### Understanding Parallel Structure

Parallel structure is the repetition of a grammatical structure that allows the poet to emphasize important ideas and add to the musical quality of the poem. For example, the repetition of "Once I spoke" and "Once I understood" emphasizes the idea of time past.

1. Name the other beginning phrases that are in parallel form with "Once I spoke."
2. Which lines are not in parallel form with "Once I spoke"? Why do you think the poet chose to begin these lines in a different way?

---

## Closure and Extension

### ANSWERS TO RESPONDING TO THE SELECTION

#### Your Response

1. Students might describe a place, an animal, an event, or a moment of reflection.

#### Recalling

2. He "understood" the speech of flowers, caterpillars, starlings, houseflies, crickets, and snowflakes.

#### Interpreting

3. The events in the poem probably took place during winter, since snowflakes are mentioned as falling.
4. Answers will differ. Suggested Response: The line has two possible meanings: (1) What were the meanings of words in this language? (2) How did my memory of this language vanish? One possible answer to the second question is that as we become adults, we lose the close contact with nature that we enjoyed as children.

#### Applying

5. Answers will differ. Suggested Response: People sometimes lose a capacity for enjoying life and a sense of wonder at the world.

### ANSWERS TO ANALYZING LITERATURE

1. "Once I understood. . . ."; "Once I smiled. . . .: "Once I heard. . . ."
2. Lines 4, 6, 8, and 9 are not in parallel form with "Once I spoke. . . ." Suggested Response:

---

He probably changed the beginning of lines 4 and 6 to make the poem more interesting by varying the pattern. He broke the pattern in the last two lines to emphasize that he no longer knows this language.

---

**Motivation/Prior Knowledge**
Ask students to remember and describe a time when they felt extremely cold. Tell them that, in this poem, Shakespeare uses images of winter to describe feelings that are even more chilling than freezing weather.

**Master Teacher Note** You may want to contrast the hopeful feeling in Tennyson's poem ''Ring Out, Wild Bells,'' page 544, with the bitterness and cynicism in this poem.

**Purpose-Setting Question** How does the poet make an abstract idea like ''man's ingratitude'' seem more concrete and specific?

**1 Enrichment** Consider playing for students some Elizabethan music so that they better understand the flavor of this song. We particularly recommend the following records from the 7-record set of the New York Pro Musica's greatest works (Everest 6145/7): Record 2— ''Thomas Morley''; Record 6— ''Children's Songs of Shakespeare's Time.'' You may also want to use the record *Glenn Gould Plays William Byrd/Orlando Gibbons* (CBS 7464-39552-1).

**2 Discussion** What is the rhyme scheme of this stanza? Basing your answer on the rhyme scheme, what can you infer about the pronunciation of ''wind'' and ''unkind'' during Shakespeare's time?

**3 Master Teacher Note** You may want to explain briefly the dramatic context in which this poem appears. In *As You Like It,* a Duke of France loses his lands to his evil younger brother and goes to live in the forest of Arden with some faithful followers. Eventually, his lands are restored to him. While he lives in the forest, however, he says that he prefers winter's cold

# Blow, Blow, Thou Winter Wind

## William Shakespeare

Blow, blow, thou winter wind.
Thou art not so unkind
  As man's ingratitude.
Thy tooth is not so keen,
5  Because thou art not seen,
  Although thy breath be rude.[1]
Heigh-ho! Sing, heigh-ho! unto the green holly.
Most friendship is feigning, most loving mere folly.
  Then, heigh-ho, the holly!
10  This life is most jolly.

Freeze, freeze, thou bitter sky,
That dost not bite so nigh
  As benefits forgot.
Though thou the waters warp,[2]
15  Thy sting is not so sharp
  As friend remembered not.
Heigh-ho! Sing, heigh-ho! unto the green holly.
Most friendship is feigning, most loving mere folly.
  Then, heigh-ho, the holly!
20  This life is most jolly.

---

**1. rude** *adj.*: Rough, harsh.
**2. warp** *v.*: Freeze.

to the lying and flattery he found at court. This song, which is sung at the end of the second act, expresses the same idea.

You may want to encourage **more advanced** students to read Shakespeare's play.

**Reader's Response** Do you share the poet's views on friendship?

**Thematic Response** How does the speaker view nature? What aspects of nature does the poet describe?

**Audiocassette** Use the **Listening to Literature** Audiocassette recordings of ''Silver'' and ''Blow, Blow, Thou Winter Wind'' (Side 5) to help students appreciate sound devices. Ask students to listen for alliteration, repetition, and parallelism.

LES TRÈS RICHES HEURES DU DUC DE BERRY: FEBRUARY
Chantilly—Musée Condé

## Humanities Note

Fine art, *February* from *Les Très Riches Heures du Duc de Berry*, 1413–16, by Pol de Limbourg (?–1416) and his brothers. Pol de Limbourg and his two brothers were Flemings who had settled in France. They produced an illuminated manuscript called *Les Très Riches Heures* for the Duc de Berry, the brother of the French king. The most important pages of this manuscript are those depicting scenes typical of the various months of the year.

1. What do you think the women in the lower left corner are doing?
2. What other winter activities can you identify?
3. Do you think this picture goes well with the poem? Explain.

**Multicultural Focus** Clearly the emphasis in Shakespeare's poem lies in the speaker's view of human behavior, rather than on winter itself. Stress that humans throughout the world—whether in torrid or frigid climates—share powerful emotions, such as the pain of betrayal. However, the imagery and metaphors a poet chooses to express those emotions may be as various as an individual's experiences in a particular culture.

Ask students to write their own poems expressing an emotion with seasonal imagery. Have them research a particular region and then use imagery relating to that region.

## RESPONDING TO THE SELECTION

### Your Response

1. Do you agree with the poet's statement that love is "mere folly"? Why or why not?

### Recalling

2. What is more unkind than the winter wind? Why is the wind's "tooth . . . not so keen"?
3. What is sharper than the sting of the bitter sky?

### Interpreting

4. Explain what the poem suggests about the harshness of nature compared to the pain of human relationships.
5. Keeping in mind the poet's views of human relationships, what do the phrases "Sing, heigh-ho!" and "This life is most jolly" tell you about the poet's attitude?

### Applying

6. Do you agree with the poet that ingratitude is painful? Explain your answer.

## LEARNING OPTION

**Performance.** With a partner practice reading the poem aloud. Try to achieve a tone that expresses the poet's cynical, or negative, attitudes toward human relationships. Keep in mind that the last four lines in each stanza should be spoken with added irony.

*Blow, Blow, Thou Winter Wind* 567

## Closure and Extension

### ANSWERS TO RESPONDING TO THE SELECTION
#### Your Response

1. Ask students to support their opinions with reasons.

#### Recalling

2. More unkind than the winter wind is "man's ingratitude." The wind's "tooth is not so keen" because the wind is invisible—it is not a human foe.
3. People's ingratitude is more painful.

### Interpreting

4. Answers will differ. Suggested Response: The poem indicates that the harshness of nature is not as painful as people's cruelty.
5. Answers will differ. Suggested Response: If the poem is read by itself, the poet's attitude in these phrases seems to be ironical. Even though he is saying "This life is most jolly," he really means that it is bitter and cruel. However, especially insightful students may see that, in dramatic context, the words "This life. . . ." may refer to the life in the forest, which *is* "jolly" by contrast with the life in court.

### Applying

6. Answers will differ. Suggested Response: Most students will say that it is painful, because it involves rejection and the violation of trust.

### LEARNING OPTION

This activity will appeal especially to students with interest and ability in drama and oral interpretation. You might vary the activity by having interested students set the poem to music that reflects its tone.

## Preparation

**More About the Author** The humorous poetry of **Morris Bishop** appeared in a volume entitled *The Best of Bishop: Light Verse From the New Yorker and Elsewhere* (1980). You might want to ask students why a professor engaged in serious scholarship would also want to write humorous verse.

**Literary Focus** Consider telling students that Edward Lear included many limericks in *A Book of Nonsense* (1846) and contributed to the popularity of the form. Lear always began his limericks with the statement that someone came from a certain place—for example, ''There was a young lady of Wilts. . . .''

You might want to encourage students to read other light verse by Lear *(The Nonsense Books of Edward Lear.* New York: The New American Library. 1964).

**Prereading Focus** You might encourage students to look for ways to make adjustments in rhythm and word choice to improve their jokes.

**Vocabulary** Consider asking less advanced students to find three synonyms for the word *applaud* in a thesaurus.

**Spelling Tip** The spelling of *meets* should not be confused with *meats,* meaning ''types of flesh from animals.''

# GUIDE FOR READING

## Hog Calling

**Morris Bishop** (1893–1973) was born in Willard, New York, and lived most of his life in Ithaca, New York. He attended Cornell University and went on to teach there from 1921 to 1973. Bishop translated plays by Molière and edited numerous collections of short stories. His diverse writings include histories, critical biographies, and light verse such as "Hog Calling."

## I Raised a Great Hullabaloo

**Anonymous.** No one knows for sure how limericks came into being. It is believed that they were originally passed down by word of mouth.

## Limerick

A **limerick** is a kind of light or humorous verse. Generally, every limerick has five lines: three long lines (the first, second, and fifth) that rhyme with one another and two short lines (the third and fourth) that rhyme. The lines also follow a particular rhythm. Each of the three long lines has three accented, or stressed, syllables; each of the two short lines has two stressed syllables.

## Focus

To develop your skill in reciting limericks, think of a funny joke and tell it to a classmate. Have your partner listen critically for ways in which you can make your telling more entertaining. After you have commented on each other's jokes, revise them and retell them. Then try out your skills on the limericks that follow.

## Vocabulary

Knowing the following words will help you as you read these limericks.

**meets** (mēts) *n.*: A series of events held during a period of days at a certain place (p. 569)
**applaud** (ə plôd′) *v.*: To show approval or enjoyment by clapping the hands (p. 569)

**awed** (ôd) *adj.*: Filled with reverence, fear, and wonder (p. 569)
**appalling** (ə pôl′ iŋ) *adj.*: Causing horror or shock (p. 569)

### Objectives

1 To understand the features of a limerick
2 To write limericks
3 To express individual interests and abilities through optional activities

## Support Material

**Teaching Portfolio**
Teacher Backup, pp. 767–769
Usage and Mechanics Worksheet, p. 770
Vocabulary Check, p. 771
Analyzing Literature Worksheet, *Understanding Limericks,* p. 772
Language Worksheet, *Using Rhythmic Language,* p. 773
Selection Test, pp. 774–775

**Listening to Literature**
Two Limericks

**Prentice Hall Literature Writing Studio**

**HOG HEAVEN**
*Mike Patrick*

# Two Limericks

A bull-voiced young fellow of Pawling
Competes in the meets for hog-calling;
   The people applaud,
   And the judges are awed,
But the hogs find it simply appalling.
                 **Morris Bishop**

I raised a great hullabaloo[1]
When I found a large mouse in my stew,
   Said the waiter, "Don't shout
   And wave it about,
Or the rest will be wanting one, too!"
                 **Anonymous**

---

**1. hullabaloo** (hul′ ə bə loo′) *n*.: Loud noise and confusion; hubbub.

*Two Limericks*    569

**Audiocassettes** Use the **Listening to Literature** Audiocassette recordings of these two limericks (Side 5) to enhance students' appreciation of the poems' humor. Have students listen for the ways in which rhythm and rhyme contribute to the humor.

569

# Closure and Extension

## ANSWERS TO RESPONDING TO THE SELECTION

### Your Response

1. Encourage students to offer specific reasons for their preferences.

### Recalling

2. He finds a mouse in his stew.
3. He takes part in hog-calling meets.

### Interpreting

4. Answers will differ. Suggested Response: An embarrassed reply might have further enraged the customer. Instead, the waiter uses surprise and humor to get his point across—he wants the customer to stop making a fuss.
5. The people "applaud," showing that they approve, and the judges are very impressed. The hogs, however, think the young man is terrible.

### Applying

6. Answers will differ. Suggested Response: Students may think of ridiculous situations involving a bowl of soup, a beard, and a bathtub. Particularly clever students may combine all the elements so that, for instance, a man taking a bath gets his beard in a bowl of soup.

## ANALYZING LITERATURE

1. In "Hog Calling" the humorous twist is that the young man's talents are appreciated by everyone *except* those who really matter—the hogs.
2. The surprise is that the waiter acts as if it is a privilege to have a mouse in one's stew.

## THINKING AND WRITING

**Publishing Student Writing** You may want to collect students' work to create an anthology of limericks.

## LEARNING OPTIONS

1. This activity will appeal to students with interest or abilities in art. You might vary the activity by having students write a limerick after viewing an illustration or a cartoon.

---

## RESPONDING TO THE SELECTION

### Your Response

1. Which of the two limericks did you enjoy more? Why?

### Recalling

2. In "I Raised a Great Hullabaloo," what does the speaker find in his stew?
3. What does the "young fellow" in "Hog Calling" do?

### Interpreting

4. In "I Raised a Great Hullabaloo," how does the waiter's reply show cleverness and presence of mind?
5. Contrast the responses of the people and the judges with those of the hogs in "Hog Calling."

### Applying

6. Humorists have a talent for looking at the everyday and seeing the ridiculous. Allow yourself to be silly for a few minutes. What would be ridiculous about an everyday bowl of soup? What could be ridiculous about a person with a beard? What could be ridiculous about a bathtub?

## ANALYZING LITERATURE

### Understanding Limericks

Limericks are meant to be funny, even foolish. Their writers observe, then poke good-natured fun at, human weaknesses and silly behavior. Generally, the humor of a limerick is delivered in a kind of "punch line"—a surprising and comical twist that comes at the end.

---

1. Explain the comical twist at the end of "Hog Calling."
2. What is surprising about the last line of "I Raised a Great Hullabaloo"?

## THINKING AND WRITING

### Writing a Limerick

Now that you are in a silly mood, choose a topic for a limerick. A good way to start a limerick is to introduce a character by name: for example, "There once was a fellow named Mo." When you revise your limerick, make sure you have followed the correct pattern. Share your completed limerick with your classmates.

## LEARNING OPTIONS

1. **Art.** Draw or paint an illustration for the limerick "I Raised a Great Hullabaloo." The style of your drawing or painting should reflect the humor found in this poetic form. Display your finished illustration in the classroom.
2. **Speaking and Listening.** Write a limerick about a classmate, and then have your classmate answer it with another limerick. Keep up this exchange as long as you can. When you are finished, recite your limericks for your class.
3. **Language.** See what you can find out about the history, or etymology, of the word *hullabaloo* and its Irish cousin, *hubbub*. What is similar about the origins of these words? Can you think of other words that originated in the same way? Give an oral presentation of your findings to your class.

---

2. This activity will appeal to verbal students. You might extend the activity by having student volunteers transcribe poems into a booklet.
3. This activity will interest students with interest in language and culture. You could vary the activity by having students also research the Irish associations of the word *limerick.*

**Multicultural Focus** Limericks often intend to ridicule silly or offensive human behavior. Metaphorically, Bishop's hog offers a shift in cultural perspective, an alternative viewpoint on human behavior toward those we consider inferior because we are ignorant of their ways. Suggest that the "young fellow" exhibits qualities associated with stereotypical "ugly American tourists," who deem themselves superior to the natives of other lands through ignorance of others' languages and customs.

Ask students to research satirical works from other cultures and bring in examples for class discussion.

# Facets of Nature

**SHADOWS OF EVENING, 1921-23**
*Rockwell Kent*
*Collection of Whitney Museum of American Art*

*Facets of Nature* 571

## Preparation

**More About the Authors** The poet **Matsuo Bashō** was born a *samurai* (warrior). At the age of twenty-two, he abandoned this honored status to devote himself wholly to writing poetry. What advantages are there of a poet's being able to spend all of his or her time writing poetry instead of having to work at a job at the same time?

**F. Arakida Moritake** was a Shinto priest. The word *Shinto* means the way of the gods. The gods, called *kami,* are believed to live in rocks, trees, rivers, mountains, and so on. Prayers and offerings are offered to the kami at shrines in homes and along the roadsides. About 33 million people practice Shinto, which is the oldest surviving religion in Japan. Why might being a Shinto priest inspire a person to write haiku?

**Literary Focus** It is not always possible to translate exactly a haiku written in Japanese into English. The strict rule requiring five syllables in the first and third lines and seven syllables in the second line makes it difficult to translate them from one language to another. If you have any bilingual students, they might attempt to write the same haiku in both languages, keeping the syllable count as it should be.

**Prereading Focus** You might encourage students to study the picture for a minute or two in order to tap the essence of it when they do begin to write.

**Thematic Focus** In two haiku Bashō and Moritake admire the fine details of our living earth.

🎧 **Audiocassette** To help students appreciate the subtle rhythms and meanings in these poems, play the **Listening to Literature** Audiocassette recordings of "Two Haiku" (Side 5).

**THEME:
OUR LIVING
EARTH**

# GUIDE FOR READING

## Haiku

**Matsuo Bashō** (1644–1694) of Japan is generally regarded as the greatest of all haiku poets. At the age of eight, he entered the service of a nobleman in Iga, in southern Japan. There he is believed to have composed his first poem when he was only nine. Later, he lived for a time in a monastery. By the age of thirty, he had founded a school for the study of haiku, and he was revered as a master of the art.

**Moritake** (1452–1540) was a priest as well as one of the leading Japanese poets of the sixteenth century.

## Haiku

**Haiku** is a special type of poetry from Japan. A haiku consists of seventeen syllables arranged in three lines. The first line has five syllables, the second has seven, and the third has five.

Generally, in a haiku, the poet describes a fleeting moment in nature—usually something he has observed and that has moved him. Through the haiku's simple image or series of images, the poet tries to arouse in the reader the same sensation that he experienced.

## Focus

Because a haiku contains only three lines, its subject is necessarily limited to a kind of "snapshot" that captures a passing moment of interest. By providing just enough detail and leaving certain feelings unexpressed, the haiku poet invites you to imagine what is left out so that you actively participate in the experience. Flip through the poetry unit of this book to find a picture that appeals to you. Jot down a few words or phrases that capture what is happening in the picture without stating it directly. See if a classmate can find the picture you are describing.

## Vocabulary

Haiku uses seemingly simple words that suggest vivid images, as do the following words from the haiku by Bashō.

**slashing** (slash′ iŋ) *v.*: Cutting with a sweeping stroke (p. 573)

**screech** (skrēch) *n.*: A shrill, high-pitched shriek or sound (p. 573)

*572    Poetry*

---

**Support Material**

**Teaching Portfolio**
Teacher Backup, p. 777
Usage and Mechanics Worksheet, p. 780
Vocabulary Check, p. 781
Analyzing Literature Worksheet, *Understanding Haiku,* p. 782
Language Worksheet, *Choosing Words,* p. 783
Selection Test, p. 784

**Listening to Literature**
Two Haiku

**Prentice Hall Literature Writing Studio**

# Two Haiku

1
The lightning flashes!
And slashing through the darkness,
A night-heron's[1] screech.
**Bashō**

The falling flower
I saw drift back to the branch
Was a butterfly.
**Moritake**

---

**1. night-heron** (nīt′ her′ ən) *n.*: A large wading bird with a long neck and long legs that is active at night.

*Japanese Lacquered Box (19th century)*
*Inside Top Cover (detail)*
The Metropolitan Museum of Art

## RESPONDING TO THE SELECTION

### Your Response

1. Which of the two haiku appeals to you more? Why?

### Recalling

2. What is the subject in the haiku by Bashō?
3. What is the subject in the haiku by Moritake?

### Interpreting

4. How does the image in Bashō's haiku change by the third line?
5. How does the image in Moritake's haiku change by the third line?

### Applying

6. Choose one of these two haiku and another poem about nature in this book. Compare and contrast the two views of nature.

## THINKING AND WRITING

### Writing a Haiku

A haiku presents a moment in nature. It has three lines with five syllables in the first line, seven syllables in the second line, and five syllables in the third line.

Choose one of your freewritten impressions and observations about nature. Try to communicate your impression in a single image or two. Write a haiku to describe the image. As you write, keep in mind the emotion or sensation you felt. Try to involve at least two of your senses. Revise your haiku, making sure you have followed the correct form for a haiku. Proofread it and prepare a final draft that you illustrate. Place your illustrated haiku on the bulletin board.

**More About the Authors** In 1982 **John Updike** won the Pulitzer Prize for fiction for *Rabbit Is Rich,* a continuation of the story that started with *Rabbit Run* and *Rabbit Redux.* Much of Updike's fiction is about middle-class suburban life. Updike is known for his careful attention to details in his writing. The poem "January" shows how careful choice of words and attention to line and stanza length all work together to describe a day in the month of January. You might ask students what words they might use to describe a day in the month of January. You might write the list of words on the chalkboard and see if any duplicate those used by Updike.

**Langston Hughes's** early poetry advocated humor and self-control as defenses against unjust social and economic conditions. His later works reflected the increased demand for social justice. In 1960 Langston Hughes won the Spingarn Medal, a gold medal with a figure of justice on it that is awarded by the National Association for the Advancement of Colored People for highest achievement in the recipient's field.

The **Tewa Indians** believe their people ascended from the underworld from the center of the cosmos, a lake in Colorado. As Pueblos, living in a dry climate, dependent upon scarce water for their crops, the rhythms of nature were of utmost importance to them. Their religious observances and their poetry both reflect this. You could ask students in what ways their religious observances and poetry might show this concern with nature.

Because **N. Scott Momaday** spent his boyhood on a number of different reservations in the Southwest, he gained a vast knowledge of Native American history and

574　Poetry

## January

**John Updike** (1932–　　) was born in Shillington, Pennsylvania. In 1954 he graduated from Harvard, where he won numerous writing honors, and then studied art in England for a year. From 1955 to 1957 he was a cartoonist and staff writer for *The New Yorker,* where many of his short stories appeared. Also a distinguished essayist and respected poet, Updike is well known for such novels as *Rabbit Run* (1960) and *Rabbit Redux* (1971). In "January" he uses stark language to portray the coldness of a winter day.

## Winter Moon

**Langston Hughes** (1902–1967) was born in Joplin, Missouri, and grew up in Lincoln, Illinois, and Cleveland, Ohio. He left Columbia University after a year to travel and write. In 1925 he met the poet Vachel Lindsay, who helped Hughes publish his first poetry collection, *The Weary Blues* (1926). Hughes also wrote two autobiographical works and humorous sketches about African American city life called *The Best of Simple* (1961). "Winter Moon" depicts the moon as it might appear on a city night.

## Song of the Sky Loom

The **Tewa Indians** were among the many Native Americans who flourished on the North American continent before the first European explorers arrived. The Tewa expressed their close relationship with nature through poetry. Native American poetry, like "Song of the Sky Loom," was not written; rather, it was chanted or sung along with music, dance, and colorful costumes. Native Americans believed this kind of poetry had magical power, and they performed it hoping to cause some good for the community.

## New World

**N. Scott Momaday** (1934–　　), a Kiowa Indian, was born in Lawton, Oklahoma. Momaday was educated on Indian reservations and in 1952 entered the University of New Mexico. Today he is professor of English at Stanford University, California. He is best known for *The Way to Rainy Mountain* (1969). In 1968 his novel *House Made of Dawn* was awarded a Pulitzer Prize. In poems like "New World," Momaday reveals the Native Americans' rapport with nature.

culture. N. Scott Momaday has had two books of poems published and considers himself primarily a poet. You might ask your students for ways in which living in a number of different places among different people might help an author with his or her writing.

## Objectives

1　To recognize sensory language
2　To use sensory language in writing a description
3　To write a poem creating a vivid image
4　To paraphrase a poem
5　To express individual interests and abilities through optional activities

## Support Material

**Teaching Portfolio**
Teacher Backup, p. 787
Grammar in Action Worksheet, *Understanding Verb Tense,* p. 791
Usage and Mechanics Worksheet, p. 793
Vocabulary Check, p. 794
Analyzing Literature Worksheet, *Recognizing Sensory Language,* p. 795
Language Worksheet, *Writing*

## Sensory Language

**Sensory language,** or language that appeals to the senses—sight, hearing, smell, touch, and taste—is an important part of any kind of descriptive writing. A description of the visible features of a landscape, of a sound (or of a silence), of the taste or smell of an exotic food, of the way a fabric feels—all these involve the writer's use of sensory language.

For example, in "January" John Updike gives you images of "Fat snowy footsteps" and "trees of lace," word pictures that appeal to your sense of sight. N. Scott Momaday describes winds that "lean upon mountains" and foxes that "stiffen in cold," images that appeal to your sense of touch. These examples of sensory language are used to create pictures in your imagination and help you experience what the poet describes.

## Focus

Recall an experience you had in which several of your senses were affected. It could be anything from a hike in the woods to a visit to a shopping mall. Try to recapture your experience by filling in a chart like the following one with as many sensory details as you can remember.

| Experience: | | | | |
|---|---|---|---|---|
| SIGHT | SOUND | SMELL | TASTE | TOUCH |
|  |  |  |  |  |

## Vocabulary

Knowing the following words will help you as you read these poems.

**fittingly** (fit′ iŋ lē) *adv.*: Properly (p. 579)
**glistens** (glis′ 'nz) *v.*: Shines (p. 580)
**borne** (bôrn) *v.*: Carried (p. 580)

**low** (lō) *v.*: Make the typical sound that a cow makes (p. 580)
**hie** (hī) *v.*: Hurry (p. 580)
**recede** (ri sēd′) *v.*: Move farther away (p. 581)

*Guide for Reading* 575

---

*Sensory Language,* p. 796
Selection Test, p. 797
Art Transparency 14, *Aurora Borealis,* by Frederic Church

**Listening to Literature**
"January," "Winter Moon," "Song of the Sky Loom," "New World"

**Audio Prose Library**
N. Scott Momaday: Interview and Reading

**Prentice Hall Literature Writing Studio**

🎧 **Audiocassette** Use the **Listening to Literature** Audiocassette recordings of "January," "Winter Moon," "Song of the Sky Loom," and "New World" (Side 5) to help students appreciate sensory language. Have students listen for images deriving from each of the five senses.

**Literary Focus** At this point your students may need to be told that sensory language can include figures of speech. Sensory language often creates images and, to be effective, uses vivid language. In other words, figures of speech, imagery, vivid language, and sensory language are overlapping categories, not discrete ones. You might want to have your students find, in this or other books or magazines, examples of sensory language that appeals to each of the five senses. They could then present them to the class.

**Prereading Focus** Students, especially less advanced ones, might benefit from discussing their sensory experiences in groups before they start to write about them.

**Vocabulary** You might want to discuss with your students the spelling of the word *borne* in "New World" and the meaning of the word *low* as it is used in "New World."

**Spelling Tip** Note that the ending of *recede* is regular, as in *precede, secede, impede,* etc. Only four words end differently: *exceed, proceed, succeed, supersede.*

**Thematic Focus** In "January" Updike evokes life amid midwinter stillness; in "Winter Moon" Hughes expresses wonder at the earth's lunar "companion"; in "Song of the Sky Loom," the poet praises nature in a prayer; and in "New World," Momaday celebrates the origins of our living earth. Which facet of nature expressed in these poems do students find most awe-inspiring?

# January

## John Updike

1. The days are short,
    The sun a spark
Hung thin between
2.     The dark and dark.

  5 Fat snowy footsteps
    Track the floor.
3. Milk bottles burst
    Outside the door.

  The river is
4.   10  A frozen place
Held still beneath
    The trees of lace.

5. The sky is low.
    The wind is gray.
  15 The radiator
6.   Purrs all day.

**WINTER TWILIGHT NEAR ALBANY, NEW YORK, 1858**
*George Henry Boughton*
*Courtesy of The New York Historical Society*

576   *Poetry*

**Making Connections** Another selection that deals with winter is "Blow, Blow, Thou Winter Wind," on page 566.

**Multicultural Focus** January is different around the world. In Israel it is a rainy time that precedes warm weather. For New Zea-landers January marks summer's beginning. Thus (in a New Zealander's poem) the radiator's comforting "purr" might be replaced by a barbecue's hot sizzle.

Have students research a country whose seasons differ from ours. Have them prepare a short report on the different ways that country experiences its seasons.

## RESPONDING TO THE SELECTION

### Your Response

1. Which image in the poem best conveys your own impression of January? Why?

### Recalling

2. How does Updike describe the sun?
3. How does the poet describe the sky?
4. What sound fills the air at the poem's end?

### Interpreting

5. Explain the image "dark and dark" in line 4.
6. Why do the trees appear to be made of lace?
7. Why did Updike write such short lines?

### Applying

8. The poet uses the color gray to describe wind in winter. What colors do you associate with the other seasons? Explain your choices.

## ANALYZING LITERATURE

### Recognizing Sensory Language

"January" gives the poet's impressions of the month. For example, he refers to the sun as "a spark / Hung thin . . ." This image of the sun as a spark barely hanging in the sky between morning and night is a visual impression.

1. To what sense does "purrs all day" appeal?
2. What does "fat snowy footsteps" mean?
3. To what senses does the last stanza appeal?
4. What impression do you form from this poem?

## THINKING AND WRITING

### Using Sensory Language

List impressions of your favorite month. Include impressions experienced through all your senses. Using this list, write a description of the month. Include sensory language, but do not state the name of the month. Check your description and make sure it portrays the month clearly. Then read your description to your classmates and let them guess which month you have described.

*January 577*

---

3. The poet describes the sky as "low"—heavy with clouds.
4. The purring of the radiator fills the air at the end of the poem.

*Interpreting*

5. The "dark and dark" refers to the shortness of the day, which starts with early morning darkness and ends in late afternoon with darkness.
6. The trees appear to be made of lace because each branch and twig is covered with snow.

7. Updike wrote such short lines to imitate the shortness of January's days.

*Applying*

8. Answers will differ. A possible student response would be pink for spring because of the pink blossoms on so many trees then, green for summer because the leaves are covering the trees then, and orange for fall because the leaves have turned color then.

### ANSWERS TO ANALYZING LITERATURE

1. "Purrs all day" appeals to the sense of hearing.
2. "Fat snowy footsteps" suggests that the snow is deep and heavy. Boots or shoes look several sizes larger than they really are when covered with snow.
3. The last stanza appeals to the sense of sight ("sky is low" and

"wind is gray"), the sense of touch ("wind" and heat from the "radiator"), and the sense of hearing ("radiator / Purrs all day").
4. Answers will differ. Suggested Response: The impression is that January is a rather unpleasant month with short days; snowy, cold, cloudy, and gray.

**Challenge** Instead of writing a prose description of a month as called for in the Thinking and Writing section, you might want your **more advanced** students to write their descriptions in poetry form. Have them consider the month they have chosen when they decide on line and stanza length and meter for their poem.

**Enrichment** Students might be asked to write contrasting images similar to the one used by Updike in the last stanza of "January." They could write images of a hot day contrasted with a method of cooling off, or images of a rainy day contrasted with a method of drying off, and so on.

### THINKING AND WRITING

**Writing Transparency** A graphic organizer may help students with their lists of impressions. Use the *Sensory Language Chart* graphic organizer in **Transparencies for Writing.**

**Alternative Assessment** *Protocol:* Have students assess their own work by responding to the following questions:

About what month did you write?

What impressions did you wish to convey in your description?

What sensory details helped to make the description vivid?

How did you develop the description?

What did you learn about using sensory language from this assignment?

You might have students use the information they gained from their protocols as a guide for revising their descriptions.

**Motivation/Prior Knowledge**
Bring to class pictures of the moon in its various phases. Tell students they are going to read a poem about one of these phases.

**Master Teacher Note** Students might benefit from a class discussion about what constitutes a poem. Langston Hughes's poem "Winter Moon" is extremely short. Discuss with students why it is still considered a poem.

**Making Connections** Another poem that presents an image of the moon is "Silver" by Walter de la Mare on page 564. Students might want to compare poems and to speculate about the phase of the moon represented in that poem.

**Purpose-Setting Question** What phase of the moon is Hughes describing?

**1 Language** What two adjectives does Hughes use to describe the moon in this line?

**2 Discussion** To what senses does this description appeal? How is it similar to line 1? How is it different from line 1?

**Reader's Response** Have you ever seen a moon like this? How did it make you feel?

**Thematic Response** How would you describe the speaker's relationship with nature?

# Winter Moon

**Langston Hughes**

1 How thin and sharp is the moon tonight!
2 How thin and sharp and ghostly white
   Is the slim curved crook of the moon tonight!

4. The moon goes through several phases during a month. What phase of the moon does the poet see?
5. What qualities of the moon seem to appeal to the poet? Look at the exclamation mark at the end of the third line.
6. What is the poet's tone, or attitude, toward what he sees?

### Applying

7. What are some of your own impressions of the moon?
8. Notice the word *ghostly* in line 2. What is it about the moon that has suggested mystery to people throughout the ages?

## THINKING AND WRITING

### Writing a Poem

Reread "Winter Moon." Notice the pattern of the lines. Line 1 is a complete sentence. Lines 2 and 3. which make a second complete sentence, repeat the idea of line 1—but add to it.

Choose an aspect of nature and freewrite about it. Then use your freewriting to compose three lines of poetry following the pattern of "Winter Moon." Revise your poem, making sure you have created a vivid picture. Proofread your poem and share it with your classmates.

## RESPONDING TO THE SELECTION

### Your Response

1. What words would you use to describe a winter moon? Why?

### Recalling

2. What precisely does the poet describe?

### Interpreting

3. What phrase is repeated? What effect does the poet achieve by repeating this phrase?

*578   Poetry*

**Closure and Extension**

**ANSWERS TO RESPONDING TO THE SELECTION**
*Your Response*
1. Encourage students to choose sensory words to describe the moon.

*Recalling*
2. The poet describes a new moon.

578

*Interpreting*
3. "How thin and sharp" is the repeated phrase. The effect is emphasis and perhaps a feeling of mystery.
4. The poet sees a new moon.
5. The thinness, sharpness, and shape like a curved crook are qualities of the moon that seem to appeal to the poet.
6. The poet's tone seems to be that of a surprised exclamation.

*Applying*
7. Answers will differ. Suggested Response: the full moon's radiance, the appearance of features on the moon.
8. Answers will differ. Suggested Response: Although the moon is visible, we have not known exactly of what it was made or how it controlled the tides until recently. Therefore, there has always been an element of mystery surrounding the moon.

**THINKING AND WRITING**
**Publishing Student Writing** Student poems could be duplicated if a copying machine is available. Each student could add them to their individual booklets of student writing.
**Writing Across the Curriculum** You might want to tell science teachers about your students' investigation of the moon's phases in case they wish to conduct similar investigations in their classes.

# Song of the Sky Loom

## Tewa Indian

Oh our Mother the Earth, oh our Father the Sky,   **1**
Your children are we, and with tired backs   **2**
We bring you the gifts that you love.   **3**
Then weave for us a garment of brightness;
5  May the warp[1] be the white light of morning,
May the weft[2] be the red light of evening,   **4**
May the fringes be the falling rain,
May the border be the standing rainbow.
Thus weave for us a garment of brightness
10  That we may walk fittingly where birds sing,   **5**
That we may walk fittingly where grass is green,
Oh our Mother the Earth, oh our Father the Sky!   **6**

---

**1. warp** (wôrp) *n.*: The threads running lengthwise in a loom.
**2. weft** (weft) *n.*: The threads carried horizontally by the shuttle back and forth across the warp in weaving.

## RESPONDING TO THE SELECTION

### Your Response

1. What does the image of the "garment of brightness" convey to you? Explain.

### Recalling

2. Who are the Mother, Father, and children?
3. What do the children bring? What do they want?

### Interpreting

4. How is one's climate like a "garment"?
5. Explain the title of the poem.

### Applying

6. Do you consider a close relationship to nature important? Explain your answer.

## CRITICAL THINKING AND READING

### Paraphrasing a Poem

**Paraphrasing a poem,** or restating it in your own words, can help you understand it. In "Song of the Sky Loom," the first three lines might be paraphrased: "Dear Mother Earth and Father Sky, we, your children, honor you with gifts."

1. How would you paraphrase lines 5–11?
2. What is the theme of this poem?

*Song of the Sky Loom*    579

## Presentation

**Motivation/Prior Knowledge**
The Pueblo Indians (of which the Tewa were a group) have practiced weaving since about A.D. 700. Native Americans of Southwestern United States are still known for the beauty of their weaving. You might bring in pictures of actual artifacts woven by Native Americans, such as baskets, rugs, and wall hangings.

**Purpose-Setting Question** To what does the title refer?

1 **Discussion** Who is the audience to whom this poem is addressed?

2 **Discussion** Who offers this poem?

3 **Discussion** What might be the gifts offered? What might "tired backs" have to do with the gifts?

4 **Discussion** What is really being requested? What metaphor appears in these lines?

5 **Discussion** Why are these gifts being requested?

6 **Discussion** Why is the first line repeated at the end of the poem?

**Reader's Response** How does the idea of "Mother Earth" and "Father Sky" affect you? Why?

**Thematic Response** What is the speaker's attitude toward nature? How involved is the speaker with the natural world?

**Alternative Assessment** You may assess your students' understanding of this poem by having them write a response paper in which they react to the personification and world view in the poem. How does the poem make them feel about nature?

---

## Closure and Extension

### ANSWERS TO RESPONDING TO THE SELECTION
#### Your Response
1. Encourage students to respond as instinctively as possible.

#### Recalling
2. The Mother is the Earth; the Father is the Sky; the children are the Tewa Indians.
3. The children bring gifts that will be loved by Mother Earth and Father Sky. The children want a garment, or environment, with white light of morning, red light of evening, falling rain, and rainbows so that there will be birds singing and green grass.

#### Interpreting
4. One's climate is all around one, affecting the environment and the way the environment looks.
5. The title refers to the metaphor of weaving for the creation of their climate, much of which seems to come from the sky.

#### Applying
6. Suggested Response: We need pure water, fertile soil, and fresh air to survive, making a close relationship to nature essential.

### ANSWERS TO CRITICAL THINKING AND READING

1. Suggested Response: May the day be started with sunshine and end with a beautiful sunset. May there be rain around the edges followed by a beautiful rainbow. Thus we will have a beautiful and bountiful environment with singing birds and green grass.
2. The theme is that if we show nature the proper respect and care, we will be rewarded with the kind of environment we need in order to live.

**Master Teacher Note** You might want to discuss this poem as an account of the creation of the Earth and compare it to the Book of Genesis in the Bible and any other accounts of the creation you may have available.

**Master Teacher Note** Spectacular natural phenomena have been the subject of much poetry, art, and photography. Place Art Transparency 14, *Aurora Borealis* by Frederic Church, located in the Teaching Portfolio, on an overhead projector. Ask students what other majestic, awe-inspiring natural scenes have been captured in poetry, art, or photography.

In "New World" the poet addresses what could be the beginning of the world or of a new day.

**Purpose-Setting Question** To what does the title of this poem refer?

**1 Discussion** To whom is this poem addressed?

**2 Discussion** Keeping in mind the Biblical account of creation, why do you think the poet talks of rain in this stanza? Why is it appropriate for him to mention pollen here?

**3 Discussion** What geographical phenomenon does Momaday mention here?

**4 Discussion** What form of plant life does the poet mention here?

# New World

### N. Scott Momaday

**1.**

1    First Man,
      behold:
      the earth
      glitters
5     with leaves;
      the sky
      glistens
      with rain.
      Pollen[1]
10    is borne
2     on winds
      that low
      and lean
      upon
15    mountains.
      Cedars
      blacken
      the slopes—
      and pines.

**2.**

20    At dawn
      eagles
      hie and
      hover
      above
3  25  the plain
      where light
      gathers
      in pools.
4     Grasses
  30  shimmer
      and shine.

---

1. **pollen** (pǎl′ ən) *n.*: The yellow, powderlike male cells formed in the stamen of a flower.

**Electronic Handbook** You might want students to review verb tense before completing the Grammar in Action activities. If students have access to the Language Master 6000, have them enter *verb, tense,* or *regular* and press the GRAMMAR key with each entry to review verb tenses.

## Grammar in Action

In both prose and poetry, writers must be careful to keep the **verb tense** consistent within a passage. In this poem Scott Momaday uses the present tense to express his ideas. Notice the verbs he uses in the first stanza: *behold, glitters, glistens, is borne, low, lean, blacken.* These verbs are all in the same tense because the author wants to say that the events all occur at once, now, in the present. The meaning of the poem is dependent upon the idea that these actions all occur now and will continue to occur; they didn't happen only in the past, nor will they happen only in the future. The use of the present tense in this poem is crucial.

Shadows
withdraw
and lie
35 away
like smoke.

**3.**

At noon
turtles
enter
40 slowly
into
the warm
dark loam.[2]
Bees hold
45 the swarm.
Meadows
recede
through planes
of heat
50 and pure
distance.

**4.**

At dusk
the gray
foxes
55 stiffen
in cold;
blackbirds
are fixed
in the
60 branches.
Rivers
follow
the moon,
the long
65 white track
of the
full moon.

5

6

7

8

9

10

_____
**2. loam** (lōm) *n.*: Rich, dark soil.

*New World*    581

5 **Literary Focus** What two things are being compared in this simile?

6 **Discussion** What forms of life does Momaday mention here?

7 **Discussion** What type of geographical features are mentioned here?

8 **Discussion** What span of time has elapsed?

9 **Discussion** How do the living creatures here compare with those mentioned in the previous stanza?

10 **Discussion** What geographical features are described?

**Reader's Response** Has some aspect of nature ever seemed awesome or spectacular to you?

**Thematic Response** What range of living things does the poet describe? What is the tone of the poet's response to nature?

**Audiocassette** You might wish to use the recordings featuring N. Scott Momaday in the **Audio Prose Library.** The recordings contain an interview with the author and his readings of selected prose and poetry. Have students listen for ways in which Momaday's oral renderings bring new meanings to the poems.

**Student Activity 1.** List all of the verbs in the remaining three stanzas. In what tense are they?

**Student Activity 2.** Reconstruct this poem by changing all of the verbs to past tense. Begin as follows:

First man,
beheld:
the earth
glittered
with leaves;

Continue through the entire poem.

**Student Activity 3.** Write your own contrasting poem. Begin as follows:

Present man,
behold:
the earth

Continue telling how the earth is now.

## ANSWERS TO RESPONDING TO THE SELECTION

### Your Response

1. Be sure students make specific comparisons and contrasts.
2. Encourage students to support their preferences with reasons.

### Recalling

3. The poet speaks to "First Man."
4. The poem takes place anywhere in the world on any day.
5. The poem moves from before daybreak through dawn, noon, and dusk.

### Interpreting

6. Three details are addressing the poem to "First Man," the use of the words *glitters* and *glistens,* and the mention of pollen from which new plants arise.
7. In the second stanza, graceful eagles hover above a flat plain shining with light. In the third stanza, slow-moving turtles burrow into rich, black soil, while bees swarm, and the heat extends as far as one can envision. In the last stanza, cold comes with the darkness and even the "foxes stiffen in cold," blackbirds huddle on the branches, and rivers seem to follow the full moon's "long white track."
8. The title could mean that each new day seems to dawn on a new world that is fresh and alive. The title might refer to the creation of the world in the first place.

### Applying

9. The world is new every day because we see it after resting and after it has been hidden by the darkness of night. An awakening seems like a rebirth. Renewing ourselves means wiping out disappointments and failures of the past and meeting the new with a rested, peaceful mind and body.

## LEARNING OPTIONS

1. Students may wish to present their choral reading of "New World" to another class.
2. This activity will appeal to students who enjoy poetry. You may extend the activity by having poems read aloud.
3. This activity will appeal to students

## RESPONDING TO THE SELECTION

### Your Response

1. In what ways is the world you live in different from and similar to the one described in the poem? Explain your answer.
2. Of the four time periods described in the poem, which appeals to you most? Why?

### Recalling

3. To whom does the poet speak?
4. Where and when does the poem take place?
5. Explain the progression of time throughout the poem.

### Interpreting

6. Find three details that suggest newness in the first stanza. Why are these details appropriate in this stanza?
7. What impression is created in the second stanza? In the third? In the last? Explain which details in each stanza help to create these impressions.
8. Explain the two meanings suggested by the title.

### Applying

9. In what way is the world new every day? In what way are people new every day? What do we mean when we speak of renewing ourselves?

## LEARNING OPTIONS

1. **Speaking and Listening.** The earliest poetry was chanted or sung aloud. Even today, poems gain in force and meaning when read aloud. A choral reading is one performed by a group, or chorus, of readers.

   Give a choral reading of "New World." Your teacher may split the class into four groups, each reading one section of the poem in turn. Read with a tone of voice that communicates wonder at the beauty of the natural world seen for the first time.
2. **Writing.** Using this poem as a model, write an original poem about the "new world" that you experience or would like to experience. Use a style and structure similar to those used by Momaday. For example, use short lines, and divide the poem into stanzas describing different time periods. Choose your words carefully to create images that truly capture the experience you want to convey.
3. **Cross-curricular Connection.** Try to find some information about the Kiowa people from an encyclopedia or a reference book in your library. See whether your findings help you to appreciate the poem more fully.
4. **Art.** Create a drawing, painting, collage, or other work of visual art to illustrate all or part of the poem "New World." You may wish to review the poem and the photograph beforehand to help you generate ideas for your illustration.

interested in history and other cultures. You may extend the activity by having students make oral reports to their class.
4. This activity will appeal to artistic students. You could extend the activity by exhibiting the poem and illustration in your classroom.

**Multicultural Focus** Many cultures have accounts of the world's creation. Students may be most familiar with the Biblical account and with the "Big Bang theory" of the planets' formation.

Many Native Americans believe that humans—as part of nature—are responsible for the earth's care. An old Onondaga legend tells of Handsome Lake being granted a vision of the future. Four spiritual "protectors" show him a river and ask him to drink, but it is too polluted. They predict that the clear waters he knows will also become filthy and foretell other environmental crises. The only hope is for each generation to renew its commitment to preventing such destruction.

Have students research different cultures' accounts of Earth's creation.

# Perceptions

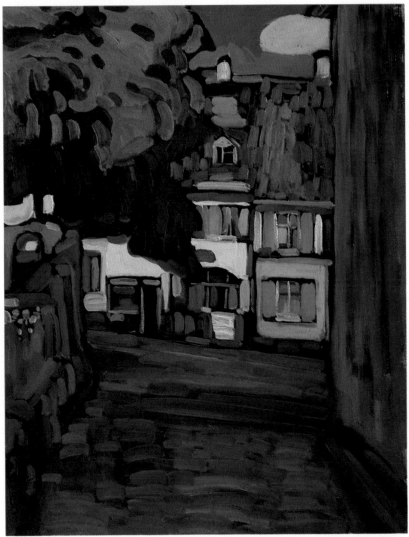

**HOUSES OF MURNAU AT OBERMARKT, 1908**
*Wassily Kandinsky*
*Lugano-Thyssen-Bornemisza Collection*

## Humanities Note

Fine art, *Houses of Murnau at Obermarkt,* by Wassily Kandinsky. Wassily Kandinsky (1866–1944) was a Russian painter who began as a legal expert in his native country. The bright peasant folk art of Russia and Impressionist paintings he saw on a visit to France convinced Kandinsky that his true interest was in art. He went to Munich, Germany, where he studied painting at the Munich Academy under Franz von Stuck. Kandinsky is important to modern art as the first European artist to paint in a totally abstract fashion. A dynamic personality, he greatly influenced his contemporaries with his writings on modern art, his teachings, and his work.

Kandinsky was not immediately committed to abstraction in art. He arrived at this stage through a series of evolutionary phases in his work. His initial paintings were Impressionistic. As his focus changed, his style became what he termed "improvisational." These works of vibrant color and simple form are related to Fauvism (a movement in art based on the exaltation of pure color). The painting *Houses of Murnau at Obermarkt* falls into this category. Painted in 1908, just two years before his first completely nonobjective work, his direction is apparent. He uses a recognizable subject, but he has simplified the forms into geometric shapes and used colors that have no basis in reality. Kandinsky's innovative genius changed the course of twentieth-century art.

**Master Teacher Note** To introduce the theme of perceptions in poetry, show Art Transparency 15, *La chiave dei campi* by René Magritte, in the Teaching Portfolio. Tell students that the way one views the world can affect the way one thinks about it. Discuss the fact that the broken shards of glass from the window reflect the trees, grass, and sky seen from the window. What statement do they think the artist is making? Explain that poets sometimes write poems in free verse—a nontraditional approach using irregular rhythms and varied line lengths. Why might free verse be appropriate for a poem about this painting?

**More About the Authors** *My Aunt Otilia's Spirits,* by **Richard García,** has been published in a bilingual edition that is printed in both English and Spanish. How might authors who can write in more than one language and who are familiar with more than one culture help other people to improve their understanding of cultures other than their own?

**Patricia Hubbell** Born in Bridgeport, Connecticut, Patricia Hubbell was raised in, and still lives in, Easton, Connecticut. Easton is a small town of about 6,000 people in southeastern Connecticut. How might living in a small town near a large metropolitan area help a poet see ordinary city sights in new and creative ways?

**May Swenson** lectured and gave readings at more than thirty American colleges and universities. Swenson received a Guggenheim Fellowship, the William Rose Benét Prize of the Poetry Society of America, a Ford Foundation grant, a Rockefeller Writing fellowship, and many others. Often literary honors and awards involve money as well as prestige. Why might it be especially important for a poet to receive awards of money? Speaking of poetry, Swenson said "by bringing into play the sensual apparatus of the reader, the poem causes him to realize the content eye-wise, ear-wise, taste, touch, and muscle-wise. . . . The analyzing intellect . . . applied alone . . . can . . . bypass initial curiosity and individual exploration, resulting in little more than a mechanistic contact with the poem." What do you think Swenson meant by this statement?

# GUIDE FOR READING

## The City Is So Big

**Richard García** (1941–    ) writes poetry for adults and children. He has published *Selected Poetry* (1973) and a contemporary folk tale for children, *My Aunt Otilia's Spirits* (1978). García is the director of the Poets in the Schools program in Marin County, California. Born in San Francisco, California, he has also lived in Mexico and Israel. In "The City Is So Big" he describes the city as a child might see it.

## Concrete Mixers

**Patricia Hubbell** (1928–    ) is a freelance journalist as well as a poet. She was born in Bridgeport, Connecticut, and attended the University of Connecticut. Her books include *The Apple Vendor's Fair* (1963), *8 A.M. Shadows* (1965), and *Catch Me a Wind* (1968). In "Concrete Mixers," she imagines these machines as elephants.

## Southbound on the Freeway

**May Swenson** (1919–1989) was born in Logan, Utah, and attended Utah State University. After working for a while as a newspaper reporter, she moved to New York City, where she found employment as an editor and as a lecturer at colleges and universities. Her poems have been published in such magazines as *The New Yorker, Harper's,* and *The Nation.* Swenson believed that poetry is based on the desire to see things as they are, rather than as they appear. In "Southbound on the Freeway," however, she portrays an aspect of our culture as it might appear to an alien creature.

*584   Poetry*

## Objectives

1 To understand free verse
2 To read free verse
3 To write free verse

## Support Material

**Teaching Portfolio**
Teacher Backup, p. 799
Usage and Mechanics Worksheet, p. 803
Vocabulary Check, p. 804
Analyzing Literature Worksheet, *Understanding Free Verse,* p. 805
Critical Thinking and Reading Worksheet, *Reading Free Verse,* p. 806
Selection Test, p. 807

**Listening to Literature**
"The City Is So Big," "Concrete Mixers," "Southbound on the Freeway"

**Prentice Hall Literature Writing Studio**

## Free Verse

**Free verse** is poetry with irregular rhythms and varied line lengths. It is "free" of the traditional forms of poetry. Since it is written in a way that is similar to ordinary speech, if it uses rhyme, the rhymes are loose and also irregular.

A poem written in free verse may be long or short. It may or may not have stanzas. The stanzas may be long or short, or both. Sometimes, as in "Southbound on the Freeway," the stanzas may be regular. In general, the lines in free verse are organized according to the flow of the poet's thoughts, ideas, and images. For example, "Concrete Mixers" is arranged according to the natural pauses one makes when speaking normally.

> They rid the trunk-like trough of concrete,
> Direct the spray to the bulging sides,
> Turn and start the monsters moving.

## Focus

With a partner take turns reading aloud the three lines from "Concrete Mixers" that appear above. Keep in mind that free verse finds its music in the sounds and rhythms of natural speech, so try to speak as naturally as possible. Use a conversational tone—as though you were speaking to a friend. As you read and listen, jot down the poetic qualities you notice in these lines. What consonant or vowel sounds are repeated? How does the rhythm help to convey the action described? Share your ideas with your partner.

## Vocabulary

Knowing the following words will help you as you read these poems.

**ponderous** (pän′ dər əs) *adj.*: Heavy; massive (p. 587)

**perch** (pʉrch) *v.*: Rest upon (p. 587)

**trough** (trôf) *n.*: Long, narrow container for holding water or food for animals (p. 587)

**bellow** (bel′ ō) *v.*: Roar powerfully (p. 587)

**Literary Focus** Although free verse does not exhibit the traditional forms of poetry, it is still poetry, not prose. You might want to have your students list elements that they think free verse might have, which distinguishes it from prose.

**Prereading Focus** After students have discussed the lines' poetic qualities, you might have several students read the lines as conversationally as possible for the whole class.

**Vocabulary** Your less advanced students might benefit from pronouncing and discussing the meaning of each of the vocabulary words before the students read the poems.

**Thematic Focus** In "The City Is So Big," "Concrete Mixers," and "Southbound on the Freeway," three poets bring fresh, creative eyes to bear on "ordinary" urban landscapes. Which of the poets' views do students find most unusual?

# The City Is So Big

### Richard García

1  The city is so big
   Its bridges quake with fear
   I know, I have seen at night

2  The lights sliding from house to house
5  And trains pass with windows shining
   Like a smile full of teeth

3  I have seen machines eating houses
   And stairways walk all by themselves
   And elevator doors opening and closing
10 And people disappear.

## RESPONDING TO THE SELECTION

### Your Response
1. Do you think the voice in this poem is child-like? Why or why not?

### Recalling
2. What has the speaker seen the bridges doing?
3. What do the passing trains resemble?

### Interpreting
4. Describe the mood of this poem. Find five details that help create this mood.
5. Interpret lines 7–10. Explain how each of the three details is possible.

### Applying
6. This poem presents one side of living in a big city. Discuss with your classmates the pros and cons of city living.

## ANALYZING LITERATURE

### Understanding Free Verse
   Poetry that is written in free verse often follows its own form. In attempting to capture the sounds of natural speech, free verse often abandons any precise rhythmic pattern and regular rhyme scheme.

1. Read the poem aloud. How would you describe its rhythm?
2. What do you notice about the length of the lines?
3. How do these two features add to the mood of the poem?

586   Poetry

# Concrete Mixers

## Patricia Hubbell

CITY AT THE SEA
*Helmut Kies*

The drivers are washing the concrete mixers;
Like elephant tenders[1] they hose them down.
Tough gray-skinned monsters standing ponderous,
Elephant-bellied and elephant-nosed,
5  Standing in muck up to their wheel-caps,
Like rows of elephants, tail to trunk.
Their drivers perch on their backs like mahouts,[2]
Sending the sprays of water up.
They rid the trunk-like trough of concrete,
10  Direct the spray to the bulging sides,
Turn and start the monsters moving.
        Concrete mixers
        Move like elephants
        Bellow like elephants
15       Spray like elephants
Concrete mixers are urban elephants,
Their trunks are raising a city.

1. **elephant tenders:** People in charge of elephants.
2. **mahouts** (mə houts') *n.*: Elephant drivers or keepers.

---

## RESPONDING TO THE SELECTION

### Your Response

1 Do you think that it is appropriate to compare an elephant to a concrete mixer? Explain.

### Recalling

2. What scene is being described in this poem?

### Interpreting

3. An extended metaphor is a figurative comparison carried throughout a poem. Describe how the two items here are alike.

### Applying

4. Cars are often named after animals. Think of two such examples and explain the intended effect of the car's name.

## CRITICAL THINKING AND READING

### Reading Free Verse

Let punctuation marks help you when you read free verse. Pause at commas and take a slightly longer pause at semicolons. Stop when you come to periods, question marks, and exclamation marks. If a line does not have a punctuation mark at the end of it, read on to the next line without pausing.

1. The punctuation marks in lines 1–11 tell you that these lines should be read one by one, pausing or stopping at the end of each. Given the subject, why do you suppose the poet chose this "step-by-step" arrangement?
2. How should lines 12–15 be read? Why?

*Concrete Mixers*  587

**Motivation/Prior Knowledge**
Lead a discussion about point of view. Elicit from students that different people will interpret events in different ways, depending on their point of view. Tell students the speaker in this poem has an unusual view of what he or she sees.

**Master Teacher Note** If your students are from rural areas, you might want to show them pictures of elaborate freeway systems. An alternative would be to have those who have visited California describe the freeways they saw there.

**Purpose-Setting Question** Why is the point of view of the speaker in this poem unusual?

1 **Discussion** From where does the tourist come?

2 **Discussion** What are the creatures referred to here?

3 **Discussion** What are the transparent parts?

4 **Discussion** What are their feet?

5 **Discussion** What are the measuring tapes?

6 **Discussion** What is the special one?

7 **Discussion** What are the soft shapes?

**Literary Focus** Why do you think the poet chose to write this poem in couplets, stanzas of two lines each?

**Reader's Response** Choose a subject and describe it as if you were a visitor from outer space seeing the subject for the first time.

# Southbound on the Freeway

May Swenson

1    A tourist came in from Orbitville,
parked in the air, and said:

2    The creatures of this star
are made of metal and glass.

3    5   Through the transparent parts
you can see their guts.

4    Their feet are round and roll
on diagrams—or long

5    10   measuring tapes—dark
with white lines.

They have four eyes.
The two in the back are red.

Sometimes you can see a five-eyed
one, with a red eye turning

15   on the top of his head.
6    He must be special—

the others respect him,
and go slow,

when he passes, winding
20   among them from behind.

They all hiss as they glide,
like inches, down the marked

7    tapes. Those soft shapes,
shadowy inside.

25   the hard bodies—are they
their guts or their brains?

**Thematic Response** Which aspects of the freeway does the "tourist" notice? Does any passage of the poem give you a new understanding about modern life?

**Making Connections** The short story "Rain, Rain, Go Away" by Isaac Asimov, page 13, is also about extraterrestrials.

**Enrichment** You might have students write poems about the Sakkaro family as seen by the Wrights in "Rain, Rain, Go Away," page 13. Another possibility might be to have artistic students illustrate the poems they write for the Thinking and Writing activity.

**Audiocassette** To help students appreciate the strange viewpoints of these three poems, use the **Listening to Literature** Audiocassette recordings of "The City Is So Big," "Concrete Mixers," and "Southbound on the Freeway" (Side 5). As they listen, have students note the ways in which the readers indicate unusual descriptions, comparisons, or word choices.

## RESPONDING TO THE SELECTION

### Your Response

1. As you read this poem, did you get the sense that you were an outsider looking down at the scene or that you were one of the creatures described in the poem? Why?

### Recalling

2. Who is the tourist in this poem?
3. According to the title, what does the tourist see?

### Interpreting

4. Part of the humor in this poem comes from the tourist's misinterpreting what he or she sees. How does the tourist misinterpret the creatures of this star?
5. What is the five-eyed creature? In what way is the tourist's analysis of the five-eyed creature actually correct?
6. Explain the question that the tourist asks. How would you answer this question?

### Applying

7. Put yourself in the place of this tourist. For example, if this tourist were to see a parking lot, he or she might interpret it as a hotel. How might this tourist interpret a drive-through window at a fast-food restaurant? List three other items and explain how this tourist might misinterpret them.

## THINKING AND WRITING

### Writing Free Verse

Imagine the tourist from Orbitville parked in the air above a football game. Freewrite about what the tourist would see and how the tourist might interpret what he or she sees. Then use your freewriting as the basis for writing a poem in free verse. When you revise your poem, make sure you have consistently described the game from the tourist's point of view. Then proofread your poem and share it with your classmates.

*Southbound on the Freeway* 589

inside are the brains of the creature.

### Applying

7. Answers will differ. Possible responses might be that a drive-through window at a fast-food restaurant might be where the creatures eat; a drive-in movie might be the creatures' school. Three other possibilities might be a school misinterpreted as a zoo; a gas station misinterpreted as a hospital; and a ship misinterpreted as a large fish.

**Challenge** You might have students write poems about people on earth seeing the tourist from outer space and misinterpreting what he or she is.

### THINKING AND WRITING

◆ **Software** If your students are working on computers, they might find it helpful to use the **Writer's Helper** activities *Lists, Five W's, Crazy Contrasts,* or *Three Ways of Seeing.*

**Alternative Assessment** You may vary the Thinking and Writing assignment as follows: Have students complete one of the Alternate Composition Assignments on pages 820 and 821 of the Teaching Portfolio.

**Publishing Student Writing** If a copying machine is available, students' poems could be added to booklets of creative writing kept by each student. If no copying machines are available, students' poems might be displayed on a bulletin board.

**Writing Across the Curriculum** You might want to tell the art teachers if you plan to have students illustrate poems they have written. They might want to guide students in illustrating their poems.

## Closure and Extension

### ANSWERS TO RESPONDING TO THE SELECTION

#### Your Response

1. Encourage students to offer clear explanations for why they identified with either the poem's speaker or its subjects.

#### Recalling

2. The tourist is someone from outer space.
3. According to the title, the tourist

sees the southbound lane of a freeway.

#### Interpreting

4. The tourist thinks the automobiles are the living creatures of this star.
5. The five-eyed creature is a police car or an ambulance. The tourist is correct in saying that the other cars respect it and go slow when he passes.
6. The tourist asks whether the soft shapes inside are the creature's guts or brains. Students will probably respond that the soft shapes

# GUIDE FOR READING

## Preparation

**More About the Author** The poet **Maxine Kumin** received an American Academy and Institute of Arts and Letters award in 1980 and became a consultant in poetry to the Library of Congress in 1981. Why do you think the Library of Congress would hire a consultant in poetry?

**Literary Focus** Concrete poetry should not be noteworthy only for its shape. In the case of "400-Meter Free Style," for example, the description of a swimmer's movements that Kumin gives is a complete and accurate one about swimming such a race. Why do you think it is important for poets not to depend completely upon the shape of a concrete poem to communicate to readers?

**Prereading Focus** You may want to lead **less advanced** students in a group discussion of the meaning of the poem's shape.

**Vocabulary** You might want to go over the vocabulary words and the footnoted words with your **less advanced** students before they read the poem.

**Spelling Tip** Note that there is no rule to determine whether *-ence* or *-ance* is correct. If a word ends in *-ance*, however, like *extravagance,* then parallel forms like *extravagant* use the same letter.

## Maxine Kumin

(1925–     ) was born in Philadelphia, Pennsylvania. She attended Radcliffe College and taught there and at Tufts University, both in Massachusetts. Kumin has written novels, essays, and children's books, as well as several volumes of poetry. In 1973 she was awarded a Pulitzer Prize for *Up Country: Poems of New England.* In her poem "400-Meter Free Style," Kumin describes a swim race not only in words but also in shape.

## 400-Meter Free Style

### Concrete Poetry

**Concrete poetry** is poetry in which the shape of the poem on the page resembles the subject of the poem. With concrete poetry, poets experiment with the way a poem *looks* on the page. They arrange the words so as to form a concrete, or actual, shape that is recognizable. Poems have been written in many shapes, including hearts, trees, wings, and even falling rain.

For example, the arrangement of the lines of "400-Meter Free Style" may confuse you at first. If so, just think about the poem's subject: a swimmer in a race.

### Focus

With your classmates brainstorm to list possible subjects for concrete poems. An appropriate subject would have an aspect to it that could be represented clearly in visual terms: a shape, a design, or a pattern. For example, suppose you wanted to write a concrete poem about a chess game. One way to convey the idea of chess would be to arrange the text on the page in the black-and-white pattern of a chessboard. As you brainstorm, list your ideas in a chart like the one that follows.

| Subject | Shape or Pattern |
| --- | --- |
| chess game | text in alternating black-and-white squares |

### Vocabulary

Knowing the following words will help you as you read "400-Meter Free Style."

**catapults** (kat′ ə pults′) *v.*: Launches (p. 591)

**cunningly** (kun′ iŋ lē) *adv.*: Skillfully (p. 591)

**extravagance** (ik strav′ ə gəns) *n.*: Waste (p. 591)

**compensation** (käm′ pən sā′ shən) *n.*: Here, equal reaction (p. 591)

**nurtures** (nʉr′ chərz) *v.*: Nourishes (p. 591)

**tick** (tik) *v.*: Operate smoothly (p. 593)

**expended** (ik spend′ id) *v.*: Used up (p. 593)

**plum** (plum) *adj.*: Here, first-class (p. 593)

---

### Objectives

1 To understand concrete poetry
2 To write a concrete poem
3 To express individual interests and abilities through optional activities

### Support Material

**Teaching Portfolio**
Teacher Backup, p. 809
Usage and Mechanics Worksheet, p. 811
Vocabulary Check, p. 812
Analyzing Literature Worksheet, *Understanding Concrete Poetry,* p. 813

Language Worksheet, *Choosing the Meaning That Fits the Context,* p. 814
Selection Test, p. 815

**Listening to Literature**
"400-Meter Free Style"

**Prentice Hall Literature Writing Studio**

# 400-Meter Free Style

Maxine Kumin

The gun full swing the swimmer catapults and cracks
        s
        i
        x
feet away onto that perfect glass he catches at    ] **1**
a
n
d
throws behind him scoop¹ after scoop cunningly moving
        t
        h
        e
water back to move him forward. Thrift is his wonderful
    s
    e                ] **2**
    c
5  ret; he has schooled out all extravagance. No muscle
        r
        i
        p
ples without compensation wrist cock² to heel snap to
h
i
s
mobile mouth that siphons³ in the air that nurtures
        h
        i    ] **3**
        m
at half an inch above sea level so to speak.
T
h
e
astonishing whites of the soles of his feet rise
        a
        n
        d

---

**1. scoop** (skōōp) *n.*: The amount taken up, in this case with a cupped hand.
**2. wrist cock:** The tilted position of the wrist.
**3. siphons** (sī′ fənz) *v.*: Draws; pulls.

*400-Meter Free Style*    591

**Multicultural Focus** Various nations and cultures have developed different aspects of and uses for swimming and other water skills.

Synchronized swimming, or water ballet, is a popular dance-like sport among American women. As a test of endurance, distance swimming in Western Europe has produced many well-publicized attempts to cross the English Channel. Fancy competitive diving is said to have begun in seventeenth-century Sweden and Germany, and cliff diving remains an internationally popular sport for many thrill seekers. Pearl cultivation in Asia and the Pacific once relied on sustained sessions of diving for oysters.

Have students research swimming (or other water activity) in other cultures and settle on one culture and style. Then have them write a poem like Kumin's in which form mirrors content. Explain that the poem's content will stem from their imagination and world view, as well as from what they have learned about the culture and type of water sport they chose. Thus lines about Japanese pearl diving might dip up and down across a page; a cliff-diving poem might consist of a single vertical line; whereas a poem about distance swimming might appear as a straight, unbroken line over several pages.

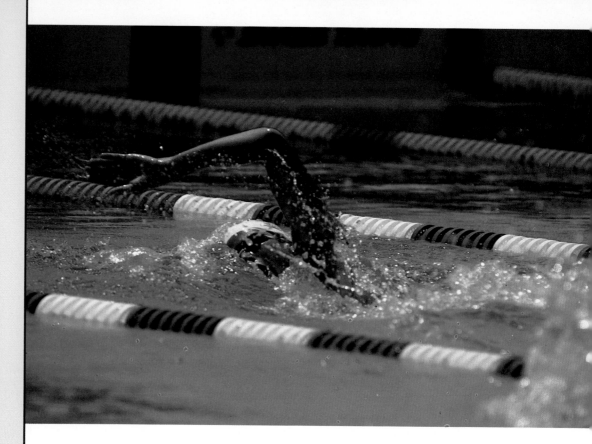

592 *Poetry*

10 salute us on the turns. He flips, converts, and is gone
a
l
l
in one. We watch him for signs. His arms are steady at
t
h
e
catch, his cadent⁴ feet tick in the stretch, they know
t
h
e
lesson well. Lungs know, too; he does not list⁵ for
a
i
r
he drives along on little sips carefully expended │ 4
b
u
t
15 that plum red heart pumps hard cries hurt how soon
i
t
s
near one more and makes its final surge        TIME 4:25:9

---

**4. cadent** (kā′ dənt) *adj.*: Rhythmic; beating.
**5. list** (list) *v.*: Wish; crave.

4 **Discussion** Explain why the swimmer's air supply is described as ''little sips carefully expended.''

**Reader's Response** What object or activity can you think of that could be described in the shape of its motion?

**Thematic Response** How can you tell that the poem portrays a competitive rather than a recreational swimmer? How does the swimmer respond to conflict and challenge?

400-Meter Free Style   593

# Closure and Extension

### Your Response

1. Encourage students to describe their responses to the challenges and delights of a concrete poem.

### Recalling

2. The poet mentions the swimmer's arm movements, breathing technique, and kicking.

3. In lines 3–6, the poet admires the thrift of the swimmer's motion, with no unnecessary movement, with only movements that produce the desired result.

4. The swimmer's heart hurts as he nears the end of the race and makes his final surge to the finish.

### Interpreting

5. At the end the poet moves "inside" the swimmer by talking about his heart hurting and by mentioning his thoughts.

6. The shape of the poem shows the laps of the pool that the swimmer swims.

7. By finishing the poem with the swimmer's racing time, the poet makes the race in the poem appear to be actually taking place as you read it.

### Applying

8. Answers will differ. Suggested Response: The swimmer's training and discipline can be helpful in daily living because the swimmer is used to finishing difficult tasks, trying his hardest despite discomfort, and constantly working to improve his performance.

## ANSWERS TO ANALYZING LITERATURE

1. Answers will differ. Suggested Response: It takes longer to read aloud because you have to concentrate on when to go to the left of each line.

2. Answers will differ. Suggested Response: You have to concentrate on how to read the poem in the same way the swimmer has to concentrate on how to move in order to win the race.

## RESPONDING TO THE SELECTION

### Your Response

1. How did the poem's shape affect you as you read? Did it add to or detract from your reading experience? Explain.

### Recalling

2. What three aspects of the swimmer's movements does the poet mention?

3. In lines 3–6, what does the poet admire about the swimmer's motion?

4. What hurts the swimmer?

### Interpreting

5. Until the last four lines, the poet confines her observations to the swimmer's external movement. How does the poet move "inside" the swimmer at the end?

6. What does the shape of the poem show?

7. What is the effect of ending the poem with the swimmer's racing time?

### Applying

8. How can the swimmer's training and discipline be helpful in daily living?

## ANALYZING LITERATURE

### Understanding Concrete Poetry

A **concrete poem** gives you another element—shape—to think about. The shape of a concrete poem not only reinforces the subject but may also give you another way of understanding its meaning. Both the title and the shape tell you that "400-Meter Free Style" is about the idea of a swimming race.

In a concrete poem, punctuation may occur in places other than at the end of a line, and words may be placed other than horizontally. This may make the poem more difficult to read but is meant to surprise you by the way the poem looks and sounds.

1. Read the poem aloud. What do you notice about your reading of a poem in this shape?

2. How might reading this poem aloud require the kind of concentration and effort that the swimmer has?

## THINKING AND WRITING

### Writing a Concrete Poem

Write a short concrete poem. You may choose your subject from the list that you created earlier, or you may choose some other subject. Think of a shape or a pattern that in some way relates to your subject. For instance, if you wanted to write about the destruction of a fire, you could shape your poem like a flame. Then draw the shape or pattern. Freewrite about the subject you chose. Use this information to write your lines of poetry. Finally, fit the lines to the shape or pattern.

## LEARNING OPTIONS

1. **Writing.** Interview a member of a swim team about his or her experiences during competition. Ask questions such as these:

   What events do you swim in? Why?
   What does it feel like—physically and emotionally—when you compete?
   What do you think about as you swim?
   How do you prepare yourself psychologically for a meet?

   Based on your interview, write a brief article for a school newspaper or magazine in which you profile this athlete and show readers what it's like to compete in a swimming event.

2. **Cross-curricular Connection.** What makes the 400-meter freestyle unique and particularly challenging to a swimmer? What is the world record for the 400-meter freestyle? How does the time in this poem compare? You can find answers to these questions with the help of a physical education teacher or a library resource such as an almanac.

## THINKING AND WRITING

**Software** If your students have access to computers, have them use **Bank Street Writer** to complete all stages of the assignment. Using the program's cut-and-paste features, students will be able to easily incorporate ideas from their prewriting into their concrete poems.

## Publishing Student Writing

These concrete poems could be included in a class booklet of the students' creative writing or could be displayed on a bulletin board.

## LEARNING OPTIONS

1. This activity will appeal especially to students with interest and abilities in journalism. You might vary the activity by having students interview athletes from other competitive sports.

2. Students interested in athletics will enjoy this activity. You might extend the activity by having students present their research findings to their class in an oral report.

# Choices

**ON THE PROMENADE**
*August Macke*

**Humanities Note**
Fine art, *On the Promenade,* by August Macke. August Macke (1887–1914) was a German Expressionist artist who received his academic training at the Düsseldorf Academy and the Arts and Crafts School. He is placed in the Blue Rider (*Blaue-Reiter*) Movement, a vital and influential movement by a group of German painters concerned with the spiritualism of nature in modern art. Macke's art involved spontaneous, happy, and colorful studies of the human figure. His death, on the front in World War I, was a severe loss to the world of modern art.

The painting *On The Promenade* is a study of the effect of people on a landscape. The simplified elongated figures appear in a park setting broken into geometric shapes and lit with fresh, pleasant color. Linear patterns produce a curving rhythm and give a sense of movement to the canvas. A woman's white parasol and a man's jaunty straw hat add compositional interest. The scene is a pleasant, harmonious observation of city life, just the sort of scene that Macke liked to paint.

**Master Teacher Note** To introduce the theme of choices in poetry, show students Art Transparency 16, *Wood's Edge* by Henri Rousseau, in the Teaching Portfolio. Explain to students that the speaker in a poem—the person who addresses the reader—has a great impact on the effect of the poem. The speaker can be the poet or some other character. Discuss what the woman in the painting might be thinking as she stands in the middle of the road, poised at the edge of the woods. If she were the speaker in a poem about choices, what might she say? Based on her appearance, how might she say it? What choice might she make?

**More About the Author** The poet **Julio Noboa Polanco** has worked as a leadership trainer with the Latino Institute in Chicago. He has also been an editor for *The Rican, Journal of Puerto Rican Thought,* where a number of his poems have been published. He writes poetry both in Spanish and in English. If there are any bilingual students in your class, you might invite them to tell what it is like to speak, write, and think in two languages. They might also answer their classmates' questions about the experience of bilingualism.

**Robert Frost's** first published book, *A Boy's Will,* did not appear until he was thirty-nine years old, and it was published in England, where he lived for several years. Much of Frost's life was shadowed by loneliness, family sorrows, depression, and fear of mental unbalance. You might wish to discuss with your class whether happiness or unhappiness is more likely to inspire literary creativity.

# GUIDE FOR READING

## Identity

**Julio Noboa Polanco** (1949–    ) was born in the Bronx, New York, of Puerto Rican parents. The family moved to Chicago, and "Identity" was written while the poet was an eighth grader at a school on the west side of Chicago. As a bilingual poet who values his parents' Hispanic heritage, Julio Noboa Polanco has developed an interest in the variety of cultures in the world and has received a bachelor's degree in anthropology as well as a master's degree in education. Currently living in San Antonio, Texas, he administers a dropout prevention program in a barrio school in the city.

## The Road Not Taken

**Robert Frost** (1874–1963) was born in San Francisco. In 1885, following the death of his father, his family moved to New England. There Frost attended school in Lawrence, Massachusetts, and then went on to Dartmouth and Harvard colleges. His experiences as a farmer and schoolteacher provided the material for many of his most famous poems. For twelve years, Frost met with little success in getting his poetry published. However, in 1913 and 1914 he put together two of his major collections, *A Boy's Will* and *North of Boston,* and these works brought him critical acclaim. Between 1913 and 1962, he won a Pulitzer Prize four times. In 1960 Congress gave him a special gold medal "in recognition of his poetry, which has enriched the culture of the United States and the philosophy of the world."

## Objectives

1  To hear the speaker's voice
2  To interpret differences in metaphors

## Support Material

**Teaching Portfolio**
Teacher Backup, p. 817
Usage and Mechanics Worksheet, p. 820
Vocabulary Check, p. 821
Analyzing Literature Worksheet, *Hearing the Speaker's Voice,* p. 822
Language Worksheet, *Finding Synonyms,* p. 823
Selection Test, p. 824

**Listening to Literature**
"Identity," "The Road Not Taken"

**Prentice Hall Literature Writing Studio**

## The Speaker

If you read a poem carefully, you will notice that someone—a speaker—is addressing you. Sometimes the speaker is the poet. Other times, however, the speaker is a character the poet has created. This character may be a man or a woman, a child, an animal, or even an inanimate object to whom the poet has chosen to give human qualities. For example, the poet may create a princess, a boxer, a baseball player, a cat, or even mushrooms that speak—all tell their own story from their unique point of view.

## Focus

The poems in this section are about choices. We all make choices every day, from choosing which clothes to put on in the morning to choosing when to go to bed at night. Suppose that you had to choose, according to your tastes and interests, between the items listed in comparable pairs below. What would your choices be? Why?

| List A | List B |
| --- | --- |
| listening to classical music | listening to rock-and-roll |
| having a cat for a pet | having a bird for a pet |
| emptying the garbage | doing the dishes |
| swimming in the ocean | swimming in a swimming pool |
| watching a horror film | watching a comedy |
| becoming an actor | becoming a teacher |

Compare your choices with those of your classmates. Discuss the types of choices people make every day. Why is making choices so difficult at times?

## Vocabulary

Knowing the following words will help you as you read these poems.

**harnessed** (här′ nist) *v.*: Tied (p. 598)

**abyss** (ə bis′) *n.*: Great depth (p. 598)

**shunned** (shund) *v.*: Avoided (p. 598)

**fertile** (fur′ t'l) *adj.*: Rich; productive (p. 598)

**musty** (mus′ tē) *adj.*: With a stale, damp smell (p. 598)

**stench** (stench) *n.*: Bad smell (p. 598)

**diverged** (də vurjd′) *v.*: Branched off (p. 600)

*Guide for Reading* 597

**Literary Focus** To make the distinction between the speaker and the poet unmistakably clear, you might read a few of the poems in *Spoon River Anthology* or, with **more advanced** students, passages from Browning's dramatic monologues. Since at least some students think of poetry as nothing more than direct self-expression, you might discuss why poets might choose to create speakers who are clearly distinguishable from themselves.

**Prereading Focus** You might wish to lead your whole class in a discussion of students' responses to the two lists. Have students articulate the reasons behind their choice of items from List A or List B.

**Vocabulary** When discussing "Identity," you may wish to question students on the suggestions and associations they see in these words (excluding *diverged*) and others. The vocabulary of Frost's poem is not likely to require discussion.

**Spelling Tip** Note that a one-syllable word in which the last three letters are consonant-vowel-consonant doubles the final consonant before adding a suffix beginning with a vowel: *shunned*.

**Alternative Assessment** Polanco and Frost express their individuality by the choices they make. Polanco says that he would rather be an ugly weed apart from the crowd than a flower "always watered, fed, guarded, admired." In "The Road Not Taken," Frost says that choice is a part of life, and he "took the road less traveled by."

Have students decide what metaphor expresses their individuality and explain their choice in a short paper.

**Thematic Focus** In "Identity" the speaker finds his place in an "unpopular" and surprising form; in "The Road Not Taken," Frost celebrates the "consequences" of the paths he has chosen in his life. Ask students how difficult they think it may be to live with the consequences of unpopular choices.

**Motivation/Prior Knowledge**
Ask your students, "What do we mean by identity? Is it just one's name and the various numbers assigned to us by computers?" Lead them to see that learning who one really is presents a problem with which poets and other thinkers have long grappled.

**Master Teacher Note** Polanco has said the following about his poem: "The whole poem is essentially a search for my individuality—finding myself as a person, as opposed to being one of the crowd." Before reading the poem, you might wish to discuss how people go about finding themselves and separating themselves from the crowd.

**Purpose-Setting Question** What has the speaker decided about his own identity?

**1 Discussion** The "them" is the crowd, whom the speaker likens to flowers harnessed to a pot of dirt. In contrast there is the "I" of the poem, likened to a weed. By questioning lead your students to see the contrast established in these stanzas. Ask them to point out the implications of the two figurative comparisons.

**2 Clarification** This stanza consists of two incomplete sentences. You can help your students' comprehension by suggesting that they imagine each sentence beginning with the phrase *It would be better* . . . Ask how this stanza continues the image of the speaker as a weed.

**3 Discussion** Ask students what is undesirable about being a pleasant-smelling flower? Then direct students' attention to the last two lines, especially the words *handled, plucked,* and *greedy.*

# Identity

## Julio Noboa Polanco

**1**

Let them be as flowers,
always watered, fed, guarded, admired,
but harnessed to a pot of dirt.

5  I'd rather be a tall, ugly weed,
clinging on cliffs, like an eagle
wind-wavering above high, jagged rocks.

**2**

To have broken through the surface of stone,
to live, to feel exposed to the madness
of the vast, eternal sky.
10  To be swayed by the breezes of an ancient sea,
carrying my soul, my seed, beyond the mountains of time
or into the abyss of the bizarre.

**3**

I'd rather be unseen, and if
then shunned by everyone,
15  than to be a pleasant-smelling flower,
growing in clusters in the fertile valley,
where they're praised, handled, and plucked
by greedy, human hands.

**4**

I'd rather smell of musty, green stench
20  than of sweet, fragrant lilac.
If I could stand alone, strong and free,
I'd rather be a tall, ugly weed.

**4 Discussion** Have students restate in their own words the meaning of the last two lines.

**Challenge** Return to the purpose-setting question and encourage your students to answer it with the ideas developed in the poem.

**Reader's Response** What does Polanco's poem mean to you? Do you ever share the narrator's desires?

**Thematic Response** What are the qualities of the "place" the speaker admires? What are the speaker's feelings about community?

**Audiocassette** Use the **Listening to Literature** Audiocassette recordings of "Identity" and "The Road Not Taken" (Side 5) to enhance students' appreciation of the poems. Ask students to listen for ways in which the readers convey the speakers' viewpoints and feelings.

**SEASHORE AT PALAVAS, 1854**
*Gustave Courbet*
*Musée Fabre, Montpellier*

ESPONDING TO THE SELECTION

### Your Response

1. Based on this poem, which would you rather be, a flower or a weed? Why?

### Recalling

2. According to the speaker, what benefits do flowers have? What two drawbacks make beings like flowers unattractive?
3. What would the speaker rather be? What benefit makes this choice extremely attractive to the speaker?

### Interpreting

4. Explain what the speaker is really choosing between in this poem.
5. Which choice would be the easier to make? Support your answer.
6. What do you think is the theme of this poem? Explain how the title of the poem relates to the theme.

### Applying

7. Provide three examples of how people, in their daily lives, make the choice the speaker makes.

## ANALYZING LITERATURE

### Hearing the Speaker's Voice

Hearing the speaker's voice when you read can help you understand the poem. In "Identity" the speaker is an individual who has made a choice about what kind of person to be.

1. Find three adjectives you think describe the speaker. Explain your reason for selecting each adjective.
2. Name three people from history or current affairs you think the speaker would admire. Explain the reason for each choice.
3. Look at the art that accompanies this poem. In what way does the figure in the painting capture the identity of the speaker?

*Identity 599*

## Humanities Note

Fine art, *Seashore at Palavas,* 1854, by Gustave Courbet. Courbet (1819–1877) was a French painter who advanced the Realist movement in art. He believed that art should show the people and events of the time realistically and honestly. In politics he was sympathetic to the revolutionary movements of his day and spent time in prison for his political activities. His paintings influenced later art movements, such as Naturalism and Impressionism.

1. Which says more to you about the meaning of individualism and personal identity, the poem or the painting? Give reasons for your opinion.
2. What does a painting such as this express that a poem cannot?

6. Answers will differ. Suggested Response: Individuality and independence are preferable to conformity within a group. The title denotes what individuality and independence can enhance and confirm—one's identity.

### Applying

7. Answers will differ. Suggested Response: Choosing not to follow fads in clothing, music, behavior, and career ambitions are examples.

### ANSWERS TO ANALYZING LITERATURE

1. Answers will differ. Suggested Response: Independent, nonconformist, unpopular, private, and unattractive are three possibilities. Such adjectives are implicit in the image of the speaker as an isolated, ugly weed alone on a cliff.
2. Answers will differ. Suggested Response: Possibilities include Christ, Socrates, Joan of Arc, Abraham Lincoln, Martin Luther King, and Mother Teresa.
3. Like the speaker in the poem, the figure in the painting is alone, removed from the crowd, and exposed to "the breezes of an ancient sea."

## Closure and Extension

### ANSWERS TO RESPONDING TO THE SELECTION
### Your Response

1. Encourage students to explain their choices with specific information about the qualities of flowers and weeds.

### Recalling

2. Flowers are watered, fed, guarded, and admired. The drawbacks are that they are harnessed to a pot of dirt, and that they are plucked by greedy hands.
3. The speaker would rather be a tall, ugly weed clinging to a cliff. The benefit is that he could be independent, strong, and free.

### Interpreting

4. The speaker is choosing between conformity and independence.
5. Answers will differ. Suggested Response: Conformity would be the easier choice; conformity brings support, protection, approval, and praise.

**Motivation/Prior Knowledge**
It is quite common for people to wonder what their lives might have been like had they made different choices at crucial moments. *What might have been* teases our imaginations. Suggest that your students imagine how their lives might have been had some moment of the past been different.

**Master Teacher Note** At some point in your discussion of this poem, you may wish to point out that if the last stanza were dropped, there would be no strong reason for believing that the poem is anything other than a literal account of the speaker's choosing one path in the woods instead of another. What is said in the fourth stanza makes it clear that the poem is symbolic of a choice in life that determines the course of one's experience and excludes the course that might have been.

**Purpose-Setting Question** What does this poem reveal about the important choices in life that people must make?

**1 Clarification** The syntax of these lines may seem difficult to some. A paraphrase like the following may help **less advanced** students: And—feeling sorry that I could not travel both and still remain one person—I stood for a long time. Ask students to summarize the situation presented in this stanza.

**2 Discussion** Compare the two roads as the speaker describes them. How different are they?

**3 Discussion** Ask your **less advanced** students to paraphrase what the speaker says about the road not taken.

# The Road Not Taken

Robert Frost

**1**
Two roads diverged in a yellow wood,
And sorry I could not travel both
And be one traveler, long I stood
And looked down one as far as I could
5  To where it bent in the undergrowth;

**2**
Then took the other, as just as fair,
And having perhaps the better claim,
Because it was grassy and wanted wear;
Though as for that, the passing there
10  Had worn them really about the same,

**3**
And both that morning equally lay
In leaves no step had trodden black.
Oh, I kept the first for another day!
Yet knowing how way leads on to way,
15  I doubted if I should ever come back.

**4**
I shall be telling this with a sigh
Somewhere ages and ages hence:
Two roads diverged in a wood, and I—
I took the one less traveled by,
20  And that has made all the difference.

600  Poetry

**4 Critical Thinking and Reading** Which details indicate that the diverging roads are symbolic of choices that change forever the course of one's life? What might a reader infer from the pause in the speaker's voice at the end of line 18?

**Reader's Response** How do you make choices about routes to travel? What factors are important to consider?

**Thematic Response** Did the speaker know the consequences of each path when he made his decision? What choice would you have made?

**Challenge** Why might Frost have decided against titling his poem "The Road Taken"? Wouldn't this title be just as appropriate?

## Your Response

1. Describe a time when you had to make a choice between two equally good alternatives. How did you choose?

### Recalling

2. At the beginning of the poem, the speaker is faced with a choice between two roads. Which choice does he make?
3. What reason does the speaker give for making this choice? Which lines tell you that he is not certain his reason is valid?

### Interpreting

4. Find two details suggesting that the speaker feels this decision is significant.
5. What do the roads seem to symbolize? Find details from the poem to support your answer.
6. Explain the theme of the poem.

### Applying

7. An old proverb states that opportunity is a short-lived visitor. Another old saying says that opportunity never knocks twice. How do these sayings relate to the poem? Do you agree with the sayings? Why or why not?

## CRITICAL THINKING AND READING

### Interpreting Differences in Metaphors

Many writers have used metaphors to describe life. Read each of the common metaphors below. Explain how each suggests a specific attitude toward life. For example, one common metaphor says that life is just a bowl of cherries. This metaphor suggests an optimistic view. However, the comedian Rodney Dangerfield has responded to this metaphor by saying that life is just a bowl of pits. His metaphor suggests a more pessimistic outlook.

1. Life is a long, hard road.
2. Life is a journey of discovery.
3. Life is a merry-go-round.
4. Life is an endless feast.

*The Road Not Taken* 601

## Recalling

2. He chooses the road that has "perhaps the better claim."
3. His reason is that the chosen road is grassy and not worn down by passersby. Lines 9 and 10 indicate he is not certain that his reason is valid.

### Interpreting

4. He shall be telling about his choice in the future, and he says that the road he took "has made all the difference."
5. The roads symbolize the irreversible, life-changing choices that people make. Lines 14 and 15 indicate that such choices are irreversible; the last line indicates that they are life-changing.
6. Answers will differ. Suggested Response: The theme is basically that people make choices that establish a particular course for their lives and that the course that might have been can never be known.

### Applying

7. The ideas contained in these sayings are similar to those of the poem. However, Frost's poem emphasizes the sadness of never knowing what might have been had a different choice been made. The sayings emphasize the need to act and to make positive choices. It is possible to agree or to disagree with the sayings. Students should offer good examples from real life to support their opinions.

### ANSWERS TO CRITICAL THINKING AND READING

1. This metaphor suggests the attitude that life is unpleasant and difficult.
2. This metaphor suggests the attitude that life pleases and surprises with what we learn as we live.
3. This metaphor suggests the attitude that life is continually amusing.
4. This metaphor suggests the attitude that life is a series of pleasures.

## Closure and Extension

### ANSWERS TO RESPONDING TO THE SELECTION
#### Your Response

1. Check to see that students explain the thoughts and feelings that informed their decisions.

# Preparation

**More About the Authors Naomi Long Madgett's** books of poetry include *Octavia and Other Poems* (1988), *Phantom Nightingale: Juvenilia* (1981), and *Pink Ladies in the Afternoon* (1972). Madgett, who has claimed that she "would rather be a good poet than anything else I can imagine," has earned dozens of awards, including the Robert Hayden Runagate Award and a citation from the Black Caucus of the National Council of Teachers of English. What do you think might be the satisfaction of being "a good poet"?

Very little is known about the poet **Roberto Félix Salazar.** In his writing he aims to dramatize his Mexican American heritage as well as challenge his readers' assumptions about the nation's beginnings.

**Literary Focus** Nearly all the elements of poetry—imagery, syntax, rhythm, metaphor, simile, rhyme, length and structure of lines—contribute to a poem's tone. For instance, using a simile that compares a grocer to a fire hydrant will probably lend a comic or playful tone to a poem. Help students see how a poet's choices have an effect on a reader's perception of tone.

**Prereading Focus** You might encourage students to perform group readings of the poem in either tone of voice. For instance, a group of four students could alternate reading lines in a somber tone, then another group could alternate reading in a lighthearted tone.

**Thematic Focus** In "Woman With Flower," Madgett explores living things' need for independence in order to be appreciated; in "The Other Pioneers," Salazar praises unsung pioneers who form part of our American heritage.

602

# GUIDE FOR READING

## Woman With Flower

**Naomi Long Madgett** (1923–     ) was born in Norfolk, Virginia, the daughter of a clergyman and a teacher. As a child, she discovered, simultaneously, Langston Hughes and Alfred, Lord Tennyson, in her father's library; and her poetry is influenced by their two divergent styles. She has spent much of her career as a teacher of writing and has written textbooks about writing and literature. Of poetry she has said, "To me a good poem is one that continues to give pleasure (and perhaps provide new insight) no matter how many times it is read."

## The Other Pioneers

**Roberto Félix Salazar** is a poet of Mexican American descent. In his poem "The Other Pioneers," Salazar celebrates his heritage and, more specifically, commemorates the contributions made by his Spanish ancestors in colonizing Texas and the Southwest. According to Philip Ortego, a professor of Chicano Studies, "The Other Pioneers" was written to remind Mexican Americans and others that the first pioneers to settle the Southwest had Spanish names and that their descendants still do, although they are American citizens.

## Tone

The **tone** of any piece of writing is the attitude the writer takes toward the subject and audience. Just as you can hear someone's tone of voice in speech, you can infer it when reading. Usually the speaker of the poem expresses the tone. The tone of a work can be formal or informal, angry or playful, sad or joyful. To understand a poem, you must listen for the tone as you read it.

## Focus

In expressing the speaker's attitude toward the subject, the tone of a poem also gives you a clue to the poet's purpose. Turn to page 542 and read the poem "Reflections Dental" by Phyllis McGinley. The tone of the poem is humorous and ironic. As an exercise in appreciating the importance of tone, read the poem aloud in a solemn voice. Notice how the poem loses its punch and meaning as well as its comic purpose. Then read it aloud in a lighthearted, tone of voice. How is the poet's purpose served by the poem's tone?

*602   Poetry*

## Objectives

1 To make inferences about a speaker
2 To write a poem or paragraph using several tones
3 To understand tone in a poem
4 To express individual interests and abilities through optional activities

## Support Material

**Teaching Portfolio**
Teacher Backup, p. 827
Usage and Mechanics Worksheet, p. 830
Vocabulary Check, p. 831
Analyzing Literature Worksheet, *Understanding Tone,* p. 832
Critical Thinking and Reading, *Making Inferences About a Speaker,* p. 833
Selection Test, p. 834

**Prentice Hall Literature Writing Studio**

# Woman With Flower

Naomi Long Madgett

MAUDELL SLEET'S MAGIC GARDEN, 1978
*Romare Bearden*
*Private Collection*

1   I wouldn't coax the plant if I were you.
    Such watchful nurturing may do it harm.
    Let the soil rest from so much digging
    And wait until it's dry before you water it.
5   The leaf's inclined to find its own direction;
2   Give it a chance to seek the sunlight for itself.

    Much growth is stunted by too careful prodding.
    Too eager tenderness.
3   The things we love we have to learn to leave alone.

## RESPONDING TO THE SELECTION

### Your Response
1. How do your gardening experiences compare with the one described in this poem?

### Recalling
2. What does the speaker say can stunt growth?

### Interpreting
3. What kind of harm would "such watchful nurturing" do?
4. What is the benefit of leaving the things we love alone?

### Applying
5. How can the advice given by the speaker be applied to human relationships?

## CRITICAL THINKING AND READING

### Making Inferences About a Speaker
We do not learn much about the speaker in this poem except that he or she feels qualified to give advice about life, expressed in terms of gardening. We can assume, however, that he or she is speaking from life experience. Based on the advice given, we can infer some of what that experience has been.

1. What do you think has happened to the speaker in the past? Find evidence to support your answer.
2. How do you think the experience has changed the speaker?

## THINKING AND WRITING

### Experimenting With Tone
Write a poem or a brief paragraph about a simple subject using one of these tones: angry, loving, solemn, sarcastic, playful, or envious. Then rewrite the poem or paragraph using one of the other tones. How does the tone help to determine meaning?

*Woman With Flower* 603

# Preparation

Before students read this feature, have them discuss how Naomi Long Madgett might have written her poem "Woman With Flower." Have students offer speculations on where Madgett got her ideas and how she decided which details to use and which to omit. You might have them jot down their ideas in their journals, or you might write them on the chalkboard for reference.

**Prereading Focus** Point out to students that Madgett's poem grew out of several real-life situations, not one: The poet synthesized her impressions of "nurturing" as they related to several different people over the course of time. Ask students to think about poetry they have read. Did they imagine that they were reading exact representations of the poets' own lives? Suggest that students jot down in their journals their thoughts about how poems come to be written.

# Presentation

**Discussion questions:**

1. What factors allowed Madgett to write "Woman With Flowers" in a single sitting?

2. What are the differences between Madgett's methods of writing poetry and prose?

3. What are the differences between the first and second drafts of Madgett's poem? Do you think her changes made the poem better? Explain.

4. What information about Madgett's writing habits can you apply to your own writing? Explain why you think they will be useful to you.

# Naomi Long Madgett and "Woman With Flower"

## PREWRITING

**A Fluff of Cloud** Poet Naomi Long Madgett once said that writing poetry is like "trying to catch a fluff of cloud/with open-fingered hands." Where does inspiration come from? According to Madgett, from our "hidden" memories, which come to light when we need them.

An idea for a poem can strike Madgett anytime, often when she doesn't have time to work on it—late at night, perhaps, or when she's rushing to do something else. "But," she says, "I have discovered that I must make the time somehow, no matter how inconvenient it is, or the poem will be lost."

**Mixing the Ingredients** The inspiration for "Woman With Flower" came from several different places. One was Madgett's memory of the different ways in which her mother and her daughter tended plants. Although her mother paid little attention to hers, they thrived, while her daughter's plants, continually fussed over, withered and died.

Once, when Madgett was interested in winning a particular man's interest, she kept prodding at him, but it did no good. The observations she had made about plant care popped into her mind. "Wait until it's dry before you water it," she realized, was good advice for human relationships too—and a good subject for a poem. "One doesn't write a poem, then, in one day or two or ten; the ingredients gather over a lifetime and wait for the right time to be mixed."

## DRAFTING

**Two Ways of Working** Once Madgett had all the necessary ingredients for "Woman

With Flower," she didn't have much trouble mixing them together. As she remembers it, she wrote the poem in one sitting. Her advice about writing poetry is that "Letting it all spill out in the first draft is important."

However, Madgett doesn't rely on the inspiration of the moment when she writes prose. Instead, she sets herself a quota of only a few pages a day, then usually ends up exceeding her quota.

## REVISING

**Prose and Poetry** Both poetry and prose, Madgett finds, can call for a lot of revising. Once she finishes the first draft of a piece of prose, she goes back to the beginning to start "the long process of revision through a second draft. The third time around, I simply work on trouble spots, not the entire manuscript."

Revising a poem brings the difficult job of deciding "what is worth keeping and what ought to be let go." Madgett confesses that it's "hard to resist the temptation to keep an especially good line or phrase and admit that it just doesn't belong there."

**"Grand Circus Park"** Although "Woman With Flower" didn't need much revision, some of her other poems did. She worked on one called "Grand Circus Park" for nine years. The box on page 605 contains two versions of the poem's first stanza. Notice what stayed the same and what was changed.

**Changes** When she wrote version 1, Madgett still wasn't sure just what her poem meant. Later, she began to see the old men as symbols of a dying city, so she made changes in the poem to increase the refer-

*604 Poetry*

ences to death. The benches became gray, and "new leaves" became "dying branches."

During the time Madgett worked on "Grand Circus Park," she was constantly learning more about her craft, especially "the importance of strong action verbs." The word *sit* became *drowse* because "drowsing carried a lot of weight that sitting didn't."

Notice the other verb change. What do you think was her reason for making it?

**Additions** Madgett also added some biblical words to her poem. At a choir rehearsal, the words and rhythm "started singing in my brain," she says. Since they seemed to fit the poem, she put them in.

---

**GRAND CIRCUS PARK**
**(Twenty Years Later)**

| (Version 1) | (Version 2) |
|---|---|
| Old men still sit on park benches watching the sun shine through new leaves. | Old men still drowse on gray park benches watching a dubious sun leak through the dying branches of elms. |
| It is hard to realize they are not the same old men, grizzled and bleary-eyed as memories. | "The axe shall be laid (Hew, hew!) to the root of the trees . . ." |
| | It is hard to realize they are not the same old men, grizzled and bleary-eyed as memories. |

---

### PUBLISHING

**Different Interpretations** Madgett hears from readers about many of her poems, including "Grand Circus Park" and "Woman With Flower." For instance, some readers have interpreted "Woman With Flower" as a comment on a romantic relationship. Most readers, however, see the poem as a criticism of an overprotective parent or teacher. Madgett doesn't mind, nor does she think it "important for readers to know the details of what the poet had in mind. The poem should be able to stand on its own feet."

**African American Poets** In the late 1960's and 1970's Madgett had trouble getting her work published. Her poems, she says, didn't suit publishers' ideas of what African Americans should write. Now, as the owner of a small publishing company, Lotus Press, she publishes her own work as well as the work of other African American poets.

Some of Madgett's poems are about race, and others, like "Woman With Flower," are not. "While I am constantly aware of my racial identity, that is only a part of who I am," Madgett says. "It is unfortunate that many readers have come to believe that black writers have nothing to write about except being black. It just isn't true."

Poems that directly reflect the black experience, she adds, can speak to people of other cultures, too. "I believe that people, whatever their racial, religious, or ethnic differences, are more alike in their experiences than they are different."

### ▌THINKING ABOUT THE PROCESS

1. How important is a writer's racial, religious, national, or gender identity to his or her writing? Should a writer focus on this aspect of identity? How important is it in your writing?
2. **Writing.** Naomi Long Madgett knows the importance of strong action verbs. Write a list of strong action verbs that describe different ways of moving. Consult your list whenever you revise a first draft.

*One Writer's Process* 605

### THINKING ABOUT THE PROCESS

1. Answers will differ. Students may say that a writer's race, religion, nationality, or gender is often central to a writer's work. Certainly this is an appropriate focus for writing if the writer is engaged by the subject in an authentic way.
2. Students' lists might include words such as *stir, budge, drift, wave, circle, sweep, toss, run, skip, meander, stray, crawl, jump, fade, turn, gyrate, lean, reel, pitch, leap, hurtle, swagger, stride, shuffle, dance, wend, wiggle,* and *squirm.*

◆ **Software** If students are working on computers, they might enjoy using the **Writer's Helper** activity *Lists* as they complete the Thinking About the Process writing activity.

**Motivation/Prior Knowledge**
Ask students to describe their perceptions of the early inhabitants of North America. What do they know about early exploration of North America by western Europeans? Explain that in this poem the speaker praises some "forgotten" American heroes.

**Master Teacher Note** You might ask students to comment on the distinction between cultural pride and cultural insensitivity. It is possible to detect in Salazar's speaker a lack of sensitivity toward both Native Americans and women. Have students offer their ideas about the ideal form of racial or cultural pride.

**Purpose-Setting Question**
What were some of the names of the first western European settlers in America?

**1 Discussion** Why do you think they decided that "here" was the place to settle?

## Humanities Note

Fine art, *The Market Plaza,* by Thomas Allen. The American artist Thomas Allen (1849–1924) studied painting at Washington University in St. Louis and later at the Royal Academy in Düsseldorf, Germany.

He is best known for the New England pastoral scenes of his later years, but several notable western landscapes emerged from the two winters he spent in Texas (1878–1879). For example, *The Market Place, San Antonio* is executed in a flowing style and contains a slow, dreamlike quality despite its active composition. Allen's formal training is evident in the elegant draftsmanship of both landscape and inhabitants.

You may wish to use these questions to discuss the art:

# The Other Pioneers

Roberto Félix Salazar

**THE MARKET PLAZA**
**(San Antonio, 1878–1924)**
*Thomas Allen*
*The San Antonio Museum*
*Association*

Now I must write
Of those of mine who rode these plains
Long years before the Saxon[1] and the Irish came.
Of those who plowed the land and built the towns
5    And gave the towns soft-woven Spanish names.
Of those who moved across the Rio Grande
Toward the hiss of Texas snake and Indian yell.
Of men who from the earth made thick-walled homes
And from the earth raised churches to their God.
10   And of the wives who bore them sons
And smiled with knowing joy.

They saw the Texas sun rise golden-red with promised
   wealth
And saw the Texas sun sink golden yet, with wealth
   unspent.
"Here," they said. "Here to live and here to love."
15   "Here is the land for our sons and the sons of our sons."
And they sang the songs of ancient Spain

──────────

**1. Saxon** (sak'sən) *n.*: English.

1. Which lines from the poem might make appropriate captions for the painting?
2. How might this plaza look today?

And they made new songs to fit new needs.
They cleared the brush and planted the corn
And saw green stalks turn black from lack of rain.
20　They roamed the plains behind the herds
And stood the Indian's cruel attacks.
There was dust and there was sweat.
And there were tears and the women prayed. ⎤
　　　　　　　　　　　　　　　　　　　　　 ⎦ 2

And the years moved on.
25　Those who were first placed in graves
Beside the broad mesquite[2] and the tall nopal.[3]
Gentle mothers left their graces and their arts
And stalwart fathers pride and manly strength.
Salinas, de la Garza, Sánchez, García,
30　Uribe, González, Martinez, de León:[4] ⎤
Such were the names of the fathers. 　　⎥ 3
Salinas, de la Garza, Sánchez, García, 　⎦
Uribe, González, Martinez, de León:
Such are the names of the sons.

_____

2. **mesquite** (mes kēt') *n.*: Thorny tree or shrub common in the southwestern United States and Mexico.
3. **nopal** (nō'pəl) *n.*: Cactus with red flowers.
4. **Salinas** (sä lē'näs), **de la Garza** (dä lä gär'sä), **Sánchez** (sän'chäs), **García** (gär sē'ä), **Uribe** (o͞o rē'bä), **Gonzáles** (gōn sä'läs), **Martinez** (mär tē'näs), **de León** (dä lä ōn')

## RESPONDING TO THE SELECTION

### Your Response

1. What feelings toward these pioneers does the poem evoke in you? Why?

### Recalling

2. Who are the other pioneers?
3. What did they accomplish?

### Interpreting

4. What motivated these pioneers?
5. What does the repetition of the names in the last six lines signify? Explain.

### Applying

6. The poem describes the pioneers' legacy to their children. What do you think is the most valuable thing a parent can leave to a child?

## ANALYZING LITERATURE

### Understanding Tone

**Tone** in a poem is the speaker's attitude toward the subject. Like tone of voice in conversation, a poem's tone can be inferred from the way the speaker says what he or she says. Tone can also give you hints about the poet's purpose. In "The Other Pioneers," the tone and the poet's purpose are closely related.

1. Who is the speaker in "The Other Pioneers"?
2. How does the speaker feel about the other pioneers? How can you tell?
3. How would you describe the poem's tone?
4. What does the tone suggest about Salazar's purpose in writing "The Other Pioneers"?

2 **Reading Strategy** You might wish to have students summarize the pioneers' character traits.

3 **Literary Concept** What is the tone of these lines? What clues tell you about the poem's tone?

**Reader's Response** What do you know about early settlers in your region? What are some common local surnames?

**Thematic Response** What is the speaker's attitude toward ''those who plowed the land and built the towns''? Why do you think he ''must write''?

## Closure and Extension

### ANSWERS TO RESPONDING TO THE SELECTION
#### Your Response

1. Ask students to describe their feelings with reference to specific images in the poem.

#### Recalling

2. They are those who preceded ''the Saxon and Irish'' in the American Southwest.

3. They established roads, towns, churches, and other facets of community.

#### Interpreting

4. Suggested Response: They may have been motivated by cultural pride and belief in God.
5. Suggested Response: It signifies the continuation of families through succeeding generations.

#### Applying

6. Answers will differ. Encourage students to share their responses with classmates or to write them in a journal.

### ANSWERS TO ANALYZING LITERATURE

1. The speaker is a descendant of ''the other pioneers.''
2. The speaker's heroic portrait of them indicates that he admires them.

3. The poem's tone could be described as celebratory yet serious.
4. The tone suggests that Salazar's purpose was to praise and celebrate the achievements of the ''other pioneers.''

# Preparation

**Reading and Responding** This lesson will help students to review what they have learned about poetry. Then they may test their knowledge in reading Mark Van Doren's poem "The Story-Teller."

**Poetry** Review with students the idea that poetry is language at its most concentrated and intense. Tell students that the intensity of a poem requires a method of reading different from that they would use for a newspaper article or even a short story. To fully enjoy a poem, they may want to read it several times, both quietly and aloud.

**Language** Remind students that figurative language consists of words used beyond their dictionary meanings. The words assume more imaginative implications.

**Appearance** Remind students that a concrete poem's shape echoes its subject, and a haiku will always consist of three lines.

**Imagery** Remind students that imagery can appeal to the senses of hearing, touch, taste, and smell as well as sight. Poets use imagery so that a reader can experience what they are describing.

**Sound** Suggest to students that poets use repetition, alliteration, and onomatopoeia to create sound patterns that are pleasing in themselves and to reinforce the meaning of the poem.

**Theme** Consider telling students that the theme of the poem is not always stated directly. A reader must sometimes infer the poet's insight into life from the poem as a whole, taking into account the imagery, figurative language, and sound devices.

# READING AND RESPONDING

## Poetry

The poet A. E. Housman has written: "I could no more define poetry than a terrier can define a rat." Although poetry resists being precisely defined, it has qualities that set it apart from other forms of literature. The language is compact, imaginative, and musical. The structure may be specific to a standard poetic form. Also, the use of sound devices and sensory details is usually more common in poetry than in other forms of literature.

Use your active reading strategies to help you respond fully to poetry.

**RESPONDING TO LANGUAGE** Poets use language to create new ways of seeing things. They often use figures of speech, or figurative language, language that is not intended to be understood literally. Figures of speech enable you to see or think about something in a new and imaginative way. What thoughts and feelings do these figures of speech call up in you?

**RESPONDING TO APPEARANCE** Poetry can take a variety of forms. What does it look like on the page? Is its appearance related to the type of poetry it is, such as a concrete poem or haiku? How does its appearance affect your expectations as you read it?

**RESPONDING TO IMAGERY** Poets appeal to your senses in creating images. Use your imagination and your five senses to respond to the images the poet has created.

**RESPONDING TO SOUND** The music of poetry is created by sound devices. Read poems aloud and listen to the rhythm and the rhyme. Listen to the repetition of consonant sounds and other devices. How do the effects of these devices contribute to the meaning of the poem?

**RESPONDING TO THEME** Many poems convey an important idea or insight about life. What do you think is the message of the poem? What special meaning does the poem have for you?

On pages 609–610 is an example of active reading and responding by Howard Jow of Eisenhower School in Albuquerque, New Mexico. The notes in the side column include Howard's comments as he read "The Story-Teller." Your thoughts as you read may be different because you bring your own experiences to your reading.

*608   Poetry*

## Objectives

1 To appreciate a poem by responding to elements of it
2 To understand rhyme
3 To define poetry
4 To retell a story
5 To express individual interests and abilities through optional activities

## Support Material

**Teaching Portfolio**
Teacher Backup, p. 837
Reading and Responding, pp. 840–841
Usage and Mechanics Worksheet, p. 842
Analyzing Literature Worksheet, *Understanding Rhyme,* p. 843
Critical Thinking and Reading Worksheet, *Defining Poetry,* p. 844

Selection Test, pp. 845–846
Art Transparency 18, *The Fantasy World,* by Alain Thomas

**Listening to Literature**
"The Story-Teller"

**Prentice Hall Literature Writing Studio**

### Humanities Note

Fine Art, *Green Violinist,* 1923–24, by Marc Chagall. Mark Chagall (1897–1985) was born in Russia. He studied painting at the Pen Academy in his native town of Vitebsk, at the Imperial School of Fine Art in St. Petersburg, and with the famous stage designer Leon Bakst. In France, where he was to live for most of his life, he was exposed to all of the new trends in modern art. Chagall studied each but developed his own unique style that remains un-classifiable.

*Green Violinist* was painted in France in the years 1923–1924. Haunted by memories of his life in Russia, Chagall painted images of this small village and its people, over and over. The dreamlike image of a violinist appears in many of his paintings. This painting appeals directly to the viewers' emotions with its bright colors and nostalgic vision.

You might use the following for discussion:
1. Describe the details of this painting.
2. What qualities of "The Story-Teller" are evident in *Green Violinist?*

**GREEN VIOLINIST, 1923–24**
*Marc Chagall*
*Solomon R. Guggenheim Museum*

# The Story-Teller

Mark Van Doren

He talked, and as he talked
Wallpaper came alive;
Suddenly ghosts walked,
And four doors were five;

**Theme:** *The title makes me think that the theme of this poem is going to have something to do with telling stories.*

**Language:** *The language is used creatively and playfully, which is how the storyteller would use it to make things come alive.*

*The Story-Teller 609*

### Motivation/Prior Knowledge
Consider asking students to re-call a time when they heard a well-told story. Have them briefly describe the occasion and ex-plain why the storyteller was ef-fective. Then tell them that the poem they will read is about the art of storytelling.

**Purpose-Setting Question** How does the poet use surprise to communicate his theme?

**Thematic Focus** In this poem Van Doren celebrates a storytell-er's creative spirit.

**Audiocassettes** Use the **Listening to Literature** Audiocassette recording of "The Story-Teller" (Side 6) to enhance students' appreciation of all the poem's elements. Ask students to listen for how the reader treats figurative language and theme.

**Master Teacher Note** Look at Art Transparency 18, *The Fantasy World* by Alain Thomas, in the Teaching Portfolio. Ask students what aspects of this painting seem fantastic or otherworldly. What are other examples of fantasy or magic in literature or the movies?

"The Story-Teller" de-scribes the magical effects of a story well told.

**Making Connections** You might want to use the essay "Talking About Writing," page 485, with this selection. In this piece Ursula K. Le Guin tells how she discovers within herself the ideas for her tales of fantasy and science fic-tion.

**Sound:** *The regular rhyme, lively rhythm, and short lines all contribute toward building momentum. The world seems to become more animated as the storyteller talks.*

**Imagery:** *The images in this stanza are even more fantastic than the ones in the previous stanzas. They appeal to several different senses at the same time: sight, touch, and taste.*

**Appearance:** *The poem's appearance is very regular and ordinary, but its language describes unusual things happening.*

**Theme:** *The storyteller is like a magician who can enliven our ordinary lives by making wonderful things happen in our imaginations.*

5   Calendars ran backward,
    And maps had mouths;
    Ships went tackward[1]
    In a great drowse;[2]

    Trains climbed trees,
10  And soon dripped down
    Like honey of bees
    On the cold brick town.

    He had wakened a worm
    In the world's brain,
15  And nothing stood firm
    Until day again.

---

1. **tackward** (tak′ wərd) *adv.*: Against the wind.
2. **drowse** (drouz) *n.*: Sluggishness; doze.

**Mark Van Doren** (1894–1972) was a poet, a critic, a novelist, an editor, and a teacher. Born in Hope, Illinois, Van Doren began his literary career as an instructor and later a professor of English at Columbia University in New York City. He went on to serve as editor and film critic of a publication called *The Nation*. Throughout these busy years, Van Doren wrote many books, including *The Poetry of John Dryden, Jonathan Gentry,* and *Shakespeare*. In 1940 he was awarded the Pulitzer Prize for Poetry for his anthology entitled *Collected Poems, 1922–38*.

## RESPONDING TO THE SELECTION

### Your Response

1. Which of the images in the poem appealed to you most? Why?
2. Describe a time when you heard a story told in such a way that it kept you riveted. What things did the storyteller do to make the story so interesting?

### Recalling

3. Find seven magical things that the storyteller is able to accomplish.
4. According to the last line, when do things return to normal?

### Interpreting

5. What is the "worm" referred to in line 13? What is the "world's brain" in line 14?
6. Interpret lines 15–16.
7. Express the theme of this poem.

### Applying

8. Why do you think that people like stories? Use details from life to support your answer.

## ANALYZING LITERATURE

### Understanding Rhyme

**Rhyme** is created by words sounding alike. In a poem, rhyme often occurs at the end of lines. The rhyme pattern of a poem helps give it a musical quality.

1. Look at the first stanza. Which words at the end of lines rhyme?
2. Look at the second stanza. Which words at the end of lines rhyme?
3. What conclusion do you draw about the rhyme pattern of this poem?

## CRITICAL THINKING AND READING

### Defining Poetry

**Defining** means giving the distinguishing characteristics of something. Read each definition of poetry below. Explain which one you think best captures the essential meaning of a poem.

1. Samuel Johnson: "Poetry is the art of uniting pleasure with truth."
2. Edgar Allan Poe: "Poetry is the rhythmical creation of beauty in words."
3. Gwyn Thomas: "Poetry is trouble dunked in tears."

## THINKING AND WRITING

### Retelling a Story

Think about the best story you have ever heard. What made this story come alive for you? Brainstorm, listing all the qualities that made this story special. Then retell the story in your own words. When you revise, make sure you have included the features that made this story magical for you. Proofread your story and share it with your classmates.

## LEARNING OPTIONS

1. **Art.** The painting by Marc Chagall on page 609 and the images in "The Story-Teller" represent a movement in art and literature known as Surrealism. Surrealist painters and writers depict the impossible as possible, showing familiar objects and images in unusual surroundings or doing extraordinary things. In the Surrealists' world, green people fly and trains climb trees. Look on page 477 for a famous example of Surrealist art, *The Persistence of Memory* by Salvador Dali.

   Illustrate "The Story-Teller" in the Surrealist style. Use the two paintings mentioned above as models.
2. **Writing.** Write a poem about something that has the same effect on you that the storyteller has on his listeners. Whatever you choose to write your poem about, think carefully about the images that would best describe the feeling of being transported and the "world" to which you are transported.

### Applying

8. Answers will differ. Suggested Response: People like the excitement, glamour, and romance of stories. Listening to ghost stories around a campfire, people can experience an enjoyable shiver of fear.

**Challenge** What makes a person a good storyteller?

### ANALYZING LITERATURE

1. The first stanza contains the following end rhymes: talked-walked, alive-five.
2. The second stanza contains the following end rhymes: backward-tackward, mouths-drowse (an approximate rhyme).
3. Each stanza has the rhyme scheme *abab*.

### CRITICAL THINKING AND READING

Answers will differ. Suggested Response: Most students will probably choose #1 or #2, especially since "The Story-Teller" does not seem at all like "trouble dunked in tears." Students who remember that "The Story-Teller" has a theme will probably choose #1, because it makes allowance for "truth" in a poem. No matter which definition they select, students should be able to justify their choice.

### THINKING AND WRITING

**Alternative Assessment** You may vary the Thinking and Writing assignment as follows: Have students complete one of the Alternate Composition Assignments on page 828 of the Teaching Portfolio.

### LEARNING OPTIONS

1. This activity will interest artistic students. Extend the activity by exhibiting illustrations publicly.
2. This activity will appeal to students who enjoy writing. You can vary the activity by having students tell a story about a time when they were "transported."

## Closure and Extension

### ANSWERS TO RESPONDING TO THE SELECTION

#### Your Response

1. Have students offer reasons for their choices.
2. Encourage students to be specific about the storyteller's techniques.

#### Recalling

3. The story-teller accomplishes the following magic things—wallpaper comes alive; ghosts walk; four doors turn into five; calendars go backward; maps have mouths; ships sail against the wind very lazily (this maneuver is usually brisk); trains climb trees and drip down like honey.
4. Things return to normal at dawn.

#### Interpreting

5. Answers will differ. Suggested Response: The "worm" might stand for the story-teller's ability to undermine the ordinary world and make it seem strange and mysterious. The "world's brain" might be either the everyday world or our usual ideas about it.
6. Answers will differ. Suggested Response: The story-teller made the world seem like a strange place where anything could happen. Not until the next day did the world appear normal again.
7. Answers will differ. Suggested Response: A well-told story can make the world seem surprising, miraculous, and alive with possibilities.

## Preparation

### Motivation/Prior Knowledge

Put students at ease with this assignment by pointing out that they have been using similes and metaphors for most of their lives. Explain that the assignment simply requires them to continue the process. Allow the class to experiment with extending common metaphors and similes such as the *fabric of society, swims like a fish, an ocean of love,* and *the mainstream of life.*

**Focus** Students should strive to avoid clichés in their descriptions. Assist them in surfacing comparisons that are apt but unusual.

## Presentation

**Prewriting** Some students may find it helps to begin by listing similes for different attributes of their subject. Once they have made some connections, they can determine which images they feel best capture the essence of their subject, and expand on one of these.

Suggest that students consider using animate descriptions for an inanimate object or using personification to describe a tree, a house, or a pet.

**Software** If students have access to computers, they can use the *Random Revelations* and *Connections* activities in **Writer's Helper** to stimulate ideas for comparisons.

**Drafting** Remind students that the style of their writing can help to strengthen their imagery. Demonstrate the different effects of short, staccato sentences and long, meandering ones. Most students will be accustomed to the manipulation of rhythm in poetry; encourage them to try it in prose as well. Tell the students to record all their ideas.

*"Poetry is a spot about half-way between where you listen and where you wonder what it was you heard."*
**Carl Sandburg**

## WRITING A DESCRIPTION

For centuries, poets have described familiar subjects in unfamiliar, and often very surprising, ways. Consider how Maxine Kumin in "400-Meter Free Style" uses a concrete poem to imitate the movements of a swimmer or how Richard García's poem "The City Is So Big" describes machines as if they were alive. These leaps of imagination help to give us another perspective on people, places, and things.

### Focus

**Assignment:** Write a description, in poetry or prose, of a familiar person, place, or object.
**Purpose:** To surprise a reader into seeing your subject in a new light.
**Audience:** Fellow classmates.

### Prewriting

**1. Choose a subject that you care about and know well.** Since you are going to be stretching the boundaries of your readers' perceptions, it is best to be thoroughly familiar with the person, place, or thing you will write about.

**2. Brainstorm to gather details.** Use a cluster diagram to help you gather details that describe your subject. Think in terms of your five senses: sight, sound, smell, taste, and touch.

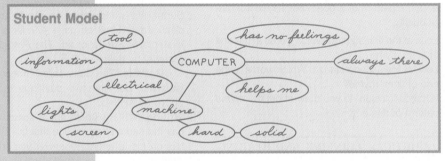

Student Model

**3. Create a comparison.** Review your diagram and think about a different subject with similar qualities. In fact, the more unusual the comparison seems, the greater the element of surprise will be for your reader!

*612  Poetry*

**Revising and Editing** Assist students in identifying comparisons that may need to be clarified. In the metaphors, especially, they may need to revise a sentence to establish the basis for the comparison.

**Grammar Tip** Caution students to make pronouns agree with their antecedents. This can be especially tricky in comparisons. If personification is used, make sure students choose a gender for their subject and stick to it. Refer students to the Handbook of Grammar and Revising Strategies for further guidance in pronoun agreement.

**4. Freewrite about your comparison.** Be creative as you write about how the two subjects are alike. Don't worry at this point about whether the connections you make are accurate. Just have fun exploring all the possibilities.

## Drafting

**1. Decide which form your writing will take.** Will you write in poetry or prose? One way to decide is to ask yourself which form might result in the better description—and, of course, which form you are more comfortable with. You might want to experiment with both forms.

**2. Use variety in your comparison.** Remember that writers may use both similes and metaphors when comparing two different subjects. A simile is a comparison that uses the words "like" or "as." A metaphor is a description of one thing as if it were another—for example, "all the world's a stage." By using similes, metaphors, or both, you can make your writing fresh and interesting.

---

### Student Model

Each afternoon when I come home from school, my computer is there in my room, anticipating my arrival like a loyal friend. It's quiet—waiting for me to say hello on the keyboard. Then, in a flash of excitement, it greets me with its ever-predictable hums, whirrs, and blinks on its screen. As fast as my fingers can move, it talks back, as if it hadn't seen me in ages and were dying to tell me the latest news. We talk like this for hours—until my parents say it's time for dinner. Then it's goodbye for now.

---

## Revising and Editing

**1. Check your description for the "surprise" factor.** Is your comparison as fresh as it can be? Put yourself in your reader's place. Do you get a clear and interesting picture of the chosen subject? Do you see that subject in a new light?

**2. Test your description on one or more peer editors.** Exchange your poem or your prose piece with one or more classmates. Consider the following questions as you review one another's work:
• Is the description surprising?
• Does the comparison make sense?

**3. Proofread your writing.** Remember, the "surprise" factor shouldn't include unforeseen mistakes in grammar, spelling, or punctuation.

**Writer's Hint**

Surprise your readers with an unusual comparison, but also convince them of the similarities between the two things being compared.

---

**Grammar Tip**

Make sure you are consistent in your use of pronouns. For instance, if you have begun your description by speaking in the first person—using the pronoun *I*—refer to yourself as *I* throughout.

---

**Options for Publishing**

• Create a bulletin board display of descriptions along with illustrations of each piece.
• Create a class anthology of descriptions and circulate it among your class and other classes at school.

---

**Reviewing Your Writing Process**

1. How did you decide which person, place, or object to describe?
2. How might you use those same decision-making strategies in other writing assignments?

*Your Writing Process* 613

---

## Closure and Extension

**Guidelines for Evaluation** The following guidelines may help you to evaluate each student's description:
1. Has the writer chosen a unique perspective on the subject?
2. Does the writer use both similes and metaphors?
3. Is the comparison developed consistently?
4. Is the comparison apt?
5. Does the writer avoid using clichés?
6. Is the description free of errors in spelling, punctuation, and grammar?

**Alternative Assessment** *Collaborative Evaluation:* In groups of four, ask your students to evaluate one another's work by responding to the following questions:

What familiar person, place, or object does the writer describe in poetry or prose?

Do the writer's descriptions appeal to the senses of sight, sound, smell, taste, and touch?

Does the writer present a clear and interesting picture of his or her subject?

Does the writer create unusual similes and metaphors? Do they surprise the reader?

Is the writer consistent in the use of pronouns?

Is the description free of errors in spelling, punctuation, and grammar?

Based on your evaluation, what do you think is an appropriate grade for this description?

After the descriptions have been evaluated, you may ask students to write protocols summarizing what they have learned about descriptive writing from writing their own descriptions and evaluating one another's work.

**Publishing** You might have students share their work by reading it aloud in small groups. Circulate among the groups and stimulate discussion about the different techniques used to describe inanimate objects, animals, people, and so forth.

**Student Portfolios** You might have students include their descriptions in their writing portfolios.

**Enrichment** Have students look up the definition of *anthropomorphism.* Discuss how different societies have anthropomorphized their deities, the weather, and the sea. Help students use the derivation to find the relationship to words like *anthropology* and *metamorphosis.*

# Preparation

## Motivation/Prior Knowledge

Stimulate students' awareness of the historical content of the poems by creating a literary timeline. In one color mark the date of the event that is the subject of the poem. In another color mark the date that the poem was written. In a third color, note any significant historical events or literary trends that correspond with these dates. Lead the students in comparing and contrasting the styles, time periods, themes, and perspectives. Keep the timeline posted during the writing lesson.

## Focus

Point out to students that they can probably recite the lyrics to many popular songs. Interest level and enjoyment have had a powerful positive impact on their memories. In recommending a particular poem, students should focus on the positive qualities that will make it an effective teaching tool, as well as on the historic content.

## Presentation

**Prewriting** Ask students to comment on their responses to meter, rhyme, alliteration, free verse, figurative language, end rhyme, and internal rhyme.

Give each student a photocopy of their chosen poem, which they can annotate during discussion. They can highlight examples of the techniques discussed and record random thoughts that might prompt them in drafting.

**Writing Transparency** You might wish to model form and style for this assignment by using *Model 7: Responding to Literature,* in **Transparencies for Writing.**

---

*"Poetry is to prose as dancing is to walking."*
**John Wain**

# YOUR WRITING PROCESS

## WRITING A RECOMMENDATION

This unit contains many interesting poems, some of which give readers insights into specific periods of American history. Suppose a group of teachers who were designing a course in American history asked you to recommend one of these poems to be included in their curriculum. Which one would you choose? Why?

### Focus

**Assignment:** Write a recommendation suggesting a poem to accompany the study of American history.
**Purpose:** To persuade readers that this poem would be a good choice.
**Audience:** A group of teachers who are designing a course in American history.

### Prewriting

**1. Select the poem that you find most interesting.** To some people, history can be very boring if all they are asked to learn are dates and facts. However, history will come alive when those same dates and facts are presented as part of an exciting story. Review the poems you read in this unit. Which one stands out in your mind as the most vivid account of historic events?

**2. Brainstorm to list reasons for your choice.** You can use the following chart to help you sort out your ideas. Because you are discussing a work of literature as well as a piece of historical "evidence," you might want to consider the poem's literary merits as well. A word or phrase next to each heading is enough to state your case.

| Title of poem: _____ | Historical event covered: _____ |
|---|---|
| Interesting/important facts conveyed: _____ _____ _____ | Literary merits: _____ _____ _____ |

---

**Drafting** Assist students in organizing the arrangement of assertions and supporting evidence. Watch for students that make generalizations too broad to substantiate. Help them to use their annotated copy and prewriting chart to formulate focused statements that can be supported by specific references.

Check that all students are including indications of the historic content of the poem, as well as commenting on the appeal of its literary merits.

**Revising and Editing** Emphasize that when quoting lines of poetry, students should not alter the poet's punctuation or capitalization.

Prompt students to replace any vague descriptions of the poem's literary merits with specific literary terms that identify the technique or device.

## Drafting

**1. Keep your writing brief and to the point.** The chart that you filled out in your prewriting stage can serve as a good outline for your recommendation. Your entries for the first two headings can appear in the opening paragraph, along with a brief sentence explaining why you are recommending the poem. You can then support your recommendation with specific details from the poem.

**2. Make your writing interesting.** Prove that poetry can make history come alive! Quote from the poem and give examples of vivid description or narrative. Demonstrate how the language reflects a memorable moment in history. Show off the dramatic strategies of your chosen poem to convince your readers that poetry can be an effective teaching tool.

## Revising and Editing

**1. Back up your reasons for choosing the poem.** Make sure you have backed up your choice with specific references to the poem and with direct quotations.

---

### Student Model

Another reason Longfellow's poem would be a good choice is that it includes specific information about the battle that followed Paul Revere's midnight ride. *The following lines are part of a vivid description of this battle:* "You know the rest. In the books you have read,/ How the British Regulars fired and fled,—"

---

**2. Test your recommendation on a peer editor.** Exchange recommendations with a classmate. Consider the following questions as you review each other's work:
- Is the recommendation clearly written?
- Does the writer keep to the point?
- Is the argument convincing?
- Is the recommendation interesting to read?

**3. Proofread your work.** Your recommendation should be error-free so that your readers aren't distracted.

## Writing Hint

Use the following devices to vary your sentences:
- Include different sentence types: declarative, interrogative, or imperative.
- Switch the position of the sentence's predicate and subject.

## Options for Publishing

- Read your recommendation to the class as a whole and invite comments about it.
- Submit your recommendation to a "committee" of several classmates, who will then vote on it.

## Reviewing Your Writing Process

1. How did your chart help you to formulate convincing arguments for using the poem you chose?
2. Did having your recommendation reviewed by a peer editor help you to revise? Explain.

**Enrichment** With the assistance of a Social Studies teacher, have your students plan a lesson around one of the chosen poems. They might present their lesson to another group of students and solicit comments on how the use of the poem enhanced the lesson.

## Closure and Extension

**Guidelines for Evaluation** The following questions can guide you in evaluating each student's recommendation:
1. Does the recommendation highlight significant historic and literary features of the poem?
2. Does the writer point out several literary techniques or devices that heighten the appeal of the poem?
3. Does the recommendation use direct quotations to illustrate some features of the poem?
4. Is the recommendation free of errors in punctuation, grammar, and usage?

**Alternative Assessment** *Collaborative Evaluation:* In groups of four, ask students to evaluate one another's work by responding to the following questions:

What poem does the writer recommend to the history teachers?

Are the reasons offered for the selection logical and relevant to the history course?

Does the writer quote from the poem and cite vivid descriptions?

Has the writer varied his or her sentences?

Based on your evaluation, what do you think is the appropriate grade for this recommendation?

After the recommendations have been evaluated, you may ask students to write protocols summarizing what they have learned about persuasive writing from completing their own recommendations and evaluating one another's work.

**Publishing** Your students can submit their recommendations to a Social Studies teacher. If time permits, have a Social Studies teacher visit the class and discuss his or her comments on the recommendations.

**Student Portfolios** You may want students to include this recommendation in their writing portfolios.

**THE WOODCUTTER, 1891**
*Winslow Homer*
*Private Collection*

# THE AMERICAN FOLK TRADITION

The American folk tradition includes myths, legends, folk tales, and tall tales that were originally passed down through oral storytelling. The authors of these tales are unknown, though someone has written down the stories to preserve them. Myths usually explain early people's ideas about nature. Their subjects are gods, goddesses, and other supernatural heroes who serve as models for us. Legends differ from myths in that they are often about heroes and heroines who actually existed. Folk tales present the customs and beliefs of a culture but do not generally involve gods and goddesses. Tall tales are stories in which exaggeration is used for entertainment. All cultures have their own folklore, and the folklore in this unit is uniquely American. Some of the tales were told in early Native American cultures, whereas others are more recent.

## Humanities Note

Fine art, *Woodcutter on a Rock,* by Winslow Homer. The painter and illustrator Winslow Homer (1836–1910) is one of America's best-known artists. Influenced at a young age by his mother, a talented watercolor painter, Homer wanted to become an artist. Without any formal training, he worked as an illustrator, an occupation he pursued for most of his life. Success in this field enabled him to paint. He is known today for the marine, genre, and landscape paintings, which he produced in great number during his lifetime.

*Woodcutter on a Rock,* c. 1891, is a watercolor painted in the Adirondack region of New York State. Homer often spent time in this area camping, fishing, and hunting. His years as an illustrator gave him the keen sense of observation and quick sketching ability necessary to handle the difficult medium of watercolor. During the end of the nineteenth century, Homer became increasingly interested in the effects of atmosphere. The attention he has given to the sky in this painting is an example of his exploration in this area. The sky provides a dramatic backdrop for the figure of the woodsman in the foreground. The figure seems to represent American ruggedness and a connection with the land.

617

**Alternative Assessment** *Portfolio Assignment:* To enable you and your students to assess their own learning, you may ask them to create a portfolio of their responses to the entire American Folk Tradition unit. They may include the following:

The reader's response journals
Selected Thinking and Writing assignments
Selected Alternate Composition assignments
Selected responses to the Learning Options
An essay from the Unit Test on page 981 in the Teaching Portfolio

Have your students write a protocol for their portfolios in which they explain the rationale for their selections and the learning that is reflected.

# READING ACTIVELY

## The American Folk Tradition

**BACKGROUND** The American folk tradition is older than recorded history. Folklore has been passed down orally from generation to generation. People have always told stories to entertain, to explain the mysterious, and to teach lessons or prove points. The stories recorded here are the stories that were first heard around campfires or first told to pass the time on long winter nights or in wagons heading west.

Although the divisions are blurred, there are differences between myths, legends, folk tales, and tall tales. Myths often explain how the world and its phenomena were created. Legends are rooted in historical events, even though their heroes frequently perform superhuman deeds. They are set in real places and in relatively recent times. Folk tales are stories about animals or people. They are not set in any particular time or place, and they usually teach a lesson. Tall tales are exaggerated stories about larger-than-life heroes, invented for sheer entertainment.

**READING STRATEGY** You may find colloquial language and clichés in American folk stories difficult to understand. Remember that in each tale, the flavor of the people who first told the story comes through. Identify the source of the story or the region of the country from which it comes. You will better understand the action and characters if you know whether it's a Native American tale, a southern story, or a western story, for example.

Finally, interact with the literature by using the active reading strategies: question, visualize, predict, connect, and respond. You may find the questioning strategy particularly useful here. Ask yourself why the story was first told. Ask yourself why events are exaggerated, for example, or why the characters have superhuman powers. Using this strategy as you read will help you appreciate American folklore more fully.

**THEMES** You will encounter the following themes:

- Conflicts and Challenges
- Our Living Earth
- Rites of Passage
- Our American Heritage
- The Lighter Side

618    *The American Folk Tradition*

# In the Beginning

**NORTH MOUNTAIN**
*Harrison Begay*
*Museum of Northern Arizona*

## Humanities Note

Fine art, *North Mountain,* by Harrison Begay. Born in 1917 Begay is a Native American painter of the Navajo tribe. Although he studied art at the famous Santa Fe Indian School, he did not adopt the typical "Santa Fe" style that so many students of this school favor. Instead, he developed a serene, precise folk-art style all his own.

The composition of *North Mountain* has a dynamic symmetry created by the man and the woman and the various pairs of animals flanking the center. The symmetry is relieved by the rainbow curving through the picture plane. The stylized figures, the lyrical design, and the naturalistic palette create a decorative work that seems to celebrate life itself.

You might use these questions for discussion:

1. In what ways might this painting represent the creation of life on earth?
2. Turn back to this painting from time to time as you read the selections in this section. Notice how many details from the stories seem to find representation in Begay's work. What does this tell you about the universal nature of folklore and folk art?

## Preparation

**More About the Authors** José Griego y Maestas contacted his friend Rudolfo Anaya with a very special project in mind. Griego had collected a select group of old folk tales that were part of the oral tradition of New Mexico. He had adapted them in Spanish from literal transcriptions of oral tellings and was interested in having them translated into English. Anaya and Griego worked together to ensure that these folk tales, "The Four Elements" among them, retained their spontaneity yet were accessible to readers outside the southwestern Hispanic culture. In his introduction to the collection, titled *Cuentos: Tales From the Hispanic Southwest,* Anaya suggests that the tales reveal "the foibles of mankind." What foible of humankind does this tale expose?

**Literary Focus** Which human characteristic does this myth explain?

**Prereading Focus** Suggest that pairs of students define the word *honor* before they compile their lists. Remind them that even the smallest act or gesture can reveal a person's sense of honor.

**ESL Teaching Strategy** Have a Spanish-speaking ESL student or teacher read "Los cuatro elementos" aloud in Spanish so that students can also *hear* the similarities between certain words in the two languages. Encourage students to imagine that they are listening to an original oral telling.

**José Griego y Maestas**

lives in New Mexico. An expert in Spanish literature, Griego is presently the director of the Guadalupe Historic Foundation in Santa Fe and is well known as a leading authority in bilingual education.

**Rudolfo A. Anaya**

(1937–    ) has earned popular acclaim as a writer of short stories, novels, and articles that strongly evoke the spirit and culture of the Hispanic people.

# GUIDE FOR READING

## The Four Elements

### Myth

A **myth** is a story that is invented to explain a natural phenomenon, a belief, or any idea that is not easily explained by reason. Handed down by word of mouth from generation to generation, most myths express beliefs, traditions, and experiences of a people or a region. By reflecting customs and values, a myth reveals the culture of the people who created it.

### Focus

Why is honor valued by people of every religion, race, and ethnic background? With a partner, discuss what honor means to you. Then list the different ways that people you know exhibit honor. Keep their ideals in mind as you read "The Four Elements."

### Vocabulary

"The Four Elements" was originally told in Spanish. Here is the tale in its original language:

#### Los cuatro elementos

Cuatro elementos tiene el mundo, son el agua, la lumbre, el viento y la vergüenza. Cuando ya transitaron muchos años, se juntaron para ganar cada uno su rumbo y el agua dijo primero:

"Pues ya nos vamos a apartar del todo, y a mí me van a necesitar algún día. Me hallarán en el centro de la tierra y en los mares."

Entonces la lumbre dijo:

"Ya nos vamos a apartar para siempre. Si a mí me necesitan, me encontrarán en el acero o en el sol."

Luego habló el viento:

"Si a mí me necesitan, me encontrarán en los cielos entre las nubes."

La vergüenza fue la última que habló y así les dijo:

"Pues ahora sí, si me pierden a mí, no me vayan a buscar porque no me encontrarán."

Which Spanish words can you recognize? Work with a partner and make a list of words that are similar in English.

**Objective**

To understand a myth

**Support Material**

**Teaching Portfolio**
Teacher Backup, p. 865
Usage and Mechanics Worksheet, p. 868
Analyzing Literature Worksheet, *Understanding a Myth,* p. 869
Critical Thinking and Reading Worksheet, *Personification,* p. 870
Selection Test, p. 871

**Audio Prose Library**
An Interview With Rudolfo Anaya

**Prentice Hall Literature Writing Studio**

**Audiocassette** You may wish to have students listen to the Audio Prose Library interview with Rudolfo Anaya, in which Anaya discusses his own experiences as a writer and the Hispanic tradition in literature.

# The Four Elements

Adapted in Spanish by José Griego y Maestas
Retold in English by Rudolfo A. Anaya

In the beginning there were four elements on this earth, as well as in man. These basic elements were Water, Fire, Wind and Honor. When the work of the creation was completed, the elements decided to separate, with each one seeking its own way.

1 ☐ Water spoke first and said:

"Our work in the creation of earth and man is done. Now it is proper to go our own ways, but if you should ever need me, look for me under the earth and in the oceans."

Fire then said:

"We will separate forever, but if you should need me you will find me in steel and in the power of the sun." ☐ 2

Wind whispered:

"If you should need me, I will be in the heavens among the clouds."

Honor was the last to speak, and it said:

"I am the bond of life.[1] If once you lose me don't look for me again—you will not find me!" ☐ 3

_____

1. **bond of life** _n._: That which holds all living things together.

---

## ▮ RESPONDING TO THE SELECTION

### Your Response

1. What part of this myth do you like best? Why?

### Recalling

2. According to this myth, what are the original four elements on Earth?

### Interpreting

3. Why does Water say it can be found under the Earth and in the ocean?
4. Why does Fire say that it will be in the sun and in steel?

### Applying

5. Do you believe that honor, once lost, can be found again? Explain. Try to include an example.

## ▮ ANALYZING LITERATURE

### Understanding a Myth

A **myth** is a traditional story that tries to explain the different qualities of nature and human beings. When you read a myth, you can learn a great deal about the culture from which it comes. "The Four Elements" reveals several characteristics of the Hispanic people of the Southwest.

1. According to this myth, what three natural elements are valued by the Hispanic people of the Southwest?
2. What human quality is highly valued in the Southwest? What part of the myth reveals this value?
3. By showing that the people of the Hispanic Southwest are made of the same elements as the Earth, what does this myth suggest about the importance of the Earth in their culture?

_The Four Elements_ 621

**Motivation/Prior Knowledge**
Have students answer the following questions and compare their answers with a partner: What do you consider the four most basic elements of life on Earth? Why?

**Purpose-Setting Question** According to this myth, what is the most important element of life?

**Thematic Focus** In this myth the elements of earth are personified. What words portray the earth as human?

**Making Connections** Another selection in which personification is used in the representation of elements of nature is the Tewa Indian poem "Song of the Sky Loom," on page 579.

**1 Discussion** When the elements give their speeches, to whom are they speaking?

**2 Enrichment** The reference to steel may seem out of place in a myth about the earth's beginnings. Not a natural element, steel is an alloy of iron and other materials. Use of steel became widespread during the Industrial Revolution of the 1700's. Why do you think this reference to relatively modern technology is included?

**3 Discussion** How does honor hold living things together?

**Multicultural Focus** Many cultures personify or deify forces of nature. The Efik-Ibibio people of Africa tell a story that in the beginning, Water never visited his friends Sun and Moon because Water was too large to fit in Sun's house; Sun built a bigger home, but still Water filled the entire house, forcing Sun and Moon to sit on the roof, the heavens of today. Among some native peoples of Siberia, the Wind Master and Fire Mistress are harsh disciplinarians. These elements are seen as adversaries to be defended against, if not conquered.

---

## Closure and Extension

### ANSWERS TO RESPONDING TO THE SELECTION
Your Response
1. Encourage students to give reasons to support their opinions.

### Recalling
2. Water, Fire, Wind, and Honor

### Interpreting
3. Water's remark explains the cre-
ation of all bodies of water and the supply of water found beneath the earth's crust.
4. Fire's comment explains the creation of sources of heat and energy.

### Applying
5. Answers will differ. Encourage students to share their responses in a discussion.

### ANSWERS TO ANALYZING LITERATURE

1. Water, Fire, and Wind
2. The Hispanic people value Honor. The last paragraph reveals the fact that Honor is the one element that cannot be recovered if it is lost.
3. Answers will differ. Lead students to understand that cultures in which people earn their livelihood by working the earth develop a close affinity with the earth.

621

## Preparation

**More About the Author** In 1912 Christine Quintasket began her novel *Cowegea* and assumed the pen name "Morning Dove." The name commemorated the ever-faithful wife of Salmon, who, according to Colville legend, welcomes his wife's return each spring. In the next decade, the writer experienced much sadness due to deaths in her family. Then in 1921 during a visit to the Spokane museum, she saw a mounted bird with the label "mourning dove." From that point on, she added the *u* to her pen name, the only name she ever used with outsiders. Why do you think a writer like Mourning Dove might use a pen name at all?

**Literary Focus** What aspects of the animal world—and the human world—does this myth explain?

**Prereading Focus** You may extend the Focus activity by asking students to come up with new names for animals they are familiar with, such as the elephant, the eagle, or the rattlesnake. Have students give reasons for their choices.

**Vocabulary Electronic Handbook** All the vocabulary words are verbs. If students have access to the Language Master 6000, encourage them to review information about verbs and apply it to these words. For example, are they linking verbs or action verbs, transitive or intransitive?

# GUIDE FOR READING

## The Spirit Chief Names the Animal People

### Creation Myth

A myth is an ancient tale invented to explain a natural phenomenon, often involving the supernatural. Every culture, for example, has its own myths to explain such universal mysteries as the creation of the world and the beginning of human civilization. These myths are called **creation myths.** Usually these myths answer timeless questions, such as why birds fly, why the oceans are salty, or why animals have the names they do.

### Focus

Have you ever named a pet or a doll or a stuffed animal? Why was it important to find the right name? As you read "The Spirit Chief Names the Animal People," think about the characteristics of the different types of animals. If you were in charge of the world, how would you assign animal names? Brainstorm for ideas with your classmates. Then compare your ideas with the method used by the Spirit Chief in this myth.

### Vocabulary

Knowing the following words will help you as you read "The Spirit Chief Names the Animal People."

**despise** (di spīz´) *v.*: Scorn; look on with contempt (p. 623)
**scoffed** (skôft) *v.*: Mocked; made fun of (p. 624)

**arouse** (ə rouz´) *v.*: Awaken; stir from sleep (p. 624)
**purify** (pyoor´ ə fī´) *v.*: Make pure; remove all evil (p. 625)

### Mourning Dove

(1885 or 1888–1936) is the pen name of Christine Quintaskat. An Okanogan Indian, she was an enrolled member of the Colville Reservation of north-central Washington. While earning a living as a migrant worker, Quintasket became a writer and political activist. Always interested in the stories she had heard all her life from relatives and visitors, she collected and recorded the folklore of her people to preserve it for posterity. "The Spirit Chief Names the Animal People" is from her collection *Coyote Stories,* originally published in 1933.

### Objectives

1 To understand creation myths
2 To understand cause and effect
3 To write a myth
4 To express individual interests and abilities through an optional activity

### Support Material

**Teaching Portfolio**
Teacher Backup, p. 874
Usage and Mechanics Worksheet, p. 876
Vocabulary Check, p. 877
Analyzing Literature Worksheet, *Understanding Creation Myths,* p. 878
Critical Thinking and Reading Worksheet, *Understanding Cause and Effect,* p. 879

Selection Test, p. 880

**Prentice Hall Literature Writing Studio**

# The Spirit Chief Names the Animal People

## Mourning Dove

1    *Hah-ah' Eel-me'-whem,* the great Spirit Chief,[1] called the Animal People together. They came from all parts of the world. Then the Spirit Chief told them there was to be a change, that a new kind of people was coming to live on the earth.

2    "All of you *Chip-chap-tiqulk*—Animal People—must have names," the Spirit Chief said. "Some of you have names now, some of you haven't. But tomorrow all will have names that shall be kept by you and your descendants forever. In the morning, as the first light of day shows in the sky, come to my lodge and choose your names. The first to come may choose any name that he or she wants. The next person may take any other name. That is the way it will go until all the names are taken. And to each person I will give work to do."

   That talk made the Animal People very excited. Each wanted a proud name and the power to rule some tribe or some part of the world, and everyone determined to get up early and hurry to the Spirit Chief's lodge.

   *Sin-ka-lip'*—Coyote—boasted that no one would be ahead of him. He walked among the people and told them that he would be the first. Coyote did not like his name; he wanted another. Nobody respected his name, Imitator, but it fitted him. He was called *Sin-ka-lip'* because he liked to imitate people. He thought that he could do anything that other persons did, and he pretended to know everything. He would ask a question, and when the answer was given he would say:

   "I knew that before. I did not have to be told."

3    Such smart talk did not make friends for Coyote. Nor did he make friends by the foolish things he did and the rude tricks he played on people.

   "I shall have my choice of the three biggest names," he boasted. "Those names are: *Kee-lau-naw,* the Mountain Person—Grizzly Bear, who will rule the four-footed people; *Milka-noups*—Eagle, who will rule the birds; and *En-tee-tee-ueh,* the Good Swimmer—Salmon. Salmon will be the chief of all the fish that the New People use for food."

4    Coyote's twin brother, Fox, who at the next sun took the name *Why-ay'-looh*—Soft Fur, laughed. "Do not be so sure, *Sin-ka-lip'*," said Fox. "Maybe you will have to keep the name you have. People despise that name. No one wants it."

   "I am tired of that name," Coyote said in an angry voice. "Let someone else carry it. Let some old person take it—someone who cannot win in war. I am going to be a great warrior. My smart brother, I will make you

---

**1. Spirit Chief:** Many Indian tribes firmly believed in a Spirit Chief, an all-powerful god.

*The Spirit Chief Names the Animal People*    623

**Master Teacher Note** Students may enjoy discussing modern practices of naming. For example, do students feel that women should take their husbands' last names when they marry? Do they know anyone who has changed names for another reason? If so, what was it? Do students know anyone who has a hyphenated name? What are the advantages and disadvantages of this practice?

**Making Connections** For a survey of Native American names (and other words) that have become part of the English language, have students read Bernard DeVoto's essay "The Indian All Around Us," on page 457.

**Motivation/Prior Knowledge** Have students brainstorm to list the characteristics they associate with coyotes, based on fictional and nonfictional information. To get students started, you might ask them questions such as the following:
- Name any coyote characters from stories, cartoons, or movies.
- What personality traits do these characters have?
- What do they look like?
- What sounds do they make?
- What do coyotes eat?
- Where do coyotes live?

**Purpose-Setting Question** As students read, have them answer this question: "What can a name reveal about the character of an animal or a person?"

**Thematic Focus** The animal kingdom is an essential part of our living earth. What relationship exists between animals and people in this myth?

1 **Reading Strategy** Suggest that students pause and try to say the Native American names aloud as they read, to help them hear the rhythm of the language.

2 **Literary Focus: Creation Myths** What do you think this change is going to be? Why?

3 **Discussion** What is your opinion of Coyote? Why?

4 **Clarification** The three "biggest names" are also the most revered animals in each of the three realms of nature: the land, the air, and the sea.

**Discussion** Based on the description of her personality and behavior, does Mole fit your description of a "good woman"? Why or why not?

6 **Discussion** Is Coyote a good father? Why or why not?

7 **Critical Thinking and Reading** What effect do you think Mole's action will have? Why?

8 **Reading Strategy** What touched the Spirit Chief's heart? Give reasons for your answer.

**Multicultural Focus** Students may be interested in discussing traditions of naming in various cultures. Point out that many names in this story describe specific physical qualities—for example, *soft fur* is a name that describes the fox. By comparison, in much of English history, surnames were considered necessary only to distinguish people living in the same region who shared the same first name. When this tradition changed, names were usually derived from just a few sources: physical attributes (Armstrong), place names (Kent), trade names (Goldsmith), or familial relationships (Johnson).

Have interested students find a book of names that lists genealogies and have them research the history of their favorite names (or perhaps their own names).

beg of me when I am called Grizzly Bear, Eagle, or Salmon."

"Your strong words mean nothing," scoffed Fox. "Better go to your *swool'-hu* (tepee) and get some sleep, or you will not wake up in time to choose any name."

Coyote stalked off to his tepee. He told himself that he would not sleep any that night; he would stay wide awake. He entered the lodge, and his three sons called as if with one voice:

*"Le-ee'-oo!"* ("Father!")

They were hungry, but Coyote had brought them nothing to eat. Their mother, who after the naming day was known as *Pul'-laqu-whu*—Mole, the Mound Digger—sat on her foot at one side of the doorway.

5 Mole was a good woman, always loyal to her husband in spite of his mean ways, his mischief-making, and his foolishness. She never was jealous, never talked back, never replied to his words of abuse. She looked up and said:

6 "Have you no food for the children? They are starving. I can find no roots to dig."

"*Eh-ha!*" Coyote grunted. "I am no common person to be addressed in that manner. I am going to be a great chief tomorrow. Did you know that? I will have a new name. I will be Grizzly Bear. Then I can devour my enemies with ease. And I shall need you no longer. You are growing too old and homely to be the wife of a great warrior and chief."

Mole said nothing. She turned to her corner of the lodge and collected a few old bones, which she put into a *klek'-chin* (cooking-basket). With two sticks she lifted hot stones from the fire and dropped them into the basket. Soon the water boiled, and there was weak soup for the hungry children.

"Gather plenty of wood for the fire," Coyote ordered. "I am going to sit up all night."

Mole obeyed. Then she and the children went to bed.

Coyote sat watching the fire. Half of the night passed. He got sleepy. His eyes grew heavy. So he picked up two little sticks and braced his eyelids apart. "Now I can stay awake," he thought, but before long he was fast asleep, although his eyes were wide open.

The sun was high in the sky when Coyote awoke. But for Mole he would not have wakened then. Mole called him. She called him after she returned with her name from the Spirit Chief's lodge. Mole loved her husband. She did not want him to have a big name and be a powerful chief. For then, she feared, he would leave her. That was why she did not arouse him at daybreak. Of this she said nothing.

7 Only half-awake and thinking it was early morning, Coyote jumped at the sound of Mole's voice and ran to the lodge of the Spirit Chief. None of the other *Chip-chap-tiqulk* were there. Coyote laughed. Blinking his sleepy eyes, he walked into the lodge. "I am going to be *Kee-lau-naw*," he announced in a strong voice. "That shall be my name."

"The name Grizzly Bear was taken at dawn," the Spirit Chief answered.

"Then I shall be *Milka-noups*," said Coyote, and his voice was not so loud.

"Eagle flew away at sunup," the other replied.

"Well, I shall be called *En-tee-tee-ueh*," Coyote said in a voice that was not loud at all.

"The name Salmon also has been taken," explained the Spirit Chief. "All the names except your own have been taken. No one wished to steal your name."

8 Poor Coyote's knees grew weak. He sank down beside the fire that blazed in the great tepee, and the heart of *Hah-ah' Eel-me'-whem* was touched.

## Commentary

At the Walla Walla Frontier Days celebration, probably in 1915, Mourning Dove met Lucullus Virgil McWhorter, a businessman and Indian-rights advocate who was so impressed by her that he charged her with primary responsibility for preserving her people's traditions. He described his vision for her: "a future of renown: a name that will live through the ages." It was McWhorter who encouraged her to collect and write down traditional stories that were fast disappearing in their original versions. McWhorter hand- ed over the task of editing these tales to his friend Heister Dean Guie, and the three collaborated to create a collection that would appeal to a popular audience.

"*Sin-ka-lip*'," said that Person, "you must keep your name. It is a good name for you. You slept long because I wanted you to be the last one here. I have important work for you, much for you to do before the New People come. You are to be chief of all the tribes.

"Many bad creatures inhabit the earth. They bother and kill people, and the tribes cannot increase as I wish. These *En-alt-na Skil-ten*—People-Devouring Monsters—cannot keep on like that. They must be stopped. It is for you to conquer them. For doing that, for all the good things you do, you will be honored and praised by the people that are here now and that come afterward. But, for the foolish and mean things you do, you will be laughed at and despised. That you cannot help. It is your way.

"To make your work easier, I give you *squas-tenk'*. It is your own special magic power. No one else ever shall have it. When you are in danger, whenever you need help, call to your power. It will do much for you, and with it you can change yourself into any form, into anything you wish.

"To your twin brother, *Why-ay'-looh*, and to others I have given *shoo'-mesh*.[2] It is strong power. With that power Fox can restore your life should you be killed. Your bones may be scattered but, if there is one hair of your body left, Fox can make you live again. Others of the people can do the same with their *shoo'-mesh*. Now, go, *Sin-ka-lip*'! Do well the work laid for your trail!"

Well, Coyote was a chief after all, and he felt good again. After that day his eyes were different. They grew slant from being propped open that night while he sat by his fire. The New People, the Indians, got their slightly slant eyes from Coyote.

---

**2. *shoo'-mesh*** (shōo' mĕsh) *n.*: Medicine, or strong magic power, provided by the Spirit Chief.

After Coyote had gone, the Spirit Chief thought it would be nice for the Animal People and the coming New People to have the benefit of the spiritual sweat-house.[3] But all of the Animal People had names, and there was no one to take the name of Sweat-house—*Quil'-sten*, the Warmer. So the wife of the Spirit Chief took the name. She wanted the people to have the sweat-house, for she pitied them. She wanted them to have a place to go to purify themselves, a place where they could pray for strength and good luck and strong medicine-power, and where they could fight sickness and get relief from their troubles.

The ribs, the frame poles, of the sweat-house represent the wife of *Hah-ah' Eel-me'-whem*. As she is a spirit, she cannot be seen, but she always is near. Songs to her are sung by the present generation. She hears them. She hears what her people say, and in her heart there is love and pity.

---

**3. sweat-house:** A mound-shaped lodge where bathers cleanse themselves physically and spiritually.

HIS HAIR FLOWS LIKE A RIVER
*T. C. Cannon*
*Philbrook Museum of Art, Tulsa, Oklahoma*

9 **Discussion** Does this description apply more to people or animals? Why?

10 **Reading Strategy** What other characters from folklore or mythology have such a power?

11 **Reading Strategy** What does Coyote have in common with the New People besides the shape of his eyes?

12 **Enrichment** Inside these "sweat-houses," heated stones were sprinkled with water to create steam. People would sing songs and pray as they bathed in the steam. The ritual would be followed by a swim in a cool stream.

## Humanities Note

Fine art, *His Hair Flows Like a River,* by T. C. Cannon. Cannon was born in Lawton, Oklahoma, in 1946. He studied art at the American Indian Art Institute in Santa Fe, New Mexico. Cannon's art was featured in a 1972 exhibit at the Smithsonian Institution and is shown in galleries throughout the United States.

Characterized by the use of saturated colors and stylized images from American Western tradition, Cannon's work is distinctive and innovative. *His Hair Flows Like a River* is a woodblock print created during the 1970's. This portrait of a Native American man, though boldly contemporary in style, is traditional in its subject matter. Works such as this earned T. C. Cannon the title *The* Contemporary Artist of the Southwest.

You might use these questions for discussion:

1. Which character from the story could this portrait represent? Why?

2. In what ways does this portrait visually convey the relationship between Coyote and the New People?

## ANSWERS TO RESPONDING TO THE SELECTION

### Your Response

1. Answers will differ. Encourage students to be specific and to support their answers with examples.
2. Answers will differ. Suggest that students include their own criteria for an entertaining story.

### Recalling

3. The Spirit Chief convenes the council to say that a new kind of people are coming and all of the animals must choose new names.
4. Coyote sleeps late on the day designated for choosing names; by the time he sees the Spirit Chief, his old name is the only name left.

### Interpreting

5. Coyote wants any of these names because they are the names of the most powerful animals.
6. Suggested Response: Coyote, determined to be the first one to choose a name, tries to stay up all night. Ironically, he falls asleep and sleeps so late that all the names (except his own) have been chosen by the time he sees the Spirit Chief.
7. Suggested Response: The Spirit Chief has given Coyote the dangerous job of conquering the People-Devouring Monsters. To protect him he provides a way for Coyote's life to be restored should he die.

### Applying

8. Answers will differ. Lead students to understand that though it is very difficult for people to change negative behaviors, it is not impossible.

## ANSWERS TO ANALYZING LITERATURE

1. The world's first inhabitants were the Animal People.
2. This tale is intended to explain how the characteristics of Coyote and other animals have earned them their names. It also explains how the New People got slanted eyes.
3. Suggested Response: The Spirit Chief seems wise, just, and compassionate.
4. Suggested Response: The Spirit Chief wants to give the Animal People and the New People a place to purify themselves, a place where

# RESPONDING TO THE SELECTION

## Your Response

1. What, if anything, do you admire about Coyote? What do you dislike about him?
2. Did you find the story entertaining? Explain.

## Recalling

3. Why does the Spirit Chief convene a council of the Animal People?
4. Explain why Coyote keeps his name.

## Interpreting

5. Why does Coyote want to be named Grizzly Bear, Eagle, or Salmon?
6. How does Coyote's behavior lead to his own misfortune?
7. Why do you think the Spirit Chief gives Fox the power to restore Coyote's life?

## Applying

8. When the Spirit Chief tells Coyote that he will have important work to do, he also reminds Coyote that he will always be despised for the foolish and mean things he does. The Spirit Chief says that Coyote cannot help it because it is "his way." Do you think people can change negative behaviors that interfere with their success? Why or why not?

# ANALYZING LITERATURE

## Understanding Creation Myths

A **creation myth** is a traditional tale designed to make sense of a chaotic world in a prescientific age. Creation myths give explanations for the way things are. "The Spirit Chief Names the Animal People" is an Okanogan myth that explains animal names and attributes. At the same time, it provides insight into Okanogan ideas, beliefs, and customs.

1. According to Okanogan tradition, who were the first inhabitants of the world?
2. What is this tale intended to explain?
3. Describe the qualities of the Spirit Chief.

4. Why does the Spirit Chief want the Animal People and the New People to have a spiritual sweat-house to go to? What does the sweat-house represent about the Okanogan belief in the relationship between the body and the spirit?

# CRITICAL THINKING AND READING

## Understanding Cause and Effect

To understand our world, we look for causality, or cause and effect. A **cause** makes something happen. An **effect** is the outcome, or what happens. Ancient myths present imaginative causes for effects that seem to lack explanation. To identify a cause, ask yourself, "Why did this happen?" To identify an effect, ask yourself, "What happened?"

What explanation or cause is suggested in "The Spirit Chief Names the Animal People" for each of the following effects?

1. There is an order in the animal kingdom.
2. The coyote helps humans by destroying animals that hurt people.
3. The coyote has slanted eyes.

# THINKING AND WRITING

## Writing a Myth

Mourning Dove recorded Okanogan myths that explain why Spider has such long legs, why Badger is so humble, and why Mosquitoes bite people. Invent a myth of your own to explain one of these mysteries or some other natural phenomenon. You might give your animals both human and superhuman characteristics.

# LEARNING OPTION

**Performance.** What's in a name? Find out by investigating the meaning of your given name and deciding if it suits you. If it does not, choose a name that better reflects who you are or who you would like to be. Plan and hold a naming ceremony with your classmates.

---

they could get relief from sickness and their troubles. The sweat-house provides evidence of the Okanogan belief that the body and spirit are one. To purify the body is to purify the spirit as well.

## ANSWERS TO CRITICAL THINKING AND READING

1. The order is because the Spirit Chief oversees the entire kingdom and each animal has been assigned its own distinct job.

2. This is the job that the Spirit Chief assigned to Coyote.
3. The Coyote propped his eyelids open one night in an attempt to stay awake.

## THINKING AND WRITING

**Writing Transparency** As students write their myths, direct them to the Paragraph Exercise on *Chronological Order*, Model 4: *Short Story*, and the graphic orga-

nizer *Series of Events Chain* in **Transparencies for Writing**.

## LEARNING OPTION

Students may wish to do research on naming ceremonies and customs from various cultures to get ideas for their own ceremony. Encourage students to divide up the many different tasks involved in this group activity according to their own interests.

# MULTICULTURAL CONNECTION

## *Coyote the Trickster*

### *By Joseph Bruchac*

**Who is Coyote?** The coyote, a smaller cousin of the wolf, is one of the most adaptable and widespread animals in North America. From the seashores to the mountains, from the deserts to the forests, coyotes survive and thrive. They will eat almost anything—snowshoe rabbits in the northern forests, watermelons in Hopi gardens, scraps from dumpsters in Los Angeles. Although Coyote the trickster has much in common with these resourceful predators of the same name, the Coyote of Native American tales is a combination of human and animal characteristics.

**Native American stories.** Coyote appears in many kinds of Native American tales, but he is especially popular in stories of how things came to be. In some of these stories, Coyote is simply a fool; in others, a mixture of clown and hero, as in the Yakima story "The Spirit Chief Names the Animal People."

Coyote is always bringing things into existence through his powers and his mistakes. The Nez Percé of Washington tell how Coyote turned a monster into a hill. To this day they will point out that very hill. In a tale told by the Miwok people of the West Coast, Coyote actually creates the Earth with the help of his brother Silver Fox by singing it into existence.

In a tale told by the Wishram people of Oregon, Coyote goes to the land of the dead to bring back his wife. He carries her back toward the land of the living in a box. When his curiosity grows too much for him, however, he opens the box too soon and she vanishes. If Coyote had been patient and waited, the Wishram say, then death would not have seemed so final.

**A universal character.** This trickster, so popular in Native American origin stories, may be seen to represent all people. By doing great things almost in spite of himself, Coyote teaches the lesson that all of us are capable of both good and evil.

## Further Reading

Caduto, Michael, and Joseph Bruchac. *Keepers of the Animals: Native American Stories and Wildlife Activities for Children* (Golden, Colorado: Fulcrum, 1991).

*Coyote Was Going There*, edited and compiled by Jarold Ramsey (Seattle, Washington: University of Washington Press, 1977). Included in this book is the Nez Percé version of "Coyote and the Swallowing Monster."

*The Maidu Indian Myths and Stories of Hanc'ibyjim*, edited by William Shipley (Berkeley, California: Heyday Books, 1991).

*Joseph Bruchac is a storyteller and writer of Abenaki, English, and Slovak descent. He has published a number of books, and his poems, articles, and stories have appeared in hundreds of magazines, from* Cricket *to* National Geographic.

*Multicultural Connection* 627

## Presentation

**Motivation/Prior Knowledge**
Ask students to share ideas they had about coyotes before and after they read "The Spirit Chief Names the Animal People." Have them consider why the coyote is characterized as a trickster. What other popular trickster characters can students name?

**Discussion** As students read this feature, have them list Coyote's positive and negative traits. Have them share their personal responses to Coyote's complex character. Do students see any of their own qualities in Coyote?

## Closure and Extension

Have students write original stories about Coyote the Trickster. Some students may wish to become more familiar with Coyote by reading some of the stories listed at the end of the feature. Others may wish to invent their own version of the crafty character.

**More About the Author** Zora Neale Hurston is acknowledged as the first American to collect and publish African American folklore. Her use of dialect in folk tales was questioned by early critics who felt that capturing the spoken language called attention to cultural differences and reinforced negative stereotypes. Today many critics, writers, and readers admire Hurston's use of dialect. Have students notice the dialect as they read.

**Literary Focus** Ask students what these two folk tales have in common. Have them compare them in terms of characterization, imagery, plot, and theme.

**Prereading Focus** To review personification, repetition, and dialogue, you may wish to have students identify the use of each in the following nursery rhyme:

Pussy Cat, Pussy Cat,
where have you been?''
''I've been to London to
visit the Queen.''
''Pussy Cat, Pussy Cat,
what did you there?''
''I   frightened   a   little
mouse under her chair.

**Vocabulary Electronic Handbook** Students will be more familiar with the noun *ornament* than the verb. If students have access to the Language Master 6000, they can see that *ornament* has two entries, one a noun, the other a verb.

**Videocassette** The Library of Video Classics work *Zora Is My Name!* provides dramatizations of folk tales that Hurston collected and recorded as well as dramatizations of Hurston's own memories. This production offers a cultural and historical context of Hurston's life and work. You might show relevant parts of it after students have read these stories.

# GUIDE FOR READING

## Zora Neale Hurston

(1901–1960) was a multitalented woman. As a cultural anthropologist, she introduced New York concert-goers to African American spirituals, work songs, and folk dance. As a writer of novels, short stories, and magazine articles, she re-created and interpreted the folklore that she had grown up with in Eatonville, Florida. In addition, she was a writer at Paramount Studios in Hollywood and headed the drama department of the North Carolina College for Negroes.

## How the Snake Got Poison
## Why the Waves Have Whitecaps

### African American Folklore

**African American folklore,** like the myths, legends, and tales of other cultures, had its beginnings in the oral traditions of community storytellers. The dialect in Hurston's tales emphasizes the oral beginnings of these tales. Told as much for instruction as for entertainment, these stories illustrate explanations for the causes of certain natural phenomena, expressions of human fears and desires, insights into the human condition, and practical advice for survival in difficult life situations.

### Focus

As an anthropologist it was important to Zora Neale Hurston to record accurately the folk tales that she had heard as a child. In "How the Snake Got Poison" and "Why the Waves Have Whitecaps," she effectively uses dialect to record local speech variations. Dialect is the regional variety of a language distinguished by its pronunciation, grammar, and vocabulary. As you read the two folk tales by Zora Neale Hurston, see if you can also find these other typical characteristics of folklore: personification, in which an aspect of nature or an animal is made to seem alive or human; repetition of words, phrases, and sentence structure to create rhythm, build suspense, and add emphasis; dialogue as a way to establish indirectly the personalities of the characters in the tales.

### Vocabulary

Knowing the following words will help you as you read "How the Snake Got Poison" and "Why the Waves Have Whitecaps."
**ornament** (ôr′ nə mənt) *v.*: To decorate (p. 630)
**immensity** (i men′ si tē) *n.*:
Something extremely large or immeasurably vast (p. 630)

628   *The American Folk Tradition*

## Objectives
1  To understand African American folklore
2  To appreciate imagination
3  To write an imaginative folk tale
4  To express individual interests and abilities through optional activities

## Support Material

**Teaching Portfolio**
Teacher Backup, p. 883
Usage and Mechanics Worksheet, p. 886
Analyzing Literature Worksheet, *Understanding African American Folklore,* p. 887
Critical  Thinking  and  Reading Worksheet, *Appreciating Imagination,* p. 888
Selection Test, p. 889

**Library of Video Classics**
*Zora Is My Name!*

**Prentice Hall Literature Writing Studio**

# How the Snake Got Poison

## Zora Neale Hurston

Well, when God made de snake he put him in de bushes to ornament de ground. But things didn't suit de snake so one day he got on de ladder and went up to see God.

"Good mawnin', God."

"How do you do, Snake?"

"Ah[1] ain't so many, God, you put me down there on my belly in de dust and everything trods upon me and kills off my generations. Ah ain't got no kind of protection at all."

God looked off towards immensity and thought about de subject for awhile, then he said, "Ah didn't mean for nothin' to be stompin' you snakes lak dat. You got to have some kind of a protection. Here, take dis poison and put it in yo' mouf and when they tromps on you, protect yo'self."

So de snake took de poison in his mouf and went on back.

So after awhile all de other varmints went up to God.

"Good evenin', God."

"How you makin' it, varmints?"

"God, please do somethin' 'bout dat snake. He' layin' in de bushes there wid poison in his mouf and he's strikin' everything dat shakes de bush. He's killin' up our generations. Wese skeered to walk de earth."

So God sent for de snake and tole him:

"Snake, when Ah give you dat poison, Ah didn't mean for you to be hittin' and killin' everything dat shake de bush. I give you dat poison and tole you to protect yo'self when they tromples on you. But you killin' everything dat moves. Ah didn't mean for you to do dat."

De snake say, "Lawd, you know Ah'm down here in de dust. Ah ain't got no claws to fight wid, and Ah ain't got no feets to git me out de way. All Ah kin see is feets comin' to tromple me. Ah can't tell who my enemy is and who is my friend. You gimme dis protection in my mouf and Ah uses it."

God thought it over for a while then he says:

"Well, snake, I don't want yo' generations all stomped out and I don't want you killin' everything else dat moves. Here take dis bell and tie it to yo' tail. When you hear feets comin' you ring yo' bell and if it's yo' friend, he'll be keerful. If it's yo' enemy, it's you and him."

So dat's how de snake got his poison and dat's how come he got rattles.

Biddy, biddy, bend my story is end.
Turn loose de rooster and hold de hen.

RATTLESNAKE NO. 3, 1988
*William Hawkins*
*Edward Thorp Gallery, New York*

---

**1. Ah** *n.*: Dialect for "I."

**Making Connections** Two selections in which dialect is also used to establish authenticity are "Davy Crockett's Dream," on page 681, and "Tussle With a Bear," on page 683. You might have students compare and contrast the dialect in these selections with that in the Hurston tales.

## Humanities Note

Fine art, *Rattlesnake No. 3*, 1988, by William Hawkins. Born in 1895, Hawkins did not begin to paint until 1979. Because of the nature of his media and themes, Hawkins is classified as a folk artist.

The simple, bold composition of *Rattlesnake No. 3* has a great deal of charm and vigor. Painted on a large panel (4 feet by 5 feet), the stylized image of the snake fills the picture plane to the decorative border.

You might use these questions for discussion:
1. In the story God created the snake to ornament the earth. How is this attitude toward the snake expressed in this painting?
2. How might the term "folk artist" apply to both Hurston and Hawkins? Explain.

## Presentation

**Motivation/Prior Knowledge** Have students use either their knowledge or their imagination to answer the following questions:

Why do waves have whitecaps?
Why do rattlesnakes have venom and rattles?

**Master Teacher Note** It may interest students to note that the two main characters in "How the Snake Got Poison" are male and the two main characters in "Why the Waves Have Whitecaps" are female. Would the tales be significantly different if the genders were reversed? Why or why not?

**Purpose-Setting Question** What do these folk tales tell you about the culture from which they come?

**Thematic Focus** Have students think about the attitudes toward the earth and the natural world that are revealed in these folk tales. What do these interpretations of the inner workings of the natural world reveal about human nature?

1 **Reading Strategy** What does the snake mean by "kills off my generations"?

2 **Reading Strategy** What do you think *immensity* means in this sentence? Use the context of the sentence to support your answer.

3 **Discussion** What human qualities do God's behavior and words reveal?

4 **Discussion** Do you think that the snake's explanation for his aggressive behavior is reasonable? Why or why not?

5 **Enrichment** The rattlesnake sends out poison through two long upper fangs that are folded back in the mouth when they are not in use. The rattle is a set of interlocking horny segments at the end of the snake's body that produces a rattling or buzzing sound when shaken.

630

## Humanities Note

Fine art, *Untitled (Mermaid)*, 1983, by Amos Ferguson. A self-taught painter, Ferguson is a native of the Bahamas, where he continues to reside. His paintings portray sunny images of island life. This painting depicts a mermaid, surrounded by sea birds, combing her hair. In the foreground is a fisherman in a small boat. The palette is one of bright primary colors, flatly applied. Only the whitecaps on the water reveal the artist's brush strokes.

Ferguson is considered a "folk artist" because of his technically uncomplicated style. The artist is pleased that the simplicity of his work can be understood and enjoyed by people of all ages.

You might use the following questions for discussion:
1. In what ways is Ferguson's painting an appropriate illustration for this folk tale?
2. How do the whitecaps on the water affect the otherwise calm and peaceful atmosphere of this painting?

**1 Discussion** Do you agree with the speaker's generalization about women? Why or why not?

**2 Reading Strategy** What feature of the ocean is Mrs. Water calling her children?

**3 Reading Strategy** What features of the wind and the weather are Mrs. Wind calling her children?

**4 Reading Strategy** Ask students to define the word *squinch,* based on the sentence's context.

**5 Literary Focus: African American Folklore** In what sense are whitecaps truly the result of a "dialogue" between wind and water?

# Why the Waves Have Whitecaps

## Zora Neale Hurston

De wind is a woman, and de water is a woman too. They useter[1] talk together a whole heap. Mrs. Wind useter go set down by de ocean and talk and patch and crochet.

**1** They was jus' like all lady people. They loved to talk about their chillun, and brag on 'em.

**2** Mrs. Water useter say, "Look at *my* chillun! Ah[2] got de biggest and de littlest in de world. All kinds of chillun. Every color in de world, and every shape!"

De wind lady bragged louder than de water woman:

**3** "Oh, but Ah got mo' different chilluns than anybody in de world. They flies, they walks, they swims, they sings, they talks, they cries. They got all de colors from de sun. Lawd, my chillun sho is a pleasure. 'Tain't nobody got no babies like mine."

Mrs. Water got tired of hearin' 'bout Mrs. Wind's chillun so she got so she hated 'em.

One day a whole passle[3] of her chillun come to Mrs. Wind and says: "Mama, wese thirsty. Kin we go git us a cool drink of water?"

She says, "Yeah chillun. Run on over to Mrs. Water and hurry right back soon."

**4** When them chillun went to squinch they thirst Mrs. Water grabbed 'em all and drowned 'em.

When her chillun didn't come home, de wind woman got worried. So she went on down to de water and ast for her babies.

---
**1. useter** (yoo′ stə) *v.*: Dialect for "used to."
**2. Ah** *pron.*: Dialect for "I."
**3. passle** *n.*: Dialect for "group."

"Good evenin' Mis' Water, you see my chillun today?"

De water woman tole her, "No-oo-oo."

Mrs. Wind knew her chillun had come down to Mrs. Water's house, so she passed over de ocean callin' her chillun, and every time she call de white feathers would come up on top of de water. And dat's how come **5** we got white caps on waves. It's de feathers comin' up when de wind woman calls her lost babies.

When you see a storm on de water, it's de wind and de water fightin' over dem chillun.

UNTITLED (MERMAID), 1983
*Amos Ferguson*
*The Museum of International Folk Art*

## Commentary

Hurston discusses her work collecting African American folklore as follows: "When I pitched headforemost into the world I landed in the crib of Negroism. From the earliest rocking of my cradle, I had known about the capers Br'er Rabbit is apt to cut and what the Squinch Owl says from the housetop. But it was fitting me like a tight chemise. I couldn't see it for wearing it. It was only when I was off in college, away from my native surroundings, that I could see myself like somebody else and stand off and look at my garment. Then I had to have the spyglass of anthropology to look through at that."

# RESPONDING TO THE SELECTIONS

## Your Response

1. Do these explanations for natural occurrences seem simplistic, or do they seem natural and logical? What makes them seem so?
2. Which of these two folk tales did you enjoy more? Why?

## Recalling

3. How does the snake explain his excessive use of the poison God gave him?
4. Why does Mrs. Water hate Mrs. Wind's children?

## Interpreting

5. In what ways are Mrs. Wind and Mrs. Water like real women?
6. What do the characters and situations in these two folk tales illustrate about people and their ways of interacting?

## Applying

7. Folklore provides an opportunity to communicate social rules and values. Discuss what these two folk tales reflect about the society that created them.

# ANALYZING LITERATURE

## Understanding African American Folklore

A characteristic of **African American folklore** is its use of repetition. Repetition within a folk tale probably arose first as a memory aid. Before tales were written down, storytellers needed to be certain that the tales were passed correctly from generation to generation. Repetition serves another purpose, however: It involves the listener or reader more actively in the tale by establishing a certain rhythm, by building suspense, and by emphasizing important ideas.

1. Reread the conversation between God and the other varmints and then compare it with God's words to the snake on page 629. Pick out words and phrases that are repeated, and explain the effect of the repetition.
2. Select several examples of repetition in "Why the Waves Have Whitecaps," and explain the effect of the repetition. How does the effect here differ from that of "How the Snake Got Poison"?

# CRITICAL THINKING AND READING

## Appreciating Imagination

If you were to research the facts about snakes, you'd probably discover that a rattlesnake rarely warns an enemy before it strikes. When a rattlesnake does rattle, it has been frightened by something. Why, then, do you suppose that folk tales such as "How the Snake Got Poison" manipulate scientific fact with imaginative results?

# THINKING AND WRITING

## Writing an Imaginative Folk Tale

If your family has a folk tale that has been told through several generations, write it as a narrative story. As an alternative, ask a question about a natural phenomenon, such as why there is lightning, and provide an imaginative explanation in an original folk tale.

# LEARNING OPTIONS

1. **Art.** Select a scene from either tale and illustrate it. Your illustration may take the form of a drawing, a diorama, or a collage. Use appropriate lines from the tale as a caption for your art.
2. **Performance.** Work with a small group of your classmates to prepare a skit based on one of the tales. You may prepare a script and make or find the necessary costumes and props. When you are ready, present the skit for your classmates.

*Why the Waves Have Whitecaps* 631

mouf'' are repeated in these speeches. The repeated phrases establish a rhythm that builds as the story progresses and, in effect, creates suspense.

2. Suggested Response: The word ''chillun'' and the phrase ''in de world'' are repeated many times. The effect is to mimic the boastful prattle of the main characters.

## ANSWERS TO CRITICAL THINKING AND READING

Suggested Response: Folk tales are meant to entertain us as they inform us about human nature, and in order to do that, they must capture our imagination.

## THINKING AND WRITING

**Writing Transparencies** As students write their folk tales, direct them to the Paragraph Exercise on *Chronological Order, Model 4: Short Story,* and the *Series of Events Chain* in the Graphic Organizers of **Transparencies for Writing.**

**Alternative Assessment** *Protocol:* Ask students to assess their own work by responding to the following questions:

What natural phenomenon is your folk tale about?

What is your general explanation of the phenomenon?

How do you use personification in your tale?

In what ways does your use of repetition create rhythm, build suspense, or add emphasis?

How do you incorporate dialogue in your tale?

You may have students use the information they have gained from their protocols as a guide for revising their folk tales.

## LEARNING OPTIONS

1. The art activity will appeal to visual and artistically inclined learners.
2. The performance activity will appeal to kinesthetic learners, as well as to those who enjoy expressing their creativity either onstage or offstage.

---

## Closure and Extension

### ANSWERS TO RESPONDING TO THE SELECTION

#### Your Response

1. Encourage students to cite specific details and images.
2. Encourage students to give reasons for their preferences and to share their opinions in a discussion.

#### Recalling

3. The snake claims that he can't tell his enemies from his friends, so he uses the poison on everyone.
4. Mrs. Water gets tired of listening to Mrs. Wind brag about her children.

#### Interpreting

5. They both talk about their children; they worry about their children; they talk while they patch and crochet.
6. Answers will differ. Lead students to understand that in both tales, the personified characters have trouble getting along with their neighbors.

#### Applying

7. Answers will differ. Lead students to understand that society values living in harmony and peace.

### ANSWERS TO ANALYZING LITERATURE

1. Suggested Response: Phrases such as ''strikin' everything dat shakes de bush,'' ''killin' up our generations,'' and ''poison in his

## Presentation

**Motivation/Prior Knowledge**
Have students discuss their favorite folk tales or fairy tales. Ask them to consider why these tales have such universal appeal and why they have endured for so many years. For examples of age-old tales that are currently popular, you may wish to cite the films *Beauty and the Beast* and *Aladdin*.

**Discussion** As students read this feature, have them jot down information about the type of folklore that appeals to them most. Ask them to consider how they might find out more information about these tales or songs.

## Closure and Extension

To give students an idea of how universal the tradition of storytelling is, suggest that they go to a library and research the different versions of a given folk tale or fairy tale. For example, how many versions of "Cinderella" can students find? How are these versions different? What elements of the story stay the same in each version? Interested students may wish to present their findings to their class.

# MULTICULTURAL CONNECTION
## *Folklore, a Worldwide Tradition*

Folklore, the collection of traditional customs, beliefs, and stories, can be found around the world and is probably as old as civilization itself. Folklore is usually passed along by telling stories, singing songs, or performing dances.

A folk tale is perhaps the form of folklore with which people are most familiar. It is usually distinguished from a myth or legend because it has a general setting and characters instead of being very specific. A popular form of folk tale is the animal tale, such as those by Zora Neale Hurston, which feature animals that talk and act like people. Animal tales that have a moral are known as fables.

**American folklore.** The United States has developed a rich folklore tradition. One popular form is the tall tale, in which things are greatly exaggerated and often quite funny. Folklore thrived in the Appalachian Mountain region of the Southeast, producing special music, great storytellers, and a distinctive way of speaking. The African American culture in the South has also played a big role in American folklore, through songs and chants sung by slaves and sharecroppers and through a rich storytelling tradition. The southern writer Joel Chandler Harris created many folk tales based on black folklore in his highly popular *Uncle Remus* stories.

The many legends of Native Americans have also been an important part of our folklore tradition. The nineteenth-century writer James Fenimore Cooper used Native American legends in his *Leatherstocking Tales,* which included the famous novel *The Last of the Mohicans.*

**Folklore around the world.** Writers and scholars have been gathering folklore for a very long time. The eighth-century B.C. Greek poet Homer based much of his famous epic poems, the *Iliad* and the *Odyssey,* on Greek folklore that dated from 1000 B.C. or earlier. In the nineteenth century, the German writers Jakob and Wilhelm Grimm traveled through Europe collecting folk tales exactly as people still told them and not from books. Folklore societies began to form in Europe in the nineteenth century. The American Folklore Society was founded in 1888, focusing mainly on the beliefs and tales of Native Americans.

**John and Alan Lomax.** In the early part of the twentieth century, a father and son named John and Alan Lomax gathered an enormous amount of American folklore in the form of folk songs. Like the Grimm brothers, they got their songs straight from the source: the performers. With the tape recorder and recording equipment, folk music was soon being recorded and played for much larger audiences.

**Zora Neale Hurston.** Zora Neale Hurston continued this tradition. In the late 1920's, she collected African American folklore in her native Florida. Her collection of folklore, *Of Mules and Men,* was published in 1935.

**Sharing**

Have students think of the folklore they are familiar with—from folk music to folk-tale heroes or even superstitions. Discuss this in class.

# Heroes and Legends

MISS ANNIE OAKLEY, THE PEERLESS LADY WING-SHOT, c. 1890
*Buffalo Bill Historical Center, Cody, Wyoming*

*Heroes and Legends* 633

## Humanities Note

Poster, *Miss Annie Oakley, The Peerless Lady Wing-Shot*, c. 1890. Using a celebrity to endorse a product was as popular a technique in nineteenth-century advertising as it is in advertising today. Poster art was a forerunner of contemporary advertising, using ornate typefaces, outlandish images, and bright colors to catch people's attention.

In *Miss Annie Oakley, The Peerless Lady Wing-Shot*, the colorful lady of the Wild West is used to advertise both Buffalo Bill's Wild West Show and the Peerless Company's "wing-shot" shotgun pellets. This poster would have been particularly eye-catching in its time because of Annie's shooting and her wearing what would have been considered a scandalously short dress.

Like some of the heroes and heroines in this section, Annie Oakley was a real person whose abilities and exploits were exaggerated in stories about her adventures. Like all the heroes and heroines in this unit, Annie Oakley is part of the American folk tradition. Stories about her life highlight characteristics and skills that are valued as an integral part of our American heritage.

You might want to use the following questions for discussion:

1. What skills and qualities does this poster of Annie Oakley highlight? Why would these traits be good for advertising?

2. Do you think Annie would have been successful in giving endorsements for ladies' dresses? Face cream? Why or why not?

3. How are women portrayed in contemporary advertising? What qualities and skills are highlighted?

**More About the Legend** Zuñi Indians are descendants of the cliff-dwelling Anasazi Indians. Their first contact with outsiders was in 1539, when a Spanish expedition discovered six of their villages. Today, many Zuñi Indians still live in adobe and stone houses. They raise livestock and produce fine jewelry from coral, silver, and turquoise.

**Literary Focus** You might want to point out to students that, unlike myths, legends are not meant to explain natural phenomena. Also, they usually have some basis, however slight, in fact.

**Prereading Focus** Lead students to recognize that it is not lack of fear that makes a person brave, but the determination to overcome fear. Have students review their lists and assess how the qualities they have listed might help someone overcome fear.

**Vocabulary** You might have your more advanced students create a sentence that includes at least three of the vocabulary words.

**Spelling Tip** The ending *-ious*, as in *voracious*, is much more common than *-eous*, which is used often in technical and scientific terms like *gaseous*, *cutaneous*, or *vitreous*.

# GUIDE FOR READING

### The Zuñi Indians

live in a harsh and unforgiving land, in northwestern New Mexico near Arizona. The early Zuñis were farmers. Their territory, governed by the United States after 1848, is parched by sun in summer and swept by wind and snow in winter. Yet there is beauty in the land: towering cliffs flaming red in the sunset; deep, cool canyons; and wide-open vistas. "The Girl Who Hunted Rabbits" tells of a courageous girl who faces the harsh elements to bring food home to her family.

## The Girl Who Hunted Rabbits

### Legend

A **legend** is an imaginative story believed to be based on an actual person or event, rather than on the supernatural. The story is passed from generation to generation, often by word of mouth. With retelling, the character's actions or the event may become more fantastic. The character becomes larger than life—a hero or heroine.

Legends also give you information about the people who tell them. "The Girl Who Hunted Rabbits" tells you how the Zuñis lived and some of the gods they believed in.

### Focus

This legend tells of the bravery of a young Native American woman. What does the concept of bravery mean to you? Do you know someone who you think is brave? Why do you consider that person brave? List the qualities that person has that make him or her brave. After you read "The Girl Who Hunted Rabbits," compare the qualities on your list with the qualities the young woman in the story is said to have.

### Vocabulary

Knowing the following words will help you as you read "The Girl Who Hunted Rabbits."

**procured** (prō kyoord') *v.:* Obtained by some effort (p. 635)
**sinew** (sin' yōō) *n.:* A tendon, a band of fibrous tissue that connects muscles to bones or to other parts and can also be used as thread for sewing (p. 636)
**mantle** (man' t'l) *n.:* Sleeveless cloak or cape (p. 636)

**unwonted** (un wän' tid) *adj.:* Not usual (p. 636)
**bedraggled** (bi drag' 'ld) *adj.:* Dirty and wet (p. 638)
**voracious** (vô rā' shəs) *adj.:* Eager to devour large quantities of food (p. 639)
**devoured** (di vourd') *v.:* Ate greedily (p. 639)

### Objectives

1 To understand legends
2 To make inferences from legends
3 To retell a legend
4 To express individual interests and abilities through optional activities

## Support Material

**Teaching Portfolio**
Teacher Backup, p. 891
Grammar in Action Worksheets, *Using Conjunctions*, p. 895; *Understanding Prepositional Phrases*, p. 897
Usage and Mechanics Worksheet, p. 899
Vocabulary Check, p. 900
Critical Thinking and Reading Worksheet, *Making Inferences*

*From a Legend*, p. 901
Language Worksheet, *Choosing Meaning to Fit Context*, p. 902
Selection Test, p. 903

**Prentice Hall Literature Writing Studio**

# The Girl Who Hunted Rabbits

## Zuñi Indian Legend

It was long ago, in the days of the ancients, that a poor maiden lived at "Little Gateway of Zuñi River." You know there are black stone walls of houses standing there on the tops of the cliffs of lava, above the narrow place through which the river runs, to this day.

In one of these houses there lived this poor maiden alone with her feeble old father and her aged mother. She was unmarried, and her brothers had all been killed in wars, or had died gently; so the family lived there helplessly, so far as many things were concerned, from the lack of men in their house.

It is true that in making the gardens— the little plantings of beans, pumpkins, squashes, melons, and corn—the maiden was able to do very well; and thus mainly on the products of these things the family were supported. But, as in those days of our ancients we had neither sheep nor cattle, the hunt was depended upon to supply the meat; or sometimes it was procured by barter[1] of the products of the fields to those who hunted mostly. Of these things this little family had barely enough for their own subsistence; hence, they could not procure their supplies of meat in this way.

Long before, it had been a great house, for many were the brave and strong young

men who had lived in it; but the rooms were now empty, or at best contained only the leavings of those who had lived there, much used and worn out.

One autumn day, near wintertime, snow fell, and it became very cold. The maiden had gathered brush and firewood in abundance, and it was piled along the roof of the house and down underneath the ladder which descended from the top. She saw the young men issue forth the next morning in great numbers, their feet protected by long stockings of deerskin, the fur turned inward, and they carried on their shoulders and stuck in their belts stone axes and rabbit sticks. As she gazed at them from the roof, she said to herself, "O that I were a man and could go forth, as do these young men, hunting rabbits! Then my poor old mother and father would not lack for flesh with which to duly season their food and nourish their lean bodies." Thus ran her thoughts, and before night, as she saw these same young men coming in, one after another, some of them bringing long strings of rabbits, others short ones, but none of them empty-handed, she decided that she would set forth on the morrow to try what luck she might find in the killing of rabbits herself.

It may seem strange that, although this maiden was beautiful and young, the youths did not give her some of their rabbits. But

---

1. **barter** (bär′ tər) *v.*: To exchange goods.

*The Girl Who Hunted Rabbits* 635

3 **Reading Strategy** You might have students summarize what they discover about the way Zuñis lived at the time of this legend. What did Zuñis eat? What were the roles of men and women? What types of shelter did they live in?

4 **Discussion** How do her parents feel about their daughter hunting? What do their preparations indicate about their feelings toward her?

their feelings were not friendly, for no one of them would she accept as a husband, although one after another of them had offered himself for marriage.

Fully resolved, the girl that evening sat down by the fireplace, and turning toward her aged parents, said, "O my mother and father, I see that the snow has fallen, whereby easily rabbits are tracked, and the young men who went out this morning returned long before evening heavily laden with strings of this game. Behold, in the other rooms of our house are many rabbit sticks, and there hang on the walls stone axes, and with these I might perchance strike down a rabbit on his trail, or, if he runs into a log, split the log and dig him out. So I have thought during the day, and have decided to go tomorrow and try my fortunes in the hunt."

"*Naiya*, my daughter," quavered the feeble, old mother, "you would surely be very cold, or you would lose your way, or grow so tired that you could not return before night, and you must not go out to hunt rabbits."

"Why, certainly not," insisted the old man, rubbing his lean knees and shaking his head over the days that were gone. "No, no; let us live in poverty rather than that you should run such risks as these, O my daughter."

But, say what they would, the girl was determined. And the old man said at last, "Very well! You will not be turned from your course. Therefore, O daughter, I will help you as best I may." He hobbled into another room, and found there some old deerskins covered thickly with fur; and drawing them out, he moistened and carefully softened them, and cut out for the maiden long stockings, which he sewed up with sinew and the fiber of the yucca[2] leaf. Then he selected

for her from among the old possessions of his brothers and sons, who had been killed or perished otherwise, a number of rabbit sticks and a fine, heavy stone ax. Meanwhile, the old woman busied herself in preparing a lunch for the girl, which was composed of little cakes of cornmeal, spiced with pepper and wild onions, pierced through the middle, and baked in the ashes. When she had made a long string of these by threading them like beads on a rope of yucca fiber, she laid them down not far from the ladder on a little bench, with the rabbit sticks, the stone ax, and the deerskin stockings.

That night the maiden planned and planned, and early on the following morning, even before the young men had gone out from the town, she had put on a warm, short-skirted dress, knotted a mantle over her shoulder and thrown another and larger one over her back, drawn on the deerskin stockings, had thrown the string of corn-cakes over her shoulder, stuck the rabbit sticks in her belt, and carrying the stone ax in her hand sallied[3] forth eastward through the Gateway of Zuñi and into the plain of the valley beyond, called the Plain of the Burnt River, on account of the black, roasted-looking rocks along some parts of its sides. Dazzlingly white the snow stretched out before her—not deep, but unbroken—and when she came near the cliffs with many little canyons in them, along the northern side of the valley, she saw many a trail of rabbits running out and in among the rocks and between the bushes.

Warm and excited by her unwonted exercise, she did not heed a coming snowstorm, but ran about from one place to another, following the trails of the rabbits, sometimes up into the canyons where the forests of pine and cedar stood, and where

---

2. **yucca** (yuk' ə) *n.*: A desert plant with stiff leaves and white flowers.

---

3. **sallied** (sal' ēd) *v.*: Set out energetically.

## Grammar in Action

**Conjunctions** connect individual words or groups of words, holding the sentence together. There are three categories of conjunctions: **coordinating, correlative,** and **subordinating.** Coordinating conjunctions connect words of a similar kind. For example, two or more verbs can be connected by a coordinating conjunction. Similarly, coordinating conjunctions connect larger groups of words, such as prepositional phrases, or even entire sentences. Examples of coordinating conjunctions are *and, but,*

*for, nor, or, so,* and *yet.* Notice how the coordinating conjunctions in the following sentence from "The Girl Who Hunted Rabbits" hold the sentence together:

It was little work to split these logs, *for* they were small, as you know, *and* to dig out the rabbits *and* slay them by a blow of the hand on the nape of the neck, back of the ears; *and* as she killed each rabbit she raised it reverently to her lips, *and* breathed from its nostrils its expiring breath *and,* tying its legs together, placed it on the string . . ."

Correlative conjunctions also connect the same kinds of words or groups of words, but unlike coordinating conjunctions, correlative conjunctions come in pairs—*both . . . and, either . . .*

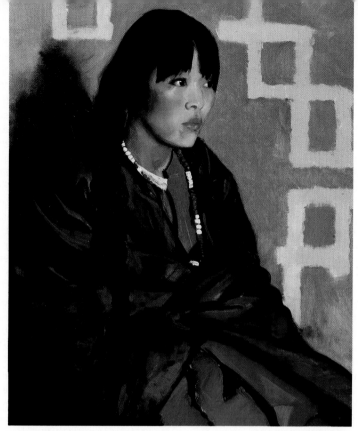

**INDIAN GIRL (1917)**
*Robert Henri*
Indianapolis Museum of Art

5 **Literary Focus** You might point out to students that the legend to this point could easily have been a true story.

## Humanities Note

Fine art, *Indian Girl*, by Robert Henri. Robert Henri (1865–1929) was an innovative painter and teacher of art. As a founding member of the "Ashcan" school of American painting (so called because of its unglamorous subject matter), Henri worked with "the Eight," a group of free-thinking painters whose work was a radical departure from the approved academic style of American painting. Their paintings of the ordinary life around them were initially scorned as "mundane" and "ugly" but eventually won public acclaim.

*Indian Girl* was one of the fourteen canvases produced by Henri on a trip to Santa Fe. The canvases chronicle his admiration and respect for Native Americans. Each of these paintings displays an Indian blanket as a decorative motif. In *Indian Girl* the flat abstract design of the blanket curiously enhances the living presence of the girl. The color palette, while not harmonious, is given continuity by repetition of the soft, vibrant reds.

This painting affirms Henri's desire to show the world "his people." He did so again and again in his numerous portraits of poor, foreign, and minority peoples.

You might want to use the following questions to discuss the art:
1. Is this how you pictured the girl in the selection? Explain.
2. How does Henri's painting affect your interpretation of the selection?

here and there she had the good fortune sometimes to run two, three, or four rabbits into a single hollow log. It was little work to split these logs, for they were small, as you know, and to dig out the rabbits and slay them by a blow of the hand on the nape of the neck, back of the ears; and as she killed each rabbit she raised it reverently to her lips, and breathed from its nostrils its expiring breath[4] and, tying its legs together, placed it on the string, which after a while began to grow heavy on her shoulders. Still

she kept on, little heeding the snow which was falling fast; nor did she notice that it was growing darker and darker, so intent was she on the hunt, and so glad was she to capture so many rabbits. Indeed, she followed the trails until they were no longer visible, as the snow fell all around her, thinking all the while, "How happy will be my poor old father and mother that they shall now have flesh to eat! How strong will they grow! And when this meat is gone, that which is dried and preserved of it also, lo! another snowstorm will no doubt come, and I can go out hunting again."

At last the twilight came, and, looking

5

---

4. **expiring** (ik spīr′ ing) **breath:** Air breathed out as the rabbit dies.

*The Girl Who Hunted Rabbits*  637

---

*or, neither . . . nor, not only . . . but also, whether . . . or.*

Subordinating conjunctions connect two ideas by making one idea dependent on the other. Some examples of frequently used subordinating conjunctions are *after, although, as if, because, before, since, though, unless, until, whenever,* and *while.* In the following sentence from "The Girl Who Hunted Rabbits," the subordinating conjunction *although* connects the dependent clause to the main idea: "But their feelings were not friendly, for no one of them would she accept as a husband, although one after another of them had offered himself for marriage."

**Student Activity.** Locate five more examples of conjunctions in the selection and identify each one as either coordinating, correlative, or subordinating.

**Electronic Handbook** You may wish to review the use of conjunctions with students before having them complete the Grammar in Action activities. If students are using the Language Master 6000, have them enter the access word *conjunction* and press the GRAMMAR key to review facts about conjunctions.

**Discussion** Do you think the girl would have been this fortunate in real life, or is her good fortune one of the events that was changed in the retelling of the legend? Support your answer.

**Multicultural Focus** Remind students that Native Americans comprise numerous tribes and nations and that there is no single standard tradition or culture among them. The methods and lore of hunting vary widely, depending on cultural and geographical factors. For example, fishing rituals and legends are central to some peoples living close to water; hunting lore in the Plains area may depend on the seasonal migration of the buffalo.

However diverse, the traditions share the view that hunting is for survival, not recreation. Skilled hunters are greatly honored, and hunting heroes are generally deified in legend. Among the Micmacs of the northeastern United States and Canada, it was the divine being Glooscap who taught humankind the art of hunting. In a Tewa legend, Deer Hunter is borne aloft on a great spirit's arrow, thus creating a new star.

Students may enjoy researching and comparing methods, rituals, and legends of hunting in the various Native American cultures—from the northernmost Eskimo cultures to the southern Maya. Have them focus on the hunter's relationship with the prey, which often is reverent and spiritual, reflecting the Native American respect for nature.

around, she found that the snow had fallen deeply, there was no trail, and that she had lost her way. True, she turned about and started in the direction of her home, as she supposed, walking as fast as she could through the soft, deep snow. Yet she reckoned not rightly, for instead of going eastward along the valley, she went southward across it, and entering the mouth of the Descending Plain of the Pines, she went on and on, thinking she was going homeward, until at last it grew dark and she knew not which way to turn.

"What harm," thought she, "if I find a sheltered place among the rocks? What harm if I remain all night, and go home in the morning when the snow has ceased falling, and by the light I shall know my way?"

So she turned about to some rocks which appeared, black and dim, a short distance away. Fortunately, among these rocks is the cave which is known as Taiuma's[5] Cave. This she came to, and peering into that black hole, she saw in it, back some distance, a little glowing light. "Ha, ha!" thought she, "perhaps some rabbit hunters like myself, belated yesterday, passed the night here and left the fire burning. If so, this is greater good fortune than I could have looked for." So, lowering the string of rabbits which she carried on her shoulder, and throwing off her mantle, she crawled in, peering well into the darkness, for fear of wild beasts; then, returning, she drew in the string of rabbits and the mantle.

Behold! there was a bed of hot coals buried in the ashes in the very middle of the cave, and piled up on one side were fragments of broken wood. The girl, happy in her good fortune, issued forth and gathered more sticks from the cliffside, where dead

5. **Taiuma's** (tī ōō′ məz)

pines are found in great numbers, and bringing them in little armfuls one after another, she finally succeeded in gathering a store sufficient to keep the fire burning brightly all the night through. Then she drew off her snow-covered stockings of deer-skin and the bedraggled mantles, and, building a fire, hung them up to dry and sat down to rest herself. The fire burned up and glowed brightly, so that the whole cave was as light as a room at night when a dance is being celebrated. By and by, after her clothing had dried, she spread a mantle on the floor of the cave by the side of the fire, and, sitting down, dressed one of her rabbits and roasted it, and, untying the string of corn-cakes her mother had made for her, feasted on the roasted meat and cakes.

She had just finished her evening meal, and was about to recline and watch the fire for awhile, when she heard away off in the distance a long, low cry of distress—*"Ho-o-o-o thlaia-a!"*

"Ah!" thought the girl, "someone, more belated than myself, is lost; doubtless one of the rabbit-hunters." She got up, and went nearer to the entrance of the cavern.

*"Ho-o-o-o thlaia-a!"* sounded the cry, nearer this time. She ran out, and, as it was repeated again, she placed her hand to her mouth, and cried, as loudly as possible, *"Li-i thlaia-a!"* ("Here!")

The cry was repeated near at hand, and presently the maiden, listening first, and then shouting, and listening again, heard the clatter of an enormous rattle. In dismay and terror she threw her hands into the air, and, crouching down, rushed into the cave and retreated to its farthest limits, where she sat shuddering with fear, for she knew that one of the Cannibal Demons of those days, perhaps the renowned Atahsaia[6] of

6. **Atahsaia** (ah'tə si′ ə)

## Grammar in Action

**Prepositional phrases** begin with a preposition and end with a noun or pronoun called the object of the preposition. A prepositional phrase can act as an adjective and modify a noun or pronoun. It can also act as an adverb and modify a verb, an adjective, or an adverb. A prepositional phrase that acts as an adjective is called an adjective phrase. It modifies a noun or pronoun by telling what kind or which one. A prepositional phrase that acts as an adverb modifying a verb, an adjective, or an adverb is an adverb phrase. Adverb phrases point out where, when, in what manner, or to what extent.

The following sentence from "The Girl Who Hunted Rabbits" has several prepositional phrases:

Behold! there was a bed *of hot coals* buried *in the ashes in the very middle of the cave,* and piled up *on one side* were fragments *of broken wood.*

*Of hot coals* and *of broken wood* are adjective phrases, modifying bed and fragments respectively, while *in the ashes, in the very middle, of the cave,* and *on one side* are adverb phrases. *In* the east, had seen the light of her fire through the cave entrance, with his terrible staring eyes, and assuming it to be a lost wanderer, had cried out, and so led her to guide him to her place of concealment.

On came the Demon, snapping the twigs under his feet and shouting in a hoarse, loud voice, *"Ho lithlsh tâ ime!"* ("Ho, there! So you are in here, are you?") *Kothl!* clanged his rattle, while, almost fainting with terror, closer to the rock crouched the maiden.

The old Demon came to the entrance of the cave and bawled out, "I am cold, I am hungry! Let me in!" Without further ado, he stooped and tried to get in; but, behold! the entrance was too small for his giant shoulders to pass. Then he pretended to be wonderfully civil, and said, "Come out, and bring me something to eat."

"I have nothing for you," cried the maiden. "I have eaten my food."

"Have you no rabbits?"

"Yes."

"Come out and bring me some of them."

But the maiden was so terrified that she dared not move toward the entrance.

"Throw me a rabbit!" shouted the old Demon.

The maiden threw him one of her precious rabbits at last, when she could rise and go to it. He clutched it with his long, horny hand, gave one gulp and swallowed it. Then he cried out, "Throw me another!" She threw him another, which he also immediately swallowed; and so on until the poor maiden had thrown all the rabbits to the voracious old monster. Every one she threw him he caught in his huge, yellow-tusked mouth, and swallowed, hair and all, at one gulp.

"Throw me another!" cried he, when the last had already been thrown to him.

So the poor maiden was forced to say, "I have no more."

"Throw me your overshoes!" cried he.

She threw the overshoes of deerskin, and these like the rabbits he speedily devoured. Then he called for her moccasins, and she threw them; for her belt, and she threw it; and finally, wonderful to tell, she threw even her mantle, and blanket, and her overdress, until, behold, she had nothing left!

Now, with all he had eaten, the old Demon was swollen hugely at the stomach, and, though he tried and tried to squeeze himself through the mouth of the cave, he could not by any means succeed. Finally, lifting his great flint ax, he began to shatter the rock about the entrance to the cave, and slowly but surely he enlarged the hole and the maiden now knew that as soon as he could get in he would devour her also, and she almost fainted at the sickening thought. Pound, pound, pound, pound, went the great ax of the Demon as he struck the rocks.

In the distance the two war-gods were sitting in their home at the Shrine amid the Bushes beyond Thunder Mountain, and though far off, they heard thus in the middle of the night the pounding of the Demon's hammer ax against the rocks. And of course they knew at once that a poor maiden, for the sake of her father and mother, had been out hunting—that she had lost her way and, finding a cave where there was a little fire, entered it, rebuilt the fire, and rested herself; that, attracted by the light of her fire, the Cannibal Demon had come and besieged her retreat,[7] and only a little time hence would he so enlarge the entrance to the cave that he could squeeze even his great overfilled paunch through it and come at the maiden to destroy her. So, catching up their wonderful weapons, these two

---

7. **besieged** (bi sējd') **her retreat:** Attacked her place of refuge.

*The Girl Who Hunted Rabbits* 639

7 **Literary Focus: Legends** The legend now takes on a fantastic element. This element is made believable by setting the story in the time of the "ancients."

8 **Reading Strategy** You might have students, based on what they know about legends, predict the outcome of this seemingly hopeless situation.

**Electronic Handbook** You may wish to review prepositional phrases with students before having them complete the Grammar in Action activities. If students have access to the Language Master 6000, have them enter the access word *prepositional* and press the GRAMMAR key to review information about prepositional phrases.

*the ashes, in the very middle, of the cave* are all adverb phrases telling where the coal was buried; *on one side* is an adverb phrase modifying *piled*.

**Student Activity.** Determine whether the prepositional phrases in the following sentence are adjective or adverb phrases:

In dismay and terror she threw her hands into the air, and, crouching down, rushed into the cave and retreated to its farthest limits, where she sat shuddering with fear, for she knew that one of the Cannibal Demons of those days, perhaps the renowned Atahsaia of the east, had seen the light of her fire through the cave entrance, with his terrible staring eyes, and assuming it to be a lost wanderer, had cried out, and so led her to guide him to her place of concealment.

Explain what each modifies and what information each gives.

**Discussion** What qualities does the girl display that make her worthy of the war-gods' help?

10 **Critical Thinking and Reading** The war-gods "slay" the rabbits that they had taken from the Cannibal Demon's belly. The girl had hunted and killed these rabbits the day before. What power does this indicate in the war-gods?

11 **Critical Thinking and Reading** Based on the two incidents in the legend, have students make inferences about the cultural meaning of the girl breathing on the hands of the gods.

**Reader's Response** Legends are often changed as they are passed on from generation to generation. If you were to retell this legend, what, if anything, would you change? Why?

**Thematic Response** What fears does the girl face and overcome? How has it changed her? What generalization can you make about overcoming fears and about rites of passage?

## Closure and Extension

### ANSWERS TO RESPONDING TO THE SELECTION
#### Your Response

1. Students might admire the girl's courage and love. Others might disapprove of her carelessness in the storm.
2. You might have students on opposite sides of the question meet in groups to discuss the reasons for their answers.

#### Recalling

3. The reasons the girl goes hunting are that there was no one else to get meat for the family, as her brothers are dead and her father is too old to hunt. Also, the male hunters did not give her any of their rabbits because she has refused to marry them.
4. Her parents resist because they think she will get lost or become too tired to return.

---

war-gods flew away into the darkness and in no time they were approaching the Descending Plain of the Pines.

Just as the Demon was about to enter the cavern, and the maiden had fainted at seeing his huge face and gray shock of hair and staring eyes, his yellow, protruding tusks, and his horny, taloned hand, they came upon the old beast. Each one hitting him a blow with his war club, they "ended his daylight," and then hauled him forth into the open space. They opened his huge paunch and withdrew from it the maiden's garments, and even the rabbits which had been slain. The rabbits they cast away among the soap-weed plants that grew on the slope at the foot of the cliff. The garments they spread out on the snow, and cleansed and made them perfect, even more perfect than they had been before. Then, flinging the huge body of the giant Demon down into the depths of the canyon, they turned them about and, calling out gentle words to the maiden, entered and restored her. She, seeing in them not their usual ugly persons, but handsome youths, was greatly comforted; and bending low, and breathing upon their hands, thanked them over and over for the rescue they had brought her. But she crouched herself low with shame that her garments were but few, when, behold! the youths went out and brought in to her the garments they had cleaned, restoring them to her.

Then, spreading their mantles by the door of the cave, they slept there that night, in order to protect the maiden, and on the morrow wakened her. They told her many things, and showed her many things which she had not known before, and counseled her thus, "It is not fearful that a maiden should marry; therefore, O maiden, return unto thy people in the Village of the Gateway of the River of Zuñi. This morning

we will slay rabbits unnumbered for you, and start you on your way, guarding you down the snow-covered valley. When you are in sight of your home we will leave you, telling you our names."

So, early in the morning the two gods went forth, flinging their sticks among the soap-weed plants. Behold! as though the soap-weed plants were rabbits, so many lay killed on the snow before these mighty hunters. And they gathered together great numbers of these rabbits, a string for each one of the party. When the Sun had risen clearer in the sky, and his light sparkled on the snow around them, they took the rabbits to the maiden and presented them, saying, "We will carry each one of us a string of these rabbits." Then taking her hand, they led her out of the cave and down the valley, until, beyond on the high black mesas[8] at the Gateway of the River of Zuñi, she saw the smoke rise from the houses of her village. Then turned the two war-gods to her, and they told her their names. And again she bent low, and breathed on their hands. Then, dropping the strings of rabbits which they had carried close beside the maiden, they swiftly disappeared.

Thinking much of all she had learned, she continued her way to the home of her father and mother. As she went into the town, staggering under her load of rabbits, the young men and the old men and women and children beheld her with wonder; and no hunter in that town thought of comparing himself with the Maiden Hunter of Zuñi River. The old man and the old woman, who had mourned the night through and sat up anxiously watching, were overcome with happiness when they saw their daughter had returned.

---

**8. mesas** (mā′ səz) *n*.: Small mountains with flat tops and steep sides.

5. The girl is rescued by two war-gods who see her plight, rush to her aid, and kill the Cannibal Demon.
6. The villagers regard her with wonder and think that she is a great hunter. Her parents are overjoyed at her return.

#### Interpreting

7. Her parents help her because they realize that she will go even if they do not want her to. Therefore, they want to help her as best

they can because they care for her.
8. The war-gods help the girl because they know that she is hunting for the sake of her parents and became lost as a result.
9. Answers will differ. Suggested Responses: The war-gods chose to appear before her as handsome youths so that she would not be frightened. Also, they might be ugly only during war, and since they were not at war, they did not appear ugly. They later tell her not

to be afraid to marry, and make themselves handsome so that she will not be afraid to do so. Possibly, the girl's happiness and gratitude over being saved by the war-gods affects her view of them.
10. The maiden learned many things that she had not known before, including the gods' names and the fact that she should marry. A suggested response is that she will be affected by what she has learned because she was "thinking much of all she had learned,"

# RESPONDING TO THE SELECTION

## Your Response

1. Do you admire the actions of the maiden hunter? Why or why not?
2. Would you like to be like the maiden hunter? Explain.

## Recalling

3. For what reasons does the girl go hunting?
4. Why do the girl's parents at first resist her plans?
5. How is the girl rescued?
6. How do the villagers regard the girl when she returns?

## Interpreting

7. Why do the girl's parents help her when they really do not want her to go?
8. Why does the war god help the girl?
9. Why does the girl see the two "usually ugly" war gods as handsome youths?
10. What does the girl learn from the war gods? Do you think what she learns will affect the way she behaves in the future? Explain.

## Applying

11. In this legend the girl demonstrates bravery. Select one other character you have read about who is brave. Compare and contrast the girl and this character.

# ANALYZING LITERATURE

## Understanding a Legend

**Legends** are imaginative stories based on real people or events. As the story is passed down, it often changes. Sometimes the retelling may result in downplaying the factual and highlighting the imaginative. "The Girl Who Hunted Rabbits" is probably based on a real incident.

1. What details of the legend could be based on fact?
2. What parts seem purely imaginative?

# CRITICAL THINKING AND READING

## Making Inferences From a Legend

An **inference** is a reasonable conclusion that can be drawn from evidence. In "The Girl Who Hunted Rabbits," you can infer that Zuñi girls were not expected to hunt based on the girl's statement, "O that I were a man and could go forth, as do these young men, hunting rabbits!"

1. Find evidence in this legend that suggests that young girls were expected to get married.
2. Find evidence that the Zuñi placed high value on children's taking care of their parents.

# THINKING AND WRITING

## Retelling a Legend

Imagine you are the girl in this legend. Think about your feelings when the demon tried to devour you. Retell this episode from the girl's point of view. Use the pronoun *I* to identify yourself as the girl. Revise, making sure you have told events through the girl's eyes. Finally, proofread your story and share it with your classmates.

# LEARNING OPTIONS

1. **Cross-curricular Connection.** Find several pieces of music to accompany "The Girl Who Hunted Rabbits." Choose music that expresses the mood or feeling of the various sections of the story. Arrange for your teacher to play the music you have chosen in class. As the music plays, read aloud parts of the story. Explain the connection between the music and the story.
2. **Art.** Make an illustrated map of the landscape described and places named in "The Girl Who Hunted Rabbits." Indicate the maiden's path, and illustrate scenes along the way.

*The Girl Who Hunted Rabbits* 641

so that her parents would have meat and her unwillingness to marry and leave her parents.

**Challenge** Find evidence in this legend that indicates that women did not normally hunt rabbits.

## THINKING AND WRITING

◆ **Software** If students have access to computers, they can use the *Three Ways of Seeing* activity in **Writer's Helper** to explore alternative points of view.

**Alternative Assessment** *Protocol:* Ask students to assess their own work by responding to the following questions:

What feelings do you express as the girl when you are confronted by the demon?

What details of the story do you retell from the girl's point of view?

What details do you add to show her feelings when faced with the demon?

What insight into the girl's feelings have you gained from retelling the story from her point of view?

Students can use their answers to the protocol to revise their stories.

**Writing Across the Curriculum** You might want to have students research and report on the way of life and the history of the Zuñi Indians. If you assign this, perhaps inform the social studies department. Social studies teachers might provide guidance and assistance for students in conducting their research.

## LEARNING OPTIONS

1. This activity will help auditory and musical learners to internalize the structure of the plot as they choose the fundamental elements they wish to represent through music. Students might also use music to examine the characters. Ask students to identify the essential qualities of each character and choose music that reflects these qualities.
2. Mathematical and visual learners will benefit from organizing the elements of setting and plot in a pictorial presentation.

as she returned to the village and the people looked on her with wonder.

## Applying

11. Answers will differ depending on the character the student chooses. Be sure that students contrast their characters with the maiden, as well as compare them.

## ANSWERS TO ANALYZING LITERATURE

1. The details that were probably based on fact include any of the details concerning the girl, her family, the hunt, and the village.
2. The parts that seem purely imaginative are those about the Cannibal Demon and the two war-gods.

## ANSWERS TO CRITICAL THINKING AND READING

1. The evidence that girls were expected to marry includes the following: The other hunters would not give her rabbits because she had refused to marry them; and the war-gods advise her that "It is not fearful that a maiden should marry."
2. The evidence that suggests that the Zuñi placed high value on children caring for their parents is the maiden's willingness to risk her life

# Preparation

**More About the Legend** This legend may be based on a true incident. The only differences between the legend and the actuality were the length of the contest between John Henry and a steam drill, and the way he died. The contest was arranged to last thirty-five minutes rather than the entire day, and the real John Henry was said to have been killed by a falling rock after he beat the engine. Why do you think these details were changed as the story was told?

**Literary Focus: Folk Hero** You might want to point out to your students that as the frontier of the United States disappeared, the frontier folk hero began to be replaced by another type of folk hero. These heroes retained the extraordinary gifts of the frontiersmen but could now be found working in factories, in mines, and on the railroad. This change reflected the change of the United States into an industrial nation.

**Prereading Focus** Some students might compile a list of technological advances in the classroom. How do these advances make a contemporary classroom different from one of fifty years ago? A hundred years ago? Have students who compiled a classroom list compare their results to the more general lists of their classmates.

**Vocabulary** Students should not have any difficulty understanding and pronouncing these vocabulary words.

### John Henry

called **Hammerman** in folk tales, was a black laborer who in the early 1870's helped to build the Big Bend Tunnel on the Chesapeake & Ohio Railroad. He was a huge man, capable of deeds that ordinary workers could only dream of doing. At the time, railroad workers used long-handled hammers to pound steel drills into rocks. One day a man arrived with a steam-powered drill, claiming it could drill faster than twenty men could using hammers. John Henry successfully raced the steam drill.

The tale "Hammerman" is retold by **Adrien Stoutenburg** (1916– ), a poet, biographer, and writer, who was born in Darfur, Minnesota.

# GUIDE FOR READING

## Hammerman
## John Henry

### The Folk Hero in the Oral Tradition

A **folk hero** is an extraordinary person who appears in folk tales. Folk tales glorify the hero for any of his or her superior qualities, such as strength, bravery, or intelligence. Many folk tales are part of the **oral tradition,** passed down by word of mouth from generation to generation. The stories can be related as yarns, ballads, myths, or legends. Though many of the stories have been written down to be remembered, they are usually shared orally. Here "Hammerman" is written as a story to be read and enjoyed, whereas "John Henry" is presented as a ballad to be sung.

### Focus

This story and song about John Henry center on one man's struggle against a machine. For a variety of reasons, people sometimes resist new technology when it is introduced into society. With a small group of your classmates, think of several reasons people might resist new machines or technologies. Then make a chart like the one that follows. For the technologies given, list the services these technologies perform and the benefits they provide. Then list reasons people might have resisted these technologies when they were first introduced. You add other technologies to your chart.

|  | Services | Benefits | Reasons for Resistance |
|---|---|---|---|
| Computers |  |  |  |
| Fax Machines |  |  |  |

### Vocabulary

Knowing the following words will help you as you read "Hammerman" and "John Henry."

**whirl** (hwurl) v.: To drive with a rotating motion (p. 644)

**hefted** (hef′ tid) v.: Lifted; tested the weight of (p. 645)

**drive** (drīv) v.: To force by hitting (p. 650)

**yonder** (yän′ dər) adj.: In the distance (p. 652)

**flagged** (flagd) v.: Signaled to a train to stop so that a passenger could board (p. 653)

---

## Objectives

1 To understand a folk hero
2 To make inferences about characters
3 To write another adventure of John Henry
4 To understand the oral tradition
5 To express individual interests and abilities through optional activities

## Support Material

**Teaching Portfolio**
Teacher Backup, p. 905
Usage and Mechanics Worksheet, p. 908
Vocabulary Check, p. 909
Analyzing Literature Worksheet, *Understanding the Oral Tradition,* p. 910
Critical Thinking and Reading Worksheet, *Making Inferences About Characters,* p. 911

Language Worksheet, *Choosing Effective Synonyms,* p. 912
Selection Test, p. 913
Art Transparency 19, *John Henry's Hand,* by Fred Becker

**Prentice Hall Literature Writing Studio**

# Hammerman

### Adrien Stoutenburg

People down South still tell stories about John Henry, how strong he was, and how he could whirl a big sledge[1] so lightning-fast you could hear thunder behind it. They even say he was born with a hammer in his hand. John Henry himself said it, but he probably didn't mean it exactly as it sounded.

The story seems to be that when John Henry was a baby, the first thing he reached out for was a hammer, which was hung nearby on the cabin wall.

John Henry's father put his arm around his wife's shoulder. "He's going to grow up to be a steel-driving man. I can see it plain as rows of cotton running uphill."

As John Henry grew a bit older, he practiced swinging the hammer, not hitting at things, but just enjoying the feel of it whooshing against the air. When he was old enough to talk, he told everyone, "I was born with a hammer in my hand."

John Henry was still a boy when the Civil War started, but he was a big, hard-muscled boy, and he could outwork and outplay all the other boys on the plantation.

"You're going to be a mighty man, John Henry," his father told him.

"A man ain't nothing but a man," young John Henry said. "And I'm a natural man, born to swing a hammer in my hand."

At night, lying on a straw bed on the floor, John Henry listened to a far-off train whistling through the darkness. Railroad tracks had been laid to carry trainloads of Southern soldiers to fight against the armies of the North. The trains had a lonesome, longing sound that made John Henry want to go wherever they were going.

When the war ended, a man from the North came to John Henry where he was working in the field. He said, "The slaves are free now. You can pack up and go wherever you want, young fellow."

"I'm craving to go where the trains go," said John Henry.

The man shook his head. "There are too many young fellows trailing the trains around now. You better settle down to doing what you know, like handling a cotton hook or driving a mule team."

John Henry thought to himself, there's a big hammer waiting for me somewhere, because I know I'm a steel-driving man. All I have to do is hunt 'til I find it.

That night, he told his folks about a dream he had had.

"I dreamed I was working on a railroad somewhere," he said, "a big, new railroad called the C. & O., and I had a mighty hammer in my hand. Every time I swung it, it made a whirling flash around my shoulder. And every time my hammer hit a spike,[2] the sky lit up from the sparks."

---

1. **sledge** (slej) *n.*: A heavy hammer, usually held with both hands.

2. **spike** (spīk) *n.*: A long, thick metal nail used for splitting rock.

*Hammerman* 643

**HAMMER IN HIS HAND**
*Palmer C. Hayden*
*Museum of African American Art*

"I believe it," his father said. "You were born to drive steel."

"That ain't all of the dream," John Henry said. "I dreamed that the railroad was going to be the end of me and I'd die with the hammer in my hand."

The next morning, John Henry bundled up some food in a red bandanna handkerchief, told his parents good-by, and set off into the world. He walked until he heard the clang-clang of hammers in the distance. He followed the sound to a place where gangs of men were building a railroad. John Henry watched the men driving steel spikes down into the crossties[3] to hold the rails in place. Three men would stand around a spike, then each, in turn, would swing a long hammer.

John Henry's heart beat in rhythm with the falling hammers. His fingers ached for the feel of a hammer in his own hands. He walked over to the foreman.

"I'm a natural steel-driving man," he said. "And I'm looking for a job."

---

**3. crossties** (krôs′ tīz) *n.:* Beams laid crosswise under railroad tracks to support them.

"How much steel-driving have you done?" the foreman asked.

"I was born knowing how," John Henry said.

The foreman shook his head. "That ain't good enough, boy. I can't take any chances. Steel-driving's dangerous work, and you might hit somebody."

"I wouldn't hit anybody," John Henry said, "because I can drive one of those spikes all by myself."

The foreman said sharply, "The one kind of man I don't need in this outfit is a bragger. Stop wasting my time."

John Henry didn't move. He got a stubborn look around his jaw. "You loan me a hammer, mister, and if somebody will hold the spike for me, I'll prove what I can do."

The three men who had just finished driving in a spike looked toward him and laughed. One of them said, "Anybody who would hold a spike for a greenhorn⁴ don't want to live long."

"I'll hold it," a fourth man said.

John Henry saw that the speaker was a small, dark-skinned fellow about his own age.

The foreman asked the small man, "D'you aim to get yourself killed, Li'l Willie?"

Li'l Willie didn't answer. He knelt and set a spike down through the rail on the crosstie. "Come on, big boy," he said.

John Henry picked up one of the sheepnose hammers lying in the cinders. He hefted it and decided it was too light. He picked up a larger one which weighed twelve pounds. The handle was lean and limber and greased with tallow⁵ to make it smooth.

Everyone was quiet, watching, as he stepped over to the spike.

---
**4. greenhorn** (grēn' hôrn) *n.*: An inexperienced person; a beginner.
**5. tallow** (tal' ō) *n.*: Solid fat obtained from sheep or cattle.

John Henry swung the hammer over his shoulder so far that the hammer head hung down against the back of his knees. He felt a thrill run through his arms and chest.

"Tap it down gentle, first," said Li'l Willie.

But John Henry had already started to swing. He brought the hammer flashing down, banging the spike squarely on the head. Before the other men could draw a breath of surprise, the hammer flashed again, whirring through the air like a giant hummingbird. One more swing, and the spike was down, its steel head smoking from the force of the blow.

The foreman blinked, swallowed, and blinked again. "Man," he told John Henry, "you're hired!"

That's the way John Henry started steel-driving. From then on, Li'l Willie was always with him, setting the spikes, or placing the drills⁶ that John Henry drove with his hammer. There wasn't another steel-driving man in the world who could touch John Henry for speed and power. He could hammer every which way, up or down or sidewise. He could drive for ten hours at a stretch and never miss a stroke.

After he'd been at the work for a few years, he started using a twenty-pound hammer in each hand. It took six men, working fast, to carry fresh drills to him. People would come for miles around to watch John Henry.

Whenever John Henry worked, he sang. Li'l Willie sang with him, chanting the rhythm of the clanging hammer strokes.

Those were happy days for John Henry. One of the happiest days came when he met a black-eyed, curly-haired girl called Polly Ann. And, on the day that Polly Ann said

---
**6. drills** (drilz) *n.*: Pointed tools used for making holes in hard substances.

**5 Literary Focus: Folk Hero** Point out that John Henry knows he has the strength and skill to drive steel even before he tries, despite the danger and difficulty involved. How did Henry's father know this as well? How does this help to glorify his deeds?

**6 Literary Focus: Folk Hero** What qualities does John Henry exhibit by this action?

**ESL Teaching Strategy** Students who are learning English as a second language will encounter several words in this selection that look and sound familiar but are used in this selection in a new context. On this page they will find *driving, sharply, outfit, aim, lean, light,* and *head.* Ask students to use context clues to try to infer an approximate meaning. Then have a student volunteer read aloud the passage in which the word appears to check the suggested meaning. How do these new meanings relate to known definitions? Encourage students to search the tale and the ballad for other examples of words with more than one meaning.

7 **Critical Thinking and Reading**
You might have students make inferences about the character of John Henry based on this event. Are these qualities extraordinary, or do all people possess them? Support your answer.

8 **Reading Strategy** You might have students question why this dream continues to recur in the tale.

9 **Critical Thinking and Reading** What do the statements of both men and the fact that they go together indicate about the characters of John and Willie? What do they indicate about their friendship?

**Multicultural Focus** The building of America's railroads was a multicultural effort. Americans of African, European, Asian, and Hispanic descent, among others, participated in laying the tracks that connected east to west and north to south.

Point out that although many ethnic groups played a significant role in building the railroads, their contribution went largely unrecognized and was poorly rewarded. Workers were forced to endure harsh living and working conditions, received low pay, and were excluded from better-paying jobs in the railroad company hierarchy. Separated from their families, they lived in camps, often segregated.

Discuss how progress for one group is sometimes achieved at the expense of another group. The exploitation of minorities and immigrants in building the railroads is one example. Today, industrial progress must be balanced against the importance of protecting the environment for future generations. Ask students to suggest ways that progress can be made with justice.

7
she would marry him, John Henry almost burst his throat with singing.

8
Every now and then, John Henry would remember the strange dream he had had years before, about the C. & O. Railroad and dying with a hammer in his hand. One night, he had the dream again. The next morning, when he went to work, the steel gang gathered round him, hopping with excitement.

"The Chesapeake and Ohio Railroad wants men to drive a tunnel through a mountain in West Virginia!" they said.

"The C. & O. wants the best hammermen there are!" they said. "And they'll pay twice as much as anybody else."

9
Li'l Willie looked at John Henry. "If they want the best, John Henry, they're goin' to need you."

John Henry looked back at his friend. "They're going to need you, too, Li'l Willie. I ain't going without you." He stood a minute, looking at the sky. There was a black thundercloud way off, with sunlight flashing behind it. John Henry felt a small chill between his shoulder blades. He shook himself, put his hammer on his shoulder, and said, "Let's go, Willie!"

When they reached Summers County where the Big Bend Tunnel was to be built, John Henry sized up the mountain standing in the way. It was almost solid rock.

"Looks soft," said John Henry. "Hold a drill up there, Li'l Willie."

Li'l Willie did. John Henry took a seventy-pound hammer and drove the drill in with one mountain-cracking stroke. Then he settled down to working the regular way, pounding in the drills with four or five strokes of a twenty-pound sledge. He worked so fast that his helpers had to keep buckets of water ready to pour on his hammers so they wouldn't catch fire.

Polly Ann, who had come along to West Virginia, sat and watched and cheered him on. She sang along with him, clapping her hands to the rhythm of his hammer, and the sound echoed around the mountains. The songs blended with the rumble of dynamite where the blasting crews were at work. For every time John Henry drilled a hole in the mountain's face, other men poked dynamite and black powder into the hole and then lighted a fuse to blow the rock apart.

One day the tunnel boss Cap'n Tommy Walters was standing watching John Henry, when a stranger in city clothes walked up to him.

"Howdy, Cap'n Tommy," said the stranger. "I'd like to talk to you about a steam engine[7] I've got for sale. My engine can drive a drill through rock so fast that not even a crew of your best men can keep up with it."

"I don't need any machine," Cap'n Tommy said proudly. "My man John Henry can out-drill any machine ever built."

"I'll place a bet with you, Cap'n," said the salesman. "You race your man against my machine for a full day. If he wins, I'll give you the steam engine free."

Cap'n Tommy thought it over. "That sounds fair enough, but I'll have to talk to John Henry first." He told John Henry what the stranger had said. "Are you willing to race a steam drill?" Cap'n Tommy asked.

John Henry ran his big hands over the handle of his hammer, feeling the strength in the wood and in his own great muscles.

"A man's a man," he said, "but a machine ain't nothing but a machine. I'll beat that steam drill, or I'll die with my hammer in my hand!"

"All right, then," said Cap'n Tommy. "We'll set a day for the contest."

---

**7. steam engine:** Here, a machine that drives a drill by means of steam power.

Polly Ann looked worried when John Henry told her what he had promised to do.

"Don't you worry, honey," John Henry said. It was the end of the workday, with the sunset burning across the mountain, and the sky shining like copper. He tapped his chest. "I've got a man's heart in here. All a machine has is a metal engine." He smiled and picked Polly Ann up in his arms, as if she were no heavier than a blade of grass.

On the morning of the contest, the slopes around the tunnel were crowded with people. At one side stood the steam engine, its gears and valves and mechanical drill gleaming. Its operators rushed around, giving it final spurts of grease and oil and shoving fresh pine knots into the fire that fed the steam boiler.

John Henry stood leaning on his hammer, as still as the mountain rock, his shoulders shining like hard coal in the rising sun.

"How do you feel, John Henry?" asked Li'l Willie. Li'l Willie's hands trembled a bit as he held the drill ready.

"I feel like a bird ready to bust out of a nest egg," John Henry said. "I feel like a rooster ready to crow. I feel pride hammering at my heart, and I can hardly wait to get started against that machine." He sucked in the mountain air. "I feel powerful free, Li'l Willie."

Cap'n Tommy held up the starting gun. For a second everything was as silent as the dust in a drill hole. Then the gun barked, making a yelp that bounced against mountain and sky.

John Henry swung his hammer, and it rang against the drill.

At the same time, the steam engine gave a roar and a hiss. Steam whistled through its escape valve. Its drill crashed down, gnawing into the granite.

John Henry paid no attention to any-thing except his hammer, nor to any sound except the steady pumping of his heart. At the end of an hour, he paused long enough to ask, "How are we doing, Li'l Willie?"

Willie licked his lips. His face was pale with rock dust and with fear. "The machine's ahead, John Henry."

John Henry tossed his smoking hammer aside and called to another helper, "Bring me two hammers! I'm only getting warmed up."

He began swinging a hammer in each hand. Sparks flew so fast and hot they singed his face. The hammers heated up until they glowed like torches.

"How're we doing now, Li'l Willie?" John Henry asked at the end of another hour.

Li'l Willie grinned. "The machine's drill busted. They have to take time to fix up a new one. You're almost even now, John Henry! How're you feeling?"

"I'm feeling like sunrise," John Henry took time to say before he flashed one of his hammers down against the drill. "Clean out the hole, Willie, and we'll drive right down to China."

Above the clash of his hammers, he heard the chug and hiss of the steam engine starting up again and the whine of its rotary drill biting into rock. The sound hurt John Henry's ears.

"Sing me a song, Li'l Willie!" he gasped. "Sing me a natural song for my hammers to sing along with."

Li'l Willie sang, and John Henry kept his hammers going in time. Hour after hour, he kept driving, sweat sliding from his forehead and chest.

The sun rolled past noon and toward the west.

"How're you feeling, John Henry?" Li'l Willie asked.

"I ain't tired yet," said John Henry and

10 **Discussion** Whom do you think the people are going to root for, John Henry or the machine? Support your answer.

11 **Literary Focus: Folk Hero** The image of John Henry standing "as still as a mountain rock" heightens the impression of his being extraordinary or larger than life. What image do students have of his physical appearance—his height, weight, and frame?

12 **Discussion** What image is created by this description and the one several paragraphs earlier of the steam drill? How does it contrast with descriptions of John Henry?

13 **Discussion** Why does the sound of the drill hurt John Henry's ears?

stood back, gasping, while Willie put a freshly sharpened drill into the rock wall. ''Only, I have a kind of roaring in my ears.''

''That's only the steam engine,'' Li'l Willie said, but he wet his lips again. ''You're gaining on it, John Henry. I reckon you're at least two inches ahead.''

John Henry coughed and slung his hammer back. ''I'll beat it by a mile, before the sun sets.''

At the end of another hour, Li'l Willie called out, his eyes sparkling, ''You're going to win, John Henry, if you can keep on drivin'!''

John Henry ground his teeth together and tried not to hear the roar in his ears or the racing thunder of his heart. ''I'll go until I drop,'' he gasped. ''I'm a steel-driving man and I'm bound to win, because a machine ain't nothing but a machine.''

The sun slid lower. The shadows of the crowd grew long and purple.

''John Henry can't keep it up,'' someone said.

''The machine can't keep it up,'' another said.

Polly Ann twisted her hands together and waited for Cap'n Tommy to fire the gun to mark the end of the contest.

''Who's winning?'' a voice cried.

''Wait and see,'' another voice answered.

There were only ten minutes left.

''How're you feeling, John Henry?'' Li'l Willie whispered, sweat dripping down his own face.

John Henry didn't answer. He just kept slamming his hammers against the drill, his mouth open.

Li'l Willie tried to go on singing. ''Flash that hammer—uh! Wham that drill—uh!'' he croaked.

Out beside the railroad tracks, Polly beat her hands together in time, until they were numb.

The sun flared an instant, then died behind the mountain. Cap'n Tommy's gun cracked. The judges ran forward to measure the depth of the holes drilled by the steam engine and by John Henry. At last, the judges came walking back and said something to Cap'n Tommy before they turned to announce their findings to the crowd.

Cap'n Tommy walked over to John Henry, who stood leaning against the face of the mountain.

''John Henry,'' he said, ''you beat that steam engine by four feet!'' He held out his hand and smiled.

John Henry heard a distant cheering. He held his own hand out, and then he staggered. He fell and lay on his back, staring up at the mountain and the sky, and then he saw Polly Ann and Li'l Willie leaning over him.

''Oh, how do you feel, John Henry?'' Polly Ann asked.

''I feel a bit tuckered out,'' said John Henry.

''Do you want me to sing to you?'' Li'l Willie asked.

''I got a song in my own heart, thank you, Li'l Willie,'' John Henry said. He raised up on his elbow and looked at all the people and the last sunset light gleaming like the edge of a golden trumpet. ''I was a steel-driving man,'' he said, and lay back and closed his eyes forever.

Down South, and in the North, too, people still talk about John Henry and how he beat the steam engine at the Big Bend Tunnel. They say, if John Henry were alive today, he could beat almost every other kind of machine, too.

Maybe so. At least, John Henry would die trying.

# RESPONDING TO THE SELECTION

## Your Response

1. If you had known John Henry, would you have encouraged him to compete against the steam engine? Explain.
2. Describe your feelings as you read the part of the story that told of the competition between John Henry and the steam engine.

## Recalling

3. Describe John Henry's dream.
4. Explain how John Henry wins his first job hammering steel.
5. What events bring about John Henry's death?

## Interpreting

6. Why is Li'l Willie willing to hold the spike for John Henry—a dangerous task—when no one else will?
7. What are the goal and the purpose of the quest?
8. What clues in the tale hint at the outcome?

## Applying

9. Ever since the invention of machines, some people have felt threatened by them. Why? What machines today cause this reaction?

# ANALYZING LITERATURE

## Understanding the Folk Hero

A **folk hero** is an extraordinary person whose qualities are glorified in folk tales.

1. What qualities of John Henry are glorified in the following sentences from "Hammerman"?
   a. "He brought the hammer flashing down, banging the spike squarely on the head . . . One more swing, and the spike was down, its steel head smoking from the force of the blow."
   b. "It took six men, working fast, to carry fresh drills to him."
2. What do these qualities say about the type of person who was admired on the frontier?

# CRITICAL THINKING AND READING

## Making Inferences About Characters

**Inferences** are conclusions drawn from evidence in a story. You make inferences about a character's traits and personality from clues given in the character's words and actions.

For example, L'il Willie goes with John Henry to work on the railroad, joins him in his competition against the machine, and sings to John Henry to urge him along. From these actions you can conclude that L'il Willie is a loyal friend.

What inferences about John Henry's character can you draw from the following?

1. "I feel like a rooster ready to crow. I feel pride hammering at my heart, and I can hardly wait to get started against that machine."
2. "I'll go until I drop."

# THINKING AND WRITING

## Writing Another Adventure

Brainstorm and write down your ideas for other adventures that John Henry could have had. Select one to write about for your class. First, freewrite about the adventure, including descriptions of John Henry, the challenge that confronts him, and what happens. Use this information to write about the adventure, including dialogue when necessary. Revise your story, making sure you have used the qualities that John Henry exhibits in "Hammerman." Read the adventure aloud to your class.

# LEARNING OPTION

**Performance.** Prepare and dramatize a skit based on "Hammerman" for your class. List the cast of characters, and devise simple dialogue and stage directions. Choose the cast and director from your classmates. After you rehearse, perform the skit for your class.

---

## Applying

9. People have always felt threatened by machines because they perceive them as a threat to their jobs, and therefore a threat to their income and to their sense of worth. It is difficult for people to accept the idea that a mindless, heartless machine might be superior to humans. New machines today that cause this reaction could be computers or robots on assembly lines.

## ANSWERS TO ANALYZING LITERATURE

1. a. Qualities that are glorified are strength, speed, and accuracy.
   b. Glorified qualities include power, speed, tirelessness, and hard work.
2. These qualities indicate that the type of person admired on the frontier worked hard, had strength and endurance, and took great pride in doing a job well.

**Challenge** How do the qualities of John Henry compare and contrast with those of Pecos Bill?

## ANSWERS TO CRITICAL THINKING AND READING

1. Inferences about John Henry's character include a great pride in and enthusiasm for his work, as well as determination.

2. Inferences about John Henry's character include a strong will, a willingness to sacrifice, and a tremendous pride.

## THINKING AND WRITING

**Alternative Assessment** *Peer Review:* In pairs or groups of four, have students assess one another's work by responding to the following questions:

What challenge confronts John Henry in the writer's adventure?

How does the writer have John Henry meet the challenge?

What qualities does John Henry exhibit in the new adventure that he also exhibited in "Hammerman"?

How effectively does the writer incorporate dialogue in the new adventure?

What suggestions can you offer the writer to improve his or her story?

What corrections do you suggest the writer make to improve the language mechanics, especially paragraphing and punctuating the dialogue?

Students can incorporate their peers' suggestions as they revise their work.

**Publishing Student Writing** You might display the additional adventures of John Henry on a bulletin board so that all class members can read them.

## LEARNING OPTION

You might want to arrange to have your class perform their skit in front of the entire school. Additional skits dramatizing some of the other folk tales, myths, and legends from this unit could be added to include the entire class.

You might have students make their own costumes and design their own scenery for their dramatic presentations of the folk tale. If you choose to do this, you might inform the art department. Art teachers might provide guidance and materials for the completion of this assignment.

**Motivation/Prior Knowledge**
Have students imagine that they were witnesses to the contest between John Henry and the steam drill recounted in "Hammerman." What would they tell others about John Henry? What would they say about the contest? How would they portray the struggle?

**Master Teacher Note** Check your local library's collection of American folk music for an audio recording of "John Henry." What other folk songs in the collection are familiar to the students? What are the subjects of the other songs in the collection?

**Making Connections** To compare and contrast selections from the American folk music heritage, you may want to use the Tewa Indian prayer "Song of the Sky Loom" on page 579.

**Purpose-Setting Question** What kind of people might have been responsible for the creation of this song?

1 **Discussion** How is this action inconsistent with the other qualities John Henry demonstrates?

2 **Critical Thinking and Reading** You might want to point out that this is the third stanza that foreshadows the death of John Henry. How do these repeated references to his death affect the mood of the song?

3 **Literary Focus: Folk Hero** The folk ballad, like other forms of folk stories, exaggerates the qualities of its characters. You might want to point out that John Henry's wife is also portrayed as a larger-than-life character because women did not drive steel in the 1800's.

# John Henry

## Traditional

John Henry was a lil baby,
Sittin' on his mama's knee,
Said: 'The Big Bend Tunnel on the C. & O. road
Gonna cause the death of me,
5　Lawd, Lawd, gonna cause the death of me.'

Cap'n says to John Henry,
'Gonna bring me a steam drill 'round,
Gonna take that steam drill out on the job,
Gonna whop that steel on down,
10　Lawd, Lawd, gonna whop that steel on down.

John Henry tol' his cap'n,
Lightnin' was in his eye:
'Cap'n, bet yo' las' red cent on me,
Fo' I'll beat it to the bottom or I'll die,
15　Lawd, Lawd, I'll beat it to the bottom or I'll die.'

Sun shine hot an' burnin',
Wer'n't no breeze a-tall,
Sweat ran down like water down a hill,
That day John Henry let his hammer fall,
20　Lawd, Lawd, that day John Henry let his hammer fall.

John Henry went to the tunnel,
An' they put him in the lead to drive,
The rock so tall an' John Henry so small,
That he lied down his hammer an' he cried,
25　Lawd, Lawd, that he lied down his hammer an' he cried.

John Henry started on the right hand,
The steam drill started on the lef'—
'Before I'd let this steam drill beat me down,
I'd hammer my fool self to death,
30　Lawd, Lawd, I'd hammer my fool self to death.'

John Henry had a lil woman,
Her name were Polly Ann,
John Henry took sick an' had to go to bed,
Polly Ann drove steel like a man,
35　Lawd, Lawd, Polly Ann drove steel like a man.

**A MAN AIN'T NOTHIN' BUT A MAN**
*Palmer C. Hayden*
*Museum of African American Art*

## Humanities Note

Fine art, *A Man Ain't Nothin' but a Man,* by Palmer C. Hayden. For information about the artist, refer to the Humanities Note on page 644.

This painting, *A Man Ain't Nothin' but a Man,* is one of a group done about John Henry. The style is the same as that of *Hammer in His Hand* on page 644. This group is considered to be Hayden's finest work. Each work in the group depicts a scene from the legend of John Henry. Here John Henry is shown holding a hammer and smiling at his boss, having just accepted the bet pitting himself against a machine.

You may want to use the following questions to generate discussion:

1. What are the similarities and differences between this painting and the one of John Henry on page 644?
2. Do you think that John Henry was driven by fate to accept the bet, or was he acting foolishly or with too much pride?

John Henry said to his shaker,[1]
'Shaker, why don' you sing?
I'm throwin' twelve poun's from my hips on down,
Jes' listen to the col' steel ring,
40  Lawd, Lawd, jes' listen to the col' steel ring.'

Oh, the captain said to John Henry,
'I b'lieve this mountain's sinkin' in.'
John Henry said to his captain, oh my!
'Ain' nothin' but my hammer suckin' win',
45  Lawd, Lawd, ain' nothin' but my hammer suckin' win'.'

John Henry tol' his shaker,
'Shaker, you better pray,
For, if I miss this six-foot steel,
Tomorrow'll be yo' buryin' day,
50  Lawd, Lawd, tomorrow'll be yo' buryin' day.'

John Henry tol' his captain,
'Look yonder what I see—
Yo' drill's done broke an' yo' hole's done choke,
An' you cain' drive steel like me,
55  Lawd, Lawd, an' you cain' drive steel like me.'

The man that invented the steam drill,
Thought he was mighty fine.
John Henry drove his fifteen feet,
An' the steam drill only made nine,
60  Lawd, Lawd, an' the steam drill only made nine.

The hammer that John Henry swung,
It weighed over nine pound;
He broke a rib in his lef'-han' side,
An' his intrels[2] fell on the groun',
65  Lawd, Lawd, an' his intrels fell on the groun'.

All the womens in the Wes',
When they heared of John Henry's death,
Stood in the rain, flagged the eas'-boun' train,
Goin' where John Henry fell dead,
70  Lawd, Lawd, goin' where John Henry fell dead.

4

---

**1. shaker** (shā′ kər) *n.*: Person who sets the spikes and places the drills for a steel-driver to hammer.
**2. intrels: entrails** (en′ trālz) *n.*: Inner organs.

John Henry's lil mother,
She was all dressed in red,
She jumped in bed, covered up her head,
Said she didn' know her son was dead,
75 Lawd, Lawd, didn' know her son was dead.

Dey took John Henry to the graveyard,
An' they buried him in the san',
An' every locomotive come roarin' by,
Says, 'There lays a steel-drivin' man,
80 Lawd, Lawd, there lays a steel-drivin' man.'

## RESPONDING TO THE SELECTION

### Your Response

1. What title would you give to the ballad of John Henry?

### Recalling

2. At what point in his life does John Henry make his prediction about his own death?
3. What tribute do trains give John Henry when they roll by his grave?

### Interpreting

4. State what we learn from this tale about John Henry that explains why he is a folk hero.

### Applying

5. What jobs today are as dangerous as driving steel was in John Henry's day? Give two examples. Explain why they are dangerous.

## ANALYZING LITERATURE

### Understanding the Oral Tradition

**Oral tradition** is the passing down by word of mouth stories, beliefs, and customs from generation to generation. Ballads, for example, are usually sung long before they are ever written down. A ballad's refrain—phrase or verse re-peated at intervals—emphasizes a point and sounds like a chorus.

A ballad passed down in the oral tradition may have several different versions. It may often include the dialect, or particular manner of speaking, of its creators. For example, "Gonna whop that steel on down" is the way black laborers in the South in the late 1800's might have said, "I will hammer that spike into the ground." To get the full flavor of the dialect, you should read the ballad aloud.

Read "John Henry" aloud. Then answer the following questions.

1. What lines contain a refrain?
2. What are two other examples of dialect from "John Henry"?
3. What feelings for John Henry does this ballad arouse?

## LEARNING OPTION

**Cross-curricular Connection.** John Henry is not the only folk hero about whom ballads have been written. Working with a group of students, think of a ballad you know about another American folk hero, or find one in your library. Read it aloud to the class.

*John Henry* 653

**More About the Legend** The tales of Johnny Appleseed became widely known following the publication of an article by W. D. Haley, called "Johnny Appleseed, a Pioneer Hero," in *Harper's New Monthly Magazine* in 1871. Although many stories, novels, and poems were written about John Chapman's deeds, none has ever been proven true.

**Literary Focus** You might point out to students that characterization is important in literature because all readers are interested in what other people are like. Readers usually identify as hero the character who possesses the character traits they admire most.

**Prereading Focus** After students have completed their individual webs, you might have them compare the qualities they included and try to make generalizations about the qualities of legendary characters.

**Vocabulary** Have your **more advanced** students use each vocabulary word in an original sentence.

**Spelling Tip** The silent *g* in *gnarled* is also found in words like *gnaw*. Other silent initial consonants include *k (knife, knave), p (psalm, psaltery),* and *w (wring, wretch)*.

## Johnny Appleseed

(1774–1845) was a frontiersman whose real name was John Chapman. Chapman was born in Leominster, Massachusetts. His life was so extraordinary that he became a folklore hero. In stories about him that blend truth and fantasy, he scattered apple seeds throughout Pennsylvania along the Allegheny River. His apple orchards actually spread through Ohio to northern Indiana.

This poem about him was written by the poet and editor **Rosemary Carr Benét** (1898–1962).

## Johnny Appleseed

### Characterization

**Characterization** is the way a writer shows you what a character is like. A writer can give you an idea of a character's personality through a description of his or her appearance and actions, through dialogue, or through direct statements. In "Johnny Appleseed," the writer portrays the character through his appearance and actions.

### Focus

The legend of Johnny Appleseed describes a character who planted apple trees for the public good. Look in your local newspaper and find a public figure who could become a legendary character. Make a web diagram in which you present the characteristics of the local figure you have chosen.

As you read "Johnny Appleseed," notice the characteristics that made him a legend.

### Vocabulary

Knowing the following words will help you as you read "Johnny Appleseed."

**gnarled** (närld) *adj.:* Knotty and twisted, as the trunk of an old tree (p. 655)

**ruddy** (rud′ ē) *adj.:* Healthy color (p. 655)

**encumber** (in kum′ bər) *v.:* Weigh down (p. 655)

**stalking** (stôk′ iŋ) *v.:* Secretly approaching (p. 656)

**tendril** (ten′ drəl) *n.:* Thin shoot from a plant (p. 656)

**lair** (ler) *n.:* Den of a wild animal (p. 656)

### Objectives

1 To understand characterization
2 To make inferences about characters
3 To compare and contrast the character
4 To express individual interests and abilities through optional activities

### Support Material

**Teaching Portfolio**
Teacher Backup, p. 915
Usage and Mechanics Worksheet, p. 918
Vocabulary Check, p. 919
Analyzing Literature Worksheet, *Understanding Characterization,* p. 920
Critical Thinking and Reading Worksheet, *Making Inferences About Characters,* p. 921

Selection Test, p. 922

**Prentice Hall Literature Writing Studio**

# Johnny Appleseed

### Rosemary Carr Benét

JOHN CHAPMAN, 1871

1
Of Jonathan Chapman
Two things are known,
That he loved apples,
That he walked alone.

At seventy-odd
He was gnarled as could be,
But ruddy and sound
As a good apple tree.

2
For fifty years over
Of harvest and dew,
He planted his apples
Where no apples grew.

The winds of the prairie
Might blow through his rags,
But he carried his seeds
In the best deerskin bags.

From old Ashtabula
To frontier Fort Wayne,
He planted and pruned
And he planted again.

3
He had not a hat
To encumber his head.
He wore a tin pan
On his white hair instead.

He nested with owl,
And with bear-cub and possum,

*Johnny Appleseed* 655

**Thematic Focus** Ask students to explain the expression "as American as apple pie." As students read the selection, have them identify the qualities Johnny exemplifies that make him as much a part of our American heritage as the apple trees he planted.

**Enrichment** The apple is one of the most important and popular fruits that grow on trees. There are thousands of varieties of apples that have been eaten by humans since prehistoric times. Apple trees are part of the rose family and can be grown anywhere but the hottest and coldest regions on earth.

## Presentation

### Humanities Note

Colored engraving, *John Chapman,* 1871. This engraving of John Chapman, known as Johnny Appleseed, was done a quarter century after Chapman's death. As students read the poem and look at the engraving, you might discuss how legends grow.

You might use the following questions to generate discussion:
1. What details of this illustration reflect details of the poem?
2. Why might an illustration like this show a man with characteristics different from those described in the poem?

**Motivation/Prior Knowledge**
Have students imagine what it might be like to meet Johnny Appleseed in person. How would he appear? What would his personality be like?

**Master Teacher Note** You might ask students how easy it is today for one person to make "a difference."

**Purpose-Setting Question** What actions or qualities of Johnny Appleseed have made him into a folk hero?

1 **Literary Focus** What do the first two stanzas reveal about Johnny Appleseed's character?

2 **Discussion** Why do you think he did this? What characteristics does a person need to accomplish such a task?

3 **Critical Thinking and Reading** You might have students make inferences about Johnny's character based on this stanza.

## Left margin (teacher notes)

**Challenge** How do you think society would view a person like Johnny Appleseed today?

**4 Discussion** Why does the author compare Johnny to an apple?

**5 Discussion** Do you think that this is a "marvelous story"? Do you think that Johnny Appleseed is or is not a folk hero? Support your answers.

**Reader's Response** If there were a modern John Chapman, what might he plant, where, and why?

**Thematic Response** What do you think are the advantages of living a life like Johnny Appleseed's? What are the disadvantages?

## Poem

And knew all his orchards
Root, tendril and blossom.

4
A fine old man,
As ripe as a pippin,[1]
His heart still light,
And his step still skipping.

The stalking Indian,
The beast in its lair
Did no hurt
While he was there.

For they could tell,
As wild things can,
That Jonathan Chapman
Was God's own man.

Why did he do it?
We do not know.
He wished that apples
Might root and grow.

He has no statue.
He has no tomb.
He has his apple trees
Still in bloom.

5
Consider, consider,
Think well upon
The marvelous story
Of Appleseed John.

---

1. **pippin** (pip' in) *n.*: An apple.

## Closure and Extension

### ANSWERS TO RESPONDING TO THE SELECTION
*Your Response*

1. You might list students' questions on a chart for independent research.
2. Ask students to support their opinions with specific examples from current events.

*Recalling*

3. His life is a simple one. He dresses in rags, carries seeds with him, and plants wherever he goes. He sleeps out-of-doors and only knows and cares for his apple orchards. He lived this way for about fifty years.
4. Chapman's monuments are the apple orchards that he planted and that remain today.

# RESPONDING TO THE SELECTION

## Your Response

1. After reading this poem, what else would you like to know about Johnny Appleseed?
2. Would the work of Johnny Appleseed be appreciated today? Why or why not?

## Recalling

3. Describe Chapman's life on the frontier.
4. What monument to Chapman stands today?

## Interpreting

5. What is Chapman's most important possession?
6. How does Chapman feel about nature?

## Applying

7. What areas in today's world would benefit from having someone provide help in growing food? Explain what those areas most need.

# ANALYZING LITERATURE

## Understanding Characterization

**Characterization** is the way a writer presents a character. A character's personality can be shown through his or her appearance, actions, and thoughts; through dialogue; or through the writer's direct statements about him or her.

1. Find a detail that shows that Chapman did not care about his appearance.
2. Find a detail that shows that Chapman did not care to live in town.
3. Find details that indicate Chapman's health.

# CRITICAL THINKING AND READING

## Making Inferences About Characters

An **inference** is a reasonable conclusion you draw from given evidence. You can make inferences about a character from his or her appear-

ance and actions. For example, from "He nested with owl, and with bear-cub and possum," you can infer that Johnny Appleseed liked animals.

What can you infer from the following?

1. Although he wore rags, he carried his apple seeds in the best deerskin bags.
2. He has no tombstone or memorial, but the apple trees he planted still thrive.

# THINKING AND WRITING

## Comparing and Contrasting

Write what you know about John Chapman. Also write what you know about Johnny Appleseed. Then list the similarities and differences between the actual man and the legend he became. Use these lists to write an essay comparing and contrasting the two for your school literary magazine. Revise your essay, making sure you state your points clearly and support them with examples. Proofread your work and share it with your classmates.

# LEARNING OPTIONS

1. **Community Connections.** Johnny Appleseed performed a great service for his country. With your classmates, design a monument for your town or city that will honor the legacy of Johnny Appleseed. Sketch the monument and suggest a location for it. Write a paragraph about Johnny's achievements to be engraved on a plaque. Finally, prepare speeches for a ceremony to unveil the monument in your community.
2. **Art.** Design a poster advertising all the uses and benefits of apples. You may need to do a little research to explore the variety of possible uses. Then go beyond your research and present creative uses, such as dried-apple dolls.

*Johnny Appleseed* 657

**More About the Authors. José Griego y Maestas** received a master's degree from the University of New Mexico. He lives in New Mexico where he is director of the Guadalupe Historic Foundation in Santa Fe. How does this tale reflect his interest in history?

**Rudolfo Anaya** was born in Pastura, New Mexico, where he attended public schools in Santa Rosa and graduated from the University of New Mexico. "Chicoria" is from *Cuentos, Tales From the Hispanic Southwest.* Ask students to discuss the responsibilities of a translator.

🎧 **Audiocassette** Give students the opportunity to listen to the **Audio Prose Library** interview with Rudolfo Anaya, in which he talks about his place in the Chicano tradition.

**Literary Focus** A clever character charms readers. You may wish to have students volunteer characteristics that a clever person might have. Encourage students to draw from their own experience.

**Prereading Focus** After students have had their discussion and before they read, ask them to watch for clues about how the New Mexicans were usually treated by the rich rancher. Have them predict the role of the clever character.

**Vocabulary** Using the adjective form *cordial* instead of *cordially*, ask students to list a series of behaviors that are cordial or haughty.

**Spelling Tip** You may want to point out to your students that the *gh* sound is silent in *haughty* even though it can sound like *f* in other words like *laugh*.

**José Griego y Maestas**

directed and administered the bilingual education program for New Mexico. Griego adapted the folk tale "Chicoria" in Spanish from literal transcriptions of oral tellings.

**Rudolfo A. Anaya**

grew up hearing *cuentos* (kwän′ tôs), stories passed down orally for generations. His translations of *cuentos,* such as "Chicoria," are testaments to his interest in preserving and celebrating the Hispanic oral tradition.

# GUIDE FOR READING

## Chicoria

### The Clever Character in Folk Tales

One of the most popular protagonists in folk tales is the **clever character,** who becomes a hero by outsmarting the selfish, cruel, and powerful characters. Sometimes this character is an animal, such as the trickster coyote in Native American tales. In "Chicoria," it is a person who must use his wits to prove his point and get what he wants. Whether animal or human in form, the clever character uses ingenuity and wisdom to achieve his goals, rather than relying on physical strength or material wealth.

### Focus

In this tale, a character who is clever but is in a position of weakness outwits a powerful character. This theme occurs again and again in literature, as it does in life. In small groups, discuss stories you have read or experiences you have had in which intelligence triumphs over might. How was the victory achieved? What ingenious thing did the person do or say in order to achieve it? Then read "Chicoria" to find out how one clever character outwits the person in power.

### Vocabulary

Knowing the following words will help you as you read the folk tale "Chicoria."

**cordially** (kôr′ jə lē) *adv.*: Warmly, sincerely, and graciously (p. 659)

**haughty** (hôt′ ē) *adj.*: Scornfully proud; arrogant (p. 659)

### Objectives

1 To appreciate the clever character
2 To make inferences about culture
3 To write a folk tale
4 To express individual interests and abilities through an optional activity

## Support Material

**Teaching Portfolio**
Teacher Backup, p. 925
Usage and Mechanics Worksheet, p. 928
Vocabulary Check, p. 929
Analyzing Literature Worksheet, *Appreciating the Clever Character in Folklore,* p. 930
Critical Thinking and Reading Worksheet, *Making Inferences about Culture,* p. 931

Selection Test, p. 932

**Audio Prose Library**
An Interview with Rudolfo Anaya

**Prentice Hall Literature Writing Studio**

# Chicoria[1]

### Adapted in Spanish by José Griego y Maestas
### Retold in English by Rudolfo A. Anaya

There were once many big ranches in California, and many New Mexicans went to work there. One day one of the big ranch owners asked his workers if there were any poets in New Mexico.

"Of course, we have many fine poets," they replied. "We have old Vilmas,[2] Chicoria, Cinfuegos,[3] to say nothing of the poets of Cebolleta[4] and the Black Poet."

"Well, when you return next season, why don't you bring one of your poets to compete with Gracia[5]—here none can compare with him!"

When the harvest was done the New Mexicans returned home. The following season when they returned to California they took with them the poet Chicoria, knowing well that in spinning a rhyme or in weaving wit there was no *Californio*[6] who could beat him.

As soon as the rancher found out that the workers had brought Chicoria with them, he sent his servant to invite his good neighbor and friend to come and hear the new poet. Meanwhile, the cooks set about

---

1. **Chicoria** (chē cō̆ rē′ ä)
2. **Vilmas** (vēl′ mäs)
3. **Cinfuegos** (sin fwä′ gōs)
4. **Cebolleta** (sā bō yä′ tä)
5. **Gracia** (grä′ syä)
6. *Californio* (kä lē fōr′ nyō) *n.*: Spanish for "person from California."

preparing a big meal. When the maids began to dish up the plates of food, Chicoria turned to one of the servers and said, "Ah, my friends, it looks like they are going to feed us well tonight!"

The servant was surprised. "No, my friend," he explained, "the food is for *them*. We don't eat at the master's table. It is not permitted. We eat in the kitchen."

"Well, I'll bet I can sit down and eat with them," Chicoria boasted.

"If you beg or if you ask, perhaps, but if you don't ask they won't invite you," replied the servant.

"I never beg," the New Mexican answered. "The master will invite me of his own accord, and I'll bet you twenty dollars he will!"

So they made a twenty-dollar bet and they instructed the serving maid to watch if this self-confident New Mexican had to ask the master for a place at the table. Then the maid took Chicoria into the dining room. Chicoria greeted the rancher cordially, but the rancher appeared haughty and did not invite Chicoria to sit with him and his guest at the table. Instead, he asked that a chair be brought and placed by the wall where Chicoria was to sit. The rich ranchers began to eat without inviting Chicoria.

So it is just as the servant predicted, Chicoria thought. The poor are not invited to share the rich man's food!

*Chicoria* 659

---

## Primary Source

As a widely respected Chicano author, Anaya speaks from the heart and mind of a native New Mexican. He writes, "If we as Chicanos do have a distinctive perspective on life, I believe that perspective will be defined when we challenge the very basic questions which mankind has always asked itself: What is my relationship to the universe, the cosmos? Who am I and why am I here?"

---

## Presentation

**Motivation/Prior Knowledge** Have students give their definitions of the word *poet*. Because Chicoria is called a poet, have them consider their definition as they read the selection.

**Master Teacher Note** If students are unfamiliar with the early ranches, explain that because they covered thousands of acres, each rancher needed dozens of hired hands, most of whom were only statistics in the ranchers' financial books.

**Purpose-Setting Question** Although Chicoria is invited to participate in a poetry contest, what is the real contest in the folk tale?

**Thematic Focus** The selection focuses on a person's meeting a challenge with a clever solution. It has been said that wit is a weapon. How does Chicoria use his wit?

**Making Connections** You might want to compare Chicoria's battle of wit with Davy Crockett's battle of brawn in "Tussle with a Bear," p. 683.

**1 Critical Thinking and Reading** What inference can you make about the workers?

**2 Critical Thinking and Reading** What inference can you make about the rancher?

**3 Reading Strategy** What do you think will happen to this self-confident poet?

**4 Visualization** You may want to have students visualize the setting and describe the dining room. Where is Chicoria sitting?

**5 Discussion** How does Chicoria feel now?

**ESL Teaching Strategy** To help students with their understanding of a clever character, you might ask them to reread carefully the dialogue between Chicoria and the master. Have students paraphrase the examples of the spoon and the goats. Then have students tell in their own words why they think Chicoria is clever by using these stories.

Fine art, *Fiesta Near Santa Barbara,* unknown artist. This painting depicts one of the vast ranches that operated near Santa Barbara, in southwestern California, in the eighteenth and nineteenth centuries. The owner of the ranch, on horseback, doffs his sombrero in greeting to his guests. Fiestas often lasted a week, and rodeos were one of the many types of entertainment provided to guests. The Santa Ynez Mountains are in the background.

You might use the following questions for discussion:
1. How many activities can you name at the fiesta?
2. How does the ranchero's attitude toward his guests in this painting compare with the master's attitude toward Chicoria?

**6 Literary Focus: Clever Character** What does Chicoria imply by relating this custom?

**7 Critical Thinking and Reading** What does Chicoria's singing and reciting imply about his culture?

**Challenge** Did the New Mexicans really know that no Californian could beat Chicoria in spinning a rhyme or in weaving wit? Explain.

**Reader's Response** What effect do you think Chicoria's visit will have on the future of the New Mexicans at the ranch?

**Thematic Response** Have you ever observed a situation in which brains were a more effective weapon that brawn? Explain.

**Alternative Assessment** The poet Chicoria uses his wits to outsmart the powerful rancher and retain his pride. Using "Chicoria" as a model, have students write a tale in which a young

**FIESTA NEAR SANTA BARBARA**
*Unknown Artist*
*Courtesy of Mr. and Mrs. Edwin Gledhill*

Then the master spoke: "Tell us about the country where you live. What are some of the customs of New Mexico?"

**6** "Well, in New Mexico when a family sits down to eat each member uses one spoon for each biteful of food," Chicoria said with a twinkle in his eyes.

The ranchers were amazed that the New Mexicans ate in that manner, but what Chicoria hadn't told them was that each spoon was a piece of tortilla:[7] one fold and it became a spoon with which to scoop up the meal.

"Furthermore," he continued, "our goats are not like yours."

_____

**7. tortilla** (tôr tē' yä) *n.:* A thin, flat, round cake made of unleavened cornmeal or flour.

"How are they different?" the rancher asked.

"Here your nannies[8] give birth to two kids, in New Mexico they give birth to three!"

"What a strange thing!" the master said. "But tell us, how can the female nurse three kids?"

"Well, they do it exactly as you're doing it now: While two of them are eating the third one looks on."

The rancher then realized his lack of manners and took Chicoria's hint. He apologized and invited his New Mexican guest to dine at the table. After dinner, Chicoria sang and recited his poetry, putting Gracia to shame. And he won his bet as well. **7**

_____

**8. nannies** (nan' ēz) *n.:* Female goats.

person feels powerless but cleverly manipulates the situation to preserve his or her self-esteem. In telling the story, students should write in the third person, include dialogue, and end with the triumph of the young hero.

*Peer review:* In pairs or groups of four, have students assess each other's stories by responding to the following questions:

What makes the young person feel powerless?

What details does the writer include to reveal the young person's predicament?

What does the hero do to turn the situation to his or her advantage?

How effective is the dialogue?

What details would you suggest the writer include to enhance the tale?

What, if anything, should the writer delete?

To validate the peer review, have your students revise their work, incorporating those suggestions they think will enhance their final product.

# RESPONDING TO THE SELECTION

## Your Response

1. Were you entertained by "Chicoria"? Why or why not?
2. If you were Chicoria, how would you have persuaded the master rancher to invite you to the table?

## Recalling

3. Why do the New Mexicans bring Chicoria to California?
4. Why does Chicoria disagree with the servant's prediction about the feast?

## Interpreting

5. Why is Chicoria distressed as he watches the ranchers eat the feast?
6. In what way is Chicoria like the third goat in the story he tells to the ranchers?

## Applying

7. Rather than confronting the ranchers, Chicoria invents a funny story to point out their poor manners. In this way, the ranchers recognize their mistake and correct it without being directly told to do so. When is it best to use an indirect method, such as storytelling, to point out another person's faults?

# ANALYZING LITERATURE

## Appreciating the Clever Character

The **clever character** arouses our sympathy and gives us hope. Like many of us, he is not particularly strong or heroic and is usually being mistreated by someone who is powerful. Yet he triumphs over his foe by using his brain, giving us hope that we, too, can achieve our goals by means of our intelligence.

1. What is the significance of the two stories Chicoria chooses to tell the ranchers?

2. What effect do his stories have on the California ranchers?
3. How does Chicoria's cleverness pay off?

# CRITICAL THINKING AND READING

## Making Inferences About Culture

An **inference** is a conclusion drawn from information given in a story. "Chicoria" is a folk tale that has been told for generations by the Hispanic people of New Mexico. You can make inferences about the culture and history of these people from information found within it.

What inferences can you make from the following facts from the story?

a. The New Mexicans travel to California to work on the ranches.

b. The New Mexicans bring Chicoria to California when they return.

# THINKING AND WRITING

## Writing a Folk Tale

Write a folk tale of your own about a clever character. Begin by brainstorming a list of ideas for a plot in which a clever character tricks and triumphs over one or more mean, powerful characters. Use "Chicoria" as a model. Then choose one of the plot ideas and write a first draft. Exchange drafts with a partner and share your reactions to each other's work. After revising, read your folk tale to the class.

# LEARNING OPTION

**Speaking and Listening.** Folk tales come to us through a tradition of oral storytelling. Try telling your class the story "Chicoria." Reread the story until you are very familiar with it. Take turns telling the story with your classmates. Notice how each person tells the story differently.

*Chicoria* 661

---

## ANSWERS TO ANALYZING LITERATURE

1. Both stories portray the New Mexican culture as thoughtful of others.
2. The ranchers see the connection between the stories and themselves, and they invite Chicoria to join them at the table.
3. Chicoria feasts with the ranchers and wins his bet.

## ANSWERS TO CRITICAL THINKING AND READING

Suggested Responses:
a. The New Mexicans are migrant workers who travel to find the nearest suitable employment.
b. The workers are proud of Chicoria and want to show him off.

## THINKING AND WRITING

**Writing Transparency**
Your students may find it helpful to use the Story Map graphic organizer in **Transparencies for Writing.**

**Software** If students are working at computers, you might have them use *Brainstorms* from *Writer's Helper* to help them generate ideas for a folk tale.

**Teaching to Ability Levels** Ask a group of **more advanced** students to rewrite the story as a skit and perform it for the class. Ask peers to analyze whether or not the spoken parts are in keeping with the story.

## LEARNING OPTION

Students who are auditory learners or verbally skilled will respond well to this activity. To help **less advanced** students, develop a chronological list of important details with the class.

**Speaking and Listening** As students participate in the storytelling activity, ask peers to keep a list of key points to check for completeness and accuracy.

## Closure and Extension

### ANSWERS TO RESPONDING TO THE SELECTION
#### Your Response

1. Some students who found the story entertaining may say that using the goat story to make the rancher invite him to the table showed that Chicoria was smart and inventive. Others may say they don't like Chicoria's cleverness.
2. Lead your students to suggest other means of persuasion, such as reason or shame. Some students may suggest that Chicoria should have joined the table uninvited.

#### Recalling

3. They want to show the rancher a great New Mexican poet.
4. Chicoria believes he can get the rancher to invite him to the table.

#### Interpreting

5. Suggested Response: Chicoria's distress may come from his sense of what is right, of what good manners demand, and from his own frustrations with how his people are being treated.
6. Suggested Response: Like the third goat, Chicoria is waiting to eat.

#### Applying

7. Students should consider the fact that no one likes to be directly criticized.

661

## Preparation

Before students read this feature, discuss the meaning of translation with them. Make sure they understand that since the work of a translator is both literal and subjective, a translator should be fluent in and sensitive to both languages. Hispanic writer Rudolfo Anaya was well suited to translate the *cuentos,* including the tale "Chicoria."

## Presentation

### Discussion Questions

1. Why do you think it was important for Anaya to translate the collection of *cuentos* into English?
2. Why was it essential that the friend to whom Anaya showed his draft be fluent in Spanish?
3. How would you go about translating a favorite story or poem into another language? Describe the process, or steps, you would go through.

## Closure and Extension

### Thinking About the Process

1. Suggested Response: Students should realize that to do an effective job of translating the *cuentos,* it was necessary for Anaya to understand them thoroughly, and to be very familiar with their language.

2. **Reflecting on Your Writing** As an extension, you might want to list on the board students' suggestions for making writing assignments easier. As students brainstorm suggestions, encourage them to specifically address different kinds of assignments (a poem, a story, a book review, and so on). Students can keep the list in their portfolios for future reference.

# *Rudolfo Anaya and "Chicoria"*

### PREWRITING

**The Assignment Finds the Writer** The assignment to retell "Chicoria" began with a phone call. Anaya explains, "My friend José Griego called me and said he had a collection of *cuentos.* These folk tales are very old. They are part of the oral tradition of New Mexico. They are all told in Spanish and recorded in Spanish. I agreed to translate them into English."

Anaya was already familiar with these tales. "I heard many *cuentos* when I was growing up," he says. "The oral tradition of telling stories was part of my culture. I heard all the stories in Spanish. I didn't learn to speak English until I went to first grade."

**Taking Nothing for Granted** Even though Anaya had heard many of these tales before, he made sure that he knew them thoroughly. He says, "I read the *cuentos* many times and became very familiar with them before I started the translation." Anaya also wanted to make sure they had a story line the reader from another culture could follow.

### DRAFTING

**Clear Your Mind** For Anaya, the most important part of drafting is concentration. "When I write I try to put other things out of my mind." Then, when he feels ready, he jumps in and starts writing.

**Early Practice** Anaya confesses that he didn't spend much time writing when *he* was a student; however, he did enjoy writing book reviews for his English class, and this type of writing was probably good practice for retelling *cuentos:* "I liked to read a book, then figure out if I could put the story in my own words."

### REVISING

**Help From a Friend** Anaya believes that "a writer always has to revise his work" and that such revision always improves the original draft. In revising "Chicoria" and the other *cuentos,* he worked closely with the friend who gave him the assignment. "José Griego read all the translations, and from time to time he would make suggestions."

### PUBLISHING

**An Important Lesson** It is important to Anaya that readers understand the lesson that "Chicoria" teaches: "At first, the large ranch owners think they are better than the workers from New Mexico, but when Chicoria points out their arrogance, they see their foolish ways. They invite him to eat with them as an equal. The *cuento* teaches us we are all equal."

### THINKING ABOUT THE PROCESS

1. Why was it valuable for Anaya to study the *cuentos* even though he knew them?
2. **Reflecting on Your Writing** As a student, Anaya especially enjoyed retelling stories that he had read. Reflect on your own preferences by jotting down your answers to the following questions. Which type of writing do you find most enjoyable? Least enjoyable? Why?

*662 The American Folk Tradition*

# Tall Tales

THE LEGEND OF PECOS BILL, 1948
*Harold von Schmidt*
Museum of Texas Tech University

## Humanities Note

Fine art, *The Legend of Pecos Bill,* by Harold von Schmidt (1893–1982). Western painter, illustrator, and educator Harold von Schmidt was born in Alameda, California. His grandfather, one of the original Forty-Niners, inspired him with his tall tales of the California gold rush. Von Schmidt's own experience as a cowhand and lumberjack added to his knowledge of western images, traditions, and folk tales that would give him an understanding of the style and tone of the life and lore he would later become famous for illustrating.

Harold von Schmidt's study of art began at age nineteen at the California College of Arts and Crafts in San Francisco. While there, he emulated the style of western painter Frederick Remington, an artist whom von Schmidt greatly admired. After teaching for a time at the San Francisco Art Institute, he traveled to New York City to study with famous illustrator Harvey Dunn. Dunn's advice was to "paint the epic not the incident," a lesson von Schmidt never forgot.

*The Legend of Pecos Bill* celebrates the great cowboy tradition of telling stories around the campfire. The storyteller, lit by firelight, is giving an animated rendition of the antics of the legendary Pecos Bill. Instead of focusing on a close-up view of the group around the fire, von Schmidt "paints the epic," letting the figure of Pecos Bill and the legends and lore he represents dominate the scene.

You may wish to use the following questions for discussion:
1. What features of this painting reflect the exaggeration of tall tales?
2. Why do you think the artist uses only shades of blue, gray, and white for the figure of Pecos Bill?
3. How do you think the storyteller feels about the character of Pecos Bill? Why do you think as you do?

**Literary Focus: Yarns** Humor is the main characteristic of many yarns. It helps to suspend the listener's belief and creates interest in the tale.

**Prereading Focus** Prompt students to identify characteristics of their school by discussing memorable or unusual events, outstanding achievements by individuals or teams, unique activities, clubs, or service groups.

**Writing Transparency** If you wish to brainstorm with your entire class before allowing students to divide into groups, you can use the graphic organizer *Cluster Map* in **Transparencies for Writing** to record student responses.

**Vocabulary** If some of your **less advanced** students are having trouble, you might have them pronounce each word aloud.

**Spelling Tip** The word *flue* should not be confused with its homophone *flew*.

**Master Teacher Note** The images evoked in this selection are taken from a wide range of the American landscape. Students might appreciate some of the images more if they saw photographs of the actual places or things. For example, photographs of the Mississippi River, a redwood forest, the Rocky Mountains, a cyclone, the landscape of Nebraska, or some of the other states mentioned could be helpful.

664

# GUIDE FOR READING

## Carl Sandburg

(1878–1967), born in Galesburg, Illinois, is best known for his poetry. Sandburg became a journalist, an author of children's books, and a historian, and he also wrote and sang his own songs and ballads. He won the Pulitzer Prize in 1940 for his biography of Abraham Lincoln, and in 1950 for his *Complete Poems*. Sandburg's poetry celebrates the lives of ordinary people. In "The People, Yes," he uses the words, style, and rhythms of common speech to celebrate the tall tales of the American people.

## *from* The People, Yes

### Yarn

A **yarn** is a **tall tale,** a story filled with exaggeration. The subject of a yarn is the tallest, fastest, strongest, longest, or most unusual of its kind. The yarn teller describes characteristics or actions that the listener knows are impossible but which, with only a small leap of the imagination, are fun to imagine as true.

### Focus

The verses of "The People, Yes" contain many humorous exaggerations found in the myths, legends, and folk tales of America. With two or three other classmates, brainstorm for ideas for legends about your school. Make a word web like the one that follows and use it to help you think of ideas. Jot down the words and concepts you think of that relate to the word *school*. After reading this excerpt from "The People, Yes," work with your classmates to exaggerate your school's characteristics captured in your word web. You may wish to apply the style used by Sandburg as you write a few humorous verses. Present your yarn to your class.

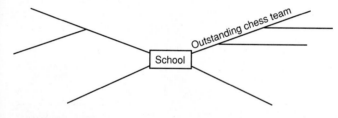

### Vocabulary

Knowing the following words will help you as you read this selection from "The People, Yes."

**shingled** (shiŋ′ g'ld) *v.*: Covered the roof with shingles (p. 665)

**mutineers** (myo͞ot′ 'n irz′) *n.*: People on a ship who revolt against their officers (p. 665)

**runt** (runt) *n.*: The smallest animal in a litter (p. 665)

**flue** (flo͞o) *n.*: The pipe in a chimney that leads smoke outside (p. 665)

**hook-and-eye:** A fastening device in which a metal hook catches onto a loop (p. 665)

664    *The American Folk Tradition*

## Objectives

1 To understand and identify yarns
2 To write a yarn
3 To express individual interests and abilities through optional activities

## Support Material

**Teaching Portfolio**
Teacher Backup, p. 935
Usage and Mechanics Worksheet, p. 938
Vocabulary Check, p. 939
Analyzing Literature Worksheet, *Understanding a Yarn,* p. 940
Language Worksheet, *Appreciating Compound Words,* p. 941
Selection Test, p. 942

**Prentice Hall Literature Writing Studio**

# from The People, Yes

### Carl Sandburg

They have yarns

**1** Of a skyscraper so tall they had to put hinges
On the two top stories so to let the moon go by,
Of one corn crop in Missouri when the roots
Went so deep and drew off so much water
The Mississippi riverbed that year was dry,

**2** Of pancakes so thin they had only one side,
Of "a fog so thick we shingled the barn and six feet out on the fog,"
Of Pecos Pete straddling a cyclone in Texas and riding it to the west coast where "it rained out under him,"
Of the man who drove a swarm of bees across the Rocky Mountains and the Desert "and didn't lose a bee,"
Of a mountain railroad curve where the engineer in his cab can touch the caboose and spit in the conductor's eye,
Of the boy who climbed a cornstalk growing so fast he would have starved to death if they hadn't shot biscuits up to him,
Of the old man's whiskers: "When the wind was with him his whiskers arrived a day before he did,"
Of the hen laying a square egg and cackling, "Ouch!" and of hens laying eggs with the dates printed on them,
Of the ship captain's shadow: it froze to the deck one cold winter night,
Of mutineers on that same ship put to chipping rust with rubber hammers,

**3** Of the sheep counter who was fast and accurate: "I just count their feet and divide by four,"
Of the man so tall he must climb a ladder to shave himself,
Of the runt so teeny-weeny it takes two men and a boy to see him,
Of mosquitoes: one can kill a dog, two of them a man,
Of a cyclone that sucked cookstoves out of the kitchen, up the chimney flue, and on to the next town,
Of the same cyclone picking up wagon-tracks in Nebraska and dropping them over in the Dakotas,
Of the hook-and-eye snake unlocking itself into forty pieces, each piece two inches long, then in nine seconds flat snapping itself together again,
Of the watch swallowed by the cow—when they butchered her a year later the watch was running and had the correct time,
Of horned snakes, hoop snakes that roll themselves where they want to go, and rattlesnakes carrying bells instead of rattles on their tails,
Of the herd of cattle in California getting lost in a giant redwood tree that had hollowed out,
**4** Of the man who killed a snake by putting its tail in its mouth so it swallowed itself,
Of railroad trains whizzing along so fast they reach the station before the whistle,
Of pigs so thin the farmer had to tie knots in

## Presentation

**Motivation/Prior Knowledge**
Have students imagine that they are listening to a championship yarn-telling match. Two speakers are swapping tales, each one more fabulous and incredible than the one before. Would students enjoy such an event? What kinds of tales might be told?

**Thematic Focus** Have students experiment with exaggerating the details of a story for humorous effect. Story chains lend themselves to outrageous plots and exaggerated events. Have students create a story chain, with each student taking a turn creating a portion of a story, then stopping at a crucial point in the action to allow the next student to continue. Ask students to identify specific elements that add humor to the story they create.

**Purpose-Setting Question** What similar characteristics do all of these yarns have?

**1** **Discussion** *The People, Yes* was published in 1936. How would the teller of this yarn feel if he or she saw cities today? Why was the yarn just as effective in 1936 when the buildings were not nearly as tall as they are today?

**2** **Literary Focus: Yarns** Point out that these yarns can be visualized. Ask students to try to visualize this image. Is it possible to imagine a one-sided pancake? Why?

**3** **Dicussion** What is humorous about this method?

**4** **Literary Focus: Yarns** You might point out the form presenting brief, one-sentence versions of these yarns. This technique is used to summarize the kinds of yarns and to give the reader an idea of the types of people who told them. Do the short passages make you want to hear the yarns in their entirety? Do they create an interest in hearing more yarns?

**Multicultural Focus** The yarn, or tall tale, is featured in the folk literature of many cultures. A Burmese tale tells of three brothers renowned for their yarns and exaggeration. They challenge a prince to a game in which the participants tell one another stories. The first person to express disbelief becomes the slave of the storyteller. The brothers tell three outrageous stories, but they fail to elicit any response from the prince. The prince then turns the tables on the brothers by telling a story of his own. He is searching for three escaped slaves—who he claims are the brothers. They are trapped. If they do not challenge the story, they agree they are the prince's slaves. If they deny the story, they lose the wager and become slaves. The prince releases them on the condition that they tell no more yarns. Ask students to consider the kinds of tales the Burmese brothers might have told the prince. Which of the tales listed in the excerpt from *The People, Yes* might be similar to the tales told by the brothers? Which do the students feel are uniquely American?

**Reader's Response** Which of these yarns would you like to hear or read? Why?

**Thematic Response** Which parts of the poem did you find most humorous? Why?

## Humanities Note

Fine art, *Baseball Player and Circus Performers,* by John Zielinski. The American illustrator John Zielinski has used bizarre symbolism in *Baseball Player and Circus Performers.* Zielinski's symbolism is reminiscent of surrealism, a modern art technique that depicts the workings of the unconscious mind. The incongruities of this piece are puzzling and prompt the viewer to think more carefully and look more closely. The fact that the viewer is prompted to wonder about the artist's meaning is an indication that the work is a success.

You might want to use the following questions to discuss the art:
1. Why do you think the baseball diamond is in a circus tent?
2. What symbols can you identify in *Baseball Player and Circus Performers?*
3. How does the content of this work relate to yarns?

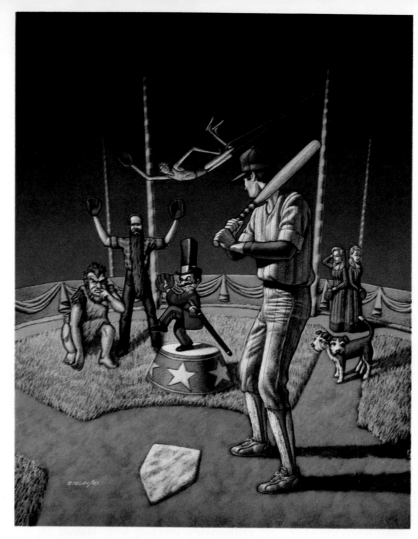

BASEBALL PLAYER AND
CIRCUS PERFORMERS
*John Zielinski*

their tails to keep them from crawling
through the cracks in their pens,
Of Paul Bunyan's big blue ox, Babe, mea-
    suring between the eyes forty-two
    ax-handles and a plug of Star tobacco
    exactly,
5   Of John Henry's hammer and the curve of
    its swing and his singing of it as "a
    rainbow round my shoulder."

## Closure and Extension

### ANSWERS TO RESPONDING TO THE SELECTION
#### Your Response

1. Ask students to identify particular yarns they would be interested in reading. Students may already be familiar with several of the yarns to which Sandburg refers. Does knowledge of the tales enhance or detract from their interest in read-ing the rest of Sandburg's poem and other yarns?
2. Encourage students to explain how they arrive at the title they choose.

#### Recalling

3. Two of the yarns that exaggerate height are the yarn about the sky-scraper that had to be hinged to let the moon go by and the yarn about the man so tall that he had to climb a ladder to shave. Yarns involving fantastic speed include the yarn

## RESPONDING TO THE SELECTION

### Your Response

1. Would you be interested in reading the rest of "The People, Yes" or yarns invented by other authors? Why or why not?
2. Suggest another title for this work. Explain why your title is appropriate.

### Recalling

3. Find two yarns that involve exaggerated heights and two yarns that involve fantastic speed.

### Interpreting

4. What did John Henry mean when he described the swing of his hammer as "a rainbow round my shoulder"?
5. Who are the people ("they") who told these yarns? What do these yarns suggest about these people?
6. Upon what characteristics of people, animals, or nature are these yarns built?

### Applying

7. Why do you think people take pleasure in spinning yarns?

## ANALYZING LITERATURE

### Understanding a Yarn

A **yarn** is a tale or story that is exaggerated or incredible. Yarns usually start with everyday situations that then become so exaggerated as to be fantastic. For example, corn crops might have deep roots (true), but not actually so deep that the Mississippi riverbed would go dry (exaggerated).

1. What might a yarn exaggerate about the following topics?
   a. cats fighting
   b. a river overflowing
2. "The People, Yes" tells you about the way of life of Americans on the frontier. Find two yarns that reveal the dangers of nature. Find two yarns that reveal the need for hard work.

## THINKING AND WRITING

### Writing a Yarn

Make a list of subjects and experiences related to life in the 1990's that are conducive to being developed as yarns. First freewrite about these subjects, including details that are as wild and exaggerated as you like. Then use these ideas to add eight lines to "The People, Yes." Revise your writing, making sure you have used exaggeration effectively. Finally, proofread your work and share it with your classmates.

## LEARNING OPTIONS

1. **Art.** Form a group with several other classmates. Draw pictures to illustrate six or seven verses of "The People, Yes." You may wish to try your hand at drawing cartoons for some of the illustrations. Then create a collage of your illustrations to display on a bulletin board in your classroom.
2. **Writing.** Write a yarn, or a tall tale, about your school. Use the ideas you developed in the Focus section on page 664.

## Preparation

**More About the Tale** Some historians suggest that the legend of Paul Bunyan can be traced to French-Canadian lumberjacks who may have related old French folk tales about giants. It is possible that these tales were transformed in the New World and developed into the legend of Paul Bunyan. The first references to Paul Bunyan in print were stories written by James McGillivray for a Detroit newspaper in 1910. These stories were based on tales he had heard from Michigan lumberjacks.

**Literary Focus** Point out to students that authentic folk tales last because they continue to appeal to people through the years. For folk tales to be considered authentic, they must have at least two versions. For example, the tale Cinderella has more than a thousand versions developed over hundreds of years in many different countries.

**Prereading Focus** Allow time for students to meet in groups to discuss contemporary heroes.

◆ **Software** If students have access to computers, they can use the *Questioner* or *Associations* activity in **Writer's Helper** to explore their potential choices.

**Vocabulary** The words for this selection are fairly easy to grasp, and students should have little difficulty with them.

**Spelling Tip** *Shanties* is the plural of *shanty*. If the final *y* is preceded by a consonant, the *y* usually changes to *i* when a suffix is added.
Example: *carry    carried*
*merry    merriment*

# GUIDE FOR READING

**Paul Bunyan**

is a legendary frontiersman— a gigantic lumberjack known for his tremendous strength and fantastic logging feats. According to folklore, Paul Bunyan invented the idea of logging in the Pacific Northwest. He created the Great Lakes—to provide drinking water for his enormous blue ox, Babe.

Folk tales about Paul Bunyan have been recorded by numerous writers, among them **Carl Sandburg** (1878–1967). (For more information on Carl Sandburg, see page 664.)

## Paul Bunyan of the North Woods

### Folk Tales

**Folk tales,** like legends and myths, are stories that have been passed down orally, but today have been preserved in written form. They are not about gods and goddesses but often involve a hero who performs amazing feats of strength or daring or solves problems. Folk tales often may last because they highlight qualities that a culture values.

### Focus

As you read "Paul Bunyan of the North Woods," look for Paul's traits—strength, size, and cleverness—that make people enjoy hearing tales about him. How do his traits reflect the values of the American frontier? What traits would you find in a contemporary folk hero? Copy the following graphic organizer. Fill in traits that could help define each type of person as a modern folk hero. At the bottom, indicate the values of today's American culture that are reflected in the list of traits.

|  | Athlete | Scientist | Artist |
|---|---|---|---|
| Traits |  |  |  |
|  |  |  |  |
|  |  |  |  |
|  |  |  |  |
|  |  |  |  |
| Values shown |  |  |  |
|  |  |  |  |

### Vocabulary

Knowing the following words will help you as you read "Paul Bunyan of the North Woods."

**lumberjack** (lum′ bər jak′) *n.*: A person employed to cut down timber (p. 669)

**shanties** (sʰan′ tēz) *n.*: Huts or shacks in which loggers lived (p. 669)

**granite** (gran′ it) *adj.*: Made of a type of very hard rock (p. 669)

**hobnailed** (häb′ nāld′) *adj.*: Having short nails put on the soles to provide greater traction (p. 669)

**commotion** (kə mō′ sʰən) *n.*: Noisy movement (p. 670)

**bellowing** (bel′ ō iŋ) *v.*: Roaring (p. 670)

668    *The American Folk Tradition*

---

### Objectives

1 To understand folk tales
2 To make generalizations about folk tales
3 To respond to a critical comment
4 To express individual interests and abilities through an optional activity

### Support Material

**Teaching Portfolio**
Teacher Backup, p. 945
Usage and Mechanics Worksheet, p. 948
Vocabulary Check, p. 949
Critical Thinking and Reading Worksheet, *Making Generalizations About a Folk Tale,* p. 950
Language Worksheet, *Appreciating Homophones,* p. 951
Selection Test, p. 952

**Prentice Hall Literature Writing Studio**

# Paul Bunyan
## of the North Woods

### Carl Sandburg

Who made Paul Bunyan, who gave him birth as a myth, who joked him into life as the Master Lumberjack, who fashioned him forth as an apparition[1] easing the hours of men amid axes and trees, saws and lumber? The people, the bookless people, they made Paul and had him alive long before he got into the books for those who read. He grew up in shanties, around the hot stoves of winter, among socks and mittens drying, in the smell of tobacco smoke and the roar of laughter mocking the outside weather. And some of Paul came overseas in wooden bunks below decks in sailing vessels. And some of Paul is old as the hills, young as the alphabet.

The Pacific Ocean froze over in the winter of the Blue Snow and Paul Bunyan had long teams of oxen hauling regular white snow over from China. This was the winter Paul gave a party to the Seven Axmen. Paul fixed a granite floor sunk two hundred feet deep for them to dance on. Still, it tipped and tilted as the dance went on. And because the Seven Axmen

**PAUL BUNYAN CARRYING A TREE
ON HIS SHOULDER AND AN AX IN HIS HAND**

refused to take off their hobnailed boots, the sparks from the nails of their dancing feet lit up the place so that Paul didn't light the kerosene lamps. No women being on the Big Onion river at that time the Seven Axmen had to dance

---

**1. apparition** (ap'ə rish'ən) *n.*: A strange figure appearing suddenly or in an extraordinary way.

**Multicultural Focus** The hyperbolic descriptions of Paul Bunyan's might and his mastery of nature highlight the qualities valued among the early settlers of the American frontier. The Paul Bunyan legend may have originated with tales of giants told by French-Canadian lumberjacks, but the stories about him were well known and often told by diverse groups of immigrant settlers in many territories. In the state of Washington, once populated by Russian fur traders, Paul was credited with scooping out Puget Sound. Settlers in North and South Dakota—Germans, Norwegians, and Russians—claimed that Paul Bunyan cleared their land of trees. German, Norwegian, and Swedish iron miners in Minnesota's early days said that when Babe the ox needed new shoes, Paul's friend Big Ole had to open a new iron mine. The Paul Bunyan character was popularized in booklets and magazines by an advertising agency trying to boost the logging industry, but he nonetheless embodied the spirit of independence and determination shared by all the early settlers.

What does Sandburg think of the theory that Paul was created by an advertising agency? How do you know?

## Presentation

### Humanities Note

Fine art, *Paul Bunyan Carrying a Tree on His Shoulder and an Ax in His Hand*, artist unknown. Paul Bunyan is depicted in folk art, statues, and illustrations. All portray one or more of his amazing qualities. The work on this page focuses on his size and strength.

You may wish to use the following questions for discussion:
1. How do the perspective and lighting in this work contribute to the impression of Paul Bunyan's great size?
2. What features of this work reinforce the perceptions you have of Paul Bunyan?
3. What is the mood of this work? How does the mood relate to the mood conveyed in the folk tales about Paul Bunyan?

**Motivation/Prior Knowledge** Have students discuss what they know about Paul Bunyan and his companion, Babe the blue ox. What impressions do students have of Paul?

**Master Teacher Note** Have students recall comic strip or cartoon heroes. What qualities do they share with Paul Bunyan? What common themes are in the stories?

**Thematic Focus** Instruct students to focus on identifying which of Paul Bunyan's characteristics reflect current cultural values.

**Purpose-Setting Question** What character traits are exaggerated in these tales?

**1 Discussion** What does the author mean by "bookless people"?

**2 Critical Thinking and Reading** You might have students infer who might be the people that the author is discussing. What do they all seem to have in common?

with each other, the one left over in each set taking Paul as a partner. The commotion of the dancing that night brought on an earthquake and the Big Onion river moved over three counties to the east.

One year when it rained from St. Patrick's Day till the Fourth of July, Paul Bunyan got disgusted because his celebration on the Fourth was spoiled. He dived into Lake Superior and swam to where a solid pillar of water was coming down. He dived under this pillar, swam up into it and climbed with powerful swimming strokes, was gone about an hour, came splashing down, and as the rain stopped, he explained, "I turned the dam thing off." This is told in the Big North Woods and on the Great Lakes, with many particulars.

Two mosquitoes lighted on one of Paul Bunyan's oxen, killed it, ate it, cleaned the bones, and sat on a grub shanty picking their teeth as Paul came along. Paul sent to Australia for two special bumblebees to kill these mosquitoes. But the bees and the mosquitoes intermarried; their children had stingers on both ends. And things kept getting worse till Paul brought a big boatload of sorghum[2] up from Louisiana and while all the bee-

---

2. **sorghum** (sor'gəm) *n.*: Tropical grasses bearing flowers and seeds that are grown for use as grain or syrup.

mosquitoes were eating at the sweet sorghum he floated them down to the Gulf of Mexico. They got so fat that it was easy to drown them all between New Orleans and Galveston.

Paul logged on the Little Gimlet in Oregon one winter. The cookstove at that camp covered an acre of ground. They fastened the side of a hog on each snowshoe and four men used to skate on the griddle while the cook flipped the pancakes. The eating table was three miles long; elevators carried the cakes to the ends of the table where boys on bicycles rode back and forth on a path down the center of the table dropping the cakes where called for.

Benny, the Little Blue Ox of Paul Bunyan, grew two feet every time Paul looked at him, when a youngster. The barn was gone one morning and they found it on Benny's back; he grew out of it in a night. One night he kept pawing and bellowing for more pancakes, till there were two hundred men at the cook-shanty stove trying to keep him fed. About breakfast time Benny broke loose, tore down the cook-shanty, ate all the pancakes piled up for the loggers' breakfast. And after that Benny made his mistake; he ate the red hot stove; and that finished him. This is only one of the hot-stove stories told in the North Woods.

## RESPONDING TO THE SELECTION

### Your Response

1. Which tall tale about Paul Bunyan do you like best? Why?
2. In what ways would you like the real world to be more like the world described in these tall tales?

### Recalling

3. How did Paul Bunyan show his cleverness?
4. How did Paul Bunyan use his strength?

### Interpreting

5. Interpret the following statement: "And some of Paul is old as the hills, young as the alphabet."
6. What qualities and abilities seem to be valued in this selection?

### Applying

7. Explain how Paul's qualities of strength, cleverness, and size might be valuable for real lumberjacks.

## ANALYZING LITERATURE

### Understanding a Folk Tale

Before **folk tales** were preserved in written form, they were simply stories retold whenever a group of people with the same interests gathered. Many times the storyteller would claim to have witnessed the tale in order to make it seem more authentic. The tales that people chose to recount indicate something about what their lives were like. For example, this selection shows you the rugged lives that loggers lived.

1. Find three details that indicate the ruggedness of the loggers' lives.
2. Find two details that indicate the need for courage.
3. Think about the landscape of the Pacific Northwest. Why would the people telling these folk tales make Paul so big?

## CRITICAL THINKING AND READING

### Making Generalizations About a Folk Tale

A **generalization** is a general idea or statement derived from particular instances. For example, if every book you have read by a certain author is science fiction, you can generalize that the author is a science-fiction writer.

1. What generalization can you make about folk tales based on the tales you read in "Paul Bunyan of the North Woods"?
2. Give some examples from "Paul Bunyan of the North Woods" on which this generalization is based.

## THINKING AND WRITING

### Writing a Response to Critical Comment

A writer has said that the Paul Bunyan folk tales were told matter-of-factly, as if by an eyewitness of commonly known events. This gives the tales a feeling of truthfulness. Choose which tales in this selection are told in a matter-of-fact manner. Then write an essay for your classmates explaining in what ways they seem matter-of-fact. Use examples to support your view. Revise your paragraphs to make sure your opinion is stated clearly. Finally, proofread your essay and share it with your classmates.

## LEARNING OPTION

**Writing.** Create a folk tale about the greatest football player, the most brilliant scientist, the finest musician, or some other imaginary hero. Be sure to exaggerate his or her talents beyond what could normally be expected. Try to be as humorous as possible in the way you "stretch the truth." You may wish to illustrate your folk tale with a colorful drawing or a cartoon.

2. Details include the harsh weather and the ferocious mosquitoes.
3. Many things found in the Northwest are large, such as the mountains, the trees, and the rugged, wild areas. Largeness can also be associated with strength.

**Challenge** Why would the work of a lumberjack be a likely topic out of which tall tales emerge?

### ANSWERS TO CRITICAL THINKING AND READING

1. A generalization about folk tales based on "Paul Bunyan of the North Woods" is that folk tales are humorous, exaggerated stories glorifying the values necessary for living and working on the American frontier.
2. The aspect of humor is found in the tale of the three-mile-long table, among others. The aspect of exaggeration can be found in all of the tales, including the tale about the winter that was so cold that the Pacific Ocean froze over. Values, including solving difficult problems, are shown in the tale of the ferocious mosquitoes.

**Challenge** What generalization do you make about yarns and tall tales based on the excerpt from *The People, Yes* and "Paul Bunyan of the North Woods"?

### THINKING AND WRITING

**Publishing Student Writing** Ask for student volunteers to read their essays aloud. Have students in the audience record one important feature of each essay. Finally, using these notes and their own essays as a guide, have students discuss their impressions of "Paul Bunyan of the North Woods".

### LEARNING OPTION

Interpersonal and auditory learners may benefit from role-playing and discussion during prewriting time.

### Recalling

3. Bunyan showed his cleverness in the tale in which he got rid of the bee-mosquitoes.
4. Bunyan used his strength when he swam up the pillar of water to turn off the rain.

### Interpreting

Suggested Responses:
5. Some of the material that was the source of the stories about Paul was very old and some was added more recently.

6. Qualities include strength, resolve, cleverness, the ability to eat a great deal, and the ability to enjoy oneself under difficult conditions.

### Applying

7. Answers will differ. Suggested Responses: The qualities of strength and size are important for the handling and transportation of large trees. Cleverness is important for solving difficult problems in remote areas with limited resources.

### ANSWERS TO ANALYZING LITERATURE

Suggested Responses:
1. The Seven Axmen wore hobnailed boots; there were no women in the area for the party; the mosquitoes were so ferocious that they could kill an ox; and the weather was sometimes severe (the winter of the Blue Snow, the year it rained from St. Patrick's Day until July Fourth).

**More About the Tale** The folk tales of Pecos Bill originated in a magazine article written by an American journalist named Edward O'Reilly in 1923. The author patterned his hero after other frontier folk heroes such as Paul Bunyan. How might a folk tale about a cowboy differ from one about a lumberjack?

**Literary Focus: Conflict** Point out to students that folk heroes like Pecos Bill are endowed with all of the qualities considered valuable on the frontier. In these tales the conflicts the hero encounters tend to test these skills. By triumphing, the folk hero reaffirms the value of such skills.

**Prereading Focus** Remind students that there are internal and external conflicts. Folk tales usually describe an external conflict, often between the hero or heroine and a force of nature. Encourage students to focus their charts on these kinds of external conflicts. Contemporary problems caused by conflicts with nature might include car trouble in bad weather, property damage, suburban garden pests, sports events or leisure activities canceled because of bad weather.

**Vocabulary** Have your **more advanced** students write original sentences using each of the vocabulary words.

**Spelling Tip** The adjective ending -*ible*, meaning "capable of," as in words like *invincible*, is the less common spelling of the ending. Most adjectives take -*able*.

672

# GUIDE FOR READING

## Pecos Bill: The Cyclone

### Conflict in a Folk Tale

A **conflict** is a struggle between opposing sides or forces. A conflict can be that of a person against another person, nature, fate, or society; or it can be between two opposing forces within a person.

The hero in a folk tale may be in conflict with the fastest runner, the hardest worker, the best shot, the most courageous person, or the quickest thinker. Folk tales are full of conflicts and competitions, such as shooting and boxing matches and encounters with nature, that the heroes win because of their extraordinary daring, skill, or strength.

### Focus

In "Pecos Bill: The Cyclone," you will read about a folk hero who solves problems by directly confronting them. On a chart like the following one, state a conflict that you or someone you know has confronted. Then list the problems the conflict has caused. At the bottom, write possible solutions to resolve the conflict.

Conflict: _____

    Problems: _____

                _____

            Solutions: _____

                _____

                _____

**Pecos Bill**

is a legendary American cowboy. He is credited with several inventions: the six-shooter and the processes of branding and roping cattle. He is said to have taught broncos how to buck. The tales tell that Pecos Bill was born in Texas in the 1830's. One of the most famous tales about Pecos Bill tells of the time he rode a cyclone in Oklahoma. That exploit is recounted by **Harold W. Felton** (1902–    ), born in Neola, Iowa, who collected folklore of the West.

### Vocabulary

Knowing the following words will help you as you read "Pecos Bill: The Cyclone."

**usurped** (yo͞o sʉrpt′) *v.*: Took power or authority away from (p. 675)

**invincible** (in vin′ sə b'l) *adj.*: Unbeatable (p. 677)

**futile** (fyo͞ot′ 'l) *adj.*: Useless; hopeless (p. 677)

**inexplicable** (in eks′ pli kə b'l) *adj.*: Without explanation (p. 678)

**skeptics** (skep′ tiks) *n.*: Persons who doubt (p. 678)

1 To understand conflict in folk tales
2 To identify reasons
3 To write a description of a conflict
4 To express individual interests and abilities through an optional activity

## Support Material

**Teaching Portfolio**
Teacher Backup, p. 955
Grammar in Action Worksheet, *Using Precise Words*, p. 958
Usage and Mechanics Worksheet, p. 960
Vocabulary Check, p. 961
Analyzing Literature Worksheet, *Understanding Conflict in a Folk Tale*, p. 962

Critical Thinking and Reading Worksheet, *Identifying Reasons*, p. 963
Selection Test, p. 964

**Prentice Hall Literature Writing Studio**

# Pecos Bill: The Cyclone

### Harold W. Felton

1 One of Bill's greatest feats, if not the greatest feat of all time, occurred unexpectedly one Fourth of July. He had invented the Fourth of July some years before. It was a great day for the cowpunchers.[1] They had taken to it right off like the real Americans they were. But the celebration had always ended on a dismal note. Somehow it seemed to be spoiled by a cyclone.

2 Bill had never minded the cyclone much. The truth is he rather liked it. But the other celebrants ran into caves for safety. He invented cyclone cellars for them. He even named the cellars. He called them "'fraid holes." Pecos wouldn't even say the word "afraid." The cyclone was something like he was. It was big and strong too. He always stood by musing[2] pleasantly as he watched it.

The cyclone caused Bill some trouble, though. Usually it would destroy a few hundred miles of fence by blowing the postholes away. But it wasn't much trouble for him to fix it. All he had to do was to go and get the postholes and then take them back and put the fence posts in them. The holes were rarely ever blown more than twenty or thirty miles.

In one respect Bill even welcomed the cyclone, for it blew so hard it blew the earth away from his wells. The first time this happened, he thought the wells would be a total loss. There they were, sticking up several hundred feet out of the ground. As wells they were useless. But he found he could cut them up into lengths and sell them for postholes to farmers in Iowa and Nebraska. It was very profitable, especially after he invented a special posthole saw to cut them with. He didn't use that type of posthole himself. He got the prairie dogs to dig his for him. He simply caught a few gross[3] of prairie dogs and set them down at proper intervals. 3 The prairie dog would dig a hole. Then Bill would put a post in it. The prairie dog would get disgusted and go down the row ahead of the others and dig another hole. Bill fenced all of Texas and parts of New Mexico and Arizona in this manner. He took a few contracts and fenced most of the Southern Pacific right of way too. That's the reason it is so crooked. He had trouble getting the prairie dogs to run a straight fence.

As for his wells, the badgers dug them. The system was the same as with the prairie dogs. The labor was cheap so it didn't make much difference if the cyclone did spoil some of the wells. The badgers were digging all of the time anyway. They didn't seem to care whether they dug wells or just badger holes.

One year he tried shipping the prairie dog holes up north, too, for postholes. It was not successful. They didn't keep in storage

---

1. **cowpunchers** (kou′ pun chərz) *n.*: Cowboys.
2. **musing** (my$\overline{oo}$z′ ing) *adv.*: Thinking deeply.

---

3. **gross** (grōs) *n.*: Twelve dozen.

*Pecos Bill: The Cyclone* 673

## Presentation

**Motivation/Prior Knowledge** You might have students visualize someone actually climbing onto and riding a tornado. What would that person look like? What similar actions are portrayed in cartoons like "Bugs Bunny"?

**Thematic Focus** Ask students to suggest skills that would have been very important on the American frontier. What exaggerated skills does Pecos Bill have that exemplify the value placed on these skills?

**Purpose-Setting Question** What is the conflict in this folk tale?

**1 Clarification** The cyclone in this folk tale is more commonly known as a tornado. Tornadoes are powerful, twisting storms with winds that reach speeds of more than 300 miles per hour. The winds are the most violent that occur on earth and often cause great destruction and death. About 700 tornadoes are reported annually in the United States, with most striking the Midwest and the states that border the Gulf of Mexico. One of the largest and fastest tornadoes in history went through Missouri, Illinois, and Indiana on March 18, 1925, leaving 689 people dead. It measured up to a mile wide and traveled at about sixty miles per hour over a distance of 220 miles.

**2 Discussion** Why won't Bill even say the word "afraid"?

**3 Critical Thinking and Reading** What is the reason that Bill does not use the same postholes as other men?

**Master Teacher Note** Like other authentic folk tales, "Pecos Bill: The Cyclone" has more than one version. Another version of this story has Pecos Bill riding the cyclone to win a bet. There are also several variations of other tales, including the death of Bill. According to one he laughed himself to death listening to a man from Boston who asked silly questions about the West.

**Making Connections** Another tale about a folk hero in conflict with a force of nature is Davy Crockett's "Tussle With a Bear," page 683. Other stories that offer explanations for the origins of natural phenomena are "How the Snake Got Poison," page 629, and "Why the Waves Have Whitecaps," page 630. You may want to have students compare and contrast the style and content of these selections.

4 **Discussion** What is the purpose of setting the story during "those days"? How does this compare with other folk tales, such as that of Paul Bunyan?

5 **Reading Strategy** You might have students question when these references to "old days" might be. Why does the writer refer to other incidents?

6 **Literary Focus: Conflict** The conflict is now established between Bill and the biggest and most terrible, original cyclone.

and they couldn't stand the handling in shipping. After they were installed they seemed to wear out quickly. Bill always thought the difference in climate had something to do with it.

4 It should be said that in those days there was only one cyclone. It was the first and original cyclone, bigger and more terrible by far than the small cyclones of today. It usually stayed by itself up north around Kansas and Oklahoma and didn't bother anyone much. But it was attracted by the noise of the Fourth of July celebration and without fail managed to put in an appearance before the close of the day.

On this particular Fourth of July, the celebration had gone off fine. The speeches were loud and long. The contests and games were hard fought. The high point of the day was Bill's exhibition with Widow Maker, which came right after he showed off Scat and Rat. People seemed never to tire of seeing them in action. The mountain lion was almost useless as a work animal after his accident, and the snake had grown old and somewhat infirm, and was troubled with rheumatism in his rattles. But they too enjoyed the Fourth of July and liked to make a public appearance. They relived the old days.

5 Widow Maker had put on a good show, bucking as no ordinary horse could ever buck. Then Bill undertook to show the gaits[4] he had taught the palomino.[5] Other mustangs[6] at that time had only two gaits. Walking and running. Only Widow Maker could pace. But now Bill had developed and taught him other gaits. Twenty-seven in all. Twenty-three forward and three reverse. He

---

**4. gaits** (gāts) *n.*: Any of the various foot movements of a horse.
**5. palomino** (pal′ə mē′ nō) *n.*: A light tan or golden brown horse with a cream-colored mane and tail.
**6. mustangs** (mus′ taŋz) *n.*: Wild horses of the American plains.

was very proud of the achievement. He showed off the slow gaits and the crowd was eager for more.

He showed the walk, trot, canter, lope, jog, slow rack, fast rack, single foot, pace, stepping pace, fox trot, running walk and the others now known. Both men and horses confuse the various gaits nowadays. Some of the gaits are now thought to be the same, such as the rack and the single foot. But with Widow Maker and Pecos Bill, each one was different. Each was precise and to be distinguished from the others. No one had ever imagined such a thing.

6 Then the cyclone came! All of the people except Bill ran into the 'fraid holes. Bill was annoyed. He stopped the performance. The remaining gaits were not shown. From that day to this horses have used no more than the gaits Widow Maker exhibited that day. It is unfortunate that the really fast gaits were not shown. If they were, horses might be much faster today than they are.

Bill glanced up at the cyclone and the quiet smile on his face faded into a frown. He saw the cyclone was angry. Very, very angry indeed.

The cyclone had always been the center of attention. Everywhere it went people would look up in wonder, fear and amazement. It had been the undisputed master of the country. It had observed Bill's rapid climb to fame and had seen the Fourth of July celebration grow. It had been keeping an eye on things all right.

In the beginning, the Fourth of July crowd had aroused its curiosity. It liked nothing more than to show its superiority and power by breaking the crowd up sometime during the day. But every year the crowd was larger. This preyed on the cyclone's mind. This year it did not come to watch. It deliberately came to spoil the celebration. Jealous of Bill and of his success,

## Grammar in Action

Writers have all the words in the English language at their disposal. The more specific or **precise** the **word** they choose, the more vivid will be the word picture they create.

Consider the precise words in the following passage:

Other mustangs at that time had only two gaits. Walking and running. Only Widow Maker could *pace*. But now Bill had developed and taught him other gaits. Twenty-seven in all. Twenty-three forward and three reverse. . . . He showed the *walk, trot, canter, lope, jog, slow rack, fast rack, single foot, pace, stepping pace, fox trot, running walk* and the others now known . . . Each was precise and to be distinguished from the others.

Notice all the words that describe types of walks. What does each word mean precisely?

**Student Activity 1.** Working with a group of five students, compile a list of words that name types of walking.

it resolved to do away with the whole institution of the Fourth of July once and for all. So much havoc and destruction would be wrought that there would never be another Independence Day Celebration. On that day, in future years, it would circle around the horizon leering[7] and gloating. At least, so it thought.

The cyclone was resolved, also, to do away with this bold fellow who did not hold it in awe and run for the 'fraid hole at its approach. For untold years it had been the most powerful thing in the land. And now, here was a mere man who threatened its position. More! Who had usurped its position!

When Bill looked at the horizon and saw the cyclone coming, he recognized the anger and rage. While a cyclone does not often smile, Bill had felt from the beginning that it was just a grouchy fellow who never had a pleasant word for anyone. But now, instead of merely an unpleasant character, Bill saw all the viciousness of which an angry cyclone is capable. He had no way of knowing that the cyclone saw its kingship tottering and was determined to stop this man who threatened its supremacy.

But Bill understood the violence of the onslaught even as the monster came into view. He knew he must meet it. The center of the cyclone was larger than ever before. The fact is, the cyclone had been training for this fight all winter and spring. It was in best form and at top weight. It headed straight for Bill intent on his destruction. In an instant it was upon him. Bill had sat quietly and silently on the great pacing mustang. But his mind was working rapidly. In the split second between his first sight of the monster and the time for action he had made his plans. Pecos Bill was ready! Ready and waiting!

Green clouds were dripping from the cyclone's jaws. Lightning flashed from its eyes as it swept down upon him. Its plan was to envelop Bill in one mighty grasp. Just as it was upon him, Bill turned Widow Maker to its left. This was a clever move for the cyclone was right-handed, and while it had been training hard to get its left in shape, that was not its best side. Bill gave rein to his mount. Widow Maker wheeled and turned on a dime which Pecos had, with great foresight[8] and accuracy, thrown to the ground to mark the exact spot for this maneuver. It was the first time that anyone had thought of turning on a dime. Then he urged the great horse forward. The cyclone, filled with surprise, lost its balance and rushed forward at an increased speed. It went so fast that it met itself coming back. This confused the cyclone, but it did not confuse Pecos Bill. He had expected that to happen. Widow Maker went into his twenty-first gait and edged up close to the whirlwind. Soon they were running neck and neck.

At the proper instant Bill grabbed the cyclone's ears, kicked himself free of the stirrups and pulled himself lightly on its back. Bill never used spurs on Widow Maker. Sometimes he wore them for show and because he liked the jingling sound they made. They made a nice accompaniment for his cowboy songs. But he had not been singing, so he had no spurs. He did not have his rattlesnake for a quirt.[9] Of course there was no bridle. It was man against monster! There he was! Pecos Bill astride a raging cyclone, slick heeled and without a saddle!

---

**7. leering** (lir′ing) *adv.*: Looking with malicious triumph.

**8. foresight** (fôr′ sīt) *n.*: The act of seeing beforehand.

**9. quirt** (kwurt) *n.*: A short-handled riding whip with a braided rawhide lash.

*Pecos Bill: The Cyclone* 675

**7 Discussion** Why does the cyclone have thoughts and actions like humans? How does this affect the conflict?

**8 Reading Strategy** Have students summarize the reasons that the cyclone is angry with Bill. How do these reasons heighten the conflict?

**9 Discussion** How is this description similar to the description of a boxing match?

**10 Literary Focus: Conflict** You might want to point out that this sentence directly states the conflict.

**Student Activity 2.** Working with a group of five students, compile a list of words that name types of dancing.

**Student Activity 3.** Working with a group of five students, compile a list of words that name types of running.

**Electronic Handbook** If students have access to the Language Master 6000, they can compare their lists of precise words to synonyms offered in the LM 6000 Thesaurus. If students are uncertain about the precise definition of a word, they can verify it using the LM 6000 Dictionary.

**11 Discussion** Does this illustration represent Pecos Bill accurately? Is this how you imagined him? Support your answer with details from the illustration.

**ESL Teaching Strategy** If you have any Spanish-speaking students, ask them to confirm that *Llano Estacado* is the translation of "Staked Plain." Review the selection for other words and phrases that describe terrain, weather, and other natural features. Allow students with limited proficiency to exchange information with students whose native language is English. Record the different translations on a chart and post it where it is visible to all students. Challenge all students to research words from other languages to add to the chart. You might want to have some students create key illustrations to be included as visual cues on the chart.

11

The cyclone was taken by surprise at this sudden turn of events. But it was undaunted. It was sure of itself. Months of training had given it a conviction that it was invincible. With a mighty heave, it twisted to its full height. Then it fell back suddenly, twisting and turning violently, so that before it came back to earth, it had turned around a thousand times. Surely no rider could ever withstand such an attack. No rider ever had. Little wonder. No one had ever ridden a cyclone before. But Pecos Bill did! He fanned the tornado's ears with his hat and dug his heels into the demon's flanks and yelled, "Yipee-ee!"

The people who had run for shelter began to come out. The audience further enraged the cyclone. It was bad enough to be disgraced by having a man astride it. It was unbearable not to have thrown him. To have all the people see the failure was too much! It got down flat on the ground and rolled over and over. Bill retained his seat throughout this ruse.[10] Evidence of this desperate but futile stratagem[11] remains today. The great Staked Plains, or as the Mexicans call it, *Llano Estacado* is the result. Its small, rugged mountains were covered with trees at the time. The rolling of the cyclone destroyed the mountains, the trees, and almost everything else in the area. The destruction was so complete, that part of the country is flat and treeless to this day. When the settlers came, there were no landmarks to guide them across the vast unmarked space, so they drove stakes in the ground to mark the trails. That is the reason it is called "Staked Plains." Here is an example of the proof of the events of history by

---

**10. ruse** (rōōz), *n.*: Trick.
**11. stratagem** (stra′ tə jəm) *n.*: Plan for defeating an opponent.

*Pecos Bill: The Cyclone* 677

**Multicultural Focus** The story of Pecos Bill's encounter with the cyclone offers an explanation for the origin of cyclones, thunderstorms, Death Valley, and the Grand Canyon. All cultures have stories that offer explanations for natural phenomena. The ancient Greeks explained winter as Demeter's period of mourning. Demeter was the goddess of the harvest. Her daughter, Persephone, was kidnapped by Hades, god of the underworld. Persephone was finally released from the underworld but was required to return there for several months each year. Demeter allowed nothing to grow on the earth while Persephone was in the underworld. When Persephone returned and mother and daughter were reunited, the world was warm and fertile again.

The Greeks also had an explanation for fire. Prometheus, cousin to Zeus, took pity on humankind. He stole some fire from the gods and gave it to the people. The folklore of the Native American Crow nation gives a similar explanation. Coyote, taking pity on the plight of humans during the cold winter months, stole an ember from the fire that was jealously guarded by the "Fire Beings" and delivered it to the humans. He also showed them how to "pull" the fire out of wood by using friction to create sparks.

An Australian Aboriginal legend reports that Narran Lake was created in the struggles between the hero Baiame and two giant crocodiles. Irish tradition credits Finn MaCumhaill (Finn MacCool) with erecting the 40,000 columns of the Giant's Causeway to build a bridge between Scotland and Ireland.

Encourage students to research tales from other cultures that offer explanations for topographical features or forces of nature. How do the tales reflect the values and customs of the culture from which they come?

## 12 Critical Thinking and Reading

This folk tale explains the geographical peculiarity of the Staked Plains, as "The Origin of Fire" explained how Indians first got fire. What other things is Bill given credit for inventing or creating in this folk tale?

## 13 Discussion What does Bill's reaction indicate about his character?

## 14 Literary Focus: Conflict The outcome of the conflict of this and most folk tales is the same. The hero succeeds in overcoming a seemingly invincible foe. What qualities of frontier life are illustrated in Bill's victory?

## 15 Discussion Do you agree with this logic? How is the writer's argument flawed?

**Reader's Response** The folk tale about Pecos Bill could only have originated in an area where cyclones are a common problem. What natural phenomena might inspire a folk tale in your region of the country? Your region may have its own tales. If so, what are they?

careful and painstaking research. It is also an example of how seemingly inexplicable geographical facts can be explained.

It was far more dangerous for the rider when the cyclone shot straight up to the sky. Once there, the twister tried the same thing it had tried on the ground. It rolled on the sky. It was no use. Bill could not be unseated. He kept his place, and he didn't have a sky hook with him either.

As for Bill, he was having the time of his life, shouting at the top of his voice, kicking his opponent in the ribs and jabbing his thumb in its flanks. It responded and went on a wild bucking rampage over the entire West. It used all the bucking tricks known to the wildest broncos as well as those known only to cyclones. The wind howled furiously and beat against the fearless rider. The rain poured. The lightning flashed around his ears. The fight went on and on. Bill enjoyed himself immensely. In spite of the elements he easily kept his place. . . .

The raging cyclone saw this out of the corner of its eye. It knew then who the victor was. It was twisting far above the Rocky Mountains when the awful truth came to it. In a horrible heave it disintegrated! Small pieces of cyclone flew in all directions. Bill still kept his seat on the main central portion until that rained out from under him. Then he jumped to a nearby streak of lightning and slid down it toward earth. But it was raining so hard that the rain put out the lightning. When it fizzled out from under him, Bill dropped the rest of the way. He lit in what is now called Death Valley. He hit quite hard, as is apparent from the fact that he so compressed the place that it is still two hundred and seventy-six feet below sea level. The Grand Canyon was washed out by the rain, though it must be understood that this happened after Paul Bunyan had given it a good start

by carelessly dragging his ax behind him when he went west a short time before.

The cyclones and the hurricanes and the tornadoes nowadays are the small pieces that broke off of the big cyclone Pecos Bill rode. In fact, the rainstorms of the present day came into being in the same way. There are always skeptics, but even they will recognize the logic of the proof of this event. They will recall that even now it almost always rains on the Fourth of July. That is because the rainstorms of today still retain some of the characteristics of the giant cyclone that met its comeuppance at the hands of Pecos Bill.

Bill lay where he landed and looked up at the sky, but he could see no sign of the cyclone. Then he laughed softly as he felt the warm sand of Death Valley on his back. . . .

It was a rough ride though, and Bill had resisted unusual tensions and pressures. When he got on the cyclone he had a twenty-dollar gold piece and a bowie knife[12] in his pocket. The tremendous force of the cyclone was such that when he finished the ride he found that his pocket contained a plugged nickel[13] and a little pearl-handled penknife. His two giant six-shooters were compressed and transformed into a small water pistol and a popgun.

It is a strange circumstance that lesser men have monuments raised in their honor. Death Valley is Bill's monument. Sort of a monument in reverse. Sunk in his honor, you might say. Perhaps that is as it should be. After all, Bill was different. He made his own monument. He made it with his hips, as is evident from the great depth of the valley. That is the hard way.

---

**12. bowie** (bō′ ē) **knife:** A strong, single-edged hunting knife named after James Bowie (1799–1836), U.S. soldier.
**13. plugged nickel:** Fake nickel.

## Closure and Extension

### ANSWERS TO RESPONDING TO THE SELECTION
#### Your Response

1. Students might cite Bill's determination, flamboyance, cleverness, or fearlessness in making their comparisons with people they know.
2. Remind students that Bill likes the cyclone because it is big and strong, as he is. They might compare the cyclone's self-centered attitude and anger at being controlled with the behavior of young children. The cyclone's fiercely competitive nature may be compared with the aggressive style required of football players, boxers, and other sports figures.

#### Recalling

3. The cyclone wants to spoil the celebration because it is jealous of Pecos Bill and his success. The cyclone had been the center of attention and the most powerful thing in the land. Now it is threat-

ened by Pecos Bill and his Fourth of July celebration.
4. The cyclone disintegrates into small cyclones when it realizes Bill is the victor.
5. The Staked Plains, Death Valley, and the Grand Canyon were caused by Bill or the cyclone.

#### Interpreting

6. The cyclone and Bill are similar in that they both are big and strong; they both are the center of attention; and they both like to display their superiority.

# RESPONDING TO THE SELECTION

## Your Response

1. Do you know a person who has characteristics similar to those attributed to Pecos Bill? Describe the characteristics of this person. Do you like this person? Why or why not?
2. Do you know a person who has characteristics similar to those attributed to the cyclone? Describe the characteristics of this person. Do you like this person? Why or why not?

## Recalling

3. Why does the cyclone want to spoil the Fourth of July celebration?
4. What happens when the cyclone realizes that Pecos Bill is the victor?
5. What natural wonders or geographical sites are caused by Pecos Bill or the cyclone?

## Interpreting

6. How is the cyclone similar to Pecos Bill?
7. Bill laughs when he sees the cyclone is gone. What does this tell you about Bill?
8. Why does the writer call Death Valley a "monument in reverse" to Pecos Bill?

## Applying

9. Bill makes his plans for this battle in "the split second between his first sight of the monster and the time for action." Do you believe anyone can think that quickly? Support your answer with examples of quick (or slow) thinking that you know about.

# ANALYZING LITERATURE

## Understanding Conflict in a Folk Tale

A **conflict,** or struggle between opposing sides or forces, is usually what a folk tale is about. Often the hero of a folk tale is thrown into conflict with another person or a natural force. After a significant struggle, the hero emerges as the winner.

1. What is the conflict in this folk tale?

2. List your ideas for variations of this conflict.

# CRITICAL THINKING AND READING

## Identifying Reasons

A **reason** is the information that explains or justifies a decision, an action, or a conclusion. A reason may be a fact, an opinion, a situation, or an occurrence. For example, in "Pecos Bill: The Cyclone," the reason for Bill's welcoming the cyclone is that it blew the earth away from his wells, which Bill then sold for postholes.

Give the reasons for the following situations from "Pecos Bill: The Cyclone."

1. The cyclone wants to do away with Pecos Bill.
2. The cyclone is in top form.
3. The cyclone disintegrates.

# THINKING AND WRITING

## Writing a Description of a Conflict

Choose one of the ideas about variations of the conflict that you wrote down earlier. Freewrite about how Pecos Bill might handle this conflict. Then use this information to write a description of the conflict and Pecos Bill's solution to it. Imagine that you are writing for a group of young children who are hearing about Pecos Bill for the first time. Revise your description, making sure you have used exaggeration effectively. Finally, proofread your description and share it with your classmates.

# LEARNING OPTION

**Cross-curricular Connection.** In this folk tale, Pecos Bill is said to have caused many of the natural wonders in the United States. Use your school or public library to research the scientific explanations of the origins of the Great Plains, Death Valley, and the Grand Canyon. Share the results of your research with your class.

7. Answers will differ. Suggested Response: His laughter tells you that Bill enjoys taking on and overcoming such challenges and that this feat has not affected him that greatly. It might also indicate that he finds humor in overcoming these challenges.
8. The writer calls Death Valley a monument in reverse because most monuments rise up from the ground so that they can be seen. Death Valley is cut into the ground to a great depth.

## Applying

9. Answers will differ. Suggested Response: Some thoughts can be made in split seconds, such as those associated with sporting events when athletes make quick decisions. Other thoughts cannot be made so quickly, especially those involving many factors and possible outcomes, such as strategies for battles, and decisions that affect many lives.

## ANSWERS TO ANALYZING LITERATURE

1. The conflict in this folk tale is a struggle between Pecos Bill and the original cyclone.
2. Answers will differ. Suggested Responses: A conflict between Bill and the cyclone in which Bill is trying to harness the cyclone's power for his own purposes or in which Bill is trying to stop the cyclone from destroying something, a

conflict between Bill and the original earthquake, a conflict between Bill and the largest bear in the West.

## ANSWERS TO CRITICAL THINKING AND READING

1. The reasons that the cyclone wants to get rid of Pecos Bill include that it is jealous of Bill and his success, and it feels threatened by him.
2. The cyclone is in top form because it has been training all through the winter and spring in anticipation of this conflict.
3. The cyclone disintegrates because it realizes that it cannot defeat and destroy Pecos Bill.

**Challenge** Ask your **less advanced** students to give the reasons that Pecos Bill welcomed the cyclone before their encounter in this tale.

## THINKING AND WRITING

**Publishing Student Writing** You might want to put together a collection of Pecos Bill folk tales created by your class. Each student could have his or her tale on a page with original artwork. You could also have some students design and create front and back covers for the collection.

## LEARNING OPTION

Allow students to choose from a variety of presentation styles. Visual and mathematical learners might choose to use charts, diagrams, and other visual aids in sharing their findings. Auditory and interpersonal learners might prefer to give a brief oral presentation and then lead a question-and-answer session. Intrapersonal learners might prepare written reports to be displayed in your classroom. They can answer questions from classmates on an informal, one-on-one basis.

**More About the Legend** Books and magazines elevated Crockett to a legendary status even before his death. After his death the tales lost all basis in reality. Tales were told of his riding up Niagara Falls on the back of an alligator and escaping from a tornado by sliding down a streak of lightning. One publication, the *Davy Crockett Almanac,* was especially popular and is among the forerunners of comic books.

**Literary Focus: Yarn** The etymology of the word *yarn* may interest students. The expression "to spin a yarn" means to tell a tale. Just as yarn is made by drawing out and twisting fibers of material such as wool, a tall tale is made by stretching out, extending, or exaggerating the original facts of a story.

**Prereading Focus** Students might use features of tall tales they have read in this unit to make generalized associations with *dream* and *reality.*

 **Software** If students have access to computers, they can use the *Associations* activity in **Writer's Helper** to help them make associations for their word webs.

**Vocabulary** Students may need help with the following words: *varmints* (p. 681), *sallied* (p. 683).

**Spelling Tip** Students may use a mnemonic to remember the first *c* in *acquaintance:* You recognize *acquaintances* when you *c* (see) them.

# GUIDE FOR READING

### Davy Crockett

(1786–1836) was a Tennessee frontiersman with both refined and wild qualities. He served with honor in the U.S. Army, the Tennessee militia, and Congress, but as America's first comic superman, he personified the untamed, comic spirit of the western frontier. In 1836 he died heroically at the Alamo, fighting Mexican troops for Texan independence. "Davy Crockett's Dream" and "Tussle with a Bear" are entries from his *Almanacs* that reflect the humor and peculiarity of his boisterous character.

## Davy Crockett's Dream
## Tussle with a Bear

### Tall Tales

A **tall tale,** or yarn, is an exaggerated, or overstated, story that captures the spirit and language of the times in which it was told. Tall tales were commonly told on the American frontier for entertainment; a good yarn teller could hold an audience spellbound for hours. A tall tale can be about any subject. It may include several anecdotes about the hero, mixing fact with imagination and exaggeration.

### Focus

Have you ever had a dream that seemed almost real? Has a friend ever told you about such a dream? In a small group, describe your dream. What made it seem real? Make a word web around the word *dream* and another around the word *reality,* similar to the following ones. Write down all the concepts you associate with each of these words. As you read Davy Crockett's *Almanac* entries, add other words to your webs. Use Davy Crockett's yarns to stimulate your verbal associations with *dream* and *reality.*

### Vocabulary

Knowing the following words will help you as you read these two yarns from *The Crockett Almanacs.*

**parson** (pär' sən) *n.:* A clergyman (p. 683)

**acquaintance** (ə kwänt' 'ns) *n.:* A person one has met (p. 683)

**disposition** (dis' pə zish' ən) *n.:* One's nature or temperament (p. 685)

**caper** (kā' pər) *n.:* Slang term for criminal act (p. 685)

### Objectives

1 To understand yarns
2 To recognize exaggeration
3 To create a yarn
4 To express individual interests and abilities through optional activities

## Support Material

**Teaching Portfolio**
Teacher Backup, p. 967
Usage and Mechanics Worksheet, p. 970
Vocabulary Check, p. 971
Analyzing Literature Worksheet, *Understanding a Yarn,* p. 972
Language Worksheet, *Appreciating Dialect,* p. 973
Selection Test, p. 974

**Prentice Hall Literature Writing Studio**

# Davy Crockett's Dream

## Davy Crockett

One day when it was so cold that I was afeard to open my mouth, lest I should freeze my tongue, I took my little dog named Grizzle and cut out for Salt River Bay to kill something for dinner. I got a good ways from home afore I knowed where I was, and as I had swetted some before I left the house my hat froze fast to my head, and I like to have put my neck out of joint in trying to pull it off. When I sneezed the icicles crackled all up and down the inside of my nose, like when you walk over a bog in winter time. The varmints was so scarce that I couldn't find one, and so when I come to an old log hut that had belonged to some squatter that had ben reformed out by the nabors, I stood my rifle up agin one of the door posts and went in. I kindled up a little fire and told Grizzle I was going to take a nap. I piled up a heap of chestnut burs for a pillow and straitened myself out on the ground, for I can curl closer than a rattle-snake and lay straiter than a log. I laid with the back of my head agin the hearth, and my eyes looking up chimney so that I could see when it was noon by the sun, for Mrs. Crockett was always rantankerous[1] when I staid out over

the time. I got to sleep before Grizzle had done warming the eend of his nose, and I had swallowed so much cold wind that it laid hard on my stomach, and as I laid gulping and belching the wind went out of me and roared up chimney like a young whirlwind. So I had a pesky dream, and kinder thought, till I waked up, that I was floating down the Massassippy in a holler tree, and I hadn't room to stir my legs and arms no more than they were withed together with young saplings. While I was there and want able to help myself a feller called Oak Wing that lived about twenty miles off, and that I had give a most almighty licking once, cum and looked in with his blind eye that I had gouged out five years before, and I saw him looking in one end of the hollow log, and he axed me if I wanted to get out. I told him to tie a rope to one of my legs and draw me out as soon as God would let him and as much sooner as he was a mind to. But he said he wouldn't do it that way, he would ram me out with a pole. So he took a long pole and rammed it down agin my head as if he was ramming home the cattridge in a cannon. This didn't make me budge an inch, but it pounded my head down in between my shoulders till I look'd like a turcle with his head drawn in. This started my temper a

---

1. **rantankerous** (ran′ tān′ kər əs) *adj.*: Dialect for "cantankerous," meaning "wildly and noisily upset."

*Davy Crockett's Dream* 681

## Presentation

**Motivation/Prior Knowledge**
You might lead your class in a discussion about all of the yarns covered in the previous selections. Based on what they have learned so far, what do students expect these tales to be like? What qualities will be glorified in the character of this frontiersman? What might some of his adventures include?

**Purpose-Setting Question**
Which events in these tales are exaggerations and which may be real?

**Thematic Focus** Ask students to share what they know about Davy Crockett. Post a record of students' knowledge to be compared with the impressions they have after reading the selection.

1 **Critical Thinking and Reading** What parts of this passage are realistic? What parts are exaggerated? Try reading the passage without the exaggerations. How does exaggeration enhance the passage?

2 **Clarification** A squatter is a person who lives on land that he has no rights to.

3 **Literary Focus: Yarn** Chestnut burs are hard and prickly. In what way is Davy Crockett boasting by claiming that he used them for a pillow? What does this tell you about his audience? What kinds of human qualities do you think they admired?

**ESL Teaching Strategy** The many nonstandard spellings and pronunciations in this selection may present difficulties for students with limited English proficiency. A group of students may want to compile a list of all the nonstandard words in the selection with their standard spellings for use by any student having difficulty with the dialect.

**Master Teacher Note** To give your students a better idea of the widespread popularity that the legend of Davy Crockett enjoys today, you might play them the recording "Davy Crockett, King of the Wild Frontier" from the soundtrack of the Walt Disney movie of the same name that was popular in the 1950's. You might also tell them about the popular television series that was based on his life.

**Making Connections** Another selection whose subject was an actual person who became a part of folklore is "Paul Revere's Ride" on page 509.

**4 Literary Focus: Yarn** Notice that Crockett did not write in standard English, but in the dialect of the Tennessee frontier. Try rereading this passage as if it had been written in standard English. What is lost? How does the use of dialect enhance the yarn?

**5 Literary Focus: Yarn** Because a yarn's main purpose is to entertain, humor is one of its main elements. What makes this sentence humorous?

**Reader's Response** After reading this yarn, do you think you would have enjoyed living on the frontier in Davy Crockett's day? What might you find attractive about this life? What would you find unappealing?

**Thematic Response** Ask students how the impressions they formed while reading the selection compare with the ideas they had before reading the selection. Why do people in modern times enjoy stories about Davy Crockett?

## Closure and Extension

### ANSWERS TO RESPONDING TO THE SELECTION
*Your Response*
1. Encourage students to identify specific character traits that influence their responses.

*Recalling*
2. He says the weather was so cold that his hat froze to his head, he fell asleep before his dog could warm his nose, and his breath went up the chimney like a whirlwind.
3. The next time Oak Wing has a dream, he must apologize for his actions in Crockett's dream.

*Interpreting*
4. Students may answer that respect for an individual's rights was valued highly.
5. Students may answer that the use of dialect makes it seem as though Crockett is actually speaking to us. The standard English version would have been less colorful and less entertaining.

682

---

**4** trifle, and I ript and swore till the breath boiled out of the end of the log like the steam out of the funnel pipe of a steemboat. Jest then I woke up, and seed my wife pulling my leg, for it was enermost sundown and she had cum arter me. There was a long icicle hanging to her nose, and when she tried to kiss me, she run it right into my eye. I telled her my dreem, and sed I would have revenge on Oak Wing for pounding my head. She said it was all a dreem and that Oak was not

to blame; but I had a very diffrent idee of the matter. So I went and talked to him, and telled him what he had done to me in a dreem, and it was settled that he should make me an apology in his next dreem, and that wood make us square,[2] for I don't like to be run upon when I'm asleep, any more than I do when I'm awake.

**5**

---
2. **square:** Even.

## RESPONDING TO THE SELECTION

### Your Response
1. Do you think you would want to be friends with Davy Crockett? Why or why not?

### Recalling
2. Give three examples of details that Crockett exaggerates.
3. What does Crockett decide will settle his differences with Oak Wing?

### Interpreting
4. At the end of the tale, Crockett and Oak Wing come to a fantastic and humorous settlement. What does their agreement tell you about respect in frontier life?
5. Explain how Crockett's dialect affects his tale. Had he written his tale in standard English, what would have been lost?

### Applying
6. Crockett's audience must be careful not to take him literally. What other examples of writing should you examine carefully before taking at face value?

## ANALYZING LITERATURE

### Understanding a Tall Tale
A **tall tale** is an exaggerated story that captures the spirit and language of the times in which it was told. A tall tale is told for entertainment, it does not have a "lesson." Through descriptions

of fantastic events or heroic feats, a tall tale can help you imagine what life was like at that time.

1. In what ways do you think the information you learn about Davy Crockett from a biographical account differs from the information you learn about him from a tall tale?
2. Are there any ways in which the information would be similar? Explain your answer.

## CRITICAL THINKING AND READING

### Recognizing Exaggeration
In his tall tale Crockett takes an ordinary event and transforms it into a bizarre experience. Through exaggerated comparisons and elaborate language, Crockett inflates the actions of his story to capture his audience. By comparing his breath to a whirlwind out of a chimney, for example, Crockett stretches the facts of his adventures out of proportion to amaze his audience.

1. Cite other examples of exaggerations of facts that lead to fantastic descriptions.
2. Do these exaggerations enhance or detract from Crockett's tales? Explain.

## LEARNING OPTION

**Art.** Choose a portion of "Davy Crockett's Dream" and draw a cartoon sequence of it. Create comic-book style dialogue to accompany it. You may enjoy imitating Davy Crockett's dialect in the dialogue you write.

682   The American Folk Tradition

---

*Applying*
6. Students may mention persuasive writing, such as propaganda or advertising copy, or figurative writing found in poetry or fiction.

### ANSWERS TO ANALYZING LITERATURE
1. A biographical account provides the reader with more accurate, factual information. A yarn may

give the reader a more vivid picture of a character's personality and sense of humor.
2. A biographer may attempt to convey to readers the personality traits that come across directly in a yarn.

### ANSWERS TO CRITICAL THINKING AND READING
1. Some examples are "I was afeard to open my mouth, lest I should

freeze my tongue" (p. 681), ". . . my hat froze fast to me head, and I like to have put my neck out of joint in trying to pull it off" (p. 681), "When I sneezed the icicles crackled all up and down the inside of my nose . . ." (p. 681), or "There was a long icicle hanging to her nose . . ." (p. 682).
2. Students might respond that the exaggerations enhance the tale by making ordinary experiences both amazing and amusing.

# Tussle with a Bear

### Davy Crockett

1 I salled out from hum, one rainy arternoon, to go down to Rattle-snake Swamp to git a squint at a turkey-buzzard, for thar war a smart chance of them down that way, and I had hered how thar war to be a Methodist parson at my house on the next day, and my wife wanted me to git sumthing nice for his tooth. She said it would help out his sarment[1] almighty much. So I took my dog and rifle and sallied out rite away. I had got down about as fur as where the wood opens at the Big Gap, when I seed it war so dark and mucilaginous[2] that I coodn't hardly see at all. 2 I went on, howsever, and intarmined[3] in my own mind, to keep on, tho I 3 shood run afoul of an earthquake, for thar is no more give back to me than thar is to a flying bullet when a painter stares it rite in the face. I war going ahead like the devil on a 4 gambler's trail, when, all at once, or I might say, all at twice, for it war done in double quick time, I felt sumthing ketch me around the middle, and it squeezed me like it war an old acquaintance. So I looked up and seed pretty quick it war no relation of mine. It was a great bear that war hugging me like a brother, and sticking as close to me as a turcle to his shell. So he squeezed an idee

---

**1. sarment** (sär′mənt) *n*.: Dialect term for "sermon."
**2. mucilaginous** (myōō′ si läj′ ə nəs) *adj*.: Thick and sticky.
**3. intarmined** (in tär′ mənd) *v*.: Dialect for "determined."

into my hed that if I got him as ded as common, and his hide off of his pesky body, he would do as well for the parson as any thing else. So I felt pretty well satisfied when I cum to think I had my Sunday's dinner so close to me. But when he railly seemed to be cuming closer and closer, I telled him to be patient for he wood git into me arter he war cooked; but he didn't seem to take a hint, and to tell the truth, I begun to think that although there war to be won dinner made out between us, it war amazing uncertain 5 which of us would be the dinner and which would be the eater. So I seed I ought to hav ben thinking about other matters. I coodn't get my knife out, and my rifle had dropped down. He put up won of his hind claws agin my side, and I seed it war cuming to the *scratch* amazing sudden. So I called to my dog, and he cum up pretty slow till he seed what war the matter, and then he jumped a 6 rod rite towards the bear. The bear got a notion that the dog was unfriendly to him, before he felt his teeth in his throat, and 7 when Rough begun to gnaw his windpipe, the varmint ment there should be no love 8 lost. But the bear had no notion of loosening his grip on me. He shoved his teeth so near my nose that I tried to cock it up out of his way, and then he drew his tongue across my throat to mark out the place where he should put in his teeth. All this showed that he had no regard for my feelings. He shook

*Tussle with a Bear* 683

---

## Presentation

1 **Clarification** Ask students how they would translate the following words from this passage from dialect to standard English: *salled, hum, arternoon, git, thar, war, hered, sumthing.*

2 **Clarification** Crockett is referring to the Cumberland Gap, a natural pass through the Appalachian mountains at the meeting point of Virginia, Kentucky, and Tennessee. The Cumberland Gap is narrow and has steep sides about 500 feet high. This scenic area is now Cumberland Gap National Historical Park, one of the largest historical parks in the United States.

3 **Discussion** "Give back" is dialect for giving up; "painter" is dialect for panther. What does Davy Crockett want his audience to think about him?

4 **Reading Strategy** Crockett uses colorful language to make this passage humorous and vivid. Look for examples of simile ("like the devil on a gambler's trail"); play on words ("all at once, or I might say, all at twice"); understatement ("it war no relation of mine"); and exaggeration ("sticking as close to me as a turcle to his shell").

5 **Reading Strategy** How does Crockett make a dangerous situation seem funny?

6 **Clarification** A rod is 16.5 feet or 5.029 meters. Could a dog jump this far?

7 **Discussion** How do people usually choose names for pets? What does the name Crockett chose for his dog tell you about the qualities he admired in pets?

8 **Discussion** What is Crockett's purpose in speaking of the bear as though he were acting intelligently, or as if he could have regard for someone's feelings?

---

off the dog three or four times, like nothing at all, and once he trod on his head; but Rough stood up to his lick log and bit at him, but the varmint's hairs set his teeth on edge. All this passed in quicker time than a blind hoss can run agin a post, when he can't see whar to find it. The varmint made a lounge and caught hold of my rite ear, and so I made a grab at his ear too, and caught it between my teeth. So we held on to each others' ears, till my teeth met through his ear. Then I tripped him down with one leg, and the cretur's back fell acrost a log, and I war on top of him. He lay so oncomfortable that he rolled off the log, and loosened his grip so much that I had a chance to get hold of my nife, and Rough dove into him at the same time. Seeing thar war two of us, he

DAVY CROCKETT, WITH THE HELP OF HIS DOG, FIGHTING A BEAR
*Cover of the Crockett Almanac, 1841*

thought he would use one paw for each one. The varmint cocked one eye at me as much as to ax me stay whar I war till he could let go of me with one paw, and finish the dog. No man can say I am of a contrary disposition, though it come so handy for me to feel the haft of my big butcher, as soon as my rite hand war at liberty, that I pulled it out. The way it went into the bowels of the varmint war nothing to nobody. It astonished him most mightily. He looked as if he thought it war a mean caper, and he turned pale. If he didn't die in short time arterwards, then the Methodist parson eat him alive, that's all. When I cum to strip, arter the affair war over, the marks of the bear's claws war up and down on my hide to such a rate that I might have been hung out for an American flag. The stripes showed most beautiful.

## RESPONDING TO THE SELECTION

### Your Response

1. Now that you have read a second tall tale by Davy Crockett, do you still feel about him as you did after reading his dream? Would you want to be friends with him now? Why or why not?

### Recalling

2. Describe Crockett's struggle with the bear.
3. Crockett describes himself in superhuman terms. Give examples from the tale.

### Interpreting

4. Are Crockett's actions heroic? Explain.
5. What effect do Crockett's exaggerations and outrageous comparisons have on the mood?
6. What does Crockett's final remark, "The stripes showed most beautiful," indicate about his feelings about killing the bear?

### Applying

7. Crockett's accounts of his outrageous experiences helped shape his image as a frontier hero. Give examples of how you shape your image.

## CRITICAL THINKING AND READING

### Appreciating Dialect

**Dialect** is the pronunciation, grammar, spelling, and vocabulary used by a particular group of people in a region. Dialect adds humor to the tall tales and makes the settings seem authentic. An example of dialect is "I salled out from hum . . ." In standard English we might say: I set out from home.

Rewrite the following sentences in standard English:

1. "I went on, howsever, and intarmined in my own mind, to keep on, tho I shood run afoul of an earthquake, for thar is no more give back to me than thar is to a flying bullet when a painter stares it rite in the face."
2. "He put up won of his hind claws agin my side, and I seed it war cuming to the *scratch* amazing sudden."

## THINKING AND WRITING

### Creating a Tall Tale

Think of an adventurous experience you have had and write about it in the same style as Davy Crockett's tall tales. Exaggerate the details of your story by using fantastic descriptions and comparisons. Like Davy Crockett, reveal something about your character by the end of your story. Revise your tale, making sure it is well organized. Proofread your tale and share it with classmates.

## LEARNING OPTION

**Cross-curricular Connection.** Use your school or public library to find out about Davy Crockett's congressional term. What policies did he support? What actions did he take? Present your findings to your class in an oral report.

*Tussle with a Bear* 685

6. Crockett was proud of his victory.

### Applying

7. Ask students how they would like others to see them. Then ask them how they might project this image.

### ANSWERS TO CRITICAL THINKING AND READING

Students' rewritten passages should be similar to the following:

1. I went on, however, and made up my mind to continue, even if there should be an earthquake, for I don't give any more than a flying bullet would if it were headed for a panther.
2. He put one of his hind claws against my side, and I saw he was about to scratch.

### THINKING AND WRITING

◆ **Software** Students can use **Bank Street Writer** to complete this assignment. They can easily incorporate prewriting notes and ideas in several drafts, experimenting with exaggeration and dialect in different sections of their tales.

**Writing Across the Curriculum** Have students write reports on other frontier figures such as Daniel Boone, Mary Jemison, or James Bowie. You might inform a social studies teacher of this assignment.

**Challenge** Some students might want to try writing their yarns in dialect.

### LEARNING OPTION

You might make research and presentation teams by grouping students of different learning styles. Ask students to work together to create a presentation that includes visual aids, written work, and an oral component. The oral component might be one of Davy Crockett's speeches or tales recited in character.

## Closure and Extension

### ANSWERS TO RESPONDING TO THE SELECTION
#### Your Response

1. Ask students to identify elements of the second tale that changed or reinforced their perceptions of Davy Crockett.

#### Recalling

2. The bear squeezed Crockett, scratched him, bit his ear. Crockett bit the bear's ear, tripped him. Crockett killed the bear with his knife.
3. Suggested Responses: Crockett bit the bear; tripped him; didn't feel the scratches.

#### Interpreting

4. His fearlessness may seem heroic to some; boastful and clownish to others.
5. They lighten the mood of the tale, making it amusing rather than frightening.

## Preparation

**Motivation/Prior Knowledge**
**Prewriting** Discuss the heroes of the tall tales in this unit. Ask students to describe the "super-powers" of each hero. Which amazing powers do students think it would be fun to have? How would they use these powers in their own lives? Are there any powers other than those mentioned in the tales that students would like to have? What would they do with these powers?

**Focus** Point out to students that the more outrageous they make the tale, the more entertaining it will be to their audience. Encourage them to stretch the limits of their imaginations in creating powers and feats for their heroes.

## Presentation

**Prewriting** Making a list of the subject's actual abilities and accomplishments may help students to get started. Have students imagine the results of exaggerating these abilities. What would the person be able to accomplish with his or her exaggerated powers?

Remind students that their tales will need to have some action. They must place their hero in a situation that requires the use of his or her special abilities.

◆ **Software** If students have access to computers, they can use the *Idea Wheel* in the **Writer's Helper** activities to generate ideas for potential situations.

**Drafting** Students may benefit from some partner interaction during drafting. Sharing their ideas orally with a partner can help students to clarify the direction of their narrative.

📖 **Writing Transparency** You might want to use *Model 4: Short*

# YOUR WRITING PROCESS

## WRITING A TALL TALE

As you know from reading the tall tales in this unit, sometimes people stretch the truth when they are trying to make an impression. Suppose your school magazine were awarding a prize for the best modern tall tale. What fabulous deeds could you imagine for the hero of such a tale?

### Focus

**Assignment:** Write a tall tale about someone in your neighborhood or school community.
**Purpose:** To entertain and to win a contest.
**Audience:** Readers of the student magazine.

### Prewriting

**1. Create a larger-than-life character.** Think about Pecos Bill or Paul Bunyan from the tall tales in this unit. How would you describe these two characters? What amazing powers do they have? You might want to use a word cluster like the one below to help you describe your own tall-tale hero. Remember that you can give your hero exaggerated powers.

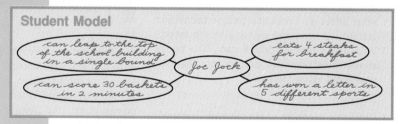

**Student Model**

- can leap to the top of the school building in a single bound
- can score 30 baskets in 2 minutes
- Joe Jock
- eats 4 steaks for breakfast
- has won a letter in 5 different sports

**2. Zero in on your setting.** Think about special landmarks in your neighborhood or school community. Remember that the events in some tall tales explain how a certain landmark came into being. The story "Pecos Bill: The Cyclone" explains the creation of Death Valley. What landmarks in your neighborhood lend themselves to funny explanations of how they came to be?

686    *The American Folk Tradition*

*Story* in **Transparencies for Writing** to demonstrate for your students the structure of a brief, fictional narrative. Call students' attention to the exposition, the climax, and the conclusion.

**Revising and Editing** Ask students to look for places where they can replace formal language with colloquial expressions. Slang expressions may be particularly effective in communicating characters' reactions to the hero's amazing powers. Point out that the nature of the tale allows some rules of grammar to be suspended. Peer editors can comment on the suitability of the language and style, making specific suggestions for improvement.

## Drafting

**1. Grab your readers' attention right away.** One way to write an opening that will really hook your audience is to arouse their curiosity about the action to come. Try to present enough information to pull them into the drama of the tale, but not so much that they have no reason to read on.

> **Student Model**
>
> If you have ever wondered why the clock on top of the Williams Bank building is always set at 12:00 and no one can fix it, you might like to hear the tale of Massie Tarbox, the woman who stopped time in its tracks.

**2. Keep your purpose in mind.** You are writing this tale to entertain your audience and to win the contest. Humor, colorful descriptions, nonsense, and fast-paced action are some possible ingredients of entertaining writing. In tall tales, exaggeration is a key component of what makes the story entertaining. Make sure your tall tale includes some clever exaggerations, but also experiment with other ways of entertaining your audience.

## Revising and Editing

**1. Read your tall tale aloud.** Remember, tall tales are part of an oral tradition—they were told before they were written down. The language in your tale should sound as natural as possible, as if you were telling a story to a friend. Do your ideas flow smoothly? Are your exaggerations funny? Is your language appropriate to your audience and purpose?

**2. Consult with a partner.** Read your tall tale to a partner or to an editing group. You might want to ask questions like these:
- Did my opening grab your attention?
- Were my exaggerations about my character's talent funny?
- Were there any points at which you were confused about the action?

**3. Root out errors.** Proofread your tall tale carefully for errors in spelling, mechanics, and punctuation. Do you have a particular kind of error you make frequently? Now is the time to catch it.

### Writer's Hint

Exclamatory sentences express strong feelings. If not overused, they can help to give your tall tale a sense of excitement. Remember to use an exclamation mark after an exclamatory sentence.

### Options for Publishing

- Hold a contest for the best tall tale in your class. Create a folder for the tales so that each student has a chance to read all the tales and vote for the winner. Display the winning tale on the bulletin board.
- Illustrate your tall tale with humorous pictures of your hero performing miraculous feats. Display your illustrated tale on the class bulletin board.

### Reviewing the Writing Process

1. What elements of entertaining writing did you use in your tall tale? Do you think your final tale succeeded in entertaining your audience? Explain.

2. Did you refer to a word cluster of your main character's powers and skills as you drafted your tale? Why or why not?

## Closure and Extension

**Guidelines for Evaluation** You may wish to consider the following questions as you evaluate each student's tall tale:

1. Has the writer used an individual's actual abilities to create amazing powers for the hero?
2. Does the tall tale place the hero in a situation that requires the use of his or her amazing powers?
3. Does the writer develop the humor of the situation?
4. Is the language used in the tale appropriate for the characters and the setting?
5. Is the tale free of errors in spelling and mechanics?

**Alternative Assessment** *Collaborative Evaluation:* In groups of four, ask your students to determine the criteria for judging the tall tales. Tell them as they develop the criteria to keep in mind what they enjoy when they read a tall tale including:

    Type of characters they expect

    Type of action they want

    Type of opening they look for

    The techniques to achieve humor they hope to find

As a class, review the criteria each group suggests and decide on those criteria you and the class will use to select the best tall tale.

**Publishing** Arrange with the teachers of younger students to have a "Tale Time." Over the course of several days, your students can take turns visiting the younger students at a designated time, sharing their tall tales and illustrations.

**Student Portfolios** You might want to have students include their tall tales in their writing portfolios.

**Enrichment** Certain American folk songs are similar to tall tales in content and style. Have your students consider songs like *Old Dan Tucker*, *The Erie Canal*, and *John Henry*, in light of what they have learned about tall tales.

## Preparation

**Motivation/Prior Knowledge**
Lead a class discussion about the folk heroes in this unit. Which characters and situations would make visually exciting subjects? Why? Elicit other reasons for commemorating a folk hero. Does the hero personify admirable qualities? Does he or she exemplify some ideal? Is the character representative of a unique facet in our cultural history?

**Focus** Artists strive to capture the essence of their subjects. Point out to students that the background they provide must go beyond a strictly physical description in order to assist the artist in his or her interpretation.

## Presentation

**Prewriting** Students who are having difficulty identifying personal qualities of a character might generate ideas by working backward from the events in the story. Have students list a few of the character's actions, then determine what these actions indicate about the character.

**Software** If students have access to computers, the *Questioner* activity in **Writer's Helper** may stimulate ideas on information about the character that can be included in the report.

Point out to students that because folk tales have their roots in the oral tradition, the details of a story will vary from version to version. As they consider the differences in detail, urge them to find the details that they think most vividly illustrate the main idea.

**Drafting** Direct students to pair each quality they list with a representative scene. In referring to their charts, students should consider the visual impact of each example. Remind students

# YOUR WRITING PROCESS

*"All morning I worked on the proof of one of my poems, and I took out a comma; in the afternoon I put it back."*

**Oscar Wilde**

## WRITING A REPORT

Reports are used as important sources of information in many fields, including the arts. Imagine it is your job to provide an artist with a report so that he or she can design a stamp commemorating a character from American folklore. Think about the characters you read about in this unit. What information would you include in your report on one of these characters?

---

**Focus**

**Assignment:** Write a report about a character who has become an American legend.
**Purpose:** To provide background for an artist who will design a stamp to honor this character.
**Audience:** The artist.

---

### Prewriting

**1. Think visually.** The information in your report will help the artist to "see" the legend who is the subject of the stamp. The better you visualize your subject, the more you will help the artist. What better way to visualize than to doodle or sketch? If your subject is John Henry ("Hammerman"), for example, draw what *you* think he looks like. Draw objects associated with him, like the famous long-handled hammer.

**2. Make a "Qualities Chart."** Think about the personal qualities of your legendary character. Decide which ones you would like to cover in your report; then list them on a chart. What actions or occurrences illustrate the qualities you chose? Organize these examples in your chart.

---

**Student Model**

**Hammerman's Qualities**

**Quality 1: Strength**
1. hammered a spike it took three men to hammer
2. could hammer for ten hours without tiring
3. caused his hammer heads to smoke from the force of his blows

**Quality 2: Determination**
1. convinced railroad foreman to hire him even though he had no experience
2. hammered even when exhausted so he could beat a drilling machine

---

688    *The American Folk Tradition*

to provide the artist with images as well as information.

**Revising and Editing** The prewriting charts can help students evaluate the structural organization of their drafts. Are images and facts grouped according to the qualities they illustrate? Are the most representative incidents emphasized?

 **Writing Transparency** You may wish to review the structure of a report using *Model 8: Report* in **Transparencies for Writing.**

**3. Read other versions of tales about your characters.** Stories about legendary characters, such as Hammerman or Johnny Appleseed, have been told through the ages. Libraries often have more than one version of a famous legend in their folk-tale collection. Read every version, and take notes about details you would like to include in your report.

## Drafting

**1. Write a strong introduction.** You want the artist who is designing the stamp to be immediately drawn to your legendary character. Make your introductory paragraph direct and inviting.

> **Student Model**
> What qualities make John Henry, otherwise known as "Hammerman," a legendary hero? He is known chiefly for the superhuman strength that enabled him to successfully compete against a machine. Strength without determination is not worth much, though. John Henry was the best steel driver on the C & O Railroad because he wanted to be the best!

**2. Don't include too many details.** Limit yourself to illustrating the hero's main qualities and achievements.

**3. Conclude your report with a recommendation.** Remember that the artist must convey the spirit of the hero through pictures, not words. Conclude your report by focusing on a scene that the artist can depict or on one or more symbolic objects that can represent the hero.

## Revising and Editing

**1. Imagine you are the artist reading the report.** Does the report give you a brief, clear account of the hero's career? Does it suggest a scene or a symbolic object that summarizes the hero's achievements?

**2. Check your facts.** If you are using facts in your report, this is the time to make sure they are accurate.

**3. Use proper nouns.** A proper noun is the name of a particular person, place, thing, or idea. In a report, use proper nouns rather than general terms. For example, write "Chesapeake and Ohio Railroad" rather than "a railroad."

**4. Aim for perfection.** Proofread your report carefully for errors in spelling and punctuation.

**Grammar Tip**

Proper nouns always begin with capital letters.

**Options for Publishing**

• Give your report to a fellow student who is an artist, and ask him or her to design a stamp. As an alternative, you may want to design a stamp yourself.

• Participate in creating a class anthology of reports on characters in American legends.

**Reviewing Your Writing Process**

1. Did organizing your character's main qualities on a chart help you during the drafting process? Explain.

2. Did you have any difficulty in thinking about your subject from a visual perspective? Explain.

*Your Writing Process* 689

## Closure and Extension

**Guidelines for Evaluation** The following questions can provide a framework for evaluating each student's report:
1. Does the report demonstrate an understanding of the character's significance?
2. Does the report identify several of the character's key qualities?
3. Does the writer provide the artist with visual images as well as factual information?
4. Is the report free of errors in capitalization, punctuation, spelling, and grammar?

**Alternative Assessment** *Collaborative Evaluation:* In groups of four, ask your students to evaluate one another's work by responding to the following questions:

On what character from American folklore does the writer report?

Does the writer describe personal qualities of the legendary character? Can the reader visualize the character from that description?

Does the writer describe actions that illustrate the character's personal qualities?

Is the introduction engaging?

Does the report conclude with a recommendation of symbols that can represent the hero?

Is the report free of errors in spelling, grammar, and punctuation?

Based on your evaluation, what do you think is an appropriate grade for this report?

After the reports have been evaluated, you may ask your students to write protocols summarizing what they have learned by completing their own reports and evaluating one another's work.

**Enrichment** Are there any philatelists in your class? This name for people who make stamp collecting their hobby was coined in France in 1864. It comes from the Greek word *philos,* meaning "loving," and *ateleia,* which means "exemption from further tax." In other words, "postage paid." Tell any students interested in exploring this hobby that most post offices offer a "starter kit" for novice philatelists.

**Grammar Tip** Students can review the folk tale to recall what proper nouns should be used in their report and where capitalization is appropriate. Refer students to the Handbook of Grammar and Revising Strategies for further guidance in distinguishing between common and proper nouns.

**Publishing** Display the stamp designs with students' written work. Use pinking shears to create a serrated edge on the paper.

**Student Portfolios** You might want the students to include this report in their writing portfolios.

**MESA AND CACTI**
*Diego Rivera*
*Detroit Institute of Arts*

# THE NOVEL

A novel is a work of fiction; that is, an author creates it from his or her imagination. Like the short story, a novel includes the elements of plot, characters, setting, theme, and point of view. However, a novel is considerably longer than a short story, allowing the writer to develop elements such as setting, plot, and character more fully. A novel usually takes place in more than one setting. Typically, the plot, or sequence of events, in a novel is more complicated than that of a short story and often includes conflicts in addition to the main conflict. Characters in a novel are usually more complex because the author has room to develop them more thoroughly.

Readers can gain greater insights about life and about a particular time and place from a novel than they can from most short stories. In *The Pearl* you will read about a time and place unfamiliar to most readers.

691

## Humanities Note

Fine art, *Mesa and Cacti,* by Diego Rivera (1886–1951). Rivera is perhaps the most well known Mexican artist. He received his formal training in Paris but returned to his native land to use his art for the glory of the Mexican people. Rivera is most notable for his murals, found around the world, which are monuments to his people and the workers of the world.

*Mesa and Cacti* is a landscape painting of terrain typical of Mexico. The handlike shapes of the cacti are counterbalanced by the mountains on the horizon. The picture plane is unified by the soft coloring of the composition. The skill of this rendering attests to the formal training Rivera underwent in Europe.

You might want to ask the following questions to discuss the art:
1. What is the atmosphere of this painting?
2. What emotion does this landscape evoke?

# READING ACTIVELY

## The Novel

On a sailing trip in 1940, John Steinbeck heard a folk tale about a fisherman who suffered great misfortune after he discovered a magnificent pearl. Inspired by the legend, Steinbeck wrote *The Pearl* four years later. Like many important novels, *The Pearl* can be interpreted on several different levels. To present his multilevel theme, Steinbeck chose to write this novel as a parable, or allegory. A parable is a short work, usually fictitious, that illustrates a lesson, often about good and evil. In his preface to *The Pearl,* Steinbeck wrote: "If the story is a parable, perhaps everyone takes his own meaning from it." Some readers see *The Pearl* as a parable about human greed, while others find it a parable about social oppression.

Steinbeck often wrote about the struggle between the wealthy and the poor, between the strong and the weak, and between different cultures. To understand *The Pearl,* you should know that when the legend originated in the early 1900's, the native peoples of Mexico had been oppressed by people of Spanish descent for more than three hundred years. In many cases, these peoples were not allowed to attend school or own land. Although Spanish culture was forced upon them, many retained elements of tribal customs, just as Juana does when she combines Catholic Hail Marys with ancient prayers.

**READING STRATEGIES** To increase your understanding of *The Pearl,* read the background and biographical information carefully. Understanding the significance of culture in the story will clarify some events in the plot. For example, many Mexicans of native origin believed that they were meant to remain in their birthplace. Therefore, leaving La Paz is an enormous step for Kino. It might also help you to appreciate the style in which Steinbeck wrote *The Pearl.* Keep in mind that he used very little dialogue and created simple rather than complex characters so that his novel would read like a parable. Finally, interact with the literature, using the active reading strategies: question, visualize, predict, connect, and respond.

**THEMES:** You will encounter the following themes in *The Pearl.*
- The struggle for survival
- Conflicts resulting from oppression and social class
- Corruption by material wealth and possessions

692   The Novel

# The Pearl

LA MOLENDERA, 1924
*Diego Rivera*
*Museo de Arte Moderno*

## Humanities Note

Fine art, *La Molendera,* by Diego Rivera. Rivera (1886–1951), a Mexican artist, studied art in Paris. Uncomfortable with the radical movements in the Parisian art world, Rivera returned to his native land. After an extended tour of his country, he took steps to bring art embodying the spirit of the Revolution to the Mexican people. He is celebrated today for the murals he created worldwide that have become monuments to both the Mexican people and to workers.

*La Molendera* means The Grinder. It is a decorative painting of a woman making tortillas. This plain, sturdy woman, absorbed in the act of preparing this humble bread, becomes almost godlike in her simplicity. She is typical of the earthy folk images that populate Rivera's art. He paints them in a stylized fashion that harks back to the art of the Aztec and Mayan civilizations. Diego Rivera's art was a dynamic force that created a distinctly Mexican style in painting.

**Alternative Assessment** *Portfolio Assignment:* To enable you and your students to assess their learning, ask them to create a portfolio of their written responses to *The Pearl.* They may select the best written responses from among the following assignments:

    Reader's response journal

    Thinking and Writing assignments (pages 715 and 743 in the student textbook)

    Selection Tests (pages 1001 and 1017 in the Teaching Portfolio)

    Your Writing Process assignment page 744 or 746 in the student textbook

    Persona story (page 1014) and either of the Alternate Composition Assignments (pages 990 and 1004) in the Teaching Portfolio

    One of the Unit Projects (page 1024 in the Teaching Portfolio)

    Have your students write a protocol for their portfolios in which they explain the reasons for their selections and the learning that is reflected.

## Preparation

**More about the Author** John Steinbeck was born in California. His knowledge of the Salinas River Valley farms and people was gained firsthand and provides the setting for many of his stories. He often used his books to point out injustice in society and to voice his concern for the oppressed. Elicit from students why Steinbeck was sympathetic to the oppressed and distressed.

**Literary Focus** Being attentive to characterization is critical in *The Pearl*. The characters in this novel are allegorical; that is, they are symbolic representations of humanity. As the reader observes the words and actions of the characters, sees their thoughts and secret hopes, and watches their interactions with nature, an image emerges of Steinbeck's view of humankind.

**Prereading Focus** Ask students to consider other stories they know that illustrate some unexpected disadvantages to sudden wealth or good fortune. Having the students compare the experiences of the characters in these stories with their own experiences may stimulate ideas for their lists of advantages and disadvantages.

◆ **Software** If students have access to computers, they can use the **Writer's Helper** activity *Questioner* to evaluate potential advantages and disadvantages under consideration for their lists.

**Vocabulary** Have your **less advanced** students read the words and their definitions. Have them participate in a discussion that allows them to use the words and demonstrate understanding of their meanings.

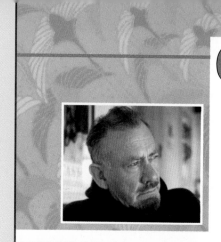

### John Steinbeck

(1902–1968) grew up in the Salinas Valley of California. As an accomplished writer, he has novels, short stories, and newspaper articles to his credit. After college he spent five years drifting and writing; he even joined a hobo camp to study the lives of its people. Steinbeck's fiction, such as his Pulitzer Prize-winning novel *The Grapes of Wrath*, shows sympathy for underprivileged people who are exploited by society. In *The Pearl* he depicts the tragic plight of socially oppressed people.

# GUIDE FOR READING

## The Pearl, Chapters 1–3

### Characters in a Parable

A **parable** is a short tale that illustrates a universal truth, a belief that appeals to all people of all civilizations. Characters in a parable are seldom complex and three-dimensional; instead, they tend to be flat, representing qualities rather than real-life people. In a parable the characters, their experiences, and the lessons they learn are meant to parallel human experience.

### Focus

*The Pearl* is the story of Kino and Juana, a poor fisherman and his wife, who find a huge pearl worth a lot of money. With your classmates, brainstorm to list the advantages and disadvantages of suddenly coming into possession of something that is very valuable in material terms. Fill in a chart like the one that follows with your ideas. As you read the first three chapters of *The Pearl*, compare your ideas to the experiences of Kino and Juana.

| Material Wealth | |
|---|---|
| Advantages | Disadvantages |
| | |

### Vocabulary

Knowing the following words will help you as you read the first three chapters of *The Pearl*.

**feinted** (fānt′ id) *v.*: Made a pretense of attack (p. 697)

**scorpion** (skôr′ pē ən) *n.*: Any of a group of poisonous arachnids found in warm regions (p. 697)

**plaintively** (plān′ tiv lē) *adv.*: Sorrowfully; mournfully (p. 697)

**undulating** (un′ dyo͞o lāt iŋ) *adj.*: Wavy in form (p. 704)

**semblance** (sem′ bləns) *n.*: Deceptive appearance (p. 706)

**avarice** (av′ ər is) *n.*: Greediness (p. 700)

**alms** (ämz) *n.*: Money given to poor people (p. 700)

**indigent** (in′ di jənt) *adj.*: Needy; poor (p. 700)

**bulwark** (bo͞ol′ wərk) *n.*: Protection; defense (p. 703)

**dissembling** (di sem′ bliŋ) *v.*: Concealing true feelings with a false appearance (p. 711)

---

## Objectives

1 To understand characterization when reading a novel
2 To write from Juana's point of view
3 To express individual interests and abilities through optional activities

## Support Material

### Teaching Portfolio

Teacher Backup, p. 989
Grammar in Action Worksheets, *Using Dashes*, pp. 993, *Understanding Intensive and Reflexive Pronouns*, pp. 995–996
Usage and Mechanics Worksheet, p. 997
Vocabulary Check, p. 998

Analyzing Literature Worksheet, *Understanding Characterization and Point of View*, p. 999
Language Worksheet, *Appreciating Words From Spanish*, p. 1000
Selection Test, p. 1001

**Library of Video Classics**
*The Pearl*

**Prentice Hall Literature Writing Studio**

# The Pearl

## John Steinbeck

1 "In the town they tell the story of the great pearl—how it was found and how it was lost again. They tell of Kino, the fisherman, and of his wife, Juana, and of the baby, Coyotito. And because the story has been told so often, it has taken root in every man's mind. And, as with all retold tales that are in people's hearts, there are only good and bad things and black and white things and good and evil things and no in-between anywhere.

"If this story is a parable, perhaps everyone takes his own meaning from it and reads his own life into it. In any case, they say in the town that . . ."

### Chapter 1

2 Kino awakened in the near dark. The stars still shone and the day had drawn only a pale wash of light in the lower sky to the east. The roosters had been crowing for some time, and the early pigs were already beginning their ceaseless turning of twigs and bits of wood to see whether anything to eat had been overlooked. Outside the brush house in the tuna[1] clump, a covey of little birds chittered and flurried with their wings.

Kino's eyes opened, and he looked first at the lightening square which was the door and then he looked at the hanging box where Coyotito slept. And last he turned his head to Juana, his wife, who lay beside him on the mat, her blue head shawl over her nose and over her breasts and around the small of her back. Juana's eyes were open too. Kino could never remember seeing them closed when he awakened. Her dark eyes made little reflected stars. She was looking at him as she was always looking at him when he awakened.

3 Kino heard the little splash of morning waves on the beach. It was very good—Kino closed his eyes again to listen to his music. Perhaps he alone did this and perhaps all of his people did it. His people had once been great makers of songs so that everything they saw or thought or did or heard became a song. That was very long ago. The songs remained; Kino knew them, but no new songs were added. That does not mean that there were no personal songs. In Kino's head there was a song now, clear and soft, and if he had been able to speak of it, he would have called it the Song of the Family.

His blanket was over his nose to protect him from the dank air. His eyes flicked to a rustle beside him. It was Juana arising, almost soundlessly. On her hard bare feet she went to the hanging box where Coyotito slept, and she leaned over and said a little reassuring word. Coyotito looked up for a moment and closed his eyes and slept again.

Juana went to the fire pit and uncovered a coal and fanned it alive while she broke little pieces of brush over it.

---

1. **tuna** (tōō′ nə) *adj.*: Prickly-pear cactus.

*The Pearl* 695

**Presentation**

**Motivation/Prior Knowledge**
For Kino the pearl represents prosperity, status, and the chance to fulfill previously impossible dreams. Lead a discussion about contemporary equivalents of the pearl—success in the stock market, inheriting great wealth, winning the lottery. Ask students what dreams these events would allow them to fulfill. What obstacles might they encounter?

**Purpose-Setting Question**
Throughout the novel Steinbeck creates sympathy for the plight of Kino. How does Steinbeck create this sympathy? What does the reader find out about Kino in the first three chapters?

1 **Enrichment** You might want to tell students that parables present stories that teach religious truths, moral lessons, or general truths by using realistic events. What are examples of other parables? Have students discuss some possible themes in parables—harmony with nature, love and family, material possessions and greed.

2 **Discussion** In this paragraph Steinbeck has Kino awaken to the sounds of animals. Through this initial description, a mood or climate is conveyed. What is the atmosphere that his description suggests?

3 **Discussion** Theme, mood, and harmony with the world are suggested by these ancient songs. When Kino is in harmony with his world, the song is melodic. What does the reader learn about Kino in this paragraph?

**Alternative Assessment** To promote active reading, have students create reader's response journals as they read Chapters 1–3 of *The Pearl*. Ask them to focus their observations on the details that reveal the poverty of Kino and Juana's life as well as those that reveal the attitude of the doctor toward the poor. Have them also note the effect on Kino and Juana of finding a great pearl.

Encourage the students to respond personally to the characters and events in the story and especially to the doctor's refusal to treat the baby until the doctor learns of Kino's good fortune in finding a giant pearl. Ask them to react to Juana's warning that the pearl "will destroy us all."

**Thematic Focus** Ask students to think about a time when they felt out of place. Why did they feel that way? What physical, societal, educational, economic, or political factors might cause people to feel out of place? How do people try to overcome these factors? As they read, students should ask themselves what circumstances give Kino a positive feeling of place and what circumstances make him feel out of place.

## Humanities Note

Fine art, *Peasant With Sombrero,* 1926, by Diego Rivera (1886–1957). Rivera trained in Mexico City. He was influenced by, among others, Cézanne, Gauguin, and Picasso. Rivera, a famous mural painter, was also a political activist. The subject matter of his murals was often the oppression suffered by Native Mexicans.

The man portrayed in this reproduction could represent the character Kino. Have students notice the positioning of the sombrero and the man's expression. Does the man appear to be at ease and looking forward to the task at hand? What might the man's eyes and the lines and shadows in the man's face reveal about his character? Has he had an easy life? As they read, have students identify points in the story when Kino most resembles the man in the painting.

**4 Clarification** Steinbeck often lived and worked with the people of a specific locale. Doing this helped him gain a better understanding to develop the characters and settings for his novels. For example, he traveled with migrants from Oklahoma to California in preparation for his novel *The Grapes of Wrath,* and he lived and worked in the Gulf of California among the Indians prior to his writing *The Pearl.*

**5 Literary Focus: Character** What is Kino feeling? How does the reader know?

**PEASANT WITH SOMBRERO (PEON), 1926**
*Diego Rivera*
Galería Arvil, Mexico City

Now Kino got up and wrapped his blanket about his head and nose and shoulders. He slipped his feet into his sandals and went outside to watch the dawn.

Outside the door he squatted down and gathered the blanket ends about his knees. **4** He saw the specks of Gulf[2] clouds flame high in the air. And a goat came near and sniffed at him and stared with its cold yellow eyes. Behind him Juana's fire leaped into flame and threw spears of light through the chinks of the brush-house wall and threw a wavering square of light out the door. A late moth blustered in to find the fire. The Song of the Family came now from behind Kino. **5** And the rhythm of the family song was the grinding stone where Juana worked the corn for the morning cakes.

The dawn came quickly now, a wash, a glow, a lightness, and then an explosion of fire as the sun arose out of the Gulf. Kino looked down to cover his eyes from the glare. He could hear the pat of the corncakes in the house and the rich smell of them on the

---

**2. Gulf:** The Gulf of California, a body of water between Baja California—a Mexican peninsula—and the main part of Mexico.

696    *The Novel*

**Master Teacher Note** The story *The Pearl* was a result of Steinbeck's ecological explorations in the Sea of Cortez. While there he was told a legend of an Indian boy who found a pearl of great size and who was imprisoned by it until he could finally rid himself of it. *The Pearl,* as it is known today, was first published in 1945 in the *Woman's Home Companion* under the title "The Pearl of the World." Prior to publication the novel was referred to as "The Pearl of La Paz" and "The Pearl of Peace." Have students consider the novel's titles as they read and have them analyze the pearl's meaning.

**Making Connections** Students might enjoy reading *Shark Beneath the Reef* in the **Prentice Hall Literature Multicultural Library.** This is a novel about Tomás, a contemporary Mexican boy, whose life and future are intricately connected with the ocean.

cooking plate. The ants were busy on the ground, big black ones with shiny bodies, and little dusty quick ants. Kino watched with the detachment of God while a dusty ant frantically tried to escape the sand trap an ant lion had dug for him. A thin, timid dog came close and, at a soft word from Kino, curled up, arranged its tail neatly over its feet, and laid its chin delicately on the pile. It was a black dog with yellow-gold spots where its eyebrows should have been.

It was a morning like other mornings and yet perfect among mornings.

Kino heard the creak of the rope when Juana took Coyotito out of his hanging box and cleaned him and hammocked him in her shawl in a loop that placed him close to her breast. Kino could see these things without looking at them. Juana sang softly an ancient song that had only three notes and yet endless variety of interval. And this was part of the family song too. It was all part. Sometimes it rose to an aching chord that caught the throat, saying this is safety, this is warmth, this is the *Whole*.

Across the brush fence were other brush houses, and the smoke came from them too, and the sound of breakfast, but those were other songs, their pigs were other pigs, their wives were not Juana. Kino was young and strong and his black hair hung over his brown forehead. His eyes were warm and fierce and bright and his mustache was thin and coarse. He lowered his blanket from his nose now, for the dark poisonous air was gone and the yellow sunlight fell on the house. Near the brush fence two roosters bowed and feinted at each other with squared wings and neck feathers ruffed out. It would be a clumsy fight. They were not game chickens. Kino watched them for a moment, and then his eyes went up to a flight of wild doves twinkling inland to the hills. The world was awake now, and Kino arose and went into his brush house.

As he came through the door Juana stood up from the glowing fire pit. She put Coyotito back in his hanging box and then she combed her black hair and braided it in two braids and tied the ends with thin green ribbon. Kino squatted by the fire pit and rolled a hot corncake and dipped it in sauce and ate it. And he drank a little pulque[3] and that was breakfast. That was the only breakfast he had ever known outside of feast days and one incredible fiesta on cookies that had nearly killed him. When Kino had finished, Juana came back to the fire and ate her breakfast. They had spoken once, but there is not need for speech if it is only a habit anyway. Kino sighed with satisfaction —and that was conversation.

The sun was warming the brush house, breaking through its crevices in long streaks. And one of the streaks fell on the hanging box where Coyotito lay, and on the ropes that held it.

It was a tiny movement that drew their eyes to the hanging box. Kino and Juana froze in their positions. Down the rope that hung the baby's box from the roof support a scorpion moved slowly. His stinging tail was straight out behind him, but he could whip it up in a flash of time.

Kino's breath whistled in his nostrils and he opened his mouth to stop it. And then the startled look was gone from him and the rigidity from his body. In his mind a new song had come, the Song of Evil, the music of the enemy, of any foe of the family, a savage, secret, dangerous melody, and underneath, the Song of the Family cried plaintively.

The scorpion moved delicately down the rope toward the box. Under her breath Juana repeated an ancient magic to guard against such evil, and on top of that she

---

3. **pulque** (pool' kǎ) *n*.: A milky drink made from the juice of the agave, a family of Mexican desert plant.

*The Pearl* 697

**11 Critical Thinking and Reading** Comment on the behaviors of both Juana and Kino regarding the bite of the scorpion. What important differences does the reader see in these characters?

**12 Literary Focus: Character** Based on what the reader already knows about Juana, why is it surprising that she is requesting a doctor?

**13 Discussion** Juana's demand that Coyotito be seen by a doctor elicits a strong reaction from neighbors and people of the village. Discuss what the village people have said, and speculate on its importance.

muttered a Hail Mary[4] between clenched teeth. But Kino was in motion. His body glided quietly across the room, noiselessly and smoothly. His hands were in front of him, palms down, and his eyes were on the scorpion. Beneath it in the hanging box Coyotito laughed and reached up his hand toward it. It sensed danger when Kino was almost within reach of it. It stopped, and its tail rose up over its back in little jerks and the curved thorn on the tail's end glistened.

Kino stood perfectly still. He could hear Juana whispering the old magic again, and he could hear the evil music of the enemy. He could not move until the scorpion moved, and it felt for the source of the death that was coming to it. Kino's hand went forward very slowly, very smoothly. The thorned tail jerked upright. And at that moment the laughing Coyotito shook the rope and the scorpion fell.

Kino's hand leaped to catch it, but it fell past his fingers, fell on the baby's shoulder, landed and struck. Then, snarling, Kino had it, had it in his fingers, rubbing it to a paste in his hands. He threw it down and beat it into the earth floor with his fist, and Coyotito screamed with pain in his box. But Kino beat and stamped the enemy until it was only a fragment and a moist place in the dirt. His teeth were bared and fury flared in his eyes and the Song of the Enemy roared in his ears.

But Juana had the baby in her arms now. She found the puncture with redness starting from it already. She put her lips down over the puncture and sucked hard and spat and sucked again while Coyotito screamed.

Kino hovered; he was helpless, he was in the way.

The screams of the baby brought the neighbors. Out of their brush houses they poured—Kino's brother Juan Tomás and his fat wife Apolonia and their four children crowded in the door and blocked the entrance, while behind them others tried to look in, and one small boy crawled among legs to have a look. And those in front passed the word back to those behind —"Scorpion. The baby has been stung."

Juana stopped sucking the puncture for a moment. The little hole was slightly enlarged and its edges whitened from the sucking, but the red swelling extended farther around it in a hard lymphatic[5] mound. And all of these people knew about the scorpion. An adult might be very ill from the sting, but a baby could easily die from the poison. First, they knew, would come swelling and fever and tightened throat, and then cramps in the stomach, and then Coyotito might die if enough of the poison had gone in. But the stinging pain of the bite was going away. Coyotito's screams turned to moans.

Kino had wondered often at the iron in his patient, fragile wife. She, who was obedient and respectful and cheerful and patient, she could arch her back in child pain with hardly a cry. She could stand fatigue and hunger almost better than Kino himself. In the canoe she was like a strong man. And now she did a most surprising thing.

"The doctor," she said. "Go to get the doctor."

The word was passed out among the neighbors where they stood close packed in the little yard behind the brush fence. And they repeated among themselves, "Juana wants the doctor." A wonderful thing, a memorable thing, to want the doctor. To get

---

**4. Hail Mary:** A prayer to the Virgin Mary, the mother of Jesus, used in the Roman Catholic Church.

**5. lymphatic** (lim fat′ ik) *adj.*: Containing the clear liquid of inflamed body tissues.

## Primary Source

Steinbeck recorded a sketch of the germ-anecdote out of which he constructed *The Pearl* in *The Sea of Cortez* (1941):

An event which happened at La Paz in recent years is typical of such places. An Indian boy by accident found a pearl of great size, an unbelievable pearl. He knew its value was so great that he need never work again. In his one pearl he had the ability to be drunk as long as he wished, to marry any one of a number of girls, and to make

many more a little happy too. In his great pearl lay salvation, for he could in advance purchase Masses sufficient to pop him out of Purgatory like a squeezed watermelon seed. In addition he could shift a number of dead relatives a little nearer Paradise. He went to La Paz with his pearl in his hand and his future clear into eternity in his heart. He took his pearl to a broker and was offered so little that he grew angry, for he knew he was cheated. Then he carried his pearl to another broker and was offered the same amount. After a few more visits he came to know that he could not sell his pearl for more. He took it to the beach and hid it under a stone, and that night he was clubbed into

**DELFINA AND DIMAS**
*Diego Rivera*
*Private Collection*

**Humanities Note**

Fine art, *Delfina and Dimas,* Diego Rivera. The woman in this painting could represent Juana, her baby, and perhaps the special relationship between mother and child. Ask students how this painting represents that relationship. What is the role of the mother? What is the need of the child?

Point out to students that the mother's arms form a circle. Ask students to consider where circles begin and end, and to discuss their symbolic meaning. What do circles symbolize?

The following questions may generate further discussion:
1. What elements in this painting convey the simplicity of a lifestyle like Juana and Kino's?
2. What can you infer from this painting about the relationship between this mother and her child? What details from the story suggest that Juana has a similar relationship with Coyotito?
3. Do you think this painting relates most closely to the events before the scorpion bite or the events after? Why do you think as you do?

**14 Literary Focus: Character** Objects function symbolically to reveal themes and characters. Juana's shawl is her badge of womanliness and maternity. Have students note its use here and throughout the novel.

him would be a remarkable thing. The doctor never came to the cluster of brush houses. Why should he, when he had more than he could do to take care of the rich people who lived in the stone and plaster houses of the town.

"He would not come," the people in the yard said.

"He would not come," the people in the door said, and the thought got into Kino.

"The doctor would not come," Kino said to Juana.

She looked up at him, her eyes as cold as the eyes of a lioness. This was Juana's first baby—this was nearly everything there was in Juana's world. And Kino saw her determination and the music of the family sounded in his head with a steely tone.

"Then we will go to him," Juana said, and with one hand she arranged her dark blue shawl over her head and made of one end of it a sling to hold the moaning baby and made of the other end of it a shade over his eyes to protect him from the light. The people in the door pushed against those behind to let her through. Kino followed her. They went out of the gate to the rutted path and the neighbors followed them.

*The Pearl* 699

unconsciousness and his clothing was searched. The next night he slept at the house of a friend and his friend and he were injured and bound and the whole house searched. Then he went inland to lose his pursuers and he was waylaid and tortured. But he was very angry now and he knew what he must do. Hurt as he was he crept back to La Paz in the night and he skulked like a hunted fox to the beach and took out his pearl from under the stone. Then he cursed it and threw it as far as he could into the channel. He was a free man again with his soul in danger and his food and shelter insecure. And he laughed a great deal about it.

**Discussion** Throughout the story Steinbeck provides many examples of the old and new residing side by side yet never blending. Note Steinbeck's contrast of the lives of the rich and the poor.

**16 Discussion** Explain Steinbeck's reference to beggars as "experts in financial analysis."

**17 Literary Focus: Character** The reader is introduced to the doctor through the eyes of four beggars. Why does Steinbeck refer to the beggars as "these endless searchers after perfect knowledge of their fellow men"? What are the first impressions given of the doctor?

**18 Discussion** What is the significance of Kino taking his hat off in such an instance?

The thing had become a neighborhood affair. They made a quick soft-footed procession into the center of the town, first Juana and Kino, and behind them Juan Tomás and Apolonia, her big stomach jiggling with the strenuous pace, then all the neighbors with the children trotting on the flanks. And the yellow sun threw their black shadows ahead of them so that they walked on their own shadows.

**15** They came to the place where the brush houses stopped and the city of stone and plaster began, the city of harsh outer walls and inner cool gardens where a little water played and the bougainvillaea[6] crusted the walls with purple and brick-red and white. They heard from the secret gardens the singing of caged birds and heard the splash of cooling water on hot flagstones. The procession crossed the blinding plaza and passed in front of the church. It had grown now, and on the outskirts the hurrying newcomers were being softly informed how the baby had been stung by a scorpion, how the father and mother were taking it to the doctor.

**16** And the newcomers, particularly the beggars from the front of the church who were great experts in financial analysis, looked quickly at Juana's old blue skirt, saw the tears in her shawl, appraised the green ribbon on her braids, read the age of Kino's blanket and the thousand washings of his clothes, and set them down as poverty people and went along to see what kind of drama might develop. The four beggars in front of the church knew everything in the town. They were students of the expressions **17** of young women as they went in to confession, and they saw them as they came out and read the nature of the sin. They knew every little scandal and some very big

crimes. They slept at their posts in the shadow of the church so that no one crept in for consolation without their knowledge. And they knew the doctor. They knew his ignorance, his cruelty, his avarice, his appetites, his sins. They knew his clumsy operations and the little brown pennies he gave sparingly for alms. They had seen his corpses go into the church. And, since early Mass was over and business was slow, they followed the procession, these endless searchers after perfect knowledge of their fellow men, to see what the fat lazy doctor would do about an indigent baby with a scorpion bite.

The scurrying procession came at last to the big gate in the wall of the doctor's house. They could hear the splashing water and the singing of caged birds and the sweep of the long brooms on the flagstones. And they could smell the frying of good bacon from the doctor's house.

Kino hesitated a moment. This doctor was not of his people. This doctor was of a race which for nearly four hundred years had beaten and starved and robbed and despised Kino's race, and frightened it too, so that the indigene[7] came humbly to the door. And as always when he came near to one of this race, Kino felt weak and afraid and angry at the same time. Rage and terror went together. He could kill the doctor more easily than he could talk to him, for all of the doctor's race spoke to all of Kino's race as though they were simple animals. And as Kino raised his right hand to the iron ring knocker in the gate, rage swelled in him, and the pounding music of the enemy beat in his ears, and his lips drew tight against his teeth—but with his left hand he reached to take off his hat. The iron ring pounded against the gate. Kino took off his hat and stood waiting. Coyotito moaned a **18**

---

**6. bougainvillaea** (boo′ gən vil′ ē ə) n.: A tropical vine with large, colorful flowers.

---

**7. indigene** (in′ di jēn′) n.: A native.

## Grammar in Action

**Dashes** are used to set off explanations, summaries, or interruptions within a clause. They may also be used to set off appositives and modifiers that are lengthy, already punctuated, or dramatic. Look at Steinbeck's use of dashes:

Summary: They tell the story of the great pearl—how it was found and how it was lost again. (page 695)

Interruption: It was very good—Kino closed his eyes again to listen to his music. (page 695)

Explanation: Kino sighed with satisfaction —and that was conversation. (page 697)

Appositive: And those in front passed the word back to those behind—"Scorpion." (page 698)

**Student Activity 1.** On the above pages locate the sentences containing dashes. Why did Steinbeck use a dash in each case?

**Student Activity 2.** Insert dashes where needed in the following sentences:

little in Juana's arms, and she spoke softly to him. The procession crowded close the better to see and hear.

After a moment the big gate opened a few inches. Kino could see the green coolness of the garden and little splashing fountain through the opening. The man who looked out at him was one of his own race. Kino spoke to him in the old language. "The little one—the firstborn—has been poisoned by the scorpion," Kino said. "He requires the skill of the healer."

The gate closed a little, and the servant refused to speak in the old language. "A little moment," he said. "I go to inform myself," and he closed the gate and slid the bolt home. The glaring sun threw the bunched shadows of the people blackly on the white wall.

In his chamber the doctor sat up in his high bed. He had on his dressing gown of red watered silk that had come from Paris, a little tight over the chest now if it was buttoned. On his lap was a silver tray with a silver chocolate pot and a tiny cup of eggshell china, so delicate that it looked silly when he lifted it with his big hand, lifted it with the tips of thumb and forefinger and spread the other three fingers wide to get them out of the way. His eyes rested in puffy little hammocks of flesh and his mouth drooped with discontent. He was growing very stout, and his voice was hoarse with the fat that pressed on his throat. Beside him on a table was a small Oriental gong and a bowl of cigarettes. The furnishings of the room were heavy and dark and gloomy. The pictures were religious, even the large tinted photograph of his dead wife, who, if Masses willed and paid for out of her own estate could do it, was in Heaven. The doctor had once for a short time been a part of the great world and his whole subsequent life was memory and longing for France. "That," he said, "was civilized living"—by which he meant that on a small income he had been able to keep a mistress and eat in restaurants. He poured his second cup of chocolate and crumbled a sweet biscuit in his fingers. The servant from the gate came to the open door and stood waiting to be noticed.

"Yes?" the doctor asked.

"It is a little Indian with a baby. He says a scorpion stung it."

The doctor put his cup down gently before he let his anger rise.

"Have I nothing better to do than cure insect bites for 'little Indians'? I am a doctor, not a veterinary."

"Yes, *Patron*,"[8] said the servant.

"Has he any money?" the doctor demanded. "No, they never have any money. I, I alone in the world am supposed to work for nothing—and I am tired of it. See if he has any money!"

At the gate the servant opened the door a trifle and looked out at the waiting people. And this time he spoke in the old language.

"Have you money to pay for the treatment?"

Now Kino reached into a secret place somewhere under his blanket. He brought out a paper folded many times. Crease by crease he unfolded it, until at last there came to view eight small misshapen seed pearls,[9] as ugly and gray as little ulcers, flattened and almost valueless. The servant took the paper and closed the gate again, but this time he was not gone long. He opened the gate just wide enough to pass the paper back.

"The doctor has gone out," he said. "He was called to a serious case." And he shut the gate quickly out of shame.

And now a wave of shame went over the whole procession. They melted away. The

---

**8. Patron** (pä trōn'): Spanish for "master."
**9. seed pearls:** Very small pearls, often imperfect.

*The Pearl* 701

**19 Critical Thinking and Reading** Contrast the differences in the descriptions given of the doctor's house and Kino's house.

**20 Literary Focus: Character** What do these events tell the reader about the character of the doctor?

**Electronic Handbook** Before students complete the Grammar in Action activities, you may wish to review the use of dashes to make sentence fragments parts of complete sentences. If students are using the Language Master 6000, have them enter the access word *fragment* and press the GRAMMAR key to review information on sentence fragments.

1. Out of their brush houses they poured Kino's brother, his fat wife, and their four children crowded in the door and blocked the entrance.
2. Kino heard music in his head the Song of the Family, the Song of Evil, the Song of the Enemy.
3. Coyotito was Juana's first baby this was nearly everything there was in Juana's world.
4. The songs were all in Kino and in his people every song that had ever been made, even the ones forgotten.
5. A vision hung in the air to the north of the city the vision of a mountain that was over two hundred miles away.
6. . . . there were not many buyers really there was only one, and he kept these agents in separate offices to keep a semblance of competition.
7. All manner of people grew interested in Kino people with things to sell and people with favors to ask.
8. It was in the pearl the picture glowing there.

**21 Clarification** Steinbeck uses the neighbors and village people in a way similar to that of the Chorus in Greek drama. The Chorus informed the audience of how common people viewed an event. They frequently gave a foreshadowing of what was about to happen. Have students share what the procession might tell the reader in this passage.

**22 Critical Thinking and Reading** In this incident Kino strikes a crushing blow with his fist. In a previous incident, Kino crushes the scorpion with his hand in a similar style. What does this tell us about Kino and his patterns of behavior? Contrast the reactions and temperament of Juana in dealing with similar frustrations.

**23 Master Teacher Note** Steinbeck uses animals in the story in a variety of ways. In this paragraph Steinbeck describes how creatures of the sea live together and yet strive for their own survival. Have students note Steinbeck's use of animals as symbols. Have them suggest what is implied in the description of the hungry dogs and pigs.

**24 Discussion** Steinbeck's description of the Gulf has meaning for the way in which the story is developing. What do you think is meant by "There was no certainty in seeing, no proof that what you saw was there or was not there"?

**25 Discussion** The canoe is meant as a symbol. What does it represent?

**21** beggars went back to the church steps, the stragglers moved off, and the neighbors departed so that the public shaming of Kino would not be in their eyes.

**22** For a long time Kino stood in front of the gate with Juana beside him. Slowly he put his suppliant hat on his head. Then, without warning, he struck the gate a crushing blow with his fist. He looked down in wonder at his split knuckles and at the blood that flowed down between his fingers.

## Chapter 2

The town lay on a broad estuary,[1] its old yellow plastered buildings hugging the beach. And on the beach the white and blue canoes that came from Nayarit[2] were drawn up, canoes preserved for generations by a hard shell-like waterproof plaster whose making was a secret of the fishing people. They were high and graceful canoes with curving bow and stern and a braced section midships where a mast could be stepped to carry a small lateen sail.[3]

**23** The beach was yellow sand, but at the water's edge a rubble of shell and algae took its place. Fiddler crabs bubbled and sputtered in their holes in the sand, and in the shallows little lobsters popped in and out of their tiny homes in the rubble and sand. The sea bottom was rich with crawling and swimming and growing things. The brown algae waved in the gentle currents and the green eel grass swayed and little sea horses clung to its stems. Spotted botete, the poison fish, lay on the bottom in the eel-grass

---

1. **estuary** (es′ chōō er′ ē) *n*.: An inlet formed where a river enters the ocean.
2. **Nayarit** (nä′ yä rēt′): A state of western Mexico across the Gulf of California from Baja California.
3. **stepped . . . lateen** (la tēn′) **sail:** Raised and fixed in place to carry a triangular sail attached to a long rod.

beds, and the bright-colored swimming crabs scampered over them.

On the beach the hungry dogs and the hungry pigs of the town searched endlessly for any dead fish or sea bird that might have floated in on a rising tide.

**24** Although the morning was young, the hazy mirage was up. The uncertain air that magnified some things and blotted out others hung over the whole Gulf so that all sights were unreal and vision could not be trusted; so that sea and land had the sharp clarities and the vagueness of a dream. Thus it might be that the people of the Gulf trust things of the spirit and things of the imagination, but they do not trust their eyes to show them distance or clear outline or any optical exactness. Across the estuary from the town one section of mangroves stood clear and telescopically defined, while another mangrove clump was a hazy black-green blob. Part of the far shore disappeared into a shimmer that looked like water. There was no certainty in seeing, no proof that what you saw was there or was not there. And the people of the Gulf expected all places were that way, and it was not strange to them. A copper haze hung over the water, and the hot morning sun beat on it and made it vibrate blindingly.

The brush houses of the fishing people were back from the beach on the right-hand side of the town, and the canoes were drawn up in front of this area.

**25** Kino and Juana came slowly down to the beach and to Kino's canoe, which was the one thing of value he owned in the world. It was very old. Kino's grandfather had brought it from Nayarit, and he had given it to Kino's father, and so it had come to Kino. It was at once property and source of food, for a man with a boat can guarantee a woman that she will eat something. It is the bulwark against starvation. And every year Kino refinished his canoe with the hard shell-like plaster by the secret method that had also come to him from his father. Now he came to the canoe and touched the bow tenderly as he always did. He laid his diving rock and his basket and the two ropes in the sand by the canoe. And he folded his blanket and laid it in the bow.

Juana laid Coyotito on the blanket, and she placed her shawl over him so that the hot sun could not shine on him. He was quiet now, but the swelling on his shoulder had continued up his neck and under his ear and his face was puffed and feverish. Juana went to the water and waded in. She gathered some brown seaweed and made a flat damp poultice[4] of it, and this she applied to the baby's swollen shoulder, which was as good a remedy as any and probably better than the doctor could have done. But the remedy lacked his authority because it was simple and didn't cost anything. The stomach cramps had not come to Coyotito. Perhaps Juana had sucked out the poison in time, but she had not sucked out her worry over her firstborn. She had not prayed directly for the recovery of the baby—she had prayed that they might find a pearl with which to hire the doctor to cure the baby, for the minds of people are as unsubstantial as the mirage of the Gulf.

Now Kino and Juana slid the canoe down the beach to the water, and when the bow floated, Juana climbed in, while Kino pushed the stern in and waded beside it until it floated lightly and trembled on the little breaking waves. Then in coordination Juana and Kino drove their double-bladed paddles into the sea, and the canoe creased

---

**4. poultice** (pōl′ tis) *n.*: An absorbent mass applied to a sore or inflamed part of the body.

the water and hissed with speed. The other pearlers were gone out long since. In a few moments Kino could see them clustered in the haze, riding over the oyster bed.

Light filtered down through the water to the bed where the frilly pearl oysters lay fastened to the rubbly bottom, a bottom strewn with shells of broken, opened oysters. This was the bed that had raised the King of Spain to be a great power in Europe in past years, had helped to pay for his wars, and had decorated the churches for his soul's sake. The gray oysters with ruffles like skirts on the shells, the barnacle-crusted oysters with little bits of weed clinging to the skirts and small crabs climbing over them. An accident could happen to these oysters, a grain of sand could lie in the folds of muscle and irritate the flesh until in self-protection the flesh coated the grain with a layer of smooth cement. But once started, the flesh continued to coat the foreign body until it fell free in some tidal flurry or until the oyster was destroyed. For centuries men had dived down and torn the oysters from the beds and ripped them open, looking for the coated grains of sand. Swarms of fish lived near the bed to live near the oysters thrown back by the searching men and to nibble at the shining inner shells. But the pearls were accidents, and the finding of one was luck, a little pat on the back by God or the gods or both.

Kino had two ropes, one tied to a heavy stone and one to a basket. He stripped off his shirt and trousers and laid his hat in the bottom of the canoe. The water was oily smooth. He took his rock in one hand and his basket in the other, and he slipped feet first over the side and the rock carried him to the bottom. The bubbles rose behind him until the water cleared and he could see. Above, the surface of the water was an

---

**26 Critical Thinking and Reading** Steinbeck shows Juana's resourcefulness in applying primitive medicine. Have students compare this with the previous references to Kino and Juana's belief that only the doctor could cure their child.

**27 Enrichment** The pearl, the central image of the novel, is described as an accident of nature. Finding one is lucky or like ''a little pat on the back . . . by the gods.'' Some critics feel that this novel is making a statement about the need to leave nature as undisturbed as possible in order to preserve the balance of nature. Ask students what they think of this viewpoint. Do they agree or disagree? Ask them to consider their response as they continue to read. Have students consider the same question when they have completed reading *The Pearl*.

**28** **Literary Focus: Character** What can you infer about Kino and his people based on the songs that are described in this paragraph?

**29** **Enrichment** Kino and Juana are superstitious. Have students discuss present-day superstitions, for example, walking under a ladder and a black cat crossing one's path.

**Multicultural Focus** Point out to students that an unblemished pearl was an ancient symbol of perfection. Since 1500 B.C., Asian cultures have been collecting pearls and using them in jewelry and art.

Today pearls are collected all over the world—Asia, Africa, North America, South America, and Europe. Although many pearl beds lie in shallow water, not all do, and pearl diving is often hazardous work. Seed pearls like the ones Kino tries to use to pay the doctor are the least valuable and the most commonly found.

Currently most pearls are gathered by industry, but some people still dive for pearls in the traditional way. Have students research pearl diving and pearl cultivation in various parts of the world and present their findings to the class.

**Videocassette** When the students finish reading Chapter 2, you might show them the **Library of Video Classics** videotape *The Pearl* from the beginning to Kino's reaction to finding the pearl. Ask students to examine the way Steinbeck's novel translates to film. How does the film compensate for the lack of color? What devices are used to convey the mood and tone found in Steinbeck's descriptions? How do the characters compare and contrast with the way students envisioned them? After viewing the visual image of Kino silhouetted against the sky and Juana's reaction, stop the video and ask students to predict what will happen. Have

undulating mirror of brightness, and he could see the bottoms of the canoes sticking through it.

Kino moved cautiously so that the water would not be obscured with mud or sand. He hooked his foot in the loop on his rock and his hands worked quickly, tearing the oysters loose, some singly, others in clusters. He laid them in his basket. In some places the oysters clung to one another so that they came free in lumps.

Now, Kino's people had sung of everything that happened or existed. They had made songs to the fishes, to the sea in anger and to the sea in calm, to the light and the dark and the sun and the moon, and the songs were all in Kino and in his people —every song that had ever been made, even the ones forgotten. And as he filled his basket the song was in Kino, and the beat of the song was his pounding heart as it ate the oxygen from his held breath, and the melody of the song was the gray-green water and the little scuttling animals and the clouds of fish that flitted by and were gone. But in the song there was a secret little inner song, hardly perceptible, but always there, sweet and secret and clinging, almost hiding in the countermelody, and this was the Song of the Pearl That Might Be, for every shell thrown in the basket might contain a pearl. Chance was against it, but luck and the gods might be for it. And in the canoe above him Kino knew that Juana was making the magic of prayer, her face set rigid and her muscles hard to force the luck, to tear the luck out of the gods' hands, for she needed the luck for the swollen shoulder of Coyotito. And because the need was great and the desire was great, the little secret melody of the pearl that might be was stronger this morning. Whole phrases of it came clearly and softly into the Song of the Undersea.

Kino, in his pride and youth and

strength, could remain down over two minutes without strain, so that he worked deliberately, selecting the largest shells. Because they were disturbed, the oyster shells were tightly closed. A little to his right a hummock[5] of rubbly rock stuck up, covered with young oysters not ready to take. Kino moved next to the hummock, and then, beside it, under a little overhang, he saw a very large oyster lying by itself, not covered with its clinging brothers. The shell was partly open, for the overhang protected this ancient oyster, and in the liplike muscle Kino saw a ghostly gleam, and then the shell closed down. His heart beat out a heavy rhythm and the melody of the maybe pearl shrilled in his ears. Slowly he forced the oyster loose and held it tightly against his breast. He kicked his foot free from the rock loop, and his body rose to the surface and his black hair gleamed in the sunlight. He reached over the side of the canoe and laid the oyster in the bottom.

Then Juana steadied the boat while he climbed in. His eyes were shining with excitement, but in decency he pulled up his rock, and then he pulled up his basket of oysters and lifted them in. Juana sensed his excitement, and she pretended to look away. It is not good to want a thing too much. It sometimes drives the luck away. You must want it just enough, and you must be very tactful with God or the gods. But Juana stopped breathing. Very deliberately Kino opened his short strong knife. He looked speculatively at the basket. Perhaps it would be better to open *the* oyster last. He took a small oyster from the basket, cut the muscle, searched the folds of flesh, and threw it in the water. Then he seemed to see the great oyster for the first time. He squatted in the bottom of the canoe, picked up the shell

---

**5. hummock** (hum′ ək) *n*.: A low, rounded hill.

students identify whether their predictions are based on foreshadowing in the film, the novel, or both.

and examined it. The flutes were shining black to brown, and only a few small barnacles adhered to the shell. Now Kino was reluctant to open it. What he had seen, he knew, might be a reflection, a piece of flat shell accidentally drifted in or a complete illusion. In this Gulf of uncertain light there were more illusions than realities.

But Juana's eyes were on him and she could not wait. She put her hand on Coyotito's covered head. "Open it," she said softly.

Kino deftly slipped his knife into the edge of the shell. Through the knife he could feel the muscle tighten hard. He worked the blade leverwise and the closing muscle parted and the shell fell apart. The liplike flesh writhed up and then subsided. Kino lifted the flesh, and there it lay, the great pearl, perfect as the moon. It captured the light and refined it and gave it back in silver incandescence.[6] It was as large as a sea gull's egg. It was the greatest pearl in the world.

Juana caught her breath and moaned a little. And to Kino the secret melody of the maybe pearl broke clear and beautiful, rich and warm and lovely, glowing and gloating and triumphant. In the surface of the great pearl he could see dream forms. He picked the pearl from the dying flesh and held it in his palm, and he turned it over and saw that its curve was perfect. Juana came near to stare at it in his hand, and it was the hand he had smashed against the doctor's gate, and the torn flesh of the knuckles was turned grayish white by the sea water.

Instinctively Juana went to Coyotito where he lay on his father's blanket. She lifted the poultice of seaweed and looked at the shoulder. "Kino," she cried shrilly.

He looked past his pearl, and he saw that the swelling was going out of the baby's

6. **incandescence** (in' kan des' əns) *n.:* State of gleaming or shining brilliantly.

shoulder, the poison was receding from its body. Then Kino's fist closed over the pearl and his emotion broke over him. He put back his head and howled. His eyes rolled up and he screamed and his body was rigid. The men in the other canoes looked up, startled, and then they dug their paddles into the sea and raced toward Kino's canoe.

## Chapter 3

A town is a thing like a colonial animal. A town has a nervous system and a head and shoulders and feet. A town is a thing separate from all other towns, so that there are no two towns alike. And a town has a whole emotion. How news travels through a town is a mystery not easily to be solved. News seems to move faster than small boys can scramble and dart to tell it, faster than women can call it over the fences.

Before Kino and Juana and the other fishers had come to Kino's brush house, the nerves of the town were pulsing and vibrating with the news—Kino had found the Pearl of the World. Before panting little boys could strangle out the words, their mothers knew it. The news swept on past the brush houses, and it washed in a foaming wave into the town of stone and plaster. It came to the priest walking in his garden, and it put a thoughtful look in his eyes and a memory of certain repairs necessary to the church. He wondered what the pearl would be worth. And he wondered whether he had baptized Kino's baby, or married him for that matter. The news came to the shopkeepers, and they looked at men's clothes that had not sold so well.

The news came to the doctor where he sat with a woman whose illness was age, though neither she nor the doctor would admit it. And when it was made plain who Kino was, the doctor grew stern and

---

30 **Discussion** The description of the Gulf focuses on illusion. There are other references to illusion in this novel—the pearl fisherman dreams of the great pearl, the doctor dreams of Paris and his youth, and the priest dreams of a great church. Have students discuss Steinbeck's use of illusion. Why is it so effective?

31 **Discussion** What figures of speech does Steinbeck use to describe the pearl?

32 **Enrichment** Based on what you know about Kino, what dreams does he have for the pearl? What do these dreams represent?

33 **Discussion** What is Steinbeck conveying in his description of the pearl in Kino's beaten and bruised hand?

34 **Clarification** In this paragraph Steinbeck implies that every part of a complex structure relates to the whole. What happens in one part has an impact on all the other parts. Ask students to speculate what implications this might have for the finding of the pearl.

35 **Reading Strategy** Summarize the reactions of the priest and the doctor.

TWO MEXICAN WOMEN AND A CHILD
*Diego Rivera*
*The Fine Arts Museum of San Francisco*

judicious at the same time. "He is a client of mine," the doctor said. "I am treating his child for a scorpion sting." And the doctor's eyes rolled up a little in their fat hammocks and he thought of Paris. He remembered the room he had lived in there as a great and luxurious place, and he remembered the hard-faced woman who had lived with him as a beautiful and kind girl, although she had been none of these three. The doctor looked past his aged patient and saw himself sitting in a restaurant in Paris and a waiter was just opening a bottle of wine.

The news came early to the beggars in front of the church, and it made them giggle a little with pleasure, for they knew that 36 there is no almsgiver in the world like a poor man who is suddenly lucky.

37 Kino had found the Pearl of the World. In the town, in little offices, sat the men who bought pearls from the fishers. They waited in their chairs until the pearls came in, and then they cackled and fought and shouted and threatened until they reached the lowest price the fisherman would stand. But there was a price below which they dared not go, for it had happened that a fisherman in despair had given his pearls to the church. And when the buying was over, these buyers sat alone and their fingers played restlessly with the pearls, and they wished they owned the pearls. For there were not many buyers really—there was only one, and he kept these agents in separate offices to give a semblance of competition. The news came to these men, and their eyes squinted and their fingertips burned a little, and each one thought how the patron could not live forever and someone had to take his place. And each one thought how

706    *The Novel*

with some capital he could get a new start.

All manner of people grew interested in Kino—people with things to sell and people with favors to ask. Kino had found the Pearl of the World. The essence of pearl mixed with essence of men and a curious dark residue was precipitated.[1] Every man suddenly became related to Kino's pearl, and Kino's pearl went into the dreams, the speculations, the schemes, the plans, the futures, the wishes, the needs, the lusts, the hungers, of everyone, and only one person stood in the way and that was Kino, so that he became curiously every man's enemy. The news stirred up something infinitely black and evil in the town; the black distillate[2] was like the scorpion, or like hunger in the smell of food, or like loneliness when love is withheld. The poison sacs of the town began to manufacture venom, and the town swelled and puffed with the pressure of it.

But Kino and Juana did not know these things. Because they were happy and excited they thought everyone shared their joy. Juan Tomás and Apolonia did, and they were the world too. In the afternoon, when the sun had gone over the mountains of the Peninsula to sink in the outward sea, Kino squatted in his house with Juana beside him. And the brush house was crowded with neighbors. Kino held the great pearl in his hand, and it was warm and alive in his hand. And the music of the pearl had merged with the music of the family so that one beautified the other. The neighbors looked at the pearl in Kino's hand and they wondered how such luck could come to any man.

And Juan Tomás, who squatted on Kino's right hand because he was his brother, asked, "What will you do now that you have become a rich man?"

Kino looked into his pearl, and Juana cast her eyelashes down and arranged her shawl to cover her face so that her excitement could not be seen. And in the incandescence of the pearl the pictures formed of the things Kino's mind had considered in the past and had given up as impossible. In the pearl he saw Juana and Coyotito and himself standing and kneeling at the high altar, and they were being married now that they could pay. He spoke softly, "We will be married—in the church."

In the pearl he saw how they were dressed—Juana in a shawl stiff with newness and a new skirt, and from under the long skirt Kino could see that she wore shoes. It was in the pearl—the picture glowing there. He himself was dressed in new white clothes, and he carried a new hat—not of straw but of fine black felt—and he too wore shoes—not sandals but shoes that laced. But Coyotito—he was the one—he wore a blue sailor suit from the United States and a little yachting cap such as Kino had seen once when a pleasure boat put into the estuary. All of these things Kino saw in the lucent[3] pearl and he said, "We will have new clothes."

And the music of the pearl rose like a chorus of trumpets in his ears.

Then to the lovely gray surface of the pearl came the little things Kino wanted: a harpoon to take the place of one lost a year ago, a new harpoon of iron with a ring in the end of the shaft; and—his mind could hardly make the leap—a rifle—but why not, since he was so rich. And Kino saw Kino in the pearl, Kino holding a Winchester carbine. It was the wildest day-dreaming and very pleasant. His lips moved hesitantly

---

1. **precipitated** (prē sip′ ə tāt′ əd) *v.*: Formed abrubtly.
2. **distillate** (dis′ tə lāt′) *n.*: The essence of anything; here, the atmosphere of the town.

---

3. **lucent** (lōō′ sənt) *adj.*: Shining.

---

**38 Literary Focus: Theme** People's feelings and attitudes toward Kino are changing; he is resented because he has something they want. Have students discuss how this change in the town will affect Kino's attempts to find a place of security and comfort for himself and his family. What can students infer about Steinbeck's view of the human condition?

**39 Discussion** Ask students to consider Kino's dreams of what he will do with his wealth—being married in church, buying a rifle, and sending his son to school. What do these dreams tell us about how poor Kino and his people are? Which of the dreams do you think would be the greatest achievement for him?

◆ **Software** Kino's dreams seem to spring one from the other, growing increasingly ambitious. If students have access to computers, they can use the *Trees* activity in **Writer's Helper** to explore the pattern of Kino's daydreaming. Students might add suggestions of their own that would be consistent with Kino's character and situation.

**40** **Reading Strategy** Have students summarize Kino's dreams. What is the significance of the word *transfigured*?

**41** **Discussion** Why does Kino not recognize the priest's song of evil?

over this—"A rifle," he said. "Perhaps a rifle."

It was the rifle that broke down the barriers. This was an impossibility, and if he could think of having a rifle whole horizons were burst and he could rush on. For it is said that humans are never satisfied, that you give them one thing and they want something more. And this is said in disparagement, whereas it is one of the greatest talents the species has and one that has made it superior to animals that are satisfied with what they have.

The neighbors, close pressed and silent in the house, nodded their heads at his wild imaginings. And a man in the rear murmured, "A rifle. He will have a rifle."

But the music of the pearl was shrilling with triumph in Kino. Juana looked up, and her eyes were wide at Kino's courage and at his imagination. And electric strength had come to him now the horizons were kicked out. In the pearl he saw Coyotito sitting at a little desk in a school, just as Kino had once seen it through an open door. And Coyotito was dressed in a jacket, and he had on a white collar and a broad silken tie. Moreover, Coyotito was writing on a big piece of paper. Kino looked at his neighbors fiercely. "My son will go to school," he said, and the neighbors were hushed. Juana caught her breath sharply. Her eyes were bright as she watched him, and she looked quickly down at Coyotito in her arms to see whether this might be possible.

**40** But Kino's face shone with prophecy. "My son will read and open the books, and my son will write and will know writing. And my son will make numbers, and these things will make us free because he will know—he will know and through him we will know." And in the pearl Kino saw himself and Juana squatting by the little fire in the brush hut while Coyotito read from a

great book. "This is what the pearl will do," said Kino. And he had never said so many words together in his life. And suddenly he was afraid of his talking. His hand closed down over the pearl and cut the light away from it. Kino was afraid as a man is afraid who says, "I will," without knowing.

Now the neighbors knew they had witnessed a great marvel. They knew that time would now date from Kino's pearl, and that they would discuss this moment for many years to come. If these things came to pass, they would recount how Kino looked and what he said and how his eyes shone, and they would say, "He was a man transfigured. Some power was given to him, and there it started. You see what a great man he has become, starting from that moment. And I myself saw it."

And if Kino's planning came to nothing, those same neighbors would say, "There it started. A foolish madness came over him so that he spoke foolish words. God keep us from such things. Yes, God punished Kino because he rebelled against the way things are. You see what has become of him. And I myself saw the moment when his reason left him."

Kino looked down at his closed hand and the knuckles were scabbed over and tight where he had struck the gate.

Now the dusk was coming. And Juana looped her shawl under the baby so that he hung against her hip, and she went to the fire hole and dug a coal from the ashes and broke a few twigs over it and fanned a flame alive. The little flames danced on the faces of the neighbors. They knew they should go to their own dinners, but they were reluctant to leave.

The dark was almost in, and Juana's fire threw shadows on the brush walls when the whisper came in, passed from mouth to mouth. "The Father is coming—the priest **41**

## Grammar in Action

Pronouns ending in -*self* or -*selves* are either **intensive** or **reflexive**. Intensive pronouns emphasize another noun or pronoun in the sentence. Reflexive pronouns refer back to the subject of the clause. Consider Steinbeck's sentences:

Intensive: He *himself* was dressed in new white clothes.

Reflexive: The doctor looked past his aged patient and saw *himself* sitting in a restaurant in Paris.

Reflexive: Kino was already making a hard skin for *himself* against the world.

These pronouns should never be used as subjects of their own clauses. It is incorrect to say "My wife and myself found the greatest pearl."

**Student Activity 1.** Identify the pronouns in italics as either intensive or reflexive.

1. "So the doctor knew," he said, but he said it for *himself*.

is coming." The men uncovered their heads and stepped back from the door, and the women gathered their shawls about their faces and cast down their eyes. Kino and Juan Tomás, his brother, stood up. The priest came in—a graying, aging man with an old skin and a young sharp eye. Children, he considered these people, and he treated them like children.

"Kino," he said softly, "thou art named after a great man—and a great Father of the Church."[4] He made it sound like a benediction. "Thy namesake tamed the desert and sweetened the minds of thy people, didst thou know that? It is in the books."

Kino looked quickly down at Coyotito's head, where he hung on Juana's hip. Some day, his mind said, that boy would know what things were in the books and what things were not. The music had gone out of Kino's head, but now, thinly, slowly, the melody of the morning, the music of evil, of the enemy sounded, but it was faint and weak. And Kino looked at his neighbors to see who might have brought this song in.

But the priest was speaking again. "It has come to me that thou hast found a great fortune, a great pearl."

Kino opened his hand and held it out, and the priest gasped a little at the size and beauty of the pearl. And then he said, "I hope thou wilt remember to give thanks, my son, to Him who has given thee this treasure, and to pray for guidance in the future."

Kino nodded dumbly, and it was Juana who spoke softly. "We will, Father. And we will be married now. Kino has said so." She looked at the neighbors for confirmation, and they nodded their heads solemnly.

The priest said, "It is pleasant to see that your first thoughts are good thoughts.

God bless you, my children." He turned and left quietly, and the people let him through.

But Kino's hand had closed tightly on the pearl again, and he was glancing about suspiciously, for the evil song was in his ears, shrilling against the music of the pearl.

The neighbors slipped away to go to their houses, and Juana squatted by the fire and set her clay pot of boiled beans over the little flame. Kino stepped to the doorway and looked out. As always, he could smell the smoke from many fires, and he could see the hazy stars and feel the damp of the night air so that he covered his nose from it. The thin dog came to him and threshed[5] itself in greeting like a windblown flag, and Kino looked down at it and didn't see it. He had broken through the horizons into a cold and lonely outside. He felt alone and unprotected, and scraping crickets and shrilling tree frogs and croaking toads seemed to be carrying the melody of evil. Kino shivered a little and drew his blanket more tightly against his nose. He carried the pearl still in his hand, tightly closed in his palm, and it was warm and smooth against his skin.

Behind him he heard Juana patting the cakes before she put them down on the clay cooking sheet. Kino felt all the warmth and security of his family behind him, and the Song of the Family came from behind him like the purring of a kitten. But now, by saying what his future was going to be like, he had created it. A plan is a real thing, and things projected are experienced. A plan once made and visualized becomes a reality along with other realities—never to be destroyed but easily to be attacked. Thus Kino's future was real, but having set it up, other forces were set up to destroy it, and

---

**4. Father of the Church:** Eusebius Kino, a Spanish missionary and explorer in the seventeenth century.

**5. threshed** (thresht) *v.*: Tossed.

---

**42 Discussion** Explain what is happening to Kino when the priest leaves. What is meant by having the two songs "shrilling" against each other?

**43 Literary Focus: Character** What does this paragraph tell us about the way Kino is changing?

**44 Discussion** What are the forces referred to in this paragraph?

**Electronic Handbook** You may wish to review the meaning of intensive and reflexive pronouns with students before having them complete the Grammar in Action activities. If students are using the Language Master 6000, have them enter the access word *pronoun* to review facts about pronouns.

---

2. And in the pearl Kino saw *himself* and Juana squatting by the little fire in the brush hut while Coyotito read from a great book.

3. And I *myself* saw the moment when his reason left him.

4. The thin dog came to him and threshed *itself* in greeting like a windblown flag.

5. Then Kino must have thought to *himself* that he imagined the sound.

**Student Activity 2.** Add intensive or reflexive pronouns to the following sentences:

1. Kino would buy a rifle for _____ when he sold the pearl.

2. The townspeople wondered among _____ if the money would go to Kino's head.

3. The doctor helped _____ to the chocolate and cheese.

4. Juana knew that she _____ had to care for the injured baby.

5. While they didn't discuss it among _____, the agents knew exactly how much they would offer for the pearl.

## 45

**Literary Focus: Character**
Throughout the novel the doctor is portrayed as evil. The reader knows the doctor was in when Kino first visited, but the doctor now tells Kino that he has come as quickly as he could. Based on what the reader already knows about the doctor, what might one suspect are the doctor's motives and how valid might his advice be?

**46 Discussion** The symbolism of the shawl is used in this paragraph. Have students discuss what it represents.

this he knew, so that he had to prepare to meet the attack. And this Kino knew also —that the gods do not love men's plans, and the gods do not love success unless it comes by accident. He knew that the gods take their revenge on a man if he be successful through his own efforts. Consequently Kino was afraid of plans, but having made one, he could never destroy it. And to meet the attack, Kino was already making a hard skin for himself against the world. His eyes and his mind probed for danger before it appeared.

Standing in the door, he saw two men approach; and one of them carried a lantern which lighted the ground and the legs of the men. They turned in through the opening of Kino's brush fence and came to his door. And Kino saw that one was the doctor and the other the servant who had opened the gate in the morning. The split knuckles on Kino's right hand burned when he saw who they were.

The doctor said, "I was not in when you came this morning. But now, at the first chance, I have come to see the baby."

Kino stood in the door, filling it, and hatred raged and flamed in back of his eyes, and fear too, for the hundreds of years of subjugation[6] were cut deep in him.

"The baby is nearly well now," he said **45** curtly.

The doctor smiled, but his eyes in their little lymph-lined hammocks did not smile.

He said, "Sometimes, my friend, the scorpion sting has a curious effect. There will be apparent improvement, and then without warning—pouf!" He pursed his lips and made a little explosion to show how quick it could be, and he shifted his small

_____
6. **subjugation** (sub′ jə gā′ shən) *n.*: Act of being brought under control.

710    *The Novel*

black doctor's bag about so that the light of the lamp fell upon it, for he knew that Kino's race love the tools of any craft and trust them. "Sometimes," the doctor went on in a liquid tone, "sometimes there will be a withered leg or a blind eye or a crumpled back. Oh, I know the sting of the scorpion, my friend, and I can cure it."

Kino felt the rage and hatred melting toward fear. He did not know, and perhaps this doctor did. And he could not take the chance of pitting his certain ignorance against this man's possible knowledge. He was trapped as his people were always trapped, and would be until, as he had said, they could be sure that the things in the books were really in the books. He could not take a chance—not with the life or with the straightness of Coyotito. He stood aside and let the doctor and his man enter the brush hut.

Juana stood up from the fire and backed away as he entered, and she covered the baby's face with the fringe of her shawl. And when the doctor went to her and held out his hand, she clutched the baby tight and looked at Kino where he stood with the fire shadows leaping on his face.

Kino nodded, and only then did she let the doctor take the baby.

"Hold the light," the doctor said, and when the servant held the lantern high, the doctor looked for a moment at the wound on the baby's shoulder. He was thoughtful for a moment and then he rolled back the baby's eyelid and looked at the eyeball. He nodded his head while Coyotito struggled against him.

"It is as I thought," he said. "The poison has gone inward and it will strike soon. Come look!" He held the eyelid down. "See—it is blue." And Kino, looking anxiously, saw that indeed it was a little blue.

**46**

## Commentary: Symbolism

Since the students have identified *The Pearl* as a parable, it probably does not surprise them to find that some things in the story are meant to represent larger ideas and issues. What they may find surprising is Steinbeck's craftsmanship in giving almost every plot element rich layers of meaning and in incorporating every symbol as a functional element of the story. The novel is not weighted with heavy-handed instruction because the symbols are

a part of the action. They function on a literal as well as a symbolic level. The action of the story teaches a lesson, but the lesson is subliminally reinforced by images and events that represent consistent ideas and messages.

The threat to Kino's simple, peaceful life is symbolically introduced early in the story. Although Steinbeck describes a pleasant awakening, the description is accompanied by the information that Kino and his wife sleep with their blankets over their noses because there is some danger in the air. The description of the ant and the ant-lion that Kino watches suggests the adversarial relationship between the weak and the strong. Finally, the scorpion enters the baby's cradle—giving impetus to the plot and introducing a concrete element of evil into Kino's home.

And he didn't know whether or not it was always a little blue. But the trap was set. He couldn't take the chance.

The doctor's eyes watered in their little hammocks. "I will give him something to try to turn the poison aside," he said. And he handed the baby to Kino.

Then from his bag he took a little bottle of white powder and a capsule of gelatine. He filled the capsule with the powder and closed it, and then around the first capsule he fitted a second capsule and closed it. Then he worked very deftly. He took the baby and pinched its lower lip until it opened its mouth. His fat fingers placed the capsule far back on the baby's tongue, back of the point where he could spit it out, and then from the floor he picked up the little pitcher of pulque and gave Coyotito a drink, and it was done. He looked again at the baby's eyeball and he pursed his lips and seemed to think.

At last he handed the baby back to Juana, and he turned to Kino. "I think the poison will attack within the hour," he said. "The medicine may save the baby from hurt, but I will come back in an hour. Perhaps I am in time to save him." He took a deep breath and went out of the hut, and his servant followed him with the lantern.

Now Juana had the baby under her shawl, and she stared at it with anxiety and fear. Kino came to her, and he lifted the shawl and stared at the baby. He moved his hand to look under the eyelid, and only then saw that the pearl was still in his hand. Then he went to a box by the wall, and from it he brought a piece of rag. He wrapped the pearl in the rag, then went to the corner of the brush house and dug a little hole with his fingers in the dirt floor, and he put the pearl in the hole and covered it up and concealed the place. And then he went to the fire where Juana was squatting, watching the baby's face.

The doctor, back in his house, settled into his chair and looked at his watch. His people brought him a little supper of chocolate and sweet cakes and fruit, and he stared at the food discontentedly.

In the houses of the neighbors the subject that would lead all conversations for a long time to come was aired for the first time to see how it would go. The neighbors showed one another with their thumbs how big the pearl was, and they made little caressing gestures to show how lovely it was. From now on they would watch Kino and Juana very closely to see whether riches turned their heads, as riches turn all people's heads. Everyone knew why the doctor had come. He was not good at dissembling and he was very well understood.

Out in the estuary a tight woven school of small fishes glittered and broke water to escape a school of great fishes that drove in to eat them. And in the houses the people could hear the swish of the small ones and the bouncing splash of the great ones as the slaughter went on. The dampness arose out of the Gulf and was deposited on bushes and cacti and on little trees in salty drops. And the night mice crept about on the ground and the little night hawks hunted them silently.

The skinny black puppy with flame spots over his eyes came to Kino's door and looked in. He nearly shook his hind quarters loose when Kino glanced up at him, and he subsided when Kino looked away. The puppy did not enter the house, but he watched with frantic interest while Kino ate his beans from the little pottery dish and wiped it clean with a corncake and ate the cake and washed the whole down with a drink of pulque.

*The Pearl* 711

711

47 **Literary Focus: Character** Kino knows that Coyotito is well. Why does Kino allow himself to be controlled by the doctor?

48 **Discussion** Again Steinbeck uses symbolism in the shawl. Compare this reference to the preceding one.

49 **Critical Thinking and Reading** Compare and contrast the events taking place outside Kino's hut to those inside.

To a greater or lesser degree, all these symbols have prepared us to expect that Kino will experience a significant conflict, that danger and evil are entering his life. Steinbeck uses other sets of images and events to suggest oppression and greed. Ask students to watch for symbols that foreshadow events and reinforce the novel's message. You may wish to have students record their observations in their reader's response journals and pause periodically to discuss what they discover.

**50 Literary Focus: Character** How does this description support previous comments about the doctor?

**51 Reading Strategy** Summarize the doctor's behavior in these paragraphs.

Kino was finished and was rolling a cigarette when Juana spoke sharply. "Kino." He glanced at her and then got up and went quickly to her for he saw fright in her eyes. He stood over her, looking down, but the light was very dim. He kicked a pile of twigs into the fire hole to make a blaze, and then he could see the face of Coyotito. The baby's face was flushed and his throat was working and a little thick drool of saliva issued from his lips. The spasm of the stomach muscles began, and the baby was very sick.

Kino knelt beside his wife. "So the doctor knew," he said, but he said it for himself as well as for his wife, for his mind was hard and suspicious and he was remembering the white powder. Juana rocked from side to side and moaned out the little Song of the Family as though it could ward off the danger, and the baby vomited and writhed in her arms. Now uncertainty was in Kino, and the music of evil throbbed in his head and nearly drove out Juana's song.

**50** The doctor finished his chocolate and nibbled the little fallen pieces of sweet cake. He brushed his fingers on a napkin, looked at his watch, arose, and took up his little bag.

The news of the baby's illness traveled quickly among the brush houses, for sickness is second only to hunger as the enemy of poor people. And some said softly, "Luck, you see, brings bitter friends." And they nodded and got up to go to Kino's house. The neighbors scuttled with covered noses through the dark until they crowded into Kino's house again. They stood and gazed, and they made little comments on the sadness that this should happen at a time of joy, and they said, "All things are in God's hands." The old women squatted down beside Juana to try to give her aid if they could and comfort if they could not.

Then the doctor hurried in, followed by his man. He scattered the old women like chickens. He took the baby and examined it and felt its head. "The poison it has worked," he said. "I think I can defeat it. I will try my best." He asked for water, and in the cup of it he put three drops of ammonia, and he pried open the baby's mouth and poured it down. The baby spluttered and screeched under the treatment, and Juana watched him with haunted eyes. The doctor spoke a little as he worked. "It is lucky that I know about the poison of the scorpion, otherwise—" and he shrugged to show what could have happened.

But Kino was suspicious, and he could not take his eyes from the doctor's open bag, and from the bottle of white powder there. Gradually the spasms subsided and the baby relaxed under the doctor's hands. And then Coyotito sighed deeply and went to sleep, for he was very tired with vomiting.

The doctor put the baby in Juana's arms. "He will get well now," he said. "I have won the fight." And Juana looked at him with adoration.

The doctor was closing his bag now. He said, "When do you think you can pay this bill?" He said it even kindly.

"When I have sold my pearl I will pay you," Kino said.

"You have a pearl? A good pearl?" the doctor asked with interest.

And then the chorus of the neighbors broke in. "He has found the Pearl of the World," they cried, and they joined forefinger with thumb to show how great the pearl was.

**51**

"Kino will be a rich man," they clamored. "It is a pearl such as one has never seen."

The doctor looked surprised. "I had not heard of it. Do you keep this pearl in a safe place? Perhaps you would like me to put it in my safe?"

Kino's eyes were hooded now, his cheeks were drawn taut. "I have it secure," he said.

"Tomorrow I will sell it and then I will pay you."

The doctor shrugged, and his wet eyes never left Kino's eyes. He knew the pearl would be buried in the house, and he thought Kino might look toward the place where it was buried. "It would be a shame to have it stolen before you could sell it," the doctor said, and he saw Kino's eyes flick involuntarily to the floor near the side post of the brush house.

When the doctor had gone and all the neighbors had reluctantly returned to their houses, Kino squatted beside the little glowing coals in the fire hole and listened to the night sound, the soft sweep of the little waves on the shore and the distant barking of dogs, the creeping of the breeze through the brush house roof and the soft speech of his neighbors in their houses in the village. For these people do not sleep soundly all night; they awaken at intervals and talk a little and then go to sleep again. And after a while Kino got up and went to the door of his house.

He smelled the breeze and he listened for any foreign sound of secrecy or creeping, and his eyes searched the darkness, for the music of evil was sounding in his head and he was fierce and afraid. After he had probed the night with his senses he went to the place by the side post where the pearl was buried, and he dug it up and brought it to his sleeping mat, and under his sleeping mat he dug another little hole in the dirt floor and buried the pearl and covered it up again.

And Juana, sitting by the fire hole, watched him with questioning eyes, and when he had buried his pearl she asked, "Who do you fear?"

Kino searched for a true answer, and at last he said, "Everyone." And he could feel a shell of hardness drawing over him.

After a while they lay down together on the sleeping mat, and Juana did not put the baby in his box tonight, but cradled him in her arms and covered his face with her head shawl. And the last light went out of the embers in the fire hole.

But Kino's brain burned, even during his sleep, and he dreamed that Coyotito could read, that one of his own people could tell him the truth of things. And in his dream, Coyotito was reading from a book as large as a house, with letters as big as dogs, and the words galloped and played on the book. And then darkness spread over the page, and with the darkness came the music of evil again, and Kino stirred in his sleep; and when he stirred, Juana's eyes opened in the darkness. And then Kino awakened, with the evil music pulsing in him, and he lay in the darkness with his ears alert.

Then from the corner of the house came a sound so soft that it might have been simply a thought, a little furtive movement, a touch of a foot on earth, the almost inaudible purr of controlled breathing. Kino held his breath to listen, and he knew that whatever dark thing was in his house was holding its breath too, to listen. For a time no sound at all came from the corner of the brush house. Then Kino might have thought he had imagined the sound. But Juana's hand came creeping over to him in warning, and then the sound came again! the whisper of a foot on dry earth and the scratch of fingers in the soil.

And now a wild fear surged in Kino's breast, and on the fear came rage, as it always did. Kino's hand crept into his breast where his knife hung on a string, and then he sprang like an angry cat, leaped striking and spitting for the dark thing he knew was in the corner of the house. He felt cloth, struck at it with his knife and missed, and struck again and felt his knife go through cloth, and then his head crashed with

*The Pearl* 713

---

**52** **Literary Focus: Character** Kino's character gradually changes in this novel. Explain why "a shell of hardness" seems to enclose him at this point.

**53** **Discussion** Consider the dream that Kino had. What do you think this dream means?

**Videocassette** You may wish to continue viewing the Library of Video Classics videotape *The Pearl* after students finish reading Chapter 3. Ask students to be alert to how camera angles, visual imagery, background music, and other devices are used to reinforce the mood and the message of Steinbeck's novel.

**Writing Transparency** You can use the graphic organizer *Venn Diagram* in **Transparencies for Writing** to help students compare and contrast *The Pearl* as a novel and as a film. Ask students to identify similarities and differences in events, symbols, characters, and setting. How do these similarities and differences affect their interpretation of the theme?

Contrast the differing viewpoints of Juana and Kino. In view of what you have read so far, do you think Juana is right? How might the pearl destroy the family?

**Reader's Response** How can material wealth, while making health and happiness affordable, breed evil? What kinds of feelings does wealth arouse?

**Thematic Response** How is the pearl helping Kino find a place? How is it hindering him?

---

lightning and exploded with pain. There was a soft scurry in the doorway, and running steps for a moment, and then silence.

Kino could feel warm blood running from his forehead, and he could hear Juana calling to him. "Kino! Kino!" And there was terror in her voice. Then coldness came over him as quickly as the rage had, and he said, "I am all right. The thing has gone."

He groped his way back to the sleeping mat. Already Juana was working at the fire. She uncovered an ember from the ashes and shredded little pieces of cornhusk over it and blew a little flame into the cornhusks so that a tiny light danced through the hut. And then from a secret place Juana brought a little piece of consecrated[7] candle and lighted it at the flame and set it upright on a fireplace stone. She worked quickly, crooning as she moved about. She dipped the end of her head shawl in water and swabbed the blood from Kino's bruised forehead. "It is nothing," Kino said, but his eyes and his voice were hard and cold and a brooding hate was growing in him.

> Now the tension which had been growing in Juana boiled up to the surface and her lips were thin. "This thing is evil," she cried harshly. "This pearl is like a sin! It will destroy us," and her voice rose shrilly. "Throw it away, Kino. Let us break it between stones. Let us bury it and forget the place. Let us throw it back into the sea. It has brought evil. Kino, my husband, it will destroy us." And in the firelight her lips and her eyes were alive with her fear.

But Kino's face was set, and his mind and his will were set. "This is our one chance," he said. "Our son must go to school. He must break out of the pot that holds us in."

"It will destroy us all," Juana cried.

"Even our son."

"Hush," said Kino. "Do not speak any more. In the morning we will sell the pearl, and then the evil will be gone, and only the good remain. Now hush, my wife." His dark eyes scowled into the little fire, and for the first time he knew that his knife was still in his hands, and he raised the blade and looked at it and saw a little line of blood on the steel. For a moment he seemed about to wipe the blade on his trousers but then he plunged the knife into the earth and so cleansed it.

The distant roosters began to crow and the air changed and the dawn was coming. The wind of the morning ruffled the water of the estuary and whispered through the mangroves, and the little waves beat on the rubbly beach with an increased tempo. Kino raised the sleeping mat and dug up his pearl and put it in front of him and stared at it.

And the beauty of the pearl, winking and glimmering in the light of the little candle, cozened[8] his brain with its beauty. So lovely it was, so soft, and its own music came from it—its music of promise and delight, its guarantee of the future, of comfort, of security. Its warm lucence promised a poultice against illness and a wall against insult. It closed a door on hunger. And as he stared at it Kino's eyes softened and his face relaxed. He could see the little image of the consecrated candle reflected in the soft surface of the pearl, and he heard again in his ears the lovely music of the undersea, the tone of the diffused green light of the sea bottom. Juana, glancing secretly at him, saw him smile. And because they were in some way one thing and one purpose, she smiled with him.

And they began this day with hope.

---

7. **consecrated** (kän′ si krāt əd) *adj.*: Holy.

8. **cozened** (kuz′ ənd) *v.*: Deceived.

---

**Closure and Extension**

**ANSWERS TO RESPONDING TO THE SELECTION**
*Your Response*

1. Students may draw on the events in the story, predictions about what will happen next, or their own experiences in supporting their answers.

*Recalling*

2. Kino's Song of the Family is a personal song, soft and clear, made up of the familiar sounds of the home he loved. The Song of Evil is another personal song—a savage, secret, dangerous melody that Kino hears when he or his family is threatened.
3. Coyotito is bitten by the scorpion.
4. Juana wants the great pearl to pay for the expenses for medical care for Coyotito. She feels that

wanting something too much will drive the luck away.
5. The people secretly envy Kino's good fortune. The priest and the doctor suddenly treat Kino with respect.

*Interpreting*

6. The doctor has no interest in treating patients who cannot pay his fees. The doctor views Kino and his people with contempt—as uneducated people who cannot afford his services.

7. The news of the pearl stirs everyone's desires, and the only person who stands in the way of the pearl fulfilling them is Kino, so he becomes everyone's enemy.
8. The townspeople envy them, the greedy doctor and priest come to visit, and an intruder invades their hut in the night.
9. Hate is growing in Kino, and he is determined to sell the pearl to improve his family's life.

# RESPONDING TO THE SELECTION

## Your Response

1. Do you think Kino should have thrown the pearl back into the sea as Juana urged him to do? Why or why not?

## Recalling

2. Compare Kino's Song of the Family with the Song of Evil.
3. What harm comes to Coyotito?
4. Why does Juana wish for a great pearl? Why does she feel that it is "not good to want a thing too much"?
5. How do people's attitudes toward Kino change after he finds "the Pearl of the World"?

## Interpreting

6. What is the doctor's attitude toward Kino and his people?
7. Explain how the news of Kino's find stirs up something "infinitely black and evil in the town."
8. In what ways does luck bring Kino and Juana "bitter friends"?
9. By the end of Chapter 3, what changes have come about in Kino?
10. How does Juana's attitude toward the pearl change?

## Applying

11. The narrator writes, "For it is said that humans are never satisfied, that you give them one thing and they want something more." Do you agree that this is a universal trait in humans? Explain your answer.

# ANALYZING LITERATURE

## Understanding Characters in a Parable

A **parable** is a short tale told to illustrate a universal truth. In parables characters tend to be simple and flat rather than complex and three-dimensional. Characters in parables represent traits in people. For example, the doctor in *The Pearl* represents greed.

1. Explain what traits are represented by Kino, Juana, and Coyotito.
2. Consider the narrator's comment: "In tales that are in people's hearts, there are only good and bad things and black and white things and good and evil things and no in-between anywhere." What does this statement suggest about the stories people know by heart?
3. Do you agree that there are only good and evil things and no in-between? Explain your answer.

# THINKING AND WRITING

## Writing From Juana's Point of View

Choose an incident in the story and rewrite it from Juana's point of view. First, review Chapters 1–3, concentrating on aspects of Juana's character. Next, imagine that you are Juana and freewrite about the incident, describing your thoughts, feelings, and actions. Then use this information to rewrite the incident from her point of view. Revise your description to make sure that it suits Juana's character. Proofread for errors in spelling, grammar, and punctuation.

# LEARNING OPTIONS

1. **Writing.** Kino hears different songs depending on how he is feeling and what is happening around him. Review Chapters 1–3 of *The Pearl* for parts in which Kino hears a song, such as the Song of the Family or the Song of Evil. Write lyrics to one or more of these songs, matching your words to the mood and tone of each.
2. **Art.** Illustrate a scene from Chapters 1–3 of *The Pearl*. For ideas you may wish to review the paintings by Diego Rivera that accompany these chapters.

---

period. Display students' writing from Juana's point of view as a journal entry of day 1. You might want to have students write a journal entry from the point of view of Juana or another character for each of the three days.

**Alternative Assessment** *Protocol:* Ask students to assess their own work by responding to the following questions:

On what incidents in Chapters 1–3 do you focus?

What personality do you give Juana?

What thoughts and feelings about the incident do you attribute to Juana?

How are the first three chapters affected by being told from Juana's point of view?

What did you learn about point of view from completing this assignment?

Students can use their answers to the protocol to help them revise their stories.

**Writing Across the Curriculum** Edward F. Ricketts, a marine biologist, was a close friend of John Steinbeck's. It was with Ricketts that Steinbeck explored marine life in the Sea of Cortez. Have students research their exploration and write an essay. You might want to notify social studies or geography teachers so that they could guide students in researching Ricketts and Steinbeck's exploration. Students could write an essay about their findings.

## *LEARNING OPTIONS*

1. You may wish to allow verbal and musical learners to work collaboratively on the writing assignment to create lyrics and a melody. If students have difficulty creating a melody, you might allow them to choose an existing melody to which they can set their words.
2. Encourage visual learners to experiment with color and intensity as well as line and form in conveying the mood of the scene.

---

10. Juana wants to get rid of the pearl.

## *Applying*

11. Answers will differ but should be supported by explanation or example.

## *ANSWERS TO ANALYZING LITERATURE*

1. Answers will differ. Suggested response: Kino represents ambition;

Juana, maternal love and safety; and Coyotito, innocence and hope.
2. Answers will differ but should be supported by explanation or examples.
3. Answers will differ, but explanations should be supported by examples.

**Challenge** To create an image of sound is more difficult than to create a visual image. That is why Steinbeck often uses metaphors

or similes to describe sounds. Choose a sound not presented in this novel and try writing a description of it in words. Read your description to the class—without mentioning outright what sound is being described—and see if the class can recognize the sound.

## *THINKING AND WRITING*

**Publishing Student Writing** *The Pearl* takes place over a three-day

## Preparation

**Literary Focus** Before students proceed with Chapters 4, 5, and 6, have them review the plot to this point. Have them discuss the conflicts—both internal and external—between primitive and modern societies, between Kino's desires and his traditions, and between Kino and the townspeople. Have students comment about how these conflicts relate to the theme.

**Prereading Focus** Allow time for students to discuss what they recall from Chapters 1, 2, and 3 to help **less advanced** students review the events before ordering them on a timeline. You may wish to allow students to work in pairs.

**Writing Transparency** You can use the *Series of Events Chain* graphic organizer in **Transparencies for Writing** to assist all students in organizing the events in chronological order. Encourage students to look for cause-and-effect relationships.

**Vocabulary** Have your **less advanced** students read the words and their definitions. Have them participate in a discussion that allows them to use the words and demonstrate understanding of their meanings.

# GUIDE FOR READING

## The Pearl, Chapters 4–6

### Plot and Theme

**Plot** is the sequence of related events that make up a literary work. Plot usually involves **conflict, climax,** and **resolution.** Conflict, a struggle between opposing forces, can occur between people, between nature and people, or within a person. The climax is the story's highest point of interest, after which the action winds down. In the resolution, the characters solve the conflict, and the reader learns the outcome of the plot. **Theme** is the central idea of a story, or the general insight into life that a story conveys. Writers of parables use plot to help express theme. Carefully examining the events in a parable will increase your understanding of its theme.

### Focus

Kino's life changes so dramatically after he finds the pearl that he and his neighbors begin to mark time dating from this occurrence. Review Chapters 1–3 for key events in the story. Write the events on a timeline that originates on the day Kino finds the pearl. As you read the rest of the novel, enter on your timeline each of the subsequent events that befall Kino and his family.

### Vocabulary

Knowing the following words will help you as you read Chapters 4–6 of *The Pearl.*

**benign** (bi nin') *adj.*: Good natured; harmless (p. 720)

**spurned** (spʉrnd) *v.*: Kicked; rejected (p. 721)

**lethargy** (leth' ər jē) *n.*: Laziness or indifference (p. 724)

**edifice** (ed' i fis) *n.*: Imposing structure (p. 728)

**leprosy** (lep' rə sē) *n.*: A disfiguring disease (p. 729)

**waning** (wān' iŋ) *adj.*: Shrinking to a new moon (p. 730)

**covert** (kuv' ərt) *n.*: A hiding place (p. 731)

**sentinel** (sen' ti nəl) *n.*: Guard (p. 732)

**goading** (gōd iŋ) *n.*: Urging (p. 733)

**monolithic** (män' ə lith' ik) *adj.*: Formed from a single block (p. 735)

**escarpment** (e skarp' mənt) *n.*: A long cliff (p. 736)

**intercession** (in' tər sesh' ən) *n.*: A prayer said on behalf of another person (p. 739)

**malignant** (mə lig' nənt) *adj.*: Harmful (p. 742)

716   *The Novel*

---

## Support Material

**Teaching Portfolio**
Teacher Backup, p. 1003
Grammar in Action Worksheets, *Understanding Gerunds,* pp. 1006–1007; *Understanding Participles,* p. 1008; *Using Specific Verbs,* p. 1010
Usage and Mechanics Worksheet, p. 1012

Vocabulary Check, p. 1013
Critical Thinking and Reading Worksheet, *Recognizing Cause and Effect,* p. 1015
Language Worksheet, *Appreciating Vivid Verbs,* p. 1016
Selection Test, p. 1017

**Library of Video Classics**
*The Pearl*

**Prentice Hall Literature Writing Studio**

## Chapter 4

It is wonderful the way a little town keeps track of itself and of all its units. If every single man and woman, child and baby, acts and conducts itself in a known pattern and breaks no walls and differs with no one and experiments in no way and is not sick and does not endanger the ease and peace of mind or steady unbroken flow of the town, then that unit can disappear and never be heard of. But let one man step out of the regular thought or the known and trusted pattern, and the nerves of the townspeople ring with nervousness and communication travels over the nerve lines of the town. Then every unit communicates to the whole.

Thus, in La Paz,[1] it was known in the early morning through the whole town that Kino was going to sell his pearl that day. It was known among the neighbors in the brush huts, among the pearl fishermen; it was known among the Chinese grocery-store owners; it was known in the church, for the altar boys whispered about it. Word of it crept in among the nuns; the beggars in front of the church spoke of it, for they would be there to take the tithe[2] of the first fruits of the luck. The little boys knew about it with excitement, but most of all the pearl buyers knew about it, and when the day had come, in the offices of the pearl buyers, each man sat alone with his little black velvet tray, and each man rolled the pearls about with his fingertips and considered his part in the picture.

It was supposed that the pearl buyers were individuals acting alone, bidding against one another for the pearls the fishermen brought in. And once it had been so. But this was a wasteful method, for often, in the excitement of bidding for a fine pearl, too great a price had been paid to the fishermen. This was extravagant and not to be countenanced.[3] Now there was only one pearl buyer with many hands, and the men who sat in their offices and waited for Kino knew what price they would offer, how high they would bid, and what method each one would use. And although these men would not profit beyond their salaries, there was excitement among the pearl buyers, for there was excitement in the hunt, and if it be a man's function to break down a price, then he must take joy and satisfaction in breaking it as far down as possible. For every man in the world functions to the best of his ability, and no one does less than his best, no matter what he may think about it. Quite apart from any reward they might get, from any word of praise, from any promotion, a pearl buyer was a pearl buyer, and the best and happiest pearl buyer was he who bought for the lowest prices.

The sun was hot yellow that morning, and it drew the moisture from the estuary and from the Gulf and hung it in shimmering scarves in the air so that the air vibrated and vision was insubstantial. A vision hung in the air to the north of the city—the vision of a mountain that was over two hundred miles away, and the high slopes of this mountain were swaddled with pines and a great stone peak arose above the timber line.

And the morning of this day the canoes lay lined up on the beach; the fishermen did not go out to dive for pearls, for there would be too much happening, too many things to see when Kino went to sell the great pearl.

In the brush houses by the shore Kino's neighbors sat long over their breakfasts, and they spoke of what they would do if they had found the pearl. And one man said that

---

**1. La Paz:** City in southern Baja California.
**2. tithe** (tī *th*) *n.*: One tenth of one's income; here, a small amount given to charity.

**3. countenanced** (koun′ tə nənsd) *v.*: Approved; supported.

**Presentation**

**Motivation/Prior Knowledge**
Have students consider what they have learned about the pearl thus far. Have them consider the images that have formed in their minds of the pearl. Consider the description of how a pearl is formed and Steinbeck's use of irony—in order to get the beautiful pearl, an oyster must be killed. Have students speculate whether or not they think this might be a foreshadowing.

**Thematic Focus** Ask students to summarize the choices Kino has made up to this point. What do we learn about Kino from his decisions? Have students predict the choices that Kino will face in the remainder of the novel and discuss the consequences of each potential course of action.

**Purpose-Setting Question** Understanding the goals and desires and conflicts of a character are important in understanding story plot, climax, and resolution. How do the events in Kino's life and his character relate to the plot of the story?

**1 Discussion** In previous chapters Steinbeck has compared the town to a living organism. How is Kino changing and what effect does this have on the town?

**2 Reading Strategy** Summarize the climate in the town.

**3 Reading Strategy** Summarize the climate in the pearl buyers' offices. What are the implications of their attitudes?

**4 Enrichment** Steinbeck has become philosophical here about the nature of humans. Have students tell whether they agree or disagree with his statement that "every man in the world functions to the best of his ability . . ."

**Master Teacher Note** *The Pearl* was not favorably received when it was first published. In one review Maxwell Geismar wrote that ". . . the quality that has marked Steinbeck's work as a whole is . . . the sense of black and white things and good and bad things—that is to say, the sense of a fabulist or a propagandist rather than the insight of an artist." You might want to read this to students and have them consider whether they agree or disagree after they have completed the reading.

## Humanities Note

Fine art, *Group*, by Jesus Guerrero Galván. Lead students to identify how the use of light, color, and composition create a mood that is different from that found in Rivera's work. Rivera uses families of colors so that each painting is chromatically cohesive, whereas Galván uses sharply delineated, contrasting colors. The intensity of the red-brown of the earth is highlighted by the black sky. Point out to students that the colors used for the women and children in *Group* blend with the colors of the earth.

You may wish to use the following questions for discussion:

1. What is the setting for this painting? How is it different from the setting in Rivera's works?

2. What is the mood of this painting? What elements of *Group* most strongly influence your interpretation of the mood?

3. Why do you think Galván chose to use similar colors for the people and the earth?

4. How does the mood of *Group* compare with the mood of *Two Mexican Women and a Child* on page 706?

5. What do you think these two women might be saying to each other?

6. What elements of this painting do you relate to the plot and theme of *The Pearl?*

**5 Discussion** Kino's neighbors say they would use the money from the pearl for the benefit of others. Kino has not planned to do this. Have students discuss whether they feel Steinbeck is making a judgment of right or wrong in this paragraph.

**6 Critical Thinking and Reading** There is an obvious cause-and-effect relationship here between wealth and destruction. How does this cause-and-effect relationship relate to the theme?

**GROUP**
*Jesus Guerrero Galván*
Collection IBM Corporation, Armonk, New York

he would give it as a present to the Holy Father in Rome. Another said that he would buy Masses for the souls of his family for a thousand years. Another thought he might take the money and distribute it among the poor of La Paz; and a fourth thought of all the good things one could do with the money from the pearl, of all the charities, benefits, of all the rescues one could perform if one had money. All of the neighbors hoped that sudden wealth would not turn Kino's head, would not make a rich man of him, would not graft onto him the evil limbs of greed and hatred and coldness. For Kino was a well-liked man; it would be a shame if the pearl destroyed him. "That good wife Juana," they said, "and the beautiful baby Coyotito, and the others to come. What a pity it would be if the pearl should destroy them all."

For Kino and Juana this was the morning of mornings of their lives, comparable only to the day when the baby had been born. This was to be the day from which all other days would take their arrangement. Thus they would say, "It was two years before we sold the pearl," or, "It was six weeks after we sold the pearl." Juana, considering the matter, threw caution to the winds, and she dressed Coyotito in the clothes she had prepared for his baptism, when there would be money for his bap-

**7 Discussion** Based on what is described and what the reader knows about the story thus far, what are Juana's and Kino's expectations for the day? What do they anticipate the day will be like?

tism. And Juana combed and braided her hair and tied the ends with two little bows of red ribbon, and she put on her marriage skirt and waist.[4] The sun was quarter high when they were ready. Kino's ragged white clothes were clean at least, and this was the last day of his raggedness. For tomorrow, or even this afternoon, he would have new clothes.

The neighbors, watching Kino's door through the crevices in their brush houses, were dressed and ready too. There was no self-consciousness about their joining Kino and Juana to go pearl selling. It was expected, it was an historic moment, they would be crazy if they didn't go. It would be almost a sign of unfriendship.

Juana put on her head shawl carefully, and she draped one long end under her right elbow and gathered it with her right hand so that a hammock hung under her arm, and in this little hammock she placed Coyotito, propped up against the head shawl so that he could see everything and perhaps remember. Kino put on his large straw hat and felt it with his hand to see that it was properly placed, not on the back or side of his head, like a rash, unmarried, irresponsible man, and not flat as an elder would wear it, but tilted a little forward to show aggressiveness and seriousness and vigor. There is a great deal to be seen in the tilt of a hat on a man. Kino slipped his feet into his sandals and pulled the thongs up over his heels. The great pearl was wrapped in an old soft piece of deerskin and placed in a little leather bag, and the leather bag was in a pocket in Kino's shirt. He folded his blanket carefully and draped it in a narrow strip over his left shoulder, and now they were ready.

Kino stepped with dignity out of the house, and Juana followed him, carrying Coyotito. And as they marched up the freshet-washed[5] alley toward the town, the neighbors joined them. The houses belched people; the doorways spewed out children. But because of the seriousness of the occasion, only one man walked with Kino, and that was his brother, Juan Tomás.

Juan Tomás cautioned his brother. "You must be careful to see they do not cheat you," he said.

And, "Very careful," Kino agreed.

"We do not know what prices are paid in other places," said Juan Tomás. "How can we know what is a fair price, if we do not know what the pearl buyer gets for the pearl in another place?"

"That is true," said Kino, "but how can we know? We are here, we are not there."

As they walked up toward the city the crowd grew behind them, and Juan Tomás, in pure nervousness, went on speaking.

"Before you were born, Kino," he said, "the old ones thought of a way to get more money for their pearls. They thought it would be better if they had an agent who took all the pearls to the capital and sold them there and kept only his share of the profit."

Kino nodded his head. "I know," he said. "It was a good thought."

"And so they got such a man," said Juan Tomás, "and they pooled their pearls, and they started him off. And he was never heard of again and the pearls were lost. Then they got another man, and they started him off, and he was never heard of again. And so they gave the whole thing up and went back to the old way."

"I know," said Kino. "I have heard our father tell of it. It was a good idea, but it was against religion, and the Father made that very clear. The loss of the pearl was a

---

**4. waist** (wāst) *n.*: Blouse.

**5. freshet** (fresh' it) **-washed** *adj.*: Washed by a stream.

---

**8 Enrichment** You can learn much about Kino's people through information presented about the wearing of hats. Select an item of clothing worn by people today. Tell what that item of clothing might reveal about our culture.

**9 Discussion** How does this procession differ from the first one?

**10 Discussion** What does this conversation between Kino and his brother tell the reader about their relationship?

**11 Humanities Note** This paragraph is reminiscent of Milton's sonnet "On His Blindness." Have students read the sonnet and then discuss Kino's statement "But each one must remain faithful to his post. . . ." in light of Milton's idea, "They also serve who only stand and wait."

12 **Discussion** What does this statement tell us about the priest?

13 **Discussion** What is the defensive behavior in response to?

14 **Reading Strategy** The pearl buyers are preparing for Kino's visit. Tell how they are doing this. What do their actions tell the reader? What do you think might happen?

punishment visited on those who tried to leave their station. And the Father made it clear that each man and woman is like a soldier sent by God to guard some part of the castle of the Universe. And some are in the ramparts and some far deep in the darkness of the walls. But each one must remain faithful to his post and must not go running about, else the castle is in danger from the assaults of Hell.''

**12** ''I have heard him make that sermon,'' said Juan Tomás. ''He makes it every year.''

The brothers, as they walked along, squinted their eyes a little, as they and their grandfathers and their great-grandfathers had done for four hundred years, since first the strangers came with argument and authority and gunpowder to back up both. And in the four hundred years Kino's people had learned only one defense—a slight slitting **13** of the eyes and a slight tightening of the lips and a retirement. Nothing could break down this wall, and they could remain whole within the wall.

The gathering procession was solemn, for they sensed the importance of this day, and any children who showed a tendency to scuffle, to scream, to cry out, to steal hats and rumple hair, were hissed to silence by their elders. So important was this day that an old man came to see, riding on the stalwart shoulders of his nephew. The procession left the brush huts and entered the stone and plaster city where the streets were a little wider and there were narrow pavements beside the buildings. And as before, the beggars joined them as they passed the church; the grocers looked out at them as they went by; the little saloons lost their customers and the owners closed up shop and went along. And the sun beat down on the streets of the city and even tiny stones threw shadows on the ground.

The news of the approach of the procession ran ahead of it, and in their little dark offices the pearl buyers stiffened and grew alert. They got out papers so that they could be at work when Kino appeared, and they put their pearls in the desks, for it is not good to let an inferior pearl be seen beside a beauty. And word of the loveliness of Kino's pearl had come to them. The pearl buyers' offices were clustered together in one narrow street, and they were barred at the windows, and wooden slats cut out the light so that only a soft gloom entered the offices.

A stout slow man sat in an office waiting. His face was fatherly and benign, and his eyes twinkled with friendship. He was a caller of good mornings, a ceremonious shaker of hands, a jolly man who knew all jokes and yet who hovered close to sadness, for in the midst of a laugh he could remember the death of your aunt, and his eyes could become wet with sorrow for your loss. **14** This morning he had placed a flower in a vase on his desk, a single scarlet hibiscus, and the vase sat beside the black velvet-lined pearl tray in front of him. He was shaved close to the blue roots of his beard, and his hands were clean and his nails polished. His door stood open to the morning, and he hummed under his breath while his right hand practiced legerdemain.[6] He rolled a coin back and forth over his knuckles and made it appear and disappear, made it spin and sparkle. The coin winked into sight and as quickly slipped out of sight, and the man did not even watch his own performance. The fingers did it all mechanically, precisely, while the man hummed to himself and peered out the door. Then he heard the tramp of feet of the approaching crowd, and the fingers of his right hand worked faster and faster until, as the figure of Kino filled

---

**6. legerdemain** (lej′ ər də mān′) *n.*: Trickery; tricks with the hand.

## Grammar in Action

**Gerunds** are verb forms ending in *-ing* used as nouns. They may assume any noun function. Consider Steinbeck's sentences:

Object of preposition: In the excitement of *bidding* for a fine pearl, too great a price had been paid to the fisherman.

Direct object: He felt the *creeping* of fate.

Subject: . . . The *whispering* went back through the crowd.

Appositive: . . . Kino's people had learned only one defense—a slight *slitting* of the eyes and a slight *tightening* of the lips. . . .

Because gerunds are nouns, nouns and pronouns immediately preceding them must be in the possessive form:

There was no self-consciousness about *their* joining Kino . . . *Kino's* finding the pearl was the talk of the town.

the doorway, the coin flashed and disappeared.

"Good morning, my friend," the stout man said. "What can I do for you?"

Kino stared into the dimness of the little office, for his eyes were squeezed from the outside glare. But the buyer's eyes had become as steady and cruel and unwinking as a hawk's eyes, while the rest of his face smiled in greeting. And secretly, behind his desk, his right hand practiced with the coin.

"I have a pearl," said Kino. And Juan Tomás stood beside him and snorted a little at the understatement. The neighbors peered around the doorway, and a line of little boys clambered on the window bars and looked through. Several little boys, on their hands and knees, watched the scene around Kino's legs.

"You have a pearl," the dealer said. "Sometimes a man brings in a dozen. Well, let us see your pearl. We will value it and give you the best price." And his fingers worked furiously with the coin.

Now Kino instinctively knew his own dramatic effects. Slowly he brought out the leather bag, slowly took from it the soft and dirty piece of deerskin, and then he let the great pearl roll into the black velvet tray, and instantly his eyes went to the buyer's face. But there was no sign, no movement, the face did not change, but the secret hand behind the desk missed in its precision. The coin stumbled over a knuckle and slipped silently into the dealer's lap. And the fingers behind the desk curled into a fist. When the right hand came out of hiding, the forefinger touched the great pearl, rolled it on the black velvet; thumb and forefinger picked it up and brought it near to the dealer's eyes and twirled it in the air.

Kino held his breath, and the neighbors held their breath, and the whispering went back through the crowd. "He is inspecting it—No price has been mentioned yet —They have not come to a price."

Now the dealer's hand had become a personality. The hand tossed the great pearl back in the tray, the forefinger poked and insulted it, and on the dealer's face there came a sad and contemptuous smile.

"I am sorry, my friend," he said, and his shoulders rose a little to indicate that the misfortune was no fault of his.

"It is a pearl of great value," Kino said.

The dealer's fingers spurned the pearl so that it bounced and rebounded softly from the side of the velvet tray.

"You have heard of fool's gold," the dealer said. "This pearl is like fool's gold. It is too large. Who would buy it? There is no market for such things. It is a curiosity only. I am sorry. You thought it was a thing of value, and it is only a curiosity."

Now Kino's face was perplexed and worried. "It is the Pearl of the World," he cried. "No one has ever seen such a pearl."

"On the contrary," said the dealer, "it is large and clumsy. As a curiosity it has interest; some museum might perhaps take it to place in a collection of seashells. I can give you, say, a thousand pesos."[7]

Kino's face grew dark and dangerous. "It is worth fifty thousand," he said. "You know it. You want to cheat me."

And the dealer heard a little grumble go through the crowd as they heard his price. And the dealer felt a little tremor of fear.

"Do not blame me," he said quickly. "I am only an appraiser. Ask the others. Go to their offices and show your pearl—or better let them come here, so that you can see there is no collusion.[8] Boy," he called. And when his servant looked through the rear

---

7. **pesos** (pā′ sōz) n.: Mexican unit of money.
8. **collusion** (kə lōō′ zhən) n.: A secret agreement for an illegal purpose.

*The Pearl* 721

**15 Discussion** How does the pearl buyer attempt to minimize and devalue Kino's pearl?

**16 Literary Focus: Plot** Students must be attentive to detail in this paragraph if they are not to be misled later on in the story. What do the actions of the dealer indicate about the value of pearl?

**17 Reading Strategy** Why do you think the dealer is showing contempt for the pearl?

**18 Literary Focus: Parable** What do you think the dishonest pearl dealers represent? What other characters serve a related symbolic function in this parable?

**19 Discussion** The crowd is more distanced and quiet than it has been on previous occasions. What is the significance of this?

**Electronic Handbook** You may wish to review gerunds with students before having them complete the Grammar in Action activities. If students are using the Language Master 6000, have them enter the access word *verb* and press the GRAMMAR key to review facts about verbs.

**Student Activity 1.** Locate the gerunds in each of the following sentences and explain how each gerund is used.

1. He must take joy and satisfaction in breaking it down as far as possible.
2. Juan Tomás, in pure nervousness, continued speaking.
3. But each one must remain faithful to his post and must not go running about.
4. The buyer's eyes had become as steady and cruel and unwinking as a hawk's eyes, while the rest of his face smiled in greeting.
5. When the right hand came out of hiding, the forefinger touched the great pearl.
6. He felt a little tugging at his back.
7. She knew she could help him best by being silent and by being near.

**Student Activity 2.** Some words like *morning* and *evening* may not seem like gerunds because their verb forms have become obsolete. Use your dictionary to find the original verbs from which *morning* and *evening* were derived.

**20 Discussion** The coin becomes a symbol. What does the coin represent?

**21 Reading Strategy** Summarize the behavior of the three pearl buyers. How could their reactions have been predicted from previous actions?

**22 Literary Focus: Conflict** This statement reflects one of Kino's external conflicts—the struggle to get justice from his oppressors. How does Kino's personal conflict represent the societal conflict that is a significant part of Steinbeck's message in this novel?

door, "Boy, go to such a one, and such another one and such a third one. Ask them to step in here and do not tell them why. Just say that I will be pleased to see them." And his right hand went behind the desk and pulled another coin from his pocket, and the coin rolled back and forth over the knuckles.

**20**

Kino's neighbors whispered together. They had been afraid of something like this. The pearl was large, but it had a strange color. They had been suspicious of it from the first. And after all, a thousand pesos was not to be thrown away. It was comparative wealth to a man who was not wealthy. And suppose Kino took a thousand pesos. Only yesterday he had nothing.

But Kino had grown tight and hard. He felt the creeping of fate, the circling of wolves, the hover of vultures. He felt the evil coagulating[9] about him, and he was helpless to protect himself. He heard in his ears the evil music. And on the black velvet the great pearl glistened, so that the dealer could not keep his eyes from it.

The crowd in the doorway wavered and broke and let the three pearl dealers through. The crowd was silent now, fearing to miss a word, to fail to see a gesture or an expression. Kino was silent and watchful. He felt a little tugging at his back, and he turned and looked in Juana's eyes, and when he looked away he had renewed strength.

**21**

The dealers did not glance at one another nor at the pearl. The man behind the desk said, "I have put a value on this pearl. The owner here does not think it fair. I will ask you to examine this—this thing and make an offer. Notice," he said to Kino, "I have not mentioned what I have offered."

The first dealer, dry and stringy, seemed

---

**9. coagulating** (kō ag′ yoo lāt′ iŋ) *v.*: Becoming solid.

now to see the pearl for the first time. He took it up, rolled it quickly between thumb and forefinger, and then cast it contemptuously back into the tray.

"Do not include me in the discussion," he said dryly. "I will make no offer at all. I do not want it. This is not a pearl—it is a monstrosity." His thin lips curled.

Now the second dealer, a little man with a shy soft voice, took up the pearl, and he examined it carefully. He took a glass from his pocket and inspected it under magnification. Then he laughed softly.

"Better pearls are made of paste," he said. "I know these things. This is soft and chalky, it will lose its color and die in a few months. Look—." He offered the glass to Kino, showed him how to use it, and Kino, who had never seen a pearl's surface magnified, was shocked at the strange-looking surface.

The third dealer took the pearl from Kino's hands. "One of my clients likes such things," he said. "I will offer five hundred pesos, and perhaps I can sell it to my client for six hundred."

Kino reached quickly and snatched the pearl from his hand. He wrapped it in the deerskin and thrust it inside his shirt.

The man behind the desk said, "I'm a fool, I know, but my first offer stands. I still offer one thousand. What are you doing?" he asked, as Kino thrust the pearl out of sight.

"I am cheated," Kino cried fiercely. "My pearl is not for sale here. I will go, perhaps even to the capital."

**22**

Now the dealers glanced quickly at one another. They knew they had played too hard; they knew they would be disciplined for their failure, and the man at the desk said quickly, "I might go to fifteen hundred."

But Kino was pushing his way through the crowd. The hum of talk came to him dimly, his rage blood pounded in his ears, and he burst through and strode away. Juana followed, trotting after him.

When the evening came, the neighbors in the brush houses sat eating their corncakes and beans, and they discussed the great theme of the morning. They did not know, it seemed a fine pearl to them, but they had never seen such a pearl before, and surely the dealers knew more about the value of pearls than they. "And mark this," they said. "Those dealers did not discuss these things. Each of the three knew the pearl was valueless."

"But suppose they had arranged it before?"

"If that is so, then all of us have been cheated all of our lives."

Perhaps, some argued, perhaps it would have been better if Kino took the one thousand five hundred pesos. That is a great deal of money, more than he has ever seen. Maybe Kino is being a pigheaded fool. Suppose he should really go to the capital and find no buyer for his pearl. He would never live that down.

And now, said other fearful ones, now that he had defied them, those buyers will not want to deal with him at all. Maybe Kino has cut off his own head and destroyed himself.

And others said, Kino is a brave man, and a fierce man; he is right. From his courage we may all profit. These were proud of Kino.

In his house Kino squatted on his sleeping mat, brooding. He had buried his pearl under a stone of the fire hole in his house, and he stared at the woven tules[10] of his sleeping mat until the crossed design danced in his head. **23** He had lost one world and had not gained another. And Kino was afraid. Never in his life had he been far from home. He was afraid of strangers and of strange places. He was terrified of that monster of strangeness they called the capital. It lay over the water and through the mountains, over a thousand miles, and every strange terrible mile was frightening. But Kino had lost his old world and he must clamber on to a new one. For his dream of the future was real and never to be destroyed, and he had said "I will go," and that made a real thing too. To determine to go and to say it was to be halfway there.

Juana watched him while he buried his pearl, and she watched him while she cleaned Coyotito and nursed him, and Juana made the corncakes for supper.

Juan Tomás came in and squatted down beside Kino and remained silent for a long time, until at last Kino demanded, "What else could I do? They are cheats."

**24** Juan Tomás nodded gravely. He was the elder, and Kino looked to him for wisdom. "It is hard to know," he said. "We do know that we are cheated from birth to the overcharge on our coffins. But we survive. You have defied not the pearl buyers, but the whole structure, the whole way of life, and I am afraid for you."

"What have I to fear but starvation?" Kino asked.

But Juan Tomás shook his head slowly. "That we must all fear. But suppose you are correct—suppose your pearl is of great value—do you think then the game is over?"

"What do you mean?"

**25** "I don't know," said Juan Tomás, "but I am afraid for you. It is new ground you are walking on, you do not know the way."

"I will go. I will go soon," said Kino.

"Yes," Juan Tomás agreed. "That you must do. But I wonder if you will find it any different in the capital. Here, you have friends and me, your brother. There, you will have no one."

---

**10. tules** (tōō′ lēz) *n*.: Grasslike plants.

**23 Literary Focus: Theme** The sentence "He had lost one world and had not gained another" is a very important one. It reflects one of Kino's internal conflicts. Kino's dreams—to get married in a church and to send his son to school—reflect his choosing the modern world of the town over the traditional world of the brush houses. The injustice of the pearl buyers prevents him from moving forward to a new life, and the possession of the pearl prevents him from returning to the old. What choices have led Kino to this point? What choices does he still have to make? How do the consequences of Kino's choices reflect Steinbeck's message about the plight of Kino's people?

**24 Critical Thinking and Reading** What do you think might be the effects of Kino's defiance of the whole system?

**25 Discussion** What do you think Juan Tomás believes Kino should do? Do you think that Juan Tomás feels that the dealer is lying?

"What can I do?" Kino cried. "Some deep outrage is here. My son must have a chance. That is what they are striking at. My friends will protect me."

"Only so long as they are not in danger or discomfort from it," said Juan Tomás. He arose, saying, "Go with God."

And Kino said, "Go with God," and did not even look up, for the words had a strange chill in them.

Long after Juan Tomás had gone Kino sat brooding on his sleeping mat. A lethargy had settled on him, and a little gray hopelessness. Every road seemed blocked against him. In his head he heard only the dark music of the enemy. His senses were burningly alive, but his mind went back to the deep participation with all things, the gift he had from his people. He heard every little sound of the gathering night, the sleepy complaint of settling birds, the love agony of cats, the strike and withdrawal of little waves on the beach, and the simple hiss of distance. And he could smell the sharp odor of exposed kelp[11] from the receding tide. The little flare of the twig fire made the design on his sleeping mat jump before his entranced eyes.

Juana watched him with worry, but she knew him and she knew she could help him best by being silent and by being near. And as though she too could hear the Song of Evil, she fought it, singing softly the melody of the family, of the safety and warmth and wholeness of the family. She held Coyotito in her arms and sang the song to him, to keep the evil out, and her voice was brave against the threat of the dark music.

Kino did not move nor ask for his supper. She knew he would ask when he wanted it. His eyes were entranced, and he could sense the wary, watchful evil outside the brush house; he could feel the dark creeping things waiting for him to go out into the night. It was shadowy and dreadful, and yet it called to him and threatened him and challenged him. His right hand went into his shirt and felt his knife; his eyes were wide; he stood up and walked to the doorway.

Juana willed to stop him; she raised her hand to stop him, and her mouth opened with terror. For a long moment Kino looked out into the darkness and then he stepped outside. Juana heard the little rush, the grunting struggle, the blow. She froze with terror for a moment, and then her lips drew back from her teeth like a cat's lips. She set Coyotito down on the ground. She seized a stone from the fireplace and rushed outside, but it was over by then. Kino lay on the ground, struggling to rise, and there was no one near him. Only the shadows and the strike and rush of waves and the hiss of distance. But the evil was all about, hidden behind the brush fence, crouched beside the house in the shadow, hovering in the air.

Juana dropped her stone, and she put her arms around Kino and helped him to his feet and supported him into the house. Blood oozed down from his scalp and there was a long deep cut in his cheek from ear to chin, a deep, bleeding slash. And Kino was only half conscious. He shook his head from side to side. His shirt was torn open and his clothes half pulled off. Juana sat him down on his sleeping mat and she wiped the thickening blood from his face with her skirt. She brought him pulque to drink in a little pitcher, and still he shook his head to clear out the darkness.

"Who?" Juana asked.

"I don't know," Kino said. "I didn't see."

Now Juana brought her clay pot of water and she washed the cut on his face while he stared dazed ahead of him.

"Kino, my husband," she cried, and his

26

_____
11. **kelp** *n.*: Seaweed.

MEXICAN PEASANT WITH SOMBRERO AND SERAPE
*Diego Rivera*
*Harry Ransom Humanities Research Center*
*The University of Texas at Austin*

eyes stared past her. "Kino, can you hear me?"

"I hear you," he said dully.

"Kino, this pearl is evil. Let us destroy it before it destroys us. Let us crush it between two stones. Let us—let us throw it back in the sea where it belongs. Kino, it is evil, it is evil!"

And as she spoke the light came back in Kino's eyes so that they glowed fiercely and his muscles hardened and his will hardened.

"No," he said. "I will fight this thing. I will win over it. We will have our chance." His fist pounded the sleeping mat. "No one shall take our good fortune from us," he said. His eyes softened then and he raised a gentle hand to Juana's shoulder. "Believe me," he said. "I am a man." And his face grew crafty.

"In the morning we will take our canoe and we will go over the sea and over the mountains to the capital, you and I. We will not be cheated. I am a man."

"Kino," she said huskily, "I am afraid. A man can be killed. Let us throw the pearl back into the sea."

"Hush," he said fiercely. "I am a man. Hush." And she was silent, for his voice was command. "Let us sleep a little," he said. "In the first light we will start. You are not afraid to go with me?"

"No, my husband."

His eyes were soft and warm on her then, his hand touched her cheek. "Let us sleep a little," he said.

*The Pearl* 725

27

---

**Master Teacher Note** Students may find the attitudes described on this page to be alternately demeaning and patronizing by contemporary standards. Caution students to consider Kino's and Juana's thoughts and actions within the context of their culture. Lead students to recognize the strength, loyalty, and love expressed in Juana's reflections about men and women, Kino and herself.

## Chapter 5

The late moon arose before the first rooster crowed. Kino opened his eyes in the darkness, for he sensed movement near him, but he did not move. Only his eyes searched the darkness, and in the pale light of the moon that crept through the holes in the brush house Kino saw Juana arise silently from beside him. He saw her move toward the fireplace. So carefully did she work that he heard only the lightest sound when she moved the fireplace stone. And then like a shadow she glided toward the door. She paused for a moment beside the hanging box where Coyotito lay, then for a second she was black in the doorway, and then she was gone.

And rage surged in Kino. He rolled up to his feet and followed her as silently as she had gone, and he could hear her quick footsteps going toward the shore. Quietly he tracked her, and his brain was red with anger. She burst clear out of the brush line and stumbled over the little boulders toward the water, and then she heard him coming and she broke into a run. Her arm was up to throw when he leaped at her and caught her arm and wrenched the pearl from her. He struck her in the face with his clenched fist and she fell among the boulders, and he kicked her in the side. In the pale light he could see the little waves break over her, and her skirt floated about and clung to her legs as the water receded.

Kino looked down at her and his teeth were bared. He hissed at her like a snake, and Juana stared at him with wide unfrightened eyes, like a sheep before the butcher. She knew there was murder in him, and it was all right; she had accepted it, and she would not resist or even protest. And then the rage left him and a sick disgust took its place. He turned away from her and walked up the beach and through the brush line. His senses were dulled by his emotion.

He heard the rush, got his knife out and lunged at one dark figure and felt his knife go home, and then he was swept to his knees and swept again to the ground. Greedy fingers went through his clothes, frantic figures searched him, and the pearl, knocked from his hand, lay winking behind a little stone in the pathway. It glinted in the soft moonlight.

Juana dragged herself up from the rocks on the edge of the water. Her face was a dull pain and her side ached. She steadied herself on her knees for a while and her wet skirt clung to her. There was no anger in her for Kino. He had said, "I am a man," and that meant certain things to Juana. It meant that he was half insane and half god. It meant that Kino would drive his strength against a mountain and plunge his strength against the sea. Juana, in her woman's soul, knew that the mountain would stand while the man broke himself; that the sea would surge while the man drowned in it. And yet it was this thing that made him a man, half insane and half god, and Juana had need of a man; she could not live without a man. Although she might be puzzled by these differences between man and woman, she knew them and accepted them and needed them. Of course she would follow him, there was no question of that. Sometimes the quality of woman, the reason, the caution, the sense of preservation, could cut through Kino's manness and save them all. She climbed painfully to her feet, and she dipped her cupped palms in the little waves and washed her bruised face with the stinging salt water, and then she went creeping up the beach after Kino.

A flight of herring clouds had moved over the sky from the south. The pale moon dipped in and out of the strands of clouds so that Juana walked in darkness for a moment and in light the next. Her back was bent with pain and her head was low. She went through the line of brush when the moon was covered, and when it looked through she saw the glimmer of the great pearl in the path behind the rock. She sank to her knees and picked it up, and the moon went into the darkness of the clouds again. Juana remained on her knees while she considered whether to go back to the sea and finish her job, and as she considered, the light came again, and she saw two dark figures lying in the path ahead of her. She leaped forward and saw that one was Kino and the other a stranger with dark shiny fluid leaking from his throat.

Kino moved sluggishly, arms and legs stirred like those of a crushed bug, and a thick muttering came from his mouth. Now, in an instant, Juana knew that the old life was gone forever. A dead man in the path and Kino's knife, dark bladed beside him, convinced her. All of the time Juana had been trying to rescue something of the old peace, of the time before the pearl. But now it was gone, and there was no retrieving it. And knowing this, she abandoned the past instantly. There was nothing to do but to save themselves.

Her pain was gone now, her slowness. Quickly she dragged the dead man from the pathway into the shelter of the brush. She went to Kino and sponged his face with her wet skirt. His senses were coming back and he moaned.

"They have taken the pearl. I have lost it. Now it is over," he said. "The pearl is gone."

Juana quieted him as she would quiet a sick child. "Hush," she said. "Here is your pearl. I found it in the path. Can you hear me now? Here is your pearl. Can you understand? You have killed a man. We must go away. They will come for us, can you understand? We must be gone before the daylight comes."

"I was attacked," Kino said uneasily. "I struck to save my life."

"Do you remember yesterday?" Juana asked. "Do you think that will matter? Do you remember the men of the city? Do you think your explanation will help?"

Kino drew a great breath and fought off his weakness. "No," he said. "You are right." And his will hardened and he was a man again.

"Go to our house and bring Coyotito," he said, "and bring all the corn we have. I will drag the canoe into the water and we will go."

He took his knife and left her. He stumbled toward the beach and he came to his canoe. And when the light broke through again he saw that a great hole had been knocked in the bottom. And a searing rage came to him and gave him strength. Now the darkness was closing in on his family; now the evil music filled the night, hung over the mangroves, skirled[1] in the wave beat. The canoe of his grandfather, plastered over and over, and a splintered hole broken in it. This was an evil beyond thinking. The killing of a man was not so evil as the killing of a boat. For a boat does not have sons, and a boat cannot protect itself, and a wounded boat does not heal. There was sorrow in Kino's rage, but this last thing had tightened him beyond breaking. He was an animal now, for hiding, for attacking, and he lived only to preserve himself and his family. He was not conscious of the pain in his head. He leaped up the beach, through the brush line toward his brush house, and it did not occur to him to take one of the canoes of his neighbors. Never once did the

---

**1. skirled** (skʉrld) *v.*: Made a shrill, piercing sound.

**31 Literary Focus: Theme** When Juana "abandoned the past," the future was determined for her and her family. One might argue that the climax of the novel has been reached, for the ending is now inevitable. How might the killing of the man lying beside Kino be considered the climax of the novel?

**32 Reading Strategy** In previous references the reader has seen the importance of the canoe—it has served as a symbol of the family and its heritage. What predictions might you make regarding the destruction of the canoe?

**Cooperative Learning** Have students work in groups of three or four to compose lyrics for a "Song of the Boat." Encourage them to include images that reflect their ideas about what the boat symbolizes. Groups might use their prewriting time to explore their ideas through discussion, art, or freewriting. When all groups have finished, ask a volunteer from each group to read the completed lyrics to the class.

**33 Discussion** Less than twenty-four hours have elapsed since Kino and Juana awoke and longingly anticipated the events of this day. Unlike their expectations, the day has been filled with destruction. Recount the events of the day. Discuss the changes that have occurred in both Juana's and Kino's lives in the course of this time.

**Writing Transparency** You can use the graphic organizer *Outline* in **Transparencies for Writing** to help students organize the events of the day and establish the significance of each. If you wish to emphasize cause-and-effect relationships, you might use the *Series of Events Chain.*

**34 Discussion** Again Steinbeck keeps the intruders unnamed. Why do you think Juana refers to them as "the dark ones"?

**35 Reading Strategy** Based on what you know about Juan Tomás, how do you think Kino, Juana, and Coyotito will be received by him?

thought enter his head, any more than he could have conceived breaking a boat.

The roosters were crowing and the dawn was not far off. Smoke of the first fires seeped out through the walls of the brush houses, and the first smell of cooking corn-cakes was in the air. Already the dawn birds were scampering in the bushes. The weak moon was losing its light and the clouds thickened and curdled to the southward. The wind blew freshly into the estuary, a nervous, restless wind with the smell of storm on its breath, and there was change and uneasiness in the air.

Kino, hurrying toward his house, felt a surge of exhilaration. Now he was not confused, for there was only one thing to do, and Kino's hand went first to the great pearl in his shirt and then to his knife hanging under his shirt.

He saw a little glow ahead of him, and then without interval a tall flame leaped up in the dark with a crackling roar, and a tall edifice of fire lighted the pathway. Kino broke into a run; it was his brush house, he knew. And he knew that these houses could burn down in a very few moments. And as he ran a scuttling figure ran toward him —Juana, with Coyotito in her arms and Kino's shoulder blanket clutched in her hand. The baby moaned with fright, and Juana's eyes were wide and terrified. Kino could see the house was gone, and he did not question Juana. He knew, but she said, "It was torn up and the floor dug—even the baby's box turned out, and as I looked they put the fire to the outside."

The fierce light of the burning house lighted Kino's face strongly. "Who?" he demanded.

"I don't know," she said. "The dark ones."

The neighbors were tumbling from their houses now, and they watched the falling sparks and stamped them out to save their own houses. Suddenly Kino was afraid. The light made him afraid. He remembered the man lying dead in the brush beside the path, and he took Juana by the arm and drew her into the shadow of a house away from the light, for light was danger to him. For a moment he considered and then he worked among the shadows until he came to the house of Juan Tomás, his brother, and he slipped into the doorway and drew Juana after him. Outside, he could hear the squeal of children and the shouts of the neighbors, for his friends thought he might be inside the burning house.

The house of Juan Tomás was almost exactly like Kino's house; nearly all the brush houses were alike, and all leaked light and air, so that Juana and Kino, sitting in the corner of the brother's house, could see the leaping flames through the wall. They saw the flames tall and furious, they saw the roof fall and watched the fire die down as quickly as a twig fire dies. They heard the cries of warning of their friends, and the shrill, keening[2] cry of Apolonia, wife of Juan Tomás. She, being the nearest woman relative, raised a formal lament for the dead of the family.

Apolonia realized that she was wearing her second-best head shawl and she rushed to her house to get her fine new one. As she rummaged in a box by the wall, Kino's voice said quietly, "Apolonia, do not cry out. We are not hurt."

"How do you come here?" she demanded.

"Do not question," he said. "Go now to Juan Tomás and bring him here and tell no one else. This is important to us, Apolonia."

She paused, her hands helpless in front

_____
**2. keening** (kēn' iŋ) *adj.*: Wailing for the dead.

728    *The Novel*

## Grammar in Action

Sometimes a verb form acts as an adjective. This form of the verb is called a **participle.** The present participle ends in *-ing;* the past participle usually ends in *-ed, -t,* or *-n.* Using participles adds action and drama to your writing. Notice the participles in these sentences:

   . . . She washed her *bruised* face with the *stinging* salt water. . . .

A *searing* rage came to him and gave him strength.

   . . . A *wounded* boat does not heal.

Notice also that participles can be used to compress your writing. The third sentence might have read:

   A boat *that has been wounded* does not heal.

**Student Activity 1.** Locate the participles in the following sentences:

1. He struck her in the face with his clenched fist.

of her, and then, "Yes, my brother-in-law," she said.

In a few moments Juan Tomás came back with her. He lighted a candle and came to them where they crouched in a corner and he said, "Apolonia, see to the door, and do not let anyone enter." He was older, Juan Tomás, and he assumed the authority. "Now, my brother," he said.

"I was attacked in the dark," said Kino. "And in the fight I have killed a man."

"Who?" asked Juan Tomás quickly.

"I do not know. It is all darkness—all darkness and shape of darkness."

"It is the pearl," said Juan Tomás. "There is a devil in this pearl. You should have sold it and passed on the devil. Perhaps you can still sell it and buy peace for yourself."

And Kino said, "Oh, my brother, an insult has been put on me that is deeper than my life. For on the beach my canoe is broken, my house is burned, and in the brush a dead man lies. Every escape is cut off. You must hide us, my brother."

And Kino, looking closely, saw deep worry come into his brother's eyes and he forestalled him in a possible refusal. "Not for long," he said quickly. "Only until a day has passed and the new night has come. Then we will go."

"I will hide you," said Juan Tomás.

"I do not want to bring danger to you," Kino said. "I know I am like a leprosy. I will go tonight and then you will be safe."

"I will protect you," said Juan Tomás, and he called, "Apolonia, close up the door. Do not even whisper that Kino is here."

They sat silently all day in the darkness of the house, and they could hear the neighbors speaking of them. Through the walls of the house they could watch their neighbors raking through the ashes to find the bones. Crouching in the house of Juan Tomás, they heard the shock go into their neighbors' minds at the news of the broken boat. Juan Tomás went out among the neighbors to divert their suspicions, and he gave them theories and ideas of what had happened to Kino and to Juana and to the baby. To one he said, "I think they have gone south along the coast to escape the evil that was on them." And to another, "Kino would never leave the sea. Perhaps he found another boat." And he said, "Apolonia is ill with grief."

And in that day the wind rose up to beat the Gulf and tore the kelps and weeds that lined the shore, and the wind cried through the brush houses and no boat was safe on the water. Then Juan Tomás told among the neighbors, "Kino is gone. If he went to the sea, he is drowned by now." And after each trip among the neighbors Juan Tomás came back with something borrowed. He brought a little woven straw bag of red beans and a gourd full of rice. He borrowed a cup of dried peppers and a block of salt, and he brought in a long working knife, eighteen inches long and heavy, as a small ax, a tool and a weapon. And when Kino saw this knife his eyes lighted up, and he fondled the blade and his thumb tested the edge.

The wind screamed over the Gulf and turned the water white, and the mangroves plunged like frightened cattle, and a fine sandy dust arose from the land and hung in a stifling cloud over the sea. The wind drove off the clouds and skimmed the sky clean and drifted the sand of the country like snow.

Then Juan Tomás, when the evening approached, talked long with his brother. "Where will you go?"

"To the north," said Kino. "I have heard that there are cities in the north."

"Avoid the shore," said Juan Tomás. "They are making a party to search the

**36 Discussion** Based on what you know about the pearl, do you think the pearl can bring Juana and Kino peace?

**37 Discussion** How does Juan Tomás protect his brother and Juana?

**Electronic Handbook** You may wish to review participle form with students before having them complete the Grammar in Action activities. If students are using the Language Master 6000, have them enter the access word *verb* or *verbal* and press the GRAMMAR key to review facts about verbs or verb phrases.

2. Kino's arms and legs stirred like those of a crushed bug.
3. The canoe of his grandfather, plastered over and over, now had a splintered hole in it.
4. A tall flame leaped up in the dark with a crackling roar.
5. And as he ran a scuttling figure ran toward him.
6. The fierce light of the burning house lighted Kino's face strongly.
7. Juana and Kino could see the leaping flames.

**Student Activity 2.** Use participles to combine or compress the following sentences: Compare the sentences you created to the ones Steinbeck wrote.

1. They heard the shock go into their neighbors' minds at the news of the boat which had been broken.
2. He brought a little straw bag of red beans. The straw bag was woven.
3. He borrowed a cup of peppers and a block of salt. The peppers had been dried.
4. The mangroves plunged like cattle which had been frightened.
5. A fine sandy dust arose from the land and hung over the sea in a cloud which was stifling.

shore. The men in the city will look for you. Do you still have the pearl?"

**38** "I have it," said Kino. "And I will keep it. I might have given it as a gift, but now it is my misfortune and my life and I will keep it." His eyes were hard and cruel and bitter.

Coyotito whimpered and Juana muttered little magics over him to make him silent.

"The wind is good," said Juan Tomás. "There will be no tracks."

They left quietly in the dark before the moon had risen. The family stood formally in the house of Juan Tomás. Juana carried Coyotito on her back, covered and held in by her head shawl, and the baby slept, cheek turned sideways against her shoulder. The head shawl covered the baby, and one end of it came across Juana's nose to protect her from the evil night air. Juan Tomás embraced his brother with the double embrace and kissed him on both cheeks. "Go with God," he said, and it was like a death. "You will not give up the pearl?"

**39** "This pearl has become my soul," said Kino. "If I give it up I shall lose my soul. Go thou also with God."

## Chapter 6

The wind blew fierce and strong, and it pelted them with bits of sticks, sand, and little rocks. Juana and Kino gathered their clothing tighter about them, and covered their noses and went out into the world. The sky was brushed clean by the wind and the stars were cold in a black sky. The two walked carefully, and they avoided the center of the town where some sleeper in a doorway might see them pass. For the town closed itself in against the night, and anyone who moved about in the darkness would be noticeable. Kino threaded his way around the edge of the city and turned north, north

by the stars, and found the rutted sandy road that led through the brushy country toward Loreto[1] where the miraculous Virgin has her station.[2]

Kino could feel the blown sand against his ankles and he was glad, for he knew there would be no tracks. The little light from the stars made out for him the narrow road through the brushy country. And Kino could hear the pad of Juana's feet behind him. He went quickly and quietly, and Juana trotted behind him to keep up.

**40** Some ancient thing stirred in Kino. Through his fear of dark and the devils that haunt the night, there came a rush of exhilaration; some animal thing was moving in him so that he was cautious and wary and dangerous; some ancient thing out of the past of his people was alive in him. The wind was at his back and the stars guided him. The wind cried and whisked in the brush, and the family went on monotonously, hour after hour. They passed no one and saw no one. At last, to their right, the waning moon arose, and when it came up the wind died down, and the land was still.

Now they could see the little road ahead of them, deep cut with sand-drifted wheel tracks. With the wind gone there would be footprints, but they were a good distance from the town and perhaps their tracks might not be noticed. Kino walked carefully in a wheel rut, and Juana followed in his path. One big cart, going to the town in the morning, could wipe out every trace of their passage.

All night they walked and never changed their pace. Once Coyotito awakened, and Juana shifted him in front of her and soothed him until he went to sleep again.

---

**1. Loreto** (lō rä′ tō): A town on the western coast of Baja California.
**2. station:** Religious shrine.

And the evils of the night were about them. The coyotes cried and laughed in the brush, and the owls screeched and hissed over their heads. And once some large animal lumbered away, crackling the undergrowth as it went. And Kino gripped the handle of the big working knife and took a sense of protection from it.

41 The music of the pearl was triumphant in Kino's head, and the quiet melody of the family underlay it, and they wove themselves into the soft padding of sandaled feet in the dust. All night they walked, and in the first dawn Kino searched the roadside for a covert to lie in during the day. He found his place near to the road, a little clearing where deer might have lain, and it was curtained thickly with the dry brittle trees that lined the road. And when Juana had seated herself and had settled to nurse the baby, Kino went back to the road. He broke a branch and carefully swept the footprints where they had turned from the roadway. And then, in the first light, he heard the creak of a wagon, and he crouched beside the road and watched a heavy two-wheeled cart go by, drawn by slouching oxen. And when it had passed out of sight, he went back to the roadway and looked at the rut and found that the footprints were gone. And again he swept out his traces and went back to Juana.

She gave him the soft corncakes Apolonia had packed for them, and after a while she slept a little. But Kino sat on the ground and stared at the earth in front of him. He watched the ants moving, a little column of them near to his foot, and he put his foot in their path. Then the column climbed over his instep and continued on its way, and Kino left his foot there and watched them move over it.

42 The sun arose hotly. They were not near the Gulf now, and the air was dry and hot so that the brush cricked[3] with heat and a good resinous smell[4] came from it. And when Juana awakened, when the sun was high, Kino told her things she knew already.

"Beware of that kind of tree there," he said, pointing. "Do not touch it, for if you do and then touch your eyes, it will blind you. And beware of the tree that bleeds. See, that one over there. For if you break it the red blood will flow from it, and it is evil luck." And she nodded and smiled a little at him, for she knew these things.

"Will they follow us?" she asked. "Do you think they will try to find us?"

"They will try," said Kino. "Whoever finds us will take the pearl. Oh, they will try."

And Juana said, "Perhaps the dealers were right and the pearl has no value. Perhaps this has all been an illusion." 43

Kino reached into his clothes and brought out the pearl. He let the sun play on it until it burned in his eyes. "No," he said, "they would not have tried to steal it if it had been valueless."

"Do you know who attacked you? Was it the dealers?"

"I do not know," he said. "I didn't see them."

He looked into his pearl to find his vision. "When we sell it at last, I will have a rifle," he said, and he looked into the shining surface for his rifle, but he saw only a huddled dark body on the ground with shining blood dripping from its throat. And he said quickly, "We will be married in a great church." And in the pearl he saw Juana with her beaten face crawling home through the night. "Our son must learn to read," he 44

---

**3. cricked** (krikt) *v.*: Twisted.
**4. resinous** (rez′ 'n əs) **smell:** Odor of the pitchy substance that is discharged from some trees, such as evergreens.

*The Pearl* 731

41 **Discussion** How is the music of the pearl triumphant? Why does Kino believe it is triumphant?

42 **Critical Thinking and Reading** What examples of Juana's past actions are consistent with her knowledge and her silence?

43 **Discussion** Juana wonders if the value of the pearl has been an illusion. Certainly the pearl and all that it represents has been an illusion to Kino and those in the town closely connected with it. Discuss Steinbeck's use of illusion. Have students comment on other stories they have read that were based on illusion.

44 **Discussion** Steinbeck now helps the reader to see the signs of illusion and reality. How does he do this?

**45 Critical Thinking and Reading**
Why are the trackers hunting for Kino?

**46 Discussion** Discuss the animal imagery. How is Kino similar to prey?

said frantically. And there in the pearl Coyotito's face, thick and feverish from the medicine.

And Kino thrust the pearl back into his clothing, and the music of the pearl had become sinister in his ears, and it was interwoven with the music of evil.

The hot sun beat on the earth so that Kino and Juana moved into the lacy shade of the brush, and small gray birds scampered on the ground in the shade. In the heat of the day Kino relaxed and covered his eyes with his hat and wrapped his blanket about his face to keep the flies off, and he slept.

But Juana did not sleep. She sat quiet as a stone and her face was quiet. Her mouth was still swollen where Kino had struck her, and big flies buzzed around the cut on her chin. But she sat as still as a sentinel, and when Coyotito awakened she placed him on the ground in front of her and watched him wave his arms and kick his feet, and he smiled and gurgled at her until she smiled too. She picked up a little twig from the ground and tickled him, and she gave him water from the gourd she carried in her bundle.

Kino stirred in a dream, and he cried out in a guttural voice, and his hand moved in symbolic fighting. And then he moaned and sat up suddenly, his eyes wide and his nostrils flaring. He listened and heard only the cricking heat and the hiss of distance.

"What is it?" Juana asked.

"Hush," he said.

"You were dreaming."

"Perhaps." But he was restless, and when she gave him a corncake from her store he paused in his chewing to listen. He was uneasy and nervous; he glanced over his shoulder; he lifted the big knife and felt its edge. When Coyotito gurgled on the ground Kino said, "Keep him quiet."

"What is the matter?" Juana asked.

"I don't know."

He listened again, an animal light in his eyes. He stood up then, silently; and crouched low, he threaded his way through the brush toward the road. But he did not step into the road; he crept into the cover of a thorny tree and peered out along the way he had come.

And then he saw them moving along. His body stiffened and he drew down his head and peeked out from under a fallen branch. In the distance he could see three figures, two on foot and one on horseback. But he knew what they were, and a chill of fear went through him. Even in the distance he could see the two on foot moving slowly along, bent low to the ground. Here, one would pause and look at the earth, while the other joined him. They were the trackers, they could follow the trail of a bighorn sheep in the stone mountains. They were as sensitive as hounds. Here, he and Juana might have stepped out of the wheel rut, and these people from the inland, these hunters, could follow, could read a broken straw or a little tumbled pile of dust. Behind them, on a horse, was a dark man, his nose covered with a blanket, and across his saddle a rifle gleamed in the sun.

Kino lay as rigid as the tree limb. He barely breathed, and his eyes went to the place where he had swept out the track. Even the sweeping might be a message to the trackers. He knew these inland hunters. In a country where there was little game they managed to live because of their ability to hunt, and they were hunting him. They scuttled over the ground like animals and found a sign and crouched over it while the horseman waited.

The trackers whined a little, like excited dogs on a warming trail. Kino slowly drew his big knife to his hand and made it ready. He knew what he must do. If the trackers found the swept place, he must leap for the horseman, kill him quickly and take the rifle. That was his only chance in the world. And as the three drew nearer on the road, Kino dug little pits with his sandaled toes so that he could leap without warning, so that his feet would not slip. He had only a little vision under the fallen limb.

Now Juana, back in her hidden place, heard the pad of the horse's hoofs, and Coyotito gurgled. She took him up quickly and put him under her shawl and gave him her breast and he was silent.

When the trackers came near, Kino could see only their legs and only the legs of the horse from under the fallen branch. He saw the dark horny feet of the men and their ragged white clothes, and he heard the creak of leather of the saddle and the clink of spurs. The trackers stopped at the swept place and studied it, and the horseman stopped. The horse flung his head up against the bit and the bit-roller clicked under his tongue and the horse snorted. Then the dark trackers turned and studied the horse and watched his ears.

Kino was not breathing, but his back arched a little and the muscles of his arms and legs stood out with tension and a line of sweat formed on his upper lip. For a long moment the trackers bent over the road, and then they moved on slowly, studying the ground ahead of them, and the horseman moved after them. The trackers scuttled along, stopping, looking, and hurrying on. They would be back, Kino knew. They would be circling and searching, peeping, stooping, and they would come back sooner or later to his covered track.

He slid backward and did not bother to cover his tracks. He could not; too many little signs were there, too many broken twigs and scuffed places and displaced stones. And there was a panic in Kino now, a panic of flight. The trackers would find his trail, he knew it. There was no escape, except in flight. He edged away from the road and went quickly and silently to the hidden place where Juana was. She looked up at him in question.

"Trackers," he said. "Come!"

And then a helplessness and a hopelessness swept over him, and his face went black and his eyes were sad. "Perhaps I should let them take me."

Instantly Juana was on her feet and her hand lay on his arm. "You have the pearl," she cried hoarsely. "Do you think they would take you back alive to say they had stolen it?"

His hand strayed limply to the place where the pearl was hidden under his clothes. "They will find it," he said weakly.

"Come," she said. "Come!"

And when he did not respond, "Do you think they would let me live? Do you think they would let the little one here live?"

Her goading struck into his brain; his lips snarled and his eyes were fierce again. "Come," he said. "We will go into the mountains. Maybe we can lose them in the mountains."

Frantically he gathered the gourds and the little bags that were their property. Kino carried a bundle in his left hand, but the big knife swung free in his right hand. He parted the brush for Juana and they hurried to the west, toward the high stone mountains. They trotted quickly through the tangle of the undergrowth. This was panic flight. Kino did not try to conceal his passage as he trotted, kicking the stones, knocking the telltale leaves from the little trees. The high sun streamed down on the dry creaking

**47**

**48**

**47 Discussion** How do these sounds create the mood of this scene?

**48 Discussion** Discuss the dialogue between Kino and Juana. What do their words convey?

**Cooperative Learning** Hold a press conference! Tell students to imagine themselves as Kino's advisors. The reporters will be arriving soon asking the advisors' opinions about Kino's escape. Allow students to meet in groups and evaluate Kino's options. Encourage students to brainstorm for options Kino has not considered. Finally, have each group prepare a brief statement summarizing their conclusions about an advised course of action and their predictions about Kino's chances for survival. After each group makes its statement, allow the members of other groups to act as reporters and ask questions.

## Humanities Note

Fine art, *Cactus on the Plains (Hands)*, 1931, by Diego Rivera. Point out to students that this work is more consciously symbolic than Rivera's other works that they have seen and discussed. The title of the work clearly indicates that the work is not completely literal.

You may wish to use the following questions to generate discussion:

1. What is the mood of this painting? What elements most strongly affect your perception of the mood?
2. What do you think the hands symbolize?
3. How does this painting relate to the action of *The Pearl*?
4. How does this painting relate to Kino's personal internal conflict?
5. How does this painting relate to the societal conflict resulting from oppression?

**CACTUS ON THE PLAINS (HANDS), 1931**
*Diego Rivera*
Edsel and Eleanor Ford House
Grosse Pointe Shores, Michigan

734    *The Novel*

earth so that even the vegetation ticked in protest. But ahead were the naked granite mountains, rising out of erosion rubble and standing monolithic against the sky. And Kino ran for the high place, as nearly all animals do when they are pursued.

This land was waterless, furred with the cacti which could store water and with the great-rooted brush which could reach deep into the earth for a little moisture and get along on very little. And underfoot was not soil but broken rock, split into small cubes, great slabs, but none of it water-rounded. Little tufts of sad dry grass grew between the stones, grass that had sprouted with one single rain and headed,[5] dropped its seed, and died. Horned toads watched the family go by and turned their little pivoting dragon heads. And now and then a great jackrabbit, disturbed in his shade, bumped away and hid behind the nearest rock. The singing heat lay over this desert country, and ahead the stone mountains looked cool and welcoming.

And Kino fled. He knew what would happen. A little way along the road the trackers would become aware that they had missed the path, and they would come back, searching and judging, and in a little while they would find the place where Kino and Juana had rested. From there it would be easy for them—these little stones, the fallen leaves and the whipped branches, the scuffed places where a foot had slipped. Kino could see them in his mind, slipping along the track, whining a little with eagerness, and behind them, dark and half disinterested, the horseman with the rifle. His work would come last, for he would not take them back. Oh, the music of evil sang loud in Kino's head now, it sang with the whine of heat and with the dry ringing of snake rattles. It was not large and overwhelming now, but secret and poisonous, and the pounding of his heart gave it undertone and rhythm.

The way began to rise, and as it did the rocks grew larger. But now Kino had put a little distance between his family and the trackers. Now, on the first rise, he rested. He climbed a great boulder and looked back over the shimmering country, but he could not see his enemies, not even the tall horseman riding through the brush. Juana had squatted in the shade of the boulder. She raised her bottle of water to Coyotito's lips; his little dried tongue sucked greedily at it. She looked up at Kino when he came back; she saw him examine her ankles, cut and scratched from the stones and brush, and she covered them quickly with her skirt. Then she handed the bottle to him, but he shook his head. Her eyes were bright in her tired face. Kino moistened his cracked lips with his tongue.

"Juana," he said, "I will go on and you will hide. I will lead them into the mountains, and when they have gone past, you will go north to Loreto or to Santa Rosalia.[6] Then, if I can escape them, I will come to you. It is the only safe way."

She looked full into his eyes for a moment. "No," she said. "We go with you."

"I can go faster alone," he said harshly. "You will put the little one in more danger if you go with me."

"No," said Juana.

"You must. It is the wise thing and it is my wish," he said.

"No," said Juana.

He looked then for weakness in her face,

---

**5. headed** (hed′ əd) v.: Grew to maturity.

**6. Santa Rosalia** (san′ tə rō zaˈ lē ə): A town on the western coast of Baja California.

49 **Reading Strategy** Summarize the description of the terrain. How is the terrain fitting with the development of the story? How might this act as a foreshadowing?

50 **Discussion** How is this description of the music of evil different from any other?

51 **Discussion** What does this conversation tell the reader about Juana? How is she changing?

**52 Discussion** Why is their flight no longer one of "panic"?

**53 Reading Strategy** Steinbeck uses symbolism to convey meaning throughout the story *The Pearl*. Summarize what the message of this paragraph is; be attentive to the symbolism, particulary in the last sentence.

**Cooperative Learning** Students might clarify the meaning of symbols in this section and elsewhere in the novel by working in groups of three or four to create symbolism charts. Instruct students to first identify a few basic issues being addressed by Steinbeck in *The Pearl*. Then group members can divide the novel into sections and take notes on the symbols used. Students should identify the literal image, character, or event, the symbolic meaning, and its relationship to one or more of the major issues. Encourage group members to discuss their findings as they record them on the charts.

**52** for fear or irresolution,[7] and there was none. Her eyes were very bright. He shrugged his shoulders helplessly then, but he had taken strength from her. When they moved on it was no longer panic flight.

The country, as it rose toward the mountains, changed rapidly. Now there were long outcroppings of granite with deep crevices between, and Kino walked on bare unmarkable stone when he could and leaped from ledge to ledge. He knew that wherever the trackers lost his path they must circle and lose time before they found it again. And so he did not go straight for the mountains any more; he moved in zigzags, and sometimes he cut back to the south and left a sign and then went toward the mountains over bare stone again. And the path rose steeply now, so that he panted a little as he went.

The sun moved downward toward the bare stone teeth of the mountains, and Kino set his direction for a dark and shadowy cleft in the range. If there were any water at all, it would be there where he could see, even in the distance, a hint of foliage. And if there were any passage through the smooth stone range, it would be by this same deep cleft. It had its danger, for the trackers would think of it too, but the empty water bottle did not let that consideration enter. And as the sun lowered, Kino and Juana struggled wearily up the steep slope toward the cleft.

High in the gray stone mountains, under a frowning peak, a little spring bubbled out of a rupture in the stone. It was fed by shade-preserved snow in the summer, and now and then it died completely and bare rocks and dry algae were on its bottom. But nearly always it gushed out, cold and clean and lovely. In the times when the quick rains fell, it might become a freshet and send its column of white water crashing down the mountain cleft, but nearly always it was a lean little spring. It bubbled out into a pool and then fell a hundred feet to another pool, and this one, overflowing, dropped again, so that it continued, down and down, until it came to the rubble of the upland, and there it disappeared altogether. There wasn't much left of it then anyway, for every time it fell over an escarpment the thirsty air drank it, and it splashed from the pools to the dry vegetation. The animals from miles around came to drink from the little pools, and the wild sheep and the deer, the pumas and raccoons, and the mice—all came to drink. And the birds which spent the day in the brushland came at night to the little pools that were like steps in the mountain cleft. Beside this tiny stream, wherever enough earth collected for roothold, colonies of plants grew, wild grape and little palms, maidenhair fern, hibiscus, and tall pampas grass[8] with feathery rods raised above the spike leaves. And in the pool lived frogs and water-skaters, and waterworms crawled on the bottom of the pool. Everything that loved water came to these few shallow places. The cats took their prey there, and strewed feathers and lapped water through their bloody teeth. The little pools were places of life because of the water, and places of killing because of the water, too.

**53** The lowest step, where the stream collected before it tumbled down a hundred feet and disappeared into the rubbly desert, was a little platform of stone and sand. Only a pencil of water fell into the pool, but it was enough to keep the pool full and to keep the ferns green in the underhang of the cliff, and wild grape climbed the stone mountain

---

**7. irresolution** (ir rez′ ə loo′ shən) *n.*: Indecisiveness.

**8. pampas** (pam′ pəs) **grass:** Grass that grows on treeless plains in certain areas of the south.

and all manner of little plants found comfort here. The freshets had made a small sandy beach through which the pool flowed, and bright green watercress grew in the damp sand. The beach was cut and scarred and padded by the feet of animals that had come to drink and to hunt.

The sun had passed over the stone mountains when Kino and Juana struggled up the steep broken slope and came at last to the water. From this step they could look out over the sunbeaten desert to the blue Gulf in the distance. They came utterly weary to the pool, and Juana slumped to her knees and first washed Coyotito's face and then filled her bottle and gave him a drink. And the baby was weary and petulant,[9] and he cried softly until Juana gave him her breast, and then he gurgled and clucked against her. Kino drank long and thirstily at the pool. For a moment, then, he stretched out beside the water and relaxed all his muscles and watched Juana feeding the baby, and then he got to his feet and went to the edge of the step where the water slipped over, and he searched the distance carefully. His eyes set on a point and he became rigid. Far down the slope he could see the two trackers; they were little more than dots or scurrying ants and behind them a larger ant.

Juana had turned to look at him and she saw his back stiffen.

"How far?" she asked quietly.

"They will be here by evening," said Kino. He looked up the long steep chimney of the cleft where the water came down. "We must go west," he said, and his eyes searched the stone shoulder behind the cleft. And thirty feet up on the gray shoulder he saw a series of little erosion caves. He slipped off his sandals and clambered up to them, gripping the bare stone with his toes, and he looked into the shallow caves. They were only a few feet deep, wind-hollowed scoops, but they sloped slightly downward and back. Kino crawled into the largest one and lay down and knew that he could not be seen from the outside. Quickly he went back to Juana.

"You must go up there. Perhaps they will not find us there," he said.

Without question she filled her water bottle to the top, and then Kino helped her up to the shallow cave and brought up the packages of food and passed them to her. And Juana sat in the cave entrance and watched him. She saw that he did not try to erase their tracks in the sand. Instead, he climbed up the brush cliff beside the water, clawing and tearing at the ferns and wild grape as he went. And when he had climbed a hundred feet to the next bench, he came down again. He looked carefully at the smooth rock shoulder toward the cave to see that there was no trace of passage, and last he climbed up and crept into the cave beside Juana.

"When they go up," he said, "we will slip away, down to the lowlands again. I am afraid only that the baby may cry. You must see that he does not cry."

"He will not cry," she said, and she raised the baby's face to her own and looked into his eyes and he stared solemnly back at her.

"He knows," said Juana.

Now Kino lay in the cave entrance, his chin braced on his crossed arms, and he watched the blue shadow of the mountain move out across the brushy desert below until it reached the Gulf, and the long twilight of the shadow was over the land.

The trackers were long in coming, as though they had trouble with the trail Kino had left. It was dusk when they came at last

---

**9. petulant** (pech′ ə lənt) *adj.*: Impatient; irritable.

54 **Discussion** Kino is becoming more and more like a hunted animal. What images does Steinbeck use to convey this?

55 **Discussion** What does this conversation between Kino and Juana tell the reader?

*The Pearl* 737

**Critical Thinking and Reading** Why does Kino decide to get the rifle from one of the trackers?

**Enrichment** What do you think Juana and Kino feel as Kino departs?

**Discussion** In previous chapters Juana combines prayer and magic. Does it seem fitting that she would use both of these now? Why or why not?

to the little pool. And all three were on foot now, for a horse could not climb the last steep slope. From above they were thin figures in the evening. The two trackers scurried about on the little beach, and they saw Kino's progress up the cliff before they drank. The man with the rifle sat down and rested himself, and the trackers squatted near him, and in the evening the points of their cigarettes glowed and receded. And then Kino could see that they were eating, and the soft murmur of their voices came to him.

Then darkness fell, deep and black in the mountain cleft. The animals that used the pool came near and smelled men there and drifted away again into the darkness.

He heard a murmur behind him. Juana was whispering, "Coyotito." She was begging him to be quiet. Kino heard the baby whimper, and he knew from the muffled sounds that Juana had covered his head with her shawl.

Down on the beach a match flared, and in its momentary light Kino saw that two of the men were sleeping, curled up like dogs, while the third watched, and he saw the glint of the rifle in the match light. And then the match died, but it left a picture on Kino's eyes. He could see it, just how each man was, two sleeping curled up and the third squatting in the sand with the rifle between his knees.

Kino moved silently back into the cave. Juana's eyes were two sparks reflecting a low star. Kino crawled quietly close to her and he put his lips near to her cheek.

"There is a way," he said.

"But they will kill you."

"If I get first to the one with the rifle," Kino said, "I must get to him first, then I will be all right. Two are sleeping."

Her hand crept out from under her shawl and gripped his arm. "They will see your white clothes in the starlight."

"No," he said. "And I must go before moonrise."

He searched for a soft word and then gave it up. "If they kill me," he said, "lie quietly. And when they are gone away, go to Loreto."

Her hand shook a little, holding his wrist.

"There is no choice," he said. "It is the only way. They will find us in the morning."

Her voice trembled a little. "Go with God," she said.

He peered closely at her and he could see her large eyes. His hand fumbled out and found the baby, and for a moment his palm lay on Coyotito's head. And then Kino raised his hand and touched Juana's cheek, and she held her breath.

Against the sky in the cave entrance Juana could see that Kino was taking off his white clothes, for dirty and ragged though they were, they would show up against the dark night. His own brown skin was a better protection for him. And then she saw how he hooked his amulet[10] neck-string about the horn handle of his great knife, so that it hung down in front of him and left both hands free. He did not come back to her. For a moment his body was black in the cave entrance, crouched and silent, and then he was gone.

Juana moved to the entrance and looked out. She peered like an owl from the hole in the mountain, and the baby slept under the blanket on her back, his face turned sideways against her neck and shoulder. She could feel his warm breath against her skin, and Juana whispered her combination of

---

10. **amulet** (am′ yə lit) *adj.*: Charm worn to protect against evil.

738 *The Novel*

---

## Grammar in Action

Using **specific verbs** that are both colorful and vivid will make your meaning clear and your sentences interesting. Study the following pairs of sentences. The first uses a common, less specific verb; the second is Steinbeck's.

The wind hit them with bits of sticks. . . .
[The wind] *pelted* them with bits of sticks . . .

Kino found his way around the edge of the city . . .
Kino *threaded* his way around the edge of the city . . .

*Pelted* tells us that they were hit repeatedly; *threaded* tells us Kino moved in a winding, complicated manner.

**Student Activity 1.** Choose verbs from the list to complete the following sentences:

| | | |
|---|---|---|
| hissed | gurgled | scampered |
| lumbered | gripped | burned |
| screeched | | |

prayer and magic, her Hail Marys and her ancient intercession, against the black un-human things.

The night seemed a little less dark when she looked out, and to the east there was a lightening in the sky, down near the horizon where the moon would show. And, looking down, she could see the cigarette of the man on watch.

Kino edged like a slow lizard down the smooth rock shoulder. He had turned his neck-string so that the great knife hung down from his back and could not clash against the stone. His spread fingers gripped the mountain, and his bare toes found support through contact, and even his chest lay against the stone so that he would not slip. For any sound, a rolling pebble or a sigh, a little slip of flesh on rock, would rouse the watchers below. Any sound that was not germane[11] to the night would make them alert. But the night was not silent; the little tree frogs that lived near the stream twittered like birds, and the high metallic ringing of the cicadas filled the mountain cleft. And Kino's own music was in his head, the music of the enemy, low and pulsing, nearly asleep. But the Song of the Family had become as fierce and sharp and feline as the snarl of a female puma. The family song was alive now and driving him down on the dark enemy. The harsh cicada seemed to take up its melody, and the twittering tree frogs called little phrases of it.

And Kino crept silently as a shadow down the smooth mountain face. One bare foot moved a few inches and the toes touched the stone and gripped, and the other foot a few inches, and then the palm of one hand a little downward, and then the

_____
**11. germane** (jər mān') *adj.*: Truly related.

other hand, until the whole body, without seeming to move, had moved. Kino's mouth was open so that even his breath would make no sound, for he knew that he was not invisible. If the watcher, sensing movement, looked at the dark place against the stone which was his body, he could see him. Kino must move so slowly he would not draw the watcher's eyes. It took him a long time to reach the bottom and to crouch behind a little dwarf palm. His heart thundered in his chest and his hands and face were wet with sweat. He crouched and took great slow long breaths to calm himself.

Only twenty feet separated him from the enemy now, and he tried to remember the ground between. Was there any stone which might trip him in his rush? He kneaded his legs against cramp and found that his muscles were jerking after their long tension. And then he looked apprehensively to the east. The moon would rise in a few moments now, and he must attack before it rose. He could see the outline of the watcher, but the sleeping men were below his vision. It was the watcher Kino must find—must find quickly and without hesitation. Silently he drew the amulet string over his shoulder and loosened the loop from the horn handle of his great knife.

He was too late, for as he rose from his crouch the silver edge of the moon slipped above the eastern horizon, and Kino sank back behind his bush.

It was an old and ragged moon, but it threw hard light and hard shadow into the mountain cleft, and now Kino could see the seated figure of the watcher on the little beach beside the pool. The watcher gazed full at the moon, and then he lighted another cigarette, and the match illumined his dark face for a moment. There could be no waiting now; when the watcher turned his

*The Pearl* 739

**59** **Literary Focus: Plot** Note the vivid description of nature. How does this emphasize Kino's predicament?
**60** **Reading Strategy** Summarize these paragraphs. Tell the importance of time and timing.

**Electronic Handbook** You may wish to review the use of specific verbs with students before having them complete the Grammar in Action activities. If students are using the Language Master 6000, have them enter the access word *verbal* or *verb* and press the GRAMMAR key to review information about verbal phrases or facts about verbs.

1. When Coyotito _____ on the ground Kino said, "Keep him quiet."

2. The owls _____ and _____ over Kino's head.

3. He let the sun play on the pearl until it _____ in his eyes.

4. Some large animal _____ away, crackling the undergrowth as it went.

5. Small gray birds _____ on the ground in the shade.

6. Kino _____ the handle of the big working knife.

**Student Activity 2.** Rewrite the following sentences, substituting a more specific, vivid verb for the italicized verb:

1. The two trackers *moved* about on the little beach.
2. Her voice *shook* a little.
3. She *watched* like an owl from the hole in the mountain.
4. Kino *moved* like a slow lizard down the smooth rock shoulder.
5. His heart *beat* in his chest.
6. The match *lit up* his dark face for a moment.

61 **Enrichment** Coyotito's name means "little coyote." What do you think the significance might be of the trackers thinking Coyotito's cry is that of a coyote pup?

62 **Literary Focus: Conflict** Discuss the role of sound in the resolution of the conflict between Kino and the trackers.

63 **Reading Strategy** What do you think has happened?

64 **Discussion** Reread Steinbeck's description of Kino and Juana as they return to their village. How has their relationship changed? What does Steinbeck mean when he writes that "they had gone through pain and had come out on the other side"? Does it mean that Kino and Juana will be all right now that the experience is over? Why or why not?

**Videocassette** You may wish to view the conclusion of the **Library of Video Classics** videotape of *The Pearl* when students have finished reading Chapter 6. Lead students to compare and contrast the two treatments of the work. What feature of the film do they feel best captures the essence of the novel? In what areas do they feel the film is weak? What features unique to the film did they enjoy?

head, Kino must leap. His legs were as tight as wound springs.

And then from above came a little murmuring cry. The watcher turned his head to listen and then he stood up, and one of the sleepers stirred on the ground and awakened and asked quietly, "What is it?"

"I don't know," said the watcher. "It sounded like a cry, almost like a human —like a baby."

The man who had been sleeping said, "You can't tell. Some coyote bitch with a litter. I've heard a coyote pup cry like a baby."

The sweat rolled in drops down Kino's forehead and fell into his eyes and burned them. The little cry came again and the watcher looked up the side of the hill to the dark cave.

"Coyote maybe," he said, and Kino heard the harsh click as he cocked the rifle.

"If it's a coyote, this will stop it," the watcher said as he raised the gun.

Kino was in midleap when the gun crashed and the barrel-flash made a picture on his eyes. The great knife swung and crunched hollowly. It bit through neck and deep into chest, and Kino was a terrible machine now. He grasped the rifle even as he wrenched free his knife. His strength and his movement and his speed were a machine. He whirled and struck the head of the seated man like a melon. The third man scrabbled away like a crab, slipped into the pool, and then he began to climb frantically, to climb up the cliff where the water penciled down. His hands and feet threshed in the tangle of the wild grapevine, and he whimpered and gibbered as he tried to get up. But Kino had become as cold and deadly as steel. Deliberately he threw the lever of the rifle, and then he raised the gun and aimed deliberately and fired. He saw his enemy tumble backward into the pool, and

Kino strode to the water. In the moonlight he could see the frantic frightened eyes, and Kino aimed and fired between the eyes.

And then Kino stood uncertainly. Something was wrong, some signal was trying to get through to his brain. Tree frogs and cicadas were silent now. And then Kino's brain cleared from its red concentration and he knew the sound—the keening, moaning, rising hysterical cry from the little cave in the side of the stone mountain, the cry of death.

Everyone in La Paz remembers the return of the family; there may be some old ones who saw it, but those whose fathers and whose grandfathers told it to them remember it nevertheless. It is an event that happened to everyone.

It was late in the golden afternoon when the first little boys ran hysterically in the town and spread the word that Kino and Juana were coming back. And everyone hurried to see them. The sun was settling toward the western mountains and the shadows on the ground were long. And perhaps that was what left the deep impression on those who saw them.

The two came from the rutted country road into the city, and they were not walking in single file, Kino ahead and Juana behind, as usual, but side by side. The sun was behind them and their long shadows stalked ahead, and they seemed to carry two towers of darkness with them. Kino had a rifle across his arm and Juana carried her shawl like a sack over her shoulder. And in it was a small limp heavy bundle. The shawl was crusted with dried blood, and the bundle swayed a little as she walked. Her face was hard and lined and leathery with fatigue and with the tightness with which she fought fatigue. And her wide eyes stared inward on herself. She was as remote and as removed as Heaven. Kino's lips were thin

---

## Primary Source

In *Twentieth Century Views,* Harry Morris draws the following comparisons and contrasts between *The Pearl* and the legend from which it sprang:

We see in Steinbeck's source all the major elements of his expanded version: the Mexican peasant, the discovered pearl, the belief that the pearl will make the finder free, the corrupt brokers, the attacks, the flight, the return, and the

disposal of the pearl. But there are also additions and alterations. The episodes of the doctor and the priest are added; the motives for retaining the pearl are changed. While the additions add perhaps some realism at the same time that they increase the impact of the allegory, the alterations tend to diminish the realistic aspects of the hero. Kino becomes almost unbelievably sophisticated. The boy wants only to be drunk forever; Kino wants his son educated. The boy wants to buy prayers for his own soul and for the souls of his relatives in Purgatory; Kino distrusts the priest who asks that the church be remembered when and his jaws tight, and the people say that he carried fear with him, that he was as dangerous as a rising storm. The people say that the two seemed to be removed from human experience; that they had gone through pain and had come out on the other side; that there was almost a magical protection about them. And those people who had rushed to see them crowded back and let them pass and did not speak to them.

Kino and Juana walked through the city as though it were not there. Their eyes glanced neither right nor left nor up nor down, but stared only straight ahead. Their legs moved a little jerkily, like well-made wooden dolls, and they carried pillars of black fear about them. And as they walked through the stone and plaster city brokers peered at them from barred windows and servants put one eye to a slitted gate and mothers turned the faces of their youngest children inward against their skirts. Kino and Juana strode side by side through the stone and plaster city and down among the brush houses, and the neighbors stood back and let them pass. Juan Tomás raised his hand in greeting and did not say the greeting and left his hand in the air for a moment uncertainly.

In Kino's ears the Song of the Family was as fierce as a cry. He was immune and terrible, and his song had become a battle cry. They trudged past the burned square where their house had been without even looking at it. They cleared the brush that edged the beach and picked their way down the shore toward the water. And they did not look toward Kino's broken canoe.

And when they came to the water's edge they stopped and stared out over the Gulf. And then Kino laid the rifle down, and he dug among his clothes, and then he held the great pearl in his hand. He looked into its surface and it was gray and ulcerous. Evil faces peered from it into his eyes, and he saw the light of burning. And in the surface of the pearl he saw the frantic eyes of the man in the pool. And in the surface of the

**THE SOB, 1939**
*David Alfaro Siqueiros*
*The Museum of Modern Art, New York*

*The Pearl* 741

the pearl is sold, closes his fist only more tightly about the pearl, determined instead to buy a rifle. The boy's desires are primitive; they are consonant with his origins and his intellect, crafty and wise as he may be. Kino's wants are sophisticated; he sees in the pearl not the objects that can be bought, but beyond. Coyotito's education will make the Indians free, a social, political, and economic sophistication; new clothes and a church wedding will give Kino and Juana position and respectability, again a social sophistication. With the rifle all other things were possible . . . Later, ironically, all that the rifle gives to Kino is the power to destroy human life; and in this irony, the symbolic import of the pearl-rifle fusion gives to the allegory the very complication that . . . is lacking. The pearl is not clearly good or evil, black or white.

**Discussion** Why do you think Juana wants Kino to throw the pearl away?

**68 Enrichment** What do you think lies ahead for Kino and Juana now that they have thrown the pearl away? Discuss their future in light of the tragedy they have experienced.

**69 Literary Focus: Conflict** The conflict in the novel is paralleled by the sounds in the novel. Trace the changes in sounds and compare these to the action of the conflict. What is meant by the last line of the novel, "And the music of the pearl drifted to a whisper and disappeared"?

**Reader's Response** Of *The Pearl* Steinbeck said, "If this story is a parable, perhaps everyone takes his own meaning from it and reads his own life into it." What meaning do you take from *The Pearl*? How do you read your life into the allegory?

**Thematic Response** What choices does Kino now face? What advice would you give him?

## Closure and Extension

### ANSWERS TO RESPONDING TO THE SELECTION
*Your Response*

1. Encourage students to consider how their answers were affected by the benefit of hindsight.

### Recalling

2. They say the pearl is like "fool's gold" and that it is too big and no one would buy it. Kino decides to go to the capital to try to sell it for more money.
3. Kino has killed one of the "dark ones"; he is afraid the trackers will seek revenge and in doing so will kill him and get the pearl. Kino hears the cry of death after he kills the trackers.
4. Kino throws the pearl into the Gulf.

pearl he saw Coyotito lying in the little cave with the top of his head shot away. And the pearl was ugly; it was gray, like a malignant growth. And Kino heard the music of the pearl, distorted and insane. Kino's hand shook a little, and he turned slowly to Juana and held the pearl out to her. She stood beside him, still holding her dead bundle over her shoulder. She looked at the pearl in his hand for a moment and then she looked into Kino's eyes and said softly, "No, you."

And Kino drew back his arm and flung the pearl with all his might. Kino and Juana watched it go, winking and glimmering under the setting sun. They saw the little splash in the distance, and they stood side by side watching the place for a long time.

And the pearl settled into the lovely green water and dropped toward the bottom. The waving branches of the algae called to it and beckoned to it. The lights on its surface were green and lovely. It settled down to the sand bottom among the fernlike plants. Above, the surface of the water was a green mirror. And the pearl lay on the floor of the sea. A crab scampering over the bottom raised a little cloud of sand, and when it settled the pearl was gone.

And the music of the pearl drifted to a whisper and disappeared.

## RESPONDING TO THE SELECTION

### Your Response

1. If you were Kino, would you have accepted the pearl dealer's offer? Why or why not?

### Recalling

2. What do the pearl dealers tell Kino about his pearl? Explain Kino's decision after visiting the pearl dealers.
3. For what reason does Kino fear the trackers? What sound does Kino hear after he kills the trackers?
4. What does Kino do with the pearl at the end of the story?

### Interpreting

5. Why does Kino hear "evil music" after the pearl dealer names his price?

6. Compare and contrast reactions to Kino's turning down the 1,500 pesos.
7. What does Kino mean at the end of Chapter 4 when he says: "I am a man"?
8. What does Kino mean when he says: "This pearl has become my soul. If I give it up I shall lose my soul"?
9. When Kino hands Juana the pearl to dispose of, why does she insist that he throw it away?

### Applying

10. Do you agree with Kino's decision to go to the capital to sell his pearl instead of accepting one of the pearl dealers' offers? Give reasons for your answer.
11. If Kino and Juana had never found the pearl, their life probably would not have changed. Do you think any good came of their discovery? Give reasons for your answer.

742    The Novel

### Interpreting

5. He feels that the pearl dealer is cheating him.
6. The neighbors are divided in regard to what they think Kino should do—some think he is being cheated by the pearl buyers; others think that Kino is fighting the established procedures. The comments of the pearl buyers influence their views regarding the value of the pearl.
7. Answers will differ. Suggested response: Kino means that as a man and the head of his family he will do anything in his determination to protect them and improve their lives.
8. Answers will differ. Suggested response: Kino means that he has identified so strongly with his dreams that the pearl can fulfill that his self-image would be damaged if he gave up his dreams.
9. She wants him to prove that he no longer wants it.

### Applying

10. Answers will differ. Some students might say that if Kino had taken the 1,500 pesos that were offered him, less harm would have come his way; others might say that by not allowing himself to be cheated by the pearl buyers, Kino made a powerful—and perhaps admirable statement—about his rejection of that dishonest system.
11. Answers will differ. Some students might say that since Kino and

# ANALYZING LITERATURE

## Understanding Plot and Theme

**Plot,** the sequence of related events or incidents that make up a literary work, usually involves conflict, climax, and resolution. The first conflict in *The Pearl* is the problem caused by Coyotito's scorpion sting. The sting generates the conflicts that follow throughout the plot. The climax, or the story's highest point of interest, comes near the end of the novel. It is followed by the resolution, when the characters resolve the conflict, and the writer reveals the outcome of the plot.

**Theme** is the universal truth or message the author conveys. A novel may have several themes. Analyzing the plot can often lead you to a better understanding of these themes.

1. List the major events that make up the plot in Chapters 4–6 of *The Pearl*.
2. What is the major conflict in *The Pearl*?
3. What is the climax of *The Pearl*?
4. How is the conflict resolved?
5. In their minds Kino and Juana hear the "song" of the family, of evil, and of the pearl. How does the writer use these "songs" to give clues to the theme?
6. When Kino and Juana set out to sell the pearl, what do they feel? How does what they feel reveal theme?
7. What do you think is the main theme of *The Pearl*? What minor themes can you identify?

# CRITICAL THINKING AND READING

## Recognizing Cause and Effect

When writing about cause and effect, you attempt to explain relationships. A **cause** makes something occur; an **effect** is the outcome of the cause.

To identify an effect, ask yourself, "What happened?" To identify its cause, ask, "Why?"

1. What causes the following events?
   a. Kino decides to go to the capital.
   b. The watcher shoots into the cave.
2. What are the effects of the following events?
   a. Juana returns the pearl to Kino after it has been knocked from his hand in the pathway by the beach.
   b. Kino kills a man in self-defense.

# THINKING AND WRITING

## Responding to Literary Criticism

It has been said of Steinbeck, "He wanted to be an individualist; he admired individualists; yet he also had a strong social conscience and a strong sense of right and wrong."

Write an essay explaining how this quotation is true of Steinbeck's writing in *The Pearl*. First, list the ways in which Steinbeck shows his admiration for individualists, or people who choose to go their own way. Then describe his strong social conscience—his caring for people who are downtrodden—and his strong sense of right and wrong. Then use this information to write your essay. Revise your essay to include examples that support your statements. Proofread for errors in spelling, grammar, and punctuation.

# LEARNING OPTIONS

1. **Writing.** The story of Kino and Juana and the pearl has a profound effect on the people of La Paz. Write a diary entry that describes the day Kino and Juana return home, from the point of view of one of the following people: Juan Tomás, the doctor, or the pearl dealer.
2. **Cross-curricular Connection.** In your library look for further information about pearls. What qualities make a pearl valuable? On what points and against what standards are they judged? Then review the novel for descriptions of the pearl. Based on your research findings, do you think that the pearl Kino found was valuable? Why or why not?

*The Pearl   743*

about making their fortune. This feeling turns out to be ironic because they are disappointed—the pearl buyers try to cheat them. It helps reveal theme by showing the conflict between their desire to improve their lives and the obstacles they encounter.

7. Many interpretations have been made regarding the central idea of the story or its insight about life—for the possibility of gaining the privileges of the modern world, Kino gives up his soul and his heritage; it is about the search for happiness and one's need to choose between the simple, natural life and the sophisticated, opulent life.

## ANSWERS TO CRITICAL THINKING AND READING

1. a. Kino feels cheated by the pearl buyers.
   b. The watcher hears the sound of what he thinks is a coyote pup.
2. a. Because Kino still has the pearl, Juana, Kino, and Coyotito must flee from the people who envy and hate him.
   b. Juana, Kino, and Coyotito take flight to Loreto.

## THINKING AND WRITING

For help in writing an essay, students may use the practice sheet Writing an Essay in the Writing Process Activities section of the Teaching Portfolio, Volume II.

## LEARNING OPTIONS

1. Allowing time for role-playing and discussion may help kinesthetic and interactive learners to prepare for the writing activity.
2. Students that complete research on pearls may give an oral report, prepare a visual presentation, or lead a question-and-answer session with their classmates.

**Writing Across the Curriculum**
You might want to notify social studies teachers and then have students read John Steinbeck's nonfiction book *America and Americans*. Have them write an essay telling how their viewpoints of Americans are the same as, or different from, Steinbeck's.

Juana are still young and can have more children, it will help them in the future to know how greed can change other people and themselves.

## ANSWERS TO ANALYZING LITERATURE

1. The major events include the visit with the pearl buyers, the intruder's striking a blow at Kino, Juana's being struck by Kino for attempting to throw the pearl back into the Gulf, Kino's killing the man on the path, their flight to Loreto, running from the trackers, the killing of the three trackers, the death of Coyotito, the return to La Paz, and the throwing of the pearl back into the Gulf.
2. Literally, the major conflict is between Kino, who wants the life the pearl can buy for him, and people like the doctor, the pearl buyers, and the thieves, who want to get the pearl from Kino through dishonest means. As a parable, the major conflict is between the virtues of a simple life and the envy and greed that is fostered by material wealth.
3. Once Juana abandoned the past, the future was determined for her and her family. At this point the climax of the story has been reached and the ending is now inevitable.
4. The conflict is resolved when the pearl is thrown back into the Gulf.
5. The songs tell the reader how Kino feels; they describe Kino's comfort level with the opposing forces.
6. When Kino and Juana set out to sell the pearl, they are hopeful

743

## Preparation

### Motivation/Prior Knowledge

You might begin by having student volunteers role-play the parts of Kino and his young relative. Prompt the student who is playing the young relative to ask questions about Kino's feelings and motives. Encourage the student playing Kino to combine imagination and knowledge of the character to formulate answers.

**Focus** Discuss the quotation from Shakespeare. Most students will be able to appreciate the desire to know why things happen, particularly when things go wrong. Ask them to express the desire to "... find out the cause of this effect ..." in their own words. Is that desire always satisfied? Do they sometimes find out much later why things happened as they did? Emphasize the need to consider how Kino might respond to these questions as they write his reminiscence.

## Presentation

**Prewriting** Discuss the improvised reminiscences from the role-playing exercise. How do students feel each reminiscence could be improved? Does the reminiscence need more details? Does the character of Kino need further development? What details from the story support the interpretation? Do any of the thoughts expressed seem to be in conflict with Kino's personality? You might wish to allow students to form "search" groups to examine the story for the answers to these and other relevant questions.

**Writing Transparency** The *Series of Events Chain* graphic organizer in **Transparencies for Writing** can help you guide the groups in organizing their information.

**Drafting** Point out to students that Kino's reminiscence will need

# YOUR WRITING PROCESS

## WRITING A REMINISCENCE

*"Find out the cause of this effect . . ."*
**William Shakespeare**

Reminiscing is a way to remember things that have happened, and to share these experiences with others. Imagine that you are writing a play about Kino, set years after Steinbeck's novel *The Pearl*. In this play, Kino reminisces with a young relative, relating events that occurred after he discovered the pearl. How would Kino tell about his experiences?

### Focus

**Assignment:** Write a reminiscence that Kino might share with a young relative.
**Purpose:** To show how one event led to another in a chain of causes and effects.
**Audience:** The young relative.

### Prewriting

**1. Discover examples of cause and effect.** Brainstorm to list causes and effects that help to explain the experience Kino had with the pearl. A *cause* makes something happen; an *effect* is the outcome of the cause. To discover an effect, ask yourself, "What happened?" To discover a cause, ask yourself, "Why did this happen?"

**2. Chart causes and effects from *The Pearl*.** In the reminiscence you write, you will want Kino to explain what happened and why. Here are the first few entries on a chart one writer developed to help with these ideas.

**Student Model**

| CAUSE | EFFECT |
| --- | --- |
| Scorpion stings Coyotito. | Kino needs money for a doctor. |
| Kino discovers the pearl. | Kino thinks the family's problems are now solved. |
| Kino refuses to sell the pearl. | Kino must make a difficult journey to the capital. |
| Kino kills an unknown man on the beach. | Kino is now considered a criminal. |

744    *The Novel*

to be told in a modified chronological order. Some events that Kino is remembering may not have had immediate effects, but in order to communicate the cause-and-effect relationship that Kino has discovered over time, the effect will be related immediately following the cause. Instruct students to use their notes and charts to create a well-organized draft.

**Revising and Editing** Prompt students to use transitional expressions between paragraphs and sentences to clarify cause-and-effect relationships. Elicit students' reactions to the different words and phrases they might use. Are some too formal for Kino to use in speaking? Are some too rhetorical? Encourage students to choose words and phrases that are consistent with the diction they are using for Kino's speech.

**Software** If students have access to computers, allow them to use the **Writer's Helper** activity *Diction Level* to assist them in establishing an appropriate voice for Kino.

**3. Experiment until you find the right voice for Kino.** Skim through the novel to reacquaint yourself with the character of Kino and the way he speaks. Try out the voice you develop by writing a few sentences as Kino. Ask yourself: How would Kino express an idea differently from the way I would?

## Drafting

**1. Begin by expressing Kino's feelings about the events.** Put yourself in Kino's shoes. How does he feel about his life today? How does he feel about his experiences with the pearl long ago? What would Kino say to make a young relative want to listen to a story about his life?

> ### Student Model
> You say you hope luck finds you one day and blesses you with great wealth. When I was young and hopeful, I wished just as you wish, and I hoped just as you now hope. Let me tell you how my wishes and hopes took strange turns that changed me into the sad old man you see before you today.

**2. Use your chart as a guide to causes and effects.** To help keep track of the correct sequence of events and explain the cause-and-effect relationships among them, refer to your chart.

**3. Create a way of speaking for Kino.** Each person speaks in a way unique to his or her personality and experience. Keep this in mind when writing in the character of Kino. Vary the vocabulary and sentence structure to keep readers' interest, but also make sure the sentences are believable as Kino's actual speech.

## Revising and Editing

**1. How have you organized your ideas?** The ideas in your reminiscence should be presented clearly so that the reader understands their cause-and-effect relationships. Refer to your chart to make sure you have described these relationships accurately.

**2. Get Kino's voice right.** Show your draft to a classmate. Have your partner point out any sentences that do not seem consistent with the voice you have established. Also, ask your partner to evaluate whether or not this is the way Kino would address a young relative.

**3. Go for zero mistakes.** Proofread your speech carefully for errors in spelling, grammar, and punctuation.

**Grammar Tip**

Use precise nouns and verbs to add interest and believability to your writing.

**Options for Publishing**

• Read your reminiscence aloud to the class.
• With a partner, expand the reminiscence into a full scene between Kino and the young relative.

**Reviewing Your Writing Process**

1. Were you able to show how one event led to another in a chain of causes and effects? Explain.
2. How were you able to produce a believable voice for Kino?

## Closure and Extension

**Guidelines for Evaluation** The following questions may help you to evaluate each student's reminiscence:
1. Does the writer establish a cause-and-effect relationship between events?
2. Are the events accurately related?
3. Does the reminiscence include Kino's emotional reactions to the events?
4. Does the writer relate the events in an organized fashion?
5. Is the diction appropriate to the speaker?
6. Is the reminiscence free of errors in spelling, punctuation, and grammar?

**Alternative Assessment** *Collaborative Evaluation:* In groups of four, ask students to evaluate one another's work by responding to the following questions:

   What is the reminiscence that the writer has Kino share with the young relative?

   Are the details organized to show a cause-and-effect relationship?

   Has the writer captured Kino's voice? Is that voice consistent?

   Does the writer use precise nouns and verbs?

   Is the reminiscence free from errors in spelling, grammar, and punctuation?

   Based on your evaluation, what is an appropriate grade for this reminiscence?

   After the reminiscences have been evaluated, you may ask students to write protocols summarizing what they have learned about cause and effect in literature from completing this assignment and evaluating one another's work.

**Student Portfolios** You might have students keep their reminiscences in their writing portfolios.

**Grammar Tip** In choosing precise nouns and verbs, students must again be cautioned to consider the speaker's voice. Have the students search the story for clues to appropriate vocabulary.

**Enrichment** Have students interview relatives or neighbors about a significant event in their lives. Students may use audio- or videotape to record the interview. Allow time for students to share the interviews with their classmates.

**Motivation/Prior Knowledge** Encourage students to bring in copies of the novels they are considering as subjects for reviews. You might have students read representative passages from their novels and solicit comments from the class.

**Focus** Provide samples of several professionally written reviews of novels, television programs, and movies that are familiar to students. Discuss the different criteria used. What questions did the reviewer ask when setting standards by which to evaluate the work? Point out examples of how the writer supports his or her opinion. Ask the students whether they agree or disagree with the review. How can they support their opinions?

## Presentation

**Prewriting** You may wish to duplicate charts for students to use in developing their evaluations. Discussion groups can formulate questions that might be used as standards against which each element can be judged. Circulate among the groups and assist students in assessing whether the standards are relevant.

**Writing Transparency** You can use the Graphic Organizer *Outline* in **Transparencies for Writing** to assist students in organizing the information that they wish to include in their reviews.

**Drafting** Students can seek peer assistance in evaluating the effectiveness of their topic sentences. Is the topic sentence clear? Will it stimulate a reader's interest?

Encourage students to create a balance between summarizing ideas and using direct quotations. Emphasize the need to establish a clear relationship between the quoted material and the assertions being made in the review.

746

> *"All good books have one thing in common—they are truer than if they had really happened."*
> **Ernest Hemingway**

# YOUR WRITING PROCESS

## WRITING A BOOK REVIEW

If you read a book that contains entertaining writing or an important message, how can you best share your enthusiasm for it? If you read a book that puts you to sleep, how can you warn other readers? A book review can spread the good or bad news.

> **Focus**
>
> **Assignment:** Write a book review for your school magazine.
> **Purpose:** To evaluate a novel.
> **Audience:** Readers of the magazine.

### Prewriting

**1. Review the literary elements of the novel.** After you have chosen a novel you would like to review, identify each of the following elements: plot, character, theme, setting, point of view. Do you think one element is more important to the story than another?

**2. Chart criteria to evaluate the novel.** If you are going to judge a novel in a book review, you need to evaluate its success or failure based on certain standards. Look at the partially developed chart that helped one reviewer evaluate John Steinbeck's novel *The Pearl.* Then create a chart and develop your own standards for judging each element.

**Student Model**

Evaluation of *The Pearl*

| ELEMENT | STANDARD | EVALUATION |
|---|---|---|
| Plot | Is it original? | Yes; it's a unique tale with an important message. |
| Main Character | Is he believable? | Yes; his problems are very human. |
| Setting | Does it contribute to the plot? | Yes; this society has special pressures and conflicts. |

**Writing Transparency** You might wish to use *Model 7: Responding to Literature* in **Transparencies for Writing** to demonstrate form and content for this assignment.

**Revising and Editing** Peer reviewers might give a rating from 1 to 5 for each of the questions listed on students' page 749. Allow time for students to meet and discuss the ratings and the reasons for them.

**Grammar Tip** Using examples from *The Pearl,* review the correct procedure for setting off direct quotations. Refer students to the Handbook of Grammar and Revising Strategies for further guidance in citing quotations.

**Software** If students have access to computers, have them use the *Outline Document* activity in **Writer's Helper** to revise the organization and structure of their drafts.

**3. Organize your ideas into an outline.** As you look over your chart, think about the order in which you want to present your ideas. Use that order to create an outline. Under each point of evaluation, list story details to support your opinion. Finally, state your opinion in a topic sentence.

## Drafting

**1. Hook your readers with a strong opening.** Use the opening to grab the readers' attention and to focus on the most important aspects of the book.

> ### Student Model
>
> Through the moving story of Kino and Juana, John Steinbeck shows readers that conflicts between poor and rich exist in any society. We may all share a sense of justice and decency, but certain events can turn our natural optimism into fear and terror. Steinbeck succeeds in revealing this truth in *The Pearl*.

**2. Use your outline as a blueprint.** Use your outline to help you present your opinions. At times you may want to summarize ideas from Steinbeck's novel. Direct quotations can also make for strong supporting arguments.

## Revising and Editing

**1. Consult with your classmates.** Ask a small group of peers to answer these questions:
- Are you persuaded by my opinion?
- Have I logically supported my opinions with details?
- Is my writing lively and to the point?

**2. Make sure you have used direct quotations from the text effectively.** Check for accuracy and relevance.

> ### Student Model
>
> Although Juana lacks the formal education of the rich, her understanding of human nature is rich indeed. She comprehends the troubles the pearl will bring to her family. Notice how she responds to Kino's incident with ~~the intruder:~~ ^(at one point, for instance, she declares,) "This thing is evil," she cried harshly. "This pearl is like a sin. It will destroy us."

## Grammar Tip

Make sure to use correct punctuation to set off direct quotations.

## Options for Publishing

- Submit your book review to the school literary magazine or newspaper.
- With a group of classmates, create a book review magazine that includes reviews of novels, short stories, nonfiction, and poetry.

## Reviewing Your Writing Process

1. How did you develop standards by which to judge the novel you reviewed?

2. Did you use your evaluation chart and outline as you drafted your review? Why or why not?

## Closure and Extension

**Guidelines for Evaluation** The following questions can serve as a guide in assessing each student's book review:
1. Does the review demonstrate a knowledge of plot, character, theme, setting, and point of view?
2. Does the reviewer use appropriate criteria and relevant standards in assessing the novel?
3. Are the details organized around the main points?
4. Are the assertions made in the review supported with specific examples from the novel?
5. Is the review free of errors in spelling, grammar, and mechanics?

**Alternative Assessment** *Protocol:* Ask students to assess their own work by responding to the following questions:

What book have you chosen to review?

How do you try to engage your readers in the opening paragraph?

For what general reason do you recommend or not recommend the book?

What specific elements of plot, character, theme, setting, and point of view have you cited to support your evaluation of the book?

What direct quotations from the text have you cited in your review?

What have you learned about the book you read from writing this review?

**Student Portfolios** You may wish to have students include their reviews in their writing portfolios.

**Enrichment** Have students trade novels with a partner. Partners can work together to prepare a team presentation, in dialogue form, of their responses to the novels. Partners may alternately support each other's viewpoints, or the presentation may take the form of a debate, in which partners present their contrasting opinions.

# INDEX OF LITERATURE IN AMERICAN HISTORY

BUFFALO BILL'S WILD WEST
CONGRESS, ROUGH RIDERS OF THE WORLD.

MISS ANNIE OAKLEY.
THE PEERLESS LADY WING-SHOT.

Reading literature is another way to learn history. Stories, poems, and plays show you how people lived and what they thought in different periods in time. The following chart presents selections from this book according to periods in American history.

## THE NEW WORLD (PREHISTORY–1750)

## THE STRUGGLE FOR INDEPENDENCE (1750–1775)

## A GROWING NATION (1776–1860)

## THE NATION DIVIDED (1860–1865)

# HANDBOOK OF THE WRITING PROCESS

## Lesson 1: Prewriting

The writing process can be divided into five stages, as follows:

1. *Prewriting:* planning the writing project
2. *Drafting:* writing your ideas in sentences and paragraphs
3. *Revising:* making improvements in your draft
4. *Proofreading:* checking for errors in spelling and mechanics
5. *Publishing or sharing:* allowing others to read your writing

In this lesson you will learn about the steps involved in prewriting.

### STEP 1: ANALYZE THE SITUATION

A writing situation can be analyzed in six parts: topic, purpose, audience, voice, content, and form. As you begin thinking about a writing project, ask yourself the following questions about these six parts:

1. *Topic* (the subject you will be writing about): What, exactly, is this subject? Can you state it in a sentence? Is your subject too broad or too narrow?
2. *Purpose* (what you want your writing to accomplish): Is your purpose to explain? to describe? to persuade? to tell a story? What do you want the reader to take away from the writing?
3. *Audience* (the people who will be reading or listening to your work): What are the backgrounds of these people? Do they already know a great deal about your subject, or will you have to provide basic information?
4. *Voice* (the way your writing will sound to the reader): What impression do you want to make on your readers? What tone should the writing have? Should it be formal or informal? Should

it be cool and reasoned or charged with emotion?
5. *Content* (the subject and all the information provided about the subject): How much do you already know about the subject? What will you have to find out? Will you have to do some research? What people, books, magazines, newspapers, or other sources should you consult?
6. *Form* (the shape that the writing will take, including its organization and length): What will the final piece of writing look like? How long will it be? Will it be a single paragraph or several paragraphs? Will it take some special form such as verse or drama? In what order will the content be presented?

The answers to some of these questions will usually be obvious from the start. For example, your teacher may assign you a particular topic and may require that your writing be of a specified length or form. However, the answers to many of these questions will be up to you to decipher. Writing always involves making decisions, setting goals, and then making a plan for achieving these goals.

### STEP 2: MAKE A PLAN

Your answers to the questions listed under Step 1 will help you determine what your plan of action will be. For example, if you discover that you are undecided about your topic, your plan of action will have to include clarifying what your topic will be. Your plan of action might also include doing research to find out more about your topic. Depending on what you need to know before you begin writing, choose one or more of the prewriting techniques described in the next section to help you.

## STEP 3: GATHER INFORMATION

The following are some techniques for gathering ideas and information for use in your writing:

1. *Freewriting:* Think about your topic, and as you do so, write down everything that comes to your mind. Do not pause to think about proper spelling, grammar, or punctuation. Just write, nonstop, for one to five minutes. Then read your freewriting to find ideas that you can use in your paper.
2. *Clustering:* Write your topic in the middle of a piece of paper and circle it. Then, in the space around your topic, write down ideas that are related to it and circle these ideas. Draw lines to show how the ideas are connected to one another and to the main topic. This technique is especially useful for broadening or narrowing a topic. If your topic is too broad, you might use one of the related ideas as a new main topic. If your topic is too narrow, you might include some of the related ideas in your main topic.
3. *Analyzing:* Divide your topic into parts. Then think about each part separately and write down your thoughts about it in your notes. Also think about how the parts relate to one another and how they relate to the topic as a whole.
4. *Questioning:* Make a list of questions about your topic in your notes. Begin your questions with the words *who, what, when, where, why,* and *how.* Then do some research to find the answers to your questions.
5. *Using outside sources:* Consult books, magazines, newspapers, pamphlets, and reference works such as encyclopedias and atlases. Talk to people who are knowledgeable about your topic. Record in your notes any information that you gather from these sources.
6. *Making charts or lists:* Create charts or lists of information related to your topic. For example, you might list all the parts or characteristics of your topic, or you might make a timeline or a pros-and-cons chart.

## STEP 4: ORGANIZE YOUR NOTES

To make sense of the information you have gathered, you will need to put it into some kind of logical order. The following are ways to organize your notes:

1. *Chronological order,* or *time order:* the order in which events occur
2. *Spatial order:* the order in which objects appear in space, as from left to right, top to bottom, or near to far
3. *Degree order:* in increasing or decreasing order, as of size, importance, or familiarity

After you have organized your notes, make a rough outline for your paper.

## CASE STUDY: PREWRITING

Mia's English teacher asked the class to write a paragraph on the topic of animals. Mia knew that the topic was too broad for a one-paragraph composition, so she tried clustering to narrow the topic. See her chart on the next page.

Since Mia had two cats of her own, she decided that the topic of her paper would be *Why Cats Make Good Pets.* Her purpose would be to explain why it is worthwhile to own a cat, and her audience would be her classmates and her teacher. She decided that her tone would be informal, since a very formal, serious tone would not suit her topic.

Mia's next plan of action was to gather ideas about why she thought cats made good house pets. She made a list in her notes of the reasons why she believed this:

- They don't take up the whole chair like big dogs.

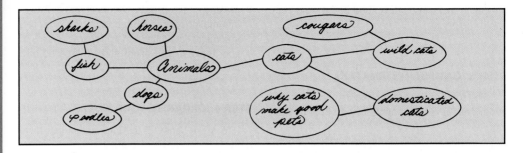

- They don't make a lot of noise.

- You don't have to walk them.

- They clean themselves and don't have to be bathed.

- They're easy to clean up after.

- They're cuddly.

- They can play with each other and not be too mad at you when you're out all day.

Mia made a rough outline for her paper. She showed in the outline that she would first introduce her topic, then would give three reasons why cats make good house pets, and finally would conclude with a summarizing sentence. She also decided that she would organize her three reasons by degree, from least to most important.

## ACTIVITIES AND ASSIGNMENTS

A. Answer the following questions about the case study:

1. How did Mia analyze the writing situation? What was her plan of action after she had analyzed it?
2. Why did Mia use the clustering technique? How did it help her?
3. Why did Mia make a list in her notes?

B. Choose one of the following topics or think of one of your own:

| | |
|---|---|
| School | Weekends |
| Hobbies | Writing |

Prepare to write a paragraph on the topic by following these steps:

1. Analyze the writing situation by answering the questions listed in this lesson.
2. Make a plan of action for gathering information and ideas to use in your paper. Use one of the prewriting techniques described in this lesson to gather information. Record this information in your notes.
3. Organize your notes and make a rough outline for your paragraph. Save your notes and outline in a folder.

# Lesson 2: Drafting and Revising

## CHOOSING A METHOD FOR DRAFTING

*Drafting* is the second stage in the writing process. After you have gathered information and made a rough outline, the next step is to put your ideas down on paper. As you draft, keep the following points in mind:

1. Choose a drafting method that feels right to you. There are many different ways of writing a draft. Some writers like to work from a detailed outline and to write very slowly and carefully. Other writers prefer to make only a very brief outline and to write quickly. Then they go back over their work and take care of the details. Whichever method works best for you is the method you should use.

2. Do not expect your first draft to be a finished product. Drafting gives you the chance to work out your ideas on paper. At this stage you should not worry about proper spelling, grammar, punctuation, and so on. You can take care of these details later.

3. Refer to your prewriting notes and to your outline as you write. Work from your notes and outline, keeping your audience and your purpose in mind.

4. Be flexible. Do not be afraid to discard old ideas as better ones come to mind. You may need to stop in the middle of your draft and do some more prewriting to develop your new ideas.

5. Write as many rough drafts as you need. You may have to make several attempts at drafting before you come up with a draft that is satisfactory. If you write a draft that does not seem to have a well-defined purpose or doesn't contain enough information to support your main idea, go back to the prewriting stage. Define your purpose more clearly, review your notes to discard irrelevant ideas, and gather any additional ideas and facts that you need.

## REVISING YOUR DRAFT

Once you have a draft that pleases you, you can begin refining and polishing it. This process of reworking a draft is known as *revising.* As you revise, ask yourself the questions in the Checklist

---

### CHECKLIST FOR REVISION

*Topic and Purpose*
- ☐ Is my topic clear?
- ☐ Does my writing have a specific purpose?
- ☐ Does my writing achieve its purpose?

*Audience*
- ☐ Will everything that I have written be clear to my audience?
- ☐ Will my audience find the writing interesting?
- ☐ Will my audience respond in the way that I would like?

*Voice and Word Choice*
- ☐ Is the impression that my writing conveys the one I intended it to convey?
- ☐ Is my language appropriately formal or informal?
- ☐ Have I avoided vague, undefined terms?
- ☐ Have I avoided jargon that my audience will not understand?
- ☐ Have I avoided clichés?
- ☐ Have I avoided slang, odd connotations, euphemisms, and gobbledygook except for novelty or humor?

*Content/Development*
- ☐ Have I avoided including unnecessary or unrelated ideas?
- ☐ Have I developed my topic completely?
- ☐ Have I supplied examples or details that support the statements I have made?
- ☐ Are my sources of information unbiased, up-to-date, and authoritative?

*Form*
- ☐ Have I followed a logical method of organization?
- ☐ Have I used transitions, or connecting words, to make the organization clear?
- ☐ Does the writing have a clear introduction, body, and conclusion?

---

*Drafting and Revising* 753

for Revision on page 753. If your answer to any of the questions is no, revise your draft until you can answer yes.

**Editorial Symbols**

Use the following symbols to edit, or revise, your draft:

| SYMBOL | MEANING | EXAMPLE |
|--------|---------|---------|
| ↻ | move text | She however was not at home. |
| ℯ | delete | I also went, too. |
| ∧ | insert | OUR of ∧car |
| ⌢ | close up; no space | every⌣where |
| ⊙ | insert period | ran⊙ I |
| ⋏ | insert comma | mice, bats⋏and rats |
| ∨ | add apostrophe | they're here |
| ⌄ ⌄ | add quotation marks | The Tell-Tale Heart |
| ⌐⌐ | transpose | to clearly see |
| ¶ | begin paragraph | crash. The man |
| / | make lower case | the Ꞵasketball player |
| ≡ | capitalize | president Truman ≡ |

**CASE STUDY: DRAFTING AND REVISING**

Mia used her prewriting notes from the preceding lesson to begin drafting her paragraph. Here is her first draft:

> Cats are grate housepets. They don't bark, you can take care of them easy and they're cuddly. I love my two cats.

Mia stopped writing and looked at her draft. She had given the three reasons why she thought cats were good pets, and now she had nothing more to say. She set a goal for her next draft: to give examples that would support each of her reasons.

Mia wrote several more drafts. Here is the last draft that she wrote, which she revised using standard editorial symbols:

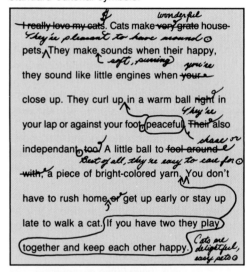

**ACTIVITIES AND ASSIGNMENTS**

A. Answer the following questions about the revised draft in the case study:

1. Why hasn't Mia corrected all of her grammar and spelling errors? When will these errors be corrected?
2. Why did Mia delete material in the first two sentences?

754   *Handbook of the Writing Process*

3. Why did Mia add the sentence "They're pleasant to have around"?
4. Why did Mia change the words "fool around with"?
5. What transitional words did Mia add to indicate that she was about to tell the last reason why cats are good house pets?
6. Why did Mia move the original last sentence in her paragraph?
7. Why did Mia add a new last sentence?
8. What other revisions did Mia make? Why did she make them?

B. Using your prewriting notes from the last lesson, write a draft of a paragraph on your topic. Then revise your draft. Follow these steps:

1. Read over your outline to see how your paragraph will be organized. Then write a thesis statement of one or two sentences to introduce your topic.
2. Write the rest of your draft, based on your outline and your prewriting notes. Make sure that you support your statements with evidence from your notes. Do not worry about spelling and mechanics at this point.
3. Write a conclusion that sums up the main point of your paragraph.
4. Revise your draft, using the Checklist for Revision in this lesson. If you answer no to any of the questions on the checklist, use standard editorial symbols to make the necessary corrections.

# Lesson 3: Proofreading and Publishing

## PROOFREADING YOUR FINAL DRAFT

Before a draft is ready to be shared with a reader, it must be checked for errors in grammar and usage, spelling, punctuation, capitalization, and manuscript form. This process of final checking is called *proofreading.* When you proofread, ask yourself the questions in the checklist at the left. If your answer to any of the questions is no, make the necessary corrections on your revised draft.

If you need to check your spelling or to review rules for mechanics, refer to a dictionary, writing textbook, or handbook of style.

> ### CHECKLIST FOR PROOFREADING
>
> *Grammar and Usage*
> ☐ Are all of my sentences complete? That is, have I avoided sentence fragments?
> ☐ Does each of my sentences express only one complete thought? That is, have I avoided run-on sentences?
> ☐ Do the verbs I have used agree with their subjects?
> ☐ Have all the words in my paper been used correctly? Am I sure about the meanings of all of these words?
> ☐ Is the person or thing being referred to by each pronoun clear?
> ☐ Have I used adjectives and adverbs correctly?
>
> *Spelling*
> ☐ Am I absolutely sure that each word has been spelled correctly?
>
> *Punctuation*
> ☐ Does every sentence end with a punctuation mark?
> ☐ Have I correctly used commas, semicolons, colons, hyphens, dashes, parentheses, quotation marks, and apostrophes?
>
> *Capitalization*
> ☐ Have I capitalized any words that should not be capitalized?
> ☐ Should I capitalize any words that I have not capitalized?
>
> *Manuscript Form*
> ☐ Have I indented the first line(s) of my paragraph(s)?
> ☐ Have I written my name and the page number in the top right-hand corner of each page?
> ☐ Have I double-spaced the manuscript?
> ☐ Is my draft neat and legible?

## PUBLISHING OR SHARING YOUR WORK

After you have proofread your revised draft, you are ready to share your writing with other people. When you write for school, you generally submit your work to your teachers. However, there are many other ways to share or publish your writing. The following is a list of possibilities:

1. Share your work in a small discussion group.
2. Read your work aloud to the class.
3. Share copies of your writing with members of your family or with friends.
4. Display your work on the class bulletin board.
5. Save your work in a folder for later publication. At the end of the year, work from the entire class can be bound together into a booklet.
6. Submit your writing to the school literary magazine, or start a literary magazine for your school or for your class.
7. Submit your writing to your school or community newspaper.
8. Enter your writing in literary contests for student writers.
9. Submit your writing to a magazine that publishes work by young people.

## CASE STUDY: PROOFREADING AND PUBLISHING

After revising her final draft, Mia made a fresh, clean copy for proofreading. She read the Checklist for Proofreading in this lesson and applied each question to her revised draft. Here is Mia's paragraph, with the proofreading corrections that she made, marked with editorial symbols:

> ¶ Cats make wonderful housepets. They're
> pleasant to have around. They make soft,
> purring sounds when ~~their~~ *they're* happy; they sound
> like little engines when you're close up. They
> curl up peaceful*ly* in a warm ball in your lap or
> against your foot. They're also independant
> — *all they need is*
> a little ball to chase or a piece of bright*ly*
> colored yarn. Best of all, they're easy to care
> for. *If you have two they play together and keep each other happy.* You don't have to rush home, get up ear-
> ly or stay up late to walk a cat. Cats are
> delightful, easy pets.

Mia made a clean final copy of her paragraph. Then she read it aloud to a few of her classmates in a small discussion group.

## ACTIVITIES AND ASSIGNMENTS

A. Answer the following questions about the case study:

1. What errors in spelling did Mia correct during proofreading?
2. Why did Mia change "peaceful" to "peacefully"?
3. What sentence fragment did Mia correct? How did she do this?
4. What punctuation error did Mia correct?
5. What error in manuscript form did Mia make? How did she correct it?
6. Are there any changes you think should still be made in Mia's paragraph? Explain.

B. Make a clean copy of your revised paragraph from the preceding lesson. Then use the Checklist for Proofreading to correct any errors in grammar and usage, spelling, punctuation, capitalization, and manuscript form that remain in your draft.

Make a final copy of your paragraph, and share this copy with your classmates and with your teacher.

# HANDBOOK OF GRAMMAR AND REVISING STRATEGIES

# STRATEGIES FOR REVISING PROBLEMS IN GRAMMAR AND STANDARD USAGE
## Problems of Sentence Structure

### ■ Run-on Sentences

**GUIDE FOR REVISING:**   A run-on sentence results when no punctuation or coordinating conjunction separates two or more independent clauses. A run-on sentence also occurs when only a comma is used to join two or more independent clauses.

**Strategy 1:**   **Create two sentences by using a period to separate independent clauses.**

**First Draft**   Roberto Clemente was a kind and caring friend, he was also a man of principle and great determination.

**Revision**   Roberto Clemente was a kind and caring friend. He was also a man of principle and great determination.

**Strategy 2:**   **Separate independent clauses with a semicolon.**

**First Draft**   Mrs. Flowers wanted Marguerite to read aloud, she also encouraged her to make a sentence sound in as many different ways as possible.

**Revision**   Mrs. Flowers wanted Marguerite to read aloud; she also encouraged her to make a sentence sound in as many different ways as possible.

**Strategy 3:**   **Use a comma and then a coordinating conjunction (*and, but, or, for, yet, so*) to join two sentences.**

**First Draft**   Charles often misbehaved in class, the teacher punished him.

**Revision**   Charles misbehaved in class, and the teacher punished him.

### ■ Fragments

**GUIDE FOR REVISING:**   A fragment is a group of words that does not express a complete thought. Although a fragment may begin with a capital letter and end with a period, it is only part of a sentence because it lacks a subject, a verb, or both.

| | |
|---|---|
| **Strategy 1:** | **Add a subject or predicate when necessary.** |
| First Draft | Debbie is a thin, bedraggled stray cat. Lives outdoors and occasionally visits Mrs. Ainsworth's house. |
| Revision | Debbie is a thin, bedraggled stray cat. She lives outdoors and occasionally visits Mrs. Ainsworth's house. |
| First Draft | A list of familiar foods and implements with roots in Indian culture. |
| Revision | A list of familiar foods and implements with roots in Indian culture would include several hundred items. |

| | |
|---|---|
| **Strategy 2:** | **Correct a phrase fragment by adding both a subject and a verb.** |
| First Draft | A form of argument in which the conclusion must be true if the premises are true. |
| Revision | Deduction is a form of argument in which the conclusion must be true if the premises are true. |

| | |
|---|---|
| **Strategy 3:** | **Correct a clause fragment by omitting the subordinating conjunction or by connecting the fragment to a nearby sentence.** |
| First Draft | Because Don Anselmo is in no hurry to sell his house and land. It takes months to reach the first agreement with him. |
| Revision | Because Don Anselmo is in no hurry to sell his house and land, it takes months to reach the first agreement with him. |

## Problems of Clarity and Coherence

■ **Effective Transitions**

**GUIDE FOR REVISING:** You can help your readers by using transition words and phrases to signal connections and relationships between words, sentences, and paragraphs.

| | |
|---|---|
| **Strategy 1:** | **Use transitions to indicate chronological order.** |
| First Draft | The Sakkaros dissolve, and the Wrights understand the reasons for their neighbor's odd behavior. |
| Revision | After the Sakkaros dissolve, the Wrights finally understand the reasons for their neighbors' odd behavior. |
| Model From Literature | After that the woman said, "Pick up my pocketbook, boy, and give it here."                   —*Hughes, p. 179* |

| | |
|---|---|
| **Strategy 2:** | **Use transitions to indicate spatial relationships.** |
| **First Draft** | When Lizzie and Bethany see the burnt grass, they know they have escaped the grass fire. |
| **Revision** | When Lizzie and Bethany see the burnt grass ahead of them, they know they have escaped the grass fire. |
| **Model From Literature** | Then he shook hands all around, put on his ragged gloves, took his stick and walked out with the boy behind him.<br>—*Sedillo, p. 94* |

| | |
|---|---|
| **Strategy 3:** | **Use transitions to indicate the order of importance of your ideas.** |
| **First Draft** | One theme suggested by *The Diary of Anne Frank* is that humans need hope and courage if they are to cope with troubles successfully. |
| **Revision** | The most important theme suggested by *The Diary of Anne Frank* is that humans need hope and courage if they are to cope with troubles successfully. |
| **Model From Literature** | And most of all, those cold numbers won't begin to delineate the man Roberto Clemente was.  —*Izenberg, p. 393* |

| | |
|---|---|
| **Strategy 4:** | **Use transitions to signal other logical relationships, such as introducing another item in a series, an illustration or an example, a result or a cause, a restatement, a conclusion or a summary, or an opposing point.** |
| **First Draft** | Sancho learns a number of lessons from his early experiences on the ranch. He acquires a liking for tamales and peppers, and he makes his regular bed ground under a mesquite tree just outside the gate. |
| **Revision** | Sancho learns a number of lessons from his early experiences on the ranch. For example, he acquires a liking for tamales and peppers, and he makes his regular bed ground under a mesquite tree just outside the gate. |

### ■ Vivid Modifiers

**GUIDE FOR REVISING:**  Modifiers such as adjectives, adverbs, and prepositional phrases describe subjects, verbs, objects, or other modifiers. Try to make your modifiers as clear, vivid, and specific as possible.

| Strategy 1: | Replace vague or abstract modifiers with specific, concrete ones. |
|---|---|
| First Draft | The doctor who attended Eliza Barnes was not very nice. |
| Revision | The doctor who attended Eliza Barnes was gruff, unsympathetic, and deeply prejudiced. |
| Model From Literature | She clung to the moist rail and breathed the damp salt air deep into her lungs. —*Uchida, p. 3* |

| Strategy 2: | Try to use fresh, original modifiers instead of stale, trite ones. |
|---|---|
| First Draft | Twain says he was proud to be a crew member on such a good boat. |
| Revision | Twain says he was proud to be a member of the executive family of so fast and famous a boat. |
| Model From Literature | The large woman simply turned around and kicked him right square in his blue-jeaned sitter. —*Hughes, p. 179* |

## ■ Pronoun-Antecedent Agreement

| Strategy 1: | Check to see that any personal pronoun you use agrees in number (singular or plural) with the noun that it replaces. |
|---|---|
| First Draft | Every five hundred years or so, the mythical phoenix bird would burn themselves up and rise from their ashes anew. |
| Revision | Every five hundred years or so, the mythical phoenix bird would burn itself up and rise from its ashes anew. |
| Model From Literature | She was a large woman with a large purse that had everything in it but hammer and nails. It had a long strap and she carried it slung across her shoulder. —*Hughes, p. 179* |

| Strategy 2: | Be sure to use a singular personal pronoun when its antecedent is a singular indefinite pronoun. |
|---|---|
| First Draft | Eudora Welty and Maya Angelou are celebrated contemporary writers; each emphasizes in their essay the importance of language and learning. |
| Revision | Eudora Welty and Maya Angelou are celebrated contemporary writers; each emphasizes in her essay the importance of language and learning. |
| Model From Literature | Everything was just as he had left it. —*O. Henry, p. 62* |

## ■ Misplaced Modifiers

**GUIDE FOR REVISING:** A modifier placed too far away from the word it modifies is called a misplaced modifier. Misplaced modifiers may seem to modify the wrong word in a sentence. Always place a modifier as close as possible to the word it modifies.

| | |
|---|---|
| **Strategy:** | **Move the modifying word, phrase, or clause closer to the word it should logically modify.** |
| **First Draft** | Professor Shlemiel consulted the telephone book for his own number in the drugstore. |
| **Revision** | In the drugstore, Professor Shlemiel consulted the telephone book for his own number. |
| **Model From Literature** | Hardly believing that she heard him aright, she unpinned the bud from the bosom of her dress, and placed it in his hand.<br>—*O. Henry, p. 66* |

## Problems of Consistency

## ■ Subject-Verb Agreement

**GUIDE FOR REVISING:** Subject and verb must agree in number. A singular subject needs a singular verb, and a plural subject needs a plural verb.

| | |
|---|---|
| **Strategy 1:** | **If the subject is singular (it names only one thing), then the verb must also be singular. If the subject is plural (it names two or more things), then the verb must be plural.** |
| **First Draft** | The narrator are the speaker or character telling a story. |
| **Revision** | The narrator is the speaker or character telling a story. |
| **Model From Literature** | The children of the village were overrunning their property.<br>—*Sedillo, p. 94* |

| | |
|---|---|
| **Strategy 2:** | **When a word group such as a subordinate clause or a prepositional phrase comes between the subject and the verb, the verb must still agree with its subject and not with a noun in the word group.** |
| **First Draft** | One of O. Henry's favorite devices in his short stories are the surprise ending. |
| **Revision** | One of O. Henry's favorite devices in his short stories is the surprise ending. |
| **Model From Literature** | Business in all lines was fairly good.     —*O. Henry, p. 63* |

| | |
|---|---|
| **Strategy 3:** | Use a singular verb with two or more singular subjects joined by *or* or *nor*. When singular and plural subjects are joined by *or* or *nor*, the verb must agree with the subject closest to it. |
| **First Draft** | Neither the Van Daans nor Mr. Dussel seem able to adjust very well to life in the attic. |
| **Revision** | Neither the Van Daans nor Mr. Dussel seems able to adjust very well to life in the attic. |

| | |
|---|---|
| **Strategy 4:** | Make sure that when a subject follows the verb, the subject and verb still agree with each other in number. |
| **First Draft** | There is always more candidates than baby dragons present on Hatching Day. |
| **Revision** | There are always more candidates than baby dragons present on Hatching Day. |

| | |
|---|---|
| **Strategy 5:** | Many indefinite pronouns can agree with either a singular or plural verb. The choice depends on the meaning given to the pronoun. |
| **First Draft** | Almost all the metaphors in Mimi Sheraton's essay involves the names of foods. |
| **Revision** | Almost all the metaphors in Mimi Sheraton's essay involve the names of foods. |
| **Model From Literature** | All I have to do in life is mind my brother Raymond, which is enough.     —*Bambara, p. 97* |

### ■ Confusion of Adjectives and Adverbs

**GUIDE FOR REVISING:**  Adjectives modify nouns and pronouns. Adverbs modify verbs, adjectives, or other adverbs.

| | |
|---|---|
| **Strategy 1:** | Use an adjective to modify a noun or a pronoun. |
| **First Draft** | During one remarkably meteor shower on a November night in 1833, an observer saw 240,000 meteors in nine hours. |
| **Revision** | During one remarkable meteor shower on a November night in 1833, an observer saw 240,000 meteors in nine hours. |

| | |
|---|---|
| **Strategy 2:** | Use an adverb to modify a verb, an adjective, or another adverb. |
| **First Draft** | Eugenie Roberts played the piano so beautiful that Miss Crosman hugged her. |

| **Revision** | Eugenie Roberts played the piano so beautifully that Miss Crosman hugged her. |
|---|---|

---

| **Strategy 3:** | **Be careful to make the correct use of troublesome adjective and adverb pairs such as bad/badly, fewer/less, and good/well.** |
|---|---|
| **First Draft** | Mitch feels badly when he learns more about Bridgie's life in Belfast. |
| **Revision** | Mitch feels bad when he learns more about Bridgie's life in Belfast. |
| **Model From Literature** | When Miss Crosman finally allowed me to start playing I played extra well, as well as I possibly could.  —*Jen, p. 87* |

### ■ Inconsistencies in Verb Tense

**GUIDE FOR REVISING:** Check to see that you maintain consistent verb tenses from sentence to sentence. Verb tenses should not shift unnecessarily.

---

| **Strategy 1:** | **Be sure that the main verbs in a single sentence or in a group of related sentences are in the same tense.** |
|---|---|
| **First Draft** | Paul Revere patted his horse's side. Then he gazed at the landscape and watches with special eagerness the belfry of the Old North Church. |
| **Revision** | Paul Revere patted his horse's side. Then he gazed at the landscape and watched with special eagerness the belfry of the Old North Church. |
| **Model From Literature** | He got up out of bed and put on his slippers and bathrobe and went softly upstairs to the attic and found the box of Christmas-tree decorations.  —*Buck, p. 24* |

---

| **Strategy 2:** | **When you want to describe the earlier of two actions that occurred at different times in the past, use a verb in the past perfect tense. This tense is formed with the helping verb *had* and the past participle of the main verb.** |
|---|---|
| **First Draft** | Before Harriet Tubman started out to Canada with the band of fugitives in December 1851, she planned the trip carefully for days. |
| **Revision** | Before Harriet Tubman started out to Canada with the band of fugitives in December 1851, she had planned the trip carefully for days. |
| **Model From Literature** | To the Bassets, Buster's arrival was rather like the intrusion of an irreverent outsider into an exclusive London club. For a long |

*Handbook of Grammar and Revising Strategies*   765

time they had led a life of measured grace; regular sedate walks with their mistress, superb food in ample quantities and long snoring sessions on the rugs and armchairs.

—Herriot, p. 442

## Problems With Incorrect Words or Phrases

### ■ Nonstandard Pronoun Cases

**GUIDE FOR REVISING:**  Use the nominative case for a personal pronoun that is either the subject of a sentence or a predicate nominative. Use the objective case for a personal pronoun when it is a direct object, an indirect object, or an object of a preposition.

| | |
|---|---|
| **Strategy 1:** | **Be sure to identify the case of a personal pronoun correctly when the pronoun is part of a compound subject or a compound object. It is often helpful to reword the sentence in your mind.** |
| **First Draft** | The students assigned to analyze the setting of "Crime on Mars" were Matt and me. |
| **Revision** | The students assigned to analyze the setting of "Crime on Mars" were Matt and I. (Could be reworded as follows: Matt and I were the students . . .) |
| **Strategy 2:** | **Personal pronouns in the possessive case show possession in two ways. Possessive pronouns show possession when they come before nouns. Certain personal pronouns also show possession when used by themselves. Notice that these pronouns sometimes have different forms (*mine, yours, his, hers, its, ours, yours, theirs*).** |
| **First Draft** | In "Gentleman of Río en Medio," the Americans believe that by the terms of Don Anselmo's sale, the trees as well as the land should be their. |
| **Revision** | In "Gentleman of Río en Medio," the Americans believe that by the terms of Don Anselmo's sale, the trees as well as the land should be theirs. |
| **Model From Literature** | "She was but thirty at the time of her death, and yet her hair had already begun to whiten, even as mine has." |

—Doyle, p. 31

### ■ Wrong Words or Phrases

**GUIDE FOR REVISING:**  Words or phrases that are suitable in one context may be inappropriate in another.

| | |
|---|---|
| **Strategy 1:** | **Check to see that you have not mistaken one word for another because the words sound alike, are spelled similarly, or are easily confused.** |
| First Draft | Robert MacNeil's essay deals with the affect of television on our ability to concentrate. |
| Revision | Robert MacNeil's essay deals with the effect of television on our ability to concentrate. |

| | |
|---|---|
| **Strategy 2:** | **Be sure that the words and phrases you use express your exact meaning.** |
| First Draft | Miss Moray uses many unclear words and phrases that hide things. |
| Revision | Miss Moray uses many euphemisms that conceal her true meaning and her feelings. |

| | |
|---|---|
| **Strategy 3:** | **Be sure that your language is appropriately formal or informal, depending on the context, subject, and audience of your writing.** |
| First Draft | Charles behaves like a bratty kid at home and sasses the teacher at school. |
| Revision | Charles behaves like a spoiled child at home and insults the teacher at school. |

| | |
|---|---|
| **Strategy 4:** | **Jargon is the use of words with specialized meanings in a particular trade or profession. Do not use jargon if you are writing for a general audience.** |
| First Draft | The custodial engineering team will terminate its assigned duties at 1 A.M. |
| Revision | The cleanup crew will finish work at 1 A.M. |
| Model From Literature | And though some Italians refer to a big mess as a big minestrone, the more popular metaphor is pasticci, a mess derived from the complicated preparations of the pastry chef, or pasticcere. —*Sheraton, pp. 493–494* |

### ■ Double Negatives

**GUIDE FOR REVISING:** A double negative is the use of two or more negative words in one clause to express a negative meaning.

| | |
|---|---|
| **Strategy:** | **Use only one negative word to give a clause or sentence a negative meaning.** |
| **First Draft** | Hardly no one in our class has never seen a woodcut print by Hokusai. |
| **Revision** | Hardly anyone in our class has ever seen a woodcut print by Hokusai. |
| **Model From Literature** | Laurie regarded his father coldly. "I didn't learn nothing ," he said.<br>"Anything," I said. " Didn't learn anything."<br>—*Jackson, p. 79* |

## Problems of Readability

■ **Sentence Variety**

**GUIDE FOR REVISING:** Varying the length and structure of your sentences will improve your writing and help you to hold your readers' attention.

| | |
|---|---|
| **Strategy 1:** | **Add details to the subject, verb, or complement of short simple sentences.** |
| **First Draft** | Kino heard the waves. |
| **Revision** | Awakening in his hut on the beach, Kino heard the splash of gentle waves. |

| | |
|---|---|
| **Strategy 2:** | **Combine two or more short simple sentences to make a longer simple sentence, a compound sentence, or a complex sentence.** |
| **First Draft** | A folk hero is a remarkable person. The qualities of a folk hero are often glorified in folk tales. |
| **Revision** | A folk hero is a remarkable person whose qualities are often glorified in folk tales. |

| | |
|---|---|
| **Strategy 3:** | **Separate rambling compound or complex sentences into two or more shorter sentences.** |
| **First Draft** | After teaching in China and the United States for some years, Pearl Buck became a full-time writer, and her novel *The Good Earth* won a Pulitzer Prize, and then in 1938 she won the Nobel Prize for Literature. |
| **Revision** | After teaching in China and the United States for some years, Pearl Buck became a full-time writer. Her novel *The Good Earth* won a Pulitzer Prize in 1932. In 1938 she won the Nobel Prize for Literature. |

| | |
|---|---|
| **Strategy 4:** | **Begin your sentences with different openers: subjects, adjectives and adverbs, phrases, and clauses.** |
| **First Draft** | The Franks and the Van Daans hid from the Nazis in a warehouse in Amsterdam, Holland. Mr. Frank returns to the warehouse in the first scene of the play. He returns after the end of the war in 1945. He starts to read Anne's diary. His voice is joined by that of Anne. The time shifts to 1942. |
| **Revision** | The Franks and the Van Daans hid from the Nazis in a warehouse in Amsterdam, Holland. In the first scene of the play, Mr. Frank returns to the warehouse after the end of the war in 1945. After he starts to read Anne's diary, his voice is joined by that of Anne. The time shifts to 1942. |
| **Model From Literature** | Although he took everything in stride, he was a hard and diligent worker. Even on holidays, he was always mending things or tending to our house and animals. He would not wait to be asked for help if he saw someone in trouble. |

—*Hayslip, p. 421*

## Problems of Conciseness

### ■ Wordy Phrases

**GUIDE FOR REVISING:** Wordy phrases and clauses weaken your writing by diminishing the focus and impact of your ideas.

| | |
|---|---|
| **Strategy 1:** | **You may often be able to shorten a wordy phrase by substituting an adverb.** |
| **First Draft** | Squeaky loves her brother Raymond and treats him in a protective fashion. |
| **Revision** | Squeaky loves her brother Raymond and treats him protectively. |

| | |
|---|---|
| **Strategy 2:** | **You may be able to eliminate a wordy clause by rewriting the sentence without changing the meaning.** |
| **First Draft** | Limericks, which are humorous poems, contain five lines and use two rhymes. |
| **Revision** | Limericks are humorous poems with five lines and two rhymes. |

### ■ Redundancy

**GUIDE FOR REVISING:** Redundancy is the unnecessary repetition of an idea. Redundancy makes writing heavy and dull.

| Strategy: | Eliminate redundant modifiers in your sentences. |
|---|---|
| **First Draft** | The exposition is the part of a story that introduces the basic, fundamental elements of the plot. |
| **Revision** | The exposition is the part of a story that introduces the basic elements of the plot. |

## Problems of Appropriateness

### ■ Inappropriate Diction

**GUIDE FOR REVISING:** There are two levels of standard English usage: formal English and informal English. The problem of inappropriate diction results when words or phrases that are generally accepted in informal conversation or writing are included in formal writing.

| Strategy: | Choose the appropriate level of diction based on your subject, audience, and writing occasion. |
|---|---|
| **First Draft** | In "The Adventure of the Speckled Band," Sherlock Holmes, like most good private eyes, uses his smarts to figure things out. |
| **Revision** | In "The Adventure of the Speckled Band," Sherlock Holmes, like most good detectives, uses his powers of reasoning to solve the mystery. |

### ■ Clichés and Slang

**GUIDE FOR REVISING:** Clichés are expressions that were once fresh and vivid but are now stale. People often use clichés in casual conversation, but in writing, expressions like cold as ice or pale as a ghost sound vague and tired. Like clichés, slang is often used in conversation. Slang words and expressions tend to be popular only for a short time among certain groups of people. In formal writing slang should be avoided.

| Strategy: | Replace clichés with clear, direct words or with a fresh expression of your own. |
|---|---|
| **First Draft** | During the 1971 World Series between the Pittsburgh Pirates and the Baltimore Orioles, Roberto Clemente rolled up his sleeves and led the Pirates to the thrill of victory. |
| **Revision** | During the 1971 World Series between the Pittsburgh Pirates and the Baltimore Orioles, Roberto Clemente worked hard and led the Pirates to victory. |

# SUMMARY OF GRAMMAR

**Nouns**    A **noun** is the name of a person, place, or thing.

A **common noun** names any one of a class of people, places, or things. A **proper noun** names a specific person, place, or thing.

| Common nouns | Proper nouns |
|---|---|
| poet | May Swenson, José Garcia Villa |
| state | Phoenix, Arizona |

**Pronouns**    **Pronouns** are words that stand for nouns or for words that take the place of nouns.

**Personal pronouns** refer to (1) the person speaking, (2) the person spoken to, or (3) the person, place, or thing spoken about.

| **First Person** | I, me, my, mine | we, us, our, ours |
|---|---|---|
| **Second Person** | you, your, yours | you, your, yours |
| **Third Person** | he, him, his, she, her, hers, it, its | they, them, their, theirs |

**Demonstrative pronouns** direct attention to specific people, places, or things.

*this   that     these   those*
*That* is a brilliant idea!

An **interrogative** pronoun is used to begin a question.

"*What* did he do?" I asked. "*Who* was it?"
—*Jackson, p. 79*

**Indefinite pronouns** refer to people, places, or things, often without specifying which ones.

*Somebody* wildly suggested dynamite.
—*O. Henry, p. 66*

It wasn't *anything* of a drop—*all* you had to watch was the patch of poison ivy.    —*Grau, p. 125*

**Verbs**    A **verb** is a word that expresses time while showing an action, a condition, or the fact that something exists.

An **action verb** is a verb that tells what action someone or something is performing.

Jimmy *collared* a boy that *was loafing* on the steps of the bank . . .    —*O. Henry, p. 63*

A **linking verb** is a verb that connects a word at or near the beginning of a sentence with a word at or near the end.

Socially he *was* also a success, . . .
—*O. Henry, p. 63*

Finally my mother *got* tired of standing on the end of the dock . . .    —*Grau, p. 121*

He *grew* more and more silent, . . .
—*Hale, p. 196*

**Helping verbs** are verbs that can be added to another verb to make a single verb phrase.

"We *shall* soon set matters right, I have no doubt. You *have* come in by train this morning. I see."
—*Doyle, p. 28*

**Adjectives**    An **adjective** is a word used to describe a noun or a pronoun or to give a noun or a pronoun a more specific meaning. Adjectives answer these questions:

| What kind? | *gray* coat | *clear* skies |
|---|---|---|
| Which one? | *that* sign | *these* trees |
| How many? | *nine* lives | *few* chances |
| How much? | *much* luck | *less* skill |

The articles *the, a,* and *an* are adjectives. *An* is used before a word beginning with a vowel sound. A noun may sometimes be used as an adjective.

*business* trip      *pleasure* boat

**Adverbs**    An adverb is a word that modifies a verb, an adjective, or another adverb. Adverbs answer the questions Where? When? In what manner? To what extent?

They fell *down*. (modifies verb *fell*)
He *seldom* laughed. (modifies verb *laughed*)
Speak *softly*, please. (modifies verb *speak*)
I was *too* angry. (modifies adjective *angry*)
It happened *very* fast. (modifies adverb *fast*)

**Prepositions**    A **preposition** is a word that relates a noun or pronoun that appears with it to another word in the sentence. Prepositions are almost always followed by nouns or pronouns.

| *at* the end | *before* lunch | *between* us |
|---|---|---|
| *on* the grass | *over* the hill | *without* you |

**Conjunctions**    A **conjunction** is a word used to connect other words or groups of words.

**Coordinating conjunctions** connect similar kinds or groups of words.

bacon *and* eggs      gentle *but* firm

**Correlative conjunctions** are used in pairs to connect similar words or groups of words.

*both* Josie *and* Elena      *neither* you *nor* I

*Handbook of Grammar and Revising Strategies*    771

**Interjections** An **interjection** is a word that expresses feeling or emotion and functions independently of a sentence.

> "*Ha!* I am glad to see that Mrs. Hudson has had the good sense to light the fire." —*Doyle, p. 28*
> "*Oh, no,*" laughed the warden. —*O. Henry, p. 61*

**Sentences** A **sentence** is a group of words with two main parts: a complete subject and a complete predicate. Together these parts express a complete thought.

> Lillian greeted him jubilantly. —*Asimov, p. 14*
> Anyway, meeting writers is always so disappointing. —*LeGuin, p. 485*

A **fragment** is a group of words that does not express a complete thought.

**Subject-Verb Agreement** To make a **subject** and **verb** agree, make sure that both are singular or both are plural. Two or more singular subjects joined by *or* or *nor* must have a singular verb. When singular and plural subjects are joined by *or* or *nor*, the verb must agree with the closest subject.

> *Juan is* here.
> *Sal or Gordon drives.*
> *We speak* next.
> Both *girls are* tired.

> Either the *radio or the stereo is* too loud.
> Neither the *stores nor the theater was* open.
> Much of the *crop was* ruined.
> Some of those *waves are* huge.

**Phrases** A **phrase** is a group of words, without a subject and verb, that functions in a sentence as one part of speech.

A **prepositional phrase** is a group of words that includes a preposition and a noun or a pronoun.

> *beyond* the horizon    *inside* the gate
> *near* us    *without* their skates

An **adjective phrase** is a prepositional phrase that modifies a noun or a pronoun by telling what kind or which one.

> It shook the whole line *of windows in the kitchen* and knocked over every single pot *of geraniums on the back porch.* —*Grau, p. 122*

An **adverb phrase** is a prepositional phrase that modifies a verb, an adjective, or an adverb by pointing out where, when, in what manner, or to what extent.

> She had baked a huge cake and decorated it *with birthday candles.* —*Singer, p. 114*

An **appositive phrase** is a noun or a pronoun with modifiers, placed next to a noun or a pronoun to add information and details.

> Five little livid spots, *the marks of four fingers and a thumb,* were printed upon the white wrist. —*Doyle, p. 33*

A **participial phrase** is a participle modified by an adjective or an adverb phrase or accompanied by a complement. The entire phrase acts as an adjective.

> Violence of temper *approaching to mania* has been hereditary in the men of the family, . . . —*Doyle, p. 30*
> *Drawn by a common sadness,* the people of San Juan began to make their way toward the beach . . . —*Izenberg, p. 395*

An **infinitive phrase** is an infinitive with modifiers, complements, or a subject, all acting together as a single part of speech.

> "To determine its exact meaning I have been obliged *to work out the present prices of the investments with which it is concerned.*" —*Doyle, p. 36*

A **gerund phrase** is a gerund with modifiers or a complement, all acting together as a noun.

> *Putting the replica into the case, checking its appearance against the photos he'd thoughtfully brought with him,* and *covering up his traces* might take most of Sunday but that didn't worry him in the least. —*Clarke, p. 140*

**Clauses** A **clause** is a group of words with its own subject and verb. An **independent clause** can stand by itself as a complete sentence. A **subordinate clause** cannot stand by itself as a complete sentence; it can only be part of a sentence. An **adjective clause** is a subordinate clause that modifies a noun or a pronoun by telling what kind or which one.

> Our client of the morning had hurried forward to meet us with a face *which spoke her joy.* —*Doyle, p. 37*

Subordinate **adverb clauses** modify verbs, adjectives, or adverbs by telling where, when, in what manner, to what extent, under what condition, or why.

> *When he came home* Nephew Tatsuo ran to the car. —*Mori, p.176*
> *If Nolan was thirty then,* he must have been near eighty *when he died.* —*Hale, p. 193*
> Some started backfiring up the mountain *so that the ascending flames could counteract the descending ones.* —*Nin, p. 454*

# SUMMARY OF CAPITALIZATION AND PUNCTUATION

## CAPITALIZATION

Capitalize the first word in sentences.
"You might as well tell them," she said. "They'll know anyway."　　　　　　*—Grau, p. 125*

Capitalize all proper nouns and adjectives.

| Toshio Mori | Colorado River | Labor Day |
|---|---|---|
| Kansas | January | Vietnam Memorial |
| Canadian | Special Olympics | Portuguese |

Capitalize a person's title when it is followed by the person's name or when it is used in direct address.

| General | Dr. Grimesby Roylott | Chief Seattle |
|---|---|---|
| Don Anselmo | Professor Shlemiel | |

Capitalize titles showing family relationships when they refer to a specific person unless they are preceded by a possessive noun or pronoun.

| Nephew Tatsuo | Charles's mother | my niece |
|---|---|---|

Capitalize the first word and all other key words in the titles of books, periodicals, poems, stories, plays, paintings, and other works of art.

| *The Pearl* | *The Diary of Anne Frank* |
|---|---|
| "Thank You, M'am" | "Song of the Sky Loom" |

Capitalize the first word and all nouns in letter salutations and the first word in letter closings.
Dear Fred,
Your old friend,

## PUNCTUATION

**End Marks** Use a **period** to end a declarative sentence, an imperative sentence, and most abbreviations.
The boy shut up his eyes, to hide inside himself, but it was too late.　　　　　*—Bradbury, p. 153*

Use a **question mark** to end a direct question or an incomplete question in which the rest of the question is understood.
"Is Dr. Motherhead at home?"　　*—Singer, p. 114*
"All the newspapers said so, eh?"　*—Asimov, p. 15*

Use an **exclamation mark** after a statement showing strong emotion, an urgent imperative sentence, or an interjection expressing strong emotion.
Strange how the habits of his youth clung to him still!　　　　　　　　　　　*—Buck, p. 21*
"Shut up! Leave him alone!"　　　*—Keyes, p. 215*

**Commas** Use a comma before the conjunction to separate two independent clauses in a compound sentence.
So my visits to the Ainsworth home were frequent but undemanding, and I had ample opportunity to look out for the little cat that had intrigued me.
　　　　　　　　　　　　　　*—Herriot, p. 439*

Use commas to separate three or more words, phrases, or clauses in a series.
Margot is eighteen, beautiful, quiet, shy.
　　　　　　　　*—Goodrich and Hackett, p. 307*
"The sight of the safe, the saucer of milk, and the loop of whipcord were enough to finally dispel any doubts which may have remained."
　　　　　　　　　　　　　　*—Doyle, p. 44*
He unbuttoned his shirt, pulled out the leather pouch, and lifted it over his head.
　　　　　　　　　　　　　　*—Sneve, p. 234*

Use commas to separate adjectives of equal rank. Do not use commas to separate adjectives that must stay in a specific order.
Its serial, kaleidoscopic exposures force us to follow its lead.　　　　　　*—MacNeil, p. 463*
. . . her life fell into a pattern which remained unchanged for the next six years.　*—Petry, p. 390*

Use a comma after an introductory word, phrase, or clause.
"Oh, Pim. I dreamed that they came to get us!"
　　　　　　　　*—Goodrich and Hackett, p. 332*
Every time Hokusai changed his name, he changed his style.　　　　　　*—Longstreet, p. 481*

Use commas to set off parenthetical and nonessential expressions.
Of all these varied cases, however, I cannot recall any which presented more singular features than that which was associated with the well-known Surrey family of the Roylotts of Stoke Moran.
　　　　　　　　　　　　　　*—Doyle, p. 27*

Use commas with places and dates made up of two or more parts.
Florida, Missouri.
September 23, 1807

Use commas after items in addresses, after the salutation in a personal letter, after the closing in all letters, and in numbers of more than three digits.

| Bay Avenue, Islip, N.Y. | Dear Aunt Jo, |
|---|---|
| All best wishes, | 54,673,529 |

Use commas to set off a direct quotation.
"Don't believe I do," said the woman, "unless you just want sweet milk yourself." *—Hughes, p. 182*

*Handbook of Grammar and Revising Strategies*　　**773**

**Semicolons** Use a semicolon to join independent clauses that are not already joined by a conjunction.

During the third and fourth weeks it looked like a reformation in Charles; Laurie reported grimly at lunch on Thursday of the third week, "Charles was so good today the teacher gave him an apple."
—*Jackson, p. 80*

Use semicolons to avoid confusion when independent clauses or items in a series already contain commas.

It was a beautiful day at Murphy's Park; hot and dry without being too hot; and with a cheerfully bright sun in a blue, blue sky. —*Asimov, p. 16*

**Colons** Use a colon before a list of items following an independent clause.

Look at a few: tobacco, corn, potatoes, beans (kidney, string and lima and therefore succotash), tomatoes, sweet potatoes, . . .
—*DeVoto, p. 457*

Use a colon in numbers giving the time, in salutations in business letters, and in labels used to signal important ideas.

3:45 P.M. Dear Mr. Buxton:
Caution: Road Work Danger: Falling Rock
Ahead Zone

**Quotation Marks** A **direct quotation** represents a person's exact speech or thoughts and is enclosed in quotation marks.

"I must find a nice young bride," he had said, startling Hana with blunt talk of marriage in her presence. —*Uchida, p. 3*

An **indirect quotation** reports only the general meaning of what a person said or thought and does not require quotation marks.

He said he had come to Elmore to look for a location to go into business. —*O. Henry, p. 71*

Always place a comma or a period inside the final quotation mark.

I said: "You lie, yourself. He did tell you."
—*Twain, p. 416*

Place a question mark or an exclamation mark inside the final quotation mark if the end mark is part of the quotation; if it is not part of the quotation, place it outside the final quotation mark.

"Oh, poor little thing!" she sobbed and stroked the cat's head again and again . . .
—*Herriot, p. 441*

And even if we do convert to decimal time, what will we do about "clockwise," "counterclockwise," and locating things at "eleven o'clock"?
—*Asimov, p. 478*

Use quotation marks around the titles of short written works, episodes in a series, songs, and titles of works mentioned as parts of collections.

"Harlem Night Song"
"The Indian All Around Us"
"Over the Rainbow"

Underline the titles of long written works, movies, television and radio shows, lengthy works of music, paintings, and sculptures.

I Know Why the Caged Bird Sings
Family Ties
The Last Judgment
Washington Crossing the Delaware
Ghost
Highway to Heaven
Michelangelo's David
Suspense

**Hyphens** Use a hyphen with certain numbers, after certain prefixes, with two or more words used as one word, and with a compound modifier that comes before a noun.

eighty-nine ex-Chairperson pro-British
jack-o'-lantern a never-to-be-
forgotten visit

**Apostrophes** Add an apostrophe and -*s* to show the possessive case of most singular nouns.

Asimov's stories the poet's theme

Add an apostrophe to show the possessive case of plural nouns ending in -*s* and -*es*.

the zebras' territory the Simses' house

Add an apostrophe and -*s* to show the possessive case of plural nouns that do not end in -*s* or -*es*.

the oxen's horns the deer's antlers

Use an apostrophe in a contraction to indicate the position of the missing letter or letters.

"It's hard to predict a local thunderstorm, but even if it were to come, and it mightn't, it wouldn't last more than half an hour on the outside."
—*Asimov, p. 18*

# GLOSSARY OF COMMON USAGE

**accept, except**
Accept is a verb that means "to receive" or "to agree to." *Except* is a preposition that means "other than" or "leaving out." Do not confuse these two words.

Helen Stoner begged Sherlock Holmes to *accept* her case.

No one in Elmore *except* Ben Price knew Jimmy Valentine's true identity.

**affect, effect**
Affect is normally a verb meaning "to influence" or "to bring about a change in." *Effect* is usually a noun, meaning "result."

When Walt Whitman wrote "O Captain! My Captain!" he showed how deeply the assassination of President Lincoln had *affected* him.

Reading poems aloud often has the *effect* of making their sound patterns clearer.

**bad, badly**
Use the predicate adjective *bad* after linking verbs such as *feel, look,* and *seem.* Use *badly* whenever an adverb is required.

When Mrs. Jones is kind to him, the boy starts to feel *bad* about his attempt to steal her purse.

Storms at sea must have *badly* frightened many of Columbus's men.

**can, may**
The verb *can* generally refers to the ability to do something. The verb *may* generally refers to permission to do something.

Isaac Asimov's essay shows that the invention of new electronic devices *can* have an important impact on the English language.

Mr. Frank says that no one *may* make any noise between the hours of 8 A.M. and 6 P.M.

**compare, contrast**
The verb *compare* can involve both similarities and differences. The verb *contrast* always involves differences. Use *to* or *with* after *compare.* Use *with* after *contrast.*

Lucas's report compared John Updike's "January" *to* Langston Hughes's "Winter Moon."

At one point in "The Medicine Bag," Martin's attitude toward his grandfather contrasts strikingly *with* that of his friends.

**farther, further**
Use *farther* when you refer to distance. Use *further* when you mean "to a greater degree or extent" or "additional."

Harriet Tubman encouraged the fugitives when they thought they could travel no *farther.*

Uncle Hiroshi decides that Nephew Tatsuo needs *further* training.

**fewer, less**
Use *fewer* for things that can be counted. Use *less* for amounts or quantities that cannot be counted.

The painter Hokusai lived in no *fewer* than a hundred different houses and changed his name thirty times.

It might have cost the speaker in Frost's poem *less* effort to choose the other road.

**good, well**
Use the predicate adjective *good* after linking verbs such as *feel, look, smell, taste,* and *seem.* Use *well* whenever you need an adverb.

At the end of "Raymond's Run," Squeaky feels *good* about Gretchen and realizes that her competitor is entitled to respect.

As he writes the letter to his wife, Robert recalls how *well* pleased his father had been by his gift of love on Christmas morning long ago.

**hopefully**
You should not loosely attach this adverb to a sentence, as in "Hopefully, the rain will stop by noon." Rewrite the sentence so that *hopefully* modifies a specific verb. Other possible ways of revising such sentences include using the adjective *hopeful* or a phrase like *everyone hopes that.*

Robert MacNeil does not write *hopefully* about the effects of television on viewers.

Ursula K. LeGuin is *hopeful* that would-be writers realize what they're in for.

**in, into**
*In* refers to position and means "within" or "inside." *Into* suggests motion from outside to inside.

Maya Angelou was born Marguerite Johnson *in* St. Louis, Missouri.

With a loud yell, the murderer leaped *into* the room.

**its, it's**
Do not confuse the possessive pronoun *its* with the contraction *it's,* standing for "it is" or "it has."

The snowhare twitched *its* nose, causing *its* whiskers to dance.

*It's* easy to see how Charlie's development parallels that of Algernon in Daniel Keyes's story "Flowers for Algernon."

### lay, lie

Do not confuse these verbs. *Lay* is a transitive verb meaning "to set or put something down." Its principal parts are *lay, laying, laid, laid*. *Lie* is an intransitive verb meaning "to recline." Its principal parts are *lie, lying, lay, lain*.

> After she enters the attic room, Miep *lays* the cake, the books, and the newspapers on the table.
> I often *lie* on the living room couch when I read poetry.

### like

*Like* is a preposition that usually means "similar to" or "in the same way as." *Like* should always be followed by an object. Do not use *like* before a subject and a verb. Use *as* or *that* instead.

> Do you think that you would have enjoyed an experience *like* Mark Twain's job as a cub pilot on the Mississippi?
> If you had been in Joby's shoes, would you have felt *as* he did?

### many, much

Use *many* to refer to a specific quantity. Use *much* for an indefinite amount or for an abstract concept.

> It takes *many* months for the Americans to buy back the trees from the descendants of Don Anselmo.
> According to Eudora Welty, children, artists, and animals have *much* in common.

### of, have

Do not use *of* in place of *have* after auxiliary verbs like *would, could, should, may, might,* or *must*.

> The speaker says that the first man *would have* given her material wealth.

### raise, rise

*Raise* is a transitive verb that usually takes a direct object. *Rise* is intransitive and never takes a direct object.

> When she meets the kindergarten teacher, Laurie's mother cautiously *raises* the subject of Charles.
> Every morning Robert and his father *rise* at four o'clock to milk the cows.

### set, sit

Do not confuse these verbs. *Set* is a transitive verb meaning "to put (something) in a certain place." Its principal parts are *set, setting, set, set*. *Sit* is an intransitive verb meaning "to be seated." Its principal parts are *sit, sitting, sat, sat*.

> Jimmy Valentine *sets* his suitcase on the table and opens it.
> Grandfather *sits* on the bed in his room while he tells Martin about the vision quest.

### than, then

The conjunction *than* is used to connect the two parts of a comparison. Do not confuse *than* with the adverb *then*, which usually refers to time.

> A round character is nearly always more interesting and complex *than* a flat character.
> Buster seized the rubber ball in his teeth and *then* brought it back to Mrs. Ainsworth.

### that, which, who

Use the relative pronoun *that* to refer to things or people. Use *which* only for things and *who* only for people.

> The Texas longhorn *that* J. Frank Dobie describes is named Sancho.
> The program included May Pole dancing, *which* Squeaky could do without.
> Frances Goodrich and Albert Hackett, *who* spent two years writing *The Diary of Anne Frank,* visited with Anne's father as part of their background work.

### their, there, they're

Do not confuse the spelling of these three words. *Their* is a possessive adjective and always modifies a noun. *There* is usually used either at the beginning of a sentence or as an adverb. *They're* is a contraction for *they are*.

> Pecos Bill, John Henry, and Paul Bunyan are American folk heroes, and many well-known legends tell of *their* deeds.
> Paul Revere's next destination was Concord, and he arrived *there* at exactly two by the village clock.
> The Sakkaros are strange in that *they're* obsessed with the weather report.

### unique

Since *unique* means "one of a kind," you should not use it carelessly instead of the words "interesting" or "unusual." Avoid such illogical expressions as "most unique," "very unique," and "extremely unique."

> Most folk tales are not *unique,* since their plots and characters have parallels in stories from various cultures throughout the world.

### who, whom

In formal writing remember to use *who* only as a subject in clauses and sentences and *whom* only as an object.

> Langston Hughes, *who* wrote "Harlem Night Song," was born in Missouri.
> The character *whom* I admired most in the play was Anne Frank.

# HANDBOOK OF LITERARY TERMS AND TECHNIQUES

**ACT**   See *Drama.*

**ALLITERATION**   *Alliteration* is the repetition of initial consonant sounds. Advertisers use alliteration to catch the ear of the reader or viewer, as in "*B*ooks for a *B*uck." In poetry alliteration is used to create a musical or rhythmic effect, to emphasize key words, or to imitate sounds. Consider the alliteration in Kenyan poet John Roberts's "The Searchers":

> I remember a dog ran out from an alley,
> *S*niffed my trousers, *s*cented rags
> And as I stopped to pat him ran back,
> *Cl*aws *cl*icking on the asphalt.

In these lines alliteration of the *s* sounds links two images of smell, while the consecutive *cl* sounds in the last line mimic the "clicking" of the dog's claws.
See *Onomatopoeia* and. *Repetition.*

**ALLUSION**   An *allusion* is a reference to a well-known person, place, event, literary work, or work of art. The title of Maya Angelou's book *I Know Why the Caged Bird Sings,* excerpted on page 403, alludes to a line from the poem "Sympathy," by Paul Laurence Dunbar. The allusion invites the reader to compare Angelou's experience growing up as an African American to the experience of the caged bird in the poem. The Bible and classical mythology provide two of the most common sources of literary allusions. In the poem "Runagate Runagate," on page 517, fleeing slaves are described as heading toward the "Bible city." This allusion sets up a comparison between the North and the Biblical city of deliverance.

Writers usually do not explain their allusions. They expect that their readers will be familiar with the things to which they refer. An active reader will think about the meaning of every allusion that he or she encounters.

**ANAPEST**   See *Meter.*

**ANECDOTE**   An *anecdote* is a brief story about an interesting, amusing, or strange event. Writers and speakers use anecdotes to entertain and to make specific points. In the entries from *Davy Crockett's Almanacs,* on page 681, legendary American folk hero Davy Crockett tells anecdotes about his outrageous frontier adventures. In "Tussle with a Bear," Crockett describes how he heroically killed a bear. "Davy Crockett's Dream" features the bizarre events in Crockett's dream.

**ANTAGONIST**   An *antagonist* is a character or force in conflict with the main character, or protagonist. A character who acts as an antagonist usually desires some goal that is at odds with the goals of the protagonist. The struggle between the two, or central conflict, is the foundation of the story's plot. In Anne McCaffrey's "The Smallest Dragonboy," on page 159, the protagonist, Keevan, wants to be chosen to be a dragonrider. Beterli, the antagonist, wants to break Keevan's spirit in order to improve his own chances of being chosen.

**ATMOSPHERE**   See *Mood.*

**AUTOBIOGRAPHY**   *Autobiography* is a form of nonfiction in which a person tells his or her own life story. An autobiographer may tell his or her entire life story or may concentrate on only part of it. Maya Angelou writes about her childhood in *I Know Why the Caged Bird Sings.* Eudora Welty's *One Writer's Beginnings* describes how she became a writer. Autobiographies often include most of the elements of good fiction: interesting stories and events, well-developed characters, and vivid descriptions of settings.

**BALLAD**   A *ballad* is a songlike poem that tells a story, often one dealing with adventure and romance. Ballads have four- to six-line stanzas, with regular rhythms and rhyme schemes. Many ballads have a *refrain,* a line or group of lines repeated at the end of each stanza.

The earliest ballads, such as "Lord Randall" and "Barbara Allan," were not written down but rather were composed orally and then sung. Then they were passed by word of mouth from singer to singer and from generation to generation. Thus the ballads often changed dramatically over the course of time. By the time modern scholars began to collect folk ballads, most ballads existed in many different versions. Many writers of the modern era have created *literary ballads,* imitating the simplicity, structure, and diction of the ancient ballads. For example, Henry Wadsworth Longfellow's "Paul Revere's Ride," on page 509, borrows many elements from the folk-ballad tradition.

**BIOGRAPHY**   *Biography* is a form of nonfiction in which a writer tells the life story of another person. People often write biographies of people who are famous for their achievements. Ann Petry's *Harriet Tubman: Guide to Freedom* is an example of biography. Biographies are considered nonfiction because they deal with real people and events. Still, a good biography shares many of the qualities of all good narrative writing. See *Autobiography.*

**BLANK VERSE**   *Blank verse* is poetry written in unrhymed iambic pentameter lines. This form should not be confused with *free verse,* which is poetry that has no regular meter. A great deal of English poetry is written in blank verse because its meter is natural to the English language and because serious subjects are often best dealt with in unrhymed lines. William Wordsworth's "There Was a Boy" is in blank verse:

> There was a boy; ye knew him well, ye cliffs
> And islands of Winander! Many a time,
> At, evening, when the earliest stars began
> To move along the edges of the hills,
> Rising or setting, would he stand alone.

**CENTRAL CONFLICT**   See *Conflict.*

**CHARACTER**   A *character* is a person or an animal who takes part in the action of a literary work. The *main character,* or protagonist, is the most important character in the story, the focus of the reader's attention. Often the protagonist changes in some important way during the course of the story. A *minor character* takes part in the story's events but is not the main focus of attention. Minor characters sometimes help the reader learn about the main character.

Fictional characters are sometimes described as either round or flat. A *round character* is fully developed. The writer reveals the character's background and his or her personality traits, both good and bad. A *flat character,* on the other hand, seems to possess only one or two personality traits and little, if any, personal history. Characters can also be described as dynamic or static. A *dynamic character* changes in the course of a story. A *static character* does not change. Philip Nolan, in Edward Everett Hale's "The Man Without a Country," on page 185, is a round, dynamic character. In contrast, Paul Revere, in Longfellow's poem, on page 509, is flat and static.
See *Characterization, Hero/Heroine,* and *Motivation.*

**CHARACTERIZATION**   *Characterization* is the act of creating and developing a character. Writers use two methods to create and develop characters—direct and indirect. When using *direct characterization,* the writer actually states a character's traits, or characteristics. Edward Everett Hale uses direct characterization in the following passage from "The Man Without a Country," on page 185:

> Philip Nolan was as fine a young officer as there was in the "Legion of the West," as the Western division of our army was then called. When Aaron Burr made his first dashing expedition down to New Orleans in 1805, he met this gay, dashing, bright young fellow.

When using *indirect characterization,* the writer allows the reader to draw his or her own conclusions based on information presented by the author. In "The Adventure of the Speckled Band," on page 35, Arthur Conan Doyle provides indirect characterization of Dr. Roylott by means of his appearance, words, and actions:

> He stepped swiftly forward, seized the poker, and bent it into a curve with his huge brown hands.
> "See that you keep yourself out of my grip," he snarled, and hurling the twisted poker into the fireplace he strode out of the room.

**CINQUAIN**   See *Stanza.*

**CLIMAX**   See *Plot.*

**CONCRETE POEM**   A *concrete poem* is one with a shape that suggests its subject. The poet arranges the letters, punctuation, and lines to create a visual image on the page. Guillaume Apollinaire's "Crown" is a concrete poem. Its letters and words are arranged in the shape of a jeweled crown.

**CONFLICT**   A *conflict* is a struggle between opposing forces. Conflict is one of the most important elements of stories, novels, and dramas because it causes the actions that form the plot. In an *external conflict,* a character struggles against some outside person or force, such as a storm, a jealous enemy, or a social convention. The conflict between Keevan and Beterli in "The Smallest Dragonboy," on page 159, is an external conflict.

In an *internal conflict,* the struggle takes place within the protagonist's mind. The character struggles to reach some new understanding or to make an important decision. Philip Nolan, in "The Man Without a Country," on page 185, experiences an inner conflict as he comes to realize the importance of home and country. Literary works can have at the same time several conflicts, both internal and external. The most important conflict in a work is called the *central conflict.* See *Plot.*

**COUPLET**   See *Stanza.*

**DACTYL**   See *Meter.*

**DENOUEMENT**   See *Plot.*

**DESCRIPTION**   A *description* is a portrait, in words, of a person, a place, or an object. Descriptive writing uses images that appeal to the five senses—sight, hearing, taste, smell, and touch.

In her poem "Desert Noon," Elizabeth Coatsworth uses images of sight to create a description of a desert scene in southwestern California:

> When the desert lies
> Pulsating with heat
> And even the rattlesnakes
> Coil among the roots of the mesquite
> And the coyotes pant at the waterholes—
> Far above,
> Against the sky,
> Shines the summit of San Jacinto,
> Blue-white and cool as a hyacinth
> With snow.

See *Image.*

**DEVELOPMENT**   See *Plot.*

**DIALECT**   A *dialect* is a form of a language spoken by people in a particular region or group.

English, for example, has numerous dialects. The English spoken in London differs from the English spoken in Liverpool. Likewise, the English spoken in Boston differs from the English spoken in Texas. Dialects differ in pronunciation, grammar, and word choice. Often they reflect the economic, geographic, and cultural differences among speakers of the same language.

Writers use dialects to make their characters seem true to life. For example, in "Tussle with a Bear," on page 684, Davy Crockett narrates in the dialect of the Tennessee frontier:

> I had got down about as fur as where the wood opens at the Big Gap, when I seed it war so dark and mucilaginous that I coodn't hardly see at all.

Mark Twain, Rudyard Kipling, and Zora Neale Hurston are three well-known writers who make effective use of dialect in their works.

**DIALOGUE**   *Dialogue* is conversation between characters. Dialogue helps make stories more interesting and more realistic. In poems, novels, and short stories, dialogue is usually set off by quotation marks, as in this example from "Tears of Autumn," by Yoshiko Uchida:

> Almost before she realized what she was doing, she spoke to her uncle. "Oji San, perhaps I should go to America to make this lonely man a good wife."
> "You Hana Chan?" Her uncle observed her with startled curiosity. "You would go all alone to a foreign land so far away from your mother and family?"
> "I would not allow it." Her mother spoke fiercely.

In a play, dialogue simply follows the name of the character who is speaking, as in these lines from *The House of Dies Drear,* by Richard Wesley:

> SHEILA: Thomas! Are you all right, chile?
> THOMAS: [*finally catching his breath*] Somethin's in there, Mama. It . . . it tried to kill me.

See *Dialect* and *Drama.*

**DIMETER**   See *Meter.*

**DRAMA**   A *drama* is a story written to be performed by actors. Although a drama is meant to be performed, one can also read the written version, or script, which contains the dialogue and stage directions. *Dialogue* is the words spoken by the actors. *Stage directions,* usually printed within brackets or parentheses and in italics, tell how the actors should look, move, and speak. They also describe the setting and desired effects of sound and lighting. Dramas are often divided into major sections called *acts.* These acts are then further divided into smaller sections called *scenes.*

In contemporary usage the term *drama* is often used to refer to serious or tragic plays, as opposed to lighter, comic plays.
See *Character, Dialogue,* and *Plot.*

**DRAMATIC IRONY**   See *Irony.*

**DYNAMIC CHARACTER**   See *Character.*

**ESSAY**   An *essay* is a short, nonfiction work about a particular subject. An *expository essay* presents information, discusses ideas, or explains a process. "The Indian All Around Us,' on page 457, is an example of an expository essay. A *narrative essay* tells a true story. "Forest Fire," on page 453, tells the story of Anaïs Nin's actual experiences during a forest fire near her Sierra Madre home. A *persuasive essay* tries to convince the reader to do something or to accept a particular conclusion. Robert MacNeil's "The Trouble with Television," on page 463, tries to convince the reader that television is a harmful influence. Finally, a *descriptive essay* presents a portrait, in words, of a person, a place, or an object. Travel writing provides many examples of descriptive essays. Few essays, however, are purely descriptive. It is important to remember, too, that an essay may combine elements of all four types of writing.

See *Description, Exposition, Narration,* and *Persuasion.*

**EXPOSITION** *Exposition* is writing or speech that explains or informs. Exposition may occur in both fiction and nonfiction writing. This Handbook of Literary Terms is an example of expository nonfiction because it explains the meanings of important literary terms and ideas.

The term *exposition* is also used to refer to the part of the story that introduces the basic elements of the plot: the characters, the setting, and the initial situation leading to the conflict. The exposition of Asimov's "Rain, Rain, Go Away," on page 13, occurs in the opening conversation between Lillian and George Wright. Here the reader learns the identity of these characters and learns, too, that the Wrights' new neighbors have been displaying some very odd behavior.
See *Plot.*

**EXTENDED METAPHOR** In an *extended metaphor,* as in a regular metaphor, a subject is spoken or written of as though it were something else. However, an extended metaphor differs from a regular metaphor in that several points of comparisons are suggested by the writer or speaker. Naoshi Koriyama uses extended metaphor in his poem "Jetliner," on page 536, to compare a jet plane to a runner.
See *Metaphor.*

**FABLE** A *fable* is a brief story, usually with animal characters, that teaches a lesson, or moral. The moral is usually stated at the end of the fable. The Greek slave Aesop wrote many fables in the sixth century B.C. that are still widely read today. Many familiar expressions, such as "cry wolf" and "sour grapes," come from Aesop's fables. Modern writers such as James Thurber and Mark Twain have also written fables.
See *Irony* and *Moral.*

**FANTASY** *Fantasy* is highly imaginative writing that contains elements not found in real life. Fantasy involves invented characters, invented situations, and sometimes invented worlds and creatures. Many science-fiction stories, such as Isaac Asimov's "Rain, Rain, Go Away," on page 13, contain elements of fantasy.
See *Science Fiction.*

**FICTION** *Fiction* is prose writing that tells about imaginary characters and events. Short stories and novels are works of fiction. Some writers base their fictional tales on actual experiences and real people, to which they add invented characters, dialogue, and settings. Other writers of fiction work entirely from their own imaginations.
See *Narration, Nonfiction,* and *Prose.*

**FIGURATIVE LANGUAGE** *Figurative language* is writing or speech that is not meant to be taken literally. The many types of figurative language are called *figures of speech.* These types include hyperbole, simile, metaphor, and personification. Writers use figurative language to express their meanings in fresh, vivid, surprising ways.
See *Hyperbole, Metaphor, Personification, Simile,* and *Symbol.*

**FIGURE OF SPEECH** See *Figurative Language.*

**FLASHBACK** A *flashback* is a section of a literary work that interrupts the sequence of events to relate an event from an earlier time. All the action in *The Diary of Anne Frank,* on page 303, except for the first and last scenes, is a flashback to events that occurred more than three years before the opening scene. Pearl Buck's "Christmas Day in the Morning," on page 21, is largely flashback. The story begins and ends with Rob as an elderly man, but the story's main action is a flashback to the Christmas of Rob's fifteenth year.

**FLAT CHARACTER** See *Character.*

**FOLK BALLAD**   See *Ballad.*

**FOLK TALE**   A *folk tale* is a story that was composed orally and then passed from person to person by word of mouth. Types of folk tales include fables, legends, myths, and tall tales. Most folk tales are *anonymous:* No one knows who first composed them. In fact, folk tales originated among people who could neither read nor write. These people entertained themselves by telling stories aloud, often ones dealing with heroes, adventure, romance, and magic.

In the modern era, scholars like the brothers Wilhelm and Jakob Grimm began collecting folk tales and writing them down. Their collection, published as *Grimm's Fairy Tales,* includes such famous tales as "Cinderella," "Rapunzel," and "The Bremen Town Musicians."

American scholars have also collected folk tales, often ones dealing with fanciful heroes such as Pecos Bill, Paul Bunyan, and Davy Crockett. See Carl Sandburg's retelling, "Paul Bunyan of the North Woods," on page 669.
See *Fable, Legend, Myth,* and *Oral Tradition.*

**FOOT**   See *Meter.*

**FORESHADOWING**   *Foreshadowing* is the use, in a literary work, of clues that suggest events that have yet to occur. Foreshadowing creates *suspense* by making the reader wonder what will happen next. In the short story "A Retrieved Reformation," on page 61, O. Henry foreshadows later events in the story by means of certain details earlier in the tale. That Jimmy is no ordinary criminal but is rather an expert safecracker will become an important detail. The fact that he falls in love with a banker's daughter is a clue that his former trade might play a role in his new life. The fact that the prison warden told Jimmy, "You're not a bad fellow at heart," is another clue. Thus foreshadowing is a means of linking seemingly minor or unconnected details with important developments later in a work.

**FREE VERSE**   *Free verse* is poetry not written in a regular rhythmical pattern, or meter. The following lines, from the South African poet Mongameli Mabona's "The Sea," are in free verse:

> Ocean,
> Green or blue or iron-gray,
> As the light
> Strikes you.
> Primordial flood,
> Relentless and remorseless
> Like a woman in a rage.

In a free-verse poem the poet is free to write lines of any length or with any number of rhythmic stresses, or beats. Thus free verse is less constraining than *metrical verse,* which requires set patterns of stresses.
See *Meter.*

**GENRE**   A *genre* is a division or type of literature. Literature is generally divided into three major genres: poetry, prose, and drama. Each, in turn, is further divided into such standard literary categories as the following:
1. *Poetry:* lyric, epic, narrative, and dramatic poetry
2. *Prose:* fiction (novels, short stories) and nonfiction (essays, letters, biographies, autobiographies, and reports)
3. *Drama:* serious drama and tragedy, comic drama, farce, and melodrama
See *Drama, Poetry,* and *Prose.*

**HAIKU**   *Haiku* is a three-line Japanese verse form. The first and third lines of a haiku have five syllables; the second line has seven syllables. A haiku usually presents a single, vivid image drawn from nature. See the two examples by Bashō and Moritake, on page 573.

**HEPTAMETER**   See *Meter.*

**HEPTASTITCH**   See *Stanza.*

**HERO/HEROINE** A *hero* or *heroine* is a character whose actions are inspiring or noble. In very old myths and stories, heroes and heroines often have superhuman powers. Hercules and Achilles are two examples of this type of hero. In modern literature heroes and heroines tend to be ordinary people. All heroes and heroines struggle to overcome some great obstacle or problem. In "The Finish of Patsy Barnes," on page 69, Patsy is a hero because he risks racing the horse that killed his father so that he might use the winnings toward medical care for his mother. In Beryl Markham's story "The Captain and His Horse," on page 47, the hero is the Baron, the horse. The Baron helps save the lives of two of its riders in the story. By the end of the story, we learn that the Baron was decorated for bravery.

The word *hero* was originally used for male characters and *heroine* for females. However, it is now acceptable to use the term *hero* to refer both to males and to female characters.

**HEXAMETER** See *Meter*.

**HUBRIS** *Hubris* is the fault of excessive pride. In tragic works the hubris of the main character is usually the cause of the protagonist's downfall. In the famous Greek play *Oedipus Rex,* the hero's downfall is partly caused by his hubris. Likewise, in the contemporary novel *Things Fall Apart,* by the Nigerian writer Chinua Achebe, the hubris of the main character, Okonkwo, leads to his exile and eventual death.

**HYPERBOLE** *Hyperbole* is an exaggeration for effect. Because it makes a statement that is not meant to be taken literally, hyperbole is considered a figure of speech. Everyday speech is full of examples of hyperbole, such as "I'm so hungry I could eat a horse." Writers use hyperboles to create humor, to emphasize particular points, and to create dramatic effects. For example, a famous novel by Ralph Ellison begins with this powerful example of hyperbole, which gives his book its name:

I am an invisible man.

See *Figurative Language*.

**IAMB** See *Meter*.

**IMAGE** An *image* is a word or a phrase that appeals to one or more of the five senses. Writers use images to create specific descriptions—to show how their subjects look, sound, smell, taste, and feel. The following lines from "Nightsong City," by the South African poet Dennis Brutus, contain several images of sound:

The sound begins again:
The siren in the night
The thunder at the door
The shriek of nerves in pain.
Then the keen crescendo
Of faces split by pain
The wordless, endless wail
Only the unfree know.

**IMAGERY** See *Image*.

**INCITING INCIDENT** See *Plot*.

**IRONY** *Irony* is the general name given to literary techniques that involve surprising, interesting, or amusing contradictions. In *verbal irony* words are used to suggest the opposite of their usual meaning, as when a weak person is called "a born leader." In *dramatic irony* there is a contradiction between what a character thinks and what the audience or reader knows to be true. An example can be found in "The Tell-Tale Heart," on page 145, in which the reader knows that the beating heart exists only in the main character's imagination. In *irony of situation,* an event occurs that directly contradicts the expectations of the characters or the reader. Shirley Jackson's story "Charles," on page 79, provides an example of irony of situation. Laurie's mother and father have been hearing their son's wild stories about a boy named Charles since his first day in kindergarten. Curious to meet the mother of this outrageous little boy, Laurie's mother goes to the PTA meeting. When she meets Laurie's teacher, she and the reader are surprised and amused to learn that there is no Charles: Charles is Laurie.

**IRONY OF SITUATION**   See *Irony.*

**LEGEND**   A *legend* is a widely told story about the past, one that may or may not have a foundation in fact. The stories of King Arthur of Britain and his knights of the Round Table are legends. Likewise, the stories that have survived about American folk heroes such as Pecos Bill and Paul Bunyan are legends. Legends usually contain fantastic details, such as incredible feats of strength or supernatural beings. "The Girl Who Hunted Rabbits," on page 635, is a Zuñi Indian legend about a brave young maiden who risks her life to find food for her family. In this legend the maiden is menaced by a cannibal demon, but she is saved by two war gods.
See *Folk Tale, Myth,* and *Oral Tradition.*

**LIMERICK**   A *limerick* is a humorous, rhyming, five-line poem with a specific meter and rhyme scheme. Most limericks have three strong stresses in lines one, two, and five, and two strong stresses in lines three and four. Most follow the rhyme scheme *aabba.* See the two limericks on page 569.

**LYRIC POEM**   A *lyric poem* is a highly musical verse that expresses the observations and feelings of a single speaker. They are called lyrics because they were, in ancient times, sung to the accompaniment of a lyre, a stringed instrument. Langston Hughes's "Harlem Night Song," on page 558, and Shakespeare's "Blow, Blow, Thou Winter Wind," on page 566 are examples of lyric poetry.

**MAIN CHARACTER**   See *Character.*

**METAMORPHOSIS**   A *metamorphosis* is a change in shape or form. In many ancient Greek and Roman myths, humans are transformed by the gods into animals, trees, or flowers, as in the story of Daphne and Apollo. Daphne, a beautiful huntress who was being chased one day by the god Apollo, was transformed into a laurel tree by her father, the river god Peneus. The Roman poet Ovid incorporated many of these myths into his great Latin poem, *The Metamorphoses.* This poem is an important source of literary allusions to classical mythology.

Metamorphosis remains an important theme in contemporary literature as well. For example, the Australian writer B. Wongar begins his short story "Babaru, the Family" with this metamorphosis:

> Our mother has left us. She has not died or run away but has changed into a crocodile. Maybe it is better that way—not that we will see much of her, but it helps to know that she is not far off; should anything like that happen to any of us, we will be around in the bush together again.

See *Allusion* and *Myth.*

**METAPHOR**   A *metaphor* is a figure of speech in which something is described as though it were something else. A metaphor, like a simile, works by pointing out a similarity between two things. For example, in Robert Frost's "The Road Not Taken," on page 600, the diverging roads are a metaphor for the major choices that people must make in their lives.

An *extended metaphor* is one that makes more than one point of comparison. Walt Whitman uses extended metaphor in his poem "O Captain! My Captain!" on page 534. He compares the United States to a ship, President Lincoln (who is not actually named in the poem) to the ship's captain, and national events to a ship's voyage.
See *Extended Metaphor* and *Figurative Language.*

**METER** The *meter* of a poem is its rhythmical pattern. This pattern is determined by the number and types of stresses, or beats, in each line. To describe the meter of a poem, you must *scan* its lines. Scanning involves marking the stressed and unstressed syllables of a poem. A slash mark ( ´ ) is used to signify a strong stress, while a weak stress is marked with a horseshoe symbol ( ˘ ). Here is an example of *scansion* using Elizabeth Barrett Browning's "The Cry of the Children":

Do ye hear the children weeping, O my
  brothers,
Ere the sorrow comes with years?
They are leaning their young heads against
  their mothers,
And that cannot stop their tears.

Each group of stresses within a line is called a *foot.* The following types of feet are common in English poetry:

1. *Iamb:* a foot with one weak stress followed by one strong stress, as in the word "reform"
2. *Trochee:* a foot with one strong stress followed by one weak stress, as in the word "flower"
3. *Anapest:* a foot with two weak stresses followed by one strong stress, as in the phrase "to the store"
4. *Dactyl:* a foot with one strong stress followed by two weak stresses, as in the word "formula"
5. *Spondee:* a foot with two strong stresses, as in the word "eighteen"
6. *Pyrrhic:* a foot with two weak stresses, as in the last foot of the word "fortu|nately"
7. *Amphibrach:* a foot with a weak syllable, one strong syllable, and another weak syllable, as in "the wandering minstrel"
8. *Amphimacer:* a foot with one strong syllable, one weak syllable, and another strong syllable, as in "black and white"

Depending on the type of foot that is most common in them, lines of poetry are described as being *iambic, trochaic, anapestic,* or *dactylic.*

Lines of poetry are also described in terms of the number of feet they contain:

1. *Monometer:* verse written in one-foot lines

One crow
melting snow
  —Elizabeth Coatsworth, "March"

2. *Dimeter:* verse written in two-foot lines
The pitch | pines fade
into a | whiteness
that has blot|ted the marsh.
  —Marge Piercy, "The Quiet Fog"

3. *Trimeter:* verse written in three-foot lines
A sat|urat|ed meadow,
  Sun-shaped | and jew|el small
A cir|cle scarce|ly wider
  Than the trees | around | were tall
  —Robert Frost, "Rose Pogonias"

4. *Tetrameter:* verse written in four-foot lines
I have wrapped | my dreams in | silken | cloth,
And laid | them away | in a box | of gold;
Where long | will cling | the lips | of the moth,
I have wrapped | my dreams | in silken | cloth.
  —Countee Cullen, "For a Poet"

5. *Pentameter:* verse written in five-foot lines

All things | within | this fad|ing world | hath
  end,
Adver|sity | doth still | our joys | attend;
No ties | so strong, | no friends | so dear |
  and sweet,
But with | death's part|ing blow | is sure | to
  meet.
  —Anne Bradstreet, "Before the Birth of
    One of Her Children"

A six-foot line is called a *hexameter.* A seven-foot line is called a *heptameter.* The meter of a poem tells both how many feet each line contains and what kind of foot occurs most often. Thus the lines from Anne Bradstreet's poem would be called *iambic pentameter.* Poetry that does not have a regular meter is called *free verse.* See *Blank Verse* and *Free Verse.*

**MINOR CHARACTER**   See *Character.*

**MONOMETER**   See *Meter.*

**MOOD**   *Mood,* or *atmosphere,* is the feeling created by a literary work. Writers use many methods to create mood, including images, dialogue, description, characterization, and plot. Often a writer creates a mood at the beginning of a work and sustains this mood throughout. For example, the mood of Edgar Allan Poe's "The Tell-Tale Heart," on page 145, is one of nervous dread and terror. Sometimes, however, the mood of a work will change with each new twist of the plot. For example, the mood of "Flowers for Algernon," on page 201, changes according to the main character's fortunes. Notice how the mood of the following poem by Mari Evans changes in the last three lines:

> If you have had
> your midnights
> and they have drenched
> your barren guts
> with tears
> I sing you sunrise
> and love
> and someone to touch

**MORAL**   A *moral* is a lesson taught by a literary work. A fable usually ends with a moral that is directly stated. For example, the moral of Aesop's famous fable of the hare and the tortoise is this: "Sure and steady wins the race."

Novels, short stories, and poems often suggest certain lessons or morals, but these are rarely stated directly. Such morals must be inferred by readers from details contained in the works.
See *Fable.*

**MOTIVATION**   A *motivation* is a reason that explains or partially explains a character's thoughts, feelings, actions, or speech. Writers try to make their characters' motivations, or motives, as clear as possible so that the characters will seem believable and lifelike. If a character's motives are not clear, then the character will seem flat and unconvincing.

Characters are often motivated by such common human feelings as love, greed, hunger, revenge, and friendship. For example, in "The Adventure of the Speckled Band," on page 27, fear motivates Miss Stoner to ask for Holmes's help. Holmes, in turn, is motivated by his intellectual interest in the case and by his sympathy for Miss Stoner.
See *Character.*

**MYTH**   A *myth* is a fictional tale that explains the actions of gods or heroes or the origins of the elements of nature. Myths were generally handed down by word of mouth for generations. "The Spirit Chief Names the Animal People," on page 623, is a Native American myth that explains how the Animal People got their names. According to the beliefs of the Okanogan people, the Animal People inhabited the earth before humans.

Every ancient culture has its own *mythology,* or collection of myths. Those of the Greeks and the Romans are called *classical mythology.* Myths often reflect the values of the cultures that give birth to them.
See *Oral Tradition.*

**NARRATION**   *Narration* is writing that tells a story. Novels, short stories, biographies, histories, and autobiographies are common types of *prose narration,* or narrative. Epics and ballads are standard types of *verse narrative.* Whether in verse or prose, a good narrative usually contains interesting events, settings, and characters.
See *Narrative Poem* and *Narrator.*

**NARRATIVE**   See *Narration.*

**NARRATIVE POEM**   A *narrative poem* is a story told in verse. It often possesses the elements of fiction, such as characters, conflict, and plot. The events are usually told in *chronological order,* the order in which they happen. Narrative poems are often based on historical events, as is Longfellow's "Paul Revere's Ride," on page 509.

**NARRATOR**    A *narrator* is a speaker or character who tells a story. There are several types of narrator, and the type that a writer chooses determines the story's *point of view.* If the narrator is a character who takes part in the story and who refers to herself or himself as *I,* this is *first-person narration.* The first-person narrator of Gish Jen's "The White Umbrella," on page 85, is the older of the two sisters. If the narrator stands outside the action of the story, then this speaker is a *third-person narrator.* Paul Laurence Dunbar's "The Finish of Patsy Barnes," on page 69, uses a third-person narrator.
See *Point of View.*

**NONFICTION**    *Nonfiction* is prose writing that presents and explains ideas or that tells about real people, places, objects, or events. Histories, biographies, autobiographies, essays, and newspaper articles are all types of nonfiction.
See *Fiction.*

**NOVEL**    A *novel* is a long work of fiction. Novels, like short stories, contain plot, character, conflict, and setting, but they are much longer than short stories. Thus they usually contain more characters, a greater variety of settings, and more complicated plots than do most short stories. A novel often contains, in addition to its major plot, one or more lesser stories, or subplots. Some famous novels include *Moby-Dick, David Copperfield,* and the *Red Badge of Courage.* John Steinbeck's novel *The Pearl* is included in this book.
See *Fiction.*

**OCTAVE**    See *Stanza.*

**ONOMATOPOEIA**    *Onomatopoeia* is the use of words that imitate sounds. *Hiss, crash, buzz,* *neigh, ring,* and *jingle* are examples of onomatopoeia. In William Shakespeare's "Full Fathom Five," onomatopoeia is used to imitate the sound of a bell:

> Sea nymphs hourly ring the knell:
> Ding-Dong.
> Hark! Now I hear them.
> Ding-dong, bell.

**ORAL TRADITION**    The *oral tradition* is the passing of songs, stories, and poems from generation to generation by word of mouth. Folk songs, ballads, fables, and myths are often the products of oral tradition. No one knows who created them. That is, they are *anonymous.* The ballad "John Henry," on page 650, is a product of the oral tradition. No one knows who first wrote this ballad. It has been passed from singer to singer for many years and, like most products of the oral tradition, exists in many different versions.
See *Folk Tale, Legend,* and *Myth.*

**PARALLELISM**    See *Repetition.*

**PENTAMETER**    See *Meter.*

**PERSONIFICATION**    *Personification* is a type of figurative language in which a nonhuman subject is given human characteristics. The expressions "Father Time" and "Mother Earth" are examples of personification. Naoshi Koriyama's poem "Jetliner," on page 536, uses personification, likening an airplane to an athlete:

> then . . . after a few . . . tense moments . . . of pondering
> he roars at his utmost
> and slowly begins to jog
> kicking the earth hard
> and now he begins to run
> kicking the earth harder

See *Figurative Language.*

**PERSUASION**    *Persuasion* is writing or speech that attempts to convince the reader to adopt an opinion or a course of action. Advertisements are the most common forms of persuasion; they try to persuade people to buy certain products or services. Newspaper editorials, political speeches, and essays are other common forms of persuasive writing. In his essay "Dial Versus Digital," on page 477, Isaac Asimov tries to persuade his readers that something important has been lost in the change from dial to digital clocks and watches.

**PLOT** *Plot* is the sequence of events in a literary work. In most novels, short stories, dramas, and narrative poems, the plot involves two basic elements—characters and conflict. The plot usually begins with the *exposition,* which establishes the setting, identifies the characters, and introduces the basic situation. This is usually followed by the *inciting incident,* which introduces the *central conflict.* The *development* of the central conflict shows how the characters are affected by it. Eventually, the development reaches a high point of interest or suspense, the *climax.* The *falling action* of the conflict then follows. Any events that occur during the falling action make up the *resolution,* or *denouement.*

Some plots do not contain all of these parts. Short stories, for example, often do not include an exposition and a denouement. Sometimes, too, the inciting incident in a short story or novel has occurred before the opening of the story.

All the events that occur before the climax of a story make up its *rising action.* All the events that occur after the climax make up the *falling action.*
See *Conflict.*

**POETRY** *Poetry* is one of the three major types of literature, the others being prose and drama. Poetry is not easy to define, but we might say that poetry is language used in special ways. Most poems make use of concise, rhythmic, and emotionally charged language. The language of poetry usually emphasizes the re-creation of experiences over analysis of these experiences.

Traditionally, poetry has differed from prose in making use of formal structural devices such as rhyme, meter, and stanzas. Some poems, however, are written out just like prose.

Major types of poetry include lyric poems, narrative poems, dramatic poems, and epics. Walter de la Mare's "Silver," on page 564, and Lew Sarett's "Four Little Foxes," on page 556, are lyric poems. Joaquin Miller's "Columbus," on page 521, and John Greenleaf Whittier's "Barbara Frietchie," on page 525, are narrative poems. In dramatic poetry, characters speak the poem in their own voices. An epic poem, such as Homer's *Iliad,* is a long, involved narrative poem about the exploits of gods and heroes.

**POINT OF VIEW** *Point of view* is the perspective, or vantage point, from which a story is told. The three most common points of view in narrative literature are first person, omniscient third person, and limited third person.

In a story from the *first-person point of view,* the narrator is a character in the story. We see the story through his or her eyes. Most of the Sherlock Holmes stories, such as "The Adventure of the Speckled Band," on page 27, are told from a first-person point of view—that of Dr. Watson.

In a story written from the *omniscient,* or "all knowing," *third-person point of view,* the narrator is not a character in the story but views the events of the story through the eyes of more than one of the characters. Isaac Asimov's "Rain Rain, Go Away," on page 13, uses the third-person omniscient point of view.

In a *third-person limited point of view,* the narrator is not a character, but he or she presents the story from the perspective of one of the characters. That character's thoughts, feelings, and experiences are the focus of attention. Pearl S. Buck's "Christmas Day in the Morning," on page 21, is an example of limited third-person narration.
See *Narrator.*

**PROSE** *Prose* is the ordinary form of written language. Most writing that is not poetry, drama, or song is considered prose. Prose fiction includes novels and short stories. Nonfiction prose includes essays, biography, autobiography, journalism, scientific reports, and historical writing. See *Fiction, Genre,* and *Nonfiction.*

**PROTAGONIST** The *protagonist* is the main character in a literary work. Normally, the reader sympathizes with or at least learns to understand the protagonist. For example, in "The Man Without a Country," on page 185, the reader sympathizes with the protagonist, Philip Nolan, who has been exiled for life to a ship. In *The Diary of Anne Frank,* on page 303, the reader sympathizes with the protagonist, Anne Frank, who must deal with many hardships.

**PYRRHIC** See *Meter.*

**QUATRAIN** See *Stanza.*

**REFRAIN** A *refrain* is a regularly repeated line or group of lines in a poem or song. In Joaquin Miller's "Columbus," on page 521, the refrain is "Sail on! sail on! sail on!"

**REPETITION** *Repetition* is the use, more than once, of any element of language—a sound, a word, a phrase, a sentence, a grammatical pattern, or a rhythmical pattern. Repetition is used both in prose and in poetry. In prose fiction, a plot may be repeated, with variations, in a subplot, or a minor character may be similar to a major character in important ways. In poetry, repetition often involves the recurring use of certain words, images, structures, and devices. Rhyme and alliteration, for example, repeat sounds. A repeating rhyme pattern is called a *rhyme scheme.* A *refrain* is a repeated line or group of lines.

Another form of repetition, used in both prose and poetry, is *parallelism,* in which a grammatical pattern is repeated, though with some changes over time. José Garcia Villa's poem "Lyric 17," which appears on page 532, contains parallel repetition of the phrase "It must":

> It must be slender as a bell,
> And it must hold fire as a well.
> It must have the wisdom of bows
> And it must kneel like a rose.

**RESOLUTION** See *Plot.*

**RHYME** *Rhyme* is the repetition of sounds at the ends of words. Poets use rhyme to create musical effects, and to emphasize and to link certain words and ideas. The most traditional type of rhyme is *end rhyme,* or rhyming words at the end of the lines. Alfred, Lord Tennyson, uses end rhyme in "Ring Out, Wild Bells" on page 544:

> Ring out, wild bells, to the wild *sky,*
>   The flying cloud, the frosty *light:*
>   The year is dying in the *night;*
> Ring out, wild bells, and let him *die.*

*Internal rhyme* occurs when rhymes occur within lines. Notice, for example, the internal rhymes in this poem by Oliver Wendell Holmes:

> In the street I heard a *thumping;* and I knew it
>   was the *stumping*
> Of the Corporal, our old *neighbor,* on that leg
>   he *wore,*
> With a knot of women *round him,*—it was lucky
>   I had *found him,*
> So I followed with the others, and the Corporal
>   marched *before.*

**RHYME SCHEME** A *rhyme scheme* is a regular pattern of rhyming words in a poem. To indicate the rhyme scheme of a poem, one uses lowercase letters. For example, the following stanza, from Robert Frost's "Blue-Butterfly Day," on page 559, has an *abab* rhyme scheme:

> It is blue-butterfly day here in *spring*          a
> And with these sky-flakes down in flurry
>   on *flurry*                                       b
> There is more unmixed color on the *wing*         a
> Than flowers will show for days unless
>   they *hurry.*                                     b

**RHYTHM**  *Rhythm* is the pattern of stresses, or beats, in spoken or written language.
See *Meter.*

**ROUND CHARACTER**  See *Character.*

**SCAN/SCANNING**  See *Meter.*

**SCENE**  See *Drama.*

**SCIENCE FICTION**  *Science fiction* is writing that tells about imaginary events that involve science or technology. Much science fiction is set in the future, often on planets other than Earth. Arthur C. Clarke's "Crime on Mars," on page 137, is a science-fiction story about a crime that takes place in a large Earth colony on Mars.
See *Fiction.*

**SENSORY LANGUAGE**  *Sensory language* is writing or speech that appeals to one or more of the five senses. Writers use sensory language to make the ideas and events they describe more vivid and clear.
See *Image.*

**SESTET**  See *Stanza.*

**SETTING**  The *setting* of a literary work is the time and place of the action. The time includes not only the historical period—past, present, or future—but also the year, the season, the time of day, and even the weather. The place may be a specific country, state, region, community, neighborhood, building, institution, or home. Details such as dialects, clothing, customs and modes of transportation are often used to establish setting. In most stories, the setting serves as a backdrop against which the characters act out the actions of the narrative. The setting of Ray Bradbury's "The Drummer Boy of Shiloh," on page 151, is an April night in 1862, during the Civil War, at a place named "Shiloh" near the Tennessee River, close to a church.

The setting of a story often helps to create a particular mood, or feeling. The mood of Ray Bradbury's story is one of nervous expectation—of fear mingled with resolve.
See *Conflict, Plot,* and *Theme.*

**SHORT STORY**  A *short story* is a brief work of fiction. Like novels, most short stories contain a central conflict and one or more characters, the most important of which is the protagonist. Like lyric poems, short stories usually create a single effect, or dominant impression. The main idea, message, or subject of a short story is its *theme.*
See *Fiction.*

**SIMILE**  A *simile* is a figure of speech that makes a direct comparison between two unlike subjects using *like* or *as.* Everyday speech contains many similes, as in "quiet as a mouse," "like a duck out of water," "good as gold," and "old as the hills."

Writers use similes to create vivid, telling descriptions. Poetry, especially, relies on similes to point out new and interesting ways of looking at the world. For example, Richard García's poem "The City Is So Big," on page 586, contains this striking simile:

And trains pass with windows shining
Like a smile full of teeth.

**SPEAKER**  The *speaker* is the imaginary voice assumed by the writer of a poem. In other words, the speaker is the character who tells the poem. Sometimes this speaker will identify himself or herself by name. At other times the speaker is more vague. Interpreting a poem often depends on inferring what the speaker is like based on the details that he or she provides.

**SPONDEE**  See *Meter.*

**STAGE DIRECTIONS**  *Stage directions* are notes included in a drama to describe how the work is to be performed or staged. Stage directions are usually printed in italics and enclosed within parentheses or brackets. They may indicate how the actors should speak their lines, how they should move, how the characters should be dressed, what the stage should look like, or what special effects of lighting or sound should be used. Here is an excerpt from Frances Goodrich and Albert Hackett's play *The Diary of Anne Frank,* on page 303, which includes stage directions:

MR. FRANK: [*Quietly, to the group*] it's safe now. The last workman has left.
[*There is an immediate stir of relief.*]
ANNE: [*Her pent-up energy explodes.*] WHEE!
MRS. FRANK: [*Startled, amused*] Anne!

See *Drama.*

**STANZA**  A *stanza* is a group of lines in a poem, considered as a unit. Many poems are divided into stanzas of equal length, with the stanzas separated by spaces. Stanzas are often like paragraphs in prose; each presents a single thought or idea.

Stanzas are usually named according to the number of lines they contain, as follows:

1. *Couplet:* a two-line stanza
2. *Tercet:* a three-line stanza
3. *Quatrain:* a four-line stanza
4. *Cinquain:* a five-line stanza
5. *Sestet:* a six-line stanza
6. *Heptastich:* a seven-line stanza
7. *Octave:* an eight-line stanza

In traditional poetry stanzas are often rhymed. However, not all rhyming poems use stanzas, nor do all poems that are divided into stanzas rhyme. Less traditional poetry contains stanzas of varying length, sometimes with, sometimes without, rhyme.

**STATIC CHARACTER**  See *Character.*

**SUBPLOT**  See *Novel.*

**SURPRISE ENDING**  A *surprise ending* is a conclusion that violates the expectations of the reader. For example, the ending of Shirley Jackson's short story "Charles," on page 79, is a complete surprise to the reader. Laurie's parents are so convinced that Charles exists that the reader is as astonished as the narrator to discover that there is no Charles. The stories that Laurie has been telling to his parents are probably stories about himself. Often a writer will *foreshadow* the surprise ending by including seemingly minor details earlier in the story that make the later surprise appear a fair, if unexpected, ending.
See *Foreshadowing* and *Plot.*

**SUSPENSE**  *Suspense* is a feeling of anxious uncertainty about the outcome of events in a literary work. Writers create suspense by raising questions in the minds of their readers. For example, in Beryl Markham's "The Captain and His Horse," on page 47, suspense peaks when the buffaloes trap the narrator and the Baron. The reader worries and wonders whether they will escape and, if so, how. Suspense in a story can be especially intense if there are convincing, interesting characters about whom the reader cares strongly.
See *Plot.*

**SYMBOL**  A *symbol* is anything that stands for or represents something else. Symbols are usually concrete objects or images that represent abstract ideas. For example, the eagle is often used as a symbol of freedom. Likewise, chains can symbolize slavery and oppression. In literature concrete images are often used to represent, or symbolize, the themes of a literary work. For example, in Edgar Allan Poe's "The Tell-Tale Heart," on page 145, the beating heart of the old man could be a symbol of the old man's vengeance or of the main character's guilt. Symbols generally differ from metaphors or similes in that the reader or listener must infer what the symbol

stands for. The writer or speaker does not explicitly make the comparison.
See *Figurative Language.*

**TERCET**   See *Stanza.*

**TETRAMETER**   See *Meter.*

**THEME**   A *theme* is a central message, concern, or insight into life expressed in a literary work. A theme can usually be expressed by a one- or two-sentence statement about human beings or about life. For example, the theme of Edward Everett Hale's short story "The Man Without a Country," on page 185, might be this: "Every man needs to feel allegiance to his native country, whether he always appreciates that country or not."

A theme may be stated directly or may be implied. In poems and in works of prose fiction, the theme is rarely stated directly. More often, the other elements of the work—its language, imagery, plot, tone, and structure—suggest the theme. *Interpretation* involves uncovering the theme of a literary work by carefully considering the parts, or elements, of the work.

In nonfiction works, and especially in essays, the theme is often stated directly. The title of Robert MacNeil's "The Trouble with Television," on page 463, suggests in a general way what the theme of the essay is, and the essay itself states the theme explicitly: Television oversimplifies, distorts, and ultimately "decivilizes" human existence.

**TONE**   *Tone* is the attitude toward the subject and audience conveyed by the language and rhythm of the speaker in a literary work. For example, the tone of Edgar Allan Poe's "The Tell-Tale Heart," on page 145, is frantic and sinister. The narrator of the story reveals, by his tone and by his actions, that he is dangerously insane. In contrast, the tone of John Updike's poem "January," on page 576, is light and humorous.
See *Mood.*

**TRIMETER**   See *Meter.*

**TROCHEE**   See *Meter.*

**VERBAL IRONY**   See *Irony.*

# GLOSSARY

## READING THE GLOSSARY ENTRIES

The words in this glossary are from selections appearing in your textbook. Each entry in the glossary contains the following parts:

**1. The Entry Word.** This word appears at the beginning of the entry in boldface type.

**2. The Pronunciation.** The symbols in parentheses tell how the entry word is pronounced. If a word has more than one possible pronunciation, the most common of these pronunciations is given first.

**3. The Part of Speech.** Appearing after the pronunciation, in italics, is an abbreviation that tells the part of speech of the entry word. The following abbreviations have been used:

**n.** noun      **p.** pronoun      **v.** verb
**adj.** adjective    **adv.** adverb    **conj.** conjunction

**4. The Definition.** This part of the entry follows the part-of-speech abbreviation and gives the meaning of the entry word as used in the selection in which it appears.

## KEY TO PRONUNCIATION SYMBOLS USED IN THE GLOSSARY

The following symbols are used in the pronunciations that follow the entry words:

| Symbol | Key Words | Symbol | Key Words |
|---|---|---|---|
| a | asp, fat, parrot | b | bed, fable, dub |
| ā | ape, date, play | d | dip, beadle, had |
| ä | ah, car, father | f | fall, after, off |
| | | g | get, haggle, dog |
| e | elf, ten, berry | h | he, ahead, hotel |
| ē | even, meet, money | j | joy, agile, badge |
| | | k | kill, tackle, bake |
| i | is, hit, mirror | l | let, yellow, ball |
| ī | ice, bite, high | m | met, camel, trim |
| | | n | not, flannel, ton |
| ō | open, tone, go | p | put, apple, tap |
| ô | all, horn, law | r | red, port, dear |
| oo | look, pull, moor | s | sell, castle, pass |
| ōō | ooze, tool, crew | t | top, cattle, hat |
| yōō | use, cute, few | v | vat, hovel, have |
| yoo | united, cure, globule | w | will, always, swear |
| oi | oil, point, toy | y | yet, onion, yard |
| ou | out, crowd, plow | z | zebra, dazzle, haze |
| u | up, cut, color | ch | chin, catcher, arch |
| ʉr | urn, fur, deter | sh | she, cushion, dash |
| | | th | thin, nothing, truth |
| ə | a in ago | th | then, father, lathe |
| | e in agent | zh | azure, leisure |
| | i in sanity | ŋ | ring, anger, drink |
| | o in comply | ʼ | [indicates that a following l or n is a syllabic consonant, as in cattle (kat′ ′l)] |
| | u in focus | | |
| ər | perhaps, murder | | |

## FOREIGN SOUNDS

à   This symbol, representing the a in French salle, can best be described as intermediate between (a) and (ä).

ë   This symbol represents the sound of the vowel cluster in french coeur and can be approximated by rounding the lips as for (ō) and pronouncing (e).

ö   This symbol variously represents the sound of eu in French feu or of ö or oe in German blöd or Goethe and can be approximated by rounding lips as for (ō) and pronouncing (ā).

ō̤   This symbol represents a range of sounds between (ô) and (u); it occurs typically in the sound of the o in French tonne or German korrekt; in Italian poco and Spanish torero, it is almost like English (ô), as in horn.

ü   This symbol variously represents the sound of u in French duc and in German grun and can be approximated by rounding the lips as for (ō) and pronouncing (ē).

kh   This symbol represents the voiceless velar or uvular fricative as in the ch of German doch or Scots English loch. It can be approximated by placing the tongue as for (ʻ:) but allowing the breath to escape in a stream, as in pronouncing (h).

r   This symbol represents any of various sounds used in languages other than English for the consonant r. It may represent the tongue-point trill or uvular trill of the r in French reste or sur, German Reuter, Italian ricotta, Russian gorod, etc.

b̵   This symbol represents the sound made by the letter v between vowels. It is pronounced like a b sound but without letting the lips come together.

This pronunciation key is from *Webster's New World Dictionary*, Third College Edition. Copyright © 1988 by Simon & Schuster. Used by permission.

## A

**abalone** (ab′ ə lō′ nē)    **shell** *n.* An oval shell with a pearly lining

**abandonment** (ə ban′ dən mənt)    *n.* Unrestrained freedom of actions or emotions

**abduction** (ab duk′ shən)    *n.* Kidnapping

**aboriginal** (ab′ ə rij′ ə nəl)    *adj.* First; native

**abstain** (ab stān′)    *v.* To refrain voluntarily

**absurdity** (ab sʉr′ də tē)    *n.* Ridiculousness

**abyss** (ə bis′)    *n.* Great depth

**acquaintance** (ə kwānt′ ′ns)    *n.* A person one has met

**acquiescent** (ak′ wē es′ nt)    *adj.* Agreeing without protest

**acrid** (ak′ rid)    *adj.* Sharp; bitter

**acute** (ə kyōōt′)    *adj.* Sensitive

**ad-lib** (ad′ lib′)    *v.* To say or do things not in a script

**adroitness** (ə droit′ nes)    *n.* Skill; dexterity

**adversary** (ad′ vər ser′ ē)    *n.* Enemy

**affectation** (af′ ek tā′ shən)    *n.* Behavior not natural to a person intended to impress others

**aghast** (ə gast′)    *adj.* Horrified

**agitated** (aj′ i tāt id)    *adj.* Upset; disturbed

**airy** (er′ ē)    *adj.* Lightness

**alkaloid** (al' kə loid') *adj.* Referring to certain bitter substances found chiefly in plants

**allure** (ə loor') *v.* To tempt; attract

**ally** (ə lī') *v.* To join or to unite, connection between country, person, or group for a common purpose

**alms** (ämz) *n.* Money given to poor people

**alterative** (ôl' tər āt' iv) *adj.* Causing a change

**amble** (am' bəl) *v.* To move at a smooth, easy pace

**ambuscade** (am' bəs kād') *n.* Place of surprise attack

**amends** (ə mendz') *n.pl.* Payment made for an injury or loss

**amenity** (ə men' ə tē) *n.* Pleasant quality

**anachronism** (ə nak' rə niz' əm) *n.* Anything that seems to be out of its proper place in history

**anemometer** (an' ə mäm' ət ər) *n.* An instrument that determines wind speed

**anguish** (aŋ' gwish) *n.* Extreme pain; torture; torment

**antagonist** (an tag' ə nist) *n.* Opponent

**anxious** (aŋk' shəs) *adj.* Eagerly wishing

**apathetic** (ap' ə thet' ik) *adv.* Indifferent

**apertures** (ap' ər chərz) *n.pl.* Openings; holes

**apex** (ā' peks') *n.* Highest point; peak

**appall** (ə pôl') *v.* To overwhelm with horror or shock

**apparition** (ap' ə rish' ən) *n.* A strange figure appearing suddenly or in an extraordinary way

**applaud** (ə plôd') *v.* To show approval or enjoyment by clapping the hands

**appraisal** (ə prāz' el) *n.* Evaluation; judgment

**apprehension** (ap' rə hen' shən) *n.* A fearful feeling about the future; dread

**apprentice** (ə pren' tis) *v.* To contract to learn a trade under a skilled worker

**arbitrary** (är' bə trer' ē) *adj.* Based on one's preference or whim

**archaeologist** (är' kē äl' ə jist) *n.* Scientist who studies the life and culture of ancient people

**archer** (är' chər) *n.* A person who shoots with bow and arrow

**archipelago** (är' kə pel' ə gō') *n.* A chain of many islands

**ardent** (ärd' 'nt) *adj.* Passionate

**aristocrat** (ə ris' tə krat') *n.* A person belonging to the upper class

**armory** (är' mər ē) *n.* A storehouse for weapons

**arouse** (ə rouz') *v.* To awaken; to stir from sleep

**articulated** (är tik' yoo lā' əd) *adj.* Connected by joints

**artifact** (ärt' ə fakt') *n.* Any object made by human work, left behind by a civilization

**ascend** (ə send') *v.* To move upward

**askew** (ə skyoo') *adv.* Crookedly

**assiduous** (ə sij' oo əs) *adj.* Careful and busy

**atone** (ə tōn') *v.* Make amends for wrongdoing

**attribute** (ə trib' yoot) *v.* To think of as belonging to or appropriate to

**august** (ô' gust') *adj.* Honored

**aura** (ô' rə) *n.* An atmosphere or quality

**austere** (ô stir') *adj.* Stern; lacking in warmth or joy

**avail** (ə vāl') *v.* To be of use

**avarice** (av' ə ris) *n.* Greediness

**avenge** (ə venj') *v.* To take revenge for or on behalf of

**aver** (ə vɝr') *v.* To declare

**awed** (ôd) *adj.* Having a mixed feeling of reverence, fear, and wonder

**axioms** (ak' sē əmz) *n.* Truths or principles that are widely accepted

**B**

**babel** (bā' bəl) *n.* A confusion of sounds

**backfire** (bak' fīr') *n.* A fire started to stop an advancing fire

**baleful** (bāl' fəl) *adj.* Threatening; harmful in effect

**banal** (bā' nəl) *adj.* Commonplace; ordinary

**bane** (bān) *n.* Ruin

**bank** (baŋk) *v.* To tilt an airplane to the side when turning

**banner** (ban' ər) *n.* Flag

**barter** (bärt' ər) *v.* To exchange goods

**becalm** (bē käm') *v.* Not to move

**beckon** (bek' 'n) *v.* To gesture for someone to come, as by nodding or waving

**bedraggle** (bē drag' əl) *v.* To wet and soil

**beguile** (bē gīl') *v.* To charm

**belfry** (bel' frē) *n.* The part of a tower that holds the bells

**bellow** (bel' ō) *v.* Roar powerfully

**benediction** (ben' ə dik' shən) *n.* A blessing

**benevolent** (bə nev' ə lənt) *adj.* Kindly

**benign** (bi nīn') *adj.* Kindly

**billow** (bil' ō) *n.* Large; spread out

**bleating** (blēt' iŋ) *n.* The sound made by sheep

**blunder** (blun' dər) *n.* A foolish or stupid mistake

**bode** (bōd) *v.* To foretell a future event

**borne** (bôrn) *v.* Carried

**brace** (brās) *n.* A pair of like things

**bravado** (brə vä' dō) *n.* Bold, bragging behavior

**bridle** (brīd' 'l) *n.* A head harness for guiding a horse

**brimstone** (brim' stōn') *n.* Another name for sulfur, a foul-smelling mineral

**brine** (brīn) *n.* Water full of salt and used for pickling

**broach** (brōch) *v.* To start a discussion about a topic

**buffet** (buf' it) *v.* To strike against forcefully; batter

**bullpen** (bool' pen') *n.* A barred room in a jail, where prisoners are kept temporarily

**bulwark** (bool' wərk) *n.* Protection; defense

**buoyant** (boi' ənt) *adj.* Lighthearted

**C**

**cadence** (kād' 'ns) *n.* Rhythmic flow of sound

**cajole** (kə jōl') *v.* To coax gently

**calamity** (kə lam' ə tē) *n.* A great misfortune or disaster

**callous** (kal' əs) *adj.* Unfeeling

**callowness** (kal' ō nəs) *n.* Youth and inexperience; immaturity

**caper** (kā' pər) *n.* Slang term for criminal act

**capitulation** (kə pich' yoo lā' shən) *n.* Surrender

**carcass** (kär′ kəs)   *n.* The dead body of an animal

**carillon** (kar′ ə län′)   *n.* A set of stationary bells, each producing one note of the scale

**catapult** (kat′ ə pult′)   *v.* To launch

**celestial** (sə les′ chəl)   *adj.* Of the sky

**centrifugal** (sen trif′ yo͞o gəl)   *adj.* Describing something that tends to move away from the center

**cessation** (se sā′ shən)   *n.* A stopping

**chancellor** (chan′ sə lər)   *n.* An official secretary

**civic** (siv′ ik)   *adj.* Of a city

**clairvoyant** (kler voi′ ənt)   *adj.* Having the ability to see what cannot be seen; keenly perceptive

**coherence** (kō hir′ əns)   *n.* The quality of being connected in an intelligible way

**commission** (kə mish′ ən)   *n.* Authority given to make something

**commotion** (kə mō′ shən)   *n.* Noisy movement

**communal** (käm′ yoo nəl)   *adj.* Shared by members of a group

**compassionate** (kəm pash′ ən it)   *adj.* Sympathizing deeply

**compensation** (käm′ pən sā′ shən)   *n.* Equal reaction

**compliance** (kəm plī′ əns)   *n.* Agreeing to a request

**compound** (käm pound′)   *adj.* Mix

**compulsory** (kəm pul′ sə rē)   *adj.* Required

**conciliate** (kən sil′ ē āt′)   *v.* To make friends with

**concoction** (kən käk′ shən)   *n.* A substance made up of many, sometimes unknown, ingredients

**condemn** (kən dem′)   *v.* To disapprove of

**confederate** (kən fed′ ər it)   *n.* Accomplice; partner in crime

**conjecture** (kən jek′ chər)   *v.* To guess from very little evidence

**conjuration** (kän′ jo͞o rā′ shən)   *n.* The making of a magic spell

**connote** (kə nōt′)   *v.* To suggest or imply

**conspicuous** (kən spik′ yo͞o əs)   *adj.* Noticeable

**conspiratorial** (kən spir′ ə tôr′ ē əl)   *adj.* Secretive

**conspire** (kən spīr′)   *v.* To work together secretly

**constellation** (kän′ stə lā′ shən)   *n.* 1 A group of stars named after and thought to resemble an object, animal, or mythological character in outline 2 A brilliant cluster

**consternation** (kän′ stər nā′ shən)   *n.* Dismay

**contradict** (kön′ trə dikt′)   *v.* To assert the opposite of

**convent** (kän′ vənt)   *n.* A girls′ boarding school run by nuns

**conviction** (kən vik′ shən)   *n.* Strong belief

**convolutions** (kän′ və lo͞o shənz)   *n.* Uneven ridges on the brain′s surface

**convulse** (kən vuls′)   *v.* To suffer a violent, involuntary spasm

**cosseted** (käs′ it əd)   *adj.* Pampered; indulged

**couch** (kouch)   *v.* To put into words

**countenance** (koun′ tə nəns)   *n.* The face

**covert** (kuv′ ərt)   *adj.* Concealed; hidden

**cower** (kou′ ər)   *v.* To crouch or huddle from fear

**cowling** (koul′ iŋ)   *n.* A removable metal covering for an engine

**cowpuncher** (kou′ pun chər)   *n.* Cowboy

**crane** (krān)   *n.* A large, slender bird with very long legs and neck

**cranny** (kran′ ē)   *n.* Small, narrow opening

**credibility** (kred′ ə bil′ i tē)   *n.* Something that can be believed; reliability

**credo** (krē′ dō)   *n.* Set of personal beliefs

**crestfallen** (krest′ fôl′ ən)   *adj.* Made sad or humble; disheartened

**crevice** (krev′ is)   *n.* A narrow opening

**crooner** (kro͞on′ ər)   *n.* Singer

**crosstie** (krôs′ tī)   *n.* Beam laid crosswise under railroad tracks to support them

**crustaceans** (krus tā′ shənz)   *n.* Shellfish, such as lobsters, crabs, or shrimp

**crypt** (kript)   *n.* An underground vault, used as a burial place

**cryptic** (krip′ tik)   *adj.* Having hidden meaning

**crystal** (kris′ təl)   *n.* The transparent covering over the face of a watch

**cultivate** (kul′ tə vāt′)   *v.* To prepare and use for the raising of crops; to till

**cunning** (kun′ iŋ)   *adj.* Skillful

**cursory** (kʉr′ sə rē)   *adj.* Hastily, often superficially done

**cynical** (sin′ i kəl)   *adj.* Disbelief as to the sincerity of people′s intentions or actions

## D

**daunt** (dônt)   *v.* To intimidate or discourage

**deference** (def′ ər əns)   *n.* Courteous respect

**defilers** (dē fīl′ ərz)   *n.* Those who corrupt or make unclean

**defray** (dē frā′)   *v.* To pay the money for the cost of

**deign** (dān)   *v.* To lower oneself

**dejected** (dē jek′ tid)   *adj.* In low spirits, depressed

**delineate** (di lin′ ē āt)   *v.* To describe in detail

**demise** (dē mīz′)   *n.* Death

**derision** (di rizh′ ən)   *n.* Contempt; ridicule

**desolation** (des′ ə lā′ shən)   *n.* Decay; a state of extreme neglect

**despise** (di spīz′)   *v.* To scorn; to look on with contempt

**destine** (des′ tin)   *v.* To determine by fate

**devour** (di vour′)   *v.* To eat up greedily

**digital** (dij′ i təl)   *adj.* Giving a reading in digits, which are the numerals from 0 to 9

**diligent** (dil′ ə jənt)   *adj.* Hard-working; industrious

**diplomatic** (dip′ lə mat′ ik)   *adj.* Tactful

**discreet** (di skrēt′)   *adj.* Careful about what one says or does

**discreet surveillance** (di skrēt′ sər vā′ləns)   *n.* Careful unobserved watch kept over a person

**disheveled** (di shev′ əld)   *adj.* Untidy; messy

**dispel** (di spel′)   *v.* To drive away

**disposition** (dis′ pə zish′ ən)   *n.* One′s nature or temperament

**dissemble** (di sem′ bəl)   *v.* To conceal under a false appearance

**dissentient** (di sen′ shənt)   *adj.* Differing from the majority

**dissimulation** (di sim′ yoo lā′ shən)   *n.* The hiding of one's feelings or purposes

**dissolute** (dis′ ə loot′)   *adj.* Unrestrained

**dissolution** (dis′ ə loo′ shən)   *n.* The act of breaking down and crumbling

**distend** (di stend′)   *v.* To stretch out; to become swollen

**diverge** (dī vurj′)   *v.* To branch off

**divert** (də vurt′)   *v.* To distract

**divest** (də vest′)   *v.* To strip; to get rid of

**doggedness** (dôg′ id nis)   *n.* Stubborness

**dogie** (dō′ gē) **calves**   *n.* Motherless calves

**douse** (dous)   *v.* To put out; extinguish

**drill** (dril)   *n.* Pointed tool used for making holes in hard substances

**drive** (drīv)   *v.* To force by hitting

**drowse** (drouz)   *n.* Sluggishness; doze

**drove** (drōv)   *n.* Large number; crowd

**dugout** (dug′ out′)   *n.* A shelter built into a hillside

**E**

**edifice** (ed′ i fis)   *n.* Imposing structure

**elaborate** (ē lab′ ə rit)   *adj.* Careful; painstaking

**elder** (el′ dər)   *n.* Shrub or small tree

**elixir** (ē liks′ ər)   *n.* Magic potion

**eloquent** (el′ ə kwənt)   *adj.* Very expressive

**elusive** (ē loo′ siv)   *adj.* Hard to grasp mentally

**emanate** (em′ ə nāt′)   *v.* To come or send forth

**emancipate** (ē man′ sə pāt)   *v.* To free from the control or power of another

**eminent** (em′ ə nənt)   *adj.* Well-known

**empathize** (em′ pə thīz′)   *v.* To feel empathy for; share the feelings of

**empathy** (em′ pə thē′)   *n.* Capacity for participating in another's feelings or ideas

**encumber** (en kum′ bər)   *v.* To weigh down

**engulf** (en gulf′)   *v.* To flow over; to swallow up

**enigma** (i nig′ mə)   *n.* An unexplainable event

**enthusiasm** (en thoo′ zē az′ em)   *n.* Intense or eager interest

**enunciate** (ē nun′ sē āt′)   *v.* To speak clearly and carefully

**escarpment** (e skärp′ mənt)   *n.* A long cliff

**esophagus** (i säf′ ə gəs)   *n.* The tube through which food passes to the stomach

**eternal** (ē tur′ nəl)   *adj.* Everlasting

**euphemism** (yoo′ fə miz′ əm)   *n.* A less direct term that substitutes for a distasteful or offensive word or phrase

**evacuee** (ē vak′ yoo ē′)   *n.* One who leaves a place because of danger

**evasion** (ē vā′ zhən)   *n.* Avoidance

**evasive** (ē vā′ siv)   *adj.* Tending to avoid or escape by deceit or cleverness; intentionally vague

**exception** (ek sep′ shən)   *n.* Exlusion

**excrescence** (eks kres′ əns)   *n.* A natural outgrowth

**exodus** (eks′ ə dəs)   *n.* Departure

**expend** (ek spend′)   *v.* To use up

**expound** (eks pound′)   *v.* To explain in careful detail

**extravagence** (ek strav′ ə gəns)   *n.* Waste

**extremity** (ek strem′ ə tē)   *n.* Dying stage

**exult** (eg zult′)   *v.* To rejoice

**F**

**fastidious** (fas tid′ ē əs)   *adj.* Not easy to please

**fatalist** (fāt′ 'l ist)   *n.* One who believes that all events are determined by fate

**fatuous** (fach′ oo əs)   *adj.* Foolish; blandly inane

**feign** (fān)   *v.* To make a false show of

**feint** (fānt)   *v.* Make a pretense of attack

**fell** (fel)   *n.* Rocky or barren hill

**fertile** (furt′ 'l)   *adj.* Rich; productive

**fiscal** (fis′ kəl)   *adj.* Having to do with finances

**fissure** (fish′ ər)   *n.* Narrow opening

**fitting** (fit′ iŋ)   *adj.* Proper

**flag** (flag)   *v.* To signal to a train to stop

**flamboyant** (flam boi′ ənt)   *adj.* Too showy; extravagant

**fleece** (flēs)   *n.* Soft, warm covering made of sheep's wool

**fluctuate** (fluk′ choo āt′)   *v.* To be constantly changing

**flue** (floo)   *n.* The pipe in a chimney

**flush** (flush)   *n.* A blush or glow

**forbear** (fôr ber′)   *v.* To refrain from

**foresight** (fôr′ sīt′)   *n.* The act of seeing beforehand

**forestall** (fôr stôl′)   *v.* To prevent

**forsaken** (fər sāk′ ən)   *adj.* Abandoned

**fragrant** (frā′ grənt)   *adj.* Covered with the odor of something

**fretted** (fret′ əd)   *adj.* Decoratively arranged

**friction** (frik′ shən)   *n.* The rubbing of the surface of one body against another

**furrow** (fur′ ō)   *n.* A deep wrinkle

**furtive** (fur′ tiv)   *adj.* Sly or done in secret

**futile** (fyoot′ 'l)   *adj.* Useless; hopeless

**G**

**galley** (gal′ ē)   *n.* Cooking area on a ship

**garnet** (gär′ nit)   *n.* Deep red gem

**garrison** (gar′ ə sən)   *n.* Military post or station

**gesticulation** (jes tik′ yoo lā′ shən)   *n.* Energetic hand or arm gesture

**gingerly** (jin′ jər′ lē)   *adv.* In a careful way

**glean** (glēn)   *v.* To find out gradually bit by bit

**gleeful** (glē′ fəl)   *adj.* Merry

**glisten** (glis′ ən)   *v.* To shine

**glockenspiel** (gläk′ ən spēl′)   *n.* Musical instrument like xylophone

**gnarled** (närld)   *adj.* Knotty and twisted

**goad** (gōd)   *v.* To urge to action

**gossamer**   (gäs′ ə mər)   *adj.* Delicate, light, or flimsy

**gout**   (gout)   *n.* Inflammation of the joints

**gracious**   (grā′ shəs)   *adj.* Kind and generous

**granite**   (gran′ it)   *adj.* Made of a type of very hard rock

**gratification**   (grat′ i fi kā′ shən)   *n.* The act of pleasing

**gross**   (grōs)   *n.* Twelve dozen

**guffaw**   (gu fô′)   *v.* To laugh in a loud, coarse way

**guffaws**   (gu fôz′)   *n.* Hearty bursts of laughter

**guile**   (gīl)   *n.* Craftiness

**gumption**   (gump′ shən)   *n.* Courage, boldness

**guttural**   (gut′ ər əl)   *adj.* Made in back of the throat; *n.* Sound produced in the throat

**gyration**   (jī ra ′ shən)   *n.* Circling or spiral movement

**H**

**habitable**   (hab′ it ə bəl)   *adj.* Fit to live in

**haggard**   (hag′ ərd)   *adj.* Having a tired look

**harness**   (här′ nis)   *v.* To tie

**hasp**   (hasp)   *n.* Hinged metal fastening of a window

**heft**   (heft)   *v.* To lift; test the weight of

**hie**   (hī)   *v.* To hurry

**hoarse**   (hôrs)   *adj.* Sounding harsh

**hobnailed**   (häb′ nāld)   *adj.* Having short nails put on the soles to provide greater traction

**homage**   (häm′ ij)   *n.* Public expression of honor

**hook and eye**   (hook and ī)   *n.* A fastening device

**horde**   (hôrd)   *n.* Large moving group

**horizon**   (hə rī′ zən)   *n.* The line that forms the apparent boundary between the earth and the sky

**host**   (hōst)   *n.* An army; a multitude

**hover**   (huv′ ər)   *v.* To stay suspended in the air

**hurtle**   (hurt′ 'l)   *v.* To move quickly

**hybrid**   (hī′ brid)   *adj.* Grown from different varieties

**I**

**ignominious**   (ig′ nə min′ ē əs)   *adj.* 1 Humiliating; degrading 2 Dishonorable

**immensity**   (im men′ si tē)   *n.* Something extremely large or immeasurably vast

**imminent**   (im′ ə nənt)   *adj.* About to happen

**impenetrable**   (im pen′ i trə bəl)   *adj.* Not able to be passed through

**imperious**   (im pir′ ē əs)   *adj.* Overbearing, arrogant

**imperturbable**   (im′ pər tur′ bə bəl)   *adj.* Unexcited; calm

**impetuous**   (im pech′ oo əs)   *adj.* Impulsive

**improvise**   (im′ prə viz′)   *v.* To do on the spur of the moment

**inarticulate**   (in′ är tik′ yoo lit)   *adj.* Speechless or unable to express oneself

**incarcerate**   (in kär′ sər āt′)   *v.* Jail; imprison

**incentive**   (in sent′ iv)   *n.* Something that stirs up people or urges them on

**incessant**   (in ses′ ənt)   *adj.* Without interruption

**incisors**   (in sī′ zərz)   *n.* The front teeth

**incorrigible**   (in kôr′ ə jə bəl)   *adj.* Incapable of being reformed

**incredulous**   (in krej′ oo ləs)   *adj.* Showing disbelief

**incredulously**   (in krej′ oo ləs lē)   *adv.* In a disbelieving way

**indigent**   (in′ di jənt)   *adj.* Needy; poor

**indignant**   (in dig′ nənt)   *adj.* Filled with anger over some injustice

**indignation**   (in′ dig nā′ shən)   *n.* Righteous anger

**indiscretion**   (in di skresh′ ən)   *n.* Lack of good judgment

**indiscriminate**   (in′ di skrim′ ə nit)   *adj.* Random

**indomitable**   (in däm′ it ə bəl)   *adj.* Not easily discouraged

**indulgent**   (in dul′ jənt)   *adj.* Very tolerant

**ineffectual**   (in′ ə fek′ choo əl)   *adj.* Without any effect

**inevitable**   (in ev′ i tə bəl)   *adj.* Unavoidable

**inexorable**   (in eks′ ər ə bəl)   *adj.* Unwilling to give in

**inexplicable**   (in eks′ pli kə bəl)   *adj.* Without explanation

**inferiority complex**   (in fir′ ē or′ ə tē käm′ pleks)   *n.* Constant sense of worthlessness

**inflammation**   (in′ flə mā′ shən)   *n.* A state of redness, pain and swelling

**infuse**   (in fyōōz′)   *v.* To put into

**infusion**   (in fyōō′ zhən)   *n.* Introduction of one thing into another

**inherent**   (in hir′ ənt)   *adj.* Natural

**initiation**   (i nish′ ē ā′ shən)   *n.* The events during which a person becomes admitted as a member of a club

**innumerable**   (i nōō′ mər ə bəl)   *adj.* Too many to be counted

**inordinately**   (in ôr′ də nit lē)   *adv.* Extremely

**inquest**   (in′ kwest)   *n.* Investigation

**inquisitive**   (in kwiz′ ə tiv)   *adj.* Curious

**insidious**   (in sid′ ē əs)   *adj.* Sly; crafty

**insolent**   (in′ sə lənt)   *n.* One who is boldly disrespectful; *adj.* In a bold disrespectful way

**insubordination**   (in′ sə bor′ d'n ā′ shən)   *n.* Disobedience

**insufferable**   (in suf′ ər ə bəl)   *adj.* Unbearable

**insular**   (in′ sə lər)   *adj.* Isolated; detached

**intercession**   (in′ tər sesh′ ən)   *n.* A prayer said on behalf of another person

**intercourse**   (int′ ər kôrs′)   *n.* Communication between people

**intern**   (in′ turn)   *n.* A doctor serving a training period

**intimation**   (in′ tə mā′ shən)   *n.* Hint or suggestion

**introspective**   (in′ trō spekt′ iv)   *adj.* Looking into one's own thoughts and feelings

**intuition**   (in′ too ish′ ən)   *n.* Ability to know immediately without reasoning

**invariable**   (in ver′ ē ə bəl)   *adj.* Not changing

**invincible**   (in vin′ sə bəl)   *adj.* Unbeatable

**J**

**jaded**   (jā′ did)   *adj.* Worn-out

**jocund**   (jäk′ ənd)   *adj.* Cheerful; merry

**K**

**kaleidoscopic** (kə lī′ də skäp′ ik)   *adj.* Constantly changing

**keel** (kēl)   *n.* The chief structural beam extending along the entire length of the bottom of a boat or ship supporting the frame

**keen** (kēn)   *adj.* Having a sharp cutting edge

**kindle** (kin′ dəl)   *v.* To ignite

**kitchenette-furnished** (kich′ ə net′ fʉr′ nisht)   *adj.* Having a small, compact kitchen

**knell** (nel)   *n.* The sound of a bell slowly ringing

**knothole** (nät′ hōl)   *n.* A hole in a board where a knot has fallen out

**L**

**lag** (lag)   *v.* To fall behind

**lair** (ler)   *n.* Den of a wild animal

**languorous** (laŋ′ gər əs)   *adj.* Slow and lazy

**lateral** (lat′ ər əl)   *adj.* Toward the side

**lee** (lē)   *n.* Sheltered place; the side away from the wind

**leer** (lir)   *v.* To look with malicious triumph

**legacy** (leg′ ə sē)   *n.* Anything handed down, as from an ancestor

**leprosy** (lep′ rə sē)   *n.* An infectious, disfiguring disease

**lethargy** (leth′ ər jē)   *n.* Laziness or indifference

**lichen** (lī′ kən)   *n.* Small plants of fungus and algae growing on rocks, wood, or soil

**lilting** (lilt′ iŋ)   *adj.* With a light, graceful rhythm

**limned** (lim′d)   *adj.* Outlined

**loam** (lōm)   *n.* Rich, dark soil

**lobulated** (läb′ yōō lāt′ əd)   *adj.* Subdivided

**lockjaw** (läk′ jô′)   *n.* A disease that causes jaw and neck muscles to become rigid

**low** (lō)   *v.* To make the typical sound that a cow makes

**lugubrious** (lə gōō′ brē əs)   *adj.* Sad

**lumberjack** (lum′ bər jak′)   *n.* A person employed to cut down timber

**luminance** (loo′ mə nəns)   *n.* Brightness

**luminous** (loo′ mə nəs)   *adj.* Glowing in the dark

**M**

**macabre** (mə käb′ rə)   *adj.* Gruesome

**malignant** (mə lig′ nənt)   *adj.* Harmful; likely to cause death

**malingerer** (mə liŋ′ gər ər)   *n.* One who pretends to be ill in order to escape work

**maneuver** (mə nōō′ vər)   *v.* To move in a planned way

**mania** (mā′ nē ə)   *n.* Uncontrollable enthusiasm

**manifold** (man′ ə fōld′)   *adj.* Many and varied

**mantle** (man′ təl)   *n.* Sleeveless cloak or cape

**meager** (mē′ gər)   *adj.* Lacking in some way

**meander** (mē an′ dər)   *v.* To follow a winding course

**meditate** (med′ ə tāt′)   *v.* To think deeply

**medium** (mē′ dē əm)   *n.* Means of communication

**meets** (mētz)   *n.* A series of races or competitions

**menacing** (men′ əs iŋ)   *adj.* Threatening

**mercurial** (mər kyoor′ ē əl)   *adj.* Quick or changeable in behavior

**Mercury** (mʉr′ kyoo rē)   *n.* In Roman mythology, the messenger of the gods

**metamorphose** (met′ ə môr′ fōz′)   *v.* To change or transform

**meticulous** (mə tik′ yoo ləs)   *adj.* Extremely careful about details

**mire** (mīr)   *n.* Deep mud

**miscreants** (mis′ krē ənts)   *n.* Criminals

**moccasin** (mäk′ ə sən)   *n.* Heelless slipper of soft flexible leather

**mode** (mōd)   *n.* Way; form

**molding** (mōl′ diŋ)   *n.* Ornamental woodwork

**monolithic** (män′ ə lith′ ik)   *adj.* Formed from a single block

**morose** (mə rōs′)   *adj.* Gloomy

**mote** (mōt)   *n.* A speck of dust or other tiny particle

**mucilage** (myōō′ si lij′)   *n.* Any watery solution of gum, glue, etc., used as an adhesive

**muse** (myōōz)   *v.* To think deeply

**musty** (mus′ tē)   *adj.* Having a stale, damp smell

**muted** (myōōt′ əd)   *adj.* Muffled; subdued

**mutineers** (myōōt′ ′n irz′)   *n.* People on a ship who revolt against their officers

**mutinous** (myōōt′ ′n əs)   *adj.* Rebellious

**mutual** (myōō′ chōō əl)   *adj.* Having the same relationship toward each other

**N**

**narcotic** (när kät′ ik)   *n.* Something that has a soothing effect

**nebulous** (neb′ yə ləs)   *adj.* Vague; unclear and indefinite

**negotiation** (ni gō′ shē ā′ shən)   *n.* Bargaining or discussing to reach an agreement

**neurosurgeon** (noo′ rō sʉr′ jən)   *n.* A doctor who operates on the nervous system

**nonchalant** (nän′ shə länt′)   *adj.* Casual

**notify** (nōt′ ə fī′)   *v.* To give notice to (someone); to inform

**nurture** (nʉr′ chər)   *v.* To nourish

**nuzzle** (nuz′ əl)   *v.* To rub with the nose

**O**

**obdurate** (äb′ door it)   *adj.* Stubborn; unyielding

**obliterate** (ə blit′ ər āt)   *v.* To wipe out; leaving no traces

**obscure** (əb skyoor′)   *adj.* Hidden; *v.* Hide

**officiously** (ə fish′ əs lē)   *adv.* Offering unwanted help

**omen** (ō′ mən)   *n.* A thing or happening supposed to foretell a future event

**ominous** (äm′ ə nəs)   *adj.* Threatening

**oratorical** (ôr′ ə tôr′ i kəl)   *adj.* Of or characteristic of an orator, lofty, high-sounding

**ornament** (ôr′ nə mənt′)  *v.* To decorate
**ornate** (ôr nāt′)  *adj.* Having fancy decorations
**orthodontist** (ôr′ thō dän′ tist)  *n.* A dentist who straightens teeth
**ostentatious** (äs′ ten tā′ shəs)  *adj.* Showy

**P**

**paleontologist** (pā′ lē ən täl′ ə jist)  *n.* Scientist who investigates prehistoric forms of life
**palmated** (pal′ māt′ əd)  *adj.* Shaped like a hand with the fingers spread
**palpate** (pal′ pāt′)  *v.* To examine by touch
**palpitant** (pal′ pə tənt)  *adj.* Quivering
**pandemonium** (pan′ də mō′ nē əm)  *n.* A scene of wild disorder
**panoply** (pan′ ə plē)  *n.* Magnificent covering or array
**paradox** (par′ ə däks′)  *n.* A situation that seems to have contradictory qualities
**paraphernalia** (par′ ə fər nāl′ yə)  *n.* Equipment
**paroxysm** (par′ əks iz′ əm)  *n.* Outburst or convulsion
**parson** (pär′ sən)  *n.* A minister
**pelt** (pelt)  *n.* The skin and fur of an animal
**perambulating** (per am′ byōō lāt′ iŋ)  *adj.* Walking
**perch** (pʉrch)  *v.* To rest upon
**peremptory** (pər emp′ tə rē)  *adj.* Absolute; without question
**periscope** (per′ i skōp′)  *n.* An instrument containing mirrors and lenses to see objects not in a direct line from the viewer; often used in submarines
**pertinacity** (pʉr′ tə nas′ ə tē)  *n.* Stubbornness
**pervade** (pər vād′)  *v.* To spread throughout
**petulant** (pech′ ə lənt)  *adj.* Impatient
**phantasmagorical** (fan taz′ mə gôr′ i kəl)  *adj.* A rapid change, as in a dream
**phantom** (fan′ təm)  *n.* Ghostlike figure
**phoenix** (fē′ niks)  *n.* In Egyptian mythology, a beautiful bird
**pinafore** (pin′ ə fôr′)  *n.* A sleeveless garment worn by little girls over a dress
**pittance** (pit′ 'ns)  *n.* A small or barely sufficient allowance of money
**placid** (plas′ id)  *adj.* Calm; quiet
**plaintive** (plān′ tiv)  *adj.* Sorrowful; mournful
**platform** (plat′ fôrm′)  *n.* Statement of intention
**plebeian** (plē bē′ ən)  *n.* A common, ordinary person or animal
**plethoric** (plə thôr′ ik)  *adj.* Too full
**plum** (plum)  *adj.* Here, first-class
**poach** (pōch)  *v.* To cook gently in near-boiling water
**pollen** (päl′ ən)  *n.* The yellow, powderlike cells formed in the stamen of a flower
**ponder** (pän′ dər)  *v.* To think deeply
**ponderous** (pän′ dər əs)  *adj.* Heavy; massive
**portentous** (pôr ten′ təs)  *adj.* Pompous
**portly** (pôrt′ lē)  *adj.* Large, heavy, and dignified
**posterity** (päs ter′ ə tē)  *n.* Future generations
**posthaste** (pōst′ hāst′)  *adv.* With great quickness

**precarious** (prē ker′ ē əs)  *adj.* Insecure and dangerous
**precipitate** (prē sip′ ə tāt′)  *v.* To cause to happen
**predecessor** (pred′ ə ses′ ər)  *n.* Someone who comes before another in a position
**preeminent** (prē em′ ə nənt)  *adj.* Dominant
**premonition** (prē mə nish′ ən)  *n.* An omen
**prerequisite** (pri rek′ wə zit)  *n.* An initial requirement
**presentable** (prē zent′ ə bəl)  *adj.* Suitable to be seen by others
**pretext** (prē′ tekst′)  *n.* A false reason or motive given to hide a real intention
**primordial** (prī môr′ dē əl)  *adj.* Primitive
**privation** (prī vā′ shən)  *n.* Lack of common comfort
**procure** (prō kyoor′)  *v.* To obtain by some effort
**prodigy** (präd′ ə jē)  *n.* A child of extraordinary genius
**proffer** (präf′ ər)  *v.* To offer
**profound** (prō found′)  *adj.* Deep
**progeny** (präj′ ə nē)  *n.* Children
**promote** (prō mōt′)  *v.* To give a higher position
**propound** (prō pound′)  *v.* To propose; put forward for consideration
**prospect** (prä′ spekt′)  *n.* A likely candidate
**protestation** (prät′ es tā′ shən)  *n.* Formal declaration or assertion
**prow** (prou)  *n.* The frontmost part of a ship
**prowess** (prou′ is)  *n.* Superior ability
**pungent** (pun′ jənt)  *adj.* Sharp and stinging to the smell
**purchase** (pʉr′ chəs)  *n.* A tight hold to keep from slipping
**purgatory** (pʉr′ gə tôr′ ē)  *n.* A state or place of temporary punishment
**purify** (pyoor′ ə fī′)  *v.* To make pure; to remove all evil

**Q**

**quaint** (kwānt)  *adj.* Charmingly curious in an old-fashioned way; strange

**R**

**rafter** (raf′ tər)  *n.* One of the beams that slopes from the ridge of a roof to the eaves and supports the roof
**ram** (ram)  *n.* A heavy beam used to break down gates
**rampage** (ram′ pāj)  *n.* An outbreak of violent behavior
**rampant** (ram′ pənt)  *adj.* Unrestrained
**raucous** (rô′ kəs)  *adj.* Boisterous; disorderly
**ravaging** (rav′ ij iŋ)  *adj.* Severely damaging or destroying
**recede** (ri sēd′)  *v.* To move farther away
**reconnoiter** (rek′ ə noit′ ər)  *v.* To make an exploratory examination to get information about a place
**recrudescence** (rē′ krōō des′ əns)  *n.* A fresh outbreak of something that has been inactive
**redress** (rē′ dres′)  *n.* The righting of wrongs
**refute** (ri fyoot′)  *v.* To disprove
**regimen** (rej′ ə mən)  *n.* A regulated system of diet and exercise

**remote**   (ri mōt′)   *adj.* Distant
**renounce**   (ri nouns′)   *v.* To give up
**repertoire**   (rep′ ər twär′)   *n.* A stock of songs, tricks, or other talents one has readily on hand
**replica**   (rep′ li kə)   *n.* A copy of a work of art
**replicate**   (rep′ li kāt′)   *v.* To duplicate; to copy
**reprehensible**   (rep′ ri hen′ sə bəl)   *adj.* Deserving blame
**repugnance**   (ri pug′ nəns)   *n.* Extreme dislike
**resolute**   (rez′ ə lōōt′)   *adj.* Showing a firm purpose; determined
**retribution**   (re′ trə byōō′ shən)   *n.* A punishment deserved for a wrong done
**retrogression**   (re′ trə gresh′ ən)   *n.* A moving backward to a more primitive state
**revelation**   (rev′ ə lā′ shən)   *n.* Something revealed; a disclosure of something not previously known or realized
**reverie**   (rev′ ər ē)   *n.* Daydream
**revue**   (ri vyōō′)   *n.* A musical show with loosely connected skits, songs and dances
**riveted**   (riv′ it əd)   *adj.* Fastened or made firm
**rivulet**   (riv′ yoo lit)   *n.* A little stream
**rollicking**   (räl′ ik iŋ)   *adj.* Lively
**ruction**   (ruk′ shən)   *n.* Quarrel or noisy disturbance
**ruddy**   (rud′ ē)   *adj.* Having a healthy color
**runt**   (runt)   *n.* The smallest animal in a litter
**ruse**   (rōōz)   *n.* A trick or plan for fooling someone

**S**

**sagacity**   (sə gas′ ə tē)   *n.* High intelligence and sound judgment
**sage**   (sāj)   *n.* A plant used to flavor food
**salient**   (sāl′ yənt)   *adj.* Noticeable; prominent
**sap**   (sap)   *v.* To drain; to exhaust
**sarcastic**   (sär kas′ tik)   *adj.* Having a sharp, mocking tone intended to hurt another
**sash**   (sash)   *n.* The frame holding the glass panes of the window
**sated**   (sāt′ əd)   *adj.* Fully satisfied
**savor**   (sā′ vər)   *v.* To enjoy; appreciate
**scoff**   (skäf)   *v.* To mock; to make fun of
**score**   (skôr)   *n.* The music for a stage production or film, apart from the lyrics and dialogue
**scorpion**   (skôr′ pē ən)   *n.* Any of a group of poisonous arachnids found in warm regions
**screech**   (skrēch)   *n.* A shrill, high-pitched shriek or sound
**scuttle**   (skut′ ′l)   *v.* To run or move quickly
**sect**   (sekt)   *n.* Small group of people with the same leader and belief
**semblance**   (sem′ bləns)   *n.* Likeness; image
**sensory**   (sen′ sər ē)   *adj.* Of receiving sense impressions
**sentinel**   (sen′ ti nəl)   *n.* Guard
**shanty**   (shan′ tē)   *n.* Hut or shack
**sheen**   (shēn)   *n.* Shininess
**shingle**   (shiŋ′ gəl)   *v.* To cover the roof with shingles

**shinny**   (shin′ ē)   *v.* To climb by gripping with both hands and legs
**shoal**   (shōl)   *n.* Sand bar
**shoon**   (shōōn)   *n.* Old-fashioned word for shoes
**shun**   (shun)   *v.* To avoid
**simultaneous**   (si′ məl tā′ nē əs)   *adj.* Taking place at the same time
**sinew**   (sin′ yōō)   *n.* A band of fibrous tissue that connects muscles to bones or to other parts and can also be used as thread for sewing
**singular**   (siŋ′ gyə lər)   *adj.* Exceptional; peculiar
**sinister**   (sin′ is tər)   *adj.* Threatening harm, evil, or misfortune
**skeptic**   (skep′ tik)   *n.* Person who doubts
**slander**   (slan′ dər)   *n.* Lies
**slash**   (slash)   *v.* To cut with a sweeping stroke
**sloth**   (slōth)   *n.* Laziness
**smolder**   (smōl′ dər)   *v.* To exist in a suppressed state
**smoldering**   (smōl′ dər iŋ)   *adj.* Fiery
**snicker**   (snik′ ər)   *v.* To laugh in a mean way
**snide**   (snīd)   *adj.* Intentionally mean
**soliloquize**   (sə lil′ ə kwīz′)   *v.* To talk to oneself
**somber**   (säm′ bər)   *adj.* Dark; gloomy
**sonorous**   (sə nôr′ əs)   *adj.* Having a powerful, impressive sound
**specious**   (spē′ shəs)   *adj.* Seeming to be true without really being so
**specter**   (spek′ tər)   *n.* 1 Ghostly figure; apparition 2 A disturbing thought
**spectral**   (spek′ trəl)   *adj.* Ghostly
**spike**   (spīk)   *n.* A long thick metal nail used for splitting rock
**spume**   (spyōōm)   *n.* Foam; froth
**spurn**   (spʉrn)   *v.* To reject scornfully
**squall**   (skwôl)   *v.* To cry out or scream
**stalk**   (stôk)   *v.* To secretly approach
**starboard**   (stär′ bərd)   *adj.* The right side of a ship, as one faces forward
**starling**   (stär′ liŋ)   *n.* Dark-colored bird
**static**   (stat′ ik)   *adj.* Not changing or progressing
**stealthily**   (stelth′ i lē)   *adv.* In a secretive manner
**stealthy**   (stel′ thē)   *adj.* Secret; quiet
**steep**   (stēp)   *adj.* Having a sharp rise or inclined slope
**stench**   (stench)   *n.* An offensive smell
**stifled**   (stī′ fəld)   *adj.* Muffled; suppressed
**stilted**   (stil′ tid)   *adj.* Unnatural; very formal
**stimulus**   (stim′ yōō ləs)   *n.* Something that rouses to action
**stoic**   (stō′ ik)   *adj.* Showing indifference to pleasure or pain; impassive
**stolid**   (stäl′ id)   *adj.* Showing little or no emotion
**stratagem**   (strat′ ə jəm)   *n.* Plan for defeating an opponent
**strife**   (strīf)   *n.* Conflict
**suavity**   (swäv′ ə tē)   *n.* Graceful politeness
**subjunctive**   (səb juŋk′ tiv)   *n.* A particular form of a verb

**subtle** (sut′ ′l) *adj.* Delicate; fine

**successor** (sək ses′ ər) *n.* A person that follows or comes after another

**suckle** (suk′ əl) *v.* To nurse at the breast

**suitor** (sōōt′ ər) *n.* A man courting a woman

**sultry** (sul′ trē) *adj.* Hot and humid

**summoning** (sum′ ən iŋ) *n.* A calling; a request to appear or attend

**superfluous** (sə pʉr′ floo əs) *adj.* More than is necessary

**surcharged** (sʉr′ chärjd) *adj.* Overcharged

**surge** (sʉrj) *v.* To move with a sudden, strong increase of power

**surveillance** (sər vā′ ləns) *n.* Watch; inspection

**swagger** (swag′ ər) *n.* Arrogance or boastfulness; *v.* To strut; walk with a bold step

**swamp** (swämp) *v.* To sink by filling with water

**swarthy** (swôr′ *th*ē) *adj.* Having a dark complexion

**swoon** (swōōn) *v.* Faint

## T

**taciturn** (tas′ ə tʉrn′) *adj.* Not likely to talk

**tangible** (tan′ jə bəl) *adj.* Observable; understandable

**taunt** (tônt) *v.* To jeer at; to mock

**taut** (tôt) *adj.* Tightly stretched

**teem** (tēm) *v.* To swarm

**tenacious** (tə nā′ shəs) *adj.* Holding on firmly

**tendril** (ten′ drəl) *n.* Thin shoot from a plant

**tenement** (ten′ ə mənt) *n.* A run-down apartment building

**tenure** (ten′ yər) *n.* Time of residence

**tepee** (tē′ pē) *n.* A cone-shaped tent of animal skins

**thesis** (thē′ sis) *n.* Statement of position or proposition

**tick** (tik) *v.* To operate smoothly

**tint** (tint) *v.* To color

**tolerate** (täl′ ər āt′) *v.* To allow; permit

**tortuous** (tôr′ chōō əs) *adj.* Winding with repeated twists and turns

**tousled-looking** (tou′ zəld look′ iŋ) *adj.* Rumpled or mussed

**transient** (tran′ shənt) *adj.* Not permanet

**tread** (tred) *n.* Step

**treatise** (trēt′ is) *n.* A formal writing on some subject

**tremor** (trem′ ər) *n.* Shaking or vibration

**tremulous** (trem′ yoo ləs) *adj.* Trembling or quivering

**trivial** (triv′ ē əl) *adj.* Of little importance

**troubadour** (trōō′ bə dôr′) *n.* Traveling singer, usually accompanying himself on a stringed instrument

**trough** (trôf) *n.* Long and narrow container for holding water or food for animals

## U

**unabashed** (un ə bash′ əd) *adj.* Unashamed

**uncanny** (un kan′ ē) *adj.* Strange

**undulate** (un′ dyōō lāt′) *v.* To move in waves

**unfurled** (un fʉrld′) *adj.* Unfolded

**unobtrusive** (un əb trōō′ siv) *adj.* Not calling attention to oneself

**unweildy** (un wēl′ dē) *adj.* Hard to handle because of size

**unwonted** (un wän′ tid) *adj.* Not usual

**uproariously** (up rôr′ ē əs lē) *adv.* Loudly and boisterously

**usurp** (yōō zʉrp′) *v.* To take over

## V

**vacuous** (vak′ yoo əs) *adj.* Empty; shallow

**venture** (ven′ chər) *v.* To express oneself at the risk of criticism, objection, or denial

**veranda** (və ran′ də) *n.* A porch or balcony, usually roofed, that extends along the outside of a building

**versatile** (vʉr′ sə təl) *adj.* Having many uses

**vicarage** (vik′ ər ij) *n.* A place where a member of the clergy lives

**vicarious** (vī kər′ ē əs) *adj.* Experienced by one person or animal in place of another

**vigil** (vij′ əl) *n.* Period of watching

**vigorous** (vig′ ər əs) *adj.* Strong and energetic

**viscera** (vis′ ər ə) *n.* Internal organs

**vituperation** (vī tōō′ pər ā′ shən) *n.* Abusive language

**voile** (voil) *n.* A light cotton fabric

**voracious** (vô rā′ shəs) *adj.* Eager to devour large quantities of food

## W

**waft** (wäft) *v.* To move lightly through the air

**wan** (wän) *adj.* Pale

**waning** (wān′ iŋ) *adj.* A full moon shrinking to a new moon

**wantonness** (wän′ tən nəs) *n.* Lack of discipline

**wary** (wer′ ē) *adj.* Cautious or careful about

**whirl** (hwʉrl) *v.* To drive with a rotating motion

**willow-wild** (wil′ ō wild′) *adj.* Slender and pliant, like a reed blowing in the wind

**winch** (winch) *n.* A machine used for lifting

**wistful** (wist′ fəl) *adj.* Expressing vague yearnings

**wizened** (wiz′ ənd) *adj.* Shrunken, and wrinkled with age

**wormwood** (wʉrm′ wood) *n.* A plant that produces a bitter oil

**wraith** (rāth) *n.* Ghost

## Y

**yearling** (yir′ liŋ) *n.* An animal that is between one and two years old

**yonder** (yän′ dər) *adj.* In the distance

**yucca** (yuk′ ə) *n.* A desert plant with stiff leaves and white flowers

*Glossary* 801

# INDEX OF FINE ART

# INDEX OF SKILLS

## CRITICAL READING AND THINKING

## LEARNING OPTIONS

## READING IN THE CONTENT AREAS

## THINKING AND WRITING

# INDEX OF TITLES BY THEMES

*Index of Titles by Themes* 809

# INDEX OF AUTHORS AND TITLES

Page numbers in *italics* refer to biographical information.

## ACKNOWLEDGMENTS (continued)

**Atheneum Publishers, an imprint of Macmillan Publishing Company**
Lines from "Concrete Mixers" from *8 A.M. Shadows* by Patricia Hubbell, Copyright © 1965 Patricia Hubbell. Reprinted with the permission of Atheneum Publishers, an imprint of Macmillan Publishing Company.

**Ayer Company Publishers**
"The Finish of Patsy Barnes" from *Strength of Gideon and Other Stories* by Paul Laurence Dunbar. Reprinted by permission of Ayer Company Publishers, Inc., P.O. Box 958, Salem, NH 03079.

**Borden Publishing Company**
From "Hokusai: The Old Man Mad About Drawing" reproduced from *The Drawings of Hokusai* by Stephen Longstreet published by Borden Publishing Co., Alhambra, California.

**Brandt & Brandt Literary Agents, Inc.**
"Johnny Appleseed" from *A Book of Americans,* copyright 1933 by Rosemary and Stephen Vincent Benét; copyright renewed 1961 by Rosemary Carr Benét. "The Land and the Water" from *The Wind Shifting West* by Shirley Ann Grau, copyright © 1973 by Shirley Ann Grau. Reprinted by permission of Brandt & Brandt Literary Agents, Inc.

**The Caxton Printers, Ltd.**
"The Six Rows of Pompons" from *Yokohama, California* by Toshio Mori. The Caxton Printers, Ltd., Caldwell, Idaho.

**Coward-McCann, Inc.**
"Desert Noon" by Elizabeth Coatsworth, reprinted by permission of Coward-McCann, Inc., from *Compass Rose* by Elizabeth Coatsworth, copyright 1929 by Coward-McCann, Inc.; copyright renewed © 1957 by Elizabeth Coatsworth.

**Don Congdon Associates Inc.**
"The Drummer Boy of Shiloh" by Ray Bradbury was originally published in the *Saturday Evening Post,* 1960, by the Curtis Publishing Company. Copyright © 1960, renewed 1988 by Ray Bradbury. Reprinted by permission.

**Doubleday, A division of Bantam Doubleday Dell Publishing Group, Inc.**
"Fathers and Daughters" from *When Heaven and Earth Changed Places* by Le Ly Hayslip. Copyright © 1989 by Le Ly Hayslip and Charles Jay Wurts. "Rain, Rain, Go Away" by Isaac Asimov copyright © 1959 by King-Size Publishing, Inc. from *Buy Jupiter and Other Stories.* "A Retrieved Reformation" from *Roads of Destiny* by O. Henry. Reprinted by permission of Doubleday, a division of Bantam Doubleday Dell Publishing Group, Inc.

**Mari Evans**
"if you have had your midnights" from *Nightstar* by Mari Evans, published by CAAS, the University of California at Los Angeles, 1981. Reprinted by permission of the author.

**Farrar, Straus & Giroux, Inc.**
"Animal Craftsmen" from *Nature by Design* by Bruce Brooks. Copyright © 1991 by the Educational Broadcasting Corporation and Bruce Brooks. Adapted from "Charles" from *The Lottery* by Shirley Jackson. Copyright © 1948, 1949 by Shirley Jackson; copyright © renewed 1976, 1977 by Laurence Hyman, Barry Hyman, Mrs. Sarah Webster, and Mrs. Joanne Schnurer. Reprinted by special permission of Farrar, Straus & Giroux, Inc. "The Day I Got Lost" from *Stories for Children* by Isaac Bashevis Singer. Copyright © 1962, 1967, 1968, 1970, 1972, 1973, 1974, 1975, 1976, 1979, 1980, 1984 by Isaac Bashevis Singer. Reprinted by permission of Farrar, Straus & Giroux, Inc.

**Richard García**
"The City Is So Big" by Richard García, © 1973 by Richard García. Reprinted by permission of the author.

**GRM Associates, Inc., Agents for the Estate of Ida M. Cullen**
Lines from "For a Poet" from *On These I Stand: The Best-Loved Poems of Countee Cullen.* Copyright © 1925 by Harper & Brothers; copyright renewed 1953 by Ida M. Cullen. Reprinted by permission of GRM Associates, Inc., Agents for the Estate of Ida M. Cullen.

**Harcourt Brace Jovanovich, Inc.**
"Crime on Mars" copyright © 1960 by Davis Publications. Reprinted from *The Nine Billion Names of God* by Arthur C. Clarke. Excerpt from "Forest Fire" from *The Diary of Anaïs Nin 1947–1955* by Anaïs Nin, edited by Gunther Stuhlmann, copyright © 1974 by Anaïs Nin. "Paul Bunyan of the North Woods" and "They Have Yarns" from *The People, Yes* by Carl Sandburg, copyright 1936 by Harcourt Brace Jovanovich, Inc.; renewed 1964 by Carl Sandburg. From "For My Sister Molly Who in The Fifties" copyright © 1972 by Alice Walker, in her volume *Revolutionary Petunias & Other Poems.* Reprinted by permission of Harcourt Brace Jovanovich, Inc.

**HarperCollins Publishers Inc.**
"How the Snake Got Poison" and "Why the Waves Have Whitecaps" from *Mules and Men* by Zora Neale Hurston. Copyright © 1935 by Zora Neale Hurston. Copyright renewed 1963 by John C. Hurston. Text of "Shooting Stars" from *This World of Wonder* by Hal Borland (J.B. Lippincott), copyright © 1972, 1973 by Hal Borland. Haiku, "The Falling Flower," by Moritake from *Poetry Handbook: A Dictionary of Terms,* 4th edition, by Babette Deutsch. Copyright © 1957, 1962, 1969, 1974 by Babette Deutsch. Reprinted by permission of HarperCollins Publishers Inc.

**Harvard University Press**
"The Tell-Tale Heart" by Edgar Allan Poe from *Collected Works of Edgar Allan Poe* edited by Thomas Ollive Mabbott, copyright © 1978 by the President and Fellows of Harvard College. From *One Writer's Beginnings* by Eudora Welty, copyright © 1983, 1984 by Eudora Welty. Reprinted by permission of Harvard University Press.

**Hill and Wang, a division of Farrar, Straus & Giroux, Inc.**
"The Story-Teller" from *Collected and New Poems 1924–1963* by Mark Van Doren, copyright © 1963 by Mark Van Doren. Reprinted by permission of Hill and Wang, a division of Farrar, Straus & Giroux, Inc.

**Henry Holt and Company, Inc.**
"Blue-Butterfly Day" and "The Road Not Taken" copyright 1916, 1923 by Holt, Rinehart and Winston, Inc. and renewed 1944, 1951 by Robert Frost. Reprinted from *The Poetry of Robert Frost* edited by Edward Connery Lathem. Lines from "Rose Pogonias" copyright © 1969 by Holt, Rinehart and Winston, Inc. Reprinted from *The Poetry of Robert Frost* edited by Edward Connery Lathem, by permission of Henry Holt and Company, Inc.

**Evelyn Tooley Hunt and Negro Digest**
"Taught Me Purple" by Evelyn Tooley Hunt from *Negro Digest,* February 1964 © 1964 by Johnson Publishing Company, Inc. Reprinted by permission of Evelyn Tooley Hunt and *Negro Digest.*

**Gish Jen**
"The White Umbrella" by Gish Jen. Copyright © 1984 by Gish Jen. First published in *The Yale Review.* Reprinted by permission of the author.

**Daniel Keyes**
"Flowers for Algernon" (short story version) by Daniel Keyes. Copyright © 1959 and 1987 by Daniel Keyes. Reprinted by permission of the author. Edited for this edition.

**Alfred A. Knopf, Inc.**
"The Cyclone" from *Pecos Bill: Texas Cowpuncher* by Harold W. Felton. Copyright 1949 by Alfred A. Knopf, Inc. "Harlem Night Song" and "Winter Moon" from *Selected Poems of Langston Hughes* by Langston Hughes. Copyright 1926 by Alfred A. Knopf, Inc. and renewed 1954 by Langston Hughes. Lines from "The Quiet Fog" copyright © 1975 by Marge Piercy, reprinted from *The Twelve Spoked Wheel Flashing* by Marge Piercy. "January" from *A Child's Calendar* by John Updike. Copyright © 1965 by John Updike and Nancy Burkert. Reprinted by permission of Alfred A. Knopf, Inc.

**Alfred A. Knopf, Inc. and Pierre Berton**
Two maps ("The Country of the Klondike Fever" and "The Trail of '98") from *The Klondike Fever* by Pierre Berton. Copyright © 1958 by Pierre Berton. Reprinted by permission.

**Naoshi Koriyama**
"Jetliner" by Naoshi Koriyama is reprinted from *Poetry Nippon* (Summer 1970) by permission of the author. Copyright © 1970 by The Poetry Society of Japan, Nagoya, Japan.

**Ursula K. Le Guin and her agent, Virginia Kidd**
"Talking About Writing" from *The Language of the Night: Essays on Fantasy and Science Fiction* by Ursula K. Le Guin, copyright © 1979 by Ursula K. Le Guin. Reprinted by permission of the author and the author's agent, Virginia Kidd.

**The Literary Trustees of Walter de la Mare and The Society of Authors as their representative**
"Silver" from *Collected Poems 1901–1918* by Walter de la Mare. Reprinted by permission.

**Little, Brown and Company**
"Sancho" from *The Longhorns* by J. Frank Dobie. Copyright 1941 by J. Frank Dobie. Copyright © renewed 1969 by J. Frank Dobie. *The Man Without a Country* by Edward Everett Hale. By permission of Little, Brown and Company.

**Liveright Publishing Corporation**
"Runagate Runagate" is reprinted from *Collected Poems* of Robert Hayden, edited by Frederick Glaysher, by permission of Liveright Publishing Corporation. Copyright © 1985 by Erma Hayden.

**Longman Group UK Limited**
"Tears of the Sea" from *Arrival of the Snake-Woman and Other Stories* by Olive Senior. © Longman Group UK Limited 1989. Reprinted by permission of the publisher, Longman Group, UK Limited.

**The LULAC National**
"The Other Pioneers" by Roberto Félix Salazar, published in *The LULAC News,* July 1939. Reprinted by permission of LULAC National.

**Macmillan Publishing Company**
Lines from "March" from *Summer Green* by Elizabeth Coatsworth. Copyright 1948 by Macmillan Publishing Company, renewed 1976 by Elizabeth Coatsworth Beston. Reprinted with permission of Macmillan Publishing Company.

**Naomi Long Madgett**
"Woman With Flower" by Naomi Long Madgett from *Star by Star* by Naomi Long Madgett. Copyright © 1965, 1970. Reprinted by permission of the author.

**N. Scott Momaday**
"New World" from *The Gourd Dancer* by N. Scott Momaday, copyright © 1976 by N. Scott Momaday. Reprinted by permission of the author.

**William Morris Agency, Inc. on behalf of the authors**
"Roberto Clemente: A Bittersweet Memoir" from *Great Latin Sports Figures* by Jerry Izenberg. Copyright © 1976 by Jerry Izenberg. Reprinted by permission of William Morris Agency, Inc. on behalf of the author.

**Museum of New Mexico Press**
"Chicoria" (English only) and "Los cuatro elementos" (Spanish and English), translated by Rudolfo Anaya, reprinted with permission of the Museum of New Mexico Press, from *Cuentos: Tales From the Hispanic Southwest* by José Griego y Maestas and Rudolfo Anaya, copyright 1980.

**New Directions Publishing Corporation**
"The Term" from *The Collected Poems of William Carlos Williams, 1909–1939,* Vol. 1 by William Carlos Williams. Copyright 1938 by New Directions Publishing Corporation. Reprinted by permission of New Directions Publishing Corporation.

**The New York Times**
"A to Z in Foods as Metaphors: Or, a Stew Is a Stew, Is a Stew" by Mimi Sheraton, September 3, 1983. Copyright © 1983 by The New York Times Company. Reprinted by permission.

**The New Yorker Magazine, Inc.**
"Hog-Calling Competition" by Morris Bishop from "Limericks Long After Lear" from *The New Yorker,* October 3, 1936. Reprinted by permission; © 1936, 1964 The New Yorker Magazine, Inc.

**Harold Ober Associates Inc.**
"Christmas Day in the Morning" by Pearl S. Buck, published in *Collier's,* December 23, 1955. Copyright © 1955 by Pearl S. Buck. Copyright renewed 1983. "Thank You, M'am" from *The Langston Hughes Reader* by Langston Hughes. Copyright © 1958 by Langston Hughes. Copyright renewed 1986 by George Houston Bass. Reprinted by permission of Harold Ober Associates Inc.

**Julio Noboa Polanco**
"Identity" by Julio Noboa Polanco from *The Rican,* Journal of Contemporary Puerto Rican Thought, copyright 1973. Reprinted by permission of the author.

**Lawrence Pollinger Limited**
"The Captain and His Horse" by Beryl Markham from *The Splendid Outcast: Beryl Markham's African Stories,* compiled by Mary S. Lovell. Copyright © 1987 by the Beryl Markham Estate. Reprinted by permission of Lawrence Pollinger Limited.

**Prentice-Hall, Inc.**
"Blow, Blow, Thou Winter Wind" (from *As You Like It,* II,vii, 174) by William Shakespeare, published in *Renaissance Poetry* edited by Leonard Dean. Reprinted by permission.

**Présence Africaine, Paris**
Lines from "The Sea" by Mongameli Mabona from *Présence Africaine* published in No. 57 (1st Quarterly, 1966). Reprinted by permission.

**The Putnam Publishing Group**
"The Girl Who Hunted Rabbits" from *Zuñi Folk Tales,* translated by Frank H. Cushing with an introduction by J. W. Powell.

**Random House, Inc.**
From *I Know Why the Caged Bird Sings* by Maya Angelou. Copyright © 1969 by Maya Angelou. "Raymond's Run" copyright © 1971 by Toni Cade Bambara. Reprinted from *Gorilla, My Love* by Toni Cade Bambara. From *The Diary of Anne Frank* by Frances Goodrich and Albert Hackett. Copyright 1954, 1956 as an unpublished work. Reprinted by permission of Random House, Inc. CAUTION: *The Diary of Anne Frank* is the sole property of the dramatists and is fully protected by copyright. It may not be acted by professionals or amateurs without written permission and the payment of a royalty. All rights, including professional, amateur, stock, radio broadcasting, television, motion picture, recitation, lecturing, public reading, and the rights of translation into foreign languages are reserved.

**Reader's Digest**
"The Indian All Around Us" by Bernard DeVoto. Reprinted with permission from the April 1953 *Reader's Digest.* Copyright © 1953 by The Reader's Digest Association, Inc.

**Reader's Digest and Robert MacNeil**
"The Trouble with Television" by Robert MacNeil (condensed from a speech delivered November 13, 1984, at the President's Leadership Forum, State University of New York at Purchase). Reprinted with permission from the March 1985 *Readers' Digest.*

**Andrea Reynolds, attorney-in-fact for André Milos**
"The Adventure of the Speckled Band" from *The Complete Sherlock Holmes"* by Sir Arthur Conan Doyle.

**Russell and Volkening, Inc. as agents for the author**
"Harriet Tubman: Guide to Freedom" from *Harriet Tubman: Conductor on the Underground Railroad* by Ann Petry. Copyright © 1955, renewed 1983 by Ann Petry. Reprinted by permission of Russell and Volkening, Inc. as agents for the author.

**St. Martin's Press, Inc., New York, and Harold Ober Associates Inc.**
"Debbie" from *All Things Wise and Wonderful* by James Herriot. Copyright © 1976, 1977 by James Herriot. Reprinted by permission.

**Argelia Sedillo**
"Gentleman of Río en Medio" by Juan A. A. Sedillo, published in *New Mexico Quarterly,* 1939. Reprinted by permission.

**Simon & Schuster, Inc.**
Pronunciation key from *Webster's New World Dictionary—Third College Edition.* Copyright © 1988 by Simon & Schuster, Inc. Reprinted by permission of Simon & Schuster, Inc.

**Virginia Driving Hawk Sneve**
"The Medicine Bag" by Virginia Driving Hawk Sneve, published in *Boy's Life,* March 1975. Reprinted by permission of the author.

**Lloyd Sarett Stockdale**
"Four Little Foxes" from *Slow Smoke* by Lew Sarett, copyright 1953 by Lew Sarett; Henry Holt and Company. Reprinted by permission of Lloyd Sarett Stockdale.

# ART CREDITS

Boldface numbers refer to the page on which the art is found.

**Cover and Title Page:** *Taos Valley,* 1932–1935, Oil on canvas, 54 x 60", Victor Higgins, Gift of Mr. John T. Higgins, Snite Museum of Art, University of Notre Dame, 63.53.3; **v:** *The Sacristan of Trampas* (detail), ca. 1915–1920, Paul Burlin, Oil on canvas, 24 x 20", Museum of Fine Arts, Museum of New Mexico; **vi:** *Memories of the Meadow* (detail), 22 x 28", John Holyfield, Courtesy of Essence Art; **vii:** Painted Bowl: Deer Figure, Mimbres, New Mexico, Museum of the American Indian; **viii:** *Maudell Sleet's Magic Garden* (detail), 1978, Romare Bearden, from the *Profile/Part I: The Twenties Series (Mecklenburg County),* Private collection, Courtesy of the Estate of Romare Bearden; **ix:** *Untitled (mermaid)* (detail), 1983, Amos Ferguson, House paint on cardboard, Courtesy of the International Folk Art Foundation Collections, in the Museum of International Folk Art, a unit of the Museum of New Mexico, Photo by John Lei/Omni-Photo Communications, Inc.; **x:** (top) *Two Mexican Women and a Child* (detail), Diego Rivera, The Fine Arts Museums of San Francisco, Gift of Albert M. Bender, 1926.122; (bottom) *Cactus on the Plains (Hands),* 1931, Diego Rivera, Edsel and Eleanor Ford House, Grosse Pointe Shores, Michigan, Photo by R. H. Hensleigh; **1:** *Children and Pigeons in the Park, Central Park,* 1907, Millard Sheets, Photograph courtesy of Kennedy Galleries, New York; **6:** *Untitled,* 1990, Kinuko Y. Craft, Illustration for *Behind the Waterfall, Three Novellas,* by Chinatsu Nakayama, published by Macmillan; **11:** *James Folly General Store and Post Office,* Winfield Scott Clime, Superstock; **20:** *Pearl S. Buck* (detail), Vita Solomon, The National Portrait Gallery, Smithsonian Institution; **23:** *Albert's Son,* 1959, Andrew Wyeth, Nasjonalgalleriet, Oslo; **26:** *Sir Arthur Conan Doyle* (detail), H. L.

*Old Theme,* 1939, Joseph Stella, Oil on canvas, 70 x 42″, Collection of Whitney Museum of American Art, Purchase, Acq. #42.15; **533:** *Still Life: Flowers,* 1855, Severin Roesen, The Metropolitan Museum of Art, Purchase, Charles Allen Munn Bequest; Fosburgh Fund, Inc., Gift; Mr. and Mrs. J. William Middendorf II and Henry G. Keasbey Bequest, 1967, © Copyright 1980 by The Metropolitan Museum of Art; **535:** *Abraham Lincoln,* William Willard, Oil on canvas, The National Portrait Gallery, Smithsonian Institution, Gift of Mr. and Mrs. David A. Morse; **538:** *Baron Alfred Tennyson* (detail), c. 1840, S. Laurence, By courtesy of the National Portrait Gallery, London; **541:** *Windy Day in Atchison,* 1952, John Phillip Falter, Oil on canvas, 25 1/4 x 23″, Nebraska Art Association Collection, Sheldon Memorial Art Gallery, University of Nebraska, Lincoln, 1980.N-575.A; **548:** *Portrait of Vulnerability,* Diogenes Ballester, Courtesy of the artist; **551:** *Summer Millinery,* 1915, Charles Webster Hawthorne, The Chrysler Museum, Norfolk, Virginia, Gift of Walter P. Chrysler, Jr; **553:** *Invitation to the Sideshow (La Parade),* Georges Pierre Seurat, The Metropolitan Museum of Art, Bequest of Stephen C. Clark, 1960, © Copyright 1981 by The Metropolitan Museum of Art; **554:** *Langston Hughes* (detail), 1925, Winold Reiss, The National Portrait Gallery, Smithsonian Institution, Gift of W. Tjark Reiss, In memory of his father, Winold Reiss; **562:** *William Shakespeare* (detail), Artist unknown, By courtesy of the National Portrait Gallery, London; **567:** *Les Trés Riches Heures Du Duc De Berry: February,* Chantilly—Musée Condé, Giraudon/Art Resource, New York; **569:** *Hog Heaven,* Mike Patrick, Courtesy of Mike Patrick; **571:** *Shadows of Evening* (detail), 1921–1923, Rockwell Kent, Oil on canvas, 38 x 44″, Collection of Whitney Museum of American Art, Acq. #31.257; **572, 573:** Box, Manuscript, with tray inside top cover lacquer (detail), Meiji Period, XIX Century Japanese Lacquers, The Metropolitan Museum of Art, Bequest of Benjamin Altman, 1913, © Copyright by The Metropolitan Museum of Art; **574:** (center top) *Langston Hughes* (detail), 1925, Winold Reiss, The National Portrait Gallery, Smithsonian Institution, Gift of W. Tjark Reiss, In memory of his father, Winold Reiss; (center bottom) *Shadows of Evening* (detail), 1921–1923, Rockwell Kent, Oil on canvas, 38 x 44″, Collection of Whitney Museum of American Art, Acq. #31-257; **576:** *Winter Twilight Near Albany, New York,* 1858, George Henry Boughton, Courtesy of The New York Historical Society, New York City; **583:** *Houses of Murnau at Obermarkt,* 1908, Wassily Kandinsky, Lugano-Thyssen-Bornemisza Collection, Art Resource, New York; **586:** *City at the Sea,* Helmut Kies, Superstock; **595:** *On the Promenade,* August Macke, Superstock; **598:** *Seashore at Palavas,* 1854, Gustave Courbet, Musée Fabre, Montpellier; **603:** *Maudell Sleet's Magic Garden,* 1978, Romare Bearden, from the *Profile/Part I: The Twenties Series (Mecklenburg County),* Private collection, Courtesy of the Estate of Romare Bearden; **606:** *The Market Plaza, San Antonio,* Thomas Allen, 1878–1924, Oil on canvas mounted on panel, 26 x 39 3/4″, Courtesy of the San Antonio Museum Association, San Antonio, Texas; **609:** *Green Violinist,* 1923–1924, Marc Chagall, Solomon R. Guggenheim Museum, New York, Photo by David Heald; **616:** *The Woodcutter,* 1891, Winslow Homer, Private collection; **619:** *North Mountain,* Harrison Begay (Haskay Yah Ne Yah), Museum of Northern Arizona, Fine Arts Collection, C659; **625:** *His Hair Flows Like a River,* T. C. Cannon, The Philbrook Museum of Art, Tulsa, Oklahoma; **629:** *Rattlesnake No. 3,* 1988, William Hawkins, Enameled paint and collage on Masonite, Courtesy of the Edward Thorp Gallery, New York; **630:** *Untitled (mermaid),* 1983, Amos Ferguson, House paint on cardboard, Courtesy of the International Folk Art Foundation Collections, in the Museum of International Folk Art, a unit of the Museum of New Mexico, Photo by John Lei/Omni-Photo Communications, Inc.; **633:** *Miss Annie Oakley, the Peerless Lady Wing-Shot,* c. 1890, Color lithograph, poster, Buffalo Bill Historical Center, Cody, Wyoming, Gift of the Coe Foundation; **634:** *Indian Girl* (detail), 1917, Robert Henri, © 1989 Indianapolis Museum of Art, Gift of Mrs. John N. Carey; **637:** *Indian Girl,* 1917, Robert Henri, © 1989 Indianapolis Museum of Art, Gift of Mrs. John N. Carey; **642:** *Hammer in His Hand* (detail), Palmer C. Hayden, Museum of African American Art, Palmer C. Hayden Collection, Gift of Miriam A. Hayden, Photo by Armando Solis; **644:** *Hammer in His Hand,* Palmer C. Hayden, Museum of African American Art, Palmer C. Hayden Collection, Gift of Miriam A. Hayden, Photo by Armando Solis; **651:** *A Man Ain't Nothin' but a Man,* Palmer C. Hayden, From the collection of the Museum of African American Art, Palmer C. Hayden Collection, Gift of Miriam A. Hayden, Photo by Armando Solis; **654:** *Johnny Appleseed,* New York Public Library, Picture Collection; **655:** *John Chapman,* Artist Unknown, The Granger Collection, New York; **660:** *Fiesta Near Santa Barbara,* Artist unknown, Photo by Henry Groskinsky; **663:** *The Legend of Pecos Bill,* 1948, Harold von Schmidt, Oil on canvas, 32 1/8 x 38 1/8″, Museum of Texas Tech University, Photo by Nicky L. Olson; **664:** *Carl Sandburg* (detail), Miriam Svet, The National Portrait Gallery, Smithsonian Institution; **666:** *Baseball Player and Circus Performers,* John Zielinski, Sal Barracca & Associates; **668:** *Paul Bunyan,* Richard Bennett, From *Legends of Paul Bunyan,* Collected by Harold W. Felton, Illustrated by Richard Bennett, New York Public Library; **669:** *Paul Bunyan Carrying a Tree on His Shoulder and an Ax in His Hand,* Artist unknown, The Bettmann Archive; **680:** *Davy Crockett,* Artist unknown, The Granger Collection, New York; **684:** *Davy Crockett, With the Help of His Dog, Fighting a Bear,* 1841, Cover of *The Crockett Almanac,* The Granger Collection, New York; **690:** *Mesa and Cacti,* 1930, Diego Rivera, © 1987 The Detroit Institute of Arts, City of Detroit Purchase, 31.24; **693:** *La Molendera,* 1924, Diego Rivera, Museo de Arte Moderno, Reproduction Authorized by El Instituto Nacional de Bellas Artes y Literatura; **696:** *Peasant With Sombrero (Peon),* 1926, Diego Rivera, Galeria Arvil, Mexico City; **699:** *Delfina and Dimas,* Diego Rivera, Private Collection; **706:** *Two Mexican Women and a Child,* 1926, Diego Rivera, The Fine Arts Museums of San Francisco, Gift of Albert M. Bender, 1926.122; **718:** *Group,* Jesus Guerrero Galván, Collection IBM Corporation, Armonk, New York; **725:** *Mexican Peasant With Sombrero and Serape,* Diego Rivera, Mr. and Mrs. Dudley Smith Collection, Harry Ransom Humanities Research Center, The University of Texas at Austin; **734:** *Cactus on the Plains (Hands),* 1931, Diego Rivera, Edsel and Eleanor Ford House, Grosse

Pointe Shores, Michigan, Photo by R. H. Hensleigh; **741:** *The Sob,* 1939, David Alfaro Siqueiros, Duco on composition board, 481/2 x 24 3/4″, Collection, The Museum of Modern Art, New York, Given anonymously; **748:** (top) *Miss Annie Oakley, the Peerless Lady Wing-Shot,* c. 1890, Color lithograph, poster, Buffalo Bill Historical Center, Cody, Wyoming, Gift of the Coe Foundation; (bottom right) *The Battle of Shiloh,* *Tennessee (6–7 April, 1862),* 1886, Kurz and Allison, The Granger Collection, New York; **749:** (top) *James Folly General Store and Post Office,* Winfield Scott Clime, Superstock; (center right) Painted Buffalo Hide Shield, Jémez, New Mexico, Museum of the American Indian; (bottom right) *The Great Mississippi Steamboat Race,* 1870, Currier & Ives, The Granger Collection, New York.

## PHOTOGRAPH CREDITS

**2:** Courtesy of Mathew Frary; **12:** Thomas Victor; **14:** Jock Pottle/Design Conceptions; **16:** Ann and Myron Sutton/Superstock; **46:** The Bettmann Archive; **78, 84:** AP/Wide World Photos; **96:** © Nikky Finney; **97:** Cliff Feulner/The Image Bank; **98:** Co Rentmeester/The Image Bank; **101:** Audrey Gottlieb/Monkmeyer Press; **103:** Steven E. Sutton/Duomo Photography, Inc.; **106:** The Granger Collection, New York; **112:** Thomas Victor; **113:** Ken Karp; **118:** AP/Wide World Photos; **128:** Courtesy of Longman International Education; **136, 144:** UPI/Bettmann Newsphotos; **150:** Thomas Victor; **158:** Edmund Ross; **172:** Steven Y. Mori; **174:** Steve Solum/Bruce Coleman, Inc.; **200:** Harry Snaveley; **203:** Memory Shop; **208, 217:** Photofest; **210:** Georgia McInnis; **221:** Memory Shop; **224:** Courtesy of Dustin Brumbaugh; **229:** Ken Karp; **233:** Tom Bean/The Stock Market; **301, 302:** UPI/Bettmann Newsphotos; **304:** © 1994, Copyright by COSMOPRESS, Geneva & Anne FRANK Fonds, The Bettmann Archive; **306, 308, 316, 318:** © 1994, Copyright by COSMOPRESS, Geneva & Anne FRANK Fonds; **324:** UPI/Bettmann Newsphotos; **328:** © 1994, Copyright by COSMOPRESS, Geneva & Anne FRANK Fonds; **333:** UPI/Bettmann Newsphotos; **337, 345, 349, 352, 358:** © 1994, Copyright by COSMOPRESS, Geneva & Anne FRANK Fonds; **363:** © 1994, Copyright by COSMOPRESS, Geneva & Anne FRANK Fonds, The Granger Collection, New York; **377:** Courtesy of Danica Wilson; **378:** J. P. Nacivet/Leo de Wys, Inc.; **379:** Thomas Victor; **392:** Courtesy of Jerry Izenberg; **395:** Ken McVey/After Image, Inc.; **398:** Jerry Wachter/Focus on Sports; **402:** Wake Forest University; **414:** Samuel Clemens, Age 15, Anonymous, Courtesy, Mark Twain Papers, The Bancroft Library; **420:** Courtesy of Le Ly Hayslip; **422:** Courtesy of East Meets West Foundation; **424:** Geoffrey Clifford; **426:** Courtesy of East Meets West Foundation; **427:** Geoffrey Clifford; **430:** The Bettmann Archive; **438:** John Wyand; **444:** Penelope Winslow Brooks; **447:** © Pat and Tom Leeson/Photo Researchers, Inc.; **449:** © Monique Claye/EXPLORER/Photo Researchers, Inc.; **452:** AP/Wide World Photos; **462:** The Bettmann Archive; **468:** Les Line; **469:** Dennis Di Cicco/Peter Arnold, Inc.; **472:** UPI/Bettmann Newsphotos; **476:** Thomas Victor; **480:** AP/Wide World Photos; **484:** Thomas Victor; **486:** Simon Warner/The Bronte Society; **490:** Courtesy of Jennifer Dugliss; **494:** AP/Wide World Photos; **502:** Courtesy of Tham Dang; **505:** Photo by Pat Wolk, Courtesy of Wendy Rose; **516:** The Bettmann Archive; **520:** The Granger Collection, New York; **524:** William Notman/The National Portrait Gallery, Smithsonian Institution; **526:** © Henri Cartier-Bresson/Magnum Photos, Inc; **530:** (top) NYT Pictures; (center) UPI/Bettmann Newsphotos; **537:** George Hall/Woodfin Camp & Associates; **538:** (top) The National Portrait Gallery, Smithsonian Institution; (center) AP/Wide World Photos; **542:** Joel Gordon; **543:** (left) Roy Morsch/The Stock Market; (right) Richard Dunoff/The Stock Market; **545:** G. Cigolini/The Image Bank; **546:** (top) Arte Público Press, University of Houston, Houston, Texas; (center) UPI/Bettmann Newsphotos; **554:** (top) Courtesy of Helen Sarett Stockdale and Lloyd Sarett Stockdale; (center) Dmitri Kessel/*Life* Magazine © Time, Inc.; (bottom) Thomas Victor; **557:** Kenneth W. Fink/Bruce Coleman, Inc.; **559:** Jane Burton/Bruce Coleman, Inc.; **562:** (top) © Faber & Faber, LTD; (center) AP/Wide World Photos; **564:** Agram Gesar/The Image Bank; **574:** Thomas Victor; **578:** A. and J. Verkaik/The Stock Market; **580:** David Fitzgerald/After Image, Inc.; **584:** (center) Harold Hornstein; (bottom) Thomas Victor; **588:** Tardos Camesi/The Stock Market; **590:** AP/Wide World Photos; **592:** Focus on Sports; **596:** (bottom) Dmitri Kessel/*Life* Magazine © Time, Inc.; **600:** Julius Fekete/The Stock Market; **602:** Courtesy of Naomi Long Madgett; **608:** Courtesy of Howard Jow; **610:** Thomas Victor; **620:** (top) Chuck Slade; (bottom) Courtesy of Rudolfo Anaya; **622:** John Lei/Omni-Photo Communications, Inc.; **628:** Courtesy of the Estate of Carl Van Vechten, Joseph Solomon, EXECUTOR, The National Portrait Gallery, Smithsonian Institution, Washington, D.C./Art Resource, New York; **658:** (top) Chuck Slade; (center) Courtesy of Rudolfo Anaya; **694:** UPI/Bettmann Newsphotos; **748:** (bottom left) Steven E. Sutton/Duomo Photography, Inc.; **749:** (bottom left) Tom Bean/The Stock Market.

## ILLUSTRATION CREDITS

**pp. 28–29, 34, 38–39:** The Art Source; **pp. 48–49, 54–55, 57:** Joel Spector; **pp. 140–141, 146, 509, 512–513, 672, 676–677:** The Art Source.

*818    Photograph Credits*